THE DATE SELECTION COMPENDIUM

THE 60 JIA ZI ATTRIBUTES

BOOK 1

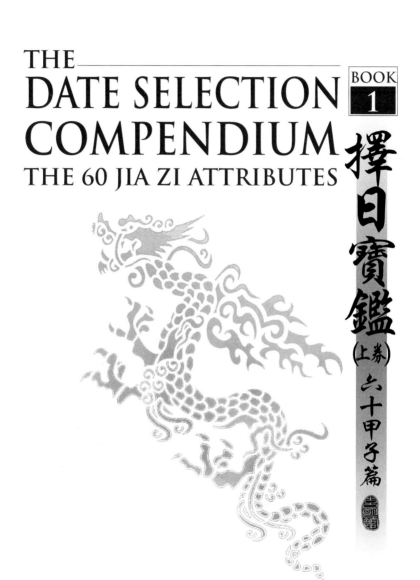

擇日寶鑑
(上券)
六十甲子篇

The Date Selection Compendium (Book 1)
The 60 Jia Zi Attributes

The author can be reached at:

Mastery Academy of Chinese Metaphysics Sdn. Bhd. (611143-A)
19-3, The Boulevard, Mid Valley City,
59200 Kuala Lumpur, Malaysia.
Tel   : +603-2284 8080
Fax   : +603-2284 1218
Email   : info@masteryacademy.com
Website: www.masteryacademy.com

DISCLAIMER:

The author, Joey Yap and the publisher, JY Books Sdn Bhd, have made their best efforts to produce this high quality, informative and helpful book. They have verified the technical accuracy of the information and contents of this book. Any information pertaining to the events, occurrences, dates and other details relating to the person or persons, dead or alive, and to the companies have been verified to the best of their abilities based on information obtained or extracted from various websites, newspaper clippings and other public media. However, they make no representation or warranties of any kind with regard to the contents of this book and accept no liability of any kind for any losses or damages caused or alleged to be caused directly or indirectly from using the information contained herein.

Published by JY Books Sdn. Bhd. (659134-T)

Table of Contents (According to Stem Groups)

Index of 60 Jia Zi

The 60 Jia Zi Year Pillar Reference Table

#	Pillar						#	Pillar				
1.	甲子 (Jia Zi) Wood Rat Year	1864	1924	1984	2044		31.	甲午 (Jia Wu) Wood Horse Year	1894	1954	2014	2074
2.	乙丑 (Yi Chou) Wood Ox Year	1865	1925	1985	2045		32.	乙未 (Yi Wei) Wood Goat Year	1895	1955	2015	2075
3.	丙寅 (Bing Yin) Fire Tiger Year	1866	1926	1986	2046		33.	丙申 (Bing Shen) Fire Monkey Year	1896	1956	2016	2076
4.	丁卯 (Ding Mao) Fire Rabbit Year	1867	1927	1987	2047		34.	丁酉 (Ding You) Fire Rooster Year	1897	1957	2017	2077
5.	戊辰 (Wu Chen) Earth Dragon Year	1868	1928	1988	2048		35.	戊戌 (Wu Xu) Earth Dog Year	1898	1958	2018	2078
6.	己巳 (Ji Si) Earth Snake Year	1869	1929	1989	2049		36.	己亥 (Ji Hai) Earth Pig Year	1899	1959	2019	2079
7.	庚午 (Geng Wu) Metal Horse Year	1870	1930	1990	2050		37.	庚子 (Geng Zi) Metal Rat Year	1900	1960	2020	2080
8.	辛未 (Xin Wei) Metal Goat Year	1871	1931	1991	2051		38.	辛丑 (Xin Chou) Metal Ox Year	1901	1961	2021	2081
9.	壬申 (Ren Shen) Water Monkey Year	1872	1932	1992	2052		39.	壬寅 (Ren Yin) Water Tiger Year	1902	1962	2022	2082
10.	癸酉 (Gui You) Water Rooster Year	1873	1933	1993	2053		40.	癸卯 (Gui Mao) Water Rabbit Year	1903	1963	2023	2083
11.	甲戌 (Jia Xu) Wood Dog Year	1874	1934	1994	2054		41.	甲辰 (Jia Chen) Wood Dragon Year	1904	1964	2024	2084
12.	乙亥 (Yi Hai) Wood Pig Year	1875	1935	1995	2055		42.	乙巳 (Yi Si) Wood Snake Year	1905	1965	2025	2085
13.	丙子 (Bing Zi) Fire Rat Year	1876	1936	1996	2056		43.	丙午 (Bing Wu) Fire Horse Year	1906	1966	2026	2086
14.	丁丑 (Ding Chou) Fire Ox Year	1877	1937	1997	2057		44.	丁未 (Ding Wei) Fire Goat Year	1907	1967	2027	2087
15.	戊寅 (Wu Yin) Earth Tiger Year	1878	1938	1998	2058		45.	戊申 (Wu Shen) Earth Monkey Year	1908	1968	2028	2088
16.	己卯 (Ji Mao) Earth Rabbit Year	1879	1939	1999	2059		46.	己酉 (Ji You) Earth Rooster Year	1909	1969	2029	2089
17.	庚辰 (Geng Chen) Metal Dragon Year	1880	1940	2000	2060		47.	庚戌 (Geng Xu) Metal Dog Year	1910	1970	2030	2090
18.	辛巳 (Xin Si) Metal Snake Year	1881	1941	2001	2061		48.	辛亥 (Xin Hai) Metal Pig Year	1911	1971	2031	2091
19.	壬午 (Ren Wu) Water Horse Year	1882	1942	2002	2062		49.	壬子 (Ren Zi) Water Rat Year	1912	1972	2032	2092
20.	癸未 (Gui Wei) Water Goat Year	1883	1943	2003	2063		50.	癸丑 (Gui Chou) Water Ox Year	1913	1973	2033	2093
21.	甲申 (Jia Shen) Wood Monkey Year	1884	1944	2004	2064		51.	甲寅 (Jia Yin) Wood Tiger Year	1914	1974	2034	2094
22.	乙酉 (Yi You) Wood Rooster Year	1885	1945	2005	2065		52.	乙卯 (Yi Mao) Wood Rabbit Year	1915	1975	2035	2095
23.	丙戌 (Bing Xu) Fire Dog Year	1886	1946	2006	2066		53.	丙辰 (Bing Chen) Fire Dragon Year	1916	1976	2036	2096
24.	丁亥 (Ding Hai) Fire Pig Year	1887	1947	2007	2067		54.	丁巳 (Ding Si) Fire Snake Year	1917	1977	2037	2097
25.	戊子 (Wu Zi) Earth Rat Year	1888	1948	2008	2068		55.	戊午 (Wu Wu) Earth Horse Year	1918	1978	2038	2098
26.	己丑 (Ji Chou) Earth Ox Year	1889	1949	2009	2069		56.	己未 (Ji Wei) Earth Goat Year	1919	1979	2039	2099
27.	庚寅 (Geng Yin) Metal Tiger Year	1890	1950	2010	2070		57.	庚申 (Geng Shen) Metal Monkey Year	1920	1980	2040	2100
28.	辛卯 (Xin Mao) Metal Rabbit Year	1891	1951	2011	2071		58.	辛酉 (Xin You) Metal Rooster Year	1921	1981	2041	2101
29.	壬辰 (Ren Chen) Water Dragon Year	1892	1952	2012	2072		59.	壬戌 (Ren Xu) Water Dog Year	1922	1982	2042	2102
30.	癸巳 (Gui Si) Water Snake Year	1893	1953	2013	2073		60.	癸亥 (Gui Hai) Water Pig Year	1923	1983	2043	2103

About The Chinese Metaphysics Reference Series

Reference Series

The Chinese Metaphysics Reference Series of books are designed primarily to be used as complimentary textbooks for scholars, students, researchers, teachers and practitioners of Chinese Metaphysics.

The goal is to provide quick easy reference tables, diagrams and charts, facilitating the study and practice of various Chinese Metaphysics subjects including Feng Shui, BaZi, Yi Jing, Zi Wei, Liu Ren, Ze Ri, Ta Yi, Qi Men and Mian Xiang.

This series of books are intended as <u>reference text and educational materials</u> principally for the academic syllabuses of the **Mastery Academy of Chinese Metaphysics**. The contents have also been formatted so that Feng Shui Masters and other teachers of Chinese Metaphysics will always have a definitive source of reference at hand, when teaching or applying their art.

Because each school of Chinese Metaphysics is different, the Reference Series of books usually do not contain any specific commentaries, application methods or explanations on the theory behind the formulas presented in its contents. This is to ensure that the contents can be used freely and independently by all Feng Shui Masters and teachers of Chinese Metaphysics without conflict.

If you would like to study or learn the applications of any of the formulas presented in the Reference Series of books, we recommend that you undertake the courses offered by Joey Yap and his team of Instructors at the Mastery Academy of Chinese Metaphysics.

Titles offers in the Reference Series:

1. The Chinese Metaphysics Compendium
2. Dong Gong Date Selection
3. Earth Study Discern Truth
4. Xuan Kong Da Gua Structure Reference Book
5. San Yuan Dragon Gate Eight Formations Water Method
6. Xuan Kong Da Gua Ten Thousand Year Calendar
7. Plum Blossom Divination Reference Book
8. The Date Selection Compendium (Book 1) - The 60 Jia Zi Attributes
9. The Date Selection Compendium (Book 2) - The Month, Day and Hourly Stars

Preface

The idea of this book came about when I was thinking about the current state of Date Selection research. For the person keen on learning and discovering more information on the subject, the selection of traditional source materials available presents a vast and mind-boggling array of choices. Some of the key traditional texts that are commonly-used include *Guo Lao Astronomy* (*Gou Lao Xing Cong* 果老星宗), *The Tome of Heaven & Earth* (*Qian Kun Bao Dian* 乾坤寶典), *The Heavenly Precious Calendar* (*Tian Bao Li* 天寶曆), *The Broad Saint Calendar* (*Guang Sheng Li* 廣聖曆), *The Central Spirit Classics* (*Shen Qu Jing* 神樞經), and the Dong Gong text on Date Selection. That's a lot of books right there!

The central text that has become the definitive traditional reference on Date Selection, however, is *The Book of Unifying Times & Discerning Dimensions* (*Xie Ji Bian Fang Shu* 協紀辨方書). This epic tome was commissioned by the renowned emperor of the Qing Dynasty, Qian Long (1711 – 1799). Due to its comprehensiveness, it is the one traditional text serious Date Selection practitioners and specialists have turned to since the time it was written!

Suffice to say, it has had a significant impact on the study and practice of Date Selection, and will continue to do so. But it is often a difficult and confusing process to search for something within the book, as the information is presented in a somewhat disorderly manner. This is compounded by the fact that most people have to go back and forth between several of these traditional texts, making the process an even more bewildering one – especially for those who are just starting out in Date Selection studies.

The seeds of this book were also sown during my Date Selection classes, where for the sake of easier edification to my students I had to compile most of this information into tables and charts. I received a favourable response from them, as they found the material easier to follow when it was presented as such. In that sense, I thought that if it could benefit my students and facilitate their understanding on Date Selection, then it could do the same for others. So I improved on the existing compilation of information and developed it further to transform it into the book you're having in your hands right now.

I compiled everything based on the Year, Month, Day and Hour Pillars to make it easier for the reader and researcher without having to cross-reference between so many books and sources that can make it sometimes quite impossible to do a proper process of Date Selection. However, it was also impossible to put all this information into one single book! Hence, the idea of coming up with two books arose, with this being the Date Selection Compendium Book 1, focusing solely on the Annual Stars for the 60 Jia Zi (Year Pillars).

However, it is important to bear in mind that even though it's based on the Year Pillar, it's not *only* directly relevant to the current and upcoming years. You can just as comfortably use this book to refer to events that took place in the past, such as for astrological purposes

that entails looking for Auxiliary Stars and Directional and Location-based Stars that have influenced a certain birth date or location in the past. In that sense, this book serves as a reference point not only for looking forward to the future, but as a means of looking back at previous periods of time and understanding what went on in those times.

As this book was primarily designed for my ZeRi Mastery Series (Date Selection) classes and its content meant to facilitate our teachings and complement our existing syllabus, it is highly recommended that you attend the class. However, any good, qualified teacher on Date Selection can guide you in your studies and research, and indeed it will be best to use this book with some expert guidance if you are new to Date Selection studies and practice.

Date Selection is a vital but highly-underrated and often overlooked component of many branches of Chinese Metaphysics, particularly Feng Shui and BaZi. It is a factor that activates or deactivates a Feng Shui setup, or puts in motion the hidden talents in your astrology chart. In essence, if you know and understand your Feng Shui or BaZi, but do not have the all-important switch to turn things on or off, you will miss out on a crucial chunk of your practice and studies. Hence, it becomes clear why Date Selection is the key to making your Feng Shui or Astrology practice and studies work.

To that end, I hope that you find this book a useful reference for your practice and studies of Date Selection, and a starting point that sets you off on many hours of pleasurable and absorbing research. All the best in your pursuit of further knowledge!

Warm regards,

Joey Yap
November 2008

Author's personal website: www.joeyyap.com | www.fengshuilogy.com (Personal blog)
Academy website: www.masteryacademy.com | www.masteryjournal.com | www.maelearning.com

MASTERY ACADEMY
OF CHINESE METAPHYSICS™

At **www.masteryacademy.com**, you will find some useful tools to ascertain key information about the Feng Shui of a property or for the study of Astrology.

The Joey Yap Flying Stars Calculator can be utilised to plot your home or office Flying Stars chart. To find out your personal best directions, use the 8 Mansions Calculator. To learn more about your personal Destiny, you can use the Joey Yap BaZi Ming Pan Calculator to plot your Four Pillars of Destiny – you just need to have your date of birth (day, month, year) and time of birth.

For more information about BaZi, Xuan Kong or Flying Star Feng Shui, or if you wish to learn more about these subjects with Joey Yap, logon to the Mastery Academy of Chinese Metaphysics website at **www.masteryacademy.com.**

MASTERY ACADEMY
E-LEARNING CENTER
www.maelearning.com

www.maelearning.com

Bookmark this address on your computer, and visit this newly-launched website today. With the E-Learning Center, knowledge of Chinese Metaphysics is a mere 'click' away!

Our E-Learning Center consists of 3 distinct components.

1. Online Courses
These shall comprise of 3 Programs: our Online Feng Shui Program, Online BaZi Program, and Online Mian Xiang Program. Each lesson contains a video lecture, slide presentation and downloadable course notes.

2. MA Live!
With MA Live!, Joey Yap's workshops, tutorials, courses and seminars on various Chinese Metaphysics subjects broadcasted right to your computer screen. Better still, participants will not only get to see and hear Joey talk 'live', but also get to engage themselves directly in the event and more importantly, TALK to Joey via the MA Live! interface. All the benefits of a live class, minus the hassle of actually having to attend one!

3. Video-On-Demand (VOD)
Get immediate streaming-downloads of the Mastery Academy's wide range of educational DVDs, right on your computer screen. No more shipping costs and waiting time to be incurred!

Study at your own pace, and interact with your Instructor and fellow students worldwide… at your own convenience and privacy. With our E-Learning Center, knowledge of Chinese Metaphysics is brought DIRECTLY to you in all its clarity, with illustrated presentations and comprehensive notes expediting your learning curve!

Welcome to the Mastery Academy's E-LEARNING CENTER…YOUR virtual gateway to Chinese Metaphysics mastery!

Using the Date Selection Compendium (Book 1)
The 60 Jia Zi Attributes

Welcome to another extraordinary compilation of Chinese Metaphysics knowledge, the Compendium for Date Selection. Essentially used for the study of Date Selection (ZeRi), the information available here is the cumulative essence extracted primarily from the 'Book of Unifying Times & Discerning Dimensions' (Xie Ji Bian Fang Shu 協 紀辨方書), a tome commissioned by Emperor Qian Long during the Qing Dynasty. The contents of this important book include planetary positions and movements, stars and constellations, and their correlation to earthly events.

Supporting crucial information used in this Compendium is also extracted from the following ZeRi classics: 'Guo Lao Astronomy' (果老星宗), 'Tome of Heaven & Earth' (乾 坤寶典), and 'Heavenly Precious Calendar' (天寶曆). The goal of the Compendium is to collect as well as to organize the wealth of information that is available from these classics.

Using the Date Selection Compendium starts with the intention or objective of the practitioner: 'What kind of information do you need?'

The collection of information is categorized under the '60 Jia Zi' (六十甲子), arranged in chapters according to their respective Stem Groups, and each chapter can be used for the following purposes:
- Date Selection (ZeRi)
    1. Year based (Location based) Date Selection
    2. Month based Date Selection
- BaZi Astrology
- Qi Men Dun Jia

At the start of each Jia Zi section, the general information for that year is presented:
- Heavenly Stem
- Earthly Branch
- Hidden Stem
- Na Yin (Harmonic Melody)
- Grand Duke
- Xuan Kong Element
- Year Hexagram
- Xuan Kong Period Luck

This is followed by information regarding the year with its corresponding locations, such as:

- Annual Positive Stars for Opening Mountain, Establishing Facing, and Commencing Repairs
- Annual Negative Stars for Opening Mountain, Establishing Facing, and Commencing Repairs
- Annual San Yuan Purple White Stars
- Mountain Covering Yellow Path
- Four Advantages Three Cycles
- And many more

The second half of each Jia Zi section is followed by Month based information, such as:

- Positive Auxiliary Stars (12 Months)
- Negative Auxiliary Stars (12 Months)
- Monthly Purple White Stars
- Qi Men Three Nobles
- Monthly Negative Sectors (Renovation)

The monthly Auxiliary Stars (Shen Sha 神煞) are non-location based, and used primarily for Personal Date Selection purposes. For example: marriage, starting a new business, ground-breaking, burial, and other events of significant importance.

As this Date Selection Compendium is meant to function as a reference guide or teaching aid, it does not instruct on the science and application of Date Selection – for which a proper class and teacher becomes necessary to understand the how's, when's and why's of Date Selection.

甲子 (Jia Zi)
Wood Rat

甲子 (Jia Zi) Wood Rat

Heavenly Stem 天干	甲 **Yang Wood (陽木)**
Earthly Branch 地支	子 **Rat (Yang Water 陽水)**
Hidden Stem 藏干	癸 **Yin Water**
Na Yin 納音	海中金 **Water from the sea**
Grand Duke 太歲	子 **Rat**
Xuan Kong Five Element 玄空五行	1 水 **Water**
Gua Name 卦名	坤爲地 **Earth**
Xuan Kong Period Luck 玄空卦運	1

Annual Positive Stars for Opening Mountain, Establishing Facing and Commencing Repairs 開山立向修方吉星：

歲德 **Duke Virtue**	甲 *Jia* Yang Wood	
歲德合 **Duke Virtue Combo**	己 *Ji* Yin Earth	
歲枝德 **Duke Branch Virtue**	巳 *Si* Snake	
陽貴人 **Yang Nobleman**	未 *Wei* Goat	
陰貴人 **Yin Nobleman**	丑 *Chou* Ox	
歲祿 **Duke Prosperous**	寅 *Yin* Tiger	
歲馬 **Duke Horse**	寅 *Yin* Tiger	
奏書 **Decree**	乾 *Qian*	
博士 **Professor**	巽 *Xun*	

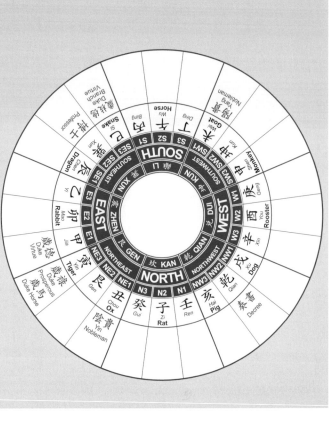

2

Annual Negative Stars for Opening Mountain, Establishing Facing and Commencing Repairs 開山立向修方凶星：

太歲 Grand Duke	歲破 Year Breaker	三煞 Three Killings			坐煞向煞 Sitting Sha Facing Sha				浮天空亡 Floating Heaven Emptiness	
子 Zi Rat	午 Wu Horse	巳 Si Snake	午 Wu Horse	未 Wei Goat	丙 Bing Yang Fire	丁 Ding Yin Fire	壬 Ren Yang Water	癸 Gui Yin Water	離 Li	壬 Ren Yang Water

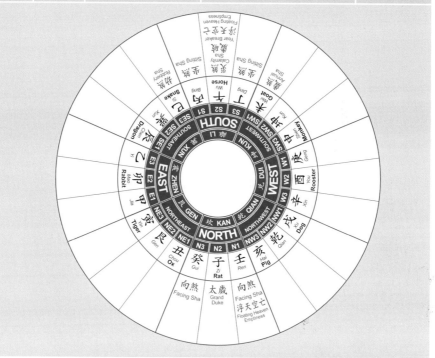

Annual San Yuan Purple White Stars 三元紫白九星：

上元 Upper Period Period 1, 2, 3	中元 Middle Period Period 4, 5, 6	下元 Lower Period Period 7, 8, 9

上元 Upper Period — Period 1, 2, 3

巽SE	離S	坤SW
9	5	7
震E 8	1 甲子 Jia Zi Wood Rat	3 兌W
4	6	2
艮NE	坎N	乾NW

中元 Middle Period — Period 4, 5, 6

巽SE	離S	坤SW
3	8	1
震E 2	4 甲子 Jia Zi Wood Rat	6 兌W
7	9	5
艮NE	坎N	乾NW

下元 Lower Period — Period 7, 8, 9

巽SE	離S	坤SW
6	2	4
震E 5	7 甲子 Jia Zi Wood Rat	9 兌W
1	3	8
艮NE	坎N	乾NW

Mountain Covering Yellow Path 蓋山黃道：

貪狼 *Tan Lang* **Greedy Wolf**				巨門 *Ju Men* **Huge Door**				武曲 *Wu Qu* **Military Arts**		文曲 *Wen Qu* **Literary Arts**	
震 *Zhen* **E2**	庚 *Geng* **W1**	亥 *Hai* **NW3**	未 *Wei* **SW1**	兌 *Dui* **W2**	丁 *Ding* **S3**	巳 *Si* **SE3**	丑 *Chou* **NE1**	巽 *Xun* **SE2**	辛 *Xin* **W3**	坤 *Kun* **SW2**	乙 *Yi* **E3**

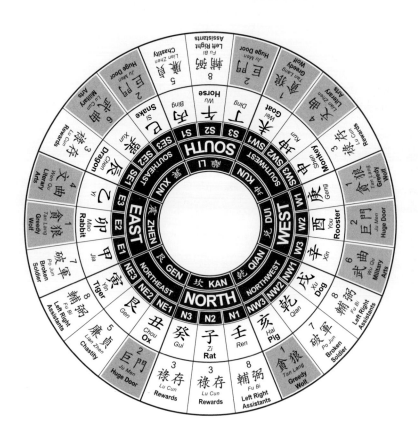

Heaven Penetrating Force 通天竅:			
三合前方 **Facing Three Harmony**	艮寅 Gen Yin	甲卯 Jia Mao	乙辰 Yi Chen
三合後方 **Sitting Three Harmony**	坤申 Kun Shen	庚酉 Geng You	辛戌 Xin Xu

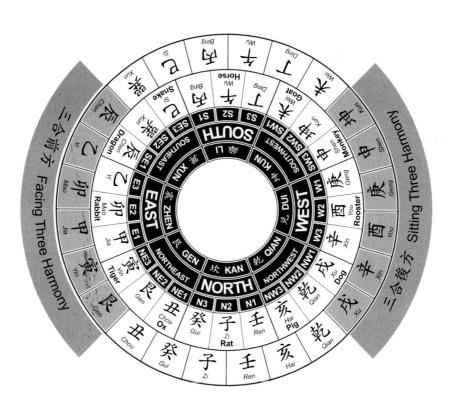

Moving Horse Six Ren Assessment 走馬六壬：					
神后 *Shen Hou* **Holy Empress**	功曹 *Gong Cao* **Marshall**	天罡 *Tian Gang* **Heavenly Dipper**	勝光 *Sheng Guang* **Subliminal Bright**	傳送 *Chuan Song* **Great General**	河魁 *He Kui* **River Scholar**
壬子 *Ren Zi*	艮寅 *Gen Yin*	乙辰 *Yi Chen*	丙午 *Bing Wu*	坤申 *Kun Shen*	辛戌 *Xin Xu*

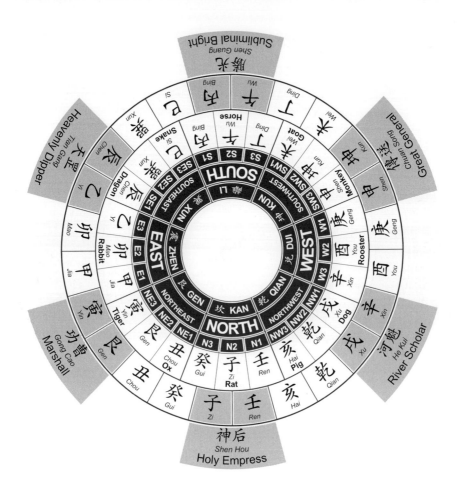

Four Advantages Three Cycles Star Plate 四利三元：

太陽 Tai Yang **Sun**	太陰 Tai Yin **Moon**	龍德 Long De **Dragon Virtue**	福德 Fu De **Fortune Virtue**
丑 Chou Ox	卯 Mao Rabbit	未 Wei Goat	酉 You Rooster

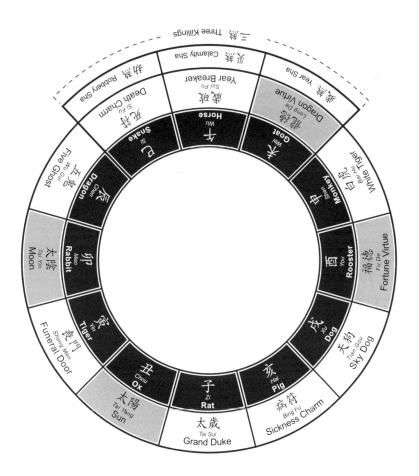

Negative Sectors For Opening Mountain 開山凶位：

年剋山家 Year Countering Sitting

甲	寅	辰	巽	戌	坎	辛	申	丑	癸	坤	庚	未
Jia	Yin	Chen	Xun	Xu	Kan	Xin	Shen	Chou	Gui	Kun	Geng	wei
E1	NE3	SE1	SE2	NW1	N2	W3	SW3	NE1	N3	SW2	W1	SW1

陰府太歲	六害	死符	灸退
Yin Fu Tai Sui	Liu Hai	Si Fu	Zhi Tui
Yin Mansion Grand Duke	**Six Harm**	**Death Charm**	**Roasting Star**
艮寅	未	巳	卯
Gen Yin	Wei	Si	Mao
NE2 NE3	SW1	SE3	E2

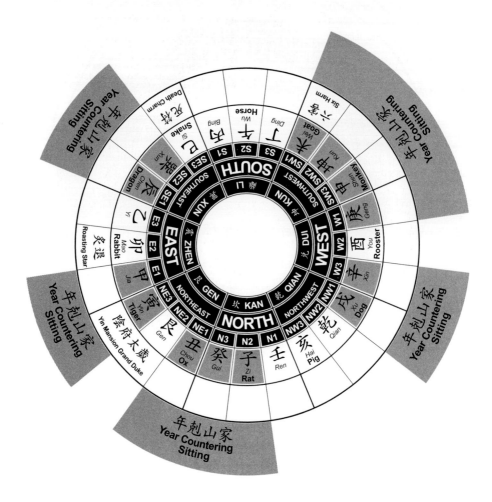

Negative Directions to Establish Facing 立向凶方：

巡山羅喉 *Xun Shan Luo Hou* **Mountain Patrol Luo Hou Star**	病符 *Bing Fu* **Sickness Charm**
癸 *Gui* **N3**	亥 *Hai* **NW3**

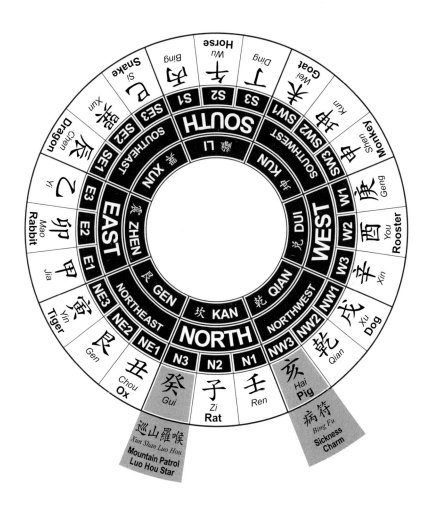

Negative Repair / Renovation Sectors Table 修方凶位表：

天官符 **Heavenly Officer Charm**	亥 *Hai* Pig	飛廉 **Flying Chaste**	申 *Shen* Monkey
地官符 **Earthly Officer Charm**	辰 *Chen* Dragon	喪門 **Funeral Door**	寅 *Yin* Tiger
大煞 **Great Sha**	子 *Zi* Rat	弔客 **Suspended Guest**	戌 *Xu* Dog
大將軍 **Big General**	酉 *You* Rooster	白虎 **White Tiger**	申 *Shen* Monkey
力士 **Strong Man**	艮 *Gen*	金神 **Golden God**	午 *Wu* Horse 未 *Wei* Goat 申 *Shen* Monkey 酉 *You* Rooster
蠶室 **Silkworm Room**	坤 *Kun*		
蠶官 **Silkworm Officer**	未 *Wei* Goat		
蠶命 **Silkworm Life**	申 *Shen* Monkey		
歲刑 **Duke Punishment**	卯 *Mao* Rabbit	獨火 **Lonely Fire**	艮 *Gen*
黃幡 **Yellow Flag**	辰 *Chen* Dragon	五鬼 **Five Ghost**	辰 *Chen* Dragon
豹尾 **Leopard Tail**	戌 *Xu* Dog	破敗五鬼 **Destructive Five Ghost**	巽 *Xun*

Negative Repair / Renovation Sectors Diagram 修方凶位圖：

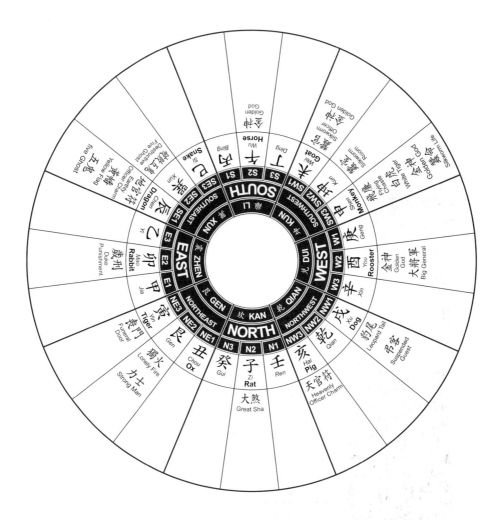

12-Month Auxiliary Stars Reference Table :
甲子年十二月，開山立向修方星表

Positive Monthly Stars 吉星方

月 **MONTH**	寅 **Tiger** (Feb 4 - Mar 5) 正月 **1st Month**	卯 **Rabbit** (Mar 6 - Apr 4) 二月 **2nd Month**	辰 **Dragon** (Apr 5 - May 5) 三月 **3rd Month**	巳 **Snake** (May 6 - Jun 5) 四月 **4th Month**	午 **Horse** (Jun 6 - July 6) 五月 **5th Month**	未 **Goat** (July 7 - Aug 7) 六月 **6th Month**
天道 **Heavenly Path**	南 South	西南 Southwest	北 North	西 West	西北 Northwest	東 East
天德 **Heavenly Virtue**	丁 Ding Yin Fire	坤 Kun (申)	壬 Ren Yang Water	辛 Xin Yin Metal	乾 Qian (亥)	甲 Jia Yang Wood
天德合 **Heavenly Virtue Combo**	壬 Ren Yang Water	(巳)	丁 Ding Yin Fire	丙 Bing Yang Fire	(寅)	己 Ji Yin Earth
月德 **Monthly Virtue**	丙 Bing Yang Fire	甲 Jia Yang Wood	壬 Ren Yang Water	庚 Geng Yang Metal	丙 Bing Yang Fire	甲 Jia Yang Wood
月德合 **Monthly Virtue Combo**	辛 Xin Yin Metal	己 Ji Yin Earth	丁 Ding Yin Fire	乙 Yi Yin Wood	辛 Xin Yin Metal	己 Ji Yin Earth
月空 **Month Emptiness**	壬 Ren Yang Water	庚 Geng Yang Metal	丙 Bing Yang Fire	甲 Jia Yang Wood	壬 Ren Yang Water	庚 Geng Yang Metal
陽貴人 **Yang Nobleman**	坎 Kan	離 Li	艮 Gen	兌 Dui	乾 Qian	中 Middle
陰貴人 **Yin Nobleman**	兌 Dui	乾 Qian	中 Middle	巽 Xun	震 Zhen	坤 Kun
飛天祿 **Flying Heavenly Wealth**	中 Middle	坎 Kan	離 Li	艮 Gen	兌 Dui	乾 Qian
飛天馬 **Flying Heavenly Horse**	中 Middle	坎 Kan	離 Li	艮 Gen	兌 Dui	乾 Qian

12-Month Auxiliary Stars Reference Table :
甲子年十二月，開山立向修方星表

申 Monkey (Aug 8 - Sept 7) 七月 7th Month	酉 Rooster (Sept 8 - Oct 7) 八月 8th Month	戌 Dog (Oct 8 - Nov 6) 九月 9th Month	亥 Pig (Nov 7 - Dec 6) 十月 10th Month	子 Rat (Dec 7 - Jan 5) 十一月 11th Month	丑 Ox (Jan 6 - Feb 3) 十二月 12th Month	月 MONTH
北 North	東北 Northeast	南 South	東 East	東南 Southeast	西 West	天道 Heavenly Path
癸 Gui Yin Water	艮 Gen (寅)	丙 Bing Yang Fire	乙 Yi Yin Wood	巽 Xun (巳)	庚 Geng Yang Metal	天德 Heavenly Virtue
戊 Wu Yang Earth	(亥)	辛 Xin Yin Metal	庚 Geng Yang Metal	(申)	乙 Yi Yin Wood	天德合 Heavenly Virtue Combo
壬 Ren Yang Water	庚 Geng Yang Metal	丙 Bing Yang Fire	甲 Jia Yang Wood	壬 Ren Yang Water	庚 Geng Yang Metal	月德 Monthly Virtue
丁 Ding Yin Fire	乙 Yi Yin Wood	辛 Xin Yin Metal	己 Ji Yin Earth	丁 Ding Yin Fire	乙 Yi Yin Wood	月德合 Monthly Virtue Combo
丙 Bing Yang Fire	甲 Jia Yang Wood	壬 Ren Yang Water	庚 Geng Yang Metal	丙 Bing Yang Fire	甲 Jia Yang Wood	月空 Month Emptiness
坎 Kan	離 Li	艮 Gen	兌 Dui	乾 Qian	中 Middle	陽貴人 Yang Nobleman
坎 Kan	離 Li	艮 Gen	兌 Dui	乾 Qian	中 Middle	陰貴人 Yin Nobleman
中 Middle	巽 Xun	震 Zhen	坤 Kun	坎 Kan	離 Li	飛天祿 Flying Heavenly Wealth
中 Middle	巽 Xun	震 Zhen	坤 Kun	坎 Kan	離 Li	飛天馬 Flying Heavenly Horse

Monthly Purple White Stars 月紫白九星 :

寅 Tiger (Feb 4 - Mar 5) 正月 1st Month

巽 SE	離 S	坤 SW
7 Red 七赤	3 Jade 三碧	5 Yellow 五黄
震 E — 6 White 六白	8 White 八白	1 White 一白 — 兌 W
2 Black 二黑	4 Green 四綠	9 Purple 九紫
艮 NE	坎 N	乾 NW

卯 Rabbit (Mar 6 - Apr 4) 二月 2nd Month

巽 SE	離 S	坤 SW
6 White 六白	2 Black 二黑	4 Green 四綠
震 E — 5 Yellow 五黄	7 Red 七赤	9 Purple 九紫 — 兌 W
1 White 一白	3 Jade 三碧	8 White 八白
艮 NE	坎 N	乾 NW

辰 Dragon (Apr 5 - May 5) 三月 3rd Month

巽 SE	離 S	坤 SW
5 Yellow 五黄	1 White 一白	3 Jade 三碧
震 E — 4 Green 四綠	6 White 六白	8 White 八白 — 兌 W
9 Purple 九紫	2 Black 二黑	7 Red 七赤
艮 NE	坎 N	乾 NW

巳 Snake (May 6 - Jun 5) 四月 4th Month

巽 SE	離 S	坤 SW
4 Green 四綠	9 Purple 九紫	2 Black 二黑
震 E — 3 Jade 三碧	5 Yellow 五黄	7 Red 七赤 — 兌 W
8 White 八白	1 White 一白	6 White 六白
艮 NE	坎 N	乾 NW

午 Horse (Jun 6 - July 6) 五月 5th Month

巽 SE	離 S	坤 SW
3 Jade 三碧	8 White 八白	1 White 一白
震 E — 2 Black 二黑	4 Green 四綠	6 White 六白 — 兌 W
7 Red 七赤	9 Purple 九紫	5 Yellow 五黄
艮 NE	坎 N	乾 NW

未 Goat (July 7 - Aug 7) 六月 6th Month

巽 SE	離 S	坤 SW
2 Black 二黑	7 Red 七赤	9 Purple 九紫
震 E — 1 White 一白	3 Jade 三碧	5 Yellow 五黄 — 兌 W
6 White 六白	8 White 八白	4 Green 四綠
艮 NE	坎 N	乾 NW

申 Monkey (Aug 8 - Sept 7) 七月 7th Month

巽 SE	離 S	坤 SW
1 White 一白	6 White 六白	8 White 八白
震 E — 9 Purple 九紫	2 Black 二黑	4 Green 四綠 — 兌 W
5 Yellow 五黄	7 Red 七赤	3 Jade 三碧
艮 NE	坎 N	乾 NW

酉 Rooster (Sept 8 - Oct 7) 八月 8th Month

巽 SE	離 S	坤 SW
9 Purple 九紫	5 Yellow 五黄	7 Red 七赤
震 E — 8 White 八白	1 White 一白	3 Jade 三碧 — 兌 W
4 Green 四綠	6 White 六白	2 Black 二黑
艮 NE	坎 N	乾 NW

戌 Dog (Oct 8 - Nov 6) 九月 9th Month

巽 SE	離 S	坤 SW
8 White 八白	4 Green 四綠	6 White 六白
震 E — 7 Red 七赤	9 Purple 九紫	2 Black 二黑 — 兌 W
3 Jade 三碧	5 Yellow 五黄	1 White 一白
艮 NE	坎 N	乾 NW

亥 Pig (Nov 7 - Dec 6) 十月 10th Month

巽 SE	離 S	坤 SW
7 Red 七赤	3 Jade 三碧	5 Yellow 五黄
震 E — 6 White 六白	8 White 八白	1 White 一白 — 兌 W
2 Black 二黑	4 Green 四綠	9 Purple 九紫
艮 NE	坎 N	乾 NW

子 Rat (Dec 7 - Jan 5) 十一月 11th Month

巽 SE	離 S	坤 SW
6 White 六白	2 Black 二黑	4 Green 四綠
震 E — 5 Yellow 五黄	7 Red 七赤	9 Purple 九紫 — 兌 W
1 White 一白	3 Jade 三碧	8 White 八白
艮 NE	坎 N	乾 NW

丑 Ox (Jan 6 - Feb 3) 十二月 12th Month

巽 SE	離 S	坤 SW
5 Yellow 五黄	1 White 一白	3 Jade 三碧
震 E — 4 Green 四綠	6 White 六白	8 White 八白 — 兌 W
9 Purple 九紫	2 Black 二黑	7 Red 七赤
艮 NE	坎 N	乾 NW

Qi Men Three Nobles 三奇 :

Three Nobles 三奇 / Seasons	乙 *Yi*	丙 *Bing*	丁 *Ding*
立春 **Coming of Spring** Feb 4 - Feb 18	艮 *Gen*	艮 *Gen*	離 *Li*
春分 **Spring Equinox** Mar 21 - Apr 4	震 *Zhen*	震 *Zhen*	巽 *Xun*
立夏 **Coming of Summer** May 6 - May 20	巽 *Xun*	巽 *Xun*	中 **Middle**
夏至 **Summer Solstice** Jun 22 - Jul 6	離 *Li*	離 *Li*	艮 *Gen*
立秋 **Coming of Autumn** Aug 8 - Aug 23	坤 *Kun*	坤 *Kun*	坎 *Kan*
秋分 **Autumn Equinox** Sept 23 - Oct 7	兌 *Dui*	兌 *Dui*	乾 *Qian*
立冬 **Coming of Winter** Nov 7 - Nov 22	乾 *Qian*	乾 *Qian*	中 **Middle**
冬至 **Winter Solstice** Dec 22 - Jan 5	坎 *Kan*	坎 *Kan*	坤 *Kun*

Sectors to Avoid Opening Mountain 開山凶位 :

月 MONTH	月建 Month Establishment	月破 Month Destruction	月剋山家 Month Countering Sitting		陰府太歲 Yin Mansion Grand Duke	
寅 Tiger (Feb 4 - Mar 5) 正月 1st Month	寅 Yin Tiger	申 Shen Monkey	乾 Qian	兌 Dui	坎 Kan	坤 Kun
卯 Rabbit (Mar 6 - Apr 4) 二月 2nd Month	卯 Mao Rabbit	酉 You Rooster	亥 Hai Pig	丁 Ding Yin Fire	乾 Qian	離 Li
辰 Dragon (Apr 5 - May 5) 三月 3rd Month	辰 Chen Dragon	戌 Xu Dog	震 Zhen	巳 Si Snake	坤 Kun	震 Zhen
巳 Snake (May 6 - Jun 5) 四月 4th Month	巳 Si Snake	亥 Hai Pig	艮 Gen		巽 Xun	艮 Gen
午 Horse (Jun 6 - July 6) 五月 5th Month	午 Wu Horse	子 Zi Rat	–		乾 Qian	兌 Dui
未 Goat (July 7 - Aug 7) 六月 6th Month	未 Wei Goat	丑 Chou Ox	–		坤 Kun	坎 Kan
申 Monkey (Aug 8 - Sept 7) 七月 7th Month	申 Shen Monkey	寅 Yin Tiger	水 Water	山 Mountain	離 Li	乾 Qian
酉 Rooster (Sept 8 - Oct 7) 八月 8th Month	酉 You Rooster	卯 Mao Rabbit	土 Earth		震 Zhen	坤 Kun
戌 Dog (Oct 8 - Nov 6) 九月 9th Month	戌 Xu Dog	辰 Chen Dragon	乾 Qian	兌 Dui	艮 Gen	巽 Xun
亥 Pig (Nov 7 - Dec 6) 十月 10th Month	亥 Hai Pig	巳 Si Snake	亥 Hai Pig	丁 Ding Yin Fire	兌 Dui	乾 Qian
子 Rat (Dec 7 - Jan 5) 十一月 11th Month	子 Zi Rat	午 Wu Horse	離 Li	丙 Bing Yang Fire	坎 Kan	坤 Kun
丑 Ox (Jan 6 - Feb 3) 十二月 12th Month	丑 Chou Ox	未 Wei Goat	壬 Ren Yang Water	乙 Yi Yin Wood	乾 Qian	離 Li

Negative Repair / Renovation Sectors 修方凶位 :

月 MONTH	天官符 Heavenly Officer Charm			地官符 Earth Officer Charm			小月建 Small Month Establishment		
寅 **Tiger** (Feb 4 - Mar 5) 正月 **1st Month**	中 Middle			庚 Geng Yang Metal	兌 Dui	辛 Xin Yin Metal	中 Middle		
卯 **Rabbit** (Mar 6 - Apr 4) 二月 **2nd Month**	辰 Chen Dragon	巽 Xun	巳 Si Snake	戌 Xu Dog	乾 Qian	亥 Hai Pig	戌 Xu Dog	乾 Qian	亥 Hai Pig
辰 **Dragon** (Apr 5 - May 5) 三月 **3rd Month**	甲 Jia Yang Wood	震 Zhen	乙 Yi Yin Wood	中 Middle			庚 Geng Yang Metal	兌 Dui	辛 Xin Yin Metal
巳 **Snake** (May 6 - Jun 5) 四月 **4th Month**	未 Wei Goat	坤 Kun	申 Shen Monkey	庚 Geng Yang Metal	兌 Dui	辛 Xin Yin Metal	丑 Chou Ox	艮 Gen	寅 Yin Tiger
午 **Horse** (Jun 6 - July 6) 五月 **5th Month**	壬 Ren Yang Water	坎 Kan	癸 Gui Yin Water	戌 Xu Dog	乾 Qian	亥 Hai Pig	丙 Bing Yang Fire	離 Li	丁 Ding Yin Fire
未 **Goat** (July 7 - Aug 7) 六月 **6th Month**	丙 Bing Yang Fire	離 Li	丁 Ding Yin Fire	中 Middle			壬 Ren Yang Water	坎 Kan	癸 Gui Yin Water
申 **Monkey** (Aug 8 - Sept 7) 七月 **7th Month**	丑 Chou Ox	艮 Gen	寅 Yin Tiger	辰 Chen Dragon	巽 Xun	巳 Si Snake	未 Wei Goat	坤 Kun	申 Shen Monkey
酉 **Rooster** (Sept 8 - Oct 7) 八月 **8th Month**	庚 Geng Yang Metal	兌 Dui	辛 Xin Yin Metal	甲 Jia Yang Wood	震 Zhen	乙 Yi Yin Wood	甲 Jia Yang Wood	震 Zhen	乙 Yi Yin Wood
戌 **Dog** (Oct 8 - Nov 6) 九月 **9th Month**	戌 Xu Dog	乾 Qian	亥 Hai Pig	未 Wei Goat	坤 Kun	申 Shen Monkey	辰 Chen Dragon	巽 Xun	巳 Si Snake
亥 **Pig** (Nov 7 - Dec 6) 十月 **10th Month**	中 Middle			壬 Ren Yang Water	坎 Kan	癸 Gui Yin Water	中 Middle		
子 **Rat** (Dec 7 - Jan 5) 十一月 **11th Month**	庚 Geng Yang Metal	兌 Dui	辛 Xin Yin Metal	丙 Bing Yang Fire	離 Li	丁 Ding Yin Fire	戌 Xu Dog	乾 Qian	辛 Xin Yin Metal
丑 **Ox** (Jan 6 - Feb 3) 十二月 **12th Month**	戌 Xu Dog	乾 Qian	亥 Hai Pig	丑 Chou Ox	艮 Gen	寅 Yin Tiger	庚 Geng Yang Metal	兌 Dui	亥 Hai Pig

Negative Repair / Renovation Sectors 修方凶位 :

月 MONTH	大月建 Big Month Establishment			飛大煞 Flying Great Sha			丙丁獨火 Bing Ding Lonely Fire	
寅 **Tiger** (Feb 4 - Mar 5) 正月 **1st Month**	丑 Chou Ox	艮 Gen	寅 Yin Tiger	戌 Xu Dog	乾 Qian	亥 Hai Pig	中 Middle	乾 Qian
卯 **Rabbit** (Mar 6 - Apr 4) 二月 **2nd Month**	庚 Geng Yang Metal	兌 Dui	辛 Xin Yin Metal	中 Middle			中 Middle	
辰 **Dragon** (Apr 5 - May 5) 三月 **3rd Month**	戌 Xu Dog	乾 Qian	亥 Hai Pig	辰 Chen Dragon	巽 Xun	巳 Si Snake	巽 Xun	中 Middle
巳 **Snake** (May 6 - Jun 5) 四月 **4th Month**		中 Middle		甲 Jia Yang Wood	震 Zhen	乙 Yi Yin Wood	震 Zhen	巽 Xun
午 **Horse** (Jun 6 - July 6) 五月 **5th Month**	辰 Chen Dragon	巽 Xun	巳 Si Snake	未 Wei Goat	坤 Kun	申 Shen Monkey	坤 Kun	震 Zhen
未 **Goat** (July 7 - Aug 7) 六月 **6th Month**	甲 Jia Yang Wood	震 Zhen	乙 Yi Yin Wood	壬 Ren Yang Water	坎 Kan	癸 Gui Yin Water	坎 Kan	坤 Kun
申 **Monkey** (Aug 8 - Sept 7) 七月 **7th Month**	未 Wei Goat	坤 Kun	申 Shen Monkey	丙 Bing Yang Fire	離 Li	丁 Ding Yin Fire	離 Li	坎 Kan
酉 **Rooster** (Sept 8 - Oct 7) 八月 **8th Month**	壬 Ren Yang Water	坎 Kan	癸 Gui Yin Water	丑 Chou Ox	艮 Gen	寅 Yin Tiger	艮 Gen	離 Li
戌 **Dog** (Oct 8 - Nov 6) 九月 **9th Month**	丙 Bing Yang Fire	離 Li	丁 Ding Yin Fire	庚 Geng Yang Metal	兌 Dui	辛 Xin Yin Metal	兌 Dui	艮 Gen
亥 **Pig** (Nov 7 - Dec 6) 十月 **10th Month**	丑 Chou Ox	艮 Gen	寅 Yin Tiger	戌 Xu Dog	乾 Qian	亥 Hai Pig	乾 Qian	兌 Dui
子 **Rat** (Dec 7 - Jan 5) 十一月 **11th Month**	庚 Geng Yang Metal	兌 Dui	辛 Xin Yin Metal	中 Middle			中 Middle	乾 Qian
丑 **Ox** (Jan 6 - Feb 3) 十二月 **12th Month**	戌 Xu Dog	乾 Qian	亥 Hai Pig	庚 Geng Yang Metal	兌 Dui	辛 Xin Yin Metal	中 Middle	

Negative Repair / Renovation Sectors 修方凶位 :

月 MONTH	月遊火 Month Wondering Fire	三煞 Monthly 3 Killings		
		劫煞 Robbery Sha	災煞 Calamity Sha	月煞 Month Sha
寅 **Tiger** (Feb 4 - Mar 5) 正月 1st Month	艮 Gen	亥 Hai **Pig**	子 Zi **Rat**	丑 Chou **Ox**
卯 **Rabbit** (Mar 6 - Apr 4) 二月 2nd Month	離 Li	申 Shen **Monkey**	酉 You **Rooster**	戌 Xu **Dog**
辰 **Dragon** (Apr 5 - May 5) 三月 3rd Month	坎 Kan	巳 Si **Snake**	午 Wu **Horse**	未 Wei **Goat**
巳 **Snake** (May 6 - Jun 5) 四月 4th Month	坤 Kun	寅 Yin **Tiger**	卯 Mao **Rabbit**	辰 Chen **Dragon**
午 **Horse** (Jun 6 - July 6) 五月 5th Month	震 Zhen	亥 Hai **Pig**	子 Zi **Rat**	丑 Chou **Ox**
未 **Goat** (July 7 - Aug 7) 六月 6th Month	巽 Xun	申 Shen **Monkey**	酉 You **Rooster**	戌 Xu **Dog**
申 **Monkey** (Aug 8 - Sept 7) 七月 7th Month	中 Middle	巳 Si **Snake**	午 Wu **Horse**	未 Wei **Goat**
酉 **Rooster** (Sept 8 - Oct 7) 八月 8th Month	乾 Qian	寅 Yin **Tiger**	卯 Mao **Rabbit**	辰 Chen **Dragon**
戌 **Dog** (Oct 8 - Nov 6) 九月 9th Month	兌 Dui	亥 Hai **Pig**	子 Zi **Rat**	丑 Chou **Ox**
亥 **Pig** (Nov 7 - Dec 6) 十月 10th Month	艮 Gen	申 Shen **Monkey**	酉 You **Rooster**	戌 Xu **Dog**
子 **Rat** (Dec 7 - Jan 5) 十一月 11th Month	離 Li	巳 Si **Snake**	午 Wu **Horse**	未 Wei **Goat**
丑 **Ox** (Jan 6 - Feb 3) 十二月 12th Month	坎 Kan	寅 Yin **Tiger**	卯 Mao **Rabbit**	辰 Chen **Dragon**

Negative Repair / Renovation Sectors 修方凶位 :

月 MONTH	月刑 Month Punishment	月害 Month Harm	月厭 Month Detest
寅 **Tiger** (Feb 4 - Mar 5) 正月 **1st Month**	巳 *Si* Snake	巳 *Si* Snake	戌 *Xu* Dog
卯 **Rabbit** (Mar 6 - Apr 4) 二月 **2nd Month**	子 *Zi* Rat	辰 *Chen* Dragon	酉 *You* Rooster
辰 **Dragon** (Apr 5 - May 5) 三月 **3rd Month**	辰 *Chen* Dragon	卯 *Mao* Rabbit	申 *Shen* Monkey
巳 **Snake** (May 6 - Jun 5) 四月 **4th Month**	申 *Shen* Monkey	寅 *Yin* Tiger	未 *Wei* Goat
午 **Horse** (Jun 6 - July 6) 五月 **5th Month**	午 *Wu* Horse	丑 *Chou* Ox	午 *Wu* Horse
未 **Goat** (July 7 - Aug 7) 六月 **6th Month**	丑 *Chou* Ox	子 *Zi* Rat	巳 *Si* Snake
申 **Monkey** (Aug 8 - Sept 7) 七月 **7th Month**	寅 *Yin* Tiger	亥 *Hai* Pig	辰 *Chen* Dragon
酉 **Rooster** (Sept 8 - Oct 7) 八月 **8th Month**	酉 *You* Rooster	戌 *Xu* Dog	卯 *Mao* Rabbit
戌 **Dog** (Oct 8 - Nov 6) 九月 **9th Month**	未 *Wei* Goat	酉 *You* Rooster	寅 *Yin* Tiger
亥 **Pig** (Nov 7 - Dec 6) 十月 **10th Month**	亥 *Hai* Pig	申 *Shen* Monkey	丑 *Chou* Ox
子 **Rat** (Dec 7 - Jan 5) 十一月 **11th Month**	卯 *Mao* Rabbit	未 *Wei* Goat	子 *Zi* Rat
丑 **Ox** (Jan 6 - Feb 3) 十二月 **12th Month**	戌 *Xu* Dog	午 *Wu* Horse	亥 *Hai* Pig

甲寅 (Jia Yin)
Wood Tiger

甲寅 (Jia Yin) Wood Tiger

Heavenly Stem 天干	甲 **Yang Wood** (陽木)
Earthly Branch 地支	寅 **Tiger** (Yang Wood 陽木)
Hidden Stem 藏干	甲 **Yang Wood**, 丙 **Yang Fire**, 戊 **Yang Earth**
Na Yin 納音	大溪水 **Water from the canal**
Grand Duke 太歲	寅 **Tiger**
Xuan Kong Five Element 玄空五行	7 火 **Fire**
Gua Name 卦名	䷾ 水火既濟 **Accomplished**
Xuan Kong Period Luck 玄空卦運	9

Annual Positive Stars for Opening Mountain, Establishing Facing and Commencing Repairs 開山立向修方吉星:

歲德 **Duke Virtue**	甲 *Jia* Yang Wood
歲德合 **Duke Virtue Combo**	己 *Ji* Yin Earth
歲枝德 **Duke Branch Virtue**	未 *Wei* Goat
陽貴人 **Yang Nobleman**	未 *Wei* Goat
陰貴人 **Yin Nobleman**	丑 *Chou* Ox
歲祿 **Duke Prosperous**	寅 *Yin* Tiger
歲馬 **Duke Horse**	申 *Shen* Monkey
奏書 **Decree**	艮 *Gen*
博士 **Professor**	坤 *Kun*

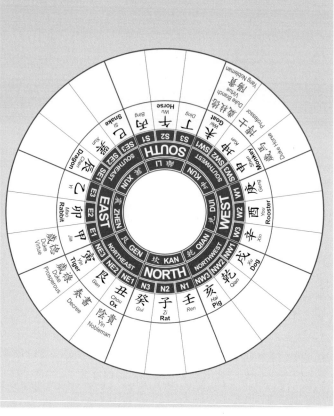

Annual Negative Stars for Opening Mountain, Establishing Facing and Commencing Repairs 開山立向修方凶星：

太歲 Grand Duke	歲破 Year Breaker	三煞 Three Killings			坐煞向煞 Sitting Sha Facing Sha				浮天空亡 Floating Heaven Emptiness	
寅 Yin Tiger	申 Shen Monkey	亥 Hai Pig	子 Zi Rat	丑 Chou Ox	壬 Ren Yang Water	癸 Gui Yin Water	丙 Bing Yang Fire	丁 Ding Yin Fire	離 Li	壬 Ren Yang Water

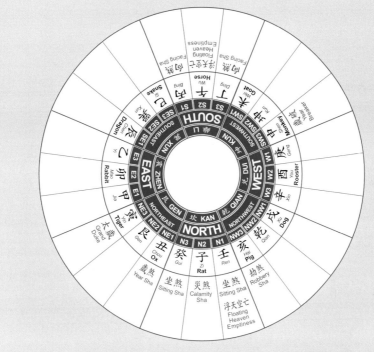

Annual San Yuan Purple White Stars 三元紫白九星：

上元 Upper Period Period 1, 2, 3			中元 Middle Period Period 4, 5, 6			下元 Lower Period Period 7, 8, 9		
巽SE	離S	坤SW	巽SE	離S	坤SW	巽SE	離S	坤SW
4	9	2	7	3	5	1	6	8
震E 3	5 甲寅 Jia Yin Wood Tiger	兌W 7	震E 6	8 甲寅 Jia Yin Wood Tiger	兌W 1	震E 9	2 甲寅 Jia Yin Wood Tiger	兌W 4
艮NE 8	坎N 1	乾NW 6	艮NE 2	坎N 4	乾NW 9	艮NE 5	坎N 7	乾NW 3

Mountain Covering Yellow Path 蓋山黃道：

貪狼 *Tan Lang* **Greedy Wolf**		巨門 *Ju Men* **Huge Door**		武曲 *Wu Qu* **Military Arts**				文曲 *Wen Qu* **Literary Arts**			
艮 *Gen* NE2	丙 *Bing* S1	巽 *Xun* SE2	辛 *Xin* W3	兌 *Dui* W2	丁 *Ding* S3	巳 *Si* SE3	丑 *Chou* NE1	離 *Li* S2	壬 *Ren* N1	寅 *Yin* NE3	戊 *Xu* NW1

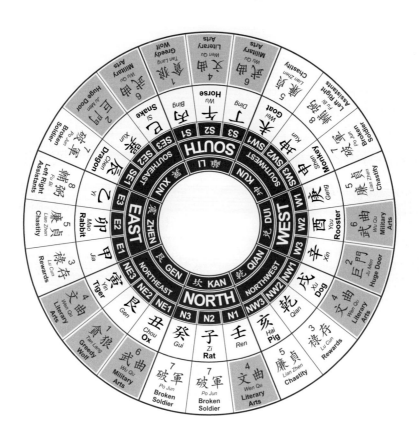

Heaven Penetrating Force 通天竅:

三合前方 **Facing Three Harmony**	坤申 Kun Shen	庚酉 Geng You	辛戌 Xin Xu
三合後方 **Sitting Three Harmony**	艮寅 Gen Yin	甲卯 Jia Mao	乙辰 Yi Chen

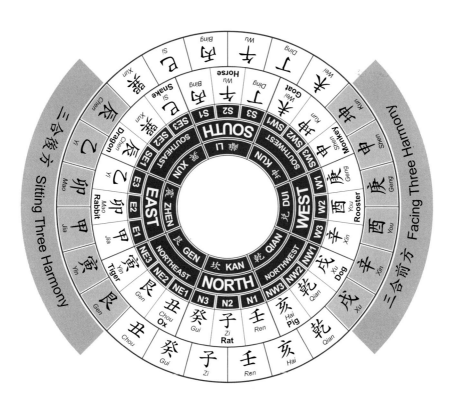

Moving Horse Six Ren Assessment 走馬六壬：

神后 Shen Hou Holy Empress	功曹 Gong Cao Marshall	天罡 Tian Gang Heavenly Dipper	勝光 Sheng Guang Subliminal Bright	傳送 Chuan Song Great General	河魁 He Kui River Scholar
辛戌 Xin Xu	壬子 Ren Zi	艮寅 Gen Yin	乙辰 Yi Chen	丙午 Bing Wu	坤申 Kun Shen

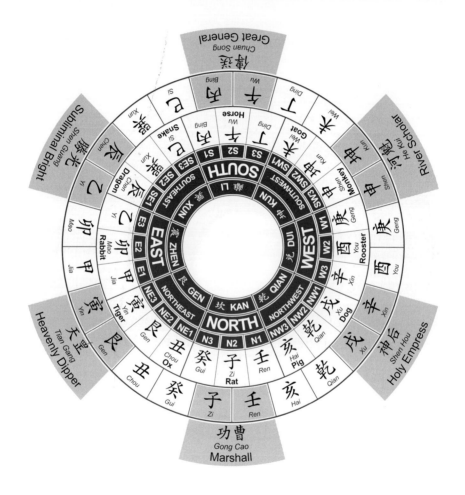

Four Advantages Three Cycles Star Plate 四利三元：

太陽 *Tai Yang* **Sun**	太陰 *Tai Yin* **Moon**	龍德 *Long De* **Dragon Virtue**	福德 *Fu De* **Fortune Virtue**
卯 *Mao* **Rabbit**	巳 *Si* **Snake**	酉 *You* **Rooster**	亥 *Hai* **Pig**

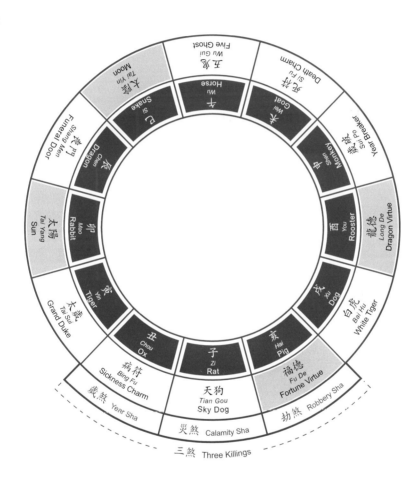

Negative Sectors For Opening Mountain 開山凶位：

年剋山家 Year Countering Sitting

離	壬	丙	乙			
Li	Ren	Bing	Yi			
S2	N1	S1	E3			

陰府太歲	六害	死符	炙退
Yin Fu Tai Sui	Liu Hai	Si Fu	Zhi Tui
Yin Mansion Grand Duke	**Six Harm**	**Death Charm**	**Roasting Star**
艮	巽	巳	未	酉
Gen	Xun	Si	Wei	You
NE2	SE2	SE3	SW1	W2

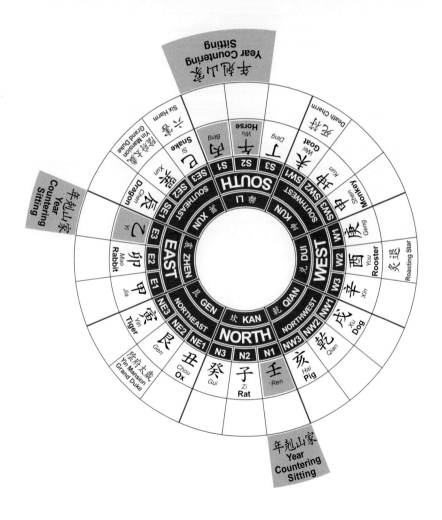

Negative Directions to Establish Facing 立向凶方：

巡山羅喉 *Xun Shan Luo Hou* **Mountain Patrol Luo Hou Star**	病符 *Bing Fu* **Sickness Charm**
甲 *Jia* **E1**	丑 *Chou* **NE1**

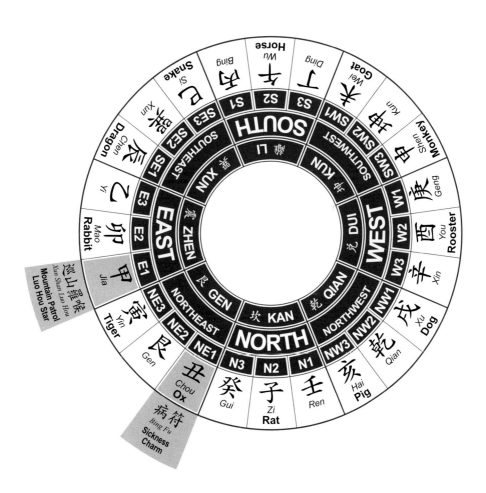

Negative Repair / Renovation Sectors Table 修方凶位表：

天官符 Heavenly Officer Charm	巳 Si Snake	飛廉 Flying Chaste	戌 Xu Dog
地官符 Earthly Officer Charm	午 Wu Horse	喪門 Funeral Door	辰 Chen Dragon
大煞 Great Sha	子 Zi Rat	弔客 Suspended Guest	子 Zi Rat
大將軍 Big General	子 Zi Rat	白虎 White Tiger	申 Shen Monkey
力士 Strong Man	巽 Xun	金神 Golden God	午 Wu Horse
蠶室 Silkworm Room	乾 Qian		未 Wei Goat
蠶官 Silkworm Officer	未 Wei Goat		申 Shen Monkey
蠶命 Silkworm Life	亥 Hai Pig		酉 You Rooster
歲刑 Duke Punishment	巳 Si Snake	獨火 Lonely Fire	震 Zhen
黃幡 Yellow Flag	戌 Xu Dog	五鬼 Five Ghost	寅 Yin Tiger
豹尾 Leopard Tail	戌 Xu Dog	破敗五鬼 Destructive Five Ghost	巽 Xun

Negative Repair / Renovation Sectors Diagram 修方凶位圖：

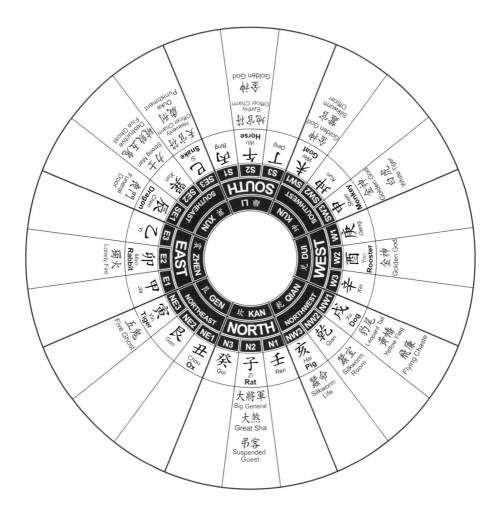

12-Month Auxiliary Stars Reference Table :
甲寅年十二月，開山立向修方星表

Positive Monthly Stars 吉星方

月 MONTH	寅 Tiger (Feb 4 - Mar 5) 正月 1st Month	卯 Rabbit (Mar 6 - Apr 4) 二月 2nd Month	辰 Dragon (Apr 5 - May 5) 三月 3rd Month	巳 Snake (May 6 - Jun 5) 四月 4th Month	午 Horse (Jun 6 - July 6) 五月 5th Month	未 Goat (July 7 - Aug 7) 六月 6th Month
天道 Heavenly Path	南 South	西南 Southwest	北 North	西 West	西北 Northwest	東 East
天德 Heavenly Virtue	丁 Ding Yin Fire	坤 Kun (申)	壬 Ren Yang Water	辛 Xin Yin Metal	乾 Qian (亥)	甲 Jia Yang Wood
天德合 Heavenly Virtue Combo	壬 Ren Yang Water	(巳)	丁 Ding Yin Fire	丙 Bing Yang Fire	(寅)	己 Ji Yin Earth
月德 Monthly Virtue	丙 Bing Yang Fire	甲 Jia Yang Wood	壬 Ren Yang Water	庚 Geng Yang Metal	丙 Bing Yang Fire	甲 Jia Yang Wood
月德合 Monthly Virtue Combo	辛 Xin Yin Metal	己 Ji Yin Earth	丁 Ding Yin Fire	乙 Yi Yin Wood	辛 Xin Yin Metal	己 Ji Yin Earth
月空 Month Emptiness	壬 Ren Yang Water	庚 Geng Yang Metal	丙 Bing Yang Fire	甲 Jia Yang Wood	壬 Ren Yang Water	庚 Geng Yang Metal
陽貴人 Yang Nobleman	坎 Kan	離 Li	艮 Gen	兌 Dui	乾 Qian	中 Middle
陰貴人 Yin Nobleman	兌 Dui	乾 Qian	中 Middle	巽 Xun	震 Zhen	坤 Kun
飛天祿 Flying Heavenly Wealth	中 Middle	坎 Kan	離 Li	艮 Gen	兌 Dui	乾 Qian
飛天馬 Flying Heavenly Horse	坤 Kun	坎 Kan	離 Li	艮 Gen	兌 Dui	乾 Qian

12-Month Auxiliary Stars Reference Table :
甲寅年十二月，開山立向修方星表

申 Monkey (Aug 8 - Sept 7) 七月 7th Month	酉 Rooster (Sept 8 - Oct 7) 八月 8th Month	戌 Dog (Oct 8 - Nov 6) 九月 9th Month	亥 Pig (Nov 7 - Dec 6) 十月 10th Month	子 Rat (Dec 7 - Jan 5) 十一月 11th Month	丑 Ox (Jan 6 - Feb 3) 十二月 12th Month	月 MONTH
北 North	東北 Northeast	南 South	東 East	東南 Southeast	西 West	天道 Heavenly Path
癸 Gui Yin Water	艮 Gen （寅）	丙 Bing Yang Fire	乙 Yi Yin Wood	巽 Xun （巳）	庚 Geng Yang Metal	天德 Heavenly Virtue
戊 Wu Yang Earth	（亥）	辛 Xin Yin Metal	庚 Geng Yang Metal	（申）	乙 Yi Yin Wood	天德合 Heavenly Virtue Combo
壬 Ren Yang Water	庚 Geng Yang Metal	丙 Bing Yang Fire	甲 Jia Yang Wood	壬 Ren Yang Water	庚 Geng Yang Metal	月德 Monthly Virtue
丁 Ding Yin Fire	乙 Yi Yin Wood	辛 Xin Yin Metal	己 Ji Yin Earth	丁 Ding Yin Fire	乙 Yi Yin Wood	月德合 Monthly Virtue Combo
丙 Bing Yang Fire	甲 Jia Yang Wood	壬 Ren Yang Water	庚 Geng Yang Metal	丙 Bing Yang Fire	甲 Jia Yang Wood	月空 Month Emptiness
坎 Kan	離 Li	艮 Gen	兌 Dui	乾 Qian	中 Middle	陽貴人 Yang Nobleman
坎 Kan	離 Li	艮 Gen	兌 Dui	乾 Qian	中 Middle	陰貴人 Yin Nobleman
中 Middle	巽 Xun	震 Zhen	坤 Kun	坎 Kan	離 Li	飛天祿 Flying Heavenly Wealth
中 Middle	坎 Kan	離 Li	艮 Gen	兌 Dui	乾 Qian	飛天馬 Flying Heavenly Horse

甲寅 (Jia Yin) Wood Tiger

Monthly Purple White Stars 月紫白九星 :

寅 Tiger (Feb 4 - Mar 5) 正月 1st Month

巽SE	離S	坤SW
1 White 一白	6 White 六白	8 White 八白
9 Purple 九紫 (震E)	2 Black 二黑	4 Green 四綠 (兌W)
5 Yellow 五黃	7 Red 七赤	3 Jade 三碧
艮NE	坎N	乾NW

卯 Rabbit (Mar 6 - Apr 4) 二月 2nd Month

巽SE	離S	坤SW
9 Purple 九紫	5 Yellow 五黃	7 Red 七赤
8 White 八白 (震E)	1 White 一白	3 Jade 三碧 (兌W)
4 Green 四綠	6 White 六白	2 Black 二黑
艮NE	坎N	乾NW

辰 Dragon (Apr 5 - May 5) 三月 3rd Month

巽SE	離S	坤SW
8 White 八白	4 Green 四綠	6 White 六白
7 Red 七赤 (震E)	9 Purple 九紫	2 Black 二黑 (兌W)
3 Jade 三碧	5 Yellow 五黃	1 White 一白
艮NE	坎N	乾NW

巳 Snake (May 6 - Jun 5) 四月 4th Month

巽SE	離S	坤SW
7 Red 七赤	3 Jade 三碧	5 Yellow 五黃
6 White 六白 (震E)	8 White 八白	1 White 一白 (兌W)
2 Black 二黑	4 Green 四綠	9 Purple 九紫
艮NE	坎N	乾NW

午 Horse (Jun 6 - July 6) 五月 5th Month

巽SE	離S	坤SW
6 White 六白	2 Black 二黑	4 Green 四綠
5 Yellow 五黃 (震E)	7 Red 七赤	9 Purple 九紫 (兌W)
1 White 一白	3 Jade 三碧	8 White 八白
艮NE	坎N	乾NW

未 Goat (July 7 - Aug 7) 六月 6th Month

巽SE	離S	坤SW
5 Yellow 五黃	1 White 一白	3 Jade 三碧
4 Green 四綠 (震E)	6 White 六白	8 White 八白 (兌W)
9 Purple 九紫	2 Black 二黑	7 Red 七赤
艮NE	坎N	乾NW

申 Monkey (Aug 8 - Sept 7) 七月 7th Month

巽SE	離S	坤SW
4 Green 四綠	9 Purple 九紫	2 Black 二黑
3 Jade 三碧 (震E)	5 Yellow 五黃	7 Red 七赤 (兌W)
8 White 八白	1 White 一白	6 White 六白
艮NE	坎N	乾NW

酉 Rooster (Sept 8 - Oct 7) 八月 8th Month

巽SE	離S	坤SW
3 Jade 三碧	8 White 八白	1 White 一白
2 Black 二黑 (震E)	4 Green 四綠	6 White 六白 (兌W)
7 Red 七赤	9 Purple 九紫	5 Yellow 五黃
艮NE	坎N	乾NW

戌 Dog (Oct 8 - Nov 6) 九月 9th Month

巽SE	離S	坤SW
2 Black 二黑	7 Red 七赤	9 Purple 九紫
1 White 一白 (震E)	3 Jade 三碧	5 Yellow 五黃 (兌W)
6 White 六白	8 White 八白	4 Green 四綠
艮NE	坎N	乾NW

亥 Pig (Nov 7 - Dec 6) 十月 10th Month

巽SE	離S	坤SW
1 White 一白	6 White 六白	8 White 八白
9 Purple 九紫 (震E)	2 Black 二黑	4 Green 四綠 (兌W)
5 Yellow 五黃	7 Red 七赤	3 Jade 三碧
艮NE	坎N	乾NW

子 Rat (Dec 7 - Jan 5) 十一月 11th Month

巽SE	離S	坤SW
9 Purple 九紫	5 Yellow 五黃	7 Red 七赤
8 White 八白 (震E)	1 White 一白	3 Jade 三碧 (兌W)
4 Green 四綠	6 White 六白	2 Black 二黑
艮NE	坎N	乾NW

丑 Ox (Jan 6 - Feb 3) 十二月 12th Month

巽SE	離S	坤SW
8 White 八白	4 Green 四綠	6 White 六白
7 Red 七赤 (震E)	9 Purple 九紫	2 Black 二黑 (兌W)
3 Jade 三碧	5 Yellow 五黃	1 White 一白
艮NE	坎N	乾NW

Qi Men Three Nobles 三奇 :

Three Nobles 三奇 / Seasons	乙 Yi	丙 Bing	丁 Ding
立春 **Coming of Spring** Feb 4 - Feb 18	巽 Xun	巽 Xun	中 **Middle**
春分 **Spring Equinox** Mar 21 - Apr 4	艮 Gen	艮 Gen	離 Li
立夏 **Coming of Summer** May 6 - May 20	離 Li	離 Li	坎 Kan
夏至 **Summer Solstice** Jun 22 - Jul 6	巽 Xun	巽 Xun	震 Zhen
立秋 **Coming of Autumn** Aug 8 - Aug 23	乾 Qian	乾 Qian	中 **Middle**
秋分 **Autumn Equinox** Sept 23 - Oct 7	坤 Kun	坤 Kun	坎 Kan
立冬 **Coming of Winter** Nov 7 - Nov 22	坎 Kan	坎 Kan	離 Li
冬至 **Winter Solstice** Dec 22 - Jan 5	乾 Qian	乾 Qian	兌 Dui

甲寅 (Jia Yin) Wood Tiger

Sectors to Avoid Opening Mountain 開山凶位 :

月 MONTH	月建 Month Establishment	月破 Month Destruction	月剋山家 Month Countering Sitting		陰府太歲 Yin Mansion Grand Duke	
寅 Tiger (Feb 4 - Mar 5) 正月 1st Month	寅 Yin Tiger	申 Shen Monkey	乾 Qian	兌 Dui	坎 Kan	坤 Kun
卯 Rabbit (Mar 6 - Apr 4) 二月 2nd Month	卯 Mao Rabbit	酉 You Rooster	亥 Hai Pig	丁 Ding Yin Fire	乾 Qian	離 Li
辰 Dragon (Apr 5 - May 5) 三月 3rd Month	辰 Chen Dragon	戌 Xu Dog	震 Zhen	巳 Si Snake	坤 Kun	震 Zhen
巳 Snake (May 6 - Jun 5) 四月 4th Month	巳 Si Snake	亥 Hai Pig	艮 Gen		巽 Xun	艮 Gen
午 Horse (Jun 6 - July 6) 五月 5th Month	午 Wu Horse	子 Zi Rat	−		乾 Qian	兌 Dui
未 Goat (July 7 - Aug 7) 六月 6th Month	未 Wei Goat	丑 Chou Ox	−		坤 Kun	坎 Kan
申 Monkey (Aug 8 - Sept 7) 七月 7th Month	申 Shen Monkey	寅 Yin Tiger	水 Water	山 Mountain	離 Li	乾 Qian
酉 Rooster (Sept 8 - Oct 7) 八月 8th Month	酉 You Rooster	卯 Mao Rabbit	土 Earth		震 Zhen	坤 Kun
戌 Dog (Oct 8 - Nov 6) 九月 9th Month	戌 Xu Dog	辰 Chen Dragon	乾 Qian	兌 Dui	艮 Gen	巽 Xun
亥 Pig (Nov 7 - Dec 6) 十月 10th Month	亥 Hai Pig	巳 Si Snake	亥 Hai Pig	丁 Ding Yin Fire	兌 Dui	乾 Qian
子 Rat (Dec 7 - Jan 5) 十一月 11th Month	子 Zi Rat	午 Wu Horse	離 Li	丙 Bing Yang Fire	坎 Kan	坤 Kun
丑 Ox (Jan 6 - Feb 3) 十二月 12th Month	丑 Chou Ox	未 Wei Goat	壬 Ren Yang Water	乙 Yi Yin Wood	乾 Qian	離 Li

Negative Repair / Renovation Sectors 修方凶位 :

月 MONTH	天官符 Heavenly Officer Charm			地官符 Earth Officer Charm			小月建 Small Month Establishment		
寅 **Tiger** (Feb 4 - Mar 5) 正月 1st Month	丑 Chou Ox	艮 Gen	寅 Yin Tiger	丙 Bing Yang Fire	離 Li	丁 Ding Yin Fire		中 Middle	
卯 **Rabbit** (Mar 6 - Apr 4) 二月 2nd Month	庚 Geng Yang Metal	兑 Dui	辛 Xin Yin Metal	丑 Chou Ox	艮 Gen	寅 Yin Tiger	戌 Xu Dog	乾 Qian	亥 Hai Pig
辰 **Dragon** (Apr 5 - May 5) 三月 3rd Month	戌 Xu Dog	乾 Qian	亥 Hai Pig	庚 Geng Yang Metal	兑 Dui	辛 Xin Yin Metal	庚 Geng Yang Metal	兑 Dui	辛 Xin Yin Metal
巳 **Snake** (May 6 - Jun 5) 四月 4th Month		中 Middle		戌 Xu Dog	乾 Qian	亥 Hai Pig	丑 Chou Ox	艮 Gen	寅 Yin Tiger
午 **Horse** (Jun 6 - July 6) 五月 5th Month	庚 Geng Yang Metal	兑 Dui	辛 Xin Yin Metal		中 Middle		丙 Bing Yang Fire	離 Li	丁 Ding Yin Fire
未 **Goat** (July 7 - Aug 7) 六月 6th Month	戌 Xu Dog	乾 Qian	亥 Hai Pig	庚 Geng Yang Metal	兑 Dui	辛 Xin Yin Metal	壬 Ren Yang Water	坎 Kan	癸 Gui Yin Water
申 **Monkey** (Aug 8 - Sept 7) 七月 7th Month		中 Middle		戌 Xu Dog	乾 Qian	亥 Hai Pig	未 Wei Goat	坤 Kun	申 Shen Monkey
酉 **Rooster** (Sept 8 - Oct 7) 八月 8th Month	辰 Chen Dragon	巽 Xun	巳 Si Snake		中 Middle		甲 Jia Yang Wood	震 Zhen	乙 Yi Yin Wood
戌 **Dog** (Oct 8 - Nov 6) 九月 9th Month	甲 Jia Yang Wood	震 Zhen	乙 Yi Yin Wood	辰 Chen Dragon	巽 Xun	巳 Si Snake	辰 Chen Dragon	巽 Xun	巳 Si Snake
亥 **Pig** (Nov 7 - Dec 6) 十月 10th Month	未 Wei Goat	坤 Kun	申 Shen Monkey	甲 Jia Yang Wood	震 Zhen	乙 Yi Yin Wood		中 Middle	
子 **Rat** (Dec 7 - Jan 5) 十一月 11th Month	壬 Ren Yang Water	坎 Kan	癸 Gui Yin Water	未 Wei Goat	坤 Kun	申 Shen Monkey	戌 Xu Dog	乾 Qian	亥 Hai Pig
丑 **Ox** (Jan 6 - Feb 3) 十二月 12th Month	丙 Bing Yang Fire	離 Li	丁 Ding Yin Fire	壬 Ren Yang Water	坎 Kan	癸 Gui Yin Water	庚 Geng Yang Metal	兑 Dui	辛 Xin Yin Metal

Negative Repair / Renovation Sectors 修方凶位 :

月 MONTH	大月建 Big Month Establishment			飛大煞 Flying Great Sha			丙丁獨火 Bing Ding Lonely Fire	
寅 Tiger (Feb 4 - Mar 5) 正月 1st Month	未 Wei Goat	坤 Kun	申 Shen Monkey	丙 Bing Yang Fire	離 Li	丁 Ding Yin Fire	中 Middle	乾 Qian
卯 Rabbit (Mar 6 - Apr 4) 二月 2nd Month	壬 Ren Yang Water	坎 Kan	癸 Gui Yin Water	丑 Chou Ox	艮 Gen	寅 Yin Tiger	中 Middle	
辰 Dragon (Apr 5 - May 5) 三月 3rd Month	丙 Bing Yang Fire	離 Li	丁 Ding Yin Fire	庚 Geng Yang Metal	兌 Dui	辛 Xin Yin Metal	巽 Xun	中 Middle
巳 Snake (May 6 - Jun 5) 四月 4th Month	丑 Chou Ox	艮 Gen	寅 Yin Tiger	戌 Xu Dog	乾 Qian	亥 Hai Pig	震 Zhen	巽 Xun
午 Horse (Jun 6 - July 6) 五月 5th Month	庚 Geng Yang Metal	兌 Dui	辛 Xin Yin Metal	中 Middle			坤 Kun	震 Zhen
未 Goat (July 7 - Aug 7) 六月 6th Month	戌 Xu Dog	乾 Qian	亥 Hai Pig	庚 Geng Yang Metal	兌 Dui	辛 Xin Yin Metal	坎 Kan	坤 Kun
申 Monkey (Aug 8 - Sept 7) 七月 7th Month	中 Middle			戌 Xu Dog	乾 Qian	亥 Hai Pig	離 Li	坎 Kan
酉 Rooster (Sept 8 - Oct 7) 八月 8th Month	辰 Chen Dragon	巽 Xun	巳 Si Snake	中 Middle			艮 Gen	離 Li
戌 Dog (Oct 8 - Nov 6) 九月 9th Month	甲 Jia Yang Wood	震 Zhen	乙 Yi Yin Wood	辰 Chen Dragon	巽 Xun	巳 Si Snake	兌 Dui	艮 Gen
亥 Pig (Nov 7 - Dec 6) 十月 10th Month	未 Wei Goat	坤 Kun	申 Shen Monkey	甲 Jia Yang Wood	震 Zhen	乙 Yi Yin Wood	乾 Qian	兌 Dui
子 Rat (Dec 7 - Jan 5) 十一月 11th Month	壬 Ren Yang Water	坎 Kan	癸 Gui Yin Water	未 Wei Goat	坤 Kun	申 Shen Monkey	中 Middle	乾 Qian
丑 Ox (Jan 6 - Feb 3) 十二月 12th Month	丙 Bing Yang Fire	離 Li	丁 Ding Yin Fire	壬 Ren Yang Water	坎 Kan	癸 Gui Yin Water	中 Middle	

Negative Repair / Renovation Sectors 修方凶位 :

月 MONTH	月遊火 Month Wondering Fire	三煞 Monthly 3 Killings		
		劫煞 Robbery Sha	災煞 Calamity Sha	月煞 Month Sha
寅 **Tiger** (Feb 4 - Mar 5) 正月 **1st Month**	震 Zhen	亥 Hai Pig	子 Zi Rat	丑 Chou Ox
卯 **Rabbit** (Mar 6 - Apr 4) 二月 **2nd Month**	巽 Xun	申 Shen Monkey	酉 You Rooster	戌 Xu Dog
辰 **Dragon** (Apr 5 - May 5) 三月 **3rd Month**	中 Middle	巳 Si Snake	午 Wu Horse	未 Wei Goat
巳 **Snake** (May 6 - Jun 5) 四月 **4th Month**	乾 Qian	寅 Yin Tiger	卯 Mao Rabbit	辰 Chen Dragon
午 **Horse** (Jun 6 - July 6) 五月 **5th Month**	兌 Dui	亥 Hai Pig	子 Zi Rat	丑 Chou Ox
未 **Goat** (July 7 - Aug 7) 六月 **6th Month**	艮 Gen	申 Shen Monkey	酉 You Rooster	戌 Xu Dog
申 **Monkey** (Aug 8 - Sept 7) 七月 **7th Month**	離 Li	巳 Si Snake	午 Wu Horse	未 Wei Goat
酉 **Rooster** (Sept 8 - Oct 7) 八月 **8th Month**	坎 Kan	寅 Yin Tiger	卯 Mao Rabbit	辰 Chen Dragon
戌 **Dog** (Oct 8 - Nov 6) 九月 **9th Month**	坤 Kun	亥 Hai Pig	子 Zi Rat	丑 Chou Ox
亥 **Pig** (Nov 7 - Dec 6) 十月 **10th Month**	震 Zhen	申 Shen Monkey	酉 You Rooster	戌 Xu Dog
子 **Rat** (Dec 7 - Jan 5) 十一月 **11th Month**	巽 Xun	巳 Si Snake	午 Wu Horse	未 Wei Goat
丑 **Ox** (Jan 6 - Feb 3) 十二月 **12th Month**	中 Middle	寅 Yin Tiger	卯 Mao Rabbit	辰 Chen Dragon

Negative Repair / Renovation Sectors 修方凶位 :

月 MONTH	月刑 Month Punishment	月害 Month Harm	月厭 Month Detest
寅 Tiger (Feb 4 - Mar 5) 正月 1st Month	巳 Si Snake	巳 Si Snake	戌 Xu Dog
卯 Rabbit (Mar 6 - Apr 4) 二月 2nd Month	子 Zi Rat	辰 Chen Dragon	酉 You Rooster
辰 Dragon (Apr 5 - May 5) 三月 3rd Month	辰 Chen Dragon	卯 Mao Rabbit	申 Shen Monkey
巳 Snake (May 6 - Jun 5) 四月 4th Month	申 Shen Monkey	寅 Yin Tiger	未 Wei Goat
午 Horse (Jun 6 - July 6) 五月 5th Month	午 Wu Horse	丑 Chou Ox	午 Wu Horse
未 Goat (July 7 - Aug 7) 六月 6th Month	丑 Chou Ox	子 Zi Rat	巳 Si Snake
申 Monkey (Aug 8 - Sept 7) 七月 7th Month	寅 Yin Tiger	亥 Hai Pig	辰 Chen Dragon
酉 Rooster (Sept 8 - Oct 7) 八月 8th Month	酉 You Rooster	戌 Xu Dog	卯 Mao Rabbit
戌 Dog (Oct 8 - Nov 6) 九月 9th Month	未 Wei Goat	酉 You Rooster	寅 Yin Tiger
亥 Pig (Nov 7 - Dec 6) 十月 10th Month	亥 Hai Pig	申 Shen Monkey	丑 Chou Ox
子 Rat (Dec 7 - Jan 5) 十一月 11th Month	卯 Mao Rabbit	未 Wei Goat	子 Zi Rat
丑 Ox (Jan 6 - Feb 3) 十二月 12th Month	戌 Xu Dog	午 Wu Horse	亥 Hai Pig

甲辰 (Jia Chen)
Wood Dragon

Heavenly Stem 天干	甲 Yang Wood (陽木)
Earthly Branch 地支	辰 Dragon (Yang Earth 陽土)
Hidden Stem 藏干	戊 Yang Earth, 乙 Yin Wood, 癸 Yin Water
Na Yin 納音	覆燈火 Fire from the lamps
Grand Duke 太歲	辰 Dragon
Xuan Kong Five Element 玄空五行	3 木 Wood
Gua Name 卦名	䷥ 火澤睽 Opposition
Xuan Kong Period Luck 玄空卦運	2

Annual Positive Stars for Opening Mountain, Establishing Facing and Commencing Repairs 開山立向修方吉星：

歲德 Duke Virtue	甲 Jia Yang Wood	
歲德合 Duke Virtue Combo	己 Ji Yin Earth	
歲枝德 Duke Branch Virtue	酉 You Rooster	
陽貴人 Yang Nobleman	未 Wei Goat	
陰貴人 Yin Nobleman	丑 Chou Ox	
歲祿 Duke Prosperous	寅 Yin Tiger	
歲馬 Duke Horse	寅 Yin Tiger	
奏書 Decree	艮 Gen	
博士 Professor	坤 Kun	

Annual Negative Stars for Opening Mountain, Establishing Facing and Commencing Repairs 開山立向修方凶星：

太歲 Grand Duke	歲破 Year Breaker	三煞 Three Killings			坐煞向煞 Sitting Sha Facing Sha				浮天空亡 Floating Heaven Emptiness	
辰 *Chen* Dragon	戌 *Xu* Dog	巳 *Si* Snake	午 *Wu* Horse	未 *Wei* Goat	丙 *Bing* Yang Fire	丁 *Ding* Yin Fire	壬 *Ren* Yang Water	癸 *Gui* Yin Water	離 *Li*	壬 *Ren* Yang Water

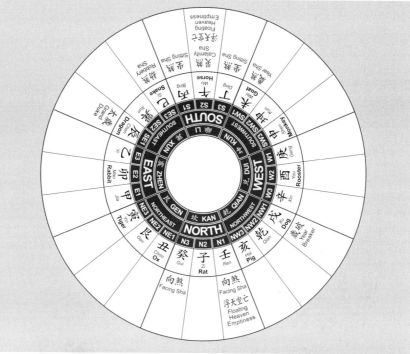

Annual San Yuan Purple White Stars 三元紫白九星：

上元 Upper Period Period 1, 2, 3			中元 Middle Period Period 4, 5, 6			下元 Lower Period Period 7, 8, 9		
巽SE **5**	離S **1**	坤SW **3**	巽SE **8**	離S **4**	坤SW **6**	巽SE **2**	離S **7**	坤SW **9**
震E **4**	**6** 甲辰 *Jia Chen* **Wood Dragon**	兑W **8**	震E **7**	**9** 甲辰 *Jia Chen* **Wood Dragon**	兑W **2**	震E **1**	**3** 甲辰 *Jia Chen* **Wood Dragon**	兑W **5**
艮NE **9**	坎N **2**	乾NW **7**	艮NE **3**	坎N **5**	乾NW **1**	艮NE **6**	坎N **8**	乾NW **4**

Mountain Covering Yellow Path 蓋山黃道：

貪狼 *Tan Lang* **Greedy Wolf**				巨門 *Ju Men* **Huge Door**				武曲 *Wu Qu* **Military Arts**		文曲 *Wen Qu* **Literary Arts**			
兌 *Dui* W2	丁 *Ding* S3	巳 *Si* SE3	丑 *Chou* NE1	震 *Zhen* E2	庚 *Geng* W1	亥 *Hai* NW3	未 *Wei* SW1	艮 *Gen* NE2	丙 *Bing* S1	坎 *Kan* N2	癸 *Gui* N3	申 *Shen* SW3	辰 *Chen* SE1

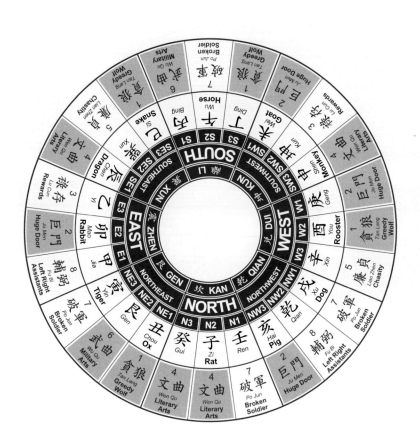

Heaven Penetrating Force 通天竅:

三合前方 Facing Three Harmony	艮寅 Gen Yin	甲卯 Jia Mao	乙辰 Yi Chen
三合後方 Sitting Three Harmony	坤申 Kun Shen	庚酉 Geng You	辛戌 Xin Xu

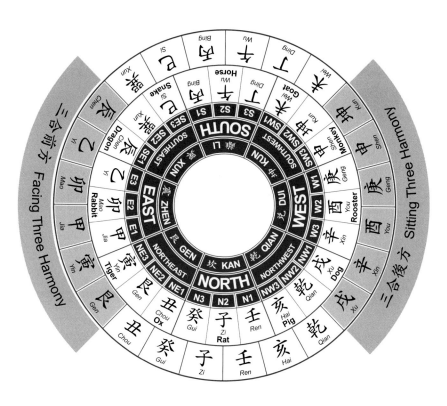

Moving Horse Six Ren Assessment 走馬六壬：

神后 Shen Hou **Holy Empress**	功曹 Gong Cao **Marshall**	天罡 Tian Gang **Heavenly Dipper**	勝光 Sheng Guang **Subliminal Bright**	傳送 Chuan Song **Great General**	河魁 He Kui **River Scholar**
坤申 Kun Shen	辛戌 Xin Xu	壬子 Ren Zi	艮寅 Gen Yin	乙辰 Yi Chen	丙午 Bing Wu

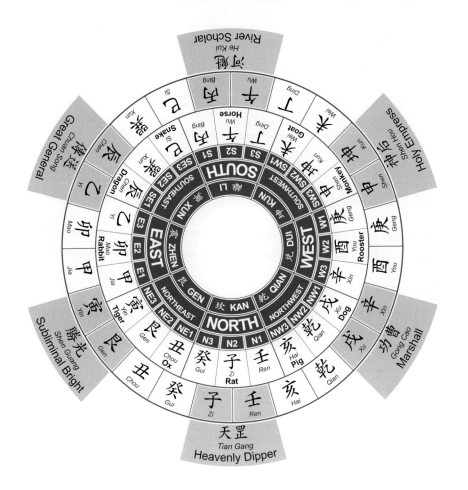

Four Advantages Three Cycles Star Plate 四利三元：

太陽 Tai Yang **Sun**	太陰 Tai Yin **Moon**	龍德 Long De **Dragon Virtue**	福德 Fu De **Fortune Virtue**
巳 Si **Snake**	未 Wei **Goat**	亥 Hai **Pig**	丑 Chou **Ox**

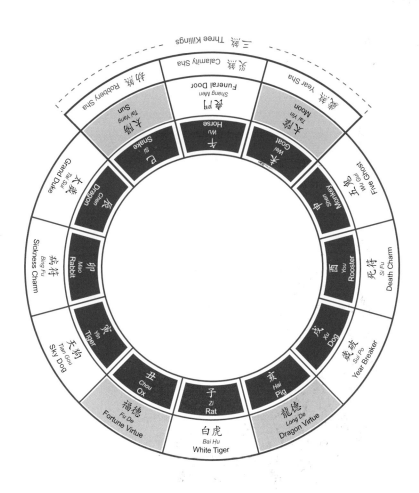

Negative Sectors For Opening Mountain 開山凶位：

年剋山家 Year Countering Sitting

乾	亥	兌	丁
Qian	*Hai*	*Dui*	*Ding*
NW2	**NW3**	**W2**	**S3**

陰府太歲 *Yin Fu Tai Sui* **Yin Mansion Grand Duke**	六害 *Liu Hai* **Six Harm**	死符 *Si Fu* **Death Charm**	炙退 *Zhi Tui* **Roasting Star**
艮 巽 *Gen* *Xun* **NE2** **SE2**	卯 *Mao* **E2**	酉 *You* **W2**	卯 *Mao* **E2**

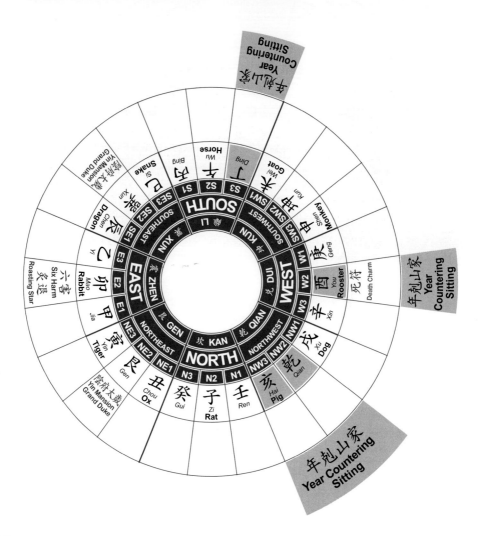

Negative Directions to Establish Facing 立向凶方：

巡山羅喉 *Xun Shan Luo Hou* **Mountain Patrol Luo Hou Star**	病符 *Bing Fu* **Sickness Charm**
巽 *Xun* **SE2**	卯 *Mao* **E2**

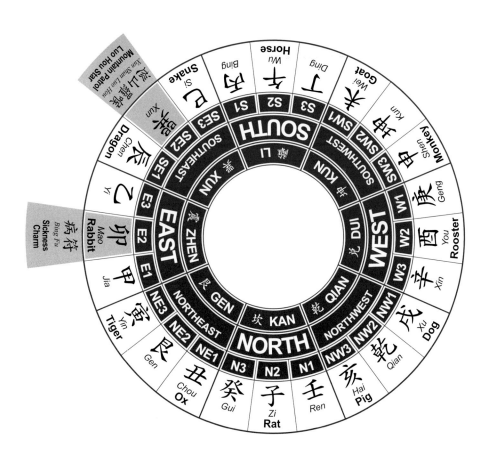

Negative Repair / Renovation Sectors Table 修方凶位表：

天官符 Heavenly Officer Charm	亥 Hai Pig	飛廉 Flying Chaste	午 Wu Horse
地官符 Earthly Officer Charm	申 Shen Monkey	喪門 Funeral Door	午 Wu Horse
大煞 Great Sha	子 Zi Rat	弔客 Suspended Guest	寅 Yin Tiger
大將軍 Big General	子 Zi Rat	白虎 White Tiger	子 Zi Rat
力士 Strong Man	巽 Xun	金神 Golden God	午 Wu Horse 未 Wei Goat 申 Shen Monkey 酉 You Rooster
蠶室 Silkworm Room	乾 Qian		
蠶官 Silkworm Officer	戌 Xu Dog		
蠶命 Silkworm Life	亥 Hai Pig		
歲刑 Duke Punishment	辰 Chen Dragon	獨火 Lonely Fire	巽 Xun
黃幡 Yellow Flag	辰 Chen Dragon	五鬼 Five Ghost	子 Zi Rat
豹尾 Leopard Tail	戌 Xu Dog	破敗五鬼 Destructive Five Ghost	巽 Xun

Negative Repair / Renovation Sectors Diagram 修方凶位圖：

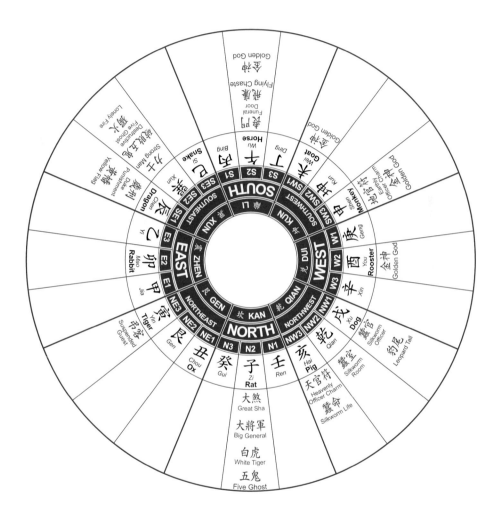

12-Month Auxiliary Stars Reference Table :
甲辰年十二月，開山立向修方星表

Positive Monthly Stars 吉星方

月 MONTH	寅 Tiger (Feb 4 - Mar 5) 正月 1st Month	卯 Rabbit (Mar 6 - Apr 4) 二月 2nd Month	辰 Dragon (Apr 5 - May 5) 三月 3rd Month	巳 Snake (May 6 - Jun 5) 四月 4th Month	午 Horse (Jun 6 - July 6) 五月 5th Month	未 Goat (July 7 - Aug 7) 六月 6th Month
天道 Heavenly Path	南 South	西南 Southwest	北 North	西 West	西北 Northwest	東 East
天德 Heavenly Virtue	丁 Ding Yin Fire	坤 Kun (申)	壬 Ren Yang Water	辛 Xin Yin Metal	乾 Qian (亥)	甲 Jia Yang Wood
天德合 Heavenly Virtue Combo	壬 Ren Yang Water	(巳)	丁 Ding Yin Fire	丙 Bing Yang Fire	(寅)	己 Ji Yin Earth
月德 Monthly Virtue	丙 Bing Yang Fire	甲 Jia Yang Wood	壬 Ren Yang Water	庚 Geng Yang Metal	丙 Bing Yang Fire	甲 Jia Yang Wood
月德合 Monthly Virtue Combo	辛 Xin Yin Metal	己 Ji Yin Earth	丁 Ding Yin Fire	乙 Yi Yin Wood	辛 Xin Yin Metal	己 Ji Yin Earth
月空 Month Emptiness	壬 Ren Yang Water	庚 Geng Yang Metal	丙 Bing Yang Fire	甲 Jia Yang Wood	壬 Ren Yang Water	庚 Geng Yang Metal
陽貴人 Yang Nobleman	坎 Kan	離 Li	艮 Gen	兌 Dui	乾 Qian	中 Middle
陰貴人 Yin Nobleman	兌 Dui	乾 Qian	中 Middle	巽 Xun	震 Zhen	坤 Kun
飛天祿 Flying Heavenly Wealth	中 Middle	坎 Kan	離 Li	艮 Gen	兌 Dui	乾 Qian
飛天馬 Flying Heavenly Horse	中 Middle	坎 Kan	離 Li	艮 Gen	兌 Dui	乾 Qian

12-Month Auxiliary Stars Reference Table :
甲辰年十二月，開山立向修方星表

申 Monkey (Aug 8 - Sept 7)	酉 Rooster (Sept 8 - Oct 7)	戌 Dog (Oct 8 - Nov 6)	亥 Pig (Nov 7 - Dec 6)	子 Rat (Dec 7 - Jan 5)	丑 Ox (Jan 6 - Feb 3)	月 MONTH
七月 7th Month	八月 8th Month	九月 9th Month	十月 10th Month	十一月 11th Month	十二月 12th Month	
北 North	東北 Northeast	南 South	東 East	東南 Southeast	西 West	天道 Heavenly Path
癸 Gui Yin Water	艮 Gen (寅)	丙 Bing Yang Fire	乙 Yi Yin Wood	巽 Xun (巳)	庚 Geng Yang Metal	天德 Heavenly Virtue
戊 Wu Yang Earth	(亥)	辛 Xin Yin Metal	庚 Geng Yang Metal	(申)	乙 Yi Yin Wood	天德合 Heavenly Virtue Combo
壬 Ren Yang Water	庚 Geng Yang Metal	丙 Bing Yang Fire	甲 Jia Yang Wood	壬 Ren Yang Water	庚 Geng Yang Metal	月德 Monthly Virtue
丁 Ding Yin Fire	乙 Yi Yin Wood	辛 Xin Yin Metal	己 Ji Yin Earth	丁 Ding Yin Fire	乙 Yi Yin Wood	月德合 Monthly Virtue Combo
丙 Bing Yang Fire	甲 Jia Yang Wood	壬 Ren Yang Water	庚 Geng Yang Metal	丙 Bing Yang Fire	甲 Jia Yang Wood	月空 Month Emptiness
坎 Kan	離 Li	艮 Gen	兌 Dui	乾 Qian	中 Middle	陽貴人 Yang Nobleman
坎 Kan	離 Li	艮 Gen	兌 Dui	乾 Qian	中 Middle	陰貴人 Yin Nobleman
中 Middle	巽 Xun	震 Zhen	坤 Kun	坎 Kan	離 Li	飛天祿 Flying Heavenly Wealth
中 Middle	巽 Xun	震 Zhen	坤 Kun	坎 Kan	離 Li	飛天馬 Flying Heavenly Horse

甲辰 (Jia Chen) Wood Dragon

Monthly Purple White Stars 月紫白九星 :

寅 Tiger (Feb 4 - Mar 5) 正月 1st Month

巽 SE	離 S	坤 SW
4 Green 四綠	9 Purple 九紫	2 Black 二黑
震 E 3 Jade 三碧	5 Yellow 五黄	7 Red 七赤 兌 W
8 White 八白	1 White 一白	6 White 六白
艮 NE	坎 N	乾 NW

卯 Rabbit (Mar 6 - Apr 4) 二月 2nd Month

巽 SE	離 S	坤 SW
3 Jade 三碧	8 White 八白	1 White 一白
震 E 2 Black 二黑	4 Green 四綠	6 White 六白 兌 W
7 Red 七赤	9 Purple 九紫	5 Yellow 五黄
艮 NE	坎 N	乾 NW

辰 Dragon (Apr 5 - May 5) 三月 3rd Month

巽 SE	離 S	坤 SW
2 Black 二黑	7 Red 七赤	9 Purple 九紫
震 E 1 White 一白	3 Jade 三碧	5 Yellow 五黄 兌 W
6 White 六白	8 White 八白	4 Green 四綠
艮 NE	坎 N	乾 NW

巳 Snake (May 6 - Jun 5) 四月 4th Month

巽 SE	離 S	坤 SW
1 White 一白	6 White 六白	8 White 八白
震 E 9 Purple 九紫	2 Black 二黑	4 Green 四綠 兌 W
5 Yellow 五黄	7 Red 七赤	3 Jade 三碧
艮 NE	坎 N	乾 NW

午 Horse (Jun 6 - July 6) 五月 5th Month

巽 SE	離 S	坤 SW
9 Purple 九紫	5 Yellow 五黄	7 Red 七赤
震 E 8 White 八白	1 White 一白	3 Jade 三碧 兌 W
4 Green 四綠	6 White 六白	2 Black 二黑
艮 NE	坎 N	乾 NW

未 Goat (July 7 - Aug 7) 六月 6th Month

巽 SE	離 S	坤 SW
8 White 八白	4 Green 四綠	6 White 六白
震 E 7 Red 七赤	9 Purple 九紫	2 Black 二黑 兌 W
3 Jade 三碧	5 Yellow 五黄	1 White 一白
艮 NE	坎 N	乾 NW

申 Monkey (Aug 8 - Sept 7) 七月 7th Month

巽 SE	離 S	坤 SW
7 Red 七赤	3 Jade 三碧	5 Yellow 五黄
震 E 6 White 六白	8 White 八白	1 White 一白 兌 W
2 Black 二黑	4 Green 四綠	9 Purple 九紫
艮 NE	坎 N	乾 NW

酉 Rooster (Sept 8 - Oct 7) 八月 8th Month

巽 SE	離 S	坤 SW
6 White 六白	2 Black 二黑	4 Green 四綠
震 E 5 Yellow 五黄	7 Red 七赤	9 Purple 九紫 兌 W
1 White 一白	3 Jade 三碧	8 White 八白
艮 NE	坎 N	乾 NW

戌 Dog (Oct 8 - Nov 6) 九月 9th Month

巽 SE	離 S	坤 SW
5 Yellow 五黄	1 White 一白	3 Jade 三碧
震 E 4 Green 四綠	6 White 六白	8 White 八白 兌 W
9 Purple 九紫	2 Black 二黑	7 Red 七赤
艮 NE	坎 N	乾 NW

亥 Pig (Nov 7 - Dec 6) 十月 10th Month

巽 SE	離 S	坤 SW
4 Green 四綠	9 Purple 九紫	2 Black 二黑
震 E 3 Jade 三碧	5 Yellow 五黄	7 Red 七赤 兌 W
8 White 八白	1 White 一白	6 White 六白
艮 NE	坎 N	乾 NW

子 Rat (Dec 7 - Jan 5) 十一月 11th Month

巽 SE	離 S	坤 SW
3 Jade 三碧	8 White 八白	1 White 一白
震 E 2 Black 二黑	4 Green 四綠	6 White 六白 兌 W
7 Red 七赤	9 Purple 九紫	5 Yellow 五黄
艮 NE	坎 N	乾 NW

丑 Ox (Jan 6 - Feb 3) 十二月 12th Month

巽 SE	離 S	坤 SW
2 Black 二黑	7 Red 七赤	9 Purple 九紫
震 E 1 White 一白	3 Jade 三碧	5 Yellow 五黄 兌 W
6 White 六白	8 White 八白	4 Green 四綠
艮 NE	坎 N	乾 NW

54

Qi Men Three Nobles 三奇 :

Three Nobles 三奇 / Seasons	乙 Yi	丙 Bing	丁 Ding
立春 **Coming of Spring** Feb 4 - Feb 18	震 Zhen	震 Zhen	巽 Xun
春分 **Spring Equinox** Mar 21 - Apr 4	兌 Dui	兌 Dui	艮 Gen
立夏 **Coming of Summer** May 6 - May 20	艮 Gen	艮 Gen	離 Li
夏至 **Summer Solstice** Jun 22 - Jul 6	中 **Middle**	中 **Middle**	巽 Xun
立秋 **Coming of Autumn** Aug 8 - Aug 23	兌 Dui	兌 Dui	乾 Qian
秋分 **Autumn Equinox** Sept 23 - Oct 7	震 Zhen	震 Zhen	坤 Kun
立冬 **Coming of Winter** Nov 7 - Nov 22	坤 Kun	坤 Kun	坎 Kan
冬至 **Winter Solstice** Dec 22 - Jan 5	中 **Middle**	中 **Middle**	乾 Qian

Sectors to Avoid Opening Mountain 開山凶位 :

月 MONTH	月建 Month Establishment	月破 Month Destruction	月剋山家 Month Countering Sitting		陰府太歲 Yin Mansion Grand Duke	
寅 Tiger (Feb 4 - Mar 5) 正月 1st Month	寅 Yin Tiger	申 Shen Monkey	乾 Qian	兌 Dui	坎 Kan	坤 Kun
卯 Rabbit (Mar 6 - Apr 4) 二月 2nd Month	卯 Mao Rabbit	酉 You Rooster	亥 Hai Pig	丁 Ding Yin Fire	乾 Qian	離 Li
辰 Dragon (Apr 5 - May 5) 三月 3rd Month	辰 Chen Dragon	戌 Xu Dog	震 Zhen	巳 Si Snake	坤 Kun	震 Zhen
巳 Snake (May 6 - Jun 5) 四月 4th Month	巳 Si Snake	亥 Hai Pig	艮 Gen		巽 Xun	艮 Gen
午 Horse (Jun 6 - July 6) 五月 5th Month	午 Wu Horse	子 Zi Rat	—		乾 Qian	兌 Dui
未 Goat (July 7 - Aug 7) 六月 6th Month	未 Wei Goat	丑 Chou Ox	—		坤 Kun	坎 Kan
申 Monkey (Aug 8 - Sept 7) 七月 7th Month	申 Shen Monkey	寅 Yin Tiger	水 Water	山 Mountain	離 Li	乾 Qian
酉 Rooster (Sept 8 - Oct 7) 八月 8th Month	酉 You Rooster	卯 Mao Rabbit	土 Earth		震 Zhen	坤 Kun
戌 Dog (Oct 8 - Nov 6) 九月 9th Month	戌 Xu Dog	辰 Chen Dragon	乾 Qian	兌 Dui	艮 Gen	巽 Xun
亥 Pig (Nov 7 - Dec 6) 十月 10th Month	亥 Hai Pig	巳 Si Snake	亥 Hai Pig	丁 Ding Yin Fire	兌 Dui	乾 Qian
子 Rat (Dec 7 - Jan 5) 十一月 11th Month	子 Zi Rat	午 Wu Horse	離 Li	丙 Bing Yang Fire	坎 Kan	坤 Kun
丑 Ox (Jan 6 - Feb 3) 十二月 12th Month	丑 Chou Ox	未 Wei Goat	壬 Ren Yang Water	乙 Yi Yin Wood	乾 Qian	離 Li

Negative Repair / Renovation Sectors 修方凶位 ：

月 MONTH	天官符 Heavenly Officer Charm			地官符 Earth Officer Charm			小月建 Small Month Establishment		
寅 **Tiger** (Feb 4 - Mar 5) 正月 1st Month	中 Middle			未 *Wei* Goat	坤 *Kun*	申 *Shen* Monkey	中 Middle		
卯 **Rabbit** (Mar 6 - Apr 4) 二月 2nd Month	辰 *Chen* Dragon	巽 *Xun*	巳 *Si* Snake	壬 *Ren* Yang Water	坎 *Kan*	癸 *Gui* Yin Water	戌 *Xu* Dog	乾 *Qian*	亥 *Hai* Pig
辰 **Dragon** (Apr 5 - May 5) 三月 3rd Month	甲 *Jia* Yang Wood	震 *Zhen*	乙 *Yi* Yin Wood	丙 *Bing* Yang Fire	離 *Li*	丁 *Ding* Yin Fire	庚 *Geng* Yang Metal	兌 *Dui*	辛 *Xin* Yin Metal
巳 **Snake** (May 6 - Jun 5) 四月 4th Month	未 *Wei* Goat	坤 *Kun*	申 *Shen* Monkey	丑 *Chou* Ox	艮 *Gen*	寅 *Yin* Tiger	丑 *Chou* Ox	艮 *Gen*	寅 *Yin* Tiger
午 **Horse** (Jun 6 - July 6) 五月 5th Month	壬 *Ren* Yang Water	坎 *Kan*	癸 *Gui* Yin Water	庚 *Geng* Yang Metal	兌 *Dui*	辛 *Xin* Yin Metal	丙 *Bing* Yang Fire	離 *Li*	丁 *Ding* Yin Fire
未 **Goat** (July 7 - Aug 7) 六月 6th Month	丙 *Bing* Yang Fire	離 *Li*	丁 *Ding* Yin Fire	戌 *Xu* Dog	乾 *Qian*	亥 *Hai* Pig	壬 *Ren* Yang Water	坎 *Kan*	癸 *Gui* Yin Water
申 **Monkey** (Aug 8 - Sept 7) 七月 7th Month	丑 *Chou* Ox	艮 *Gen*	寅 *Yin* Tiger	中 Middle			未 *Wei* Goat	坤 *Kun*	申 *Shen* Monkey
酉 **Rooster** (Sept 8 - Oct 7) 八月 8th Month	庚 *Geng* Yang Metal	兌 *Dui*	辛 *Xin* Yin Metal	庚 *Geng* Yang Metal	兌 *Dui*	辛 *Xin* Yin Metal	甲 *Jia* Yang Wood	震 *Zhen*	乙 *Yi* Yin Wood
戌 **Dog** (Oct 8 - Nov 6) 九月 9th Month	戌 *Xu* Dog	乾 *Qian*	亥 *Hai* Pig	戌 *Xu* Dog	乾 *Qian*	亥 *Hai* Pig	辰 *Chen* Dragon	巽 *Xun*	巳 *Si* Snake
亥 **Pig** (Nov 7 - Dec 6) 十月 10th Month	中 Middle			中 Middle			中 Middle		
子 **Rat** (Dec 7 - Jan 5) 十一月 11th Month	庚 *Geng* Yang Metal	兌 *Dui*	辛 *Xin* Yin Metal	辰 *Chen* Dragon	巽 *Xun*	巳 *Si* Snake	戌 *Xu* Dog	乾 *Qian*	亥 *Hai* Pig
丑 **Ox** (Jan 6 - Feb 3) 十二月 12th Month	戌 *Xu* Dog	乾 *Qian*	亥 *Hai* Pig	甲 *Jia* Yang Wood	震 *Zhen*	乙 *Yi* Yin Wood	庚 *Geng* Yang Metal	兌 *Dui*	辛 *Xin* Yin Metal

甲辰 (Jia Chen) Wood Dragon

Negative Repair / Renovation Sectors 修方凶位：

月 MONTH	大月建 Big Month Establishment			飛大煞 Flying Great Sha			丙丁獨火 Bing Ding Lonely Fire	
寅 **Tiger** (Feb 4 - Mar 5) 正月 **1st Month**		中 Middle		戌 *Xu* Dog	乾 *Qian*	亥 *Hai* Pig	巽 中 Middle	乾 *Qian*
卯 **Rabbit** (Mar 6 - Apr 4) 二月 **2nd Month**	辰 *Chen* Dragon	巽 *Xun*	巳 *Si* Snake		中 Middle			中 Middle
辰 **Dragon** (Apr 5 - May 5) 三月 **3rd Month**	甲 *Jia* Yang Wood	震 *Zhen*	乙 *Yi* Yin Wood	辰 *Chen* Dragon	巽 *Xun*	巳 *Si* Snake	巽 *Xun*	中 Middle
巳 **Snake** (May 6 - Jun 5) 四月 **4th Month**	未 *Wei* Goat	坤 *Kun*	申 *Shen* Monkey	甲 *Jia* Yang Wood	震 *Zhen*	乙 *Yi* Yin Wood	震 *Zhen*	巽 *Xun*
午 **Horse** (Jun 6 - July 6) 五月 **5th Month**	壬 *Ren* Yang Water	坎 *Kan*	癸 *Gui* Yin Water	未 *Wei* Goat	坤 *Kun*	申 *Shen* Monkey	坤 *Kun*	震 *Zhen*
未 **Goat** (July 7 - Aug 7) 六月 **6th Month**	丙 *Bing* Yang Fire	離 *Li*	丁 *Ding* Yin Fire	壬 *Ren* Yang Water	坎 *Kan*	癸 *Gui* Yin Water	坎 *Kan*	坤 *Kun*
申 **Monkey** (Aug 8 - Sept 7) 七月 **7th Month**	丑 *Chou* Ox	艮 *Gen*	寅 *Yin* Tiger	丙 *Bing* Yang Fire	離 *Li*	丁 *Ding* Yin Fire	離 *Li*	坎 *Kan*
酉 **Rooster** (Sept 8 - Oct 7) 八月 **8th Month**	庚 *Geng* Yang Metal	兌 *Dui*	辛 *Xin* Yin Metal	丑 *Chou* Ox	艮 *Gen*	寅 *Yin* Tiger	艮 *Gen*	離 *Li*
戌 **Dog** (Oct 8 - Nov 6) 九月 **9th Month**	戌 *Xu* Dog	乾 *Qian*	亥 *Hai* Pig	庚 *Geng* Yang Metal	兌 *Dui*	辛 *Xin* Yin Metal	兌 *Dui*	艮 *Gen*
亥 **Pig** (Nov 7 - Dec 6) 十月 **10th Month**		中 Middle		戌 *Xu* Dog	乾 *Qian*	亥 *Hai* Pig	乾 *Qian*	兌 *Dui*
子 **Rat** (Dec 7 - Jan 5) 十一月 **11th Month**	辰 *Chen* Dragon	巽 *Xun*	巳 *Si* Snake		中 Middle		中 Middle	乾 *Qian*
丑 **Ox** (Jan 6 - Feb 3) 十二月 **12th Month**	甲 *Jia* Yang Wood	震 *Zhen*	乙 *Yi* Yin Wood	庚 *Geng* Yang Metal	兌 *Dui*	辛 *Xin* Yin Metal		中 Middle

58

Negative Repair / Renovation Sectors 修方凶位 :

月 MONTH	月遊火 Month Wondering Fire	三煞 Monthly 3 Killings		
		劫煞 Robbery Sha	災煞 Calamity Sha	月煞 Month Sha
寅 Tiger (Feb 4 - Mar 5) 正月 1st Month	巽 Xun	亥 Hai Pig	子 Zi Rat	丑 Chou Ox
卯 Rabbit (Mar 6 - Apr 4) 二月 2nd Month	中 Middle	申 Shen Monkey	酉 You Rooster	戌 Xu Dog
辰 Dragon (Apr 5 - May 5) 三月 3rd Month	乾 Qian	巳 Si Snake	午 Wu Horse	未 Wei Goat
巳 Snake (May 6 - Jun 5) 四月 4th Month	兌 Dui	寅 Yin Tiger	卯 Mao Rabbit	辰 Chen Dragon
午 Horse (Jun 6 - July 6) 五月 5th Month	艮 Gen	亥 Hai Pig	子 Zi Rat	丑 Chou Ox
未 Goat (July 7 - Aug 7) 六月 6th Month	離 Li	申 Shen Monkey	酉 You Rooster	戌 Xu Dog
申 Monkey (Aug 8 - Sept 7) 七月 7th Month	坎 Kan	巳 Si Snake	午 Wu Horse	未 Wei Goat
酉 Rooster (Sept 8 - Oct 7) 八月 8th Month	坤 Kun	寅 Yin Tiger	卯 Mao Rabbit	辰 Chen Dragon
戌 Dog (Oct 8 - Nov 6) 九月 9th Month	震 Zhen	亥 Hai Pig	子 Zi Rat	丑 Chou Ox
亥 Pig (Nov 7 - Dec 6) 十月 10th Month	巽 Xun	申 Shen Monkey	酉 You Rooster	戌 Xu Dog
子 Rat (Dec 7 - Jan 5) 十一月 11th Month	中 Middle	巳 Si Snake	午 Wu Horse	未 Wei Goat
丑 Ox (Jan 6 - Feb 3) 十二月 12th Month	乾 Qian	寅 Yin Tiger	卯 Mao Rabbit	辰 Chen Dragon

Negative Repair / Renovation Sectors 修方凶位 :

月 MONTH	月刑 Month Punishment	月害 Month Harm	月厭 Month Detest
寅 **Tiger** (Feb 4 - Mar 5) 正月 **1st Month**	巳 Si Snake	巳 Si Snake	戌 Xu Dog
卯 **Rabbit** (Mar 6 - Apr 4) 二月 **2nd Month**	子 Zi Rat	辰 Chen Dragon	酉 You Rooster
辰 **Dragon** (Apr 5 - May 5) 三月 **3rd Month**	辰 Chen Dragon	卯 Mao Rabbit	申 Shen Monkey
巳 **Snake** (May 6 - Jun 5) 四月 **4th Month**	申 Shen Monkey	寅 Yin Tiger	未 Wei Goat
午 **Horse** (Jun 6 - July 6) 五月 **5th Month**	午 Wu Horse	丑 Chou Ox	午 Wu Horse
未 **Goat** (July 7 - Aug 7) 六月 **6th Month**	丑 Chou Ox	子 Zi Rat	巳 Si Snake
申 **Monkey** (Aug 8 - Sept 7) 七月 **7th Month**	寅 Yin Tiger	亥 Hai Pig	辰 Chen Dragon
酉 **Rooster** (Sept 8 - Oct 7) 八月 **8th Month**	酉 You Rooster	戌 Xu Dog	卯 Mao Rabbit
戌 **Dog** (Oct 8 - Nov 6) 九月 **9th Month**	未 Wei Goat	酉 You Rooster	寅 Yin Tiger
亥 **Pig** (Nov 7 - Dec 6) 十月 **10th Month**	亥 Hai Pig	申 Shen Monkey	丑 Chou Ox
子 **Rat** (Dec 7 - Jan 5) 十一月 **11th Month**	卯 Mao Rabbit	未 Wei Goat	子 Zi Rat
丑 **Ox** (Jan 6 - Feb 3) 十二月 **12th Month**	戌 Xu Dog	午 Wu Horse	亥 Hai Pig

甲午 (Jia Wu)
Wood Horse

Heavenly Stem 天干	甲 **Yang Wood** (陽木)
Earthly Branch 地支	午 **Horse** (Yang Fire 陽火)
Hidden Stem 藏干	丁 **Yin Fire**, 己 **Yin Earth**
Na Yin 納音	沙中金 **Metal from sand**
Grand Duke 太歲	午 **Horse**
Xuan Kong Five Element 玄空五行	9 金 **Metal**
Gua Name 卦名	☰ 乾爲天 **Heaven**
Xuan Kong Period Luck 玄空卦運	**1**

Annual Positive Stars for Opening Mountain, Establishing Facing and Commencing Repairs 開山立向修方吉星：

歲德 **Duke Virtue**	甲 *Jia* **Yang Wood**
歲德合 **Duke Virtue Combo**	己 *Ji* **Yin Earth**
歲枝德 **Duke Branch Virtue**	亥 *Hai* **Pig**
陽貴人 **Yang Nobleman**	未 *Wei* **Goat**
陰貴人 **Yin Nobleman**	丑 *Chou* **Ox**
歲祿 **Duke Prosperous**	寅 *Yin* **Tiger**
歲馬 **Duke Horse**	申 *Shen* **Monkey**
奏書 **Decree**	巽 *Xun*
博士 **Professor**	乾 *Qian*

Annual Negative Stars for Opening Mountain, Establishing Facing and Commencing Repairs 開山立向修方凶星：

太歲 Grand Duke	歲破 Year Breaker	三煞 Three Killings			坐煞向煞 Sitting Sha Facing Sha				浮天空亡 Floating Heaven Emptiness	
午 *Wu* Horse	子 *Zi* Rat	亥 *Hai* Pig	子 *Zi* Rat	丑 *Chou* Ox	壬 *Ren* Yang Water	癸 *Gui* Yin Water	丙 *Bing* Yang Fire	丁 *Ding* Yin Fire	離 *Li*	壬 *Ren* Yang Water

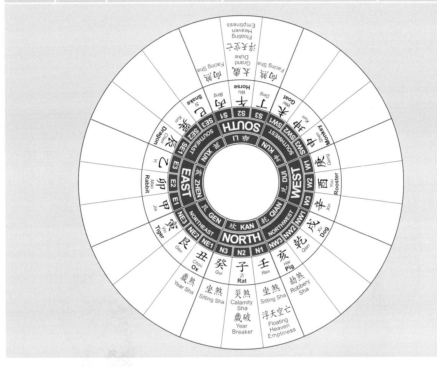

Annual San Yuan Purple White Stars 三元紫白九星：

上元 Upper Period Period 1, 2, 3	中元 Middle Period Period 4, 5, 6	下元 Lower Period Period 7, 8, 9

上元 Upper Period — Period 1, 2, 3

巽SE	離S	坤SW
6	2	4
5	**7** 甲午 *Jia Wu* Wood Horse	9
1	3	8

震E / 兌W · 艮NE 坎N 乾NW

中元 Middle Period — Period 4, 5, 6

巽SE	離S	坤SW
9	5	7
8	**1** 甲午 *Jia Wu* Wood Horse	3
4	6	2

下元 Lower Period — Period 7, 8, 9

巽SE	離S	坤SW
3	8	1
2	**4** 甲午 *Jia Wu* Wood Horse	6
7	9	5

Mountain Covering Yellow Path 蓋山黃道：

貪狼 *Tan Lang* **Greedy Wolf**	巨門 *Ju Men* **Huge Door**	武曲 *Wu Qu* **Military Arts**	文曲 *Wen Qu* **Literary Arts**
巽 *Xun* SE2 辛 *Xin* W3	艮 *Gen* NE2 丙 *Bing* S1	震 *Zhen* E2 庚 *Geng* W1 亥 *Hai* NW3 未 *Wei* SW1	乾 *Qian* NW2 甲 *Jia* E1

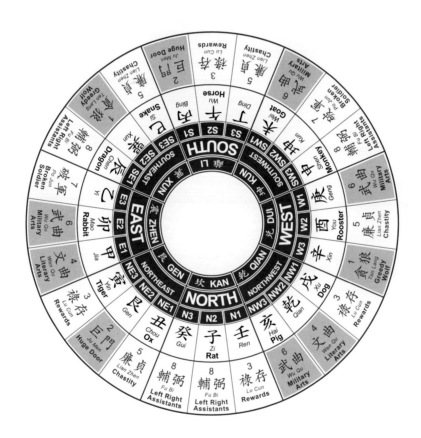

Heaven Penetrating Force 通天竅：

三合前方 **Facing Three Harmony**	坤申 *Kun Shen*	庚酉 *Geng You*	辛戌 *Xin Xu*
三合後方 **Sitting Three Harmony**	艮寅 *Gen Yin*	甲卯 *Jia Mao*	乙辰 *Yi Chen*

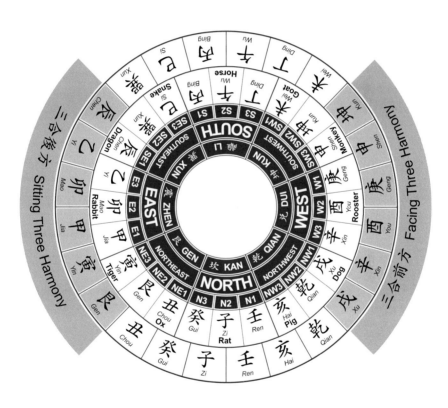

Moving Horse Six Ren Assessment 走馬六壬:

神后 Shen Hou **Holy Empress**	功曹 Gong Cao **Marshall**	天罡 Tian Gang **Heavenly Dipper**	勝光 Sheng Guang **Subliminal Bright**	傳送 Chuan Song **Great General**	河魁 He Kui **River Scholar**
丙午 Bing Wu	坤申 Kun Shen	辛戌 Xin Xu	壬子 Ren Zi	艮寅 Gen Yin	乙辰 Yi Chen

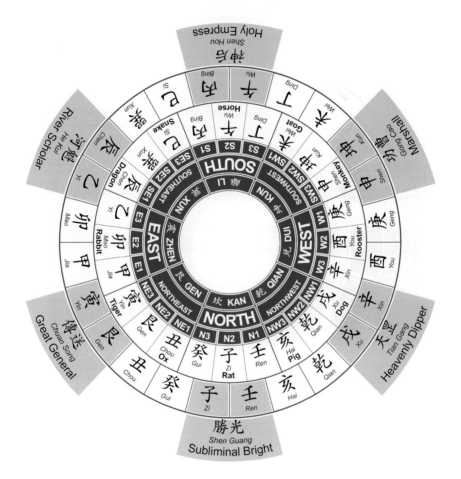

Four Advantages Three Cycles Star Plate 四利三元：

太陽 *Tai Yang* **Sun**	太陰 *Tai Yin* **Moon**	龍德 *Long De* **Dragon Virtue**	福德 *Fu De* **Fortune Virtue**
未 *Wei* Goat	酉 *You* Rooster	丑 *Chou* Ox	卯 *Mao* Rabbit

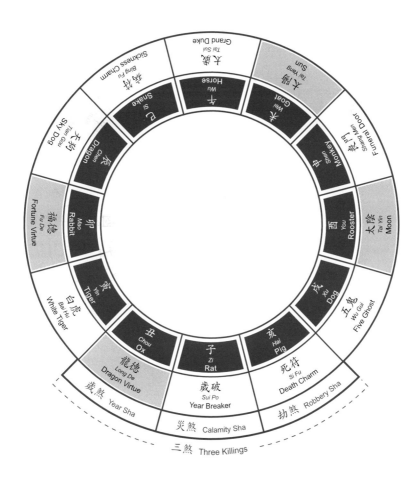

Negative Sectors For Opening Mountain 開山凶位：

年剋山家 Year Countering Sitting

甲	寅	辰	巽	戌	坎	辛	申	丑	癸	坤	庚	未
Jia E1	*Yin* NE3	*Chen* SE1	*Xun* SE2	*Xu* NW1	*Kan* N2	*Xin* W3	*Shen* SW3	*Chou* NE1	*Gui* N3	*Kun* SW2	*Geng* W1	*Wei* SW1

陰府太歲 *Yin Fu Tai Sui* **Yin Mansion Grand Duke**		六害 *Liu Hai* **Six Harm**	死符 *Si Fu* **Death Charm**	炙退 *Zhi Tui* **Roasting Star**
艮 *Gen* NE2	巽 *Xun* SE2	丑 *Chou* NE1	亥 *Hai* NW3	酉 *You* W2

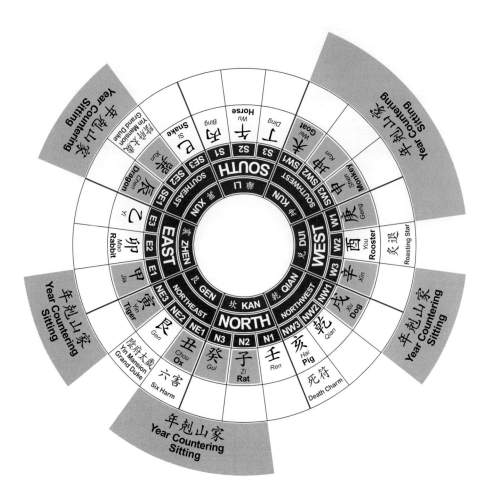

Negative Directions to Establish Facing 立向凶方：

巡山羅喉 *Xun Shan Luo Hou* **Mountain Patrol Luo Hou Star**	病符 *Bing Fu* **Sickness Charm**
丁 *Ding* **S3**	巳 *Si* **SE3**

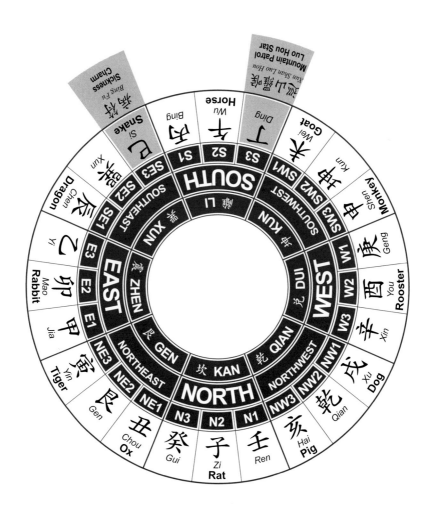

Negative Repair / Renovation Sectors Table 修方凶位表:

天官符 **Heavenly Officer Charm**	巳 *Si* Snake	飛廉 **Flying Chaste**	寅 *Yin* Tiger
地官符 **Earthly Officer Charm**	戌 *Xu* Dog	喪門 **Funeral Door**	申 *Shen* Monkey
大煞 **Great Sha**	午 *Wu* Horse	弔客 **Suspended Guest**	辰 *Chen* Dragon
大將軍 **Big General**	卯 *Mao* Rabbit	白虎 **White Tiger**	寅 *Yin* Tiger
力士 **Strong Man**	坤 *Kun*	金神 **Golden God**	午 *Wu* Horse
蠶室 **Silkworm Room**	艮 *Gen*		未 *Wei* Goat
蠶官 **Silkworm Officer**	丑 *Chou* Ox		申 *Shen* Monkey
蠶命 **Silkworm Life**	寅 *Yin* Tiger		酉 *You* Rooster
歲刑 **Duke Punishment**	午 *Wu* Horse	獨火 **Lonely Fire**	兌 *Dui*
黃幡 **Yellow Flag**	戌 *Xu* Dog	五鬼 **Five Ghost**	戌 *Xu* Dog
豹尾 **Leopard Tail**	辰 *Chen* Dragon	破敗五鬼 **Destructive Five Ghost**	巽 *Xun*

Negative Repair / Renovation Sectors Diagram 修方凶位圖：

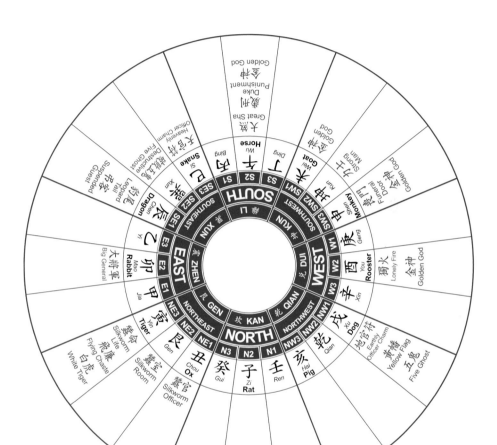

12-Month Auxiliary Stars Reference Table :
甲午年年十二月，開山立向修方星表

Positive Monthly Stars 吉星方

月 MONTH	寅 Tiger (Feb 4 - Mar 5) 正月 1st Month	卯 Rabbit (Mar 6 - Apr 4) 二月 2nd Month	辰 Dragon (Apr 5 - May 5) 三月 3rd Month	巳 Snake (May 6 - Jun 5) 四月 4th Month	午 Horse (Jun 6 - July 6) 五月 5th Month	未 Goat (July 7 - Aug 7) 六月 6th Month
天道 Heavenly Path	南 South	西南 Southwest	北 North	西 West	西北 Northwest	東 East
天德 Heavenly Virtue	丁 Ding Yin Fire	坤 Kun (申)	壬 Ren Yang Water	辛 Xin Yin Metal	乾 Qian (亥)	甲 Jia Yang Wood
天德合 Heavenly Virtue Combo	壬 Ren Yang Water	(巳)	丁 Ding Yin Fire	丙 Bing Yang Fire	(寅)	己 Ji Yin Earth
月德 Monthly Virtue	丙 Bing Yang Fire	甲 Jia Yang Wood	壬 Ren Yang Water	庚 Geng Yang Metal	丙 Bing Yang Fire	甲 Jia Yang Wood
月德合 Monthly Virtue Combo	辛 Xin Yin Metal	己 Ji Yin Earth	丁 Ding Yin Fire	乙 Yi Yin Wood	辛 Xin Yin Metal	己 Ji Yin Earth
月空 Month Emptiness	壬 Ren Yang Water	庚 Geng Yang Metal	丙 Bing Yang Fire	甲 Jia Yang Wood	壬 Ren Yang Water	庚 Geng Yang Metal
陽貴人 Yang Nobleman	坎 Kan	離 Li	艮 Gen	兌 Dui	乾 Qian	中 Middle
陰貴人 Yin Nobleman	兌 Dui	乾 Qian	中 Middle	巽 Xun	震 Zhen	坤 Kun
飛天祿 Flying Heavenly Wealth	中 Middle	坎 Kan	離 Li	艮 Gen	兌 Dui	乾 Qian
飛天馬 Flying Heavenly Horse	坤 Kun	坎 Kan	離 Li	艮 Gen	兌 Dui	乾 Qian

12-Month Auxiliary Stars Reference Table :
甲午年十二月，開山立向修方星表

申 Monkey (Aug 8 - Sept 7)	酉 Rooster (Sept 8 - Oct 7)	戌 Dog (Oct 8 - Nov 6)	亥 Pig (Nov 7 - Dec 6)	子 Rat (Dec 7 - Jan 5)	丑 Ox (Jan 6 - Feb 3)	月 MONTH
七月 7th Month	八月 8th Month	九月 9th Month	十月 10th Month	十一月 11th Month	十二月 12th Month	
北 North	東北 Northeast	南 South	東 East	東南 Southeast	西 West	天道 Heavenly Path
癸 Gui Yin Water	艮 Gen (寅)	丙 Bing Yang Fire	乙 Yi Yin Wood	巽 Xun (巳)	庚 Geng Yang Metal	天德 Heavenly Virtue
戊 Wu Yang Earth	(亥)	辛 Xin Yin Metal	庚 Geng Yang Metal	(申)	乙 Yi Yin Wood	天德合 Heavenly Virtue Combo
壬 Ren Yang Water	庚 Geng Yang Metal	丙 Bing Yang Fire	甲 Jia Yang Wood	壬 Ren Yang Water	庚 Geng Yang Metal	月德 Monthly Virtue
丁 Ding Yin Fire	乙 Yi Yin Wood	辛 Xin Yin Metal	己 Ji Yin Earth	丁 Ding Yin Fire	乙 Yi Yin Wood	月德合 Monthly Virtue Combo
丙 Bing Yang Fire	甲 Jia Yang Wood	壬 Ren Yang Water	庚 Geng Yang Metal	丙 Bing Yang Fire	甲 Jia Yang Wood	月空 Month Emptiness
坎 Kan	離 Li	艮 Gen	兌 Dui	乾 Qian	中 Middle	陽貴人 Yang Nobleman
坎 Kan	離 Li	艮 Gen	兌 Dui	乾 Qian	中 Middle	陰貴人 Yin Nobleman
中 Middle	巽 Xun	震 Zhen	坤 Kun	坎 Kan	離 Li	飛天祿 Flying Heavenly Wealth
中 Middle	坎 Kan	離 Li	艮 Gen	兌 Dui	乾 Qian	飛天馬 Flying Heavenly Horse

Monthly Purple White Stars 月紫白九星 :

寅 Tiger (Feb 4 - Mar 5) 正月 1st Month

巽 SE	離 S	坤 SW
7 Red 七赤	3 Jade 三碧	5 Yellow 五黃
震 E 6 White 六白	8 White 八白	1 White 一白 兌 W
2 Black 二黑	4 Green 四綠	9 Purple 九紫
艮 NE	坎 N	乾 NW

卯 Rabbit (Mar 6 - Apr 4) 二月 2nd Month

巽 SE	離 S	坤 SW
6 White 六白	2 Black 二黑	4 Green 四綠
震 E 5 Yellow 五黃	7 Red 七赤	9 Purple 九紫 兌 W
1 White 一白	3 Jade 三碧	8 White 八白
艮 NE	坎 N	乾 NW

辰 Dragon (Apr 5 - May 5) 三月 3rd Month

巽 SE	離 S	坤 SW
5 Yellow 五黃	1 White 一白	3 Jade 三碧
震 E 4 Green 四綠	6 White 六白	8 White 八白 兌 W
9 Purple 九紫	2 Black 二黑	7 Red 七赤
艮 NE	坎 N	乾 NW

巳 Snake (May 6 - Jun 5) 四月 4th Month

巽 SE	離 S	坤 SW
4 Green 四綠	9 Purple 九紫	2 Black 二黑
震 E 3 Jade 三碧	5 Yellow 五黃	7 Red 七赤 兌 W
8 White 八白	1 White 一白	6 White 六白
艮 NE	坎 N	乾 NW

午 Horse (Jun 6 - July 6) 五月 5th Month

巽 SE	離 S	坤 SW
3 Jade 三碧	8 White 八白	1 White 一白
震 E 2 Black 二黑	4 Green 四綠	6 White 六白 兌 W
7 Red 七赤	9 Purple 九紫	5 Yellow 五黃
艮 NE	坎 N	乾 NW

未 Goat (July 7 - Aug 7) 六月 6th Month

巽 SE	離 S	坤 SW
2 Black 二黑	7 Red 七赤	9 Purple 九紫
震 E 1 White 一白	3 Jade 三碧	5 Yellow 五黃 兌 W
6 White 六白	8 White 八白	4 Green 四綠
艮 NE	坎 N	乾 NW

申 Monkey (Aug 8 - Sept 7) 七月 7th Month

巽 SE	離 S	坤 SW
1 White 一白	6 White 六白	8 White 八白
震 E 9 Purple 九紫	2 Black 二黑	4 Green 四綠 兌 W
5 Yellow 五黃	7 Red 七赤	3 Jade 三碧
艮 NE	坎 N	乾 NW

酉 Rooster (Sept 8 - Oct 7) 八月 8th Month

巽 SE	離 S	坤 SW
9 Purple 九紫	5 Yellow 五黃	7 Red 七赤
震 E 8 White 八白	1 White 一白	3 Jade 三碧 兌 W
4 Green 四綠	6 White 六白	2 Black 二黑
艮 NE	坎 N	乾 NW

戌 Dog (Oct 8 - Nov 6) 九月 9th Month

巽 SE	離 S	坤 SW
8 White 八白	4 Green 四綠	6 White 六白
震 E 7 Red 七赤	9 Purple 九紫	2 Black 二黑 兌 W
3 Jade 三碧	5 Yellow 五黃	1 White 一白
艮 NE	坎 N	乾 NW

亥 Pig (Nov 7 - Dec 6) 十月 10th Month

巽 SE	離 S	坤 SW
7 Red 七赤	3 Jade 三碧	5 Yellow 五黃
震 E 6 White 六白	8 White 八白	1 White 一白 兌 W
2 Black 二黑	4 Green 四綠	9 Purple 九紫
艮 NE	坎 N	乾 NW

子 Rat (Dec 7 - Jan 5) 十一月 11th Month

巽 SE	離 S	坤 SW
6 White 六白	2 Black 二黑	4 Green 四綠
震 E 5 Yellow 五黃	7 Red 七赤	9 Purple 九紫 兌 W
1 White 一白	3 Jade 三碧	8 White 八白
艮 NE	坎 N	乾 NW

丑 Ox (Jan 6 - Feb 3) 十二月 12th Month

巽 SE	離 S	坤 SW
5 Yellow 五黃	1 White 一白	3 Jade 三碧
震 E 4 Green 四綠	6 White 六白	8 White 八白 兌 W
9 Purple 九紫	2 Black 二黑	7 Red 七赤
艮 NE	坎 N	乾 NW

Qi Men Three Nobles 三奇 :

Three Nobles 三奇 / Seasons	乙 Yi	丙 Bing	丁 Ding
立春 **Coming of Spring** Feb 4 - Feb 18	坤 Kun	坤 Kun	震 Zhen
春分 **Spring Equinox** Mar 21 - Apr 4	乾 Qian	乾 Qian	兌 Dui
立夏 **Coming of Summer** May 6 - May 20	兌 Dui	兌 Dui	艮 Gen
夏至 **Summer Solstice** Jun 22 - Jul 6	乾 Qian	乾 Qian	中 **Middle**
立秋 **Coming of Autumn** Aug 8 - Aug 23	艮 Gen	艮 Gen	兌 Dui
秋分 **Autumn Equinox** Sept 23 - Oct 7	巽 Xun	巽 Xun	震 Zhen
立冬 **Coming of Winter** Nov 7 - Nov 22	震 Zhen	震 Zhen	坤 Kun
冬至 **Winter Solstice** Dec 22 - Jan 5	巽 Xun	巽 Xun	中 **Middle**

Sectors to Avoid Opening Mountain 開山凶位：

月 MONTH	月建 Month Establishment	月破 Month Destruction	月剋山家 Month Countering Sitting		陰府太歲 Yin Mansion Grand Duke	
寅 Tiger (Feb 4 - Mar 5) 正月 1st Month	寅 Yin Tiger	申 Shen Monkey	乾 Qian	兌 Dui	坎 Kan	坤 Kun
卯 Rabbit (Mar 6 - Apr 4) 二月 2nd Month	卯 Mao Rabbit	酉 You Rooster	亥 Hai Pig	丁 Ding Yin Fire	乾 Qian	離 Li
辰 Dragon (Apr 5 - May 5) 三月 3rd Month	辰 Chen Dragon	戌 Xu Dog	震 Zhen	巳 Si Snake	坤 Kun	震 Zhen
巳 Snake (May 6 - Jun 5) 四月 4th Month	巳 Si Snake	亥 Hai Pig	艮 Gen		巽 Xun	艮 Gen
午 Horse (Jun 6 - July 6) 五月 5th Month	午 Wu Horse	子 Zi Rat	—		乾 Qian	兌 Dui
未 Goat (July 7 - Aug 7) 六月 6th Month	未 Wei Goat	丑 Chou Ox	—		坤 Kun	坎 Kan
申 Monkey (Aug 8 - Sept 7) 七月 7th Month	申 Shen Monkey	寅 Yin Tiger	水 Water	山 Mountain	離 Li	乾 Qian
酉 Rooster (Sept 8 - Oct 7) 八月 8th Month	酉 You Rooster	卯 Mao Rabbit	土 Earth		震 Zhen	坤 Kun
戌 Dog (Oct 8 - Nov 6) 九月 9th Month	戌 Xu Dog	辰 Chen Dragon	乾 Qian	兌 Dui	艮 Gen	巽 Xun
亥 Pig (Nov 7 - Dec 6) 十月 10th Month	亥 Hai Pig	巳 Si Snake	亥 Hai Pig	丁 Ding Yin Fire	兌 Dui	乾 Qian
子 Rat (Dec 7 - Jan 5) 十一月 11th Month	子 Zi Rat	午 Wu Horse	離 Li	丙 Bing Yang Fire	坎 Kan	坤 Kun
丑 Ox (Jan 6 - Feb 3) 十二月 12th Month	丑 Chou Ox	未 Wei Goat	壬 Ren Yang Water	乙 Yi Yin Wood	乾 Qian	離 Li

Negative Repair / Renovation Sectors 修方凶位 :

月 MONTH	天官符 Heavenly Officer Charm			地官符 Earth Officer Charm			小月建 Small Month Establishment		
寅 **Tiger** (Feb 4 - Mar 5) 正月 **1st Month**	丑 Chou Ox	艮 Gen	寅 Yin Tiger	辰 Chen Dragon	巽 Xun	巳 Si Snake	中 Middle		
卯 **Rabbit** (Mar 6 - Apr 4) 二月 **2nd Month**	庚 Geng Yang Metal	兌 Dui	辛 Xin Yin Metal	甲 Jia Yang Wood	震 Zhen	乙 Yi Yin Wood	戌 Xu Dog	乾 Qian	亥 Hai Pig
辰 **Dragon** (Apr 5 - May 5) 三月 **3rd Month**	戌 Xu Dog	乾 Qian	亥 Hai Pig	未 Wei Goat	坤 Kun	申 Shen Monkey	庚 Geng Yang Metal	兌 Dui	辛 Xin Yin Metal
巳 **Snake** (May 6 - Jun 5) 四月 **4th Month**	中 Middle			壬 Ren Yang Water	坎 Kan	癸 Gui Yin Water	丑 Chou Ox	艮 Gen	寅 Yin Tiger
午 **Horse** (Jun 6 - July 6) 五月 **5th Month**	庚 Geng Yang Metal	兌 Dui	辛 Xin Yin Metal	丙 Bing Yang Fire	離 Li	丁 Ding Yin Fire	丙 Bing Yang Fire	離 Li	丁 Ding Yin Fire
未 **Goat** (July 7 - Aug 7) 六月 **6th Month**	戌 Xu Dog	乾 Qian	亥 Hai Pig	丑 Chou Ox	艮 Gen	寅 Yin Tiger	壬 Ren Yang Water	坎 Kan	癸 Gui Yin Water
申 **Monkey** (Aug 8 - Sept 7) 七月 **7th Month**	中 Middle			庚 Geng Yang Metal	兌 Dui	辛 Xin Yin Metal	未 Wei Goat	坤 Kun	申 Shen Monkey
酉 **Rooster** (Sept 8 - Oct 7) 八月 **8th Month**	辰 Chen Dragon	巽 Xun	巳 Si Snake	戌 Xu Dog	乾 Qian	亥 Hai Pig	甲 Jia Yang Wood	震 Zhen	乙 Yi Yin Wood
戌 **Dog** (Oct 8 - Nov 6) 九月 **9th Month**	甲 Jia Yang Wood	震 Zhen	乙 Yi Yin Wood	中 Middle			辰 Chen Dragon	巽 Xun	巳 Si Snake
亥 **Pig** (Nov 7 - Dec 6) 十月 **10th Month**	未 Wei Goat	坤 Kun	申 Shen Monkey	庚 Geng Yang Metal	兌 Dui	辛 Xin Yin Metal	中 Middle		
子 **Rat** (Dec 7 - Jan 5) 十一月 **11th Month**	壬 Ren Yang Water	坎 Kan	癸 Gui Yin Water	戌 Xu Dog	乾 Qian	亥 Hai Pig	戌 Xu Dog	乾 Qian	亥 Hai Pig
丑 **Ox** (Jan 6 - Feb 3) 十二月 **12th Month**	丙 Bing Yang Fire	離 Li	丁 Ding Yin Fire	中 Middle			庚 Geng Yang Metal	兌 Dui	辛 Xin Yin Metal

Negative Repair / Renovation Sectors 修方凶位 :

月 MONTH	大月建 Big Month Establishment			飛大煞 Flying Great Sha			丙丁獨火 Bing Ding Lonely Fire	
寅 Tiger (Feb 4 - Mar 5) 正月 1st Month	丑 Chou Ox	艮 Gen	寅 Yin Tiger	丙 Bing Yang Fire	離 Li	丁 Ding Yin Fire	中 Middle	乾 Qian
卯 Rabbit (Mar 6 - Apr 4) 二月 2nd Month	庚 Geng Yang Metal	兌 Dui	辛 Xin Yin Metal	丑 Chou Ox	艮 Gen	寅 Yin Tiger	中 Middle	
辰 Dragon (Apr 5 - May 5) 三月 3rd Month	戌 Xu Dog	乾 Qian	亥 Hai Pig	庚 Geng Yang Metal	兌 Dui	辛 Xin Yin Metal	巽 Xun	中 Middle
巳 Snake (May 6 - Jun 5) 四月 4th Month		中 Middle		戌 Xu Dog	乾 Qian	亥 Hai Pig	震 Zhen	巽 Xun
午 Horse (Jun 6 - July 6) 五月 5th Month	辰 Chen Dragon	巽 Xun	巳 Si Snake		中 Middle		坤 Kun	震 Zhen
未 Goat (July 7 - Aug 7) 六月 6th Month	甲 Jia Yang Wood	震 Zhen	乙 Yi Yin Wood	庚 Geng Yang Metal	兌 Dui	辛 Xin Yin Metal	坎 Kan	坤 Kun
申 Monkey (Aug 8 - Sept 7) 七月 7th Month	未 Wei Goat	坤 Kun	申 Shen Monkey	戌 Xu Dog	乾 Qian	亥 Hai Pig	離 Li	坎 Kan
酉 Rooster (Sept 8 - Oct 7) 八月 8th Month	壬 Ren Yang Water	坎 Kan	癸 Gui Yin Water		中 Middle		艮 Gen	離 Li
戌 Dog (Oct 8 - Nov 6) 九月 9th Month	丙 Bing Yang Fire	離 Li	丁 Ding Yin Fire	辰 Chen Dragon	巽 Xun	巳 Si Snake	兌 Dui	艮 Gen
亥 Pig (Nov 7 - Dec 6) 十月 10th Month	丑 Chou Ox	艮 Gen	寅 Yin Tiger	甲 Jia Yang Wood	震 Zhen	乙 Yi Yin Wood	乾 Qian	兌 Dui
子 Rat (Dec 7 - Jan 5) 十一月 11th Month	庚 Geng Yang Metal	兌 Dui	辛 Xin Yin Metal	未 Wei Goat	坤 Kun	申 Shen Monkey	中 Middle	乾 Qian
丑 Ox (Jan 6 - Feb 3) 十二月 12th Month	戌 Xu Dog	乾 Qian	亥 Hai Pig	壬 Ren Yang Water	坎 Kan	癸 Gui Yin Water	中 Middle	

Negative Repair / Renovation Sectors 修方凶位 :

月 MONTH	月遊火 Month Wondering Fire	三煞 Monthly 3 Killings		
		劫煞 Robbery Sha	災煞 Calamity Sha	月煞 Month Sha
寅 **Tiger** (Feb 4 - Mar 5) 正月 **1st Month**	坤 Kun	亥 Hai Pig	子 Zi Rat	丑 Chou Ox
卯 **Rabbit** (Mar 6 - Apr 4) 二月 **2nd Month**	震 Zhen	申 Shen Monkey	酉 You Rooster	戌 Xu Dog
辰 **Dragon** (Apr 5 - May 5) 三月 **3rd Month**	巽 Xun	巳 Si Snake	午 Wu Horse	未 Wei Goat
巳 **Snake** (May 6 - Jun 5) 四月 **4th Month**	中 Middle	寅 Yin Tiger	卯 Mao Rabbit	辰 Chen Dragon
午 **Horse** (Jun 6 - July 6) 五月 **5th Month**	乾 Qian	亥 Hai Pig	子 Zi Rat	丑 Chou Ox
未 **Goat** (July 7 - Aug 7) 六月 **6th Month**	兌 Dui	申 Shen Monkey	酉 You Rooster	戌 Xu Dog
申 **Monkey** (Aug 8 - Sept 7) 七月 **7th Month**	艮 Gen	巳 Si Snake	午 Wu Horse	未 Wei Goat
酉 **Rooster** (Sept 8 - Oct 7) 八月 **8th Month**	離 Li	寅 Yin Tiger	卯 Mao Rabbit	辰 Chen Dragon
戌 **Dog** (Oct 8 - Nov 6) 九月 **9th Month**	坎 Kan	亥 Hai Pig	子 Zi Rat	丑 Chou Ox
亥 **Pig** (Nov 7 - Dec 6) 十月 **10th Month**	坤 Kun	申 Shen Monkey	酉 You Rooster	戌 Xu Dog
子 **Rat** (Dec 7 - Jan 5) 十一月 **11th Month**	震 Zhen	巳 Si Snake	午 Wu Horse	未 Wei Goat
丑 **Ox** (Jan 6 - Feb 3) 十二月 **12th Month**	巽 Xun	寅 Yin Tiger	卯 Mao Rabbit	辰 Chen Dragon

Negative Repair / Renovation Sectors 修方凶位 :

月 MONTH	月刑 Month Punishment	月害 Month Harm	月厭 Month Detest
寅 **Tiger** (Feb 4 - Mar 5) 正月 **1st Month**	巳 *Si* Snake	巳 *Si* Snake	戌 *Xu* Dog
卯 **Rabbit** (Mar 6 - Apr 4) 二月 **2nd Month**	子 *Zi* Rat	辰 *Chen* Dragon	酉 *You* Rooster
辰 **Dragon** (Apr 5 - May 5) 三月 **3rd Month**	辰 *Chen* Dragon	卯 *Mao* Rabbit	申 *Shen* Monkey
巳 **Snake** (May 6 - Jun 5) 四月 **4th Month**	申 *Shen* Monkey	寅 *Yin* Tiger	未 *Wei* Goat
午 **Horse** (Jun 6 - July 6) 五月 **5th Month**	午 *Wu* Horse	丑 *Chou* Ox	午 *Wu* Horse
未 **Goat** (July 7 - Aug 7) 六月 **6th Month**	丑 *Chou* Ox	子 *Zi* Rat	巳 *Si* Snake
申 **Monkey** (Aug 8 - Sept 7) 七月 **7th Month**	寅 *Yin* Tiger	亥 *Hai* Pig	辰 *Chen* Dragon
酉 **Rooster** (Sept 8 - Oct 7) 八月 **8th Month**	酉 *You* Rooster	戌 *Xu* Dog	卯 *Mao* Rabbit
戌 **Dog** (Oct 8 - Nov 6) 九月 **9th Month**	未 *Wei* Goat	酉 *You* Rooster	寅 *Yin* Tiger
亥 **Pig** (Nov 7 - Dec 6) 十月 **10th Month**	亥 *Hai* Pig	申 *Shen* Monkey	丑 *Chou* Ox
子 **Rat** (Dec 7 - Jan 5) 十一月 **11th Month**	卯 *Mao* Rabbit	未 *Wei* Goat	子 *Zi* Rat
丑 **Ox** (Jan 6 - Feb 3) 十二月 **12th Month**	戌 *Xu* Dog	午 *Wu* Horse	亥 *Hai* Pig

甲申 (Jia Shen)
Wood Monkey

Heavenly Stem 天干	甲 **Yang Wood** (陽木)
Earthly Branch 地支	申 **Monkey (Yang Metal** 陽金**)**
Hidden Stem 藏干	庚 **Yang Metal,** 壬 **Yang Water,** 戊 **Yang Earth**
Na Yin 納音	泉中水 **Water from the spring**
Grand Duke 太歲	申 **Monkey**
Xuan Kong Five Element 玄空五行	3 木 **Wood**
Gua Name 卦名	䷻ 火水未濟 **Not Yet Accomplished**
Xuan Kong Period Luck 玄空卦運	9

Annual Positive Stars for Opening Mountain, Establishing Facing and Commencing Repairs 開山立向修方吉星：

歲德 **Duke Virtue**	甲 *Jia* **Yang Wood**	
歲德合 **Duke Virtue Combo**	己 *Ji* **Yin Earth**	
歲枝德 **Duke Branch Virtue**	丑 *Chou* **Ox**	
陽貴人 **Yang Nobleman**	未 *Wei* **Goat**	
陰貴人 **Yin Nobleman**	丑 *Chou* **Ox**	
歲祿 **Duke Prosperous**	寅 *Yin* **Tiger**	
歲馬 **Duke Horse**	寅 *Yin* **Tiger**	
奏書 **Decree**	坤 *Kun*	
博士 **Professor**	艮 *Gen*	

Annual Negative Stars for Opening Mountain, Establishing Facing and Commencing Repairs 開山立向修方凶星：

太歲 Grand Duke	歲破 Year Breaker	三煞 Three Killings			坐煞向煞 Sitting Sha Facing Sha				浮天空亡 Floating Heaven Emptiness	
申 *Shen* Monkey	寅 *Yin* Tiger	巳 *Si* Snake	午 *Wu* Horse	未 *Wei* Goat	丙 *Bing* Yang Fire	丁 *Ding* Yin Fire	壬 *Ren* Yang Water	癸 *Gui* Yin Water	離 *Li*	壬 *Ren* Yang Water

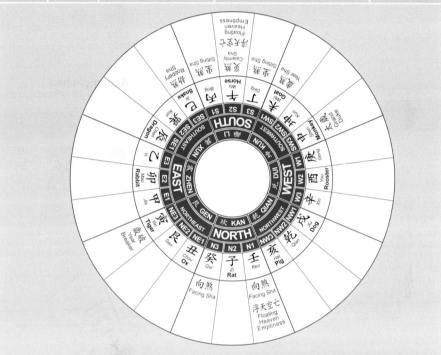

Annual San Yuan Purple White Stars 三元紫白九星：

上元 Upper Period Period 1, 2, 3			中元 Middle Period Period 4, 5, 6			下元 Lower Period Period 7, 8, 9		
巽SE **7**	離S **3**	坤SW **5**	巽SE **1**	離S **6**	坤SW **8**	巽SE **4**	離S **9**	坤SW **2**
震E **6**	**8** 甲申 *Jia Shen* Wood Monkey	兌W **1**	震E **9**	**2** 甲申 *Jia Shen* Wood Monkey	兌W **4**	震E **3**	**5** 甲申 *Jia Shen* Wood Monkey	兌W **7**
艮NE **2**	坎N **4**	乾NW **9**	艮NE **5**	坎N **7**	乾NW **3**	艮NE **8**	坎N **1**	乾NW **6**

Mountain Covering Yellow Path 蓋山黃道:

貪狼 *Tan Lang* **Greedy Wolf**		巨門 *Ju Men* **Huge Door**				武曲 *Wu Qu* **Military Arts**		文曲 *Wen Qu* **Literary Arts**			
坤 *Kun* SW2	乙 *Yi* E3	坎 *Kan* N2	癸 *Gui* N3	申 *Shen* SW3	辰 *Chen* SE1	乾 *Qian* NW2	甲 *Jia* E1	震 *Zhen* E2	庚 *Geng* W1	亥 *Hai* NW3	未 *Wei* SW1

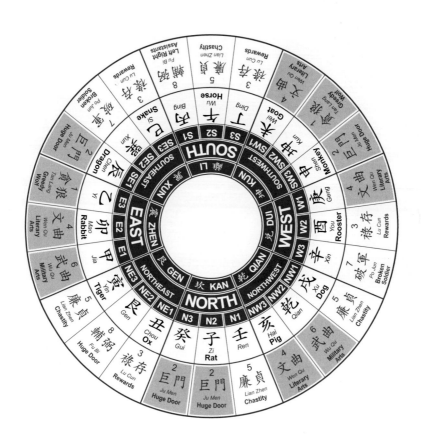

Heaven Penetrating Force 通天竅：			
三合前方 **Facing Three Harmony**	艮寅 Gen Yin	甲卯 Jia Mao	乙辰 Yi Chen
三合後方 **Sitting Three Harmony**	坤申 Kun Shen	庚酉 Geng You	辛戌 Xin Xu

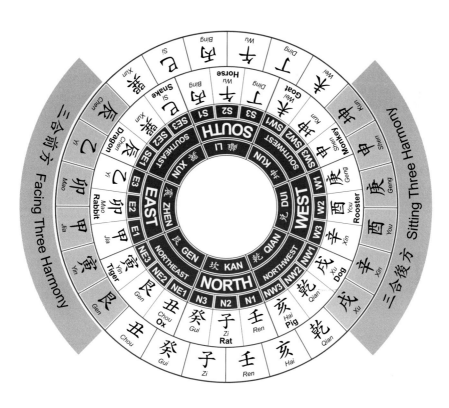

Moving Horse Six Ren Assessment 走馬六壬：					
神后 *Shen Hou* **Holy Empress**	功曹 *Gong Cao* **Marshall**	天罡 *Tian Gang* **Heavenly Dipper**	勝光 *Sheng Guang* **Subliminal Bright**	傳送 *Chuan Song* **Great General**	河魁 *He Kui* **River Scholar**
乙辰 *Yi Chen*	丙午 *Bing Wu*	坤申 *Kun Shen*	辛戌 *Xin Xu*	壬子 *Ren Zi*	艮寅 *Gen Yin*

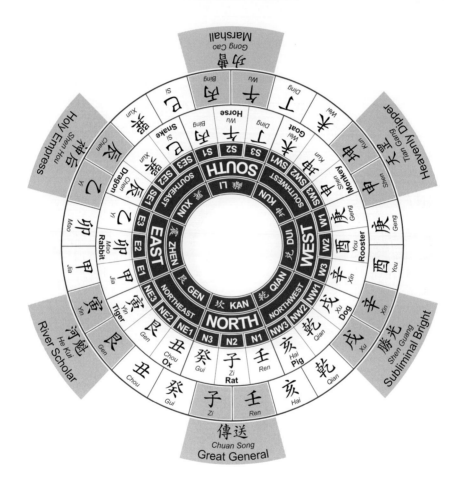

Four Advantages Three Cycles Star Plate 四利三元：

太陽 *Tai Yang* **Sun**	太陰 *Tai Yin* **Moon**	龍德 *Long De* **Dragon Virtue**	福德 *Fu De* **Fortune Virtue**
酉 *You* **Rooster**	亥 *Hai* **Pig**	卯 *Mao* **Rabbit**	巳 *Si* **Snake**

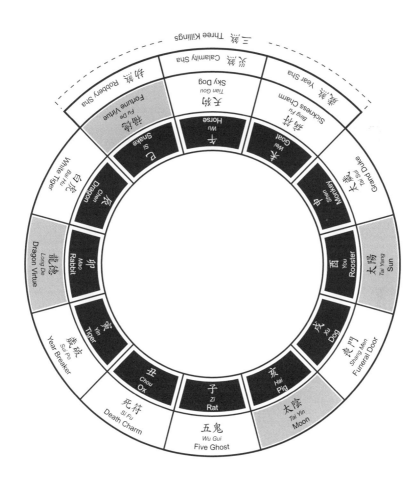

Negative Sectors For Opening Mountain 開山凶位：

年剋山家 Year Countering Sitting

離	壬	丙	乙
Li	*Ren*	*Bing*	*Yi*
S2	N1	S1	E3

陰府太歲 Yin Fu Tai Sui		六害 Liu Hai	死符 Si Fu	炙退 Zhi Tui
Yin Mansion Grand Duke		**Six Harm**	**Death Charm**	**Roasting Star**
艮	巽	亥	丑	卯
Gen	*Xun*	*Hai*	*Chou*	*Mao*
NE2	SE2	NW3	NE1	E2

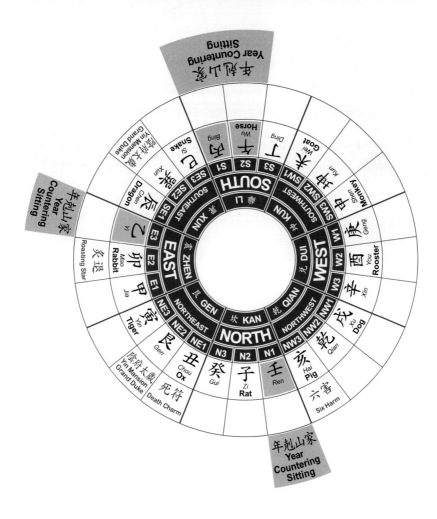

Negative Directions to Establish Facing 立向凶方：

巡山羅喉 *Xun Shan Luo Hou* **Mountain Patrol Luo Hou Star**	病符 *Bing Fu* **Sickness Charm**
庚 *Geng* **W1**	未 *Wei* **SW1**

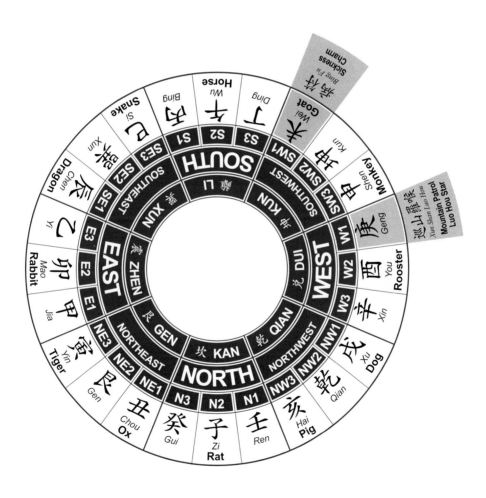

Negative Repair / Renovation Sectors Table 修方凶位表：

天官符 Heavenly Officer Charm	亥 *Hai* Pig	飛廉 Flying Chaste	辰 *Chen* Dragon
地官符 Earthly Officer Charm	子 *Zi* Rat	喪門 Funeral Door	戌 *Xu* Dog
大煞 Great Sha	子 *Zi* Rat	弔客 Suspended Guest	午 *Wu* Horse
大將軍 Big General	午 *Wu* Horse	白虎 White Tiger	辰 *Chen* Dragon
力士 Strong Man	乾 *Qian*	金神 Golden God	午 *Wu* Horse
蠶室 Silkworm Room	巽 *Xun*		未 *Wei* Goat
蠶官 Silkworm Officer	辰 *Chen* Dragon		申 *Shen* Monkey
蠶命 Silkworm Life	巳 *Si* Snake		酉 *You* Rooster
歲刑 Duke Punishment	寅 *Yin* Tiger	獨火 Lonely Fire	離 *Li*
黃幡 Yellow Flag	辰 *Chen* Dragon	五鬼 Five Ghost	申 *Shen* Monkey
豹尾 Leopard Tail	戌 *Xu* Dog	破敗五鬼 Destructive Five Ghost	巽 *Xun*

Negative Repair / Renovation Sectors Diagram 修方凶位圖：

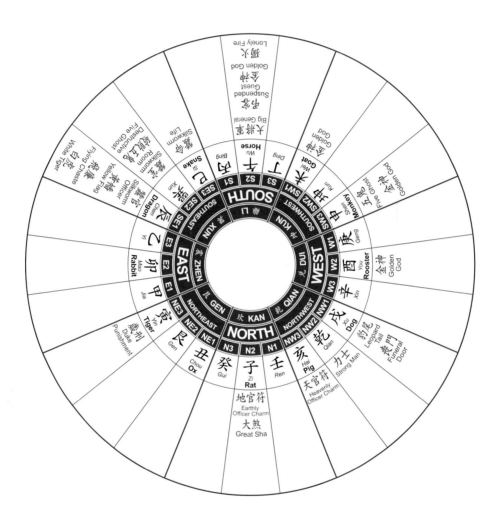

12-Month Auxiliary Stars Reference Table :
甲申年十二月，開山立向修方星表

Positive Monthly Stars 吉星方

月 MONTH	寅 Tiger (Feb 4 - Mar 5) 正月 1st Month	卯 Rabbit (Mar 6 - Apr 4) 二月 2nd Month	辰 Dragon (Apr 5 - May 5) 三月 3rd Month	巳 Snake (May 6 - Jun 5) 四月 4th Month	午 Horse (Jun 6 - July 6) 五月 5th Month	未 Goat (July 7 - Aug 7) 六月 6th Month
天道 Heavenly Path	南 South	西南 Southwest	北 North	西 West	西北 Northwest	東 East
天德 Heavenly Virtue	丁 Ding Yin Fire	坤 Kun （申）	壬 Ren Yang Water	辛 Xin Yin Metal	乾 Qian （亥）	甲 Jia Yang Wood
天德合 Heavenly Virtue Combo	壬 Ren Yang Water	（巳）	丁 Ding Yin Fire	丙 Bing Yang Fire	（寅）	己 Ji Yin Earth
月德 Monthly Virtue	丙 Bing Yang Fire	甲 Jia Yang Wood	壬 Ren Yang Water	庚 Geng Yang Metal	丙 Bing Yang Fire	甲 Jia Yang Wood
月德合 Monthly Virtue Combo	辛 Xin Yin Metal	己 Ji Yin Earth	丁 Ding Yin Fire	乙 Yi Yin Wood	辛 Xin Yin Metal	己 Ji Yin Earth
月空 Month Emptiness	壬 Ren Yang Water	庚 Geng Yang Metal	丙 Bing Yang Fire	甲 Jia Yang Wood	壬 Ren Yang Water	庚 Geng Yang Metal
陽貴人 Yang Nobleman	坎 Kan	離 Li	艮 Gen	兌 Dui	乾 Qian	中 Middle
陰貴人 Yin Nobleman	兌 Dui	乾 Qian	中 Middle	巽 Xun	震 Zhen	坤 Kun
飛天祿 Flying Heavenly Wealth	中 Middle	坎 Kan	離 Li	艮 Gen	兌 Dui	乾 Qian
飛天馬 Flying Heavenly Horse	中 Middle	坎 Kan	離 Li	艮 Gen	兌 Dui	乾 Qian

12-Month Auxiliary Stars Reference Table :
甲申年十二月，開山立向修方星表

申 Monkey (Aug 8 - Sept 7) 七月 7th Month	酉 Rooster (Sept 8 - Oct 7) 八月 8th Month	戌 Dog (Oct 8 - Nov 6) 九月 9th Month	亥 Pig (Nov 7 - Dec 6) 十月 10th Month	子 Rat (Dec 7 - Jan 5) 十一月 11th Month	丑 Ox (Jan 6 - Feb 3) 十二月 12th Month	月 MONTH
北 North	東北 Northeast	南 South	東 East	東南 Southeast	西 West	天道 Heavenly Path
癸 Gui Yin Water	艮 Gen (寅)	丙 Bing Yang Fire	乙 Yi Yin Wood	巽 Xun (巳)	庚 Geng Yang Metal	天德 Heavenly Virtue
戊 Wu Yang Earth	(亥)	辛 Xin Yin Metal	庚 Geng Yang Metal	(申)	乙 Yi Yin Wood	天德合 Heavenly Virtue Combo
壬 Ren Yang Water	庚 Geng Yang Metal	丙 Bing Yang Fire	甲 Jia Yang Wood	壬 Ren Yang Water	庚 Geng Yang Metal	月德 Monthly Virtue
丁 Ding Yin Fire	乙 Yi Yin Wood	辛 Xin Yin Metal	己 Ji Yin Earth	丁 Ding Yin Fire	乙 Yi Yin Wood	月德合 Monthly Virtue Combo
丙 Bing Yang Fire	甲 Jia Yang Wood	壬 Ren Yang Water	庚 Geng Yang Metal	丙 Bing Yang Fire	甲 Jia Yang Wood	月空 Month Emptiness
坎 Kan	離 Li	艮 Gen	兌 Dui	乾 Qian	中 Middle	陽貴人 Yang Nobleman
坎 Kan	離 Lii	艮 Gen	兌 Dui	乾 Qian	中 Middle	陰貴人 Yin Nobleman
中 Middle	巽 Xun	震 Zhen	坤 Kun	坎 Kan	離 Lii	飛天祿 Flying Heavenly Wealth
中 Middle	巽 Xun	震 Zhen	坤 Kun	坎 Kan	離 Lii	飛天馬 Flying Heavenly Horse

Monthly Purple White Stars 月紫白九星 ：

寅 Tiger (Feb 4 - Mar 5) 正月 1st Month

巽 SE	離 S	坤 SW
1 White 一白	6 White 六白	8 White 八白
震 E — 9 Purple 九紫	2 Black 二黑	4 Green 四綠 — 兌 W
5 Yellow 五黃	7 Red 七赤	3 Jade 三碧
艮 NE	坎 N	乾 NW

卯 Rabbit (Mar 6 - Apr 4) 二月 2nd Month

巽 SE	離 S	坤 SW
9 Purple 九紫	5 Yellow 五黃	7 Red 七赤
震 E — 8 White 八白	1 White 一白	3 Jade 三碧 — 兌 W
4 Green 四綠	6 White 六白	2 Black 二黑
艮 NE	坎 N	乾 NW

辰 Dragon (Apr 5 - May 5) 三月 3rd Month

巽 SE	離 S	坤 SW
8 White 八白	4 Green 四綠	6 White 六白
震 E — 7 Red 七赤	9 Purple 九紫	2 Black 二黑 — 兌 W
3 Jade 三碧	5 Yellow 五黃	1 White 一白
艮 NE	坎 N	乾 NW

巳 Snake (May 6 - Jun 5) 四月 4th Month

巽 SE	離 S	坤 SW
7 Red 七赤	3 Jade 三碧	5 Yellow 五黃
震 E — 6 White 六白	8 White 八白	1 White 一白 — 兌 W
2 Black 二黑	4 Green 四綠	9 Purple 九紫
艮 NE	坎 N	乾 NW

午 Horse (Jun 6 - July 6) 五月 5th Month

巽 SE	離 S	坤 SW
6 White 六白	2 Black 二黑	4 Green 四綠
震 E — 5 Yellow 五黃	7 Red 七赤	9 Purple 九紫 — 兌 W
1 White 一白	3 Jade 三碧	8 White 八白
艮 NE	坎 N	乾 NW

未 Goat (July 7 - Aug 7) 六月 6th Month

巽 SE	離 S	坤 SW
5 Yellow 五黃	1 White 一白	3 Jade 三碧
震 E — 4 Green 四綠	6 White 六白	8 White 八白 — 兌 W
9 Purple 九紫	2 Black 二黑	7 Red 七赤
艮 NE	坎 N	乾 NW

申 Monkey (Aug 8 - Sept 7) 七月 7th Month

巽 SE	離 S	坤 SW
4 Green 四綠	9 Purple 九紫	2 Black 二黑
震 E — 3 Jade 三碧	5 Yellow 五黃	7 Red 七赤 — 兌 W
8 White 八白	1 White 一白	6 White 六白
艮 NE	坎 N	乾 NW

酉 Rooster (Sept 8 - Oct 7) 八月 8th Month

巽 SE	離 S	坤 SW
3 Jade 三碧	8 White 八白	1 White 一白
震 E — 2 Black 二黑	4 Green 四綠	6 White 六白 — 兌 W
7 Red 七赤	9 Purple 九紫	5 Yellow 五黃
艮 NE	坎 N	乾 NW

戌 Dog (Oct 8 - Nov 6) 九月 9th Month

巽 SE	離 S	坤 SW
2 Black 二黑	7 Red 七赤	9 Purple 九紫
震 E — 1 White 一白	3 Jade 三碧	5 Yellow 五黃 — 兌 W
6 White 六白	8 White 八白	4 Green 四綠
艮 NE	坎 N	乾 NW

亥 Pig (Nov 7 - Dec 6) 十月 10th Month

巽 SE	離 S	坤 SW
1 White 一白	6 White 六白	8 White 八白
震 E — 9 Purple 九紫	2 Black 二黑	4 Green 四綠 — 兌 W
5 Yellow 五黃	7 Red 七赤	3 Jade 三碧
艮 NE	坎 N	乾 NW

子 Rat (Dec 7 - Jan 5) 十一月 11th Month

巽 SE	離 S	坤 SW
9 Purple 九紫	5 Yellow 五黃	7 Red 七赤
震 E — 8 White 八白	1 White 一白	3 Jade 三碧 — 兌 W
4 Green 四綠	6 White 六白	2 Black 二黑
艮 NE	坎 N	乾 NW

丑 Ox (Jan 6 - Feb 3) 十二月 12th Month

巽 SE	離 S	坤 SW
8 White 八白	4 Green 四綠	6 White 六白
震 E — 7 Red 七赤	9 Purple 九紫	2 Black 二黑 — 兌 W
3 Jade 三碧	5 Yellow 五黃	1 White 一白
艮 NE	坎 N	乾 NW

Qi Men Three Nobles 三奇 :

Three Nobles 三奇 / Seasons	乙 Yi	丙 Bing	丁 Ding
立春 **Coming of Spring** Feb 4 - Feb 18	坎 Kan	坎 Kan	坤 Kun
春分 **Spring Equinox** Mar 21 - Apr 4	中 Middle	中 Middle	乾 Qian
立夏 **Coming of Summer** May 6 - May 20	乾 Qian	乾 Qian	兌 Dui
夏至 **Summer Solstice** Jun 22 - Jul 6	兌 Dui	兌 Dui	乾 Qian
立秋 **Coming of Autumn** Aug 8 - Aug 23	離 Li	離 Li	艮 Gen
秋分 **Autumn Equinox** Sept 23 - Oct 7	中 Middle	中 Middle	巽 Xun
立冬 **Coming of Winter** Nov 7 - Nov 22	巽 Xun	巽 Xun	震 Zhen
冬至 **Winter Solstice** Dec 22 - Jan 5	震 Zhen	震 Zhen	巽 Xun

Sectors to Avoid Opening Mountain 開山凶位 :

月 MONTH	月建 Month Establishment	月破 Month Destruction	月剋山家 Month Countering Sitting		陰府太歲 Yin Mansion Grand Duke	
寅 Tiger (Feb 4 - Mar 5) 正月 1st Month	寅 Yin Tiger	申 Shen Monkey	乾 Qian	兌 Dui	坎 Kan	坤 Kun
卯 Rabbit (Mar 6 - Apr 4) 二月 2nd Month	卯 Mao Rabbit	酉 You Rooster	亥 Hai Pig	丁 Ding Yin Fire	乾 Qian	離 Li
辰 Dragon (Apr 5 - May 5) 三月 3rd Month	辰 Chen Dragon	戌 Xu Dog	震 Zhen	巳 Si Snake	坤 Kun	震 Zhen
巳 Snake (May 6 - Jun 5) 四月 4th Month	巳 Si Snake	亥 Hai Pig	艮 Gen		巽 Xun	艮 Gen
午 Horse (Jun 6 - July 6) 五月 5th Month	午 Wu Horse	子 Zi Rat	—		乾 Qian	兌 Dui
未 Goat (July 7 - Aug 7) 六月 6th Month	未 Wei Goat	丑 Chou Ox	—		坤 Kun	坎 Kan
申 Monkey (Aug 8 - Sept 7) 七月 7th Month	申 Shen Monkey	寅 Yin Tiger	水 Water	山 Mountain	離 Li	乾 Qian
酉 Rooster (Sept 8 - Oct 7) 八月 8th Month	酉 You Rooster	卯 Mao Rabbit	土 Earth		震 Zhen	坤 Kun
戌 Dog (Oct 8 - Nov 6) 九月 9th Month	戌 Xu Dog	辰 Chen Dragon	乾 Qian	兌 Dui	艮 Gen	巽 Xun
亥 Pig (Nov 7 - Dec 6) 十月 10th Month	亥 Hai Pig	巳 Si Snake	亥 Hai Pig	丁 Ding Yin Fire	兌 Dui	乾 Qian
子 Rat (Dec 7 - Jan 5) 十一月 11th Month	子 Zi Rat	午 Wu Horse	離 Li	丙 Bing Yang Fire	坎 Kan	坤 Kun
丑 Ox (Jan 6 - Feb 3) 十二月 12th Month	丑 Chou Ox	未 Wei Goat	壬 Ren Yang Water	乙 Yi Yin Wood	乾 Qian	離 Li

Negative Repair / Renovation Sectors 修方凶位：

月 MONTH	天官符 Heavenly Officer Charm			地官符 Earth Officer Charm			小月建 Small Month Establishment		
寅 **Tiger** (Feb 4 - Mar 5) 正月 **1st Month**		中 Middle		戌 Xu Dog	乾 Qian	亥 Hai Pig		中 Middle	
卯 **Rabbit** (Mar 6 - Apr 4) 二月 **2nd Month**	辰 Chen Dragon	巽 Xun	巳 Si Snake		中 Middle		戌 Xu Dog	乾 Qian	亥 Hai Pig
辰 **Dragon** (Apr 5 - May 5) 三月 **3rd Month**	甲 Jia Yang Wood	震 Zhen	乙 Yi Yin Wood	辰 Chen Dragon	巽 Xun	巳 Si Snake	庚 Geng Yang Metal	兌 Dui	辛 Xin Yin Metal
巳 **Snake** (May 6 - Jun 5) 四月 **4th Month**	未 Wei Goat	坤 Kun	申 Shen Monkey	甲 Jia Yang Wood	震 Zhen	乙 Yi Yin Wood	丑 Chou Ox	艮 Gen	寅 Yin Tiger
午 **Horse** (Jun 6 - July 6) 五月 **5th Month**	壬 Ren Yang Water	坎 Kan	癸 Gui Yin Water	未 Wei Goat	坤 Kun	申 Shen Monkey	丙 Bing Yang Fire	離 Li	丁 Ding Yin Fire
未 **Goat** (July 7 - Aug 7) 六月 **6th Month**	丙 Bing Yang Fire	離 Li	丁 Ding Yin Fire	壬 Ren Yang Water	坎 Kan	癸 Gui Yin Water	壬 Ren Yang Water	坎 Kan	癸 Gui Yin Water
申 **Monkey** (Aug 8 - Sept 7) 七月 **7th Month**	丑 Chou Ox	艮 Gen	寅 Yin Tiger	丙 Bing Yang Fire	離 Li	丁 Ding Yin Fire	未 Wei Goat	坤 Kun	申 Shen Monkey
酉 **Rooster** (Sept 8 - Oct 7) 八月 **8th Month**	庚 Geng Yang Metal	兌 Dui	辛 Xin Yin Metal	丑 Chou Ox	艮 Gen	寅 Yin Tiger	甲 Jia Yang Wood	震 Zhen	乙 Yi Yin Wood
戌 **Dog** (Oct 8 - Nov 6) 九月 **9th Month**	戌 Xu Dog	乾 Qian	亥 Hai Pig	庚 Geng Yang Metal	兌 Dui	辛 Xin Yin Metal	辰 Chen Dragon	巽 Xun	巳 Si Snake
亥 **Pig** (Nov 7 - Dec 6) 十月 **10th Month**		中 Middle		戌 Xu Dog	乾 Qian	亥 Hai Pig		中 Middle	
子 **Rat** (Dec 7 - Jan 5) 十一月 **11th Month**	庚 Geng Yang Metal	兌 Dui	辛 Xin Yin Metal		中 Middle		戌 Xu Dog	乾 Qian	亥 Hai Pig
丑 **Ox** (Jan 6 - Feb 3) 十二月 **12th Month**	戌 Xu Dog	乾 Qian	亥 Hai Pig	庚 Geng Yang Metal	兌 Dui	辛 Xin Yin Metal	庚 Geng Yang Metal	兌 Dui	辛 Xin Yin Metal

Negative Repair / Renovation Sectors 修方凶位 :

月 MONTH	大月建 Big Month Establishment			飛大煞 Flying Great Sha			丙丁獨火 Bing Ding Lonely Fire	
寅 **Tiger** (Feb 4 - Mar 5) 正月 **1st Month**	未 *Wei* **Goat**	坤 *Kun*	申 *Shen* **Monkey**	戌 *Xu* **Dog**	乾 *Qian*	亥 *Hai* **Pig**	中 **Middle**	乾 *Qian*
卯 **Rabbit** (Mar 6 - Apr 4) 二月 **2nd Month**	壬 *Ren* **Yang Water**	坎 *Kan*	癸 *Gui* **Yin Water**	中 **Middle**			中 **Middle**	
辰 **Dragon** (Apr 5 - May 5) 三月 **3rd Month**	丙 *Bing* **Yang Fire**	離 *Li*	丁 *Ding* **Yin Fire**	辰 *Chen* **Dragon**	巽 *Xun*	巳 *Si* **Snake**	巽 *Xun*	中 **Middle**
巳 **Snake** (May 6 - Jun 5) 四月 **4th Month**	丑 *Chou* **Ox**	艮 *Gen*	寅 *Yin* **Tiger**	甲 *Jia* **Yang Wood**	震 *Zhen*	乙 *Yi* **Yin Wood**	震 *Zhen*	巽 *Xun*
午 **Horse** (Jun 6 - July 6) 五月 **5th Month**	庚 *Geng* **Yang Metal**	兌 *Dui*	辛 *Xin* **Yin Metal**	未 *Wei* **Goat**	坤 *Kun*	申 *Shen* **Monkey**	坤 *Kun*	震 *Zhen*
未 **Goat** (July 7 - Aug 7) 六月 **6th Month**	戌 *Xu* **Dog**	乾 *Qian*	亥 *Hai* **Pig**	壬 *Ren* **Yang Water**	坎 *Kan*	癸 *Gui* **Yin Water**	坎 *Kan*	坤 *Kun*
申 **Monkey** (Aug 8 - Sept 7) 七月 **7th Month**	中 **Middle**			丙 *Bing* **Yang Fire**	離 *Li*	丁 *Ding* **Yin Fire**	離 *Li*	坎 *Kan*
酉 **Rooster** (Sept 8 - Oct 7) 八月 **8th Month**	辰 *Chen* **Dragon**	巽 *Xun*	巳 *Si* **Snake**	丑 *Chou* **Ox**	艮 *Gen*	寅 *Yin* **Tiger**	艮 *Gen*	離 *Li*
戌 **Dog** (Oct 8 - Nov 6) 九月 **9th Month**	甲 *Jia* **Yang Wood**	震 *Zhen*	乙 *Yi* **Yin Wood**	庚 *Geng* **Yang Metal**	兌 *Dui*	辛 *Xin* **Yin Metal**	兌 *Dui*	艮 *Gen*
亥 **Pig** (Nov 7 - Dec 6) 十月 **10th Month**	未 *Wei* **Goat**	坤 *Kun*	申 *Shen* **Monkey**	戌 *Xu* **Dog**	乾 *Qian*	亥 *Hai* **Pig**	乾 *Qian*	兌 *Dui*
子 **Rat** (Dec 7 - Jan 5) 十一月 **11th Month**	壬 *Ren* **Yang Water**	坎 *Kan*	癸 *Gui* **Yin Water**	中 **Middle**			中 **Middle**	乾 *Qian*
丑 **Ox** (Jan 6 - Feb 3) 十二月 **12th Month**	丙 *Bing* **Yang Fire**	離 *Li*	丁 *Ding* **Yin Fire**	庚 *Geng* **Yang Metal**	兌 *Dui*	辛 *Xin* **Yin Metal**	中 **Middle**	

Negative Repair / Renovation Sectors 修方凶位 ：

月 MONTH	月遊火 Month Wondering Fire	三煞 Monthly 3 Killings		
		劫煞 Robbery Sha	災煞 Calamity Sha	月煞 Month Sha
寅 Tiger (Feb 4 - Mar 5) 正月 1st Month	兌 Dui	亥 Hai Pig	子 Zi Rat	丑 Chou Ox
卯 Rabbit (Mar 6 - Apr 4) 二月 2nd Month	艮 Gen	申 Shen Monkey	酉 You Rooster	戌 Xu Dog
辰 Dragon (Apr 5 - May 5) 三月 3rd Month	離 Li	巳 Si Snake	午 Wu Horse	未 Wei Goat
巳 Snake (May 6 - Jun 5) 四月 4th Month	坎 Kan	寅 Yin Tiger	卯 Mao Rabbit	辰 Chen Dragon
午 Horse (Jun 6 - July 6) 五月 5th Month	坤 Kun	亥 Hai Pig	子 Zi Rat	丑 Chou Ox
未 Goat (July 7 - Aug 7) 六月 6th Month	震 Zhen	申 Shen Monkey	酉 You Rooster	戌 Xu Dog
申 Monkey (Aug 8 - Sept 7) 七月 7th Month	巽 Xun	巳 Si Snake	午 Wu Horse	未 Wei Goat
酉 Rooster (Sept 8 - Oct 7) 八月 8th Month	中 Middle	寅 Yin Tiger	卯 Mao Rabbit	辰 Chen Dragon
戌 Dog (Oct 8 - Nov 6) 九月 9th Month	乾 Qian	亥 Hai Pig	子 Zi Rat	丑 Chou Ox
亥 Pig (Nov 7 - Dec 6) 十月 10th Month	兌 Dui	申 Shen Monkey	酉 You Rooster	戌 Xu Dog
子 Rat (Dec 7 - Jan 5) 十一月 11th Month	艮 Gen	巳 Si Snake	午 Wu Horse	未 Wei Goat
丑 Ox (Jan 6 - Feb 3) 十二月 12th Month	離 Li	寅 Yin Tiger	卯 Mao Rabbit	辰 Chen Dragon

Negative Repair / Renovation Sectors 修方凶位 ：

月 MONTH	月刑 Month Punishment	月害 Month Harm	月厭 Month Detest
寅 **Tiger** (Feb 4 - Mar 5) 正月 **1st Month**	巳 *Si* Snake	巳 *Si* Snake	戌 *Xu* Dog
卯 **Rabbit** (Mar 6 - Apr 4) 二月 **2nd Month**	子 *Zi* Rat	辰 *Chen* Dragon	酉 *You* Rooster
辰 **Dragon** (Apr 5 - May 5) 三月 **3rd Month**	辰 *Chen* Dragon	卯 *Mao* Rabbit	申 *Shen* Monkey
巳 **Snake** (May 6 - Jun 5) 四月 **4th Month**	申 *Shen* Monkey	寅 *Yin* Tiger	未 *Wei* Goat
午 **Horse** (Jun 6 - July 6) 五月 **5th Month**	午 *Wu* Horse	丑 *Chou* Ox	午 *Wu* Horse
未 **Goat** (July 7 - Aug 7) 六月 **6th Month**	丑 *Chou* Ox	子 *Zi* Rat	巳 *Si* Snake
申 **Monkey** (Aug 8 - Sept 7) 七月 **7th Month**	寅 *Yin* Tiger	亥 *Hai* Pig	辰 *Chen* Dragon
酉 **Rooster** (Sept 8 - Oct 7) 八月 **8th Month**	酉 *You* Rooster	戌 *Xu* Dog	卯 *Mao* Rabbit
戌 **Dog** (Oct 8 - Nov 6) 九月 **9th Month**	未 *Wei* Goat	酉 *You* Rooster	寅 *Yin* Tiger
亥 **Pig** (Nov 7 - Dec 6) 十月 **10th Month**	亥 *Hai* Pig	申 *Shen* Monkey	丑 *Chou* Ox
子 **Rat** (Dec 7 - Jan 5) 十一月 **11th Month**	卯 *Mao* Rabbit	未 *Wei* Goat	子 *Zi* Rat
丑 **Ox** (Jan 6 - Feb 3) 十二月 **12th Month**	戌 *Xu* Dog	午 *Wu* Horse	亥 *Hai* Pig

甲戌 (Jia Xu)
Wood Dog

Heavenly Stem 天干	甲 **Yang Wood** (陽木)
Earthly Branch 地支	戌 **Dog** (Yang Earth 陽土)
Hidden Stem 藏干	戊 **Yang Earth,** 辛 **Yin Metal ,** 丁 **Yin Fire**
Na Yin 納音	山頭火 **Fire from the mountain**
Grand Duke 太歲	戌 **Dog**
Xuan Kong Five Element 玄空五行	7 火 **Fire**
Gua Name 卦名	水山蹇 **Obstruction**
Xuan Kong Period Luck 玄空卦運	**2**

Annual Positive Stars for Opening Mountain, Establishing Facing and Commencing Repairs 開山立向修方吉星:

歲德 **Duke Virtue**	甲	*Jia* **Yang Wood**
歲德合 **Duke Virtue Combo**	己	*Ji* **Yin Earth**
歲枝德 **Duke Branch Virtue**	卯	*Mao* **Rabbit**
陽貴人 **Yang Nobleman**	未	*Wei* **Goat**
陰貴人 **Yin Nobleman**	丑	*Chou* **Ox**
歲祿 **Duke Prosperous**	寅	*Yin* **Tiger**
歲馬 **Duke Horse**	申	*Shen* **Monkey**
奏書 **Decree**	坤	*Kun*
博士 **Professor**	艮	*Gen*

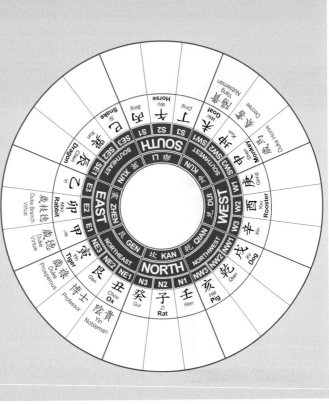

Annual Negative Stars for Opening Mountain, Establishing Facing and Commencing Repairs 開山立向修方凶星:

太歲 Grand Duke	歲破 Year Breaker	三煞 Three Killings			坐煞向煞 Sitting Sha Facing Sha				浮天空亡 Floating Heaven Emptiness	
戌 *Xu* Dog	辰 *Chen* Dragon	亥 *Hai* Pig	子 *Zi* Rat	丑 *Chou* Ox	壬 *Ren* Yang Water	癸 *Gui* Yin Water	丙 *Bing* Yang Fire	丁 *Ding* Yin Fire	離 *Li*	壬 *Ren* Yang Water

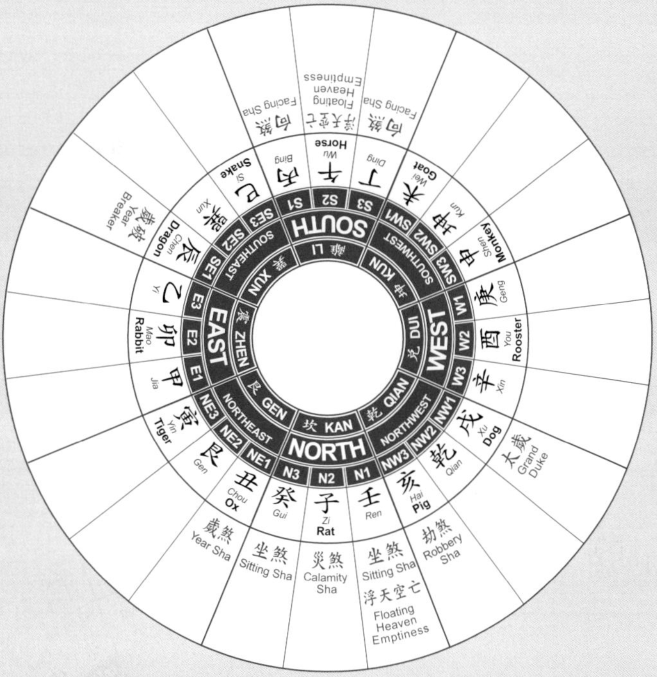

Annual San Yuan Purple White Stars 三元紫白九星:

上元 Upper Period Period 1, 2, 3

巽SE	離S	坤SW
8	4	6
震E 7	9 甲戌 Jia Xu Wood Dog	2 兌W
3	5	1
艮NE	坎N	乾NW

中元 Middle Period Period 4, 5, 6

巽SE	離S	坤SW
2	7	9
震E 1	3 甲戌 Jia Xu Wood Dog	5 兌W
6	8	4
艮NE	坎N	乾NW

下元 Lower Period Period 7, 8, 9

巽SE	離S	坤SW
5	1	3
震E 4	6 甲戌 Jia Xu Wood Dog	8 兌W
9	2	7
艮NE	坎N	乾NW

Mountain Covering Yellow Path 蓋山黄道：

貪狼 *Tan Lang* **Greedy Wolf**				巨門 *Ju Men* **Huge Door**		武曲 *Wu Qu* **Military Arts**				文曲 *Wen Qu* **Literary Arts**			
坎 *Kan* N2	癸 *Gui* N3	申 *Shen* SW3	辰 *Chen* SE1	坤 *Kun* SW2	乙 *Yi* E3	離 *Li* S2	壬 *Ren* N1	寅 *Yin* NE3	戌 *Xu* NW1	兌 *Dui* W2	丁 *Ding* S3	巳 *Si* SE3	丑 *Chou* NE1

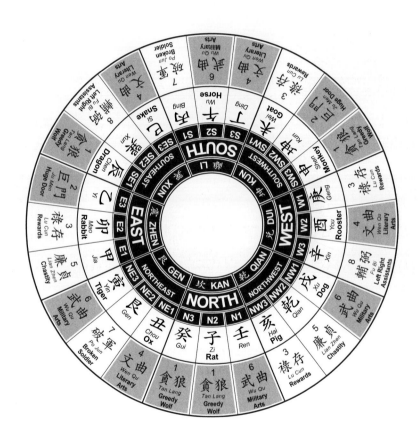

Heaven Penetrating Force 通天竅：

三合前方 **Facing Three Harmony**	坤申 *Kun Shen*	庚酉 *Geng You*	辛戌 *Xin Xu*
三合後方 **Sitting Three Harmony**	艮寅 *Gen Yin*	甲卯 *Jia Mao*	乙辰 *Yi Chen*

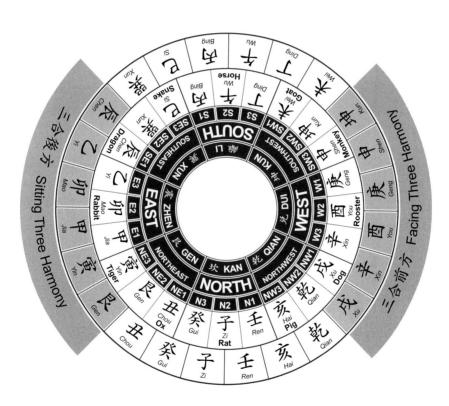

Moving Horse Six Ren Assessment 走馬六壬:

神后 *Shen Hou* **Holy Empress**	功曹 *Gong Cao* **Marshall**	天罡 *Tian Gang* **Heavenly Dipper**	勝光 *Sheng Guang* **Subliminal Bright**	傳送 *Chuan Song* **Great General**	河魁 *He Kui* **River Scholar**
艮寅 *Gen Yin*	乙辰 *Yi Chen*	丙午 *Bing Wu*	坤申 *Kun Shen*	辛戌 *Xin Xu*	壬子 *Ren Zi*

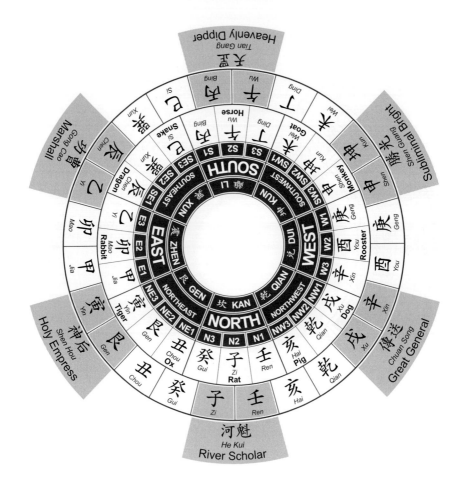

Four Advantages Three Cycles Star Plate 四利三元：

太陽 *Tai Yang* **Sun**	太陰 *Tai Yin* **Moon**	龍德 *Long De* **Dragon Virtue**	福德 *Fu De* **Fortune Virtue**
亥 *Hai* **Pig**	丑 *Chou* **Ox**	巳 *Si* **Snake**	未 *Wei* **Goat**

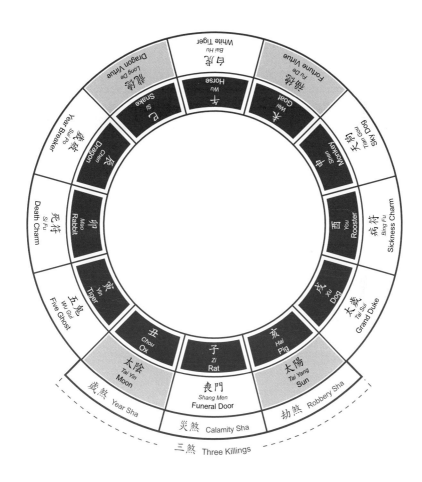

Negative Sectors For Opening Mountain 開山凶位:

年尅山家 Year Countering Sitting

乾 Qian NW2	亥 Hai NW3	兌 Dui W2	丁 Ding S3

陰府太歲 Yin Fu Tai Sui **Yin Mansion Grand Duke**	六害 Liu Hai **Six Harm**	死符 Si Fu **Death Charm**	炙退 Zhi Tui **Roasting Star**
艮 Gen NE2	巽 Xun SE2	酉 You W2	卯 Mao E2	酉 You W2

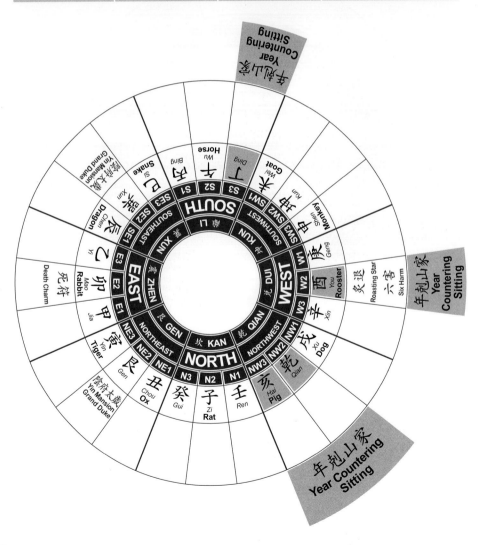

Negative Directions to Establish Facing 立向凶方：

巡山羅喉 *Xun Shan Luo Hou* **Mountain Patrol Luo Hou Star**	病符 *Bing Fu* **Sickness Charm**
乾 *Qian* **NW2**	酉 *You* **W2**

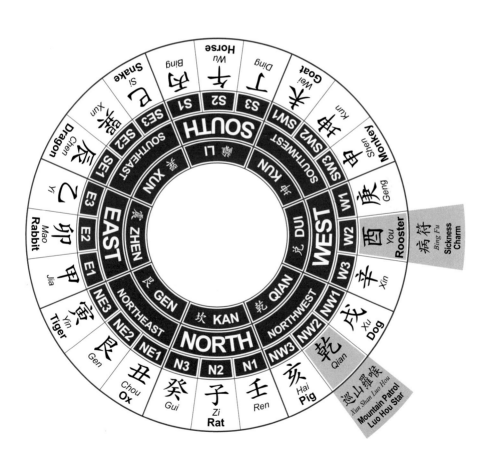

Negative Repair / Renovation Sectors Table 修方凶位表：

天官符 **Heavenly Officer Charm**	巳 *Si* Snake		飛廉 **Flying Chaste**	子 *Zi* Rat
地官符 **Earthly Officer Charm**	寅 *Yin* Tiger		喪門 **Funeral Door**	子 *Zi* Rat
大煞 **Great Sha**	午 *Wu* Horse		弔客 **Suspended Guest**	申 *Shen* Monkey
大將軍 **Big General**	午 *Wu* Horse		白虎 **White Tiger**	午 *Wu* Horse
力士 **Strong Man**	乾 *Qian*			午 *Wu* Horse
蠶室 **Silkworm Room**	巽 *Xun*			未 *Wei* Goat
蠶官 **Silkworm Officer**	辰 *Chen* Dragon		金神 **Golden God**	申 *Shen* Monkey
蠶命 **Silkworm Life**	巳 *Si* Snake			酉 *You* Rooster
歲刑 **Duke Punishment**	未 *Wei* Goat		獨火 **Lonely Fire**	乾 *Qian*
黃幡 **Yellow Flag**	戌 *Xu* Dog		五鬼 **Five Ghost**	午 *Wu* Horse
豹尾 **Leopard Tail**	辰 *Chen* Dragon		破敗五鬼 **Destructive Five Ghost**	巽 *Xun*

Negative Repair / Renovation Sectors Diagram 修方凶位圖：

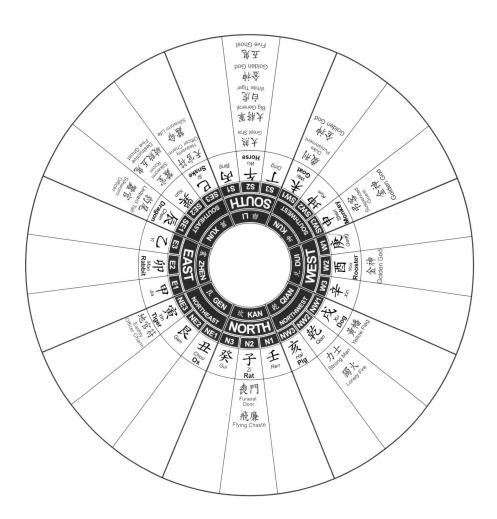

12-Month Auxiliary Stars Reference Table :
甲戌年十二月，開山立向修方星表

Positive Monthly Stars 吉星方

月 MONTH	寅 Tiger (Feb 4 - Mar 5) 正月 1st Month	卯 Rabbit (Mar 6 - Apr 4) 二月 2nd Month	辰 Dragon (Apr 5 - May 5) 三月 3rd Month	巳 Snake (May 6 - Jun 5) 四月 4th Month	午 Horse (Jun 6 - July 6) 五月 5th Month	未 Goat (July 7 - Aug 7) 六月 6th Month
天道 Heavenly Path	南 South	西南 Southwest	北 North	西 West	西北 Northwest	東 East
天德 Heavenly Virtue	丁 Ding Yin Fire	坤 Kun (申)	壬 Ren Yang Water	辛 Xin Yin Metal	乾 Qian (亥)	甲 Jia Yang Wood
天德合 Heavenly Virtue Combo	壬 Ren Yang Water	(巳)	丁 Ding Yin Fire	丙 Bing Yang Fire	(寅)	己 Ji Yin Earth
月德 Monthly Virtue	丙 Bing Yang Fire	甲 Jia Yang Wood	壬 Ren Yang Water	庚 Geng Yang Metal	丙 Bing Yang Fire	甲 Jia Yang Wood
月德合 Monthly Virtue Combo	辛 Xin Yin Metal	己 Ji Yin Earth	丁 Ding Yin Fire	乙 Yi Yin Wood	辛 Xin Yin Metal	己 Ji Yin Earth
月空 Month Emptiness	壬 Ren Yang Water	庚 Geng Yang Metal	丙 Bing Yang Fire	甲 Jia Yang Wood	壬 Ren Yang Water	庚 Geng Yang Metal
陽貴人 Yang Nobleman	坎 Kan	離 Li	艮 Gen	兌 Dui	乾 Qian	中 Middle
陰貴人 Yin Nobleman	兌 Dui	乾 Qian	中 Middle	巽 Xun	震 Zhen	坤 Kun
飛天祿 Flying Heavenly Wealth	中 Middle	坎 Kan	離 Li	艮 Gen	兌 Dui	乾 Qian
飛天馬 Flying Heavenly Horse	坤 Kun	坎 Kan	離 Li	艮 Gen	兌 Dui	乾 Qian

12-Month Auxiliary Stars Reference Table :
甲戌年十二月，開山立向修方星表

申 Monkey (Aug 8 - Sept 7) 七月 7th Month	酉 Rooster (Sept 8 - Oct 7) 八月 8th Month	戌 Dog (Oct 8 - Nov 6) 九月 9th Month	亥 Pig (Nov 7 - Dec 6) 十月 10th Month	子 Rat (Dec 7 - Jan 5) 十一月 11th Month	丑 Ox (Jan 6 - Feb 3) 十二月 12th Month	月 MONTH
北 North	東北 Northeast	南 South	東 East	東南 Southeast	西 West	天道 Heavenly Path
癸 Gui Yin Water	艮 Gen (寅)	丙 Bing Yang Fire	乙 Yi Yin Wood	巽 Xun (巳)	庚 Geng Yang Metal	天德 Heavenly Virtue
戊 Wu Yang Earth	(亥)	辛 Xin Yin Metal	庚 Geng Yang Metal	(申)	乙 Yi Yin Wood	天德合 Heavenly Virtue Combo
壬 Ren Yang Water	庚 Geng Yang Metal	丙 Bing Yang Fire	甲 Jia Yang Wood	壬 Ren Yang Water	庚 Geng Yang Metal	月德 Monthly Virtue
丁 Ding Yin Fire	乙 Yi Yin Wood	辛 Xin Yin Metal	己 Ji Yin Earth	丁 Ding Yin Fire	乙 Yi Yin Wood	月德合 Monthly Virtue Combo
丙 Bing Yang Fire	甲 Jia Yang Wood	壬 Ren Yang Water	庚 Geng Yang Metal	丙 Bing Yang Fire	甲 Jia Yang Wood	月空 Month Emptiness
坎 Kan	離 Li	艮 Gen	兌 Dui	乾 Qian	中 Middle	陽貴人 Yang Nobleman
坎 Kan	離 Li	艮 Gen	兌 Dui	乾 Qian	中 Middle	陰貴人 Yin Nobleman
中 Middle	巽 Xun	震 Zhen	坤 Kun	坎 Kan	離 Li	飛天祿 Flying Heavenly Wealth
中 Middle	坎 Kan	離 Li	艮 Gen	兌 Dui	乾 Qian	飛天馬 Flying Heavenly Horse

甲戌 (Jia Xu) Wood Dog

Monthly Purple White Stars 月紫白九星：

寅 Tiger (Feb 4 - Mar 5) 正月 1st Month

巽SE	離S	坤SW
4 Green 四綠	**9** Purple 九紫	**2** Black 二黑
震E **3** Jade 三碧	**5** Yellow 五黃	**7** Red 七赤 兌W
艮NE **8** White 八白	坎N **1** White 一白	乾NW **6** White 六白

卯 Rabbit (Mar 6 - Apr 4) 二月 2nd Month

巽SE	離S	坤SW
3 Jade 三碧	**8** White 八白	**1** White 一白
震E **2** Black 二黑	**4** Green 四綠	**6** White 六白 兌W
艮NE **7** Red 七赤	坎N **9** Purple 九紫	乾NW **5** Yellow 五黃

辰 Dragon (Apr 5 - May 5) 三月 3rd Month

巽SE	離S	坤SW
2 Black 二黑	**7** Red 七赤	**9** Purple 九紫
震E **1** White 一白	**3** Jade 三碧	**5** Yellow 五黃 兌W
艮NE **6** White 六白	坎N **8** White 八白	乾NW **4** Green 四綠

巳 Snake (May 6 - Jun 5) 四月 4th Month

巽SE	離S	坤SW
1 White 一白	**6** White 六白	**8** White 八白
震E **9** Purple 九紫	**2** Black 二黑	**4** Green 四綠 兌W
艮NE **5** Yellow 五黃	坎N **7** Red 七赤	乾NW **3** Jade 三碧

午 Horse (Jun 6 - July 6) 五月 5th Month

巽SE	離S	坤SW
9 Purple 九紫	**5** Yellow 五黃	**7** Red 七赤
震E **8** White 八白	**1** White 一白	**3** Jade 三碧 兌W
艮NE **4** Green 四綠	坎N **6** White 六白	乾NW **2** Black 二黑

未 Goat (July 7 - Aug 7) 六月 6th Month

巽SE	離S	坤SW
8 White 八白	**4** Green 四綠	**6** White 六白
震E **7** Red 七赤	**9** Purple 九紫	**2** Black 二黑 兌W
艮NE **3** Jade 三碧	坎N **5** Yellow 五黃	乾NW **1** White 一白

申 Monkey (Aug 8 - Sept 7) 七月 7th Month

巽SE	離S	坤SW
7 Red 七赤	**3** Jade 三碧	**5** Yellow 五黃
震E **6** White 六白	**8** White 八白	**1** White 一白 兌W
艮NE **2** Black 二黑	坎N **4** Green 四綠	乾NW **9** Purple 九紫

酉 Rooster (Sept 8 - Oct 7) 八月 8th Month

巽SE	離S	坤SW
6 White 六白	**2** Black 二黑	**4** Green 四綠
震E **5** Yellow 五黃	**7** Red 七赤	**9** Purple 九紫 兌W
艮NE **1** White 一白	坎N **3** Jade 三碧	乾NW **8** White 八白

戌 Dog (Oct 8 - Nov 6) 九月 9th Month

巽SE	離S	坤SW
5 Yellow 五黃	**1** White 一白	**3** Jade 三碧
震E **4** Green 四綠	**6** White 六白	**8** White 八白 兌W
艮NE **9** Purple 九紫	坎N **2** Black 二黑	乾NW **7** Red 七赤

亥 Pig (Nov 7 - Dec 6) 十月 10th Month

巽SE	離S	坤SW
4 Green 四綠	**9** Purple 九紫	**2** Black 二黑
震E **3** Jade 三碧	**5** Yellow 五黃	**7** Red 七赤 兌W
艮NE **8** White 八白	坎N **1** White 一白	乾NW **6** White 六白

子 Rat (Dec 7 - Jan 5) 十一月 11th Month

巽SE	離S	坤SW
3 Jade 三碧	**8** White 八白	**1** White 一白
震E **2** Black 二黑	**4** Green 四綠	**6** White 六白 兌W
艮NE **7** Red 七赤	坎N **9** Purple 九紫	乾NW **5** Yellow 五黃

丑 Ox (Jan 6 - Feb 3) 十二月 12th Month

巽SE	離S	坤SW
2 Black 二黑	**7** Red 七赤	**9** Purple 九紫
震E **1** White 一白	**3** Jade 三碧	**5** Yellow 五黃 兌W
艮NE **6** White 六白	坎N **8** White 八白	乾NW **4** Green 四綠

Qi Men Three Nobles 三奇 :

Three Nobles 三奇 / Seasons	乙 Yi	丙 Bing	丁 Ding
立春 **Coming of Spring** Feb 4 - Feb 18	離 Li	離 Li	坎 Kan
春分 **Spring Equinox** Mar 21 - Apr 4	巽 Xun	巽 Xun	中 **Middle**
立夏 **Coming of Summer** May 6 - May 20	中 **Middle**	中 **Middle**	乾 Qian
夏至 **Summer Solstice** Jun 22 - Jul 6	艮 Gen	艮 Gen	兑 Dui
立秋 **Coming of Autumn** Aug 8 - Aug 23	坎 Kan	坎 Kan	離 Li
秋分 **Autumn Equinox** Sept 23 - Oct 7	乾 Qian	乾 Qian	中 **Middle**
立冬 **Coming of Winter** Nov 7 - Nov 22	中 **Middle**	中 **Middle**	巽 Xun
冬至 **Winter Solstice** Dec 22 - Jan 5	坤 Kun	坤 Kun	震 Zhen

Sectors to Avoid Opening Mountain 開山凶位 :

月 MONTH	月建 Month Establishment	月破 Month Destruction	月剋山家 Month Countering Sitting		陰府太歲 Yin Mansion Grand Duke	
寅 **Tiger** (Feb 4 - Mar 5) 正月 **1st Month**	寅 *Yin* **Tiger**	申 *Shen* **Monkey**	乾 *Qian*	兌 *Dui*	坎 *Kan*	坤 *Kun*
卯 **Rabbit** (Mar 6 - Apr 4) 二月 **2nd Month**	卯 *Mao* **Rabbit**	酉 *You* **Rooster**	亥 *Hai* **Pig** / 丁 *Ding* **Yin Fire**		乾 *Qian*	離 *Li*
辰 **Dragon** (Apr 5 - May 5) 三月 **3rd Month**	辰 *Chen* **Dragon**	戌 *Xu* **Dog**	震 *Zhen*	巳 *Si* **Snake**	坤 *Kun*	震 *Zhen*
巳 **Snake** (May 6 - Jun 5) 四月 **4th Month**	巳 *Si* **Snake**	亥 *Hai* **Pig**	艮 *Gen*		巽 *Xun*	艮 *Gen*
午 **Horse** (Jun 6 - July 6) 五月 **5th Month**	午 *Wu* **Horse**	子 *Zi* **Rat**	–		乾 *Qian*	兌 *Dui*
未 **Goat** (July 7 - Aug 7) 六月 **6th Month**	未 *Wei* **Goat**	丑 *Chou* **Ox**	–		坤 *Kun*	坎 *Kan*
申 **Monkey** (Aug 8 - Sept 7) 七月 **7th Month**	申 *Shen* **Monkey**	寅 *Yin* **Tiger**	水 **Water**	山 **Mountain**	離 *Li*	乾 *Qian*
酉 **Rooster** (Sept 8 - Oct 7) 八月 **8th Month**	酉 *You* **Rooster**	卯 *Mao* **Rabbit**	土 **Earth**		震 *Zhen*	坤 *Kun*
戌 **Dog** (Oct 8 - Nov 6) 九月 **9th Month**	戌 *Xu* **Dog**	辰 *Chen* **Dragon**	乾 *Qian*	兌 *Dui*	艮 *Gen*	巽 *Xun*
亥 **Pig** (Nov 7 - Dec 6) 十月 **10th Month**	亥 *Hai* **Pig**	巳 *Si* **Snake**	亥 *Hai* **Pig**	丁 *Ding* **Yin Fire**	兌 *Dui*	乾 *Qian*
子 **Rat** (Dec 7 - Jan 5) 十一月 **11th Month**	子 *Zi* **Rat**	午 *Wu* **Horse**	離 *Li*	丙 *Bing* **Yang Fire**	坎 *Kan*	坤 *Kun*
丑 **Ox** (Jan 6 - Feb 3) 十二月 **12th Month**	丑 *Chou* **Ox**	未 *Wei* **Goat**	壬 *Ren* **Yang Water**	乙 *Yi* **Yin Wood**	乾 *Qian*	離 *Li*

Negative Repair / Renovation Sectors 修方凶位 :

月 MONTH	天官符 Heavenly Officer Charm			地官符 Earth Officer Charm			小月建 Small Month Establishment		
寅 Tiger (Feb 4 - Mar 5) 正月 1st Month	丑 Chou Ox	艮 Gen	寅 Yin Tiger	中 Middle			中 Middle		
卯 Rabbit (Mar 6 - Apr 4) 二月 2nd Month	庚 Geng Yang Metal	兌 Dui	辛 Xin Yin Metal	庚 Geng Yang Metal	兌 Dui	辛 Xin Yin Metal	戌 Xu Dog	乾 Qian	亥 Hai Pig
辰 Dragon (Apr 5 - May 5) 三月 3rd Month	戌 Xu Dog	乾 Qian	亥 Hai Pig	戌 Xu Dog	乾 Qian	亥 Hai Pig	庚 Geng Yang Metal	兌 Dui	辛 Xin Yin Metal
巳 Snake (May 6 - Jun 5) 四月 4th Month	中 Middle			中 Middle			丑 Chou Ox	艮 Gen	寅 Yin Tiger
午 Horse (Jun 6 - July 6) 五月 5th Month	庚 Geng Yang Metal	兌 Dui	辛 Xin Yin Metal	辰 Chen Dragon	巽 Xun	巳 Si Snake	丙 Bing Yang Fire	離 Li	丁 Ding Yin Fire
未 Goat (July 7 - Aug 7) 六月 6th Month	戌 Xu Dog	乾 Qian	亥 Hai Pig	甲 Jia Yang Wood	震 Zhen	乙 Yi Yin Wood	壬 Ren Yang Water	坎 Kan	癸 Gui Yin Water
申 Monkey (Aug 8 - Sept 7) 七月 7th Month	中 Middle			未 Wei Goat	坤 Kun	申 Shen Monkey	未 Wei Goat	坤 Kun	申 Shen Monkey
酉 Rooster (Sept 8 - Oct 7) 八月 8th Month	辰 Chen Dragon	巽 Xun	巳 Si Snake	壬 Ren Yang Water	坎 Kan	癸 Gui Yin Water	甲 Jia Yang Wood	震 Zhen	乙 Yi Yin Wood
戌 Dog (Oct 8 - Nov 6) 九月 9th Month	甲 Jia Yang Wood	震 Zhen	乙 Yi Yin Wood	丙 Bing Yang Fire	離 Li	丁 Ding Yin Fire	辰 Chen Dragon	巽 Xun	巳 Si Snake
亥 Pig (Nov 7 - Dec 6) 十月 10th Month	未 Wei Goat	坤 Kun	申 Shen Monkey	丑 Chou Ox	艮 Gen	寅 Yin Tiger	中 Middle		
子 Rat (Dec 7 - Jan 5) 十一月 11th Month	壬 Ren Yang Water	坎 Kan	癸 Gui Yin Water	庚 Geng Yang Metal	兌 Dui	辛 Xin Yin Metal	戌 Xu Dog	乾 Qian	亥 Hai Pig
丑 Ox (Jan 6 - Feb 3) 十二月 12th Month	丙 Bing Yang Fire	離 Li	丁 Ding Yin Fire	戌 Xu Dog	乾 Qian	亥 Hai Pig	庚 Geng Yang Metal	兌 Dui	辛 Xin Yin Metal

Negative Repair / Renovation Sectors 修方凶位 :

月 MONTH	大月建 Big Month Establishment			飛大煞 Flying Great Sha			丙丁獨火 Bing Ding Lonely Fire	
寅 **Tiger** (Feb 4 - Mar 5) 正月 1st Month	中 Middle			丙 Bing Yang Fire	離 Li	丁 Ding Yin Fire	中 Middle	乾 Qian
卯 **Rabbit** (Mar 6 - Apr 4) 二月 2nd Month	辰 Chen Dragon	巽 Xun	巳 Si Snake	丑 Chou Ox	艮 Gen	寅 Yin Tiger	中 Middle	
辰 **Dragon** (Apr 5 - May 5) 三月 3rd Month	甲 Jia Yang Wood	震 Zhen	乙 Yi Yin Wood	庚 Geng Yang Metal	兌 Dui	辛 Xin Yin Metal	巽 Xun	中 Middle
巳 **Snake** (May 6 - Jun 5) 四月 4th Month	未 Wei Goat	坤 Kun	申 Shen Monkey	戌 Xu Dog	乾 Qian	亥 Hai Pig	震 Zhen	巽 Xun
午 **Horse** (Jun 6 - July 6) 五月 5th Month	壬 Ren Yang Water	坎 Kan	癸 Gui Yin Water	中 Middle			坤 Kun	震 Zhen
未 **Goat** (July 7 - Aug 7) 六月 6th Month	丙 Bing Yang Fire	離 Li	丁 Ding Yin Fire	庚 Geng Yang Metal	兌 Dui	辛 Xin Yin Metal	坎 Kan	坤 Kun
申 **Monkey** (Aug 8 - Sept 7) 七月 7th Month	丑 Chou Ox	艮 Gen	寅 Yin Tiger	戌 Xu Dog	乾 Qian	亥 Hai Pig	離 Li	坎 Kan
酉 **Rooster** (Sept 8 - Oct 7) 八月 8th Month	庚 Geng Yang Metal	兌 Dui	辛 Xin Yin Metal	中 Middle			艮 Gen	離 Li
戌 **Dog** (Oct 8 - Nov 6) 九月 9th Month	戌 Xu Dog	乾 Qian	亥 Hai Pig	辰 Chen Dragon	巽 Xun	巳 Si Snake	兌 Dui	艮 Gen
亥 **Pig** (Nov 7 - Dec 6) 十月 10th Month	中 Middle			甲 Jia Yang Wood	震 Zhen	乙 Yi Yin Wood	乾 Qian	兌 Dui
子 **Rat** (Dec 7 - Jan 5) 十一月 11th Month	辰 Chen Dragon	巽 Xun	巳 Si Snake	未 Wei Goat	坤 Kun	申 Shen Monkey	中 Middle	乾 Qian
丑 **Ox** (Jan 6 - Feb 3) 十二月 12th Month	甲 Jia Yang Wood	震 Zhen	乙 Yi Yin Wood	壬 Ren Yang Water	坎 Kan	癸 Gui Yin Water	中 Middle	

Negative Repair / Renovation Sectors 修方凶位 :

月 MONTH	月遊火 Month Wondering Fire	三煞 Monthly 3 Killings		
		劫煞 Robbery Sha	災煞 Calamity Sha	月煞 Month Sha
寅 Tiger (Feb 4 - Mar 5) 正月 1st Month	乾 Qian	亥 Hai Pig	子 Zi Rat	丑 Chou Ox
卯 Rabbit (Mar 6 - Apr 4) 二月 2nd Month	兌 Dui	申 Shen Monkey	酉 You Rooster	戌 Xu Dog
辰 Dragon (Apr 5 - May 5) 三月 3rd Month	艮 Gen	巳 Si Snake	午 Wu Horse	未 Wei Goat
巳 Snake (May 6 - Jun 5) 四月 4th Month	離 Li	寅 Yin Tiger	卯 Mao Rabbit	辰 Chen Dragon
午 Horse (Jun 6 - July 6) 五月 5th Month	坎 Kan	亥 Hai Pig	子 Zi Rat	丑 Chou Ox
未 Goat (July 7 - Aug 7) 六月 6th Month	坤 Kun	申 Shen Monkey	酉 You Rooster	戌 Xu Dog
申 Monkey (Aug 8 - Sept 7) 七月 7th Month	震 Zhen	巳 Si Snake	午 Wu Horse	未 Wei Goat
酉 Rooster (Sept 8 - Oct 7) 八月 8th Month	巽 Xun	寅 Yin Tiger	卯 Mao Rabbit	辰 Chen Dragon
戌 Dog (Oct 8 - Nov 6) 九月 9th Month	中 Middle	亥 Hai Pig	子 Zi Rat	丑 Chou Ox
亥 Pig (Nov 7 - Dec 6) 十月 10th Month	乾 Qian	申 Shen Monkey	酉 You Rooster	戌 Xu Dog
子 Rat (Dec 7 - Jan 5) 十一月 11th Month	兌 Dui	巳 Si Snake	午 Wu Horse	未 Wei Goat
丑 Ox (Jan 6 - Feb 3) 十二月 12th Month	艮 Gen	寅 Yin Tiger	卯 Mao Rabbit	辰 Chen Dragon

Negative Repair / Renovation Sectors 修方凶位 :

月 MONTH	月刑 Month Punishment	月害 Month Harm	月厭 Month Detest
寅 **Tiger** (Feb 4 - Mar 5) 正月 **1st Month**	巳 *Si* Snake	巳 *Si* Snake	戌 *Xu* Dog
卯 **Rabbit** (Mar 6 - Apr 4) 二月 **2nd Month**	子 *Zi* Rat	辰 *Chen* Dragon	酉 *You* Rooster
辰 **Dragon** (Apr 5 - May 5) 三月 **3rd Month**	辰 *Chen* Dragon	卯 *Mao* Rabbit	申 *Shen* Monkey
巳 **Snake** (May 6 - Jun 5) 四月 **4th Month**	申 *Shen* Monkey	寅 *Yin* Tiger	未 *Wei* Goat
午 **Horse** (Jun 6 - July 6) 五月 **5th Month**	午 *Wu* Horse	丑 *Chou* Ox	午 *Wu* Horse
未 **Goat** (July 7 - Aug 7) 六月 **6th Month**	丑 *Chou* Ox	子 *Zi* Rat	巳 *Si* Snake
申 **Monkey** (Aug 8 - Sept 7) 七月 **7th Month**	寅 *Yin* Tiger	亥 *Hai* Pig	辰 *Chen* Dragon
酉 **Rooster** (Sept 8 - Oct 7) 八月 **8th Month**	酉 *You* Rooster	戌 *Xu* Dog	卯 *Mao* Rabbit
戌 **Dog** (Oct 8 - Nov 6) 九月 **9th Month**	未 *Wei* Goat	酉 *You* Rooster	寅 *Yin* Tiger
亥 **Pig** (Nov 7 - Dec 6) 十月 **10th Month**	亥 *Hai* Pig	申 *Shen* Monkey	丑 *Chou* Ox
子 **Rat** (Dec 7 - Jan 5) 十一月 **11th Month**	卯 *Mao* Rabbit	未 *Wei* Goat	子 *Zi* Rat
丑 **Ox** (Jan 6 - Feb 3) 十二月 **12th Month**	戌 *Xu* Dog	午 *Wu* Horse	亥 *Hai* Pig

乙丑 (Yi Chou)
Wood Ox

Heavenly Stem 天干	乙 **Yin Wood** (陰木)
Earthly Branch 地支	丑 **Ox (Yin Earth** 陰土)
Hidden Stem 藏干	己 **Yin Earth**, 癸 **Yin Water**, 辛 **Yin Metal**
Na Yin 納音	海中金 **Metal from the sea**
Grand Duke 太歲	丑 **Ox**
Xuan Kong Five Element 玄空五行	3 木 **Wood**
Gua Name 卦名	火雷噬嗑 **Biting**
Xuan Kong Period Luck 玄空卦運	6

Annual Positive Stars for Opening Mountain, Establishing Facing and Commencing Repairs 開山立向修方吉星：

歲德 **Duke** **Virtue**	庚 *Geng* **Yang Metal**
歲德合 **Duke Virtue** **Combo**	乙 *Yi* **Yin Wood**
歲枝德 **Duke Branch** **Virtue**	午 *Wu* **Horse**
陽貴人 **Yang** **Nobleman**	申 *Shen* **Monkey**
陰貴人 **Yin** **Nobleman**	子 *Zi* **Rat**
歲祿 **Duke** **Prosperous**	卯 *Mao* **Rabbit**
歲馬 **Duke** **Horse**	亥 *Hai* **Pig**
奏書 **Decree**	乾 *Qian*
博士 **Professor**	巽 *Xun*

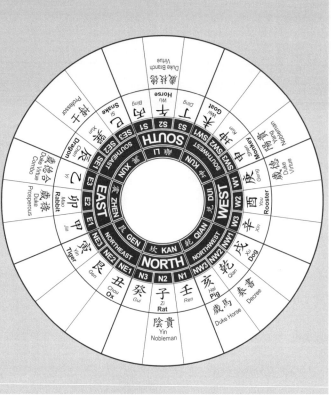

Annual Negative Stars for Opening Mountain, Establishing Facing and Commencing Repairs 開山立向修方凶星：

太歲 Grand Duke	歲破 Year Breaker	三煞 Three Killings			坐煞向煞 Sitting Sha Facing Sha				浮天空亡 Floating Heaven Emptiness	
丑 Chou Ox	未 Wei Goat	寅 Yin Tiger	卯 Mao Rabbit	辰 Chen Dragon	甲 Jia Yang Wood	乙 Yi Yin Wood	庚 Geng Yang Metal	辛 Xin Yin Metal	坎 Kan	癸 Gui Yin Water

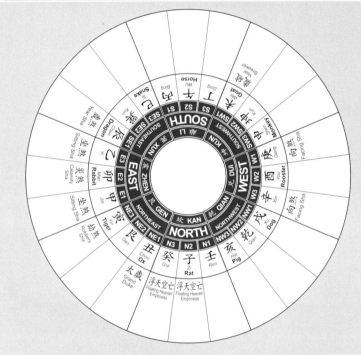

Annual San Yuan Purple White Stars 三元紫白九星：

	上元 Upper Period Period 1, 2, 3			中元 Middle Period Period 4, 5, 6			下元 Lower Period Period 7, 8, 9	

Upper Period (Period 1, 2, 3)

巽SE	離S	坤SW
8	4	6
震E 7	9 乙丑 Yi Chou Wood Ox	2 兌W
3	5	1
艮NE	坎N	乾NW

Middle Period (Period 4, 5, 6)

巽SE	離S	坤SW
2	7	9
震E 1	3 乙丑 Yi Chou Wood Ox	5 兌W
6	8	4
艮NE	坎N	乾NW

Lower Period (Period 7, 8, 9)

巽SE	離S	坤SW
5	1	3
震E 4	6 乙丑 Yi Chou Wood Ox	8 兌W
9	2	7
艮NE	坎N	乾NW

Mountain Covering Yellow Path 蓋山黃道：

貪狼 *Tan Lang* **Greedy Wolf**		巨門 *Ju Men* **Huge Door**		武曲 *Wu Qu* **Military Arts**				文曲 *Wen Qu* **Literary Arts**			
艮 *Gen* NE2	丙 *Bing* S1	巽 *Xun* SE2	辛 *Xin* W3	兌 *Dui* W2	丁 *Ding* S3	巳 *Si* SE3	丑 *Chou* NE1	離 *Li* S2	壬 *Ren* N1	寅 *Yin* NE3	戌 *Xu* NW1

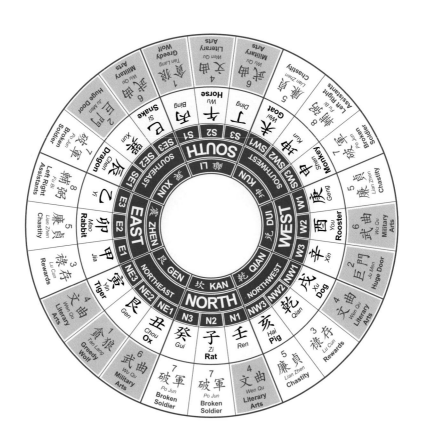

Heaven Penetrating Force 通天竅：			
三合前方 **Facing Three Harmony**	乾亥 Qian Hai	壬子 Ren Zi	癸丑 Gui Chou
三合後方 **Sitting Three Harmony**	巽巳 Xun Si	丙午 Bing Wu	丁未 Ding Wei

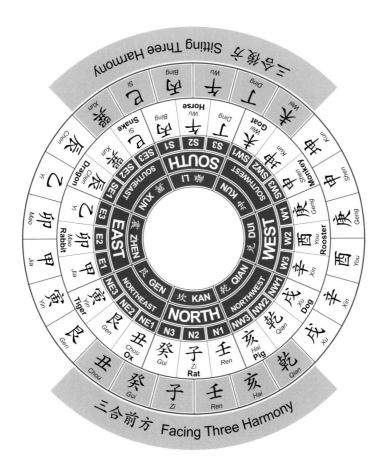

Moving Horse Six Ren Assessment 走馬六壬：

神后 *Shen Hou* **Holy Empress**	功曹 *Gong Cao* **Marshall**	天罡 *Tian Gang* **Heavenly Dipper**	勝光 *Sheng Guang* **Subliminal Bright**	傳送 *Chuan Song* **Great General**	河魁 *He Kui* **River Scholar**
乾亥 *Qian Hai*	癸丑 *Gui Chou*	甲卯 *Jia Mao*	巽巳 *Xun Si*	丁未 *Ding Wei*	庚酉 *Geng You*

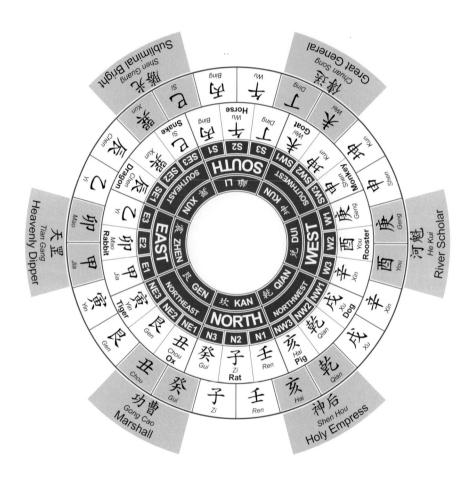

Four Advantages Three Cycles Star Plate 四利三元：

太陽 *Tai Yang* **Sun**	太陰 *Tai Yin* **Moon**	龍德 *Long De* **Dragon Virtue**	福德 *Fu De* **Fortune Virtue**
寅 *Yin* Tiger	辰 *Chen* Dragon	申 *Shen* Monkey	戌 *Xu* Dog

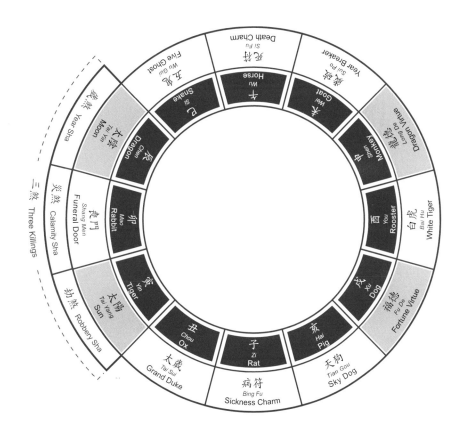

Negative Sectors For Opening Mountain 開山凶位：

年剋山家 Year Countering Sitting

震 *Zhen* **E2**	艮 *Gen* **NE2**	巳 *Si* **SE3**		

陰府太歲 *Yin Fu Tai Sui* **Yin Mansion Grand Duke**	六害 *Liu Hai* **Six Harm**	死符 *Si Fu* **Death Charm**	炙退 *Zhi Tui* **Roasting Star**
兌 乾 *Dui* *Qian* **W2** **NW2**	午 *Wu* **S2**	午 *Wu* **S2**	子 *Zi* **N2**

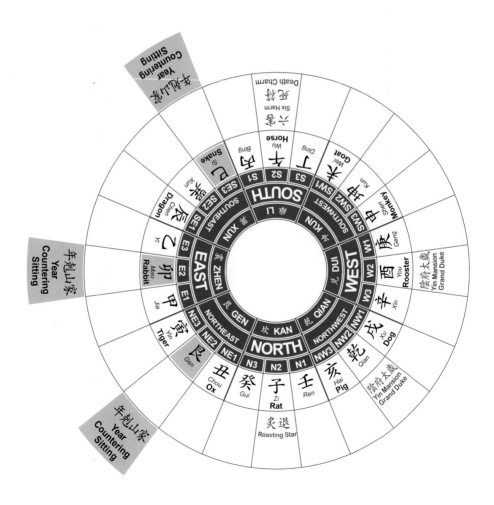

Negative Directions to Establish Facing 立向凶方：

巡山羅喉 *Xun Shan Luo Hou* **Mountain Patrol Luo Hou Star**	病符 *Bing Fu* **Sickness Charm**
艮 *Gen* **NE2**	子 *Zi* **N2**

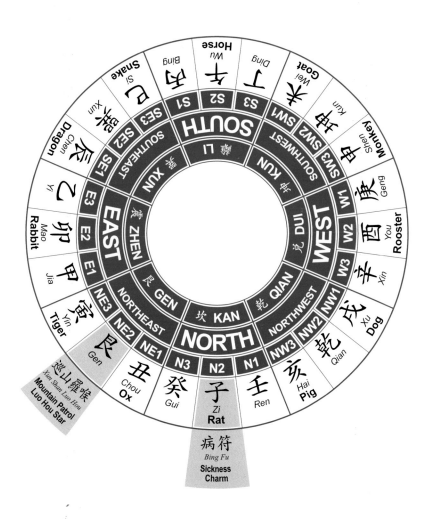

Negative Repair / Renovation Sectors Table 修方凶位表：

天官符 Heavenly Officer Charm	申 *Shen* Monkey	豹尾 Leopard Tail	未 *Wei* Goat
地官符 Earthly Officer Charm	巳 *Si* Snake	飛廉 Flying Chaste	酉 *You* Rooster
大煞 Great Sha	酉 *You* Rooster	喪門 Funeral Door	卯 *Mao* Rabbit
大將軍 Big General	酉 *You* Rooster	弔客 Suspended Guest	亥 *Hai* Pig
力士 Strong Man	艮 *Gen*	白虎 White Tiger	酉 *You* Rooster
蠶室 Silkworm Room	坤 *Kun*	金神 Golden God	辰 *Chen* Dragon 巳 *Si* Snake
蠶官 Silkworm Officer	未 *Wei* Goat		
蠶命 Silkworm Life	申 *Shen* Monkey	獨火 Lonely Fire	震 *Zhen*
歲刑 Duke Punishment	戌 *Xu* Dog	五鬼 Five Ghost	卯 *Mao* Rabbit
黃幡 Yellow Flag	丑 *Chou* Ox	破敗五鬼 Destructive Five Ghost	艮 *Gen*

Negative Repair / Renovation Sectors Diagram 修方凶位圖：

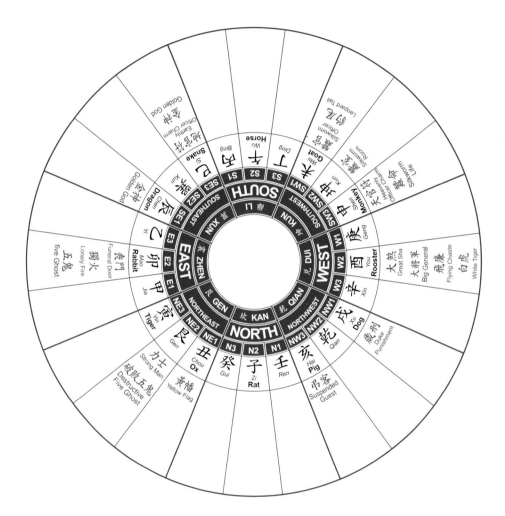

131

12-Month Auxiliary Stars Reference Table :
乙丑年十二月，開山立向修方星表

Positive Monthly Stars 吉星方

月 MONTH	寅 Tiger (Feb 4 - Mar 5) 正月 1st Month	卯 Rabbit (Mar 6 - Apr 4) 二月 2nd Month	辰 Dragon (Apr 5 - May 5) 三月 3rd Month	巳 Snake (May 6 - Jun 5) 四月 4th Month	午 Horse (Jun 6 - July 6) 五月 5th Month	未 Goat (July 7 - Aug 7) 六月 6th Month
天道 Heavenly Path	南 South	西南 Southwest	北 North	西 West	西北 Northwest	東 East
天德 Heavenly Virtue	丁 Ding Yin Fire	坤 Kun （申）	壬 Ren Yang Water	辛 Xin Yin Metal	乾 Qian （亥）	甲 Jia Yang Wood
天德合 Heavenly Virtue Combo	壬 Ren Yang Water	（巳）	丁 Ding Yin Fire	丙 Bing Yang Fire	（寅）	己 Ji Yin Earth
月德 Monthly Virtue	丙 Bing Yang Fire	甲 Jia Yang Wood	壬 Ren Yang Water	庚 Geng Yang Metal	丙 Bing Yang Fire	甲 Jia Yang Wood
月德合 Monthly Virtue Combo	辛 Xin Yin Metal	己 Ji Yin Earth	丁 Ding Yin Fire	乙 Yi Yin Wood	辛 Xin Yin Metal	己 Ji Yin Earth
月空 Month Emptiness	壬 Ren Yang Water	庚 Geng Yang Metal	丙 Bing Yang Fire	甲 Jia Yang Wood	壬 Ren Yang Water	庚 Geng Yang Metal
陽貴人 Yang Nobleman	坤 Kun	坎 Kan	離 Li	艮 Gen	兌 Dui	乾 Qian
陰貴人 Yin Nobleman	乾 Qian	中 Middle	巽 Xun	震 Zhen	坤 Kun	坎 Kan
飛天祿 Flying Heavenly Wealth	乾 Qian	中 Middle	坎 Kan	離 Li	艮 Gen	兌 Dui
飛天馬 Flying Heavenly Horse	中 Middle	巽 Xun	震 Zhen	坤 Kun	坎 Kan	離 Li

12-Month Auxiliary Stars Reference Table :
乙丑年十二月，開山立向修方星表

申 Monkey (Aug 8 - Sept 7) 七月 7th Month	酉 Rooster (Sept 8 - Oct 7) 八月 8th Month	戌 Dog (Oct 8 - Nov 6) 九月 9th Month	亥 Pig (Nov 7 - Dec 6) 十月 10th Month	子 Rat (Dec 7 - Jan 5) 十一月 11th Month	丑 Ox (Jan 6 - Feb 3) 十二月 12th Month	月 MONTH
北 North	東北 Northeast	南 South	東 East	東南 Southeast	西 West	天道 Heavenly Path
癸 Gui Yin Water	艮 Gen (寅)	丙 Bing Yang Fire	乙 Yi Yin Wood	巽 Xun (巳)	庚 Geng Yang Metal	天德 Heavenly Virtue
戊 Wu Yang Earth	(亥)	辛 Xin Yin Metal	庚 Geng Yang Metal	(申)	乙 Yi Yin Wood	天德合 Heavenly Virtue Combo
壬 Ren Yang Water	庚 Geng Yang Metal	丙 Bing Yang Fire	甲 Jia Yang Wood	壬 Ren Yang Water	庚 Geng Yang Metal	月德 Monthly Virtue
丁 Ding Yin Fire	乙 Yi Yin Wood	辛 Xin Yin Metal	己 Ji Yin Earth	丁 Ding Yin Fire	乙 Yi Yin Wood	月德合 Monthly Virtue Combo
丙 Bing Yang Fire	甲 Jia Yang Wood	壬 Ren Yang Water	庚 Geng Yang Metal	丙 Bing Yang Fire	甲 Jia Yang Wood	月空 Month Emptiness
中 Middle	坎 Kan	離 Li	艮 Gen	兌 Dui	乾 Qian	陽貴人 Yang Nobleman
離 Li	艮 Gen	兌 Dui	乾 Qian	中 Middle	坎 Kan	陰貴人 Yin Nobleman
乾 Qian	中 Middle	巽 Xun	震 Zhen	坤 Kun	坎 Kan	飛天祿 Flying Heavenly Wealth
艮 Gen	兌 Dui	乾 Qian	中 Middle	坎 Kan	離 Li	飛天馬 Flying Heavenly Horse

Monthly Purple White Stars 月紫白九星 :

寅 Tiger (Feb 4 - Mar 5) 正月 1st Month

巽 SE	離 S	坤 SW
4 Green 四綠	9 Purple 九紫	2 Black 二黑
震 E · 3 Jade 三碧	5 Yellow 五黃	7 Red 七赤 · 兌 W
8 White 八白	1 White 一白	6 White 六白
艮 NE	坎 N	乾 NW

卯 Rabbit (Mar 6 - Apr 4) 二月 2nd Month

巽 SE	離 S	坤 SW
3 Jade 三碧	8 White 八白	1 White 一白
震 E · 2 Black 二黑	4 Green 四綠	6 White 六白 · 兌 W
7 Red 七赤	9 Purple 九紫	5 Yellow 五黃
艮 NE	坎 N	乾 NW

辰 Dragon (Apr 5 - May 5) 三月 3rd Month

巽 SE	離 S	坤 SW
2 Black 二黑	7 Red 七赤	9 Purple 九紫
震 E · 1 White 一白	3 Jade 三碧	5 Yellow 五黃 · 兌 W
6 White 六白	8 White 八白	4 Green 四綠
艮 NE	坎 N	乾 NW

巳 Snake (May 6 - Jun 5) 四月 4th Month

巽 SE	離 S	坤 SW
1 White 一白	6 White 六白	8 White 八白
震 E · 9 Purple 九紫	2 Black 二黑	4 Green 四綠 · 兌 W
5 Yellow 五黃	7 Red 七赤	3 Jade 三碧
艮 NE	坎 N	乾 NW

午 Horse (Jun 6 - July 6) 五月 5th Month

巽 SE	離 S	坤 SW
9 Purple 九紫	5 Yellow 五黃	7 Red 七赤
震 E · 8 White 八白	1 White 一白	3 Jade 三碧 · 兌 W
4 Green 四綠	6 White 六白	2 Black 二黑
艮 NE	坎 N	乾 NW

未 Goat (July 7 - Aug 7) 六月 6th Month

巽 SE	離 S	坤 SW
8 White 八白	4 Green 四綠	6 White 六白
震 E · 7 Red 七赤	9 Purple 九紫	2 Black 二黑 · 兌 W
3 Jade 三碧	5 Yellow 五黃	1 White 一白
艮 NE	坎 N	乾 NW

申 Monkey (Aug 8 - Sept 7) 七月 7th Month

巽 SE	離 S	坤 SW
7 Red 七赤	3 Jade 三碧	5 Yellow 五黃
震 E · 6 White 六白	8 White 八白	1 White 一白 · 兌 W
2 Black 二黑	4 Green 四綠	9 Purple 九紫
艮 NE	坎 N	乾 NW

酉 Rooster (Sept 8 - Oct 7) 八月 8th Month

巽 SE	離 S	坤 SW
6 White 六白	2 Black 二黑	4 Green 四綠
震 E · 5 Yellow 五黃	7 Red 七赤	9 Purple 九紫 · 兌 W
1 White 一白	3 Jade 三碧	8 White 八白
艮 NE	坎 N	乾 NW

戌 Dog (Oct 8 - Nov 6) 九月 9th Month

巽 SE	離 S	坤 SW
5 Yellow 五黃	1 White 一白	3 Jade 三碧
震 E · 4 Green 四綠	6 White 六白	8 White 八白 · 兌 W
9 Purple 九紫	2 Black 二黑	7 Red 七赤
艮 NE	坎 N	乾 NW

亥 Pig (Nov 7 - Dec 6) 十月 10th Month

巽 SE	離 S	坤 SW
4 Green 四綠	9 Purple 九紫	2 Black 二黑
震 E · 3 Jade 三碧	5 Yellow 五黃	7 Red 七赤 · 兌 W
8 White 八白	1 White 一白	6 White 六白
艮 NE	坎 N	乾 NW

子 Rat (Dec 7 - Jan 5) 十一月 11th Month

巽 SE	離 S	坤 SW
3 Jade 三碧	8 White 八白	1 White 一白
震 E · 2 Black 二黑	4 Green 四綠	6 White 六白 · 兌 W
7 Red 七赤	9 Purple 九紫	5 Yellow 五黃
艮 NE	坎 N	乾 NW

丑 Ox (Jan 6 - Feb 3) 十二月 12th Month

巽 SE	離 S	坤 SW
2 Black 二黑	7 Red 七赤	9 Purple 九紫
震 E · 1 White 一白	3 Jade 三碧	5 Yellow 五黃 · 兌 W
6 White 六白	8 White 八白	4 Green 四綠
艮 NE	坎 N	乾 NW

Qi Men Three Nobles 三奇 :

Three Nobles 三奇 / Seasons	乙 Yi	丙 Bing	丁 Ding
立春 **Coming of Spring** Feb 4 - Feb 18	兌 Dui	艮 Gen	離 Li
春分 **Spring Equinox** Mar 21 - Apr 4	坤 Kun	震 Zhen	巽 Xun
立夏 **Coming of Summer** May 6 - May 20	震 Zhen	巽 Xun	中 **Middle**
夏至 **Summer Solstice** Jun 22 - Jul 6	坎 Kan	離 Li	艮 Gen
立秋 **Coming of Autumn** Aug 8 - Aug 23	震 Zhen	坤 Kun	坎 Kan
秋分 **Autumn Equinox** Sept 23 - Oct 7	艮 Gen	兌 Dui	乾 Qian
立冬 **Coming of Winter** Nov 7 - Nov 22	兌 Dui	乾 Qian	中 **Middle**
冬至 **Winter Solstice** Dec 22 - Jan 5	離 Li	坎 Kan	坤 Kun

Sectors to Avoid Opening Mountain 開山凶位 :

月 MONTH	月建 Month Establishment	月破 Month Destruction	月剋山家 Month Countering Sitting		陰府太歲 Yin Mansion Grand Duke	
寅 **Tiger** (Feb 4 - Mar 5) 正月 **1st Month**	寅 Yin **Tiger**	申 Shen **Monkey**	乾 Qian	兌 Dui	坤 Kun	震 Zhen
卯 **Rabbit** (Mar 6 - Apr 4) 二月 **2nd Month**	卯 Mao **Rabbit**	酉 You **Rooster**	亥 Hai **Pig**	丁 Ding **Yin Fire**	巽 Xun	艮 Gen
辰 **Dragon** (Apr 5 - May 5) 三月 **3rd Month**	辰 Chen **Dragon**	戌 Xu **Dog**	震 Zhen	巳 Si **Snake**	乾 Qian	兌 Dui
巳 **Snake** (May 6 - Jun 5) 四月 **4th Month**	巳 Si **Snake**	亥 Hai **Pig**	艮 Gen		坤 Kun	坎 Kan
午 **Horse** (Jun 6 - July 6) 五月 **5th Month**	午 Wu **Horse**	子 Zi **Rat**	離 Li	丙 Bing **Yang Fire**	離 Li	乾 Qian
未 **Goat** (July 7 - Aug 7) 六月 **6th Month**	未 Wei **Goat**	丑 Chou **Ox**	壬 Ren **Yang Water**	乙 Yi **Yin Wood**	震 Zhen	坤 Kun
申 **Monkey** (Aug 8 - Sept 7) 七月 **7th Month**	申 Shen **Monkey**	寅 Yin **Tiger**	—		艮 Gen	巽 Xun
酉 **Rooster** (Sept 8 - Oct 7) 八月 **8th Month**	酉 You **Rooster**	卯 Mao **Rabbit**	—		兌 Dui	乾 Qian
戌 **Dog** (Oct 8 - Nov 6) 九月 **9th Month**	戌 Xu **Dog**	辰 Chen **Dragon**	乾 Qian	兌 Dui	坎 Kan	坤 Kun
亥 **Pig** (Nov 7 - Dec 6) 十月 **10th Month**	亥 Hai **Pig**	巳 Si **Snake**	亥 Hai **Pig**	丁 Ding **Yin Fire**	乾 Qian	離 Li
子 **Rat** (Dec 7 - Jan 5) 十一月 **11th Month**	子 Zi **Rat**	午 Wu **Horse**	水 **Water**	山 **Mountain**	坤 Kun	震 Zhen
丑 **Ox** (Jan 6 - Feb 3) 十二月 **12th Month**	丑 Chou **Ox**	未 Wei **Goat**	土 **Earth**		巽 Xun	艮 Gen

Negative Repair / Renovation Sectors 修方凶位 :

月 MONTH	天官符 Heavenly Officer Charm			地官符 Earth Officer Charm			小月建 Small Month Establishment		
寅 Tiger (Feb 4 - Mar 5) 正月 1st Month	未 Wei Goat	坤 Kun	申 Shen Monkey	丑 Chou Ox	艮 Gen	寅 Yin Tiger	丙 Bing Yang Fire	離 Li	丁 Ding Yin Fire
卯 Rabbit (Mar 6 - Apr 4) 二月 2nd Month	壬 Ren Yang Water	坎 Kan	癸 Gui Yin Water	庚 Geng Yang Metal	兌 Dui	辛 Xin Yin Metal	壬 Ren Yang Water	坎 Kan	癸 Gui Yin Water
辰 Dragon (Apr 5 - May 5) 三月 3rd Month	丙 Bing Yang Fire	離 Li	丁 Ding Yin Fire	戌 Xu Dog	乾 Qian	亥 Hai Pig	未 Wei Goat	坤 Kun	申 Shen Monkey
巳 Snake (May 6 - Jun 5) 四月 4th Month	丑 Chou Ox	艮 Gen	寅 Yin Tiger	中 Middle			甲 Jia Yang Wood	震 Zhen	乙 Yi Yin Wood
午 Horse (Jun 6 - July 6) 五月 5th Month	庚 Geng Yang Metal	兌 Dui	辛 Xin Yin Metal	庚 Geng Yang Metal	兌 Dui	辛 Xin Yin Metal	辰 Chen Dragon	巽 Xun	巳 Si Snake
未 Goat (July 7 - Aug 7) 六月 6th Month	戌 Xu Dog	乾 Qian	亥 Hai Pig	戌 Xu Dog	乾 Qian	亥 Hai Pig	中 Middle		
申 Monkey (Aug 8 - Sept 7) 七月 7th Month	中 Middle			中 Middle			戌 Xu Dog	乾 Qian	亥 Hai Pig
酉 Rooster (Sept 8 - Oct 7) 八月 8th Month	庚 Geng Yang Metal	兌 Dui	辛 Xin Yin Metal	辰 Chen Dragon	巽 Xun	巳 Si Snake	庚 Geng Yang Metal	兌 Dui	辛 Xin Yin Metal
戌 Dog (Oct 8 - Nov 6) 九月 9th Month	戌 Xu Dog	乾 Qian	亥 Hai Pig	甲 Jia Yang Wood	震 Zhen	乙 Yi Yin Wood	丑 Chou Ox	艮 Gen	寅 Yin Tiger
亥 Pig (Nov 7 - Dec 6) 十月 10th Month	中 Middle			未 Wei Goat	坤 Kun	申 Shen Monkey	丙 Bing Yang Fire	離 Li	丁 Ding Yin Fire
子 Rat (Dec 7 - Jan 5) 十一月 11th Month	辰 Chen Dragon	巽 Xun	巳 Si Snake	壬 Ren Yang Water	坎 Kan	癸 Gui Yin Water	壬 Ren Yang Water	坎 Kan	癸 Gui Yin Water
丑 Ox (Jan 6 - Feb 3) 十二月 12th Month	甲 Jia Yang Wood	震 Zhen	乙 Yi Yin Wood	丙 Bing Yang Fire	離 Li	丁 Ding Yin Fire	未 Wei Goat	坤 Kun	申 Shen Monkey

Negative Repair / Renovation Sectors 修方凶位：

月 MONTH	大月建 Big Month Establishment			飛大煞 Flying Great Sha			丙丁獨火 Bing Ding Lonely Fire	
寅 **Tiger** (Feb 4 - Mar 5) 正月 **1st Month**	中 Middle			甲 Jia Yang Wood	震 Zhen	乙 Yi Yin Wood	巽 Xun	中 Middle
卯 **Rabbit** (Mar 6 - Apr 4) 二月 **2nd Month**	辰 Chen Dragon	巽 Xun	巳 Si Snake	未 Wei Goat	坤 Kun	申 Shen Monkey	震 Zhen	巽 Xun
辰 **Dragon** (Apr 5 - May 5) 三月 **3rd Month**	甲 Jia Yang Wood	震 Zhen	乙 Yi Yin Wood	壬 Ren Yang Water	坎 Kan	癸 Gui Yin Water	坤 Kun	震 Zhen
巳 **Snake** (May 6 - Jun 5) 四月 **4th Month**	未 Wei Goat	坤 Kun	申 Shen Monkey	丙 Bing Yang Fire	離 Li	丁 Ding Yin Fire	坎 Kan	坤 Kun
午 **Horse** (Jun 6 - July 6) 五月 **5th Month**	壬 Ren Yang Water	坎 Kan	癸 Gui Yin Water	丑 Chou Ox	艮 Gen	寅 Yin Tiger	離 Li	坎 Kan
未 **Goat** (July 7 - Aug 7) 六月 **6th Month**	丙 Bing Yang Fire	離 Li	丁 Ding Yin Fire	庚 Geng Yang Metal	兌 Dui	辛 Xin Yin Metal	艮 Gen	離 Li
申 **Monkey** (Aug 8 - Sept 7) 七月 **7th Month**	丑 Chou Ox	艮 Gen	寅 Yin Tiger	戌 Xu Dog	乾 Qian	亥 Hai Pig	兌 Dui	艮 Gen
酉 **Rooster** (Sept 8 - Oct 7) 八月 **8th Month**	庚 Geng Yang Metal	兌 Dui	辛 Xin Yin Metal	中 Middle			乾 Qian	兌 Dui
戌 **Dog** (Oct 8 - Nov 6) 九月 **9th Month**	戌 Xu Dog	乾 Qian	亥 Hai Pig	庚 Geng Yang Metal	兌 Dui	辛 Xin Yin Metal	中 Middle	乾 Qian
亥 **Pig** (Nov 7 - Dec 6) 十月 **10th Month**	中 Middle			戌 Xu Dog	乾 Qian	亥 Hai Pig	中 Middle	
子 **Rat** (Dec 7 - Jan 5) 十一月 **11th Month**	辰 Chen Dragon	巽 Xun	巳 Si Snake	中 Middle			巽 Xun	中 Middle
丑 **Ox** (Jan 6 - Feb 3) 十二月 **12th Month**	甲 Jia Yang Wood	震 Zhen	乙 Yi Yin Wood	辰 Chen Dragon	巽 Xun	巳 Si Snake	震 Zhen	巽 Xun

Negative Repair / Renovation Sectors 修方凶位：

月 MONTH	月遊火 Month Wondering Fire	三煞 Monthly 3 Killings		
		劫煞 Robbery Sha	災煞 Calamity Sha	月煞 Month Sha
寅 Tiger (Feb 4 - Mar 5) 正月 1st Month	艮 Gen	亥 Hai Pig	子 Zi Rat	丑 Chou Ox
卯 Rabbit (Mar 6 - Apr 4) 二月 2nd Month	離 Li	申 Shen Monkey	酉 You Rooster	戌 Xu Dog
辰 Dragon (Apr 5 - May 5) 三月 3rd Month	坎 Kan	巳 Si Snake	午 Wu Horse	未 Wei Goat
巳 Snake (May 6 - Jun 5) 四月 4th Month	坤 Kun	寅 Yin Tiger	卯 Mao Rabbit	辰 Chen Dragon
午 Horse (Jun 6 - July 6) 五月 5th Month	震 Zhen	亥 Hai Pig	子 Zi Rat	丑 Chou Ox
未 Goat (July 7 - Aug 7) 六月 6th Month	巽 Xun	申 Shen Monkey	酉 You Rooster	戌 Xu Dog
申 Monkey (Aug 8 - Sept 7) 七月 7th Month	中 Middle	巳 Si Snake	午 Wu Horse	未 Wei Goat
酉 Rooster (Sept 8 - Oct 7) 八月 8th Month	乾 Qian	寅 Yin Tiger	卯 Mao Rabbit	辰 Chen Dragon
戌 Dog (Oct 8 - Nov 6) 九月 9th Month	兌 Dui	亥 Hai Pig	子 Zi Rat	丑 Chou Ox
亥 Pig (Nov 7 - Dec 6) 十月 10th Month	艮 Gen	申 Shen Monkey	酉 You Rooster	戌 Xu Dog
子 Rat (Dec 7 - Jan 5) 十一月 11th Month	離 Li	巳 Si Snake	午 Wu Horse	未 Wei Goat
丑 Ox (Jan 6 - Feb 3) 十二月 12th Month	坎 Kan	寅 Yin Tiger	卯 Mao Rabbit	辰 Chen Dragon

Negative Repair / Renovation Sectors 修方凶位 :

月 MONTH	月刑 Month Punishment	月害 Month Harm	月厭 Month Detest
寅 **Tiger** (Feb 4 - Mar 5) 正月 **1st Month**	巳 Si Snake	巳 Si Snake	戌 Xu Dog
卯 **Rabbit** (Mar 6 - Apr 4) 二月 **2nd Month**	子 Zi Rat	辰 Chen Dragon	酉 You Rooster
辰 **Dragon** (Apr 5 - May 5) 三月 **3rd Month**	辰 Chen Dragon	卯 Mao Rabbit	申 Shen Monkey
巳 **Snake** (May 6 - Jun 5) 四月 **4th Month**	申 Shen Monkey	寅 Yin Tiger	未 Wei Goat
午 **Horse** (Jun 6 - July 6) 五月 **5th Month**	午 Wu Horse	丑 Chou Ox	午 Wu Horse
未 **Goat** (July 7 - Aug 7) 六月 **6th Month**	丑 Chou Ox	子 Zi Rat	巳 Si Snake
申 **Monkey** (Aug 8 - Sept 7) 七月 **7th Month**	寅 Yin Tiger	亥 Hai Pig	辰 Chen Dragon
酉 **Rooster** (Sept 8 - Oct 7) 八月 **8th Month**	酉 You Rooster	戌 Xu Dog	卯 Mao Rabbit
戌 **Dog** (Oct 8 - Nov 6) 九月 **9th Month**	未 Wei Goat	酉 You Rooster	寅 Yin Tiger
亥 **Pig** (Nov 7 - Dec 6) 十月 **10th Month**	亥 Hai Pig	申 Shen Monkey	丑 Chou Ox
子 **Rat** (Dec 7 - Jan 5) 十一月 **11th Month**	卯 Mao Rabbit	未 Wei Goat	子 Zi Rat
丑 **Ox** (Jan 6 - Feb 3) 十二月 **12th Month**	戌 Xu Dog	午 Wu Horse	亥 Hai Pig

乙卯 (Yi Mao)
Wood Rabbit

乙卯 (Yi Mao) Wood Rabbit

Heavenly Stem 天干	乙 Yin Wood (陰木)
Earthly Branch 地支	卯 Rabbit (Yin Wood 陰木)
Hidden Stem 藏干	乙 Yin Wood
Na Yin 納音	大溪水 Water from the canal
Grand Duke 太歲	卯 Rabbit
Xuan Kong Five Element 玄空五行	1 水 Water
Gua Name 卦名	☷☱ 地澤臨 Arriving
Xuan Kong Period Luck 玄空卦運	4

Annual Positive Stars for Opening Mountain, Establishing Facing and Commencing Repairs 開山立向修方吉星：

歲德 Duke Virtue	庚 Geng Yang Metal
歲德合 Duke Virtue Combo	乙 Yi Yin Wood
歲枝德 Duke Branch Virtue	申 Shen Monkey
陽貴人 Yang Nobleman	申 Shen Monkey
陰貴人 Yin Nobleman	子 Zi Rat
歲祿 Duke Prosperous	卯 Mao Rabbit
歲馬 Duke Horse	巳 Si Snake
奏書 Decree	艮 Gen
博士 Professor	坤 Kun

142

Annual Negative Stars for Opening Mountain, Establishing Facing and Commencing Repairs 開山立向修方凶星：

太歲 Grand Duke	歲破 Year Breaker	三煞 Three Killings			坐煞向煞 Sitting Sha Facing Sha				浮天空亡 Floating Heaven Emptiness	
卯 Mao Rabbit	酉 You Rooster	申 Shen Monkey	酉 You Rooster	戌 Xu Dog	庚 Geng Yang Metal	辛 Xin Yin Metal	甲 Jia Yang Wood	乙 Yi Yin Wood	坎 Kan	癸 Gui Yin Water

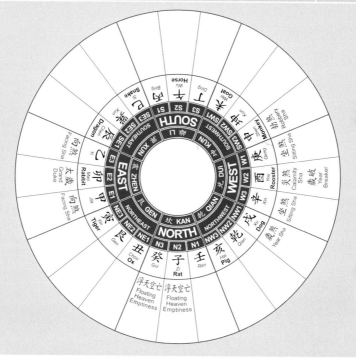

Annual San Yuan Purple White Stars 三元紫白九星：

上元 Upper Period Period 1, 2, 3	中元 Middle Period Period 4, 5, 6	下元 Lower Period Period 7, 8, 9

Upper Period (Period 1, 2, 3):

巽SE	離S	坤SW
3	8	1
2 (震E)	4 乙卯 Yi Mao Wood Rabbit	6 (兌W)
7	9	5
艮NE	坎N	乾NW

Middle Period (Period 4, 5, 6):

巽SE	離S	坤SW
6	2	4
5 (震E)	7 乙卯 Yi Mao Wood Rabbit	9 (兌W)
1	3	8
艮NE	坎N	乾NW

Lower Period (Period 7, 8, 9):

巽SE	離S	坤SW
9	5	7
8 (震E)	1 乙卯 Yi Mao Wood Rabbit	3 (兌W)
4	6	2
艮NE	坎N	乾NW

Mountain Covering Yellow Path 蓋山黃道：

貪狼 *Tan Lang* **Greedy Wolf**	巨門 *Ju Men* **Huge Door**	武曲 *Wu Qu* **Military Arts**	文曲 *Wen Qu* **Literary Arts**
乾 甲 *Qian*　*Jia* NW2　E1	離 壬 寅 戌 *Li*　*Ren*　*Yin*　*Xu* S2　N1　NE3　NW1	坤 乙 *Kun*　*Yi* SW2　E3	巽 辛 *Xun*　*Xin* SE2　W3

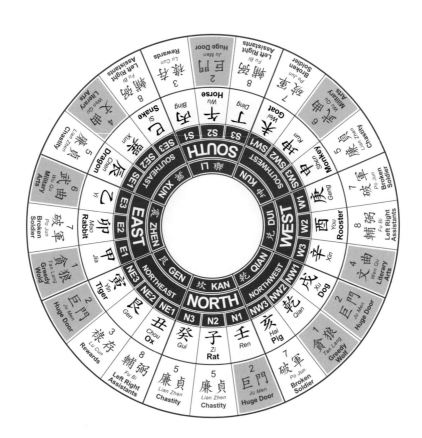

Heaven Penetrating Force 通天竅：			
三合前方 **Facing Three Harmony**	巽巳 _{Xun Si}	丙午 _{Bing Wu}	丁未 _{Ding Wei}
三合後方 **Sitting Three Harmony**	乾亥 _{Qian Hai}	壬子 _{Ren Zi}	癸丑 _{Gui Chou}

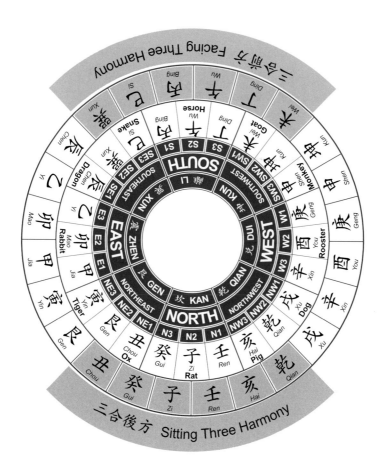

Moving Horse Six Ren Assessment 走馬六壬：

神后 Shen Hou Holy Empress	功曹 Gong Cao Marshall	天罡 Tian Gang Heavenly Dipper	勝光 Sheng Guang Subliminal Bright	傳送 Chuan Song Great General	河魁 He Kui River Scholar
庚酉 Geng You	乾亥 Qian Hai	癸丑 Gui Chou	甲卯 Jia Mao	巽巳 Xun Si	丁未 Ding Wei

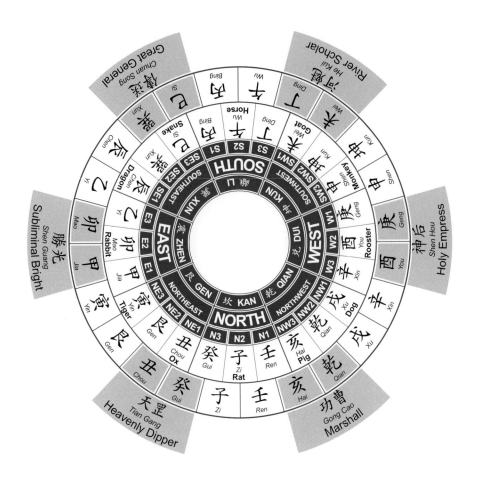

Four Advantages Three Cycles Star Plate 四利三元：

太陽 *Tai Yang* **Sun**	太陰 *Tai Yin* **Moon**	龍德 *Long De* **Dragon Virtue**	福德 *Fu De* **Fortune Virtue**
辰 *Chen* **Dragon**	午 *Wu* **Horse**	戌 *Xu* **Dog**	子 *Zi* **Rat**

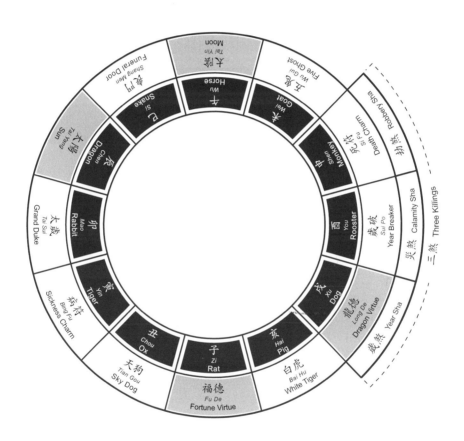

Negative Sectors For Opening Mountain 開山凶位：

年剋山家 Year Countering Sitting (冬至後 After Winter Solstice)

乾 Qian NW2	亥 Hai NW3	兌 Dui W2	丁 Ding S3

陰府太歲 Yin Fu Tai Sui **Yin Mansion Grand Duke**	六害 Liu Hai **Six Harm**	死符 Si Fu **Death Charm**	炙退 Zhi Tui **Roasting Star**
兌 Dui W2　　乾 Qian NW2	辰 Chen SE1	申 Shen SW3	午 Wu S2

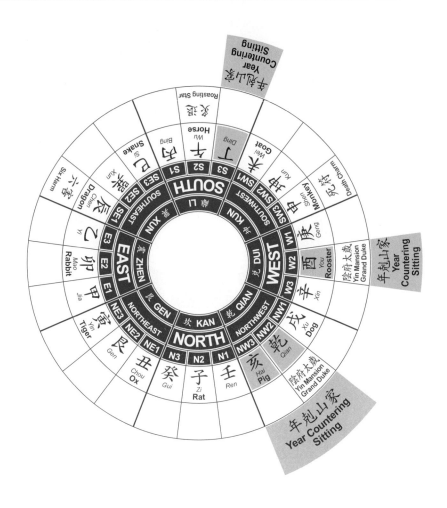

Negative Directions to Establish Facing 立向凶方：

巡山羅喉 *Xun Shan Luo Hou* **Mountain Patrol Luo Hou Star**	病符 *Bing Fu* **Sickness Charm**
乙 *Yi* **E3**	寅 *Yin* **NE3**

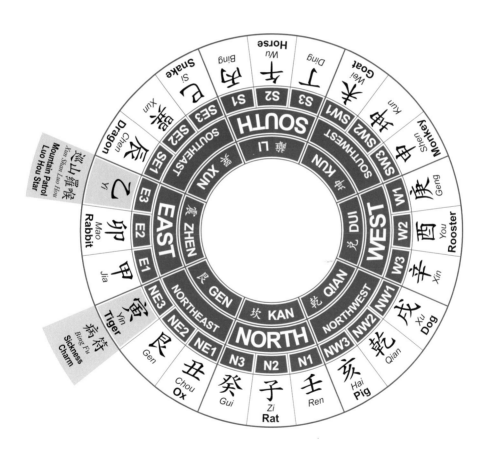

Negative Repair / Renovation Sectors Table 修方凶位表:

天官符 Heavenly Officer Charm	寅 *Yin* Tiger	豹尾 Leopard Tail	丑 *Chou* Ox
地官符 Earthly Officer Charm	未 *Wei* Goat	飛廉 Flying Chaste	巳 *Si* Snake
大煞 Great Sha	卯 *Mao* Rabbit	喪門 Funeral Door	巳 *Si* Snake
大將軍 Big General	子 *Zi* Rat	弔客 Suspended Guest	丑 *Chou* Ox
力士 Strong Man	巽 *Xun*	白虎 White Tiger	亥 *Hai* Pig
蠶室 Silkworm Room	乾 *Qian*	金神 Golden God	辰 *Chen* Dragon / 巳 *Si* Snake
蠶官 Silkworm Officer	戌 *Xu* Dog		
蠶命 Silkworm Life	亥 *Hai* Pig	獨火 Lonely Fire	坎 *Kan*
歲刑 Duke Punishment	子 *Zi* Rat	五鬼 Five Ghost	丑 *Chou* Ox
黃幡 Yellow Flag	未 *Wei* Goat	破敗五鬼 Destructive Five Ghost	艮 *Gen*

Negative Repair / Renovation Sectors Diagram 修方凶位圖：

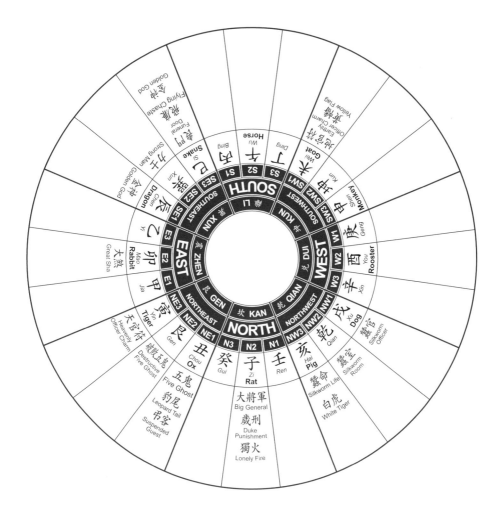

16-Month Auxiliary Stars Reference Table :
乙卯年十二月，開山立向修方星表

Positive Monthly Stars 吉星方

月 MONTH	寅 Tiger (Feb 4 - Mar 5) 正月 1st Month	卯 Rabbit (Mar 6 - Apr 4) 二月 2nd Month	辰 Dragon (Apr 5 - May 5) 三月 3rd Month	巳 Snake (May 6 - Jun 5) 四月 4th Month	午 Horse (Jun 6 - July 6) 五月 5th Month	未 Goat (July 7 - Aug 7) 六月 6th Month
天道 Heavenly Path	南 South	西南 Southwest	北 North	西 West	西北 Northwest	東 East
天德 Heavenly Virtue	丁 Ding Yin Fire	坤 Kun (申)	壬 Ren Yang Water	辛 Xin Yin Metal	乾 Qian (亥)	甲 Jia Yang Wood
天德合 Heavenly Virtue Combo	壬 Ren Yang Water	(巳)	丁 Ding Yin Fire	丙 Bing Yang Fire	(寅)	己 Ji Yin Earth
月德 Monthly Virtue	丙 Bing Yang Fire	甲 Jia Yang Wood	壬 Ren Yang Water	庚 Geng Yang Metal	丙 Bing Yang Fire	甲 Jia Yang Wood
月德合 Monthly Virtue Combo	辛 Xin Yin Metal	己 Ji Yin Earth	丁 Ding Yin Fire	乙 Yi Yin Wood	辛 Xin Yin Metal	己 Ji Yin Earth
月空 Month Emptiness	壬 Ren Yang Water	庚 Geng Yang Metal	丙 Bing Yang Fire	甲 Jia Yang Wood	壬 Ren Yang Water	庚 Geng Yang Metal
陽貴人 Yang Nobleman	坤 Kun	坎 Kan	離 Li	艮 Gen	兌 Dui	乾 Qian
陰貴人 Yin Nobleman	乾 Qian	中 Middle	巽 Xun	震 Zhen	坤 Kun	坎 Kan
飛天祿 Flying Heavenly Wealth	乾 Qian	中 Middle	坎 Kan	離 Li	艮 Gen	兌 Dui
飛天馬 Flying Heavenly Horse	艮 Gen	兌 Dui	乾 Qian	中 Middle	坎 Kan	離 Li

16-Month Auxiliary Stars Reference Table :
乙卯年十二月，開山立向修方星表

申 Monkey (Aug 8 - Sept 7) 七月 7th Month	酉 Rooster (Sept 8 - Oct 7) 八月 8th Month	戌 Dog (Oct 8 - Nov 6) 九月 9th Month	亥 Pig (Nov 7 - Dec 6) 十月 10th Month	子 Rat (Dec 7 - Jan 5) 十一月 11th Month	丑 Ox (Jan 6 - Feb 3) 十二月 12th Month	月 MONTH
北 North	東北 Northeast	南 South	東 East	東南 Southeast	西 West	天道 Heavenly Path
癸 Gui Yin Water	艮 Gen (寅)	丙 Bing Yang Fire	乙 Yi Yin Wood	巽 Xun (巳)	庚 Geng Yang Metal	天德 Heavenly Virtue
戊 Wu Yang Earth	(亥)	辛 Xin Yin Metal	庚 Geng Yang Metal	(申)	乙 Yi Yin Wood	天德合 Heavenly Virtue Combo
壬 Ren Yang Water	庚 Geng Yang Metal	丙 Bing Yang Fire	甲 Jia Yang Wood	壬 Ren Yang Water	庚 Geng Yang Metal	月德 Monthly Virtue
丁 Ding Yin Fire	乙 Yi Yin Wood	辛 Xin Yin Metal	己 Ji Yin Earth	丁 Ding Yin Fire	乙 Yi Yin Wood	月德合 Monthly Virtue Combo
丙 Bing Yang Fire	甲 Jia Yang Wood	壬 Ren Yang Water	庚 Geng Yang Metal	丙 Bing Yang Fire	甲 Jia Yang Wood	月空 Month Emptiness
中 Middle	坎 Kan	離 Li	艮 Gen	兌 Dui	乾 Qian	陽貴人 Yang Nobleman
離 Li	艮 Gen	兌 Dui	乾 Qian	中 Middle	坎 Kan	陰貴人 Yin Nobleman
乾 Qian	中 Middle	巽 Xun	震 Zhen	坤 Kun	坎 Kan	飛天祿 Flying Heavenly Wealth
艮 Gen	兌 Dui	乾 Qian	中 Middle	巽 Xun	震 Zhen	飛天馬 Flying Heavenly Horse

Monthly Purple White Stars 月紫白九星 ：

寅 Tiger (Feb 4 - Mar 5) 正月 1st Month

巽 SE	離 S	坤 SW
7 Red 七赤	3 Jade 三碧	5 Yellow 五黄
震 E 6 White 六白	8 White 八白	1 White 一白 兌 W
2 Black 二黑	4 Green 四緑	9 Purple 九紫
艮 NE	坎 N	乾 NW

卯 Rabbit (Mar 6 - Apr 4) 二月 2nd Month

巽 SE	離 S	坤 SW
6 White 六白	2 Black 二黑	4 Green 四緑
震 E 5 Yellow 五黄	7 Red 七赤	9 Purple 九紫 兌 W
1 White 一白	3 Jade 三碧	8 White 八白
艮 NE	坎 N	乾 NW

辰 Dragon (Apr 5 - May 5) 三月 3rd Month

巽 SE	離 S	坤 SW
5 Yellow 五黄	1 White 一白	3 Jade 三碧
震 E 4 Green 四緑	6 White 六白	8 White 八白 兌 W
9 Purple 九紫	2 Black 二黑	7 Red 七赤
艮 NE	坎 N	乾 NW

巳 Snake (May 6 - Jun 5) 四月 4th Month

巽 SE	離 S	坤 SW
4 Green 四緑	9 Purple 九紫	2 Black 二黑
震 E 3 Jade 三碧	5 Yellow 五黄	7 Red 七赤 兌 W
8 White 八白	1 White 一白	6 White 六白
艮 NE	坎 N	乾 NW

午 Horse (Jun 6 - July 6) 五月 5th Month

巽 SE	離 S	坤 SW
3 Jade 三碧	8 White 八白	1 White 一白
震 E 2 Black 二黑	4 Green 四緑	6 White 六白 兌 W
7 Red 七赤	9 Purple 九紫	5 Yellow 五黄
艮 NE	坎 N	乾 NW

未 Goat (July 7 - Aug 7) 六月 6th Month

巽 SE	離 S	坤 SW
2 Black 二黑	7 Red 七赤	9 Purple 九紫
震 E 1 White 一白	3 Jade 三碧	5 Yellow 五黄 兌 W
6 White 六白	8 White 八白	4 Green 四緑
艮 NE	坎 N	乾 NW

申 Monkey (Aug 8 - Sept 7) 七月 7th Month

巽 SE	離 S	坤 SW
1 White 一白	6 White 六白	8 White 八白
震 E 9 Purple 九紫	2 Black 二黑	4 Green 四緑 兌 W
5 Yellow 五黄	7 Red 七赤	3 Jade 三碧
艮 NE	坎 N	乾 NW

酉 Rooster (Sept 8 - Oct 7) 八月 8th Month

巽 SE	離 S	坤 SW
9 Purple 九紫	5 Yellow 五黄	7 Red 七赤
震 E 8 White 八白	1 White 一白	3 Jade 三碧 兌 W
4 Green 四緑	6 White 六白	2 Black 二黑
艮 NE	坎 N	乾 NW

戌 Dog (Oct 8 - Nov 6) 九月 9th Month

巽 SE	離 S	坤 SW
8 White 八白	4 Green 四緑	6 White 六白
震 E 7 Red 七赤	9 Purple 九紫	2 Black 二黑 兌 W
3 Jade 三碧	5 Yellow 五黄	1 White 一白
艮 NE	坎 N	乾 NW

亥 Pig (Nov 7 - Dec 6) 十月 10th Month

巽 SE	離 S	坤 SW
7 Red 七赤	3 Jade 三碧	5 Yellow 五黄
震 E 6 White 六白	8 White 八白	1 White 一白 兌 W
2 Black 二黑	4 Green 四緑	9 Purple 九紫
艮 NE	坎 N	乾 NW

子 Rat (Dec 7 - Jan 5) 十一月 11th Month

巽 SE	離 S	坤 SW
6 White 六白	2 Black 二黑	4 Green 四緑
震 E 5 Yellow 五黄	7 Red 七赤	9 Purple 九紫 兌 W
1 White 一白	3 Jade 三碧	8 White 八白
艮 NE	坎 N	乾 NW

丑 Ox (Jan 6 - Feb 3) 十二月 12th Month

巽 SE	離 S	坤 SW
5 Yellow 五黄	1 White 一白	3 Jade 三碧
震 E 4 Green 四緑	6 White 六白	8 White 八白 兌 W
9 Purple 九紫	2 Black 二黑	7 Red 七赤
艮 NE	坎 N	乾 NW

Qi Men Three Nobles 三奇 :

Three Nobles 三奇 / Seasons	乙 Yi	丙 Bing	丁 Ding
立春 **Coming of Spring** Feb 4 - Feb 18	震 Zhen	巽 Xun	中 Middle
春分 **Spring Equinox** Mar 21 - Apr 4	兌 Dui	艮 Gen	離 Li
立夏 **Coming of Summer** May 6 - May 20	艮 Gen	離 Li	坎 Kan
夏至 **Summer Solstice** Jun 22 - Jul 6	中 Middle	巽 Xun	震 Zhen
立秋 **Coming of Autumn** Aug 8 - Aug 23	兌 Dui	乾 Qian	中 Middle
秋分 **Autumn Equinox** Sept 23 - Oct 7	震 Zhen	坤 Kun	坎 Kan
立冬 **Coming of Winter** Nov 7 - Nov 22	坤 Kun	坎 Kan	離 Li
冬至 **Winter Solstice** Dec 22 - Jan 5	中 Middle	乾 Qian	兌 Dui

Sectors to Avoid Opening Mountain 開山凶位 ：

月 MONTH	月建 Month Establishment	月破 Month Destruction	月剋山家 Month Countering Sitting		陰府太歲 Yin Mansion Grand Duke	
寅 **Tiger** (Feb 4 - Mar 5) 正月 **1st Month**	寅 *Yin* Tiger	申 *Shen* Monkey	乾 *Qian*	兌 *Dui*	坤 *Kun*	震 *Zhen*
卯 **Rabbit** (Mar 6 - Apr 4) 二月 **2nd Month**	卯 *Mao* Rabbit	酉 *You* Rooster	亥 *Hai* Pig	丁 *Ding* Yin Fire	巽 *Xun*	艮 *Gen*
辰 **Dragon** (Apr 5 - May 5) 三月 **3rd Month**	辰 *Chen* Dragon	戌 *Xu* Dog	震 *Zhen*	巳 *Si* Snake	乾 *Qian*	兌 *Dui*
巳 **Snake** (May 6 - Jun 5) 四月 **4th Month**	巳 *Si* Snake	亥 *Hai* Pig	艮 *Gen*		坤 *Kun*	坎 *Kan*
午 **Horse** (Jun 6 - July 6) 五月 **5th Month**	午 *Wu* Horse	子 *Zi* Rat	離 *Li*	丙 *Bing* Yang Fire	離 *Li*	乾 *Qian*
未 **Goat** (July 7 - Aug 7) 六月 **6th Month**	未 *Wei* Goat	丑 *Chou* Ox	壬 *Ren* Yang Water	乙 *Yi* Yin Wood	震 *Zhen*	坤 *Kun*
申 **Monkey** (Aug 8 - Sept 7) 七月 **7th Month**	申 *Shen* Monkey	寅 *Yin* Tiger	—		艮 *Gen*	巽 *Xun*
酉 **Rooster** (Sept 8 - Oct 7) 八月 **8th Month**	酉 *You* Rooster	卯 *Mao* Rabbit	—		兌 *Dui*	乾 *Qian*
戌 **Dog** (Oct 8 - Nov 6) 九月 **9th Month**	戌 *Xu* Dog	辰 *Chen* Dragon	乾 *Qian*	兌 *Dui*	坎 *Kan*	坤 *Kun*
亥 **Pig** (Nov 7 - Dec 6) 十月 **10th Month**	亥 *Hai* Pig	巳 *Si* Snake	亥 *Hai* Pig	丁 *Ding* Yin Fire	乾 *Qian*	離 *Li*
子 **Rat** (Dec 7 - Jan 5) 十一月 **11th Month**	子 *Zi* Rat	午 *Wu* Horse	水 Water	山 Mountain	坤 *Kun*	震 *Zhen*
丑 **Ox** (Jan 6 - Feb 3) 十二月 **12th Month**	丑 *Chou* Ox	未 *Wei* Goat	土 Earth		巽 *Xun*	艮 *Gen*

Negative Repair / Renovation Sectors 修方凶位 :

月 MONTH	天官符 Heavenly Officer Charm			地官符 Earth Officer Charm			小月建 Small Month Establishment		
寅 **Tiger** (Feb 4 - Mar 5) 正月 1st Month	中 Middle			壬 Ren Yang Water	坎 Kan	癸 Gui Yin Water	丙 Bing Yang Fire	離 Li	丁 Ding Yin Fire
卯 **Rabbit** (Mar 6 - Apr 4) 二月 2nd Month	庚 Geng Yang Metal	兌 Dui	辛 Xin Yin Metal	丙 Bing Yang Fire	離 Li	丁 Ding Yin Fire	壬 Ren Yang Water	坎 Kan	癸 Gui Yin Water
辰 **Dragon** (Apr 5 - May 5) 三月 3rd Month	戊 Xu Dog	乾 Qian	亥 Hai Pig	丑 Chou Ox	艮 Gen	寅 Yin Tiger	未 Wei Goat	坤 Kun	申 Shen Monkey
巳 **Snake** (May 6 - Jun 5) 四月 4th Month	中 Middle			庚 Geng Yang Metal	兌 Dui	辛 Xin Yin Metal	甲 Jia Yang Wood	震 Zhen	乙 Yi Yin Wood
午 **Horse** (Jun 6 - July 6) 五月 5th Month	辰 Chen Dragon	巽 Xun	巳 Si Snake	戊 Xu Dog	乾 Qian	亥 Hai Pig	辰 Chen Dragon	巽 Xun	巳 Si Snake
未 **Goat** (July 7 - Aug 7) 六月 6th Month	甲 Jia Yang Wood	震 Zhen	乙 Yi Yin Wood	中 Middle			中 Middle		
申 **Monkey** (Aug 8 - Sept 7) 七月 7th Month	未 Wei Goat	坤 Kun	申 Shen Monkey	庚 Geng Yang Metal	兌 Dui	辛 Xin Yin Metal	戊 Xu Dog	乾 Qian	亥 Hai Pig
酉 **Rooster** (Sept 8 - Oct 7) 八月 8th Month	壬 Ren Yang Water	坎 Kan	癸 Gui Yin Water	戊 Xu Dog	乾 Qian	亥 Hai Pig	庚 Geng Yang Metal	兌 Dui	辛 Xin Yin Metal
戌 **Dog** (Oct 8 - Nov 6) 九月 9th Month	丙 Bing Yang Fire	離 Li	丁 Ding Yin Fire	中 Middle			丑 Chou Ox	艮 Gen	寅 Yin Tiger
亥 **Pig** (Nov 7 - Dec 6) 十月 10th Month	丑 Chou Ox	艮 Gen	寅 Yin Tiger	辰 Chen Dragon	巽 Xun	巳 Si Snake	丙 Bing Yang Fire	離 Li	丁 Ding Yin Fire
子 **Rat** (Dec 7 - Jan 5) 十一月 11th Month	庚 Geng Yang Metal	兌 Dui	辛 Xin Yin Metal	甲 Jia Yang Wood	震 Zhen	乙 Yi Yin Wood	壬 Ren Yang Water	坎 Kan	癸 Gui Yin Water
丑 **Ox** (Jan 6 - Feb 3) 十二月 12th Month	戊 Xu Dog	乾 Qian	亥 Hai Pig	未 Wei Goat	坤 Kun	申 Shen Monkey	未 Wei Goat	坤 Kun	申 Shen Monkey

乙卯 (Yi Mao) Wood Rabbit

Negative Repair / Renovation Sectors 修方凶位：

月 MONTH	大月建 Big Month Establishment			飛大煞 Flying Great Sha			丙丁獨火 Bing Ding Lonely Fire	
寅 Tiger (Feb 4 - Mar 5) 正月 1st Month	丑 Chou Ox	艮 Gen	寅 Yin Tiger	戌 Xu Dog	乾 Qian	亥 Hai Pig	巽 Xun	中 Middle
卯 Rabbit (Mar 6 - Apr 4) 二月 2nd Month	庚 Geng Yang Metal	兑 Dui	辛 Xin Yin Metal	中 Middle			震 Zhen	巽 Xun
辰 Dragon (Apr 5 - May 5) 三月 3rd Month	戌 Xu Dog	乾 Qian	亥 Hai Pig	庚 Geng Yang Metal	兑 Dui	辛 Xin Yin Metal	坤 Kun	震 Zhen
巳 Snake (May 6 - Jun 5) 四月 4th Month	中 Middle			戌 Xu Dog	乾 Qian	亥 Hai Pig	坎 Kan	坤 Kun
午 Horse (Jun 6 - July 6) 五月 5th Month	辰 Chen Dragon	巽 Xun	巳 Si Snake	中 Middle			離 Li	坎 Kan
未 Goat (July 7 - Aug 7) 六月 6th Month	甲 Jia Yang Wood	震 Zhen	乙 Yi Yin Wood	辰 Chen Dragon	巽 Xun	巳 Si Snake	艮 Gen	離 Li
申 Monkey (Aug 8 - Sept 7) 七月 7th Month	未 Wei Goat	坤 Kun	申 Shen Monkey	甲 Jia Yang Wood	震 Zhen	乙 Yi Yin Wood	兑 Dui	艮 Gen
酉 Rooster (Sept 8 - Oct 7) 八月 8th Month	壬 Ren Yang Water	坎 Kan	癸 Gui Yin Water	未 Wei Goat	坤 Kun	申 Shen Monkey	乾 Qian	兑 Dui
戌 Dog (Oct 8 - Nov 6) 九月 9th Month	丙 Bing Yang Fire	離 Li	丁 Ding Yin Fire	壬 Ren Yang Water	坎 Kan	癸 Gui Yin Water	中 Middle	乾 Qian
亥 Pig (Nov 7 - Dec 6) 十月 10th Month	丑 Chou Ox	艮 Gen	寅 Yin Tiger	丙 Bing Yang Fire	離 Li	丁 Ding Yin Fire	中 Middle	
子 Rat (Dec 7 - Jan 5) 十一月 11th Month	庚 Geng Yang Metal	兑 Dui	辛 Xin Yin Metal	丑 Chou Ox	艮 Gen	寅 Yin Tiger	巽 Xun	中 Middle
丑 Ox (Jan 6 - Feb 3) 十二月 12th Month	戌 Xu Dog	乾 Qian	亥 Hai Pig	庚 Geng Yang Metal	兑 Dui	辛 Xin Yin Metal	震 Zhen	巽 Xun

Negative Repair / Renovation Sectors 修方凶位 :

月 MONTH	月遊火 Month Wondering Fire	三煞 Monthly 3 Killings		
		劫煞 Robbery Sha	災煞 Calamity Sha	月煞 Month Sha
寅 **Tiger** (Feb 4 - Mar 5) 正月 **1st Month**	巽 Xun	亥 Hai Pig	子 Zi Rat	丑 Chou Ox
卯 **Rabbit** (Mar 6 - Apr 4) 二月 **2nd Month**	中 Middle	申 Shen Monkey	酉 You Rooster	戌 Xu Dog
辰 **Dragon** (Apr 5 - May 5) 三月 **3rd Month**	乾 Qian	巳 Si Snake	午 Wu Horse	未 Wei Goat
巳 **Snake** (May 6 - Jun 5) 四月 **4th Month**	兌 Dui	寅 Yin Tiger	卯 Mao Rabbit	辰 Chen Dragon
午 **Horse** (Jun 6 - July 6) 五月 **5th Month**	艮 Gen	亥 Hai Pig	子 Zi Rat	丑 Chou Ox
未 **Goat** (July 7 - Aug 7) 六月 **6th Month**	離 Li	申 Shen Monkey	酉 You Rooster	戌 Xu Dog
申 **Monkey** (Aug 8 - Sept 7) 七月 **7th Month**	坎 Kan	巳 Si Snake	午 Wu Horse	未 Wei Goat
酉 **Rooster** (Sept 8 - Oct 7) 八月 **8th Month**	坤 Kun	寅 Yin Tiger	卯 Mao Rabbit	辰 Chen Dragon
戌 **Dog** (Oct 8 - Nov 6) 九月 **9th Month**	震 Zhen	亥 Hai Pig	子 Zi Rat	丑 Chou Ox
亥 **Pig** (Nov 7 - Dec 6) 十月 **10th Month**	巽 Xun	申 Shen Monkey	酉 You Rooster	戌 Xu Dog
子 **Rat** (Dec 7 - Jan 5) 十一月 **11th Month**	中 Middle	巳 Si Snake	午 Wu Horse	未 Wei Goat
丑 **Ox** (Jan 6 - Feb 3) 十二月 **12th Month**	乾 Qian	寅 Yin Tiger	卯 Mao Rabbit	辰 Chen Dragon

乙卯 (Yi Mao) Wood Rabbit

Negative Repair / Renovation Sectors 修方凶位 :

月 MONTH	月刑 Month Punishment	月害 Month Harm	月厭 Month Detest
寅 **Tiger** (Feb 4 - Mar 5) 正月 **1st Month**	巳 *Si* Snake	巳 *Si* Snake	戌 *Xu* Dog
卯 **Rabbit** (Mar 6 - Apr 4) 二月 **2nd Month**	子 *Zi* Rat	辰 *Chen* Dragon	酉 *You* Rooster
辰 **Dragon** (Apr 5 - May 5) 三月 **3rd Month**	辰 *Chen* Dragon	卯 *Mao* Rabbit	申 *Shen* Monkey
巳 **Snake** (May 6 - Jun 5) 四月 **4th Month**	申 *Shen* Monkey	寅 *Yin* Tiger	未 *Wei* Goat
午 **Horse** (Jun 6 - July 6) 五月 **5th Month**	午 *Wu* Horse	丑 *Chou* Ox	午 *Wu* Horse
未 **Goat** (July 7 - Aug 7) 六月 **6th Month**	丑 *Chou* Ox	子 *Zi* Rat	巳 *Si* Snake
申 **Monkey** (Aug 8 - Sept 7) 七月 **7th Month**	寅 *Yin* Tiger	亥 *Hai* Pig	辰 *Chen* Dragon
酉 **Rooster** (Sept 8 - Oct 7) 八月 **8th Month**	酉 *You* Rooster	戌 *Xu* Dog	卯 *Mao* Rabbit
戌 **Dog** (Oct 8 - Nov 6) 九月 **9th Month**	未 *Wei* Goat	酉 *You* Rooster	寅 *Yin* Tiger
亥 **Pig** (Nov 7 - Dec 6) 十月 **10th Month**	亥 *Hai* Pig	申 *Shen* Monkey	丑 *Chou* Ox
子 **Rat** (Dec 7 - Jan 5) 十一月 **11th Month**	卯 *Mao* Rabbit	未 *Wei* Goat	子 *Zi* Rat
丑 **Ox** (Jan 6 - Feb 3) 十二月 **12th Month**	戌 *Xu* Dog	午 *Wu* Horse	亥 *Hai* Pig

乙巳 (Yi Si)
Wood Snake

Heavenly Stem 天干	乙 Yin Wood (陰木)
Earthly Branch 地支	巳 Snake (Yin Fire 陰火)
Hidden Stem 藏干	丙 Yang Fire, 戊 Yang Earth, 庚 Yang Metal
Na Yin 納音	覆燈火 Fire from the lamps
Grand Duke 太歲	巳 Snake
Xuan Kong Five Element 玄空五行	7 火 Fire
Gua Name 卦名	䷄ 水天需 Waiting
Xuan Kong Period Luck 玄空卦運	3

Annual Positive Stars for Opening Mountain, Establishing Facing and Commencing Repairs 開山立向修方吉星：

歲德 Duke Virtue	庚 Geng Yang Metal	
歲德合 Duke Virtue Combo	乙 Yi Yin Wood	
歲枝德 Duke Branch Virtue	戊 Xu Dog	
陽貴人 Yang Nobleman	申 Shen Monkey	
陰貴人 Yin Nobleman	子 Zi Rat	
歲祿 Duke Prosperous	卯 Mao Rabbit	
歲馬 Duke Horse	亥 Hai Pig	
奏書 Decree	巽 Xun	
博士 Professor	乾 Qian	

Annual Negative Stars for Opening Mountain, Establishing Facing and Commencing Repairs 開山立向修方凶星：

太歲 Grand Duke	歲破 Year Breaker	三煞 Three Killings			坐煞向煞 Sitting Sha Facing Sha				浮天空亡 Floating Heaven Emptiness	
巳 Si Snake	亥 Hai Pig	寅 Yin Tiger	卯 Mao Rabbit	辰 Chen Dragon	甲 Jia Yang Wood	乙 Yi Yin Wood	庚 Geng Yang Metal	辛 Xin Yin Metal	坎 Kan	癸 Gui Yin Water

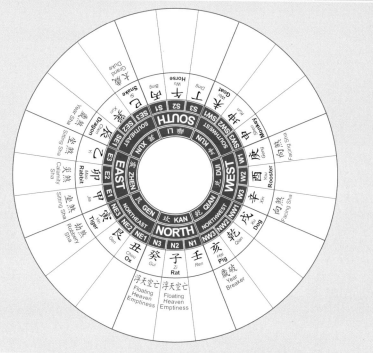

Annual San Yuan Purple White Stars 三元紫白九星：

上元 Upper Period Period 1, 2, 3	中元 Middle Period Period 4, 5, 6	下元 Lower Period Period 7, 8, 9

上元 Upper Period — Period 1, 2, 3

巽SE	離S	坤SW
4	9	2
震E 3	5 乙巳 Yi Si Wood Snake	7 兌W
8	1	6
艮NE	坎N	乾NW

中元 Middle Period — Period 4, 5, 6

巽SE	離S	坤SW
7	3	5
震E 6	8 乙巳 Yi Si Wood Snake	1 兌W
2	4	9
艮NE	坎N	乾NW

下元 Lower Period — Period 7, 8, 9

巽SE	離S	坤SW
1	6	8
震E 9	2 乙巳 Yi Si Wood Snake	4 兌W
5	7	3
艮NE	坎N	乾NW

Mountain Covering Yellow Path 蓋山黃道：

貪狼 *Tan Lang* **Greedy Wolf**				巨門 *Ju Men* **Huge Door**				武曲 *Wu Qu* **Military Arts**		文曲 *Wen Qu* **Literary Arts**			
兌 *Dui* W2	丁 *Ding* S3	巳 *Si* SE3	丑 *Chou* NE1	震 *Zhen* E2	庚 *Geng* W1	亥 *Hai* NW3	未 *Wei* SW1	艮 *Gen* NE2	丙 *Bing* S1	坎 *Kan* N2	癸 *Gui* N3	申 *Shen* SW3	辰 *Chen* SE1

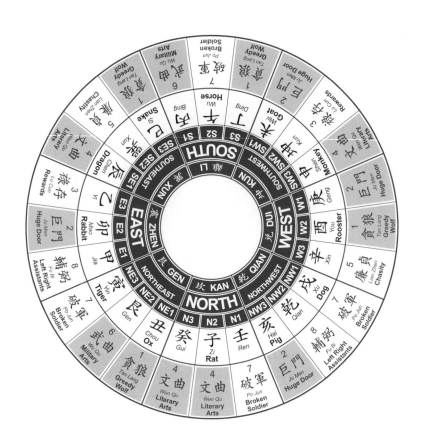

Heaven Penetrating Force 通天竅：

三合前方 **Facing Three Harmony**	乾亥 _{Qian Hai}	壬子 _{Ren Zi}	癸丑 _{Gui Chou}
三合後方 **Sitting Three Harmony**	巽巳 _{Xun Si}	丙午 _{Bing Wu}	丁未 _{Ding Wei}

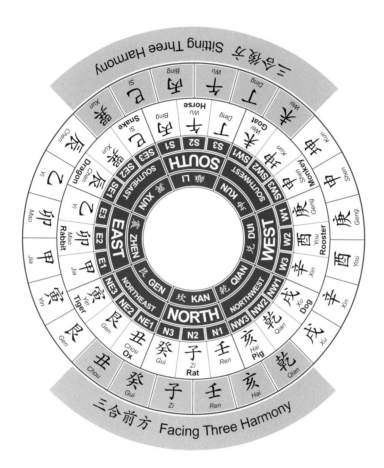

Moving Horse Six Ren Assessment 走馬六壬:

神后 *Shen Hou* **Holy Empress**	功曹 *Gong Cao* **Marshall**	天罡 *Tian Gang* **Heavenly Dipper**	勝光 *Sheng Guang* **Subliminal Bright**	傳送 *Chuan Song* **Great General**	河魁 *He Kui* **River Scholar**
丁未 *Ding Wei*	庚酉 *Geng You*	乾亥 *Qian Hai*	癸丑 *Gui Chou*	甲卯 *Jia Mao*	巽巳 *Xun Si*

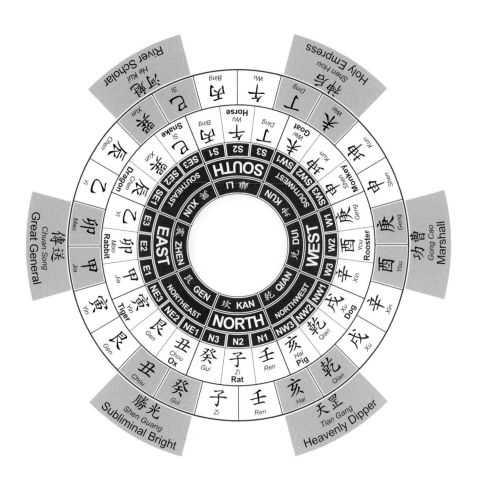

Four Advantages Three Cycles Star Plate 四利三元：

太陽 *Tai Yang* **Sun**	太陰 *Tai Yin* **Moon**	龍德 *Long De* **Dragon Virtue**	福德 *Fu De* **Fortune Virtue**
午 *Wu* **S2**	申 *Shen* **SW3**	子 *Zi* **N2**	寅 *Yin* **NE3**

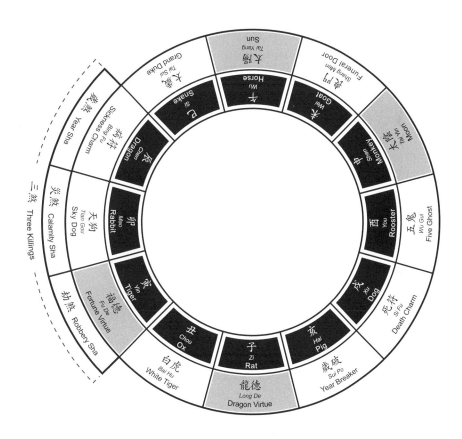

Negative Sectors For Opening Mountain 開山凶位：

年剋山家 Year Countering Sitting

甲 Jia E1	寅 Yin NE3	辰 Chen SE1	巽 Xun SE2	戌 Xu NW1	坎 Kan N1	辛 Xin W3	申 Shen SW3	丑 Chou NE1	癸 Gui N3	坤 Kun SW2	庚 Geng W1	未 Wei SW1

陰府太歲 *Yin Fu Tai Sui* **Yin Mansion Grand Duke**		六害 *Liu Hai* **Six Harm**	死符 *Si Fu* **Death Charm**	炙退 *Zhi Tui* **Roasting Star**
兌 Dui W2	乾 Qian NW2	寅 Yin NE3	戌 Xu NW1	子 Zi N2

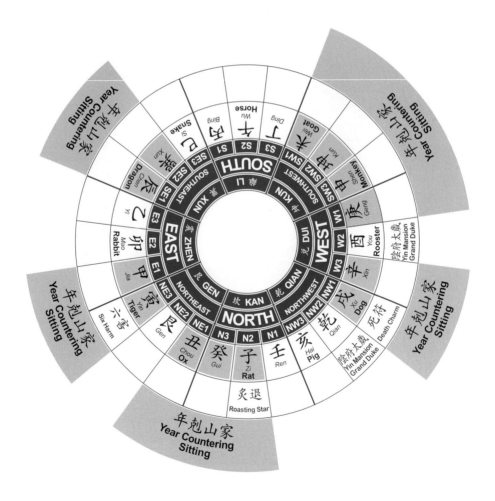

Negative Directions to Establish Facing 立向凶方：

巡山羅喉 *Xun Shan Luo Hou* **Mountain Patrol Luo Hou Star**	病符 *Bing Fu* **Sickness Charm**
丙 *Bing* **S1**	辰 *Chen* **SE1**

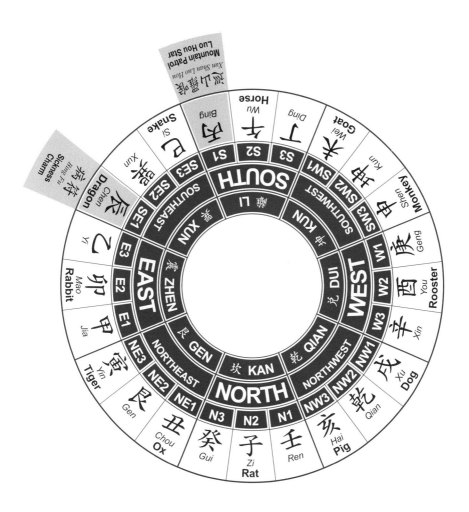

Negative Repair / Renovation Sectors Table 修方凶位表：

天官符 Heavenly Officer Charm	寅 *Yin* Tiger		豹尾 Leopard Tail	未 *Wei* Goat
地官符 Earthly Officer Charm	酉 *You* Rooster		飛廉 Flying Chaste	未 *Wei* Goat
大煞 Great Sha	酉 *You* Rooster		喪門 Funeral Door	未 *Wei* Goat
大將軍 Big General	卯 *Mao* Rabbit		弔客 Suspended Guest	卯 *Mao* Rabbit
力士 Strong Man	坤 *Kun*		白虎 White Tiger	丑 *Chou* Ox
蠶室 Silkworm Room	艮 *Gen*		金神 Golden God	辰 *Chen* Dragon 巳 *Si* Snake
蠶官 Silkworm Officer	丑 *Chou* Ox			
蠶命 Silkworm Life	寅 *Yin* Tiger		獨火 Lonely Fire	巽 *Xun*
歲刑 Duke Punishment	申 *Shen* Monkey		五鬼 Five Ghost	亥 *Hai* Pig
黃幡 Yellow Flag	丑 *Chou* Ox		破敗五鬼 Destructive Five Ghost	艮 *Gen*

Negative Repair / Renovation Sectors Diagram 修方凶位圖：

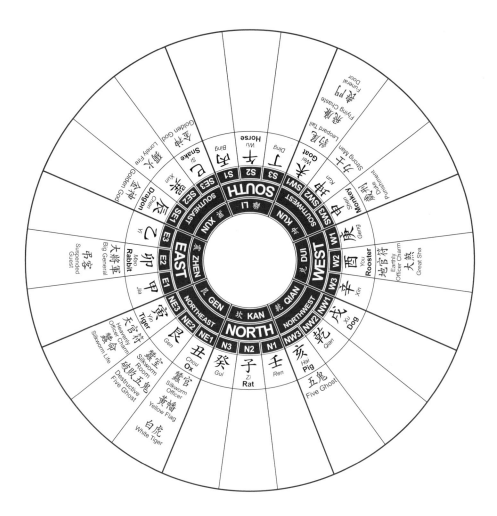

171

12-Month Auxiliary Stars Reference Table :
乙巳年十二月，開山立向修方星表

Positive Monthly Stars 吉星方

月 MONTH	寅 Tiger (Feb 4 - Mar 5) 正月 1st Month	卯 Rabbit (Mar 6 - Apr 4) 二月 2nd Month	辰 Dragon (Apr 5 - May 5) 三月 3rd Month	巳 Snake (May 6 - Jun 5) 四月 4th Month	午 Horse (Jun 6 - July 6) 五月 5th Month	未 Goat (July 7 - Aug 7) 六月 6th Month
天道 Heavenly Path	南 South	西南 Southwest	北 North	西 West	西北 Northwest	東 East
天德 Heavenly Virtue	丁 Ding Yin Fire	坤 Kun (申)	壬 Ren Yang Water	辛 Xin Yin Metal	乾 Qian (亥)	甲 Jia Yang Wood
天德合 Heavenly Virtue Combo	壬 Ren Yang Water	(巳)	丁 Ding Yin Fire	丙 Bing Yang Fire	(寅)	己 Ji Yin Earth
月德 Monthly Virtue	丙 Bing Yang Fire	甲 Jia Yang Wood	壬 Ren Yang Water	庚 Geng Yang Metal	丙 Bing Yang Fire	甲 Jia Yang Wood
月德合 Monthly Virtue Combo	辛 Xin Yin Metal	己 Ji Yin Earth	丁 Ding Yin Fire	乙 Yi Yin Wood	辛 Xin Yin Metal	己 Ji Yin Earth
月空 Month Emptiness	壬 Ren Yang Water	庚 Geng Yang Metal	丙 Bing Yang Fire	甲 Jia Yang Wood	壬 Ren Yang Water	庚 Geng Yang Metal
陽貴人 Yang Nobleman	坤 Kun	坎 Kan	離 Li	艮 Gen	兌 Dui	乾 Qian
陰貴人 Yin Nobleman	乾 Qian	中 Middle	巽 Xun	震 Zhen	坤 Kun	坎 Kan
飛天祿 Flying Heavenly Wealth	乾 Qian	中 Middle	坎 Kan	離 Li	艮 Gen	兌 Dui
飛天馬 Flying Heavenly Horse	中 Middle	巽 Xun	震 Zhen	坤 Kun	坎 Kan	離 Li

12-Month Auxiliary Stars Reference Table :
乙巳年十二月，開山立向修方星表

申 Monkey (Aug 8 - Sept 7) 七月 7th Month	酉 Rooster (Sept 8 - Oct 7) 八月 8th Month	戌 Dog (Oct 8 - Nov 6) 九月 9th Month	亥 Pig (Nov 7 - Dec 6) 十月 10th Month	子 Rat (Dec 7 - Jan 5) 十一月 11th Month	丑 Ox (Jan 6 - Feb 3) 十二月 12th Month	月 MONTH
北 North	東北 Northeast	南 South	東 East	東南 Southeast	西 West	天道 Heavenly Path
癸 Gui Yin Water	艮 Gen (寅)	丙 Bing Yang Fire	乙 Yi Yin Wood	巽 Xun (巳)	庚 Geng Yang Metal	天德 Heavenly Virtue
戊 Wu Yang Earth	(亥)	辛 Xin Yin Metal	庚 Geng Yang Metal	(申)	乙 Yi Yin Wood	天德合 Heavenly Virtue Combo
壬 Ren Yang Water	庚 Geng Yang Metal	丙 Bing Yang Fire	甲 Jia Yang Wood	壬 Ren Yang Water	庚 Geng Yang Metal	月德 Monthly Virtue
丁 Ding Yin Fire	乙 Yi Yin Wood	辛 Xin Yin Metal	己 Ji Yin Earth	丁 Ding Yin Fire	乙 Yi Yin Wood	月德合 Monthly Virtue Combo
丙 Bing Yang Fire	甲 Jia Yang Wood	壬 Ren Yang Water	庚 Geng Yang Metal	丙 Bing Yang Fire	甲 Jia Yang Wood	月空 Month Emptiness
中 Middle	坎 Kan	離 Li	艮 Gen	兌 Dui	乾 Qian	陽貴人 Yang Nobleman
離 Li	艮 Gen	兌 Dui	乾 Qian	中 Middle	坎 Kan	陰貴人 Yin Nobleman
乾 Qian	中 Middle	巽 Xun	震 Zhen	坤 Kun	坎 Kan	飛天祿 Flying Heavenly Wealth
艮 Gen	兌 Dui	乾 Qian	中 Middle	坎 Kan	離 Li	飛天馬 Flying Heavenly Horse

Monthly Purple White Stars 月紫白九星 :

寅 Tiger (Feb 4 - Mar 5) 正月 1st Month

巽SE	離S	坤SW
1 White 一白	6 White 六白	8 White 八白
震E 9 Purple 九紫	2 Black 二黑	4 Green 四綠 兌W
艮NE 5 Yellow 五黃	坎N 7 Red 七赤	3 Jade 三碧 乾NW

卯 Rabbit (Mar 6 - Apr 4) 二月 2nd Month

巽SE	離S	坤SW
9 Purple 九紫	5 Yellow 五黃	7 Red 七赤
震E 8 White 八白	1 White 一白	3 Jade 三碧 兌W
艮NE 4 Green 四綠	坎N 6 White 六白	2 Black 二黑 乾NW

辰 Dragon (Apr 5 - May 5) 三月 3rd Month

巽SE	離S	坤SW
8 White 八白	4 Green 四綠	6 White 六白
震E 7 Red 七赤	9 Purple 九紫	2 Black 二黑 兌W
艮NE 3 Jade 三碧	坎N 5 Yellow 五黃	1 White 一白 乾NW

巳 Snake (May 6 - Jun 5) 四月 4th Month

巽SE	離S	坤SW
7 Red 七赤	3 Jade 三碧	5 Yellow 五黃
震E 6 White 六白	8 White 八白	1 White 一白 兌W
艮NE 2 Black 二黑	坎N 4 Green 四綠	9 Purple 九紫 乾NW

午 Horse (Jun 6 - July 6) 五月 5th Month

巽SE	離S	坤SW
6 White 六白	2 Black 二黑	4 Green 四綠
震E 5 Yellow 五黃	7 Red 七赤	9 Purple 九紫 兌W
艮NE 1 White 一白	坎N 3 Jade 三碧	8 White 八白 乾NW

未 Goat (July 7 - Aug 7) 六月 6th Month

巽SE	離S	坤SW
5 Yellow 五黃	1 White 一白	3 Jade 三碧
震E 4 Green 四綠	6 White 六白	8 White 八白 兌W
艮NE 9 Purple 九紫	坎N 2 Black 二黑	7 Red 七赤 乾NW

申 Monkey (Aug 8 - Sept 7) 七月 7th Month

巽SE	離S	坤SW
4 Green 四綠	9 Purple 九紫	2 Black 二黑
震E 3 Jade 三碧	5 Yellow 五黃	7 Red 七赤 兌W
艮NE 8 White 八白	坎N 1 White 一白	6 White 六白 乾NW

酉 Rooster (Sept 8 - Oct 7) 八月 8th Month

巽SE	離S	坤SW
3 Jade 三碧	8 White 八白	1 White 一白
震E 2 Black 二黑	4 Green 四綠	6 White 六白 兌W
艮NE 7 Red 七赤	坎N 9 Purple 九紫	5 Yellow 五黃 乾NW

戌 Dog (Oct 8 - Nov 6) 九月 9th Month

巽SE	離S	坤SW
2 Black 二黑	7 Red 七赤	9 Purple 九紫
震E 1 White 一白	3 Jade 三碧	5 Yellow 五黃 兌W
艮NE 6 White 六白	坎N 8 White 八白	4 Green 四綠 乾NW

亥 Pig (Nov 7 - Dec 6) 十月 10th Month

巽SE	離S	坤SW
1 White 一白	6 White 六白	8 White 八白
震E 9 Purple 九紫	2 Black 二黑	4 Green 四綠 兌W
艮NE 5 Yellow 五黃	坎N 7 Red 七赤	3 Jade 三碧 乾NW

子 Rat (Dec 7 - Jan 5) 十一月 11th Month

巽SE	離S	坤SW
9 Purple 九紫	5 Yellow 五黃	7 Red 七赤
震E 8 White 八白	1 White 一白	3 Jade 三碧 兌W
艮NE 4 Green 四綠	坎N 6 White 六白	2 Black 二黑 乾NW

丑 Ox (Jan 6 - Feb 3) 十二月 12th Month

巽SE	離S	坤SW
8 White 八白	4 Green 四綠	6 White 六白
震E 7 Red 七赤	9 Purple 九紫	2 Black 二黑 兌W
艮NE 3 Jade 三碧	坎N 5 Yellow 五黃	1 White 一白 乾NW

Qi Men Three Nobles 三奇 :

Three Nobles 三奇 / Seasons	乙 Yi	丙 Bing	丁 Ding
立春 **Coming of Spring** Feb 4 - Feb 18	坤 Kun	震 Zhen	巽 Xun
春分 **Spring Equinox** Mar 21 - Apr 4	乾 Qian	兌 Dui	艮 Gen
立夏 **Coming of Summer** May 6 - May 20	兌 Dui	艮 Gen	離 Li
夏至 **Summer Solstice** Jun 22 - Jul 6	乾 Qian	中 Middle	巽 Xun
立秋 **Coming of Autumn** Aug 8 - Aug 23	艮 Gen	兌 Dui	乾 Qian
秋分 **Autumn Equinox** Sept 23 - Oct 7	巽 Xun	震 Zhen	坤 Kun
立冬 **Coming of Winter** Nov 7 - Nov 22	震 Zhen	坤 Kun	坎 Kan
冬至 **Winter Solstice** Dec 22 - Jan 5	巽 Xun	中 Middle	乾 Qian

Sectors to Avoid Opening Mountain 開山凶位 :

月 MONTH	月建 Month Establishment	月破 Month Destruction	月剋山家 Month Countering Sitting		陰府太歲 Yin Mansion Grand Duke	
寅 **Tiger** (Feb 4 - Mar 5) 正月 **1st Month**	寅 *Yin* **Tiger**	申 *Shen* **Monkey**	乾 *Qian*	兌 *Dui*	坤 *Kun*	震 *Zhen*
卯 **Rabbit** (Mar 6 - Apr 4) 二月 **2nd Month**	卯 *Mao* **Rabbit**	酉 *You* **Rooster**	亥 *Hai* **Pig**	丁 *Ding* **Yin Fire**	巽 *Xun*	艮 *Gen*
辰 **Dragon** (Apr 5 - May 5) 三月 **3rd Month**	辰 *Chen* **Dragon**	戌 *Xu* **Dog**	震 *Zhen*	巳 *Si* **Snake**	乾 *Qian*	兌 *Dui*
巳 **Snake** (May 6 - Jun 5) 四月 **4th Month**	巳 *Si* **Snake**	亥 *Hai* **Pig**	艮 *Gen*		坤 *Kun*	坎 *Kan*
午 **Horse** (Jun 6 - July 6) 五月 **5th Month**	午 *Wu* **Horse**	子 *Zi* **Rat**	離 *Li*	丙 *Bing* **Yang Fire**	離 *Li*	乾 *Qian*
未 **Goat** (July 7 - Aug 7) 六月 **6th Month**	未 *Wei* **Goat**	丑 *Chou* **Ox**	壬 *Ren* **Yang Water**	乙 *Yi* **Yin Wood**	震 *Zhen*	坤 *Kun*
申 **Monkey** (Aug 8 - Sept 7) 七月 **7th Month**	申 *Shen* **Monkey**	寅 *Yin* **Tiger**	–		艮 *Gen*	巽 *Xun*
酉 **Rooster** (Sept 8 - Oct 7) 八月 **8th Month**	酉 *You* **Rooster**	卯 *Mao* **Rabbit**	–		兌 *Dui*	乾 *Qian*
戌 **Dog** (Oct 8 - Nov 6) 九月 **9th Month**	戌 *Xu* **Dog**	辰 *Chen* **Dragon**	乾 *Qian*	兌 *Dui*	坎 *Kan*	坤 *Kun*
亥 **Pig** (Nov 7 - Dec 6) 十月 **10th Month**	亥 *Hai* **Pig**	巳 *Si* **Snake**	亥 *Hai* **Pig**	丁 *Ding* **Yin Fire**	乾 *Qian*	離 *Li*
子 **Rat** (Dec 7 - Jan 5) 十一月 **11th Month**	子 *Zi* **Rat**	午 *Wu* **Horse**	水 **Water**	山 **Mountain**	坤 *Kun*	震 *Zhen*
丑 **Ox** (Jan 6 - Feb 3) 十二月 **12th Month**	丑 *Chou* **Ox**	未 *Wei* **Goat**	土 **Earth**		巽 *Xun*	艮 *Gen*

Negative Repair / Renovation Sectors 修方凶位 :

月 MONTH	天官符 Heavenly Officer Charm			地官符 Earth Officer Charm			小月建 Small Month Establishment		
寅 Tiger (Feb 4 - Mar 5) 正月 1st Month	未 Wei Goat	坤 Kun	申 Shen Monkey	甲 Jia Yang Wood	震 Zhen	乙 Yi Yin Wood	丙 Bing Yang Fire	離 Li	丁 Ding Yin Fire
卯 Rabbit (Mar 6 - Apr 4) 二月 2nd Month	壬 Ren Yang Water	坎 Kan	癸 Gui Yin Water	未 Wei Goat	坤 Kun	申 Shen Monkey	壬 Ren Yang Water	坎 Kan	癸 Gui Yin Water
辰 Dragon (Apr 5 - May 5) 三月 3rd Month	丙 Bing Yang Fire	離 Li	丁 Ding Yin Fire	壬 Ren Yang Water	坎 Kan	癸 Gui Yin Water	未 Wei Goat	坤 Kun	申 Shen Monkey
巳 Snake (May 6 - Jun 5) 四月 4th Month	丑 Chou Ox	艮 Gen	寅 Yin Tiger	丙 Bing Yang Fire	離 Li	丁 Ding Yin Fire	甲 Jia Yang Wood	震 Zhen	乙 Yi Yin Wood
午 Horse (Jun 6 - July 6) 五月 5th Month	庚 Geng Yang Metal	兌 Dui	辛 Xin Yin Metal	丑 Chou Ox	艮 Gen	寅 Yin Tiger	辰 Chen Dragon	巽 Xun	己 Ji Yin Earth
未 Goat (July 7 - Aug 7) 六月 6th Month	戌 Xu Dog	乾 Qian	亥 Hai Pig	庚 Geng Yang Metal	兌 Dui	辛 Xin Yin Metal	中 Middle		
申 Monkey (Aug 8 - Sept 7) 七月 7th Month	中 Middle			戌 Xu Dog	乾 Qian	亥 Hai Pig	戌 Xu Dog	乾 Qian	亥 Hai Pig
酉 Rooster (Sept 8 - Oct 7) 八月 8th Month	庚 Geng Yang Metal	兌 Dui	辛 Xin Yin Metal	中 Middle			庚 Geng Yang Metal	兌 Dui	辛 Xin Yin Metal
戌 Dog (Oct 8 - Nov 6) 九月 9th Month	戌 Xu Dog	乾 Qian	亥 Hai Pig	庚 Geng Yang Metal	兌 Dui	辛 Xin Yin Metal	丑 Chou Ox	艮 Gen	寅 Yin Tiger
亥 Pig (Nov 7 - Dec 6) 十月 10th Month	中 Middle			戌 Xu Dog	乾 Qian	亥 Hai Pig	丙 Bing Yang Fire	離 Li	丁 Ding Yin Fire
子 Rat (Dec 7 - Jan 5) 十一月 11th Month	辰 Chen Dragon	巽 Xun	巳 Si Snake	中 Middle			壬 Ren Yang Water	坎 Kan	癸 Gui Yin Water
丑 Ox (Jan 6 - Feb 3) 十二月 12th Month	甲 Jia Yang Wood	震 Zhen	乙 Yi Yin Wood	辰 Chen Dragon	巽 Xun	巳 Si Snake	未 Wei Goat	坤 Kun	申 Shen Monkey

Negative Repair / Renovation Sectors 修方凶位 ：

月 MONTH	大月建 Big Month Establishment			飛大煞 Flying Great Sha			丙丁獨火 Bing Ding Lonely Fire	
寅 **Tiger** (Feb 4 - Mar 5) 正月 **1st Month**	未 *Wei* Goat	坤 *Kun*	申 *Shen* Monkey	甲 *Jia* Yang Wood	震 *Zhen*	乙 *Yi* Yin Wood	巽 *Xun*	中 Middle
卯 **Rabbit** (Mar 6 - Apr 4) 二月 **2nd Month**	壬 *Ren* Yang Water	坎 *Kan*	癸 *Gui* Yin Water	未 *Wei* Goat	坤 *Kun*	申 *Shen* Monkey	震 *Zhen*	巽 *Xun*
辰 **Dragon** (Apr 5 - May 5) 三月 **3rd Month**	丙 *Bing* Yang Fire	離 *Li*	丁 *Ding* Yin Fire	壬 *Ren* Yang Water	坎 *Kan*	癸 *Gui* Yin Water	坤 *Kun*	震 *Zhen*
巳 **Snake** (May 6 - Jun 5) 四月 **4th Month**	丑 *Chou* Ox	艮 *Gen*	寅 *Yin* Tiger	丙 *Bing* Yang Fire	離 *Li*	丁 *Ding* Yin Fire	坎 *Kan*	坤 *Kun*
午 **Horse** (Jun 6 - July 6) 五月 **5th Month**	庚 *Geng* Yang Metal	兑 *Dui*	辛 *Xin* Yin Metal	丑 *Chou* Ox	艮 *Gen*	寅 *Yin* Tiger	離 *Li*	坎 *Kan*
未 **Goat** (July 7 - Aug 7) 六月 **6th Month**	戌 *Xu* Dog	乾 *Qian*	亥 *Hai* Pig	庚 *Geng* Yang Metal	兑 *Dui*	辛 *Xin* Yin Metal	艮 *Gen*	離 *Li*
申 **Monkey** (Aug 8 - Sept 7) 七月 **7th Month**		中 Middle		戌 *Xu* Dog	乾 *Qian*	亥 *Hai* Pig	兑 *Dui*	艮 *Gen*
酉 **Rooster** (Sept 8 - Oct 7) 八月 **8th Month**	辰 *Chen* Dragon	巽 *Xun*	巳 *Si* Snake		中 Middle		乾 *Qian*	兑 *Dui*
戌 **Dog** (Oct 8 - Nov 6) 九月 **9th Month**	甲 *Jia* Yang Wood	震 *Zhen*	乙 *Yi* Yin Wood	庚 *Geng* Yang Metal	兑 *Dui*	辛 *Xin* Yin Metal	中 Middle	乾 *Qian*
亥 **Pig** (Nov 7 - Dec 6) 十月 **10th Month**	未 *Wei* Goat	坤 *Kun*	申 *Shen* Monkey	戌 *Xu* Dog	乾 *Qian*	亥 *Hai* Pig		中 Middle
子 **Rat** (Dec 7 - Jan 5) 十一月 **11th Month**	壬 *Ren* Yang Water	坎 *Kan*	癸 *Gui* Yin Water		中 Middle		巽 *Xun*	中 Middle
丑 **Ox** (Jan 6 - Feb 3) 十二月 **12th Month**	丙 *Bing* Yang Fire	離 *Li*	丁 *Ding* Yin Fire	辰 *Chen* Dragon	巽 *Xun*	巳 *Si* Snake	震 *Zhen*	巽 *Xun*

Negative Repair / Renovation Sectors 修方凶位 :

月 MONTH	月遊火 Month Wondering Fire	三煞 Monthly 3 Killings		
		劫煞 Robbery Sha	災煞 Calamity Sha	月煞 Month Sha
寅 **Tiger** (Feb 4 - Mar 5) 正月 **1st Month**	離 Li	亥 Hai Pig	子 Zi Rat	丑 Chou Ox
卯 **Rabbit** (Mar 6 - Apr 4) 二月 **2nd Month**	坎 Kan	申 Shen Monkey	酉 You Rooster	戌 Xu Dog
辰 **Dragon** (Apr 5 - May 5) 三月 **3rd Month**	坤 Kun	巳 Si Snake	午 Wu Horse	未 Wei Goat
巳 **Snake** (May 6 - Jun 5) 四月 **4th Month**	震 Zhen	寅 Yin Tiger	卯 Mao Rabbit	辰 Chen Dragon
午 **Horse** (Jun 6 - July 6) 五月 **5th Month**	巽 Xun	亥 Hai Pig	子 Zi Rat	丑 Chou Ox
未 **Goat** (July 7 - Aug 7) 六月 **6th Month**	中 Middle	申 Shen Monkey	酉 You Rooster	戌 Xu Dog
申 **Monkey** (Aug 8 - Sept 7) 七月 **7th Month**	乾 Qian	巳 Si Snake	午 Wu Horse	未 Wei Goat
酉 **Rooster** (Sept 8 - Oct 7) 八月 **8th Month**	兌 Dui	寅 Yin Tiger	卯 Mao Rabbit	辰 Chen Dragon
戌 **Dog** (Oct 8 - Nov 6) 九月 **9th Month**	艮 Gen	亥 Hai Pig	子 Zi Rat	丑 Chou Ox
亥 **Pig** (Nov 7 - Dec 6) 十月 **10th Month**	離 Li	申 Shen Monkey	酉 You Rooster	戌 Xu Dog
子 **Rat** (Dec 7 - Jan 5) 十一月 **11th Month**	坎 Kan	巳 Si Snake	午 Wu Horse	未 Wei Goat
丑 **Ox** (Jan 6 - Feb 3) 十二月 **12th Month**	坤 Kun	寅 Yin Tiger	卯 Mao Rabbit	辰 Chen Dragon

Negative Repair / Renovation Sectors 修方凶位 :

月 MONTH	月刑 Month Punishment	月害 Month Harm	月厭 Month Detest
寅 **Tiger** (Feb 4 - Mar 5) 正月 **1st Month**	巳 *Si* Snake	巳 *Si* Snake	戌 *Xu* Dog
卯 **Rabbit** (Mar 6 - Apr 4) 二月 **2nd Month**	子 *Zi* Rat	辰 *Chen* Dragon	酉 *You* Rooster
辰 **Dragon** (Apr 5 - May 5) 三月 **3rd Month**	辰 *Chen* Dragon	卯 *Mao* Rabbit	申 *Shen* Monkey
巳 **Snake** (May 6 - Jun 5) 四月 **4th Month**	申 *Shen* Monkey	寅 *Yin* Tiger	未 *Wei* Goat
午 **Horse** (Jun 6 - July 6) 五月 **5th Month**	午 *Wu* Horse	丑 *Chou* Ox	午 *Wu* Horse
未 **Goat** (July 7 - Aug 7) 六月 **6th Month**	丑 *Chou* Ox	子 *Zi* Rat	巳 *Si* Snake
申 **Monkey** (Aug 8 - Sept 7) 七月 **7th Month**	寅 *Yin* Tiger	亥 *Hai* Pig	辰 *Chen* Dragon
酉 **Rooster** (Sept 8 - Oct 7) 八月 **8th Month**	酉 *You* Rooster	戌 *Xu* Dog	卯 *Mao* Rabbit
戌 **Dog** (Oct 8 - Nov 6) 九月 **9th Month**	未 *Wei* Goat	酉 *You* Rooster	寅 *Yin* Tiger
亥 **Pig** (Nov 7 - Dec 6) 十月 **10th Month**	亥 *Hai* Pig	申 *Shen* Monkey	丑 *Chou* Ox
子 **Rat** (Dec 7 - Jan 5) 十一月 **11th Month**	卯 *Mao* Rabbit	未 *Wei* Goat	子 *Zi* Rat
丑 **Ox** (Jan 6 - Feb 3) 十二月 **12th Month**	戌 *Xu* Dog	午 *Wu* Horse	亥 *Hai* Pig

乙未 (Yi Wei)
Wood Goat

Heavenly Stem 天干	乙 **Yin Wood** (陰木)
Earthly Branch 地支	未 **Goat** (Yin Earth 陰土)
Hidden Stem 藏干	己 **Yin Earth**, 丁 **Yin Fire**, 乙 **Yin Wood**
Na Yin 納音	沙中金 **Metal from sand**
Grand Duke 太歲	未 **Goat**
Xuan Kong Five Element 玄空五行	**7** 火 **Fire**
Gua Name 卦名	䷯ 水風井 **Well**
Xuan Kong Period Luck 玄空卦運	**6**

Annual Positive Stars for Opening Mountain, Establishing Facing and Commencing Repairs 開山立向修方吉星:

歲德 **Duke Virtue**	庚 *Geng* **Yang Metal**
歲德合 **Duke Virtue Combo**	乙 *Yi* **Yin Wood**
歲枝德 **Duke Branch Virtue**	子 *Zi* **Rat**
陽貴人 **Yang Nobleman**	申 *Shen* **Monkey**
陰貴人 **Yin Nobleman**	子 *Zi* **Rat**
歲祿 **Duke Prosperous**	卯 *Mao* **Rabbit**
歲馬 **Duke Horse**	巳 *Si* **Snake**
奏書 **Decree**	巽 *Xun*
博士 **Professor**	乾 *Qian*

Annual Negative Stars for Opening Mountain, Establishing Facing and Commencing Repairs 開山立向修方凶星：

太歲 Grand Duke	歲破 Year Breaker	三煞 Three Killings			坐煞向煞 Sitting Sha Facing Sha				浮天空亡 Floating Heaven Emptiness	
未 *Wei* Goat	丑 *Chou* Ox	申 *Shen* Monkey	酉 *You* Rooster	戌 *Xu* Dog	庚 *Geng* Yang Metal	辛 *Xin* Yin Metal	甲 *Jia* Yang Wood	乙 *Yi* Yin Wood	坎 *Kan*	癸 *Gui* Yin Water

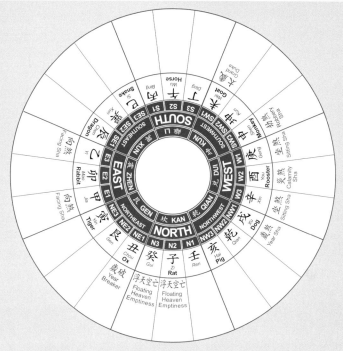

Annual San Yuan Purple White Stars 三元紫白九星：

上元 **Upper Period** **Period 1, 2, 3**			中元 **Middle Period** **Period 4, 5, 6**			下元 **Lower Period** **Period 7, 8, 9**		
巽**SE** 5	離**S** 1	坤**SW** 3	巽**SE** 8	離**S** 4	坤**SW** 6	巽**SE** 2	離**S** 7	坤**SW** 9
震**E** 4	6 乙未 *Yi Wei* **Wood Goat**	兌**W** 8	震**E** 7	9 乙未 *Yi Wei* **Wood Goat**	兌**W** 2	震**E** 1	3 乙未 *Yi Wei* **Wood Goat**	兌**W** 5
艮**NE** 9	坎**N** 2	乾**NW** 7	艮**NE** 3	坎**N** 5	乾**NW** 1	艮**NE** 6	坎**N** 8	乾**NW** 4

Mountain Covering Yellow Path 蓋山黃道：

貪狼 *Tan Lang* **Greedy Wolf**		巨門 *Ju Men* **Huge Door**				武曲 *Wu Qu* **Military Arts**		文曲 *Wen Qu* **Literary Arts**			
坤 *Kun* SW2	乙 *Yi* E3	坎 *Kan* N2	癸 *Gui* N3	申 *Shen* SW3	辰 *Chen* SE1	乾 *Qian* NW2	甲 *Jia* E1	震 *Zhen* E2	庚 *Geng* W1	亥 *Hai* NW3	未 *Wei* SW1

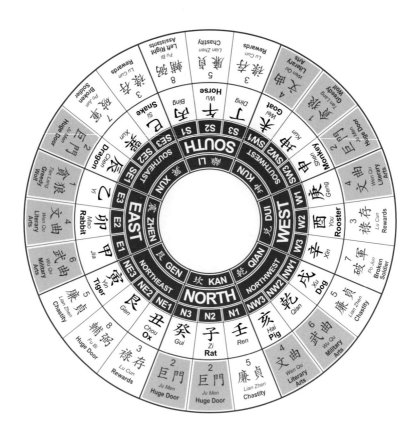

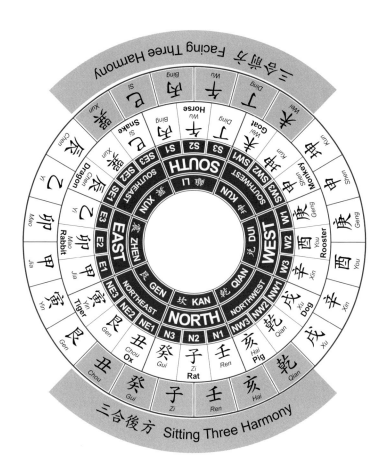

Heaven Penetrating Force 通天竅 :

三合前方 **Facing Three** **Harmony**	巽巳 Xun Si	丙午 Bing Wu	丁未 Ding Wei
三合後方 **Sitting Three** **Harmony**	乾亥 Qian Hai	壬子 Ren Zi	癸丑 Gui Chou

Moving Horse Six Ren Assessment 走馬六壬：

神后 *Shen Hou* **Holy Empress**	功曹 *Gong Cao* **Marshall**	天罡 *Tian Gang* **Heavenly Dipper**	勝光 *Sheng Guang* **Subliminal Bright**	傳送 *Chuan Song* **Great General**	河魁 *He Kui* **River Scholar**
巽巳 *Xun Si*	丁未 *Ding Wei*	庚酉 *Geng You*	乾亥 *Qian Hai*	癸丑 *Gui Chou*	甲卯 *Jia Mao*

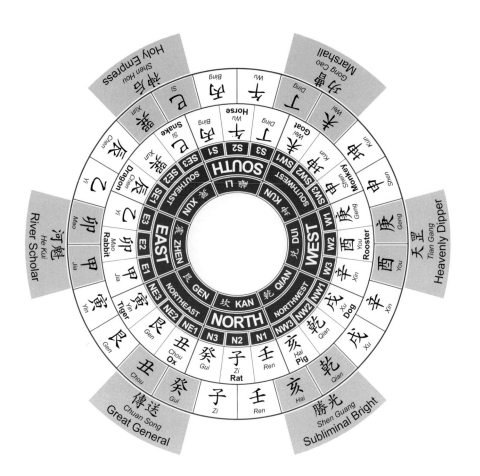

乙未 (Yi Wei) Wood Goat

Four Advantages Three Cycles Star Plate 四利三元：

太陽 *Tai Yang* **Sun**	太陰 *Tai Yin* **Moon**	龍德 *Long De* **Dragon Virtue**	福德 *Fu De* **Fortune Virtue**
申 *Shen* **Monkey**	戌 *Xu* **Dog**	寅 *Yin* **Tiger**	辰 *Chen* **Dragon**

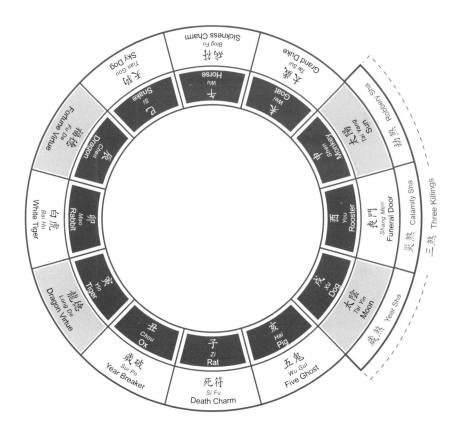

187

Negative Sectors For Opening Mountain 開山凶位：

年剋山家 Year Countering Sitting

震 Zhen E2	艮 Gen NE2	巳 Si SE3	

陰府太歲 Yin Fu Tai Sui **Yin Mansion Grand Duke**		六害 Liu Hai **Six Harm**	死符 Si Fu **Death Charm**	炙退 Zhi Tui **Roasting Star**
兌 Dui W2	乾 Qian NW2	子 Zi N2	子 Zi N2	午 Wu Horse

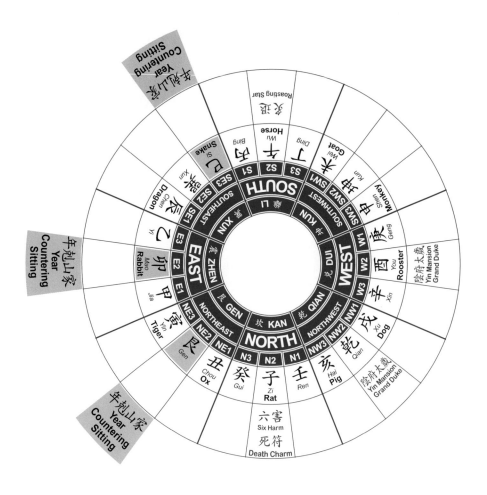

Negative Directions to Establish Facing 立向凶方：	
巡山羅喉 *Xun Shan Luo Hou* **Mountain Patrol Luo Hou Star**	病符 *Bing Fu* **Sickness Charm**
坤 *Kun* **SW2**	午 *Wu* **S2**

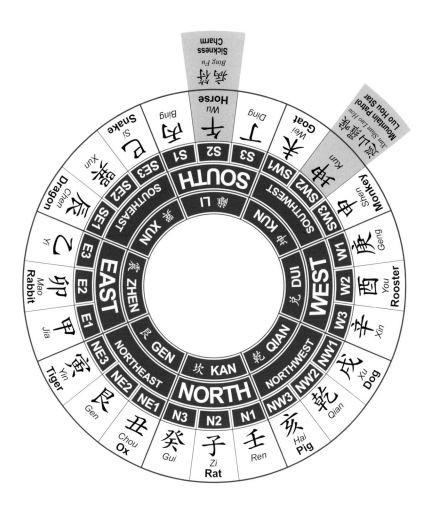

Negative Repair / Renovation Sectors Table 修方凶位表：

天官符 Heavenly Officer Charm	寅 *Yin* Tiger	豹尾 Leopard Tail	丑 *Chou* Ox
地官符 Earthly Officer Charm	亥 *Hai* Pig	飛廉 Flying Chaste	卯 *Mao* Rabbit
大煞 Great Sha	卯 *Mao* Rabbit	喪門 Funeral Door	酉 *You* Rooster
大將軍 Big General	卯 *Mao* Rabbit	弔客 Suspended Guest	巳 *Si* Snake
力士 Strong Man	坤 *Kun*	白虎 White Tiger	卯 *Mao* Rabbit
蠶室 Silkworm Room	艮 *Gen*	金神 Golden God	辰 *Chen* Dragon 巳 *Si* Snake
蠶官 Silkworm Officer	丑 *Chou* Ox		
蠶命 Silkworm Life	寅 *Yin* Tiger	獨火 Lonely Fire	離 *Li*
歲刑 Duke Punishment	丑 *Chou* Ox	五鬼 Five Ghost	酉 *You* Rooster
黃幡 Yellow Flag	未 *Wei* Goat	破敗五鬼 Destructive Five Ghost	艮 *Gen*

Negative Repair / Renovation Sectors Diagram 修方凶位圖：

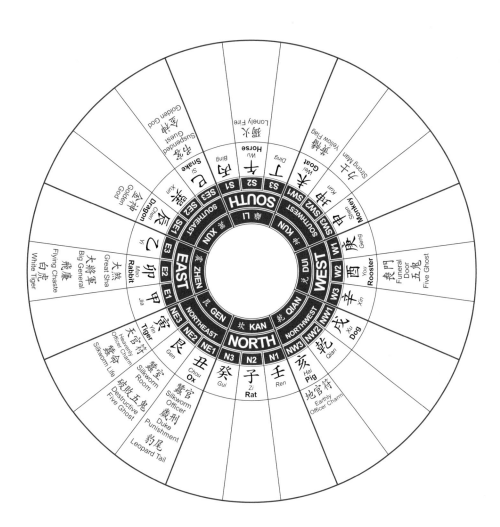

12-Month Auxiliary Stars Reference Table :
乙未年十二月，開山立向修方星表

Positive Monthly Stars 吉星方

月 MONTH	寅 Tiger (Feb 4 - Mar 5) 正月 1st Month	卯 Rabbit (Mar 6 - Apr 4) 二月 2nd Month	辰 Dragon (Apr 5 - May 5) 三月 3rd Month	巳 Snake (May 6 - Jun 5) 四月 4th Month	午 Horse (Jun 6 - July 6) 五月 5th Month	未 Goat (July 7 - Aug 7) 六月 6th Month
天道 Heavenly Path	南 South	西南 Southwest	北 North	西 West	西北 Northwest	東 East
天德 Heavenly Virtue	丁 Ding Yin Fire	坤 Kun (申)	壬 Ren Yang Water	辛 Xin Yin Metal	乾 Qian (亥)	甲 Jia Yang Wood
天德合 Heavenly Virtue Combo	壬 Ren Yang Water	(巳)	丁 Ding Yin Fire	丙 Bing Yang Fire	(寅)	己 Ji Yin Earth
月德 Monthly Virtue	丙 Bing Yang Fire	甲 Jia Yang Wood	壬 Ren Yang Water	庚 Geng Yang Metal	丙 Bing Yang Fire	甲 Jia Yang Wood
月德合 Monthly Virtue Combo	辛 Xin Yin Metal	己 Ji Yin Earth	丁 Ding Yin Fire	乙 Yi Yin Wood	辛 Xin Yin Metal	己 Ji Yin Earth
月空 Month Emptiness	壬 Ren Yang Water	庚 Geng Yang Metal	丙 Bing Yang Fire	甲 Jia Yang Wood	壬 Ren Yang Water	庚 Geng Yang Metal
陽貴人 Yang Nobleman	坤 Kun	坎 Kan	離 Li	艮 Gen	兌 Dui	乾 Qian
陰貴人 Yin Nobleman	乾 Qia	中 Middle	巽 Xun	震 Zhen	坤 Kun	坎 Kan
飛天祿 Flying Heavenly Wealth	乾 Qian	中 Middle	坎 Kan	離 Li	艮 Gen	兌 Dui
飛天馬 Flying Heavenly Horse	艮 Gen	兌 Dui	乾 Qian	中 Middle	坎 Kan	離 Li

12-Month Auxiliary Stars Reference Table :
乙未年十二月，開山立向修方星表

申 Monkey (Aug 8 - Sept 7) 七月 7th Month	酉 Rooster (Sept 8 - Oct 7) 八月 8th Month	戌 Dog (Oct 8 - Nov 6) 九月 9th Month	亥 Pig (Nov 7 - Dec 6) 十月 10th Month	子 Rat (Dec 7 - Jan 5) 十一月 11th Month	丑 Ox (Jan 6 - Feb 3) 十二月 12th Month	月 MONTH
北 North	東北 Northeast	南 South	東 East	東南 Southeast	西 West	天道 Heavenly Path
癸 Gui Yin Water	艮 Gen (寅)	丙 Bing Yang Fire	乙 Yi Yin Wood	巽 Xun (巳)	庚 Geng Yang Metal	天德 Heavenly Virtue
戊 Wu Yang Earth	(亥)	辛 Xin Yin Metal	庚 Geng Yang Metal	(申)	乙 Yi Yin Wood	天德合 Heavenly Virtue Combo
壬 Ren Yang Water	庚 Geng Yang Metal	丙 Bing Yang Fire	甲 Jia Yang Wood	壬 Ren Yang Water	庚 Geng Yang Metal	月德 Monthly Virtue
丁 Ding Yin Fire	乙 Yi Yin Wood	辛 Xin Yin Metal	己 Ji Yin Earth	丁 Ding Yin Fire	乙 Yi Yin Wood	月德合 Monthly Virtue Combo
丙 Bing Yang Fire	甲 Jia Yang Wood	壬 Ren Yang Water	庚 Geng Yang Metal	丙 Bing Yang Fire	甲 Jia Yang Wood	月空 Month Emptiness
中 Middle	坎 Kan	離 Li	艮 Gen	兌 Dui	乾 Qia	陽貴人 Yang Nobleman
離 Li	艮 Gen	兌 Dui	乾 Qian	中 Middle	坎 Kan	陰貴人 Yin Nobleman
乾 Qia	中 Middle	巽 Xun	震 Zhen	坤 Kun	坎 Kan	飛天祿 Flying Heavenly Wealth
艮 Gen	兌 Dui	乾 Qian	中 Middle	巽 Xun	震 Zhen	飛天馬 Flying Heavenly Horse

Monthly Purple White Stars 月紫白九星 ：

寅 Tiger (Feb 4 - Mar 5) 正月 1st Month

巽SE	離S	坤SW
4 Green 四綠	9 Purple 九紫	2 Black 二黑
震E 3 Jade 三碧	5 Yellow 五黄	7 Red 七赤 兌W
艮NE 8 White 八白	坎N 1 White 一白	6 White 六白 乾NW

卯 Rabbit (Mar 6 - Apr 4) 二月 2nd Month

巽SE	離S	坤SW
3 Jade 三碧	8 White 八白	1 White 一白
震E 2 Black 二黑	4 Green 四綠	6 White 六白 兌W
艮NE 7 Red 七赤	坎N 9 Purple 九紫	5 Yellow 五黄 乾NW

辰 Dragon (Apr 5 - May 5) 三月 3rd Month

巽SE	離S	坤SW
2 Black 二黑	7 Red 七赤	9 Purple 九紫
震E 1 White 一白	3 Jade 三碧	5 Yellow 五黄 兌W
艮NE 6 White 六白	坎N 8 White 八白	4 Green 四綠 乾NW

巳 Snake (May 6 - Jun 5) 四月 4th Month

巽SE	離S	坤SW
1 White 一白	6 White 六白	8 White 八白
震E 9 Purple 九紫	2 Black 二黑	4 Green 四綠 兌W
艮NE 5 Yellow 五黄	坎N 7 Red 七赤	3 Jade 三碧 乾NW

午 Horse (Jun 6 - July 6) 五月 5th Month

巽SE	離S	坤SW
9 Purple 九紫	5 Yellow 五黄	7 Red 七赤
震E 8 White 八白	1 White 一白	3 Jade 三碧 兌W
艮NE 4 Green 四綠	坎N 6 White 六白	2 Black 二黑 乾NW

未 Goat (July 7 - Aug 7) 六月 6th Month

巽SE	離S	坤SW
8 White 八白	4 Green 四綠	6 White 六白
震E 7 Red 七赤	9 Purple 九紫	2 Black 二黑 兌W
艮NE 3 Jade 三碧	坎N 5 Yellow 五黄	1 White 一白 乾NW

申 Monkey (Aug 8 - Sept 7) 七月 7th Month

巽SE	離S	坤SW
7 Red 七赤	3 Jade 三碧	5 Yellow 五黄
震E 6 White 六白	8 White 八白	1 White 一白 兌W
艮NE 2 Black 二黑	坎N 4 Green 四綠	9 Purple 九紫 乾NW

酉 Rooster (Sept 8 - Oct 7) 八月 8th Month

巽SE	離S	坤SW
6 White 六白	2 Black 二黑	4 Green 四綠
震E 5 Yellow 五黄	7 Red 七赤	9 Purple 九紫 兌W
艮NE 1 White 一白	坎N 3 Jade 三碧	8 White 八白 乾NW

戌 Dog (Oct 8 - Nov 6) 九月 9th Month

巽SE	離S	坤SW
5 Yellow 五黄	1 White 一白	3 Jade 三碧
震E 4 Green 四綠	6 White 六白	8 White 八白 兌W
艮NE 9 Purple 九紫	坎N 2 Black 二黑	7 Red 七赤 乾NW

亥 Pig (Nov 7 - Dec 6) 十月 10th Month

巽SE	離S	坤SW
4 Green 四綠	9 Purple 九紫	2 Black 二黑
震E 3 Jade 三碧	5 Yellow 五黄	7 Red 七赤 兌W
艮NE 8 White 八白	坎N 1 White 一白	6 White 六白 乾NW

子 Rat (Dec 7 - Jan 5) 十一月 11th Month

巽SE	離S	坤SW
3 Jade 三碧	8 White 八白	1 White 一白
震E 2 Black 二黑	4 Green 四綠	6 White 六白 兌W
艮NE 7 Red 七赤	坎N 9 Purple 九紫	5 Yellow 五黄 乾NW

丑 Ox (Jan 6 - Feb 3) 十二月 12th Month

巽SE	離S	坤SW
2 Black 二黑	7 Red 七赤	9 Purple 九紫
震E 1 White 一白	3 Jade 三碧	5 Yellow 五黄 兌W
艮NE 6 White 六白	坎N 8 White 八白	4 Green 四綠 乾NW

Qi Men Three Nobles 三奇 :

Three Nobles 三奇 / Seasons	乙 Yi	丙 Bing	丁 Ding
立春 **Coming of Spring** Feb 4 - Feb 18	坎 Kan	坤 Kun	震 Zhen
春分 **Spring Equinox** Mar 21 - Apr 4	中 Middle	乾 Qian	兌 Dui
立夏 **Coming of Summer** May 6 - May 20	乾 Qian	兌 Dui	艮 Gen
夏至 **Summer Solstice** Jun 22 - Jul 6	兌 Dui	乾 Qian	中 Middle
立秋 **Coming of Autumn** Aug 8 - Aug 23	離 Li	艮 Gen	兌 Dui
秋分 **Autumn Equinox** Sept 23 - Oct 7	中 Middle	巽 Xunn	震 Zhen
立冬 **Coming of Winter** Nov 7 - Nov 22	巽 Xunn	震 Zhen	坤 Kun
冬至 **Winter Solstice** Dec 22 - Jan 5	震 Zhen	巽 Xunn	中 Middle

Sectors to Avoid Opening Mountain 開山凶位 :

月 MONTH	月建 Month Establishment	月破 Month Destruction	月剋山家 Month Countering Sitting		陰府太歲 Yin Mansion Grand Duke	
寅 **Tiger** (Feb 4 - Mar 5) 正月 **1st Month**	寅 Yin Tiger	申 Shen Monkey	乾 Qian	兌 Dui	坤 Kun	震 Zhen
卯 **Rabbit** (Mar 6 - Apr 4) 二月 **2nd Month**	卯 Mao Rabbit	酉 You Rooster	亥 Hai Pig	丁 Ding Yin Fire	巽 Xun	艮 Gen
辰 **Dragon** (Apr 5 - May 5) 三月 **3rd Month**	辰 Chen Dragon	戌 Xu Dog	震 Zhen	巳 Si Snake	乾 Qian	兌 Du
巳 **Snake** (May 6 - Jun 5) 四月 **4th Month**	巳 Si Snake	亥 Hai Pig	艮 Gen		坤 Kun	坎 Kan
午 **Horse** (Jun 6 - July 6) 五月 **5th Month**	午 Wu Horse	子 Zi Rat	離 Li	丙 Bing Yang Fire	離 Li	乾 Qian
未 **Goat** (July 7 - Aug 7) 六月 **6th Month**	未 Wei Goat	丑 Chou Ox	壬 Ren Yang Water	乙 Yi Yin Wood	震 Zhen	坤 Kun
申 **Monkey** (Aug 8 - Sept 7) 七月 **7th Month**	申 Shen Monkey	寅 Yin Tiger	—		艮 Genn	巽 Xun
酉 **Rooster** (Sept 8 - Oct 7) 八月 **8th Month**	酉 You Rooster	卯 Mao Rabbit	—		兌 Duin	乾 Qian
戌 **Dog** (Oct 8 - Nov 6) 九月 **9th Month**	戌 Xu Dog	辰 Chen Dragon	乾 Qian	兌 Dui	坎 Kan	坤 Kun
亥 **Pig** (Nov 7 - Dec 6) 十月 **10th Month**	亥 Hai Pig	巳 Si Snake	亥 Hai Pig	丁 Ding Yin Fire	乾 Qian	離 Li
子 **Rat** (Dec 7 - Jan 5) 十一月 **11th Month**	子 Zi Rat	午 Wu Horse	水 Water	山 Mountain	坤 Kun	震 Zhen
丑 **Ox** (Jan 6 - Feb 3) 十二月 **12th Month**	丑 Chou Ox	未 Wei Goat	土 Earth		巽 Xun	艮 Gen

Negative Repair / Renovation Sectors 修方凶位 ：

月 MONTH	天官符 Heavenly Officer Charm	地官符 Earth Officer Charm	小月建 Small Month Establishment
寅 Tiger (Feb 4 - Mar 5) 正月 1st Month	中 Middle	中 Middle	丙 Bing Yang Fire / 離 Li / 丁 Ding Yin Fire
卯 Rabbit (Mar 6 - Apr 4) 二月 2nd Month	庚 Geng Yang Metal / 兌 Dui / 辛 Xin Yin Metal	辰 Chen Dragon / 巽 Xun / 巳 Si Snake	壬 Ren Yang Water / 坎 Kan / 癸 Gui Yin Water
辰 Dragon (Apr 5 - May 5) 三月 3rd Month	戌 Xu Dog / 乾 Qian / 亥 Hai Pig	甲 Jia Yang Wood / 震 Zhen / 乙 Yi Yin Wood	未 Wei Goat / 坤 Kun / 申 Shen Monkey
巳 Snake (May 6 - Jun 5) 四月 4th Month	中 Middle	未 Wei Goat / 坤 Kun / 申 Shen Monkey	甲 Jia Yang Wood / 震 Zhen / 乙 Yi Yin Wood
午 Horse (Jun 6 - July 6) 五月 5th Month	辰 Chen Dragon / 巽 Xun / 巳 Si Snake	壬 Ren Yang Water / 坎 Kan / 癸 Gui Yin Water	辰 Chen Dragon / 巽 Xun / 己 Ji Yin Earth
未 Goat (July 7 - Aug 7) 六月 6th Month	甲 Jia Yang Wood / 震 Zhen / 乙 Yi Yin Wood	丙 Bing Yang Fire / 離 Li / 丁 Ding Yin Fire	中 Middle
申 Monkey (Aug 8 - Sept 7) 七月 7th Month	未 Wei Goat / 坤 Kun / 申 Shen Monkey	丑 Chou Ox / 艮 Gen / 寅 Yin Tiger	戌 Xu Dog / 乾 Qian / 亥 Hai Pig
酉 Rooster (Sept 8 - Oct 7) 八月 8th Month	壬 Ren Yang Water / 坎 Kan / 癸 Gui Yin Water	庚 Geng Yang Metal / 兌 Dui / 辛 Xin Yin Metal	庚 Geng Yang Metal / 兌 Dui / 辛 Xin Yin Metal
戌 Dog (Oct 8 - Nov 6) 九月 9th Month	丙 Bing Yang Fire / 離 Li / 丁 Ding Yin Fire	戌 Xu Dog / 乾 Qian / 亥 Hai Pig	丑 Chou Ox / 艮 Gen / 寅 Yin Tiger
亥 Pig (Nov 7 - Dec 6) 十月 10th Month	丑 Chou Ox / 艮 Gen / 寅 Yin Tiger	中 Middle	丙 Bing Yang Fire / 離 Li / 丁 Ding Yin Fire
子 Rat (Dec 7 - Jan 5) 十一月 11th Month	庚 Geng Yang Metal / 兌 Dui / 辛 Xin Yin Metal	庚 Geng Yang Metal / 兌 Dui / 辛 Xin Yin Metal	壬 Ren Yang Water / 坎 Kan / 癸 Gui Yin Water
丑 Ox (Jan 6 - Feb 3) 十二月 12th Month	戌 Xu Dog / 乾 Qian / 亥 Hai Pig	戌 Xu Dog / 乾 Qian / 亥 Hai Pig	未 Wei Goat / 坤 Kun / 申 Shen Monkey

Negative Repair / Renovation Sectors 修方凶位 :

月 MONTH	大月建 Big Month Establishment			飛大煞 Flying Great Sha			丙丁獨火 Bing Ding Lonely Fire	
寅 **Tiger** (Feb 4 - Mar 5) 正月 **1st Month**		中 Middle		戌 Xu Dog	乾 Qian	亥 Hai Pig	巽 Xun	中 Middle
卯 **Rabbit** (Mar 6 - Apr 4) 二月 **2nd Month**	辰 Chen Dragon	巽 Xun	巳 Si Snake		中 Middle		震 Zhen	巽 Xun
辰 **Dragon** (Apr 5 - May 5) 三月 **3rd Month**	甲 Jia Yang Wood	震 Zhen	乙 Yi Yin Wood	庚 Geng Yang Metal	兌 Dui	辛 Xin Yin Metal	坤 Kun	震 Zhen
巳 **Snake** (May 6 - Jun 5) 四月 **4th Month**	未 Wei Goat	坤 Kun	申 Shen Monkey	戌 Xu Dog	乾 Qian	亥 Hai Pig	坎 Kan	坤 Kun
午 **Horse** (Jun 6 - July 6) 五月 **5th Month**	壬 Ren Yang Water	坎 Kan	癸 Gui Yin Water		中 Middle		離 Li	坎 Kan
未 **Goat** (July 7 - Aug 7) 六月 **6th Month**	丙 Bing Yang Fire	離 Li	丁 Ding Yin Fire	辰 Chen Dragon	巽 Xun	巳 Si Snake	艮 Gen	離 Li
申 **Monkey** (Aug 8 - Sept 7) 七月 **7th Month**	丑 Chou Ox	艮 Gen	寅 Yin Tiger	甲 Jia Yang Wood	震 Zhen	乙 Yi Yin Wood	兌 Dui	艮 Gen
酉 **Rooster** (Sept 8 - Oct 7) 八月 **8th Month**	庚 Geng Yang Metal	兌 Dui	辛 Xin Yin Metal	未 Wei Goat	坤 Kun	申 Shen Monkey	乾 Qian	兌 Dui
戌 **Dog** (Oct 8 - Nov 6) 九月 **9th Month**	戌 Xu Dog	乾 Qian	亥 Hai Pig	壬 Ren Yang Water	坎 Kan	癸 Gui Yin Water	中 Middle	乾 Qian
亥 **Pig** (Nov 7 - Dec 6) 十月 **10th Month**		中 Middle		丙 Bing Yang Fire	離 Li	丁 Ding Yin Fire		中 Middle
子 **Rat** (Dec 7 - Jan 5) 十一月 **11th Month**	辰 Chen Dragon	巽 Xun	巳 Si Snake	丑 Chou Ox	艮 Gen	寅 Yin Tiger	巽 Xun	中 Middle
丑 **Ox** (Jan 6 - Feb 3) 十二月 **12th Month**	甲 Jia Yang Wood	震 Zhen	乙 Yi Yin Wood	庚 Geng Yang Metal	兌 Dui	辛 Xin Yin Metal	震 Zhen	巽 Xun

Negative Repair / Renovation Sectors 修方凶位 :

月 MONTH	月遊火 Month Wondering Fire	三煞 Monthly 3 Killings		
		劫煞 Robbery Sha	災煞 Calamity Sha	月煞 Month Sha
寅 **Tiger** (Feb 4 - Mar 5) 正月 **1st Month**	坤 *Kun*	亥 *Hai* Pig	子 *Zi* Rat	丑 *Chou* Ox
卯 **Rabbit** (Mar 6 - Apr 4) 二月 **2nd Month**	震 *Zhen*	申 *Shen* Monkey	酉 *You* Rooster	戌 *Xu* Dog
辰 **Dragon** (Apr 5 - May 5) 三月 **3rd Month**	巽 *Xun*	巳 *Si* Snake	午 *Wu* Horse	未 *Wei* Goat
巳 **Snake** (May 6 - Jun 5) 四月 **4th Month**	中 Middle	寅 *Yin* Tiger	卯 *Mao* Rabbit	辰 *Chen* Dragon
午 **Horse** (Jun 6 - July 6) 五月 **5th Month**	乾 *Qian*	亥 *Hai* Pig	子 *Zi* Rat	丑 *Chou* Ox
未 **Goat** (July 7 - Aug 7) 六月 **6th Month**	兌 *Dui*	申 *Shen* Monkey	酉 *You* Rooster	戌 *Xu* Dog
申 **Monkey** (Aug 8 - Sept 7) 七月 **7th Month**	艮 *Gen*	巳 *Si* Snake	午 *Wu* Horse	未 *Wei* Goat
酉 **Rooster** (Sept 8 - Oct 7) 八月 **8th Month**	離 *Li*	寅 *Yin* Tiger	卯 *Mao* Rabbit	辰 *Chen* Dragon
戌 **Dog** (Oct 8 - Nov 6) 九月 **9th Month**	坎 *Kan*	亥 *Hai* Pig	子 *Zi* Rat	丑 *Chou* Ox
亥 **Pig** (Nov 7 - Dec 6) 十月 **10th Month**	坤 *Kun*	申 *Shen* Monkey	酉 *You* Rooster	戌 *Xu* Dog
子 **Rat** (Dec 7 - Jan 5) 十一月 **11th Month**	震 *Zhen*	巳 *Si* Snake	午 *Wu* Horse	未 *Wei* Goat
丑 **Ox** (Jan 6 - Feb 3) 十二月 **12th Month**	巽 *Xun*	寅 *Yin* Tiger	卯 *Mao* Rabbit	辰 *Chen* Dragon

Negative Repair / Renovation Sectors 修方凶位 :

月 MONTH	月刑 Month Punishment	月害 Month Harm	月厭 Month Detest
寅 **Tiger** (Feb 4 - Mar 5) 正月 **1st Month**	巳 *Si* **Snake**	巳 *Si* **Snake**	戌 *Xu* **Dog**
卯 **Rabbit** (Mar 6 - Apr 4) 二月 **2nd Month**	子 *Zi* **Rat**	辰 *Chen* **Dragon**	酉 *You* **Rooster**
辰 **Dragon** (Apr 5 - May 5) 三月 **3rd Month**	辰 *Chen* **Dragon**	卯 *Mao* **Rabbit**	申 *Shen* **Monkey**
巳 **Snake** (May 6 - Jun 5) 四月 **4th Month**	申 *Shen* **Monkey**	寅 *Yin* **Tiger**	未 *Wei* **Goat**
午 **Horse** (Jun 6 - July 6) 五月 **5th Month**	午 *Wu* **Horse**	丑 *Chou* **Ox**	午 *Wu* **Horse**
未 **Goat** (July 7 - Aug 7) 六月 **6th Month**	丑 *Chou* **Ox**	子 *Zi* **Rat**	巳 *Si* **Snake**
申 **Monkey** (Aug 8 - Sept 7) 七月 **7th Month**	寅 *Yin* **Tiger**	亥 *Hai* **Pig**	辰 *Chen* **Dragon**
酉 **Rooster** (Sept 8 - Oct 7) 八月 **8th Month**	酉 *You* **Rooster**	戌 *Xu* **Dog**	卯 *Mao* **Rabbit**
戌 **Dog** (Oct 8 - Nov 6) 九月 **9th Month**	未 *Wei* **Goat**	酉 *You* **Rooster**	寅 *Yin* **Tiger**
亥 **Pig** (Nov 7 - Dec 6) 十月 **10th Month**	亥 *Hai* **Pig**	申 *Shen* **Monkey**	丑 *Chou* **Ox**
子 **Rat** (Dec 7 - Jan 5) 十一月 **11th Month**	卯 *Mao* **Rabbit**	未 *Wei* **Goat**	子 *Zi* **Rat**
丑 **Ox** (Jan 6 - Feb 3) 十二月 **12th Month**	戌 *Xu* **Dog**	午 *Wu* **Horse**	亥 *Hai* **Pig**

乙酉 (Yi You)
Wood Rooster

乙酉 (Yi You) Wood Rooster

Heavenly Stem 天干	乙 **Yin Wood** (陰木)
Earthly Branch 地支	酉 **Rooster (Yin Metal** 陰金**)**
Hidden Stem 藏干	辛 **Yin Metal**
Na Yin 納音	泉中水 **Water from the spring**
Grand Duke 太歲	酉 **Rooster**
Xuan Kong Five Element 玄空五行	9 金 **Metal**
Gua Name 卦名	䷠ 天山遯 **Retreat**
Xuan Kong Period Luck 玄空卦運	4

Annual Positive Stars for Opening Mountain, Establishing Facing and Commencing Repairs 開山立向修方吉星：

歲德 **Duke Virtue**	庚 *Geng* **Yang Metal**
歲德合 **Duke Virtue Combo**	乙 *Yi* **Yin Wood**
歲枝德 **Duke Branch Virtue**	寅 *Yin* **Tiger**
陽貴人 **Yang Nobleman**	申 *Shen* **Monkey**
陰貴人 **Yin Nobleman**	子 *Zi* **Rat**
歲祿 **Duke Prosperous**	卯 *Mao* **Rabbit**
歲馬 **Duke Horse**	亥 *Hai* **Pig**
奏書 **Decree**	坤 *Kun*
博士 **Professor**	艮 *Gen*

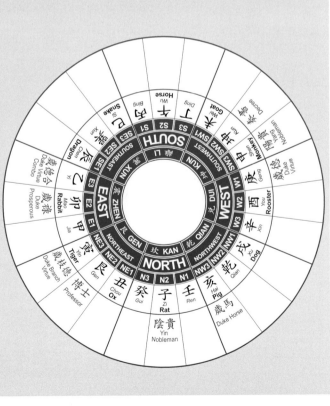

202

Annual Negative Stars for Opening Mountain, Establishing Facing and Commencing Repairs 開山立向修方凶星:

太歲 Grand Duke	歲破 Year Breaker	三煞 Three Killings			坐煞向煞 Sitting Sha Facing Sha				浮天空亡 Floating Heaven Emptiness	
酉 You Rooster	卯 Mao Rabbit	寅 Yin Tiger	卯 Mao Rabbit	辰 Chen Dragon	甲 Jia Yang Wood	乙 Yi Yin Wood	庚 Geng Yang Metal	辛 Xin Yin Metal	坎 Kan	癸 Gui Yin Water

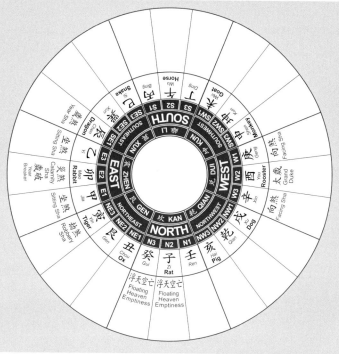

Annual San Yuan Purple White Stars 三元紫白九星:

上元 Upper Period Period 1, 2, 3			中元 Middle Period Period 4, 5, 6			下元 Lower Period Period 7, 8, 9		
巽SE 6	**離S** 2	**坤SW** 4	**巽SE** 9	**離S** 5	**坤SW** 7	**巽SE** 3	**離S** 8	**坤SW** 1
震E 5	**7** 乙酉 Yi You Wood Rooster	**兌W** 9	**震E** 8	**1** 乙酉 Yi You Wood Rooster	**兌W** 3	**震E** 2	**4** 乙酉 Yi You Wood Rooster	**兌W** 6
艮NE 1	**坎N** 3	**乾NW** 8	**艮NE** 4	**坎N** 6	**乾NW** 2	**艮NE** 7	**坎N** 9	**乾NW** 5

Mountain Covering Yellow Path 蓋山黃道：

貪狼 Tan Lang **Greedy Wolf**				巨門 Ju Men **Huge Door**		武曲 Wu Qu **Military Arts**				文曲 Wen Qu **Literary Arts**	
離 Li S2	壬 Ren N1	寅 Yin NE3	戌 Xu NW1	乾 Qian NW2	甲 Jia E1	坎 Kan N2	癸 Gui N3	申 Shen SW3	辰 Chen SE1	艮 Gen NE2	丙 Bing S1

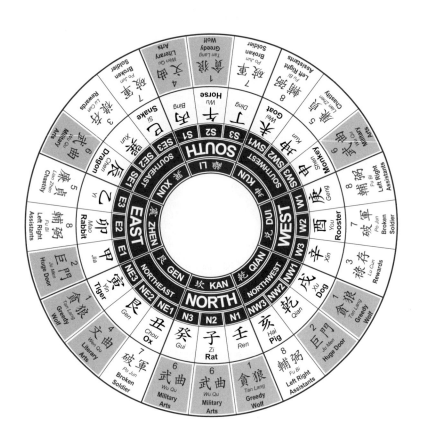

Heaven Penetrating Force 通天竅：

三合前方 Facing Three Harmony	乾亥 Qian Hai	壬子 Ren Zi	癸丑 Gui Chou
三合後方 Sitting Three Harmony	巽巳 Xun Si	丙午 Bing Wu	丁未 Ding Wei

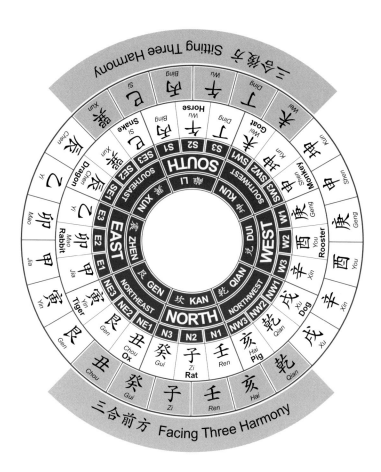

Moving Horse Six Ren Assessment 走馬六壬：

神后 Shen Hou **Holy Empress**	功曹 Gong Cao **Marshall**	天罡 Tian Gang **Heavenly Dipper**	勝光 Sheng Guang **Subliminal Bright**	傳送 Chuan Song **Great General**	河魁 He Kui **River Scholar**
甲卯 Jia Mao	巽巳 Xun Si	丁未 Ding Wei	庚酉 Geng You	乾亥 Qian Hai	癸丑 Gui Chou

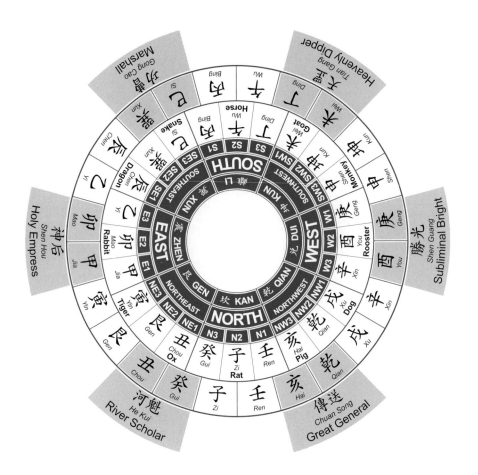

Four Advantages Three Cycles Star Plate 四利三元：

太陽 *Tai Yang* **Sun**	太陰 *Tai Yin* **Moon**	龍德 *Long De* **Dragon Virtue**	福德 *Fu De* **Fortune Virtue**
戌 *Xu* Dog	子 *Zi* Rat	辰 *Chen* Dragon	午 *Wu* Horse

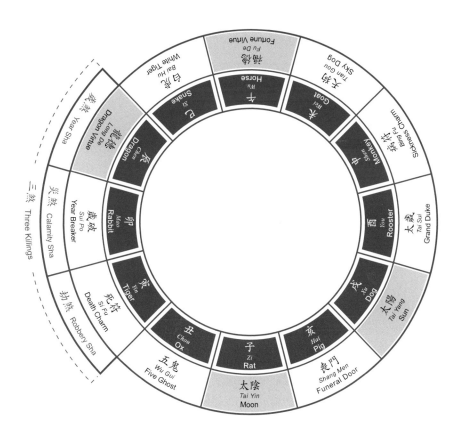

Negative Sectors For Opening Mountain 開山凶位：

年剋山家 Year Countering Sitting (冬至後 After Winter Solstice)

乾 Qian NW2	亥 Hai NW3	兌 Dui W2	丁 Ding S3

陰府太歲 Yin Fu Tai Sui **Yin Mansion Grand Duke**		六害 Liu Hai **Six Harm**	死符 Si Fu **Death Charm**	炙退 Zhi Tui **Roasting Star**
兌 Dui W2	乾 Qian NW2	戌 Xu NW1	寅 Yin NE3	子 Zi N2

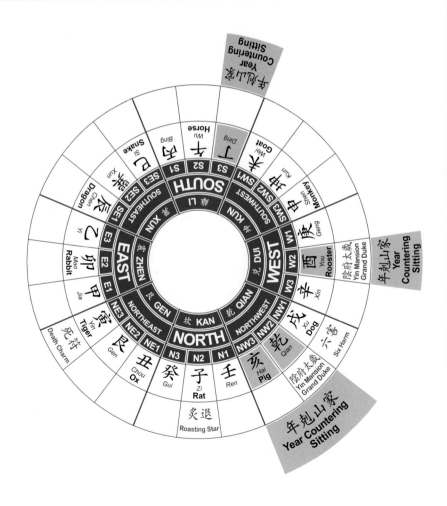

Negative Directions to Establish Facing 立向凶方：

巡山羅喉 *Xun Shan Luo Hou* **Mountain Patrol Luo Hou Star**	病符 *Bing Fu* **Sickness Charm**
辛 *Xin* **W3**	申 *Shen* **SW3**

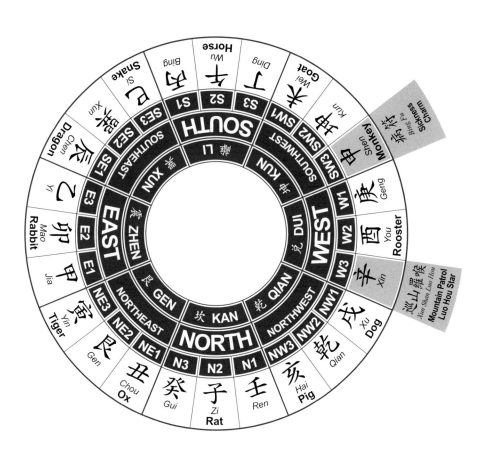

Negative Repair / Renovation Sectors Table 修方凶位表：

天官符 **Heavenly Officer Charm**	申 *Shen* Monkey	豹尾 **Leopard Tail**	未 *Wei* Goat
地官符 **Earthly Officer Charm**	丑 *Chou* Ox	飛廉 **Flying Chaste**	亥 *Hai* Pig
大煞 **Great Sha**	酉 *You* Rooster	喪門 **Funeral Door**	亥 *Hai* Pig
大將軍 **Big General**	午 *Wu* Horse	弔客 **Suspended Guest**	未 *Wei* Goat
力士 **Strong Man**	乾 *Qian*	白虎 **White Tiger**	巳 *Si* Snake
蠶室 **Silkworm Room**	巽 *Xun*	金神 **Golden God**	辰 *Chen* Dragon 巳 *Si* Snake
蠶官 **Silkworm Officer**	辰 *Chen* Dragon		
蠶命 **Silkworm Life**	巳 *Si* Snake	獨火 **Lonely Fire**	坤 *Kun*
歲刑 **Duke Punishment**	酉 *You* Rooster	五鬼 **Five Ghost**	未 *Wei* Goat
黃幡 **Yellow Flag**	丑 *Chou* Ox	破敗五鬼 **Destructive Five Ghost**	艮 *Gen*

Negative Repair / Renovation Sectors Diagram 修方凶位圖：

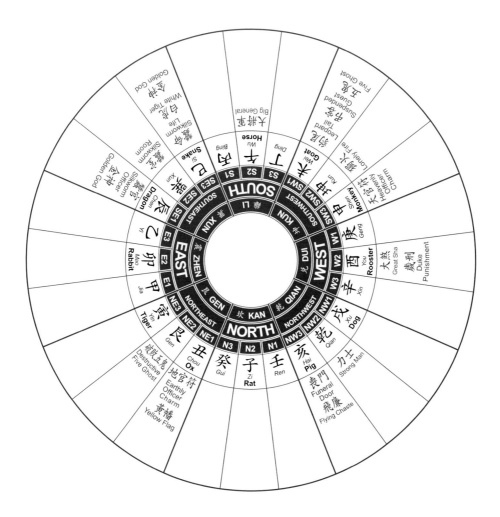

12-Month Auxiliary Stars Reference Table :
乙酉年十二月，開山立向修方星表

Positive Monthly Stars 吉星方

月 MONTH	寅 Tiger (Feb 4 - Mar 5) 正月 1st Month	卯 Rabbit (Mar 6 - Apr 4) 二月 2nd Month	辰 Dragon (Apr 5 - May 5) 三月 3rd Month	巳 Snake (May 6 - Jun 5) 四月 4th Month	午 Horse (Jun 6 - July 6) 五月 5th Month	未 Goat (July 7 - Aug 7) 六月 6th Month
天道 Heavenly Path	南 South	西南 Southwest	北 North	西 West	西北 Northwest	東 East
天德 Heavenly Virtue	丁 Ding Yin Fire	坤 Kun （申）	壬 Ren Yang Water	辛 Xin Yin Metal	乾 Qian （亥）	甲 Jia Yang Wood
天德合 Heavenly Virtue Combo	壬 Ren Yang Water	（巳）	丁 Ding Yin Fire	丙 Bing Yang Fire	（寅）	己 Ji Yin Earth
月德 Monthly Virtue	丙 Bing Yang Fire	甲 Jia Yang Wood	壬 Ren Yang Water	庚 Geng Yang Metal	丙 Bing Yang Fire	甲 Jia Yang Wood
月德合 Monthly Virtue Combo	辛 Xin Yin Metal	己 Ji Yin Earth	丁 Ding Yin Fire	乙 Yi Yin Wood	辛 Xin Yin Metal	己 Ji Yin Earth
月空 Month Emptiness	壬 Ren Yang Water	庚 Geng Yang Metal	丙 Bing Yang Fire	甲 Jia Yang Wood	壬 Ren Yang Water	庚 Geng Yang Metal
陽貴人 Yang Nobleman	坤 Kun	坎 Kan	離 Li	艮 Gen	兌 Dui	乾 Qian
陰貴人 Yin Nobleman	乾 Qian	中 Middle	巽 Xun	震 Zhen	坤 Kun	坎 Kan
飛天祿 Flying Heavenly Wealth	乾 Qian	中 Middle	坎 Kan	離 Li	艮 Gen	兌 Dui
飛天馬 Flying Heavenly Horse	中 Middle	巽 Xun	震 Zhen	坤 Kun	坎 Kan	離 Li

12-Month Auxiliary Stars Reference Table :
乙酉年十二月，開山立向修方星表

申 Monkey (Aug 8 - Sept 7) 七月 7th Month	酉 Rooster (Sept 8 - Oct 7) 八月 8th Month	戌 Dog (Oct 8 - Nov 6) 九月 9th Month	亥 Pig (Nov 7 - Dec 6) 十月 10th Month	子 Rat (Dec 7 - Jan 5) 十一月 11th Month	丑 Ox (Jan 6 - Feb 3) 十二月 12th Month	月 MONTH
北 North	東北 Northeast	南 South	東 East	東南 Southeast	西 West	天道 Heavenly Path
癸 Gui Yin Water	艮 Gen (寅)	丙 Bing Yang Fire	乙 Yi Yin Wood	巽 Xun (巳)	庚 Geng Yang Metal	天德 Heavenly Virtue
戊 Wu Yang Earth	(亥)	辛 Xin Yin Metal	庚 Geng Yang Metal	(申)	乙 Yi Yin Wood	天德合 Heavenly Virtue Combo
壬 Ren Yang Water	庚 Geng Yang Metal	丙 Bing Yang Fire	甲 Jia Yang Wood	壬 Ren Yang Water	庚 Geng Yang Metal	月德 Monthly Virtue
丁 Ding Yin Fire	乙 Yi Yin Wood	辛 Xin Yin Metal	己 Ji Yin Earth	丁 Ding Yin Fire	乙 Yi Yin Wood	月德合 Monthly Virtue Combo
丙 Bing Yang Fire	甲 Jia Yang Wood	壬 Ren Yang Water	庚 Geng Yang Metal	丙 Bing Yang Fire	甲 Jia Yang Wood	月空 Month Emptiness
中 Middle	坎 Kan	離 Li	艮 Gen	兌 Dui	乾 Qian	陽貴人 Yang Nobleman
離 Li	艮 Gen	兌 Dui	乾 Qian	中 Middle	坎 Kan	陰貴人 Yin Nobleman
乾 Qian	中 Middle	巽 Xun	震 Zhen	坤 Kun	坎 Kan	飛天祿 Flying Heavenly Wealth
艮 Gen	兌 Dui	乾 Qian	中 Middle	坎 Kan	離 Li	飛天馬 Flying Heavenly Horse

Monthly Purple White Stars 月紫白九星 ：

寅 Tiger (Feb 4 - Mar 5) 正月 1st Month

巽 SE	離 S	坤 SW
7 Red 七赤	3 Jade 三碧	5 Yellow 五黄
震 E 6 White 六白	8 White 八白	1 White 一白 兌 W
2 Black 二黑	4 Green 四綠	9 Purple 九紫
艮 NE	坎 N	乾 NW

卯 Rabbit (Mar 6 - Apr 4) 二月 2nd Month

巽 SE	離 S	坤 SW
6 White 六白	2 Black 二黑	4 Green 四綠
震 E 5 Yellow 五黄	7 Red 七赤	9 Purple 九紫 兌 W
1 White 一白	3 Jade 三碧	8 White 八白
艮 NE	坎 N	乾 NW

辰 Dragon (Apr 5 - May 5) 三月 3rd Month

巽 SE	離 S	坤 SW
5 Yellow 五黄	1 White 一白	3 Jade 三碧
震 E 4 Green 四綠	6 White 六白	8 White 八白 兌 W
9 Purple 九紫	2 Black 二黑	7 Red 七赤
艮 NE	坎 N	乾 NW

巳 Snake (May 6 - Jun 5) 四月 4th Month

巽 SE	離 S	坤 SW
4 Green 四綠	9 Purple 九紫	2 Black 二黑
震 E 3 Jade 三碧	5 Yellow 五黄	7 Red 七赤 兌 W
8 White 八白	1 White 一白	6 White 六白
艮 NE	坎 N	乾 NW

午 Horse (Jun 6 - July 6) 五月 5th Month

巽 SE	離 S	坤 SW
3 Jade 三碧	8 White 八白	1 White 一白
震 E 2 Black 二黑	4 Green 四綠	6 White 六白 兌 W
7 Red 七赤	9 Purple 九紫	5 Yellow 五黄
艮 NE	坎 N	乾 NW

未 Goat (July 7 - Aug 7) 六月 6th Month

巽 SE	離 S	坤 SW
2 Black 二黑	7 Red 七赤	9 Purple 九紫
震 E 1 White 一白	3 Jade 三碧	5 Yellow 五黄 兌 W
6 White 六白	8 White 八白	4 Green 四綠
艮 NE	坎 N	乾 NW

申 Monkey (Aug 8 - Sept 7) 七月 7th Month

巽 SE	離 S	坤 SW
1 White 一白	6 White 六白	8 White 八白
震 E 9 Purple 九紫	2 Black 二黑	4 Green 四綠 兌 W
5 Yellow 五黄	7 Red 七赤	3 Jade 三碧
艮 NE	坎 N	乾 NW

酉 Rooster (Sept 8 - Oct 7) 八月 8th Month

巽 SE	離 S	坤 SW
9 Purple 九紫	5 Yellow 五黄	7 Red 七赤
震 E 8 White 八白	1 White 一白	3 Jade 三碧 兌 W
4 Green 四綠	6 White 六白	2 Black 二黑
艮 NE	坎 N	乾 NW

戌 Dog (Oct 8 - Nov 6) 九月 9th Month

巽 SE	離 S	坤 SW
8 White 八白	4 Green 四綠	6 White 六白
震 E 7 Red 七赤	9 Purple 九紫	2 Black 二黑 兌 W
3 Jade 三碧	5 Yellow 五黄	1 White 一白
艮 NE	坎 N	乾 NW

亥 Pig (Nov 7 - Dec 6) 十月 10th Month

巽 SE	離 S	坤 SW
7 Red 七赤	3 Jade 三碧	5 Yellow 五黄
震 E 6 White 六白	8 White 八白	1 White 一白 兌 W
2 Black 二黑	4 Green 四綠	9 Purple 九紫
艮 NE	坎 N	乾 NW

子 Rat (Dec 7 - Jan 5) 十一月 11th Month

巽 SE	離 S	坤 SW
6 White 六白	2 Black 二黑	4 Green 四綠
震 E 5 Yellow 五黄	7 Red 七赤	9 Purple 九紫 兌 W
1 White 一白	3 Jade 三碧	8 White 八白
艮 NE	坎 N	乾 NW

丑 Ox (Jan 6 - Feb 3) 十二月 12th Month

巽 SE	離 S	坤 SW
5 Yellow 五黄	1 White 一白	3 Jade 三碧
震 E 4 Green 四綠	6 White 六白	8 White 八白 兌 W
9 Purple 九紫	2 Black 二黑	7 Red 七赤
艮 NE	坎 N	乾 NW

Qi Men Three Nobles 三奇 :

Three Nobles 三奇 / Seasons	乙 Yi	丙 Bing	丁 Ding
立春 **Coming of Spring** Feb 4 - Feb 18	離 Li	坎 Kan	坤 Kun
春分 **Spring Equinox** Mar 21 - Apr 4	巽 Xun	中 Middle	乾 Qian
立夏 **Coming of Summer** May 6 - May 20	中 Middle	乾 Qian	兌 Dui
夏至 **Summer Solstice** Jun 22 - Jul 6	艮 Gen	兌 Dui	乾 Qian
立秋 **Coming of Autumn** Aug 8 - Aug 23	坎 Kan	離 Li	艮 Gen
秋分 **Autumn Equinox** Sept 23 - Oct 7	乾 Qian	中 Middle	巽 Xun
立冬 **Coming of Winter** Nov 7 - Nov 22	中 Middle	巽 Xun	震 Zhen
冬至 **Winter Solstice** Dec 22 - Jan 5	坤 Kun	震 Zhen	巽 Xun

乙酉 (Yi You) Wood Rooster

Sectors to Avoid Opening Mountain 開山凶位 :

月 MONTH	月建 Month Establishment	月破 Month Destruction	月剋山家 Month Countering Sitting		陰府太歲 Yin Mansion Grand Duke	
寅 Tiger (Feb 4 - Mar 5) 正月 1st Month	寅 Yin Tiger	申 Shen Monkey	乾 Qian	兌 Dui	坤 Kun	震 Zhen
卯 Rabbit (Mar 6 - Apr 4) 二月 2nd Month	卯 Mao Rabbit	酉 You Rooster	亥 Hai Pig	丁 Ding Yin Fire	巽 Xun	艮 Gen
辰 Dragon (Apr 5 - May 5) 三月 3rd Month	辰 Chen Dragon	戌 Xu Dog	震 Zhen	巳 Si Snake	乾 Qian	兌 Dui
巳 Snake (May 6 - Jun 5) 四月 4th Month	巳 Si Snake	亥 Hai Pig	艮 Gen		坤 Kun	坎 Kan
午 Horse (Jun 6 - July 6) 五月 5th Month	午 Wu Horse	子 Zi Rat	離 Li	丙 Bing Yang Fire	離 Li	乾 Qian
未 Goat (July 7 - Aug 7) 六月 6th Month	未 Wei Goat	丑 Chou Ox	壬 Ren Yang Water	乙 Yi Yin Wood	震 Zhen	坤 Kun
申 Monkey (Aug 8 - Sept 7) 七月 7th Month	申 Shen Monkey	寅 Yin Tiger	—		艮 Gen	巽 Xun
酉 Rooster (Sept 8 - Oct 7) 八月 8th Month	酉 You Rooster	卯 Mao Rabbit	—		兌 Dui	乾 Qian
戌 Dog (Oct 8 - Nov 6) 九月 9th Month	戌 Xu Dog	辰 Chen Dragon	乾 Qian	兌 Dui	坎 Kan	坤 Kun
亥 Pig (Nov 7 - Dec 6) 十月 10th Month	亥 Hai Pig	巳 Si Snake	亥 Hai Pig	丁 Ding Yin Fire	乾 Qian	離 Li
子 Rat (Dec 7 - Jan 5) 十一月 11th Month	子 Zi Rat	午 Wu Horse	水 Water	山 Mountain	坤 Kun	震 Zhen
丑 Ox (Jan 6 - Feb 3) 十二月 12th Month	丑 Chou Ox	未 Wei Goat	土 Earth		巽 Xun	艮 Gen

Negative Repair / Renovation Sectors 修方凶位 :

月 MONTH	天官符 Heavenly Officer Charm			地官符 Earth Officer Charm			小月建 Small Month Establishment		
寅 Tiger (Feb 4 - Mar 5) 正月 1st Month	未 Wei Goat	坤 Kun	申 Shen Monkey	庚 Geng Yang Metal	兌 Dui	辛 Xin Yin Metal	丙 Bing Yang Fire	離 Li	丁 Ding Yin Fire
卯 Rabbit (Mar 6 - Apr 4) 二月 2nd Month	壬 Ren Yang Water	坎 Kan	癸 Gui Yin Water	戌 Xu Dog	乾 Qian	亥 Hai Pig	壬 Ren Yang Water	坎 Kan	癸 Gui Yin Water
辰 Dragon (Apr 5 - May 5) 三月 3rd Month	丙 Bing Yang Fire	離 Li	丁 Ding Yin Fire	中 Middle			未 Wei Goat	坤 Kun	申 Shen Monkey
巳 Snake (May 6 - Jun 5) 四月 4th Month	丑 Chou Ox	艮 Gen	寅 Yin Tiger	辰 Chen Dragon	巽 Xun	巳 Si Snake	甲 Jia Yang Wood	震 Zhen	乙 Yi Yin Wood
午 Horse (Jun 6 - July 6) 五月 5th Month	庚 Geng Yang Metal	兌 Dui	辛 Xin Yin Metal	甲 Jia Yang Wood	震 Zhen	乙 Yi Yin Wood	辰 Chen Dragon	巽 Xun	己 Ji Yin Earth
未 Goat (July 7 - Aug 7) 六月 6th Month	戌 Xu Dog	乾 Qian	亥 Hai Pig	未 Wei Goat	坤 Kun	申 Shen Monkey	中 Middle		
申 Monkey (Aug 8 - Sept 7) 七月 7th Month	中 Middle			壬 Ren Yang Water	坎 Kan	癸 Gui Yin Water	戌 Xu Dog	乾 Qian	亥 Hai Pig
酉 Rooster (Sept 8 - Oct 7) 八月 8th Month	庚 Geng Yang Metal	兌 Dui	辛 Xin Yin Metal	丙 Bing Yang Fire	離 Li	丁 Ding Yin Fire	庚 Geng Yang Metal	兌 Dui	辛 Xin Yin Metal
戌 Dog (Oct 8 - Nov 6) 九月 9th Month	戌 Xu Dog	乾 Qian	亥 Hai Pig	丑 Chou Ox	艮 Gen	寅 Yin Tiger	丑 Chou Ox	艮 Gen	寅 Yin Tiger
亥 Pig (Nov 7 - Dec 6) 十月 10th Month	中 Middle			庚 Geng Yang Metal	兌 Dui	辛 Xin Yin Metal	丙 Bing Yang Fire	離 Li	丁 Ding Yin Fire
子 Rat (Dec 7 - Jan 5) 十一月 11th Month	辰 Chen Dragon	巽 Xun	巳 Si Snake	戌 Xu Dog	乾 Qian	亥 Hai Pig	壬 Ren Yang Water	坎 Kan	癸 Gui Yin Water
丑 Ox (Jan 6 - Feb 3) 十二月 12th Month	甲 Jia Yang Wood	震 Zhen	乙 Yi Yin Wood	中 Middle			未 Wei Goat	坤 Kun	申 Shen Monkey

Negative Repair / Renovation Sectors 修方凶位 :

月 MONTH	大月建 Big Month Establishment			飛大煞 Flying Great Sha			丙丁獨火 Bing Ding Lonely Fire	
寅 **Tiger** (Feb 4 - Mar 5) 正月 **1st Month**	丑 Chou Ox	艮 Gen	寅 Yin Tiger	甲 Jia Yang Wood	震 Zhen	乙 Yi Yin Wood	巽 Xun	中 Middle
卯 **Rabbit** (Mar 6 - Apr 4) 二月 **2nd Month**	庚 Geng Yang Metal	兌 Dui	辛 Xin Yin Metal	未 Wei Goat	坤 Kun	申 Shen Monkey	震 Zhen	巽 Xun
辰 **Dragon** (Apr 5 - May 5) 三月 **3rd Month**	戊 Xu Dog	乾 Qian	亥 Hai Pig	壬 Ren Yang Water	坎 Kan	癸 Gui Yin Water	坤 Kun	震 Zhen
巳 **Snake** (May 6 - Jun 5) 四月 **4th Month**		中 Middle		丙 Bing Yang Fire	離 Li	丁 Ding Yin Fire	坎 Kan	坤 Kun
午 **Horse** (Jun 6 - July 6) 五月 **5th Month**	辰 Chen Dragon	巽 Xun	巳 Si Snake	丑 Chou Ox	艮 Gen	寅 Yin Tiger	離 Li	坎 Kan
未 **Goat** (July 7 - Aug 7) 六月 **6th Month**	甲 Jia Yang Wood	震 Zhen	乙 Yi Yin Wood	庚 Geng Yang Metal	兌 Dui	辛 Xin Yin Metal	艮 Gen	離 Li
申 **Monkey** (Aug 8 - Sept 7) 七月 **7th Month**	未 Wei Goat	坤 Kun	申 Shen Monkey	戊 Xu Dog	乾 Qian	亥 Hai Pig	兌 Dui	艮 Gen
酉 **Rooster** (Sept 8 - Oct 7) 八月 **8th Month**	壬 Ren Yang Water	坎 Kan	癸 Gui Yin Water		中 Middle		乾 Qian	兌 Dui
戌 **Dog** (Oct 8 - Nov 6) 九月 **9th Month**	丙 Bing Yang Fire	離 Li	丁 Ding Yin Fire	庚 Geng Yang Metal	兌 Dui	辛 Xin Yin Metal	中 Middle	乾 Qian
亥 **Pig** (Nov 7 - Dec 6) 十月 **10th Month**	丑 Chou Ox	艮 Gen	寅 Yin Tiger	戊 Xu Dog	乾 Qian	亥 Hai Tiger		中 Middle
子 **Rat** (Dec 7 - Jan 5) 十一月 **11th Month**	庚 Geng Yang Metal	兌 Dui	辛 Xin Yin Metal		中 Middle		巽 Xun	中 Middle
丑 **Ox** (Jan 6 - Feb 3) 十二月 **12th Month**	戊 Xu Dog	乾 Qian	亥 Hai Pig	辰 Chen Dragon	巽 Xun	巳 Si Snake	震 Zhen	巽 Xun

Negative Repair / Renovation Sectors 修方凶位 :

月 MONTH	月遊火 Month Wondering Fire	三煞 Monthly 3 Killings		
		劫煞 Robbery Sha	災煞 Calamity Sha	月煞 Month Sha
寅 Tiger (Feb 4 - Mar 5) 正月 1st Month	乾 Qian	亥 Hai Pig	子 Zi Rat	丑 Chou Ox
卯 Rabbit (Mar 6 - Apr 4) 二月 2nd Month	兌 Dui	申 Shen Monkey	酉 You Rooster	戌 Xu Dog
辰 Dragon (Apr 5 - May 5) 三月 3rd Month	艮 Gen	巳 Si Snake	午 Wu Horse	未 Wei Goat
巳 Snake (May 6 - Jun 5) 四月 4th Month	離 Li	寅 Yin Tiger	卯 Mao Rabbit	辰 Chen Dragon
午 Horse (Jun 6 - July 6) 五月 5th Month	坎 Kan	亥 Hai Pig	子 Zi Rat	丑 Chou Ox
未 Goat (July 7 - Aug 7) 六月 6th Month	坤 Kun	申 Shen Monkey	酉 You Rooster	戌 Xu Dog
申 Monkey (Aug 8 - Sept 7) 七月 7th Month	震 Zhen	巳 Si Snake	午 Wu Horse	未 Wei Goat
酉 Rooster (Sept 8 - Oct 7) 八月 8th Month	巽 Xun	寅 Yin Tiger	卯 Mao Rabbit	辰 Chen Dragon
戌 Dog (Oct 8 - Nov 6) 九月 9th Month	中 Middle	亥 Hai Pig	子 Zi Rat	丑 Chou Ox
亥 Pig (Nov 7 - Dec 6) 十月 10th Month	乾 Qian	申 Shen Monkey	酉 You Rooster	戌 Xu Dog
子 Rat (Dec 7 - Jan 5) 十一月 11th Month	兌 Dui	巳 Si Snake	午 Wu Horse	未 Wei Goat
丑 Ox (Jan 6 - Feb 3) 十二月 12th Month	艮 Gen	寅 Yin Tiger	卯 Mao Rabbit	辰 Chen Dragon

Negative Repair / Renovation Sectors 修方凶位 :

月 MONTH	月刑 Month Punishment	月害 Month Harm	月厭 Month Detest
寅 **Tiger** (Feb 4 - Mar 5) 正月 **1st Month**	巳 Si Snake	巳 Si Snake	戌 Xu Dog
卯 **Rabbit** (Mar 6 - Apr 4) 二月 **2nd Month**	子 Zi Rat	辰 Chen Dragon	酉 You Rooster
辰 **Dragon** (Apr 5 - May 5) 三月 **3rd Month**	辰 Chen Dragon	卯 Mao Rabbit	申 Shen Monkey
巳 **Snake** (May 6 - Jun 5) 四月 **4th Month**	申 Shen Monkey	寅 Yin Tiger	未 Wei Goat
午 **Horse** (Jun 6 - July 6) 五月 **5th Month**	午 Wu Horse	丑 Chou Ox	午 Wu Horse
未 **Goat** (July 7 - Aug 7) 六月 **6th Month**	丑 Chou Ox	子 Zi Rat	巳 Si Snake
申 **Monkey** (Aug 8 - Sept 7) 七月 **7th Month**	寅 Yin Tiger	亥 Hai Pig	辰 Chen Dragon
酉 **Rooster** (Sept 8 - Oct 7) 八月 **8th Month**	酉 You Rooster	戌 Xu Dog	卯 Mao Rabbit
戌 **Dog** (Oct 8 - Nov 6) 九月 **9th Month**	未 Wei Goat	酉 You Rooster	寅 Yin Tiger
亥 **Pig** (Nov 7 - Dec 6) 十月 **10th Month**	亥 Hai Pig	申 Shen Monkey	丑 Chou Ox
子 **Rat** (Dec 7 - Jan 5) 十一月 **11th Month**	卯 Mao Rabbit	未 Wei Goat	子 Zi Rat
丑 **Ox** (Jan 6 - Feb 3) 十二月 **12th Month**	戌 Xu Dog	午 Wu Horse	亥 Hai Pig

乙亥 (Yi Hai)
Wood Pig

Heavenly Stem 天干	乙 Yin Wood (陰木)
Earthly Branch 地支	亥 Pig (Yin Water 陰水)
Hidden Stem 藏干	壬 Yang Water, 甲 Yang Wood
Na Yin 納音	山頭火 Fire from the mountain
Grand Duke 太歲	亥 Pig
Xuan Kong Five Element 玄空五行	3木 Wood
Gua Name 卦名	䷢ 火地晉 Advancement
Xuan Kong Period Luck 玄空卦運	3

Annual Positive Stars for Opening Mountain, Establishing Facing and Commencing Repairs 開山立向修方吉星:

歲德 **Duke Virtue**	庚 *Geng* **Yang Metal**
歲德合 **Duke Virtue Combo**	乙 *Yi* **Yin Wood**
歲枝德 **Duke Branch Virtue**	辰 *Chen* **Dragon**
陽貴人 **Yang Nobleman**	申 *Shen* **Monkey**
陰貴人 **Yin Nobleman**	子 *Zi* **Rat**
歲祿 **Duke Prosperous**	卯 *Mao* **Rabbit**
歲馬 **Duke Horse**	巳 *Si* **Snake**
奏書 **Decree**	乾 *Qian*
博士 **Professor**	巽 *Xun*

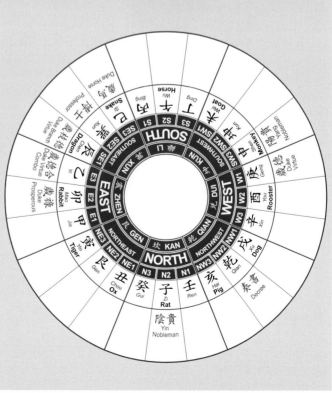

Annual Negative Stars for Opening Mountain, Establishing Facing and Commencing Repairs 開山立向修方凶星：

太歲 Grand Duke	歲破 Year Breaker	三煞 Three Killings			坐煞向煞 Sitting Sha Facing Sha				浮天空亡 Floating Heaven Emptiness	
亥 Hai Pig	巳 Si Snake	申 Shen Monkey	酉 You Rooster	戌 Xu Dog	庚 Geng Yang Metal	辛 Xin Yin Metal	甲 Jia Yang Wood	乙 Yi Yin Wood	坎 Kan	癸 Gui Yin Water

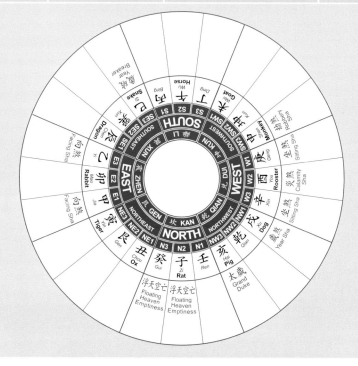

Annual San Yuan Purple White Stars 三元紫白九星：

上元 Upper Period Period 1, 2, 3	中元 Middle Period Period 4, 5, 6	下元 Lower Period Period 7, 8, 9

Upper Period (Period 1, 2, 3)

巽SE	離S	坤SW
7	3	5
6 (震E)	8 乙亥 Yi Hai Wood Pig	1 (兌W)
2	4	9
艮NE	坎N	乾NW

Middle Period (Period 4, 5, 6)

巽SE	離S	坤SW
1	6	8
9 (震E)	2 乙亥 Yi Hai Wood Pig	4 (兌W)
5	7	3
艮NE	坎N	乾NW

Lower Period (Period 7, 8, 9)

巽SE	離S	坤SW
4	9	2
3 (震E)	5 乙亥 Yi Hai Wood Pig	7 (兌W)
8	1	6
艮NE	坎N	乾NW

223

Mountain Covering Yellow Path 蓋山黃道：

貪狼 Tan Lang **Greedy Wolf**				巨門 Ju Men **Huge Door**		武曲 Wu Qu **Military Arts**				文曲 Wen Qu **Literary Arts**			
坎 Kan N2	癸 Gui N3	申 Shen SW3	辰 Chen SE1	坤 Kun SW2	乙 Yi E3	離 Li S2	壬 Ren N1	寅 Yin NE3	戌 Xu NW1	兌 Dui W2	丁 Ding S3	巳 Si SE3	丑 Chou NE1

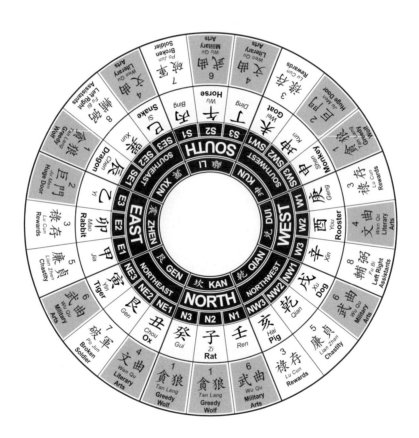

Heaven Penetrating Force 通天竅：

三合前方 **Facing Three** **Harmony**	巽巳 Xun Si	丙午 Bing Wu	丁未 Ding Wei
三合後方 **Sitting Three** **Harmony**	乾亥 Qian Hai	壬子 Ren Zi	癸丑 Gui Chou

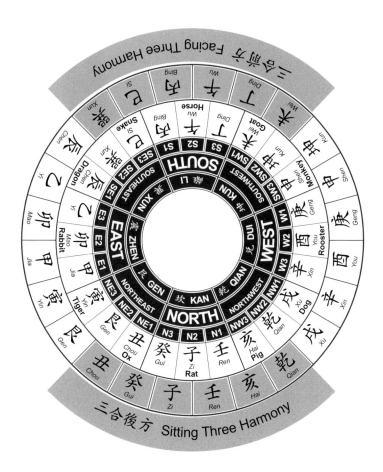

Moving Horse Six Ren Assessment 走馬六壬：

神后 Shen Hou Holy Empress	功曹 Gong Cao Marshall	天罡 Tian Gang Heavenly Dipper	勝光 Sheng Guang Subliminal Bright	傳送 Chuan Song Great General	河魁 He Kui River Scholar
癸丑 Gui Chou	甲卯 Jia Mao	巽巳 Xun Si	丁未 Ding Wei	庚酉 Geng You	乾亥 Qian Hai

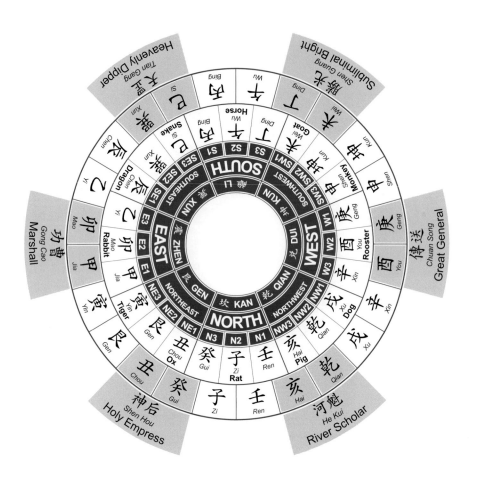

Four Advantages Three Cycles Star Plate 四利三元:

太陽 *Tai Yang* **Sun**	太陰 *Tai Yin* **Moon**	龍德 *Long De* **Dragon Virtue**	福德 *Fu De* **Fortune Virtue**
子 *Zi* **Rat**	寅 *Yin* **Tiger**	午 *Wu* **Horse**	申 *Shen* **Monkey**

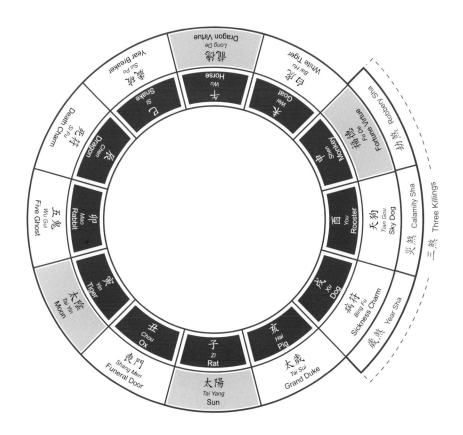

Negative Sectors For Opening Mountain 開山凶位：

年剋山家 Year Countering Sitting

甲 Jia E1	寅 Yin NE3	辰 Chen SE1	巽 Xun SE2	戌 Xu NW1	坎 Kan N2	辛 Xin W3	申 Shen SW3	丑 Chou NE1	癸 Gui N3	坤 Kun SW2	庚 Geng W1	未 Wei SW1

陰府太歲 Yin Fu Tai Sui **Yin Mansion Grand Duke**		六害 Liu Hai **Six Harm**	死符 Si Fu **Death Charm**	炙退 Zhi Tui **Roasting Star**
兌 Dui W2	乾 Qian NW2	申 Shen SW3	辰 Chen SE1	午 Wu S2

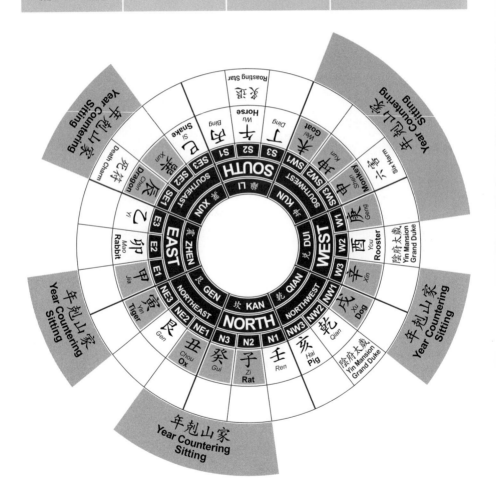

巡山羅喉 *Xun Shan Luo Hou* **Mountain Patrol Luo Hou Star**	病符 *Bing Fu* **Sickness Charm**
Negative Directions to Establish Facing 立向凶方：	
壬 *Ren* **N1**	戌 *Xu* **NW1**

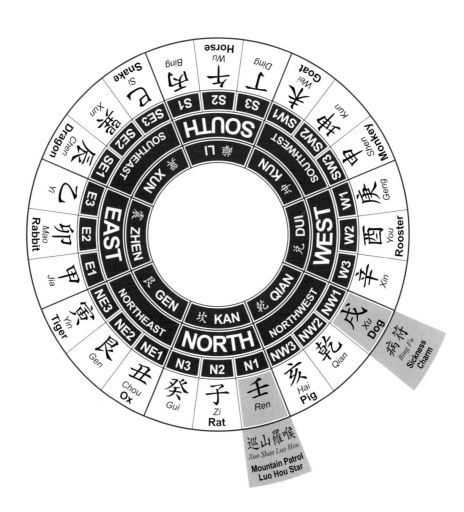

Negative Repair / Renovation Sectors Table 修方凶位表：

天官符 Heavenly Officer Charm	寅 Yin Tiger	豹尾 Leopard Tail	丑 Chou Ox
地官符 Earthly Officer Charm	卯 Mao Rabbit	飛廉 Flying Chaste	丑 Chou Ox
大煞 Great Sha	卯 Mao Rabbit	喪門 Funeral Door	丑 Chou Ox
大將軍 Big General	酉 You Rooster	弔客 Suspended Guest	酉 You Rooster
力士 Strong Man	艮 Gen	白虎 White Tiger	未 Wei Goat
蠶室 Silkworm Room	坤 Kun	金神 Golden God	辰 Chen Dragon / 巳 Si Snake
蠶官 Silkworm Officer	未 Wei Goat		
蠶命 Silkworm Life	申 Shen Monkey	獨火 Lonely Fire	乾 Qian
歲刑 Duke Punishment	亥 Hai Pig	五鬼 Five Ghost	巳 Si Snake
黃幡 Yellow Flag	未 Wei Goat	破敗五鬼 Destructive Five Ghost	艮 Gen

Negative Repair / Renovation Sectors Diagram 修方凶位圖：

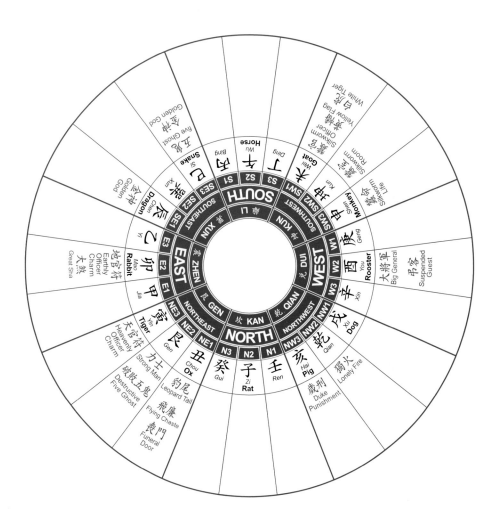

12-Month Auxiliary Stars Reference Table :
乙亥年十二月，開山立向修方星表

Positive Monthly Stars 吉星方

月 MONTH	寅 Tiger (Feb 4 - Mar 5) 正月 1st Month	卯 Rabbit (Mar 6 - Apr 4) 二月 2nd Month	辰 Dragon (Apr 5 - May 5) 三月 3rd Month	巳 Snake (May 6 - Jun 5) 四月 4th Month	午 Horse (Jun 6 - July 6) 五月 5th Month	未 Goat (July 7 - Aug 7) 六月 6th Month
天道 Heavenly Path	南 South	西南 Southwest	北 North	西 West	西北 Northwest	東 East
天德 Heavenly Virtue	丁 Ding Yin Fire	坤 Kun （申）	壬 Ren Yang Water	辛 Xin Yin Metal	乾 Qian （亥）	甲 Jia Yang Wood
天德合 Heavenly Virtue Combo	壬 Ren Yang Water	（巳）	丁 Ding Yin Fire	丙 Bing Yang Fire	（寅）	己 Ji Yin Earth
月德 Monthly Virtue	丙 Bing Yang Fire	甲 Jia Yang Wood	壬 Ren Yang Water	庚 Geng Yang Metal	丙 Bing Yang Fire	甲 Jia Yang Wood
月德合 Monthly Virtue Combo	辛 Xin Yin Metal	己 Ji Yin Earth	丁 Ding Yin Fire	乙 Yi Yin Wood	辛 Xin Yin Metal	己 Ji Yin Earth
月空 Month Emptiness	壬 Ren Yang Water	庚 Geng Yang Metal	丙 Bing Yang Fire	甲 Jia Yang Wood	壬 Ren Yang Water	庚 Geng Yang Metal
陽貴人 Yang Nobleman	坤 Kun	坎 Kan	離 Li	艮 Gen	兌 Dui	乾 Qian
陰貴人 Yin Nobleman	乾 Qian	中 Middle	巽 Xun	震 Zhen	坤 Kun	坎 Kan
飛天祿 Flying Heavenly Wealth	乾 Qian	中 Middle	坎 Kan	離 Li	艮 Gen	兌 Dui
飛天馬 Flying Heavenly Horse	艮 Gen	兌 Dui	乾 Qian	中 Middle	坎 Kan	離 Li

12-Month Auxiliary Stars Reference Table :
乙亥年十二月，開山立向修方星表

申 Monkey (Aug 8 - Sept 7) 七月 7th Month	酉 Rooster (Sept 8 - Oct 7) 八月 8th Month	戌 Dog (Oct 8 - Nov 6) 九月 9th Month	亥 Pig (Nov 7 - Dec 6) 十月 10th Month	子 Rat (Dec 7 - Jan 5) 十一月 11th Month	丑 Ox (Jan 6 - Feb 3) 十二月 12th Month	月 MONTH
北 North	東北 Northeast	南 South	東 East	東南 Southeast	西 West	天道 Heavenly Path
癸 Gui Yin Water	艮 Gen (寅)	丙 Bing Yang Fire	乙 Yi Yin Wood	巽 Xun (巳)	庚 Geng Yang Metal	天德 Heavenly Virtue
戊 Wu Yang Earth	(亥)	辛 Xin Yin Metal	庚 Geng Yang Metal	(申)	乙 Yi Yin Wood	天德合 Heavenly Virtue Combo
壬 Ren Yang Water	庚 Geng Yang Metal	丙 Bing Yang Fire	甲 Jia Yang Wood	壬 Ren Yang Water	庚 Geng Yang Metal	月德 Monthly Virtue
丁 Ding Yin Fire	乙 Yi Yin Wood	辛 Xin Yin Metal	己 Ji Yin Earth	丁 Ding Yin Fire	乙 Yi Yin Wood	月德合 Monthly Virtue Combo
丙 Bing Yang Fire	甲 Jia Yang Wood	壬 Ren Yang Water	庚 Geng Yang Metal	丙 Bing Yang Fire	甲 Jia Yang Wood	月空 Month Emptiness
中 Middle	坎 Kan	離 Li	艮 Gen	兌 Dui	乾 Qian	陽貴人 Yang Nobleman
離 Li	艮 Gen	兌 Dui	乾 Qian	中 Middle	坎 Kan	陰貴人 Yin Nobleman
乾 Qian	中 Middle	巽 Xun	震 Zhen	坤 Kun	坎 Kan	飛天祿 Flying Heavenly Wealth
艮 Gen	兌 Dui	乾 Qian	中 Middle	巽 Xun	震 Zhen	飛天馬 Flying Heavenly Horse

Monthly Purple White Stars 月紫白九星 :

寅 Tiger (Feb 4 - Mar 5) 正月 1st Month

巽 SE	離 S	坤 SW
1 White 一白	6 White 六白	8 White 八白
震 E 9 Purple 九紫	2 Black 二黑	4 Green 四綠 兌 W
艮 NE 5 Yellow 五黃	坎 N 7 Red 七赤	乾 NW 3 Jade 三碧

卯 Rabbit (Mar 6 - Apr 4) 二月 2nd Month

巽 SE	離 S	坤 SW
9 Purple 九紫	5 Yellow 五黃	7 Red 七赤
震 E 8 White 八白	1 White 一白	3 Jade 三碧 兌 W
艮 NE 4 Green 四綠	坎 N 6 White 六白	乾 NW 2 Black 二黑

辰 Dragon (Apr 5 - May 5) 三月 3rd Month

巽 SE	離 S	坤 SW
8 White 八白	4 Green 四綠	6 White 六白
震 E 7 Red 七赤	9 Purple 九紫	2 Black 二黑 兌 W
艮 NE 3 Jade 三碧	坎 N 5 Yellow 五黃	乾 NW 1 White 一白

巳 Snake (May 6 - Jun 5) 四月 4th Month

巽 SE	離 S	坤 SW
7 Red 七赤	3 Jade 三碧	5 Yellow 五黃
震 E 6 White 六白	8 White 八白	1 White 一白 兌 W
艮 NE 2 Black 二黑	坎 N 4 Green 四綠	乾 NW 9 Purple 九紫

午 Horse (Jun 6 - July 6) 五月 5th Month

巽 SE	離 S	坤 SW
6 White 六白	2 Black 二黑	4 Green 四綠
震 E 5 Yellow 五黃	7 Red 七赤	9 Purple 九紫 兌 W
艮 NE 1 White 一白	坎 N 3 Jade 三碧	乾 NW 8 White 八白

未 Goat (July 7 - Aug 7) 六月 6th Month

巽 SE	離 S	坤 SW
5 Yellow 五黃	1 White 一白	3 Jade 三碧
震 E 4 Green 四綠	6 White 六白	8 White 八白 兌 W
艮 NE 9 Purple 九紫	坎 N 2 Black 二黑	乾 NW 7 Red 七赤

申 Monkey (Aug 8 - Sept 7) 七月 7th Month

巽 SE	離 S	坤 SW
4 Green 四綠	9 Purple 九紫	2 Black 二黑
震 E 3 Jade 三碧	5 Yellow 五黃	7 Red 七赤 兌 W
艮 NE 8 White 八白	坎 N 1 White 一白	乾 NW 6 White 六白

酉 Rooster (Sept 8 - Oct 7) 八月 8th Month

巽 SE	離 S	坤 SW
3 Jade 三碧	8 White 八白	1 White 一白
震 E 2 Black 二黑	4 Green 四綠	6 White 六白 兌 W
艮 NE 7 Red 七赤	坎 N 9 Purple 九紫	乾 NW 5 Yellow 五黃

戌 Dog (Oct 8 - Nov 6) 九月 9th Month

巽 SE	離 S	坤 SW
2 Black 二黑	7 Red 七赤	9 Purple 九紫
震 E 1 White 一白	3 Jade 三碧	5 Yellow 五黃 兌 W
艮 NE 6 White 六白	坎 N 8 White 八白	乾 NW 4 Green 四綠

亥 Pig (Nov 7 - Dec 6) 十月 10th Month

巽 SE	離 S	坤 SW
1 White 一白	6 White 六白	8 White 八白
震 E 9 Purple 九紫	2 Black 二黑	4 Green 四綠 兌 W
艮 NE 5 Yellow 五黃	坎 N 7 Red 七赤	乾 NW 3 Jade 三碧

子 Rat (Dec 7 - Jan 5) 十一月 11th Month

巽 SE	離 S	坤 SW
9 Purple 九紫	5 Yellow 五黃	7 Red 七赤
震 E 8 White 八白	1 White 一白	3 Jade 三碧 兌 W
艮 NE 4 Green 四綠	坎 N 6 White 六白	乾 NW 2 Black 二黑

丑 Ox (Jan 6 - Feb 3) 十二月 12th Month

巽 SE	離 S	坤 SW
8 White 八白	4 Green 四綠	6 White 六白
震 E 7 Red 七赤	9 Purple 九紫	2 Black 二黑 兌 W
艮 NE 3 Jade 三碧	坎 N 5 Yellow 五黃	乾 NW 1 White 一白

Qi Men Three Nobles 三奇 :

Three Nobles 三奇 / Seasons	乙 Yi	丙 Bing	丁 Ding
立春 **Coming of Spring** Feb 4 - Feb 18	艮 Gen	離 Li	坎 Kan
春分 **Spring Equinox** Mar 21 - Apr 4	震 Zhen	巽 Xun	中 **Middle**
立夏 **Coming of Summer** May 6 - May 20	巽 Xun	中 **Middle**	乾 Qian
夏至 **Summer Solstice** Jun 22 - Jul 6	離 Li	艮 Gen	兌 Dui
立秋 **Coming of Autumn** Aug 8 - Aug 23	坤 Kun	坎 Kan	離 Li
秋分 **Autumn Equinox** Sept 23 - Oct 7	兌 Dui	乾 Qian	中 **Middle**
立冬 **Coming of Winter** Nov 7 - Nov 22	乾 Qian	中 **Middle**	巽 Xun
冬至 **Winter Solstice** Dec 22 - Jan 5	坎 Kan	坤 Kun	震 Zhen

乙亥 (Yi Hai) Wood Pig

Sectors to Avoid Opening Mountain 開山凶位 :

月 MONTH	月建 Month Establishment	月破 Month Destruction	月剋山家 Month Countering Sitting		陰府太歲 Yin Mansion Grand Duke	
寅 **Tiger** (Feb 4 - Mar 5) 正月 • **1st Month**	寅 *Yin* **Tiger**	申 *Shen* **Monkey**	乾 *Qian*	兌 *Dui*	坤 *Kun*	震 *Zhen*
卯 **Rabbit** (Mar 6 - Apr 4) 二月 **2nd Month**	卯 *Mao* **Rabbit**	酉 *You* **Rooster**	亥 *Hai* **Pig**	丁 *Ding* **Yin Fire**	巽 *Xun*	艮 *Gen*
辰 **Dragon** (Apr 5 - May 5) 三月 **3rd Month**	辰 *Chen* **Dragon**	戌 *Xu* **Dog**	震 *Zhen*	巳 *Si* **Snake**	乾 *Qian*	兌 *Dui*
巳 **Snake** (May 6 - Jun 5) 四月 **4th Month**	巳 *Si* **Snake**	亥 *Hai* **Pig**	艮 *Gen*		坤 *Kun*	坎 *Kan*
午 **Horse** (Jun 6 - July 6) 五月 **5th Month**	午 *Wu* **Horse**	子 *Zi* **Rat**	離 *Li*	丙 *Bing* **Yang Fire**	離 *Li*	乾 *Qian*
未 **Goat** (July 7 - Aug 7) 六月 **6th Month**	未 *Wei* **Goat**	丑 *Chou* **Ox**	壬 *Ren* **Yang Water**	乙 *Yi* **Yin Wood**	震 *Zhen*	坤 *Kun*
申 **Monkey** (Aug 8 - Sept 7) 七月 **7th Month**	申 *Shen* **Monkey**	寅 *Yin* **Tiger**	—		艮 *Gen*	巽 *Xun*
酉 **Rooster** (Sept 8 - Oct 7) 八月 **8th Month**	酉 *You* **Rooster**	卯 *Mao* **Rabbit**	—		兌 *Dui*	乾 *Qian*
戌 **Dog** (Oct 8 - Nov 6) 九月 **9th Month**	戌 *Xu* **Dog**	辰 *Chen* **Dragon**	乾 *Qian*	兌 *Dui*	坎 *Kan*	坤 *Kun*
亥 **Pig** (Nov 7 - Dec 6) 十月 **10th Month**	亥 *Hai* **Pig**	巳 *Si* **Snake**	亥 *Hai* **Pig**	丁 *Ding* **Yin Fire**	乾 *Qian*	離 *Li*
子 **Rat** (Dec 7 - Jan 5) 十一月 **11th Month**	子 *Zi* **Rat**	午 *Wu* **Horse**	水 **Water**	山 **Mountain**	坤 *Kun*	震 *Zhen*
丑 **Ox** (Jan 6 - Feb 3) 十二月 **12th Month**	丑 *Chou* **Ox**	未 *Wei* **Goat**	土 **Earth**		巽 *Xun*	艮 *Gen*

Negative Repair / Renovation Sectors 修方凶位 :

月 MONTH	天官符 Heavenly Officer Charm			地官符 Earth Officer Charm			小月建 Small Month Establishment		
寅 Tiger (Feb 4 - Mar 5) 正月 1st Month	中 Middle			戌 Xu Dog	乾 Qian	亥 Hai Pig	丙 Bing Yang Fire	離 Li	丁 Ding Yin Fire
卯 Rabbit (Mar 6 - Apr 4) 二月 2nd Month	庚 Geng Yang Metal	兌 Dui	辛 Xin Yin Metal	中 Middle			壬 Ren Yang Water	坎 Kan	癸 Gui Yin Water
辰 Dragon (Apr 5 - May 5) 三月 3rd Month	戌 Xu Dog	乾 Qian	亥 Hai Pig	庚 Geng Yang Metal	兌 Dui	辛 Xin Yin Metal	未 Wei Goat	坤 Kun	申 Shen Monkey
巳 Snake (May 6 - Jun 5) 四月 4th Month	中 Middle			戌 Xu Dog	乾 Qian	亥 Hai Pig	甲 Jia Yang Wood	震 Zhen	乙 Yi Yin Wood
午 Horse (Jun 6 - July 6) 五月 5th Month	辰 Chen Dragon	巽 Xun	巳 Si Snake	中 Middle			辰 Chen Dragon	巽 Xun	巳 Si Snake
未 Goat (July 7 - Aug 7) 六月 6th Month	甲 Jia Yang Wood	震 Zhen	乙 Yi Yin Wood	辰 Chen Dragon	巽 Xun	巳 Si Snake	中 Middle		
申 Monkey (Aug 8 - Sept 7) 七月 7th Month	未 Wei Goat	坤 Kun	申 Shen Monkey	甲 Jia Yang Wood	震 Zhen	乙 Yi Yin Wood	戌 Xu Dog	乾 Qian	亥 Hai Pig
酉 Rooster (Sept 8 - Oct 7) 八月 8th Month	壬 Ren Yang Water	坎 Kan	癸 Gui Yin Water	未 Wei Goat	坤 Kun	申 Shen Monkey	庚 Geng Yang Metal	兌 Dui	辛 Xin Yin Metal
戌 Dog (Oct 8 - Nov 6) 九月 9th Month	丙 Bing Yang Fire	離 Li	丁 Ding Yin Fire	壬 Ren Yang Water	坎 Kan	癸 Gui Yin Water	丑 Chou Ox	艮 Gen	寅 Yin Tiger
亥 Pig (Nov 7 - Dec 6) 十月 10th Month	丑 Chou Ox	艮 Gen	寅 Yin Tiger	丙 Bing Yang Fire	離 Li	丁 Ding Yin Fire	丙 Bing Yang Fire	離 Li	丁 Ding Yin Fire
子 Rat (Dec 7 - Jan 5) 十一月 11th Month	庚 Geng Yang Metal	兌 Dui	辛 Xin Yin Metal	丑 Chou Ox	艮 Gen	寅 Yin Tiger	壬 Ren Yang Water	坎 Kan	癸 Gui Yin Water
丑 Ox (Jan 6 - Feb 3) 十二月 12th Month	戌 Xu Dog	乾 Qian	亥 Hai Pig	庚 Geng Yang Metal	兌 Dui	辛 Xin Yin Metal	未 Wei Goat	坤 Kun	申 Shen Monkey

Negative Repair / Renovation Sectors 修方凶位 :

月 MONTH	大月建 Big Month Establishment			飛大煞 Flying Great Sha			丙丁獨火 Bing Ding Lonely Fire	
寅 **Tiger** (Feb 4 - Mar 5) 正月 **1st Month**	未 Wei **Goat**	坤 Kun	申 Shen **Monkey**	戌 Xu **Dog**	乾 Qian	亥 Hai **Pig**	巽 Xun	中 **Middle**
卯 **Rabbit** (Mar 6 - Apr 4) 二月 **2nd Month**	壬 Ren **Yang Water**	坎 Kan	癸 Gui **Yin Water**		中 **Middle**		震 Zhen	巽 Xun
辰 **Dragon** (Apr 5 - May 5) 三月 **3rd Month**	丙 Bing **Yang Fire**	離 Li	丁 Ding **Yin Fire**	庚 Geng **Yang Metal**	兌 Dui	辛 Xin **Yin Metal**	坤 Kun	震 Zhen
巳 **Snake** (May 6 - Jun 5) 四月 **4th Month**	丑 Chou **Ox**	艮 Gen	寅 Yin **Tiger**	戌 Xu **Dog**	乾 Qian	亥 Hai **Pig**	坎 Kan	坤 Kun
午 **Horse** (Jun 6 - July 6) 五月 **5th Month**	庚 Geng **Yang Metal**	兌 Dui	辛 Xin **Yin Metal**		中 **Middle**		離 Li	坎 Kan
未 **Goat** (July 7 - Aug 7) 六月 **6th Month**	戌 Xu **Dog**	乾 Qian	亥 Hai **Pig**	辰 Chen **Dragon**	巽 Xun	巳 Si **Snake**	艮 Gen	離 Li
申 **Monkey** (Aug 8 - Sept 7) 七月 **7th Month**		中 **Middle**		甲 Jia **Yang Wood**	震 Zhen	乙 Yi **Yin Wood**	兌 Dui	艮 Gen
酉 **Rooster** (Sept 8 - Oct 7) 八月 **8th Month**	辰 Chen **Dragon**	巽 Xun	巳 Si **Snake**	未 Wei **Goat**	坤 Kun	申 Shen **Monkey**	乾 Qian	兌 Dui
戌 **Dog** (Oct 8 - Nov 6) 九月 **9th Month**	甲 Jia **Yang Wood**	震 Zhen	乙 Yi **Yin Wood**	壬 Ren **Yang Water**	坎 Kan	癸 Gui **Yin Water**	中 **Middle**	乾 Qian
亥 **Pig** (Nov 7 - Dec 6) 十月 **10th Month**	未 Wei **Goat**	坤 Kun	申 Shen **Monkey**	丙 Bing **Yang Fire**	離 Li	丁 Ding **Yin Fire**	中 **Middle**	
子 **Rat** (Dec 7 - Jan 5) 十一月 **11th Month**	壬 Ren **Yang Water**	坎 Kan	癸 Gui **Yin Water**	丑 Chou **Ox**	艮 Gen	寅 Yin **Tiger**	巽 Xun	中 **Middle**
丑 **Ox** (Jan 6 - Feb 3) 十二月 **12th Month**	丙 Bing **Yang Fire**	離 Li	丁 Ding **Yin Fire**	庚 Geng **Yang Metal**	兌 Dui	辛 Xin **Yin Metal**	震 Zhen	巽 Xun

Negative Repair / Renovation Sectors 修方凶位 :

月 MONTH	月遊火 Month Wondering Fire	三煞 Monthly 3 Killings		
		劫煞 Robbery Sha	災煞 Calamity Sha	月煞 Month Sha
寅 Tiger (Feb 4 - Mar 5) 正月 1st Month	坎 Kan	亥 Hai Pig	子 Zi Rat	丑 Chou Ox
卯 Rabbit (Mar 6 - Apr 4) 二月 2nd Month	坤 Kun	申 Shen Monkey	酉 You Rooster	戌 Xu Dog
辰 Dragon (Apr 5 - May 5) 三月 3rd Month	震 Zhen	巳 Si Snake	午 Wu Horse	未 Wei Goat
巳 Snake (May 6 - Jun 5) 四月 4th Month	巽 Xun	寅 Yin Tiger	卯 Mao Rabbit	辰 Chen Dragon
午 Horse (Jun 6 - July 6) 五月 5th Month	中 Middle	亥 Hai Pig	子 Zi Rat	丑 Chou Ox
未 Goat (July 7 - Aug 7) 六月 6th Month	乾 Qian	申 Shen Monkey	酉 You Rooster	戌 Xu Dog
申 Monkey (Aug 8 - Sept 7) 七月 7th Month	兌 Dui	巳 Si Snake	午 Wu Horse	未 Wei Goat
酉 Rooster (Sept 8 - Oct 7) 八月 8th Month	艮 Gen	寅 Yin Tiger	卯 Mao Rabbit	辰 Chen Dragon
戌 Dog (Oct 8 - Nov 6) 九月 9th Month	離 Li	亥 Hai Pig	子 Zi Rat	丑 Chou Ox
亥 Pig (Nov 7 - Dec 6) 十月 10th Month	坎 Kan	申 Shen Monkey	酉 You Rooster	戌 Xu Dog
子 Rat (Dec 7 - Jan 5) 十一月 11th Month	坤 Kun	巳 Si Snake	午 Wu Horse	未 Wei Goat
丑 Ox (Jan 6 - Feb 3) 十二月 12th Month	震 Zhen	寅 Yin Tiger	卯 Mao Rabbit	辰 Chen Dragon

Negative Repair / Renovation Sectors 修方凶位 :

月 MONTH	月刑 Month Punishment	月害 Month Harm	月厭 Month Detest
寅 **Tiger** (Feb 4 - Mar 5) 正月 **1st Month**	巳 *Si* Snake	巳 *Si* Snake	戌 *Xu* Dog
卯 **Rabbit** (Mar 6 - Apr 4) 二月 **2nd Month**	子 *Zi* Rat	辰 *Chen* Dragon	酉 *You* Rooster
辰 **Dragon** (Apr 5 - May 5) 三月 **3rd Month**	辰 *Chen* Dragon	卯 *Mao* Rabbit	申 *Shen* Monkey
巳 **Snake** (May 6 - Jun 5) 四月 **4th Month**	申 *Shen* Monkey	寅 *Yin* Tiger	未 *Wei* Goat
午 **Horse** (Jun 6 - July 6) 五月 **5th Month**	午 *Wu* Horse	丑 *Chou* Ox	午 *Wu* Horse
未 **Goat** (July 7 - Aug 7) 六月 **6th Month**	丑 *Chou* Ox	子 *Zi* Rat	巳 *Si* Snake
申 **Monkey** (Aug 8 - Sept 7) 七月 **7th Month**	寅 *Yin* Tiger	亥 *Hai* Pig	辰 *Chen* Dragon
酉 **Rooster** (Sept 8 - Oct 7) 八月 **8th Month**	酉 *You* Rooster	戌 *Xu* Dog	卯 *Mao* Rabbit
戌 **Dog** (Oct 8 - Nov 6) 九月 **9th Month**	未 *Wei* Goat	酉 *You* Rooster	寅 *Yin* Tiger
亥 **Pig** (Nov 7 - Dec 6) 十月 **10th Month**	亥 *Hai* Pig	申 *Shen* Monkey	丑 *Chou* Ox
子 **Rat** (Dec 7 - Jan 5) 十一月 **11th Month**	卯 *Mao* Rabbit	未 *Wei* Goat	子 *Zi* Rat
丑 **Ox** (Jan 6 - Feb 3) 十二月 **12th Month**	戌 *Xu* Dog	午 *Wu* Horse	亥 *Hai* Pig

丙子 (Bing Zi)
Fire Rat

Heavenly Stem 天干	丙 Yang Fire (陽火)
Earthly Branch 地支	子 Rat (Yang Water 陽水)
Hidden Stem 藏干	癸 Yin Water
Na Yin 納音	澗下水 Water from the streams
Grand Duke 太歲	子 Rat
Xuan Kong Five Element 玄空五行	6 水 Water
Gua Name 卦名	䷚ 山雷頤 Nourish
Xuan Kong Period Luck 玄空卦運	3

Annual Positive Stars for Opening Mountain, Establishing Facing and Commencing Repairs 開山立向修方吉星：

歲德 Duke Virtue	丙 Bing Yang Fire
歲德合 Duke Virtue Combo	辛 Xin Yin Metal
歲枝德 Duke Branch Virtue	巳 Si Snake
陽貴人 Yang Nobleman	酉 You Rooster
陰貴人 Yin Nobleman	亥 Hai Pig
歲祿 Duke Prosperous	巳 Si Snake
歲馬 Duke Horse	寅 Yin Tiger
奏書 Decree	乾 Qian
博士 Professor	巽 Xun

Annual Negative Stars for Opening Mountain, Establishing Facing and Commencing Repairs 開山立向修方凶星：

太歲 Grand Duke	歲破 Year Breaker	三煞 Three Killings			坐煞向煞 Sitting Sha Facing Sha				浮天空亡 Floating Heaven Emptiness	
子 Zi Rat	午 Wu Horse	巳 Si Snake	午 Wu Horse	未 Wei Goat	丙 Bing Yang Fire	丁 Ding Yin Fire	壬 Ren Yang Water	癸 Gui Yin Water	巽 Xun	辛 Xin Yin Metal

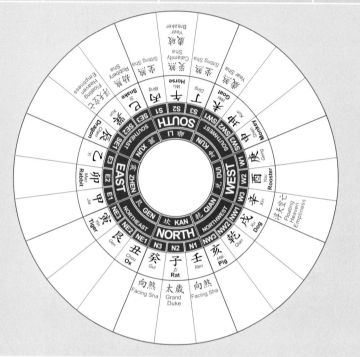

Annual San Yuan Purple White Stars 三元紫白九星：

上元 Upper Period Period 1, 2, 3			中元 Middle Period Period 4, 5, 6			下元 Lower Period Period 7, 8, 9		
巽SE **6**	離S **2**	坤SW **4**	巽SE **9**	離S **5**	坤SW **7**	巽SE **3**	離S **8**	坤SW **1**
震E **5**	**7** 丙子 Bing Zi Fire Rat	兑W **9**	震E **8**	**1** 丙子 Bing Zi Fire Rat	兑W **3**	震E **2**	**4** 丙子 Bing Zi Fire Rat	兑W **6**
艮NE **1**	坎N **3**	乾NW **8**	艮NE **4**	坎N **6**	乾NW **2**	艮NE **7**	坎N **9**	乾NW **5**

Mountain Covering Yellow Path 蓋山黃道：

貪狼 *Tan Lang* **Greedy Wolf**				巨門 *Ju Men* **Huge Door**				武曲 *Wu Qu* **Military Arts**		文曲 *Wen Qu* **Literary Arts**	
震 *Zhen* E2	庚 *Geng* W1	亥 *Hai* NW3	未 *Wei* SW1	兌 *Dui* W2	丁 *Ding* S3	巳 *Si* SE3	丑 *Chou* NE1	巽 *Xun* SE2	辛 *Xin* W3	坤 *Kun* SW2	乙 *Yi* E3

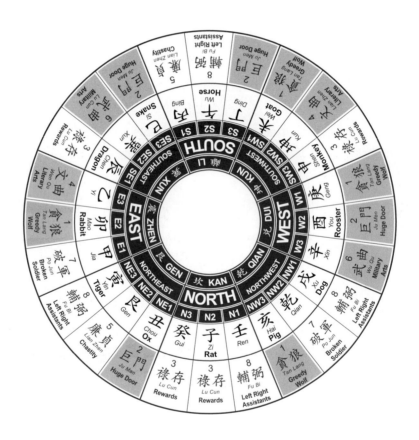

Heaven Penetrating Force 通天竅 :			
三合前方 **Facing Three Harmony**	艮寅 Gen Yin	甲卯 Jia Mao	乙辰 Yi Chen
三合後方 **Sitting Three Harmony**	坤申 Kun Shen	庚酉 Geng You	辛戌 Xin Xu

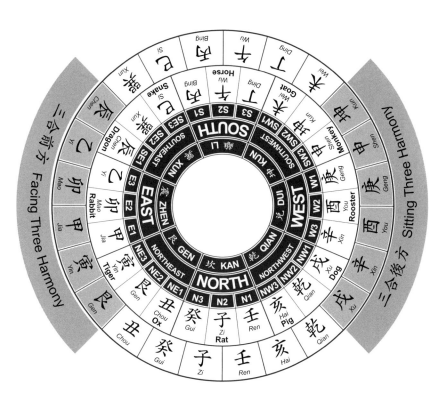

Moving Horse Six Ren Assessment 走馬六壬:

神后 Shen Hou **Holy Empress**	功曹 Gong Cao **Marshall**	天罡 Tian Gang **Heavenly Dipper**	勝光 Sheng Guang **Subliminal Bright**	傳送 Chuan Song **Great General**	河魁 He Kui **River Scholar**
壬子 Ren Zi	艮寅 Gen Yin	乙辰 Yi Chen	丙午 Bing Wu	坤申 Kun Shen	辛戌 Xin Xu

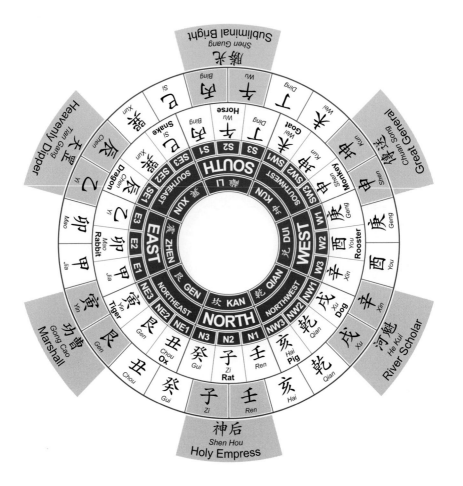

Four Advantages Three Cycles Star Plate 四利三元：

太陽 *Tai Yang* **Sun**	太陰 *Tai Yin* **Moon**	龍德 *Long De* **Dragon Virtue**	福德 *Fu De* **Fortune Virtue**
丑 *Chou* Ox	卯 *Mao* Rabbit	未 *Wei* Goat	酉 *You* Rooster

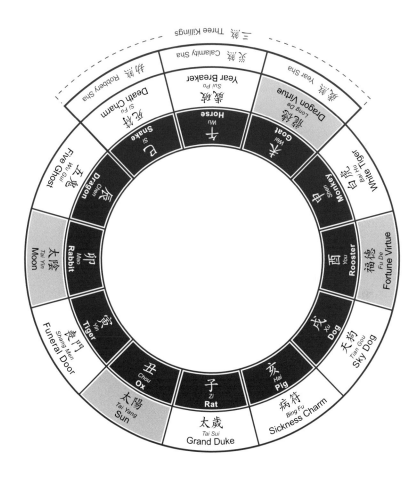

丙子 (Bing Zi) Fire Rat

Negative Sectors For Opening Mountain 開山凶位：

年尅山家 Year Countering Sitting

乾	亥	兌	丁
Qian	Hai	Dui	Ding
NW2	NW3	W2	S3

陰府太歲 Yin Fu Tai Sui **Yin Mansion Grand Duke**	六害 Liu Hai **Six Harm**	死符 Si Fu **Death Charm**	灸退 Zhi Tui **Roasting Star**
坎 坤 Kan Kun N2 SW2	未 Wei SW1	巳 Si SE3	卯 Mao E2

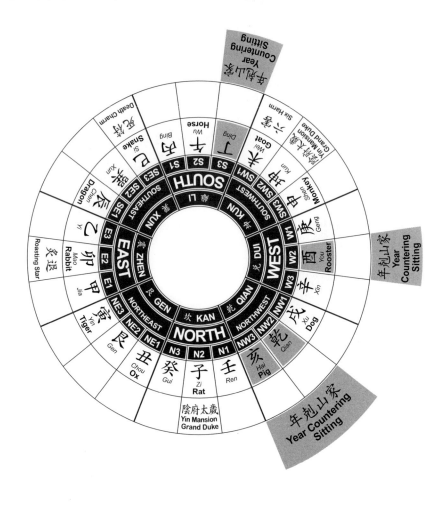

Negative Directions to Establish Facing 立向凶方：

巡山羅喉 *Xun Shan Luo Hou* **Mountain Patrol Luo Hou Star**	病符 *Bing Fu* **Sickness Charm**
癸 *Gui* **N3**	亥 *Hai* **NW3**

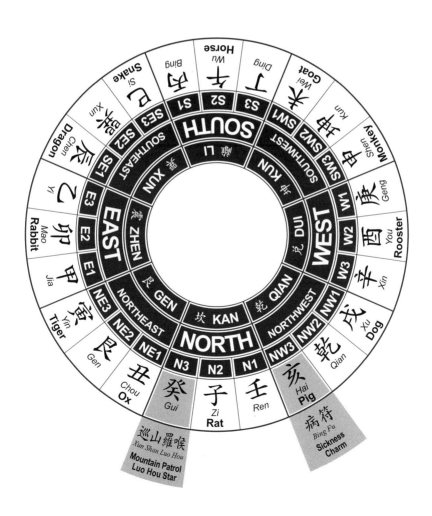

Negative Repair / Renovation Sectors Table 修方凶位表：

天官符 **Heavenly Officer Charm**	亥 *Hai* Pig	飛廉 **Flying Chaste**	申 *Shen* Monkey
地官符 **Earthly Officer Charm**	辰 *Chen* Dragon	喪門 **Funeral Door**	寅 *Yin* Tiger
大煞 **Great Sha**	子 *Zi* Rat	弔客 **Suspended Guest**	戌 *Xu* Dog
大將軍 **Big General**	酉 *You* Rooster	白虎 **White Tiger**	申 *Shen* Monkey
力士 **Strong Man**	艮 *Gen*	金神 **Golden God**	寅 *Yin* Tiger 卯 *Mao* Rabbit 午 *Wu* Horse 未 *Wei* Goat 子 *Zi* Rat 丑 *Chou* Ox
蠶室 **Silkworm Room**	坤 *Kun*		
蠶官 **Silkworm Officer**	未 *Wei* Goat		
蠶命 **Silkworm Life**	申 *Shen* Monkey		
歲刑 **Duke Punishment**	卯 *Mao* Rabbit	獨火 **Lonely Fire**	艮 *Gen*
黃幡 **Yellow Flag**	辰 *Chen* Dragon	五鬼 **Five Ghost**	辰 *Chen* Dragon
豹尾 **Leopard Tail**	戌 *Xu* Dog	破敗五鬼 **Destructive Five Ghost**	坤 *Kun*

Negative Repair / Renovation Sectors Diagram 修方凶位圖：

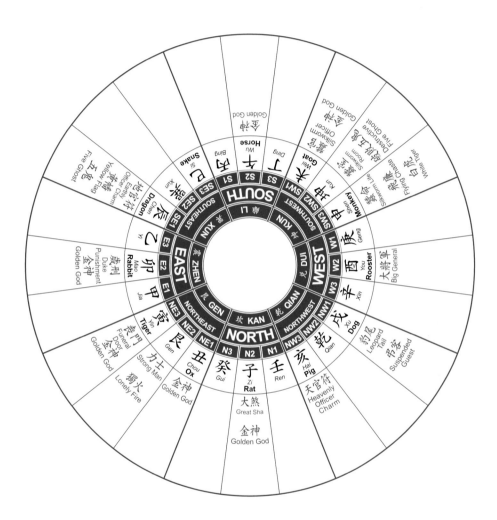

12-Month Auxiliary Stars Reference Table :
丙子年十二月，開山立向修方星表

Positive Monthly Stars 吉星方

月 MONTH	寅 Tiger (Feb 4 - Mar 5) 正月 1st Month	卯 Rabbit (Mar 6 - Apr 4) 二月 2nd Month	辰 Dragon (Apr 5 - May 5) 三月 3rd Month	巳 Snake (May 6 - Jun 5) 四月 4th Month	午 Horse (Jun 6 - July 6) 五月 5th Month	未 Goat (July 7 - Aug 7) 六月 6th Month
天道 Heavenly Path	南 South	西南 Southwest	北 North	西 West	西北 Northwest	東 East
天德 Heavenly Virtue	丁 Ding Yin Fire	坤 Kun (申)	壬 Ren Yang Water	辛 Xin Yin Metal	乾 Qian (亥)	甲 Jia Yang Wood
天德合 Heavenly Virtue Combo	壬 Ren Yang Water	(巳)	丁 Ding Yin Fire	丙 Bing Yang Fire	(寅)	己 Ji Yin Earth
月德 Monthly Virtue	丙 Bing Yang Fire	甲 Jia Yang Wood	壬 Ren Yang Water	庚 Geng Yang Metal	丙 Bing Yang Fire	甲 Jia Yang Wood
月德合 Monthly Virtue Combo	辛 Xin Yin Metal	己 Ji Yin Earth	丁 Ding Yin Fire	乙 Yi Yin Wood	辛 Xin Yin Metal	己 Ji Yin Earth
月空 Month Emptiness	壬 Ren Yang Water	庚 Geng Yang Metal	丙 Bing Yang Fire	甲 Jia Yang Wood	壬 Ren Yang Water	庚 Geng Yang Metal
陽貴人 Yang Nobleman	震 Zhen	坤 Kun	坎 Kan	離 Li	艮 Gen	兌 Dui
陰貴人 Yin Nobleman	中 Middle	巽 Xun	震 Zhen	坤 Kun	坎 Kan	離 Li
飛天祿 Flying Heavenly Wealth	艮 Gen	兌 Dui	乾 Qian	中 Middle	坎 Kan	離 Li
飛天馬 Flying Heavenly Horse	中 Middle	坎 Kan	離 Li	艮 Gen	兌 Dui	乾 Qian

12-Month Auxiliary Stars Reference Table :
丙子年十二月，開山立向修方星表

申 **Monkey** (Aug 8 - Sept 7) 七月 **7th Month**	酉 **Rooster** (Sept 8 - Oct 7) 八月 **8th Month**	戌 **Dog** (Oct 8 - Nov 6) 九月 **9th Month**	亥 **Pig** (Nov 7 - Dec 6) 十月 **10th Month**	子 **Rat** (Dec 7 - Jan 5) 十一月 **11th Month**	丑 **Ox** (Jan 6 - Feb 3) 十二月 **12th Month**	月 **MONTH**
北 North	東北 Northeast	南 South	東 East	東南 Southeast	西 West	天道 **Heavenly Path**
癸 Gui Yin Water	艮 Gen (寅)	丙 Bing Yang Fire	乙 Yi Yin Wood	巽 Xun (巳)	庚 Geng Yang Metal	天德 **Heavenly Virtue**
戊 Wu Yang Earth	(亥)	辛 Xin Yin Metal	庚 Geng Yang Metal	(申)	乙 Yi Yin Wood	天德合 **Heavenly Virtue Combo**
壬 Ren Yang Water	庚 Geng Yang Metal	丙 Bing Yang Fire	甲 Jia Yang Wood	壬 Ren Yang Water	庚 Geng Yang Metal	月德 **Monthly Virtue**
丁 Ding Yin Fire	乙 Yi Yin Wood	辛 Xin Yin Metal	己 Ji Yin Earth	丁 Ding Yin Fire	乙 Yi Yin Wood	月德合 **Monthly Virtue Combo**
丙 Bing Yang Fire	甲 Jia Yang Wood	壬 Ren Yang Water	庚 Geng Yang Metal	丙 Bing Yang Fire	甲 Jia Yang Wood	月空 **Month Emptiness**
乾 Qian	中 Middle	坎 Kan	離 Li	艮 Gen	兌 Dui	陽貴人 **Yang Nobleman**
艮 Gen	兌 Dui	乾 Qian	中 Middle	坎 Kan	離 Li	陰貴人 **Yin Nobleman**
艮 Gen	兌 Dui	乾 Qian	中 Middle	巽 Xun	震 Zhen	飛天祿 **Flying Heavenly Wealth**
中 Middle	巽 Xun	震 Zhen	坤 Kun	坎 Kan	離 Li	飛天馬 **Flying Heavenly Horse**

Monthly Purple White Stars 月紫白九星 :

寅 Tiger (Feb 4 - Mar 5) 正月 1st Month

巽SE	離S	坤SW
7 Red 七赤	3 Jade 三碧	5 Yellow 五黄
震E 6 White 六白	8 White 八白	1 White 一白 兌W
2 Black 二黑	4 Green 四綠	9 Purple 九紫
艮NE	坎N	乾NW

卯 Rabbit (Mar 6 - Apr 4) 二月 2nd Month

巽SE	離S	坤SW
6 White 六白	2 Black 二黑	4 Green 四綠
震E 5 Yellow 五黄	7 Red 七赤	9 Purple 九紫 兌W
1 White 一白	3 Jade 三碧	8 White 八白
艮NE	坎N	乾NW

辰 Dragon (Apr 5 - May 5) 三月 3rd Month

巽SE	離S	坤SW
5 Yellow 五黄	1 White 一白	3 Jade 三碧
震E 4 Green 四綠	6 White 六白	8 White 八白 兌W
9 Purple 九紫	2 Black 二黑	7 Red 七赤
艮NE	坎N	乾NW

巳 Snake (May 6 - Jun 5) 四月 4th Month

巽SE	離S	坤SW
4 Green 四綠	9 Purple 九紫	2 Black 二黑
震E 3 Jade 三碧	5 Yellow 五黄	7 Red 七赤 兌W
8 White 八白	1 White 一白	6 White 六白
艮NE	坎N	乾NW

午 Horse (Jun 6 - July 6) 五月 5th Month

巽SE	離S	坤SW
3 Jade 三碧	8 White 八白	1 White 一白
震E 2 Black 二黑	4 Green 四綠	6 White 六白 兌W
7 Red 七赤	9 Purple 九紫	5 Yellow 五黄
艮NE	坎N	乾NW

未 Goat (July 7 - Aug 7) 六月 6th Month

巽SE	離S	坤SW
2 Black 二黑	7 Red 七赤	9 Purple 九紫
震E 1 White 一白	3 Jade 三碧	5 Yellow 五黄 兌W
6 White 六白	8 White 八白	4 Green 四綠
艮NE	坎N	乾NW

申 Monkey (Aug 8 - Sept 7) 七月 7th Month

巽SE	離S	坤SW
1 White 一白	6 White 六白	8 White 八白
震E 9 Purple 九紫	2 Black 二黑	4 Green 四綠 兌W
5 Yellow 五黄	7 Red 七赤	3 Jade 三碧
艮NE	坎N	乾NW

酉 Rooster (Sept 8 - Oct 7) 八月 8th Month

巽SE	離S	坤SW
9 Purple 九紫	5 Yellow 五黄	7 Red 七赤
震E 8 White 八白	1 White 一白	3 Jade 三碧 兌W
4 Green 四綠	6 White 六白	2 Black 二黑
艮NE	坎N	乾NW

戌 Dog (Oct 8 - Nov 6) 九月 9th Month

巽SE	離S	坤SW
8 White 八白	4 Green 四綠	6 White 六白
震E 7 Red 七赤	9 Purple 九紫	2 Black 二黑 兌W
3 Jade 三碧	5 Yellow 五黄	1 White 一白
艮NE	坎N	乾NW

亥 Pig (Nov 7 - Dec 6) 十月 10th Month

巽SE	離S	坤SW
7 Red 七赤	3 Jade 三碧	5 Yellow 五黄
震E 6 White 六白	8 White 八白	1 White 一白 兌W
2 Black 二黑	4 Green 四綠	9 Purple 九紫
艮NE	坎N	乾NW

子 Rat (Dec 7 - Jan 5) 十一月 11th Month

巽SE	離S	坤SW
6 White 六白	2 Black 二黑	4 Green 四綠
震E 5 Yellow 五黄	7 Red 七赤	9 Purple 九紫 兌W
1 White 一白	3 Jade 三碧	8 White 八白
艮NE	坎N	乾NW

丑 Ox (Jan 6 - Feb 3) 十二月 12th Month

巽SE	離S	坤SW
5 Yellow 五黄	1 White 一白	3 Jade 三碧
震E 4 Green 四綠	6 White 六白	8 White 八白 兌W
9 Purple 九紫	2 Black 二黑	7 Red 七赤
艮NE	坎N	乾NW

Qi Men Three Nobles 三奇 :

Three Nobles 三奇 / Seasons	乙 *Yi*	丙 *Bing*	丁 *Ding*
立春 **Coming of Spring** Feb 4 - Feb 18	兌 Dui	艮 Gen	離 Li
春分 **Spring Equinox** Mar 21 - Apr 4	坤 Kun	震 Zhen	巽 Xun
立夏 **Coming of Summer** May 6 - May 20	震 Zhen	巽 Xun	中 **Middle**
夏至 **Summer Solstice** Jun 22 - Jul 6	坎 Kan	離 Li	艮 Gen
立秋 **Coming of Autumn** Aug 8 - Aug 23	震 Zhen	坤 Kun	坎 Kan
秋分 **Autumn Equinox** Sept 23 - Oct 7	艮 Gen	兌 Dui	乾 Qian
立冬 **Coming of Winter** Nov 7 - Nov 22	兌 Dui	乾 Qian	中 **Middle**
冬至 **Winter Solstice** Dec 22 - Jan 5	離 Li	坎 Kan	坤 Kun

Sectors to Avoid Opening Mountain 開山凶位 :

月 MONTH	月建 Month Establishment	月破 Month Destruction	月剋山家 Month Countering Sitting		陰府太歲 Yin Mansion Grand Duke	
寅 **Tiger** (Feb 4 - Mar 5) 正月 **1st Month**	寅 *Yin* **Tiger**	申 *Shen* **Monkey**	—		乾 *Qian*	兌 *Dui*
卯 **Rabbit** (Mar 6 - Apr 4) 二月 **2nd Month**	卯 *Mao* **Rabbit**	酉 *You* **Rooster**	—		坤 *Kun*	坎 *Kan*
辰 **Dragon** (Apr 5 - May 5) 三月 **3rd Month**	辰 *Chen* **Dragon**	戌 *Xu* **Dog**	乾 *Qian*	兌 *Dui*	離 *Li*	乾 *Qian*
巳 **Snake** (May 6 - Jun 5) 四月 **4th Month**	巳 *Si* **Snake**	亥 *Hai* **Pig**	亥 *Hai* **Pig**	丁 *Ding* **Yin Fire**	震 *Zhen*	坤 *Kun*
午 **Horse** (Jun 6 - July 6) 五月 **5th Month**	午 *Wu* **Horse**	子 *Zi* **Rat**	離 *Li*	丙 *Bing* **Yang Fire**	艮 *Gen*	巽 *Xun*
未 **Goat** (July 7 - Aug 7) 六月 **6th Month**	未 *Wei* **Goat**	丑 *Chou* **Ox**	壬 *Ren* **Yang Water**	乙 *Yi* **Yin Wood**	兌 *Dui*	乾 *Qian*
申 **Monkey** (Aug 8 - Sept 7) 七月 **7th Month**	申 *Shen* **Monkey**	寅 *Yin* **Tiger**	震 *Zhen*	巳 *Si* **Snake**	坎 *Kan*	坤 *Kun*
酉 **Rooster** (Sept 8 - Oct 7) 八月 **8th Month**	酉 *You* **Rooster**	卯 *Mao* **Rabbit**	艮 *Gen*		乾 *Qian*	離 *Li*
戌 **Dog** (Oct 8 - Nov 6) 九月 **9th Month**	戌 *Xu* **Dog**	辰 *Chen* **Dragon**	—		坤 *Kun*	震 *Zhen*
亥 **Pig** (Nov 7 - Dec 6) 十月 **10th Month**	亥 *Hai* **Pig**	巳 *Si* **Snake**	—		巽 *Xun*	艮 *Gen*
子 **Rat** (Dec 7 - Jan 5) 十一月 **11th Month**	子 *Zi* **Rat**	午 *Wu* **Horse**	水 **Water**	山 **Mountain**	乾 *Qian*	兌 *Dui*
丑 **Ox** (Jan 6 - Feb 3) 十二月 **12th Month**	丑 *Chou* **Ox**	未 *Wei* **Goat**	土 **Earth**		坤 *Kun*	坎 *Kan*

Negative Repair / Renovation Sectors 修方凶位 ：

月 MONTH	天官符 Heavenly Officer Charm			地官符 Earth Officer Charm			小月建 Small Month Establishment		
寅 Tiger (Feb 4 - Mar 5) 正月 1st Month		中 Middle		庚 Geng Yang Metal	兌 Dui	辛 Xin Yin Metal		中 Middle	
卯 Rabbit (Mar 6 - Apr 4) 二月 2nd Month	辰 Chen Dragon	巽 Xun	巳 Si Snake	戊 Xu Dog	乾 Qian	亥 Hai Pig	戊 Xu Dog	乾 Qian	亥 Hai Pig
辰 Dragon (Apr 5 - May 5) 三月 3rd Month	甲 Jia Yang Wood	震 Zhen	乙 Yi Yin Wood	辰 Chen Dragon	巽 Xun	巳 Si Snake	庚 Geng Yang Metal	兌 Dui	辛 Xin Yin Metal
巳 Snake (May 6 - Jun 5) 四月 4th Month	未 Wei Goat	坤 Kun	申 Shen Monkey		中 Middle		丑 Chou Ox	艮 Gen	寅 Yin Tiger
午 Horse (Jun 6 - July 6) 五月 5th Month	壬 Ren Yang Water	坎 Kan	癸 Gui Yin Water	庚 Geng Yang Metal	兌 Dui	辛 Xin Yin Metal	丙 Bing Yang Fire	離 Li	丁 Ding Yin Fire
未 Goat (July 7 - Aug 7) 六月 6th Month	丙 Bing Yang Fire	離 Li	丁 Ding Yin Fire	戊 Xu Dog	乾 Qian	亥 Hai Pig	壬 Ren Yang Water	坎 Kan	癸 Gui Yin Water
申 Monkey (Aug 8 - Sept 7) 七月 7th Month	丑 Chou Ox	艮 Gen	寅 Yin Tiger		中 Middle		未 Wei Goat	坤 Kun	申 Shen Monkey
酉 Rooster (Sept 8 - Oct 7) 八月 8th Month	庚 Geng Yang Metal	兌 Dui	辛 Xin Yin Metal	甲 Jia Yang Wood	震 Zhen	乙 Yi Yin Wood	甲 Jia Yang Wood	震 Zhen	乙 Yi Yin Wood
戌 Dog (Oct 8 - Nov 6) 九月 9th Month	戊 Xu Dog	乾 Qian	亥 Hai Pig	未 Wei Goat	坤 Kun	申 Shen Monkey	辰 Chen Dragon	巽 Xun	巳 Si Snake
亥 Pig (Nov 7 - Dec 6) 十月 10th Month		中 Middle		壬 Ren Yang Water	坎 Kan	癸 Gui Yin Water		中 Middle	
子 Rat (Dec 7 - Jan 5) 十一月 11th Month	庚 Geng Yang Metal	兌 Dui	辛 Xin Yin Metal	丙 Bing Yang Fire	離 Li	丁 Ding Yin Fire	戊 Xu Dog	乾 Qian	亥 Hai Pig
丑 Ox (Jan 6 - Feb 3) 十二月 12th Month	戊 Xu Dog	乾 Qian	亥 Hai Pig	丑 Chou Ox	艮 Gen	寅 Yin Tiger	庚 Geng Yang Metal	兌 Dui	辛 Xin Yin Metal

Negative Repair / Renovation Sectors 修方凶位 :

月 MONTH	大月建 Big Month Establishment			飛大煞 Flying Great Sha			丙丁獨火 Bing Ding Lonely Fire	
寅 **Tiger** (Feb 4 - Mar 5) 正月 **1st Month**	丑 *Chou* **Ox**	艮 *Gen*	寅 *Yin* **Tiger**	戌 *Xu* **Dog**	乾 *Qian*	亥 *Hai* **Pig**	坤 *Kun*	震 *Zhen*
卯 **Rabbit** (Mar 6 - Apr 4) 二月 **2nd Month**	庚 *Geng* **Yang Metal**	兌 *Dui*	辛 *Xin* **Yin Metal**	中 **Middle**			坎 *Kan*	坤 *Kun*
辰 **Dragon** (Apr 5 - May 5) 三月 **3rd Month**	戌 *Xu* **Dog**	乾 *Qian*	亥 *Hai* **Pig**	辰 *Chen* **Dragon**	巽 *Xun*	巳 *Si* **Snake**	離 *Li*	坎 *Kan*
巳 **Snake** (May 6 - Jun 5) 四月 **4th Month**	中 **Middle**			甲 *Jia* **Yang Wood**	震 *Zhen*	乙 *Yi* **Yin Wood**	艮 *Gen*	離 *Li*
午 **Horse** (Jun 6 - July 6) 五月 **5th Month**	辰 *Chen* **Dragon**	巽 *Xun*	巳 *Si* **Snake**	未 *Wei* **Goat**	坤 *Kun*	申 *Shen* **Monkey**	兌 *Dui*	艮 *Gen*
未 **Goat** (July 7 - Aug 7) 六月 **6th Month**	甲 *Jia* **Yang Wood**	震 *Zhen*	乙 *Yi* **Yin Wood**	壬 *Ren* **Yang Water**	坎 *Kan*	癸 *Gui* **Yin Water**	乾 *Qian*	兌 *Dui*
申 **Monkey** (Aug 8 - Sept 7) 七月 **7th Month**	未 *Wei* **Goat**	坤 *Kun*	申 *Shen* **Monkey**	丙 *Bing* **Yang Fire**	離 *Li*	丁 *Ding* **Yin Fire**	中 **Middle**	乾 *Qian*
酉 **Rooster** (Sept 8 - Oct 7) 八月 **8th Month**	壬 *Ren* **Yang Water**	坎 *Kan*	癸 *Gui* **Yin Water**	丑 *Chou* **Ox**	艮 *Gen*	寅 *Yin* **Tiger**	中 **Middle**	
戌 **Dog** (Oct 8 - Nov 6) 九月 **9th Month**	丙 *Bing* **Yang Fire**	離 *Li*	丁 *Ding* **Yin Fire**	庚 *Geng* **Yang Metal**	兌 *Dui*	辛 *Xin* **Yin Metal**	巽 *Xun*	中 **Middle**
亥 **Pig** (Nov 7 - Dec 6) 十月 **10th Month**	丑 *Chou* **Ox**	艮 *Gen*	寅 *Yin* **Tiger**	戌 *Xu* **Dog**	乾 *Qian*	亥 *Hai* **Pig**	震 *Zhen*	巽 *Xun*
子 **Rat** (Dec 7 - Jan 5) 十一月 **11th Month**	庚 *Geng* **Yang Metal**	兌 *Dui*	辛 *Xin* **Yin Metal**	中 **Middle**			坤 *Kun*	震 *Zhen*
丑 **Ox** (Jan 6 - Feb 3) 十二月 **12th Month**	戌 *Xu* **Dog**	乾 *Qian*	亥 *Hai* **Pig**	庚 *Geng* **Yang Metal**	兌 *Dui*	辛 *Xin* **Yin Metal**	坎 *Kan*	坤 *Kun*

Negative Repair / Renovation Sectors 修方凶位：

月 MONTH	月遊火 Month Wondering Fire	三煞 Monthly 3 Killings		
		劫煞 Robbery Sha	災煞 Calamity Sha	月煞 Month Sha
寅 **Tiger** (Feb 4 - Mar 5) 正月 **1st Month**	艮 Gen	亥 Hai **Pig**	子 Zi **Rat**	丑 Chou **Ox**
卯 **Rabbit** (Mar 6 - Apr 4) 二月 **2nd Month**	離 Li	申 Shen **Monkey**	酉 You **Rooster**	戌 Xu **Dog**
辰 **Dragon** (Apr 5 - May 5) 三月 **3rd Month**	坎 Kan	巳 Si **Snake**	午 Wu **Horse**	未 Wei **Goat**
巳 **Snake** (May 6 - Jun 5) 四月 **4th Month**	坤 Kun	寅 Yin **Tiger**	卯 Mao **Rabbit**	辰 Chen **Dragon**
午 **Horse** (Jun 6 - July 6) 五月 **5th Month**	震 Zhen	亥 Hai **Pig**	子 Zi **Rat**	丑 Chou **Ox**
未 **Goat** (July 7 - Aug 7) 六月 **6th Month**	巽 Xun	申 Shen **Monkey**	酉 You **Rooster**	戌 Xu **Dog**
申 **Monkey** (Aug 8 - Sept 7) 七月 **7th Month**	中 Middle	巳 Si **Snake**	午 Wu **Horse**	未 Wei **Goat**
酉 **Rooster** (Sept 8 - Oct 7) 八月 **8th Month**	乾 Qian	寅 Yin **Tiger**	卯 Mao **Rabbit**	辰 Chen **Dragon**
戌 **Dog** (Oct 8 - Nov 6) 九月 **9th Month**	兌 Dui	亥 Hai **Pig**	子 Zi **Rat**	丑 Chou **Ox**
亥 **Pig** (Nov 7 - Dec 6) 十月 **10th Month**	艮 Gen	申 Shen **Monkey**	酉 You **Rooster**	戌 Xu **Dog**
子 **Rat** (Dec 7 - Jan 5) 十一月 **11th Month**	離 Li	巳 Si **Snake**	午 Wu **Horse**	未 Wei **Goat**
丑 **Ox** (Jan 6 - Feb 3) 十二月 **12th Month**	坎 Kan	寅 Yin **Tiger**	卯 Mao **Rabbit**	辰 Chen **Dragon**

Negative Repair / Renovation Sectors 修方凶位 ：

月 MONTH	月刑 Month Punishment	月害 Month Harm	月厭 Month Detest
寅 **Tiger** (Feb 4 - Mar 5) 正月 **1st Month**	巳 *Si* Snake	巳 *Si* Snake	戌 *Xu* Dog
卯 **Rabbit** (Mar 6 - Apr 4) 二月 **2nd Month**	子 *Zi* Rat	辰 *Chen* Dragon	酉 *You* Rooster
辰 **Dragon** (Apr 5 - May 5) 三月 **3rd Month**	辰 *Chen* Dragon	卯 *Mao* Rabbit	申 *Shen* Monkey
巳 **Snake** (May 6 - Jun 5) 四月 **4th Month**	申 *Shen* Monkey	寅 *Yin* Tiger	未 *Wei* Goat
午 **Horse** (Jun 6 - July 6) 五月 **5th Month**	午 *Wu* Horse	丑 *Chou* Ox	午 *Wu* Horse
未 **Goat** (July 7 - Aug 7) 六月 **6th Month**	丑 *Chou* Ox	子 *Zi* Rat	巳 *Si* Snake
申 **Monkey** (Aug 8 - Sept 7) 七月 **7th Month**	寅 *Yin* Tiger	亥 *Hai* Pig	辰 *Chen* Dragon
酉 **Rooster** (Sept 8 - Oct 7) 八月 **8th Month**	酉 *You* Rooster	戌 *Xu* Dog	卯 *Mao* Rabbit
戌 **Dog** (Oct 8 - Nov 6) 九月 **9th Month**	未 *Wei* Goat	酉 *You* Rooster	寅 *Yin* Tiger
亥 **Pig** (Nov 7 - Dec 6) 十月 **10th Month**	亥 *Hai* Pig	申 *Shen* Monkey	丑 *Chou* Ox
子 **Rat** (Dec 7 - Jan 5) 十一月 **11th Month**	卯 *Mao* Rabbit	未 *Wei* Goat	子 *Zi* Rat
丑 **Ox** (Jan 6 - Feb 3) 十二月 **12th Month**	戌 *Xu* Dog	午 *Wu* Horse	亥 *Hai* Pig

丙寅 (Bing Yin)
Fire Tiger

丙寅 (Bing Yin) Fire Tiger

Heavenly Stem 天干	丙 Yang Fire (陽火)
Earthly Branch 地支	寅 Tiger (Yang Wood 陽木)
Hidden Stem 藏干	甲 Yang Wood, 丙 Yang Fire, 戊 Yang Earth
Na Yin 納音	爐中火 Fire from the kiln
Grand Duke 太歲	寅 Tiger
Xuan Kong Five Element 玄空五行	2 火 Fire
Gua Name 卦名	☲ 風火家人 Family
Xuan Kong Period Luck 玄空卦運	4

Annual Positive Stars for Opening Mountain, Establishing Facing and Commencing Repairs 開山立向修方吉星:

歲德 Duke Virtue	丙 Bing Yang Fire
歲德合 Duke Virtue Combo	辛 Xin Yin Metal
歲枝德 Duke Branch Virtue	未 Wei Goat
陽貴人 Yang Nobleman	酉 You Rooster
陰貴人 Yin Nobleman	亥 Hai Pig
歲祿 Duke Prosperous	巳 Si Snake
歲馬 Duke Horse	申 Shen Monkey
奏書 Decree	艮 Gen
博士 Professor	坤 Kun

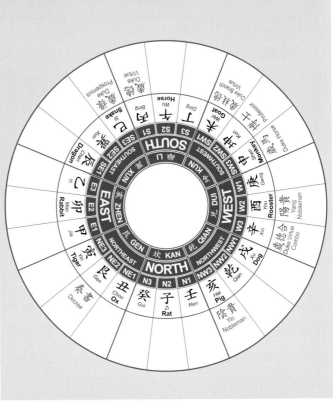

Annual Negative Stars for Opening Mountain, Establishing Facing and Commencing Repairs 開山立向修方凶星：

太歲 Grand Duke	歲破 Year Breaker	三煞 Three Killings			坐煞向煞 Sitting Sha Facing Sha				浮天空亡 Floating Heaven Emptiness	
寅 *Yin* Tiger	申 *Shen* Monkey	亥 *Hai* Pig	子 *Zi* Rat	丑 *Chou* Ox	壬 *Ren* Yang Water	癸 *Gui* Yin Water	丙 *Bing* Yang Fire	丁 *Ding* Yin Fire	巽 *Xun*	辛 *Xin* Yin Metal

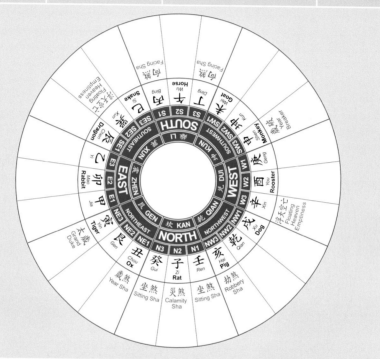

Annual San Yuan Purple White Stars 三元紫白九星：

上元 Upper Period Period 1, 2, 3			中元 Middle Period Period 4, 5, 6			下元 Lower Period Period 7, 8, 9		
巽SE	離S	坤SW	巽SE	離S	坤SW	巽SE	離S	坤SW
7	3	5	1	6	8	4	9	2
震E **6**	**8** 丙寅 *Bing Yin* Fire Tiger	**1** 兌W	震E **9**	**2** 丙寅 *Bing Yin* Fire Tiger	**4** 兌W	震E **3**	**5** 丙寅 *Bing Yin* Fire Tiger	**7** 兌W
艮NE **2**	坎N **4**	乾NW **9**	艮NE **5**	坎N **7**	乾NW **3**	艮NE **8**	坎N **1**	乾NW **6**

Mountain Covering Yellow Path 蓋山黃道：

貪狼 *Tan Lang* **Greedy Wolf**		巨門 *Ju Men* **Huge Door**		武曲 *Wu Qu* **Military Arts**				文曲 *Wen Qu* **Literary Arts**			
艮 *Gen* NE2	丙 *Bing* S1	巽 *Xun* SE2	辛 *Xin* W3	兌 *Dui* W2	丁 *Ding* S3	巳 *Si* SE3	丑 *Chou* NE1	離 *Li* S2	壬 *Ren* N1	寅 *Yin* NE3	戌 *Xu* NW1

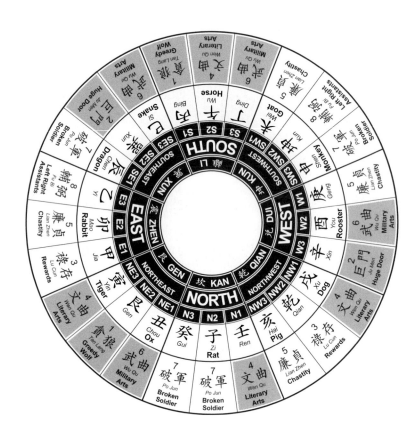

Heaven Penetrating Force 通天竅 :

三合前方 Facing Three Harmony	坤申 Kun Shen	庚酉 Geng You	辛戌 Xin Xu
三合後方 Sitting Three Harmony	艮寅 Gen Yin	甲卯 Jia Mao	乙辰 Yi Chen

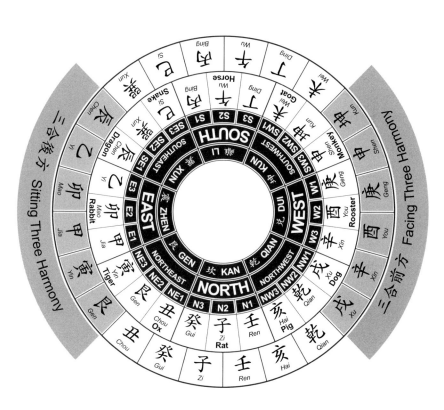

Moving Horse Six Ren Assessment 走馬六壬：

神后 Shen Hou **Holy Empress**	功曹 Gong Cao **Marshall**	天罡 Tian Gang **Heavenly Dipper**	勝光 Sheng Guang **Subliminal Bright**	傳送 Chuan Song **Great General**	河魁 He Kui **River Scholar**
辛戌 Xin Xu	壬子 Ren Zi	艮寅 Gen Yin	乙辰 Yi Chen	丙午 Bing Wu	坤申 Kun Shen

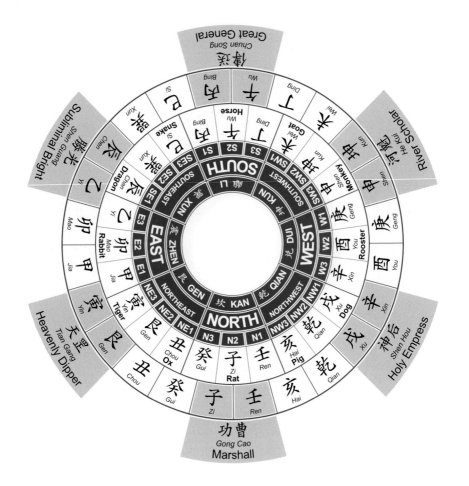

Four Advantages Three Cycles Star Plate 四利三元：

太陽 Tai Yang **Sun**	太陰 Tai Yin **Moon**	龍德 Long De **Dragon Virtue**	福德 Fu De **Fortune Virtue**
卯 Mao **Rabbit**	巳 Si **Snake**	酉 You **Rooster**	亥 Hai **Pig**

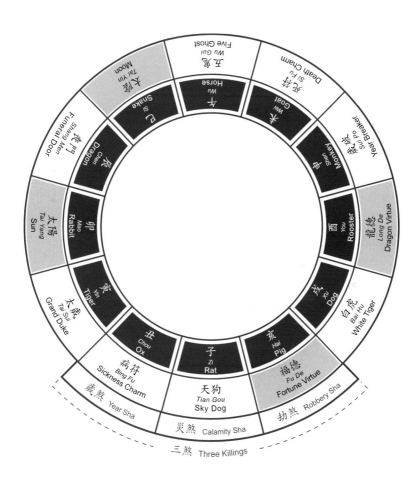

Negative Sectors For Opening Mountain 開山凶位:

年剋山家 Year Countering Sitting

震 Zhen E2	艮 Gen NE2	巳 Si SE3

陰府太歲 Yin Fu Tai Sui **Yin Mansion Grand Duke**	六害 Liu Hai **Six Harm**	死符 Si Fu **Death Charm**	炙退 Zhi Tui **Roasting Star**
坎 Kan N2 / 坤 Kun SW2	巳 Si SE3	未 Wei SW1	酉 You W2

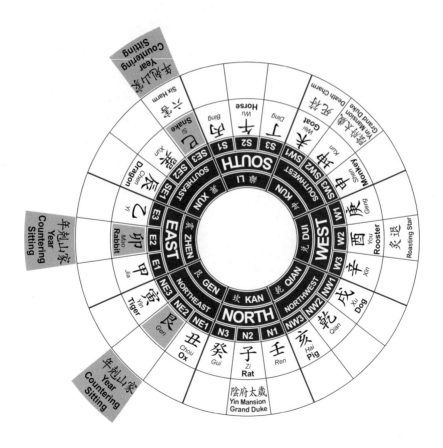

Negative Directions to Establish Facing 立向凶方：

巡山羅喉 *Xun Shan Luo Hou* **Mountain Patrol Luo Hou Star**	病符 *Bing Fu* **Sickness Charm**
甲 *Jia* **E1**	丑 *Chou* **NE1**

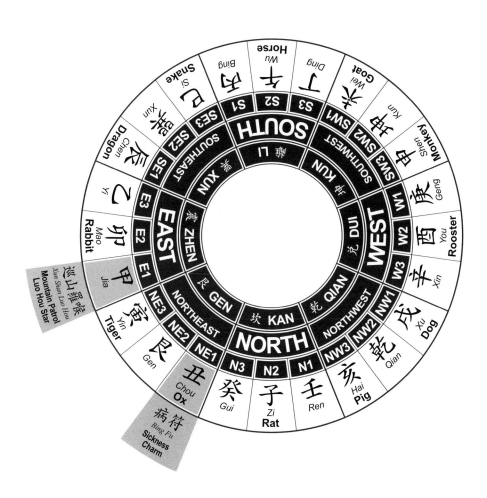

Negative Repair / Renovation Sectors Table 修方凶位表：

天官符 **Heavenly Officer Charm**	巳 *Si* Snake	飛廉 **Flying Chaste**	戌 *Xu* Dog
地官符 **Earthly Officer Charm**	午 *Wu* Horse	喪門 **Funeral Door**	辰 *Chen* Dragon
大煞 **Great Sha**	午 *Wu* Horse	弔客 **Suspended Guest**	子 *Zi* Rat
大將軍 **Big General**	子 *Zi* Rat	白虎 **White Tiger**	戌 *Xu* Dog
力士 **Strong Man**	巽 *Xun*	金神 **Golden God**	寅 *Yin* Tiger 卯 *Mao* Rabbit 午 *Wu* Horse 未 *Wei* Goat 子 *Zi* Rat 丑 *Chou* Ox
蠶室 **Silkworm Room**	乾 *Qian*		
蠶官 **Silkworm Officer**	戌 *Xu* Dog		
蠶命 **Silkworm Life**	亥 *Hai* Pig		
歲刑 **Duke Punishment**	巳 *Si* Snake	獨火 **Lonely Fire**	震 *Zhen*
黃幡 **Yellow Flag**	戌 *Xu* Dog	五鬼 **Five Ghost**	寅 *Yin* Tiger
豹尾 **Leopard Tail**	辰 *Chen* Dragon	破敗五鬼 **Destructive Five Ghost**	坤 *Kun*

Negative Repair / Renovation Sectors Diagram 修方凶位圖：

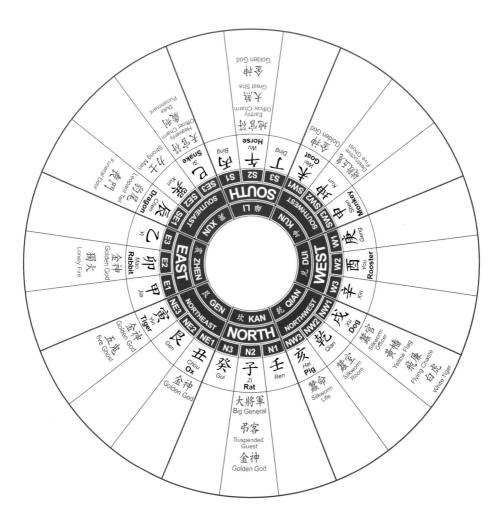

12-Month Auxiliary Stars Reference Table :
丙寅年十二月，開山立向修方星表

Positive Monthly Stars 吉星方

月 MONTH	寅 Tiger (Feb 4 - Mar 5) 正月 1st Month	卯 Rabbit (Mar 6 - Apr 4) 二月 2nd Month	辰 Dragon (Apr 5 - May 5) 三月 3rd Month	巳 Snake (May 6 - Jun 5) 四月 4th Month	午 Horse (Jun 6 - July 6) 五月 5th Month	未 Goat (July 7 - Aug 7) 六月 6th Month
天道 Heavenly Path	南 South	西南 Southwest	北 North	西 West	西北 Northwest	東 East
天德 Heavenly Virtue	丁 Ding Yin Fire	坤 Kun (申)	壬 Ren Yang Water	辛 Xin Yin Metal	乾 Qian (亥)	甲 Jia Yang Wood
天德合 Heavenly Virtue Combo	壬 Ren Yang Water	(巳)	丁 Ding Yin Fire	丙 Bing Yang Fire	(寅)	己 Ji Yin Earth
月德 Monthly Virtue	丙 Bing Yang Fire	甲 Jia Yang Wood	壬 Ren Yang Water	庚 Geng Yang Metal	丙 Bing Yang Fire	甲 Jia Yang Wood
月德合 Monthly Virtue Combo	辛 Xin Yin Metal	己 Ji Yin Earth	丁 Ding Yin Fire	乙 Yi Yin Wood	辛 Xin Yin Metal	己 Ji Yin Earth
月空 Month Emptiness	壬 Ren Yang Water	庚 Geng Yang Metal	丙 Bing Yang Fire	甲 Jia Yang Wood	壬 Ren Yang Water	庚 Geng Yang Metal
陽貴人 Yang Nobleman	震 Zhen	坤 Kun	坎 Kan	離 Li	艮 Gen	兌 Dui
陰貴人 Yin Nobleman	中 Middle	巽 Xun	震 Zhen	坤 Kun	坎 Kan	離 Li
飛天祿 Flying Heavenly Wealth	艮 Gen	兌 Dui	乾 Qian	中 Middle	坎 Kan	離 Li
飛天馬 Flying Heavenly Horse	坤 Kun	坎 Kan	離 Li	艮 Gen	兌 Dui	乾 Qian

12-Month Auxiliary Stars Reference Table :
丙寅年十二月，開山立向修方星表

申 Monkey (Aug 8 - Sept 7) 七月 **7th Month**	酉 Rooster (Sept 8 - Oct 7) 八月 **8th Month**	戌 Dog (Oct 8 - Nov 6) 九月 **9th Month**	亥 Pig (Nov 7 - Dec 6) 十月 **10th Month**	子 Rat (Dec 7 - Jan 5) 十一月 **11th Month**	丑 Ox (Jan 6 - Feb 3) 十二月 **12th Month**	月 **MONTH**
北 North	東北 Northeast	南 South	東 East	東南 Southeast	西 West	天道 **Heavenly Path**
癸 *Gui* Yin Water	艮 *Gen* (寅)	丙 *Bing* Yang Fire	乙 *Yi* Yin Wood	巽 *Xun* (巳)	庚 *Geng* Yang Metal	天德 **Heavenly Virtue**
戊 *Wu* Yang Earth	(亥)	辛 *Xin* Yin Metal	庚 *Geng* Yang Metal	(申)	乙 *Yi* Yin Wood	天德合 **Heavenly Virtue Combo**
壬 *Ren* Yang Water	庚 *Geng* Yang Metal	丙 *Bing* Yang Fire	甲 *Jia* Yang Wood	壬 *Ren* Yang Water	庚 *Geng* Yang Metal	月德 **Monthly Virtue**
丁 *Ding* Yin Fire	乙 *Yi* Yin Wood	辛 *Xin* Yin Metal	己 *Ji* Yin Earth	丁 *Ding* Yin Fire	乙 *Yi* Yin Wood	月德合 **Monthly Virtue Combo**
丙 *Bing* Yang Fire	甲 *Jia* Yang Wood	壬 *Ren* Yang Water	庚 *Geng* Yang Metal	丙 *Bing* Yang Fire	甲 *Jia* Yang Wood	月空 **Month Emptiness**
乾 *Qian*	中 Middle	坎 *Kan*	離 *Li*	艮 *Gen*	兌 *Dui*	陽貴人 **Yang Nobleman**
艮 *Gen*	兌 *Dui*	乾 *Qian*	中 Middle	坎 *Kan*	離 *Li*	陰貴人 **Yin Nobleman**
艮 *Gen*	兌 *Dui*	乾 *Qian*	中 Middle	巽 *Xun*	震 *Zhen*	飛天祿 **Flying Heavenly Wealth**
中 Middle	坎 *Kan*	離 *Li*	艮 *Gen*	兌 *Dui*	乾 *Qian*	飛天馬 **Flying Heavenly Horse**

Monthly Purple White Stars 月紫白九星 :

寅 Tiger (Feb 4 - Mar 5) 正月 1st Month

巽 SE	離 S	坤 SW
1 White 一白	6 White 六白	8 White 八白
震 E 9 Purple 九紫	2 Black 二黑	4 Green 四綠 兌 W
艮 NE 5 Yellow 五黃	坎 N 7 Red 七赤	乾 NW 3 Jade 三碧

卯 Rabbit (Mar 6 - Apr 4) 二月 2nd Month

巽 SE	離 S	坤 SW
9 Purple 九紫	5 Yellow 五黃	7 Red 七赤
震 E 8 White 八白	1 White 一白	3 Jade 三碧 兌 W
艮 NE 4 Green 四綠	坎 N 6 White 六白	乾 NW 2 Black 二黑

辰 Dragon (Apr 5 - May 5) 三月 3rd Month

巽 SE	離 S	坤 SW
8 White 八白	4 Green 四綠	6 White 六白
震 E 7 Red 七赤	9 Purple 九紫	2 Black 二黑 兌 W
艮 NE 3 Jade 三碧	坎 N 5 Yellow 五黃	乾 NW 1 White 一白

巳 Snake (May 6 - Jun 5) 四月 4th Month

巽 SE	離 S	坤 SW
7 Red 七赤	3 Jade 三碧	5 Yellow 五黃
震 E 6 White 六白	8 White 八白	1 White 一白 兌 W
艮 NE 2 Black 二黑	坎 N 4 Green 四綠	乾 NW 9 Purple 九紫

午 Horse (Jun 6 - July 6) 五月 5th Month

巽 SE	離 S	坤 SW
6 White 六白	2 Black 二黑	4 Green 四綠
震 E 5 Yellow 五黃	7 Red 七赤	9 Purple 九紫 兌 W
艮 NE 1 White 一白	坎 N 3 Jade 三碧	乾 NW 8 White 八白

未 Goat (July 7 - Aug 7) 六月 6th Month

巽 SE	離 S	坤 SW
5 Yellow 五黃	1 White 一白	3 Jade 三碧
震 E 4 Green 四綠	6 White 六白	8 White 八白 兌 W
艮 NE 9 Purple 九紫	坎 N 2 Black 二黑	乾 NW 7 Red 七赤

申 Monkey (Aug 8 - Sept 7) 七月 7th Month

巽 SE	離 S	坤 SW
4 Green 四綠	9 Purple 九紫	2 Black 二黑
震 E 3 Jade 三碧	5 Yellow 五黃	7 Red 七赤 兌 W
艮 NE 8 White 八白	坎 N 1 White 一白	乾 NW 6 White 六白

酉 Rooster (Sept 8 - Oct 7) 八月 8th Month

巽 SE	離 S	坤 SW
3 Jade 三碧	8 White 八白	1 White 一白
震 E 2 Black 二黑	4 Green 四綠	6 White 六白 兌 W
艮 NE 7 Red 七赤	坎 N 9 Purple 九紫	乾 NW 5 Yellow 五黃

戌 Dog (Oct 8 - Nov 6) 九月 9th Month

巽 SE	離 S	坤 SW
2 Black 二黑	7 Red 七赤	9 Purple 九紫
震 E 1 White 一白	3 Jade 三碧	5 Yellow 五黃 兌 W
艮 NE 6 White 六白	坎 N 8 White 八白	乾 NW 4 Green 四綠

亥 Pig (Nov 7 - Dec 6) 十月 10th Month

巽 SE	離 S	坤 SW
1 White 一白	6 White 六白	8 White 八白
震 E 9 Purple 九紫	2 Black 二黑	4 Green 四綠 兌 W
艮 NE 5 Yellow 五黃	坎 N 7 Red 七赤	乾 NW 3 Jade 三碧

子 Rat (Dec 7 - Jan 5) 十一月 11th Month

巽 SE	離 S	坤 SW
9 Purple 九紫	5 Yellow 五黃	7 Red 七赤
震 E 8 White 八白	1 White 一白	3 Jade 三碧 兌 W
艮 NE 4 Green 四綠	坎 N 6 White 六白	乾 NW 2 Black 二黑

丑 Ox (Jan 6 - Feb 3) 十二月 12th Month

巽 SE	離 S	坤 SW
8 White 八白	4 Green 四綠	6 White 六白
震 E 7 Red 七赤	9 Purple 九紫	2 Black 二黑 兌 W
艮 NE 3 Jade 三碧	坎 N 5 Yellow 五黃	乾 NW 1 White 一白

Qi Men Three Nobles 三奇 :

Three Nobles 三奇 / Seasons	乙 Yi	丙 Bing	丁 Ding
立春 **Coming of Spring** Feb 4 - Feb 18	乾 Qian	兌 Dui	艮 Gen
春分 **Spring Equinox** Mar 21 - Apr 4	坎 Kan	坤 Kun	震 Zhen
立夏 **Coming of Summer** May 6 - May 20	坤 Kun	震 Zhen	巽 Xun
夏至 **Summer Solstice** Jun 22 - Jul 6	坤 Kun	坎 Kan	離 Li
立秋 **Coming of Autumn** Aug 8 - Aug 23	巽 Xun	震 Zhen	坤 Kun
秋分 **Autumn Equinox** Sept 23 - Oct 7	離 Li	艮 Gen	兌 Dui
立冬 **Coming of Winter** Nov 7 - Nov 22	艮 Gen	兌 Dui	乾 Qian
冬至 **Winter Solstice** Dec 22 - Jan 5	艮 Gen	離 Li	坎 Kan

Sectors to Avoid Opening Mountain 開山凶位 :

月 MONTH	月建 Month Establishment	月破 Month Destruction	月剋山家 Month Countering Sitting	陰府太歲 Yin Mansion Grand Duke	
寅 Tiger (Feb 4 - Mar 5) 正月 1st Month	寅 Yin Tiger	申 Shen Monkey	—	乾 Qian	兌 Dui
卯 Rabbit (Mar 6 - Apr 4) 二月 2nd Month	卯 Mao Rabbit	酉 You Rooster	—	坤 Kun	坎 Kan
辰 Dragon (Apr 5 - May 5) 三月 3rd Month	辰 Chen Dragon	戌 Xu Dog	乾 兌 Qian Dui	離 Li	乾 Qian
巳 Snake (May 6 - Jun 5) 四月 4th Month	巳 Si Snake	亥 Hai Pig	亥 丁 Hai Ding Pig Yin Fire	震 Zhen	坤 Kun
午 Horse (Jun 6 - July 6) 五月 5th Month	午 Wu Horse	子 Zi Rat	離 丙 Li Bing Yang Fire	艮 Gen	巽 Xun
未 Goat (July 7 - Aug 7) 六月 6th Month	未 Wei Goat	丑 Chou Ox	壬 乙 Ren Yi Yang Water Yin Wood	兌 Dui	乾 Qian
申 Monkey (Aug 8 - Sept 7) 七月 7th Month	申 Shen Monkey	寅 Yin Tiger	震 巳 Zhen Si Snake	坎 Kan	坤 Kun
酉 Rooster (Sept 8 - Oct 7) 八月 8th Month	酉 You Rooster	卯 Mao Rabbit	艮 Gen	乾 Qian	離 Li
戌 Dog (Oct 8 - Nov 6) 九月 9th Month	戌 Xu Dog	辰 Chen Dragon	—	坤 Kun	震 Zhen
亥 Pig (Nov 7 - Dec 6) 十月 10th Month	亥 Hai Pig	巳 Si Snake	—	巽 Xun	艮 Gen
子 Rat (Dec 7 - Jan 5) 十一月 11th Month	子 Zi Rat	午 Wu Horse	水 山 Water Mountain	乾 Qian	兌 Dui
丑 Ox (Jan 6 - Feb 3) 十二月 12th Month	丑 Chou Ox	未 Wei Goat	土 Earth	坤 Kun	坎 Kan

Negative Repair / Renovation Sectors 修方凶位 :

月 MONTH	天官符 Heavenly Officer Charm			地官符 Earth Officer Charm			小月建 Small Month Establishment		
寅 **Tiger** (Feb 4 - Mar 5) 正月 **1st Month**	丑 Chou Ox	艮 Gen	寅 Yin Tiger	丙 Bing Yang Fire	離 Li	丁 Ding Yin Fire	中 Middle		
卯 **Rabbit** (Mar 6 - Apr 4) 二月 **2nd Month**	庚 Geng Yang Metal	兌 Dui	辛 Xin Yin Metal	丑 Chou Ox	艮 Gen	寅 Yin Tiger	戌 Xu Dog	乾 Qian	亥 Hai Pig
辰 **Dragon** (Apr 5 - May 5) 三月 **3rd Month**	戌 Xu Dog	乾 Qian	亥 Hai Pig	庚 Geng Yang Metal	兌 Dui	辛 Xin Yin Metal	庚 Geng Yang Metal	兌 Dui	辛 Xin Yin Metal
巳 **Snake** (May 6 - Jun 5) 四月 **4th Month**	中 Middle			戌 Xu Dog	乾 Qian	亥 Hai Pig	丑 Chou Ox	艮 Gen	寅 Yin Tiger
午 **Horse** (Jun 6 - July 6) 五月 **5th Month**	庚 Geng Yang Metal	兌 Dui	辛 Xin Yin Metal	中 Middle			丙 Bing Yang Fire	離 Li	丁 Ding Yin Fire
未 **Goat** (July 7 - Aug 7) 六月 **6th Month**	戌 Xu Dog	乾 Qian	亥 Hai Pig	庚 Geng Yang Metal	兌 Dui	辛 Xin Yin Metal	壬 Ren Yang Water	坎 Kan	癸 Gui Yin Water
申 **Monkey** (Aug 8 - Sept 7) 七月 **7th Month**	中 Middle			戌 Xu Dog	乾 Qian	亥 Hai Pig	未 Wei Goat	坤 Kun	申 Shen Monkey
酉 **Rooster** (Sept 8 - Oct 7) 八月 **8th Month**	辰 Chen Dragon	巽 Xun	巳 Si Snake	中 Middle			甲 Jia Yang Wood	震 Zhen	乙 Yi Yin Wood
戌 **Dog** (Oct 8 - Nov 6) 九月 **9th Month**	甲 Jia Yang Wood	震 Zhen	乙 Yi Yin Wood	辰 Chen Dragon	巽 Xun	巳 Si Snake	辰 Chen Dragon	巽 Xun	巳 Si Snake
亥 **Pig** (Nov 7 - Dec 6) 十月 **10th Month**	未 Wei Goat	坤 Kun	申 Shen Monkey	甲 Jia Yang Wood	震 Zhen	乙 Yi Yin Wood	中 Middle		
子 **Rat** (Dec 7 - Jan 5) 十一月 **11th Month**	壬 Ren Yang Water	坎 Kan	癸 Gui Yin Water	未 Wei Goat	坤 Kun	申 Shen Monkey	戌 Xu Dog	乾 Qian	亥 Hai Pig
丑 **Ox** (Jan 6 - Feb 3) 十二月 **12th Month**	丙 Bing Yang Fire	離 Li	丁 Ding Yin Fire	壬 Ren Yang Water	坎 Kan	癸 Gui Yin Water	庚 Geng Yang Metal	兌 Dui	辛 Xin Yin Metal

丙寅 (Bing Yin) Fire Tiger

Negative Repair / Renovation Sectors 修方凶位 :

月 MONTH	大月建 Big Month Establishment			飛大煞 Flying Great Sha			丙丁獨火 Bing Ding Lonely Fire	
寅 **Tiger** (Feb 4 - Mar 5) 正月 **1st Month**	未 *Wei* Goat	坤 *Kun*	申 *Shen* Monkey	丙 *Bing* Yang Fire	離 *Li*	丁 *Ding* Yin Fire	坤 *Kun*	震 *Zhen*
卯 **Rabbit** (Mar 6 - Apr 4) 二月 **2nd Month**	壬 *Ren* Yang Water	坎 *Kan*	癸 *Gui* Yin Water	丑 *Chou* Ox	艮 *Gen*	寅 *Yin* Tiger	坎 *Kan*	坤 *Kun*
辰 **Dragon** (Apr 5 - May 5) 三月 **3rd Month**	丙 *Bing* Yang Fire	離 *Li*	丁 *Ding* Yin Fire	庚 *Geng* Yang Metal	兌 *Dui*	辛 *Xin* Yin Metal	離 *Li*	坎 *Kan*
巳 **Snake** (May 6 - Jun 5) 四月 **4th Month**	丑 *Chou* Ox	艮 *Gen*	寅 *Yin* Tiger	戌 *Xu* Dog	乾 *Qian*	亥 *Hai* Pig	艮 *Gen*	離 *Li*
午 **Horse** (Jun 6 - July 6) 五月 **5th Month**	庚 *Geng* Yang Metal	兌 *Dui*	辛 *Xin* Yin Metal	中 Middle			兌 *Dui*	艮 *Gen*
未 **Goat** (July 7 - Aug 7) 六月 **6th Month**	戌 *Xu* Dog	乾 *Qian*	亥 *Hai* Pig	庚 *Geng* Yang Metal	兌 *Dui*	辛 *Xin* Yin Metal	乾 *Qian*	兌 *Dui*
申 **Monkey** (Aug 8 - Sept 7) 七月 **7th Month**		中 Middle		戌 *Xu* Dog	乾 *Qian*	亥 *Hai* Pig	中 Middle	乾 *Qian*
酉 **Rooster** (Sept 8 - Oct 7) 八月 **8th Month**	辰 *Chen* Dragon	巽 *Xun*	巳 *Si* Snake	中 Middle			中 Middle	
戌 **Dog** (Oct 8 - Nov 6) 九月 **9th Month**	甲 *Jia* Yang Wood	震 *Zhen*	乙 *Yi* Yin Wood	辰 *Chen* Dragon	巽 *Xun*	巳 *Si* Snake	巽 *Xun*	中 Middle
亥 **Pig** (Nov 7 - Dec 6) 十月 **10th Month**	未 *Wei* Goat	坤 *Kun*	申 *Shen* Monkey	甲 *Jia* Yang Wood	震 *Zhen*	乙 *Yi* Yin Wood	震 *Zhen*	巽 *Xun*
子 **Rat** (Dec 7 - Jan 5) 十一月 **11th Month**	壬 *Ren* Yang Water	坎 *Kan*	癸 *Gui* Yin Water	未 *Wei* Goat	坤 *Kun*	申 *Shen* Monkey	坤 *Kun*	震 *Zhen*
丑 **Ox** (Jan 6 - Feb 3) 十二月 **12th Month**	丙 *Bing* Yang Fire	離 *Li*	丁 *Ding* Yin Fire	壬 *Ren* Yang Water	坎 *Kan*	癸 *Gui* Yin Water	坎 *Kan*	坤 *Kun*

Negative Repair / Renovation Sectors 修方凶位：

月 MONTH	月遊火 Month Wondering Fire	三煞 Monthly 3 Killings		
		劫煞 Robbery Sha	災煞 Calamity Sha	月煞 Month Sha
寅 Tiger (Feb 4 - Mar 5) 正月 1st Month	震 Zhen	亥 Hai Pig	子 Zi Rat	丑 Chou Ox
卯 Rabbit (Mar 6 - Apr 4) 二月 2nd Month	巽 Xun	申 Shen Monkey	酉 You Rooster	戌 Xu Dog
辰 Dragon (Apr 5 - May 5) 三月 3rd Month	中 Middle	巳 Si Snake	午 Wu Horse	未 Wei Goat
巳 Snake (May 6 - Jun 5) 四月 4th Month	乾 Qian	寅 Yin Tiger	卯 Mao Rabbit	辰 Chen Dragon
午 Horse (Jun 6 - July 6) 五月 5th Month	兌 Dui	亥 Hai Pig	子 Zi Rat	丑 Chou Ox
未 Goat (July 7 - Aug 7) 六月 6th Month	艮 Gen	申 Shen Monkey	酉 You Rooster	戌 Xu Dog
申 Monkey (Aug 8 - Sept 7) 七月 7th Month	離 Li	巳 Si Snake	午 Wu Horse	未 Wei Goat
酉 Rooster (Sept 8 - Oct 7) 八月 8th Month	坎 Kan	寅 Yin Tiger	卯 Mao Rabbit	辰 Chen Dragon
戌 Dog (Oct 8 - Nov 6) 九月 9th Month	坤 Kun	亥 Hai Pig	子 Zi Rat	丑 Chou Ox
亥 Pig (Nov 7 - Dec 6) 十月 10th Month	震 Zhen	申 Shen Monkey	酉 You Rooster	戌 Xu Dog
子 Rat (Dec 7 - Jan 5) 十一月 11th Month	巽 Xun	巳 Si Snake	午 Wu Horse	未 Wei Goat
丑 Ox (Jan 6 - Feb 3) 十二月 12th Month	中 Middle	寅 Yin Tiger	卯 Mao Rabbit	辰 Chen Dragon

Negative Repair / Renovation Sectors 修方凶位 ：

月 MONTH	月刑 Month Punishment	月害 Month Harm	月厭 Month Detest
寅 Tiger (Feb 4 - Mar 5) 正月 1st Month	巳 Si Snake	巳 Si Snake	戌 Xu Dog
卯 Rabbit (Mar 6 - Apr 4) 二月 2nd Month	子 Zi Rat	辰 Chen Dragon	酉 You Rooster
辰 Dragon (Apr 5 - May 5) 三月 3rd Month	辰 Chen Dragon	卯 Mao Rabbit	申 Shen Monkey
巳 Snake (May 6 - Jun 5) 四月 4th Month	申 Shen Monkey	寅 Yin Tiger	未 Wei Goat
午 Horse (Jun 6 - July 6) 五月 5th Month	午 Wu Horse	丑 Chou Ox	午 Wu Horse
未 Goat (July 7 - Aug 7) 六月 6th Month	丑 Chou Ox	子 Zi Rat	巳 Si Snake
申 Monkey (Aug 8 - Sept 7) 七月 7th Month	寅 Yin Tiger	亥 Hai Pig	辰 Chen Dragon
酉 Rooster (Sept 8 - Oct 7) 八月 8th Month	酉 You Rooster	戌 Xu Dog	卯 Mao Rabbit
戌 Dog (Oct 8 - Nov 6) 九月 9th Month	未 Wei Goat	酉 You Rooster	寅 Yin Tiger
亥 Pig (Nov 7 - Dec 6) 十月 10th Month	亥 Hai Pig	申 Shen Monkey	丑 Chou Ox
子 Rat (Dec 7 - Jan 5) 十一月 11th Month	卯 Mao Rabbit	未 Wei Goat	子 Zi Rat
丑 Ox (Jan 6 - Feb 3) 十二月 12th Month	戌 Xu Dog	午 Wu Horse	亥 Hai Pig

丙辰 (Bing Chen)
Fire Dragon

Heavenly Stem 天干	丙 Yang Fire (陽火)
Earthly Branch 地支	辰 Dragon (Yang Earth 陽土)
Hidden Stem 藏干	戊 Yang Earth, 乙 Yin Wood, 癸 Yin Water
Na Yin 納音	沙中土 Earth from the sand
Grand Duke 太歲	辰 Dragon
Xuan Kong Five Element 玄空五行	4 金 Metal
Gua Name 卦名	兌爲澤 Marsh
Xuan Kong Period Luck 玄空卦運	1

Annual Positive Stars for Opening Mountain, Establishing Facing and Commencing Repairs 開山立向修方吉星：

歲德 Duke Virtue	丙 Bing Yang Fire	
歲德合 Duke Virtue Combo	辛 Xin Yin Metal	
歲枝德 Duke Branch Virtue	酉 You Rooster	
陽貴人 Yang Nobleman	酉 You Rooster	
陰貴人 Yin Nobleman	亥 Hai Pig	
歲祿 Duke Prosperous	巳 Si Snake	
歲馬 Duke Horse	寅 Yin Tiger	
奏書 Decree	艮 Gen	
博士 Professor	坤 Kun	

Annual Negative Stars for Opening Mountain, Establishing Facing and Commencing Repairs 開山立向修方凶星：

太歲 Grand Duke	歲破 Year Breaker	三煞 Three Killings			坐煞向煞 Sitting Sha Facing Sha				浮天空亡 Floating Heaven Emptiness	
辰 Chen Dragon	午 Wu Horse	巳 Si Snake	午 Wu Horse	未 Wei Goat	丙 Bing Yang Fire	丁 Ding Yin Fire	壬 Ren Yang Water	癸 Gui Yin Water	巽 Xun	辛 Xin Yin Metal

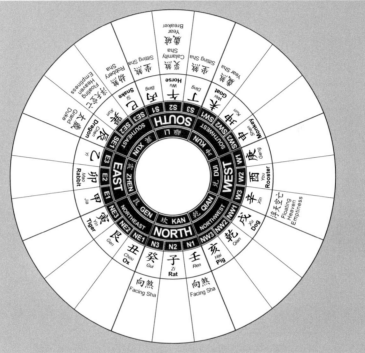

Annual San Yuan Purple White Stars 三元紫白九星：

上元 Upper Period Period 1, 2, 3	中元 Middle Period Period 4, 5, 6	下元 Lower Period Period 7, 8, 9

上元 Upper Period — Period 1, 2, 3

巽SE	離S	坤SW
2	7	9
震E 1	3 丙辰 Bing Chen Fire Dragon	兌W 5
6	8	4
艮NE	坎N	乾NW

中元 Middle Period — Period 4, 5, 6

巽SE	離S	坤SW
5	1	3
震E 4	6 丙辰 Bing Chen Fire Dragon	兌W 8
9	2	7
艮NE	坎N	乾NW

下元 Lower Period — Period 7, 8, 9

巽SE	離S	坤SW
8	4	6
震E 7	9 丙辰 Bing Chen Fire Dragon	兌W 2
3	5	1
艮NE	坎N	乾NW

Mountain Covering Yellow Path 蓋山黃道：

貪狼 *Tan Lang* **Greedy Wolf**				巨門 *Ju Men* **Huge Door**				武曲 *Wu Qu* **Military Arts**		文曲 *Wen Qu* **Literary Arts**			
兌	丁	巳	丑	震	庚	亥	未	艮	丙	坎	癸	申	辰
Duin	*Ding*	*Si*	*Chou*	*Zhen*	*Geng*	*Hai*	*Wei*	*Gen*	*Bing*	*Kan*	*Gui*	*Shen*	*Chen*
W2	S3	SE3	NE1	E2	W1	NW3	SW1	NE	S1	N2	N3	SW3	SE1

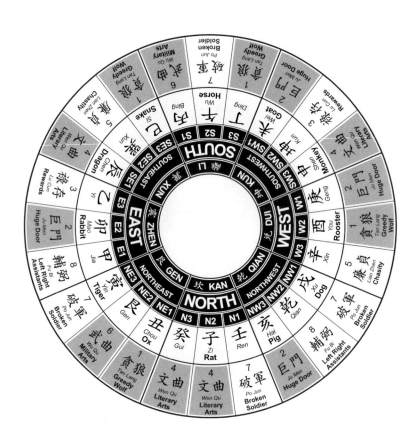

Heaven Penetrating Force 通天竅：

三合前方 **Facing Three Harmony**	艮寅 Gen Yin	甲卯 Jia Mao	乙辰 Yi Chen
三合後方 **Sitting Three Harmony**	坤申 Kun Shen	庚酉 Geng You	辛戌 Xin Xu

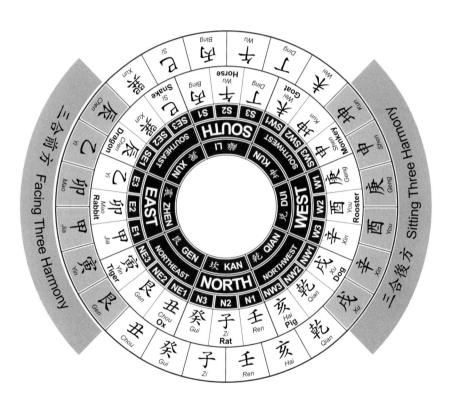

丙辰 (Bing Chen) Fire Dragon

神后 Shen Hou Holy Empress	功曹 Gong Cao Marshall	天罡 Tian Gang Heavenly Dipper	勝光 Sheng Guang Subliminal Bright	傳送 Chuan Song Great General	河魁 He Kui River Scholar
Moving Horse Six Ren Assessment 走馬六壬：					
坤申 Kun Shen	辛戌 Xin Xu	壬子 Ren Zi	艮寅 Gen Yin	乙辰 Yi Chen	丙午 Bing Wu

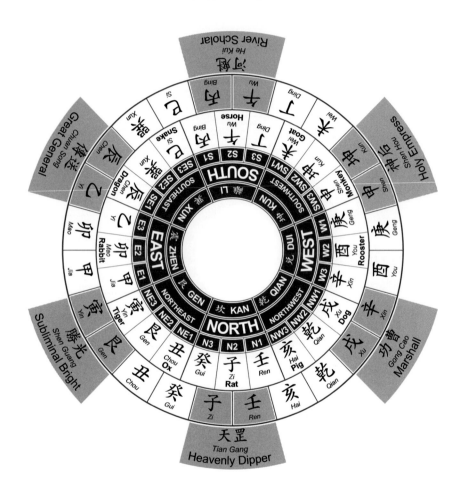

Four Advantages Three Cycles Star Plate 四利三元：

太陽 *Tai Yang* **Sun**	太陰 *Tai Yin* **Moon**	龍德 *Long De* **Dragon Virtue**	福德 *Fu De* **Fortune Virtue**
巳 *Si* **Snake**	未 *Wei* **Goat**	亥 *Hai* **Pig**	丑 *Chou* **Ox**

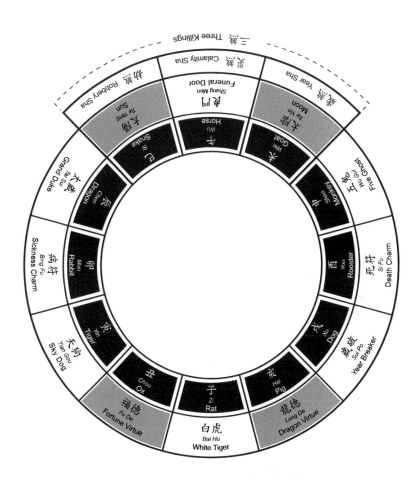

丙辰 (Bing Chen) Fire Dragon

Negative Sectors For Opening Mountain 開山凶位：

年剋山家 Year Countering Sitting

乾	亥	兌	丁
Qian	Hai	Dui	Ding
NW2	NW3	W2	S3

陰府太歲	六害	死符	炙退
Yin Fu Tai Sui	Liu Hai	Si Fu	Zhi Tui
Yin Mansion Grand Duke	**Six Harm**	**Death Charm**	**Roasting Star**

離	乾	未	巳	卯
Li	Qian	Wei	Si	Mao
S2	NW2	SW1	SE3	E2

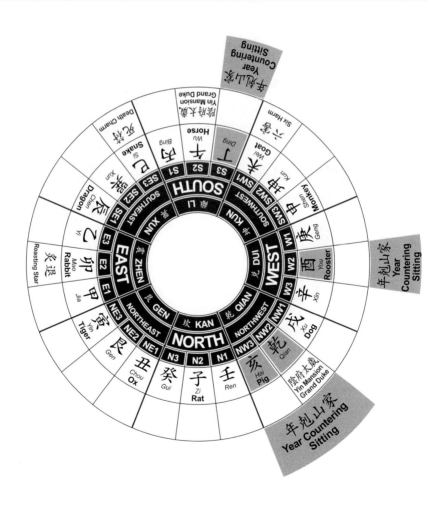

288

Negative Directions to Establish Facing 立向凶方：	
巡山羅喉 *Xun Shan Luo Hou* **Mountain Patrol Luo Hou Star**	病符 *Bing Fu* **Sickness Charm**
癸 *Gui* **N3**	亥 *Hai* **NW3**

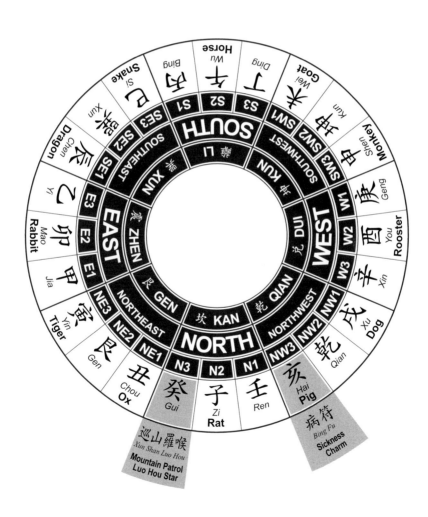

Negative Repair / Renovation Sectors Table 修方凶位表:

天官符 Heavenly Officer Charm	亥 *Hai* Pig		飛廉 Flying Chaste	申 *Shen* Monkey
地官符 Earthly Officer Charm	辰 *Chen* Dragon		喪門 Funeral Door	寅 *Yin* Tiger
大煞 Great Sha	子 *Zi* Rat		弔客 Suspended Guest	戌 *Xu* Dog
大將軍 Big General	酉 *You* Rooster		白虎 White Tiger	申 *Shen* Monkey
力士 Strong Man	艮 *Gen*		金神 Golden God	寅 *Yin* Tiger 卯 *Mao* Rabbit 戌 *Xu* Dog 亥 *Hai* Pig
蠶室 Silkworm Room	坤 *Kun*			
蠶官 Silkworm Officer	未 *Wei* Goat			
蠶命 Silkworm Life	申 *Shen* Monkey			
歲刑 Duke Punishment	卯 *Mao* Rabbit		獨火 Lonely Fire	艮 *Gen*
黃幡 Yellow Flag	辰 *Chen* Dragon		五鬼 Five Ghost	辰 *Chen* Dragon
豹尾 Leopard Tail	戌 *Xu* Dog		破敗五鬼 Destructive Five Ghost	巽 *Xun*

Negative Repair / Renovation Sectors Diagram 修方凶位圖：

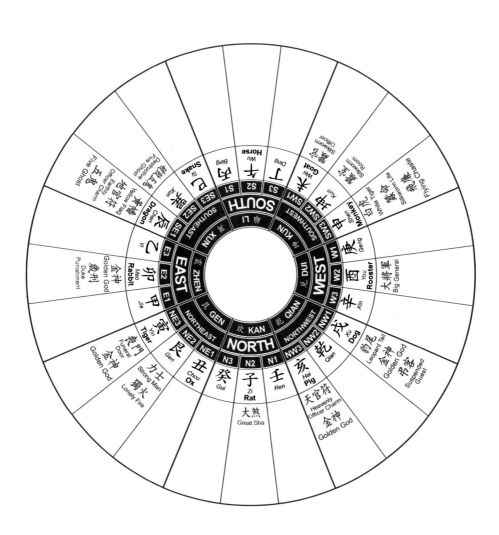

12-Month Auxiliary Stars Reference Table :
丙辰年十二月，開山立向修方星表

Positive Monthly Stars 吉星方

月 MONTH	寅 Tiger (Feb 4 - Mar 5) 正月 1st Month	卯 Rabbit (Mar 6 - Apr 4) 二月 2nd Month	辰 Dragon (Apr 5 - May 5) 三月 3rd Month	巳 Snake (May 6 - Jun 5) 四月 4th Month	午 Horse (Jun 6 - July 6) 五月 5th Month	未 Goat (July 7 - Aug 7) 六月 6th Month
天道 Heavenly Path	南 South	西南 Southwest	北 North	西 West	西北 Northwest	東 East
天德 Heavenly Virtue	丁 Ding Yin Fire	坤 Kun (申)	壬 Ren Yang Water	辛 Xin Yin Metal	乾 Qian (亥)	甲 Jia Yang Wood
天德合 Heavenly Virtue Combo	壬 Ren Yang Water	(巳)	丁 Ding Yin Fire	丙 Bing Yang Fire	(寅)	己 Ji Yin Earth
月德 Monthly Virtue	丙 Bing Yang Fire	甲 Jia Yang Wood	壬 Ren Yang Water	庚 Geng Yang Metal	丙 Bing Yang Fire	甲 Jia Yang Wood
月德合 Monthly Virtue Combo	辛 Xin Yin Metal	己 Ji Yin Earth	丁 Ding Yin Fire	乙 Yi Yin Wood	辛 Xin Yin Metal	己 Ji Yin Earth
月空 Month Emptiness	壬 Ren Yang Water	庚 Geng Yang Metal	丙 Bing Yang Fire	甲 Jia Yang Wood	壬 Ren Yang Water	庚 Geng Yang Metal
陽貴人 Yang Nobleman	震 Zhen	坤 Kun	坎 Kan	離 Li	艮 Gen	兌 Dui
陰貴人 Yin Nobleman	中 Middle	巽 Xun	震 Zhen	坤 Kun	坎 Kan	離 Li
飛天祿 Flying Heavenly Wealth	艮 Gen	兌 Dui	乾 Qian	中 Middle	坎 Kan	離 Li
飛天馬 Flying Heavenly Horse	中 Middle	坎 Kan	離 Li	艮 Gen	兌 Dui	乾 Qian

12-Month Auxiliary Stars Reference Table :
丙辰年十二月，開山立向修方星表

申 Monkey (Aug 8 - Sept 7)	酉 Rooster (Sept 8 - Oct 7)	戌 Dog (Oct 8 - Nov 6)	亥 Pig (Nov 7 - Dec 6)	子 Rat (Dec 7 - Jan 5)	丑 Ox (Jan 6 - Feb 3)	月 MONTH
七月 7th Month	八月 8th Month	九月 9th Month	十月 10th Month	十一月 11th Month	十二月 12th Month	
北 North	東北 Northeast	南 South	東 East	東南 Southeast	西 West	天道 Heavenly Path
癸 Gui Yin Water	艮 Gen (寅)	丙 Bing Yang Fire	乙 Yi Yin Wood	巽 Xun (巳)	庚 Geng Yang Metal	天德 Heavenly Virtue
戊 Wu Yang Earth	(亥)	辛 Xin Yin Metal	庚 Geng Yang Metal	(申)	乙 Yi Yin Wood	天德合 Heavenly Virtue Combo
壬 Ren Yang Water	庚 Geng Yang Metal	丙 Bing Yang Fire	甲 Jia Yang Wood	壬 Ren Yang Water	庚 Geng Yang Metal	月德 Monthly Virtue
丁 Ding Yin Fire	乙 Yi Yin Wood	辛 Xin Yin Metal	己 Ji Yin Earth	丁 Ding Yin Fire	乙 Yi Yin Wood	月德合 Monthly Virtue Combo
丙 Bing Yang Fire	甲 Jia Yang Wood	壬 Ren Yang Water	庚 Geng Yang Metal	丙 Bing Yang Fire	甲 Jia Yang Wood	月空 Month Emptiness
乾 Qian	中 Middle	坎 Kan	離 Li	艮 Gen	兌 Dui	陽貴人 Yang Nobleman
艮 Gen	兌 Dui	乾 Qian	中 Middle	坎 Kan	離 Li	陰貴人 Yin Nobleman
艮 Gen	兌 Dui	乾 Qian	中 Middle	巽 Xun	震 Zhen	飛天祿 Flying Heavenly Wealth
中 Middle	巽 Xun	震 Zhen	坤 Kun	坎 Kan	離 Li	飛天馬 Flying Heavenly Horse

Monthly Purple White Stars 月紫白九星 :

寅 Tiger (Feb 4 - Mar 5) 正月 1st Month

巽SE	離S	坤SW
4 Green 四綠	**9** Purple 九紫	**2** Black 二黑
3 Jade 三碧	**5** Yellow 五黃	**7** Red 七赤
8 White 八白	**1** White 一白	**6** White 六白

震E / 兌W / 艮NE / 坎N / 乾NW

卯 Rabbit (Mar 6 - Apr 4) 二月 2nd Month

巽SE	離S	坤SW
3 Jade 三碧	**8** White 八白	**1** White 一白
2 Black 二黑	**4** Green 四綠	**6** White 六白
7 Red 七赤	**9** Purple 九紫	**5** Yellow 五黃

震E / 兌W / 艮NE / 坎N / 乾NW

辰 Dragon (Apr 5 - May 5) 三月 3rd Month

巽SE	離S	坤SW
2 Black 二黑	**7** Red 七赤	**9** Purple 九紫
1 White 一白	**3** Jade 三碧	**5** Yellow 五黃
6 White 六白	**8** White 八白	**4** Green 四綠

震E / 兌W / 艮NE / 坎N / 乾NW

巳 Snake (May 6 - Jun 5) 四月 4th Month

巽SE	離S	坤SW
1 White 一白	**6** White 六白	**8** White 八白
9 Purple 九紫	**2** Black 二黑	**4** Green 四綠
5 Yellow 五黃	**7** Red 七赤	**3** Jade 三碧

震E / 兌W / 艮NE / 坎N / 乾NW

午 Horse (Jun 6 - July 6) 五月 5th Month

巽SE	離S	坤SW
9 Purple 九紫	**5** Yellow 五黃	**7** Red 七赤
8 White 八白	**1** White 一白	**3** Jade 三碧
4 Green 四綠	**6** White 六白	**2** Black 二黑

震E / 兌W / 艮NE / 坎N / 乾NW

未 Goat (July 7 - Aug 7) 六月 6th Month

巽SE	離S	坤SW
8 White 八白	**4** Green 四綠	**6** White 六白
7 Red 七赤	**9** Purple 九紫	**2** Black 二黑
3 Jade 三碧	**5** Yellow 五黃	**1** White 一白

震E / 兌W / 艮NE / 坎N / 乾NW

申 Monkey (Aug 8 - Sept 7) 七月 7th Month

巽SE	離S	坤SW
7 Red 七赤	**3** Jade 三碧	**5** Yellow 五黃
6 White 六白	**8** White 八白	**1** White 一白
2 Black 二黑	**4** Green 四綠	**9** Purple 九紫

震E / 兌W / 艮NE / 坎N / 乾NW

酉 Rooster (Sept 8 - Oct 7) 八月 8th Month

巽SE	離S	坤SW
6 White 六白	**2** Black 二黑	**4** Green 四綠
5 Yellow 五黃	**7** Red 七赤	**9** Purple 九紫
1 White 一白	**3** Jade 三碧	**8** White 八白

震E / 兌W / 艮NE / 坎N / 乾NW

戌 Dog (Oct 8 - Nov 6) 九月 9th Month

巽SE	離S	坤SW
5 Yellow 五黃	**1** White 一白	**3** Jade 三碧
4 Green 四綠	**6** White 六白	**8** White 八白
9 Purple 九紫	**2** Black 二黑	**7** Red 七赤

震E / 兌W / 艮NE / 坎N / 乾NW

亥 Pig (Nov 7 - Dec 6) 十月 10th Month

巽SE	離S	坤SW
4 Green 四綠	**9** Purple 九紫	**2** Black 二黑
3 Jade 三碧	**5** Yellow 五黃	**7** Red 七赤
8 White 八白	**1** White 一白	**6** White 六白

震E / 兌W / 艮NE / 坎N / 乾NW

子 Rat (Dec 7 - Jan 5) 十一月 11th Month

巽SE	離S	坤SW
3 Jade 三碧	**8** White 八白	**1** White 一白
2 Black 二黑	**4** Green 四綠	**6** White 六白
7 Red 七赤	**9** Purple 九紫	**5** Yellow 五黃

震E / 兌W / 艮NE / 坎N / 乾NW

丑 Ox (Jan 6 - Feb 3) 十二月 12th Month

巽SE	離S	坤SW
2 Black 二黑	**7** Red 七赤	**9** Purple 九紫
1 White 一白	**3** Jade 三碧	**5** Yellow 五黃
6 White 六白	**8** White 八白	**4** Green 四綠

震E / 兌W / 艮NE / 坎N / 乾NW

Qi Men Three Nobles 三奇 :

Three Nobles 三奇 / Seasons	乙 Yi	丙 Bing	丁 Ding
立春 **Coming of Spring** Feb 4 - Feb 18	坤 Kun	震 Zhen	巽 Xun
春分 **Spring Equinox** Mar 21 - Apr 4	乾 Qian	兌 Dui	艮 Gen
立夏 **Coming of Summer** May 6 - May 20	兌 Dui	艮 Gen	離 Li
夏至 **Summer Solstice** Jun 22 - Jul 6	乾 Qian	中 **Middle**	巽 Xun
立秋 **Coming of Autumn** Aug 8 - Aug 23	艮 Gen	兌 Dui	乾 Qian
秋分 **Autumn Equinox** Sept 23 - Oct 7	巽 Xun	震 Zhen	坤 Kun
立冬 **Coming of Winter** Nov 7 - Nov 22	震 Zhen	坤 Kun	坎 Kan
冬至 **Winter Solstice** Dec 22 - Jan 5	巽 Xun	中 **Middle**	乾 Qian

丙辰 (Bing Chen) Fire Dragon

Sectors to Avoid Opening Mountain 開山凶位：

月 MONTH	月建 Month Establishment	月破 Month Destruction	月剋山家 Month Countering Sitting		陰府太歲 Yin Mansion Grand Duke	
寅 **Tiger** (Feb 4 - Mar 5) 正月 **1st Month**	寅 Yin **Tiger**	申 Shen **Monkey**	–		乾 Qian	兌 Dui
卯 **Rabbit** (Mar 6 - Apr 4) 二月 **2nd Month**	卯 Mao **Rabbit**	酉 You **Rooster**	–		坤 Kun	坎 Kan
辰 **Dragon** (Apr 5 - May 5) 三月 **3rd Month**	辰 Chen **Dragon**	戌 Xu **Dog**	乾 Qian	兌 Dui	離 Li	乾 Qian
巳 **Snake** (May 6 - Jun 5) 四月 **4th Month**	巳 Si **Snake**	亥 Hai **Pig**	亥 Hai **Pig**	丁 Ding **Yin Fire**	震 Zhen	坤 Kun
午 **Horse** (Jun 6 - July 6) 五月 **5th Month**	午 Wu **Horse**	子 Zi **Rat**	離 Li	丙 Bing **Yang Fire**	艮 Gen	巽 Xun
未 **Goat** (July 7 - Aug 7) 六月 **6th Month**	未 Wei **Goat**	丑 Chou **Ox**	壬 Ren **Yang Water**	乙 Yi **Yin Wood**	兌 Dui	乾 Qian
申 **Monkey** (Aug 8 - Sept 7) 七月 **7th Month**	申 Shen **Monkey**	寅 Yin **Tiger**	震 Zhen	巳 Si **Snake**	坎 Kan	坤 Kun
酉 **Rooster** (Sept 8 - Oct 7) 八月 **8th Month**	酉 You **Rooster**	卯 Mao **Rabbit**	艮 Gen		乾 Qian	離 Li
戌 **Dog** (Oct 8 - Nov 6) 九月 **9th Month**	戌 Xu **Dog**	辰 Chen **Dragon**	–		坤 Kun	震 Zhen
亥 **Pig** (Nov 7 - Dec 6) 十月 **10th Month**	亥 Hai **Pig**	巳 Si **Snake**	–		巽 Xun	艮 Gen
子 **Rat** (Dec 7 - Jan 5) 十一月 **11th Month**	子 Zi **Rat**	午 Wu **Horse**	水 **Water**	山 **Mountain**	乾 Qian	兌 Dui
丑 **Ox** (Jan 6 - Feb 3) 十二月 **12th Month**	丑 Chou **Ox**	未 Wei **Goat**	土 **Earth**		坤 Kun	坎 Kan

Negative Repair / Renovation Sectors 修方凶位 :

月 MONTH	天官符 Heavenly Officer Charm			地官符 Earth Officer Charm			小月建 Small Month Establishment		
寅 **Tiger** (Feb 4 - Mar 5) 正月 **1st Month**		中 Middle		未 Wei Goat	坤 Kun	申 Shen Monkey		中 Middle	
卯 **Rabbit** (Mar 6 - Apr 4) 二月 **2nd Month**	辰 Chen Dragon	巽 Xun	巳 Si Snake	壬 Ren Yang Water	坎 Kan	癸 Gui Yin Water	戌 Xu Dog	乾 Qian	亥 Hai Pig
辰 **Dragon** (Apr 5 - May 5) 三月 **3rd Month**	甲 Jia Yang Wood	震 Zhen	乙 Yi Yin Wood	丙 Bing Yang Fire	離 Li	丁 Ding Yin Fire	庚 Geng Yang Metal	兌 Dui	辛 Xin Yin Metal
巳 **Snake** (May 6 - Jun 5) 四月 **4th Month**	未 Wei Goat	坤 Kun	申 Shen Monkey	丑 Chou Ox	艮 Gen	寅 Yin Tiger	丑 Chou Ox	艮 Gen	寅 Yin Tiger
午 **Horse** (Jun 6 - July 6) 五月 **5th Month**	壬 Ren Yang Water	坎 Kan	癸 Gui Yin Water	庚 Geng Yang Metal	兌 Dui	辛 Xin Yin Metal	丙 Bing Yang Fire	離 Li	丁 Ding Yin Fire
未 **Goat** (July 7 - Aug 7) 六月 **6th Month**	丙 Bing Yang Fire	離 Li	丁 Ding Yin Fire	戌 Xu Dog	乾 Qian	亥 Hai Pig	壬 Ren Yang Water	坎 Kan	癸 Gui Yin Water
申 **Monkey** (Aug 8 - Sept 7) 七月 **7th Month**	丑 Chou Ox	艮 Gen	寅 Yin Tiger		中 Middle		未 Wei Goat	坤 Kun	申 Shen Monkey
酉 **Rooster** (Sept 8 - Oct 7) 八月 **8th Month**	庚 Geng Yang Metal	兌 Dui	辛 Xin Yin Metal	庚 Geng Yang Metal	兌 Dui	辛 Xin Yin Metal	甲 Jia Yang Wood	震 Zhen	乙 Yi Yin Wood
戌 **Dog** (Oct 8 - Nov 6) 九月 **9th Month**	戌 Xu Dog	乾 Qian	亥 Hai Pig	戌 Xu Dog	乾 Qian	亥 Hai Pig	辰 Chen Dragon	巽 Xun	巳 Si Snake
亥 **Pig** (Nov 7 - Dec 6) 十月 **10th Month**		中 Middle			中 Middle			中 Middle	
子 **Rat** (Dec 7 - Jan 5) 十一月 **11th Month**	庚 Geng Yang Metal	兌 Dui	辛 Xin Yin Metal	辰 Chen Dragon	巽 Xun	巳 Si Snake	戌 Xu Dog	乾 Qian	亥 Hai Pig
丑 **Ox** (Jan 6 - Feb 3) 十二月 **12th Month**	戌 Xu Dog	乾 Qian	亥 Hai Pig	甲 Jia Yang Wood	震 Zhen	乙 Yi Yin Wood	庚 Geng Yang Metal	兌 Dui	辛 Xin Yin Metal

丙辰 (Bing Chen) Fire Dragon

月 MONTH	大月建 Big Month Establishment			飛大煞 Flying Great Sha			丙丁獨火 Bing Ding Lonely Fire	
寅 **Tiger** (Feb 4 - Mar 5) 正月 **1st Month**		中 Middle		戌 Xu Dog	乾 Qian	亥 Hai Pig	坤 Kun	震 Zhen
卯 **Rabbit** (Mar 6 - Apr 4) 二月 **2nd Month**	辰 Chen Dragon	巽 Xun	巳 Si Snake		中 Middle		坎 Kan	坤 Kun
辰 **Dragon** (Apr 5 - May 5) 三月 **3rd Month**	甲 Jia Yang Wood	震 Zhen	乙 Yi Yin Wood	辰 Chen Dragon	巽 Xun	巳 Si Snake	離 Li	坎 Kan
巳 **Snake** (May 6 - Jun 5) 四月 **4th Month**	未 Wei Goat	坤 Kun	申 Shen Monkey	甲 Jia Yang Wood	震 Zhen	乙 Yi Yin Wood	艮 Gen	離 Li
午 **Horse** (Jun 6 - July 6) 五月 **5th Month**	壬 Ren Yang Water	坎 Kan	癸 Gui Yin Water	未 Wei Goat	坤 Kun	申 Shen Monkey	兌 Dui	艮 Gen
未 **Goat** (July 7 - Aug 7) 六月 **6th Month**	丙 Bing Yang Fire	離 Li	丁 Ding Yin Fire	壬 Ren Yang Water	坎 Kan	癸 Gui Yin Water	乾 Qian	兌 Dui
申 **Monkey** (Aug 8 - Sept 7) 七月 **7th Month**	丑 Chou Ox	艮 Gen	寅 Yin Tiger	丙 Bing Yang Fire	離 Li	丁 Ding Yin Fire	中 Middle	乾 Qian
酉 **Rooster** (Sept 8 - Oct 7) 八月 **8th Month**	庚 Geng Yang Metal	兌 Dui	辛 Xin Yin Metal	丑 Chou Ox	艮 Gen	寅 Yin Tiger		中 Middle
戌 **Dog** (Oct 8 - Nov 6) 九月 **9th Month**	戌 Xu Dog	乾 Qian	亥 Hai Pig	庚 Geng Yang Metal	兌 Dui	辛 Xin Yin Metal	巽 Xun	中 Middle
亥 **Pig** (Nov 7 - Dec 6) 十月 **10th Month**		中 Middle		戌 Xu Dog	乾 Qian	亥 Hai Pig	震 Zhen	巽 Xun
子 **Rat** (Dec 7 - Jan 5) 十一月 **11th Month**	辰 Chen Dragon	巽 Xun	巳 Si Snake		中 Middle		坤 Kun	震 Zhen
丑 **Ox** (Jan 6 - Feb 3) 十二月 **12th Month**	甲 Jia Yang Wood	震 Zhen	乙 Yi Yin Wood	庚 Geng Yang Metal	兌 Dui	辛 Xin Yin Metal	坎 Kan	坤 Kun

Negative Repair / Renovation Sectors 修方凶位 :

月 MONTH	月遊火 Month Wondering Fire	三煞 Monthly 3 Killings		
		劫煞 Robbery Sha	災煞 Calamity Sha	月煞 Month Sha
寅 Tiger (Feb 4 - Mar 5) 正月 1st Month	巽 Xun	亥 Hai Pig	子 Zi Rat	丑 Chou Ox
卯 Rabbit (Mar 6 - Apr 4) 二月 2nd Month	中 Middle	申 Shen Monkey	酉 You Rooster	戌 Xu Dog
辰 Dragon (Apr 5 - May 5) 三月 3rd Month	乾 Qian	巳 Si Snake	午 Wu Horse	未 Wei Goat
巳 Snake (May 6 - Jun 5) 四月 4th Month	兌 Dui	寅 Yin Tiger	卯 Mao Rabbit	辰 Chen Dragon
午 Horse (Jun 6 - July 6) 五月 5th Month	艮 Gen	亥 Hai Pig	子 Zi Rat	丑 Chou Ox
未 Goat (July 7 - Aug 7) 六月 6th Month	離 Li	申 Shen Monkey	酉 You Rooster	戌 Xu Dog
申 Monkey (Aug 8 - Sept 7) 七月 7th Month	坎 Kan	巳 Si Snake	午 Wu Horse	未 Wei Goat
酉 Rooster (Sept 8 - Oct 7) 八月 8th Month	坤 Kun	寅 Yin Tiger	卯 Mao Rabbit	辰 Chen Dragon
戌 Dog (Oct 8 - Nov 6) 九月 9th Month	震 Zhen	亥 Hai Pig	子 Zi Rat	丑 Chou Ox
亥 Pig (Nov 7 - Dec 6) 十月 10th Month	巽 Xun	申 Shen Monkey	酉 You Rooster	戌 Xu Dog
子 Rat (Dec 7 - Jan 5) 十一月 11th Month	中 Middle	巳 Si Snake	午 Wu Horse	未 Wei Goat
丑 Ox (Jan 6 - Feb 3) 十二月 12th Month	乾 Qian	寅 Yin Tiger	卯 Mao Rabbit	辰 Chen Dragon

Negative Repair / Renovation Sectors 修方凶位 :

月 MONTH	月刑 Month Punishment	月害 Month Harm	月厭 Month Detest
寅 **Tiger** (Feb 4 - Mar 5) 正月 **1st Month**	巳 *Si* Snake	巳 *Si* Snake	戌 *Xu* Dog
卯 **Rabbit** (Mar 6 - Apr 4) 二月 **2nd Month**	子 *Zi* Rat	辰 *Chen* Dragon	酉 *You* Rooster
辰 **Dragon** (Apr 5 - May 5) 三月 **3rd Month**	辰 *Chen* Dragon	卯 *Mao* Rabbit	申 *Shen* Monkey
巳 **Snake** (May 6 - Jun 5) 四月 **4th Month**	申 *Shen* Monkey	寅 *Yin* Tiger	未 *Wei* Goat
午 **Horse** (Jun 6 - July 6) 五月 **5th Month**	午 *Wu* Horse	丑 *Chou* Ox	午 *Wu* Horse
未 **Goat** (July 7 - Aug 7) 六月 **6th Month**	丑 *Chou* Ox	子 *Zi* Rat	巳 *Si* Snake
申 **Monkey** (Aug 8 - Sept 7) 七月 **7th Month**	寅 *Yin* Tiger	亥 *Hai* Pig	辰 *Chen* Dragon
酉 **Rooster** (Sept 8 - Oct 7) 八月 **8th Month**	酉 *You* Rooster	戌 *Xu* Dog	卯 *Mao* Rabbit
戌 **Dog** (Oct 8 - Nov 6) 九月 **9th Month**	未 *Wei* Goat	酉 *You* Rooster	寅 *Yin* Tiger
亥 **Pig** (Nov 7 - Dec 6) 十月 **10th Month**	亥 *Hai* Pig	申 *Shen* Monkey	丑 *Chou* Ox
子 **Rat** (Dec 7 - Jan 5) 十一月 **11th Month**	卯 *Mao* Rabbit	未 *Wei* Goat	子 *Zi* Rat
丑 **Ox** (Jan 6 - Feb 3) 十二月 **12th Month**	戌 *Xu* Dog	午 *Wu* Horse	亥 *Hai* Pig

丙午 (Bing Wu)
Fire Horse

Heavenly Stem 天干	丙 **Yang Fire (陽火)**
Earthly Branch 地支	午 **Horse (Yang Fire 陽火)**
Hidden Stem 藏干	丁 **Yin Fire,** 己 **Yin Earth**
Na Yin 納音	天河水 **Water from heavenly river**
Grand Duke 太歲	午 **Horse**
Xuan Kong Five Element 玄空五行	4 金 **Metal**
Gua Name 卦名	䷛ 澤風大過 **Great Exceeding**
Xuan Kong Period Luck 玄空卦運	3

Annual Positive Stars for Opening Mountain, Establishing Facing and Commencing Repairs 開山立向修方吉星:

歲德 **Duke Virtue**	丙 *Bing* **Yang Fire**
歲德合 **Duke Virtue Combo**	辛 *Xin* **Yin Metal**
歲枝德 **Duke Branch Virtue**	亥 *Hai* **Pig**
陽貴人 **Yang Nobleman**	酉 *You* **Rooster**
陰貴人 **Yin Nobleman**	亥 *Hai* **Pig**
歲祿 **Duke Prosperous**	巳 *Si* **Snake**
歲馬 **Duke Horse**	申 *Shen* **Monkey**
奏書 **Decree**	巽 *Xun*
博士 **Professor**	乾 *Qian*

Annual Negative Stars for Opening Mountain, Establishing Facing and Commencing Repairs 開山立向修方凶星：

太歲 Grand Duke	歲破 Year Breaker	三煞 Three Killings			坐煞向煞 Sitting Sha Facing Sha				浮天空亡 Floating Heaven Emptiness	
午 Wu Horse	子 Zi Rat	亥 Hai Pig	子 Zi Rat	丑 Chou Ox	壬 Ren Yang Water	癸 Gui Yin Water	丙 Bing Yang Fire	丁 Ding Yin Fire	巽 Xun	辛 Xin Yin Metal

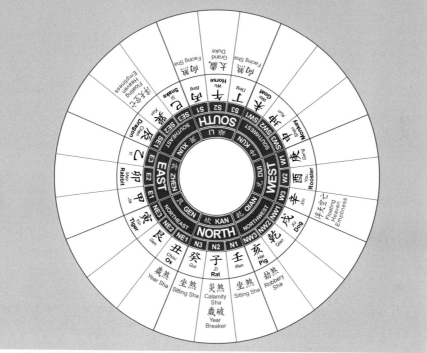

Annual San Yuan Purple White Stars 三元紫白九星：

上元 Upper Period — Period 1, 2, 3

巽SE	離S	坤SW
3	8	1
2	4 丙午 Bing Wu Fire Horse	6
7	9	5

震E · 兌W · 艮NE · 坎N · 乾NW

中元 Middle Period — Period 4, 5, 6

巽SE	離S	坤SW
6	2	4
5	7 丙午 Bing Wu Fire Horse	9
1	3	8

震E · 兌W · 艮NE · 坎N · 乾NW

下元 Lower Period — Period 7, 8, 9

巽SE	離S	坤SW
9	5	7
8	1 丙午 Bing Wu Fire Horse	3
4	6	2

震E · 兌W · 艮NE · 坎N · 乾NW

Mountain Covering Yellow Path 蓋山黃道：

貪狼 Tan Lang **Greedy Wolf**		巨門 Ju Men **Huge Door**		武曲 Wu Qu **Military Arts**				文曲 Wen Qu **Literary Arts**	
巽 Xun SE2	辛 Xin W3	艮 Gen NE2	丙 Bing S1	震 Zhen E2	庚 Geng W1	亥 Hai NW3	未 Wei SW1	乾 Qian NW2	甲 Jia E1

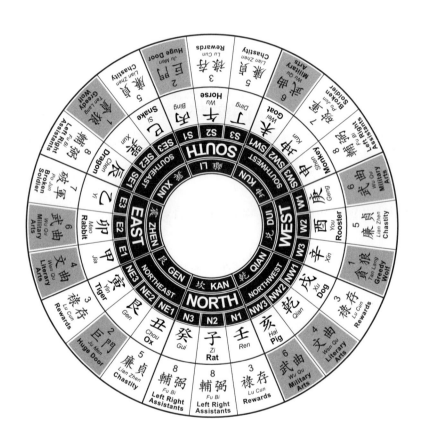

Heaven Penetrating Force 通天竅：

三合前方 Facing Three Harmony	坤申 Kun Shen	庚酉 Geng You	辛戌 Xin Xu
三合後方 Sitting Three Harmony	艮寅 Gen Yin	甲卯 Jia Mao	乙辰 Yi Chen

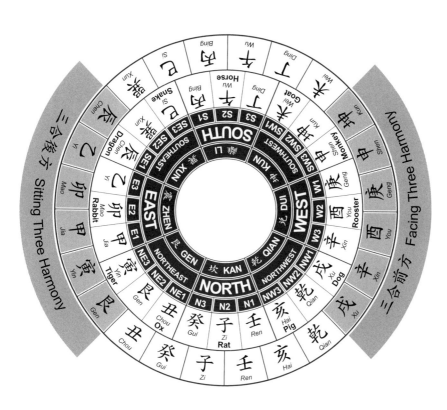

Moving Horse Six Ren Assessment 走馬六壬：

神后 *Shen Hou* **Holy Empress**	功曹 *Gong Cao* **Marshall**	天罡 *Tian Gang* **Heavenly Dipper**	勝光 *Sheng Guang* **Subliminal Bright**	傳送 *Chuan Song* **Great General**	河魁 *He Kui* **River Scholar**
丙午 *Bing Wu*	坤申 *Kun Shen*	辛戌 *Xin Xu*	壬子 *Ren Zi*	艮寅 *Gen Yin*	乙辰 *Yi Chen*

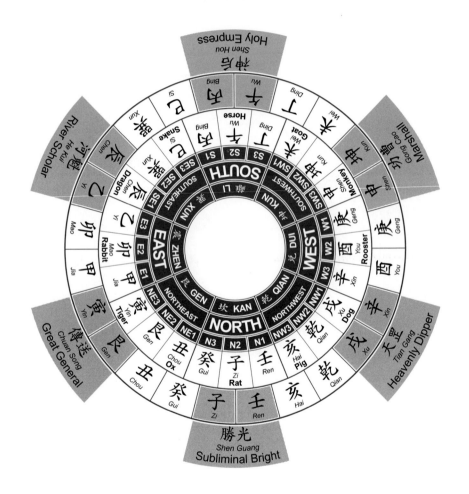

Four Advantages Three Cycles Star Plate 四利三元：

太陽 *Tai Yang* **Sun**	太陰 *Tai Yin* **Moon**	龍德 *Long De* **Dragon Virtue**	福德 *Fu De* **Fortune Virtue**
未 *Wei* **Goat**	酉 *You* **Rooster**	丑 *Chou* **Ox**	卯 *Mao* **Rabbit**

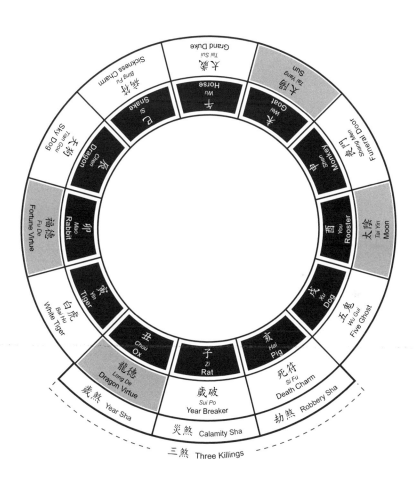

丙午 (Bing Wu) Fire Horse

Negative Sectors For Opening Mountain 開山凶位：

年剋山家 Year Countering Sitting

乾	亥	兌	丁
Qian	Hai	Dui	Ding
NW2	NW3	W2	S3

陰府太歲 Yin Fu Tai Sui **Yin Mansion Grand Duke**	六害 Liu Hai **Six Harm**	死符 Si Fu **Death Charm**	炙退 Zhi Tui **Roasting Star**
坎 Kan N2 坤 Kun SW2	丑 Chou NE1	亥 Hai NW3	酉 You W2

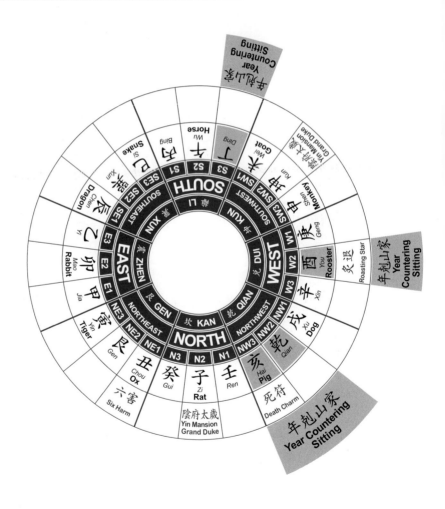

Negative Directions to Establish Facing 立向凶方：

巡山羅喉 *Xun Shan Luo Hou* **Mountain Patrol Luo Hou Star**	病符 *Bing Fu* **Sickness Charm**
丁 *Ding* **S3**	巳 *Si* **Snake**

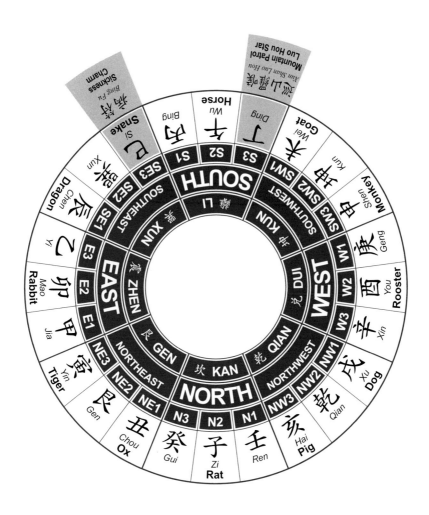

Negative Repair / Renovation Sectors Table 修方凶位表：

天官符 **Heavenly Officer Charm**	巳 *Si* Snake		飛廉 **Flying Chaste**	寅 *Yin* Tiger
地官符 **Earthly Officer Charm**	戌 *Xu* Dog		喪門 **Funeral Door**	申 *Shen* Monkey
大煞 **Great Sha**	午 *Wu* Horse		弔客 **Suspended Guest**	辰 *Chen* Dragon
大將軍 **Big General**	卯 *Mao* Rabbit		白虎 **White Tiger**	寅 *Yin* Tiger
力士 **Strong Man**	坤 *Kun*		金神 **Golden God**	寅 *Yin* Tiger 卯 *Mao* Rabbit 午 *Wu* Horse 未 *Wei* Goat 子 *Zi* Rat 丑 *Chou* Ox
蠶室 **Silkworm Room**	艮 *Gen*			
蠶官 **Silkworm Officer**	丑 *Chou* Ox			
蠶命 **Silkworm Life**	寅 *Yin* Tiger			
歲刑 **Duke Punishment**	午 *Wu* Horse		獨火 **Lonely Fire**	兌 *Dui*
黃幡 **Yellow Flag**	戌 *Xu* Dog		五鬼 **Five Ghost**	戌 *Xu* Dog
豹尾 **Leopard Tail**	辰 *Chen* Dragon		破敗五鬼 **Destructive Five Ghost**	坤 *Kun*

Negative Repair / Renovation Sectors Diagram 修方凶位圖：

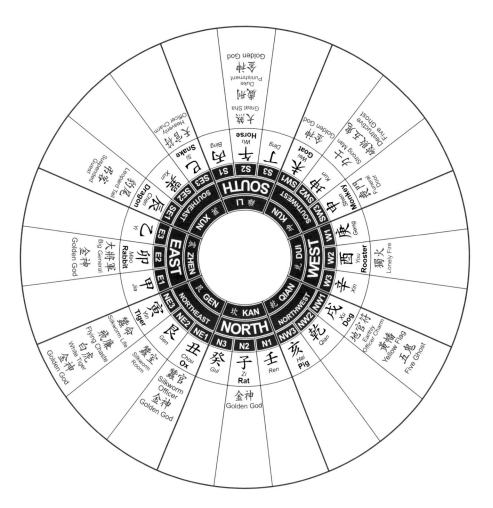

12-Month Auxiliary Stars Reference Table :
丙午年十二月，開山立向修方星表

Positive Monthly Stars 吉星方

月 MONTH	寅 **Tiger** (Feb 4 - Mar 5) 正月 **1st Month**	卯 **Rabbit** (Mar 6 - Apr 4) 二月 **2nd Month**	辰 **Dragon** (Apr 5 - May 5) 三月 **3rd Month**	巳 **Snake** (May 6 - Jun 5) 四月 **4th Month**	午 **Horse** (Jun 6 - July 6) 五月 **5th Month**	未 **Goat** (July 7 - Aug 7) 六月 **6th Month**
天道 **Heavenly Path**	南 South	西南 Southwest	北 North	西 West	西北 Northwest	東 East
天德 **Heavenly Virtue**	丁 Ding Yin Fire	坤 Kun (申)	壬 Ren Yang Water	辛 Xin Yin Metal	乾 Qian (亥)	甲 Jia Yang Wood
天德合 **Heavenly Virtue Combo**	壬 Ren Yang Water	(巳)	丁 Ding Yin Fire	丙 Bing Yang Fire	(寅)	己 Ji Yin Earth
月德 **Monthly Virtue**	丙 Bing Yang Fire	甲 Jia Yang Wood	壬 Ren Yang Water	庚 Geng Yang Metal	丙 Bing Yang Fire	甲 Jia Yang Wood
月德合 **Monthly Virtue Combo**	辛 Xin Yin Metal	己 Ji Yin Earth	丁 Ding Yin Fire	乙 Yi Yin Wood	辛 Xin Yin Metal	己 Ji Yin Earth
月空 **Month Emptiness**	壬 Ren Yang Water	庚 Geng Yang Metal	丙 Bing Yang Fire	甲 Jia Yang Wood	壬 Ren Yang Water	庚 Geng Yang Metal
陽貴人 **Yang Nobleman**	震 Zhen	坤 Kun	坎 Kan	離 Li	艮 Gen	兌 Dui
陰貴人 **Yin Nobleman**	中 Middle	巽 Xun	震 Zhen	坤 Kun	坎 Kan	離 Li
飛天祿 **Flying Heavenly Wealth**	艮 Gen	兌 Dui	乾 Qian	中 Middle	坎 Kan	離 Li
飛天馬 **Flying Heavenly Horse**	坤 Kun	坎 Kan	離 Li	艮 Gen	兌 Dui	乾 Qian

12-Month Auxiliary Stars Reference Table :
丙午年十二月，開山立向修方星表

申 Monkey (Aug 8 - Sept 7) 七月 7th Month	酉 Rooster (Sept 8 - Oct 7) 八月 8th Month	戌 Dog (Oct 8 - Nov 6) 九月 9th Month	亥 Pig (Nov 7 - Dec 6) 十月 10th Month	子 Rat (Dec 7 - Jan 5) 十一月 11th Month	丑 Ox (Jan 6 - Feb 3) 十二月 12th Month	月 MONTH
北 North	東北 Northeast	南 South	東 East	東南 Southeast	西 West	天道 Heavenly Path
癸 Gui Yin Water	艮 Gen (寅)	丙 Bing Yang Fire	乙 Yi Yin Wood	巽 Xun (巳)	庚 Geng Yang Metal	天德 Heavenly Virtue
戊 Wu Yang Earth	(亥)	辛 Xin Yin Metal	庚 Geng Yang Metal	(申)	乙 Yi Yin Wood	天德合 Heavenly Virtue Combo
壬 Ren Yang Water	庚 Geng Yang Metal	丙 Bing Yang Fire	甲 Jia Yang Wood	壬 Ren Yang Water	庚 Geng Yang Metal	月德 Monthly Virtue
丁 Ding Yin Fire	乙 Yi Yin Wood	辛 Xin Yin Metal	己 Ji Yin Earth	丁 Ding Yin Fire	乙 Yi Yin Wood	月德合 Monthly Virtue Combo
丙 Bing Yang Fire	甲 Jia Yang Wood	壬 Ren Yang Water	庚 Geng Yang Metal	丙 Bing Yang Fire	甲 Jia Yang Wood	月空 Month Emptiness
乾 Qian	中 Middle	坎 Kan	離 Li	艮 Gen	兌 Dui	陽貴人 Yang Nobleman
艮 Gen	兌 Dui	乾 Qian	中 Middle	坎 Kan	離 Li	陰貴人 Yin Nobleman
艮 Gen	兌 Dui	乾 Qian	中 Middle	巽 Xun	震 Zhen	飛天祿 Flying Heavenly Wealth
中 Middle	坎 Kan	離 Li	艮 Gen	兌 Dui	乾 Qian	飛天馬 Flying Heavenly Horse

丙午 (Bing Wu) Fire Horse

Monthly Purple White Stars 月紫白九星 :

寅 Tiger (Feb 4 - Mar 5) 正月 1st Month

巽 SE	離 S	坤 SW
7 Red 七赤	3 Jade 三碧	5 Yellow 五黄
震 E — 6 White 六白	8 White 八白	1 White 一白 — 兌 W
2 Black 二黑	4 Green 四綠	9 Purple 九紫
艮 NE	坎 N	乾 NW

卯 Rabbit (Mar 6 - Apr 4) 二月 2nd Month

巽 SE	離 S	坤 SW
6 White 六白	2 Black 二黑	4 Green 四綠
震 E — 5 Yellow 五黄	7 Red 七赤	9 Purple 九紫 — 兌 W
1 White 一白	3 Jade 三碧	8 White 八白
艮 NE	坎 N	乾 NW

辰 Dragon (Apr 5 - May 5) 三月 3rd Month

巽 SE	離 S	坤 SW
5 Yellow 五黄	1 White 一白	3 Jade 三碧
震 E — 4 Green 四綠	6 White 六白	8 White 八白 — 兌 W
9 Purple 九紫	2 Black 二黑	7 Red 七赤
艮 NE	坎 N	乾 NW

巳 Snake (May 6 - Jun 5) 四月 4th Month

巽 SE	離 S	坤 SW
4 Green 四綠	9 Purple 九紫	2 Black 二黑
震 E — 3 Jade 三碧	5 Yellow 五黄	7 Red 七赤 — 兌 W
8 White 八白	1 White 一白	6 White 六白
艮 NE	坎 N	乾 NW

午 Horse (Jun 6 - July 6) 五月 5th Month

巽 SE	離 S	坤 SW
3 Jade 三碧	8 White 八白	1 White 一白
震 E — 2 Black 二黑	4 Green 四綠	6 White 六白 — 兌 W
7 Red 七赤	9 Purple 九紫	5 Yellow 五黄
艮 NE	坎 N	乾 NW

未 Goat (July 7 - Aug 7) 六月 6th Month

巽 SE	離 S	坤 SW
2 Black 二黑	7 Red 七赤	9 Purple 九紫
震 E — 1 White 一白	3 Jade 三碧	5 Yellow 五黄 — 兌 W
6 White 六白	8 White 八白	4 Green 四綠
艮 NE	坎 N	乾 NW

申 Monkey (Aug 8 - Sept 7) 七月 7th Month

巽 SE	離 S	坤 SW
1 White 一白	6 White 六白	8 White 八白
震 E — 9 Purple 九紫	2 Black 二黑	4 Green 四綠 — 兌 W
5 Yellow 五黄	7 Red 七赤	3 Jade 三碧
艮 NE	坎 N	乾 NW

酉 Rooster (Sept 8 - Oct 7) 八月 8th Month

巽 SE	離 S	坤 SW
9 Purple 九紫	5 Yellow 五黄	7 Red 七赤
震 E — 8 White 八白	1 White 一白	3 Jade 三碧 — 兌 W
4 Green 四綠	6 White 六白	2 Black 二黑
艮 NE	坎 N	乾 NW

戌 Dog (Oct 8 - Nov 6) 九月 9th Month

巽 SE	離 S	坤 SW
8 White 八白	4 Green 四綠	6 White 六白
震 E — 7 Red 七赤	9 Purple 九紫	2 Black 二黑 — 兌 W
3 Jade 三碧	5 Yellow 五黄	1 White 一白
艮 NE	坎 N	乾 NW

亥 Pig (Nov 7 - Dec 6) 十月 10th Month

巽 SE	離 S	坤 SW
7 Red 七赤	3 Jade 三碧	5 Yellow 五黄
震 E — 6 White 六白	8 White 八白	1 White 一白 — 兌 W
2 Black 二黑	4 Green 四綠	9 Purple 九紫
艮 NE	坎 N	乾 NW

子 Rat (Dec 7 - Jan 5) 十一月 11th Month

巽 SE	離 S	坤 SW
6 White 六白	2 Black 二黑	4 Green 四綠
震 E — 5 Yellow 五黄	7 Red 七赤	9 Purple 九紫 — 兌 W
1 White 一白	3 Jade 三碧	8 White 八白
艮 NE	坎 N	乾 NW

丑 Ox (Jan 6 - Feb 3) 十二月 12th Month

巽 SE	離 S	坤 SW
5 Yellow 五黄	1 White 一白	3 Jade 三碧
震 E — 4 Green 四綠	6 White 六白	8 White 八白 — 兌 W
9 Purple 九紫	2 Black 二黑	7 Red 七赤
艮 NE	坎 N	乾 NW

Qi Men Three Nobles 三奇 :

Three Nobles 三奇 / Seasons	乙 Yi	丙 Bing	丁 Ding
立春 **Coming of Spring** Feb 4 - Feb 18	坎 Kan	坤 Kun	震 Zhen
春分 **Spring Equinox** Mar 21 - Apr 4	中 Middle	乾 Qian	兌 Dui
立夏 **Coming of Summer** May 6 - May 20	乾 Qian	兌 Dui	艮 Gen
夏至 **Summer Solstice** Jun 22 - Jul 6	兌 Dui	乾 Qian	中 Middle
立秋 **Coming of Autumn** Aug 8 - Aug 23	離 Li	艮 Gen	兌 Dui
秋分 **Autumn Equinox** Sept 23 - Oct 7	中 Middle	巽 Xun	震 Zhen
立冬 **Coming of Winter** Nov 7 - Nov 22	巽 Xun	震 Zhen	坤 Kun
冬至 **Winter Solstice** Dec 22 - Jan 5	震 Zhen	巽 Xun	中 Middle

Sectors to Avoid Opening Mountain 開山凶位 :

月 MONTH	月建 Month Establishment	月破 Month Destruction	月剋山家 Month Countering Sitting		陰府太歲 Yin Mansion Grand Duke	
寅 Tiger (Feb 4 - Mar 5) 正月 1st Month	寅 Yin Tiger	申 Shen Monkey	–		乾 Qian	兑 Dui
卯 Rabbit (Mar 6 - Apr 4) 二月 2nd Month	卯 Mao Rabbit	酉 You Rooster	–		坤 Kun	坎 Kan
辰 Dragon (Apr 5 - May 5) 三月 3rd Month	辰 Chen Dragon	戌 Xu Dog	乾 Qian	兑 Dui	離 Li	乾 Qian
巳 Snake (May 6 - Jun 5) 四月 4th Month	巳 Si Snake	亥 Hai Pig	亥 Hai Pig	丁 Ding Yin Fire	震 Zhen	坤 Kun
午 Horse (Jun 6 - July 6) 五月 5th Month	午 Wu Horse	子 Zi Rat	離 Li	丙 Bing Yang Fire	艮 Gen	巽 Xun
未 Goat (July 7 - Aug 7) 六月 6th Month	未 Wei Goat	丑 Chou Ox	壬 Ren Yang Water	乙 Yi Yin Wood	兑 Dui	乾 Qian
申 Monkey (Aug 8 - Sept 7) 七月 7th Month	申 Shen Monkey	寅 Yin Tiger	震 Zhen	巳 Si Snake	坎 Kan	坤 Kun
酉 Rooster (Sept 8 - Oct 7) 八月 8th Month	酉 You Rooster	卯 Mao Rabbit	艮 Gen		乾 Qian	離 Li
戌 Dog (Oct 8 - Nov 6) 九月 9th Month	戌 Xu Dog	辰 Chen Dragon	–		坤 Kun	震 Zhen
亥 Pig (Nov 7 - Dec 6) 十月 10th Month	亥 Hai Pig	巳 Si Snake	–		巽 Xun	艮 Gen
子 Rat (Dec 7 - Jan 5) 十一月 11th Month	子 Zi Rat	午 Wu Horse	水 Water	山 Mountain	乾 Qian	兑 Dui
丑 Ox (Jan 6 - Feb 3) 十二月 12th Month	丑 Chou Ox	未 Wei Goat	土 Earth		坤 Kun	坎 Kan

Negative Repair / Renovation Sectors 修方凶位 :

月 MONTH	天官符 Heavenly Officer Charm			地官符 Earth Officer Charm			小月建 Small Month Establishment		
寅 Tiger (Feb 4 - Mar 5) 正月 1st Month	辰 *Chen* Dragon	巽 *Xun*	巳 *Si* Snake	辰 *Chen* Dragon	巽 *Xun*	巳 *Si* Snake	中 Middle		
卯 Rabbit (Mar 6 - Apr 4) 二月 2nd Month	庚 *Geng* Yang Metal	兌 *Dui*	辛 *Xin* Yin Metal	甲 *Jia* Yang Wood	震 *Zhen*	乙 *Yi* Yin Wood	戌 *Xu* Dog	乾 *Qian*	亥 *Hai* Pig
辰 Dragon (Apr 5 - May 5) 三月 3rd Month	戌 *Xu* Dog	乾 *Qian*	亥 *Hai* Pig	未 *Wei* Goat	坤 *Kun*	申 *Shen* Monkey	庚 *Geng* Yang Metal	兌 *Dui*	辛 *Xin* Yin Metal
巳 Snake (May 6 - Jun 5) 四月 4th Month		中 Middle		壬 *Ren* Yang Water	坎 *Kan*	癸 *Gui* Yin Water	丑 *Chou* Ox	艮 *Gen*	寅 *Yin* Tiger
午 Horse (Jun 6 - July 6) 五月 5th Month	庚 *Geng* Yang Metal	兌 *Dui*	辛 *Xin* Yin Metal	丙 *Bing* Yang Fire	離 *Li*	丁 *Ding* Yin Fire	丙 *Bing* Yang Fire	離 *Li*	丁 *Ding* Yin Fire
未 Goat (July 7 - Aug 7) 六月 6th Month	戌 *Xu* Dog	乾 *Qian*	亥 *Hai* Pig	丑 *Chou* Ox	艮 *Gen*	寅 *Yin* Tiger	壬 *Ren* Yang Water	坎 *Kan*	癸 *Gui* Yin Water
申 Monkey (Aug 8 - Sept 7) 七月 7th Month		中 Middle		庚 *Geng* Yang Metal	兌 *Dui*	辛 *Xin* Yin Metal	未 *Wei* Goat	坤 *Kun*	申 *Shen* Monkey
酉 Rooster (Sept 8 - Oct 7) 八月 8th Month	辰 *Chen* Dragon	巽 *Xun*	巳 *Si* Snake	戌 *Xu* Dog	乾 *Qian*	亥 *Hai* Pig	甲 *Jia* Yang Wood	震 *Zhen*	乙 *Yi* Yin Wood
戌 Dog (Oct 8 - Nov 6) 九月 9th Month	甲 *Jia* Yang Wood	震 *Zhen*	乙 *Yi* Yin Wood		中 Middle		辰 *Chen* Dragon	巽 *Xun*	巳 *Si* Snake
亥 Pig (Nov 7 - Dec 6) 十月 10th Month	未 *Wei* Goat	坤 *Kun*	申 *Shen* Monkey	庚 *Geng* Yang Metal	兌 *Dui*	辛 *Xin* Yin Metal		中 Middle	
子 Rat (Dec 7 - Jan 5) 十一月 11th Month	壬 *Ren* Yang Water	坎 *Kan*	癸 *Gui* Yin Water	戌 *Xu* Dog	乾 *Qian*	亥 *Hai* Pig	戌 *Xu* Dog	乾 *Qian*	亥 *Hai* Pig
丑 Ox (Jan 6 - Feb 3) 十二月 12th Month	丙 *Bing* Yang Fire	離 *Li*	丁 *Ding* Yin Fire		中 Middle		庚 *Geng* Yang Metal	兌 *Dui*	辛 *Xin* Yin Metal

317

Negative Repair / Renovation Sectors 修方凶位 :

月 MONTH	大月建 Big Month Establishment			飛大煞 Flying Great Sha			丙丁獨火 Bing Ding Lonely Fire	
寅 **Tiger** (Feb 4 - Mar 5) 正月 **1st Month**	丑 Chou Ox	艮 Gen	寅 Yin Tiger	丙 Bing Yang Fire	離 Li	丁 Ding Yin Fire	坤 Kun	震 Zhen
卯 **Rabbit** (Mar 6 - Apr 4) 二月 **2nd Month**	庚 Geng Yang Metal	兌 Dui	辛 Xin Yin Metal	丑 Chou Ox	艮 Gen	寅 Yin Tiger	坎 Kan	坤 Kun
辰 **Dragon** (Apr 5 - May 5) 三月 **3rd Month**	戌 Xu Dog	乾 Qian	亥 Hai Pig	庚 Geng Yang Metal	兌 Dui	辛 Xin Yin Metal	離 Li	坎 Kan
巳 **Snake** (May 6 - Jun 5) 四月 **4th Month**		中 Middle		戌 Xu Dog	乾 Qian	亥 Hai Pig	艮 Gen	離 Li
午 **Horse** (Jun 6 - July 6) 五月 **5th Month**	辰 Chen Dragon	巽 Xun	巳 Si Snake		中 Middle		兌 Dui	艮 Gen
未 **Goat** (July 7 - Aug 7) 六月 **6th Month**	甲 Jia Yang Wood	震 Zhen	乙 Yi Yin Wood	庚 Geng Yang Metal	兌 Dui	辛 Xin Yin Metal	乾 Qian	兌 Dui
申 **Monkey** (Aug 8 - Sept 7) 七月 **7th Month**	未 Wei Goat	坤 Kun	申 Shen Monkey	戌 Xu Dog	乾 Qian	亥 Hai Pig	中 Middle	乾 Qian
酉 **Rooster** (Sept 8 - Oct 7) 八月 **8th Month**	壬 Ren Yang Water	坎 Kan	癸 Gui Yin Water		中 Middle			中 Middle
戌 **Dog** (Oct 8 - Nov 6) 九月 **9th Month**	丙 Bing Yang Fire	離 Li	丁 Ding Yin Fire	辰 Chen Dragon	巽 Xun	巳 Si Snake	巽 Xun	中 Middle
亥 **Pig** (Nov 7 - Dec 6) 十月 **10th Month**	丑 Chou Ox	艮 Gen	寅 Yin Tiger	甲 Jia Yang Wood	震 Zhen	乙 Yi Yin Wood	震 Zhen	巽 Xun
子 **Rat** (Dec 7 - Jan 5) 十一月 **11th Month**	庚 Geng Yang Metal	兌 Dui	辛 Xin Yin Metal	未 Wei Goat	坤 Kun	申 Shen Monkey	坤 Kun	震 Zhen
丑 **Ox** (Jan 6 - Feb 3) 十二月 **12th Month**	戌 Xu Dog	乾 Qian	亥 Hai Pig	壬 Ren Yang Water	坎 Kan	癸 Gui Yin Water	坎 Kan	坤 Kun

Negative Repair / Renovation Sectors 修方凶位 :

月 MONTH	月遊火 Month Wondering Fire	三煞 Monthly 3 Killings		
		劫煞 Robbery Sha	災煞 Calamity Sha	月煞 Month Sha
寅 **Tiger** (Feb 4 - Mar 5) 正月 **1st Month**	坤 *Kun*	亥 *Hai* Pig	子 *Zi* Rat	丑 *Chou* Ox
卯 **Rabbit** (Mar 6 - Apr 4) 二月 **2nd Month**	震 *Zhen*	申 *Shen* Monkey	酉 *You* Rooster	戌 *Xu* Dog
辰 **Dragon** (Apr 5 - May 5) 三月 **3rd Month**	巽 *Xun*	巳 *Si* Snake	午 *Wu* Horse	未 *Wei* Goat
巳 **Snake** (May 6 - Jun 5) 四月 **4th Month**	中 Middle	寅 *Yin* Tiger	卯 *Mao* Rabbit	辰 *Chen* Dragon
午 **Horse** (Jun 6 - July 6) 五月 **5th Month**	乾 *Qian*	亥 *Hai* Pig	子 *Zi* Rat	丑 *Chou* Ox
未 **Goat** (July 7 - Aug 7) 六月 **6th Month**	兌 *Dui*	申 *Shen* Monkey	酉 *You* Rooster	戌 *Xu* Dog
申 **Monkey** (Aug 8 - Sept 7) 七月 **7th Month**	艮 *Gen*	巳 *Si* Snake	午 *Wu* Horse	未 *Wei* Goat
酉 **Rooster** (Sept 8 - Oct 7) 八月 **8th Month**	離 *Li*	寅 *Yin* Tiger	卯 *Mao* Rabbit	辰 *Chen* Dragon
戌 **Dog** (Oct 8 - Nov 6) 九月 **9th Month**	坎 *Kan*	亥 *Hai* Pig	子 *Zi* Rat	丑 *Chou* Ox
亥 **Pig** (Nov 7 - Dec 6) 十月 **10th Month**	坤 *Kun*	申 *Shen* Monkey	酉 *You* Rooster	戌 *Xu* Dog
子 **Rat** (Dec 7 - Jan 5) 十一月 **11th Month**	震 *Zhen*	巳 *Si* Snake	午 *Wu* Horse	未 *Wei* Goat
丑 **Ox** (Jan 6 - Feb 3) 十二月 **12th Month**	巽 *Xun*	寅 *Yin* Tiger	卯 *Mao* Rabbit	辰 *Chen* Dragon

Negative Repair / Renovation Sectors 修方凶位 :

月 MONTH	月刑 Month Punishment	月害 Month Harm	月厭 Month Detest
寅 Tiger (Feb 4 - Mar 5) 正月 1st Month	巳 Si Snake	巳 Si Snake	戌 Xu Dog
卯 Rabbit (Mar 6 - Apr 4) 二月 2nd Month	子 Zi Rat	辰 Chen Dragon	酉 You Rooster
辰 Dragon (Apr 5 - May 5) 三月 3rd Month	辰 Chen Dragon	卯 Mao Rabbit	申 Shen Monkey
巳 Snake (May 6 - Jun 5) 四月 4th Month	申 Shen Monkey	寅 Yin Tiger	未 Wei Goat
午 Horse (Jun 6 - July 6) 五月 5th Month	午 Wu Horse	丑 Chou Ox	午 Wu Horse
未 Goat (July 7 - Aug 7) 六月 6th Month	丑 Chou Ox	子 Zi Rat	巳 Si Snake
申 Monkey (Aug 8 - Sept 7) 七月 7th Month	寅 Yin Tiger	亥 Hai Pig	辰 Chen Dragon
酉 Rooster (Sept 8 - Oct 7) 八月 8th Month	酉 You Rooster	戌 Xu Dog	卯 Mao Rabbit
戌 Dog (Oct 8 - Nov 6) 九月 9th Month	未 Wei Goat	酉 You Rooster	寅 Yin Tiger
亥 Pig (Nov 7 - Dec 6) 十月 10th Month	亥 Hai Pig	申 Shen Monkey	丑 Chou Ox
子 Rat (Dec 7 - Jan 5) 十一月 11th Month	卯 Mao Rabbit	未 Wei Goat	子 Zi Rat
丑 Ox (Jan 6 - Feb 3) 十二月 12th Month	戌 Xu Dog	午 Wu Horse	亥 Hai Pig

丙申 (Bing Shen)
Fire Monkey

Heavenly Stem 天干	丙 **Yang Fire (**陽火**)**
Earthly Branch 地支	申 **Monkey (Yang Metal** 陽金**)**
Hidden Stem 藏干	庚 **Yang Metal,** 壬 **Yang Water,** 戊 **Yang Earth**
Na Yin 納音	山下火 **Fire from mountain slopes**
Grand Duke 太歲	申 **Monkey**
Xuan Kong Five Element 玄空五行	8 木 **Wood**
Gua Name 卦名	雷水解 **Relief**
Xuan Kong Period Luck 玄空卦運	4

Annual Positive Stars for Opening Mountain, Establishing Facing and Commencing Repairs 開山立向修方吉星:

歲德 **Duke Virtue**	丙 _Bing_ **Yang Fire**	
歲德合 **Duke Virtue Combo**	辛 _Xin_ **Yin Metal**	
歲枝德 **Duke Branch Virtue**	丑 _Chou_ **Ox**	
陽貴人 **Yang Nobleman**	酉 _You_ **Rooster**	
陰貴人 **Yin Nobleman**	亥 _Hai_ **Pig**	
歲祿 **Duke Prosperous**	巳 _Si_ **Snake**	
歲馬 **Duke Horse**	寅 _Yin_ **Tiger**	
奏書 **Decree**	坤 _Kun_	
博士 **Professor**	艮 _Gen_	

Annual Negative Stars for Opening Mountain, Establishing Facing and Commencing Repairs 開山立向修方凶星：

太歲 Grand Duke	歲破 Year Breaker	三煞 Three Killings			坐煞向煞 Sitting Sha Facing Sha				浮天空亡 Floating Heaven Emptiness	
申 Shen Monkey	寅 Yin Tiger	巳 Si Snake	午 Wu Horse	未 Wei Goat	丙 Bing Yang Fire	丁 Ding Yin Fire	壬 Ren Yang Water	癸 Gui Yin Water	巽 Xun	辛 Xin Yin Metal

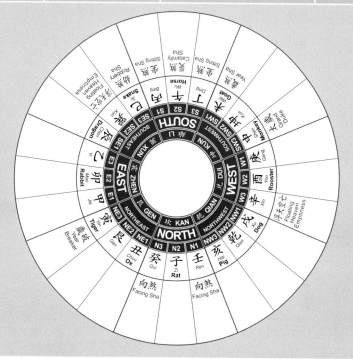

Annual San Yuan Purple White Stars 三元紫白九星：

上元 Upper Period Period 1, 2, 3			中元 Middle Period Period 4, 5, 6			下元 Lower Period Period 7, 8, 9		
巽SE **4**	離S **9**	坤SW **2**	巽SE **7**	離S **3**	坤SW **5**	巽SE **1**	離S **6**	坤SW **8**
震E **3**	**5** 丙申 Bing Shen Fire Monkey	兌W **7**	震E **6**	**8** 丙申 Bing Shen Fire Monkey	兌W **1**	震E **9**	**2** 丙申 Bing Shen Fire Monkey	兌W **4**
艮NE **8**	坎N **1**	乾NW **6**	艮NE **2**	坎N **4**	乾NW **9**	艮NE **5**	坎N **7**	乾NW **3**

Mountain Covering Yellow Path 蓋山黃道:

貪狼 Tan Lang **Greedy Wolf**		巨門 Ju Men **Huge Door**				武曲 Wu Qu **Military Arts**		文曲 Wen Qu **Literary Arts**			
坤 Kun SW2	乙 Yi E3	坎 Kan N2	癸 Gui N3	申 Shen SW3	辰 Chen SE1	乾 Qian NW2	甲 Jia E1	震 Zhen E2	庚 Geng W1	亥 Hai NW3	未 Wei SW1

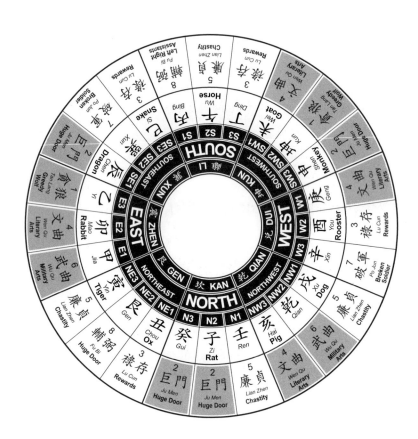

Heaven Penetrating Force 通天竅:

三合前方 **Facing Three Harmony**	艮寅 Gen Yin	甲卯 Jia Mao	乙辰 Yi Chen
三合後方 **Sitting Three Harmony**	坤申 Kun Shen	庚酉 Geng You	辛戌 Xin Xu

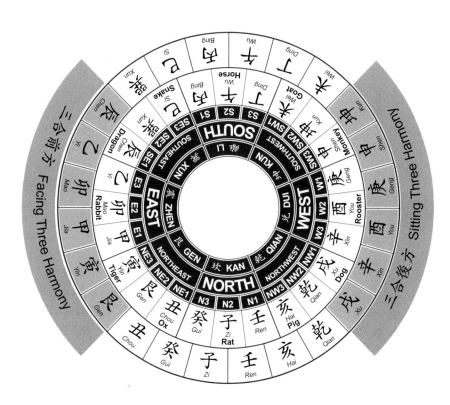

Moving Horse Six Ren Assessment 走馬六壬:

神后 Shen Hou **Holy Empress**	功曹 Gong Cao **Marshall**	天罡 Tian Gang **Heavenly Dipper**	勝光 Sheng Guang **Subliminal Bright**	傳送 Chuan Song **Great General**	河魁 He Kui **River Scholar**
乙辰 Yi Chen	丙午 Bing Wu	坤申 Kun Shen	辛戌 Xin Xu	壬子 Ren Zi	艮寅 Gen Yin

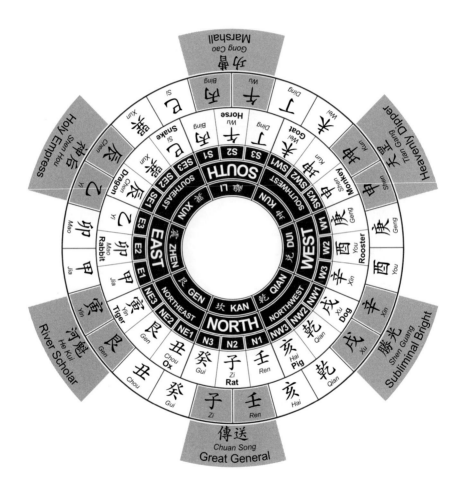

Four Advantages Three Cycles Star Plate 四利三元:

太陽 *Tai Yang* **Sun**	太陰 *Tai Yin* **Moon**	龍德 *Long De* **Dragon Virtue**	福德 *Fu De* **Fortune Virtue**
酉 *You* **Rooster**	亥 *Hai* **Pig**	卯 *Mao* **Rabbit**	巳 *Si* **Snake**

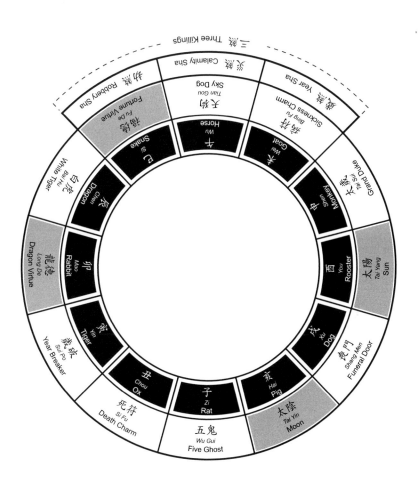

Negative Sectors For Opening Mountain 開山凶位：

年剋山家 Year Countering Sitting

震	艮	巳
Zhen	Gen	Si
E2	NE2	SE3

陰府太歲 Yin Fu Tai Sui **Yin Mansion Grand Duke**	六害 Liu Hai **Six Harm**	死符 Si Fu **Death Charm**	炙退 Zhi Tui **Roasting Star**
坎 Kan **N2** 坤 Kun **SW2**	亥 Hai **NW3**	丑 Chou **NE1**	卯 Mao **E2**

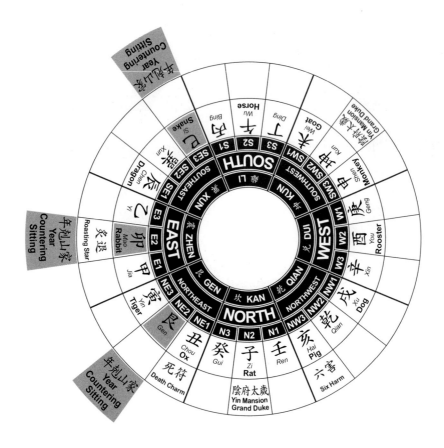

Negative Directions to Establish Facing 立向凶方:

巡山羅喉 *Xun Shan Luo Hou* **Mountain Patrol Luo Hou Star**	病符 *Bing Fu* **Sickness Charm**
庚 *Geng* **W1**	未 *Wei* **SW1**

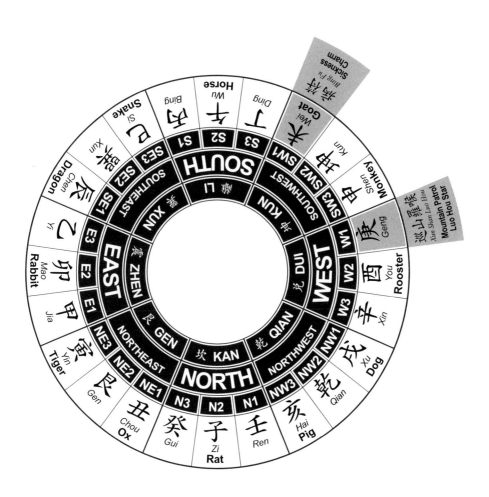

Negative Repair / Renovation Sectors Table 修方凶位表：

天官符 Heavenly Officer Charm	亥 *Hai* Pig		飛廉 Flying Chaste	辰 *Chen* Dragon
地官符 Earthly Officer Charm	子 *Zi* Rat		喪門 Funeral Door	戌 *Xu* Dog
大煞 Great Sha	子 *Zi* Rat		弔客 Suspended Guest	午 *Wu* Horse
大將軍 Big General	午 *Wu* Horse		白虎 White Tiger	辰 *Chen* Dragon
力士 Strong Man	乾 *Qian*		金神 Golden God	寅 *Yin* Tiger 卯 *Mao* Rabbit 午 *Wu* Horse 未 *Wei* Goat 子 *Zi* Rat 丑 *Chou* Ox
蠶室 Silkworm Room	巽 *Xun*			
蠶官 Silkworm Officer	辰 *Chen* Dragon			
蠶命 Silkworm Life	巳 *Si* Snake			
歲刑 Duke Punishment	寅 *Yin* Tiger		獨火 Lonely Fire	離 *Li*
黃幡 Yellow Flag	辰 *Chen* Dragon		五鬼 Five Ghost	申 *Shen* Monkey
豹尾 Leopard Tail	戌 *Xu* Dog		破敗五鬼 Destructive Five Ghost	坤 *Kun*

Negative Repair / Renovation Sectors Diagram 修方凶位圖：

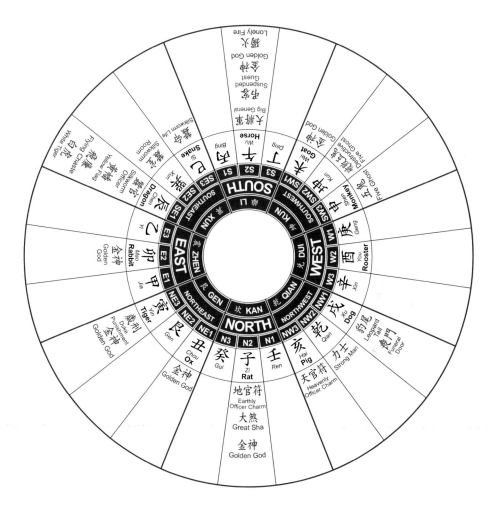

12-Month Auxiliary Stars Reference Table :
丙申年十二月，開山立向修方星表

Positive Monthly Stars 吉星方

月 MONTH	寅 Tiger (Feb 4 - Mar 5) 正月 1st Month	卯 Rabbit (Mar 6 - Apr 4) 二月 2nd Month	辰 Dragon (Apr 5 - May 5) 三月 3rd Month	巳 Snake (May 6 - Jun 5) 四月 4th Month	午 Horse (Jun 6 - July 6) 五月 5th Month	未 Goat (July 7 - Aug 7) 六月 6th Month
天道 Heavenly Path	南 South	西南 Southwest	北 North	西 West	西北 Northwest	東 East
天德 Heavenly Virtue	丁 Ding Yin Fire	坤 Kun (申)	壬 Ren Yang Water	辛 Xin Yin Metal	乾 Qian (亥)	甲 Jia Yang Wood
天德合 Heavenly Virtue Combo	壬 Ren Yang Water	(巳)	丁 Ding Yin Fire	丙 Bing Yang Fire	(寅)	己 Ji Yin Earth
月德 Monthly Virtue	丙 Bing Yang Fire	甲 Jia Yang Wood	壬 Ren Yang Water	庚 Geng Yang Metal	丙 Bing Yang Fire	甲 Jia Yang Wood
月德合 Monthly Virtue Combo	辛 Xin Yin Metal	己 Ji Yin Earth	丁 Ding Yin Fire	乙 Yi Yin Wood	辛 Xin Yin Metal	己 Ji Yin Earth
月空 Month Emptiness	壬 Ren Yang Water	庚 Geng Yang Metal	丙 Bing Yang Fire	甲 Jia Yang Wood	壬 Ren Yang Water	庚 Geng Yang Metal
陽貴人 Yang Nobleman	震 Zhen	坤 Kun	坎 Kan	離 Lii	艮 Gen	兌 Dui
陰貴人 Yin Nobleman	中 Middle	巽 Xun	震 Zhen	坤 Kun	坎 Kan	離 Lii
飛天祿 Flying Heavenly Wealth	艮 Gen	兌 Dui	乾 Qian	中 Middle	坎 Kan	離 Li
飛天馬 Flying Heavenly Horse	中 Middle	坎 Kan	離 Li	艮 Gen	兌 Dui	乾 Qian

12-Month Auxiliary Stars Reference Table :
丙申年十二月，開山立向修方星表

申 Monkey (Aug 8 - Sept 7)	酉 Rooster (Sept 8 - Oct 7)	戌 Dog (Oct 8 - Nov 6)	亥 Pig (Nov 7 - Dec 6)	子 Rat (Dec 7 - Jan 5)	丑 Ox (Jan 6 - Feb 3)	月 MONTH
七月 7th Month	八月 8th Month	九月 9th Month	十月 10th Month	十一月 11th Month	十二月 12th Month	
北 North	東北 Northeast	南 South	東 East	東南 Southeast	西 West	天道 Heavenly Path
癸 Gui Yin Water	艮 Gen (寅)	丙 Bing Yang Fire	乙 Yi Yin Wood	巽 Xun (巳)	庚 Geng Yang Metal	天德 Heavenly Virtue
戊 Wu Yang Earth	(亥)	辛 Xin Yin Metal	庚 Geng Yang Metal	(申)	乙 Yi Yin Wood	天德合 Heavenly Virtue Combo
壬 Ren Yang Water	庚 Geng Yang Metal	丙 Bing Yang Fire	甲 Jia Yang Wood	壬 Ren Yang Water	庚 Geng Yang Metal	月德 Monthly Virtue
丁 Ding Yin Fire	乙 Yi Yin Wood	辛 Xin Yin Metal	己 Ji Yin Earth	丁 Ding Yin Fire	乙 Yi Yin Wood	月德合 Monthly Virtue Combo
丙 Bing Yang Fire	甲 Jia Yang Wood	壬 Ren Yang Water	庚 Geng Yang Metal	丙 Bing Yang Fire	甲 Jia Yang Wood	月空 Month Emptiness
乾 Qian	中 Middle	坎 Kan	離 Lii	艮 Gen	兌 Dui	陽貴人 Yang Nobleman
艮 Gen	兌 Dui	乾 Qian	中 Middle	坎 Kan	離 Lii	陰貴人 Yin Nobleman
艮 Gen	兌 Dui	乾 Qian	中 Middle	巽 Xun	震 Zhen	飛天祿 Flying Heavenly Wealth
中 Middle	巽 Xun	震 Zhen	坤 Kun	坎 Kan	離 Lii	飛天馬 Flying Heavenly Horse

Monthly Purple White Stars 月紫白九星：

寅 Tiger (Feb 4 - Mar 5) 正月 1st Month

巽SE	離S	坤SW
1 White 一白	6 White 六白	8 White 八白
震E 9 Purple 九紫	2 Black 二黑	4 Green 四綠 兌W
艮NE 5 Yellow 五黃	坎N 7 Red 七赤	乾NW 3 Jade 三碧

卯 Rabbit (Mar 6 - Apr 4) 二月 2nd Month

巽SE	離S	坤SW
9 Purple 九紫	5 Yellow 五黃	7 Red 七赤
震E 8 White 八白	1 White 一白	3 Jade 三碧 兌W
艮NE 4 Green 四綠	坎N 6 White 六白	乾NW 2 Black 二黑

辰 Dragon (Apr 5 - May 5) 三月 3rd Month

巽SE	離S	坤SW
8 White 八白	4 Green 四綠	6 White 六白
震E 7 Red 七赤	9 Purple 九紫	2 Black 二黑 兌W
艮NE 3 Jade 三碧	坎N 5 Yellow 五黃	乾NW 1 White 一白

巳 Snake (May 6 - Jun 5) 四月 4th Month

巽SE	離S	坤SW
7 Red 七赤	3 Jade 三碧	5 Yellow 五黃
震E 6 White 六白	8 White 八白	1 White 一白 兌W
艮NE 2 Black 二黑	坎N 4 Green 四綠	乾NW 9 Purple 九紫

午 Horse (Jun 6 - July 6) 五月 5th Month

巽SE	離S	坤SW
6 White 六白	2 Black 二黑	4 Green 四綠
震E 5 Yellow 五黃	7 Red 七赤	9 Purple 九紫 兌W
艮NE 1 White 一白	坎N 3 Jade 三碧	乾NW 8 White 八白

未 Goat (July 7 - Aug 7) 六月 6th Month

巽SE	離S	坤SW
5 Yellow 五黃	1 White 一白	3 Jade 三碧
震E 4 Green 四綠	6 White 六白	8 White 八白 兌W
艮NE 9 Purple 九紫	坎N 2 Black 二黑	乾NW 7 Red 七赤

申 Monkey (Aug 8 - Sept 7) 七月 7th Month

巽SE	離S	坤SW
4 Green 四綠	9 Purple 九紫	2 Black 二黑
震E 3 Jade 三碧	5 Yellow 五黃	7 Red 七赤 兌W
艮NE 8 White 八白	坎N 1 White 一白	乾NW 6 White 六白

酉 Rooster (Sept 8 - Oct 7) 八月 8th Month

巽SE	離S	坤SW
3 Jade 三碧	8 White 八白	1 White 一白
震E 2 Black 二黑	4 Green 四綠	6 White 六白 兌W
艮NE 7 Red 七赤	坎N 9 Purple 九紫	乾NW 5 Yellow 五黃

戌 Dog (Oct 8 - Nov 6) 九月 9th Month

巽SE	離S	坤SW
2 Black 二黑	7 Red 七赤	9 Purple 九紫
震E 1 White 一白	3 Jade 三碧	5 Yellow 五黃 兌W
艮NE 6 White 六白	坎N 8 White 八白	乾NW 4 Green 四綠

亥 Pig (Nov 7 - Dec 6) 十月 10th Month

巽SE	離S	坤SW
1 White 一白	6 White 六白	8 White 八白
震E 9 Purple 九紫	2 Black 二黑	4 Green 四綠 兌W
艮NE 5 Yellow 五黃	坎N 7 Red 七赤	乾NW 3 Jade 三碧

子 Rat (Dec 7 - Jan 5) 十一月 11th Month

巽SE	離S	坤SW
9 Purple 九紫	5 Yellow 五黃	7 Red 七赤
震E 8 White 八白	1 White 一白	3 Jade 三碧 兌W
艮NE 4 Green 四綠	坎N 6 White 六白	乾NW 2 Black 二黑

丑 Ox (Jan 6 - Feb 3) 十二月 12th Month

巽SE	離S	坤SW
8 White 八白	4 Green 四綠	6 White 六白
震E 7 Red 七赤	9 Purple 九紫	2 Black 二黑 兌W
艮NE 3 Jade 三碧	坎N 5 Yellow 五黃	乾NW 1 White 一白

Qi Men Three Nobles 三奇 :

Three Nobles 三奇 / Seasons	乙 Yi	丙 Bing	丁 Ding
立春 **Coming of Spring** Feb 4 - Feb 18	離 Li	坎 Kan	坤 Kun
春分 **Spring Equinox** Mar 21 - Apr 4	巽 Xun	中 **Middle**	乾 Qian
立夏 **Coming of Summer** May 6 - May 20	中 **Middle**	乾 Qian	兌 Dui
夏至 **Summer Solstice** Jun 22 - Jul 6	艮 Gen	兌 Dui	乾 Qian
立秋 **Coming of Autumn** Aug 8 - Aug 23	坎 Kan	離 Li	艮 Gen
秋分 **Autumn Equinox** Sept 23 - Oct 7	乾 Qian	中 **Middle**	巽 Xun
立冬 **Coming of Winter** Nov 7 - Nov 22	中 **Middle**	巽 Xun	震 Zhen
冬至 **Winter Solstice** Dec 22 - Jan 5	坤 Kun	震 Zhen	巽 Xun

Sectors to Avoid Opening Mountain 開山凶位 :

月 MONTH	月建 Month Establishment	月破 Month Destruction	月剋山家 Month Countering Sitting		陰府太歲 Yin Mansion Grand Duke	
寅 **Tiger** (Feb 4 - Mar 5) 正月 **1st Month**	寅 *Yin* **Tiger**	申 *Shen* **Monkey**	–		乾 *Qian*	兌 *Dui*
卯 **Rabbit** (Mar 6 - Apr 4) 二月 **2nd Month**	卯 *Mao* **Rabbit**	酉 *You* **Rooster**	–		坤 *Kun*	坎 *Kan*
辰 **Dragon** (Apr 5 - May 5) 三月 **3rd Month**	辰 *Chen* **Dragon**	戌 *Xu* **Dog**	乾 *Qian*	兌 *Dui*	離 *Li*	乾 *Qian*
巳 **Snake** (May 6 - Jun 5) 四月 **4th Month**	巳 *Si* **Snake**	亥 *Hai* **Pig**	亥 *Hai* **Pig**	丁 *Ding* **Yin Fire**	震 *Zhen*	坤 *Kun*
午 **Horse** (Jun 6 - July 6) 五月 **5th Month**	午 *Wu* **Horse**	子 *Zi* **Rat**	離 *Li*	丙 *Bing* **Yang Fire**	艮 *Gen*	巽 *Xun*
未 **Goat** (July 7 - Aug 7) 六月 **6th Month**	未 *Wei* **Goat**	丑 *Chou* **Ox**	壬 *Ren* **Yang Water**	乙 *Yi* **Yin Wood**	兌 *Dui*	乾 *Qian*
申 **Monkey** (Aug 8 - Sept 7) 七月 **7th Month**	申 *Shen* **Monkey**	寅 *Yin* **Tiger**	震 *Zhen*	巳 *Si* **Snake**	坎 *Kan*	坤 *Kun*
酉 **Rooster** (Sept 8 - Oct 7) 八月 **8th Month**	酉 *You* **Rooster**	卯 *Mao* **Rabbit**	艮 *Gen*		乾 *Qian*	離 *Li*
戌 **Dog** (Oct 8 - Nov 6) 九月 **9th Month**	戌 *Xu* **Dog**	辰 *Chen* **Dragon**	–		坤 *Kun*	震 *Zhen*
亥 **Pig** (Nov 7 - Dec 6) 十月 **10th Month**	亥 *Hai* **Pig**	巳 *Si* **Snake**	–		巽 *Xun*	艮 *Gen*
子 **Rat** (Dec 7 - Jan 5) 十一月 **11th Month**	子 *Zi* **Rat**	午 *Wu* **Horse**	水 **Water**	山 **Mountain**	乾 *Qian*	兌 *Dui*
丑 **Ox** (Jan 6 - Feb 3) 十二月 **12th Month**	丑 *Chou* **Ox**	未 *Wei* **Goat**	土 **Earth**		坤 *Kun*	坎 *Kan*

Negative Repair / Renovation Sectors 修方凶位 :

月 MONTH	天官符 Heavenly Officer Charm			地官符 Earth Officer Charm			小月建 Small Month Establishment		
寅 Tiger (Feb 4 - Mar 5) 正月 1st Month		中 Middle		戌 Xu Dog	乾 Qian	亥 Hai Pig		中 Middle	
卯 Rabbit (Mar 6 - Apr 4) 二月 2nd Month	辰 Chen Dragon	巽 Xun	巳 Si Snake		中 Middle		戌 Xu Dog	乾 Qian	亥 Hai Pig
辰 Dragon (Apr 5 - May 5) 三月 3rd Month	甲 Jia Yang Wood	震 Zhen	乙 Yi Yin Wood	辰 Chen Dragon	巽 Xun	巳 Si Snake	庚 Geng Yang Metal	兌 Dui	辛 Xin Yin Metal
巳 Snake (May 6 - Jun 5) 四月 4th Month	未 Wei Goat	坤 Kun	申 Shen Monkey	甲 Jia Yang Wood	震 Zhen	乙 Yi Yin Wood	丑 Chou Ox	艮 Gen	寅 Yin Tiger
午 Horse (Jun 6 - July 6) 五月 5th Month	壬 Ren Yang Water	坎 Kan	癸 Gui Yin Water	未 Wei Goat	坤 Kun	申 Shen Monkey	丙 Bing Yang Fire	離 Li	丁 Ding Yin Fire
未 Goat (July 7 - Aug 7) 六月 6th Month	丙 Bing Yang Fire	離 Li	丁 Ding Yin Fire	壬 Ren Yang Water	坎 Kan	癸 Gui Yin Water	壬 Ren Yang Water	坎 Kan	癸 Gui Yin Water
申 Monkey (Aug 8 - Sept 7) 七月 7th Month	丑 Chou Ox	艮 Gen	寅 Yin Tiger	丙 Bing Yang Fire	離 Li	丁 Ding Yin Fire	未 Wei Goat	坤 Kun	申 Shen Monkey
酉 Rooster (Sept 8 - Oct 7) 八月 8th Month	庚 Geng Yang Metal	兌 Dui	辛 Xin Yin Metal	丑 Chou Ox	艮 Gen	寅 Yin Tiger	甲 Jia Yang Wood	震 Zhen	乙 Yi Yin Wood
戌 Dog (Oct 8 - Nov 6) 九月 9th Month	戌 Xu Dog	乾 Qian	亥 Hai Pig	庚 Geng Yang Metal	兌 Dui	辛 Xin Yin Metal	辰 Chen Dragon	巽 Xun	巳 Si Snake
亥 Pig (Nov 7 - Dec 6) 十月 10th Month		中 Middle		戌 Xu Dog	乾 Qian	亥 Hai Pig		中 Middle	
子 Rat (Dec 7 - Jan 5) 十一月 11th Month	庚 Geng Yang Metal	兌 Dui	辛 Xin Yin Metal		中 Middle		戌 Xu Dog	乾 Qian	亥 Hai Pig
丑 Ox (Jan 6 - Feb 3) 十二月 12th Month	戌 Xu Dog	乾 Qian	亥 Hai Pig	庚 Geng Yang Metal	兌 Dui	辛 Xin Yin Metal	庚 Geng Yang Metal	兌 Dui	辛 Xin Yin Metal

Negative Repair / Renovation Sectors 修方凶位 :

月 MONTH	大月建 Big Month Establishment			飛大煞 Flying Great Sha			丙丁獨火 Bing Ding Lonely Fire	
寅 Tiger (Feb 4 - Mar 5) 正月 1st Month	未 Wei Goat	坤 Kun	申 Shen Monkey	戌 Xu Dog	乾 Qian	亥 Hai Pig	坤 Kun	震 Zhen
卯 Rabbit (Mar 6 - Apr 4) 二月 2nd Month	壬 Ren Yang Water	坎 Kan	癸 Gui Yin Water	中 Middle			坎 Kan	坤 Kun
辰 Dragon (Apr 5 - May 5) 三月 3rd Month	丙 Bing Yang Fire	離 Li	丁 Ding Yin Fire	辰 Chen Dragon	巽 Xun	巳 Si Snake	離 Li	坎 Kan
巳 Snake (May 6 - Jun 5) 四月 4th Month	丑 Chou Ox	艮 Gen	寅 Yin Tiger	甲 Jia Yang Wood	震 Zhen	乙 Yi Yin Wood	艮 Gen	離 Li
午 Horse (Jun 6 - July 6) 五月 5th Month	庚 Geng Yang Metal	兌 Dui	辛 Xin Yin Metal	未 Wei Goat	坤 Kun	申 Shen Monkey	兌 Dui	艮 Gen
未 Goat (July 7 - Aug 7) 六月 6th Month	戌 Xu Dog	乾 Qian	亥 Hai Pig	壬 Ren Yang Water	坎 Kan	癸 Gui Yin Water	乾 Qian	兌 Dui
申 Monkey (Aug 8 - Sept 7) 七月 7th Month	中 Middle			丙 Bing Yang Fire	離 Li	丁 Ding Yin Fire	中 Middle	乾 Qian
酉 Rooster (Sept 8 - Oct 7) 八月 8th Month	辰 Chen Dragon	巽 Xun	巳 Si Snake	丑 Chou Ox	艮 Gen	寅 Yin Tiger	中 Middle	
戌 Dog (Oct 8 - Nov 6) 九月 9th Month	甲 Jia Yang Wood	震 Zhen	乙 Yi Yin Wood	庚 Geng Yang Metal	兌 Dui	辛 Xin Yin Metal	巽 Xun	中 Middle
亥 Pig (Nov 7 - Dec 6) 十月 10th Month	未 Wei Goat	坤 Kun	申 Shen Monkey	戌 Xu Dog	乾 Qian	亥 Hai Pig	震 Zhen	巽 Xun
子 Rat (Dec 7 - Jan 5) 十一月 11th Month	壬 Ren Yang Water	坎 Kan	癸 Gui Yin Water	中 Middle			坤 Kun	震 Zhen
丑 Ox (Jan 6 - Feb 3) 十二月 12th Month	丙 Bing Yang Fire	離 Li	丁 Ding Yin Fire	庚 Geng Yang Metal	兌 Dui	辛 Xin Yin Metal	坎 Kan	坤 Kun

Negative Repair / Renovation Sectors 修方凶位 :

月 MONTH	月遊火 Month Wondering Fire	三煞 Monthly 3 Killings		
		劫煞 Robbery Sha	災煞 Calamity Sha	月煞 Month Sha
寅 Tiger (Feb 4 - Mar 5) 正月 1st Month	兌 Dui	亥 Hai Pig	子 Zi Rat	丑 Chou Ox
卯 Rabbit (Mar 6 - Apr 4) 二月 2nd Month	艮 Gen	申 Shen Monkey	酉 You Rooster	戌 Xu Dog
辰 Dragon (Apr 5 - May 5) 三月 3rd Month	離 Li	巳 Si Snake	午 Wu Horse	未 Wei Goat
巳 Snake (May 6 - Jun 5) 四月 4th Month	坎 Kan	寅 Yin Tiger	卯 Mao Rabbit	辰 Chen Dragon
午 Horse (Jun 6 - July 6) 五月 5th Month	坤 Kun	亥 Hai Pig	子 Zi Rat	丑 Chou Ox
未 Goat (July 7 - Aug 7) 六月 6th Month	震 Zhen	申 Shen Monkey	酉 You Rooster	戌 Xu Dog
申 Monkey (Aug 8 - Sept 7) 七月 7th Month	巽 Xun	巳 Si Snake	午 Wu Horse	未 Wei Goat
酉 Rooster (Sept 8 - Oct 7) 八月 8th Month	中 Middle	寅 Yin Tiger	卯 Mao Rabbit	辰 Chen Dragon
戌 Dog (Oct 8 - Nov 6) 九月 9th Month	乾 Qian	亥 Hai Pig	子 Zi Rat	丑 Chou Ox
亥 Pig (Nov 7 - Dec 6) 十月 10th Month	兌 Dui	申 Shen Monkey	酉 You Rooster	戌 Xu Dog
子 Rat (Dec 7 - Jan 5) 十一月 11th Month	艮 Gen	巳 Si Snake	午 Wu Horse	未 Wei Goat
丑 Ox (Jan 6 - Feb 3) 十二月 12th Month	離 Li	寅 Yin Tiger	卯 Mao Rabbit	辰 Chen Dragon

Negative Repair / Renovation Sectors 修方凶位 :

月 MONTH	月刑 Month Punishment	月害 Month Harm	月厭 Month Detest
寅 Tiger (Feb 4 - Mar 5) 正月 1st Month	巳 *Si* Snake	巳 *Si* Snake	戌 *Xu* Dog
卯 Rabbit (Mar 6 - Apr 4) 二月 2nd Month	子 *Zi* Rat	辰 *Chen* Dragon	酉 *You* Rooster
辰 Dragon (Apr 5 - May 5) 三月 3rd Month	辰 *Chen* Dragon	卯 *Mao* Rabbit	申 *Shen* Monkey
巳 Snake (May 6 - Jun 5) 四月 4th Month	申 *Shen* Monkey	寅 *Yin* Tiger	未 *Wei* Goat
午 Horse (Jun 6 - July 6) 五月 5th Month	午 *Wu* Horse	丑 *Chou* Ox	午 *Wu* Horse
未 Goat (July 7 - Aug 7) 六月 6th Month	丑 *Chou* Ox	子 *Zi* Rat	巳 *Si* Snake
申 Monkey (Aug 8 - Sept 7) 七月 7th Month	寅 *Yin* Tiger	亥 *Hai* Pig	辰 *Chen* Dragon
酉 Rooster (Sept 8 - Oct 7) 八月 8th Month	酉 *You* Rooster	戌 *Xu* Dog	卯 *Mao* Rabbit
戌 Dog (Oct 8 - Nov 6) 九月 9th Month	未 *Wei* Goat	酉 *You* Rooster	寅 *Yin* Tiger
亥 Pig (Nov 7 - Dec 6) 十月 10th Month	亥 *Hai* Pig	申 *Shen* Monkey	丑 *Chou* Ox
子 Rat (Dec 7 - Jan 5) 十一月 11th Month	卯 *Mao* Rabbit	未 *Wei* Goat	子 *Zi* Rat
丑 Ox (Jan 6 - Feb 3) 十二月 12th Month	戌 *Xu* Dog	午 *Wu* Horse	亥 *Hai* Pig

丙戌 (Bing Xu)
Fire Dog

Heavenly Stem 天干	丙 Yang Fire (陽火)
Earthly Branch 地支	戌 Dog (Yang Earth 陽土)
Hidden Stem 藏干	戊 Yang Earth, 辛 Yin Metal , 丁 Yin Fire
Na Yin 納音	屋上土 Earth from the house
Grand Duke 太歲	戌 Dog
Xuan Kong Five Element 玄空五行	6 水 Water
Gua Name 卦名	☶ 艮爲山 Mountain
Xuan Kong Period Luck 玄空卦運	1

Annual Positive Stars for Opening Mountain, Establishing Facing and Commencing Repairs 開山立向修方吉星：

歲德 Duke Virtue	丙 Bing Yang Fire
歲德合 Duke Virtue Combo	辛 Xin Yin Metal
歲枝德 Duke Branch Virtue	卯 Mao Rabbit
陽貴人 Yang Nobleman	酉 You Rooster
陰貴人 Yin Nobleman	亥 Hai Pig
歲祿 Duke Prosperous	巳 Si Snake
歲馬 Duke Horse	申 Shen Monkey
奏書 Decree	坤 Kun
博士 Professor	艮 Gen

Annual Negative Stars for Opening Mountain, Establishing Facing and Commencing Repairs 開山立向修方凶星 :

太歲 Grand Duke	歲破 Year Breaker	三煞 Three Killings			坐煞向煞 Sitting Sha Facing Sha				浮天空亡 Floating Heaven Emptiness	
戌 *Xu* Dog	辰 *Chen* Dragon	亥 *Hai* Pig	子 *Zi* Rat	丑 *Chou* Ox	壬 *Ren* Yang Water	癸 *Gui* Yin Water	丙 *Bing* Yang Fire	丁 *Ding* Yin Fire	巽 *Xun*	辛 *Xin* Yin Metal

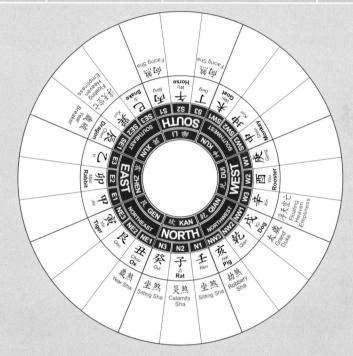

Annual San Yuan Purple White Stars 三元紫白九星 :

上元 Upper Period Period 1, 2, 3			中元 Middle Period Period 4, 5, 6			下元 Lower Period Period 7, 8, 9		
巽SE 5	離S 1	坤SW 3	巽SE 8	離S 4	坤SW 6	巽SE 2	離S 7	坤SW 9
震E 4	**6 丙戌 *Bing Xu* Fire Dog**	兌W 8	震E 7	**4 丙戌 *Bing Xu* Fire Dog**	兌W 2	震E 1	**3 丙戌 *Bing Xu* Fire Dog**	兌W 5
艮NE 9	坎N 2	乾NW 7	艮NE 3	坎N 5	乾NW 1	艮NE 6	坎N 8	乾NW 4

Mountain Covering Yellow Path 蓋山黃道：

貪狼 *Tan Lang* **Greedy Wolf**				巨門 *Ju Men* **Huge Door**		武曲 *Wu Qu* **Military Arts**				文曲 *Wen Qu* **Literary Arts**			
坎 *Kan* N2	癸 *Gui* N3	申 *Shen* SW3	辰 *Chen* SE1	坤 *Kun* SW2	乙 *Yi* E3	離 *Li* S2	壬 *Ren* N1	寅 *Yin* NE3	戌 *Xu* NW1	兌 *Dui* W2	丁 *Ding* S3	巳 *Si* SE3	丑 *Chou* NE1

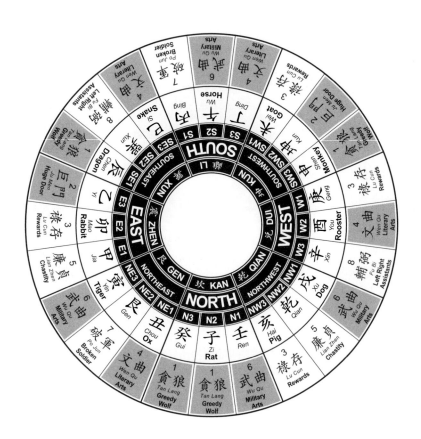

Heaven Penetrating Force 通天竅:			
三合前方 **Facing Three Harmony**	坤申 Kun Shen	庚酉 Geng You	辛戌 Xin Xu
三合後方 **Sitting Three Harmony**	艮寅 Gen Yin	甲卯 Jia Mao	乙辰 Yi Chen

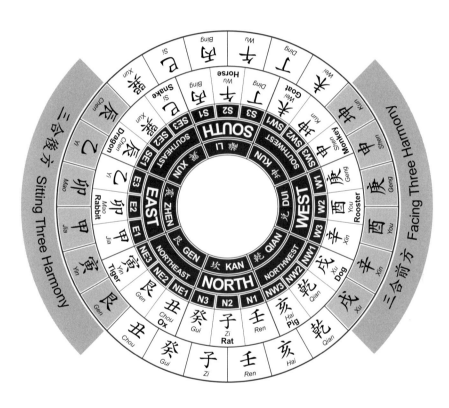

Moving Horse Six Ren Assessment 走馬六壬：

神后 Shen Hou Holy Empress	功曹 Gong Cao Marshall	天罡 Tian Gang Heavenly Dipper	勝光 Sheng Guang Subliminal Bright	傳送 Chuan Song Great General	河魁 He Kui River Scholar
艮寅 Gen Yin	乙辰 Yi Chen	丙午 Bing Wu	坤申 Kun Shen	辛戌 Xin Xu	壬子 Ren Zi

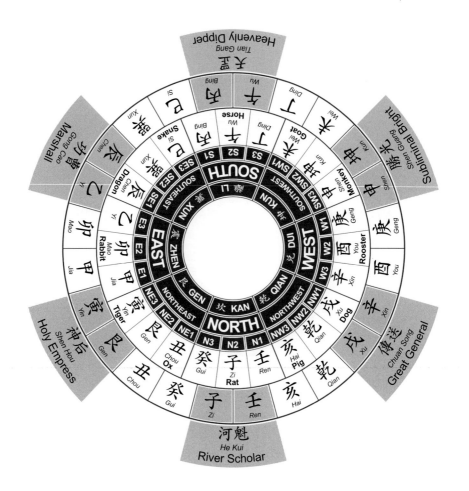

Four Advantages Three Cycles Star Plate 四利三元：

太陽 *Tai Yang* **Sun**	太陰 *Tai Yin* **Moon**	龍德 *Long De* **Dragon Virtue**	福德 *Fu De* **Fortune Virtue**
亥 *Hai* **Pig**	丑 *Chou* **Ox**	巳 *Si* **Snake**	未 *Wei* **Goat**

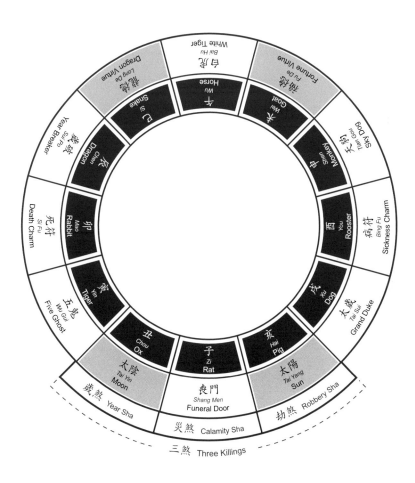

Negative Sectors For Opening Mountain 開山凶位:

年剋山家 Year Countering Sitting

甲 Jia E1	寅 Yin NE3	辰 Chen SE1	巽 Xun SE2	戌 Xu NW1	坎 Kan N	辛 Xin W3	申 Shen SW3	丑 Chou NE1	癸 Gui N3	坤 Kun SW2	庚 Geng W1	未 Wei SW1

陰府太歲 Yin Fu Tai Sui **Yin Mansion Grand Duke**		六害 Liu Hai **Six Harm**	死符 Si Fu **Death Charm**	炙退 Zhi Tui **Roasting Star**
坎 Kan N2	坤 Kun SW2	酉 You W2	卯 Mao E2	酉 You W2

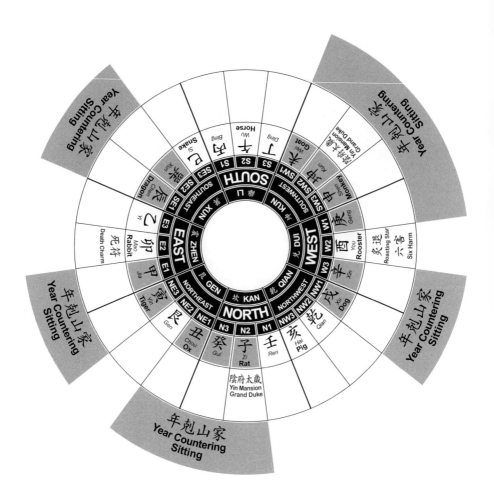

Negative Directions to Establish Facing 立向凶方：

巡山羅喉 *Xun Shan Luo Hou* **Mountain Patrol Luo Hou Star**	病符 *Bing Fu* **Sickness Charm**
乾 *Qian* **NW2**	酉 *You* **W2**

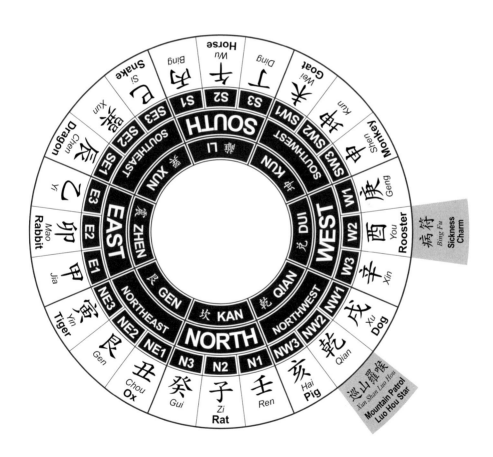

Negative Repair / Renovation Sectors Table 修方凶位表：

天官符 **Heavenly Officer Charm**	巳 *Si* Snake		飛廉 **Flying Chaste**	子 *Zi* Rat
地官符 **Earthly Officer Charm**	寅 *Yin* Tiger		喪門 **Funeral Door**	子 *Zi* Rat
大煞 **Great Sha**	午 *Wu* Horse		弔客 **Suspended Guest**	申 *Shen* Monkey
大將軍 **Big General**	午 *Wu* Horse		白虎 **White Tiger**	午 *Wu* Horse
力士 **Strong Man**	乾 *Qian*		金神 **Golden God**	寅 *Yin* Tiger / 卯 *Mao* Rabbit / 午 *Wu* Horse / 未 *Wei* Goat / 子 *Zi* Rat / 丑 *Chou* Ox
蠶室 **Silkworm Room**	巽 *Xun*			
蠶官 **Silkworm Officer**	辰 *Chen* Dragon			
蠶命 **Silkworm Life**	巳 *Si* Snake			
歲刑 **Duke Punishment**	未 *Wei* Goat		獨火 **Lonely Fire**	乾 *Qian*
黃幡 **Yellow Flag**	戌 *Xu* Dog		五鬼 **Five Ghost**	午 *Wu* Horse
豹尾 **Leopard Tail**	辰 *Chen* Dragon		破敗五鬼 **Destructive Five Ghost**	坤 *Kun*

Negative Repair / Renovation Sectors Diagram 修方凶位圖：

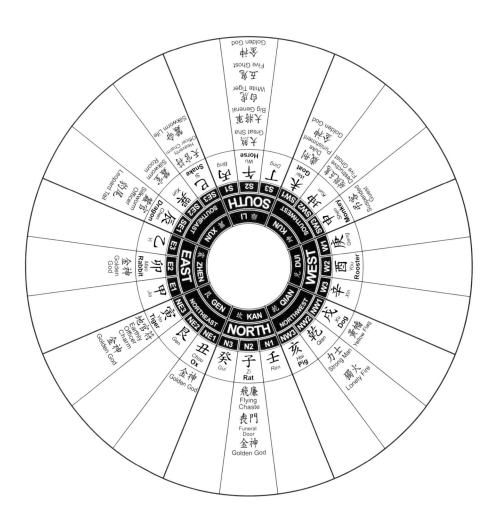

12-Month Auxiliary Stars Reference Table :
丙戌年十二月，開山立向修方星表

Positive Monthly Stars 吉星方

月 MONTH	寅 Tiger (Feb 4 - Mar 5) 正月 1st Month	卯 Rabbit (Mar 6 - Apr 4) 二月 2nd Month	辰 Dragon (Apr 5 - May 5) 三月 3rd Month	巳 Snake (May 6 - Jun 5) 四月 4th Month	午 Horse (Jun 6 - July 6) 五月 5th Month	未 Goat (July 7 - Aug 7) 六月 6th Month
天道 Heavenly Path	南 South	西南 Southwest	北 North	西 West	西北 Northwest	東 East
天德 Heavenly Virtue	丁 Ding Yin Fire	坤 Kun （申）	壬 Ren Yang Water	辛 Xin Yin Metal	乾 Qian （亥）	甲 Jia Yang Wood
天德合 Heavenly Virtue Combo	壬 Ren Yang Water	（巳）	丁 Ding Yin Fire	丙 Bing Yang Fire	（寅）	己 Ji Yin Earth
月德 Monthly Virtue	丙 Bing Yang Fire	甲 Jia Yang Wood	壬 Ren Yang Water	庚 Geng Yang Metal	丙 Bing Yang Fire	甲 Jia Yang Wood
月德合 Monthly Virtue Combo	辛 Xin Yin Metal	己 Ji Yin Earth	丁 Ding Yin Fire	乙 Yi Yin Wood	辛 Xin Yin Metal	己 Ji Yin Earth
月空 Month Emptiness	壬 Ren Yang Water	庚 Geng Yang Metal	丙 Bing Yang Fire	甲 Jia Yang Wood	壬 Ren Yang Water	庚 Geng Yang Metal
陽貴人 Yang Nobleman	震 Zhen	坤 Kun	坎 Kan	離 Li	艮 Gen	兌 Dui
陰貴人 Yin Nobleman	中 Middle	巽 Xun	震 Zhen	坤 Kun	坎 Kan	離 Li
飛天祿 Flying Heavenly Wealth	艮 Gen	兌 Dui	乾 Qian	中 Middle	坎 Kan	離 Li
飛天馬 Flying Heavenly Horse	坤 Kun	坎 Kan	離 Li	艮 Gen	兌 Dui	乾 Qian

12-Month Auxiliary Stars Reference Table :
丙戌年十二月，開山立向修方星表

申 Monkey (Aug 8 - Sept 7) 七月 7th Month	酉 Rooster (Sept 8 - Oct 7) 八月 8th Month	戌 Dog (Oct 8 - Nov 6) 九月 9th Month	亥 Pig (Nov 7 - Dec 6) 十月 10th Month	子 Rat (Dec 7 - Jan 5) 十一月 11th Month	丑 Ox (Jan 6 - Feb 3) 十二月 12th Month	月 MONTH
北 North	東北 Northeast	南 South	東 East	東南 Southeast	西 West	天道 Heavenly Path
癸 Gui Yin Water	艮 Gen (寅)	丙 Bing Yang Fire	乙 Yi Yin Wood	巽 Xun (巳)	庚 Geng Yang Metal	天德 Heavenly Virtue
戊 Wu Yang Earth	(亥)	辛 Xin Yin Metal	庚 Geng Yang Metal	(申)	乙 Yi Yin Wood	天德合 Heavenly Virtue Combo
壬 Ren Yang Water	庚 Geng Yang Metal	丙 Bing Yang Fire	甲 Jia Yang Wood	壬 Ren Yang Water	庚 Geng Yang Metal	月德 Monthly Virtue
丁 Ding Yin Fire	乙 Yi Yin Wood	辛 Xin Yin Metal	己 Ji Yin Earth	丁 Ding Yin Fire	乙 Yi Yin Wood	月德合 Monthly Virtue Combo
丙 Bing Yang Fire	甲 Jia Yang Wood	壬 Ren Yang Water	庚 Geng Yang Metal	丙 Bing Yang Fire	甲 Jia Yang Wood	月空 Month Emptiness
乾 Qian	中 Middle	坎 Kan	離 Li	艮 Gen	兌 Dui	陽貴人 Yang Nobleman
艮 Gen	兌 Dui	乾 Qian	中 Middle	坎 Kan	離 Li	陰貴人 Yin Nobleman
艮 Gen	兌 Dui	乾 Qian	中 Middle	巽 Xun	震 Zhen	飛天祿 Flying Heavenly Wealth
中 Middle	坎 Kan	離 Li	艮 Gen	兌 Dui	乾 Qian	飛天馬 Flying Heavenly Horse

353

Monthly Purple White Stars 月紫白九星 :

寅 Tiger (Feb 4 - Mar 5) 正月 1st Month

巽 SE	離 S	坤 SW
4 Green 四綠	9 Purple 九紫	2 Black 二黑
震 E 3 Jade 三碧	5 Yellow 五黃	7 Red 七赤 兌 W
8 White 八白	1 White 一白	6 White 六白
艮 NE	坎 N	乾 NW

卯 Rabbit (Mar 6 - Apr 4) 二月 2nd Month

巽 SE	離 S	坤 SW
3 Jade 三碧	8 White 八白	1 White 一白
震 E 2 Black 二黑	4 Green 四綠	6 White 六白 兌 W
7 Red 七赤	9 Purple 九紫	5 Yellow 五黃
艮 NE	坎 N	乾 NW

辰 Dragon (Apr 5 - May 5) 三月 3rd Month

巽 SE	離 S	坤 SW
2 Black 二黑	7 Red 七赤	9 Purple 九紫
震 E 1 White 一白	3 Jade 三碧	5 Yellow 五黃 兌 W
6 White 六白	8 White 八白	4 Green 四綠
艮 NE	坎 N	乾 NW

巳 Snake (May 6 - Jun 5) 四月 4th Month

巽 SE	離 S	坤 SW
1 White 一白	6 White 六白	8 White 八白
震 E 9 Purple 九紫	2 Black 二黑	4 Green 四綠 兌 W
5 Yellow 五黃	7 Red 七赤	3 Jade 三碧
艮 NE	坎 N	乾 NW

午 Horse (Jun 6 - July 6) 五月 5th Month

巽 SE	離 S	坤 SW
9 Purple 九紫	5 Yellow 五黃	7 Red 七赤
震 E 8 White 八白	1 White 一白	3 Jade 三碧 兌 W
4 Green 四綠	6 White 六白	2 Black 二黑
艮 NE	坎 N	乾 NW

未 Goat (July 7 - Aug 7) 六月 6th Month

巽 SE	離 S	坤 SW
8 White 八白	4 Green 四綠	6 White 六白
震 E 7 Red 七赤	9 Purple 九紫	2 Black 二黑 兌 W
3 Jade 三碧	5 Yellow 五黃	1 White 一白
艮 NE	坎 N	乾 NW

申 Monkey (Aug 8 - Sept 7) 七月 7th Month

巽 SE	離 S	坤 SW
7 Red 七赤	3 Jade 三碧	5 Yellow 五黃
震 E 6 White 六白	8 White 八白	1 White 一白 兌 W
2 Black 二黑	4 Green 四綠	9 Purple 九紫
艮 NE	坎 N	乾 NW

酉 Rooster (Sept 8 - Oct 7) 八月 8th Month

巽 SE	離 S	坤 SW
6 White 六白	2 Black 二黑	4 Green 四綠
震 E 5 Yellow 五黃	7 Red 七赤	9 Purple 九紫 兌 W
1 White 一白	3 Jade 三碧	8 White 八白
艮 NE	坎 N	乾 NW

戌 Dog (Oct 8 - Nov 6) 九月 9th Month

巽 SE	離 S	坤 SW
5 Yellow 五黃	1 White 一白	3 Jade 三碧
震 E 4 Green 四綠	6 White 六白	8 White 八白 兌 W
Purple 九紫	2 Black 二黑	7 Red 七赤
艮 NE	坎 N	乾 NW

亥 Pig (Nov 7 - Dec 6) 十月 10th Month

巽 SE	離 S	坤 SW
4 Green 四綠	9 Purple 九紫	2 Black 二黑
震 E 3 Jade 三碧	5 Yellow 五黃	7 Red 七赤 兌 W
8 White 八白	1 White 一白	6 White 六白
艮 NE	坎 N	乾 NW

子 Rat (Dec 7 - Jan 5) 十一月 11th Month

巽 SE	離 S	坤 SW
3 Jade 三碧	8 White 八白	1 White 一白
震 E 2 Black 二黑	4 Green 四綠	6 White 六白 兌 W
7 Red 七赤	9 Purple 九紫	5 Yellow 五黃
艮 NE	坎 N	乾 NW

丑 Ox (Jan 6 - Feb 3) 十二月 12th Month

巽 SE	離 S	坤 SW
2 Black 二黑	7 Red 七赤	9 Purple 九紫
震 E 1 White 一白	3 Jade 三碧	5 Yellow 五黃 兌 W
6 White 六白	8 White 八白	4 Green 四綠
艮 NE	坎 N	乾 NW

Qi Men Three Nobles 三奇 :

Three Nobles 三奇 / Seasons	乙 Yi	丙 Bing	丁 Ding
立春 **Coming of Spring** Feb 4 - Feb 18	艮 Gen	離 Li	坎 Kan
春分 **Spring Equinox** Mar 21 - Apr 4	震 Zhen	巽 Xun	中 **Middle**
立夏 **Coming of Summer** May 6 - May 20	巽 Xun	中 **Middle**	乾 Qian
夏至 **Summer Solstice** Jun 22 - Jul 6	離 Li	艮 Gen	兑 Dui
立秋 **Coming of Autumn** Aug 8 - Aug 23	坤 Kun	坎 Kan	離 Li
秋分 **Autumn Equinox** Sept 23 - Oct 7	兑 Dui	乾 Qian	中 **Middle**
立冬 **Coming of Winter** Nov 7 - Nov 22	乾 Qian	中 **Middle**	巽 Xun
冬至 **Winter Solstice** Dec 22 - Jan 5	坎 Kan	坤 Kun	震 Zhen

Sectors to Avoid Opening Mountain 開山凶位 :

月 MONTH	月建 Month Establishment	月破 Month Destruction	月剋山家 Month Countering Sitting		陰府太歲 Yin Mansion Grand Duke	
寅 Tiger (Feb 4 - Mar 5) 正月 1st Month	寅 Yin Tiger	申 Shen Monkey	–		乾 Qian	兌 Dui
卯 Rabbit (Mar 6 - Apr 4) 二月 2nd Month	卯 Mao Rabbit	酉 You Rooster	–		坤 Kun	坎 Kan
辰 Dragon (Apr 5 - May 5) 三月 3rd Month	辰 Chen Dragon	戌 Xu Dog	乾 Qian	兌 Dui	離 Li	乾 Qian
巳 Snake (May 6 - Jun 5) 四月 4th Month	巳 Si Snake	亥 Hai Pig	亥 Hai Pig	丁 Ding Yin Fire	震 Zhen	坤 Kun
午 Horse (Jun 6 - July 6) 五月 5th Month	午 Wu Horse	子 Zi Rat	離 Li	丙 Bing Yang Fire	艮 Gen	巽 Xun
未 Goat (July 7 - Aug 7) 六月 6th Month	未 Wei Goat	丑 Chou Ox	壬 Ren Yang Water	乙 Yi Yin Wood	兌 Dui	乾 Qian
申 Monkey (Aug 8 - Sept 7) 七月 7th Month	申 Shen Monkey	寅 Yin Tiger	震 Zhen	巳 Si Snake	坎 Kan	坤 Kun
酉 Rooster (Sept 8 - Oct 7) 八月 8th Month	酉 You Rooster	卯 Mao Rabbit	艮 Gen		乾 Qian	離 Li
戌 Dog (Oct 8 - Nov 6) 九月 9th Month	戌 Xu Dog	辰 Chen Dragon	–		坤 Kun	震 Zhen
亥 Pig (Nov 7 - Dec 6) 十月 10th Month	亥 Hai Pig	巳 Si Snake	–		巽 Xun	艮 Gen
子 Rat (Dec 7 - Jan 5) 十一月 11th Month	子 Zi Rat	午 Wu Horse	水 Water	山 Mountain	乾 Qian	兌 Dui
丑 Ox (Jan 6 - Feb 3) 十二月 12th Month	丑 Chou Ox	未 Wei Goat	土 Earth		坤 Kun	坎 Kan

Negative Repair / Renovation Sectors 修方凶位 :

月 MONTH	天官符 Heavenly Officer Charm			地官符 Earth Officer Charm			小月建 Small Month Establishment		
寅 **Tiger** (Feb 4 - Mar 5) 正月 **1st Month**	丑 *Chou* Ox	艮 *Gen*	寅 *Yin* Tiger	中 Middle			中 Middle		
卯 **Rabbit** (Mar 6 - Apr 4) 二月 **2nd Month**	庚 *Geng* Yang Metal	兌 *Dui*	辛 *Xin* Yin Metal	庚 *Geng* Yang Metal	兌 *Dui*	辛 *Xin* Yin Metal	戌 *Xu* Dog	乾 *Qian*	亥 *Hai* Pig
辰 **Dragon** (Apr 5 - May 5) 三月 **3rd Month**	戌 *Xu* Dog	乾 *Qian*	亥 *Hai* Pig	戌 *Xu* Dog	乾 *Qian*	亥 *Hai* Pig	庚 *Geng* Yang Metal	兌 *Dui*	辛 *Xin* Yin Metal
巳 **Snake** (May 6 - Jun 5) 四月 **4th Month**	中 Middle			中 Middle			丑 *Chou* Ox	艮 *Gen*	寅 *Yin* Tiger
午 **Horse** (Jun 6 - July 6) 五月 **5th Month**	庚 *Geng* Yang Metal	兌 *Dui*	辛 *Xin* Yin Metal	辰 *Chen* Dragon	巽 *Xun*	巳 *Si* Snake	丙 *Bing* Yang Fire	離 *Li*	丁 *Ding* Yin Fire
未 **Goat** (July 7 - Aug 7) 六月 **6th Month**	戌 *Xu* Dog	乾 *Qian*	亥 *Hai* Pig	甲 *Jia* Yang Wood	震 *Zhen*	乙 *Yi* Yin Wood	壬 *Ren* Yang Water	坎 *Kan*	癸 *Gui* Yin Water
申 **Monkey** (Aug 8 - Sept 7) 七月 **7th Month**	中 Middle			未 *Wei* Goat	坤 *Kun*	申 *Shen* Monkey	未 *Wei* Goat	坤 *Kun*	申 *Shen* Monkey
酉 **Rooster** (Sept 8 - Oct 7) 八月 **8th Month**	辰 *Chen* Dragon	巽 *Xun*	巳 *Si* Snake	壬 *Ren* Yang Water	坎 *Kan*	癸 *Gui* Yin Water	甲 *Jia* Yang Wood	震 *Zhen*	乙 *Yi* Yin Wood
戌 **Dog** (Oct 8 - Nov 6) 九月 **9th Month**	甲 *Jia* Yang Wood	震 *Zhen*	乙 *Yi* Yin Wood	丙 *Bing* Yang Fire	離 *Li*	丁 *Ding* Yin Fire	辰 *Chen* Dragon	巽 *Xun*	巳 *Si* Snake
亥 **Pig** (Nov 7 - Dec 6) 十月 **10th Month**	未 *Wei* Goat	坤 *Kun*	申 *Shen* Monkey	丑 *Chou* Ox	艮 *Gen*	寅 *Yin* Tiger	中 Middle		
子 **Rat** (Dec 7 - Jan 5) 十一月 **11th Month**	壬 *Ren* Yang Water	坎 *Kan*	癸 *Gui* Yin Water	庚 *Geng* Yang Metal	兌 *Dui*	辛 *Xin* Yin Metal	戌 *Xu* Dog	乾 *Qian*	亥 *Hai* Pig
丑 **Ox** (Jan 6 - Feb 3) 十二月 **12th Month**	丙 *Bing* Yang Fire	離 *Li*	丁 *Ding* Yin Fire	戌 *Xu* Dog	乾 *Qian*	亥 *Hai* Pig	庚 *Geng* Yang Metal	兌 *Dui*	辛 *Xin* Yin Metal

Negative Repair / Renovation Sectors 修方凶位 :

月 MONTH	大月建 Big Month Establishment			飛大煞 Flying Great Sha			丙丁獨火 Bing Ding Lonely Fire	
寅 **Tiger** (Feb 4 - Mar 5) 正月 **1st Month**	中 Middle			丙 Bing Yang Fire	離 Li	丁 Ding Yin Fire	坤 Kun	震 Zhen
卯 **Rabbit** (Mar 6 - Apr 4) 二月 **2nd Month**	辰 Chen Dragon	巽 Xun	巳 Si Snake	丑 Chou Ox	艮 Gen	寅 Yin Tiger	坎 Kan	坤 Kun
辰 **Dragon** (Apr 5 - May 5) 三月 **3rd Month**	甲 Jia Yang Wood	震 Zhen	乙 Yi Yin Wood	庚 Geng Yang Metal	兌 Dui	辛 Xin Yin Metal	離 Li	坎 Kan
巳 **Snake** (May 6 - Jun 5) 四月 **4th Month**	未 Wei Goat	坤 Kun	申 Shen Monkey	戌 Xu Dog	乾 Qian	亥 Hai Pig	艮 Gen	離 Li
午 **Horse** (Jun 6 - July 6) 五月 **5th Month**	壬 Ren Yang Water	坎 Kan	癸 Gui Yin Water	中 Middle			兌 Dui	艮 Gen
未 **Goat** (July 7 - Aug 7) 六月 **6th Month**	丙 Bing Yang Fire	離 Li	丁 Ding Yin Fire	庚 Geng Yang Metal	兌 Dui	辛 Xin Yin Metal	乾 Qian	兌 Dui
申 **Monkey** (Aug 8 - Sept 7) 七月 **7th Month**	丑 Chou Ox	艮 Gen	寅 Yin Tiger	戌 Xu Dog	乾 Qian	亥 Hai Pig	中 Middle	乾 Qian
酉 **Rooster** (Sept 8 - Oct 7) 八月 **8th Month**	庚 Geng Yang Metal	兌 Dui	辛 Xin Yin Metal	中 Middle			中 Middle	
戌 **Dog** (Oct 8 - Nov 6) 九月 **9th Month**	戌 Xu Dog	乾 Qian	亥 Hai Pig	辰 Chen Dragon	巽 Xun	巳 Si Snake	巽 Xun	中 Middle
亥 **Pig** (Nov 7 - Dec 6) 十月 **10th Month**	中 Middle			甲 Jia Yang Wood	震 Zhen	乙 Yi Yin Wood	震 Zhen	巽 Xun
子 **Rat** (Dec 7 - Jan 5) 十一月 **11th Month**	辰 Chen Dragon	巽 Xun	巳 Si Snake	未 Wei Goat	坤 Kun	申 Shen Monkey	坤 Kun	震 Zhen
丑 **Ox** (Jan 6 - Feb 3) 十二月 **12th Month**	甲 Jia Yang Wood	震 Zhen	乙 Yi Yin Wood	壬 Ren Yang Water	坎 Kan	癸 Gui Yin Water	坎 Kan	坤 Kun

Negative Repair / Renovation Sectors 修方凶位 :

月 MONTH	月遊火 Month Wondering Fire	三煞 Monthly 3 Killings		
		劫煞 Robbery Sha	災煞 Calamity Sha	月煞 Month Sha
寅 Tiger (Feb 4 - Mar 5) 正月 1st Month	乾 Qian	亥 Hai Pig	子 Zi Rat	丑 Chou Ox
卯 Rabbit (Mar 6 - Apr 4) 二月 2nd Month	兑 Dui	申 Shen Monkey	酉 You Rooster	戌 Xu Dog
辰 Dragon (Apr 5 - May 5) 三月 3rd Month	艮 Gen	巳 Si Snake	午 Wu Horse	未 Wei Goat
巳 Snake (May 6 - Jun 5) 四月 4th Month	離 Li	寅 Yin Tiger	卯 Mao Rabbit	辰 Chen Dragon
午 Horse (Jun 6 - July 6) 五月 5th Month	坎 Kan	亥 Hai Pig	子 Zi Rat	丑 Chou Ox
未 Goat (July 7 - Aug 7) 六月 6th Month	坤 Kun	申 Shen Monkey	酉 You Rooster	戌 Xu Dog
申 Monkey (Aug 8 - Sept 7) 七月 7th Month	震 Zhen	巳 Si Snake	午 Wu Horse	未 Wei Goat
酉 Rooster (Sept 8 - Oct 7) 八月 8th Month	巽 Xun	寅 Yin Tiger	卯 Mao Rabbit	辰 Chen Dragon
戌 Dog (Oct 8 - Nov 6) 九月 9th Month	中 Middle	亥 Hai Pig	子 Zi Rat	丑 Chou Ox
亥 Pig (Nov 7 - Dec 6) 十月 10th Month	乾 Qian	申 Shen Monkey	酉 You Rooster	戌 Xu Dog
子 Rat (Dec 7 - Jan 5) 十一月 11th Month	兑 Dui	巳 Si Snake	午 Wu Horse	未 Wei Goat
丑 Ox (Jan 6 - Feb 3) 十二月 12th Month	艮 Gen	寅 Yin Tiger	卯 Mao Rabbit	辰 Chen Dragon

Negative Repair / Renovation Sectors 修方凶位 :

月 MONTH	月刑 Month Punishment	月害 Month Harm	月厭 Month Detest
寅 Tiger (Feb 4 - Mar 5) 正月 1st Month	巳 Si Snake	巳 Si Snake	戌 Xu Dog
卯 Rabbit (Mar 6 - Apr 4) 二月 2nd Month	子 Zi Rat	辰 Chen Dragon	酉 You Rooster
辰 Dragon (Apr 5 - May 5) 三月 3rd Month	辰 Chen Dragon	卯 Mao Rabbit	申 Shen Monkey
巳 Snake (May 6 - Jun 5) 四月 4th Month	申 Shen Monkey	寅 Yin Tiger	未 Wei Goat
午 Horse (Jun 6 - July 6) 五月 5th Month	午 Wu Horse	丑 Chou Ox	午 Wu Horse
未 Goat (July 7 - Aug 7) 六月 6th Month	丑 Chou Ox	子 Zi Rat	巳 Si Snake
申 Monkey (Aug 8 - Sept 7) 七月 7th Month	寅 Yin Tiger	亥 Hai Pig	辰 Chen Dragon
酉 Rooster (Sept 8 - Oct 7) 八月 8th Month	酉 You Rooster	戌 Xu Dog	卯 Mao Rabbit
戌 Dog (Oct 8 - Nov 6) 九月 9th Month	未 Wei Goat	酉 You Rooster	寅 Yin Tiger
亥 Pig (Nov 7 - Dec 6) 十月 10th Month	亥 Hai Pig	申 Shen Monkey	丑 Chou Ox
子 Rat (Dec 7 - Jan 5) 十一月 11th Month	卯 Mao Rabbit	未 Wei Goat	子 Zi Rat
丑 Ox (Jan 6 - Feb 3) 十二月 12th Month	戌 Xu Dog	午 Wu Horse	亥 Hai Pig

丁丑 (Ding Chou)
Fire Ox

Heavenly Stem 天干	丁 **Yin Fire (陰火)**
Earthly Branch 地支	丑 **Ox (Yin Earth 陰土)**
Hidden Stem 藏干	己 **Yin Earth,** 癸 **Yin Water,** 辛 **Yin Metal**
Na Yin 納音	澗下水 **Water from the streams**
Grand Duke 太歲	丑 **Ox**
Xuan Kong Five Element 玄空五行	4 金 **Metal**
Gua Name 卦名	䷐ 澤雷隨 **Following**
Xuan Kong Period Luck 玄空卦運	7

Annual Positive Stars for Opening Mountain, Establishing Facing and Commencing Repairs 開山立向修方吉星:

歲德 Duke Virtue	壬 Ren Yang Water
歲德合 Duke Virtue Combo	丁 Ding Yin Fire
歲枝德 Duke Branch Virtue	午 Wu Horse
陽貴人 Yang Nobleman	亥 Hai Pig
陰貴人 Yin Nobleman	酉 You Rooster
歲祿 Duke Prosperous	午 Wu Horse
歲馬 Duke Horse	亥 Hai Pig
奏書 Decree	乾 Qian
博士 Professor	巽 Xun

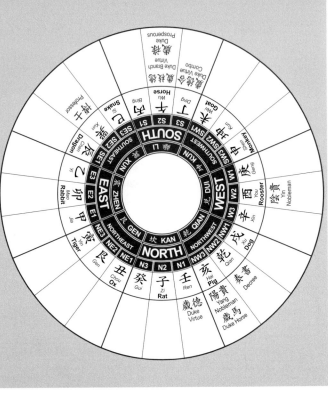

Annual Negative Stars for Opening Mountain, Establishing Facing and Commencing Repairs 開山立向修方凶星：

太歲 Grand Duke	歲破 Year Breaker	三煞 Three Killings			坐煞向煞 Sitting Sha Facing Sha				浮天空亡 Floating Heaven Emptiness	
丑 Chou Ox	未 Wei Goat	寅 Yin Tiger	卯 Mao Rabbit	辰 Chen Dragon	甲 Jia Yang Wood	乙 Yi Yin Wood	庚 Geng Yang Metal	辛 Xin Yin Metal	震 Zhen	庚 Geng Yang Metal

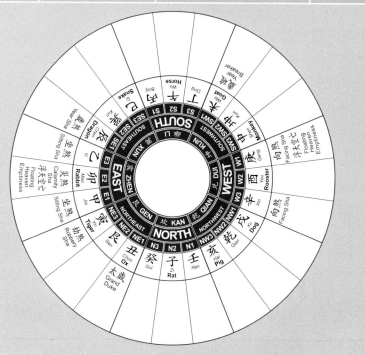

Annual San Yuan Purple White Stars 三元紫白九星：

上元 Upper Period Period 1, 2, 3			中元 Middle Period Period 4, 5, 6			下元 Lower Period Period 7, 8, 9		
巽SE	離S	坤SW	巽SE	離S	坤SW	巽SE	離S	坤SW
5	1	3	8	4	6	2	7	9
震E 4	6 丁丑 Ding Chou Fire Ox	兑W 8	震E 7	9 丁丑 Ding Chou Fire Ox	兑W 2	震E 1	3 丁丑 Ding Chou Fire Ox	兑W 5
9	2	7	3	5	1	6	8	4
艮NE	坎N	乾NW	艮NE	坎N	乾NW	艮NE	坎N	乾NW

Mountain Covering Yellow Path 蓋山黃道：

貪狼 Tan Lang **Greedy Wolf**	巨門 Ju Men **Huge Door**	武曲 Wu Qu **Military Arts**	文曲 Wen Qu **Literary Arts**
艮 丙 *Gen* *Bing* NE2 S1	巽 辛 *Xun* *Xin* SE2 W3	兌 丁 巳 丑 *Dui* *Ding* *Si* *Chou* W2 S3 SE3 NE1	離 壬 寅 戌 *Li* *Ren* *Yin* *Xu* S2 N1 NE3 NW1

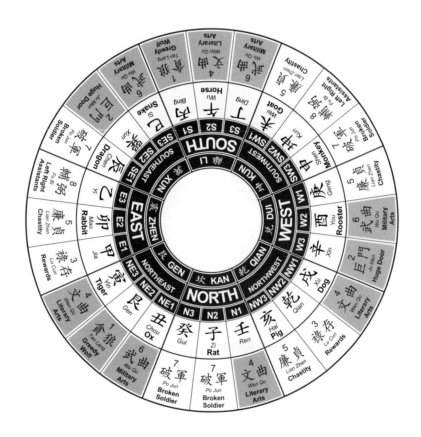

Heaven Penetrating Force 通天竅 :

三合前方 **Facing Three Harmony**	乾亥 Qian Hai	壬子 Ren Zi	癸丑 Gui Chou
三合後方 **Sitting Three Harmony**	巽巳 Xun Si	丙午 Bing Wu	丁未 Ding Wei

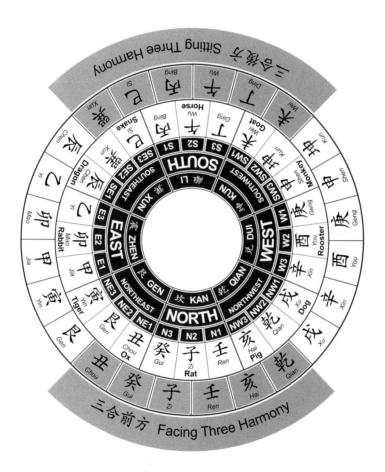

Moving Horse Six Ren Assessment 走馬六壬:

神后 *Shen Hou* **Holy Empress**	功曹 *Gong Cao* **Marshall**	天罡 *Tian Gang* **Heavenly Dipper**	勝光 *Sheng Guang* **Subliminal Bright**	傳送 *Chuan Song* **Great General**	河魁 *He Kui* **River Scholar**
乾亥 *Qian Hai*	癸丑 *Gui Chou*	甲卯 *Jia Mao*	巽巳 *Xun Si*	丁未 *Ding Wei*	庚酉 *Geng You*

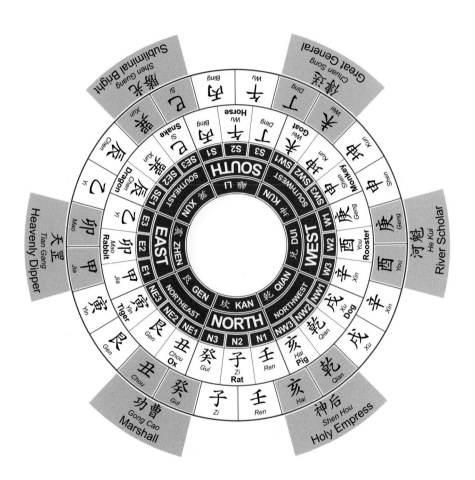

Four Advantages Three Cycles Star Plate 四利三元：

太陽 Tai Yang **Sun**	太陰 Tai Yin **Moon**	龍德 Long De **Dragon Virtue**	福德 Fu De **Fortune Virtue**
寅 Yin **Tiger**	辰 Chen **Dragon**	申 Shen **Monkey**	戌 Xu **Dog**

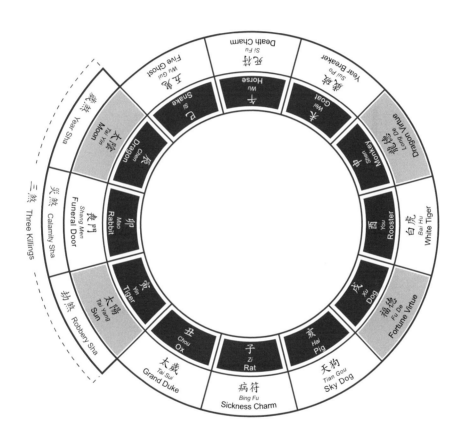

Negative Sectors For Opening Mountain 開山凶位：

年剋山家 Year Countering Sitting

甲	寅	辰	巽	戌	坎	辛	申	丑	癸	坤	艮	未
Jia	Yin	Chen	Xun	Xu	Kan	Xin	Shen	Chou	Gui	Kun	Gen	Wei
E1	NE3	SE1	SE2	NW1	N2	W3	SW3	NE1	N3	SW2	NE2	SW1

陰府太歲 Yin Fu Tai Sui **Yin Mansion Grand Duke**		六害 Liu Hai **Six Harm**	死符 Si Fu **Death Charm**	炙退 Zhi Tui **Roasting Star**
乾 Qian NW2	離 Li S2	午 Wu S2	午 Wu S2	子 Zi N2

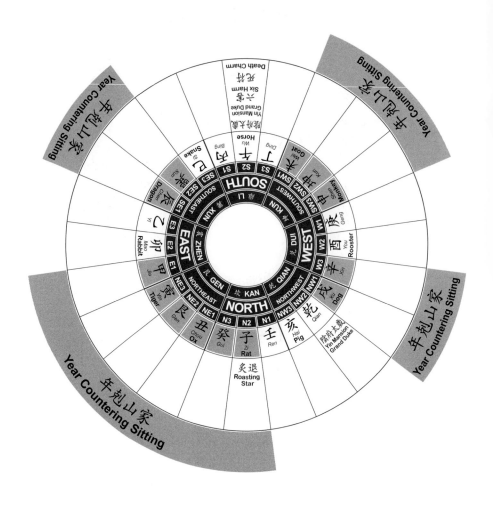

Negative Directions to Establish Facing 立向凶方：

巡山羅喉 *Xun Shan Luo Hou* **Mountain Patrol Luo Hou Star**	病符 *Bing Fu* **Sickness Charm**
艮 *Gen* **NE2**	子 *Zi* **N2**

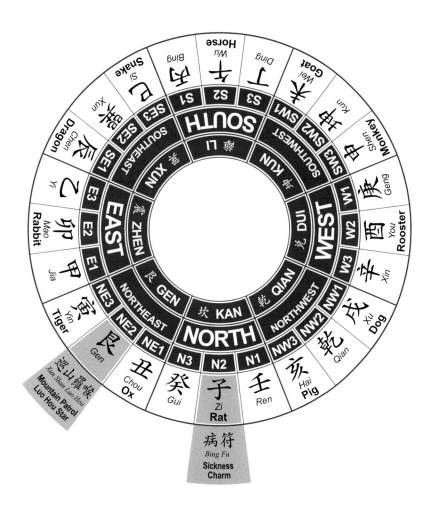

Negative Repair / Renovation Sectors Table 修方凶位表：

天官符 Heavenly Officer Charm	申 Shen Monkey	飛廉 Flying Chaste	酉 You Rooster
地官符 Earthly Officer Charm	巳 Si Snake	喪門 Funeral Door	卯 Mao Rabbit
大煞 Great Sha	酉 You Rooster	弔客 Suspended Guest	亥 Hai Pig
大將軍 Big General	酉 You Rooster	白虎 White Tiger	酉 You Rooster
力士 Strong Man	艮 Gen	金神 Golden God	寅 Yin Tiger / 卯 Mao Rabbit / 戌 Xu Dog / 亥 Hai Pig
蠶室 Silkworm Room	坤 Kun		
蠶官 Silkworm Officer	未 Wei Goat		
蠶命 Silkworm Life	申 Shen Monkey		
歲刑 Duke Punishment	戌 Xu Dog	獨火 Lonely Fire	震 Zhen
黃幡 Yellow Flag	丑 Chou Ox	五鬼 Five Ghost	卯 Mao Rabbit
豹尾 Leopard Tail	未 Wei Goat	破敗五鬼 Destructive Five Ghost	震 Zhen

Negative Repair / Renovation Sectors Diagram 修方凶位圖：

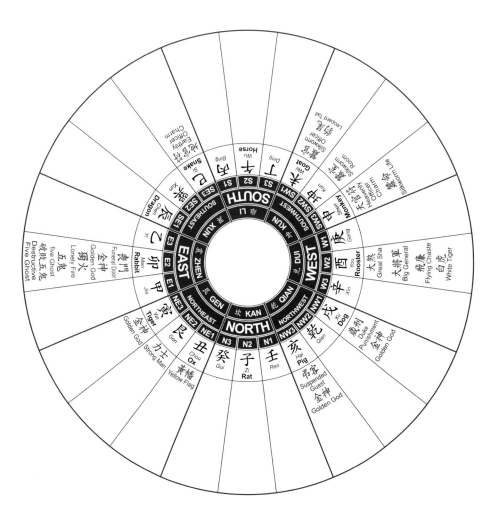

12-Month Auxiliary Stars Reference Table :
丁丑年十二月，開山立向修方星表

Positive Monthly Stars 吉星方

月 MONTH	寅 Tiger (Feb 4 - Mar 5) 正月 1st Month	卯 Rabbit (Mar 6 - Apr 4) 二月 2nd Month	辰 Dragon (Apr 5 - May 5) 三月 3rd Month	巳 Snake (May 6 - Jun 5) 四月 4th Month	午 Horse (Jun 6 - July 6) 五月 5th Month	未 Goat (July 7 - Aug 7) 六月 6th Month
天道 Heavenly Path	南 South	西南 Southwest	北 North	西 West	西北 Northwest	東 East
天德 Heavenly Virtue	丁 Ding Yin Fire	坤 Kun （申）	壬 Ren Yang Water	辛 Xin Yin Metal	乾 Qian （亥）	甲 Jia Yang Wood
天德合 Heavenly Virtue Combo	壬 Ren Yang Water	（巳）	丁 Ding Yin Fire	丙 Bing Yang Fire	（寅）	己 Ji Yin Earth
月德 Monthly Virtue	丙 Bing Yang Fire	甲 Jia Yang Wood	壬 Ren Yang Water	庚 Geng Yang Metal	丙 Bing Yang Fire	甲 Jia Yang Wood
月德合 Monthly Virtue Combo	辛 Xin Yin Metal	己 Ji Yin Earth	丁 Ding Yin Fire	乙 Yi Yin Wood	辛 Xin Yin Metal	己 Ji Yin Earth
月空 Month Emptiness	壬 Ren Yang Water	庚 Geng Yang Metal	丙 Bing Yang Fire	甲 Jia Yang Wood	壬 Ren Yang Water	庚 Geng Yang Metal
陽貴人 Yang Nobleman	中 Middle	巽 Xun	震 Zhen	坤 Kun	坎 Kan	離 Li
陰貴人 Yin Nobleman	震 Zhen	坤 Kun	坎 Kan	離 Li	艮 Gen	兌 Dui
飛天祿 Flying Heavenly Wealth	離 Li	艮 Gen	兌 Dui	乾 Qian	中 Middle	坎 Kan
飛天馬 Flying Heavenly Horse	中 Middle	巽 Xun	震 Zhen	坤 Kun	坎 Kan	離 Li

12-Month Auxiliary Stars Reference Table :
丁丑年十二月，開山立向修方星表

申 Monkey (Aug 8 - Sept 7) 七月 7th Month	酉 Rooster (Sept 8 - Oct 7) 八月 8th Month	戌 Dog (Oct 8 - Nov 6) 九月 9th Month	亥 Pig (Nov 7 - Dec 6) 十月 10th Month	子 Rat (Dec 7 - Jan 5) 十一月 11th Month	丑 Ox (Jan 6 - Feb 3) 十二月 12th Month	月 MONTH
北 North	東北 Northeast	南 South	東 East	東南 Southeast	西 West	天道 Heavenly Path
癸 Gui Yin Water	艮 Gen (寅)	丙 Bing Yang Fire	乙 Yi Yin Wood	巽 Xun (巳)	庚 Geng Yang Metal	天德 Heavenly Virtue
戊 Wu Yang Earth	(亥)	辛 Xin Yin Metal	庚 Geng Yang Metal	(申)	乙 Yi Yin Wood	天德合 Heavenly Virtue Combo
壬 Ren Yang Water	庚 Geng Yang Metal	丙 Bing Yang Fire	甲 Jia Yang Wood	壬 Ren Yang Water	庚 Geng Yang Metal	月德 Monthly Virtue
丁 Ding Yin Fire	乙 Yi Yin Wood	辛 Xin Yin Metal	己 Ji Yin Earth	丁 Ding Yin Fire	乙 Yi Yin Wood	月德合 Monthly Virtue Combo
丙 Bing Yang Fire	甲 Jia Yang Wood	壬 Ren Yang Water	庚 Geng Yang Metal	丙 Bing Yang Fire	甲 Jia Yang Wood	月空 Month Emptiness
艮 Gen	兑 Dui	乾 Qian	中 Middle	坎 Kan	離 Li	陽貴人 Yang Nobleman
乾 Qian	中 Middle	坎 Kan	離 Li	艮 Gen	兑 Dui	陰貴人 Yin Nobleman
離 Li	艮 Gen	兑 Dui	乾 Qian	中 Middle	巽 Xun	飛天祿 Flying Heavenly Wealth
艮 Gen	兑 Dui	乾 Qian	中 Middle	坎 Kan	離 Li	飛天馬 Flying Heavenly Horse

Monthly Purple White Stars 月紫白九星 :

寅 Tiger (Feb 4 - Mar 5) 正月 1st Month

巽 SE	離 S	坤 SW
4 Green 四綠	9 Purple 九紫	2 Black 二黑
3 Jade 三碧 (震 E)	5 Yellow 五黃	7 Red 七赤 (兌 W)
8 White 八白	1 White 一白	6 White 六白
艮 NE	坎 N	乾 NW

卯 Rabbit (Mar 6 - Apr 4) 二月 2nd Month

巽 SE	離 S	坤 SW
3 Jade 三碧	8 White 八白	1 White 一白
2 Black 二黑 (震 E)	4 Green 四綠	6 White 六白 (兌 W)
7 Red 七赤	9 Purple 九紫	5 Yellow 五黃
艮 NE	坎 N	乾 NW

辰 Dragon (Apr 5 - May 5) 三月 3rd Month

巽 SE	離 S	坤 SW
2 Black 二黑	7 Red 七赤	9 Purple 九紫
1 White 一白 (震 E)	3 Jade 三碧	5 Yellow 五黃 (兌 W)
6 White 六白	8 White 八白	4 Green 四綠
艮 NE	坎 N	乾 NW

巳 Snake (May 6 - Jun 5) 四月 4th Month

巽 SE	離 S	坤 SW
1 White 一白	6 White 六白	8 White 八白
9 Purple 九紫 (震 E)	2 Black 二黑	4 Green 四綠 (兌 W)
5 Yellow 五黃	7 Red 七赤	3 Jade 三碧
艮 NE	坎 N	乾 NW

午 Horse (Jun 6 - July 6) 五月 5th Month

巽 SE	離 S	坤 SW
9 Purple 九紫	5 Yellow 五黃	7 Red 七赤
8 White 八白 (震 E)	1 White 一白	3 Jade 三碧 (兌 W)
4 Green 四綠	6 White 六白	2 Black 二黑
艮 NE	坎 N	乾 NW

未 Goat (July 7 - Aug 7) 六月 6th Month

巽 SE	離 S	坤 SW
8 White 八白	4 Green 四綠	6 White 六白
7 Red 七赤 (震 E)	9 Purple 九紫	2 Black 二黑 (兌 W)
3 Jade 三碧	5 Yellow 五黃	1 White 一白
艮 NE	坎 N	乾 NW

申 Monkey (Aug 8 - Sept 7) 七月 7th Month

巽 SE	離 S	坤 SW
7 Red 七赤	3 Jade 三碧	5 Yellow 五黃
6 White 六白 (震 E)	8 White 八白	1 White 一白 (兌 W)
2 Black 二黑	4 Green 四綠	9 Purple 九紫
艮 NE	坎 N	乾 NW

酉 Rooster (Sept 8 - Oct 7) 八月 8th Month

巽 SE	離 S	坤 SW
6 White 六白	2 Black 二黑	4 Green 四綠
5 Yellow 五黃 (震 E)	7 Red 七赤	9 Purple 九紫 (兌 W)
1 White 一白	3 Jade 三碧	8 White 八白
艮 NE	坎 N	乾 NW

戌 Dog (Oct 8 - Nov 6) 九月 9th Month

巽 SE	離 S	坤 SW
5 Yellow 五黃	1 White 一白	3 Jade 三碧
4 Green 四綠 (震 E)	6 White 六白	8 White 八白 (兌 W)
9 Purple 九紫	2 Black 二黑	7 Red 七赤
艮 NE	坎 N	乾 NW

亥 Pig (Nov 7 - Dec 6) 十月 10th Month

巽 SE	離 S	坤 SW
4 Green 四綠	9 Purple 九紫	2 Black 二黑
3 Jade 三碧 (震 E)	5 Yellow 五黃	7 Red 七赤 (兌 W)
8 White 八白	1 White 一白	6 White 六白
艮 NE	坎 N	乾 NW

子 Rat (Dec 7 - Jan 5) 十一月 11th Month

巽 SE	離 S	坤 SW
3 Jade 三碧	8 White 八白	1 White 一白
2 Black 二黑 (震 E)	4 Green 四綠	6 White 六白 (兌 W)
7 Red 七赤	9 Purple 九紫	5 Yellow 五黃
艮 NE	坎 N	乾 NW

丑 Ox (Jan 6 - Feb 3) 十二月 12th Month

巽 SE	離 S	坤 SW
2 Black 二黑	7 Red 七赤	9 Purple 九紫
1 White 一白 (震 E)	3 Jade 三碧	5 Yellow 五黃 (兌 W)
6 White 六白	8 White 八白	4 Green 四綠
艮 NE	坎 N	乾 NW

Qi Men Three Nobles 三奇 :

Three Nobles 三奇 / Seasons	乙 Yi	丙 Bing	丁 Ding
立春 **Coming of Spring** Feb 4 - Feb 18	乾 Qian	兑 Dui	艮 Gen
春分 **Spring Equinox** Mar 21 - Apr 4	坎 Kan	坤 Kun	震 Zhen
立夏 **Coming of Summer** May 6 - May 20	坤 Kun	震 Zhen	巽 Xun
夏至 **Summer Solstice** Jun 22 - Jul 6	坤 Kun	坎 Kan	離 Li
立秋 **Coming of Autumn** Aug 8 - Aug 23	巽 Xun	震 Zhen	坤 Kun
秋分 **Autumn Equinox** Sept 23 - Oct 7	離 Li	艮 Gen	兑 Dui
立冬 **Coming of Winter** Nov 7 - Nov 22	艮 Gen	兑 Dui	乾 Qian
冬至 **Winter Solstice** Dec 22 - Jan 5	艮 Gen	離 Li	坎 Kan

Sectors to Avoid Opening Mountain 開山凶位 :

月 MONTH	月建 Month Establishment	月破 Month Destruction	月剋山家 Month Countering Sitting		陰府太歲 Yin Mansion Grand Duke	
寅 Tiger (Feb 4 - Mar 5) 正月 1st Month	寅 Yin Tiger	申 Shen Monkey	—		離 Li	乾 Qian
卯 Rabbit (Mar 6 - Apr 4) 二月 2nd Month	卯 Mao Rabbit	酉 You Rooster	—		震 Zhen	坤 Kun
辰 Dragon (Apr 5 - May 5) 三月 3rd Month	辰 Chen Dragon	戌 Xu Dog	離 Li	丙 Bing Yang Fire	艮 Gen	巽 Xun
巳 Snake (May 6 - Jun 5) 四月 4th Month	巳 Si Snake	亥 Hai Pig	壬 Ren Yang Water	乙 Yi Yin Wood	兌 Dui	乾 Qian
午 Horse (Jun 6 - July 6) 五月 5th Month	午 Wu Horse	子 Zi Rat	水 Water	山 Mountain	坎 Kan	坤 Kun
未 Goat (July 7 - Aug 7) 六月 6th Month	未 Wei Goat	丑 Chou Ox	土 Earth		乾 Qian	離 Li
申 Monkey (Aug 8 - Sept 7) 七月 7th Month	申 Shen Monkey	寅 Yin Tiger	震 Zhen	巳 Si Snake	坤 Kun	震 Zhen
酉 Rooster (Sept 8 - Oct 7) 八月 8th Month	酉 You Rooster	卯 Mao Rabbit	艮 Gen		巽 Xun	艮 Gen
戌 Dog (Oct 8 - Nov 6) 九月 9th Month	戌 Xu Dog	辰 Chen Dragon	—		乾 Qian	兌 Dui
亥 Pig (Nov 7 - Dec 6) 十月 10th Month	亥 Hai Pig	巳 Si Snake	—		坤 Kun	坎 Kan
子 Rat (Dec 7 - Jan 5) 十一月 11th Month	子 Zi Rat	午 Wu Horse	—		離 Li	乾 Qian
丑 Ox (Jan 6 - Feb 3) 十二月 12th Month	丑 Chou Ox	未 Wei Goat	—		震 Zhen	坤 Kun

Negative Repair / Renovation Sectors 修方凶位

月 MONTH	天官符 Heavenly Officer Charm			地官符 Earth Officer Charm			小月建 Small Month Establishment		
寅 Tiger (Feb 4 - Mar 5) 正月 1st Month	未 Wei Goat	坤 Kun	申 Shen Monkey	丑 Chou Ox	艮 Gen	寅 Yin Tiger	丙 Bing Yang Fire	離 Li	丁 Ding Yin Fire
卯 Rabbit (Mar 6 - Apr 4) 二月 2nd Month	壬 Ren Yang Water	坎 Kan	癸 Gui Yin Water	庚 Geng Yang Metal	兌 Dui	辛 Xin Yin Metal	壬 Ren Yang Water	坎 Kan	癸 Gui Yin Water
辰 Dragon (Apr 5 - May 5) 三月 3rd Month	丙 Bing Yang Fire	離 Li	丁 Ding Yin Fire	戊 Xu Dog	乾 Qian	亥 Hai Pig	未 Wei Goat	坤 Kun	申 Shen Monkey
巳 Snake (May 6 - Jun 5) 四月 4th Month	丑 Chou Ox	艮 Gen	寅 Yin Tiger	中 Middle			甲 Jia Yang Wood	震 Zhen	乙 Yi Yin Wood
午 Horse (Jun 6 - July 6) 五月 5th Month	庚 Geng Yang Metal	兌 Dui	辛 Xin Yin Metal	庚 Geng Yang Metal	兌 Dui	辛 Xin Yin Metal	辰 Chen Dragon	巽 Xun	巳 Si Snake
未 Goat (July 7 - Aug 7) 六月 6th Month	戊 Xu Dog	乾 Qian	亥 Hai Pig	戊 Xu Dog	乾 Qian	亥 Hai Pig	中 Middle		
申 Monkey (Aug 8 - Sept 7) 七月 7th Month	中 Middle			中 Middle			戊 Xu Dog	乾 Qian	亥 Hai Pig
酉 Rooster (Sept 8 - Oct 7) 八月 8th Month	庚 Geng Yang Metal	兌 Dui	辛 Xin Yin Metal	辰 Chen Dragon	巽 Xun	巳 Si Snake	庚 Geng Yang Metal	兌 Dui	辛 Xin Yin Metal
戌 Dog (Oct 8 - Nov 6) 九月 9th Month	戊 Xu Dog	乾 Qian	亥 Hai Pig	甲 Jia Yang Wood	震 Zhen	乙 Yi Yin Wood	丑 Chou Ox	艮 Gen	寅 Yin Tiger
亥 Pig (Nov 7 - Dec 6) 十月 10th Month	中 Middle			未 Wei Goat	坤 Kun	申 Shen Monkey	丙 Bing Yang Fire	離 Li	丁 Ding Yin Fire
子 Rat (Dec 7 - Jan 5) 十一月 11th Month	辰 Chen Dragon	巽 Xun	巳 Si Snake	壬 Ren Yang Water	坎 Kan	癸 Gui Yin Water	壬 Ren Yang Water	坎 Kan	癸 Gui Yin Water
丑 Ox (Jan 6 - Feb 3) 十二月 12th Month	甲 Jia Yang Wood	震 Zhen	乙 Yi Yin Wood	丙 Bing Yang Fire	離 Li	丁 Ding Yin Fire	未 Wei Goat	坤 Kun	申 Shen Monkey

丁丑 (Ding Chou) Fire Ox

Negative Repair / Renovation Sectors 修方凶位 :

月 MONTH	大月建 Big Month Establishment			飛大煞 Flying Great Sha			丙丁獨火 Bing Ding Lonely Fire	
寅 **Tiger** (Feb 4 - Mar 5) 正月 **1st Month**	中 Middle			甲 Jia Yang Wood	震 Zhen	乙 Yi Yin Wood	離 Li	坎 Kan
卯 **Rabbit** (Mar 6 - Apr 4) 二月 **2nd Month**	辰 Chen Dragon	巽 Xun	巳 Si Snake	未 Wei Goat	坤 Kun	申 Shen Monkey	艮 Gen	離 Li
辰 **Dragon** (Apr 5 - May 5) 三月 **3rd Month**	甲 Jia Yang Wood	震 Zhen	乙 Yi Yin Wood	壬 Ren Yang Water	坎 Kan	癸 Gui Yin Water	兌 Dui	艮 Gen
巳 **Snake** (May 6 - Jun 5) 四月 **4th Month**	未 Wei Goat	坤 Kun	申 Shen Monkey	丙 Bing Yang Fire	離 Li	丁 Ding Yin Fire	乾 Qian	兌 Dui
午 **Horse** (Jun 6 - July 6) 五月 **5th Month**	壬 Ren Yang Water	坎 Kan	癸 Gui Yin Water	丑 Chou Ox	艮 Gen	寅 Yin Tiger	中 Middle	乾 Qian
未 **Goat** (July 7 - Aug 7) 六月 **6th Month**	丙 Bing Yang Fire	離 Li	丁 Ding Yin Fire	庚 Geng Yang Metal	兌 Dui	辛 Xin Yin Metal	中 Middle	
申 **Monkey** (Aug 8 - Sept 7) 七月 **7th Month**	丑 Chou Ox	艮 Gen	寅 Yin Tiger	戌 Xu Dog	乾 Qian	亥 Hai Pig	巽 Xun	中 Middle
酉 **Rooster** (Sept 8 - Oct 7) 八月 **8th Month**	庚 Geng Yang Metal	兌 Dui	辛 Xin Yin Metal	中 Middle			震 Zhen	巽 Xun
戌 **Dog** (Oct 8 - Nov 6) 九月 **9th Month**	戌 Xu Dog	乾 Qian	亥 Hai Pig	庚 Geng Yang Metal	兌 Dui	辛 Xin Yin Metal	坤 Kun	震 Zhen
亥 **Pig** (Nov 7 - Dec 6) 十月 **10th Month**	中 Middle			戌 Xu Dog	乾 Qian	亥 Hai Pig	坎 Kan	坤 Kun
子 **Rat** (Dec 7 - Jan 5) 十一月 **11th Month**	辰 Chen Dragon	巽 Xun	巳 Si Snake	中 Middle			離 Li	坎 Kan
丑 **Ox** (Jan 6 - Feb 3) 十二月 **12th Month**	甲 Jia Yang Wood	震 Zhen	乙 Yi Yin Wood	辰 Chen Dragon	巽 Xun	巳 Si Snake	艮 Gen	離 Li

Negative Repair / Renovation Sectors 修方凶位 :

月 MONTH	月遊火 Month Wondering Fire	三煞 Monthly 3 Killings		
		劫煞 Robbery Sha	災煞 Calamity Sha	月煞 Month Sha
寅 Tiger (Feb 4 - Mar 5) 正月 1st Month	艮 Gen	亥 Hai Pig	子 Zi Rat	丑 Chou Ox
卯 Rabbit (Mar 6 - Apr 4) 二月 2nd Month	離 Li	申 Shen Monkey	酉 You Rooster	戌 Xu Dog
辰 Dragon (Apr 5 - May 5) 三月 3rd Month	坎 Kan	巳 Si Snake	午 Wu Horse	未 Wei Goat
巳 Snake (May 6 - Jun 5) 四月 4th Month	坤 Kun	寅 Yin Tiger	卯 Mao Rabbit	辰 Chen Dragon
午 Horse (Jun 6 - July 6) 五月 5th Month	震 Zhen	亥 Hai Pig	子 Zi Rat	丑 Chou Ox
未 Goat (July 7 - Aug 7) 六月 6th Month	巽 Xun	申 Shen Monkey	酉 You Rooster	戌 Xu Dog
申 Monkey (Aug 8 - Sept 7) 七月 7th Month	中 Middle	巳 Si Snake	午 Wu Horse	未 Wei Goat
酉 Rooster (Sept 8 - Oct 7) 八月 8th Month	乾 Qian	寅 Yin Tiger	卯 Mao Rabbit	辰 Chen Dragon
戌 Dog (Oct 8 - Nov 6) 九月 9th Month	兌 Dui	亥 Hai Pig	子 Zi Rat	丑 Chou Ox
亥 Pig (Nov 7 - Dec 6) 十月 10th Month	艮 Gen	申 Shen Monkey	酉 You Rooster	戌 Xu Dog
子 Rat (Dec 7 - Jan 5) 十一月 11th Month	離 Li	巳 Si Snake	午 Wu Horse	未 Wei Goat
丑 Ox (Jan 6 - Feb 3) 十二月 12th Month	坎 Kan	寅 Yin Tiger	卯 Mao Rabbit	辰 Chen Dragon

Negative Repair / Renovation Sectors 修方凶位 :

月 MONTH	月刑 Month Punishment	月害 Month Harm	月厭 Month Detest
寅 **Tiger** (Feb 4 - Mar 5) 正月 **1st Month**	巳 *Si* Snake	巳 *Si* Snake	戌 *Xu* Dog
卯 **Rabbit** (Mar 6 - Apr 4) 二月 **2nd Month**	子 *Zi* Rat	辰 *Chen* Dragon	酉 *You* Rooster
辰 **Dragon** (Apr 5 - May 5) 三月 **3rd Month**	辰 *Chen* Dragon	卯 *Mao* Rabbit	申 *Shen* Monkey
巳 **Snake** (May 6 - Jun 5) 四月 **4th Month**	申 *Shen* Monkey	寅 *Yin* Tiger	未 *Wei* Goat
午 **Horse** (Jun 6 - July 6) 五月 **5th Month**	午 *Wu* Horse	丑 *Chou* Ox	午 *Wu* Horse
未 **Goat** (July 7 - Aug 7) 六月 **6th Month**	丑 *Chou* Ox	子 *Zi* Rat	巳 *Si* Snake
申 **Monkey** (Aug 8 - Sept 7) 七月 **7th Month**	寅 *Yin* Tiger	亥 *Hai* Pig	辰 *Chen* Dragon
酉 **Rooster** (Sept 8 - Oct 7) 八月 **8th Month**	酉 *You* Rooster	戌 *Xu* Dog	卯 *Mao* Rabbit
戌 **Dog** (Oct 8 - Nov 6) 九月 **9th Month**	未 *Wei* Goat	酉 *You* Rooster	寅 *Yin* Tiger
亥 **Pig** (Nov 7 - Dec 6) 十月 **10th Month**	亥 *Hai* Pig	申 *Shen* Monkey	丑 *Chou* Ox
子 **Rat** (Dec 7 - Jan 5) 十一月 **11th Month**	卯 *Mao* Rabbit	未 *Wei* Goat	子 *Zi* Rat
丑 **Ox** (Jan 6 - Feb 3) 十二月 **12th Month**	戌 *Xu* Dog	午 *Wu* Horse	亥 *Hai* Pig

丁卯 (Ding Mao)
Fire Rabbit

丁卯 (Ding Mao) Fire Rabbit

Heavenly Stem 天干	丁 **Yin Fire** (陰火)
Earthly Branch 地支	卯 **Rabbit** (Yin Wood 陰木)
Hidden Stem 藏干	乙 **Yin Wood**
Na Yin 納音	爐中火 **Fire from the kiln**
Grand Duke 太歲	卯 **Rabbit**
Xuan Kong Five Element 玄空五行	6 水 **Water**
Gua Name 卦名	☶ 山澤損 **Decreasing**
Xuan Kong Period Luck 玄空卦運	9

Annual Positive Stars for Opening Mountain, Establishing Facing and Commencing Repairs 丁卯年十二月，開山立向修方吉星：

歲德 **Duke Virtue**	壬 *Ren* **Yang Water**
歲德合 **Duke Virtue Combo**	丁 *Ding* **Yin Fire**
歲枝德 **Duke Branch Virtue**	申 *Shen* **Monkey**
陽貴人 **Yang Nobleman**	亥 *Hai* **Pig**
陰貴人 **Yin Nobleman**	酉 *You* **Rooster**
歲祿 **Duke Prosperous**	午 *Wu* **Horse**
歲馬 **Duke Horse**	巳 *Si* **Snake**
奏書 **Decree**	艮 *Gen*
博士 **Professor**	坤 *Kun*

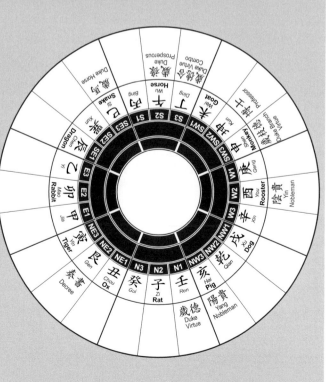

382

Annual Negative Stars for Opening Mountain, Establishing Facing and Commencing Repairs 丁卯年十二月，開山立向修方凶星：

太歲 Grand Duke	歲破 Year Breaker	三煞 Three Killings			坐煞向煞 Sitting Sha Facing Sha				浮天空亡 Floating Heaven Emptiness	
卯 Mao Rabbit	酉 You Rooster	申 Shen Monkey	酉 You Rooster	戌 Xu Dog	庚 Geng Yang Meta	辛 Xin Yin Metal	甲 Jia Yang Wood	乙 Yi Yin Wood	震 Zhen	庚 Geng Yang Metal

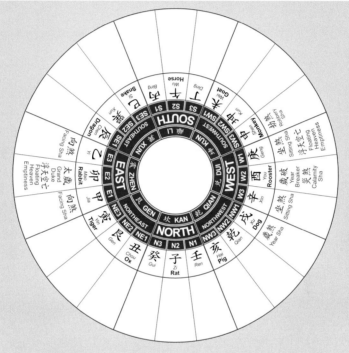

Annual San Yuan Purple White Stars 三元紫白九星：

上元 Upper Period Period 1, 2, 3	中元 Middle Period Period 4, 5, 6	下元 Lower Period Period 7, 8, 9

Upper Period (Period 1, 2, 3)

巽SE	離S	坤SW
6	2	4
5 (震E)	7 丁卯 Ding Mao Yin Wood	9 (兌W)
1 (艮NE)	3 (坎N)	8 (乾NW)

Middle Period (Period 4, 5, 6)

巽SE	離S	坤SW
9	5	7
8 (震E)	1 丁卯 Ding Mao Yin Wood	3 (兌W)
4 (艮NE)	6 (坎N)	2 (乾NW)

Lower Period (Period 7, 8, 9)

巽SE	離S	坤SW
3	8	1
2 (震E)	4 丁卯 Ding Mao Yin Wood	6 (兌W)
7 (艮NE)	9 (坎N)	5 (乾NW)

Mountain Covering Yellow Path 蓋山黃道：

貪狼 *Tan Lang* **Greedy Wolf**		巨門 *Ju Men* **Huge Door**				武曲 *Wu Qu* **Military Arts**		文曲 *Wen Qu* **Literary Arts**	
乾 *Qian* NW2	甲 *Jia* E1	離 *Li* S2	壬 *Ren* N1	寅 *Yin* NE3	戌 *Xu* NW1	坤 *Kun* SW2	乙 *Yi* E3	巽 *Xun* SE2	辛 *Xin* W3

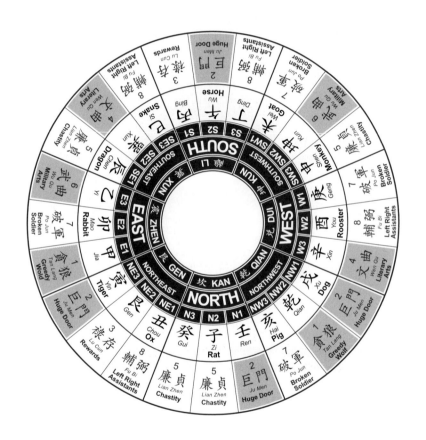

Heaven Penetrating Force 通天竅:

三合前方 **Facing Three Harmony**	巽巳 Xun Si	丙午 Bing Wu	丁未 Ding Wei
三合後方 **Sitting Three Harmony**	乾亥 Qian Hai	壬子 Ren Zi	癸丑 Gui Chou

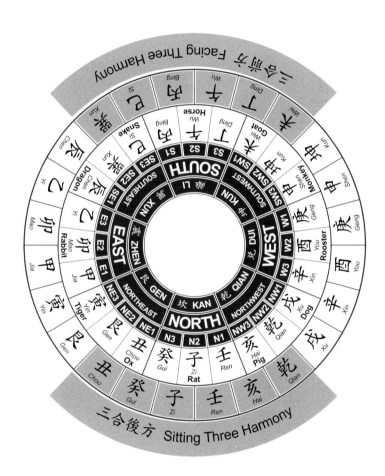

Moving Horse Six Ren Assessment 走馬六壬：

神后 Shen Hou Holy Empress	功曹 Gong Cao Marshall	天罡 Tian Gang Heavenly Dipper	勝光 Sheng Guang Subliminal Bright	傳送 Chuan Song Great General	河魁 He Kui River Scholar
庚酉 Geng You	乾亥 Qian Hai	癸丑 Gui Chou	甲卯 Jia Mao	巽巳 Xun Si	丁未 Ding Wei

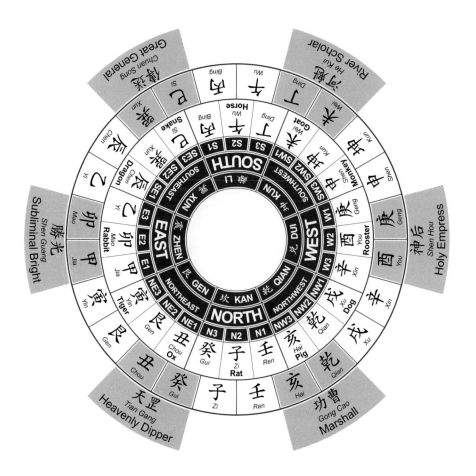

Four Advantages Three Cycles Star Plate 四利三元：

太陽 *Tai Yang* **Sun**	太陰 *Tai Yin* **Moon**	龍德 *Long De* **Dragon Virtue**	福德 *Fu De* **Fortune Virtue**
辰 *Chen* **Dragon**	午 *Wu* **Horse**	戌 *Xu* **Dog**	子 *Zi* **Rat**

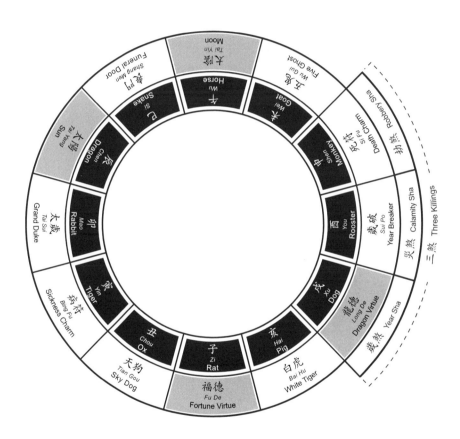

Negative Sectors For Opening Mountain 開山凶位：

年剋山家 Year Countering Sitting

離 Li S2	壬 Ren N1	丙 Bing S1	乙 Yi E3

陰府太歲 Yin Fu Tai Sui **Yin Mansion Grand Duke**		六害 Liu Hai **Six Harm**	死符 Si Fu **Death Charm**	炙退 Zhi Tui **Roasting Star**
乾 Qian NW2	離 Li S2	辰 Chen SE1	申 Shen SW3	午 Wu S2

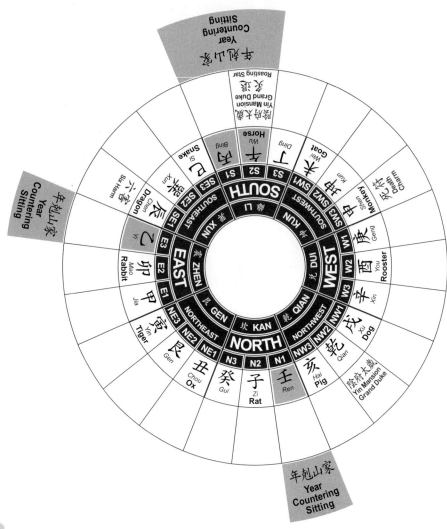

Negative Directions to Establish Facing 立向凶方：

巡山羅喉 *Xun Shan Luo Hou* **Mountain Patrol Luo Hou Star**	病符 *Bing Fu* **Sickness Charm**
乙 *Yi* **E3**	寅 *Yin* **NE3**

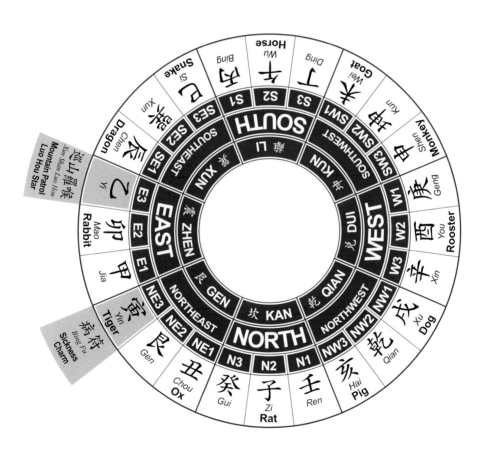

Negative Repair / Renovation Sectors Table 修方凶位表：

天官符 **Heavenly Officer Charm**	寅 *Yin* Tiger		飛廉 **Flying Chaste**	巳 *Si* Snake
地官符 **Earthly Officer Charm**	未 *Wei* Goat		喪門 **Funeral Door**	巳 *Si* Snake
大煞 **Great Sha**	卯 *Mao* Rabbit		弔客 **Suspended Guest**	丑 *Chou* Ox
大將軍 **Big General**	子 *Zi* Rat		白虎 **White Tiger**	亥 *Hai* Pig
力士 **Strong Man**	巽 *Xun*		金神 **Golden God**	寅 *Yin* Tiger
蠶室 **Silkworm Room**	乾 *Qian*			卯 *Mao* Rabbit
蠶官 **Silkworm Officer**	戌 *Xu* Dog			戌 *Xu* Dog
蠶命 **Silkworm Life**	亥 *Hai* Pig			亥 *Hai* Pig
歲刑 **Duke Punishment**	子 *Zi* Rat		獨火 **Lonely Fire**	坎 *Kan*
黃幡 **Yellow Flag**	未 *Wei* Goat		五鬼 **Five Ghost**	丑 *Chou* Ox
豹尾 **Leopard Tail**	丑 *Chou* Ox		破敗五鬼 **Destructive Five Ghost**	震 *Zhen*

Negative Repair / Renovation Sectors Diagram 修方凶位圖:

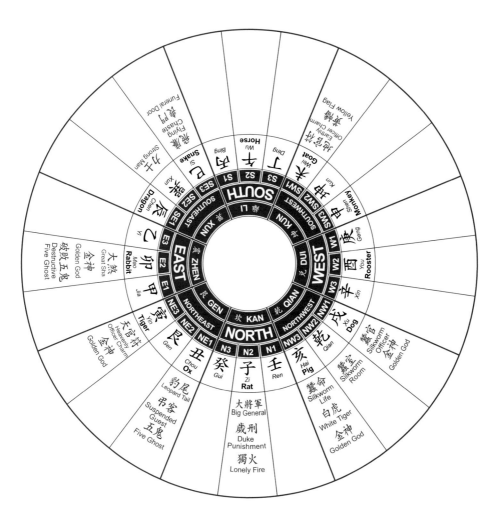

12-Month Auxiliary Stars Reference Table :
丁卯年十二月，開山立向修方星表

Positive Monthly Stars 吉星方

月 MONTH	寅 Tiger (Feb 4 - Mar 5) 正月 1st Month	卯 Rabbit (Mar 6 - Apr 4) 二月 2nd Month	辰 Dragon (Apr 5 - May 5) 三月 3rd Month	巳 Snake (May 6 - Jun 5) 四月 4th Month	午 Horse (Jun 6 - July 6) 五月 5th Month	未 Goat (July 7 - Aug 7) 六月 6th Month
天道 Heavenly Path	南 South	西南 Southwest	北 North	西 West	西北 Northwest	東 East
天德 Heavenly Virtue	丁 Ding Yin Fire	坤 Kun (申)	壬 Ren Yang Water	辛 Xin Yin Metal	乾 Qian (亥)	甲 Jia Yang Wood
天德合 Heavenly Virtue Combo	壬 Ren Yang Water	(巳)	丁 Ding Yin Fire	丙 Bing Yang Fire	(寅)	己 Ji Yin Earth
月德 Monthly Virtue	丙 Bing Yang Fire	甲 Jia Yang Wood	壬 Ren Yang Water	庚 Geng Yang Metal	丙 Bing Yang Fire	甲 Jia Yang Wood
月德合 Monthly Virtue Combo	辛 Xin Yin Metal	己 Ji Yin Earth	丁 Ding Yin Fire	乙 Yi Yin Wood	辛 Xin Yin Metal	己 Ji Yin Earth
月空 Month Emptiness	壬 Ren Yang Water	庚 Geng Yang Metal	丙 Bing Yang Fire	甲 Jia Yang Wood	壬 Ren Yang Water	庚 Geng Yang Metal
陽貴人 Yang Nobleman	中 Middle	巽 Xun	震 Zhen	坤 Kun	坎 Kan	離 Li
陰貴人 Yin Nobleman	震 Zhen	坤 Kun	坎 Kan	離 Li	艮 Gen	兌 Dui
飛天祿 Flying Heavenly Wealth	離 Li	艮 Gen	兌 Dui	乾 Qian	中 Middle	坎 Kan
飛天馬 Flying Heavenly Horse	艮 Gen	兌 Dui	乾 Qian	中 Middle	坎 Kan	離 Li

12-Month Auxiliary Stars Reference Table :
丁卯年十二月，開山立向修方星表

申 Monkey (Aug 8 - Sept 7) 七月 7th Month	酉 Rooster (Sept 8 - Oct 7) 八月 8th Month	戌 Dog (Oct 8 - Nov 6) 九月 9th Month	亥 Pig (Nov 7 - Dec 6) 十月 10th Month	子 Rat (Dec 7 - Jan 5) 十一月 11th Month	丑 Ox (Jan 6 - Feb 3) 十二月 12th Month	月 MONTH
北 North	東北 Northeast	南 South	東 East	東南 Southeast	西 West	天道 Heavenly Path
癸 Gui Yin Water	艮 Gen (寅)	丙 Bing Yang Fire	乙 Yi Yin Wood	巽 Xun (巳)	庚 Geng Yang Metal	天德 Heavenly Virtue
戊 Wu Yang Earth	(亥)	辛 Xin Yin Metal	庚 Geng Yang Metal	(申)	乙 Yi Yin Wood	天德合 Heavenly Virtue Combo
壬 Ren Yang Water	庚 Geng Yang Metal	丙 Bing Yang Fire	甲 Jia Yang Wood	壬 Ren Yang Water	庚 Geng Yang Metal	月德 Monthly Virtue
丁 Ding Yin Fire	乙 Yi Yin Wood	辛 Xin Yin Metal	己 Ji Yin Earth	丁 Ding Yin Fire	乙 Yi Yin Wood	月德合 Monthly Virtue Combo
丙 Bing Yang Fire	甲 Jia Yang Wood	壬 Ren Yang Water	庚 Geng Yang Metal	丙 Bing Yang Fire	甲 Jia Yang Wood	月空 Month Emptiness
艮 Gen	兌 Dui	乾 Qian	中 Middle	坎 Kan	離 Li	陽貴人 Yang Nobleman
乾 Qian	中 Middle	坎 Kan	離 Li	艮 Gen	兌 Dui	陰貴人 Yin Nobleman
離 Li	艮 Gen	兌 Dui	乾 Qian	中 Middle	巽 Xun	飛天祿 Flying Heavenly Wealth
艮 Gen	兌 Dui	乾 Qian	中 Middle	巽 Xun	震 Zhen	飛天馬 Flying Heavenly Horse

丁卯 (Ding Mao) Fire Rabbit

Monthly Purple White Stars 月紫白九星 :

寅 Tiger (Feb 4 - Mar 5) 正月 1st Month

巽 SE	離 S	坤 SW
7 Red 七赤	**3** Jade 三碧	**5** Yellow 五黄
6 White 六白 (震 E)	**8** White 八白	**1** White 一白 (兌 W)
2 Black 二黑	**4** Green 四綠	**9** Purple 九紫
艮 NE	坎 N	乾 NW

卯 Rabbit (Mar 6 - Apr 4) 二月 2nd Month

巽 SE	離 S	坤 SW
6 White 六白	**2** Black 二黑	**4** Green 四綠
5 Yellow 五黄 (震 E)	**7** Red 七赤	**9** Purple 九紫 (兌 W)
1 White 一白	**3** Jade 三碧	**8** White 八白
艮 NE	坎 N	乾 NW

辰 Dragon (Apr 5 - May 5) 三月 3rd Month

巽 SE	離 S	坤 SW
5 Yellow 五黄	**1** White 一白	**3** Jade 三碧
4 Green 四綠 (震 E)	**6** White 六白	**8** White 八白 (兌 W)
9 Purple 九紫	**2** Black 二黑	**7** Red 七赤
艮 NE	坎 N	乾 NW

巳 Snake (May 6 - Jun 5) 四月 4th Month

巽 SE	離 S	坤 SW
4 Green 四綠	**9** Purple 九紫	**2** Black 二黑
3 Jade 三碧 (震 E)	**5** Yellow 五黄	**7** Red 七赤 (兌 W)
8 White 八白	**1** White 一白	**6** White 六白
艮 NE	坎 N	乾 NW

午 Horse (Jun 6 - July 6) 五月 5th Month

巽 SE	離 S	坤 SW
3 Jade 三碧	**8** White 八白	**1** White 一白
2 Black 二黑 (震 E)	**4** Green 四綠	**6** White 六白 (兌 W)
7 Red 七赤	**9** Purple 九紫	**5** Yellow 五黄
艮 NE	坎 N	乾 NW

未 Goat (July 7 - Aug 7) 六月 6th Month

巽 SE	離 S	坤 SW
2 Black 二黑	**7** Red 七赤	**9** Purple 九紫
1 White 一白 (震 E)	**3** Jade 三碧	**5** Yellow 五黄 (兌 W)
6 White 六白	**8** White 八白	**4** Green 四綠
艮 NE	坎 N	乾 NW

申 Monkey (Aug 8 - Sept 7) 七月 7th Month

巽 SE	離 S	坤 SW
1 White 一白	**6** White 六白	**8** White 八白
9 Purple 九紫 (震 E)	**2** Black 二黑	**4** Green 四綠 (兌 W)
5 Yellow 五黄	**7** Red 七赤	**3** Jade 三碧
艮 NE	坎 N	乾 NW

酉 Rooster (Sept 8 - Oct 7) 八月 8th Month

巽 SE	離 S	坤 SW
9 Purple 九紫	**5** Yellow 五黄	**7** Red 七赤
8 White 八白 (震 E)	**1** White 一白	**3** Jade 三碧 (兌 W)
4 Green 四綠	**6** White 六白	**2** Black 二黑
艮 NE	坎 N	乾 NW

戌 Dog (Oct 8 - Nov 6) 九月 9th Month

巽 SE	離 S	坤 SW
8 White 八白	**4** Green 四綠	**6** White 六白
7 Red 七赤 (震 E)	**9** Purple 九紫	**2** Black 二黑 (兌 W)
3 Jade 三碧	**5** Yellow 五黄	**1** White 一白
艮 NE	坎 N	乾 NW

亥 Pig (Nov 7 - Dec 6) 十月 10th Month

巽 SE	離 S	坤 SW
7 Red 七赤	**3** Jade 三碧	**5** Yellow 五黄
6 White 六白 (震 E)	**8** White 八白	**1** White 一白 (兌 W)
2 Black 二黑	**4** Green 四綠	**9** Purple 九紫
艮 NE	坎 N	乾 NW

子 Rat (Dec 7 - Jan 5) 十一月 11th Month

巽 SE	離 S	坤 SW
6 White 六白	**2** Black 二黑	**4** Green 四綠
5 Yellow 五黄 (震 E)	**7** Red 七赤	**9** Purple 九紫 (兌 W)
1 White 一白	**3** Jade 三碧	**8** White 八白
艮 NE	坎 N	乾 NW

丑 Ox (Jan 6 - Feb 3) 十二月 12th Month

巽 SE	離 S	坤 SW
5 Yellow 五黄	**1** White 一白	**3** Jade 三碧
4 Green 四綠 (震 E)	**6** White 六白	**8** White 八白 (兌 W)
9 Purple 九紫	**2** Black 二黑	**7** Red 七赤
艮 NE	坎 N	乾 NW

Qi Men Three Nobles 三奇 :

Three Nobles 三奇 / Seasons	乙 Yi	丙 Bing	丁 Ding
立春 **Coming of Spring** Feb 4 - Feb 18	中 Middle	乾 Qian	兌 Dui
春分 **Spring Equinox** Mar 21 - Apr 4	離 Li	坎 Kan	坤 Kun
立夏 **Coming of Summer** May 6 - May 20	坎 Kan	坤 Kun	震 Zhen
夏至 **Summer Solstice** Jun 22 - Jul 6	震 Zhen	坤 Kun	坎 Kan
立秋 **Coming of Autumn** Aug 8 - Aug 23	中 Middle	巽 Xun	震 Zhen
秋分 **Autumn Equinox** Sept 23 - Oct 7	坎 Kan	離 Li	艮 Gen
立冬 **Coming of Winter** Nov 7 - Nov 22	離 Li	艮 Gen	兌 Dui
冬至 **Winter Solstice** Dec 22 - Jan 5	兌 Dui	艮 Gen	離 Li

Sectors to Avoid Opening Mountain 開山凶位 :

月 MONTH	月建 Month Establishment	月破 Month Destruction	月剋山家 Month Countering Sitting		陰府太歲 Yin Mansion Grand Duke	
寅 **Tiger** (Feb 4 - Mar 5) 正月 **1st Month**	寅 *Yin* **Tiger**	申 *Shen* **Monkey**	—		離 *Li*	乾 *Qian*
卯 **Rabbit** (Mar 6 - Apr 4) 二月 **2nd Month**	卯 *Mao* **Rabbit**	酉 *You* **Rooster**	—		震 *Zhen*	坤 *Kun*
辰 **Dragon** (Apr 5 - May 5) 三月 **3rd Month**	辰 *Chen* **Dragon**	戌 *Xu* **Dog**	離 *Li*	丙 *Bing* **Yang Fire**	艮 *Gen*	巽 *Xuni*
巳 **Snake** (May 6 - Jun 5) 四月 **4th Month**	巳 *Si* **Snake**	亥 *Hai* **Pig**	壬 *Ren* **Yang Water**	乙 *Yi* **Yin Wood**	兌 *Dui*	乾 *Qian*
午 **Horse** (Jun 6 - July 6) 五月 **5th Month**	午 *Wu* **Horse**	子 *Zi* **Rat**	水 **Water**	山 **Mountain**	坎 *Kan*	坤 *Kun*
未 **Goat** (July 7 - Aug 7) 六月 **6th Month**	未 *Wei* **Goat**	丑 *Chou* **Ox**	土 **Earth**		乾 *Qian*	離 *Li*
申 **Monkey** (Aug 8 - Sept 7) 七月 **7th Month**	申 *Shen* **Monkey**	寅 *Yin* **Tiger**	震 *Zhen*	巳 *Si* **Snake**	坤 *Kun*	震 *Zhen*
酉 **Rooster** (Sept 8 - Oct 7) 八月 **8th Month**	酉 *You* **Rooster**	卯 *Mao* **Rabbit**	艮 *Gen*		巽 *Xun*	艮 *Gen*
戌 **Dog** (Oct 8 - Nov 6) 九月 **9th Month**	戌 *Xu* **Dog**	辰 *Chen* **Dragon**	—		乾 *Qian*	兌 *Dui*
亥 **Pig** (Nov 7 - Dec 6) 十月 **10th Month**	亥 *Hai* **Pig**	巳 *Si* **Snake**	—		坤 *Kun*	坎 *Kan*
子 **Rat** (Dec 7 - Jan 5) 十一月 **11th Month**	子 *Zi* **Rat**	午 *Wu* **Horse**	—		離 *Li*	乾 *Qian*
丑 **Ox** (Jan 6 - Feb 3) 十二月 **12th Month**	丑 *Chou* **Ox**	未 *Wei* **Goat**	—		震 *Zhen*	坤 *Kun*

Negative Repair / Renovation Sectors 修方凶位 :

月 MONTH	天官符 Heavenly Officer Charm			地官符 Earth Officer Charm			小月建 Small Month Establishment		
寅 **Tiger** (Feb 4 - Mar 5) 正月 **1st Month**	中 Middle			壬 *Ren* Yang Water	坎 *Kan*	癸 *Gui* Yin Water	丙 *Bing* Yang Fire	離 *Li*	丁 *Ding* Yin Fire
卯 **Rabbit** (Mar 6 - Apr 4) 二月 **2nd Month**	庚 *Geng* Yang Metal	兑 *Dui*	辛 *Xin* Yin Metal	丙 *Bing* Yang Fire	離 *Li*	丁 *Ding* Yin Fire	壬 *Ren* Yang Water	坎 *Kan*	癸 *Gui* Yin Water
辰 **Dragon** (Apr 5 - May 5) 三月 **3rd Month**	戊 *Xu* Dog	乾 *Qian*	亥 *Hai* Pig	丑 *Chou* Ox	艮 *Gen*	寅 *Yin* Tiger	未 *Wei* Goat	坤 *Kun*	申 *Shen* Monkey
巳 **Snake** (May 6 - Jun 5) 四月 **4th Month**	中 Middle			庚 *Geng* Yang Metal	兑 *Dui*	辛 *Xin* Yin Metal	甲 *Jia* Yang Wood	震 *Zhen*	乙 *Yi* Yin Wood
午 **Horse** (Jun 6 - July 6) 五月 **5th Month**	辰 *Chen* Dragon	巽 *Xun*	巳 *Si* Snake	戊 *Xu* Dog	乾 *Qian*	亥 *Hai* Pig	辰 *Chen* Dragon	巽 *Xun*	巳 *Si* Snake
未 **Goat** (July 7 - Aug 7) 六月 **6th Month**	甲 *Jia* Yang Wood	震 *Zhen*	乙 *Yi* Yin Wood	中 Middle			中 Middle		
申 **Monkey** (Aug 8 - Sept 7) 七月 **7th Month**	未 *Wei* Goat	坤 *Kun*	申 *Shen* Monkey	庚 *Geng* Yang Metal	兑 *Dui*	辛 *Xin* Yin Metal	戊 *Xu* Dog	乾 *Qian*	亥 *Hai* Pig
酉 **Rooster** (Sept 8 - Oct 7) 八月 **8th Month**	壬 *Ren* Yang Water	坎 *Kan*	癸 *Gui* Yin Water	戊 *Xu* Dog	乾 *Qian*	亥 *Hai* Pig	庚 *Geng* Yang Metal	兑 *Dui*	辛 *Xin* Yin Metal
戌 **Dog** (Oct 8 - Nov 6) 九月 **9th Month**	丙 *Bing* Yang Fire	離 *Li*	丁 *Ding* Yin Fire	中 Middle			丑 *Chou* Ox	艮 *Gen*	寅 *Yin* Tiger
亥 **Pig** (Nov 7 - Dec 6) 十月 **10th Month**	丑 *Chou* Ox	艮 *Gen*	寅 *Yin* Tiger	辰 *Chen* Dragon	巽 *Xun*	巳 *Si* Snake	丙 *Bing* Yang Fire	離 *Li*	丁 *Ding* Yin Fire
子 **Rat** (Dec 7 - Jan 5) 十一月 **11th Month**	庚 *Geng* Yang Metal	兑 *Dui*	辛 *Xin* Yin Metal	甲 *Jia* Yang Wood	震 *Zhen*	乙 *Yi* Yin Wood	壬 *Ren* Yang Water	坎 *Kan*	癸 *Gui* Yin Water
丑 **Ox** (Jan 6 - Feb 3) 十二月 **12th Month**	戊 *Xu* Dog	乾 *Qian*	亥 *Hai* Pig	未 *Wei* Goat	坤 *Kun*	申 *Shen* Monkey	未 *Wei* Goat	坤 *Kun*	申 *Shen* Monkey

Negative Repair / Renovation Sectors 修方凶位 :

月 MONTH	大月建 Big Month Establishment			飛大煞 Flying Great Sha			丙丁獨火 Bing Ding Lonely Fire	
寅 Tiger (Feb 4 - Mar 5) 正月 1st Month	丑 Chou Ox	艮 Gen	寅 Yin Tiger	戌 Xu Dog	乾 Qian	亥 Hai Pig	離 Li	坎 Kan
卯 Rabbit (Mar 6 - Apr 4) 二月 2nd Month	庚 Geng Yang Metal	兌 Dui	辛 Xin Yin Metal	中 Middle			艮 Gen	離 Li
辰 Dragon (Apr 5 - May 5) 三月 3rd Month	戌 Xu Dog	乾 Qian	亥 Hai Pig	庚 Geng Yang Metal	兌 Dui	辛 Xin Yin Metal	兌 Dui	艮 Gen
巳 Snake (May 6 - Jun 5) 四月 4th Month	中 Middle			戌 Xu Dog	乾 Qian	亥 Hai Pig	乾 Qian	兌 Dui
午 Horse (Jun 6 - July 6) 五月 5th Month	辰 Chen Dragon	巽 Xun	巳 Si Snake	中 Middle			中 Middle	乾 Qian
未 Goat (July 7 - Aug 7) 六月 6th Month	甲 Jia Yang Wood	震 Zhen	乙 Yi Yin Wood	辰 Chen Dragon	巽 Xun	巳 Si Snake	中 Middle	
申 Monkey (Aug 8 - Sept 7) 七月 7th Month	未 Wei Goat	坤 Kun	申 Shen Monkey	甲 Jia Yang Wood	震 Zhen	乙 Yi Yin Wood	巽 Xun	中 Middle
酉 Rooster (Sept 8 - Oct 7) 八月 8th Month	壬 Ren Yang Water	坎 Kan	癸 Gui Yin Water	未 Wei Goat	坤 Kun	申 Shen Monkey	震 Zhen	巽 Xun
戌 Dog (Oct 8 - Nov 6) 九月 9th Month	丙 Bing Yang Fire	離 Li	丁 Ding Yin Fire	壬 Ren Yang Water	坎 Kan	癸 Gui Yin Water	坤 Kun	震 Zhen
亥 Pig (Nov 7 - Dec 6) 十月 10th Month	丑 Chou Ox	艮 Gen	寅 Yin Tiger	丙 Bing Yang Fire	離 Li	丁 Ding Yin Fire	坎 Kan	坤 Kun
子 Rat (Dec 7 - Jan 5) 十一月 11th Month	庚 Geng Yang Metal	兌 Dui	辛 Xin Yin Metal	丑 Chou Ox	艮 Gen	寅 Yin Tiger	離 Li	坎 Kan
丑 Ox (Jan 6 - Feb 3) 十二月 12th Month	戌 Xu Dog	乾 Qian	亥 Hai Pig	庚 Geng Yang Metal	兌 Dui	辛 Xin Yin Metal	艮 Gen	離 Li

Negative Repair / Renovation Sectors 修方凶位 :

月 MONTH	月遊火 Month Wondering Fire	三煞 Monthly 3 Killings		
		劫煞 Robbery Sha	災煞 Calamity Sha	月煞 Month Sha
寅 Tiger (Feb 4 - Mar 5) 正月 1st Month	巽 Xun	亥 Hai Pig	子 Zi Rat	丑 Chou Ox
卯 Rabbit (Mar 6 - Apr 4) 二月 2nd Month	中 Middle	申 Shen Monkey	酉 You Rooster	戌 Xu Dog
辰 Dragon (Apr 5 - May 5) 三月 3rd Month	乾 Qian	巳 Si Snake	午 Wu Horse	未 Wei Goat
巳 Snake (May 6 - Jun 5) 四月 4th Month	兑 Dui	寅 Yin Tiger	卯 Mao Rabbit	辰 Chen Dragon
午 Horse (Jun 6 - July 6) 五月 5th Month	艮 Gen	亥 Hai Pig	子 Zi Rat	丑 Chou Ox
未 Goat (July 7 - Aug 7) 六月 6th Month	離 Li	申 Shen Monkey	酉 You Rooster	戌 Xu Dog
申 Monkey (Aug 8 - Sept 7) 七月 7th Month	坎 Kan	巳 Si Snake	午 Wu Horse	未 Wei Goat
酉 Rooster (Sept 8 - Oct 7) 八月 8th Month	坤 Kun	寅 Yin Tiger	卯 Mao Rabbit	辰 Chen Dragon
戌 Dog (Oct 8 - Nov 6) 九月 9th Month	震 Zhen	亥 Hai Pig	子 Zi Rat	丑 Chou Ox
亥 Pig (Nov 7 - Dec 6) 十月 10th Month	巽 Xun	申 Shen Monkey	酉 You Rooster	戌 Xu Dog
子 Rat (Dec 7 - Jan 5) 十一月 11th Month	中 Middle	巳 Si Snake	午 Wu Horse	未 Wei Goat
丑 Ox (Jan 6 - Feb 3) 十二月 12th Month	乾 Qian	寅 Yin Tiger	卯 Mao Rabbit	辰 Chen Dragon

月 MONTH	月刑 Month Punishment	月害 Month Harm	月厭 Month Detest
寅 **Tiger** (Feb 4 - Mar 5) 正月 **1st Month**	巳 *Si* Snake	巳 *Si* Snake	戌 *Xu* Dog
卯 **Rabbit** (Mar 6 - Apr 4) 二月 **2nd Month**	子 *Zi* Rat	辰 *Chen* Dragon	酉 *You*
辰 **Dragon** (Apr 5 - May 5) 三月 **3rd Month**	辰 *Chen* Dragon	卯 *Mao* Rabbit	申 *Shen* Monkey
巳 **Snake** (May 6 - Jun 5) 四月 **4th Month**	申 *Shen* Monkey	寅 *Yin* Tiger	未 *Wei* Goat
午 **Horse** (Jun 6 - July 6) 五月 **5th Month**	午 *Wu* Horse	丑 *Chou* Ox	午 *Wu* Horse
未 **Goat** (July 7 - Aug 7) 六月 **6th Month**	丑 *Chou* Ox	子 *Zi* Rat	巳 *Si* Snake
申 **Monkey** (Aug 8 - Sept 7) 七月 **7th Month**	寅 *Yin* Tiger	亥 *Hai* Pig	辰 *Chen* Dragon
酉 **Rooster** (Sept 8 - Oct 7) 八月 **8th Month**	酉 *You* Rooster	戌 *Xu* Dog	卯 *Mao* Rabbit
戌 **Dog** (Oct 8 - Nov 6) 九月 **9th Month**	未 *Wei* Goat	酉 *You* Rooster	寅 *Yin* Tiger
亥 **Pig** (Nov 7 - Dec 6) 十月 **10th Month**	亥 *Hai* Pig	申 *Shen* Monkey	丑 *Chou* Ox
子 **Rat** (Dec 7 - Jan 5) 十一月 **11th Month**	卯 *Mao* Rabbit	未 *Wei* Goat	子 *Zi* Rat
丑 **Ox** (Jan 6 - Feb 3) 十二月 **12th Month**	戌 *Xu* Dog	午 *Wu* Horse	亥 *Hai* Pig

丁巳 (Ding Si)
Fire Snake

丁巳 (Ding Si) Fire Snake

Heavenly Stem 天干	丁 **Yin Fire (**陰火**)**
Earthly Branch 地支	巳 **Snake (Yin Fire** 陰火**)**
Hidden Stem 藏干	丙 **Yang Fire,** 戊 **Yang Earth,** 庚 **Yang Metal**
Na Yin 納音	沙中土 **Earth from the sand**
Grand Duke 太歲	巳 **Snake**
Xuan Kong Five Element 玄空五行	2 火 **Fire**
Gua Name 卦名	䷈ 風天小畜 **Small Livestock**
Xuan Kong Period Luck 玄空卦運	8

Annual Positive Stars for Opening Mountain, Establishing Facing and Commencing Repairs 開山立向修方吉星：

歲德 **Duke Virtue**	壬 *Ren* **Yang Water**	
歲德合 **Duke Virtue Combo**	丁 *Ding* **Yin Fire**	
歲枝德 **Duke Branch Virtue**	戊 *Xu* **Dog**	
陽貴人 **Yang Nobleman**	亥 *Hai* **Pig**	
陰貴人 **Yin Nobleman**	酉 *You* **Rooster**	
歲祿 **Duke Prosperous**	午 *Wu* **Horse**	
歲馬 **Duke Horse**	亥 *Hai* **Pig**	
奏書 **Decree**	巽 *Xun*	
博士 **Professor**	乾 *Qian*	

402

Annual Negative Stars for Opening Mountain, Establishing Facing and Commencing Repairs 開山立向修方凶星：

太歲 Grand Duke	歲破 Year Breaker	三煞 Three Killings			坐煞向煞 Sitting Sha Facing Sha				浮天空亡 Floating Heaven Emptiness	
巳 *Si* Snake	亥 *Hai* Pig	寅 *Yin* Tiger	卯 *Mao* Rabbit	辰 *Chen* Dragon	甲 *Jia* Yang Wood	乙 *Yi* Yin Wood	庚 *Geng* Yang Metal	辛 *Xin* Yin Metal	震 *Zhen*	庚 *Geng* Yang Metal

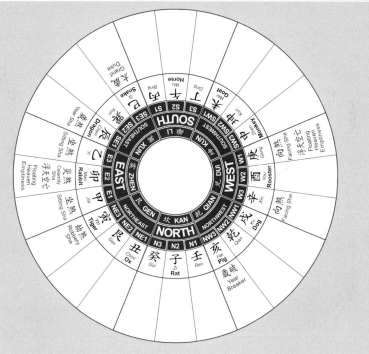

Annual San Yuan Purple White Stars 三元紫白九星：

上元 Upper Period Period 1, 2, 3			中元 Middle Period Period 4, 5, 6			下元 Lower Period Period 7, 8, 9		
巽 SE **1**	離 S **6**	坤 SW **8**	巽 SE **4**	離 S **9**	坤 SW **2**	巽 SE **7**	離 S **3**	坤 SW **5**
震 E **9**	**2** 丁巳 *Ding Si* **Fire Snake**	兌 W **4**	震 E **3**	**5** 丁巳 *Ding Si* **Fire Snake**	兌 W **7**	震 E **6**	**8** 丁巳 *Ding Si* **Fire Snake**	兌 W **1**
艮 NE **5**	坎 N **7**	乾 NW **3**	艮 NE **8**	坎 N **1**	乾 NW **6**	艮 NE **2**	坎 N **4**	乾 NW **9**

Mountain Covering Yellow Path 蓋山黃道：

貪狼 Tan Lang **Greedy Wolf**				巨門 Ju Men **Huge Door**				武曲 Wu Qu **Military Arts**		文曲 Wen Qu **Literary Arts**			
兌	丁	巳	丑	震	庚	亥	未	艮	丙	坎	癸	申	辰
Dui	Ding	Si	Chou	Zhen	Geng	Hai	Wei	Gen	Bing	Kan	Gui	Shen	Chen
W2	S3	SE3	NE1	E2	W1	NW3	SW1	NE2	S1	N2	N3	SW3	SE1

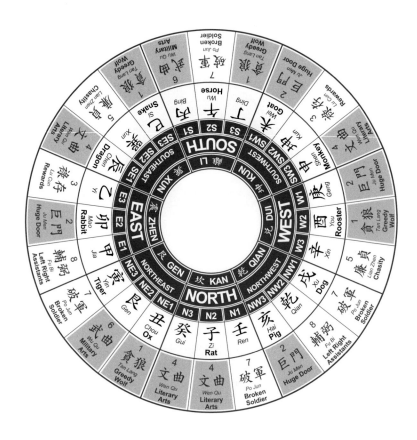

Heaven Penetrating Force 通天竅：			
三合前方 **Facing Three Harmony**	乾亥 Qian Hai	壬子 Ren Zi	癸丑 Gui Chou
三合後方 **Sitting Three Harmony**	巽巳 Xun Si	丙午 Bing Wu	丁未 Ding Wei

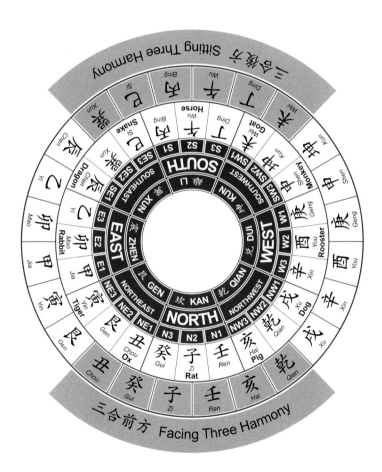

Moving Horse Six Ren Assessment 走馬六壬：

神后 Shen Hou **Holy Empress**	功曹 Gong Cao **Marshall**	天罡 Tian Gang **Heavenly Dipper**	勝光 Sheng Guang **Subliminal Bright**	傳送 Chuan Song **Great General**	河魁 He Kui **River Scholar**
丁未 Ding Wei	庚酉 Geng You	乾亥 Qian Hai	癸丑 Gui Chou	甲卯 Jia Mao	巽巳 Xun Si

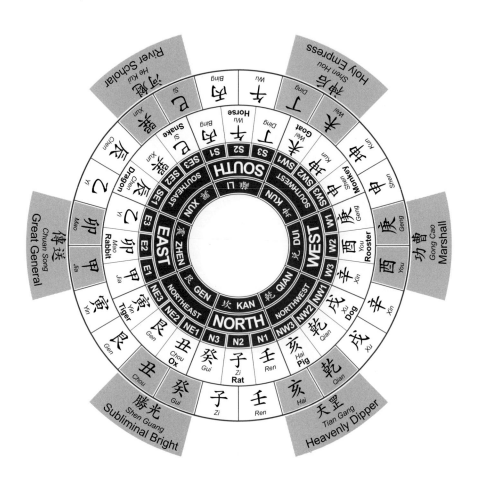

Four Advantages Three Cycles Star Plate 四利三元：

太陽 *Tai Yang* **Sun**	太陰 *Tai Yin* **Moon**	龍德 *Long De* **Dragon Virtue**	福德 *Fu De* **Fortune Virtue**
午 *Wu* **S2**	申 *Shen* **SW3**	子 *Zi* **N2**	寅 *Yin* **NE3**

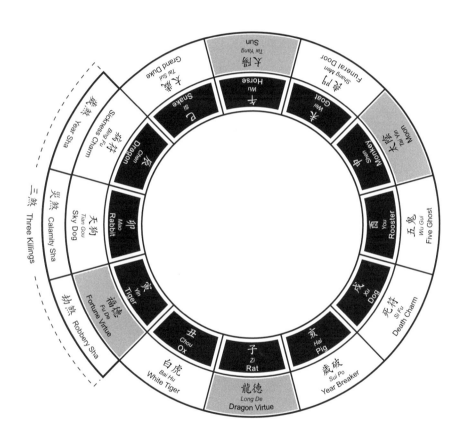

Negative Sectors For Opening Mountain 開山凶位：

年剋山家 Year Countering Sitting

震 Zhen E2	艮 Gen NE2	巳 Si SE3	

陰府太歲 Yin Fu Tai Sui **Yin Mansion Grand Duke**	六害 Liu Hai **Six Harm**	死符 Si Fu **Death Charm**	炙退 Zhi Tui **Roasting Star**
乾 Qian NW	離 Li S2	寅 Yin NE3	戌 Xu NW1	子 Zi N2

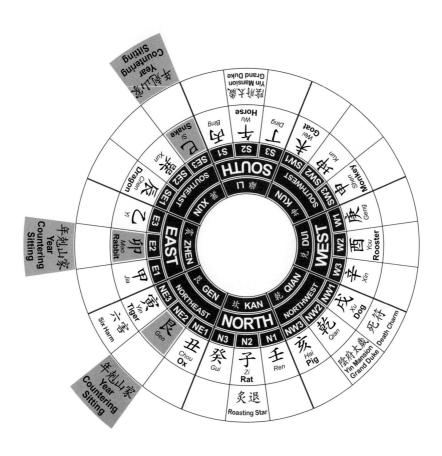

Negative Directions to Establish Facing 立向凶方：

巡山羅喉 *Xun Shan Luo Hou* **Mountain Patrol Luo Hou Star**	病符 *Bing Fu* **Sickness Charm**
丙 *Bing* **S1**	辰 *Chen* **SE1**

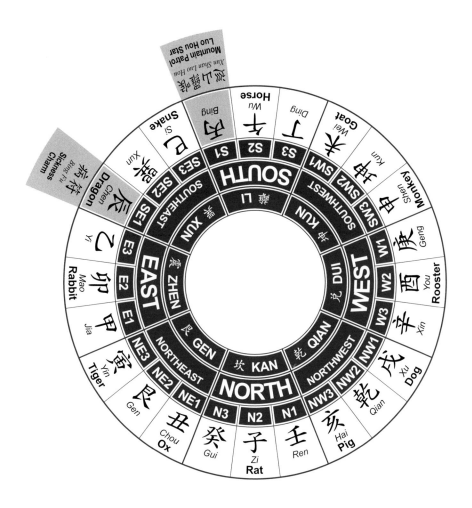

Negative Repair / Renovation Sectors Table 修方凶位表：

天官符 **Heavenly Officer Charm**	申 *Shen* **Monkey**	飛廉 **Flying Chaste**	未 *Wei* **Goat**
地官符 **Earthly Officer Charm**	酉 *You* **Rooster**	喪門 **Funeral Door**	未 *Wei* **Goat**
大煞 **Great Sha**	酉 *You* **Rooster**	弔客 **Suspended Guest**	卯 *Mao* **Rabbit**
大將軍 **Big General**	卯 *Mao* **Rabbit**	白虎 **White Tiger**	丑 *Chou* **Ox**
力士 **Strong Man**	坤 *Kun*	金神 **Golden God**	寅 *Yin* **Tiger** 卯 *Mao* **Rabbit** 戌 *Xu* **Dog** 亥 *Hai* **Pig**
蠶室 **Silkworm Room**	艮 *Gen*		
蠶官 **Silkworm Officer**	丑 *Chou* **Ox**		
蠶命 **Silkworm Life**	寅 *Yin* **Tiger**		
歲刑 **Duke Punishment**	申 *Shen* **Monkey**	獨火 **Lonely Fire**	巽 *Xun*
黃幡 **Yellow Flag**	丑 *Chou* **Ox**	五鬼 **Five Ghost**	亥 *Hai* **Pig**
豹尾 **Leopard Tail**	未 *Wei* **Goat**	破敗五鬼 **Destructive Five Ghost**	震 *Zhen*

Negative Repair / Renovation Sectors Diagram 修方凶位圖：

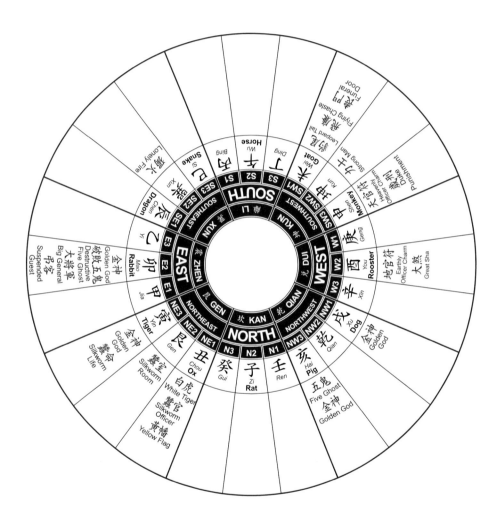

丁巳 (Ding Si) Fire Snake

Positive Monthly Stars 吉星方

月 MONTH	寅 Tiger (Feb 4 - Mar 5) 正月 1st Month	卯 Rabbit (Mar 6 - Apr 4) 二月 2nd Month	辰 Dragon (Apr 5 - May 5) 三月 3rd Month	巳 Snake (May 6 - Jun 5) 四月 4th Month	午 Horse (Jun 6 - July 6) 五月 5th Month	未 Goat (July 7 - Aug 7) 六月 6th Month
天道 Heavenly Path	南 South	西南 Southwest	北 North	西 West	西北 Northwest	東 East
天德 Heavenly Virtue	丁 Ding Yin Fire	坤 Kun (申)	壬 Ren Yang Water	辛 Xin Yin Metal	乾 Qian (亥)	甲 Jia Yang Wood
天德合 Heavenly Virtue Combo	壬 Ren Yang Water	(巳)	丁 Ding Yin Fire	丙 Bing Yang Fire	(寅)	己 Ji Yin Earth
月德 Monthly Virtue	丙 Bing Yang Fire	甲 Jia Yang Wood	壬 Ren Yang Water	庚 Geng Yang Metal	丙 Bing Yang Fire	甲 Jia Yang Wood
月德合 Monthly Virtue Combo	辛 Xin Yin Metal	己 Ji Yin Earth	丁 Ding Yin Fire	乙 Yi Yin Wood	辛 Xin Yin Metal	己 Ji Yin Earth
月空 Month Emptiness	壬 Ren Yang Water	庚 Geng Yang Metal	丙 Bing Yang Fire	甲 Jia Yang Wood	壬 Ren Yang Water	庚 Geng Yang Metal
陽貴人 Yang Nobleman	中 Middle	巽 Xun	震 Zhen	坤 Kun	坎 Kan	離 Li
陰貴人 Yin Nobleman	震 Zhen	坤 Kun	坎 Kan	離 Li	艮 Gen	兌 Dui
飛天祿 Flying Heavenly Wealth	離 Li	艮 Gen	兌 Dui	乾 Qian	中 Middle	坎 Kan
飛天馬 Flying Heavenly Horse	中 Middle	巽 Xun	震 Zhen	坤 Kun	坎 Kan	離 Li

12-Month Auxiliary Stars Reference Table :
丁巳年十二月，開山立向修方星表

申 Monkey (Aug 8 - Sept 7) 七月 7th Month	酉 Rooster (Sept 8 - Oct 7) 八月 8th Month	戌 Dog (Oct 8 - Nov 6) 九月 9th Month	亥 Pig (Nov 7 - Dec 6) 十月 10th Month	子 Rat (Dec 7 - Jan 5) 十一月 11th Month	丑 Ox (Jan 6 - Feb 3) 十二月 12th Month	月 MONTH
北 North	東北 Northeast	南 South	東 East	東南 Southeast	西 West	天道 Heavenly Path
癸 Gui Yin Water	艮 Gen (寅)	丙 Bing Yang Fire	乙 Yi Yin Wood	巽 Xun (巳)	庚 Geng Yang Metal	天德 Heavenly Virtue
戊 Wu Yang Earth	(亥)	辛 Xin Yin Metal	庚 Geng Yang Metal	(申)	乙 Yi Yin Wood	天德合 Heavenly Virtue Combo
壬 Ren Yang Water	庚 Geng Yang Metal	丙 Bing Yang Fire	甲 Jia Yang Wood	壬 Ren Yang Water	庚 Geng Yang Metal	月德 Monthly Virtue
丁 Ding Yin Fire	乙 Yi Yin Wood	辛 Xin Yin Metal	己 Ji Yin Earth	丁 Ding Yin Fire	乙 Yi Yin Wood	月德合 Monthly Virtue Combo
丙 Bing Yang Fire	甲 Jia Yang Wood	壬 Ren Yang Water	庚 Geng Yang Metal	丙 Bing Yang Fire	甲 Jia Yang Wood	月空 Month Emptiness
艮 Gen	兌 Dui	乾 Qian	中 Middle	坎 Kan	離 Li	陽貴人 Yang Nobleman
乾 Qian	中 Middle	坎 Kan	離 Li	艮 Gen	兌 Dui	陰貴人 Yin Nobleman
離 Li	艮 Gen	兌 Dui	乾 Qian	中 Middle	巽 Xun	飛天祿 Flying Heavenly Wealth
艮 Gen	兌 Dui	乾 Qian	中 Middle	坎 Kan	離 Li	飛天馬 Flying Heavenly Horse

丁巳 (Ding Si) Fire Snake

Monthly Purple White Stars 月紫白九星 :

寅 Tiger (Feb 4 - Mar 5) 正月 1st Month

巽SE	離S	坤SW
1 White 一白	**6** White 六白	**8** White 八白
震E **9** Purple 九紫	**2** Black 二黑	**4** Green 四綠 兌W
5 Yellow 五黃	**7** Red 七赤	**3** Jade 三碧
艮NE	坎N	乾NW

卯 Rabbit (Mar 6 - Apr 4) 二月 2nd Month

巽SE	離S	坤SW
9 Purple 九紫	**5** Yellow 五黃	**7** Red 七赤
震E **8** White 八白	**1** White 一白	**3** Jade 三碧 兌W
4 Green 四綠	**6** White 六白	**2** Black 二黑
艮NE	坎N	乾NW

辰 Dragon (Apr 5 - May 5) 三月 3rd Month

巽SE	離S	坤SW
8 White 八白	**4** Green 四綠	**6** White 六白
震E **7** Red 七赤	**9** Purple 九紫	**2** Black 二黑 兌W
3 Jade 三碧	**5** Yellow 五黃	**1** White 一白
艮NE	坎N	乾NW

巳 Snake (May 6 - Jun 5) 四月 4th Month

巽SE	離S	坤SW
7 Red 七赤	**3** Jade 三碧	**5** Yellow 五黃
震E **6** White 六白	**8** White 八白	**1** White 一白 兌W
2 Black 二黑	**4** Green 四綠	**9** Purple 九紫
艮NE	坎N	乾NW

午 Horse (Jun 6 - July 6) 五月 5th Month

巽SE	離S	坤SW
6 White 六白	**2** Black 二黑	**4** Green 四綠
震E **5** Yellow 五黃	**7** Red 七赤	**9** Purple 九紫 兌W
1 White 一白	**3** Jade 三碧	**8** White 八白
艮NE	坎N	乾NW

未 Goat (July 7 - Aug 7) 六月 6th Month

巽SE	離S	坤SW
5 Yellow 五黃	**1** White 一白	**3** Jade 三碧
震E **4** Green 四綠	**6** White 六白	**8** White 八白 兌W
9 Purple 九紫	**2** Black 二黑	**7** Red 七赤
艮NE	坎N	乾NW

申 Monkey (Aug 8 - Sept 7) 七月 7th Month

巽SE	離S	坤SW
4 Green 四綠	**9** Purple 九紫	**2** Black 二黑
震E **3** Jade 三碧	**5** Yellow 五黃	**7** Red 七赤 兌W
8 White 八白	**1** White 一白	**6** White 六白
艮NE	坎N	乾NW

酉 Rooster (Sept 8 - Oct 7) 八月 8th Month

巽SE	離S	坤SW
3 Jade 三碧	**8** White 八白	**1** White 一白
震E **2** Black 二黑	**4** Green 四綠	**6** White 六白 兌W
7 Red 七赤	**9** Purple 九紫	**5** Yellow 五黃
艮NE	坎N	乾NW

戌 Dog (Oct 8 - Nov 6) 九月 9th Month

巽SE	離S	坤SW
2 Black 二黑	**7** Red 七赤	**9** Purple 九紫
震E **1** White 一白	**3** Jade 三碧	**5** Yellow 五黃 兌W
6 White 六白	**8** White 八白	**4** Green 四綠
艮NE	坎N	乾NW

亥 Pig (Nov 7 - Dec 6) 十月 10th Month

巽SE	離S	坤SW
1 White 一白	**6** White 六白	**8** White 八白
震E **9** Purple 九紫	**2** Black 二黑	**4** Green 四綠 兌W
5 Yellow 五黃	**7** Red 七赤	**3** Jade 三碧
艮NE	坎N	乾NW

子 Rat (Dec 7 - Jan 5) 十一月 11th Month

巽SE	離S	坤SW
9 Purple 九紫	**5** Yellow 五黃	**7** Red 七赤
震E **8** White 八白	**1** White 一白	**3** Jade 三碧 兌W
4 Green 四綠	**6** White 六白	**2** Black 二黑
艮NE	坎N	乾NW

丑 Ox (Jan 6 - Feb 3) 十二月 12th Month

巽SE	離S	坤SW
8 White 八白	**4** Green 四綠	**6** White 六白
震E **7** Red 七赤	**9** Purple 九紫	**2** Black 二黑 兌W
3 Jade 三碧	**5** Yellow 五黃	**1** White 一白
艮NE	坎N	乾NW

Qi Men Three Nobles 三奇 :

Three Nobles 三奇 / Seasons	乙 Yi	丙 Bing	丁 Ding
立春 **Coming of Spring** Feb 4 - Feb 18	坎 Kan	坤 Kun	震 Zhen
春分 **Spring Equinox** Mar 21 - Apr 4	中 Middle	乾 Qian	兌 Dui
立夏 **Coming of Summer** May 6 - May 20	乾 Qian	兌 Dui	艮 Gen
夏至 **Summer Solstice** Jun 22 - Jul 6	兌 Dui	乾 Qian	中 Middle
立秋 **Coming of Autumn** Aug 8 - Aug 23	離 Li	艮 Gen	兌 Dui
秋分 **Autumn Equinox** Sept 23 - Oct 7	中 Middle	巽 Xun	震 Zhen
立冬 **Coming of Winter** Nov 7 - Nov 22	巽 Xun	震 Zhen	坤 Kun
冬至 **Winter Solstice** Dec 22 - Jan 5	震 Zhen	巽 Xun	中 Middle

丁巳 (Ding Si) Fire Snake

Sectors to Avoid Opening Mountain 開山凶位 :

月 MONTH	月建 Month Establishment	月破 Month Destruction	月剋山家 Month Countering Sitting		陰府太歲 Yin Mansion Grand Duke	
寅 **Tiger** (Feb 4 - Mar 5) 正月 **1st Month**	寅 *Yin* **Tiger**	申 *Shen* **Monkey**	–		離 *Li*	乾 *Qian*
卯 **Rabbit** (Mar 6 - Apr 4) 二月 **2nd Month**	卯 *Mao* **Rabbit**	酉 *You* **Rooster**	–		震 *Zhen*	坤 *Kun*
辰 **Dragon** (Apr 5 - May 5) 三月 **3rd Month**	辰 *Chen* **Dragon**	戌 *Xu* **Dog**	離 *Li*	丙 *Bing* **Yang Fire**	艮 *Gen*	巽 *Xun*
巳 **Snake** (May 6 - Jun 5) 四月 **4th Month**	巳 *Si* **Snake**	亥 *Hai* **Pig**	壬 *Ren* **Yang Water**	乙 *Yi* **Yin Wood**	兌 *Dui*	乾 *Qian*
午 **Horse** (Jun 6 - July 6) 五月 **5th Month**	午 *Wu* **Horse**	子 *Zi* **Rat**	水 **Water**	山 **Mountain**	坎 *Kan*	坤 *Kun*
未 **Goat** (July 7 - Aug 7) 六月 **6th Month**	未 *Wei* **Goat**	丑 *Chou* **Ox**	土 **Earth**		乾 *Qian*	離 *Li*
申 **Monkey** (Aug 8 - Sept 7) 七月 **7th Month**	申 *Shen* **Monkey**	寅 *Yin* **Tiger**	震 *Zhen*	巳 *Si* **Snake**	坤 *Kun*	震 *Zhen*
酉 **Rooster** (Sept 8 - Oct 7) 八月 **8th Month**	酉 *You* **Rooster**	卯 *Mao* **Rabbit**	艮 *Gen*		巽 *Xun*	艮 *Gen*
戌 **Dog** (Oct 8 - Nov 6) 九月 **9th Month**	戌 *Xu* **Dog**	辰 *Chen* **Dragon**	–		乾 *Qian*	兌 *Dui*
亥 **Pig** (Nov 7 - Dec 6) 十月 **10th Month**	亥 *Hai* **Pig**	巳 *Si* **Snake**	–		坤 *Kun*	坎 *Kan*
子 **Rat** (Dec 7 - Jan 5) 十一月 **11th Month**	子 *Zi* **Rat**	午 *Wu* **Horse**	–		離 *Li*	乾 *Qian*
丑 **Ox** (Jan 6 - Feb 3) 十二月 **12th Month**	丑 *Chou* **Ox**	未 *Wei* **Goat**	–		震 *Zhen*	坤 *Kun*

Negative Repair / Renovation Sectors 修方凶位 :

月 MONTH	天官符 Heavenly Officer Charm			地官符 Earth Officer Charm			小月建 Small Month Establishment		
寅 Tiger (Feb 4 - Mar 5) 正月 1st Month	未 Wei Goat	坤 Kun	申 Shen Monkey	甲 Jia Yang Wood	震 Zhen	乙 Yi Yin Wood	丙 Bing Yang Fire	離 Li	丁 Ding Yin Fire
卯 Rabbit (Mar 6 - Apr 4) 二月 2nd Month	壬 Ren Yang Water	坎 Kan	癸 Gui Yin Water	未 Wei Goat	坤 Kun	申 Shen Monkey	壬 Ren Yang Water	坎 Kan	癸 Gui Yin Water
辰 Dragon (Apr 5 - May 5) 三月 3rd Month	丙 Bing Yang Fire	離 Li	丁 Ding Yin Fire	壬 Ren Yang Water	坎 Kan	癸 Gui Yin Water	未 Wei Goat	坤 Kun	申 Shen Monkey
巳 Snake (May 6 - Jun 5) 四月 4th Month	丑 Chou Ox	艮 Gen	寅 Yin Tiger	丙 Bing Yang Fire	離 Li	丁 Ding Yin Fire	甲 Jia Yang Wood	震 Zhen	乙 Yi Yin Wood
午 Horse (Jun 6 - July 6) 五月 5th Month	庚 Geng Yang Metal	兌 Dui	辛 Xin Yin Metal	丑 Chou Ox	艮 Gen	寅 Yin Tiger	辰 Chen Dragon	巽 Xun	巳 Si Snake
未 Goat (July 7 - Aug 7) 六月 6th Month	戌 Xu Dog	乾 Qian	亥 Hai Pig	庚 Geng Yang Metal	兌 Dui	辛 Xin Yin Metal		中 Middle	
申 Monkey (Aug 8 - Sept 7) 七月 7th Month		中 Middle		戌 Xu Dog	乾 Qian	亥 Hai Pig	戌 Xu Dog	乾 Qian	亥 Hai Pig
酉 Rooster (Sept 8 - Oct 7) 八月 8th Month	庚 Geng Yang Metal	兌 Dui	辛 Xin Yin Metal		中 Middle		庚 Geng Yang Metal	兌 Dui	辛 Xin Yin Metal
戌 Dog (Oct 8 - Nov 6) 九月 9th Month	戌 Xu Dog	乾 Qian	亥 Hai Pig	庚 Geng Yang Metal	兌 Dui	辛 Xin Yin Metal	丑 Chou Ox	艮 Gen	寅 Yin Tiger
亥 Pig (Nov 7 - Dec 6) 十月 10th Month		中 Middle		戌 Xu Dog	乾 Qian	亥 Hai Pig	丙 Bing Yang Fire	離 Li	丁 Ding Yin Fire
子 Rat (Dec 7 - Jan 5) 十一月 11th Month	辰 Chen Dragon	巽 Xun	巳 Si Snake		中 Middle		壬 Ren Yang Water	坎 Kan	癸 Gui Yin Water
丑 Ox (Jan 6 - Feb 3) 十二月 12th Month	甲 Jia Yang Wood	震 Zhen	乙 Yi Yin Wood	辰 Chen Dragon	巽 Xun	巳 Si Snake	未 Wei Goat	坤 Kun	申 Shen Monkey

Negative Repair / Renovation Sectors 修方凶位 :

月 MONTH	大月建 Big Month Establishment			飛大煞 Flying Great Sha			丙丁獨火 Bing Ding Lonely Fire	
寅 Tiger (Feb 4 - Mar 5) 正月 1st Month	未 Wei Goat	坤 Kun	申 Shen Monkey	甲 Jia Yang Wood	震 Zhen	乙 Yi Yin Wood	離 Li	坎 Kan
卯 Rabbit (Mar 6 - Apr 4) 二月 2nd Month	壬 Ren Yang Water	坎 Kan	癸 Gui Yin Water	未 Wei Goat	坤 Kun	申 Shen Monkey	艮 Gen	離 Li
辰 Dragon (Apr 5 - May 5) 三月 3rd Month	丙 Bing Yang Fire	離 Li	丁 Ding Yin Fire	壬 Ren Yang Water	坎 Kan	癸 Gui Yin Water	兌 Dui	艮 Gen
巳 Snake (May 6 - Jun 5) 四月 4th Month	丑 Chou Ox	艮 Gen	寅 Yin Tiger	丙 Bing Yang Fire	離 Li	丁 Ding Yin Fire	乾 Qian	兌 Dui
午 Horse (Jun 6 - July 6) 五月 5th Month	庚 Geng Yang Metal	兌 Dui	辛 Xin Yin Metal	丑 Chou Ox	艮 Gen	寅 Yin Tiger	中 Middle	乾 Qian
未 Goat (July 7 - Aug 7) 六月 6th Month	戊 Xu Dog	乾 Qian	亥 Hai Pig	庚 Geng Yang Metal	兌 Dui	辛 Xin Yin Metal	中 Middle	
申 Monkey (Aug 8 - Sept 7) 七月 7th Month	中 Middle			戊 Xu Dog	乾 Qian	亥 Hai Pig	巽 Xun	中 Middle
酉 Rooster (Sept 8 - Oct 7) 八月 8th Month	辰 Chen Dragon	巽 Xun	巳 Si Snake	中 Middle			震 Zhen	巽 Xun
戌 Dog (Oct 8 - Nov 6) 九月 9th Month	甲 Jia Yang Wood	震 Zhen	乙 Yi Yin Wood	庚 Geng Yang Metal	兌 Dui	辛 Xin Yin Metal	坤 Kun	震 Zhen
亥 Pig (Nov 7 - Dec 6) 十月 10th Month	未 Wei Goat	坤 Kun	申 Shen Monkey	戊 Xu Dog	乾 Qian	亥 Hai Pig	坎 Kan	坤 Kun
子 Rat (Dec 7 - Jan 5) 十一月 11th Month	壬 Ren Yang Water	坎 Kan	癸 Gui Yin Water	中 Middle			離 Li	坎 Kan
丑 Ox (Jan 6 - Feb 3) 十二月 12th Month	丙 Bing Yang Fire	離 Li	丁 Ding Yin Fire	辰 Chen Dragon	巽 Xun	巳 Si Snake	艮 Gen	離 Li

Negative Repair / Renovation Sectors 修方凶位 :

月 MONTH	月遊火 Month Wondering Fire	三煞 Monthly 3 Killings		
		劫煞 Robbery Sha	災煞 Calamity Sha	月煞 Month Sha
寅 Tiger (Feb 4 - Mar 5) 正月 1st Month	離 Li	亥 Hai Pig	子 Zi Rat	丑 Chou Ox
卯 Rabbit (Mar 6 - Apr 4) 二月 2nd Month	坎 Kan	申 Shen Monkey	酉 You Rooster	戌 Xu Dog
辰 Dragon (Apr 5 - May 5) 三月 3rd Month	坤 Kun	巳 Si Snake	午 Wu Horse	未 Wei Goat
巳 Snake (May 6 - Jun 5) 四月 4th Month	震 Zhen	寅 Yin Tiger	卯 Mao Rabbit	辰 Chen Dragon
午 Horse (Jun 6 - July 6) 五月 5th Month	巽 Xun	亥 Hai Pig	子 Zi Rat	丑 Chou Ox
未 Goat (July 7 - Aug 7) 六月 6th Month	中 Middle	申 Shen Monkey	酉 You Rooster	戌 Xu Dog
申 Monkey (Aug 8 - Sept 7) 七月 7th Month	乾 Qian	巳 Si Snake	午 Wu Horse	未 Wei Goat
酉 Rooster (Sept 8 - Oct 7) 八月 8th Month	兌 Dui	寅 Yin Tiger	卯 Mao Rabbit	辰 Chen Dragon
戌 Dog (Oct 8 - Nov 6) 九月 9th Month	艮 Gen	亥 Hai Pig	子 Zi Rat	丑 Chou Ox
亥 Pig (Nov 7 - Dec 6) 十月 10th Month	離 Li	申 Shen Monkey	酉 You Rooster	戌 Xu Dog
子 Rat (Dec 7 - Jan 5) 十一月 11th Month	坎 Kan	巳 Si Snake	午 Wu Horse	未 Wei Goat
丑 Ox (Jan 6 - Feb 3) 十二月 12th Month	坤 Kun	寅 Yin Tiger	卯 Mao Rabbit	辰 Chen Dragon

丁巳 (Ding Si) Fire Snake

月 MONTH	月刑 Month Punishment	月害 Month Harm	月厭 Month Detest
寅 **Tiger** (Feb 4 - Mar 5) 正月 **1st Month**	巳 Si Snake	巳 Si Snake	戌 Xu Dog
卯 **Rabbit** (Mar 6 - Apr 4) 二月 **2nd Month**	子 Zi Rat	辰 Chen Dragon	酉 You Rooster
辰 **Dragon** (Apr 5 - May 5) 三月 **3rd Month**	辰 Chen Dragon	卯 Mao Rabbit	申 Shen Monkey
巳 **Snake** (May 6 - Jun 5) 四月 **4th Month**	申 Shen Monkey	寅 Yin Tiger	未 Wei Goat
午 **Horse** (Jun 6 - July 6) 五月 **5th Month**	午 Wu Horse	丑 Chou Ox	午 Wu Horse
未 **Goat** (July 7 - Aug 7) 六月 **6th Month**	丑 Chou Ox	子 Zi Rat	巳 Si Snake
申 **Monkey** (Aug 8 - Sept 7) 七月 **7th Month**	寅 Yin Tiger	亥 Hai Pig	辰 Chen Dragon
酉 **Rooster** (Sept 8 - Oct 7) 八月 **8th Month**	酉 You Rooster	戌 Xu Dog	卯 Mao Rabbit
戌 **Dog** (Oct 8 - Nov 6) 九月 **9th Month**	未 Wei Goat	酉 You Rooster	寅 Yin Tiger
亥 **Pig** (Nov 7 - Dec 6) 十月 **10th Month**	亥 Hai Pig	申 Shen Monkey	丑 Chou Ox
子 **Rat** (Dec 7 - Jan 5) 十一月 **11th Month**	卯 Mao Rabbit	未 Wei Goat	子 Zi Rat
丑 **Ox** (Jan 6 - Feb 3) 十二月 **12th Month**	戌 Xu Dog	午 Wu Horse	亥 Hai Pig

丁未 (Ding Wei)
Fire Goat

丁未 (Ding Wei) Fire Goat

Heavenly Stem 天干	丁 **Yin Fire (陰火)**
Earthly Branch 地支	未 **Goat (Yin Earth 陰土)**
Hidden Stem 藏干	己 **Yin Earth,** 丁 **Yin Fire,** 乙 **Yin Wood**
Na Yin 納音	天河水 **Water from heavenly river**
Grand Duke 太歲	未 **Goat**
Xuan Kong Five Element 玄空五行	6 水 **Water**
Gua Name 卦名	䷑ 山風蠱 **Poison**
Xuan Kong Period Luck 玄空卦運	7

Annual Positive Stars for Opening Mountain, Establishing Facing and Commencing Repairs 開山立向修方吉星:

歲德 **Duke Virtue**	壬 *Ren* **Yang Water**	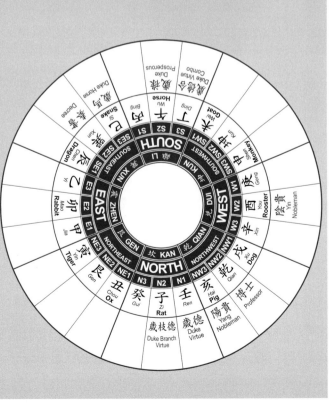
歲德合 **Duke Virtue Combo**	丁 *Ding* **Yin Fire**	
歲枝德 **Duke Branch Virtue**	子 *Zi* **Rat**	
陽貴人 **Yang Nobleman**	亥 *Hai* **Pig**	
陰貴人 **Yin Nobleman**	酉 *You* **Rooster**	
歲祿 **Duke Prosperous**	午 *Wu* **Horse**	
歲馬 **Duke Horse**	巳 *Si* **Snake**	
奏書 **Decree**	巽 *Xun*	
博士 **Professor**	乾 *Qian*	

Annual Negative Stars for Opening Mountain, Establishing Facing and Commencing Repairs 開山立向修方凶星：

太歲 Grand Duke	歲破 Year Breaker	三煞 Three Killings			坐煞向煞 Sitting Sha Facing Sha				浮天空亡 Floating Heaven Emptiness	
未 Wei Goat	丑 Chou Ox	申 Shen Monkey	酉 You Rooster	戌 Xu Dog	庚 Geng Yang Metal	辛 Xin Yin Metal	甲 Jia Yang Wood	乙 Yi Yin Wood	震 Zhen	庚 Geng Yang Metal

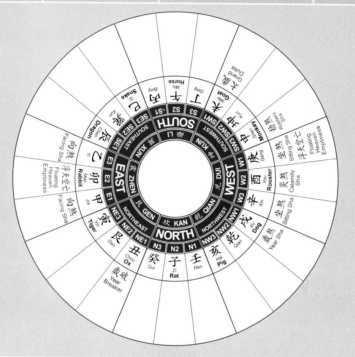

Annual San Yuan Purple White Stars 三元紫白九星：

上元 Upper Period Period 1, 2, 3			中元 Middle Period Period 4, 5, 6			下元 Lower Period Period 7, 8, 9		
巽SE **2**	離S **7**	坤SW **9**	巽SE **5**	離S **1**	坤SW **3**	巽SE **8**	離S **4**	坤SW **6**
震E **1**	**3** 丁未 Ding Wei Fire Goat	兌W **5**	震E **4**	**6** 丁未 Ding Wei Fire Goat	兌W **8**	震E **7**	**9** 丁未 Ding Wei Fire Goat	兌W **2**
艮NE **6**	坎N **8**	乾NW **4**	艮NE **9**	坎N **2**	乾NW **7**	艮NE **3**	坎N **5**	乾NW **1**

Mountain Covering Yellow Path 蓋山黃道：

貪狼 *Tan Lang* **Greedy Wolf**		巨門 *Ju Men* **Huge Door**				武曲 *Wu Qu* **Military Arts**		文曲 *Wen Qu* **Literary Arts**			
坤 *Kun* SW2	乙 *Yi* E3	坎 *Kan* N2	癸 *Gui* N3	申 *Shen* SW3	辰 *Chen* SE1	乾 *Qian* NW2	甲 *Jia* E1	震 *Zhen* E2	庚 *Geng* W1	亥 *Hai* NW3	未 *Wei* SW1

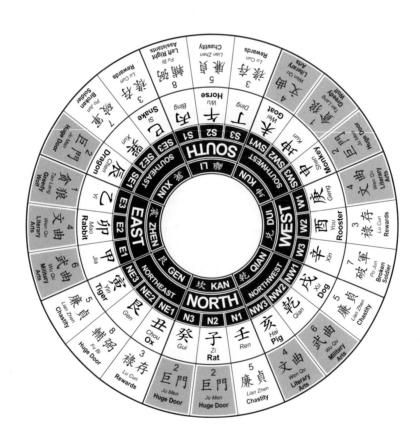

Heaven Penetrating Force 通天竅：			
三合前方 **Facing Three Harmony**	巽巳 Xun Si	丙午 Bing Wu	丁未 Ding Wei
三合後方 **Sitting Three Harmony**	乾亥 Qian Hai	壬子 Ren Zi	癸丑 Gui Chou

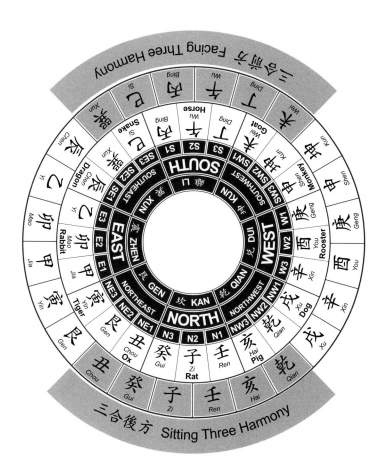

Moving Horse Six Ren Assessment 走馬六壬:

神后 Shen Hou Holy Empress	功曹 Gong Cao Marshall	天罡 Tian Gang Heavenly Dipper	勝光 Sheng Guang Subliminal Bright	傳送 Chuan Song Great General	河魁 He Kui River Scholar
巽巳 Xun Si	丁未 Ding Wei	庚酉 Geng You	乾亥 Qian Hai	癸丑 Gui Chou	甲卯 Jia Mao

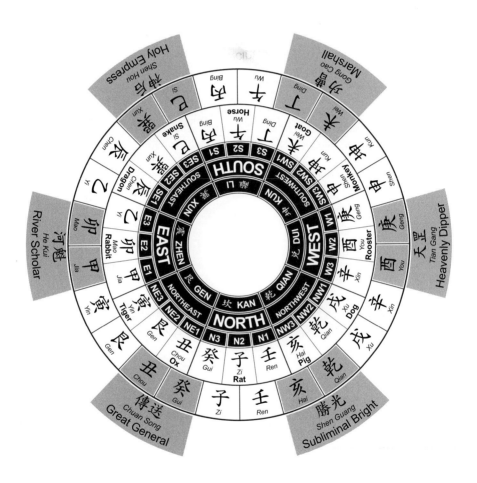

Four Advantages Three Cycles Star Plate 四利三元：

太陽 *Tai Yang* **Sun**	太陰 *Tai Yin* **Moon**	龍德 *Long De* **Dragon Virtue**	福德 *Fu De* **Fortune Virtue**
申 *Shen* **Monkey**	戌 *Xu* **Dog**	寅 *Yin* **Tiger**	辰 *Chen* **Dragon**

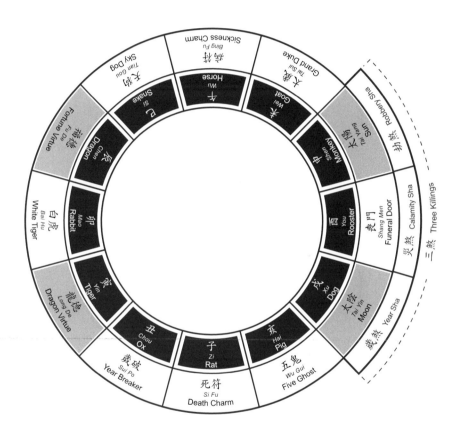

Negative Sectors For Opening Mountain 開山凶位:

年剋山家 Year Countering Sitting

甲	寅	辰	巽	戌	坎	辛	申	丑	癸	坤	庚	未
Jia	Yin	Chen	Xun	Xu	Kan	Xin	Shen	Chou	Gui	Kun	Geng	Wei
E1	NE3	SE1	SE2	NW1	N2	W3	SW3	NE1	N3	SW2	W1	SW1

陰府太歲 Yin Fu Tai Sui **Yin Mansion Grand Duke**		六害 Liu Hai **Six Harm**	死符 Si Fu **Death Charm**	炙退 Zhi Tui **Roasting Star**
乾 Qian NW2	離 Li S2	子 Zi N2	子 Zi N2	午 Wu S2

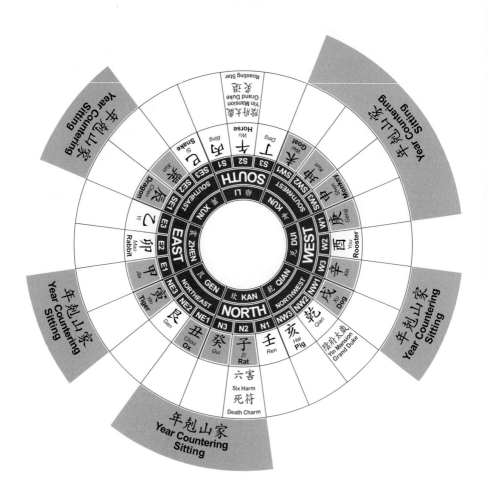

Negative Directions to Establish Facing 立向凶方:

巡山羅喉 *Xun Shan Luo Hou* **Mountain Patrol Luo Hou Star**	病符 *Bing Fu* **Sickness Charm**
坤 *Kun* **SW2**	午 *Wu* **S2**

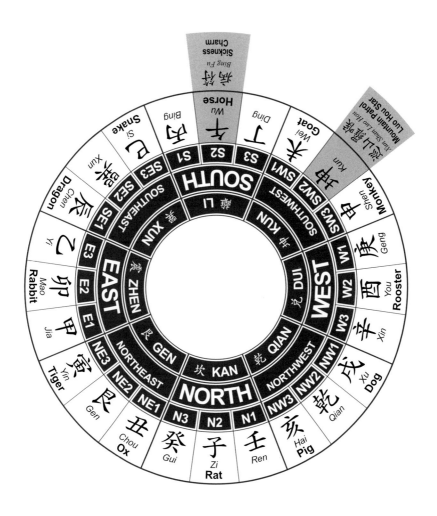

Negative Repair / Renovation Sectors Table 修方凶位表：

天官符 Heavenly Officer Charm	寅 Yin Tiger		飛廉 Flying Chaste	卯 Mao Rabbit
地官符 Earthly Officer Charm	亥 Hai Pig		喪門 Funeral Door	酉 You Rooster
大煞 Great Sha	卯 Mao Rabbit		弔客 Suspended Guest	巳 Si Snake
大將軍 Big General	卯 Mao Rabbit		白虎 White Tiger	卯 Mao Rabbit
力士 Strong Man	坤 Kun		金神 Golden God	寅 Yin Tiger 卯 Mao Rabbit 戌 Xu Dog 亥 Hai Pig
蠶室 Silkworm Room	艮 Gen			
蠶官 Silkworm Officer	丑 Chou Ox			
蠶命 Silkworm Life	寅 Yin Tiger			
歲刑 Duke Punishment	丑 Chou Ox		獨火 Lonely Fire	離 Li
黃幡 Yellow Flag	未 Wei Goat		五鬼 Five Ghost	酉 You Rooster
豹尾 Leopard Tail	丑 Chou Ox		破敗五鬼 Destructive Five Ghost	震 Zhen

Negative Repair / Renovation Sectors Diagram 修方凶位圖：

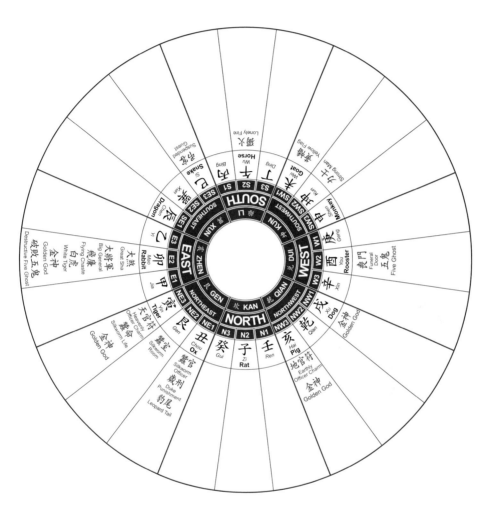

12-Month Auxiliary Stars Reference Table :
丁未年十二月，開山立向修方星表

Positive Monthly Stars 吉星方

月 MONTH	寅 Tiger (Feb 4 - Mar 5) 正月 1st Month	卯 Rabbit (Mar 6 - Apr 4) 二月 2nd Month	辰 Dragon (Apr 5 - May 5) 三月 3rd Month	巳 Snake (May 6 - Jun 5) 四月 4th Month	午 Horse (Jun 6 - July 6) 五月 5th Month	未 Goat (July 7 - Aug 7) 六月 6th Month
天道 Heavenly Path	南 South	西南 Southwest	北 North	西 West	西北 Northwest	東 East
天德 Heavenly Virtue	丁 Ding Yin Fire	坤 Kun （申）	壬 Ren Yang Water	辛 Xin Yin Metal	乾 Qian （亥）	甲 Jia Yang Wood
天德合 Heavenly Virtue Combo	壬 Ren Yang Water	（巳）	丁 Ding Yin Fire	丙 Bing Yang Fire	（寅）	己 Ji Yin Earth
月德 Monthly Virtue	丙 Bing Yang Fire	甲 Jia Yang Wood	壬 Ren Yang Water	庚 Geng Yang Metal	丙 Bing Yang Fire	甲 Jia Yang Wood
月德合 Monthly Virtue Combo	辛 Xin Yin Metal	己 Ji Yin Earth	丁 Ding Yin Fire	乙 Yi Yin Wood	辛 Xin Yin Metal	己 Ji Yin Earth
月空 Month Emptiness	壬 Ren Yang Water	庚 Geng Yang Metal	丙 Bing Yang Fire	甲 Jia Yang Wood	壬 Ren Yang Water	庚 Geng Yang Metal
陽貴人 Yang Nobleman	中 Middle	巽 Xun	震 Zhen	坤 Kun	坎 Kan	離 Li
陰貴人 Yin Nobleman	震 Zhen	坤 Kun	坎 Kan	離 Li	艮 Gen	兌 Dui
飛天祿 Flying Heavenly Wealth	離 Li	艮 Gen	兌 Dui	乾 Qian	中 Middle	坎 Kan
飛天馬 Flying Heavenly Horse	艮 Gen	兌 Dui	乾 Qian	中 Middle	坎 Kan	離 Li

12-Month Auxiliary Stars Reference Table :
丁未年十二月，開山立向修方星表

申 Monkey (Aug 8 - Sept 7) 七月 7th Month	酉 Rooster (Sept 8 - Oct 7) 八月 8th Month	戌 Dog (Oct 8 - Nov 6) 九月 9th Month	亥 Pig (Nov 7 - Dec 6) 十月 10th Month	子 Rat (Dec 7 - Jan 5) 十一月 11th Month	丑 Ox (Jan 6 - Feb 3) 十二月 12th Month	月 MONTH
北 North	東北 Northeast	南 South	東 East	東南 Southeast	西 West	天道 Heavenly Path
癸 Gui Yin Water	艮 Gen (寅)	丙 Bing Yang Fire	乙 Yi Yin Wood	巽 Xun (巳)	庚 Geng Yang Metal	天德 Heavenly Virtue
戊 Wu Yang Earth	(亥)	辛 Xin Yin Metal	庚 Geng Yang Metal	(申)	乙 Yi Yin Wood	天德合 Heavenly Virtue Combo
壬 Ren Yang Water	庚 Geng Yang Metal	丙 Bing Yang Fire	甲 Jia Yang Wood	壬 Ren Yang Water	庚 Geng Yang Metal	月德 Monthly Virtue
丁 Ding Yin Fire	乙 Yi Yin Wood	辛 Xin Yin Metal	己 Ji Yin Earth	丁 Ding Yin Fire	乙 Yi Yin Wood	月德合 Monthly Virtue Combo
丙 Bing Yang Fire	甲 Jia Yang Wood	壬 Ren Yang Water	庚 Geng Yang Metal	丙 Bing Yang Fire	甲 Jia Yang Wood	月空 Month Emptiness
艮 Gen	兌 Dui	乾 Qian	中 Middle	坎 Kan	離 Li	陽貴人 Yang Nobleman
乾 Qian	中 Middle	坎 Kan	離 Li	艮 Gen	兌 Dui	陰貴人 Yin Nobleman
離 Li	艮 Gen	兌 Dui	乾 Qian	中 Middle	坎 Kan	飛天祿 Flying Heavenly Wealth
艮 Gen	兌 Dui	乾 Qian	中 Middle	巽 Xun	震 Zhen	飛天馬 Flying Heavenly Horse

丁未 (Ding Wei) Fire Goat

Monthly Purple White Stars 月紫白九星 :

寅 Tiger (Feb 4 - Mar 5) 正月 1st Month

巽 SE	離 S	坤 SW
4 Green 四緑	9 Purple 九紫	2 Black 二黑
3 Jade 三碧 (震 E)	5 Yellow 五黃	7 Red 七赤 (兌 W)
8 White 八白	1 White 一白	6 White 六白
艮 NE	坎 N	乾 NW

卯 Rabbit (Mar 6 - Apr 4) 二月 2nd Month

巽 SE	離 S	坤 SW
3 Jade 三碧	8 White 八白	1 White 一白
2 Black 二黑 (震 E)	4 Green 四緑	6 White 六白 (兌 W)
7 Red 七赤	9 Purple 九紫	5 Yellow 五黃
艮 NE	坎 N	乾 NW

辰 Dragon (Apr 5 - May 5) 三月 3rd Month

巽 SE	離 S	坤 SW
2 Black 二黑	7 Red 七赤	9 Purple 九紫
1 White 一白 (震 E)	3 Jade 三碧	5 Yellow 五黃 (兌 W)
6 White 六白	8 White 八白	4 Green 四緑
艮 NE	坎 N	乾 NW

巳 Snake (May 6 - Jun 5) 四月 4th Month

巽 SE	離 S	坤 SW
1 White 一白	6 White 六白	8 White 八白
9 Purple 九紫 (震 E)	2 Black 二黑	4 Green 四緑 (兌 W)
5 Yellow 五黃	7 Red 七赤	3 Jade 三碧
艮 NE	坎 N	乾 NW

午 Horse (Jun 6 - July 6) 五月 5th Month

巽 SE	離 S	坤 SW
9 Purple 九紫	5 Yellow 五黃	7 Red 七赤
8 White 八白 (震 E)	1 White 一白	3 Jade 三碧 (兌 W)
4 Green 四緑	6 White 六白	2 Black 二黑
艮 NE	坎 N	乾 NW

未 Goat (July 7 - Aug 7) 六月 6th Month

巽 SE	離 S	坤 SW
8 White 八白	4 Green 四緑	6 White 六白
7 Red 七赤 (震 E)	9 Purple 九紫	2 Black 二黑 (兌 W)
3 Jade 三碧	5 Yellow 五黃	1 White 一白
艮 NE	坎 N	乾 NW

申 Monkey (Aug 8 - Sept 7) 七月 7th Month

巽 SE	離 S	坤 SW
7 Red 七赤	3 Jade 三碧	5 Yellow 五黃
6 White 六白 (震 E)	8 White 八白	1 White 一白 (兌 W)
2 Black 二黑	4 Green 四緑	9 Purple 九紫
艮 NE	坎 N	乾 NW

酉 Rooster (Sept 8 - Oct 7) 八月 8th Month

巽 SE	離 S	坤 SW
6 White 六白	2 Black 二黑	4 Green 四緑
5 Yellow 五黃 (震 E)	7 Red 七赤	9 Purple 九紫 (兌 W)
1 White 一白	3 Jade 三碧	8 White 八白
艮 NE	坎 N	乾 NW

戌 Dog (Oct 8 - Nov 6) 九月 9th Month

巽 SE	離 S	坤 SW
5 Yellow 五黃	1 White 一白	3 Jade 三碧
4 Green 四緑 (震 E)	6 White 六白	8 White 八白 (兌 W)
9 Purple 九紫	2 Black 二黑	7 Red 七赤
艮 NE	坎 N	乾 NW

亥 Pig (Nov 7 - Dec 6) 十月 10th Month

巽 SE	離 S	坤 SW
4 Green 四緑	9 Purple 九紫	2 Black 二黑
3 Jade 三碧 (震 E)	5 Yellow 五黃	7 Red 七赤 (兌 W)
8 White 八白	1 White 一白	6 White 六白
艮 NE	坎 N	乾 NW

子 Rat (Dec 7 - Jan 5) 十一月 11th Month

巽 SE	離 S	坤 SW
3 Jade 三碧	8 White 八白	1 White 一白
2 Black 二黑 (震 E)	4 Green 四緑	6 White 六白 (兌 W)
7 Red 七赤	9 Purple 九紫	5 Yellow 五黃
艮 NE	坎 N	乾 NW

丑 Ox (Jan 6 - Feb 3) 十二月 12th Month

巽 SE	離 S	坤 SW
2 Black 二黑	7 Red 七赤	9 Purple 九紫
1 White 一白 (震 E)	3 Jade 三碧	5 Yellow 五黃 (兌 W)
6 White 六白	8 White 八白	4 Green 四緑
艮 NE	坎 N	乾 NW

Qi Men Three Nobles 三奇 :

Three Nobles 三奇 / Seasons	乙 Yi	丙 Bing	丁 Ding
立春 **Coming of Spring** Feb 4 - Feb 18	離 Li	坎 Kan	坤 Kun
春分 **Spring Equinox** Mar 21 - Apr 4	巽 Xun	中 Middle	乾 Qian
立夏 **Coming of Summer** May 6 - May 20	中 Middle	乾 Qian	兌 Dui
夏至 **Summer Solstice** Jun 22 - Jul 6	艮 Gen	兌 Dui	乾 Qian
立秋 **Coming of Autumn** Aug 8 - Aug 23	坎 Kan	離 Li	艮 Gen
秋分 **Autumn Equinox** Sept 23 - Oct 7	乾 Qian	中 Middle	巽 Xun
立冬 **Coming of Winter** Nov 7 - Nov 22	中 Middle	巽 Xun	震 Zhen
冬至 **Winter Solstice** Dec 22 - Jan 5	坤 Kun	震 Zhen	巽 Xun

Sectors to Avoid Opening Mountain 開山凶位 :

月 MONTH	月建 Month Establishment	月破 Month Destruction	月剋山家 Month Countering Sitting		陰府太歲 Yin Mansion Grand Duke	
寅 **Tiger** (Feb 4 - Mar 5) 正月 **1st Month**	寅 *Yin* **Tiger**	申 *Shen* **Monkey**	−		離 *Li*	乾 *Qian*
卯 **Rabbit** (Mar 6 - Apr 4) 二月 **2nd Month**	卯 *Mao* **Rabbit**	酉 *You* **Rooster**	−		震 *Zhen*	坤 *Kun*
辰 **Dragon** (Apr 5 - May 5) 三月 **3rd Month**	辰 *Chen* **Dragon**	戌 *Xu* **Dog**	離 *Li*	丙 *Bing* **Yang Fire**	艮 *Gen*	巽 *Xun*
巳 **Snake** (May 6 - Jun 5) 四月 **4th Month**	巳 *Si* **Snake**	亥 *Hai* **Pig**	壬 *Ren* **Yang Water**	乙 *Yi* **Yin Wood**	兌 *Dui*	乾 *Qian*
午 **Horse** (Jun 6 - July 6) 五月 **5th Month**	午 *Wu* **Horse**	子 *Zi* **Rat**	水 **Water**	山 **Mountain**	坎 *Kan*	坤 *Kun*
未 **Goat** (July 7 - Aug 7) 六月 **6th Month**	未 *Wei* **Goat**	丑 *Chou* **Ox**	土 **Earth**		乾 *Qian*	離 *Li*
申 **Monkey** (Aug 8 - Sept 7) 七月 **7th Month**	申 *Shen* **Monkey**	寅 *Yin* **Tiger**	震 *Zhen*	巳 *Si* **Snake**	坤 *Kun*	震 *Zhen*
酉 **Rooster** (Sept 8 - Oct 7) 八月 **8th Month**	酉 *You* **Rooster**	卯 *Mao* **Rabbit**	艮 *Gen*		巽 *Xun*	艮 *Gen*
戌 **Dog** (Oct 8 - Nov 6) 九月 **9th Month**	戌 *Xu* **Dog**	辰 *Chen* **Dragon**	−		乾 *Qian*	兌 *Dui*
亥 **Pig** (Nov 7 - Dec 6) 十月 **10th Month**	亥 *Hai* **Pig**	巳 *Si* **Snake**	−		坤 *Kun*	坎 *Kan*
子 **Rat** (Dec 7 - Jan 5) 十一月 **11th Month**	子 *Zi* **Rat**	午 *Wu* **Horse**	−		離 *Li*	乾 *Qian*
丑 **Ox** (Jan 6 - Feb 3) 十二月 **12th Month**	丑 *Chou* **Ox**	未 *Wei* **Goat**	−		震 *Zhen*	坤 *Kun*

Negative Repair / Renovation Sectors 修方凶位 :

月 MONTH	天官符 Heavenly Officer Charm			地官符 Earth Officer Charm			小月建 Small Month Establishment		
寅 Tiger (Feb 4 - Mar 5) 正月 1st Month		中 Middle			中 Middle		丙 Bing Yang Fire	離 Li	丁 Ding Yin Fire
卯 Rabbit (Mar 6 - Apr 4) 二月 2nd Month	庚 Geng Yang Metal	兌 Dui	辛 Xin Yin Metal	辰 Chen Dragon	巽 Xun	巳 Si Snake	壬 Ren Yang Water	坎 Kan	癸 Gui Yin Water
辰 Dragon (Apr 5 - May 5) 三月 3rd Month	戊 Xu Dog	乾 Qian	亥 Hai Pig	甲 Jia Yang Wood	震 Zhen	乙 Yi Yin Wood	未 Wei Goat	坤 Kun	申 Shen Monkey
巳 Snake (May 6 - Jun 5) 四月 4th Month		中 Middle		未 Wei Goat	坤 Kun	申 Shen Monkey	甲 Jia Yang Wood	震 Zhen	乙 Yi Yin Wood
午 Horse (Jun 6 - July 6) 五月 5th Month	辰 Chen Dragon	巽 Xun	巳 Si Snake	壬 Ren Yang Water	坎 Kan	癸 Gui Yin Water	辰 Chen Dragon	巽 Xun	巳 Si Snake
未 Goat (July 7 - Aug 7) 六月 6th Month	甲 Jia Yang Wood	震 Zhen	乙 Yi Yin Wood	丙 Bing Yang Fire	離 Li	丁 Ding Yin Fire		中 Middle	
申 Monkey (Aug 8 - Sept 7) 七月 7th Month	未 Wei Goat	坤 Kun	申 Shen Monkey	丑 Chou Ox	艮 Gen	寅 Yin Tiger	戊 Xu Dog	乾 Qian	亥 Hai Pig
酉 Rooster (Sept 8 - Oct 7) 八月 8th Month	壬 Ren Yang Water	坎 Kan	癸 Gui Yin Water	庚 Geng Yang Metal	兌 Dui	辛 Xin Yin Metal	庚 Geng Yang Metal	兌 Dui	辛 Xin Yin Metal
戌 Dog (Oct 8 - Nov 6) 九月 9th Month	丙 Bing Yang Fire	離 Li	丁 Ding Yin Fire	戊 Xu Dog	乾 Qian	亥 Hai Pig	丑 Chou Ox	艮 Gen	寅 Yin Tiger
亥 Pig (Nov 7 - Dec 6) 十月 10th Month	丑 Chou Ox	艮 Gen	寅 Yin Tiger		中 Middle		丙 Bing Yang Fire	離 Li	丁 Ding Yin Fire
子 Rat (Dec 7 - Jan 5) 十一月 11th Month	庚 Geng Yang Metal	兌 Dui	辛 Xin Yin Metal	庚 Geng Yang Metal	兌 Dui	辛 Xin Yin Metal	壬 Ren Yang Water	坎 Kan	癸 Gui Yin Water
丑 Ox (Jan 6 - Feb 3) 十二月 12th Month	戊 Xu Dog	乾 Qian	亥 Hai Pig	戊 Xu Dog	乾 Qian	亥 Hai Pig	未 Wei Goat	坤 Kun	申 Shen Monkey

Negative Repair / Renovation Sectors 修方凶位 :

月 MONTH	大月建 Big Month Establishment			飛大煞 Flying Great Sha			丙丁獨火 Bing Ding Lonely Fire	
寅 **Tiger** (Feb 4 - Mar 5) 正月 **1st Month**		中 Middle		戌 *Xu* **Dog**	乾 *Qian*	亥 *Hai* **Pig**	離 *Li*	坎 *Kan*
卯 **Rabbit** (Mar 6 - Apr 4) 二月 **2nd Month**	辰 *Chen* **Dragon**	巽 *Xun*	巳 *Si* **Snake**		中 Middle		艮 *Gen*	離 *Li*
辰 **Dragon** (Apr 5 - May 5) 三月 **3rd Month**	甲 *Jia* **Yang Wood**	震 *Zhen*	乙 *Yi* **Yin Wood**	庚 *Geng* **Yang Metal**	兌 *Dui*	辛 *Xin* **Yin Metal**	兌 *Dui*	艮 *Gen*
巳 **Snake** (May 6 - Jun 5) 四月 **4th Month**	未 *Wei* **Goat**	坤 *Kun*	申 *Shen* **Monkey**	戌 *Xu* **Dog**	乾 *Qian*	亥 *Hai* **Pig**	乾 *Qian*	兌 *Dui*
午 **Horse** (Jun 6 - July 6) 五月 **5th Month**	壬 *Ren* **Yang Water**	坎 *Kan*	癸 *Gui* **Yin Water**		中 Middle		中 Middle	乾 *Qian*
未 **Goat** (July 7 - Aug 7) 六月 **6th Month**	丙 *Bing* **Yang Fire**	離 *Li*	丁 *Ding* **Yin Fire**	辰 *Chen* **Dragon**	巽 *Xun*	巳 *Si* **Snake**		中 Middle
申 **Monkey** (Aug 8 - Sept 7) 七月 **7th Month**	丑 *Chou* **Ox**	艮 *Gen*	寅 *Yin* **Tiger**	甲 *Jia* **Yang Wood**	震 *Zhen*	乙 *Yi* **Yin Wood**	巽 *Xun*	中 Middle
酉 **Rooster** (Sept 8 - Oct 7) 八月 **8th Month**	庚 *Geng* **Yang Metal**	兌 *Dui*	辛 *Xin* **Yin Metal**	未 *Wei* **Goat**	坤 *Kun*	申 *Shen* **Monkey**	震 *Zhen*	巽 *Xun*
戌 **Dog** (Oct 8 - Nov 6) 九月 **9th Month**	戌 *Xu* **Dog**	乾 *Qian*	亥 *Hai* **Pig**	壬 *Ren* **Yang Water**	坎 *Kan*	癸 *Gui* **Yin Water**	坤 *Kun*	震 *Zhen*
亥 **Pig** (Nov 7 - Dec 6) 十月 **10th Month**		中 Middle		丙 *Bing* **Yang Fire**	離 *Li*	丁 *Ding* **Yin Fire**	坎 *Kan*	坤 *Kun*
子 **Rat** (Dec 7 - Jan 5) 十一月 **11th Month**	辰 *Chen* **Dragon**	巽 *Xun*	巳 *Si* **Snake**	丑 *Chou* **Ox**	艮 *Gen*	寅 *Yin* **Tiger**	離 *Li*	坎 *Kan*
丑 **Ox** (Jan 6 - Feb 3) 十二月 **12th Month**	甲 *Jia* **Yang Wood**	震 *Zhen*	乙 *Yi* **Yin Wood**	庚 *Geng* **Yang Metal**	兌 *Dui*	辛 *Xin* **Yin Metal**	艮 *Gen*	離 *Li*

Negative Repair / Renovation Sectors 修方凶位 :

月 MONTH	月遊火 Month Wondering Fire	三煞 Monthly 3 Killings		
		劫煞 Robbery Sha	災煞 Calamity Sha	月煞 Month Sha
寅 **Tiger** (Feb 4 - Mar 5) 正月 **1st Month**	坤 Kun	亥 Hai Pig	子 Zi Rat	丑 Chou Ox
卯 **Rabbit** (Mar 6 - Apr 4) 二月 **2nd Month**	震 Zhen	申 Shen Monkey	酉 You Rooster	戌 Xu Dog
辰 **Dragon** (Apr 5 - May 5) 三月 **3rd Month**	巽 Xun	巳 Si Snake	午 Wu Horse	未 Wei Goat
巳 **Snake** (May 6 - Jun 5) 四月 **4th Month**	中 Middle	寅 Yin Tiger	卯 Mao Rabbit	辰 Chen Dragon
午 **Horse** (Jun 6 - July 6) 五月 **5th Month**	乾 Qian	亥 Hai Pig	子 Zi Rat	丑 Chou Ox
未 **Goat** (July 7 - Aug 7) 六月 **6th Month**	兌 Dui	申 Shen Monkey	酉 You Rooster	戌 Xu Dog
申 **Monkey** (Aug 8 - Sept 7) 七月 **7th Month**	艮 Gen	巳 Si Snake	午 Wu Horse	未 Wei Goat
酉 **Rooster** (Sept 8 - Oct 7) 八月 **8th Month**	離 Li	寅 Yin Tiger	卯 Mao Rabbit	辰 Chen Dragon
戌 **Dog** (Oct 8 - Nov 6) 九月 **9th Month**	坎 Kan	亥 Hai Pig	子 Zi Rat	丑 Chou Ox
亥 **Pig** (Nov 7 - Dec 6) 十月 **10th Month**	坤 Kun	申 Shen Monkey	酉 You Rooster	戌 Xu Dog
子 **Rat** (Dec 7 - Jan 5) 十一月 **11th Month**	震 Zhen	巳 Si Snake	午 Wu Horse	未 Wei Goat
丑 **Ox** (Jan 6 - Feb 3) 十二月 **12th Month**	巽 Xun	寅 Yin Tiger	卯 Mao Rabbit	辰 Chen Dragon

Negative Repair / Renovation Sectors 修方凶位 :

月 MONTH	月刑 Month Punishment	月害 Month Harm	月厭 Month Detest
寅 **Tiger** (Feb 4 - Mar 5) 正月 **1st Month**	巳 *Si* Snake	巳 *Si* Snake	戌 *Xu* Dog
卯 **Rabbit** (Mar 6 - Apr 4) 二月 **2nd Month**	子 *Zi* Rat	辰 *Chen* Dragon	酉 *You* Rooster
辰 **Dragon** (Apr 5 - May 5) 三月 **3rd Month**	辰 *Chen* Dragon	卯 *Mao* Rabbit	申 *Shen* Monkey
巳 **Snake** (May 6 - Jun 5) 四月 **4th Month**	申 *Shen* Monkey	寅 *Yin* Tiger	未 *Wei* Goat
午 **Horse** (Jun 6 - July 6) 五月 **5th Month**	午 *Wu* Horse	丑 *Chou* Ox	午 *Wu* Horse
未 **Goat** (July 7 - Aug 7) 六月 **6th Month**	丑 *Chou* Ox	子 *Zi* Rat	巳 *Si* Snake
申 **Monkey** (Aug 8 - Sept 7) 七月 **7th Month**	寅 *Yin* Tiger	亥 *Hai* Pig	辰 *Chen* Dragon
酉 **Rooster** (Sept 8 - Oct 7) 八月 **8th Month**	酉 *You* Rooster	戌 *Xu* Dog	卯 *Mao* Rabbit
戌 **Dog** (Oct 8 - Nov 6) 九月 **9th Month**	未 *Wei* Goat	酉 *You* Rooster	寅 *Yin* Tiger
亥 **Pig** (Nov 7 - Dec 6) 十月 **10th Month**	亥 *Hai* Pig	申 *Shen* Monkey	丑 *Chou* Ox
子 **Rat** (Dec 7 - Jan 5) 十一月 **11th Month**	卯 *Mao* Rabbit	未 *Wei* Goat	子 *Zi* Rat
丑 **Ox** (Jan 6 - Feb 3) 十二月 **12th Month**	戌 *Xu* Dog	午 *Wu* Horse	亥 *Hai* Pig

丁酉 (Ding You)
Fire Rooster

丁酉 (Ding You) Fire Rooster

Heavenly Stem 天干	丁 **Yin Fire (陰火)**
Earthly Branch 地支	酉 **Rooster (Yin Metal 陰金)**
Hidden Stem 藏干	辛 **Yin Metal**
Na Yin 納音	山下火 **Fire from mountain slopes**
Grand Duke 太歲	酉 **Rooster**
Xuan Kong Five Element 玄空五行	4 金 **Metal**
Gua Name 卦名	☱☶ 澤山咸 **Influence**
Xuan Kong Period Luck 玄空卦運	9

Annual Positive Stars for Opening Mountain, Establishing Facing and Commencing Repairs 開山立向修方吉星：

歲德 **Duke Virtue**	壬	Ren Yang Water
歲德合 **Duke Virtue Combo**	丁	Ding Yin Fire
歲枝德 **Duke Branch Virtue**	寅	Yin Tiger
陽貴人 **Yang Nobleman**	亥	Hai Pig
陰貴人 **Yin Nobleman**	酉	You Rooster
歲祿 **Duke Prosperous**	午	Wu Horse
歲馬 **Duke Horse**	亥	Hai Pig
奏書 **Decree**	坤	Kun
博士 **Professor**	艮	Gen

442

Annual Negative Stars for Opening Mountain, Establishing Facing and Commencing Repairs 開山立向修方凶星：

太歲 Grand Duke	歲破 Year Breaker	三煞 Three Killings			坐煞向煞 Sitting Sha Facing Sha				浮天空亡 Floating Heaven Emptiness	
酉 *You* Rooster	卯 *Mao* Rabbit	寅 *Yin* Tiger	卯 *Mao* Rabbit	辰 *Chen* Dragon	甲 *Jia* Yang Wood	乙 *Yi* Yin Wood	庚 *Geng* Yang Metal	辛 *Xin* Yin Metal	震 *Zhen*	庚 *Geng* Yang Metal

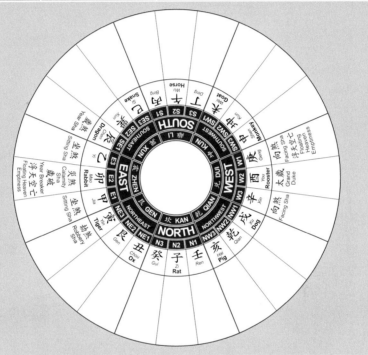

Annual San Yuan Purple White Stars 三元紫白九星：

上元 Upper Period Period 1, 2, 3			中元 Middle Period Period 4, 5, 6			下元 Lower Period Period 7, 8, 9		
巽SE **3**	離S **8**	坤SW **1**	巽SE **6**	離S **2**	坤SW **4**	巽SE **9**	離S **5**	坤SW **7**
震E **2**	**4** 丁酉 *Ding You* Fire Rooster	兌W **6**	震E **5**	**7** 丁酉 *Ding You* Fire Rooster	兌W **9**	震E **8**	**1** 丁酉 *Ding You* Fire Rooster	兌W **3**
艮NE **7**	坎N **9**	乾NW **5**	艮NE **1**	坎N **3**	乾NW **8**	艮NE **4**	坎N **6**	乾NW **2**

Mountain Covering Yellow Path 蓋山黃道：

貪狼 *Tan Lang* **Greedy Wolf**				巨門 *Ju Men* **Huge Door**		武曲 *Wu Qu* **Military Arts**				文曲 *Wen Qu* **Literary Arts**	
離 *Li* **S2**	壬 *Ren* **N1**	寅 *Yin* **NE3**	戌 *Xu* **NW1**	乾 *Qian* **NW2**	甲 *Jia* **E1**	坎 *Kan* **N2**	癸 *Gui* **N3**	申 *Shen* **SW3**	辰 *Chen* **SE1**	艮 *Gen* **NE2**	丙 *Bing* **S1**

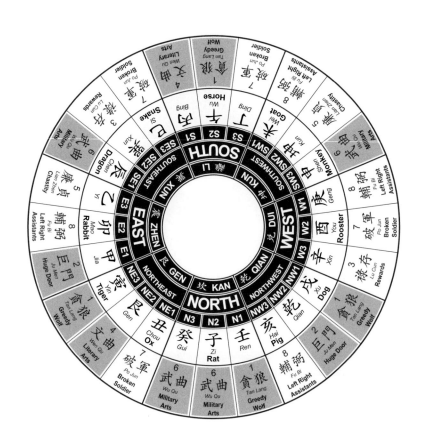

Heaven Penetrating Force 通天竅：			
三合前方 **Facing Three Harmony**	乾亥 Qian Hai	壬子 Ren Zi	癸丑 Gui Chou
三合後方 **Sitting Three Harmony**	巽巳 Xun Si	丙午 Bing Wu	丁未 Ding Wei

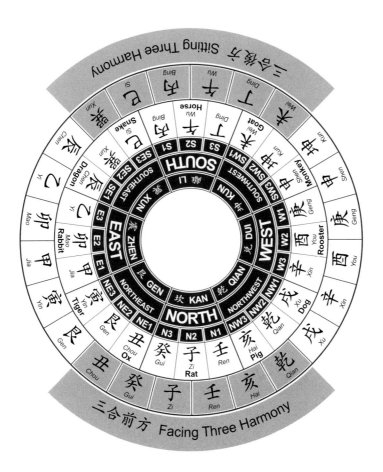

丁酉 (Ding You) Fire Rooster

Moving Horse Six Ren Assessment 走馬六壬:

神后 Shen Hou Holy Empress	功曹 Gong Cao Marshall	天罡 Tian Gang Heavenly Dipper	勝光 Sheng Guang Subliminal Bright	傳送 Chuan Song Great General	河魁 He Kui River Scholar
甲卯 Jia Mao	巽巳 Xun Si	丁未 Ding Wei	庚酉 Geng You	乾亥 Qian Hai	癸丑 Gui Chou

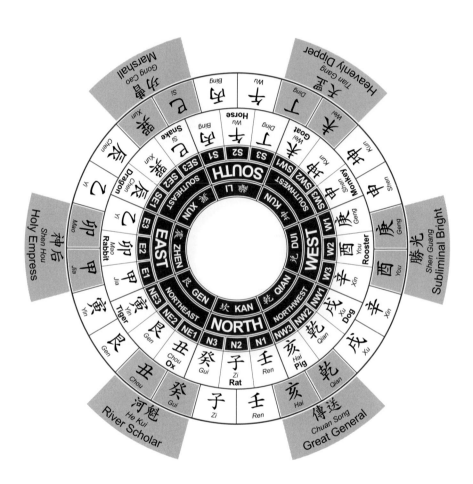

Four Advantages Three Cycles Star Plate 四利三元：

太陽 *Tai Yang* **Sun**	太陰 *Tai Yin* **Moon**	龍德 *Long De* **Dragon Virtue**	福德 *Fu De* **Fortune Virtue**
戌 *Xu* Dog	子 *Zi* Rat	辰 *Chen* Dragon	午 *Wu* Horse

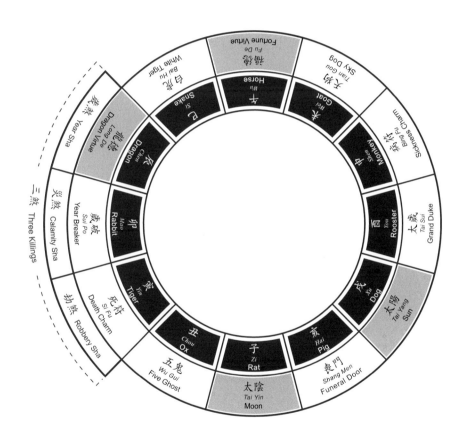

Negative Sectors For Opening Mountain 開山凶位：

年剋山家 Year Countering Sitting

離	壬	丙	乙
Li	*Ren*	*Bing*	*Yi*
S2	N1	S1	E3

陰府太歲	六害	死符	炙退
Yin Fu Tai Sui	*Liu Hai*	*Si Fu*	*Zhi Tui*
Yin Mansion Grand Duke	**Six Harm**	**Death Charm**	**Roasting Star**

乾	離	戌	寅	子
Qian	*Li*	*Xu*	*Yin*	*Zi*
NW2	S2	NW1	NE3	N2

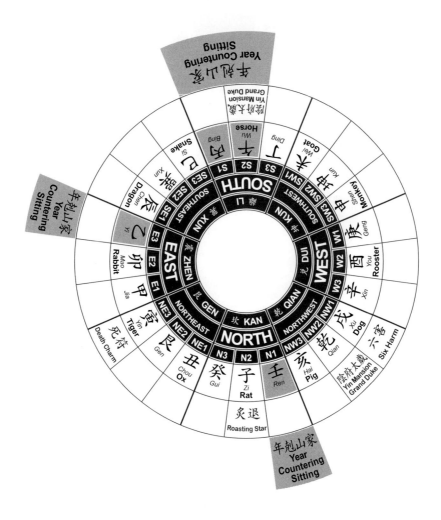

448

巡山羅喉 Xun Shan Luo Hou **Mountain Patrol Luo Hou Star**	病符 Bing Fu **Sickness Charm**
辛 Xin **W3**	申 Shen **SW3**

Negative Directions to Establish Facing 立向凶方：

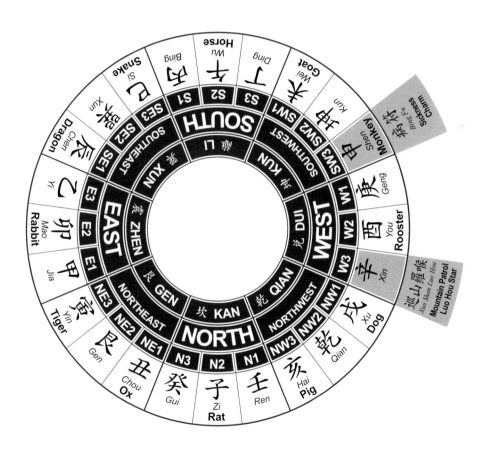

Negative Repair / Renovation Sectors Table 修方凶位表：

天官符 Heavenly Officer Charm	申 Shen Monkey	飛廉 Flying Chaste	亥 Hai Pig
地官符 Earthly Officer Charm	丑 Chou Ox	喪門 Funeral Door	亥 Hai Pig
大煞 Great Sha	酉 You Rooster	弔客 Suspended Guest	未 Wei Goat
大將軍 Big General	午 Wu Horse	白虎 White Tiger	巳 Si Snake
力士 Strong Man	乾 Qian	金神 Golden God	寅 Yin Tiger / 卯 Mao Rabbit / 戌 Xu Dog / 亥 Hai Pig
蠶室 Silkworm Room	巽 Xun		
蠶官 Silkworm Officer	辰 Chen Dragon		
蠶命 Silkworm Life	巳 Si Snake		
歲刑 Duke Punishment	酉 You Rooster	獨火 Lonely Fire	坤 Kun
黃幡 Yellow Flag	丑 Chou Ox	五鬼 Five Ghost	未 Wei Goat
豹尾 Leopard Tail	未 Wei Goat	破敗五鬼 Destructive Five Ghost	震 Zhen

Negative Repair / Renovation Sectors Diagram 修方凶位圖：

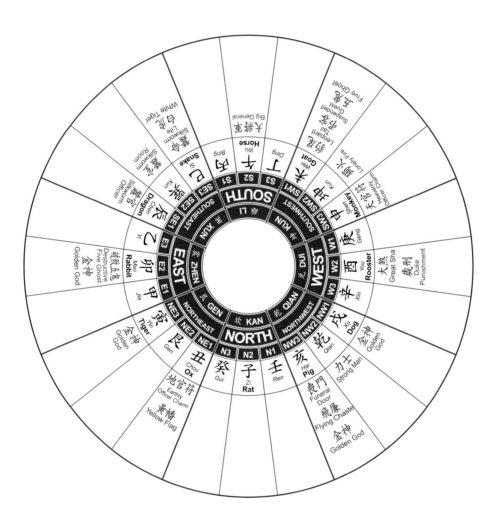

丁酉 (Ding You) Fire Rooster

12-Month Auxiliary Stars Reference Table :
丁酉年十二月，開山立向修方星表

Positive Monthly Stars 吉星方

月 MONTH	寅 Tiger (Feb 4 - Mar 5) 正月 1st Month	卯 Rabbit (Mar 6 - Apr 4) 二月 2nd Month	辰 Dragon (Apr 5 - May 5) 三月 3rd Month	巳 Snake (May 6 - Jun 5) 四月 4th Month	午 Horse (Jun 6 - July 6) 五月 5th Month	未 Goat (July 7 - Aug 7) 六月 6th Month
天道 Heavenly Path	南 South	西南 Southwest	北 North	西 West	西北 Northwest	東 East
天德 Heavenly Virtue	丁 Ding Yin Fire	坤 Kun (申)	壬 Ren Yang Water	辛 Xin Yin Metal	乾 Qian (亥)	甲 Jia Yang Wood
天德合 Heavenly Virtue Combo	壬 Ren Yang Water	(巳)	丁 Ding Yin Fire	丙 Bing Yang Fire	(寅)	己 Ji Yin Earth
月德 Monthly Virtue	丙 Bing Yang Fire	甲 Jia Yang Wood	壬 Ren Yang Water	庚 Geng Yang Metal	丙 Bing Yang Fire	甲 Jia Yang Wood
月德合 Monthly Virtue Combo	辛 Xin Yin Metal	己 Ji Yin Earth	丁 Ding Yin Fire	乙 Yi Yin Wood	辛 Xin Yin Metal	己 Ji Yin Earth
月空 Month Emptiness	壬 Ren Yang Water	庚 Geng Yang Metal	丙 Bing Yang Fire	甲 Jia Yang Wood	壬 Ren Yang Water	庚 Geng Yang Metal
陽貴人 Yang Nobleman	中 Middle	巽 Xun	震 Zhen	坤 Kun	坎 Kan	離 Li
陰貴人 Yin Nobleman	震 Zhen	坤 Kun	坎 Kan	離 Li	艮 Gen	兌 Dui
飛天祿 Flying Heavenly Wealth	離 Li	艮 Gen	兌 Dui	乾 Qian	中 Middle	坎 Kan
飛天馬 Flying Heavenly Horse	中 Middle	巽 Xun	震 Zhen	坤 Kun	坎 Kan	離 Li

12-Month Auxiliary Stars Reference Table :
丁酉年十二月，開山立向修方星表

申 Monkey (Aug 8 - Sept 7) 七月 7th Month	酉 Rooster (Sept 8 - Oct 7) 八月 8th Month	戌 Dog (Oct 8 - Nov 6) 九月 9th Month	亥 Pig (Nov 7 - Dec 6) 十月 10th Month	子 Rat (Dec 7 - Jan 5) 十一月 11th Month	丑 Ox (Jan 6 - Feb 3) 十二月 12th Month	月 MONTH
北 North	東北 Northeast	南 South	東 East	東南 Southeast	西 West	天道 Heavenly Path
癸 Gui Yin Water	艮 Gen (寅)	丙 Bing Yang Fire	乙 Yi Yin Wood	巽 Xun (巳)	庚 Geng Yang Metal	天德 Heavenly Virtue
戊 Wu Yang Earth	(亥)	辛 Xin Yin Metal	庚 Geng Yang Metal	(申)	乙 Yi Yin Wood	天德合 Heavenly Virtue Combo
壬 Ren Yang Water	庚 Geng Yang Metal	丙 Bing Yang Fire	甲 Jia Yang Wood	壬 Ren Yang Water	庚 Geng Yang Metal	月德 Monthly Virtue
丁 Ding Yin Fire	乙 Yi Yin Wood	辛 Xin Yin Metal	己 Ji Yin Earth	丁 Ding Yin Fire	乙 Yi Yin Wood	月德合 Monthly Virtue Combo
丙 Bing Yang Fire	甲 Jia Yang Wood	壬 Ren Yang Water	庚 Geng Yang Metal	丙 Bing Yang Fire	甲 Jia Yang Wood	月空 Month Emptiness
艮 Gen	兌 Dui	乾 Qian	中 Middle	坎 Kan	離 Li	陽貴人 Yang Nobleman
乾 Qian	中 Middle	坎 Kan	離 Li	艮 Gen	兌 Dui	陰貴人 Yin Nobleman
離 Li	艮 Gen	兌 Dui	乾 Qian	中 Middle	巽 Xun	飛天祿 Flying Heavenly Wealth
艮 Gen	兌 Dui	乾 Qian	中 Middle	坎 Kan	離 Li	飛天馬 Flying Heavenly Horse

Monthly Purple White Stars 月紫白九星 :

寅 Tiger (Feb 4 - Mar 5) 正月 1st Month

	巽SE	離S	坤SW	
	7 Red 七赤	3 Jade 三碧	5 Yellow 五黄	
震 E	6 White 六白	8 White 八白	1 White 一白	兌 W
	2 Black 二黑	4 Green 四綠	9 Purple 九紫	
	艮NE	坎N	乾NW	

卯 Rabbit (Mar 6 - Apr 4) 二月 2nd Month

	巽SE	離S	坤SW	
	6 White 六白	2 Black 二黑	4 Green 四綠	
震 E	5 Yellow 五黄	7 Red 七赤	9 Purple 九紫	兌 W
	1 White 一白	3 Jade 三碧	8 White 八白	
	艮NE	坎N	乾NW	

辰 Dragon (Apr 5 - May 5) 三月 3rd Month

	巽SE	離S	坤SW	
	5 Yellow 五黄	1 White 一白	3 Jade 三碧	
震 E	4 Green 四綠	6 White 六白	8 White 八白	兌 W
	9 Purple 九紫	2 Black 二黑	7 Red 七赤	
	艮NE	坎N	乾NW	

巳 Snake (May 6 - Jun 5) 四月 4th Month

	巽SE	離S	坤SW	
	4 Green 四綠	9 Purple 九紫	2 Black 二黑	
震 E	3 Jade 三碧	5 Yellow 五黄	7 Red 七赤	兌 W
	8 White 八白	1 White 一白	6 White 六白	
	艮NE	坎N	乾NW	

午 Horse (Jun 6 - July 6) 五月 5th Month

	巽SE	離S	坤SW	
	3 Jade 三碧	8 White 八白	1 White 一白	
震 E	2 Black 二黑	4 Green 四綠	6 White 六白	兌 W
	7 Red 七赤	9 Purple 九紫	5 Yellow 五黄	
	艮NE	坎N	乾NW	

未 Goat (July 7 - Aug 7) 六月 6th Month

	巽SE	離S	坤SW	
	2 Black 二黑	7 Red 七赤	9 Purple 九紫	
震 E	1 White 一白	3 Jade 三碧	5 Yellow 五黄	兌 W
	6 White 六白	8 White 八白	4 Green 四綠	
	艮NE	坎N	乾NW	

申 Monkey (Aug 8 - Sept 7) 七月 7th Month

	巽SE	離S	坤SW	
	1 White 一白	6 White 六白	8 White 八白	
震 E	9 Purple 九紫	2 Black 二黑	4 Green 四綠	兌 W
	5 Yellow 五黄	7 Red 七赤	3 Jade 三碧	
	艮NE	坎N	乾NW	

酉 Rooster (Sept 8 - Oct 7) 八月 8th Month

	巽SE	離S	坤SW	
	9 Purple 九紫	5 Yellow 五黄	7 Red 七赤	
震 E	8 White 八白	1 White 一白	3 Jade 三碧	兌 W
	4 Green 四綠	6 White 六白	2 Black 二黑	
	艮NE	坎N	乾NW	

戌 Dog (Oct 8 - Nov 6) 九月 9th Month

	巽SE	離S	坤SW	
	8 White 八白	4 Green 四綠	6 White 六白	
震 E	7 Red 七赤	9 Purple 九紫	2 Black 二黑	兌 W
	3 Jade 三碧	5 Yellow 五黄	1 White 一白	
	艮NE	坎N	乾NW	

亥 Pig (Nov 7 - Dec 6) 十月 10th Month

	巽SE	離S	坤SW	
	7 Red 七赤	3 Jade 三碧	5 Yellow 五黄	
震 E	6 White 六白	8 White 八白	1 White 一白	兌 W
	2 Black 二黑	4 Green 四綠	9 Purple 九紫	
	艮NE	坎N	乾NW	

子 Rat (Dec 7 - Jan 5) 十一月 11th Month

	巽SE	離S	坤SW	
	6 White 六白	2 Black 二黑	4 Green 四綠	
震 E	5 Yellow 五黄	7 Red 七赤	9 Purple 九紫	兌 W
	1 White 一白	3 Jade 三碧	8 White 八白	
	艮NE	坎N	乾NW	

丑 Ox (Jan 6 - Feb 3) 十二月 12th Month

	巽SE	離S	坤SW	
	5 Yellow 五黄	1 White 一白	3 Jade 三碧	
震 E	4 Green 四綠	6 White 六白	8 White 八白	兌 W
	9 Purple 九紫	2 Black 二黑	7 Red 七赤	
	艮NE	坎N	乾NW	

Qi Men Three Nobles 三奇 :

Three Nobles 三奇 / Seasons	乙 *Yi*	丙 *Bing*	丁 *Ding*
立春 **Coming of Spring** Feb 4 - Feb 18	艮 Gen	離 Li	坎 Kan
春分 **Spring Equinox** Mar 21 - Apr 4	震 Zhen	巽 Xun	中 **Middle**
立夏 **Coming of Summer** May 6 - May 20	巽 Xun	中 **Middle**	乾 Qian
夏至 **Summer Solstice** Jun 22 - Jul 6	離 Li	艮 Gen	兌 Dui
立秋 **Coming of Autumn** Aug 8 - Aug 23	坤 Kun	坎 Kan	離 Li
秋分 **Autumn Equinox** Sept 23 - Oct 7	兌 Dui	乾 Qian	中 **Middle**
立冬 **Coming of Winter** Nov 7 - Nov 22	乾 Qian	中 **Middle**	巽 Xun
冬至 **Winter Solstice** Dec 22 - Jan 5	坎 Kan	坤 Kun	震 Zhen

丁酉 (Ding You) Fire Rooster

Sectors to Avoid Opening Mountain 開山凶位 :

月 MONTH	月建 Month Establishment	月破 Month Destruction	月剋山家 Month Countering Sitting		陰府太歲 Yin Mansion Grand Duke	
寅 **Tiger** (Feb 4 - Mar 5) 正月 **1st Month**	寅 Yin **Tiger**	申 Shen **Monkey**	—		離 Li	乾 Qian
卯 **Rabbit** (Mar 6 - Apr 4) 二月 **2nd Month**	卯 Mao **Rabbit**	酉 You **Rooster**	—		震 Zhen	坤 Kun
辰 **Dragon** (Apr 5 - May 5) 三月 **3rd Month**	辰 Chen **Dragon**	戌 Xu **Dog**	離 Li	丙 Bing **Yang Fire**	艮 Gen	巽 Xun
巳 **Snake** (May 6 - Jun 5) 四月 **4th Month**	巳 Si **Snake**	亥 Hai **Pig**	壬 Ren **Yang Water**	乙 Yi **Yin Wood**	兌 Dui	乾 Qian
午 **Horse** (Jun 6 - July 6) 五月 **5th Month**	午 Wu **Horse**	子 Zi **Rat**	水 **Water**	山 **Mountain**	坎 Kan	坤 Kun
未 **Goat** (July 7 - Aug 7) 六月 **6th Month**	未 Wei **Goat**	丑 Chou **Ox**	土 **Earth**		乾 Qian	離 Li
申 **Monkey** (Aug 8 - Sept 7) 七月 **7th Month**	申 Shen **Monkey**	寅 Yin **Tiger**	震 Zhen	巳 Si **Snake**	坤 Kun	震 Zhen
酉 **Rooster** (Sept 8 - Oct 7) 八月 **8th Month**	酉 You **Rooster**	卯 Mao **Rabbit**	艮 Gen		巽 Xun	艮 Gen
戌 **Dog** (Oct 8 - Nov 6) 九月 **9th Month**	戌 Xu **Dog**	辰 Chen **Dragon**	—		乾 Qian	兌 Dui
亥 **Pig** (Nov 7 - Dec 6) 十月 **10th Month**	亥 Hai **Pig**	巳 Si **Snake**	—		坤 Kun	坎 Kan
子 **Rat** (Dec 7 - Jan 5) 十一月 **11th Month**	子 Zi **Rat**	午 Wu **Horse**	—		離 Li	乾 Qian
丑 **Ox** (Jan 6 - Feb 3) 十二月 **12th Month**	丑 Chou **Ox**	未 Wei **Goat**	—		震 Zhen	坤 Kun

Negative Repair / Renovation Sectors 修方凶位 :

月 MONTH	天官符 Heavenly Officer Charm			地官符 Earth Officer Charm			小月建 Small Month Establishment		
寅 Tiger (Feb 4 - Mar 5) 正月 1st Month	未 Wei Goat	坤 Kun	申 Shen Monkey	庚 Geng Yang Metal	兌 Dui	辛 Xin Yin Metal	丙 Bing Yang Fire	離 Li	丁 Ding Yin Fire
卯 Rabbit (Mar 6 - Apr 4) 二月 2nd Month	壬 Ren Yang Water	坎 Kan	癸 Gui Yin Water	戌 Xu Dog	乾 Qian	亥 Hai Pig	壬 Ren Yang Water	坎 Kan	癸 Gui Yin Water
辰 Dragon (Apr 5 - May 5) 三月 3rd Month	丙 Bing Yang Fire	離 Li	丁 Ding Yin Fire	中 Middle			未 Wei Goat	坤 Kun	申 Shen Monkey
巳 Snake (May 6 - Jun 5) 四月 4th Month	丑 Chou Ox	艮 Gen	寅 Yin Tiger	辰 Chen Dragon	巽 Xun	巳 Si Snake	甲 Jia Yang Wood	震 Zhen	乙 Yi Yin Wood
午 Horse (Jun 6 - July 6) 五月 5th Month	庚 Geng Yang Metal	兌 Dui	辛 Xin Yin Metal	甲 Jia Yang Wood	震 Zhen	乙 Yi Yin Wood	辰 Chen Dragon	巽 Xun	巳 Si Snake
未 Goat (July 7 - Aug 7) 六月 6th Month	戌 Xu Dog	乾 Qian	亥 Hai Pig	未 Wei Goat	坤 Kun	申 Shen Monkey	中 Middle		
申 Monkey (Aug 8 - Sept 7) 七月 7th Month	中 Middle			壬 Ren Yang Water	坎 Kan	癸 Gui Yin Water	戌 Xu Dog	乾 Qian	亥 Hai Pig
酉 Rooster (Sept 8 - Oct 7) 八月 8th Month	庚 Geng Yang Metal	兌 Dui	辛 Xin Yin Metal	丙 Bing Yang Fire	離 Li	丁 Ding Yin Fire	庚 Geng Yang Metal	兌 Dui	辛 Xin Yin Metal
戌 Dog (Oct 8 - Nov 6) 九月 9th Month	戌 Xu Dog	乾 Qian	亥 Hai Pig	丑 Chou Ox	艮 Gen	寅 Yin Tiger	丑 Chou Ox	艮 Gen	寅 Yin Tiger
亥 Pig (Nov 7 - Dec 6) 十月 10th Month	中 Middle			庚 Geng Yang Metal	兌 Dui	辛 Xin Yin Metal	丙 Bing Yang Fire	離 Li	丁 Ding Yin Fire
子 Rat (Dec 7 - Jan 5) 十一月 11th Month	辰 Chen Dragon	巽 Xun	巳 Si Snake	戌 Xu Dog	乾 Qian	亥 Hai Pig	壬 Ren Yang Water	坎 Kan	癸 Gui Yin Water
丑 Ox (Jan 6 - Feb 3) 十二月 12th Month	甲 Jia Yang Wood	震 Zhen	乙 Yi Yin Wood	中 Middle			未 Wei Goat	坤 Kun	申 Shen Monkey

丁酉 (Ding You) Fire Rooster

Negative Repair / Renovation Sectors 修方凶位 :

月 MONTH	大月建 Big Month Establishment			飛大煞 Flying Great Sha			丙丁獨火 Bing Ding Lonely Fire	
寅 Tiger (Feb 4 - Mar 5) 正月 1st Month	丑 Chou Ox	艮 Gen Yin	寅 Yin Tiger	甲 Jia Yang Wood	震 Zhen	乙 Yi Yin Wood	離 Li	坎 Kan
卯 Rabbit (Mar 6 - Apr 4) 二月 2nd Month	庚 Geng Yang Metal	兌 Dui	辛 Xin Yin Metal	未 Wei Goat	坤 Kun	申 Shen Monkey	艮 Gen	離 Li
辰 Dragon (Apr 5 - May 5) 三月 3rd Month	戌 Xu Dog	乾 Qian	亥 Hai Pig	壬 Ren Yang Water	坎 Kan	癸 Gui Yin Water	兌 Dui	艮 Gen
巳 Snake (May 6 - Jun 5) 四月 4th Month		中 Middle		丙 Bing Yang Fire	離 Li	丁 Ding Yin Fire	乾 Qian	兌 Dui
午 Horse (Jun 6 - July 6) 五月 5th Month	辰 Chen Dragon	巽 Xun	巳 Si Snake	丑 Chou Ox	艮 Gen	寅 Yin Tiger	中 Middle	乾 Qian
未 Goat (July 7 - Aug 7) 六月 6th Month	甲 Jia Yang Wood	震 Zhen	乙 Yi Yin Wood	庚 Geng Yang Metal	兌 Dui	辛 Xin Yin Metal	中 Middle	
申 Monkey (Aug 8 - Sept 7) 七月 7th Month	未 Wei Goat	坤 Kun	申 Shen Monkey	戌 Xu Dog	乾 Qian	亥 Hai Pig	巽 Xun	中 Middle
酉 Rooster (Sept 8 - Oct 7) 八月 8th Month	壬 Ren Yang Water	坎 Kan	癸 Gui Yin Water	中 Middle			震 Zhen	巽 Xun
戌 Dog (Oct 8 - Nov 6) 九月 9th Month	丙 Bing Yang Fire	離 Li	丁 Ding Yin Fire	庚 Geng Yang Metal	兌 Dui	辛 Xin Yin Metal	坤 Kun	震 Zhen
亥 Pig (Nov 7 - Dec 6) 十月 10th Month	丑 Chou Ox	艮 Gen	寅 Yin Tiger	戌 Xu Dog	乾 Qian	亥 Hai Pig	坎 Kan	坤 Kun
子 Rat (Dec 7 - Jan 5) 十一月 11th Month	庚 Geng Yang Metal	兌 Dui	辛 Xin Yin Metal	中 Middle			離 Li	坎 Kan
丑 Ox (Jan 6 - Feb 3) 十二月 12th Month	戌 Xu Dog	乾 Qian	亥 Hai Pig	辰 Chen Dragon	巽 Xun	巳 Si Snake	艮 Gen	離 Li

Negative Repair / Renovation Sectors 修方凶位 :

月 MONTH	月遊火 Month Wondering Fire	三煞 Monthly 3 Killings		
		劫煞 Robbery Sha	災煞 Calamity Sha	月煞 Month Sha
寅 Tiger (Feb 4 - Mar 5) 正月 1st Month	乾 Qian	亥 Hai Pig	子 Zi Rat	丑 Chou Ox
卯 Rabbit (Mar 6 - Apr 4) 二月 2nd Month	兌 Dui	申 Shen Monkey	酉 You Rooster	戌 Xu Dog
辰 Dragon (Apr 5 - May 5) 三月 3rd Month	艮 Gen	巳 Si Snake	午 Wu Horse	未 Wei Goat
巳 Snake (May 6 - Jun 5) 四月 4th Month	離 Li	寅 Yin Tiger	卯 Mao Rabbit	辰 Chen Dragon
午 Horse (Jun 6 - July 6) 五月 5th Month	坎 Kan	亥 Hai Pig	子 Zi Rat	丑 Chou Ox
未 Goat (July 7 - Aug 7) 六月 6th Month	坤 Kun	申 Shen Monkey	酉 You Rooster	戌 Xu Dog
申 Monkey (Aug 8 - Sept 7) 七月 7th Month	震 Zhen	巳 Si Snake	午 Wu Horse	未 Wei Goat
酉 Rooster (Sept 8 - Oct 7) 八月 8th Month	巽 Xun	寅 Yin Tiger	卯 Mao Rabbit	辰 Chen Dragon
戌 Dog (Oct 8 - Nov 6) 九月 9th Month	中 Middle	亥 Hai Pig	子 Zi Rat	丑 Chou Ox
亥 Pig (Nov 7 - Dec 6) 十月 10th Month	乾 Qian	申 Shen Monkey	酉 You Rooster	戌 Xu Dog
子 Rat (Dec 7 - Jan 5) 十一月 11th Month	兌 Dui	巳 Si Snake	午 Wu Horse	未 Wei Goat
丑 Ox (Jan 6 - Feb 3) 十二月 12th Month	艮 Gen	寅 Yin Tiger	卯 Mao Rabbit	辰 Chen Dragon

Negative Repair / Renovation Sectors 修方凶位 :

月 MONTH	月刑 Month Punishment	月害 Month Harm	月厭 Month Detest
寅 Tiger (Feb 4 - Mar 5) 正月 1st Month	巳 Si Snake	巳 Si Snake	戌 Xu Dog
卯 Rabbit (Mar 6 - Apr 4) 二月 2nd Month	子 Zi Rat	辰 Chen Dragon	酉 You Rooster
辰 Dragon (Apr 5 - May 5) 三月 3rd Month	辰 Chen Dragon	卯 Mao Rabbit	申 Shen Monkey
巳 Snake (May 6 - Jun 5) 四月 4th Month	申 Shen Monkey	寅 Yin Tiger	未 Wei Goat
午 Horse (Jun 6 - July 6) 五月 5th Month	午 Wu Horse	丑 Chou Ox	午 Wu Horse
未 Goat (July 7 - Aug 7) 六月 6th Month	丑 Chou Ox	子 Zi Rat	巳 Si Snake
申 Monkey (Aug 8 - Sept 7) 七月 7th Month	寅 Yin Tiger	亥 Hai Pig	辰 Chen Dragon
酉 Rooster (Sept 8 - Oct 7) 八月 8th Month	酉 You Rooster	戌 Xu Dog	卯 Mao Rabbit
戌 Dog (Oct 8 - Nov 6) 九月 9th Month	未 Wei Goat	酉 You Rooster	寅 Yin Tiger
亥 Pig (Nov 7 - Dec 6) 十月 10th Month	亥 Hai Pig	申 Shen Monkey	丑 Chou Ox
子 Rat (Dec 7 - Jan 5) 十一月 11th Month	卯 Mao Rabbit	未 Wei Goat	子 Zi Rat
丑 Ox (Jan 6 - Feb 3) 十二月 12th Month	戌 Xu Dog	午 Wu Horse	亥 Hai Pig

丁亥 (Ding Hai)
Fire Pig

Heavenly Stem 天干	丁 Yin Fire (陰火)
Earthly Branch 地支	亥 Pig (Yin Water 陰水)
Hidden Stem 藏干	壬 Yang Water, 甲 Yang Wood
Na Yin 納音	屋上土 Earth from the house
Grand Duke 太歲	亥 Pig
Xuan Kong Five Element 玄空五行	8木 Wood
Gua Name 卦名	䷏ 雷地豫 Delight
Xuan Kong Period Luck 玄空卦運	8

Annual Positive Stars for Opening Mountain, Establishing Facing and Commencing Repairs 開山立向修方吉星：

歲德 Duke Virtue	壬 Ren Yang Water
歲德合 Duke Virtue Combo	丁 Ding Yin Fire
歲枝德 Duke Branch Virtue	辰 Chen Dragon
陽貴人 Yang Nobleman	亥 Hai Pig
陰貴人 Yin Nobleman	酉 You Rooster
歲祿 Duke Prosperous	午 Wu Horse
歲馬 Duke Horse	巳 Si Snake
奏書 Decree	乾 Qian
博士 Professor	巽 Xun

462

Annual Negative Stars for Opening Mountain, Establishing Facing and Commencing Repairs 開山立向修方凶星：

太歲 **Grand Duke**	歲破 **Year Breaker**	三煞 **Three Killings**			坐煞向煞 **Sitting Sha Facing Sha**				浮天空亡 **Floating Heaven Emptiness**	
亥 *Hai* **Pig**	巳 *Si* **Snake**	申 *Shen* **Monkey**	酉 *You* **Rooster**	戌 *Xu* **Dog**	庚 *Geng* **Yang Metal**	辛 *Xin* **Yin Metal**	甲 *Jia* **Yang Wood**	乙 *Yi* **Yin Wood**	震 *Zhen*	庚 *Geng* **Yang Metal**

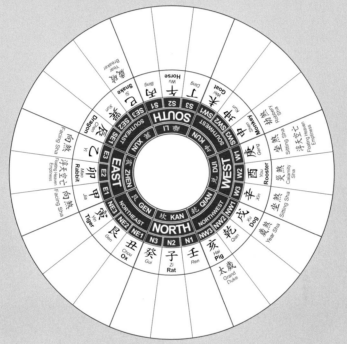

Annual San Yuan Purple White Stars 三元紫白九星：

上元 Upper Period Period 1, 2, 3			中元 Middle Period Period 4, 5, 6			下元 Lower Period Period 7, 8, 9		
巽SE 4	離S 9	坤SW 2	巽SE 7	離S 3	坤SW 5	巽SE 1	離S 6	坤SW 8
震E 3	5 丁亥 Ding Hai Fire Pig	兌W 7	震E 6	8 丁亥 Ding Hai Fire Pig	兌W 1	震E 9	2 丁亥 Ding Hai Fire Pig	兌W 4
艮NE 8	坎N 1	乾NW 6	艮NE 2	坎N 4	乾NW 9	艮NE 5	坎N 7	乾NW 3

Mountain Covering Yellow Path 蓋山黃道:

貪狼 Tan Lang **Greedy Wolf**				巨門 Ju Men **Huge Door**		武曲 Wu Qu **Military Arts**				文曲 Wen Qu **Literary Arts**			
坎	癸	申	辰	坤	乙	離	壬	寅	戌	兌	丁	巳	丑
Kan	Gui	Shen	Chen	Kun	Yi	Li	Ren	Yin	Xu	Dui	Ding	Si	Chou
N2	N3	SW3	SE1	SW2	E3	S2	N1	NE3	NW1	W2	S3	SE3	NE1

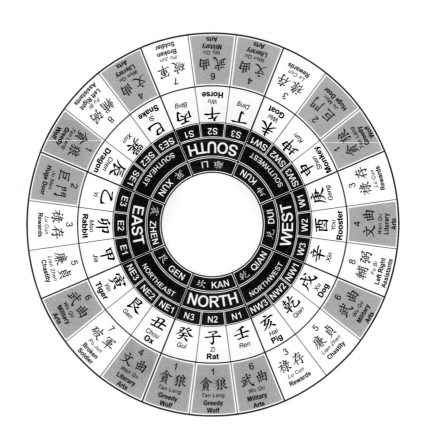

通天竅 Heaven Penetrating Force			
三合前方 **Facing Three Harmony**	巽巳 *Xun Si*	丙午 *Bing Wu*	丁未 *Ding Wei*
三合後方 **Sitting Three Harmony**	乾亥 *Qian Hai*	壬子 *Ren Zi*	癸丑 *Gui Chou*

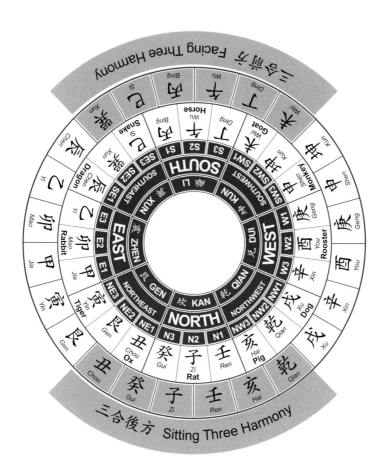

Moving Horse Six Ren Assessment 走馬六壬：

神后 Shen Hou **Holy Empress**	功曹 Gong Cao **Marshall**	天罡 Tian Gang **Heavenly Dipper**	勝光 Sheng Guang **Subliminal Bright**	傳送 Chuan Song **Great General**	河魁 He Kui **River Scholar**
癸丑 Gui Chou	甲卯 Jia Mao	巽巳 Xun Si	丁未 Ding Wei	庚酉 Geng You	乾亥 Qian Hai

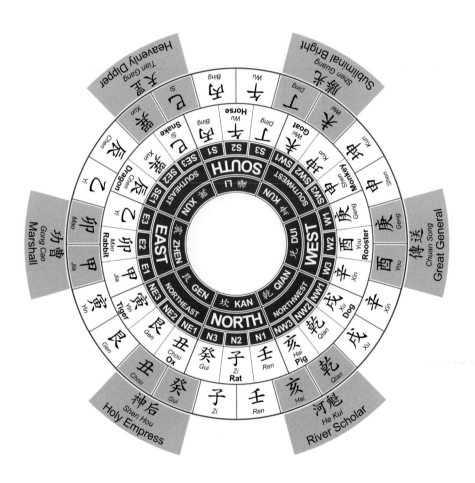

Four Advantages Three Cycles Star Plate 四利三元:

太陽 *Tai Yang* **Sun**	太陰 *Tai Yin* **Moon**	龍德 *Long De* **Dragon Virtue**	福德 *Fu De* **Fortune Virtue**
子 *Zi* Rat	寅 *Yin* Tiger	午 *Wu* Horse	申 *Shen* Monkey

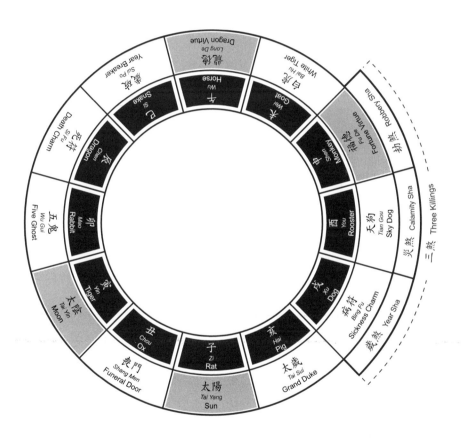

Negative Sectors For Opening Mountain 開山凶位：

年剋山家 Year Countering Sitting

震	艮	巳
Zhen	Gen	Si
E2	NE2	SE3

陰府太歲 Yin Fu Tai Sui **Yin Mansion Grand Duke**	六害 Liu Hai **Six Harm**	死符 Si Fu **Death Charm**	炙退 Zhi Tui **Roasting Star**
乾 離 Qian Li **NW2 S2**	申 Shen **SW3**	辰 Chen **SE1**	午 Wu **S2**

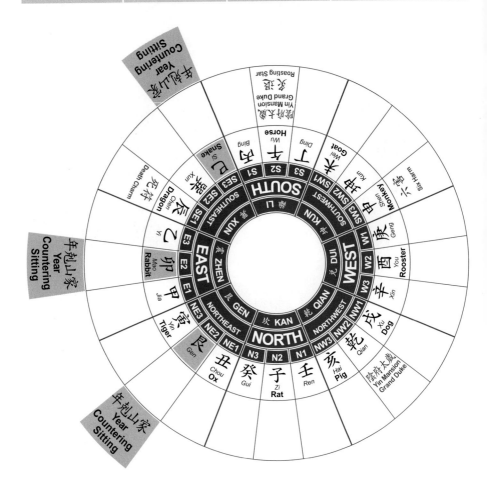

Negative Directions to Establish Facing 立向凶方：

巡山羅喉 *Xun Shan Luo Hou* **Mountain Patrol Luo Hou Star**	病符 *Bing Fu* **Sickness Charm**
壬 *Ren* **N1**	戌 *Xu* **NW1**

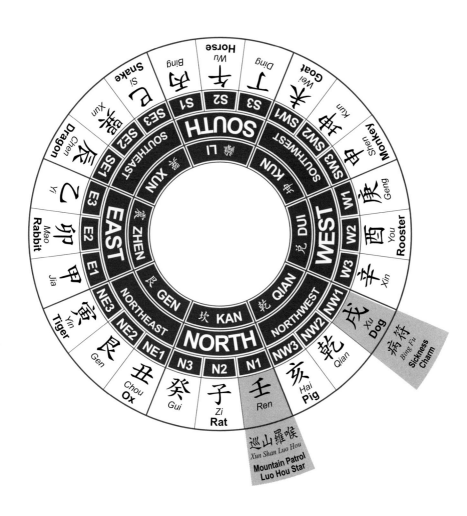

Negative Repair / Renovation Sectors Table 修方凶位表：

天官符 Heavenly Officer Charm	寅 *Yin* Tiger	飛廉 Flying Chaste	丑 *Chou* Ox	
地官符 Earthly Officer Charm	卯 *Mao* Rabbit	喪門 Funeral Door	丑 *Chou* Ox	
大煞 Great Sha	卯 *Mao* Rabbit	弔客 Suspended Guest	酉 *You* Rooster	
大將軍 Big General	酉 *You* Rooster	白虎 White Tiger	未 *Wei* Goat	
力士 Strong Man	艮 *Gen*	金神 Golden God	寅 *Yin* Tiger / 卯 *Mao* Rabbit / 戌 *Xu* Dog / 亥 *Hai* Pig	
蠶室 Silkworm Room	坤 *Kun*			
蠶官 Silkworm Officer	未 *Wei* Goat			
蠶命 Silkworm Life	申 *Shen* Monkey			
歲刑 Duke Punishment	亥 *Hai* Pig	獨火 Lonely Fire	乾 *Qian*	
黃幡 Yellow Flag	未 *Wei* Goat	五鬼 Five Ghost	巳 *Si* Snake	
豹尾 Leopard Tail	丑 *Chou* Ox	破敗五鬼 Destructive Five Ghost	震 *Zhen*	

Negative Repair / Renovation Sectors Diagram 修方凶位圖：

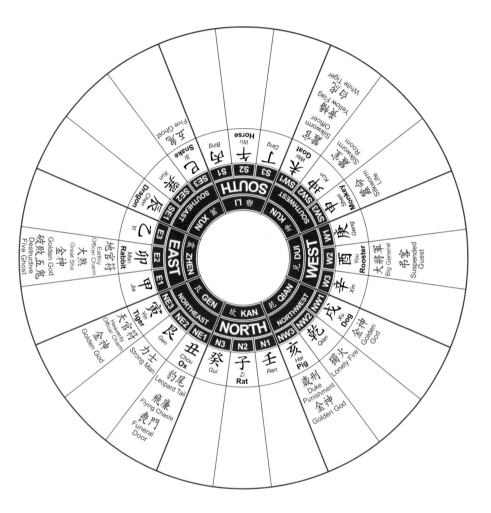

12-Month Auxiliary Stars Reference Table :
丁亥年十二月，開山立向修方星表

Positive Monthly Stars 吉星方

月 MONTH	寅 Tiger (Feb 4 - Mar 5) 正月 1st Month	卯 Rabbit (Mar 6 - Apr 4) 二月 2nd Month	辰 Dragon (Apr 5 - May 5) 三月 3rd Month	巳 Snake (May 6 - Jun 5) 四月 4th Month	午 Horse (Jun 6 - July 6) 五月 5th Month	未 Goat (July 7 - Aug 7) 六月 6th Month
天道 Heavenly Path	南 South	西南 Southwest	北 North	西 West	西北 Northwest	東 East
天德 Heavenly Virtue	丁 Ding Yin Fire	坤 Kun (申)	壬 Ren Yang Water	辛 Xin Yin Metal	乾 Qian (亥)	甲 Jia Yang Wood
天德合 Heavenly Virtue Combo	壬 Ren Yang Water	(巳)	丁 Ding Yin Fire	丙 Bing Yang Fire	(寅)	己 Ji Yin Earth
月德 Monthly Virtue	丙 Bing Yang Fire	甲 Jia Yang Wood	壬 Ren Yang Water	庚 Geng Yang Metal	丙 Bing Yang Fire	甲 Jia Yang Wood
月德合 Monthly Virtue Combo	辛 Xin Yin Metal	己 Ji Yin Earth	丁 Ding Yin Fire	乙 Yi Yin Wood	辛 Xin Yin Metal	己 Ji Yin Earth
月空 Month Emptiness	壬 Ren Yang Water	庚 Geng Yang Metal	丙 Bing Yang Fire	甲 Jia Yang Wood	壬 Ren Yang Water	庚 Geng Yang Metal
陽貴人 Yang Nobleman	中 Middle	巽 Xun	震 Zhen	坤 Kun	坎 Kan	離 Li
陰貴人 Yin Nobleman	震 Zhen	坤 Kun	坎 Kan	離 Li	艮 Gen	兌 Dui
飛天祿 Flying Heavenly Wealth	離 Li	艮 Gen	兌 Dui	乾 Qian	中 Middle	坎 Kan
飛天馬 Flying Heavenly Horse	艮 Gen	兌 Dui	乾 Qian	中 Middle	坎 Kan	離 Li

12-Month Auxiliary Stars Reference Table :
丁亥年十二月，開山立向修方星表

申 **Monkey** (Aug 8 - Sept 7) 七月 **7th Month**	酉 **Rooster** (Sept 8 - Oct 7) 八月 **8th Month**	戌 **Dog** (Oct 8 - Nov 6) 九月 **9th Month**	亥 **Pig** (Nov 7 - Dec 6) 十月 **10th Month**	子 **Rat** (Dec 7 - Jan 5) 十一月 **11th Month**	丑 **Ox** (Jan 6 - Feb 3) 十二月 **12th Month**	月 **MONTH**
北 North	東北 Northeast	南 South	東 East	東南 Southeast	西 West	天道 **Heavenly Path**
癸 Gui Yin Water	艮 Gen （寅）	丙 Bing Yang Fire	乙 Yi Yin Wood	巽 Xun （巳）	庚 Geng Yang Metal	天德 **Heavenly Virtue**
戊 Wu Yang Earth	（亥）	辛 Xin Yin Metal	庚 Geng Yang Metal	（申）	乙 Yi Yin Wood	天德合 **Heavenly Virtue Combo**
壬 Ren Yang Water	庚 Geng Yang Metal	丙 Bing Yang Fire	甲 Jia Yang Wood	壬 Ren Yang Water	庚 Geng Yang Metal	月德 **Monthly Virtue**
丁 Ding Yin Fire	乙 Yi Yin Wood	辛 Xin Yin Metal	己 Ji Yin Earth	丁 Ding Yin Fire	乙 Yi Yin Wood	月德合 **Monthly Virtue Combo**
丙 Bing Yang Fire	甲 Jia Yang Wood	壬 Ren Yang Water	庚 Geng Yang Metal	丙 Bing Yang Fire	甲 Jia Yang Wood	月空 **Month Emptiness**
艮 Gen	兌 Dui	乾 Qian	中 Middle	坎 Kan	離 Li	陽貴人 **Yang Nobleman**
乾 Qian	中 Middle	坎 Kan	離 Li	艮 Gen	兌 Dui	陰貴人 **Yin Nobleman**
離 Li	艮 Gen	兌 Dui	乾 Qian	中 Middle	巽 Xun	飛天祿 **Flying Heavenly Wealth**
艮 Gen	兌 Dui	乾 Qian	中 Middle	巽 Xun	震 Zhen	飛天馬 **Flying Heavenly Horse**

Monthly Purple White Stars 月紫白九星 :

寅 **Tiger** (Feb 4 - Mar 5) 正月 **1st Month**

巽 **SE**	離 **S**	坤 **SW**
1 White 一白	**6** White 六白	**8** White 八白
9 Purple 九紫 (震 **E**)	**2** Black 二黑	**4** Green 四綠 (兌 **W**)
5 Yellow 五黃 (艮 **NE**)	**7** Red 七赤 (坎 **N**)	**3** Jade 三碧 (乾 **NW**)

卯 **Rabbit** (Mar 6 - Apr 4) 二月 **2nd Month**

巽 **SE**	離 **S**	坤 **SW**
9 Purple 九紫	**5** Yellow 五黃	**7** Red 七赤
8 White 八白 (震 **E**)	**1** White 一白	**3** Jade 三碧 (兌 **W**)
4 Green 四綠 (艮 **NE**)	**6** White 六白 (坎 **N**)	**2** Black 二黑 (乾 **NW**)

辰 **Dragon** (Apr 5 - May 5) 三月 **3rd Month**

巽 **SE**	離 **S**	坤 **SW**
8 White 八白	**4** Green 四綠	**6** White 六白
7 Red 七赤 (震 **E**)	**9** Purple 九紫	**2** Black 二黑 (兌 **W**)
3 Jade 三碧 (艮 **NE**)	**5** Yellow 五黃 (坎 **N**)	**1** White 一白 (乾 **NW**)

巳 **Snake** (May 6 - Jun 5) 四月 **4th Month**

巽 **SE**	離 **S**	坤 **SW**
7 Red 七赤	**3** Jade 三碧	**5** Yellow 五黃
6 White 六白 (震 **E**)	**8** White 八白	**1** White 一白 (兌 **W**)
2 Black 二黑 (艮 **NE**)	**4** Green 四綠 (坎 **N**)	**9** Purple 九紫 (乾 **NW**)

午 **Horse** (Jun 6 - July 6) 五月 **5th Month**

巽 **SE**	離 **S**	坤 **SW**
6 White 六白	**2** Black 二黑	**4** Green 四綠
5 Yellow 五黃 (震 **E**)	**7** Red 七赤	**9** Purple 九紫 (兌 **W**)
1 White 一白 (艮 **NE**)	**3** Jade 三碧 (坎 **N**)	**8** White 八白 (乾 **NW**)

未 **Goat** (July 7 - Aug 7) 六月 **6th Month**

巽 **SE**	離 **S**	坤 **SW**
5 Yellow 五黃	**1** White 一白	**3** Jade 三碧
4 Green 四綠 (震 **E**)	**6** White 六白	**8** White 八白 (兌 **W**)
9 Purple 九紫 (艮 **NE**)	**2** Black 二黑 (坎 **N**)	**7** Red 七赤 (乾 **NW**)

申 **Monkey** (Aug 8 - Sept 7) 七月 **7th Month**

巽 **SE**	離 **S**	坤 **SW**
4 Green 四綠	**9** Purple 九紫	**2** Black 二黑
3 Jade 三碧 (震 **E**)	**5** Yellow 五黃	**7** Red 七赤 (兌 **W**)
8 White 八白 (艮 **NE**)	**1** White 一白 (坎 **N**)	**6** White 六白 (乾 **NW**)

酉 **Rooster** (Sept 8 - Oct 7) 八月 **8th Month**

巽 **SE**	離 **S**	坤 **SW**
3 Jade 三碧	**8** White 八白	**1** White 一白
2 Black 二黑 (震 **E**)	**4** Green 四綠	**6** White 六白 (兌 **W**)
7 Red 七赤 (艮 **NE**)	**9** Purple 九紫 (坎 **N**)	**5** Yellow 五黃 (乾 **NW**)

戌 **Dog** (Oct 8 - Nov 6) 九月 **9th Month**

巽 **SE**	離 **S**	坤 **SW**
2 Black 二黑	**7** Red 七赤	**9** Purple 九紫
1 White 一白 (震 **E**)	**3** Jade 三碧	**5** Yellow 五黃 (兌 **W**)
6 White 六白 (艮 **NE**)	**8** White 八白 (坎 **N**)	**4** Green 四綠 (乾 **NW**)

亥 **Pig** (Nov 7 - Dec 6) 十月 **10th Month**

巽 **SE**	離 **S**	坤 **SW**
1 White 一白	**6** White 六白	**8** White 八白
9 Purple 九紫 (震 **E**)	**2** Black 二黑	**4** Green 四綠 (兌 **W**)
5 Yellow 五黃 (艮 **NE**)	**7** Red 七赤 (坎 **N**)	**3** Jade 三碧 (乾 **NW**)

子 **Rat** (Dec 7 - Jan 5) 十一月 **11th Month**

巽 **SE**	離 **S**	坤 **SW**
9 Purple 九紫	**5** Yellow 五黃	**7** Red 七赤
8 White 八白 (震 **E**)	**1** White 一白	**3** Jade 三碧 (兌 **W**)
4 Green 四綠 (艮 **NE**)	**6** White 六白 (坎 **N**)	**2** Black 二黑 (乾 **NW**)

丑 **Ox** (Jan 6 - Feb 3) 十二月 **12th Month**

巽 **SE**	離 **S**	坤 **SW**
8 White 八白	**4** Green 四綠	**6** White 六白
7 Red 七赤 (震 **E**)	**9** Purple 九紫	**2** Black 二黑 (兌 **W**)
3 Jade 三碧 (艮 **NE**)	**5** Yellow 五黃 (坎 **N**)	**1** White 一白 (乾 **NW**)

Qi Men Three Nobles 三奇 :

Three Nobles 三奇 / Seasons	乙 *Yi*	丙 *Bing*	丁 *Ding*
立春 **Coming of Spring** Feb 4 - Feb 18	兑 Dui	艮 Gen	離 Li
春分 **Spring Equinox** Mar 21 - Apr 4	坤 Kun	震 Zhen	巽 Xun
立夏 **Coming of Summer** May 6 - May 20	震 Zhen	巽 Xun	中 **Middle**
夏至 **Summer Solstice** Jun 22 - Jul 6	坎 Kan	離 Li	艮 Gen
立秋 **Coming of Autumn** Aug 8 - Aug 23	震 Zhen	坤 Kunn	坎 Kan
秋分 **Autumn Equinox** Sept 23 - Oct 7	艮 Gen	兑 Dui	乾 Qian
立冬 **Coming of Winter** Nov 7 - Nov 22	兑 Dui	乾 Qian	中 **Middle**
冬至 **Winter Solstice** Dec 22 - Jan 5	離 Li	坎 Kan	坤 Kun

Sectors to Avoid Opening Mountain 開山凶位 :

月 MONTH	月建 Month Establishment	月破 Month Destruction	月剋山家 Month Countering Sitting		陰府太歲 Yin Mansion Grand Duke	
寅 Tiger (Feb 4 - Mar 5) 正月 1st Month	寅 Yin Tiger	申 Shen Monkey	—		離 Li	乾 Qian
卯 Rabbit (Mar 6 - Apr 4) 二月 2nd Month	卯 Mao Rabbit	酉 You Rooster	—		震 Zhen	坤 Kun
辰 Dragon (Apr 5 - May 5) 三月 3rd Month	辰 Chen Dragon	戌 Xu Dog	離 Li	丙 Bing Yang Fire	艮 Gen	巽 Xun
巳 Snake (May 6 - Jun 5) 四月 4th Month	巳 Si Snake	亥 Hai Pig	壬 Ren Yang Water	乙 Yi Yin Wood	兌 Dui	乾 Qian
午 Horse (Jun 6 - July 6) 五月 5th Month	午 Wu Horse	子 Zi Rat	水 Water	山 Mountain	坎 Kan	坤 Kun
未 Goat (July 7 - Aug 7) 六月 6th Month	未 Wei Goat	丑 Chou Ox	土 Earth		乾 Qian	離 Li
申 Monkey (Aug 8 - Sept 7) 七月 7th Month	申 Shen Monkey	寅 Yin Tiger	震 Zhen	巳 Si Snake	坤 Kun	震 Zhen
酉 Rooster (Sept 8 - Oct 7) 八月 8th Month	酉 You Rooster	卯 Mao Rabbit	艮 Gen		巽 Xun	艮 Gen
戌 Dog (Oct 8 - Nov 6) 九月 9th Month	戌 Xu Dog	辰 Chen Dragon	—		乾 Qian	兌 Dui
亥 Pig (Nov 7 - Dec 6) 十月 10th Month	亥 Hai Pig	巳 Si Snake	—		坤 Kun	坎 Kan
子 Rat (Dec 7 - Jan 5) 十一月 11th Month	子 Zi Rat	午 Wu Horse	—		離 Li	乾 Qian
丑 Ox (Jan 6 - Feb 3) 十二月 12th Month	丑 Chou Ox	未 Wei Goat	—		震 Zhen	坤 Kun

Negative Repair / Renovation Sectors 修方凶位 :

月 MONTH	天官符 Heavenly Officer Charm			地官符 Earth Officer Charm			小月建 Small Month Establishment		
寅 **Tiger** (Feb 4 - Mar 5) 正月 **1st Month**		中 Middle		戌 *Xu* Dog	乾 *Qian*	亥 *Hai* Pig	丙 *Bing* Yang Fire	離 *Li*	丁 *Ding* Yin Fire
卯 **Rabbit** (Mar 6 - Apr 4) 二月 **2nd Month**	庚 *Geng* Yang Metal	兌 *Dui*	辛 *Xin* Yin Metal		中 Middle		壬 *Ren* Yang Water	坎 *Kan*	癸 *Gui* Yin Water
辰 **Dragon** (Apr 5 - May 5) 三月 **3rd Month**	戌 *Xu* Dog	乾 *Qian*	亥 *Hai* Pig	庚 *Geng* Yang Metal	兌 *Dui*	辛 *Xin* Yin Metal	未 *Wei* Goat	坤 *Kun*	申 *Shen* Monkey
巳 **Snake** (May 6 - Jun 5) 四月 **4th Month**		中 Middle		戌 *Xu* Dog	乾 *Qian*	亥 *Hai* Pig	甲 *Jia* Yang Wood	震 *Zhen*	乙 *Yi* Yin Wood
午 **Horse** (Jun 6 - July 6) 五月 **5th Month**	辰 *Chen* Dragon	巽 *Xun*	巳 *Si* Snake		中 Middle		辰 *Chen* Dragon	巽 *Xun*	巳 *Si* Snake
未 **Goat** (July 7 - Aug 7) 六月 **6th Month**	甲 *Jia* Yang Wood	震 *Zhen*	乙 *Yi* Yin Wood	辰 *Chen* Dragon	巽 *Xun*	巳 *Si* Snake		中 Middle	
申 **Monkey** (Aug 8 - Sept 7) 七月 **7th Month**	未 *Wei* Goat	坤 *Kun*	申 *Shen* Monkey	甲 *Jia* Yang Wood	震 *Zhen*	乙 *Yi* Yin Wood	戌 *Xu* Dog	乾 *Qian*	亥 *Hai* Pig
酉 **Rooster** (Sept 8 - Oct 7) 八月 **8th Month**	壬 *Ren* Yang Water	坎 *Kan*	癸 *Gui* Yin Water	未 *Wei* Goat	坤 *Kun*	申 *Shen* Monkey	庚 *Geng* Yang Metal	兌 *Dui*	辛 *Xin* Yin Metal
戌 **Dog** (Oct 8 - Nov 6) 九月 **9th Month**	丙 *Bing* Yang Fire	離 *Li*	丁 *Ding* Yin Fire	壬 *Ren* Yang Water	坎 *Kan*	癸 *Gui* Yin Water	丑 *Chou* Ox	艮 *Gen*	寅 *Yin* Tiger
亥 **Pig** (Nov 7 - Dec 6) 十月 **10th Month**	丑 *Chou* Ox	艮 *Gen*	寅 *Yin* Tiger	丙 *Bing* Yang Fire	離 *Li*	丁 *Ding* Yin Fire	丙 *Bing* Yang Fire	離 *Li*	丁 *Ding* Yin Fire
子 **Rat** (Dec 7 - Jan 5) 十一月 **11th Month**	庚 *Geng* Yang Metal	兌 *Dui*	辛 *Xin* Yin Metal	丑 *Chou* Ox	艮 *Gen*	寅 *Yin* Tiger	壬 *Ren* Yang Water	坎 *Kan*	癸 *Gui* Yin Water
丑 **Ox** (Jan 6 - Feb 3) 十二月 **12th Month**	戌 *Xu* Dog	乾 *Qian*	亥 *Hai* Pig	庚 *Geng* Yang Metal	兌 *Dui*	辛 *Xin* Yin Metal	未 *Wei* Goat	坤 *Kun*	申 *Shen* Monkey

Negative Repair / Renovation Sectors 修方凶位 :

月 MONTH	大月建 Big Month Establishment			飛大煞 Flying Great Sha			丙丁獨火 Bing Ding Lonely Fire	
寅 **Tiger** (Feb 4 - Mar 5) 正月 **1st Month**	未 *Wei* Goat	坤 *Kun*	申 *Shen* Monkey	戌 *Xu* Dog	乾 *Qian*	亥 *Hai* Pig	離 *Li*	坎 *Kan*
卯 **Rabbit** (Mar 6 - Apr 4) 二月 **2nd Month**	壬 *Ren* Yang Water	坎 *Kan*	癸 *Gui* Yin Water	中 Middle			艮 *Gen*	離 *Li*
辰 **Dragon** (Apr 5 - May 5) 三月 **3rd Month**	丙 *Bing* Yang Fire	離 *Li*	丁 *Ding* Yin Fire	庚 *Geng* Yang Metal	兌 *Dui*	辛 *Xin* Yin Metal	兌 *Dui*	艮 *Gen*
巳 **Snake** (May 6 - Jun 5) 四月 **4th Month**	丑 *Chou* Ox	艮 *Gen*	寅 *Yin* Tiger	戌 *Xu* Dog	乾 *Qian*	亥 *Hai* Pig	乾 *Qian*	兌 *Dui*
午 **Horse** (Jun 6 - July 6) 五月 **5th Month**	庚 *Geng* Yang Metal	兌 *Dui*	辛 *Xin* Yin Metal	中 Middle			中 Middle	乾 *Qian*
未 **Goat** (July 7 - Aug 7) 六月 **6th Month**	戌 *Xu* Dog	乾 *Qian*	亥 *Hai* Pig	辰 *Chen* Dragon	巽 *Xun*	巳 *Si* Snake	中 Middle	
申 **Monkey** (Aug 8 - Sept 7) 七月 **7th Month**	中 Middle			甲 *Jia* Yang Wood	震 *Zhen*	乙 *Yi* Yin Wood	巽 *Xun*	中 Middle
酉 **Rooster** (Sept 8 - Oct 7) 八月 **8th Month**	辰 *Chen* Dragon	巽 *Xun*	巳 *Si* Snake	未 *Wei* Goat	坤 *Kun*	申 *Shen* Monkey	震 *Zhen*	巽 *Xun*
戌 **Dog** (Oct 8 - Nov 6) 九月 **9th Month**	甲 *Jia* Yang Wood	震 *Zhen*	乙 *Yi* Yin Wood	壬 *Ren* Yang Water	坎 *Kan*	癸 *Gui* Yin Water	坤 *Kun*	震 *Zhen*
亥 **Pig** (Nov 7 - Dec 6) 十月 **10th Month**	未 *Wei* Goat	坤 *Kun*	申 *Shen* Monkey	丙 *Bing* Yang Fire	離 *Li*	丁 *Ding* Yin Fire	坎 *Kan*	坤 *Kun*
子 **Rat** (Dec 7 - Jan 5) 十一月 **11th Month**	壬 *Ren* Yang Water	坎 *Kan*	癸 *Gui* Yin Water	丑 *Chou* Ox	艮 *Gen*	寅 *Yin* Tiger	離 *Li*	坎 *Kan*
丑 **Ox** (Jan 6 - Feb 3) 十二月 **12th Month**	丙 *Bing* Yang Fire	離 *Li*	丁 *Ding* Yin Fire	庚 *Geng* Yang Metal	兌 *Dui*	辛 *Xin* Yin Metal	艮 *Gen*	離 *Li*

Negative Repair / Renovation Sectors 修方凶位：

月 MONTH	月遊火 Month Wondering Fire	三煞 Monthly 3 Killings		
		劫煞 Robbery Sha	災煞 Calamity Sha	月煞 Month Sha
寅 Tiger (Feb 4 - Mar 5) 正月 1st Month	坎 Kan	亥 Hai Pig	子 Zi Rat	丑 Chou Ox
卯 Rabbit (Mar 6 - Apr 4) 二月 2nd Month	坤 Kun	申 Shen Monkey	酉 You Rooster	戌 Xu Dog
辰 Dragon (Apr 5 - May 5) 三月 3rd Month	震 Zhen	巳 Si Snake	午 Wu Horse	未 Wei Goat
巳 Snake (May 6 - Jun 5) 四月 4th Month	巽 Xun	寅 Yin Tiger	卯 Mao Rabbit	辰 Chen Dragon
午 Horse (Jun 6 - July 6) 五月 5th Month	中 Middle	亥 Hai Pig	子 Zi Rat	丑 Chou Ox
未 Goat (July 7 - Aug 7) 六月 6th Month	乾 Qian	申 Shen Monkey	酉 You Rooster	戌 Xu Dog
申 Monkey (Aug 8 - Sept 7) 七月 7th Month	兌 Dui	巳 Si Snake	午 Wu Horse	未 Wei Goat
酉 Rooster (Sept 8 - Oct 7) 八月 8th Month	艮 Gen	寅 Yin Tiger	卯 Mao Rabbit	辰 Chen Dragon
戌 Dog (Oct 8 - Nov 6) 九月 9th Month	離 Li	亥 Hai Pig	子 Zi Rat	丑 Chou Ox
亥 Pig (Nov 7 - Dec 6) 十月 10th Month	坎 Kan	申 Shen Monkey	酉 You Rooster	戌 Xu Dog
子 Rat (Dec 7 - Jan 5) 十一月 11th Month	坤 Kun	巳 Si Snake	午 Wu Horse	未 Wei Goat
丑 Ox (Jan 6 - Feb 3) 十二月 12th Month	震 Zhen	寅 Yin Tiger	卯 Mao Rabbit	辰 Chen Dragon

Negative Repair / Renovation Sectors 修方凶位 :

月 MONTH	月刑 Month Punishment	月害 Month Harm	月厭 Month Detest
寅 **Tiger** (Feb 4 - Mar 5) 正月 **1st Month**	巳 *Si* Snake	巳 *Si* Snake	戌 *Xu* Dog
卯 **Rabbit** (Mar 6 - Apr 4) 二月 **2nd Month**	子 *Zi* Rat	辰 *Chen* Dragon	酉 *You* Rooster
辰 **Dragon** (Apr 5 - May 5) 三月 **3rd Month**	辰 *Chen* Dragon	卯 *Mao* Rabbit	申 *Shen* Monkey
巳 **Snake** (May 6 - Jun 5) 四月 **4th Month**	申 *Shen* Monkey	寅 *Yin* Tiger	未 *Wei* Goat
午 **Horse** (Jun 6 - July 6) 五月 **5th Month**	午 *Wu* Horse	丑 *Chou* Ox	午 *Wu* Horse
未 **Goat** (July 7 - Aug 7) 六月 **6th Month**	丑 *Chou* Ox	子 *Zi* Rat	巳 *Si* Snake
申 **Monkey** (Aug 8 - Sept 7) 七月 **7th Month**	寅 *Yin* Tiger	亥 *Hai* Pig	辰 *Chen* Dragon
酉 **Rooster** (Sept 8 - Oct 7) 八月 **8th Month**	酉 *You* Rooster	戌 *Xu* Dog	卯 *Mao* Rabbit
戌 **Dog** (Oct 8 - Nov 6) 九月 **9th Month**	未 *Wei* Goat	酉 *You* Rooster	寅 *Yin* Tiger
亥 **Pig** (Nov 7 - Dec 6) 十月 **10th Month**	亥 *Hai* Pig	申 *Shen* Monkey	丑 *Chou* Ox
子 **Rat** (Dec 7 - Jan 5) 十一月 **11th Month**	卯 *Mao* Rabbit	未 *Wei* Goat	子 *Zi* Rat
丑 **Ox** (Jan 6 - Feb 3) 十二月 **12th Month**	戌 *Xu* Dog	午 *Wu* Horse	亥 *Hai* Pig

戊子 (Wu Zi)
Earth Rat

Heavenly Stem 天干	戊 Yang Earth (陽土)
Earthly Branch 地支	子 Rat (Yang Water 陽水)
Hidden Stem 藏干	癸 Yin Water
Na Yin 納音	霹靂火 Fire from thunder
Grand Duke 太歲	子 Rat
Xuan Kong Five Element 玄空五行	7 火 Fire
Gua Name 卦名	䷂ 水雷屯 Beginning
Xuan Kong Period Luck 玄空卦運	4

Annual Positive Stars for Opening Mountain, Establishing Facing and Commencing Repairs 開山立向修方吉星：

歲德 Duke Virtue	戊 Wu Yang Earth
歲德合 Duke Virtue Combo	癸 Gui Yin Water
歲枝德 Duke Branch Virtue	巳 Si Snake
陽貴人 Yang Nobleman	丑 Chou Ox
陰貴人 Yin Nobleman	未 Wei Goat
歲祿 Duke Prosperous	巳 Si Snake
歲馬 Duke Horse	寅 Yin Tiger
奏書 Decree	乾 Qian
博士 Professor	巽 Xun

Annual Negative Stars for Opening Mountain, Establishing Facing and Commencing Repairs 開山立向修方凶星:

太歲 Grand Duke	歲破 Year Breaker	三煞 Three Killings			坐煞向煞 Sitting Sha Facing Sha				浮天空亡 Floating Heaven Emptiness	
子 Zi Rat	午 Wu Horse	巳 Si Snake	午 Wu Horse	未 Wei Goat	丙 Bing Yang Fire	丁 Ding Yin Fire	壬 Ren Yang Water	癸 Gui Yin Water	坤 Kun	乙 Yi Yin Wood

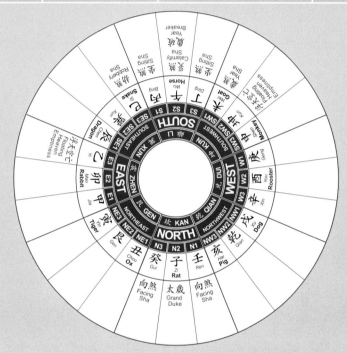

Annual San Yuan Purple White Stars 三元紫白九星:

上元 Upper Period Period 1, 2, 3			中元 Middle Period Period 4, 5, 6			下元 Lower Period Period 7, 8, 9		
巽SE 3	離S 8	坤SW 1	巽SE 6	離S 2	坤SW 4	巽SE 9	離S 5	坤SW 7
震E 2	4 戊子 Wu Zi Earth Rat	兌W 6	震E 5	7 戊子 Wu Zi Earth Rat	兌W 9	震E 8	1 戊子 Wu Zi Earth Rat	兌W 3
艮NE 7	坎N 9	乾NW 5	艮NE 1	坎N 3	乾NW 8	艮NE 4	坎N 6	乾NW 2

Mountain Covering Yellow Path 蓋山黃道:

貪狼 Tan Lang **Greedy Wolf**				巨門 Ju Men **Huge Door**				武曲 Wu Qu **Military Arts**		文曲 Wen Qu **Literary Arts**	
震 Zhen E2	庚 Geng W1	亥 Hai NW3	未 Wei SW1	兌 Dui W2	丁 Ding S3	巳 Si SE3	丑 Chou NE1	巽 Xun SE2	辛 Xin W3	坤 Kun SW2	乙 Yi E3

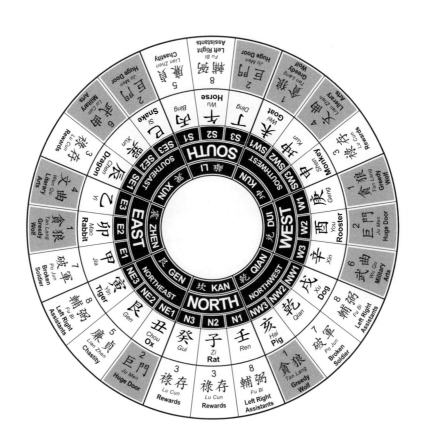

Heaven Penetrating Force 通天竅：		
三合前方 **Facing Three Harmony**	艮寅 Gen Yin	甲卯 Jia Mao	乙辰 Yi Chen
三合後方 **Sitting Three Harmony**	坤申 Kun Shen	庚酉 Geng You	辛戌 Xin Xu

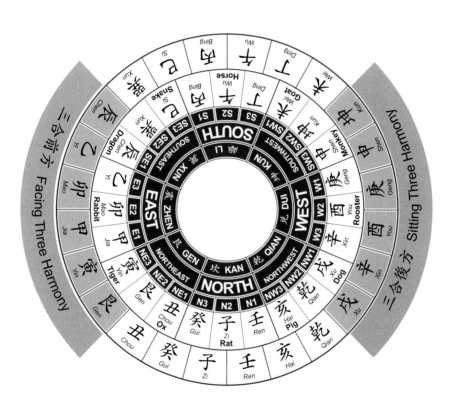

Moving Horse Six Ren Assessment 走馬六壬：

神后 Shen Hou **Holy Empress**	功曹 Gong Cao **Marshall**	天罡 Tian Gang **Heavenly Dipper**	勝光 Sheng Guang **Subliminal Bright**	傳送 Chuan Song **Great General**	河魁 He Kui **River Scholar**
壬子 Ren Zi	艮寅 Gen Yin	乙辰 Yi Chen	丙午 Bing Wu	坤申 Kun Shen	辛戌 Xin Xu

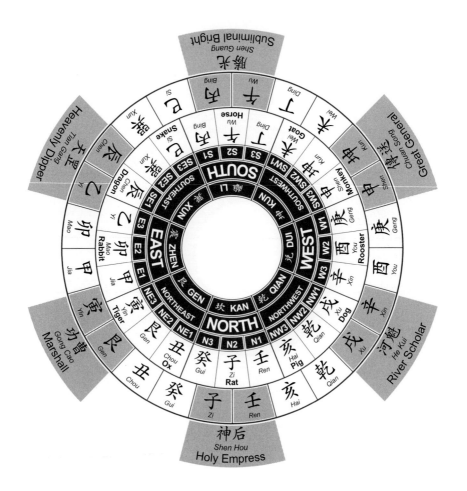

Four Advantages Three Cycles Star Plate 四利三元：

太陽 *Tai Yang* **Sun**	太陰 *Tai Yin* **Moon**	龍德 *Long De* **Dragon Virtue**	福德 *Fu De* **Fortune Virtue**
丑 *Chou* **Ox**	卯 *Mao* **Rabbit**	未 *Wei* **Goat**	酉 *You* **Rooster**

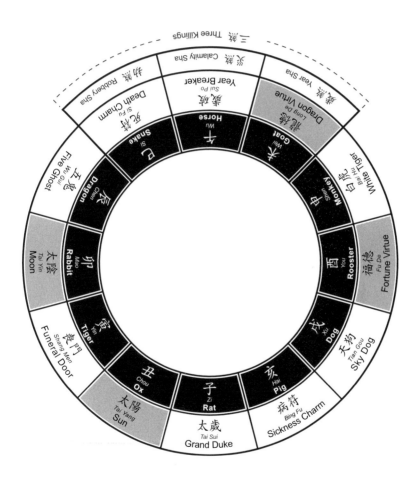

Negative Sectors For Opening Mountain 開山凶位：

年剋山家 Year Countering Sitting (冬至後 After Winter Solstice)

乾 Qian NW2	亥 Hai NW3	兌 Dui W2	丁 Ding S3

陰府太歲 Yin Fu Tai Sui **Yin Mansion Grand Duke**	六害 Liu Hai **Six Harm**	死符 Si Fu **Death Charm**	炙退 Zhi Tui **Roasting Star**
坤 Kun SW2 震 Zhen E2	未 Wei SW1	巳 Si SE3	卯 Mao E2

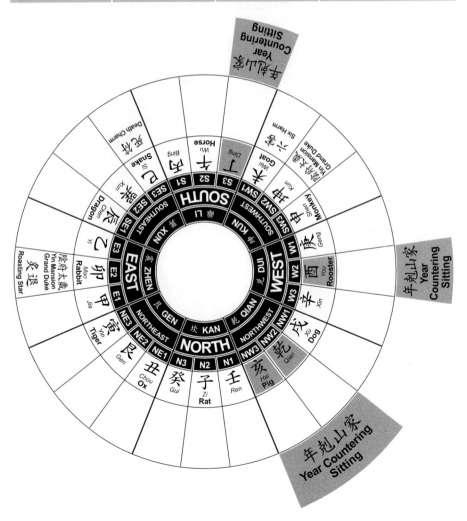

Negative Directions to Establish Facing 立向凶方：

巡山羅喉 *Xun Shan Luo Hou* **Mountain Patrol Luo Hou Star**	病符 *Bing Fu* **Sickness Charm**
癸 *Gui* **N3**	亥 *Hai* **NW3**

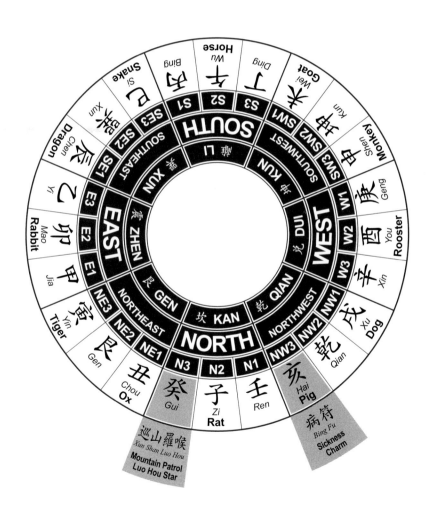

戊子 (Wu Zi) Earth Rat

Negative Repair / Renovation Sectors Table 修方凶位表：

天官符 Heavenly Officer Charm	亥 *Hai* Pig	飛廉 Flying Chaste	申 *Shen* Monkey
地官符 Earthly Officer Charm	辰 *Chen* Dragon	喪門 Funeral Door	寅 *Yin* Tiger
大煞 Great Sha	子 *Zi* Rat	弔客 Suspended Guest	戌 *Xu* Dog
大將軍 Big General	酉 *You* Rooster	白虎 White Tiger	申 *Shen* Monkey
力士 Strong Man	艮 *Gen*	金神 Golden God	申 *Shen* Monkey 酉 *You* Rooster 子 *Zi* Rat 丑 *Chou* Ox
蠶室 Silkworm Room	坤 *Kun*		
蠶官 Silkworm Officer	未 *Wei* Goat		
蠶命 Silkworm Life	申 *Shen* Monkey		
歲刑 Duke Punishment	卯 *Mao* Rabbit	獨火 Lonely Fire	艮 *Gen*
黃幡 Yellow Flag	辰 *Chen* Dragon	五鬼 Five Ghost	辰 *Chen* Dragon
豹尾 Leopard Tail	戌 *Xu* Dog	破敗五鬼 Destructive Five Ghost	離 *Li*

Negative Repair / Renovation Sectors Diagram 修方凶位圖:

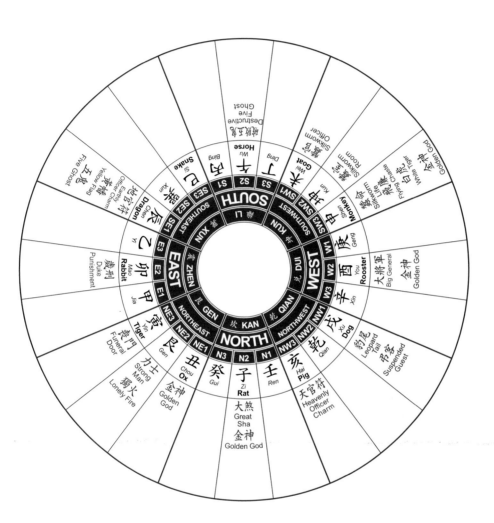

12-Month Auxiliary Stars Reference Table :
戊子年十二月，開山立向修方星表

Positive Monthly Stars 吉星方

月 MONTH	寅 Tiger (Feb 4 - Mar 5) 正月 1st Month	卯 Rabbit (Mar 6 - Apr 4) 二月 2nd Month	辰 Dragon (Apr 5 - May 5) 三月 3rd Month	巳 Snake (May 6 - Jun 5) 四月 4th Month	午 Horse (Jun 6 - July 6) 五月 5th Month	未 Goat (July 7 - Aug 7) 六月 6th Month
天道 Heavenly Path	南 South	西南 Southwest	北 North	西 West	西北 Northwest	東 East
天德 Heavenly Virtue	丁 Ding Yin Fire	坤 Kun (申)	壬 Ren Yang Water	辛 Xin Yin Metal	乾 Qian (亥)	甲 Jia Yang Wood
天德合 Heavenly Virtue Combo	壬 Ren Yang Water	(巳)	丁 Ding Yin Fire	丙 Bing Yang Fire	(寅)	己 Ji Yin Earth
月德 Monthly Virtue	丙 Bing Yang Fire	甲 Jia Yang Wood	壬 Ren Yang Water	庚 Geng Yang Metal	丙 Bing Yang Fire	甲 Jia Yang Wood
月德合 Monthly Virtue Combo	辛 Xin Yin Metal	己 Ji Yin Earth	丁 Ding Yin Fire	乙 Yi Yin Wood	辛 Xin Yin Metal	己 Ji Yin Earth
月空 Month Emptiness	壬 Ren Yang Water	庚 Geng Yang Metal	丙 Bing Yang Fire	甲 Jia Yang Wood	壬 Ren Yang Water	庚 Geng Yang Metal
陽貴人 Yang Nobleman	兌 Dui	乾 Qian	中 Middle	巽 Xun	震 Zhen	坤 Kun
陰貴人 Yin Nobleman	坎 Kan	離 Li	艮 Gen	兌 Dui	乾 Qian	中 Middle
飛天祿 Flying Heavenly Wealth	艮 Gen	兌 Dui	乾 Qian	中 Middle	坎 Kan	離 Li
飛天馬 Flying Heavenly Horse	中 Middle	坎 Kan	離 Li	艮 Gen	兌 Dui	乾 Qian

12-Month Auxiliary Stars Reference Table :
戊子年十二月，開山立向修方星表

申 Monkey (Aug 8 - Sept 7)	酉 Rooster (Sept 8 - Oct 7)	戌 Dog (Oct 8 - Nov 6)	亥 Pig (Nov 7 - Dec 6)	子 Rat (Dec 7 - Jan 5)	丑 Ox (Jan 6 - Feb 3)	月 MONTH
七月 7th Month	八月 8th Month	九月 9th Month	十月 10th Month	十一月 11th Month	十二月 12th Month	
北 North	東北 Northeast	南 South	東 East	東南 Southeast	西 West	天道 Heavenly Path
癸 Gui Yin Water	艮 Gen (寅)	丙 Bing Yang Fire	乙 Yi Yin Wood	巽 Xun (巳)	庚 Geng Yang Metal	天德 Heavenly Virtue
戊 Wu Yang Earth	(亥)	辛 Xin Yin Metal	庚 Geng Yang Metal	(申)	乙 Yi Yin Wood	天德合 Heavenly Virtue Combo
壬 Ren Yang Water	庚 Geng Yang Metal	丙 Bing Yang Fire	甲 Jia Yang Wood	壬 Ren Yang Water	庚 Geng Yang Metal	月德 Monthly Virtue
丁 Ding Yin Fire	乙 Yi Yin Wood	辛 Xin Yin Metal	己 Ji Yin Earth	丁 Ding Yin Fire	乙 Yi Yin Wood	月德合 Monthly Virtue Combo
丙 Bing Yang Fire	甲 Jia Yang Wood	壬 Ren Yang Water	庚 Geng Yang Metal	丙 Bing Yang Fire	甲 Jia Yang Wood	月空 Month Emptiness
坎 Kan	離 Li	艮 Gen	兌 Dui	乾 Qian	中 Middle	陽貴人 Yang Nobleman
坎 Kan	離 Li	艮 Gen	兌 Dui	乾 Qian	中 Middle	陰貴人 Yin Nobleman
艮 Gen	兌 Dui	乾 Qian	中 Middle	巽 Xun	震 Zhen	飛天祿 Flying Heavenly Wealth
中 Middle	巽 Xun	震 Zhen	坤 Kun	坎 Kan	離 Li	飛天馬 Flying Heavenly Horse

Monthly Purple White Stars 月紫白九星：

寅 Tiger (Feb 4 - Mar 5) 正月 1st Month

巽 SE	離 S	坤 SW
7 Red 七赤	3 Jade 三碧	5 Yellow 五黃
震 E — 6 White 六白	8 White 八白	1 White 一白 — 兌 W
2 Black 二黑	4 Green 四綠	9 Purple 九紫
艮 NE	坎 N	乾 NW

卯 Rabbit (Mar 6 - Apr 4) 二月 2nd Month

巽 SE	離 S	坤 SW
6 White 六白	2 Black 二黑	4 Green 四綠
震 E — 5 Yellow 五黃	7 Red 七赤	9 Purple 九紫 — 兌 W
1 White 一白	3 Jade 三碧	8 White 八白
艮 NE	坎 N	乾 NW

辰 Dragon (Apr 5 - May 5) 三月 3rd Month

巽 SE	離 S	坤 SW
5 Yellow 五黃	1 White 一白	3 Jade 三碧
震 E — 4 Green 四綠	6 White 六白	8 White 八白 — 兌 W
9 Purple 九紫	2 Black 二黑	7 Red 七赤
艮 NE	坎 N	乾 NW

巳 Snake (May 6 - Jun 5) 四月 4th Month

巽 SE	離 S	坤 SW
4 Green 四綠	9 Purple 九紫	2 Black 二黑
震 E — 3 Jade 三碧	5 Yellow 五黃	7 Red 七赤 — 兌 W
8 White 八白	1 White 一白	6 White 六白
艮 NE	坎 N	乾 NW

午 Horse (Jun 6 - July 6) 五月 5th Month

巽 SE	離 S	坤 SW
3 Jade 三碧	8 White 八白	1 White 一白
震 E — 2 Black 二黑	4 Green 四綠	6 White 六白 — 兌 W
7 Red 七赤	9 Purple 九紫	5 Yellow 五黃
艮 NE	坎 N	乾 NW

未 Goat (July 7 - Aug 7) 六月 6th Month

巽 SE	離 S	坤 SW
2 Black 二黑	7 Red 七赤	9 Purple 九紫
震 E — 1 White 一白	3 Jade 三碧	5 Yellow 五黃 — 兌 W
6 White 六白	8 White 八白	4 Green 四綠
艮 NE	坎 N	乾 NW

申 Monkey (Aug 8 - Sept 7) 七月 7th Month

巽 SE	離 S	坤 SW
1 White 一白	6 White 六白	8 White 八白
震 E — 9 Purple 九紫	2 Black 二黑	4 Green 四綠 — 兌 W
5 Yellow 五黃	7 Red 七赤	3 Jade 三碧
艮 NE	坎 N	乾 NW

酉 Rooster (Sept 8 - Oct 7) 八月 8th Month

巽 SE	離 S	坤 SW
9 Purple 九紫	5 Yellow 五黃	7 Red 七赤
震 E — 8 White 八白	1 White 一白	3 Jade 三碧 — 兌 W
4 Green 四綠	6 White 六白	2 Black 二黑
艮 NE	坎 N	乾 NW

戌 Dog (Oct 8 - Nov 6) 九月 9th Month

巽 SE	離 S	坤 SW
8 White 八白	4 Green 四綠	6 White 六白
震 E — 7 Red 七赤	9 Purple 九紫	2 Black 二黑 — 兌 W
3 Jade 三碧	5 Yellow 五黃	1 White 一白
艮 NE	坎 N	乾 NW

亥 Pig (Nov 7 - Dec 6) 十月 10th Month

巽 SE	離 S	坤 SW
7 Red 七赤	3 Jade 三碧	5 Yellow 五黃
震 E — 6 White 六白	8 White 八白	1 White 一白 — 兌 W
2 Black 二黑	4 Green 四綠	9 Purple 九紫
艮 NE	坎 N	乾 NW

子 Rat (Dec 7 - Jan 5) 十一月 11th Month

巽 SE	離 S	坤 SW
6 White 六白	2 Black 二黑	4 Green 四綠
震 E — 5 Yellow 五黃	7 Red 七赤	9 Purple 九紫 — 兌 W
1 White 一白	3 Jade 三碧	8 White 八白
艮 NE	坎 N	乾 NW

丑 Ox (Jan 6 - Feb 3) 十二月 12th Month

巽 SE	離 S	坤 SW
5 Yellow 五黃	1 White 一白	3 Jade 三碧
震 E — 4 Green 四綠	6 White 六白	8 White 八白 — 兌 W
9 Purple 九紫	2 Black 二黑	7 Red 七赤
艮 NE	坎 N	乾 NW

Qi Men Three Nobles 三奇 :

Three Nobles 三奇 / Seasons	乙 Yi	丙 Bing	丁 Ding
立春 **Coming of Spring** Feb 4 - Feb 18	乾 Qian	兌 Dui	艮 Gen
春分 **Spring Equinox** Mar 21 - Apr 4	坎 Kan	坤 Kun	震 Zhen
立夏 **Coming of Summer** May 6 - May 20	坤 Kun	震 Zhen	巽 Xun
夏至 **Summer Solstice** Jun 22 - Jul 6	坤 Kun	坎 Kan	離 Li
立秋 **Coming of Autumn** Aug 8 - Aug 23	巽 Xun	震 Zhen	坤 Kun
秋分 **Autumn Equinox** Sept 23 - Oct 7	離 Li	艮 Gen	兌 Dui
立冬 **Coming of Winter** Nov 7 - Nov 22	艮 Gen	兌 Dui	乾 Qian
冬至 **Winter Solstice** Dec 22 - Jan 5	艮 Gen	離 Li	坎 Kan

Sectors to Avoid Opening Mountain 開山凶位 :

月 MONTH	月建 Month Establishment	月破 Month Destruction	月剋山家 Month Countering Sitting		陰府太歲 Yin Mansion Grand Duke	
寅 **Tiger** (Feb 4 - Mar 5) 正月 **1st Month**	寅 *Yin* **Tiger**	申 *Shen* **Monkey**	震 *Zhen*	巳 *Si* **Snake**	艮 *Gen*	巽 *Xun*
卯 **Rabbit** (Mar 6 - Apr 4) 二月 **2nd Month**	卯 *Mao* **Rabbit**	酉 *You* **Rooster**	艮 *Gen*		兌 *Dui*	乾 *Qian*
辰 **Dragon** (Apr 5 - May 5) 三月 **3rd Month**	辰 *Chen* **Dragon**	戌 *Xu* **Dog**	離 *Li*	丙 *Bing* **Yang Fire**	坎 *Kan*	坤 *Kun*
巳 **Snake** (May 6 - Jun 5) 四月 **4th Month**	巳 *Si* **Snake**	亥 *Hai* **Pig**	壬 *Ren* **Yang Water**	乙 *Yi* **Yin Wood**	乾 *Qian*	離 *Li*
午 **Horse** (Jun 6 - July 6) 五月 **5th Month**	午 *Wu* **Horse**	子 *Zi* **Rat**	–		坤 *Kun*	震 *Zhen*
未 **Goat** (July 7 - Aug 7) 六月 **6th Month**	未 *Wei* **Goat**	丑 *Chou* **Ox**	–		巽 *Xun*	艮 *Gen*
申 **Monkey** (Aug 8 - Sept 7) 七月 **7th Month**	申 *Shen* **Monkey**	寅 *Yin* **Tiger**	水 **Water**	山 **Mountain**	乾 *Qian*	兌 *Dui*
酉 **Rooster** (Sept 8 - Oct 7) 八月 **8th Month**	酉 *You* **Rooster**	卯 *Mao* **Rabbit**	土 **Earth**		坤 *Kun*	坎 *Kan*
戌 **Dog** (Oct 8 - Nov 6) 九月 **9th Month**	戌 *Xu* **Dog**	辰 *Chen* **Dragon**	震 *Zhen*	巳 *Si* **Snake**	離 *Li*	乾 *Qian*
亥 **Pig** (Nov 7 - Dec 6) 十月 **10th Month**	亥 *Hai* **Pig**	巳 *Si* **Snake**	艮 *Gen*		震 *Zhen*	坤 *Kun*
子 **Rat** (Dec 7 - Jan 5) 十一月 **11th Month**	子 *Zi* **Rat**	午 *Wu* **Horse**	–		艮 *Gen*	巽 *Xun*
丑 **Ox** (Jan 6 - Feb 3) 十二月 **12th Month**	丑 *Chou* **Ox**	未 *Wei* **Goat**	–		兌 *Dui*	乾 *Qian*

Negative Repair / Renovation Sectors 修方凶位 :

月 MONTH	天官符 Heavenly Officer Charm			地官符 Earth Officer Charm			小月建 Small Month Establishment		
寅 Tiger (Feb 4 - Mar 5) 正月 1st Month		中 Middle		庚 Geng Yang Metal	兑 Dui	辛 Xin Yin Metal		中 Middle	
卯 Rabbit (Mar 6 - Apr 4) 二月 2nd Month	辰 Chen Dragon	巽 Xun	巳 Si Snake	戌 Xu Dog	乾 Qian	亥 Hai Pig	戌 Xu Dog	乾 Qian	亥 Hai Pig
辰 Dragon (Apr 5 - May 5) 三月 3rd Month	甲 Jia Yang Wood	震 Zhen	乙 Yi Yin Wood		中 Middle		庚 Geng Yang Metal	兑 Dui	辛 Xin Yin Metal
巳 Snake (May 6 - Jun 5) 四月 4th Month	未 Wei Goat	坤 Kun	申 Shen Monkey	庚 Geng Yang Metal	兑 Dui	辛 Xin Yin Metal	丑 Chou Ox	艮 Gen	寅 Yin Tiger
午 Horse (Jun 6 - July 6) 五月 5th Month	壬 Ren Yang Water	坎 Kan	癸 Gui Yin Water	戌 Xu Dog	乾 Qian	亥 Hai Pig	丙 Bing Yang Fire	離 Li	丁 Ding Yin Fire
未 Goat (July 7 - Aug 7) 六月 6th Month	丙 Bing Yang Fire	離 Li	丁 Ding Yin Fire		中 Middle		壬 Ren Yang Water	坎 Kan	癸 Gui Yin Water
申 Monkey (Aug 8 - Sept 7) 七月 7th Month	丑 Chou Ox	艮 Gen	寅 Yin Tiger	辰 Chen Dragon	巽 Xun	巳 Si Snake	未 Wei Goat	坤 Kun	申 Shen Monkey
酉 Rooster (Sept 8 - Oct 7) 八月 8th Month	庚 Geng Yang Metal	兑 Dui	辛 Xin Yin Metal	甲 Jia Yang Wood	震 Zhen	乙 Yi Yin Wood	甲 Jia Yang Wood	震 Zhen	乙 Yi Yin Wood
戌 Dog (Oct 8 - Nov 6) 九月 9th Month	戌 Xu Dog	乾 Qian	亥 Hai Pig	未 Wei Goat	坤 Kun	申 Shen Monkey	辰 Chen Dragon	巽 Xun	巳 Si Snake
亥 Pig (Nov 7 - Dec 6) 十月 10th Month		中 Middle		壬 Ren Yang Water	坎 Kan	癸 Gui Yin Water		中 Middle	
子 Rat (Dec 7 - Jan 5) 十一月 11th Month	庚 Geng Yang Metal	兑 Dui	辛 Xin Yin Metal	丙 Bing Yang Fire	離 Li	丁 Ding Yin Fire	戌 Xu Dog	乾 Qian	亥 Hai Pig
丑 Ox (Jan 6 - Feb 3) 十二月 12th Month	戌 Xu Dog	乾 Qian	亥 Hai Pig	丑 Chou Ox	艮 Gen	寅 Yin Tiger	庚 Geng Yang Metal	兑 Dui	辛 Xin Yin Metal

Negative Repair / Renovation Sectors 修方凶位 :

月 MONTH	大月建 Big Month Establishment			飛大煞 Flying Great Sha			丙丁獨火 Bing Ding Lonely Fire	
寅 **Tiger** (Feb 4 - Mar 5) 正月 **1st Month**	壬 Ren Yang Water	艮 Gen	寅 Yin Tiger	戌 Xu Dog	乾 Qian	亥 Hai Pig	兌 Dui	艮 Gen
卯 **Rabbit** (Mar 6 - Apr 4) 二月 **2nd Month**	庚 Geng Yang Metal	兌 Dui	辛 Xin Yin Metal	中 Middle			乾 Qian	兌 Dui
辰 **Dragon** (Apr 5 - May 5) 三月 **3rd Month**	戌 Xu Dog	乾 Qian	亥 Hai Pig	辰 Chen Dragon	巽 Xun	巳 Si Snake	中 Middle	乾 Qian
巳 **Snake** (May 6 - Jun 5) 四月 **4th Month**	中 Middle			甲 Jia Yang Wood	震 Zhen	乙 Yi Yin Wood	中 Middle	
午 **Horse** (Jun 6 - July 6) 五月 **5th Month**	辰 Chen Dragon	巽 Xun	巳 Si Snake	未 Wei Goat	坤 Kun	申 Shen Monkey	巽 Xun	中 Middle
未 **Goat** (July 7 - Aug 7) 六月 **6th Month**	甲 Jia Yang Wood	震 Zhen	乙 Yi Yin Wood	壬 Ren Yang Water	坎 Kan	癸 Gui Yin Water	震 Zhen	巽 Xun
申 **Monkey** (Aug 8 - Sept 7) 七月 **7th Month**	未 Wei Goat	坤 Kun	申 Shen Monkey	丙 Bing Yang Fire	離 Li	丁 Ding Yin Fire	坤 Kun	震 Zhen
酉 **Rooster** (Sept 8 - Oct 7) 八月 **8th Month**	壬 Ren Yang Water	坎 Kan	癸 Gui Yin Water	丑 Chou Ox	艮 Gen	寅 Yin Tiger	坎 Kan	坤 Kun
戌 **Dog** (Oct 8 - Nov 6) 九月 **9th Month**	丙 Bing Yang Fire	離 Li	丁 Ding Yin Fire	庚 Geng Yang Metal	兌 Dui	辛 Xin Yin Metal	離 Li	坎 Kan
亥 **Pig** (Nov 7 - Dec 6) 十月 **10th Month**	丑 Chou Ox	艮 Gen	寅 Yin Tiger	戌 Xu Dog	乾 Qian	亥 Hai Pig	艮 Gen	離 Li
子 **Rat** (Dec 7 - Jan 5) 十一月 **11th Month**	庚 Geng Yang Metal	兌 Dui	辛 Xin Yin Metal	中 Middle			兌 Dui	艮 Gen
丑 **Ox** (Jan 6 - Feb 3) 十二月 **12th Month**	戌 Xu Dog	乾 Qian	亥 Hai Pig	庚 Geng Yang Metal	兌 Dui	辛 Xin Yin Metal	乾 Qian	兌 Dui

Negative Repair / Renovation Sectors 修方凶位 :

月 MONTH	月遊火 Month Wondering Fire	三煞 Monthly 3 Killings		
		劫煞 Robbery Sha	災煞 Calamity Sha	月煞 Month Sha
寅 Tiger (Feb 4 - Mar 5) 正月 1st Month	艮 Gen	亥 Hai Pig	子 Zi Rat	丑 Chou Ox
卯 Rabbit (Mar 6 - Apr 4) 二月 2nd Month	離 Li	申 Shen Monkey	酉 You Rooster	戌 Xu Dog
辰 Dragon (Apr 5 - May 5) 三月 3rd Month	坎 Kan	巳 Si Snake	午 Wu Horse	未 Wei Goat
巳 Snake (May 6 - Jun 5) 四月 4th Month	坤 Kun	寅 Yin Tiger	卯 Mao Rabbit	辰 Chen Dragon
午 Horse (Jun 6 - July 6) 五月 5th Month	震 Zhen	亥 Hai Pig	子 Zi Rat	丑 Chou Ox
未 Goat (July 7 - Aug 7) 六月 6th Month	巽 Xun	申 Shen Monkey	酉 You Rooster	戌 Xu Dog
申 Monkey (Aug 8 - Sept 7) 七月 7th Month	中 Middle	巳 Si Snake	午 Wu Horse	未 Wei Goat
酉 Rooster (Sept 8 - Oct 7) 八月 8th Month	乾 Qian	寅 Yin Tiger	卯 Mao Rabbit	辰 Chen Dragon
戌 Dog (Oct 8 - Nov 6) 九月 9th Month	兌 Dui	亥 Hai Pig	子 Zi Rat	丑 Chou Ox
亥 Pig (Nov 7 - Dec 6) 十月 10th Month	艮 Gen	申 Shen Monkey	酉 You Rooster	戌 Xu Dog
子 Rat (Dec 7 - Jan 5) 十一月 11th Month	離 Li	巳 Si Snake	午 Wu Horse	未 Wei Goat
丑 Ox (Jan 6 - Feb 3) 十二月 12th Month	坎 Kan	寅 Yin Tiger	卯 Mao Rabbit	辰 Chen Dragon

Negative Repair / Renovation Sectors 修方凶位 :

月 MONTH	月刑 Month Punishment	月害 Month Harm	月厭 Month Detest
寅 **Tiger** (Feb 4 - Mar 5) 正月 **1st Month**	巳 *Si* Snake	巳 *Si* Snake	戌 *Xu* Dog
卯 **Rabbit** (Mar 6 - Apr 4) 二月 **2nd Month**	子 *Zi* Rat	辰 *Chen* Dragon	酉 *You* Rooster
辰 **Dragon** (Apr 5 - May 5) 三月 **3rd Month**	辰 *Chen* Dragon	卯 *Mao* Rabbit	申 *Shen* Monkey
巳 **Snake** (May 6 - Jun 5) 四月 **4th Month**	申 *Shen* Monkey	寅 *Yin* Tiger	未 *Wei* Goat
午 **Horse** (Jun 6 - July 6) 五月 **5th Month**	午 *Wu* Horse	丑 *Chou* Ox	午 *Wu* Horse
未 **Goat** (July 7 - Aug 7) 六月 **6th Month**	丑 *Chou* Ox	子 *Zi* Rat	巳 *Si* Snake
申 **Monkey** (Aug 8 - Sept 7) 七月 **7th Month**	寅 *Yin* Tiger	亥 *Hai* Pig	辰 *Chen* Dragon
酉 **Rooster** (Sept 8 - Oct 7) 八月 **8th Month**	酉 *You* Rooster	戌 *Xu* Dog	卯 *Mao* Rabbit
戌 **Dog** (Oct 8 - Nov 6) 九月 **9th Month**	未 *Wei* Goat	酉 *You* Rooster	寅 *Yin* Tiger
亥 **Pig** (Nov 7 - Dec 6) 十月 **10th Month**	亥 *Hai* Pig	申 *Shen* Monkey	丑 *Chou* Ox
子 **Rat** (Dec 7 - Jan 5) 十一月 **11th Month**	卯 *Mao* Rabbit	未 *Wei* Goat	子 *Zi* Rat
丑 **Ox** (Jan 6 - Feb 3) 十二月 **12th Month**	戌 *Xu* Dog	午 *Wu* Horse	亥 *Hai* Pig

戊寅 (Wu Yin)
Earth Tiger

Heavenly Stem 天干	戊 Yang Earth (陽土)
Earthly Branch 地支	寅 Tiger (Yang Wood 陽木)
Hidden Stem 藏干	甲 Yang Wood, 丙 Yang Fire, 戊 Yang Earth
Na Yin 納音	城頭土 Earth from the city
Grand Duke 太歲	寅 Tiger
Xuan Kong Five Element 玄空五行	8 木 Wood
Gua Name 卦名	䷶ 雷火豐 Abundance
Xuan Kong Period Luck 玄空卦運	6

Annual Positive Stars for Opening Mountain, Establishing Facing and Commencing Repairs 開山立向修方吉星：

歲德 **Duke Virtue**	戊 *Wu* Yang Earth	
歲德合 **Duke Virtue Combo**	癸 *Gui* Yin Water	
歲枝德 **Duke Branch Virtue**	未 *Wei* Goat	
陽貴人 **Yang Nobleman**	丑 *Chou* Ox	
陰貴人 **Yin Nobleman**	未 *Wei* Goat	
歲祿 **Duke Prosperous**	巳 *Si* Snake	
歲馬 **Duke Horse**	中 Middle	
奏書 **Decree**	艮 *Gen*	
博士 **Professor**	坤 *Kun*	

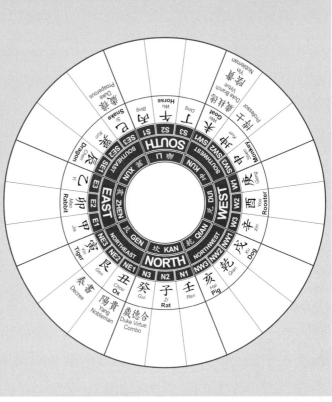

Annual Negative Stars for Opening Mountain, Establishing Facing and Commencing Repairs 開山立向修方凶星：

太歲 Grand Duke	歲破 Year Breaker	三煞 Three Killings			坐煞向煞 Sitting Sha Facing Sha				浮天空亡 Floating Heaven Emptiness	
寅 Yin Tiger	申 Shen Monkey	亥 Hai Pig	子 Zi Rat	丑 Chou Ox	壬 Ren Yang Water	癸 Gui Yin Water	丙 Bing Yang Fire	丁 Ding Yin Fire	坤 Kun	乙 Yi Yin Wood

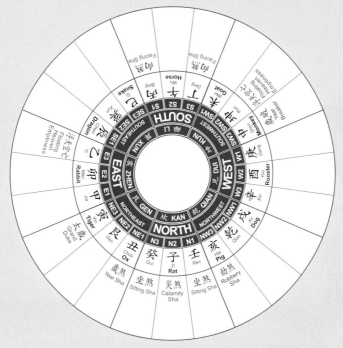

Annual San Yuan Purple White Stars 三元紫白九星：

上元 Upper Period Period 1, 2, 3	中元 Middle Period Period 4, 5, 6	下元 Lower Period Period 7, 8, 9

Upper Period:
巽SE	離S	坤SW
4	9	2
3	5 戊寅 Wu Yin Earth Tiger	7
8	1	6

Middle Period:
7	3	5
6	8 戊寅	1
2	4	9

Lower Period:
1	6	8
9	2 戊寅	4
5	7	3

503

Mountain Covering Yellow Path 蓋山黃道：

貪狼 Tan Lang **Greedy Wolf**		巨門 Ju Men **Huge Door**		武曲 Wu Qu **Military Arts**				文曲 Wen Qu **Literary Arts**			
艮 Gen NE2	丙 Bing S1	巽 Xun SE2	辛 Xin W3	兌 Dui W2	丁 Ding S3	巳 Si SE3	丑 Chou NE1	離 Li S2	壬 Ren N1	寅 Yin NE3	戌 Xu NW1

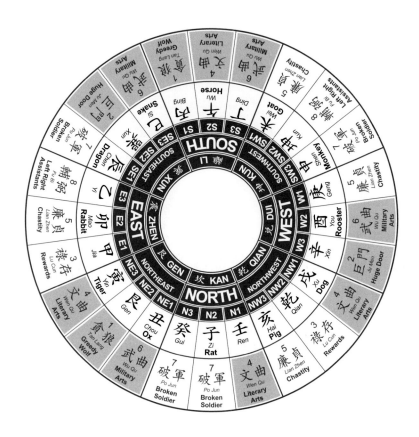

504

Heaven Penetrating Force 通天竅：

三合前方 **Facing Three Harmony**	坤申 Kun Shen	庚酉 Geng You	辛戌 Xin Xu
三合後方 **Sitting Three Harmony**	艮寅 Gen Yin	甲卯 Jia Mao	乙辰 Yi Chen

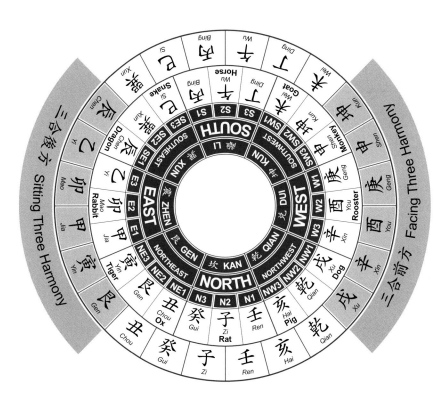

Moving Horse Six Ren Assessment 走馬六壬:

神后 Shen Hou **Holy Empress**	功曹 Gong Cao **Marshall**	天罡 Tian Gang **Heavenly Dipper**	勝光 Sheng Guang **Subliminal Bright**	傳送 Chuan Song **Great General**	河魁 He Kui **River Scholar**
辛戌 Xin Xu	壬子 Ren Zi	艮寅 Gen Yin	乙辰 Yi Chen	丙午 Bing Wu	坤申 Kun Shen

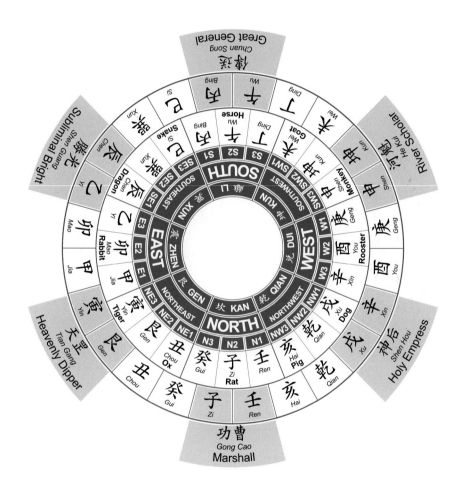

Four Advantages Three Cycles Star Plate 四利三元:

太陽 *Tai Yang* **Sun**	太陰 *Tai Yin* **Moon**	龍德 *Long De* **Dragon Virtue**	福德 *Fu De* **Fortune Virtue**
卯 *Mao* **Rabbit**	巳 *Si* **Snake**	酉 *You* **Rooster**	亥 *Hai* **Pig**

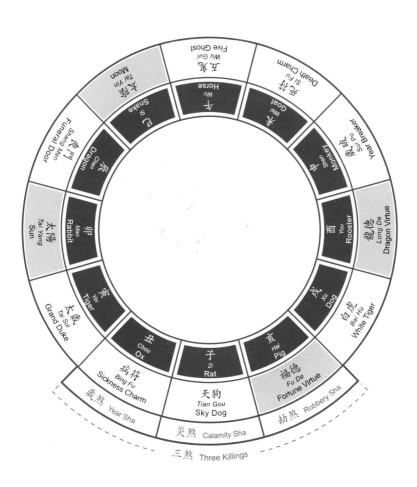

Negative Sectors For Opening Mountain 開山凶位：

年剋山家 Year Countering Sitting

離 Li S2	壬 Ren N1	丙 Bing S1	乙 Yi E3

陰府太歲 Yin Fu Tai Sui **Yin Mansion Grand Duke**	六害 Liu Hai **Six Harm**	死符 Si Fu **Death Charm**	炙退 Zhi Tui **Roasting Star**
坤 Kun SW2 震 Zhen E2	巳 Si SE3	未 Wei SW1	酉 You W2

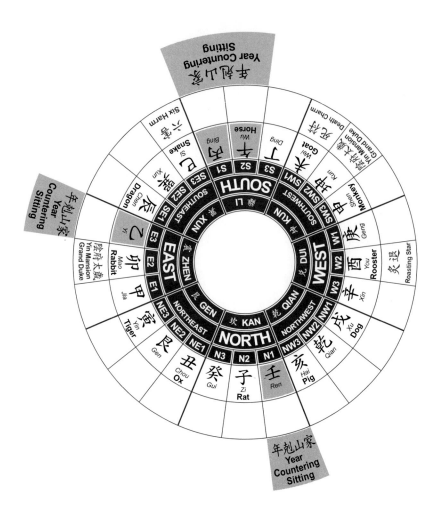

Negative Directions to Establish Facing 立向凶方：

巡山羅喉 *Xun Shan Luo Hou* **Mountain Patrol Luo Hou Star**	病符 *Bing Fu* **Sickness Charm**
甲 *Jia* **E1**	丑 *Chou* **NE1**

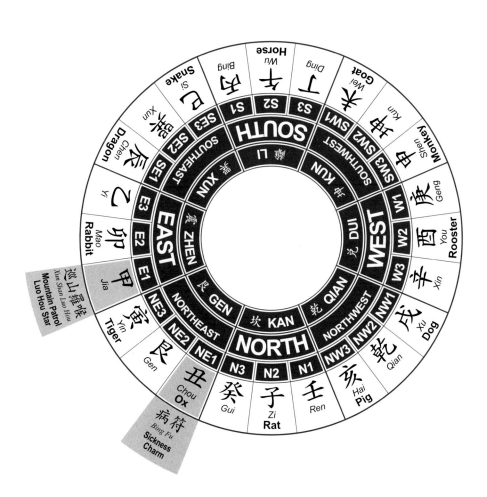

Negative Repair / Renovation Sectors Table 修方凶位表：

天官符 **Heavenly Officer Charm**	巳 *Si* Snake	飛廉 **Flying Chaste**	亥 *Hai* Pig
地官符 **Earthly Officer Charm**	午 *Wu* Horse	喪門 **Funeral Door**	辰 *Chen* Dragon
大煞 **Great Sha**	午 *Wu* Horse	弔客 **Suspended Guest**	子 *Zi* Rat
大將軍 **Big General**	子 *Zi* Rat	白虎 **White Tiger**	戌 *Xu* Dog
力士 **Strong Man**	巽 *Xun*	金神 **Golden God**	申 *Shen* Monkey
蠶室 **Silkworm Room**	乾 *Qian*		酉 *You* Rooster
蠶官 **Silkworm Officer**	戌 *Xu* Dog		子 *Zi* Rat
蠶命 **Silkworm Life**	亥 *Hai* Pig		丑 *Chou* Ox
歲刑 **Duke Punishment**	巳 *Si* Snake	獨火 **Lonely Fire**	辰 *Chen* Dragon
黃幡 **Yellow Flag**	戌 *Xu* Dog	五鬼 **Five Ghost**	寅 *Yin* Tiger
豹尾 **Leopard Tail**	辰 *Chen* Dragon	破敗五鬼 **Destructive Five Ghost**	離 *Li*

Negative Repair / Renovation Sectors Diagram 修方凶位圖：

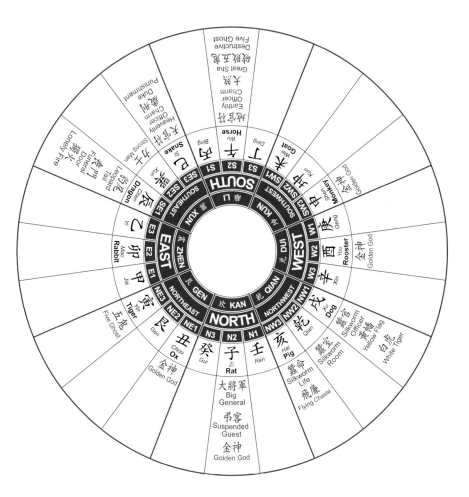

戊寅 (Wu Yin) Earth Tiger

Positive Monthly Stars 吉星方

月 MONTH	寅 Tiger (Feb 4 - Mar 5) 正月 1st Month	卯 Rabbit (Mar 6 - Apr 4) 二月 2nd Month	辰 Dragon (Apr 5 - May 5) 三月 3rd Month	巳 Snake (May 6 - Jun 5) 四月 4th Month	午 Horse (Jun 6 - July 6) 五月 5th Month	未 Goat (July 7 - Aug 7) 六月 6th Month
天道 Heavenly Path	南 South	西南 Southwest	北 North	西 West	西北 Northwest	東 East
天德 Heavenly Virtue	丁 Ding Yin Fire	坤 Kun (申)	壬 Ren Yang Water	辛 Xin Yin Metal	乾 Qian (亥)	甲 Jia Yang Wood
天德合 Heavenly Virtue Combo	壬 Ren Yang Water	(巳)	丁 Ding Yin Fire	丙 Bing Yang Fire	(寅)	己 Ji Yin Earth
月德 Monthly Virtue	丙 Bing Yang Fire	甲 Jia Yang Wood	壬 Ren Yang Water	庚 Geng Yang Metal	丙 Bing Yang Fire	甲 Jia Yang Wood
月德合 Monthly Virtue Combo	辛 Xin Yin Metal	己 Ji Yin Earth	丁 Ding Yin Fire	乙 Yi Yin Wood	辛 Xin Yin Metal	己 Ji Yin Earth
月空 Month Emptiness	壬 Ren Yang Water	庚 Geng Yang Metal	丙 Bing Yang Fire	甲 Jia Yang Wood	壬 Ren Yang Water	庚 Geng Yang Metal
陽貴人 Yang Nobleman	兌 Dui	乾 Qian	中 Middle	巽 Xun	震 Zhen	坤 Kun
陰貴人 Yin Nobleman	坎 Kan	離 Li	艮 Gen	兌 Dui	乾 Qian	中 Middle
飛天祿 Flying Heavenly Wealth	艮 Gen	兌 Dui	乾 Qian	中 Middle	坎 Kan	離 Li
飛天馬 Flying Heavenly Horse	坤 Kun	坎 Kan	離 Li	艮 Gen	兌 Dui	乾 Qian

12-Month Auxiliary Stars Reference Table :
戊寅年十二月，開山立向修方星表

申 Monkey (Aug 8 - Sept 7) 七月 7th Month	酉 Rooster (Sept 8 - Oct 7) 八月 8th Month	戌 Dog (Oct 8 - Nov 6) 九月 9th Month	亥 Pig (Nov 7 - Dec 6) 十月 10th Month	子 Rat (Dec 7 - Jan 5) 十一月 11th Month	丑 Ox (Jan 6 - Feb 3) 十二月 12th Month	月 MONTH
北 North	東北 Northeast	南 South	東 East	東南 Southeast	西 West	天道 Heavenly Path
癸 Gui Yin Water	艮 Gen (寅)	丙 Bing Yang Fire	乙 Yi Yin Wood	巽 Xun (巳)	庚 Geng Yang Metal	天德 Heavenly Virtue
戊 Wu Yang Earth	(亥)	辛 Xin Yin Metal	庚 Geng Yang Metal	(申)	乙 Yi Yin Wood	天德合 Heavenly Virtue Combo
壬 Ren Yang Water	庚 Geng Yang Metal	丙 Bing Yang Fire	甲 Jia Yang Wood	壬 Ren Yang Water	庚 Geng Yang Metal	月德 Monthly Virtue
丁 Ding Yin Fire	乙 Yi Yin Wood	辛 Xin Yin Metal	己 Ji Yin Earth	丁 Ding Yin Fire	乙 Yi Yin Wood	月德合 Monthly Virtue Combo
丙 Bing Yang Fire	甲 Jia Yang Wood	壬 Ren Yang Water	庚 Geng Yang Metal	丙 Bing Yang Fire	甲 Jia Yang Wood	月空 Month Emptiness
坎 Kan	離 Li	艮 Gen	兌 Dui	乾 Qian	中 Middle	陽貴人 Yang Nobleman
坎 Kan	離 Li	艮 Gen	兌 Dui	乾 Qian	中 Middle	陰貴人 Yin Nobleman
艮 Gen	兌 Dui	乾 Qian	中 Middle	巽 Xun	震 Zhen	飛天祿 Flying Heavenly Wealth
中 Middle	坎 Kan	離 Li	艮 Gen	兌 Dui	乾 Qian	飛天馬 Flying Heavenly Horse

513

Monthly Purple White Stars 月紫白九星 :

寅 Tiger (Feb 4 - Mar 5) 正月 1st Month

巽 SE	離 S	坤 SW
1 White 一白	6 White 六白	8 White 八白
9 Purple 九紫	2 Black 二黑	4 Green 四綠
5 Yellow 五黃	7 Red 七赤	3 Jade 三碧
艮 NE	坎 N	乾 NW

震 E · 兌 W

卯 Rabbit (Mar 6 - Apr 4) 二月 2nd Month

巽 SE	離 S	坤 SW
9 Purple 九紫	5 Yellow 五黃	7 Red 七赤
8 White 八白	1 White 一白	3 Jade 三碧
4 Green 四綠	6 White 六白	2 Black 二黑
艮 NE	坎 N	乾 NW

震 E · 兌 W

辰 Dragon (Apr 5 - May 5) 三月 3rd Month

巽 SE	離 S	坤 SW
8 White 八白	4 Green 四綠	6 White 六白
7 Red 七赤	9 Purple 九紫	2 Black 二黑
3 Jade 三碧	5 Yellow 五黃	1 White 一白
艮 NE	坎 N	乾 NW

震 E · 兌 W

巳 Snake (May 6 - Jun 5) 四月 4th Month

巽 SE	離 S	坤 SW
7 Red 七赤	3 Jade 三碧	5 Yellow 五黃
6 White 六白	8 White 八白	1 White 一白
2 Black 二黑	4 Green 四綠	9 Purple 九紫
艮 NE	坎 N	乾 NW

震 E · 兌 W

午 Horse (Jun 6 - July 6) 五月 5th Month

巽 SE	離 S	坤 SW
6 White 六白	2 Black 二黑	4 Green 四綠
5 Yellow 五黃	7 Red 七赤	9 Purple 九紫
1 White 一白	3 Jade 三碧	8 White 八白
艮 NE	坎 N	乾 NW

震 E · 兌 W

未 Goat (July 7 - Aug 7) 六月 6th Month

巽 SE	離 S	坤 SW
5 Yellow 五黃	1 White 一白	3 Jade 三碧
4 Green 四綠	6 White 六白	8 White 八白
9 Purple 九紫	2 Black 二黑	7 Red 七赤
艮 NE	坎 N	乾 NW

震 E · 兌 W

申 Monkey (Aug 8 - Sept 7) 七月 7th Month

巽 SE	離 S	坤 SW
4 Green 四綠	9 Purple 九紫	2 Black 二黑
3 Jade 三碧	5 Yellow 五黃	7 Red 七赤
8 White 八白	1 White 一白	6 White 六白
艮 NE	坎 N	乾 NW

震 E · 兌 W

酉 Rooster (Sept 8 - Oct 7) 八月 8th Month

巽 SE	離 S	坤 SW
3 Jade 三碧	8 White 八白	1 White 一白
2 Black 二黑	4 Green 四綠	6 White 六白
7 Red 七赤	9 Purple 九紫	5 Yellow 五黃
艮 NE	坎 N	乾 NW

震 E · 兌 W

戌 Dog (Oct 8 - Nov 6) 九月 9th Month

巽 SE	離 S	坤 SW
2 Black 二黑	7 Red 七赤	9 Purple 九紫
1 White 一白	3 Jade 三碧	5 Yellow 五黃
6 White 六白	8 White 八白	4 Green 四綠
艮 NE	坎 N	乾 NW

震 E · 兌 W

亥 Pig (Nov 7 - Dec 6) 十月 10th Month

巽 SE	離 S	坤 SW
1 White 一白	6 White 六白	8 White 八白
9 Purple 九紫	2 Black 二黑	4 Green 四綠
5 Yellow 五黃	7 Red 七赤	3 Jade 三碧
艮 NE	坎 N	乾 NW

震 E · 兌 W

子 Rat (Dec 7 - Jan 5) 十一月 11th Month

巽 SE	離 S	坤 SW
9 Purple 九紫	5 Yellow 五黃	7 Red 七赤
8 White 八白	1 White 一白	3 Jade 三碧
4 Green 四綠	6 White 六白	2 Black 二黑
艮 NE	坎 N	乾 NW

震 E · 兌 W

丑 Ox (Jan 6 - Feb 3) 十二月 12th Month

巽 SE	離 S	坤 SW
8 White 八白	4 Green 四綠	6 White 六白
7 Red 七赤	9 Purple 九紫	2 Black 二黑
3 Jade 三碧	5 Yellow 五黃	1 White 一白
艮 NE	坎 N	乾 NW

震 E · 兌 W

Qi Men Three Nobles 三奇 :

Three Nobles 三奇 / Seasons	乙 Yi	丙 Bing	丁 Ding
立春 **Coming of Spring** Feb 4 - Feb 18	中 Middle	乾 Qian	兌 Dui
春分 **Spring Equinox** Mar 21 - Apr 4	離 Li	坎 Kan	坤 Kun
立夏 **Coming of Summer** May 6 - May 20	坎 Kan	坤 Kun	震 Zhen
夏至 **Summer Solstice** Jun 22 - Jul 6	震 Zhen	坤 Kun	坎 Kan
立秋 **Coming of Autumn** Aug 8 - Aug 23	中 Middle	巽 Xun	震 Zhen
秋分 **Autumn Equinox** Sept 23 - Oct 7	坎 Kan	離 Li	艮 Gen
立冬 **Coming of Winter** Nov 7 - Nov 22	離 Li	艮 Gen	兌 Dui
冬至 **Winter Solstice** Dec 22 - Jan 5	兌 Dui	艮 Gen	離 Li

Sectors to Avoid Opening Mountain 開山凶位 :

月 MONTH	月建 Month Establishment	月破 Month Destruction	月剋山家 Month Countering Sitting		陰府太歲 Yin Mansion Grand Duke	
寅 Tiger (Feb 4 - Mar 5) 正月 1st Month	寅 Yin Tiger	申 Shen Monkey	震 Zhen	巳 Si Snake	艮 Gen	巽 Xun
卯 Rabbit (Mar 6 - Apr 4) 二月 2nd Month	卯 Mao Rabbit	酉 You Rooster	艮 Gen		兌 Dui	乾 Qian
辰 Dragon (Apr 5 - May 5) 三月 3rd Month	辰 Chen Dragon	戌 Xu Dog	離 Li	丙 Bing Yang Fire	坎 Kan	坤 Kun
巳 Snake (May 6 - Jun 5) 四月 4th Month	巳 Si Snake	亥 Hai Pig	壬 Ren Yang Water	乙 Yi Yin Wood	乾 Qian	離 Li
午 Horse (Jun 6 - July 6) 五月 5th Month	午 Wu Horse	子 Zi Rat	—		坤 Kun	震 Zhen
未 Goat (July 7 - Aug 7) 六月 6th Month	未 Wei Goat	丑 Chou Ox	—		巽 Xun	艮 Gen
申 Monkey (Aug 8 - Sept 7) 七月 7th Month	申 Shen Monkey	寅 Yin Tiger	水 Water	山 Mountain	乾 Qian	兌 Dui
酉 Rooster (Sept 8 - Oct 7) 八月 8th Month	酉 You Rooster	卯 Mao Rabbit	土 Earth		坤 Kun	坎 Kan
戌 Dog (Oct 8 - Nov 6) 九月 9th Month	戌 Xu Dog	辰 Chen Dragon	震 Zhen	巳 Si Snake	離 Li	乾 Qian
亥 Pig (Nov 7 - Dec 6) 十月 10th Month	亥 Hai Pig	巳 Si Snake	艮 Gen		震 Zhen	坤 Kun
子 Rat (Dec 7 - Jan 5) 十一月 11th Month	子 Zi Rat	午 Wu Horse	—		艮 Gen	巽 Xun
丑 Ox (Jan 6 - Feb 3) 十二月 12th Month	丑 Chou Ox	未 Wei Goat	—		兌 Dui	乾 Qian

Negative Repair / Renovation Sectors 修方凶位 :

月 MONTH	天官符 Heavenly Officer Charm			地官符 Earth Officer Charm			小月建 Small Month Establishment		
寅 **Tiger** (Feb 4 - Mar 5) 正月 **1st Month**	丑 *Chou* **Ox**	艮 *Gen*	寅 *Yin* **Tiger**	丙 *Bing* **Yang Fire**	離 *Li*	丁 *Ding* **Yin Fire**	中 **Middle**		
卯 **Rabbit** (Mar 6 - Apr 4) 二月 **2nd Month**	庚 *Geng* **Yang Metal**	兌 *Dui*	辛 *Xin* **Yin Metal**	丑 *Chou* **Ox**	艮 *Gen*	寅 *Yin* **Tiger**	戌 *Xu* **Dog**	乾 *Qian*	亥 *Hai* **Pig**
辰 **Dragon** (Apr 5 - May 5) 三月 **3rd Month**	戌 *Xu* **Dog**	乾 *Qian*	亥 *Hai* **Pig**	庚 *Geng* **Yang Metal**	兌 *Dui*	辛 *Xin* **Yin Metal**	庚 *Geng* **Yang Metal**	兌 *Dui*	辛 *Xin* **Yin Metal**
巳 **Snake** (May 6 - Jun 5) 四月 **4th Month**		中 **Middle**		戌 *Xu* **Dog**	乾 *Qian*	亥 *Hai* **Pig**	丑 *Chou* **Ox**	艮 *Gen*	寅 *Yin* **Tiger**
午 **Horse** (Jun 6 - July 6) 五月 **5th Month**	庚 *Geng* **Yang Metal**	兌 *Dui*	辛 *Xin* **Yin Metal**		中 **Middle**		丙 *Bing* **Yang Fire**	離 *Li*	丁 *Ding* **Yin Fire**
未 **Goat** (July 7 - Aug 7) 六月 **6th Month**	戌 *Xu* **Dog**	乾 *Qian*	亥 *Hai* **Pig**	庚 *Geng* **Yang Metal**	兌 *Dui*	辛 *Xin* **Yin Metal**	壬 *Ren* **Yang Water**	坎 *Kan*	癸 *Gui* **Yin Water**
申 **Monkey** (Aug 8 - Sept 7) 七月 **7th Month**		中 **Middle**		戌 *Xu* **Dog**	乾 *Qian*	亥 *Hai* **Pig**	未 *Wei* **Goat**	坤 *Kun*	申 *Shen* **Monkey**
酉 **Rooster** (Sept 8 - Oct 7) 八月 **8th Month**	辰 *Chen* **Dragon**	巽 *Xun*	巳 *Si* **Snake**		中 **Middle**		甲 *Jia* **Yang Wood**	震 *Zhen*	乙 *Yi* **Yin Wood**
戌 **Dog** (Oct 8 - Nov 6) 九月 **9th Month**	甲 *Jia* **Yang Wood**	震 *Zhen*	乙 *Yi* **Yin Wood**	辰 *Chen* **Dragon**	巽 *Xun*	巳 *Si* **Snake**	辰 *Chen* **Dragon**	巽 *Xun*	巳 *Si* **Snake**
亥 **Pig** (Nov 7 - Dec 6) 十月 **10th Month**	未 *Wei* **Goat**	坤 *Kun*	申 *Shen* **Monkey**	甲 *Jia* **Yang Wood**	震 *Zhen*	乙 *Yi* **Yin Wood**	中 **Middle**		
子 **Rat** (Dec 7 - Jan 5) 十一月 **11th Month**	壬 *Ren* **Yang Water**	坎 *Kan*	癸 *Gui* **Yin Water**	未 *Wei* **Goat**	坤 *Kun*	申 *Shen* **Monkey**	戌 *Xu* **Dog**	乾 *Qian*	亥 *Hai* **Pig**
丑 **Ox** (Jan 6 - Feb 3) 十二月 **12th Month**	丙 *Bing* **Yang Fire**	離 *Li*	丁 *Ding* **Yin Fire**	壬 *Ren* **Yang Water**	坎 *Kan*	癸 *Gui* **Yin Water**	庚 *Geng* **Yang Metal**	兌 *Dui*	辛 *Xin* **Yin Metal**

Negative Repair / Renovation Sectors 修方凶位 :

月 MONTH	大月建 Big Month Establishment			飛大煞 Flying Great Sha			丙丁獨火 Bing Ding Lonely Fire	
寅 **Tiger** (Feb 4 - Mar 5) 正月 **1st Month**	未 Wei Goat	坤 Kun	申 Shen Monkey	丙 Bing Yang Fire	離 Li	丁 Ding Yin Fire	兌 Dui	艮 Gen
卯 **Rabbit** (Mar 6 - Apr 4) 二月 **2nd Month**	壬 Ren Yang Water	坎 Kan	癸 Gui Yin Water	丑 Chou Ox	艮 Gen	寅 Yin Tiger	乾 Qian	兌 Dui
辰 **Dragon** (Apr 5 - May 5) 三月 **3rd Month**	丙 Bing Yang Fire	離 Li	丁 Ding Yin Fire	庚 Geng Yang Metal	兌 Dui	辛 Xin Yin Metal	中 Middle	乾 Qian
巳 **Snake** (May 6 - Jun 5) 四月 **4th Month**	丑 Chou Ox	艮 Gen	寅 Yin Tiger	戌 Xu Dog	乾 Qian	亥 Hai Pig	中 Middle	
午 **Horse** (Jun 6 - July 6) 五月 **5th Month**	庚 Geng Yang Metal	兌 Dui	辛 Xin Yin Metal		中 Middle		巽 Xun	中 Middle
未 **Goat** (July 7 - Aug 7) 六月 **6th Month**	戌 Xu Dog	乾 Qian	亥 Hai Pig	庚 Geng Yang Metal	兌 Dui	辛 Xin Yin Metal	震 Zhen	巽 Xun
申 **Monkey** (Aug 8 - Sept 7) 七月 **7th Month**		中 Middle		戌 Xu Dog	乾 Qian	亥 Hai Pig	坤 Kun	震 Zhen
酉 **Rooster** (Sept 8 - Oct 7) 八月 **8th Month**	辰 Chen Dragon	巽 Xun	巳 Si Snake		中 Middle		坎 Kan	坤 Kun
戌 **Dog** (Oct 8 - Nov 6) 九月 **9th Month**	甲 Jia Yang Wood	震 Zhen	乙 Yi Yin Wood	辰 Chen Dragon	巽 Xun	巳 Si Snake	離 Li	坎 Kan
亥 **Pig** (Nov 7 - Dec 6) 十月 **10th Month**	未 Wei Goat	坤 Kun	申 Shen Monkey	甲 Jia Yang Wood	震 Zhen	乙 Yi Yin Wood	艮 Gen	離 Li
子 **Rat** (Dec 7 - Jan 5) 十一月 **11th Month**	壬 Ren Yang Water	坎 Kan	癸 Gui Yin Water	未 Wei Goat	坤 Kun	申 Shen Monkey	兌 Dui	艮 Gen
丑 **Ox** (Jan 6 - Feb 3) 十二月 **12th Month**	丙 Bing Yang Fire	離 Li	丁 Ding Yin Fire	壬 Ren Yang Water	坎 Kan	癸 Gui Yin Water	乾 Qian	兌 Dui

Negative Repair / Renovation Sectors 修方凶位 :

月 MONTH	月遊火 Month Wondering Fire	三煞 Monthly 3 Killings		
		劫煞 Robbery Sha	災煞 Calamity Sha	月煞 Month Sha
寅 **Tiger** (Feb 4 - Mar 5) 正月 **1st Month**	震 Zhen	亥 Hai Pig	子 Zi Rat	丑 Chou Ox
卯 **Rabbit** (Mar 6 - Apr 4) 二月 **2nd Month**	巽 Xun	申 Shen Monkey	酉 You Rooster	戌 Xu Dog
辰 **Dragon** (Apr 5 - May 5) 三月 **3rd Month**	中 Middle	巳 Si Snake	午 Wu Horse	未 Wei Goat
巳 **Snake** (May 6 - Jun 5) 四月 **4th Month**	乾 Qian	寅 Yin Tiger	卯 Mao Rabbit	辰 Chen Dragon
午 **Horse** (Jun 6 - July 6) 五月 **5th Month**	兌 Dui	亥 Hai Pig	子 Zi Rat	丑 Chou Ox
未 **Goat** (July 7 - Aug 7) 六月 **6th Month**	艮 Gen	申 Shen Monkey	酉 You Rooster	戌 Xu Dog
申 **Monkey** (Aug 8 - Sept 7) 七月 **7th Month**	離 Li	巳 Si Snake	午 Wu Horse	未 Wei Goat
酉 **Rooster** (Sept 8 - Oct 7) 八月 **8th Month**	坎 Kan	寅 Yin Tiger	卯 Mao Rabbit	辰 Chen Dragon
戌 **Dog** (Oct 8 - Nov 6) 九月 **9th Month**	坤 Kun	亥 Hai Pig	子 Zi Rat	丑 Chou Ox
亥 **Pig** (Nov 7 - Dec 6) 十月 **10th Month**	震 Zhen	申 Shen Monkey	酉 You Rooster	戌 Xu Dog
子 **Rat** (Dec 7 - Jan 5) 十一月 **11th Month**	巽 Xun	巳 Si Snake	午 Wu Horse	未 Wei Goat
丑 **Ox** (Jan 6 - Feb 3) 十二月 **12th Month**	中 Middle	寅 Yin Tiger	卯 Mao Rabbit	辰 Chen Dragon

Negative Repair / Renovation Sectors 修方凶位 :

月 MONTH	月刑 Month Punishment	月害 Month Harm	月厭 Month Detest
寅 **Tiger** (Feb 4 - Mar 5) 正月 **1st Month**	巳 Si **Snake**	巳 Si **Snake**	戌 Xu **Dog**
卯 **Rabbit** (Mar 6 - Apr 4) 二月 **2nd Month**	子 Zi **Rat**	辰 Chen **Dragon**	酉 You **Rooster**
辰 **Dragon** (Apr 5 - May 5) 三月 **3rd Month**	辰 Chen **Dragon**	卯 Mao **Rabbit**	申 Shen **Monkey**
巳 **Snake** (May 6 - Jun 5) 四月 **4th Month**	申 Shen **Monkey**	寅 Yin **Tiger**	未 Wei **Goat**
午 **Horse** (Jun 6 - July 6) 五月 **5th Month**	午 Wu **Horse**	丑 Chou **Ox**	午 Wu **Horse**
未 **Goat** (July 7 - Aug 7) 六月 **6th Month**	丑 Chou **Ox**	子 Zi **Rat**	巳 Si **Snake**
申 **Monkey** (Aug 8 - Sept 7) 七月 **7th Month**	寅 Yin **Tiger**	亥 Hai **Pig**	辰 Chen **Dragon**
酉 **Rooster** (Sept 8 - Oct 7) 八月 **8th Month**	酉 You **Rooster**	戌 Xu **Dog**	卯 Mao **Rabbit**
戌 **Dog** (Oct 8 - Nov 6) 九月 **9th Month**	未 Wei **Goat**	酉 You **Rooster**	寅 Yin **Tiger**
亥 **Pig** (Nov 7 - Dec 6) 十月 **10th Month**	亥 Hai **Pig**	申 Shen **Monkey**	丑 Chou **Ox**
子 **Rat** (Dec 7 - Jan 5) 十一月 **11th Month**	卯 Mao **Rabbit**	未 Wei **Goat**	子 Zi **Rat**
丑 **Ox** (Jan 6 - Feb 3) 十二月 **12th Month**	戌 Xu **Dog**	午 Wu **Horse**	亥 Hai **Pig**

戊辰 **(Wu Chen)**
Earth Dragon

戊辰 (Wu Chen) Earth Dragon

Heavenly Stem 天干	戊 Yang Earth (陽土)
Earthly Branch 地支	辰 Dragon (Yang Earth 陽土)
Hidden Stem 藏干	戊 Yang Earth, 乙 Yin Wood, 癸 Yin Water
Na Yin 納音	大林木 Wood from the forest
Grand Duke 太歲	辰 Dragon
Xuan Kong Five Element 玄空五行	9 金 Metal
Gua Name 卦名	䷉ 天澤履 Tread
Xuan Kong Period Luck 玄空卦運	6

Annual Positive Stars for Opening Mountain, Establishing Facing and Commencing Repairs 開山立向修方吉星：

歲德 **Duke Virtue**	戊	Wu Yang Earth
歲德合 **Duke Virtue Combo**	癸	Gui Yin Water
歲枝德 **Duke Branch Virtue**	酉	You Rooster
陽貴人 **Yang Nobleman**	丑	Chou Ox
陰貴人 **Yin Nobleman**	未	Wei Goat
歲祿 **Duke Prosperous**	巳	Si Snake
歲馬 **Duke Horse**	寅	Yin Tiger
奏書 **Decree**	艮	Gen
博士 **Professor**	坤	Kun

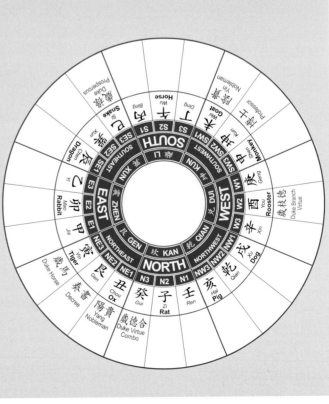

Annual Negative Stars for Opening Mountain, Establishing Facing and Commencing Repairs 開山立向修方凶星：

太歲 Grand Duke	歲破 Year Breaker	三煞 Three Killings			坐煞向煞 Sitting Sha Facing Sha				浮天空亡 Floating Heaven Emptiness	
辰 Chen Dragon	戌 Xu Dog	巳 Si Snake	午 Wu Horse	未 Wei Goat	丙 Bing Yang Fire	丁 Ding Yin Fire	壬 Ren Yang Water	癸 Gui Yin Water	坤 Kun	乙 Yi Yin Wood

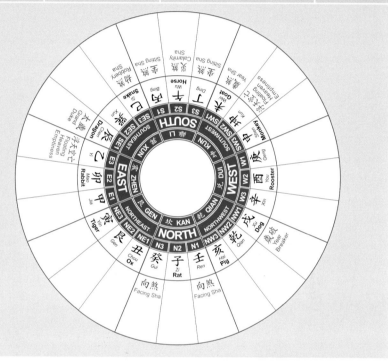

Annual San Yuan Purple White Stars 三元紫白九星：

上元 Upper Period Period 1, 2, 3			中元 Middle Period Period 4, 5, 6			下元 Lower Period Period 7, 8, 9		
巽SE 5	離S 1	坤SW 3	巽SE 8	離S 4	坤SW 6	巽SE 2	離S 7	坤SW 9
震E 4	6 戊辰 Wu Chen Earth Dragon	兌W 8	震E 7	9 戊辰 Wu Chen Earth Dragon	兌W 2	震E 1	3 戊辰 Wu Chen Earth Dragon	兌W 5
艮NE 9	坎N 2	乾NW 7	艮NE 3	坎N 5	乾NW 1	艮NE 6	坎N 8	乾NW 4

Mountain Covering Yellow Path 蓋山黃道:

貪狼				巨門				武曲		文曲			
Tan Lang				*Ju Men*				*Wu Qu*		*Wen Qu*			
Greedy Wolf				**Huge Door**				**Military Arts**		**Literary Arts**			
兌	丁	巳	丑	震	庚	亥	未	艮	丙	坎	癸	申	辰
Dui	*Ding*	*Si*	*Chou*	*Zhen*	*Geng*	*Hai*	*Wei*	*Gen*	*Bing*	*Kan*	*Gui*	*Shen*	*Chen*
W2	S3	SE3	NE1	E2	W1	NW3	SW1	NE2	S1	N2	N3	SW3	SE1

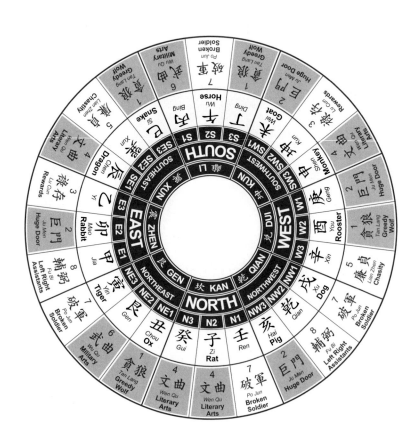

Heaven Penetrating Force 通天竅：			
三合前方 **Facing Three Harmony**	艮寅 Gen Yin	甲卯 Jia Mao	乙辰 Yi Chen
三合後方 **Sitting Three Harmony**	坤申 Kun Shen	庚酉 Geng You	辛戌 Xin Xu

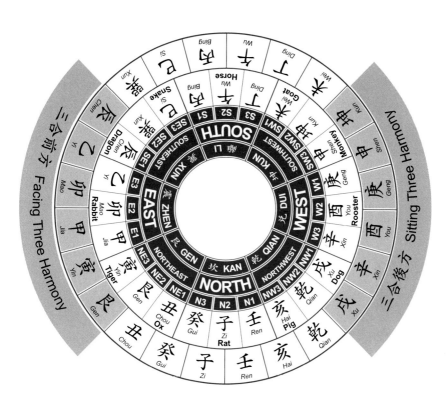

Moving Horse Six Ren Assessment 走馬六壬：

神后 Shen Hou **Holy Empress**	功曹 Gong Cao **Marshall**	天罡 Tian Gang **Heavenly Dipper**	勝光 Sheng Guang **Subliminal Bright**	傳送 Chuan Song **Great General**	河魁 He Kui **River Scholar**
坤申 Kun Shen	辛戌 Xin Xu	壬子 Ren Zi	艮寅 Gen Yin	乙辰 Yi Chen	丙午 Bing Wu

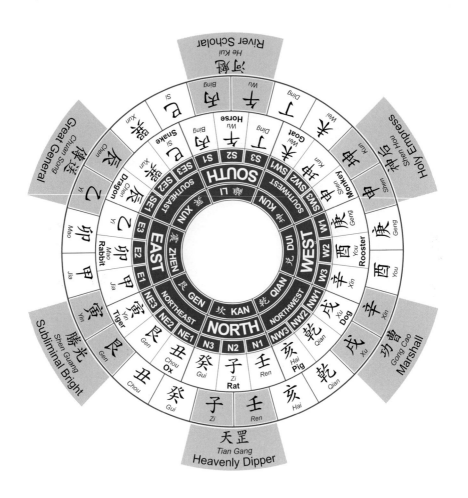

Four Advantages Three Cycles Star Plate 四利三元：

太陽 Tai Yang **Sun**	太陰 Tai Yin **Moon**	龍德 Long De **Dragon Virtue**	福德 Fu De **Fortune Virtue**
巳 Si Snake	未 Wei Goat	亥 Hai Pig	丑 Chou Ox

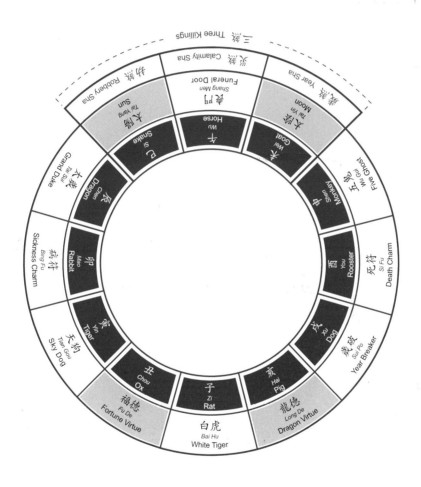

Negative Sectors For Opening Mountain 開山凶位：

年剋山家 Year Countering Sitting

甲	寅	辰	巽	戊	坎	辛	申	丑	癸	坤	庚	未
Jia	Yin	Chen	Xun	Xu	Kan	Xin	Shen	Chou	Gui	Kun	Geng	wei
E1	NE3	SE1	SE2	NW1	N2	W3	SW3	NE1	N3	SW2	W1	SW1

陰府太歲 Yin Fu Tai Sui **Yin Mansion Grand Duke**		六害 Liu Hai **Six Harm**	死符 Si Fu **Death Charm**	炙退 Zhi Tui **Roasting Star**
坤 Kun **SW2**	震 Zhen **E2**	卯 Mao **E2**	酉 You **W2**	卯 Mao **E2**

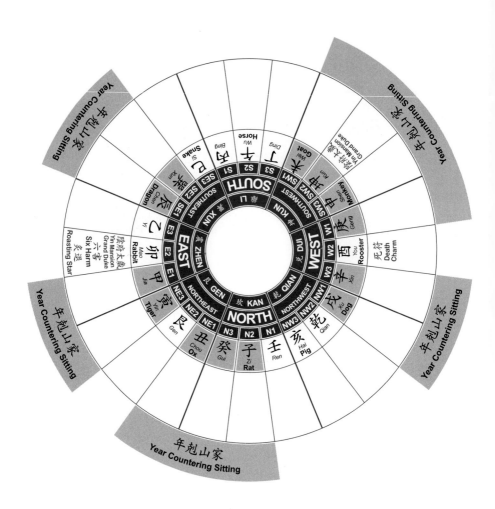

Negative Directions to Establish Facing 立向凶方：

巡山羅喉 *Xun Shan Luo Hou* **Mountain Patrol Luo Hou Star**	病符 *Bing Fu* **Sickness Charm**
巽 *Xun* **SE2**	卯 *Mao* **E2**

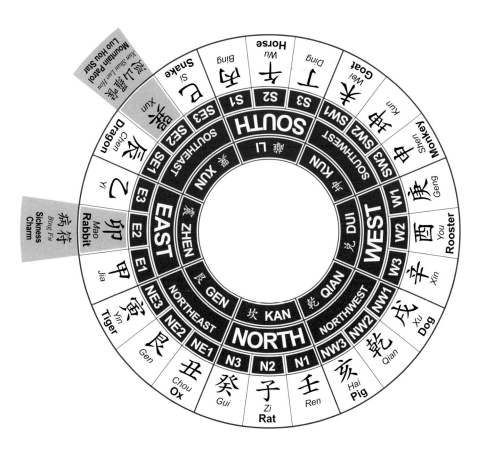

戊辰 (Wu Chen) Earth Dragon

天官符 Heavenly Officer Charm	亥 Hai Pig		飛廉 Flying Chaste	午 Wu Horse
地官符 Earthly Officer Charm	申 Shen Monkey		喪門 Funeral Door	午 Wu Horse
大煞 Great Sha	子 Zi Rat		弔客 Suspended Guest	寅 Yin Tiger
大將軍 Big General	子 Zi Rat		白虎 White Tiger	子 Zi Rat
力士 Strong Man	巽 Xun		金神 Golden God	申 Shen Monkey
蠶室 Silkworm Room	乾 Qian			酉 You Rooster
蠶官 Silkworm Officer	戌 Xu Dog			子 Zi Rat
蠶命 Silkworm Life	亥 Hai Pig			丑 Chou Ox
歲刑 Duke Punishment	辰 Chen Dragon		獨火 Lonely Fire	巽 Xun
黃幡 Yellow Flag	辰 Chen Dragon		五鬼 Five Ghost	子 Zi Rat
豹尾 Leopard Tail	戌 Xu Dog		破敗五鬼 Destructive Five Ghost	離 Li

Negative Repair / Renovation Sectors Diagram 修方凶位圖：

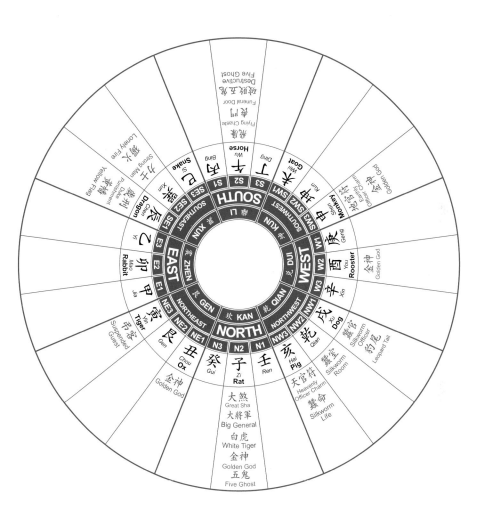

531

12-Month Auxiliary Stars Reference Table :
戊辰年十二月，開山立向修方星表

Positive Monthly Stars 吉星方

月 MONTH	寅 Tiger (Feb 4 - Mar 5) 正月 1st Month	卯 Rabbit (Mar 6 - Apr 4) 二月 2nd Month	辰 Dragon (Apr 5 - May 5) 三月 3rd Month	巳 Snake (May 6 - Jun 5) 四月 4th Month	午 Horse (Jun 6 - July 6) 五月 5th Month	未 Goat (July 7 - Aug 7) 六月 6th Month
天道 Heavenly Path	南 South	西南 Southwest	北 North	西 West	西北 Northwest	東 East
天德 Heavenly Virtue	丁 Ding Yin Fire	坤 Kun (申)	壬 Ren Yang Water	辛 Xin Yin Metal	乾 Qian (亥)	甲 Jia Yang Wood
天德合 Heavenly Virtue Combo	壬 Ren Yang Water	(巳)	丁 Ding Yin Fire	丙 Bing Yang Fire	(寅)	己 Ji Yin Earth
月德 Monthly Virtue	丙 Bing Yang Fire	甲 Jia Yang Wood	壬 Ren Yang Water	庚 Geng Yang Metal	丙 Bing Yang Fire	甲 Jia Yang Wood
月德合 Monthly Virtue Combo	辛 Xin Yin Metal	己 Ji Yin Earth	丁 Ding Yin Fire	乙 Yi Yin Wood	辛 Xin Yin Metal	己 Ji Yin Earth
月空 Month Emptiness	壬 Ren Yang Water	庚 Geng Yang Metal	丙 Bing Yang Fire	甲 Jia Yang Wood	壬 Ren Yang Water	庚 Geng Yang Metal
陽貴人 Yang Nobleman	兌 Dui	乾 Qian	中 Middle	巽 Xun	震 Zhen	坤 Kun
陰貴人 Yin Nobleman	坎 Kan	離 Li	艮 Gen	兌 Dui	乾 Qian	中 Middle
飛天祿 Flying Heavenly Wealth	艮 Gen	兌 Dui	乾 Qian	中 Middle	坎 Kan	離 Li
飛天馬 Flying Heavenly Horse	中 Middle	坎 Kan	離 Li	艮 Gen	兌 Dui	乾 Qian

12-Month Auxiliary Stars Reference Table :
戊辰年十二月，開山立向修方星表

申 Monkey (Aug 8 - Sept 7) 七月 7th Month	酉 Rooster (Sept 8 - Oct 7) 八月 8th Month	戌 Dog (Oct 8 - Nov 6) 九月 9th Month	亥 Pig (Nov 7 - Dec 6) 十月 10th Month	子 Rat (Dec 7 - Jan 5) 十一月 11th Month	丑 Ox (Jan 6 - Feb 3) 十二月 12th Month	月 MONTH
北 North	東北 Northeast	南 South	東 East	東南 Southeast	西 West	天道 Heavenly Path
癸 Gui Yin Water	艮 Gen (寅)	丙 Bing Yang Fire	乙 Yi Yin Wood	巽 Xun (巳)	庚 Geng Yang Metal	天德 Heavenly Virtue
戊 Wu Yang Earth	(亥)	辛 Xin Yin Metal	庚 Geng Yang Metal	(申)	乙 Yi Yin Wood	天德合 Heavenly Virtue Combo
壬 Ren Yang Water	庚 Geng Yang Metal	丙 Bing Yang Fire	甲 Jia Yang Wood	壬 Ren Yang Water	庚 Geng Yang Metal	月德 Monthly Virtue
丁 Ding Yin Fire	乙 Yi Yin Wood	辛 Xin Yin Metal	己 Ji Yin Earth	丁 Ding Yin Fire	乙 Yi Yin Wood	月德合 Monthly Virtue Combo
丙 Bing Yang Fire	甲 Jia Yang Wood	壬 Ren Yang Water	庚 Geng Yang Metal	丙 Bing Yang Fire	甲 Jia Yang Wood	月空 Month Emptiness
坎 Kan	離 Li	艮 Gen	兌 Dui	乾 Qian	中 Middle	陽貴人 Yang Nobleman
坎 Kan	離 Li	艮 Gen	兌 Dui	乾 Qian	中 Middle	陰貴人 Yin Nobleman
艮 Gen	兌 Dui	乾 Qian	中 Middle	巽 Xun	震 Zhen	飛天祿 Flying Heavenly Wealth
中 Middle	巽 Xun	震 Zhen	坤 Kun	坎 Kan	離 Li	飛天馬 Flying Heavenly Horse

Monthly Purple White Stars 月紫白九星 :

寅 Tiger (Feb 4 - Mar 5) 正月 1st Month

巽 SE	離 S	坤 SW
4 Green 四綠	9 Purple 九紫	2 Black 二黑
震 E 3 Jade 三碧	5 Yellow 五黃	7 Red 七赤 兑 W
8 White 八白	1 White 一白	6 White 六白
艮 NE	坎 N	乾 NW

卯 Rabbit (Mar 6 - Apr 4) 二月 2nd Month

巽 SE	離 S	坤 SW
3 Jade 三碧	8 White 八白	1 White 一白
震 E 2 Black 二黑	4 Green 四綠	6 White 六白 兑 W
7 Red 七赤	9 Purple 九紫	5 Yellow 五黃
艮 NE	坎 N	乾 NW

辰 Dragon (Apr 5 - May 5) 三月 3rd Month

巽 SE	離 S	坤 SW
2 Black 二黑	7 Red 七赤	9 Purple 九紫
震 E 1 White 一白	3 Jade 三碧	5 Yellow 五黃 兑 W
6 White 六白	8 White 八白	4 Green 四綠
艮 NE	坎 N	乾 NW

巳 Snake (May 6 - Jun 5) 四月 4th Month

巽 SE	離 S	坤 SW
1 White 一白	6 White 六白	8 White 八白
震 E 9 Purple 九紫	2 Black 二黑	4 Green 四綠 兑 W
5 Yellow 五黃	7 Red 七赤	3 Jade 三碧
艮 NE	坎 N	乾 NW

午 Horse (Jun 6 - July 6) 五月 5th Month

巽 SE	離 S	坤 SW
9 Purple 九紫	5 Yellow 五黃	7 Red 七赤
震 E 8 White 八白	1 White 一白	3 Jade 三碧 兑 W
4 Green 四綠	6 White 六白	2 Black 二黑
艮 NE	坎 N	乾 NW

未 Goat (July 7 - Aug 7) 六月 6th Month

巽 SE	離 S	坤 SW
8 White 八白	4 Green 四綠	6 White 六白
震 E 7 Red 七赤	9 Purple 九紫	2 Black 二黑 兑 W
3 Jade 三碧	5 Yellow 五黃	1 White 一白
艮 NE	坎 N	乾 NW

申 Monkey (Aug 8 - Sept 7) 七月 7th Month

巽 SE	離 S	坤 SW
7 Red 七赤	3 Jade 三碧	5 Yellow 五黃
震 E 6 White 六白	8 White 八白	1 White 一白 兑 W
2 Black 二黑	4 Green 四綠	9 Purple 九紫
艮 NE	坎 N	乾 NW

酉 Rooster (Sept 8 - Oct 7) 八月 8th Month

巽 SE	離 S	坤 SW
6 White 六白	2 Black 二黑	4 Green 四綠
震 E 5 Yellow 五黃	7 Red 七赤	9 Purple 九紫 兑 W
1 White 一白	3 Jade 三碧	8 White 八白
艮 NE	坎 N	乾 NW

戌 Dog (Oct 8 - Nov 6) 九月 9th Month

巽 SE	離 S	坤 SW
5 Yellow 五黃	1 White 一白	3 Jade 三碧
震 E 4 Green 四綠	6 White 六白	8 White 八白 兑 W
9 Purple 九紫	2 Black 二黑	7 Red 七赤
艮 NE	坎 N	乾 NW

亥 Pig (Nov 7 - Dec 6) 十月 10th Month

巽 SE	離 S	坤 SW
4 Green 四綠	9 Purple 九紫	2 Black 二黑
震 E 3 Jade 三碧	5 Yellow 五黃	7 Red 七赤 兑 W
8 White 八白	1 White 一白	6 White 六白
艮 NE	坎 N	乾 NW

子 Rat (Dec 7 - Jan 5) 十一月 11th Month

巽 SE	離 S	坤 SW
3 Jade 三碧	8 White 八白	1 White 一白
震 E 2 Black 二黑	4 Green 四綠	6 White 六白 兑 W
7 Red 七赤	9 Purple 九紫	5 Yellow 五黃
艮 NE	坎 N	乾 NW

丑 Ox (Jan 6 - Feb 3) 十二月 12th Month

巽 SE	離 S	坤 SW
2 Black 二黑	7 Red 七赤	9 Purple 九紫
震 E 1 White 一白	3 Jade 三碧	5 Yellow 五黃 兑 W
6 White 六白	8 White 八白	4 Green 四綠
艮 NE	坎 N	乾 NW

Qi Men Three Nobles 三奇 :

Three Nobles 三奇 / Seasons	乙 Yi	丙 Bing	丁 Ding
立春 **Coming of Spring** Feb 4 - Feb 18	巽 Xun	中 Middle	乾 Qian
春分 **Spring Equinox** Mar 21 - Apr 4	艮 Gen	離 Li	坎 Kan
立夏 **Coming of Summer** May 6 - May 20	離 Li	坎 Kan	坤 Kun
夏至 **Summer Solstice** Jun 22 - Jul 6	巽 Xun	震 Zhen	坤 Kun
立秋 **Coming of Autumn** Aug 8 - Aug 23	乾 Qian	中 Middle	巽 Xun
秋分 **Autumn Equinox** Sept 23 - Oct 7	坤 Kun	坎 Kan	離 Li
立冬 **Coming of Winter** Nov 7 - Nov 22	坎 Kan	離 Li	艮 Gen
冬至 **Winter Solstice** Dec 22 - Jan 5	乾 Qian	兌 Dui	艮 Gen

535

Sectors to Avoid Opening Mountain 開山凶位 :

月 MONTH	月建 Month Establishment	月破 Month Destruction	月剋山家 Month Countering Sitting		陰府太歲 Yin Mansion Grand Duke	
寅 Tiger (Feb 4 - Mar 5) 正月 1st Month	寅 Yin Tiger	申 Shen Monkey	震 Zhen	巳 Si Snake	艮 Gen	巽 Xun
卯 Rabbit (Mar 6 - Apr 4) 二月 2nd Month	卯 Mao Rabbit	酉 You Rooster	艮 Gen		兌 Dui	乾 Qian
辰 Dragon (Apr 5 - May 5) 三月 3rd Month	辰 Chen Dragon	戌 Xu Dog	離 Li	丙 Bing Yang Fire	坎 Kan	坤 Kun
巳 Snake (May 6 - Jun 5) 四月 4th Month	巳 Si Snake	亥 Hai Pig	壬 Ren Yang Water	乙 Yi Yin Wood	乾 Qian	離 Li
午 Horse (Jun 6 - July 6) 五月 5th Month	午 Wu Horse	子 Zi Rat	—		坤 Kun	震 Zhen
未 Goat (July 7 - Aug 7) 六月 6th Month	未 Wei Goat	丑 Chou Ox	—		巽 Xun	艮 Gen
申 Monkey (Aug 8 - Sept 7) 七月 7th Month	申 Shen Monkey	寅 Yin Tiger	水 Water	山 Mountain	乾 Qian	兌 Dui
酉 Rooster (Sept 8 - Oct 7) 八月 8th Month	酉 You Rooster	卯 Mao Rabbit	土 Earth		坤 Kun	坎 Kan
戌 Dog (Oct 8 - Nov 6) 九月 9th Month	戌 Xu Dog	辰 Chen Dragon	震 Zhen	巳 Si Snake	離 Li	乾 Qian
亥 Pig (Nov 7 - Dec 6) 十月 10th Month	亥 Hai Pig	巳 Si Snake	艮 Gen		震 Zhen	坤 Kun
子 Rat (Dec 7 - Jan 5) 十一月 11th Month	子 Zi Rat	午 Wu Horse	—		艮 Gen	巽 Xun
丑 Ox (Jan 6 - Feb 3) 十二月 12th Month	丑 Chou Ox	未 Wei Goat	—		兌 Dui	乾 Qian

Negative Repair / Renovation Sectors 修方凶位 :

月 MONTH	天官符 Heavenly Officer Charm			地官符 Earth Officer Charm			小月建 Small Month Establishment		
寅 **Tiger** (Feb 4 - Mar 5) 正月 **1st Month**		中 Middle		未 *Wei* Goat	坤 *Kun*	申 *Shen* Monkey		中 Middle	
卯 **Rabbit** (Mar 6 - Apr 4) 二月 **2nd Month**	辰 *Chen* Dragon	巽 *Xun*	巳 *Si* Snake	壬 *Ren* Yang Water	坎 *Kan*	癸 *Gui* Yin Water	戌 *Xu* Dog	乾 *Qian*	亥 *Hai* Pig
辰 **Dragon** (Apr 5 - May 5) 三月 **3rd Month**	甲 *Jia* Yang Wood	震 *Zhen*	乙 *Yi* Yin Wood	丙 *Bing* Yang Fire	離 *Li*	丁 *Ding* Yin Fire	庚 *Geng* Yang Metal	兌 *Dui*	辛 *Xin* Yin Metal
巳 **Snake** (May 6 - Jun 5) 四月 **4th Month**	未 *Wei* Goat	坤 *Kun*	申 *Shen* Monkey	丑 *Chou* Ox	艮 *Gen*	寅 *Yin* Tiger	丑 *Chou* Ox	艮 *Gen*	寅 *Yin* Tiger
午 **Horse** (Jun 6 - July 6) 五月 **5th Month**	壬 *Ren* Yang Water	坎 *Kan*	癸 *Gui* Yin Water	庚 *Geng* Yang Metal	兌 *Dui*	辛 *Xin* Yin Metal	丙 *Bing* Yang Fire	離 *Li*	丁 *Ding* Yin Fire
未 **Goat** (July 7 - Aug 7) 六月 **6th Month**	丙 *Bing* Yang Fire	離 *Li*	丁 *Ding* Yin Fire	戊 *Xu* Dog	乾 *Qian*	亥 *Hai* Pig	壬 *Ren* Yang Water	坎 *Kan*	癸 *Gui* Yin Water
申 **Monkey** (Aug 8 - Sept 7) 七月 **7th Month**	丑 *Chou* Ox	艮 *Gen*	寅 *Yin* Tiger		中 Middle		未 *Wei* Goat	坤 *Kun*	申 *Shen* Monkey
酉 **Rooster** (Sept 8 - Oct 7) 八月 **8th Month**	庚 *Geng* Yang Metal	兌 *Dui*	辛 *Xin* Yin Metal	庚 *Geng* Yang Metal	兌 *Dui*	辛 *Xin* Yin Metal	甲 *Jia* Yang Wood	震 *Zhen*	乙 *Yi* Yin Wood
戌 **Dog** (Oct 8 - Nov 6) 九月 **9th Month**	戊 *Xu* Dog	乾 *Qian*	亥 *Hai* Pig	戊 *Xu* Dog	乾 *Qian*	亥 *Hai* Pig	辰 *Chen* Dragon	巽 *Xun*	巳 *Si* Snake
亥 **Pig** (Nov 7 - Dec 6) 十月 **10th Month**		中 Middle			中 Middle			中 Middle	
子 **Rat** (Dec 7 - Jan 5) 十一月 **11th Month**	庚 *Geng* Yang Metal	兌 *Dui*	辛 *Xin* Yin Metal	辰 *Chen* Dragon	巽 *Xun*	巳 *Si* Snake	戊 *Xu* Dog	乾 *Qian*	亥 *Hai* Pig
丑 **Ox** (Jan 6 - Feb 3) 十二月 **12th Month**	戊 *Xu* Dog	乾 *Qian*	亥 *Hai* Pig	甲 *Jia* Yang Wood	震 *Zhen*	乙 *Yi* Yin Wood	庚 *Geng* Yang Metal	兌 *Dui*	辛 *Xin* Yin Metal

Negative Repair / Renovation Sectors 修方凶位 :

月 MONTH	大月建 Big Month Establishment			飛大煞 Flying Great Sha			丙丁獨火 Bing Ding Lonely Fire	
寅 Tiger (Feb 4 - Mar 5) 正月 1st Month	中 Middle			戌 Xu Dog	乾 Qian	亥 Hai Pig	兌 Dui	艮 Gen
卯 Rabbit (Mar 6 - Apr 4) 二月 2nd Month	辰 Chen Dragon	巽 Xun	巳 Si Snake	中 Middle			乾 Qian	兌 Dui
辰 Dragon (Apr 5 - May 5) 三月 3rd Month	甲 Jia Yang Wood	震 Zhen	乙 Yi Yin Wood	辰 Chen Dragon	巽 Xun	巳 Si Snake	中 Middle	乾 Qian
巳 Snake (May 6 - Jun 5) 四月 4th Month	未 Wei Goat	坤 Kun	申 Shen Monkey	甲 Jia Yang Wood	震 Zhen	乙 Yi Yin Wood	中 Middle	
午 Horse (Jun 6 - July 6) 五月 5th Month	壬 Ren Yang Water	坎 Kan	癸 Gui Yin Water	未 Wei Goat	坤 Kun	申 Shen Monkey	巽 Xun	中 Middle
未 Goat (July 7 - Aug 7) 六月 6th Month	丙 Bing Yang Fire	離 Li	丁 Ding Yin Fire	壬 Ren Yang Water	坎 Kan	癸 Gui Yin Water	震 Zhen	巽 Xun
申 Monkey (Aug 8 - Sept 7) 七月 7th Month	丑 Chou Ox	艮 Gen	寅 Yin Tiger	丙 Bing Yang Fire	離 Li	丁 Ding Yin Fire	坤 Kun	震 Zhen
酉 Rooster (Sept 8 - Oct 7) 八月 8th Month	庚 Geng Yang Metal	兌 Dui	辛 Xin Yin Metal	丑 Chou Ox	艮 Gen	寅 Yin Tiger	坎 Kan	坤 Kun
戌 Dog (Oct 8 - Nov 6) 九月 9th Month	戌 Xu Dog	乾 Qian	亥 Hai Pig	庚 Geng Yang Metal	兌 Dui	辛 Xin Yin Metal	離 Li	坎 Kan
亥 Pig (Nov 7 - Dec 6) 十月 10th Month	中 Middle			戌 Xu Dog	乾 Qian	亥 Hai Pig	艮 Gen	離 Li
子 Rat (Dec 7 - Jan 5) 十一月 11th Month	辰 Chen Dragon	巽 Xun	巳 Si Snake	中 Middle			兌 Dui	艮 Gen
丑 Ox (Jan 6 - Feb 3) 十二月 12th Month	甲 Jia Yang Wood	震 Zhen	乙 Yi Yin Wood	庚 Geng Yang Metal	兌 Dui	辛 Xin Yin Metal	乾 Qian	兌 Dui

Negative Repair / Renovation Sectors 修方凶位 :

月 MONTH	月遊火 Month Wondering Fire	三煞 Monthly 3 Killings		
		劫煞 Robbery Sha	災煞 Calamity Sha	月煞 Month Sha
寅 Tiger (Feb 4 - Mar 5) 正月 1st Month	巽 Xun	亥 Hai Pig	子 Zi Rat	丑 Chou Ox
卯 Rabbit (Mar 6 - Apr 4) 二月 2nd Month	中 Middle	申 Shen Monkey	酉 You Rooster	戌 Xu Dog
辰 Dragon (Apr 5 - May 5) 三月 3rd Month	乾 Qian	巳 Si Snake	午 Wu Horse	未 Wei Goat
巳 Snake (May 6 - Jun 5) 四月 4th Month	兌 Dui	寅 Yin Tiger	卯 Mao Rabbit	辰 Chen Dragon
午 Horse (Jun 6 - July 6) 五月 5th Month	艮 Gen	亥 Hai Pig	子 Zi Rat	丑 Chou Ox
未 Goat (July 7 - Aug 7) 六月 6th Month	離 Li	申 Shen Monkey	酉 You Rooster	戌 Xu Dog
申 Monkey (Aug 8 - Sept 7) 七月 7th Month	坎 Kan	巳 Si Snake	午 Wu Horse	未 Wei Goat
酉 Rooster (Sept 8 - Oct 7) 八月 8th Month	坤 Kun	寅 Yin Tiger	卯 Mao Rabbit	辰 Chen Dragon
戌 Dog (Oct 8 - Nov 6) 九月 9th Month	震 Zhen	亥 Hai Pig	子 Zi Rat	丑 Chou Ox
亥 Pig (Nov 7 - Dec 6) 十月 10th Month	巽 Xun	申 Shen Monkey	酉 You Rooster	戌 Xu Dog
子 Rat (Dec 7 - Jan 5) 十一月 11th Month	中 Middle	巳 Si Snake	午 Wu Horse	未 Wei Goat
丑 Ox (Jan 6 - Feb 3) 十二月 12th Month	乾 Qian	寅 Yin Tiger	卯 Mao Rabbit	辰 Chen Dragon

Negative Repair / Renovation Sectors 修方凶位 :

月 MONTH	月刑 Month Punishment	月害 Month Harm	月厭 Month Detest
寅 **Tiger** (Feb 4 - Mar 5) 正月 **1st Month**	巳 Si Snake	巳 Si Snake	戌 Xu Dog
卯 **Rabbit** (Mar 6 - Apr 4) 二月 **2nd Month**	子 Zi Rat	辰 Chen Dragon	酉 You Rooster
辰 **Dragon** (Apr 5 - May 5) 三月 **3rd Month**	辰 Chen Dragon	卯 Mao Rabbit	申 Shen Monkey
巳 **Snake** (May 6 - Jun 5) 四月 **4th Month**	申 Shen Monkey	寅 Yin Tiger	未 Wei Goat
午 **Horse** (Jun 6 - July 6) 五月 **5th Month**	午 Wu Horse	丑 Chou Ox	午 Wu Horse
未 **Goat** (July 7 - Aug 7) 六月 **6th Month**	丑 Chou Ox	子 Zi Rat	巳 Si Snake
申 **Monkey** (Aug 8 - Sept 7) 七月 **7th Month**	寅 Yin Tiger	亥 Hai Pig	辰 Chen Dragon
酉 **Rooster** (Sept 8 - Oct 7) 八月 **8th Month**	酉 You Rooster	戌 Xu Dog	卯 Mao Rabbit
戌 **Dog** (Oct 8 - Nov 6) 九月 **9th Month**	未 Wei Goat	酉 You Rooster	寅 Yin Tiger
亥 **Pig** (Nov 7 - Dec 6) 十月 **10th Month**	亥 Hai Pig	申 Shen Monkey	丑 Chou Ox
子 **Rat** (Dec 7 - Jan 5) 十一月 **11th Month**	卯 Mao Rabbit	未 Wei Goat	子 Zi Rat
丑 **Ox** (Jan 6 - Feb 3) 十二月 **12th Month**	戌 Xu Dog	午 Wu Horse	亥 Hai Pig

戊午 (Wu Wu)
Earth Horse

戊午 (Wu Wu) Earth Horse

Heavenly Stem 天干	戊 **Yang Earth** (陽土)
Earthly Branch 地支	午 **Horse (Yang Fire** 陽火**)**
Hidden Stem 藏干	丁 **Yin Fire,** 己 **Yin Earth**
Na Yin 納音	天上火 **Fire from the skies**
Grand Duke 太歲	午 **Horse**
Xuan Kong Five Element 玄空五行	3 木 **Wood**
Gua Name 卦名	火風鼎 **The Cauldron**
Xuan Kong Period Luck 玄空卦運	**4**

Annual Positive Stars for Opening Mountain, Establishing Facing and Commencing Repairs 開山立向修方吉星：

歲德 **Duke Virtue**	戊 Wu **Yang Earth**
歲德合 **Duke Virtue Combo**	癸 Gui **Yin Water**
歲枝德 **Duke Branch Virtue**	亥 Hai **Pig**
陽貴人 **Yang Nobleman**	丑 Chou **Ox**
陰貴人 **Yin Nobleman**	未 Wei **Goat**
歲祿 **Duke Prosperous**	巳 Si **Snake**
歲馬 **Duke Horse**	申 Shen **Monkey**
奏書 **Decree**	巽 Xun
博士 **Professor**	乾 Qian

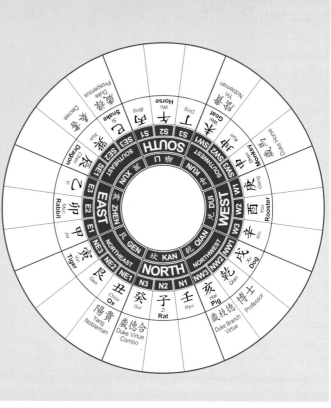

Annual Negative Stars for Opening Mountain, Establishing Facing and Commencing Repairs 開山立向修方凶星：

太歲 Grand Duke	歲破 Year Breaker	三煞 Three Killings			坐煞向煞 Sitting Sha Facing Sha				浮天空亡 Floating Heaven Emptiness	
午 Wu Horse	子 Zi Rat	亥 Hai Pig	子 Zi Rat	丑 Chou Ox	壬 Ren Yang Water	癸 Gui Yin Water	丙 Bing Yang Fire	丁 Ding Yin Fire	坤 Kun	乙 Yi Yin Wood

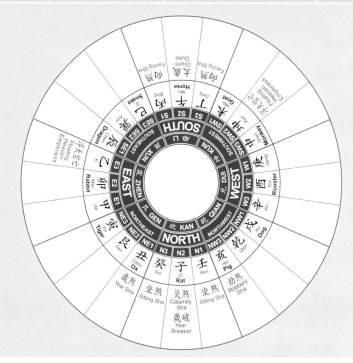

Annual San Yuan Purple White Stars 三元紫白九星：

上元 **Upper Period** **Period 1, 2, 3**			中元 **Middle Period** **Period 4, 5, 6**			下元 **Lower Period** **Period 7, 8, 9**		
巽SE	離S	坤SW	巽SE	離S	坤SW	巽SE	離S	坤SW
9	5	7	3	8	1	6	2	4
震E 8	1 戊午 Wu Wu Earth Horse	兌W 3	震E 2	4 戊午 Wu Wu Earth Horse	兌W 6	震E 5	7 戊午 Wu Wu Earth Horse	兌W 9
4	6	2	7	9	5	1	3	8
艮NE	坎N	乾NW	艮NE	坎N	乾NW	艮NE	坎N	乾NW

Mountain Covering Yellow Path 蓋山黃道：

貪狼 *Tan Lang* **Greedy Wolf**		巨門 *Ju Men* **Huge Door**		武曲 *Wu Qu* **Military Arts**				文曲 *Wen Qu* **Literary Arts**	
巽 *Xun* **SE2**	辛 *Xin* **W3**	艮 *Gen* **NE2**	丙 *Bing* **S1**	震 *Zhen* **E2**	庚 *Geng* **W1**	亥 *Hai* **NW3**	未 *Wei* **SW1**	乾 *Qian* **NW2**	甲 *Jia* **E1**

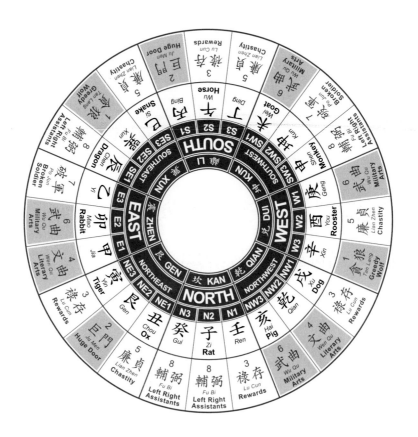

Heaven Penetrating Force 通天竅：

三合前方 **Facing Three Harmony**	坤申 Kun Shen	庚酉 Geng You	辛戌 Xin Xu
三合後方 **Sitting Three Harmony**	艮寅 Gen Yin	甲卯 Jia Mao	乙辰 Yi Chen

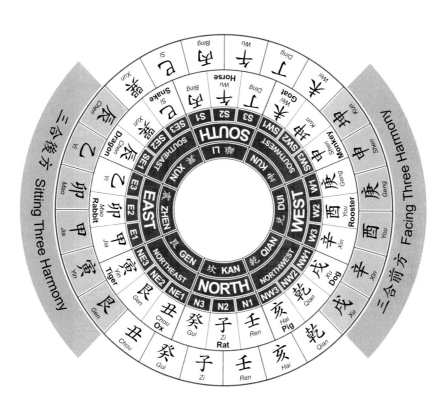

Moving Horse Six Ren Assessment 走馬六壬：

神后 Shen Hou **Holy Empress**	功曹 Gong Cao **Marshall**	天罡 Tian Gang **Heavenly Dipper**	勝光 Sheng Guang **Subliminal Bright**	傳送 Chuan Song **Great General**	河魁 He Kui **River Scholar**
丙午 Bing Wu	坤申 Kun Shen	辛戌 Xin Xu	壬子 Ren Zi	艮寅 Gen Yin	乙辰 Yi Chen

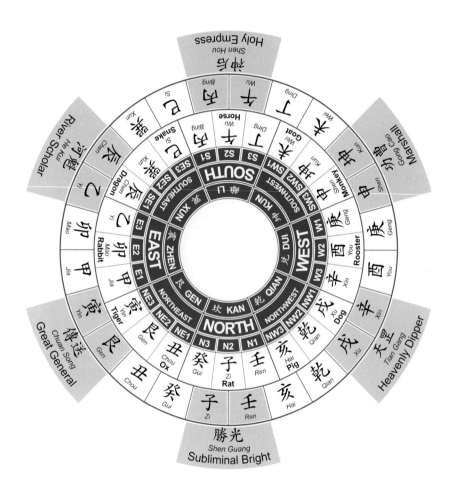

Four Advantages Three Cycles Star Plate 四利三元：

太陽 *Tai Yang* **Sun**	太陰 *Tai Yin* **Moon**	龍德 *Long De* **Dragon Virtue**	福德 *Fu De* **Fortune Virtue**
未 *Wei* **Goat**	酉 *You* **Rooster**	丑 *Chou* **Ox**	卯 *Mao* **Rabbit**

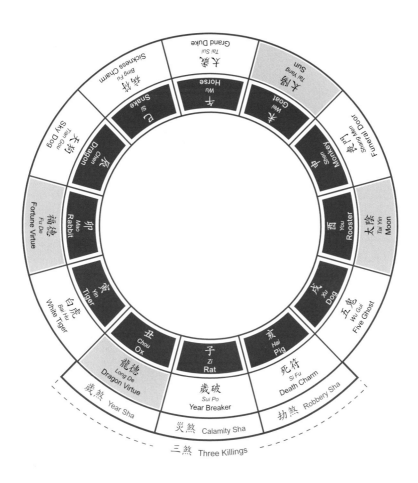

Negative Sectors For Opening Mountain 開山凶位：

年剋山家 Year Countering Sitting (冬至後 After Winter Solstice)

乾 Qian NW2	亥 Hai NW3	兌 Dui W2	丁 Ding S3

陰府太歲 Yin Fu Tai Sui **Yin Mansion Grand Duke**	六害 Liu Hai **Six Harm**	死符 Si Fu **Death Charm**	炙退 Zhi Tui **Roasting Star**
坤 Kun SW2　　震 Zhen E2	丑 Chou NE1	亥 Hai NW3	酉 You W2

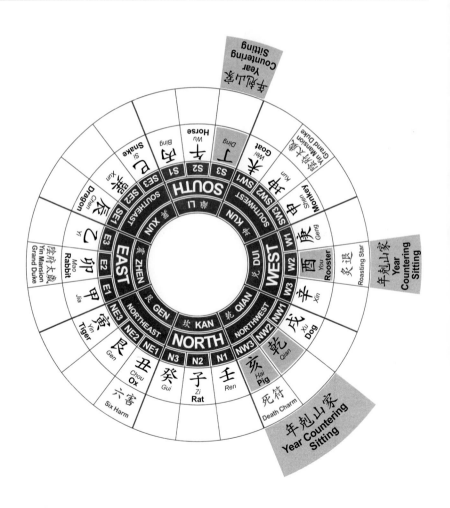

巡山羅喉 *Xun Shan Luo Hou* **Mountain Patrol Luo Hou Star**	病符 *Bing Fu* **Sickness Charm**
丁 *Ding* **S3**	巳 *Si* **Snake**

Negative Directions to Establish Facing 立向凶方：

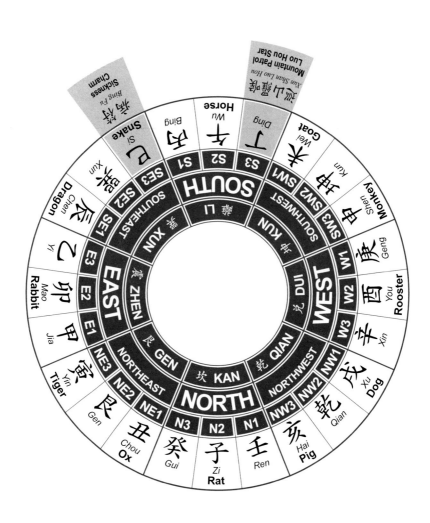

Negative Repair / Renovation Sectors Table 修方凶位表：

天官符 Heavenly Officer Charm	巳 *Si* Snake		飛廉 Flying Chaste	寅 *Yin* Tiger
地官符 Earthly Officer Charm	戌 *Xu* Dog		喪門 Funeral Door	申 *Shen* Monkey
大煞 Great Sha	午 *Wu* Horse		弔客 Suspended Guest	辰 *Chen* Dragon
大將軍 Big General	卯 *Mao* Rabbit		白虎 White Tiger	寅 *Yin* Tiger
力士 Strong Man	坤 *Kun*		金神 Golden God	申 *Shen* Monkey
蠶室 Silkworm Room	艮 *Gen*			酉 *You* Rooster
蠶官 Silkworm Officer	丑 *Chou* Ox			子 *Zi* Rat
蠶命 Silkworm Life	寅 *Yin* Tiger			丑 *Chou* Ox
歲刑 Duke Punishment	午 *Wu* Horse		獨火 Lonely Fire	兌 *Dui*
黃幡 Yellow Flag	戌 *Xu* Dog		五鬼 Five Ghost	戌 *Xu* Dog
豹尾 Leopard Tail	辰 *Chen* Dragon		破敗五鬼 Destructive Five Ghost	離 *Li*

Negative Repair / Renovation Sectors Diagram 修方凶位圖:

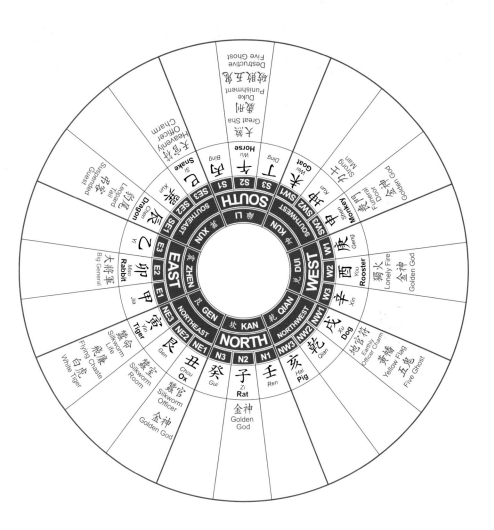

551

12-Month Auxiliary Stars Reference Table :
戊午年十二月，開山立向修方星表

Positive Monthly Stars 吉星方

月 MONTH	寅 Tiger (Feb 4 - Mar 5) 正月 1st Month	卯 Rabbit (Mar 6 - Apr 4) 二月 2nd Month	辰 Dragon (Apr 5 - May 5) 三月 3rd Month	巳 Snake (May 6 - Jun 5) 四月 4th Month	午 Horse (Jun 6 - July 6) 五月 5th Month	未 Goat (July 7 - Aug 7) 六月 6th Month
天道 Heavenly Path	南 South	西南 Southwest	北 North	西 West	西北 Northwest	東 East
天德 Heavenly Virtue	丁 Ding Yin Fire	坤 Kun （申）	壬 Ren Yang Water	辛 Xin Yin Metal	乾 Qian （亥）	甲 Jia Yang Wood
天德合 Heavenly Virtue Combo	壬 Ren Yang Water	（巳）	丁 Ding Yin Fire	丙 Bing Yang Fire	（寅）	己 Ji Yin Earth
月德 Monthly Virtue	丙 Bing Yang Fire	甲 Jia Yang Wood	壬 Ren Yang Water	庚 Geng Yang Metal	丙 Bing Yang Fire	甲 Jia Yang Wood
月德合 Monthly Virtue Combo	辛 Xin Yin Metal	己 Ji Yin Earth	丁 Ding Yin Fire	乙 Yi Yin Wood	辛 Xin Yin Metal	己 Ji Yin Earth
月空 Month Emptiness	壬 Ren Yang Water	庚 Geng Yang Metal	丙 Bing Yang Fire	甲 Jia Yang Wood	壬 Ren Yang Water	庚 Geng Yang Metal
陽貴人 Yang Nobleman	兌 Duin	乾 Qian	中 Middle	巽 Xun	震 Zhen	坤 Kun
陰貴人 Yin Nobleman	坎 Kan	離 Li	艮 Gen	兌 Dui	乾 Qian	中 Middle
飛天祿 Flying Heavenly Wealth	艮 Gen	兌 Dui	乾 Qian	中 Middle	坎 Kan	離 Li
飛天馬 Flying Heavenly Horse	坤 Kun	坎 Kan	離 Li	艮 Gen	兌 Dui	乾 Qian

12-Month Auxiliary Stars Reference Table :
戊午年十二月，開山立向修方星表

申 Monkey (Aug 8 - Sept 7)	酉 Rooster (Sept 8 - Oct 7)	戌 Dog (Oct 8 - Nov 6)	亥 Pig (Nov 7 - Dec 6)	子 Rat (Dec 7 - Jan 5)	丑 Ox (Jan 6 - Feb 3)	月 MONTH
七月 7th Month	八月 8th Month	九月 9th Month	十月 10th Month	十一月 11th Month	十二月 12th Month	
北 North	東北 Northeast	南 South	東 East	東南 Southeast	西 West	天道 Heavenly Path
癸 Gui Yin Water	艮 Gen （寅）	丙 Bing Yang Fire	乙 Yi Yin Wood	巽 Xun （巳）	庚 Geng Yang Metal	天德 Heavenly Virtue
戊 Wu Yang Earth	（亥）	辛 Xin Yin Metal	庚 Geng Yang Metal	（申）	乙 Yi Yin Wood	天德合 Heavenly Virtue Combo
壬 Ren Yang Water	庚 Geng Yang Metal	丙 Bing Yang Fire	甲 Jia Yang Wood	壬 Ren Yang Water	庚 Geng Yang Metal	月德 Monthly Virtue
丁 Ding Yin Fire	乙 Yi Yin Wood	辛 Xin Yin Metal	己 Ji Yin Earth	丁 Ding Yin Fire	乙 Yi Yin Wood	月德合 Monthly Virtue Combo
丙 Bing Yang Fire	甲 Jia Yang Wood	壬 Ren Yang Water	庚 Geng Yang Metal	丙 Bing Yang Fire	甲 Jia Yang Wood	月空 Month Emptiness
坎 Kan	離 Li	艮 Gen	兌 Dui	乾 Qian	中 Middle	陽貴人 Yang Nobleman
坎 Kan	離 Li	艮 Gen	兌 Dui	乾 Qian	中 Middle	陰貴人 Yin Nobleman
艮 Gen	兌 Dui	乾 Qian	中 Middle	巽 Xun	震 Zhen	飛天祿 Flying Heavenly Wealth
中 Middle	坎 Kan	離 Li	艮 Gen	兌 Dui	乾 Qian	飛天馬 Flying Heavenly Horse

Monthly Purple White Stars 月紫白九星：

寅 Tiger (Feb 4 - Mar 5) 正月 1st Month

巽 SE	離 S	坤 SW
7 Red 七赤	**3** Jade 三碧	**5** Yellow 五黄
6 White 六白 (震 E)	**8** White 八白	**1** White 一白 (兌 W)
2 Black 二黑 (艮 NE)	**4** Green 四綠 (坎 N)	**9** Purple 九紫 (乾 NW)

卯 Rabbit (Mar 6 - Apr 4) 二月 2nd Month

巽 SE	離 S	坤 SW
6 White 六白	**2** Black 二黑	**4** Green 四綠
5 Yellow 五黄 (震 E)	**7** Red 七赤	**9** Purple 九紫 (兌 W)
1 White 一白 (艮 NE)	**3** Jade 三碧 (坎 N)	**8** White 八白 (乾 NW)

辰 Dragon (Apr 5 - May 5) 三月 3rd Month

巽 SE	離 S	坤 SW
5 Yellow 五黄	**1** White 一白	**3** Jade 三碧
4 Green 四綠 (震 E)	**6** White 六白	**8** White 八白 (兌 W)
9 Purple 九紫 (艮 NE)	**2** Black 二黑 (坎 N)	**7** Red 七赤 (乾 NW)

巳 Snake (May 6 - Jun 5) 四月 4th Month

巽 SE	離 S	坤 SW
4 Green 四綠	**9** Purple 九紫	**2** Black 二黑
3 Jade 三碧 (震 E)	**5** Yellow 五黄	**7** Red 七赤 (兌 W)
8 White 八白 (艮 NE)	**1** White 一白 (坎 N)	**6** White 六白 (乾 NW)

午 Horse (Jun 6 - July 6) 五月 5th Month

巽 SE	離 S	坤 SW
3 Jade 三碧	**8** White 八白	**1** White 一白
2 Black 二黑 (震 E)	**4** Green 四綠	**6** White 六白 (兌 W)
7 Red 七赤 (艮 NE)	**9** Purple 九紫 (坎 N)	**5** Yellow 五黄 (乾 NW)

未 Goat (July 7 - Aug 7) 六月 6th Month

巽 SE	離 S	坤 SW
2 Black 二黑	**7** Red 七赤	**9** Purple 九紫
1 White 一白 (震 E)	**3** Jade 三碧	**5** Yellow 五黄 (兌 W)
6 White 六白 (艮 NE)	**8** White 八白 (坎 N)	**4** Green 四綠 (乾 NW)

申 Monkey (Aug 8 - Sept 7) 七月 7th Month

巽 SE	離 S	坤 SW
1 White 一白	**6** White 六白	**8** White 八白
9 Purple 九紫 (震 E)	**2** Black 二黑	**4** Green 四綠 (兌 W)
5 Yellow 五黄 (艮 NE)	**7** Red 七赤 (坎 N)	**3** Jade 三碧 (乾 NW)

酉 Rooster (Sept 8 - Oct 7) 八月 8th Month

巽 SE	離 S	坤 SW
9 Purple 九紫	**5** Yellow 五黄	**7** Red 七赤
8 White 八白 (震 E)	**1** White 一白	**3** Jade 三碧 (兌 W)
4 Green 四綠 (艮 NE)	**6** White 六白 (坎 N)	**2** Black 二黑 (乾 NW)

戌 Dog (Oct 8 - Nov 6) 九月 9th Month

巽 SE	離 S	坤 SW
8 White 八白	**4** Green 四綠	**6** White 六白
7 Red 七赤 (震 E)	**9** Purple 九紫	**2** Black 二黑 (兌 W)
3 Jade 三碧 (艮 NE)	**5** Yellow 五黄 (坎 N)	**1** White 一白 (乾 NW)

亥 Pig (Nov 7 - Dec 6) 十月 10th Month

巽 SE	離 S	坤 SW
7 Red 七赤	**3** Jade 三碧	**5** Yellow 五黄
6 White 六白 (震 E)	**8** White 八白	**1** White 一白 (兌 W)
2 Black 二黑 (艮 NE)	**4** Green 四綠 (坎 N)	**9** Purple 九紫 (乾 NW)

子 Rat (Dec 7 - Jan 5) 十一月 11th Month

巽 SE	離 S	坤 SW
6 White 六白	**2** Black 二黑	**4** Green 四綠
5 Yellow 五黄 (震 E)	**7** Red 七赤	**9** Purple 九紫 (兌 W)
1 White 一白 (艮 NE)	**3** Jade 三碧 (坎 N)	**8** White 八白 (乾 NW)

丑 Ox (Jan 6 - Feb 3) 十二月 12th Month

巽 SE	離 S	坤 SW
5 Yellow 五黄	**1** White 一白	**3** Jade 三碧
4 Green 四綠 (震 E)	**6** White 六白	**8** White 八白 (兌 W)
9 Purple 九紫 (艮 NE)	**2** Black 二黑 (坎 N)	**7** Red 七赤 (乾 NW)

Qi Men Three Nobles 三奇 :

Three Nobles 三奇 / Seasons	乙 Yi	丙 Bing	丁 Ding
立春 **Coming of Spring** Feb 4 - Feb 18	離 Li	坎 Kan	坤 Kun
春分 **Spring Equinox** Mar 21 - Apr 4	巽 Xun	中 **Middle**	乾 Qian
立夏 **Coming of Summer** May 6 - May 20	中 **Middle**	乾 Qian	兌 Dui
夏至 **Summer Solstice** Jun 22 - Jul 6	艮 Gen	兌 Dui	乾 Qian
立秋 **Coming of Autumn** Aug 8 - Aug 23	坎 Kan	離 Li	艮 Gen
秋分 **Autumn Equinox** Sept 23 - Oct 7	乾 Qian	中 **Middle**	巽 Xun
立冬 **Coming of Winter** Nov 7 - Nov 22	中 **Middle**	巽 Xun	震 Zhen
冬至 **Winter Solstice** Dec 22 - Jan 5	坤 Kun	震 Zhen	巽 Xun

Sectors to Avoid Opening Mountain 開山凶位 :

月 MONTH	月建 Month Establishment	月破 Month Destruction	月剋山家 Month Countering Sitting		陰府太歲 Yin Mansion Grand Duke	
寅 **Tiger** (Feb 4 - Mar 5) 正月 **1st Month**	寅 *Yin* **Tiger**	申 *Shen* **Monkey**	震 *Zhen*	巳 *Si* **Snake**	艮 *Gen*	巽 *Xun*
卯 **Rabbit** (Mar 6 - Apr 4) 二月 **2nd Month**	卯 *Mao* **Rabbit**	酉 *You* **Rooster**	艮 *Gen*		兌 *Dui*	乾 *Qian*
辰 **Dragon** (Apr 5 - May 5) 三月 **3rd Month**	辰 *Chen* **Dragon**	戌 *Xu* **Dog**	離 *Li*	丙 *Bing* **Yang Fire**	坎 *Kan*	坤 *Kun*
巳 **Snake** (May 6 - Jun 5) 四月 **4th Month**	巳 *Si* **Snake**	亥 *Hai* **Pig**	壬 *Ren* **Yang Water**	乙 *Yi* **Yin Wood**	乾 *Qian*	離 *Li*
午 **Horse** (Jun 6 - July 6) 五月 **5th Month**	午 *Wu* **Horse**	子 *Zi* **Rat**	–		坤 *Kun*	震 *Zhen*
未 **Goat** (July 7 - Aug 7) 六月 **6th Month**	未 *Wei*	丑 *Chou* **Ox**	–		巽 *Xun*	艮 *Gen*
申 **Monkey** (Aug 8 - Sept 7) 七月 **7th Month**	申 *Shen* **Monkey**	寅 *Yin* **Tiger**	水 **Water**	山 **Mountain**	乾 *Qian*	兌 *Dui*
酉 **Rooster** (Sept 8 - Oct 7) 八月 **8th Month**	酉 *You* **Rooster**	卯 *Mao* **Rabbit**	土 **Earth**		坤 *Kun*	坎 *Kan*
戌 **Dog** (Oct 8 - Nov 6) 九月 **9th Month**	戌 *Xu* **Dog**	辰 *Chen* **Dragon**	震 *Zhen*	巳 *Si* **Snake**	離 *Li*	乾 *Qian*
亥 **Pig** (Nov 7 - Dec 6) 十月 **10th Month**	亥 *Hai* **Pig**	巳 *Si* **Snake**	艮 *Gen*		震 *Zhen*	坤 *Kun*
子 **Rat** (Dec 7 - Jan 5) 十一月 **11th Month**	子 *Zi* **Rat**	午 *Wu* **Horse**	–		艮 *Gen*	巽 *Xun*
丑 **Ox** (Jan 6 - Feb 3) 十二月 **12th Month**	丑 *Chou* **Ox**	未 *Wei* **Goat**	–		兌 *Dui*	乾 *Qian*

Negative Repair / Renovation Sectors 修方凶位 :

月 MONTH	天官符 Heavenly Officer Charm			地官符 Earth Officer Charm			小月建 Small Month Establishment		
寅 Tiger (Feb 4 - Mar 5) 正月 1st Month	丑 Chou Ox	艮 Gen	寅 Yin Tiger	辰 Chen Dragon	巽 Xun	巳 Si Snake		中 Middle	
卯 Rabbit (Mar 6 - Apr 4) 二月 2nd Month	庚 Geng Yang Metal	兌 Dui	辛 Xin Yin Metal	甲 Jia Yang Wood	震 Zhen	乙 Yi Yin Wood	戌 Xu Dog	乾 Qian	亥 Hai Pig
辰 Dragon (Apr 5 - May 5) 三月 3rd Month	戌 Xu Dog	乾 Qian	亥 Hai Pig	未 Wei Goat	坤 Kun	申 Shen Monkey	庚 Geng Yang Metal	兌 Dui	辛 Xin Yin Metal
巳 Snake (May 6 - Jun 5) 四月 4th Month		中 Middle		壬 Ren Yang Water	坎 Kan	癸 Gui Yin Water	丑 Chou Ox	艮 Gen	寅 Yin Tiger
午 Horse (Jun 6 - July 6) 五月 5th Month	庚 Geng Yang Metal	兌 Dui	辛 Xin Yin Metal	丙 Bing Yang Fire	離 Li	丁 Ding Yin Fire	丙 Bing Yang Fire	離 Li	丁 Ding Yin Fire
未 Goat (July 7 - Aug 7) 六月 6th Month	戌 Xu Dog	乾 Qian	亥 Hai Pig	丑 Chou Ox	艮 Gen	寅 Yin Tiger	壬 Ren Yang Water	坎 Kan	癸 Gui Yin Water
申 Monkey (Aug 8 - Sept 7) 七月 7th Month		中 Middle		庚 Geng Yang Metal	兌 Dui	辛 Xin Yin Metal	未 Wei Goat	坤 Kun	申 Shen Monkey
酉 Rooster (Sept 8 - Oct 7) 八月 8th Month	辰 Chen Dragon	巽 Xun	巳 Si Snake	戌 Xu Dog	乾 Qian	亥 Hai Pig	甲 Jia Yang Wood	震 Zhen	乙 Yi Yin Wood
戌 Dog (Oct 8 - Nov 6) 九月 9th Month	甲 Jia Yang Wood	震 Zhen	乙 Yi Yin Wood		中 Middle		辰 Chen Dragon	巽 Xun	巳 Si Snake
亥 Pig (Nov 7 - Dec 6) 十月 10th Month	未 Wei Goat	坤 Kun	申 Shen Monkey	庚 Geng Yang Metal	兌 Dui	辛 Xin Yin Metal		中 Middle	
子 Rat (Dec 7 - Jan 5) 十一月 11th Month	壬 Ren Yang Water	坎 Kan	癸 Gui Yin Water	戌 Xu Dog	乾 Qian	亥 Hai Pig	戌 Xu Dog	乾 Qian	亥 Hai Pig
丑 Ox (Jan 6 - Feb 3) 十二月 12th Month	丙 Bing Yang Fire	離 Li	丁 Ding Yin Fire		中 Middle		庚 Geng Yang Metal	兌 Dui	辛 Xin Yin Metal

Negative Repair / Renovation Sectors 修方凶位：

月 MONTH	大月建 Big Month Establishment			飛大煞 Flying Great Sha			丙丁獨火 Bing Ding Lonely Fire	
寅 **Tiger** (Feb 4 - Mar 5) 正月 1st Month	丑 Chou Ox	艮 Gen	寅 Yin Tiger	丙 Bing Yang Fire	離 Li	丁 Ding Yin Fire	兌 Dui	艮 Gen
卯 **Rabbit** (Mar 6 - Apr 4) 二月 2nd Month	庚 Geng Yang Metal	兌 Dui	辛 Xin Yin Metal	丑 Chou Ox	艮 Gen	寅 Yin Tiger	乾 Qian	兌 Dui
辰 **Dragon** (Apr 5 - May 5) 三月 3rd Month	戌 Xu Dog	乾 Qian	亥 Hai Pig	庚 Geng Yang Metal	兌 Dui	辛 Xin Yin Metal	中 Middle	乾 Qian
巳 **Snake** (May 6 - Jun 5) 四月 4th Month	中 Middle			戌 Xu Dog	乾 Qian	亥 Hai Pig	中 Middle	
午 **Horse** (Jun 6 - July 6) 五月 5th Month	辰 Chen Dragon	巽 Xun	巳 Si Snake	中 Middle			巽 Xun	中 Middle
未 **Goat** (July 7 - Aug 7) 六月 6th Month	甲 Jia Yang Wood	震 Zhen	乙 Yi Yin Wood	庚 Geng Yang Metal	兌 Dui	辛 Xin Yin Metal	震 Zhen	巽 Xun
申 **Monkey** (Aug 8 - Sept 7) 七月 7th Month	未 Wei Goat	坤 Kun	申 Shen Monkey	戌 Xu Dog	乾 Qian	亥 Hai Pig	坤 Kun	震 Zhen
酉 **Rooster** (Sept 8 - Oct 7) 八月 8th Month	壬 Ren Yang Water	坎 Kan	癸 Gui Yin Water	中 Middle			坎 Kan	坤 Kun
戌 **Dog** (Oct 8 - Nov 6) 九月 9th Month	丙 Bing Yang Fire	離 Li	丁 Ding Yin Fire	辰 Chen Dragon	巽 Xun	巳 Si Snake	離 Li	坎 Kan
亥 **Pig** (Nov 7 - Dec 6) 十月 10th Month	丑 Chou Ox	艮 Gen	寅 Yin Tiger	甲 Jia Yang Wood	震 Zhen	乙 Yi Yin Wood	艮 Gen	離 Li
子 **Rat** (Dec 7 - Jan 5) 十一月 11th Month	庚 Geng Yang Metal	兌 Dui	辛 Xin Yin Metal	未 Wei Goat	坤 Kun	申 Shen Monkey	兌 Dui	艮 Gen
丑 **Ox** (Jan 6 - Feb 3) 十二月 12th Month	戌 Xu Dog	乾 Qian	亥 Hai Pig	壬 Ren Yang Water	坎 Kan	癸 Gui Yin Water	乾 Qian	兌 Dui

Negative Repair / Renovation Sectors 修方凶位 :

月 MONTH	月遊火 Month Wondering Fire	三煞 Monthly 3 Killings		
		劫煞 Robbery Sha	災煞 Calamity Sha	月煞 Month Sha
寅 **Tiger** (Feb 4 - Mar 5) 正月 **1st Month**	坤 Kun	亥 Hai Pig	子 Zi Rat	丑 Chou Ox
卯 **Rabbit** (Mar 6 - Apr 4) 二月 **2nd Month**	震 Zhen	申 Shen Monkey	酉 You Rooster	戌 Xu Dog
辰 **Dragon** (Apr 5 - May 5) 三月 **3rd Month**	巽 Xun	巳 Si Snake	午 Wu Horse	未 Wei Goat
巳 **Snake** (May 6 - Jun 5) 四月 **4th Month**	中 Middle	寅 Yin Tiger	卯 Mao Rabbit	辰 Chen Dragon
午 **Horse** (Jun 6 - July 6) 五月 **5th Month**	乾 Qian	亥 Hai Pig	子 Zi Rat	丑 Chou Ox
未 **Goat** (July 7 - Aug 7) 六月 **6th Month**	兌 Dui	申 Shen Monkey	酉 You Rooster	戌 Xu Dog
申 **Monkey** (Aug 8 - Sept 7) 七月 **7th Month**	艮 Gen	巳 Si Snake	午 Wu Horse	未 Wei Goat
酉 **Rooster** (Sept 8 - Oct 7) 八月 **8th Month**	離 Li	寅 Yin Tiger	卯 Mao Rabbit	辰 Chen Dragon
戌 **Dog** (Oct 8 - Nov 6) 九月 **9th Month**	坎 Kan	亥 Hai Pig	子 Zi Rat	丑 Chou Ox
亥 **Pig** (Nov 7 - Dec 6) 十月 **10th Month**	坤 Kun	申 Shen Monkey	酉 You Rooster	戌 Xu Dog
子 **Rat** (Dec 7 - Jan 5) 十一月 **11th Month**	震 Zhen	巳 Si Snake	午 Wu Horse	未 Wei Goat
丑 **Ox** (Jan 6 - Feb 3) 十二月 **12th Month**	巽 Xun	寅 Yin Tiger	卯 Mao Rabbit	辰 Chen Dragon

戊午 (Wu Wu) Earth Horse

Negative Repair / Renovation Sectors 修方凶位 :

月 MONTH	月刑 Month Punishment	月害 Month Harm	月厭 Month Detest
寅 **Tiger** (Feb 4 - Mar 5) 正月 **1st Month**	巳 Si Snake	巳 Si Snake	戌 Xu Dog
卯 **Rabbit** (Mar 6 - Apr 4) 二月 **2nd Month**	子 Zi Rat	辰 Chen Dragon	酉 You Rooster
辰 **Dragon** (Apr 5 - May 5) 三月 **3rd Month**	辰 Chen Dragon	卯 Mao Rabbit	申 Shen Monkey
巳 **Snake** (May 6 - Jun 5) 四月 **4th Month**	申 Shen Monkey	寅 Yin Tiger	未 Wei Goat
午 **Horse** (Jun 6 - July 6) 五月 **5th Month**	午 Wu Horse	丑 Chou Ox	午 Wu Horse
未 **Goat** (July 7 - Aug 7) 六月 **6th Month**	丑 Chou Ox	子 Zi Rat	巳 Si Snake
申 **Monkey** (Aug 8 - Sept 7) 七月 **7th Month**	寅 Yin Tiger	亥 Hai Pig	辰 Chen Dragon
酉 **Rooster** (Sept 8 - Oct 7) 八月 **8th Month**	酉 You Rooster	戌 Xu Dog	卯 Mao Rabbit
戌 **Dog** (Oct 8 - Nov 6) 九月 **9th Month**	未 Wei Goat	酉 You Rooster	寅 Yin Tiger
亥 **Pig** (Nov 7 - Dec 6) 十月 **10th Month**	亥 Hai Pig	申 Shen Monkey	丑 Chou Ox
子 **Rat** (Dec 7 - Jan 5) 十一月 **11th Month**	卯 Mao Rabbit	未 Wei Goat	子 Zi Rat
丑 **Ox** (Jan 6 - Feb 3) 十二月 **12th Month**	戌 Xu Dog	午 Wu Horse	亥 Hai Pig

560

戊申 (Wu Shen)
Earth Monkey

Heavenly Stem 天干	戊 Yang Earth (陽土)
Earthly Branch 地支	申 Monkey (Yang Metal 陽金)
Hidden Stem 藏干	庚 Yang Metal, 壬 Yang Water, 戊 Yang Earth
Na Yin 納音	大驛土 Earth from the main roads
Grand Duke 太歲	申 Monkey
Xuan Kong Five Element 玄空五行	2 火 Fire
Gua Name 卦名	䷺ 風水渙 Dispersing
Xuan Kong Period Luck 玄空卦運	6

Annual Positive Stars for Opening Mountain, Establishing Facing and Commencing Repairs 開山立向修方吉星:

歲德 Duke Virtue	戊 Wu Yang Earth
歲德合 Duke Virtue Combo	癸 Gui Yin Water
歲枝德 Duke Branch Virtue	丑 Chou Ox
陽貴人 Yang Nobleman	丑 Chou Ox
陰貴人 Yin Nobleman	未 Wei Goat
歲祿 Duke Prosperous	巳 Si Snake
歲馬 Duke Horse	寅 Yin Tiger
奏書 Decree	坤 Kun
博士 Professor	艮 Gen

Annual Negative Stars for Opening Mountain, Establishing Facing and Commencing Repairs 開山立向修方凶星：

太歲 Grand Duke	歲破 Year Breaker	三煞 Three Killings			坐煞向煞 Sitting Sha Facing Sha				浮天空亡 Floating Heaven Emptiness	
申 Shen Monkey	寅 Yin Tiger	巳 Si Snake	午 Wu Horse	未 Wei Goat	丙 Bing Yang Fire	丁 Ding Yin Fire	壬 Ren Yang Water	癸 Gui Yin Water	坤 Kun	乙 Yi Yin Wood

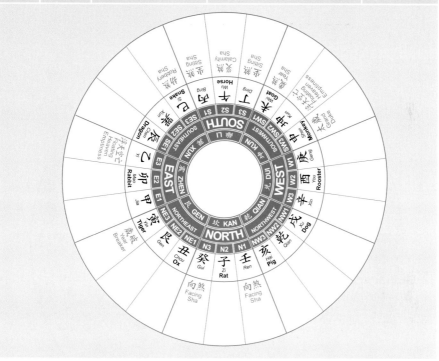

Annual San Yuan Purple White Stars 三元紫白九星：

上元 Upper Period Period 1, 2, 3			中元 Middle Period Period 4, 5, 6			下元 Lower Period Period 7, 8, 9		
巽SE 1	**離S** 6	**坤SW** 8	**巽SE** 4	**離S** 9	**坤SW** 2	**巽SE** 7	**離S** 3	**坤SW** 5
震E 9	**2** 戊申 Wu Shen Earth Monkey	**兌W** 4	**震E** 3	**5** 戊申 Wu Shen Earth Monkey	**兌W** 7	**震E** 6	**8** 戊申 Wu Shen Earth Monkey	**兌W** 1
艮NE 5	**坎N** 7	**乾NW** 3	**艮NE** 8	**坎N** 1	**乾NW** 6	**艮NE** 2	**坎N** 4	**乾NW** 9

Mountain Covering Yellow Path 蓋山黃道：

貪狼 *Tan Lang* **Greedy Wolf**		巨門 *Ju Men* **Huge Door**				武曲 *Wu Qu* **Military Arts**		文曲 *Wen Qu* **Literary Arts**			
坤 *Kun* SW2	乙 *Yi* E3	坎 *Kan* N2	癸 *Gui* N3	申 *Shen* SW3	辰 *Chen* SE1	乾 *Qian* NW2	甲 *Jia* E1	震 *Zhen* E2	庚 *Geng* W1	亥 *Hai* NW3	未 *Wei* SW1

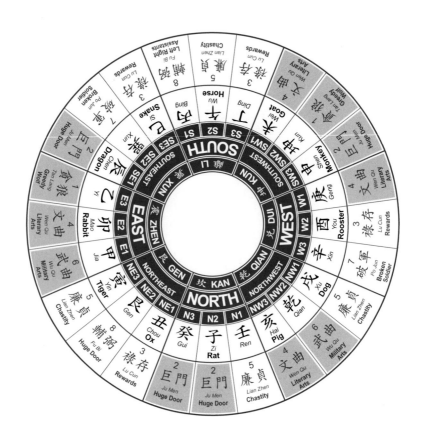

Heaven Penetrating Force 通天竅:

三合前方 **Facing Three Harmony**	艮寅 *Gen Yin*	甲卯 *Jia Mao*	乙辰 *Yi Chen*
三合後方 **Sitting Three Harmony**	坤申 *Kun Shen*	庚酉 *Geng You*	辛戌 *Xin Xu*

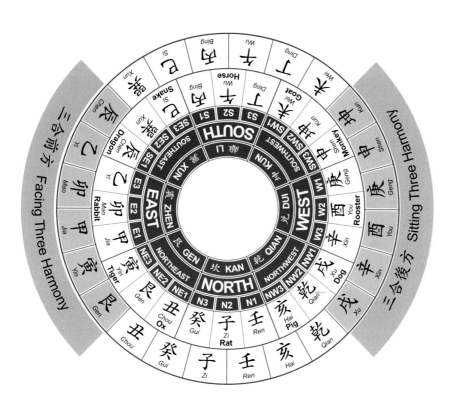

Moving Horse Six Ren Assessment 走馬六壬：

神后 *Shen Hou* **Holy Empress**	功曹 *Gong Cao* **Marshall**	天罡 *Tian Gang* **Heavenly Dipper**	勝光 *Sheng Guang* **Subliminal Bright**	傳送 *Chuan Song* **Great General**	河魁 *He Kui* **River Scholar**
乙辰 *Yi Chen*	丙午 *Bing Wu*	坤申 *Kun Shen*	辛戌 *Xin Xu*	壬子 *Ren Zi*	艮寅 *Gen Yin*

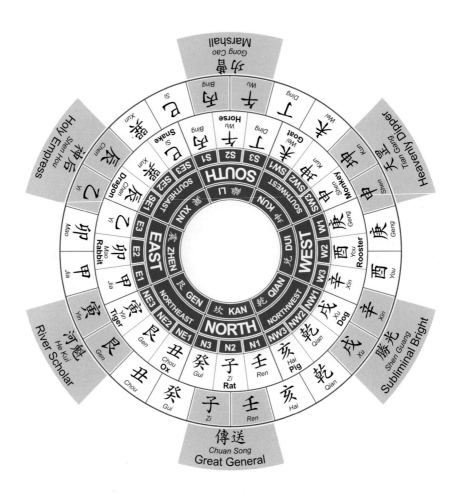

Four Advantages Three Cycles Star Plate 四利三元：

太陽 *Tai Yang* **Sun**	太陰 *Tai Yin* **Moon**	龍德 *Long De* **Dragon Virtue**	福德 *Fu De* **Fortune Virtue**
酉 *You* **Rooster**	亥 *Hai* **Pig**	卯 *Mao* **Rabbit**	巳 *Si* **Snake**

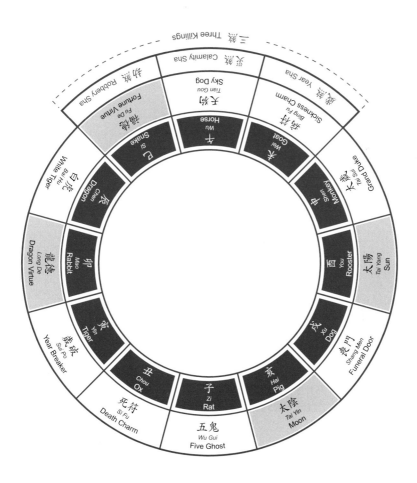

567

Negative Sectors For Opening Mountain 開山凶位：

年尅山家 Year Countering Sitting

離	壬	丙	乙
Li	*Ren*	*Bing*	*Yi*
S2	N1	S1	E3

陰府太歲		六害	死符	炙退
Yin Fu Tai Sui		*Liu Hai*	*Si Fu*	*Zhi Tui*
Yin Mansion Grand Duke		**Six Harm**	**Death Charm**	**Roasting Star**
坤	震	亥	丑	卯
Kun	*Zhen*	*Hai*	*Chou*	*Mao*
SW2	E2	NW3	NE1	E2

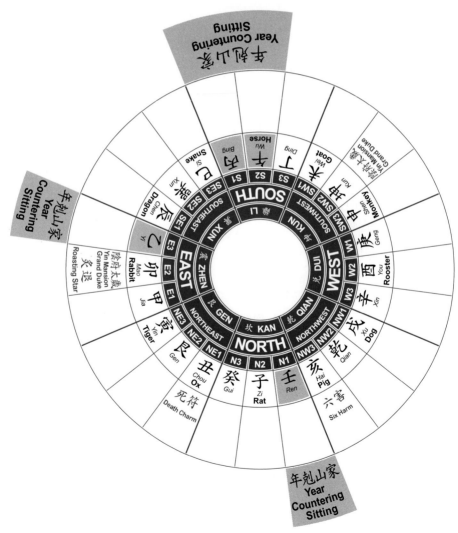

568

Negative Directions to Establish Facing 立向凶方:

巡山羅喉 *Xun Shan Luo Hou* **Mountain Patrol Luo Hou Star**	病符 *Bing Fu* **Sickness Charm**
庚 *Geng* **W1**	未 *Wei* **SW1**

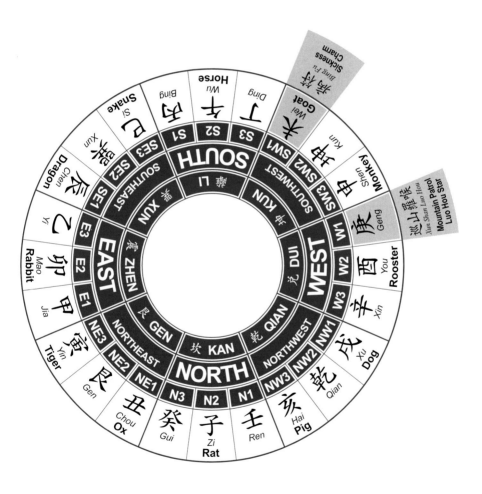

Negative Repair / Renovation Sectors Table 修方凶位表：

天官符 Heavenly Officer Charm	亥 Hai Pig	飛廉 Flying Chaste	辰 Chen Dragon
地官符 Earthly Officer Charm	子 Zi Rat	喪門 Funeral Door	戌 Xu Dog
大煞 Great Sha	子 Zi Rat	弔客 Suspended Guest	午 Wu Horse
大將軍 Big General	午 Wu Horse	白虎 White Tiger	辰 Chen Dragon
力士 Strong Man	乾 Qian	金神 Golden God	申 Shen Monkey
蠶室 Silkworm Room	巽 Xun		酉 You Rooster
蠶官 Silkworm Officer	辰 Chen Dragon		子 Zi Rat
蠶命 Silkworm Life	巳 Si Snake		丑 Chou Ox
歲刑 Duke Punishment	寅 Yin Tiger	獨火 Lonely Fire	離 Li
黃幡 Yellow Flag	辰 Chen Dragon	五鬼 Five Ghost	申 Shen Monkey
豹尾 Leopard Tail	戌 Xu Dog	破敗五鬼 Destructive Five Ghost	離 Li

Negative Repair / Renovation Sectors Diagram 修方凶位圖:

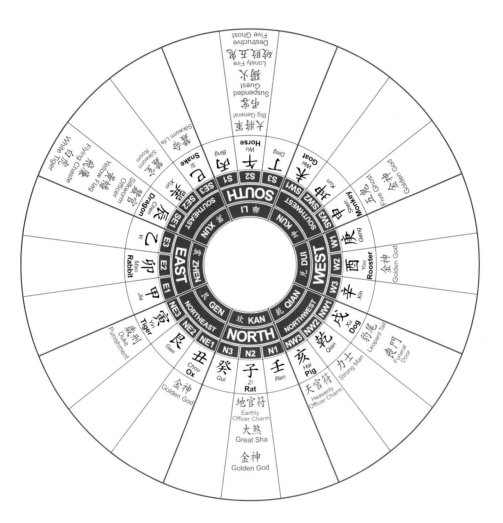

12-Month Auxiliary Stars Reference Table :
戊申年十二月，開山立向修方星表

Positive Monthly Stars 吉星方

月 MONTH	寅 Tiger (Feb 4 - Mar 5) 正月 1st Month	卯 Rabbit (Mar 6 - Apr 4) 二月 2nd Month	辰 Dragon (Apr 5 - May 5) 三月 3rd Month	巳 Snake (May 6 - Jun 5) 四月 4th Month	午 Horse (Jun 6 - July 6) 五月 5th Month	未 Goat (July 7 - Aug 7) 六月 6th Month
天道 Heavenly Path	南 South	西南 Southwest	北 North	西 West	西北 Northwest	東 East
天德 Heavenly Virtue	丁 Ding Yin Fire	坤 Kun (申)	壬 Ren Yang Water	辛 Xin Yin Metal	乾 Qian (亥)	甲 Jia Yang Wood
天德合 Heavenly Virtue Combo	壬 Ren Yang Water	(巳)	丁 Ding Yin Fire	丙 Bing Yang Fire	(寅)	己 Ji Yin Earth
月德 Monthly Virtue	丙 Bing Yang Fire	甲 Jia Yang Wood	壬 Ren Yang Water	庚 Geng Yang Metal	丙 Bing Yang Fire	甲 Jia Yang Wood
月德合 Monthly Virtue Combo	辛 Xin Yin Metal	己 Ji Yin Earth	丁 Ding Yin Fire	乙 Yi Yin Wood	辛 Xin Yin Metal	己 Ji Yin Earth
月空 Month Emptiness	壬 Ren Yang Water	庚 Geng Yang Metal	丙 Bing Yang Fire	甲 Jia Yang Wood	壬 Ren Yang Water	庚 Geng Yang Metal
陽貴人 Yang Nobleman	兌 Dui	乾 Qian	中 Middle	巽 Xun	震 Zhen	坤 Kun
陰貴人 Yin Nobleman	坎 Kan	離 Lii	艮 Gen	兌 Dui	乾 Qian	中 Middle
飛天祿 Flying Heavenly Wealth	艮 Gen	兌 Dui	乾 Qian	中 Middle	坎 Kan	離 Lii
飛天馬 Flying Heavenly Horse	中 Middle	坎 Kan	離 Li	艮 Gen	兌 Dui	乾 Qian

12-Month Auxiliary Stars Reference Table :
戊申年十二月，開山立向修方星表

申 Monkey (Aug 8 - Sept 7) 七月 7th Month	酉 Rooster (Sept 8 - Oct 7) 八月 8th Month	戌 Dog (Oct 8 - Nov 6) 九月 9th Month	亥 Pig (Nov 7 - Dec 6) 十月 10th Month	子 Rat (Dec 7 - Jan 5) 十一月 11th Month	丑 Ox (Jan 6 - Feb 3) 十二月 12th Month	月 MONTH
北 North	東北 Northeast	南 South	東 East	東南 Southeast	西 West	天道 Heavenly Path
癸 Gui Yin Water	艮 Gen (寅)	丙 Bing Yang Fire	乙 Yi Yin Wood	巽 Xun (巳)	庚 Geng Yang Metal	天德 Heavenly Virtue
戊 Wu Yang Earth	(亥)	辛 Xin Yin Metal	庚 Geng Yang Metal	(申)	乙 Yi Yin Wood	天德合 Heavenly Virtue Combo
壬 Ren Yang Water	庚 Geng Yang Metal	丙 Bing Yang Fire	甲 Jia Yang Wood	壬 Ren Yang Water	庚 Geng Yang Metal	月德 Monthly Virtue
丁 Ding Yin Fire	乙 Yi Yin Wood	辛 Xin Yin Metal	己 Ji Yin Earth	丁 Ding Yin Fire	乙 Yi Yin Wood	月德合 Monthly Virtue Combo
丙 Bing Yang Fire	甲 Jia Yang Wood	壬 Ren Yang Water	庚 Geng Yang Metal	丙 Bing Yang Fire	甲 Jia Yang Wood	月空 Month Emptiness
坎 Kan	離 Lii	艮 Gen	兌 Dui	乾 Qian	中 Middle	陽貴人 Yang Nobleman
坎 Kan	離 Lii	艮 Gen	兌 Dui	乾 Qian	中 Middle	陰貴人 Yin Nobleman
艮 Gen	兌 Dui	乾 Qian	中 Middle	巽 Xun	震 Zhen	飛天祿 Flying Heavenly Wealth
中 Middle	巽 Xun	震 Zhen	坤 Kun	坎 Kan	離 Lii	飛天馬 Flying Heavenly Horse

Monthly Purple White Stars 月紫白九星 :

寅 Tiger (Feb 4 - Mar 5) 正月 1st Month

巽 SE	離 S	坤 SW
1 White 一白	6 White 六白	8 White 八白
震 E 9 Purple 九紫	2 Black 二黑	4 Green 四綠 兌 W
艮 NE 5 Yellow 五黃	坎 N 7 Red 七赤	乾 NW 3 Jade 三碧

卯 Rabbit (Mar 6 - Apr 4) 二月 2nd Month

巽 SE	離 S	坤 SW
9 Purple 九紫	5 Yellow 五黃	7 Red 七赤
震 E 8 White 八白	1 White 一白	3 Jade 三碧 兌 W
艮 NE 4 Green 四綠	坎 N 6 White 六白	乾 NW 2 Black 二黑

辰 Dragon (Apr 5 - May 5) 三月 3rd Month

巽 SE	離 S	坤 SW
8 White 八白	4 Green 四綠	6 White 六白
震 E 7 Red 七赤	9 Purple 九紫	2 Black 二黑 兌 W
艮 NE 3 Jade 三碧	坎 N 5 Yellow 五黃	乾 NW 1 White 一白

巳 Snake (May 6 - Jun 5) 四月 4th Month

巽 SE	離 S	坤 SW
7 Red 七赤	3 Jade 三碧	5 Yellow 五黃
震 E 6 White 六白	8 White 八白	1 White 一白 兌 W
艮 NE 2 Black 二黑	坎 N 4 Green 四綠	乾 NW 9 Purple 九紫

午 Horse (Jun 6 - July 6) 五月 5th Month

巽 SE	離 S	坤 SW
6 White 六白	2 Black 二黑	4 Green 四綠
震 E 5 Yellow 五黃	7 Red 七赤	9 Purple 九紫 兌 W
艮 NE 1 White 一白	坎 N 3 Jade 三碧	乾 NW 8 White 八白

未 Goat (July 7 - Aug 7) 六月 6th Month

巽 SE	離 S	坤 SW
5 Yellow 五黃	1 White 一白	3 Jade 三碧
震 E 4 Green 四綠	6 White 六白	8 White 八白 兌 W
艮 NE 9 Purple 九紫	坎 N 2 Black 二黑	乾 NW 7 Red 七赤

申 Monkey (Aug 8 - Sept 7) 七月 7th Month

巽 SE	離 S	坤 SW
4 Green 四綠	9 Purple 九紫	2 Black 二黑
震 E 3 Jade 三碧	5 Yellow 五黃	7 Red 七赤 兌 W
艮 NE 8 White 八白	坎 N 1 White 一白	乾 NW 6 White 六白

酉 Rooster (Sept 8 - Oct 7) 八月 8th Month

巽 SE	離 S	坤 SW
3 Jade 三碧	8 White 八白	1 White 一白
震 E 2 Black 二黑	4 Green 四綠	6 White 六白 兌 W
艮 NE 7 Red 七赤	坎 N 9 Purple 九紫	乾 NW 5 Yellow 五黃

戌 Dog (Oct 8 - Nov 6) 九月 9th Month

巽 SE	離 S	坤 SW
2 Black 二黑	7 Red 七赤	9 Purple 九紫
震 E 1 White 一白	3 Jade 三碧	5 Yellow 五黃 兌 W
艮 NE 6 White 六白	坎 N 8 White 八白	乾 NW 4 Green 四綠

亥 Pig (Nov 7 - Dec 6) 十月 10th Month

巽 SE	離 S	坤 SW
1 White 一白	6 White 六白	8 White 八白
震 E 9 Purple 九紫	2 Black 二黑	4 Green 四綠 兌 W
艮 NE 5 Yellow 五黃	坎 N 7 Red 七赤	乾 NW 3 Jade 三碧

子 Rat (Dec 7 - Jan 5) 十一月 11th Month

巽 SE	離 S	坤 SW
9 Purple 九紫	5 Yellow 五黃	7 Red 七赤
震 E 8 White 八白	1 White 一白	3 Jade 三碧 兌 W
艮 NE 4 Green 四綠	坎 N 6 White 六白	乾 NW 2 Black 二黑

丑 Ox (Jan 6 - Feb 3) 十二月 12th Month

巽 SE	離 S	坤 SW
8 White 八白	4 Green 四綠	6 White 六白
震 E 7 Red 七赤	9 Purple 九紫	2 Black 二黑 兌 W
艮 NE 3 Jade 三碧	坎 N 5 Yellow 五黃	乾 NW 1 White 一白

Qi Men Three Nobles 三奇 :

Three Nobles 三奇 / Seasons	乙 Yi	丙 Bing	丁 Ding
立春 **Coming of Spring** Feb 4 - Feb 18	艮 Gen	離 Li	坎 Kan
春分 **Spring Equinox** Mar 21 - Apr 4	震 Zhen	巽 Xun	中 **Middle**
立夏 **Coming of Summer** May 6 - May 20	巽 Xun	中 **Middle**	乾 Qian
夏至 **Summer Solstice** Jun 22 - Jul 6	離 Li	艮 Gen	兌 Dui
立秋 **Coming of Autumn** Aug 8 - Aug 23	坤 Kun	坎 Kan	離 Li
秋分 **Autumn Equinox** Sept 23 - Oct 7	兌 Dui	乾 Qian	中 **Middle**
立冬 **Coming of Winter** Nov 7 - Nov 22	乾 Qian	中 **Middle**	巽 Xun
冬至 **Winter Solstice** Dec 22 - Jan 5	坎 Kan	坤 Kun	震 Zhen

Sectors to Avoid Opening Mountain 開山凶位 :

月 MONTH	月建 Month Establishment	月破 Month Destruction	月剋山家 Month Countering Sitting		陰府太歲 Yin Mansion Grand Duke	
寅 **Tiger** (Feb 4 - Mar 5) 正月 **1st Month**	寅 *Yin* **Tiger**	申 *Shen* **Monkey**	震 *Zhen*	巳 *Si* **Snake**	艮 *Gen*	巽 *Xun*
卯 **Rabbit** (Mar 6 - Apr 4) 二月 **2nd Month**	卯 *Mao* **Rabbit**	酉 *You* **Rooster**	艮 *Gen*		兌 *Dui*	乾 *Qian*
辰 **Dragon** (Apr 5 - May 5) 三月 **3rd Month**	辰 *Chen* **Dragon**	戌 *Xu* **Dog**	離 *Li*	丙 *Bing* **Yang Fire**	坎 *Kan*	坤 *Kun*
巳 **Snake** (May 6 - Jun 5) 四月 **4th Month**	巳 *Si* **Snake**	亥 *Hai* **Pig**	壬 *Ren* **Yang Water**	乙 *Yi* **Yin Wood**	乾 *Qian*	離 *Li*
午 **Horse** (Jun 6 - July 6) 五月 **5th Month**	午 *Wu* **Horse**	子 *Zi* **Rat**	–		坤 *Kun*	震 *Zhen*
未 **Goat** (July 7 - Aug 7) 六月 **6th Month**	未 *Wei* **Goat**	丑 *Chou* **Ox**	–		巽 *Xun*	艮 *Gen*
申 **Monkey** (Aug 8 - Sept 7) 七月 **7th Month**	申 *Shen* **Monkey**	寅 *Yin* **Tiger**	水 **Water**	山 **Mountain**	乾 *Qian*	兌 *Dui*
酉 **Rooster** (Sept 8 - Oct 7) 八月 **8th Month**	酉 *You* **Rooster**	卯 *Mao* **Rabbit**	土 **Earth**		坤 *Kun*	坎 *Kan*
戌 **Dog** (Oct 8 - Nov 6) 九月 **9th Month**	戌 *Xu* **Dog**	辰 *Chen* **Dragon**	震 *Zhen*	巳 *Si* **Snake**	離 *Li*	乾 *Qian*
亥 **Pig** (Nov 7 - Dec 6) 十月 **10th Month**	亥 *Hai* **Pig**	巳 *Si* **Snake**	艮 *Gen*		震 *Zhen*	坤 *Kun*
子 **Rat** (Dec 7 - Jan 5) 十一月 **11th Month**	子 *Zi* **Rat**	午 *Wu* **Horse**	–		艮 *Gen*	巽 *Xun*
丑 **Ox** (Jan 6 - Feb 3) 十二月 **12th Month**	丑 *Chou* **Ox**	未 *Wei* **Goat**	–		兌 *Dui*	乾 *Qian*

Negative Repair / Renovation Sectors 修方凶位 ：

月 MONTH	天官符 Heavenly Officer Charm			地官符 Earth Officer Charm			小月建 Small Month Establishment		
寅 Tiger (Feb 4 - Mar 5) 正月 1st Month		中 Middle		戌 Xu Dog	乾 Qian	亥 Hai Pig		中 Middle	
卯 Rabbit (Mar 6 - Apr 4) 二月 2nd Month	辰 Chen Dragon	巽 Xun	巳 Si Snake		中 Middle		戌 Xu Dog	乾 Qian	亥 Hai Pig
辰 Dragon (Apr 5 - May 5) 三月 3rd Month	甲 Jia Yang Wood	震 Zhen	乙 Yi Yin Wood	辰 Chen Dragon	巽 Xun	巳 Si Snake	庚 Geng Yang Metal	兌 Dui	辛 Xin Yin Metal
巳 Snake (May 6 - Jun 5) 四月 4th Month	未 Wei Goat	坤 Kun	申 Shen Monkey	甲 Jia Yang Wood	震 Zhen	乙 Yi Yin Wood	丑 Chou Ox	艮 Gen	寅 Yin Tiger
午 Horse (Jun 6 - July 6) 五月 5th Month	壬 Ren Yang Water	坎 Kan	癸 Gui Yin Water	未 Wei Goat	坤 Kun	申 Shen Monkey	丙 Bing Yang Fire	離 Li	丁 Ding Yin Fire
未 Goat (July 7 - Aug 7) 六月 6th Month	丙 Bing Yang Fire	離 Li	丁 Ding Yin Fire	壬 Ren Yang Water	坎 Kan	癸 Gui Yin Water	壬 Ren Yang Water	坎 Kan	癸 Gui Yin Water
申 Monkey (Aug 8 - Sept 7) 七月 7th Month	丑 Chou Ox	艮 Gen	寅 Yin Tiger	丙 Bing Yang Fire	離 Li	丁 Ding Yin Fire	未 Wei Goat	坤 Kun	申 Shen Monkey
酉 Rooster (Sept 8 - Oct 7) 八月 8th Month	庚 Geng Yang Metal	兌 Dui	辛 Xin Yin Metal	丑 Chou Ox	艮 Gen	寅 Yin Tiger	甲 Jia Yang Wood	震 Zhen	乙 Yi Yin Wood
戌 Dog (Oct 8 - Nov 6) 九月 9th Month	戌 Xu Dog	乾 Qian	亥 Hai Pig	庚 Geng Yang Metal	兌 Dui	辛 Xin Yin Metal	辰 Chen Dragon	巽 Xun	巳 Si Snake
亥 Pig (Nov 7 - Dec 6) 十月 10th Month		中 Middle		戌 Xu Dog	乾 Qian	亥 Hai Pig		中 Middle	
子 Rat (Dec 7 - Jan 5) 十一月 11th Month	庚 Geng Yang Metal	兌 Dui	辛 Xin Yin Metal		中 Middle		戌 Xu Dog	乾 Qian	亥 Hai Pig
丑 Ox (Jan 6 - Feb 3) 十二月 12th Month	戌 Xu Dog	乾 Qian	亥 Hai Pig	庚 Geng Yang Metal	兌 Dui	辛 Xin Yin Metal	庚 Geng Yang Metal	兌 Dui	辛 Xin Yin Metal

Negative Repair / Renovation Sectors 修方凶位 :

月 MONTH	大月建 Big Month Establishment			飛大煞 Flying Great Sha			丙丁獨火 Bing Ding Lonely Fire	
寅 Tiger (Feb 4 - Mar 5) 正月 1st Month	未 Wei Goat	坤 Kun	申 Shen Monkey	戌 Xu Dog	乾 Qian	亥 Hai Pig	兌 Dui	艮 Gen
卯 Rabbit (Mar 6 - Apr 4) 二月 2nd Month	壬 Ren Yang Water	坎 Kan	癸 Gui Yin Water	中 Middle			乾 Qian	兌 Dui
辰 Dragon (Apr 5 - May 5) 三月 3rd Month	丙 Bing Yang Fire	離 Li	丁 Ding Yin Fire	辰 Chen Dragon	巽 Xun	巳 Si Snake	中 Middle	乾 Qian
巳 Snake (May 6 - Jun 5) 四月 4th Month	丑 Chou Ox	艮 Gen	寅 Yin Tiger	甲 Jia Yang Wood	震 Zhen	乙 Yi Yin Wood	中 Middle	
午 Horse (Jun 6 - July 6) 五月 5th Month	庚 Geng Yang Metal	兌 Dui	辛 Xin Yin Metal	未 Wei Goat	坤 Kun	申 Shen Monkey	巽 Xun	中 Middle
未 Goat (July 7 - Aug 7) 六月 6th Month	戌 Xu Dog	乾 Qian	亥 Hai Pig	壬 Ren Yang Water	坎 Kan	癸 Gui Yin Water	震 Zhen	巽 Xun
申 Monkey (Aug 8 - Sept 7) 七月 7th Month	中 Middle			丙 Bing Yang Fire	離 Li	丁 Ding Yin Fire	坤 Kun	震 Zhen
酉 Rooster (Sept 8 - Oct 7) 八月 8th Month	辰 Chen Dragon	巽 Xun	巳 Si Snake	丑 Chou Ox	艮 Gen	寅 Yin Tiger	坎 Kan	坤 Kun
戌 Dog (Oct 8 - Nov 6) 九月 9th Month	甲 Jia Yang Wood	震 Zhen	乙 Yi Yin Wood	庚 Geng Yang Metal	兌 Dui	辛 Xin Yin Metal	離 Li	坎 Kan
亥 Pig (Nov 7 - Dec 6) 十月 10th Month	未 Wei Goat	坤 Kun	申 Shen Monkey	戌 Xu Dog	乾 Qian	亥 Hai Pig	艮 Gen	離 Li
子 Rat (Dec 7 - Jan 5) 十一月 11th Month	壬 Ren Yang Water	坎 Kan	癸 Gui Yin Water	中 Middle			兌 Dui	艮 Gen
丑 Ox (Jan 6 - Feb 3) 十二月 12th Month	丙 Bing Yang Fire	離 Li	丁 Ding Yin Fire	庚 Geng Yang Metal	兌 Dui	辛 Xin Yin Metal	乾 Qian	兌 Dui

Negative Repair / Renovation Sectors 修方凶位：

月 MONTH	月遊火 Month Wondering Fire	三煞 Monthly 3 Killings		
		劫煞 Robbery Sha	災煞 Calamity Sha	月煞 Month Sha
寅 **Tiger** (Feb 4 - Mar 5) 正月 **1st Month**	兌 Dui	亥 Hai **Pig**	子 Zi **Rat**	丑 Chou **Ox**
卯 **Rabbit** (Mar 6 - Apr 4) 二月 **2nd Month**	艮 Gen	申 Shen **Monkey**	酉 You **Rooster**	戌 Xu **Dog**
辰 **Dragon** (Apr 5 - May 5) 三月 **3rd Month**	離 Li	巳 Si **Snake**	午 Wu **Horse**	未 Wei **Goat**
巳 **Snake** (May 6 - Jun 5) 四月 **4th Month**	坎 Kan	寅 Yin **Tiger**	卯 Mao **Rabbit**	辰 Chen **Dragon**
午 **Horse** (Jun 6 - July 6) 五月 **5th Month**	坤 Kun	亥 Hai **Pig**	子 Zi **Rat**	丑 Chou **Ox**
未 **Goat** (July 7 - Aug 7) 六月 **6th Month**	震 Zhen	申 Shen **Monkey**	酉 You **Rooster**	戌 Xu **Dog**
申 **Monkey** (Aug 8 - Sept 7) 七月 **7th Month**	巽 Xun	巳 Si **Snake**	午 Wu **Horse**	未 Wei **Goat**
酉 **Rooster** (Sept 8 - Oct 7) 八月 **8th Month**	中 Middle	寅 Yin **Tiger**	卯 Mao **Rabbit**	辰 Chen **Dragon**
戌 **Dog** (Oct 8 - Nov 6) 九月 **9th Month**	乾 Qian	亥 Hai **Pig**	子 Zi **Rat**	丑 Chou **Ox**
亥 **Pig** (Nov 7 - Dec 6) 十月 **10th Month**	兌 Dui	申 Shen **Monkey**	酉 You **Rooster**	戌 Xu **Dog**
子 **Rat** (Dec 7 - Jan 5) 十一月 **11th Month**	艮 Gen	巳 Si **Snake**	午 Wu **Horse**	未 Wei **Goat**
丑 **Ox** (Jan 6 - Feb 3) 十二月 **12th Month**	離 Li	寅 Yin **Tiger**	卯 Mao **Rabbit**	辰 Chen **Dragon**

Negative Repair / Renovation Sectors 修方凶位 :

月 MONTH	月刑 Month Punishment	月害 Month Harm	月厭 Month Detest
寅 **Tiger** (Feb 4 - Mar 5) 正月 **1st Month**	巳 Si Snake	巳 Si Snake	戌 Xu Dog
卯 **Rabbit** (Mar 6 - Apr 4) 二月 **2nd Month**	子 Zi Rat	辰 Chen Dragon	酉 You Rooster
辰 **Dragon** (Apr 5 - May 5) 三月 **3rd Month**	辰 Chen Dragon	卯 Mao Rabbit	申 Shen Monkey
巳 **Snake** (May 6 - Jun 5) 四月 **4th Month**	申 Shen Monkey	寅 Yin Tiger	未 Wei Goat
午 **Horse** (Jun 6 - July 6) 五月 **5th Month**	午 Wu Horse	丑 Chou Ox	午 Wu Horse
未 **Goat** (July 7 - Aug 7) 六月 **6th Month**	丑 Chou Ox	子 Zi Rat	巳 Si Snake
申 **Monkey** (Aug 8 - Sept 7) 七月 **7th Month**	寅 Yin Tiger	亥 Hai Pig	辰 Chen Dragon
酉 **Rooster** (Sept 8 - Oct 7) 八月 **8th Month**	酉 You Rooster	戌 Xu Dog	卯 Mao Rabbit
戌 **Dog** (Oct 8 - Nov 6) 九月 **9th Month**	未 Wei Goat	酉 You Rooster	寅 Yin Tiger
亥 **Pig** (Nov 7 - Dec 6) 十月 **10th Month**	亥 Hai Pig	申 Shen Monkey	丑 Chou Ox
子 **Rat** (Dec 7 - Jan 5) 十一月 **11th Month**	卯 Mao Rabbit	未 Wei Goat	子 Zi Rat
丑 **Ox** (Jan 6 - Feb 3) 十二月 **12th Month**	戌 Xu Dog	午 Wu Horse	亥 Hai Pig

戊戌 (Wu Xu)
Earth Dog

戊戌 (Wu Xu) Earth Dog

Heavenly Stem 天干	戊 Yang Earth (陽土)
Earthly Branch 地支	戌 Dog (Yang Earth 陽土)
Hidden Stem 藏干	戊 Yang Earth, 辛 Yin Metal, 丁 Yin Fire
Na Yin 納音	平地木 Wood from the flatlands
Grand Duke 太歲	戌 Dog
Xuan Kong Five Element 玄空五行	1 水 Water
Gua Name 卦名	䷎ 地山謙 Humility
Xuan Kong Period Luck 玄空卦運	6

Annual Positive Stars for Opening Mountain, Establishing Facing and Commencing Repairs 開山立向修方吉星：

歲德 Duke Virtue	戊 Wu Yang Earth
歲德合 Duke Virtue Combo	癸 Gui Yin Water
歲枝德 Duke Branch Virtue	卯 Mao Rabbit
陽貴人 Yang Nobleman	丑 Chou Ox
陰貴人 Yin Nobleman	未 Wei Goat
歲祿 Duke Prosperous	巳 Si Snake
歲馬 Duke Horse	申 Shen Monkey
奏書 Decree	坤 Kun
博士 Professor	艮 Gen

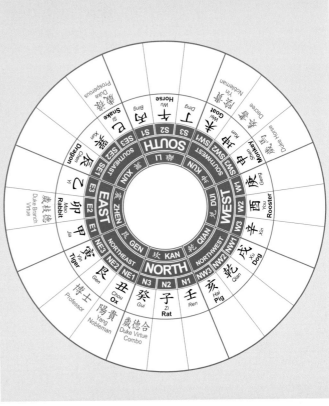

Annual Negative Stars for Opening Mountain, Establishing Facing and Commencing Repairs 開山立向修方凶星：

太歲 Grand Duke	歲破 Year Breaker	三煞 Three Killings			坐煞向煞 Sitting Sha Facing Sha				浮天空亡 Floating Heaven Emptiness	
戊 Xu Dog	辰 Chen Dragon	亥 Hai Pig	子 Zi Rat	丑 Chou Ox	壬 Ren Yang Water	癸 Gui Yin Water	丙 Bing Yang Fire	丁 Ding Yin Fire	坤 Kun	乙 Yi Yin Wood

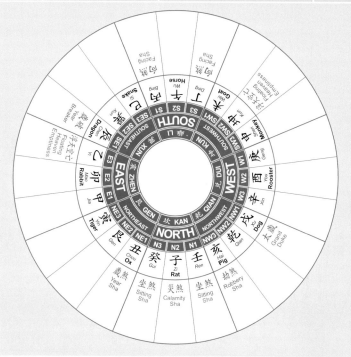

Annual San Yuan Purple White Stars 三元紫白九星：

上元 Upper Period
Period 1, 2, 3

巽SE	離S	坤SW
2	7	9
1 震E	3 戊戌 Wu Xu Earth Dog	5 兌W
6	8	4
艮NE	坎N	乾NW

中元 Middle Period
Period 4, 5, 6

巽SE	離S	坤SW
5	1	3
4 震E	6 戊戌 Wu Xu Earth Dog	8 兌W
9	2	7
艮NE	坎N	乾NW

下元 Lower Period
Period 7, 8, 9

巽SE	離S	坤SW
8	4	6
7 震E	9 戊戌 Wu Xu Earth Dog	2 兌W
3	5	1
艮NE	坎N	乾NW

Mountain Covering Yellow Path 蓋山黃道：

貪狼 *Tan Lang* **Greedy Wolf**				巨門 *Ju Men* **Huge Door**		武曲 *Wu Qu* **Military Arts**				文曲 *Wen Qu* **Literary Arts**			
坎	癸	申	辰	坤	乙	離	壬	寅	戌	兌	丁	巳	丑
Kan	*Gui*	*Shen*	*Chen*	*Kun*	*Yi*	*Li*	*Ren*	*Yin*	*Xu*	*Dui*	*Ding*	*Si*	*Chou*
N2	N3	SW3	SE1	SW2	E3	S2	N1	NE3	NW1	W2	S3	SE3	NE1

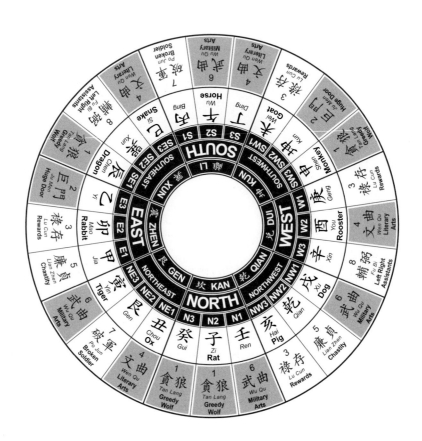

Heaven Penetrating Force 通天竅:

三合前方 **Facing Three Harmony**	坤申 Kun Shen	庚酉 Geng You	辛戌 Xin Xu
三合後方 **Sitting Three Harmony**	艮寅 Gen Yin	甲卯 Jia Mao	乙辰 Yi Chen

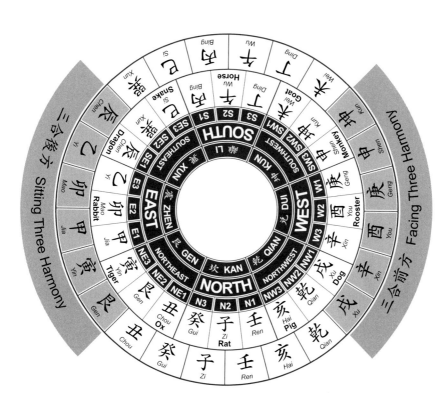

Moving Horse Six Ren Assessment 走馬六壬:

神后 Shen Hou Holy Empress	功曹 Gong Cao Marshall	天罡 Tian Gang Heavenly Dipper	勝光 Sheng Guang Subliminal Bright	傳送 Chuan Song Great General	河魁 He Kui River Scholar
艮寅 Gen Yin	乙辰 Yi Chen	丙午 Bing Wu	坤申 Kun Shen	辛戌 Xin Xu	壬子 Ren Zi

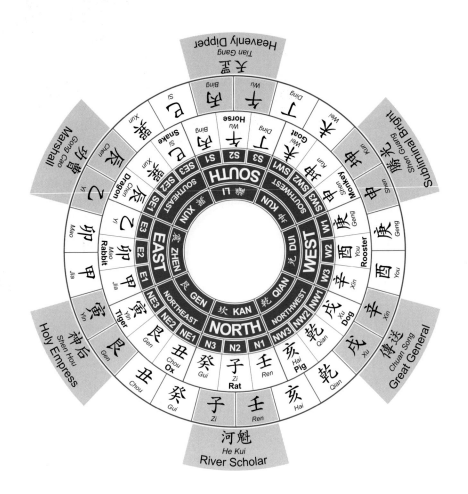

戊戌 (Wu Xu) Earth Dog

Four Advantages Three Cycles Star Plate 四利三元:

太陽 *Tai Yang* **Sun**	太陰 *Tai Yin* **Moon**	龍德 *Long De* **Dragon Virtue**	福德 *Fu De* **Fortune Virtue**
亥 *Hai* Pig	丑 *Chou* Ox	巳 *Si* Snake	未 *Wei* Goat

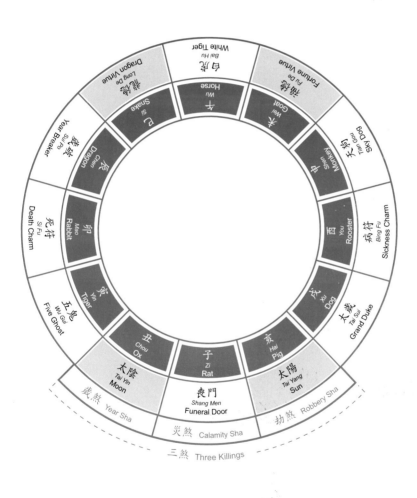

587

Negative Sectors For Opening Mountain 開山凶位：

年剋山家 Year Countering Sitting

甲	寅	辰	巽	戌	坎	辛	申	丑	癸	坤	庚	未
Jia	Yin	Chen	Xun	Xu	Kan	Xin	Shen	Chou	Gui	Kun	Geng	Wei
E1	NE3	SE1	SE2	NW1	N2	W3	SW3	NE1	N3	SW2	W1	SW1

陰府太歲		六害	死符	炙退
Yin Fu Tai Sui		Liu Hai	Si Fu	Zhi Tui
Yin Mansion Grand Duke		**Six Harm**	**Death Charm**	**Roasting Star**

坤	震	酉	卯	酉
Kun	Zhen	You	Mao	You
SW2	E2	W2	E2	W2

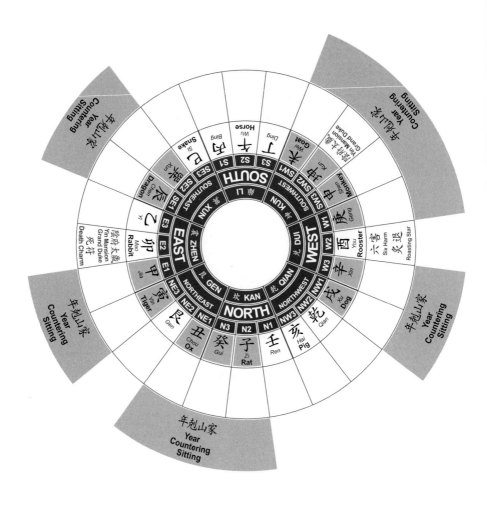

Negative Directions to Establish Facing 立向凶方：

巡山羅喉 *Xun Shan Luo Hou* **Mountain Patrol Luo Hou Star**	病符 *Bing Fu* **Sickness Charm**
乾 *Qian* **NW2**	酉 *You* **W2**

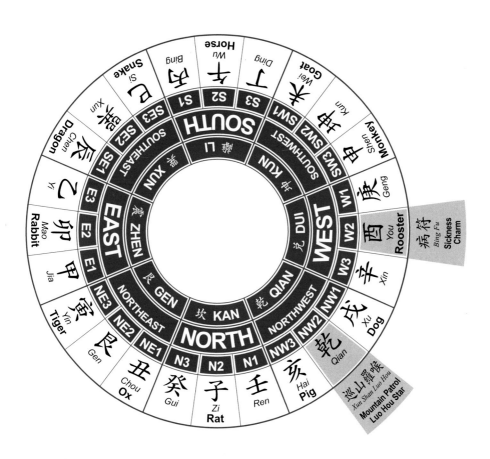

Negative Repair / Renovation Sectors Table 修方凶位表：

天官符 Heavenly Officer Charm	巳 Si Snake	飛廉 Flying Chaste	子 Zi Rat
地官符 Earthly Officer Charm	寅 Yin Tiger	喪門 Funeral Door	子 Zi Rat
大煞 Great Sha	午 Wu Horse	弔客 Suspended Guest	申 Shen Monkey
大將軍 Big General	午 Wu Horse	白虎 White Tiger	午 Wu Horse
力士 Strong Man	乾 Qian	金神 Golden God	申 Shen Monkey
蠶室 Silkworm Room	巽 Xun		酉 You Rooster
蠶官 Silkworm Officer	辰 Chen Dragon		子 Zi Rat
蠶命 Silkworm Life	巳 Si Snake		丑 Chou Ox
歲刑 Duke Punishment	未 Wei Goat	獨火 Lonely Fire	乾 Qian
黃幡 Yellow Flag	戌 Xu Dog	五鬼 Five Ghost	午 Wu Horse
豹尾 Leopard Tail	辰 Chen Dragon	破敗五鬼 Destructive Five Ghost	離 Li

Negative Repair / Renovation Sectors Diagram 修方凶位圖：

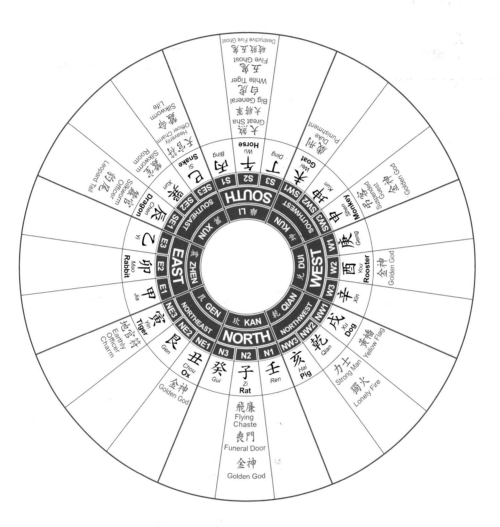

12-Month Auxiliary Stars Reference Table :
戊戌年十二月，開山立向修方星表

Positive Monthly Stars 吉星方

月 MONTH	寅 Tiger (Feb 4 - Mar 5) 正月 1st Month	卯 Rabbit (Mar 6 - Apr 4) 二月 2nd Month	辰 Dragon (Apr 5 - May 5) 三月 3rd Month	巳 Snake (May 6 - Jun 5) 四月 4th Month	午 Horse (Jun 6 - July 6) 五月 5th Month	未 Goat (July 7 - Aug 7) 六月 6th Month
天道 Heavenly Path	南 South	西南 Southwest	北 North	西 West	西北 Northwest	東 East
天德 Heavenly Virtue	丁 Ding Yin Fire	坤 Kun (申)	壬 Ren Yang Water	辛 Xin Yin Metal	乾 Qian (亥)	甲 Jia Yang Wood
天德合 Heavenly Virtue Combo	壬 Ren Yang Water	(巳)	丁 Ding Yin Fire	丙 Bing Yang Fire	(寅)	己 Ji Yin Earth
月德 Monthly Virtue	丙 Bing Yang Fire	甲 Jia Yang Wood	壬 Ren Yang Water	庚 Geng Yang Metal	丙 Bing Yang Fire	甲 Jia Yang Wood
月德合 Monthly Virtue Combo	辛 Xin Yin Metal	己 Ji Yin Earth	丁 Ding Yin Fire	乙 Yi Yin Wood	辛 Xin Yin Metal	己 Ji Yin Earth
月空 Month Emptiness	壬 Ren Yang Water	庚 Geng Yang Metal	丙 Bing Yang Fire	甲 Jia Yang Wood	壬 Ren Yang Water	庚 Geng Yang Metal
陽貴人 Yang Nobleman	兌 Dui	乾 Qian	中 Middle	巽 Xun	震 Zhen	坤 Kun
陰貴人 Yin Nobleman	坎 Kan	離 Li	艮 Gen	兌 Dui	乾 Qian	中 Middle
飛天祿 Flying Heavenly Wealth	艮 Gen	兌 Dui	乾 Qian	中 Middle	坎 Kan	離 Li
飛天馬 Flying Heavenly Horse	坤 Kun	坎 Kan	離 Li	艮 Gen	兌 Dui	乾 Qian

12-Month Auxiliary Stars Reference Table :
戊戌年十二月，開山立向修方星表

申 Monkey (Aug 8 - Sept 7)	酉 Rooster (Sept 8 - Oct 7)	戌 Dog (Oct 8 - Nov 6)	亥 Pig (Nov 7 - Dec 6)	子 Rat (Dec 7 - Jan 5)	丑 Ox (Jan 6 - Feb 3)	月 MONTH
七月 7th Month	八月 8th Month	九月 9th Month	十月 10th Month	十一月 11th Month	十二月 12th Month	
北 North	東北 Northeast	南 South	東 East	東南 Southeast	西 West	天道 Heavenly Path
癸 Gui Yin Water	艮 Gen (寅)	丙 Bing Yang Fire	乙 Yi Yin Wood	巽 Xun (巳)	庚 Geng Yang Metal	天德 Heavenly Virtue
戊 Wu Yang Earth	(亥)	辛 Xin Yin Metal	庚 Geng Yang Metal	(申)	乙 Yi Yin Wood	天德合 Heavenly Virtue Combo
壬 Ren Yang Water	庚 Geng Yang Metal	丙 Bing Yang Fire	甲 Jia Yang Wood	壬 Ren Yang Water	庚 Geng Yang Metal	月德 Monthly Virtue
丁 Ding Yin Fire	乙 Yi Yin Wood	辛 Xin Yin Metal	己 Ji Yin Earth	丁 Ding Yin Fire	乙 Yi Yin Wood	月德合 Monthly Virtue Combo
丙 Bing Yang Fire	甲 Jia Yang Wood	壬 Ren Yang Water	庚 Geng Yang Metal	丙 Bing Yang Fire	甲 Jia Yang Wood	月空 Month Emptiness
坎 Kan	離 Li	艮 Gen	兌 Dui	乾 Qian	中 Middle	陽貴人 Yang Nobleman
坎 Kan	離 Li	艮 Gen	兌 Dui	乾 Qian	中 Middle	陰貴人 Yin Nobleman
艮 Gen	兌 Dui	乾 Qian	中 Middle	巽 Xun	震 Zhen	飛天祿 Flying Heavenly Wealth
中 Middle	坎 Kan	離 Li	艮 Gen	兌 Dui	乾 Qian	飛天馬 Flying Heavenly Horse

Monthly Purple White Stars 月紫白九星：

寅 Tiger (Feb 4 - Mar 5) 正月 1st Month

巽 SE	離 S	坤 SW
4 Green 四綠	9 Purple 九紫	2 Black 二黑
3 Jade 三碧 (震 E)	5 Yellow 五黃	7 Red 七赤 (兌 W)
8 White 八白	1 White 一白	6 White 六白
艮 NE	坎 N	乾 NW

卯 Rabbit (Mar 6 - Apr 4) 二月 2nd Month

巽 SE	離 S	坤 SW
3 Jade 三碧	8 White 八白	1 White 一白
2 Black 二黑 (震 E)	4 Green 四綠	6 White 六白 (兌 W)
7 Red 七赤	9 Purple 九紫	5 Yellow 五黃
艮 NE	坎 N	乾 NW

辰 Dragon (Apr 5 - May 5) 三月 3rd Month

巽 SE	離 S	坤 SW
2 Black 二黑	7 Red 七赤	9 Purple 九紫
1 White 一白 (震 E)	3 Jade 三碧	5 Yellow 五黃 (兌 W)
6 White 六白	8 White 八白	4 Green 四綠
艮 NE	坎 N	乾 NW

巳 Snake (May 6 - Jun 5) 四月 4th Month

巽 SE	離 S	坤 SW
1 White 一白	6 White 六白	8 White 八白
9 Purple 九紫 (震 E)	2 Black 二黑	4 Green 四綠 (兌 W)
5 Yellow 五黃	7 Red 七赤	3 Jade 三碧
艮 NE	坎 N	乾 NW

午 Horse (Jun 6 - July 6) 五月 5th Month

巽 SE	離 S	坤 SW
9 Purple 九紫	5 Yellow 五黃	7 Red 七赤
8 White 八白 (震 E)	1 White 一白	3 Jade 三碧 (兌 W)
4 Green 四綠	6 White 六白	2 Black 二黑
艮 NE	坎 N	乾 NW

未 Goat (July 7 - Aug 7) 六月 6th Month

巽 SE	離 S	坤 SW
8 White 八白	4 Green 四綠	6 White 六白
7 Red 七赤 (震 E)	9 Purple 九紫	2 Black 二黑 (兌 W)
3 Jade 三碧	5 Yellow 五黃	1 White 一白
艮 NE	坎 N	乾 NW

申 Monkey (Aug 8 - Sept 7) 七月 7th Month

巽 SE	離 S	坤 SW
7 Red 七赤	3 Jade 三碧	5 Yellow 五黃
6 White 六白 (震 E)	8 White 八白	1 White 一白 (兌 W)
2 Black 二黑	4 Green 四綠	9 Purple 九紫
艮 NE	坎 N	乾 NW

酉 Rooster (Sept 8 - Oct 7) 八月 8th Month

巽 SE	離 S	坤 SW
6 White 六白	2 Black 二黑	4 Green 四綠
5 Yellow 五黃 (震 E)	7 Red 七赤	9 Purple 九紫 (兌 W)
1 White 一白	3 Jade 三碧	8 White 八白
艮 NE	坎 N	乾 NW

戌 Dog (Oct 8 - Nov 6) 九月 9th Month

巽 SE	離 S	坤 SW
5 Yellow 五黃	1 White 一白	3 Jade 三碧
4 Green 四綠 (震 E)	6 White 六白	8 White 八白 (兌 W)
9 Purple 九紫	2 Black 二黑	7 Red 七赤
艮 NE	坎 N	乾 NW

亥 Pig (Nov 7 - Dec 6) 十月 10th Month

巽 SE	離 S	坤 SW
4 Green 四綠	9 Purple 九紫	2 Black 二黑
3 Jade 三碧 (震 E)	5 Yellow 五黃	7 Red 七赤 (兌 W)
8 White 八白	1 White 一白	6 White 六白
艮 NE	坎 N	乾 NW

子 Rat (Dec 7 - Jan 5) 十一月 11th Month

巽 SE	離 S	坤 SW
3 Jade 三碧	8 White 八白	1 White 一白
2 Black 二黑 (震 E)	4 Green 四綠	6 White 六白 (兌 W)
7 Red 七赤	9 Purple 九紫	5 Yellow 五黃
艮 NE	坎 N	乾 NW

丑 Ox (Jan 6 - Feb 3) 十二月 12th Month

巽 SE	離 S	坤 SW
2 Black 二黑	7 Red 七赤	9 Purple 九紫
1 White 一白 (震 E)	3 Jade 三碧	5 Yellow 五黃 (兌 W)
6 White 六白	8 White 八白	4 Green 四綠
艮 NE	坎 N	乾 NW

Qi Men Three Nobles 三奇 :

Three Nobles 三奇 / Seasons	乙 Yi	丙 Bing	丁 Ding
立春 **Coming of Spring** Feb 4 - Feb 18	兌 Dui	艮 Gen	離 Li
春分 **Spring Equinox** Mar 21 - Apr 4	坤 Kun	震 Zhen	巽 Xun
立夏 **Coming of Summer** May 6 - May 20	震 Zhen	巽 Xun	中 Middle
夏至 **Summer Solstice** Jun 22 - Jul 6	坎 Kan	離 Li	艮 Gen
立秋 **Coming of Autumn** Aug 8 - Aug 23	震 Zhen	坤 Kun	坎 Kan
秋分 **Autumn Equinox** Sept 23 - Oct 7	艮 Gen	兌 Dui	乾 Qian
立冬 **Coming of Winter** Nov 7 - Nov 22	兌 Dui	乾 Qian	中 Middle
冬至 **Winter Solstice** Dec 22 - Jan 5	離 Li	坎 Kan	坤 Kun

Sectors to Avoid Opening Mountain 開山凶位 :

月 MONTH	月建 Month Establishment	月破 Month Destruction	月剋山家 Month Countering Sitting		陰府太歲 Yin Mansion Grand Duke	
寅 Tiger (Feb 4 - Mar 5) 正月 1st Month	寅 Yin Tiger	申 Shen Monkey	震 Zhen	巳 Si Snake	艮 Gen	巽 Xun
卯 Rabbit (Mar 6 - Apr 4) 二月 2nd Month	卯 Mao Rabbit	酉 You Rooster	艮 Gen		兌 Dui	乾 Qian
辰 Dragon (Apr 5 - May 5) 三月 3rd Month	辰 Chen Dragon	戌 Xu Dog	離 Li	丙 Bing Yang Fire	坎 Kan	坤 Kun
巳 Snake (May 6 - Jun 5) 四月 4th Month	巳 Si Snake	亥 Hai Pig	壬 Ren Yang Water	乙 Yi Yin Wood	乾 Qian	離 Li
午 Horse (Jun 6 - July 6) 五月 5th Month	午 Wu Horse	子 Zi Rat	—		坤 Kun	震 Zhen
未 Goat (July 7 - Aug 7) 六月 6th Month	未 Wei Goat	丑 Chou Ox	—		巽 Xun	艮 Gen
申 Monkey (Aug 8 - Sept 7) 七月 7th Month	申 Shen Monkey	寅 Yin Tiger	水 Water	山 Mountain	乾 Qian	兌 Dui
酉 Rooster (Sept 8 - Oct 7) 八月 8th Month	酉 You Rooster	卯 Mao Rabbit	土 Earth		坤 Kun	坎 Kan
戌 Dog (Oct 8 - Nov 6) 九月 9th Month	戌 Xu Dog	辰 Chen Dragon	震 Zhen	巳 Si Snake	離 Li	乾 Qian
亥 Pig (Nov 7 - Dec 6) 十月 10th Month	亥 Hai Pig	巳 Si Snake	艮 Gen		震 Zhen	坤 Kun
子 Rat (Dec 7 - Jan 5) 十一月 11th Month	子 Zi Rat	午 Wu Horse	—		艮 Gen	巽 Xun
丑 Ox (Jan 6 - Feb 3) 十二月 12th Month	丑 Chou Ox	未 Wei Goat	—		兌 Dui	乾 Qian

Negative Repair / Renovation Sectors 修方凶位 ：

月 MONTH	天官符 Heavenly Officer Charm			地官符 Earth Officer Charm			小月建 Small Month Establishment		
寅 Tiger (Feb 4 - Mar 5) 正月 1st Month	丑 Chou Ox	艮 Gen	寅 Yin Tiger	中 Middle			中 Middle		
卯 Rabbit (Mar 6 - Apr 4) 二月 2nd Month	庚 Geng Yang Metal	兑 Dui	辛 Xin Yin Metal	庚 Geng Yang Metal	兑 Dui	辛 Xin Yin Metal	戌 Xu Dog	乾 Qian	亥 Hai Pig
辰 Dragon (Apr 5 - May 5) 三月 3rd Month	戌 Xu Dog	乾 Qian	亥 Hai Pig	戌 Xu Dog	乾 Qian	亥 Hai Pig	庚 Geng Yang Metal	兑 Dui	辛 Xin Yin Metal
巳 Snake (May 6 - Jun 5) 四月 4th Month	中 Middle			中 Middle			丑 Chou Ox	艮 Gen	寅 Yin Tiger
午 Horse (Jun 6 - July 6) 五月 5th Month	庚 Geng Yang Metal	兑 Dui	辛 Xin Yin Metal	辰 Chen Dragon	巽 Xun	巳 Si Snake	丙 Bing Yang Fire	離 Li	丁 Ding Yin Fire
未 Goat (July 7 - Aug 7) 六月 6th Month	戌 Xu Dog	乾 Qian	亥 Hai Pig	甲 Jia Yang Wood	震 Zhen	乙 Yi Yin Wood	壬 Ren Yang Water	坎 Kan	癸 Gui Yin Water
申 Monkey (Aug 8 - Sept 7) 七月 7th Month	中 Middle			未 Wei Goat	坤 Kun	申 Shen Monkey	未 Wei Goat	坤 Kun	申 Shen Monkey
酉 Rooster (Sept 8 - Oct 7) 八月 8th Month	辰 Chen Dragon	巽 Xun	巳 Si Snake	壬 Ren Yang Water	坎 Kan	癸 Gui Yin Water	甲 Jia Yang Wood	震 Zhen	乙 Yi Yin Wood
戌 Dog (Oct 8 - Nov 6) 九月 9th Month	甲 Jia Yang Wood	震 Zhen	乙 Yi Yin Wood	丙 Bing Yang Fire	離 Li	丁 Ding Yin Fire	辰 Chen Dragon	巽 Xun	巳 Si Snake
亥 Pig (Nov 7 - Dec 6) 十月 10th Month	未 Wei Goat	坤 Kun	申 Shen Monkey	丑 Chou Ox	艮 Gen	寅 Yin Tiger	中 Middle		
子 Rat (Dec 7 - Jan 5) 十一月 11th Month	壬 Ren Yang Water	坎 Kan	癸 Gui Yin Water	庚 Geng Yang Metal	兑 Dui	辛 Xin Yin Metal	戌 Xu Dog	乾 Qian	亥 Hai Pig
丑 Ox (Jan 6 - Feb 3) 十二月 12th Month	丙 Bing Yang Fire	離 Li	丁 Ding Yin Fire	戌 Xu Dog	乾 Qian	亥 Hai Pig	庚 Geng Yang Metal	兑 Dui	辛 Xin Yin Metal

Negative Repair / Renovation Sectors 修方凶位 :

月 MONTH	大月建 Big Month Establishment			飛大煞 Flying Great Sha			丙丁獨火 Bing Ding Lonely Fire	
寅 **Tiger** (Feb 4 - Mar 5) 正月 **1st Month**	中 Middle			丙 Bing Yang Fire	離 Li	丁 Ding Yin Fire	兌 Dui	艮 Gen
卯 **Rabbit** (Mar 6 - Apr 4) 二月 **2nd Month**	辰 Chen Dragon	巽 Xun	巳 Si Snake	丑 Chou Ox	艮 Gen	寅 Yin Tiger	乾 Qian	兌 Dui
辰 **Dragon** (Apr 5 - May 5) 三月 **3rd Month**	甲 Jia Yang Wood	震 Zhen	乙 Yi Yin Wood	庚 Geng Yang Metal	兌 Dui	辛 Xin Yin Metal	中 Middle	乾 Qian
巳 **Snake** (May 6 - Jun 5) 四月 **4th Month**	未 Wei Goat	坤 Kun	申 Shen Monkey	戌 Xu Dog	乾 Qian	亥 Hai Pig	中 Middle	
午 **Horse** (Jun 6 - July 6) 五月 **5th Month**	壬 Ren Yang Water	坎 Kan	癸 Gui Yin Water	中 Middle			巽 Xun	中 Middle
未 **Goat** (July 7 - Aug 7) 六月 **6th Month**	丙 Bing Yang Fire	離 Li	丁 Ding Yin Fire	庚 Geng Yang Metal	兌 Dui	辛 Xin Yin Metal	震 Zhen	巽 Xun
申 **Monkey** (Aug 8 - Sept 7) 七月 **7th Month**	丑 Chou Ox	艮 Gen	寅 Yin Tiger	戌 Xu Dog	乾 Qian	亥 Hai Pig	坤 Kun	震 Zhen
酉 **Rooster** (Sept 8 - Oct 7) 八月 **8th Month**	庚 Geng Yang Metal	兌 Dui	辛 Xin Yin Metal	中 Middle			坎 Kan	坤 Kun
戌 **Dog** (Oct 8 - Nov 6) 九月 **9th Month**	戌 Xu Dog	乾 Qian	亥 Hai Pig	辰 Chen Dragon	巽 Xun	巳 Si Snake	離 Li	坎 Kan
亥 **Pig** (Nov 7 - Dec 6) 十月 **10th Month**	中 Middle			甲 Jia Yang Wood	震 Zhen	乙 Yi Yin Wood	艮 Gen	離 Li
子 **Rat** (Dec 7 - Jan 5) 十一月 **11th Month**	辰 Chen Dragon	巽 Xun	巳 Si Snake	未 Wei Goat	坤 Kun	申 Shen Monkey	兌 Dui	艮 Gen
丑 **Ox** (Jan 6 - Feb 3) 十二月 **12th Month**	甲 Jia Yang Wood	震 Zhen	乙 Yi Yin Wood	壬 Ren Yang Water	坎 Kan	癸 Gui Yin Water	乾 Qian	兌 Dui

Negative Repair / Renovation Sectors 修方凶位 :

月 MONTH	月遊火 Month Wondering Fire	三煞 Monthly 3 Killings		
		劫煞 Robbery Sha	災煞 Calamity Sha	月煞 Month Sha
寅 Tiger (Feb 4 - Mar 5) 正月 1st Month	乾 Qian	亥 Hai Pig	子 Zi Rat	丑 Chou Ox
卯 Rabbit (Mar 6 - Apr 4) 二月 2nd Month	兌 Dui	申 Shen Monkey	酉 You Rooster	戌 Xu Dog
辰 Dragon (Apr 5 - May 5) 三月 3rd Month	艮 Gen	巳 Si Snake	午 Wu Horse	未 Wei Goat
巳 Snake (May 6 - Jun 5) 四月 4th Month	離 Li	寅 Yin Tiger	卯 Mao Rabbit	辰 Chen Dragon
午 Horse (Jun 6 - July 6) 五月 5th Month	坎 Kan	亥 Hai Pig	子 Zi Rat	丑 Chou Ox
未 Goat (July 7 - Aug 7) 六月 6th Month	坤 Kun	申 Shen Monkey	酉 You Rooster	戌 Xu Dog
申 Monkey (Aug 8 - Sept 7) 七月 7th Month	震 Zhen	巳 Si Snake	午 Wu Horse	未 Wei Goat
酉 Rooster (Sept 8 - Oct 7) 八月 8th Month	巽 Xun	寅 Yin Tiger	卯 Mao Rabbit	辰 Chen Dragon
戌 Dog (Oct 8 - Nov 6) 九月 9th Month	中 Middle	亥 Hai Pig	子 Zi Rat	丑 Chou Ox
亥 Pig (Nov 7 - Dec 6) 十月 10th Month	乾 Qian	申 Shen Monkey	酉 You Rooster	戌 Xu Dog
子 Rat (Dec 7 - Jan 5) 十一月 11th Month	兌 Dui	巳 Si Snake	午 Wu Horse	未 Wei Goat
丑 Ox (Jan 6 - Feb 3) 十二月 12th Month	艮 Gen	寅 Yin Tiger	卯 Mao Rabbit	辰 Chen Dragon

Negative Repair / Renovation Sectors 修方凶位 :

月 MONTH	月刑 Month Punishment	月害 Month Harm	月厭 Month Detest
寅 **Tiger** (Feb 4 - Mar 5) 正月 **1st Month**	巳 *Si* Snake	巳 *Si* Snake	戌 *Xu* Dog
卯 **Rabbit** (Mar 6 - Apr 4) 二月 **2nd Month**	子 *Zi* Rat	辰 *Chen* Dragon	酉 *You* Rooster
辰 **Dragon** (Apr 5 - May 5) 三月 **3rd Month**	辰 *Chen* Dragon	卯 *Mao* Rabbit	申 *Shen* Monkey
巳 **Snake** (May 6 - Jun 5) 四月 **4th Month**	申 *Shen* Monkey	寅 *Yin* Tiger	未 *Wei* Goat
午 **Horse** (Jun 6 - July 6) 五月 **5th Month**	午 *Wu* Horse	丑 *Chou* Ox	午 *Wu* Horse
未 **Goat** (July 7 - Aug 7) 六月 **6th Month**	丑 *Chou* Ox	子 *Zi* Rat	巳 *Si* Snake
申 **Monkey** (Aug 8 - Sept 7) 七月 **7th Month**	寅 *Yin* Tiger	亥 *Hai* Pig	辰 *Chen* Dragon
酉 **Rooster** (Sept 8 - Oct 7) 八月 **8th Month**	酉 *You* Rooster	戌 *Xu* Dog	卯 *Mao* Rabbit
戌 **Dog** (Oct 8 - Nov 6) 九月 **9th Month**	未 *Wei* Goat	酉 *You* Rooster	寅 *Yin* Tiger
亥 **Pig** (Nov 7 - Dec 6) 十月 **10th Month**	亥 *Hai* Pig	申 *Shen* Monkey	丑 *Chou* Ox
子 **Rat** (Dec 7 - Jan 5) 十一月 **11th Month**	卯 *Mao* Rabbit	未 *Wei* Goat	子 *Zi* Rat
丑 **Ox** (Jan 6 - Feb 3) 十二月 **12th Month**	戌 *Xu* Dog	午 *Wu* Horse	亥 *Hai* Pig

己丑 (Ji Chou)
Earth Ox

Heavenly Stem 天干	己 Yin Earth (陰土)
Earthly Branch 地支	丑 Ox (Yin Earth 陰土)
Hidden Stem 藏干	己 Yin Earth, 癸 Yin Water, 辛 Yin Metal
Na Yin 納音	霹靂火 Fire from thunder
Grand Duke 太歲	丑 Ox
Xuan Kong Five Element 玄空五行	9 金 Metal
Gua Name 卦名	䷘ 天雷無妄 Without Wrongdoing
Xuan Kong Period Luck 玄空卦運	2

Annual Positive Stars for Opening Mountain, Establishing Facing and Commencing Repairs 開山立向修方吉星：

歲德 Duke Virtue	甲 Jia Yang Wood
歲德合 Duke Virtue Combo	己 Ji Yin Earth
歲枝德 Duke Branch Virtue	午 Wu Horse
陽貴人 Yang Nobleman	子 Zi Rat
陰貴人 Yin Nobleman	申 Shen Monkey
歲祿 Duke Prosperous	午 Wu Horse
歲馬 Duke Horse	亥 Hai Pig
奏書 Decree	乾 Qian
博士 Professor	巽 Xun

Annual Negative Stars for Opening Mountain, Establishing Facing and Commencing Repairs 開山立向修方凶星：

太歲 Grand Duke	歲破 Year Breaker	三煞 Three Killings			坐煞向煞 Sitting Sha Facing Sha				浮天空亡 Floating Heaven Emptiness	
丑 Chou Ox	未 Wei Goat	寅 Yin Tiger	卯 Mao Rabbit	辰 Chen Dragon	甲 Jia Yang Wood	乙 Yi Yin Wood	庚 Geng Yang Metal	辛 Xin Yin Metal	乾 Qian	甲 Jia Yang Wood

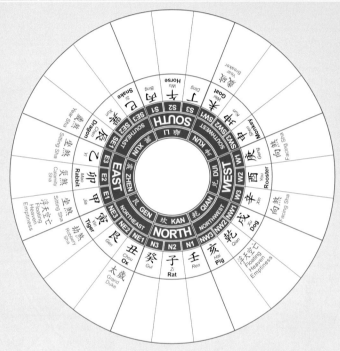

Annual San Yuan Purple White Stars 三元紫白九星：

上元 Upper Period Period 1, 2, 3			中元 Middle Period Period 4, 5, 6			下元 Lower Period Period 7, 8, 9		
巽SE **2**	離S **7**	坤SW **9**	巽SE **5**	離S **1**	坤SW **3**	巽SE **8**	離S **4**	坤SW **6**
震E **1**	**3** 己丑 Yi Chou Earth Ox	兌W **5**	震E **4**	**6** 己丑 Yi Chou Earth Ox	兌W **8**	震E **7**	**9** 己丑 Yi Chou Earth Ox	兌W **2**
艮NE **6**	坎N **8**	乾NW **4**	艮NE **9**	坎N **2**	乾NW **7**	艮NE **3**	坎N **5**	乾NW **1**

Mountain Covering Yellow Path 蓋山黃道：

貪狼 *Tan Lang* **Greedy Wolf**		巨門 *Ju Men* **Huge Door**		武曲 *Wu Qu* **Military Arts**				文曲 *Wen Qu* **Literary Arts**			
艮 *Gen* NE2	丙 *Bing* S1	巽 *Xun* SE2	辛 *Xin* W3	兌 *Dui* W2	丁 *Ding* S3	巳 *Si* SE3	丑 *Chou* NE1	離 *Li* S2	壬 *Ren* N1	寅 *Yin* NE3	戌 *Xu* NW1

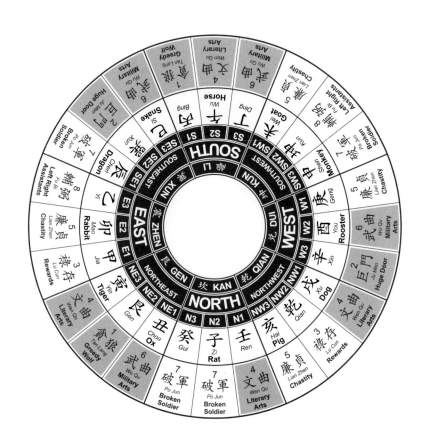

Heaven Penetrating Force 通天竅：

三合前方 **Facing Three Harmony**	乾亥 Qian Hai	壬子 Ren Zi	癸丑 Gui Chou
三合後方 **Sitting Three Harmony**	巽巳 Xun Si	丙午 Bing Wu	丁未 Ding Wei

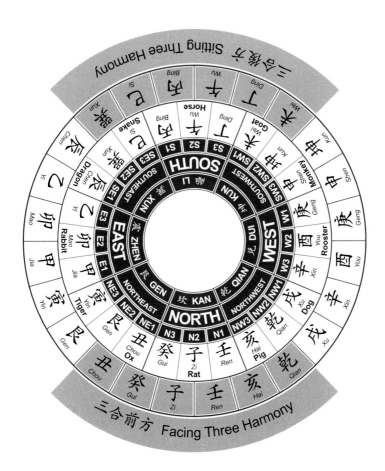

Moving Horse Six Ren Assessment 走馬六壬：

神后 *Shen Hou* **Holy Empress**	功曹 *Gong Cao* **Marshall**	天罡 *Tian Gang* **Heavenly Dipper**	勝光 *Sheng Guang* **Subliminal Bright**	傳送 *Chuan Song* **Great General**	河魁 *He Kui* **River Scholar**
乾亥 *Qian Hai*	癸丑 *Gui Chou*	甲卯 *Jia Mao*	巽巳 *Xun Si*	丁未 *Ding Wei*	庚酉 *Geng You*

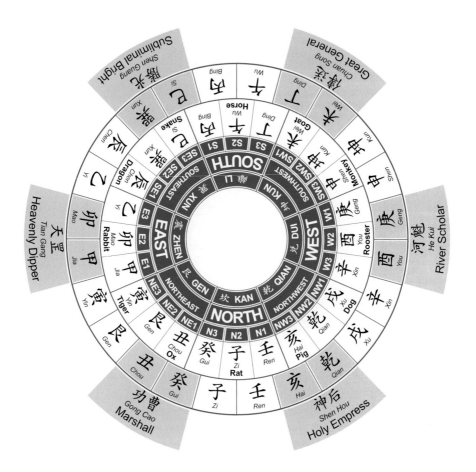

606

Four Advantages Three Cycles Star Plate 四利三元：

太陽 Tai Yang **Sun**	太陰 Tai Yin **Moon**	龍德 Long De **Dragon Virtue**	福德 Fu De **Fortune Virtue**
寅 Yin **Tiger**	辰 Chen **Dragon**	申 Shen **Monkey**	戌 Xu **Dog**

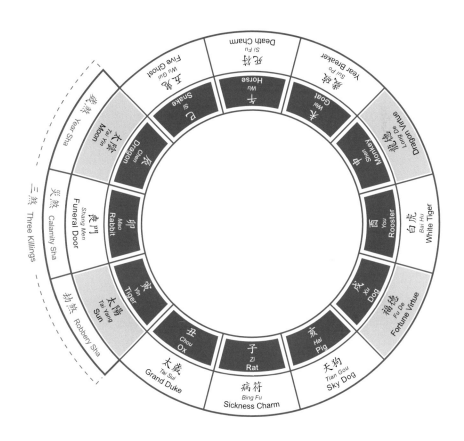

Negative Sectors For Opening Mountain 開山凶位:

年剋山家 Year Countering Sitting			
乾 *Qian* **NW2**	亥 *Hai* **NW3**	兌 *Dui* **W2**	丁 *Ding* **S3**

陰府太歲 *Yin Fu Tai Sui* **Yin Mansion Grand Duke**		六害 *Liu Hai* **Six Harm**	死符 *Si Fu* **Death Charm**	炙退 *Zhi Tui* **Roasting Star**
巽 *Xun* **SE2**	艮 *Gen* **NE2**	午 *Wu* **S2**	午 *Wu* **S2**	子 *Zi* **N2**

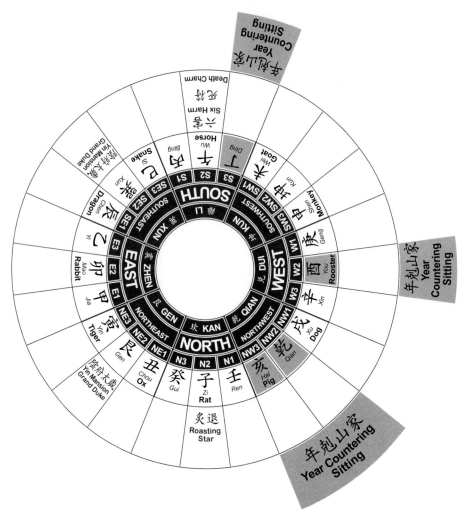

Negative Directions to Establish Facing 立向凶方：

巡山羅喉 *Xun Shan Luo Hou* **Mountain Patrol Luo Hou Star**	病符 *Bing Fu* **Sickness Charm**
艮 *Gen* **NE2**	子 *Zi* **N2**

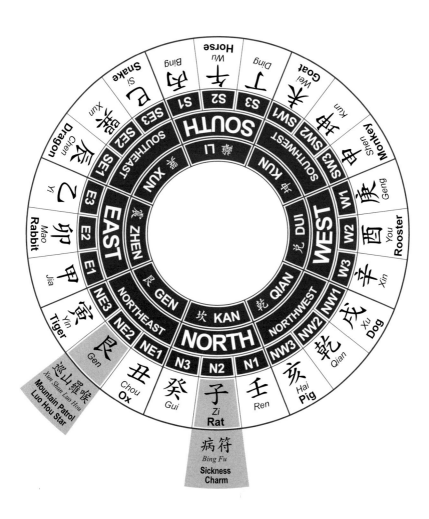

Negative Repair / Renovation Sectors Table 修方凶位表：

天官符 **Heavenly Officer Charm**	申 *Shen* Monkey		飛廉 **Flying Chaste**	酉 *You* Rooster
地官符 **Earthly Officer Charm**	巳 *Si* Snake		喪門 **Funeral Door**	卯 *Mao* Rabbit
大煞 **Great Sha**	酉 *You* Rooster		弔客 **Suspended Guest**	亥 *Hai* Pig
大將軍 **Big General**	酉 *You* Rooster		白虎 **White Tiger**	酉 *You* Rooster
力士 **Strong Man**	艮 *Gen*		金神 **Golden God**	午 *Wu* Horse
蠶室 **Silkworm Room**	坤 *Kun*			未 *Wei* Goat
蠶官 **Silkworm Officer**	未 *Wei* Goat			申 *Shen* Monkey
蠶命 **Silkworm Life**	申 *Shen* Monkey			酉 *You* Rooster
歲刑 **Duke Punishment**	戌 *Xu* Dog		獨火 **Lonely Fire**	震 *Zhen*
黃幡 **Yellow Flag**	丑 *Chou* Ox		五鬼 **Five Ghost**	卯 *Mao* Rabbit
豹尾 **Leopard Tail**	未 *Wei* Goat		破敗五鬼 **Destructive Five Ghost**	坎 *Kan*

Negative Repair / Renovation Sectors Diagram 修方凶位圖：

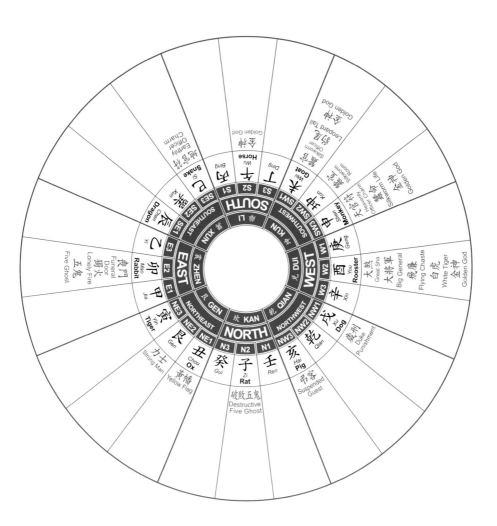

12-Month Auxiliary Stars Reference Table :
己丑年十二月，開山立向修方星表

Positive Monthly Stars 吉星方

月 MONTH	寅 Tiger (Feb 4 - Mar 5) 正月 1st Month	卯 Rabbit (Mar 6 - Apr 4) 二月 2nd Month	辰 Dragon (Apr 5 - May 5) 三月 3rd Month	巳 Snake (May 6 - Jun 5) 四月 4th Month	午 Horse (Jun 6 - July 6) 五月 5th Month	未 Goat (July 7 - Aug 7) 六月 6th Month
天道 Heavenly Path	南 South	西南 Southwest	北 North	西 West	西北 Northwest	東 East
天德 Heavenly Virtue	丁 Ding Yin Fire	坤 Kun (申)	壬 Ren Yang Water	辛 Xin Yin Metal	乾 Qian (亥)	甲 Jia Yang Wood
天德合 Heavenly Virtue Combo	壬 Ren Yang Water	(巳)	丁 Ding Yin Fire	丙 Bing Yang Fire	(寅)	己 Ji Yin Earth
月德 Monthly Virtue	丙 Bing Yang Fire	甲 Jia Yang Wood	壬 Ren Yang Water	庚 Geng Yang Metal	丙 Bing Yang Fire	甲 Jia Yang Wood
月德合 Monthly Virtue Combo	辛 Xin Yin Metal	己 Ji Yin Earth	丁 Ding Yin Fire	乙 Yi Yin Wood	辛 Xin Yin Metal	己 Ji Yin Earth
月空 Month Emptiness	壬 Ren Yang Water	庚 Geng Yang Metal	丙 Bing Yang Fire	甲 Jia Yang Wood	壬 Ren Yang Water	庚 Geng Yang Metal
陽貴人 Yang Nobleman	乾 Qian	中 Middle	巽 Xun	震 Zhen	坤 Kun	坎 Kan
陰貴人 Yin Nobleman	坤 Kun	坎 Kan	離 Li	艮 Gen	兌 Dui	乾 Qian
飛天祿 Flying Heavenly Wealth	離 Li	艮 Gen	兌 Dui	乾 Qian	中 Middle	坎 Kan
飛天馬 Flying Heavenly Horse	中 Middle	巽 Xun	震 Zhen	坤 Kun	坎 Kan	離 Li

12-Month Auxiliary Stars Reference Table :
己丑年十二月，開山立向修方星表

申 Monkey (Aug 8 - Sept 7) 七月 7th Month	酉 Rooster (Sept 8 - Oct 7) 八月 8th Month	戌 Dog (Oct 8 - Nov 6) 九月 9th Month	亥 Pig (Nov 7 - Dec 6) 十月 10th Month	子 Rat (Dec 7 - Jan 5) 十一月 11th Month	丑 Ox (Jan 6 - Feb 3) 十二月 12th Month	月 MONTH
北 North	東北 Northeast	南 South	東 East	東南 Southeast	西 West	天道 Heavenly Path
癸 Gui Yin Water	艮 Gen （寅）	丙 Bing Yang Fire	乙 Yi Yin Wood	巽 Xun （巳）	庚 Geng Yang Metal	天德 Heavenly Virtue
戊 Wu Yang Earth	（亥）	辛 Xin Yin Metal	庚 Geng Yang Metal	（申）	乙 Yi Yin Wood	天德合 Heavenly Virtue Combo
壬 Ren Yang Water	庚 Geng Yang Metal	丙 Bing Yang Fire	甲 Jia Yang Wood	壬 Ren Yang Water	庚 Geng Yang Metal	月德 Monthly Virtue
丁 Ding Yin Fire	乙 Yi Yin Wood	辛 Xin Yin Metal	己 Ji Yin Earth	丁 Ding Yin Fire	乙 Yi Yin Wood	月德合 Monthly Virtue Combo
丙 Bing Yang Fire	甲 Jia Yang Wood	壬 Ren Yang Water	庚 Geng Yang Metal	丙 Bing Yang Fire	甲 Jia Yang Wood	月空 Month Emptiness
離 Li	艮 Gen	兌 Dui	乾 Qian	中 Middle	坎 Kan	陽貴人 Yang Nobleman
中 Middle	坎 Kan	離 Li	艮 Gen	兌 Dui	乾 Qian	陰貴人 Yin Nobleman
離 Li	艮 Gen	兌 Dui	乾 Qian	中 Middle	巽 Xun	飛天祿 Flying Heavenly Wealth
艮 Gen	兌 Dui	乾 Qian	中 Middle	坎 Kan	離 Li	飛天馬 Flying Heavenly Horse

Monthly Purple White Stars 月紫白九星 :

寅 Tiger (Feb 4 - Mar 5) 正月 **1st Month**

巽 SE	離 S	坤 SW
4 Green 四綠	**9** Purple 九紫	**2** Black 二黑
3 Jade 三碧	**5** Yellow 五黃	**7** Red 七赤
8 White 八白	**1** White 一白	**6** White 六白

震 E (left) · 兌 W (right) · 艮 NE · 坎 N · 乾 NW

卯 Rabbit (Mar 6 - Apr 4) 二月 **2nd Month**

巽 SE	離 S	坤 SW
3 Jade 三碧	**8** White 八白	**1** White 一白
2 Black 二黑	**4** Green 四綠	**6** White 六白
7 Red 七赤	**9** Purple 九紫	**5** Yellow 五黃

辰 Dragon (Apr 5 - May 5) 三月 **3rd Month**

巽 SE	離 S	坤 SW
2 Black 二黑	**7** Red 七赤	**9** Purple 九紫
1 White 一白	**3** Jade 三碧	**5** Yellow 五黃
6 White 六白	**8** White 八白	**4** Green 四綠

巳 Snake (May 6 - Jun 5) 四月 **4th Month**

巽 SE	離 S	坤 SW
1 White 一白	**6** White 六白	**8** White 八白
9 Purple 九紫	**2** Black 二黑	**4** Green 四綠
5 Yellow 五黃	**7** Red 七赤	**3** Jade 三碧

午 Horse (Jun 6 - July 6) 五月 **5th Month**

巽 SE	離 S	坤 SW
9 Purple 九紫	**5** Yellow 五黃	**7** Red 七赤
8 White 八白	**1** White 一白	**3** Jade 三碧
4 Green 四綠	**6** White 六白	**2** Black 二黑

未 Goat (July 7 - Aug 7) 六月 **6th Month**

巽 SE	離 S	坤 SW
8 White 八白	**4** Green 四綠	**6** White 六白
7 Red 七赤	**9** Purple 九紫	**2** Black 二黑
3 Jade 三碧	**5** Yellow 五黃	**1** White 一白

申 Monkey (Aug 8 - Sept 7) 七月 **7th Month**

巽 SE	離 S	坤 SW
7 Red 七赤	**3** Jade 三碧	**5** Yellow 五黃
6 White 六白	**8** White 八白	**1** White 一白
2 Black 二黑	**4** Green 四綠	**9** Purple 九紫

酉 Rooster (Sept 8 - Oct 7) 八月 **8th Month**

巽 SE	離 S	坤 SW
6 White 六白	**2** Black 二黑	**4** Green 四綠
5 Yellow 五黃	**7** Red 七赤	**9** Purple 九紫
1 White 一白	**3** Jade 三碧	**8** White 八白

戌 Dog (Oct 8 - Nov 6) 九月 **9th Month**

巽 SE	離 S	坤 SW
5 Yellow 五黃	**1** White 一白	**3** Jade 三碧
4 Green 四綠	**6** White 六白	**8** White 八白
9 Purple 九紫	**2** Black 二黑	**7** Red 七赤

亥 Pig (Nov 7 - Dec 6) 十月 **10th Month**

巽 SE	離 S	坤 SW
4 Green 四綠	**9** Purple 九紫	**2** Black 二黑
3 Jade 三碧	**5** Yellow 五黃	**7** Red 七赤
8 White 八白	**1** White 一白	**6** White 六白

子 Rat (Dec 7 - Jan 5) 十一月 **11th Month**

巽 SE	離 S	坤 SW
3 Jade 三碧	**8** White 八白	**1** White 一白
2 Black 二黑	**4** Green 四綠	**6** White 六白
7 Red 七赤	**9** Purple 九紫	**5** Yellow 五黃

丑 Ox (Jan 6 - Feb 3) 十二月 **12th Month**

巽 SE	離 S	坤 SW
2 Black 二黑	**7** Red 七赤	**9** Purple 九紫
1 White 一白	**3** Jade 三碧	**5** Yellow 五黃
6 White 六白	**8** White 八白	**4** Green 四綠

Qi Men Three Nobles 三奇 :

Three Nobles 三奇 / Seasons	乙 Yi	丙 Bing	丁 Ding
立春 **Coming of Spring** Feb 4 - Feb 18	乾 Qian	乾 Qian	兌 Dui
春分 **Spring Equinox** Mar 21 - Apr 4	坎 Kan	坎 Kan	坤 Kun
立夏 **Coming of Summer** May 6 - May 20	坤 Kun	坤 Kun	震 Zhen
夏至 **Summer Solstice** Jun 22 - Jul 6	坤 Kun	坤 Kun	坎 Kan
立秋 **Coming of Autumn** Aug 8 - Aug 23	巽 Xun	巽 Xun	震 Zhen
秋分 **Autumn Equinox** Sept 23 - Oct 7	離 Li	離 Li	艮 Gen
立冬 **Coming of Winter** Nov 7 - Nov 22	艮 Gen	艮 Gen	兌 Dui
冬至 **Winter Solstice** Dec 22 - Jan 5	艮 Gen	艮 Gen	離 Li

Sectors to Avoid Opening Mountain 開山凶位 :

月 MONTH	月建 Month Establishment	月破 Month Destruction	月剋山家 Month Countering Sitting		陰府太歲 Yin Mansion Grand Duke	
寅 **Tiger** (Feb 4 - Mar 5) 正月 **1st Month**	寅 *Yin* **Tiger**	申 *Shen* **Monkey**	乾 *Qian*	兌 *Dui*	坎 *Kan*	坤 *Kun*
卯 **Rabbit** (Mar 6 - Apr 4) 二月 **2nd Month**	卯 *Mao* **Rabbit**	酉 *You* **Rooster**	亥 *Hai* **Pig**	丁 *Ding* **Yin Fire**	乾 *Qian*	離 *Li*
辰 **Dragon** (Apr 5 - May 5) 三月 **3rd Month**	辰 *Chen* **Dragon**	戌 *Xu* **Dog**	震 *Zhen*	巳 *Si* **Snake**	坤 *Kun*	震 *Zhen*
巳 **Snake** (May 6 - Jun 5) 四月 **4th Month**	巳 *Si* **Snake**	亥 *Hai* **Pig**	艮 *Gen*		巽 *Xun*	艮 *Gen*
午 **Horse** (Jun 6 - July 6) 五月 **5th Month**	午 *Wu* **Horse**	子 *Zi* **Rat**	—		乾 *Qian*	兌 *Dui*
未 **Goat** (July 7 - Aug 7) 六月 **6th Month**	未 *Wei* **Goat**	丑 *Chou* **Ox**	—		坤 *Kun*	坎 *Kan*
申 **Monkey** (Aug 8 - Sept 7) 七月 **7th Month**	申 *Shen* **Monkey**	寅 *Yin* **Tiger**	水 **Water**	山 **Mountain**	離 *Li*	乾 *Qian*
酉 **Rooster** (Sept 8 - Oct 7) 八月 **8th Month**	酉 *You* **Rooster**	卯 *Mao* **Rabbit**	土 **Earth**		震 *Zhen*	坤 *Kun*
戌 **Dog** (Oct 8 - Nov 6) 九月 **9th Month**	戌 *Xu* **Dog**	辰 *Chen* **Dragon**	乾 *Qian*	兌 *Dui*	艮 *Gen*	巽 *Xun*
亥 **Pig** (Nov 7 - Dec 6) 十月 **10th Month**	亥 *Hai* **Pig**	巳 *Si* **Snake**	亥 *Hai* **Pig**	丁 *Ding* **Yin Fire**	兌 *Dui*	乾 *Qian*
子 **Rat** (Dec 7 - Jan 5) 十一月 **11th Month**	子 *Zi* **Rat**	午 *Wu* **Horse**	離 *Li*	丙 *Bing* **Yang Fire**	坎 *Kan*	坤 *Kun*
丑 **Ox** (Jan 6 - Feb 3) 十二月 **12th Month**	丑 *Chou* **Ox**	未 *Wei* **Goat**	壬 *Ren* **Yang Water**	乙 *Yi* **Yin Wood**	乾 *Qian*	離 *Li*

Negative Repair / Renovation Sectors 修方凶位 :

月 MONTH	天官符 Heavenly Officer Charm			地官符 Earth Officer Charm			小月建 Small Month Establishment		
寅 **Tiger** (Feb 4 - Mar 5) 正月 **1st Month**	未 *Wei* Goat	坤 *Kun*	申 *Shen* Monkey	丑 *Chou* Ox	艮 *Gen*	寅 *Yin* Tiger	丙 *Bing* Yang Fire	離 *Li*	丁 *Ding* Yin Fire
卯 **Rabbit** (Mar 6 - Apr 4) 二月 **2nd Month**	壬 *Ren* Yang Water	坎 *Kan*	癸 *Gui* Yin Water	庚 *Geng* Yang Metal	兑 *Dui*	辛 *Xin* Yin Metal	壬 *Ren* Yang Water	坎 *Kan*	癸 *Gui* Yin Water
辰 **Dragon** (Apr 5 - May 5) 三月 **3rd Month**	丙 *Bing* Yang Fire	離 *Li*	丁 *Ding* Yin Fire	戌 *Xu* Dog	乾 *Qian*	亥 *Hai* Pig	未 *Wei* Goat	坤 *Kun*	申 *Shen* Monkey
巳 **Snake** (May 6 - Jun 5) 四月 **4th Month**	丑 *Chou* Ox	艮 *Gen*	寅 *Yin* Tiger	中 Middle			甲 *Jia* Yang Wood	震 *Zhen*	乙 *Yi* Yin Wood
午 **Horse** (Jun 6 - July 6) 五月 **5th Month**	庚 *Geng* Yang Metal	兑 *Dui*	辛 *Xin* Yin Metal	庚 *Geng* Yang Metal	兑 *Dui*	辛 *Xin* Yin Metal	辰 *Chen* Dragon	巽 *Xun*	巳 *Si* Snake
未 **Goat** (July 7 - Aug 7) 六月 **6th Month**	戌 *Xu* Dog	乾 *Qian*	亥 *Hai* Pig	戌 *Xu* Dog	乾 *Qian*	亥 *Hai* Pig		中 Middle	
申 **Monkey** (Aug 8 - Sept 7) 七月 **7th Month**		中 Middle			中 Middle		戌 *Xu* Dog	乾 *Qian*	亥 *Hai* Pig
酉 **Rooster** (Sept 8 - Oct 7) 八月 **8th Month**	庚 *Geng* Yang Metal	兑 *Dui*	辛 *Xin* Yin Metal	辰 *Chen* Dragon	巽 *Xun*	巳 *Si* Snake	庚 *Geng* Yang Metal	兑 *Dui*	辛 *Xin* Yin Metal
戌 **Dog** (Oct 8 - Nov 6) 九月 **9th Month**	戌 *Xu* Dog	乾 *Qian*	亥 *Hai* Pig	甲 *Jia* Yang Wood	震 *Zhen*	乙 *Yi* Yin Wood	丑 *Chou* Ox	艮 *Gen*	寅 *Yin* Tiger
亥 **Pig** (Nov 7 - Dec 6) 十月 **10th Month**		中 Middle		未 *Wei* Goat	坤 *Kun*	申 *Shen* Monkey	丙 *Bing* Yang Fire	離 *Li*	丁 *Ding* Yin Fire
子 **Rat** (Dec 7 - Jan 5) 十一月 **11th Month**	辰 *Chen* Dragon	巽 *Xun*	巳 *Si* Snake	壬 *Ren* Yang Water	坎 *Kan*	癸 *Gui* Yin Water	壬 *Ren* Yang Water	坎 *Kan*	癸 *Gui* Yin Water
丑 **Ox** (Jan 6 - Feb 3) 十二月 **12th Month**	甲 *Jia* Yang Wood	震 *Zhen*	乙 *Yi* Yin Wood	丙 *Bing* Yang Fire	離 *Li*	丁 *Ding* Yin Fire	未 *Wei* Goat	坤 *Kun*	申 *Shen* Monkey

Negative Repair / Renovation Sectors 修方凶位：

月 MONTH	大月建 Big Month Establishment			飛大煞 Flying Great Sha			丙丁獨火 Bing Ding Lonely Fire	
寅 **Tiger** (Feb 4 - Mar 5) 正月 **1st Month**		中 Middle		甲 Jia Yang Wood	震 Zhen	乙 Yi Yin Wood	中 Middle	乾 Qian
卯 **Rabbit** (Mar 6 - Apr 4) 二月 **2nd Month**	辰 Chen Dragon	巽 Xun	巳 Si Snake	未 Wei Goat	坤 Kun	申 Shen Monkey	中 Middle	
辰 **Dragon** (Apr 5 - May 5) 三月 **3rd Month**	甲 Jia Yang Wood	震 Zhen	乙 Yi Yin Wood	壬 Ren Yang Water	坎 Kan	癸 Gui Yin Water	巽 Xun	中 Middle
巳 **Snake** (May 6 - Jun 5) 四月 **4th Month**	未 Wei Goat	坤 Kun	申 Shen Monkey	丙 Bing Yang Fire	離 Li	丁 Ding Yin Fire	震 Zhen	巽 Xun
午 **Horse** (Jun 6 - July 6) 五月 **5th Month**	壬 Ren Yang Water	坎 Kan	癸 Gui Yin Water	丑 Chou Ox	艮 Gen	寅 Yin Tiger	坤 Kun	震 Zhen
未 **Goat** (July 7 - Aug 7) 六月 **6th Month**	丙 Bing Yang Fire	離 Li	丁 Ding Yin Fire	庚 Geng Yang Metal	兌 Dui	辛 Xin Yin Metal	坎 Kan	坤 Kun
申 **Monkey** (Aug 8 - Sept 7) 七月 **7th Month**	丑 Chou Ox	艮 Gen	寅 Yin Tiger	戌 Xu Dog	乾 Qian	亥 Hai Pig	離 Li	坎 Kan
酉 **Rooster** (Sept 8 - Oct 7) 八月 **8th Month**	庚 Geng Yang Metal	兌 Dui	辛 Xin Yin Metal		中 Middle		艮 Gen	離 Li
戌 **Dog** (Oct 8 - Nov 6) 九月 **9th Month**	戌 Xu Dog	乾 Qian	亥 Hai Pig	庚 Geng Yang Metal	兌 Dui	辛 Xin Yin Metal	兌 Dui	艮 Gen
亥 **Pig** (Nov 7 - Dec 6) 十月 **10th Month**		中 Middle		戌 Xu Dog	乾 Qian	亥 Hai Pig	乾 Qian	兌 Dui
子 **Rat** (Dec 7 - Jan 5) 十一月 **11th Month**	辰 Chen Dragon	巽 Xun	巳 Si Snake		中 Middle		中 Middle	乾 Qian
丑 **Ox** (Jan 6 - Feb 3) 十二月 **12th Month**	甲 Jia Yang Wood	震 Zhen	乙 Yi Yin Wood	辰 Chen Dragon	巽 Xun	巳 Si Snake		中 Middle

Negative Repair / Renovation Sectors 修方凶位 :

月 MONTH	月遊火 Month Wondering Fire	三煞 Monthly 3 Killings		
		劫煞 Robbery Sha	災煞 Calamity Sha	月煞 Month Sha
寅 Tiger (Feb 4 - Mar 5) 正月 1st Month	艮 Gen	亥 Hai Pig	子 Zi Rat	丑 Chou Ox
卯 Rabbit (Mar 6 - Apr 4) 二月 2nd Month	離 Li	申 Shen Monkey	酉 You Rooster	戌 Xu Dog
辰 Dragon (Apr 5 - May 5) 三月 3rd Month	坎 Kan	巳 Si Snake	午 Wu Horse	未 Wei Goat
巳 Snake (May 6 - Jun 5) 四月 4th Month	坤 Kun	寅 Yin Tiger	卯 Mao Rabbit	辰 Chen Dragon
午 Horse (Jun 6 - July 6) 五月 5th Month	震 Zhen	亥 Hai Pig	子 Zi Rat	丑 Chou Ox
未 Goat (July 7 - Aug 7) 六月 6th Month	巽 Xun	申 Shen Monkey	酉 You Rooster	戌 Xu Dog
申 Monkey (Aug 8 - Sept 7) 七月 7th Month	中 Middle	巳 Si Snake	午 Wu Horse	未 Wei Goat
酉 Rooster (Sept 8 - Oct 7) 八月 8th Month	乾 Qian	寅 Yin Tiger	卯 Mao Rabbit	辰 Chen Dragon
戌 Dog (Oct 8 - Nov 6) 九月 9th Month	兌 Dui	亥 Hai Pig	子 Zi Rat	丑 Chou Ox
亥 Pig (Nov 7 - Dec 6) 十月 10th Month	艮 Gen	申 Shen Monkey	酉 You Rooster	戌 Xu Dog
子 Rat (Dec 7 - Jan 5) 十一月 11th Month	離 Li	巳 Si Snake	午 Wu Horse	未 Wei Goat
丑 Ox (Jan 6 - Feb 3) 十二月 12th Month	坎 Kan	寅 Yin Tiger	卯 Mao Rabbit	辰 Chen Dragon

Negative Repair / Renovation Sectors 修方凶位 :

月 MONTH	月刑 Month Punishment	月害 Month Harm	月厭 Month Detest
寅 **Tiger** (Feb 4 - Mar 5) 正月 **1st Month**	巳 *Si* Snake	巳 *Si* Snake	戌 *Xu* Dog
卯 **Rabbit** (Mar 6 - Apr 4) 二月 **2nd Month**	子 *Zi* Rat	辰 *Chen* Dragon	酉 *You* Rooster
辰 **Dragon** (Apr 5 - May 5) 三月 **3rd Month**	辰 *Chen* Dragon	卯 *Mao* Rabbit	申 *Shen* Monkey
巳 **Snake** (May 6 - Jun 5) 四月 **4th Month**	申 *Shen* Monkey	寅 *Yin* Tiger	未 *Wei* Goat
午 **Horse** (Jun 6 - July 6) 五月 **5th Month**	午 *Wu* Horse	丑 *Chou* Ox	午 *Wu* Horse
未 **Goat** (July 7 - Aug 7) 六月 **6th Month**	丑 *Chou* Ox	子 *Zi* Rat	巳 *Si* Snake
申 **Monkey** (Aug 8 - Sept 7) 七月 **7th Month**	寅 *Yin* Tiger	亥 *Hai* Pig	辰 *Chen* Dragon
酉 **Rooster** (Sept 8 - Oct 7) 八月 **8th Month**	酉 *You* Rooster	戌 *Xu* Dog	卯 *Mao* Rabbit
戌 **Dog** (Oct 8 - Nov 6) 九月 **9th Month**	未 *Wei* Goat	酉 *You* Rooster	寅 *Yin* Tiger
亥 **Pig** (Nov 7 - Dec 6) 十月 **10th Month**	亥 *Hai* Pig	申 *Shen* Monkey	丑 *Chou* Ox
子 **Rat** (Dec 7 - Jan 5) 十一月 **11th Month**	卯 *Mao* Rabbit	未 *Wei* Goat	子 *Zi* Rat
丑 **Ox** (Jan 6 - Feb 3) 十二月 **12th Month**	戌 *Xu* Dog	午 *Wu* Horse	亥 *Hai* Pig

己卯 (Ji Mao)
Earth Rabbit

己卯 (Ji Mao) Earth Rabbit

Heavenly Stem 天干	己 **Yin Earth** (陰土)
Earthly Branch 地支	卯 **Rabbit (Yin Wood** 陰木**)**
Hidden Stem 藏干	乙 **Yin Wood**
Na Yin 納音	城頭土 **Earth from the city**
Grand Duke 太歲	卯 **Rabbit**
Xuan Kong Five Element 玄空五行	7 火 **Fire**
Gua Name 卦名	䷻ 水澤節 **Regulate**
Xuan Kong Period Luck 玄空卦運	8

Annual Positive Stars for Opening Mountain, Establishing Facing and Commencing Repairs 開山立向修方吉星：

歲德 **Duke Virtue**	甲 *Jia* **Yang Wood**	
歲德合 **Duke Virtue Combo**	己 *Ji* **Yin Earth**	
歲枝德 **Duke Branch Virtue**	申 *Shen* **Monkey**	
陽貴人 **Yang Nobleman**	子 *Zi* **Rat**	
陰貴人 **Yin Nobleman**	申 *Shen* **Monkey**	
歲祿 **Duke Prosperous**	午 *Wu* **Horse**	
歲馬 **Duke Horse**	巳 *Si* **Snake**	
奏書 **Decree**	艮 *Gen*	
博士 **Professor**	坤 *Kun*	

Annual Negative Stars for Opening Mountain, Establishing Facing and Commencing Repairs 開山立向修方凶星：

太歲 Grand Duke	歲破 Year Breaker	三煞 Three Killings			坐煞向煞 Sitting Sha Facing Sha				浮天空亡 Floating Heaven Emptiness	
卯 Mao Rabbit	酉 You Rooster	申 Shen Monkey	酉 You Rooster	戌 Xu Dog	庚 Geng Yang Metal	辛 Xin Yin Metal	甲 Jia Yang Wood	乙 Yi Yin Wood	乾 Qian	甲 Jia Yang Wood

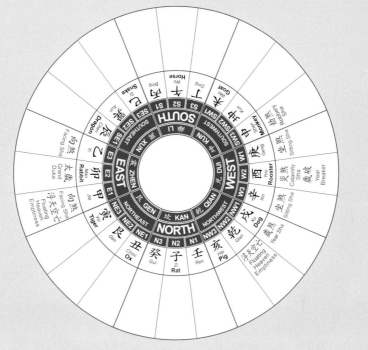

Annual San Yuan Purple White Stars 三元紫白九星：

上元 Upper Period Period 1, 2, 3			中元 Middle Period Period 4, 5, 6			下元 Lower Period Period 7, 8, 9		
巽SE	離S	坤SW	巽SE	離S	坤SW	巽SE	離S	坤SW
3	8	1	6	2	4	9	5	7
震E 2	4 己卯 Ji Mao Earth Rabbit	兌W 6	震E 5	7 己卯 Ji Mao Earth Rabbit	兌W 9	震E 8	1 己卯 Ji Mao Earth Rabbit	兌W 3
7	9	5	1	3	8	4	6	2
艮NE	坎N	乾NW	艮NE	坎N	乾NW	艮NE	坎N	乾NW

Mountain Covering Yellow Path 蓋山黃道：			
貪狼 *Tan Lang* **Greedy Wolf**	巨門 *Ju Men* **Huge Door**	武曲 *Wu Qu* **Military Arts**	文曲 *Wen Qu* **Literary Arts**
乾　甲 *Qian*　*Jia* NW2　E1	離　壬　寅　戌 *Li*　*Ren*　*Yin*　*Xu* S2　N1　NE3　NW1	坤　乙 *Kun*　*Yi* SW2　E3	巽　辛 *Xun*　*Xin* SE2　W3

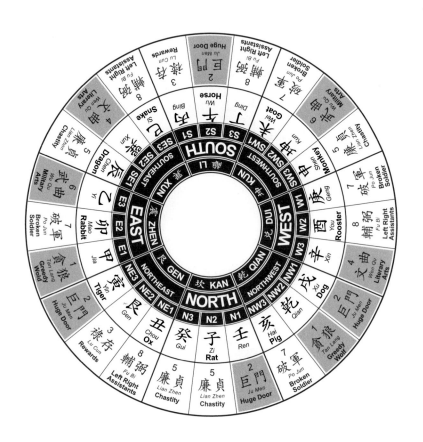

Heaven Penetrating Force 通天竅：

三合前方 **Facing Three Harmony**	巽巳 Xun Si	丙午 Bing Wu	丁未 Ding Wei
三合後方 **Sitting Three Harmony**	乾亥 Qian Hai	壬子 Ren Zi	癸丑 Gui Chou

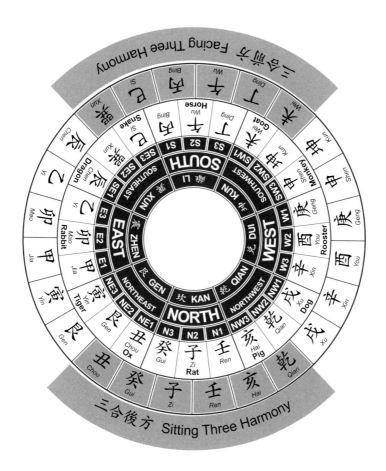

Moving Horse Six Ren Assessment 走馬六壬：

神后 *Shen Hou* **Holy Empress**	功曹 *Gong Cao* **Marshall**	天罡 *Tian Gang* **Heavenly Dipper**	勝光 *Sheng Guang* **Subliminal Bright**	傳送 *Chuan Song* **Great General**	河魁 *He Kui* **River Scholar**
庚酉 *Geng You*	乾亥 *Qian Hai*	癸丑 *Gui Chou*	甲卯 *Jia Mao*	巽巳 *Xun Si*	丁未 *Ding Wei*

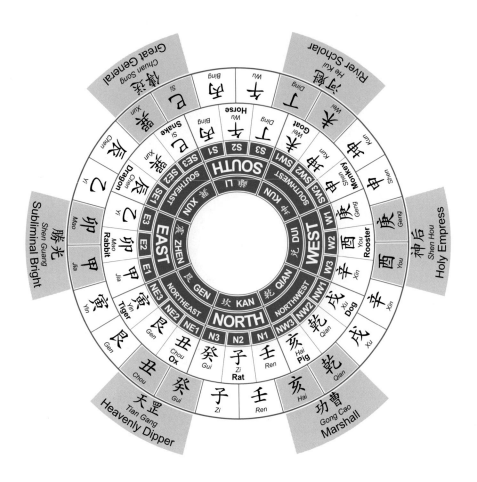

Four Advantages Three Cycles Star Plate 四利三元：

太陽 *Tai Yang* **Sun**	太陰 *Tai Yin* **Moon**	龍德 *Long De* **Dragon Virtue**	福德 *Fu De* **Fortune Virtue**
辰 *Chen* **Dragon**	午 *Wu* **Horse**	戌 *Xu* **Dog**	子 *Zi* **Rat**

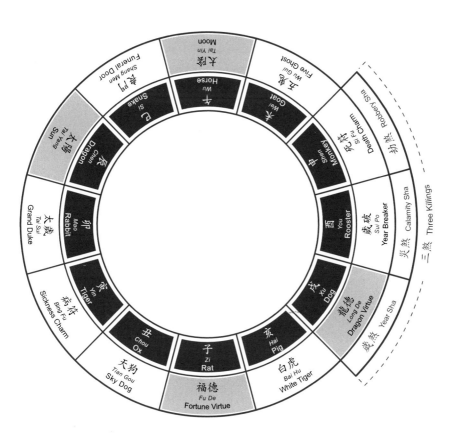

Negative Sectors For Opening Mountain 開山凶位：

年剋山家 Year Countering Sitting (冬至後 After Winter Solstice)

乾	亥	兌	丁
Qian	Hai	Dui	Ding
NW2	NW3	W2	S3

陰府太歲 Yin Fu Tai Sui **Yin Mansion Grand Duke**	六害 Liu Hai **Six Harm**	死符 Si Fu **Death Charm**	炙退 Zhi Tui **Roasting Star**
巽 艮 Xun Gen SE2 NE2	辰 Chen SE1	申 Shen SW3	午 Wu S2

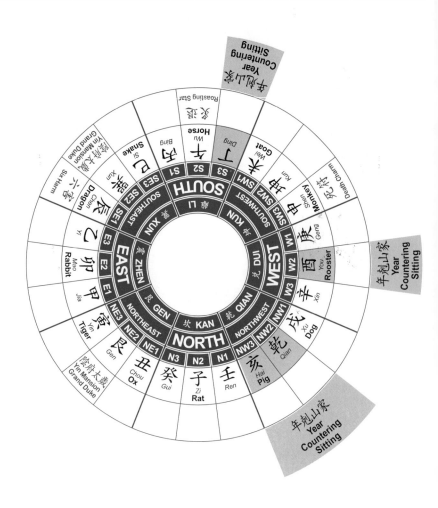

Negative Directions to Establish Facing 立向凶方：

巡山羅喉 *Xun Shan Luo Hou* **Mountain Patrol Luo Hou Star**	病符 *Bing Fu* **Sickness Charm**
乙 *Yi* **E3**	寅 *Yin* **NE3**

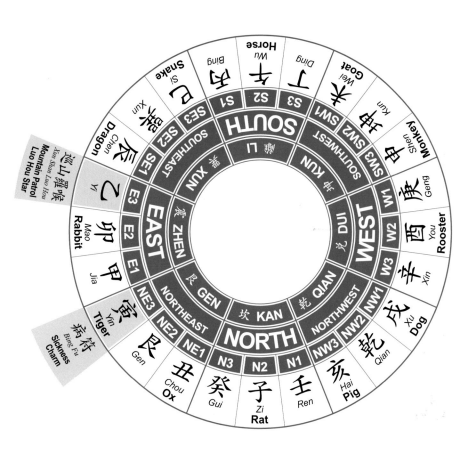

Negative Repair / Renovation Sectors Table 修方凶位表：

天官符 **Heavenly Officer Charm**	寅 *Yin* Tiger		飛廉 **Flying Chaste**	巳 *Si* Snake
地官符 **Earthly Officer Charm**	未 *Wei* Goat		喪門 **Funeral Door**	巳 *Si* Snake
大煞 **Great Sha**	卯 *Mao* Rabbit		弔客 **Suspended Guest**	丑 *Chou* Ox
大將軍 **Big General**	子 *Zi* Rat		白虎 **White Tiger**	亥 *Hai* Pig
力士 **Strong Man**	巽 *Xun*			午 *Wu* Horse
蠶室 **Silkworm Room**	乾 *Qian*			未 *Wei* Goat
蠶官 **Silkworm Officer**	戌 *Xu* Dog		金神 **Golden God**	申 *Shen* Monkey
蠶命 **Silkworm Life**	亥 *Hai* Pig			酉 *You* Rooster
歲刑 **Duke Punishment**	子 *Zi* Rat		獨火 **Lonely Fire**	坎 *Kan*
黃幡 **Yellow Flag**	未 *Wei* Goat		五鬼 **Five Ghost**	丑 *Chou* Ox
豹尾 **Leopard Tail**	丑 *Chou* Ox		破敗五鬼 **Destructive Five Ghost**	戌 *Xu* Dog

Negative Repair / Renovation Sectors Diagram 修方凶位圖：

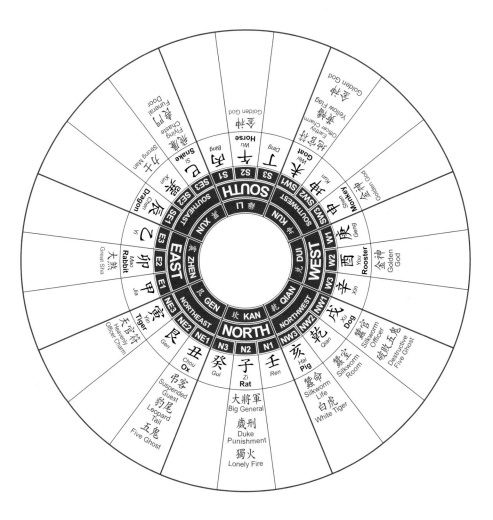

16-Month Auxiliary Stars Reference Table :
己卯年十二月，開山立向修方星表

Positive Monthly Stars 吉星方

月 MONTH	寅 Tiger (Feb 4 - Mar 5) 正月 1st Month	卯 Rabbit (Mar 6 - Apr 4) 二月 2nd Month	辰 Dragon (Apr 5 - May 5) 三月 3rd Month	巳 Snake (May 6 - Jun 5) 四月 4th Month	午 Horse (Jun 6 - July 6) 五月 5th Month	未 Goat (July 7 - Aug 7) 六月 6th Month
天道 Heavenly Path	南 South	西南 Southwest	北 North	西 West	西北 Northwest	東 East
天德 Heavenly Virtue	丁 Ding Yin Fire	坤 Kun (申)	壬 Ren Yang Water	辛 Xin Yin Metal	乾 Qian (亥)	甲 Jia Yang Wood
天德合 Heavenly Virtue Combo	壬 Ren Yang Water	(巳)	丁 Ding Yin Fire	丙 Bing Yang Fire	(寅)	己 Ji Yin Earth
月德 Monthly Virtue	丙 Bing Yang Fire	甲 Jia Yang Wood	壬 Ren Yang Water	庚 Geng Yang Metal	丙 Bing Yang Fire	甲 Jia Yang Wood
月德合 Monthly Virtue Combo	辛 Xin Yin Metal	己 Ji Yin Earth	丁 Ding Yin Fire	乙 Yi Yin Wood	辛 Xin Yin Metal	己 Ji Yin Earth
月空 Month Emptiness	壬 Ren Yang Water	庚 Geng Yang Metal	丙 Bing Yang Fire	甲 Jia Yang Wood	壬 Ren Yang Water	庚 Geng Yang Metal
陽貴人 Yang Nobleman	乾 Qian	中 Middle	巽 Xun	震 Zhen	坤 Kun	坎 Kan
陰貴人 Yin Nobleman	坤 Kun	坎 Kan	離 Li	艮 Gen	兌 Dui	乾 Qian
飛天祿 Flying Heavenly Wealth	離 Li	艮 Gen	兌 Dui	乾 Qian	中 Middle	坎 Kan
飛天馬 Flying Heavenly Horse	艮 Gen	兌 Dui	乾 Qian	中 Middle	坎 Kan	離 Li

16-Month Auxiliary Stars Reference Table :
己卯年十二月，開山立向修方星表

申 Monkey (Aug 8 - Sept 7) 七月 7th Month	酉 Rooster (Sept 8 - Oct 7) 八月 8th Month	戌 Dog (Oct 8 - Nov 6) 九月 9th Month	亥 Pig (Nov 7 - Dec 6) 十月 10th Month	子 Rat (Dec 7 - Jan 5) 十一月 11th Month	丑 Ox (Jan 6 - Feb 3) 十二月 12th Month	月 MONTH
北 North	東北 Northeast	南 South	東 East	東南 Southeast	西 West	天道 Heavenly Path
癸 Gui Yin Water	艮 Gen (寅)	丙 Bing Yang Fire	乙 Yi Yin Wood	巽 Xun (巳)	庚 Geng Yang Metal	天德 Heavenly Virtue
戊 Wu Yang Earth	(亥)	辛 Xin Yin Metal	庚 Geng Yang Metal	(申)	乙 Yi Yin Wood	天德合 Heavenly Virtue Combo
壬 Ren Yang Water	庚 Geng Yang Metal	丙 Bing Yang Fire	甲 Jia Yang Wood	壬 Ren Yang Water	庚 Geng Yang Metal	月德 Monthly Virtue
丁 Ding Yin Fire	乙 Yi Yin Wood	辛 Xin Yin Metal	己 Ji Yin Earth	丁 Ding Yin Fire	乙 Yi Yin Wood	月德合 Monthly Virtue Combo
丙 Bing Yang Fire	甲 Jia Yang Wood	壬 Ren Yang Water	庚 Geng Yang Metal	丙 Bing Yang Fire	甲 Jia Yang Wood	月空 Month Emptiness
離 Li	艮 Gen	兌 Dui	乾 Qian	中 Middle	坎 Kan	陽貴人 Yang Nobleman
中 Middle	坎 Kan	離 Li	艮 Gen	兌 Dui	乾 Qian	陰貴人 Yin Nobleman
離 Li	艮 Gen	兌 Dui	乾 Qian	中 Middle	巽 Xun	飛天祿 Flying Heavenly Wealth
艮 Gen	兌 Dui	乾 Qian	中 Middle	巽 Xun	震 Zhen	飛天馬 Flying Heavenly Horse

Monthly Purple White Stars 月紫白九星 :

寅 Tiger (Feb 4 - Mar 5) 正月 1st Month

巽 SE	離 S	坤 SW
7 Red 七赤	**3** Jade 三碧	**5** Yellow 五黄
6 White 六白 (震 E)	**8** White 八白	**1** White 一白 (兌 W)
2 Black 二黑 (艮 NE)	**4** Green 四綠 (坎 N)	**9** Purple 九紫 (乾 NW)

卯 Rabbit (Mar 6 - Apr 4) 二月 2nd Month

巽 SE	離 S	坤 SW
6 White 六白	**2** Black 二黑	**4** Green 四綠
5 Yellow 五黄 (震 E)	**7** Red 七赤	**9** Purple 九紫 (兌 W)
1 White 一白 (艮 NE)	**3** Jade 三碧 (坎 N)	**8** White 八白 (乾 NW)

辰 Dragon (Apr 5 - May 5) 三月 3rd Month

巽 SE	離 S	坤 SW
5 Yellow 五黄	**1** White 一白	**3** Jade 三碧
4 Green 四綠 (震 E)	**6** White 六白	**8** White 八白 (兌 W)
9 Purple 九紫 (艮 NE)	**2** Black 二黑 (坎 N)	**7** Red 七赤 (乾 NW)

巳 Snake (May 6 - Jun 5) 四月 4th Month

巽 SE	離 S	坤 SW
4 Green 四綠	**9** Purple 九紫	**2** Black 二黑
3 Jade 三碧 (震 E)	**5** Yellow 五黄	**7** Red 七赤 (兌 W)
8 White 八白 (艮 NE)	**1** White 一白 (坎 N)	**6** White 六白 (乾 NW)

午 Horse (Jun 6 - July 6) 五月 5th Month

巽 SE	離 S	坤 SW
3 Jade 三碧	**8** White 八白	**1** White 一白
2 Black 二黑 (震 E)	**4** Green 四綠	**6** White 六白 (兌 W)
7 Red 七赤 (艮 NE)	**9** Purple 九紫 (坎 N)	**5** Yellow 五黄 (乾 NW)

未 Goat (July 7 - Aug 7) 六月 6th Month

巽 SE	離 S	坤 SW
2 Black 二黑	**7** Red 七赤	**9** Purple 九紫
1 White 一白 (震 E)	**3** Jade 三碧	**5** Yellow 五黄 (兌 W)
6 White 六白 (艮 NE)	**8** White 八白 (坎 N)	**4** Green 四綠 (乾 NW)

申 Monkey (Aug 8 - Sept 7) 七月 7th Month

巽 SE	離 S	坤 SW
1 White 一白	**6** White 六白	**8** White 八白
9 Purple 九紫 (震 E)	**2** Black 二黑	**4** Green 四綠 (兌 W)
5 Yellow 五黄 (艮 NE)	**7** Red 七赤 (坎 N)	**3** Jade 三碧 (乾 NW)

酉 Rooster (Sept 8 - Oct 7) 八月 8th Month

巽 SE	離 S	坤 SW
9 Purple 九紫	**5** Yellow 五黄	**7** Red 七赤
8 White 八白 (震 E)	**1** White 一白	**3** Jade 三碧 (兌 W)
4 Green 四綠 (艮 NE)	**6** White 六白 (坎 N)	**2** Black 二黑 (乾 NW)

戌 Dog (Oct 8 - Nov 6) 九月 9th Month

巽 SE	離 S	坤 SW
8 White 八白	**4** Green 四綠	**6** White 六白
7 Red 七赤 (震 E)	**9** Purple 九紫	**2** Black 二黑 (兌 W)
3 Jade 三碧 (艮 NE)	**5** Yellow 五黄 (坎 N)	**1** White 一白 (乾 NW)

亥 Pig (Nov 7 - Dec 6) 十月 10th Month

巽 SE	離 S	坤 SW
7 Red 七赤	**3** Jade 三碧	**5** Yellow 五黄
6 White 六白 (震 E)	**8** White 八白	**1** White 一白 (兌 W)
2 Black 二黑 (艮 NE)	**4** Green 四綠 (坎 N)	**9** Purple 九紫 (乾 NW)

子 Rat (Dec 7 - Jan 5) 十一月 11th Month

巽 SE	離 S	坤 SW
6 White 六白	**2** Black 二黑	**4** Green 四綠
5 Yellow 五黄 (震 E)	**7** Red 七赤	**9** Purple 九紫 (兌 W)
1 White 一白 (艮 NE)	**3** Jade 三碧 (坎 N)	**8** White 八白 (乾 NW)

丑 Ox (Jan 6 - Feb 3) 十二月 12th Month

巽 SE	離 S	坤 SW
5 Yellow 五黄	**1** White 一白	**3** Jade 三碧
4 Green 四綠 (震 E)	**6** White 六白	**8** White 八白 (兌 W)
9 Purple 九紫 (艮 NE)	**2** Black 二黑 (坎 N)	**7** Red 七赤 (乾 NW)

Qi Men Three Nobles 三奇 :

Three Nobles 三奇 / Seasons	乙 Yi	丙 Bing	丁 Ding
立春 **Coming of Spring** Feb 4 - Feb 18	中 Middle	中 Middle	乾 Qian
春分 **Spring Equinox** Mar 21 - Apr 4	離 Li	離 Li	坎 Kan
立夏 **Coming of Summer** May 6 - May 20	坎 Kan	坎 Kan	坤 Kun
夏至 **Summer Solstice** Jun 22 - Jul 6	震 Zhen	震 Zhen	坤 Kun
立秋 **Coming of Autumn** Aug 8 - Aug 23	中 Middle	中 Middle	巽 Xun
秋分 **Autumn Equinox** Sept 23 - Oct 7	坎 Kan	坎 Kan	離 Li
立冬 **Coming of Winter** Nov 7 - Nov 22	離 Li	離 Li	艮 Gen
冬至 **Winter Solstice** Dec 22 - Jan 5	兌 Dui	兌 Dui	艮 Gen

Sectors to Avoid Opening Mountain 開山凶位 :

月 MONTH	月建 Month Establishment	月破 Month Destruction	月剋山家 Month Countering Sitting		陰府太歲 Yin Mansion Grand Duke	
寅 **Tiger** (Feb 4 - Mar 5) 正月 **1st Month**	寅 *Yin* Tiger	申 *Shen* Monkey	乾 *Qian*	兌 *Dui*	坎 *Kan*	坤 *Kun*
卯 **Rabbit** (Mar 6 - Apr 4) 二月 **2nd Month**	卯 *Mao* Rabbit	酉 *You* Rooster	亥 *Hai* Pig	丁 *Ding* Yin Fire	乾 *Qian*	離 *Li*
辰 **Dragon** (Apr 5 - May 5) 三月 **3rd Month**	辰 *Chen* Dragon	戌 *Xu* Dog	震 *Zhen*	巳 *Si* Snake	坤 *Kun*	震 *Zhen*
巳 **Snake** (May 6 - Jun 5) 四月 **4th Month**	巳 *Si* Snake	亥 *Hai* Pig	艮 *Gen*		巽 *Xun*	艮 *Gen*
午 **Horse** (Jun 6 - July 6) 五月 **5th Month**	午 *Wu* Horse	子 *Zi* Rat	—		乾 *Qian*	兌 *Dui*
未 **Goat** (July 7 - Aug 7) 六月 **6th Month**	未 *Wei* Goat	丑 *Chou* Ox	—		坤 *Kun*	坎 *Kan*
申 **Monkey** (Aug 8 - Sept 7) 七月 **7th Month**	申 *Shen* Monkey	寅 *Yin* Tiger	水 Water	山 Mountain	離 *Li*	乾 *Qian*
酉 **Rooster** (Sept 8 - Oct 7) 八月 **8th Month**	酉 *You* Rooster	卯 *Mao* Rabbit	土 Earth		震 *Zhen*	坤 *Kun*
戌 **Dog** (Oct 8 - Nov 6) 九月 **9th Month**	戌 *Xu* Dog	辰 *Chen* Dragon	乾 *Qian*	兌 *Dui*	艮 *Gen*	巽 *Xun*
亥 **Pig** (Nov 7 - Dec 6) 十月 **10th Month**	亥 *Hai* Pig	巳 *Si* Snake	亥 *Hai* Pig	丁 *Ding* Yin Fire	兌 *Dui*	乾 *Qian*
子 **Rat** (Dec 7 - Jan 5) 十一月 **11th Month**	子 *Zi* Rat	午 *Wu* Horse	離 *Li*	丙 *Bing* Yang Fire	坎 *Kan*	坤 *Kun*
丑 **Ox** (Jan 6 - Feb 3) 十二月 **12th Month**	丑 *Chou* Ox	未 *Wei* Goat	壬 *Ren* Yang Water	乙 *Yi* Yin Wood	兌 *Dui*	乾 *Qian*

Negative Repair / Renovation Sectors 修方凶位 :

月 MONTH	天官符 Heavenly Officer Charm			地官符 Earth Officer Charm			小月建 Small Month Establishment		
寅 **Tiger** (Feb 4 - Mar 5) 正月 **1st Month**		中 Middle		壬 Ren Yang Water	坎 Kan	癸 Gui Yin Water	丙 Bing Yang Fire	離 Li	丁 Ding Yin Fire
卯 **Rabbit** (Mar 6 - Apr 4) 二月 **2nd Month**	庚 Geng Yang Metal	兌 Dui	辛 Xin Yin Metal	丙 Bing Yang Fire	離 Li	丁 Ding Yin Fire	壬 Ren Yang Water	坎 Kan	癸 Gui Yin Water
辰 **Dragon** (Apr 5 - May 5) 三月 **3rd Month**	戊 Xu Dog	乾 Qian	亥 Hai Pig	丑 Chou Ox	艮 Gen	寅 Yin Tiger	未 Wei Goat	坤 Kun	申 Shen Monkey
巳 **Snake** (May 6 - Jun 5) 四月 **4th Month**		中 Middle		庚 Geng Yang Metal	兌 Dui	辛 Xin Yin Metal	甲 Jia Yang Wood	震 Zhen	乙 Yi Yin Wood
午 **Horse** (Jun 6 - July 6) 五月 **5th Month**	辰 Chen Dragon	巽 Xun	巳 Si Snake	戊 Xu Dog	乾 Qian	亥 Hai Pig	辰 Chen Dragon	巽 Xun	巳 Si Snake
未 **Goat** (July 7 - Aug 7) 六月 **6th Month**	甲 Jia Yang Wood	震 Zhen	乙 Yi Yin Wood		中 Middle			中 Middle	
申 **Monkey** (Aug 8 - Sept 7) 七月 **7th Month**	未 Wei Goat	坤 Kun	申 Shen Monkey	庚 Geng Yang Metal	兌 Dui	辛 Xin Yin Metal	戊 Xu Dog	乾 Qian	亥 Hai Pig
酉 **Rooster** (Sept 8 - Oct 7) 八月 **8th Month**	壬 Ren Yang Water	坎 Kan	癸 Gui Yin Water	戊 Xu Dog	乾 Qian	亥 Hai Pig	庚 Geng Yang Metal	兌 Dui	辛 Xin Yin Metal
戌 **Dog** (Oct 8 - Nov 6) 九月 **9th Month**	丙 Bing Yang Fire	離 Li	丁 Ding Yin Fire		中 Middle		丑 Chou Ox	艮 Gen	寅 Yin Tiger
亥 **Pig** (Nov 7 - Dec 6) 十月 **10th Month**	丑 Chou Ox	艮 Gen	寅 Yin Tiger	辰 Chen Dragon	巽 Xun	巳 Si Snake	丙 Bing Yang Fire	離 Li	丁 Ding Yin Fire
子 **Rat** (Dec 7 - Jan 5) 十一月 **11th Month**	庚 Geng Yang Metal	兌 Dui	辛 Xin Yin Metal	甲 Jia Yang Wood	震 Zhen	乙 Yi Yin Wood	壬 Ren Yang Water	坎 Kan	癸 Gui Yin Water
丑 **Ox** (Jan 6 - Feb 3) 十二月 **12th Month**	戊 Xu Dog	乾 Qian	亥 Hai Pig	未 Wei Goat	坤 Kun	申 Shen Monkey	未 Wei Goat	坤 Kun	申 Shen Monkey

Negative Repair / Renovation Sectors 修方凶位 :

月 MONTH	大月建 Big Month Establishment			飛大煞 Flying Great Sha			丙丁獨火 Bing Ding Lonely Fire	
寅 **Tiger** (Feb 4 - Mar 5) 正月 **1st Month**	丑 *Chou* Ox	艮 *Gen*	寅 *Yin* Tiger	戌 *Xu* Dog	乾 *Qian*	亥 *Hai* Pig	中 Middle	乾 *Qian*
卯 **Rabbit** (Mar 6 - Apr 4) 二月 **2nd Month**	庚 *Geng* Yang Metal	兌 *Dui*	辛 *Xin* Yin Metal	中 Middle			中 Middle	
辰 **Dragon** (Apr 5 - May 5) 三月 **3rd Month**	戌 *Xu* Dog	乾 *Qian*	亥 *Hai* Pig	庚 *Geng* Yang Metal	兌 *Dui*	辛 *Xin* Yin Metal	巽 *Xun*	中 Middle
巳 **Snake** (May 6 - Jun 5) 四月 **4th Month**	中 Middle			戌 *Xu* Dog	乾 *Qian*	亥 *Hai* Pig	震 *Zhen*	巽 *Xun*
午 **Horse** (Jun 6 - July 6) 五月 **5th Month**	辰 *Chen* Dragon	巽 *Xun*	巳 *Si* Snake	中 Middle			坤 *Kun*	震 *Zhen*
未 **Goat** (July 7 - Aug 7) 六月 **6th Month**	甲 *Jia* Yang Wood	震 *Zhen*	乙 *Yi* Yin Wood	辰 *Chen* Dragon	巽 *Xun*	巳 *Si* Snake	坎 *Kan*	坤 *Kun*
申 **Monkey** (Aug 8 - Sept 7) 七月 **7th Month**	未 *Wei* Goat	坤 *Kun*	申 *Shen* Monkey	甲 *Jia* Yang Wood	震 *Zhen*	乙 *Yi* Yin Wood	離 *Li*	坎 *Kan*
酉 **Rooster** (Sept 8 - Oct 7) 八月 **8th Month**	壬 *Ren* Yang Water	坎 *Kan*	癸 *Gui* Yin Water	未 *Wei* Goat	坤 *Kun*	申 *Shen* Monkey	艮 *Gen*	離 *Li*
戌 **Dog** (Oct 8 - Nov 6) 九月 **9th Month**	丙 *Bing* Yang Fire	離 *Li*	丁 *Ding* Yin Fire	壬 *Ren* Yang Water	坎 *Kan*	癸 *Gui* Yin Water	兌 *Dui*	艮 *Gen*
亥 **Pig** (Nov 7 - Dec 6) 十月 **10th Month**	丑 *Chou* Ox	艮 *Gen*	寅 *Yin* Tiger	丙 *Bing* Yang Fire	離 *Li*	丁 *Ding* Yin Fire	乾 *Qian*	兌 *Dui*
子 **Rat** (Dec 7 - Jan 5) 十一月 **11th Month**	庚 *Geng* Yang Metal	兌 *Dui*	辛 *Xin* Yin Metal	丑 *Chou* Ox	艮 *Gen*	寅 *Yin* Tiger	中 Middle	乾 *Qian*
丑 **Ox** (Jan 6 - Feb 3) 十二月 **12th Month**	戌 *Xu* Dog	乾 *Qian*	亥 *Hai* Pig	庚 *Geng* Yang Metal	兌 *Dui*	辛 *Xin* Yin Metal	中 Middle	

Negative Repair / Renovation Sectors 修方凶位 :

月 MONTH	月遊火 Month Wondering Fire	三煞 Monthly 3 Killings		
		劫煞 Robbery Sha	災煞 Calamity Sha	月煞 Month Sha
寅 **Tiger** (Feb 4 - Mar 5) 正月 **1st Month**	巽 Xun	亥 Hai Pig	子 Zi Rat	丑 Chou Ox
卯 **Rabbit** (Mar 6 - Apr 4) 二月 **2nd Month**	中 Middle	申 Shen Monkey	酉 You Rooster	戌 Xu Dog
辰 **Dragon** (Apr 5 - May 5) 三月 **3rd Month**	乾 Qian	巳 Si Snake	午 Wu Horse	未 Wei Goat
巳 **Snake** (May 6 - Jun 5) 四月 **4th Month**	兌 Dui	寅 Yin Tiger	卯 Mao Rabbit	辰 Chen Dragon
午 **Horse** (Jun 6 - July 6) 五月 **5th Month**	艮 Gen	亥 Hai Pig	子 Zi Rat	丑 Chou Ox
未 **Goat** (July 7 - Aug 7) 六月 **6th Month**	離 Li	申 Shen Monkey	酉 You Rooster	戌 Xu Dog
申 **Monkey** (Aug 8 - Sept 7) 七月 **7th Month**	坎 Kan	巳 Si Snake	午 Wu Horse	未 Wei Goat
酉 **Rooster** (Sept 8 - Oct 7) 八月 **8th Month**	坤 Kun	寅 Yin Tiger	卯 Mao Rabbit	辰 Chen Dragon
戌 **Dog** (Oct 8 - Nov 6) 九月 **9th Month**	震 Zhen	亥 Hai Pig	子 Zi Rat	丑 Chou Ox
亥 **Pig** (Nov 7 - Dec 6) 十月 **10th Month**	巽 Xun	申 Shen Monkey	酉 You Rooster	戌 Xu Dog
子 **Rat** (Dec 7 - Jan 5) 十一月 **11th Month**	中 Middle	巳 Si Snake	午 Wu Horse	未 Wei Goat
丑 **Ox** (Jan 6 - Feb 3) 十二月 **12th Month**	乾 Qian	寅 Yin Tiger	卯 Mao Rabbit	辰 Chen Dragon

Negative Repair / Renovation Sectors 修方凶位 :

月 MONTH	月刑 Month Punishment	月害 Month Harm	月厭 Month Detest
寅 **Tiger** (Feb 4 - Mar 5) 正月 1st Month	巳 *Si* Snake	巳 *Si* Snake	戌 *Xu* Dog
卯 **Rabbit** (Mar 6 - Apr 4) 二月 2nd Month	子 *Zi* Rat	辰 *Chen* Dragon	酉 *You* Rooster
辰 **Dragon** (Apr 5 - May 5) 三月 3rd Month	辰 *Chen* Dragon	卯 *Mao* Rabbit	申 *Shen* Monkey
巳 **Snake** (May 6 - Jun 5) 四月 4th Month	申 *Shen* Monkey	寅 *Yin* Tiger	未 *Wei* Goat
午 **Horse** (Jun 6 - July 6) 五月 5th Month	午 *Wu* Horse	丑 *Chou* Ox	午 *Wu* Horse
未 **Goat** (July 7 - Aug 7) 六月 6th Month	丑 *Chou* Ox	子 *Zi* Rat	巳 *Si* Snake
申 **Monkey** (Aug 8 - Sept 7) 七月 7th Month	寅 *Yin* Tiger	亥 *Hai* Pig	辰 *Chen* Dragon
酉 **Rooster** (Sept 8 - Oct 7) 八月 8th Month	酉 *You* Rooster	戌 *Xu* Dog	卯 *Mao* Rabbit
戌 **Dog** (Oct 8 - Nov 6) 九月 9th Month	未 *Wei* Goat	酉 *You* Rooster	寅 *Yin* Tiger
亥 **Pig** (Nov 7 - Dec 6) 十月 10th Month	亥 *Hai* Pig	申 *Shen* Monkey	丑 *Chou* Ox
子 **Rat** (Dec 7 - Jan 5) 十一月 11th Month	卯 *Mao* Rabbit	未 *Wei* Goat	子 *Zi* Rat
丑 **Ox** (Jan 6 - Feb 3) 十二月 12th Month	戌 *Xu* Dog	午 *Wu* Horse	亥 *Hai* Pig

己巳 (Ji Si)
Earth Snake

Heavenly Stem 天干	己 **Yin Earth** (陰土)
Earthly Branch 地支	巳 **Snake (Yin Fire** 陰火**)**
Hidden Stem 藏干	丙 **Yang Fire,** 戊 **Yang Earth,** 庚 **Yang Metal**
Na Yin 納音	大林木 **Wood from the forest**
Grand Duke 太歲	巳 **Snake**
Xuan Kong Five Element 玄空五行	8 木 **Wood**
Gua Name 卦名	雷天大壯 **Great Strength**
Xuan Kong Period Luck 玄空卦運	2

Annual Positive Stars for Opening Mountain, Establishing Facing and Commencing Repairs 開山立向修方吉星：

歲德 **Duke Virtue**	甲 *Jia* **Yang Wood**	
歲德合 **Duke Virtue Combo**	己 *Ji* **Yin Earth**	
歲枝德 **Duke Branch Virtue**	戌 *Xu* **Dog**	
陽貴人 **Yang Nobleman**	子 *Zi* **Rat**	
陰貴人 **Yin Nobleman**	申 *Shen* **Monkey**	
歲祿 **Duke Prosperous**	午 *Wu* **Horse**	
歲馬 **Duke Horse**	亥 *Hai* **Pig**	
奏書 **Decree**	巽 *Xun*	
博士 **Professor**	乾 *Qian*	

642

Annual Negative Stars for Opening Mountain, Establishing Facing and Commencing Repairs 開山立向修方凶星：

太歲 Grand Duke	歲破 Year Breaker	三煞 Three Killings			坐煞向煞 Sitting Sha Facing Sha				浮天空亡 Floating Heaven Emptiness	
巳 Si Snake	亥 Hai Pig	寅 Yin Tiger	卯 Mao Rabbit	辰 Chen Dragon	甲 Jia Yang Wood	乙 Yi Yin Wood	庚 Geng Yang Metal	辛 Xin Yin Metal	乾 Qian	甲 Jia Yang Wood

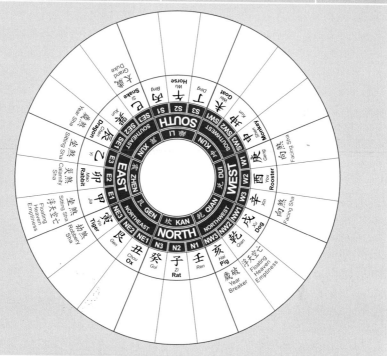

Annual San Yuan Purple White Stars 三元紫白九星：

上元 Upper Period Period 1, 2, 3	中元 Middle Period Period 4, 5, 6	下元 Lower Period Period 7, 8, 9

Upper Period (Period 1, 2, 3)

巽 SE	離 S	坤 SW
4	9	2
3 震 E	5 己巳 Ji Si Earth Snake	7 兌 W
8	1	6
艮 NE	坎 N	乾 NW

Middle Period (Period 4, 5, 6)

巽 SE	離 S	坤 SW
7	3	5
6 震 E	8 己巳 Ji Si Earth Snake	1 兌 W
2	4	9
艮 NE	坎 N	乾 NW

Lower Period (Period 7, 8, 9)

巽 SE	離 S	坤 SW
1	6	8
9 震 E	2 己巳 Ji Si Earth Snake	4 兌 W
5	7	3
艮 NE	坎 N	乾 NW

Mountain Covering Yellow Path 蓋山黃道：

貪狼 Tan Lang **Greedy Wolf**				巨門 Ju Men **Huge Door**				武曲 Wu Qu **Military Arts**		文曲 Wen Qu **Literary Arts**			
兌 Dui W2	丁 Ding S3	巳 Si SE3	丑 Chou NE1	震 Zhen E2	庚 Geng W1	亥 Hai NW3	未 Wei SW1	艮 Gen NE2	丙 Bing S1	坎 Kan N2	癸 Gui N3	申 Shen SW3	辰 Chen SE1

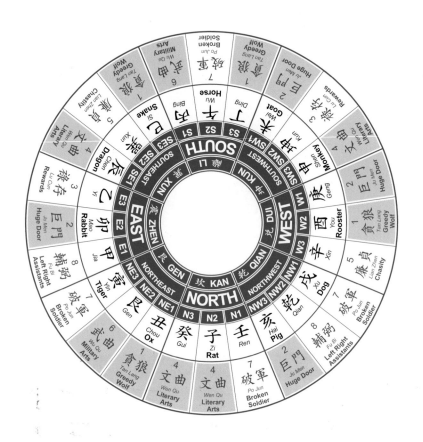

Heaven Penetrating Force 通天竅：

三合前方 Facing Three Harmony	乾亥 Qian Hai	壬子 Ren Zi	癸丑 Gui Chou
三合後方 Sitting Three Harmony	巽巳 Xun Si	丙午 Bing Wu	丁未 Ding Wei

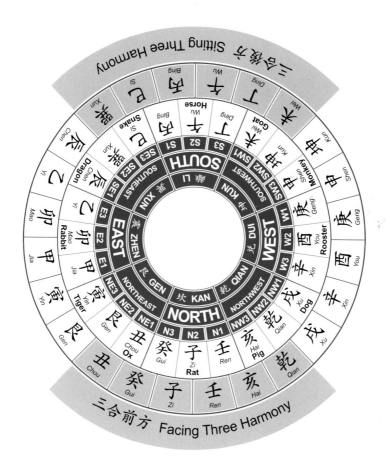

Moving Horse Six Ren Assessment 走馬六壬：

神后 Shen Hou Holy Empress	功曹 Gong Cao Marshall	天罡 Tian Gang Heavenly Dipper	勝光 Sheng Guang Subliminal Bright	傳送 Chuan Song Great General	河魁 He Kui River Scholar
丁未 Ding Wei	庚酉 Geng You	乾亥 Qian Hai	癸丑 Gui Chou	甲卯 Jia Mao	巽巳 Xun Si

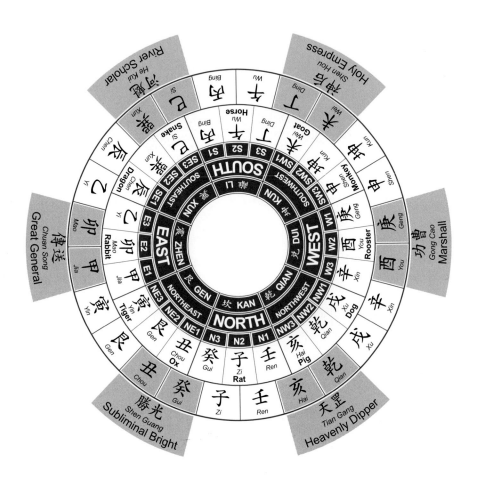

Four Advantages Three Cycles Star Plate 四利三元：

太陽 *Tai Yang* **Sun**	太陰 *Tai Yin* **Moon**	龍德 *Long De* **Dragon Virtue**	福德 *Fu De* **Fortune Virtue**
午 *Wu* **S2**	申 *Shen* **SW3**	子 *Zi* **N2**	寅 *Yin* **NE3**

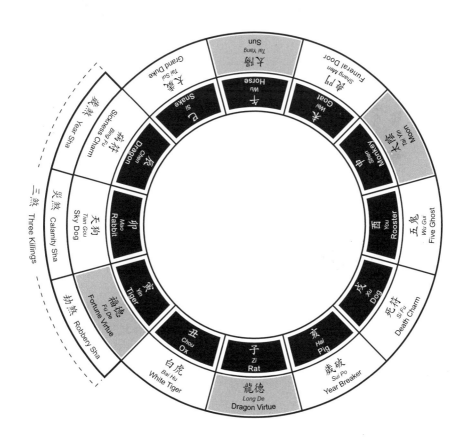

Negative Sectors For Opening Mountain 開山凶位：

年剋山家 Year Countering Sitting

震 Zhen E2	艮 Gen NE2	巳 Si SE3			

陰府太歲 Yin Fu Tai Sui **Yin Mansion Grand Duke**		六害 Liu Hai **Six Harm**	死符 Si Fu **Death Charm**	炙退 Zhi Tui **Roasting Star**
巽 Xun SE2	艮 Gen NE2	寅 Yin NE3	戌 Xu NW1	子 Zi N2

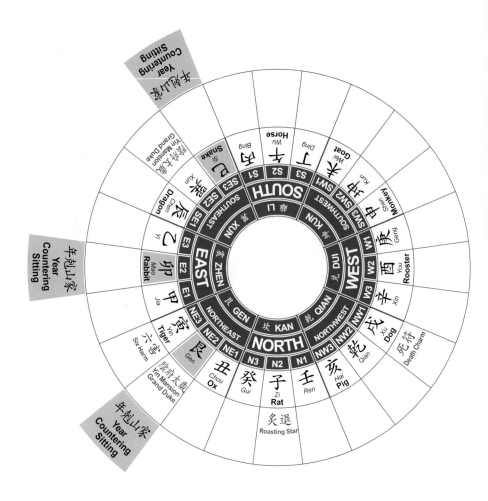

Negative Directions to Establish Facing 立向凶方:

巡山羅喉 *Xun Shan Luo Hou* **Mountain Patrol Luo Hou Star**	病符 *Bing Fu* **Sickness Charm**
丙 *Bing* **S1**	辰 *Chen* **SE1**

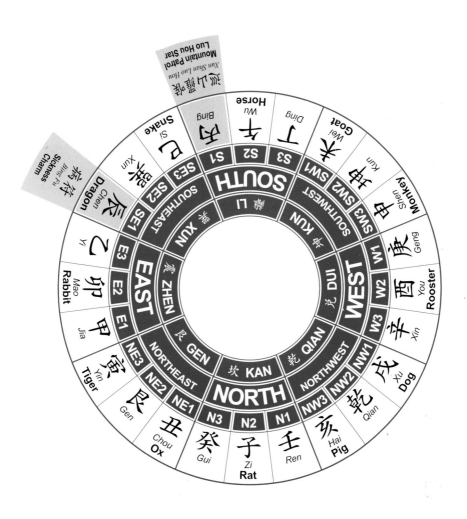

Negative Repair / Renovation Sectors Table 修方凶位表：

天官符 Heavenly Officer Charm	申 *Shen* Monkey	飛廉 Flying Chaste	未 *Wei* Goat
地官符 Earthly Officer Charm	酉 *You* Rooster	喪門 Funeral Door	未 *Wei* Goat
大煞 Great Sha	酉 *You* Rooster	弔客 Suspended Guest	卯 *Mao* Rabbit
大將軍 Big General	卯 *Mao* Rabbit	白虎 White Tiger	丑 *Chou* Ox
力士 Strong Man	坤 *Kun*	金神 Golden God	午 *Wu* Horse
蠶室 Silkworm Room	艮 *Gen*		未 *Wei* Goat
蠶官 Silkworm Officer	丑 *Chou* Ox		申 *Shen* Monkey
蠶命 Silkworm Life	寅 *Yin* Tiger		酉 *You* Rooster
歲刑 Duke Punishment	申 *Shen* Monkey	獨火 Lonely Fire	巽 *Xun*
黃幡 Yellow Flag	丑 *Chou* Ox	五鬼 Five Ghost	亥 *Hai* Pig
豹尾 Leopard Tail	未 *Wei* Goat	破敗五鬼 Destructive Five Ghost	坎 *Kan*

Negative Repair / Renovation Sectors Diagram 修方凶位圖:

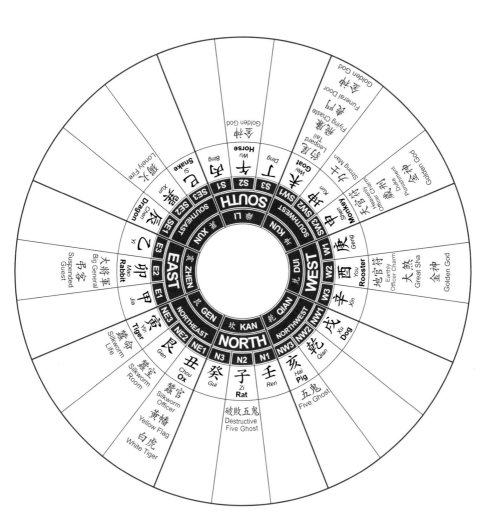

12-Month Auxiliary Stars Reference Table :
己巳年十二月，開山立向修方星表

Positive Monthly Stars 吉星方

月 MONTH	寅 Tiger (Feb 4 - Mar 5) 正月 1st Month	卯 Rabbit (Mar 6 - Apr 4) 二月 2nd Month	辰 Dragon (Apr 5 - May 5) 三月 3rd Month	巳 Snake (May 6 - Jun 5) 四月 4th Month	午 Horse (Jun 6 - July 6) 五月 5th Month	未 Goat (July 7 - Aug 7) 六月 6th Month
天道 Heavenly Path	南 South	西南 Southwest	北 North	西 West	西北 Northwest	東 East
天德 Heavenly Virtue	丁 Ding Yin Fire	坤 Kun （申）	壬 Ren Yang Water	辛 Xin Yin Metal	乾 Qian （亥）	甲 Jia Yang Wood
天德合 Heavenly Virtue Combo	壬 Ren Yang Water	（巳）	丁 Ding Yin Fire	丙 Bing Yang Fire	（寅）	己 Ji Yin Earth
月德 Monthly Virtue	丙 Bing Yang Fire	甲 Jia Yang Wood	壬 Ren Yang Water	庚 Geng Yang Metal	丙 Bing Yang Fire	甲 Jia Yang Wood
月德合 Monthly Virtue Combo	辛 Xin Yin Metal	己 Ji Yin Earth	丁 Ding Yin Fire	乙 Yi Yin Wood	辛 Xin Yin Metal	己 Ji Yin Earth
月空 Month Emptiness	壬 Ren Yang Water	庚 Geng Yang Metal	丙 Bing Yang Fire	甲 Jia Yang Wood	壬 Ren Yang Water	庚 Geng Yang Metal
陽貴人 Yang Nobleman	乾 Qian	中 Middle	巽 Xun	震 Zhen	坤 Kun	坎 Kan
陰貴人 Yin Nobleman	坤 Kun	坎 Kan	離 Li	艮 Gen	兌 Dui	乾 Qian
飛天祿 Flying Heavenly Wealth	離 Li	艮 Gen	兌 Dui	乾 Qian	中 Middle	坎 Kan
飛天馬 Flying Heavenly Horse	中 Middle	巽 Xun	震 Zhen	坤 Kun	坎 Kan	離 Li

12-Month Auxiliary Stars Reference Table :
己巳年十二月，開山立向修方星表

申 Monkey (Aug 8 - Sept 7) 七月 7th Month	酉 Rooster (Sept 8 - Oct 7) 八月 8th Month	戌 Dog (Oct 8 - Nov 6) 九月 9th Month	亥 Pig (Nov 7 - Dec 6) 十月 10th Month	子 Rat (Dec 7 - Jan 5) 十一月 11th Month	丑 Ox (Jan 6 - Feb 3) 十二月 12th Month	月 MONTH
北 North	東北 Northeast	南 South	東 East	東南 Southeast	西 West	天道 Heavenly Path
癸 Gui Yin Water	艮 Gen （寅）	丙 Bing Yang Fire	乙 Yi Yin Wood	巽 Xun （巳）	庚 Geng Yang Metal	天德 Heavenly Virtue
戊 Wu Yang Earth	（亥）	辛 Xin Yin Metal	庚 Geng Yang Metal	（申）	乙 Yi Yin Wood	天德合 Heavenly Virtue Combo
壬 Ren Yang Water	庚 Geng Yang Metal	丙 Bing Yang Fire	甲 Jia Yang Wood	壬 Ren Yang Water	庚 Geng Yang Metal	月德 Monthly Virtue
丁 Ding Yin Fire	乙 Yi Yin Wood	辛 Xin Yin Metal	己 Ji Yin Earth	丁 Ding Yin Fire	乙 Yi Yin Wood	月德合 Monthly Virtue Combo
丙 Bing Yang Fire	甲 Jia Yang Wood	壬 Ren Yang Water	庚 Geng Yang Metal	丙 Bing Yang Fire	甲 Jia Yang Wood	月空 Month Emptiness
離 Li	艮 Gen	兌 Dui	乾 Qian	中 Middle	坎 Kan	陽貴人 Yang Nobleman
中 Middle	坎 Kan	離 Li	艮 Gen	兌 Dui	乾 Qian	陰貴人 Yin Nobleman
離 Li	艮 Gen	兌 Dui	乾 Qian	中 Middle	巽 Xun	飛天祿 Flying Heavenly Wealth
艮 Gen	兌 Dui	乾 Qian	中 Middle	坎 Kan	離 Li	飛天馬 Flying Heavenly Horse

己巳 (Ji Si) Earth Snake

Monthly Purple White Stars 月紫白九星 :

寅 Tiger (Feb 4 - Mar 5) 正月 1st Month

巽SE	離S	坤SW
1 White 一白	6 White 六白	8 White 八白
震E 9 Purple 九紫	2 Black 二黑	4 Green 四綠 兌W
艮NE 5 Yellow 五黄	坎N 7 Red 七赤	乾NW 3 Jade 三碧

卯 Rabbit (Mar 6 - Apr 4) 二月 2nd Month

巽SE	離S	坤SW
9 Purple 九紫	5 Yellow 五黄	7 Red 七赤
震E 8 White 八白	1 White 一白	3 Jade 三碧 兌W
艮NE 4 Green 四綠	坎N 6 White 六白	乾NW 2 Black 二黑

辰 Dragon (Apr 5 - May 5) 三月 3rd Month

巽SE	離S	坤SW
8 White 八白	4 Green 四綠	6 White 六白
震E 7 Red 七赤	9 Purple 九紫	2 Black 二黑 兌W
艮NE 3 Jade 三碧	坎N 5 Yellow 五黄	乾NW 1 White 一白

巳 Snake (May 6 - Jun 5) 四月 4th Month

巽SE	離S	坤SW
7 Red 七赤	3 Jade 三碧	5 Yellow 五黄
震E 6 White 六白	8 White 八白	1 White 一白 兌W
艮NE 2 Black 二黑	坎N 4 Green 四綠	乾NW 9 Purple 九紫

午 Horse (Jun 6 - July 6) 五月 5th Month

巽SE	離S	坤SW
6 White 六白	2 Black 二黑	4 Green 四綠
震E 5 Yellow 五黄	7 Red 七赤	9 Purple 九紫 兌W
艮NE 1 White 一白	坎N 3 Jade 三碧	乾NW 8 White 八白

未 Goat (July 7 - Aug 7) 六月 6th Month

巽SE	離S	坤SW
5 Yellow 五黄	1 White 一白	3 Jade 三碧
震E 4 Green 四綠	6 White 六白	8 White 八白 兌W
艮NE 9 Purple 九紫	坎N 2 Black 二黑	乾NW 7 Red 七赤

申 Monkey (Aug 8 - Sept 7) 七月 7th Month

巽SE	離S	坤SW
4 Green 四綠	9 Purple 九紫	2 Black 二黑
震E 3 Jade 三碧	5 Yellow 五黄	7 Red 七赤 兌W
艮NE 8 White 八白	坎N 1 White 一白	乾NW 6 White 六白

酉 Rooster (Sept 8 - Oct 7) 八月 8th Month

巽SE	離S	坤SW
3 Jade 三碧	8 White 八白	1 White 一白
震E 2 Black 二黑	4 Green 四綠	6 White 六白 兌W
艮NE 7 Red 七赤	坎N 9 Purple 九紫	乾NW 5 Yellow 五黄

戌 Dog (Oct 8 - Nov 6) 九月 9th Month

巽SE	離S	坤SW
2 Black 二黑	7 Red 七赤	9 Purple 九紫
震E 1 White 一白	3 Jade 三碧	5 Yellow 五黄 兌W
艮NE 6 White 六白	坎N 8 White 八白	乾NW 4 Green 四綠

亥 Pig (Nov 7 - Dec 6) 十月 10th Month

巽SE	離S	坤SW
1 White 一白	6 White 六白	8 White 八白
震E 9 Purple 九紫	2 Black 二黑	4 Green 四綠 兌W
艮NE 5 Yellow 五黄	坎N 7 Red 七赤	乾NW 3 Jade 三碧

子 Rat (Dec 7 - Jan 5) 十一月 11th Month

巽SE	離S	坤SW
9 Purple 九紫	5 Yellow 五黄	7 Red 七赤
震E 8 White 八白	1 White 一白	3 Jade 三碧 兌W
艮NE 4 Green 四綠	坎N 6 White 六白	乾NW 2 Black 二黑

丑 Ox (Jan 6 - Feb 3) 十二月 12th Month

巽SE	離S	坤SW
8 White 八白	4 Green 四綠	6 White 六白
震E 7 Red 七赤	9 Purple 九紫	2 Black 二黑 兌W
艮NE 3 Jade 三碧	坎N 5 Yellow 五黄	乾NW 1 White 一白

Qi Men Three Nobles 三奇 :

Three Nobles 三奇 / Seasons	乙 Yi	丙 Bing	丁 Ding
立春 **Coming of Spring** Feb 4 - Feb 18	巽 Xun	巽 Xun	中 Middle
春分 **Spring Equinox** Mar 21 - Apr 4	艮 Gen	艮 Gen	離 Li
立夏 **Coming of Summer** May 6 - May 20	離 Li	離 Li	坎 Kan
夏至 **Summer Solstice** Jun 22 - Jul 6	巽 Xun	巽 Xun	震 Zhen
立秋 **Coming of Autumn** Aug 8 - Aug 23	乾 Qian	乾 Qian	中 Middle
秋分 **Autumn Equinox** Sept 23 - Oct 7	坤 Kun	坤 Kun	坎 Kan
立冬 **Coming of Winter** Nov 7 - Nov 22	坎 Kan	坎 Kan	離 Li
冬至 **Winter Solstice** Dec 22 - Jan 5	乾 Qian	乾 Qian	兌 Dui

Sectors to Avoid Opening Mountain 開山凶位 :

月 MONTH	月建 Month Establishment	月破 Month Destruction	月剋山家 Month Countering Sitting		陰府太歲 Yin Mansion Grand Duke	
寅 **Tiger** (Feb 4 - Mar 5) 正月 **1st Month**	寅 *Yin* **Tiger**	申 *Shen* **Monkey**	乾 *Qian*	兌 *Dui*	坎 *Kan*	坤 *Kun*
卯 **Rabbit** (Mar 6 - Apr 4) 二月 **2nd Month**	卯 *Mao* **Rabbit**	酉 *You* **Rooster**	亥 *Hai* **Pig**	丁 *Ding* **Yin Fire**	乾 *Qian*	離 *Li*
辰 **Dragon** (Apr 5 - May 5) 三月 **3rd Month**	辰 *Chen* **Dragon**	戌 *Xu* **Dog**	震 *Zhen*	巳 *Si* **Snake**	坤 *Kun*	震 *Zhen*
巳 **Snake** (May 6 - Jun 5) 四月 **4th Month**	巳 *Si* **Snake**	亥 *Hai* **Pig**	艮 *Gen*		巽 *Xun*	艮 *Gen*
午 **Horse** (Jun 6 - July 6) 五月 **5th Month**	午 *Wu* **Horse**	子 *Zi* **Rat**	–		乾 *Qian*	兌 *Dui*
未 **Goat** (July 7 - Aug 7) 六月 **6th Month**	未 *Wei* **Goat**	丑 *Chou* **Ox**	–		坤 *Kun*	坎 *Kan*
申 **Monkey** (Aug 8 - Sept 7) 七月 **7th Month**	申 *Shen* **Monkey**	寅 *Yin* **Tiger**	水 **Water**	山 **Mountain**	離 *Li*	乾 *Qian*
酉 **Rooster** (Sept 8 - Oct 7) 八月 **8th Month**	酉 *You* **Rooster**	卯 *Mao* **Rabbit**	土 **Earth**		震 *Zhen*	坤 *Kun*
戌 **Dog** (Oct 8 - Nov 6) 九月 **9th Month**	戌 *Xu* **Dog**	辰 *Chen* **Dragon**	乾 *Qian*	兌 *Dui*	艮 *Gen*	巽 *Xun*
亥 **Pig** (Nov 7 - Dec 6) 十月 **10th Month**	亥 *Hai* **Pig**	巳 *Si* **Snake**	亥 *Hai* **Pig**	丁 *Ding* **Yin Fire**	兌 *Dui*	乾 *Qian*
子 **Rat** (Dec 7 - Jan 5) 十一月 **11th Month**	子 *Zi* **Rat**	午 *Wu* **Horse**	離 *Li*	丙 *Bing* **Yang Fire**	坎 *Kan*	坤 *Kun*
丑 **Ox** (Jan 6 - Feb 3) 十二月 **12th Month**	丑 *Chou* **Ox**	未 *Wei* **Goat**	壬 *Ren* **Yang Water**	乙 *Yi* **Yin Wood**	乾 *Qian*	離 *Li*

Negative Repair / Renovation Sectors 修方凶位 :

月 MONTH	天官符 Heavenly Officer Charm			地官符 Earth Officer Charm			小月建 Small Month Establishment		
寅 **Tiger** (Feb 4 - Mar 5) 正月 **1st Month**	未 Wei Goat	坤 Kun	申 Shen Monkey	甲 Jia Yang Wood	震 Zhen	乙 Yi Yin Wood	丙 Bing Yang Fire	離 Li	丁 Ding Yin Fire
卯 **Rabbit** (Mar 6 - Apr 4) 二月 **2nd Month**	壬 Ren Yang Water	坎 Kan	癸 Gui Yin Water	未 Wei Goat	坤 Kun	申 Shen Monkey	壬 Ren Yang Water	坎 Kan	癸 Gui Yin Water
辰 **Dragon** (Apr 5 - May 5) 三月 **3rd Month**	丙 Bing Yang Fire	離 Li	丁 Ding Yin Fire	壬 Ren Yang Water	坎 Kan	癸 Gui Yin Water	未 Wei Goat	坤 Kun	申 Shen Monkey
巳 **Snake** (May 6 - Jun 5) 四月 **4th Month**	丑 Chou Ox	艮 Gen	寅 Yin Tiger	丙 Bing Yang Fire	離 Li	丁 Ding Yin Fire	甲 Jia Yang Wood	震 Zhen	乙 Yi Yin Wood
午 **Horse** (Jun 6 - July 6) 五月 **5th Month**	庚 Geng Yang Metal	兌 Dui	辛 Xin Yin Metal	丑 Chou Ox	艮 Gen	寅 Yin Tiger	辰 Chen Dragon	巽 Xun	己 Ji Yin Earth
未 **Goat** (July 7 - Aug 7) 六月 **6th Month**	戌 Xu Dog	乾 Qian	亥 Hai Pig	庚 Geng Yang Metal	兌 Dui	辛 Xin Yin Metal	中 Middle		
申 **Monkey** (Aug 8 - Sept 7) 七月 **7th Month**	中 Middle			戌 Xu Dog	乾 Qian	亥 Hai Pig	戌 Xu Dog	乾 Qian	亥 Hai Pig
酉 **Rooster** (Sept 8 - Oct 7) 八月 **8th Month**	庚 Geng Yang Metal	兌 Dui	辛 Xin Yin Metal	中 Middle			庚 Geng Yang Metal	兌 Dui	辛 Xin Yin Metal
戌 **Dog** (Oct 8 - Nov 6) 九月 **9th Month**	戌 Xu Dog	乾 Qian	亥 Hai Pig	庚 Geng Yang Metal	兌 Dui	辛 Xin Yin Metal	丑 Chou Ox	艮 Gen	寅 Yin Tiger
亥 **Pig** (Nov 7 - Dec 6) 十月 **10th Month**	中 Middle			戌 Xu Dog	乾 Qian	亥 Hai Pig	丙 Bing Yang Fire	離 Li	丁 Ding Yin Fire
子 **Rat** (Dec 7 - Jan 5) 十一月 **11th Month**	辰 Chen Dragon	巽 Xun	巳 Si Snake	中 Middle			壬 Ren Yang Water	坎 Kan	癸 Gui Yin Water
丑 **Ox** (Jan 6 - Feb 3) 十二月 **12th Month**	甲 Jia Yang Wood	震 Zhen	乙 Yi Yin Wood	辰 Chen Dragon	巽 Xun	巳 Si Snake	未 Wei Goat	坤 Kun	申 Shen Monkey

Negative Repair / Renovation Sectors 修方凶位 :

月 MONTH	大月建 Big Month Establishment			飛大煞 Flying Great Sha			丙丁獨火 Bing Ding Lonely Fire	
寅 Tiger (Feb 4 - Mar 5) 正月 1st Month	未 Wei Goat	坤 Kun	申 Shen Monkey	甲 Jia Yang Wood	震 Zhen	乙 Yi Yin Wood	中 Middle	乾 Qian
卯 Rabbit (Mar 6 - Apr 4) 二月 2nd Month	壬 Ren Yang Water	坎 Kan	癸 Gui Yin Water	未 Wei Goat	坤 Kun	申 Shen Monkey	中 Middle	
辰 Dragon (Apr 5 - May 5) 三月 3rd Month	丙 Bing Yang Fire	離 Li	丁 Ding Yin Fire	壬 Ren Yang Water	坎 Kan	癸 Gui Yin Water	巽 Xun	中 Middle
巳 Snake (May 6 - Jun 5) 四月 4th Month	丑 Chou Ox	艮 Gen	寅 Yin	丙 Bing Yang Fire	離 Li	丁 Ding Yin Fire	震 Zhen	巽 Xun
午 Horse (Jun 6 - July 6) 五月 5th Month	庚 Geng Yang Metal	兌 Dui	辛 Xin Yin Metal	丑 Chou Ox	艮 Gen	寅 Yin	坤 Kun	震 Zhen
未 Goat (July 7 - Aug 7) 六月 6th Month	戌 Xu Dog	乾 Qian	亥 Hai Pig	庚 Geng Yang Metal	兌 Dui	辛 Xin Yin Metal	坎 Kan	坤 Kun
申 Monkey (Aug 8 - Sept 7) 七月 7th Month	中 Middle			戌 Xu Dog	乾 Qian	亥 Hai Pig	離 Li	坎 Kan
酉 Rooster (Sept 8 - Oct 7) 八月 8th Month	辰 Chen Dragon	巽 Xun	巳 Si Snake	中 Middle			艮 Gen	離 Li
戌 Dog (Oct 8 - Nov 6) 九月 9th Month	甲 Jia Yang Wood	震 Zhen	乙 Yi Yin Wood	庚 Geng Yang Metal	兌 Dui	辛 Xin Yin Metal	兌 Dui	艮 Gen
亥 Pig (Nov 7 - Dec 6) 十月 10th Month	未 Wei Goat	坤 Kun	申 Shen Monkey	戌 Xu Dog	乾 Qian	亥 Hai Pig	乾 Qian	兌 Dui
子 Rat (Dec 7 - Jan 5) 十一月 11th Month	壬 Ren Yang Water	坎 Kan	癸 Gui Yin Water	中 Middle			中 Middle	乾 Qian
丑 Ox (Jan 6 - Feb 3) 十二月 12th Month	丙 Bing Yang Fire	離 Li	丁 Ding Yin Fire	辰 Chen Dragon	巽 Xun	巳 Si Snake	中 Middle	

Negative Repair / Renovation Sectors 修方凶位 :

月 MONTH	月遊火 Month Wondering Fire	三煞 Monthly 3 Killings		
		劫煞 Robbery Sha	災煞 Calamity Sha	月煞 Month Sha
寅 Tiger (Feb 4 - Mar 5) 正月 1st Month	離 Li	亥 Hai Pig	子 Zi Rat	丑 Chou Ox
卯 Rabbit (Mar 6 - Apr 4) 二月 2nd Month	坎 Kan	申 Shen Monkey	酉 You Rooster	戌 Xu Dog
辰 Dragon (Apr 5 - May 5) 三月 3rd Month	坤 Kun	巳 Si Snake	午 Wu Horse	未 Wei Goat
巳 Snake (May 6 - Jun 5) 四月 4th Month	震 Zhen	寅 Yin Tiger	卯 Mao Rabbit	辰 Chen Dragon
午 Horse (Jun 6 - July 6) 五月 5th Month	巽 Xun	亥 Hai Pig	子 Zi Rat	丑 Chou Ox
未 Goat (July 7 - Aug 7) 六月 6th Month	中 Middle	申 Shen Monkey	酉 You Rooster	戌 Xu Dog
申 Monkey (Aug 8 - Sept 7) 七月 7th Month	乾 Qian	巳 Si Snake	午 Wu Horse	未 Wei Goat
酉 Rooster (Sept 8 - Oct 7) 八月 8th Month	兌 Dui	寅 Yin Tiger	卯 Mao Rabbit	辰 Chen Dragon
戌 Dog (Oct 8 - Nov 6) 九月 9th Month	艮 Gen	亥 Hai Pig	子 Zi Rat	丑 Chou Ox
亥 Pig (Nov 7 - Dec 6) 十月 10th Month	離 Li	申 Shen Monkey	酉 You Rooster	戌 Xu Dog
子 Rat (Dec 7 - Jan 5) 十一月 11th Month	坎 Kan	巳 Si Snake	午 Wu Horse	未 Wei Goat
丑 Ox (Jan 6 - Feb 3) 十二月 12th Month	坤 Kun	寅 Yin Tiger	卯 Mao Rabbit	辰 Chen Dragon

Negative Repair / Renovation Sectors 修方凶位 :

月 MONTH	月刑 Month Punishment	月害 Month Harm	月厭 Month Detest
寅 **Tiger** (Feb 4 - Mar 5) 正月 **1st Month**	巳 Si **Snake**	巳 Si **Snake**	戌 Xu **Dog**
卯 **Rabbit** (Mar 6 - Apr 4) 二月 **2nd Month**	子 Zi **Rat**	辰 Chen **Dragon**	酉 You **Rooster**
辰 **Dragon** (Apr 5 - May 5) 三月 **3rd Month**	辰 Chen **Dragon**	卯 Mao **Rabbit**	申 Shen **Monkey**
巳 **Snake** (May 6 - Jun 5) 四月 **4th Month**	申 Shen **Monkey**	寅 Yin **Tiger**	未 Wei **Goat**
午 **Horse** (Jun 6 - July 6) 五月 **5th Month**	午 Wu **Horse**	丑 Chou **Ox**	午 Wu **Horse**
未 **Goat** (July 7 - Aug 7) 六月 **6th Month**	丑 Chou **Ox**	子 Zi **Rat**	巳 Si **Snake**
申 **Monkey** (Aug 8 - Sept 7) 七月 **7th Month**	寅 Yin **Tiger**	亥 Hai **Pig**	辰 Chen **Dragon**
酉 **Rooster** (Sept 8 - Oct 7) 八月 **8th Month**	酉 You **Rooster**	戌 Xu **Dog**	卯 Mao **Rabbit**
戌 **Dog** (Oct 8 - Nov 6) 九月 **9th Month**	未 Wei **Goat**	酉 You **Rooster**	寅 Yin **Tiger**
亥 **Pig** (Nov 7 - Dec 6) 十月 **10th Month**	亥 Hai **Pig**	申 Shen **Monkey**	丑 Chou **Ox**
子 **Rat** (Dec 7 - Jan 5) 十一月 **11th Month**	卯 Mao **Rabbit**	未 Wei **Goat**	子 Zi **Rat**
丑 **Ox** (Jan 6 - Feb 3) 十二月 **12th Month**	戌 Xu **Dog**	午 Wu **Horse**	亥 Hai **Pig**

己未 (Ji Wei)
Earth Goat

Heavenly Stem 天干	己 **Yin Earth (陰土)**
Earthly Branch 地支	未 **Goat (Yin Earth 陰土)**
Hidden Stem 藏干	己 **Yin Earth,** 丁 **Yin Fire,** 乙 **Yin Wood**
Na Yin 納音	天上火 **Fire from the skies**
Grand Duke 太歲	未 **Goat**
Xuan Kong Five Element 玄空五行	1 水 **Water**
Gua Name 卦名	☷☴ 地風升 **Rising**
Xuan Kong Period Luck 玄空卦運	**2**

Annual Positive Stars for Opening Mountain, Establishing Facing and Commencing Repairs 開山立向修方吉星：

歲德 **Duke Virtue**	甲 *Jia* **Yang Wood**	
歲德合 **Duke Virtue Combo**	己 *Ji* **Yin Earth**	
歲枝德 **Duke Branch Virtue**	子 *Zi* **Rat**	
陽貴人 **Yang Nobleman**	子 *Zi* **Rat**	
陰貴人 **Yin Nobleman**	申 *Shen* **Monkey**	
歲祿 **Duke Prosperous**	午 *Wu* **Horse**	
歲馬 **Duke Horse**	巳 *Si* **Snake**	
奏書 **Decree**	巽 *Xun*	
博士 **Professor**	乾 *Qian*	

Annual Negative Stars for Opening Mountain, Establishing Facing and Commencing Repairs 開山立向修方凶星：

太歲 Grand Duke	歲破 Year Breaker	三煞 Three Killings			坐煞向煞 Sitting Sha Facing Sha				浮天空亡 Floating Heaven Emptiness	
未 Wei Goat	丑 Chou Ox	申 Shen Monkey	酉 You Rooster	戌 Xu Dog	庚 Geng Yang Metal	辛 Xin Yin Metal	甲 Jia Yang Wood	乙 Yi Yin Wood	乾 Qian	甲 Jia Yang Wood

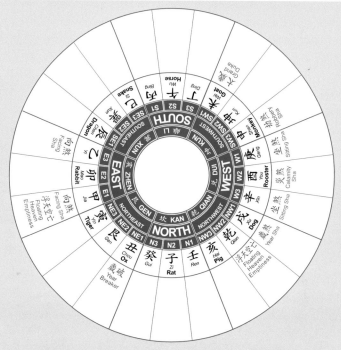

Annual San Yuan Purple White Stars 三元紫白九星：

上元 Upper Period Period 1, 2, 3	中元 Middle Period Period 4, 5, 6	下元 Lower Period Period 7, 8, 9

上元 Upper Period — Period 1, 2, 3

巽SE	離S	坤SW
8	4	6
震E 7	9 己未 Ji Wei Earth Goat	2 兌W
3	5	1
艮NE	坎N	乾NW

中元 Middle Period — Period 4, 5, 6

巽SE	離S	坤SW
2	7	9
震E 1	3 己未 Ji Wei Earth Goat	5 兌W
6	8	4
艮NE	坎N	乾NW

下元 Lower Period — Period 7, 8, 9

巽SE	離S	坤SW
5	1	3
震E 4	6 己未 Ji Wei Earth Goat	8 兌W
9	2	7
艮NE	坎N	乾NW

Mountain Covering Yellow Path 蓋山黃道:

貪狼 Tan Lang **Greedy Wolf**		巨門 Ju Men **Huge Door**				武曲 Wu Qu **Military Arts**		文曲 Wen Qu **Literary Arts**			
坤 Kun SW2	乙 Yi E3	坎 Kan N2	癸 Gui N3	申 Shen SW3	辰 Chen SE1	乾 Qian NW2	甲 Jia E1	震 Zhen E2	庚 Geng W1	亥 Hai NW3	未 Wei SW1

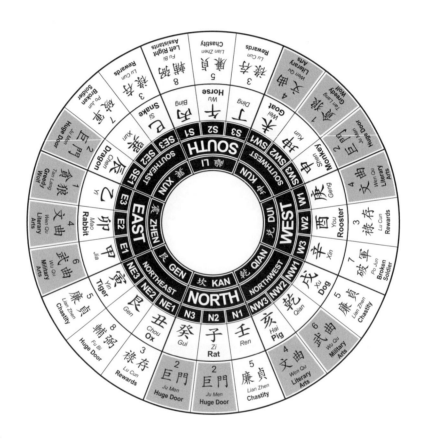

三合前方 **Facing Three Harmony**	巽巳 Xun Si	丙午 Bing Wu	丁未 Ding Wei
三合後方 **Sitting Three Harmony**	乾亥 Qian Hai	壬子 Ren Zi	癸丑 Gui Chou

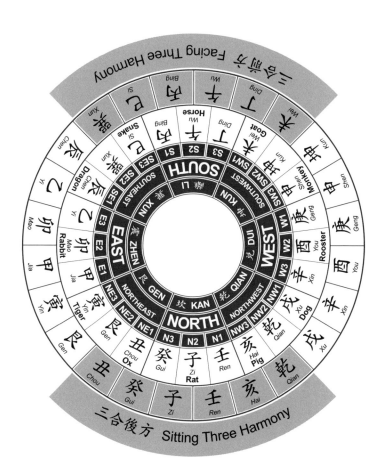

Moving Horse Six Ren Assessment 走馬六壬：

神后 Shen Hou **Holy Empress**	功曹 Gong Cao **Marshall**	天罡 Tian Gang **Heavenly Dipper**	勝光 Sheng Guang **Subliminal Bright**	傳送 Chuan Song **Great General**	河魁 He Kui **River Scholar**
巽巳 Xun Si	丁未 Ding Wei	庚酉 Geng You	乾亥 Qian Hai	癸丑 Gui Chou	甲卯 Jia Mao

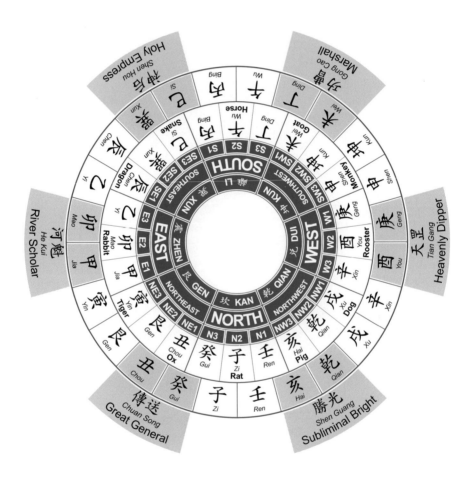

Four Advantages Three Cycles Star Plate 四利三元：

太陽 Tai Yang Sun	太陰 Tai Yin Moon	龍德 Long De Dragon Virtue	福德 Fu De Fortune Virtue
申 Shen Monkey	戌 Xu Dog	寅 Yin Tiger	辰 Chen Dragon

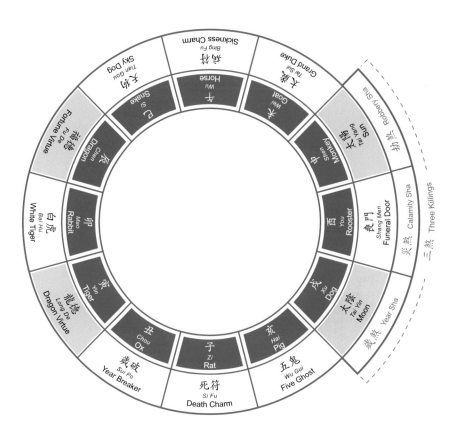

Negative Sectors For Opening Mountain 開山凶位:

年剋山家 Year Countering Sitting

乾	亥	兌	丁
Qian	Hai	Dui	Ding
NW2	NW3	W2	S3

陰府太歲 Yin Fu Tai Sui		六害 Liu Hai	死符 Si Fu	炙退 Zhi Tui
Yin Mansion Grand Duke		**Six Harm**	**Death Charm**	**Roasting Star**
巽	艮	子	子	午
Xun	Gen	Zi	Zi	Wu
SE2	NE2	N2	N2	S2

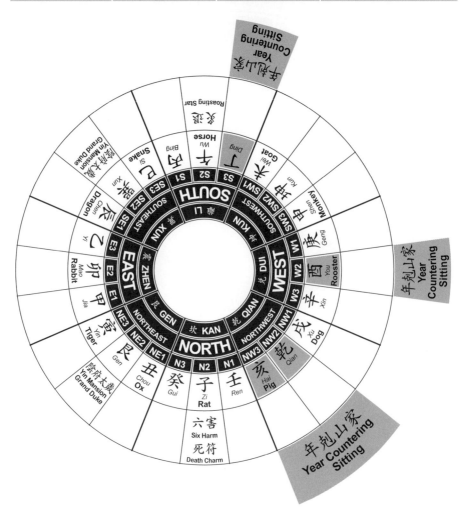

巡山羅喉 *Xun Shan Luo Hou* **Mountain Patrol Luo Hou Star**	病符 *Bing Fu* **Sickness Charm**
坤 *Kun* **SW2**	午 *Wu* **S2**

Negative Directions to Establish Facing 立向凶方：

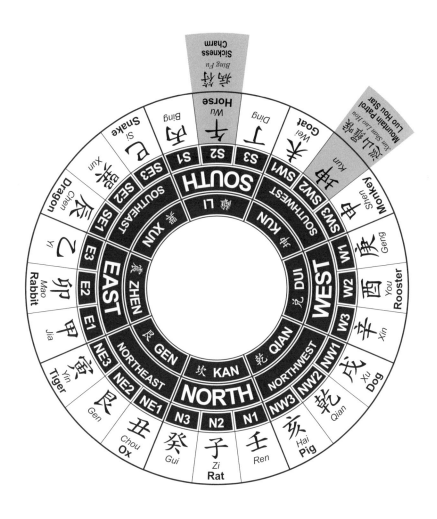

Negative Repair / Renovation Sectors Table 修方凶位表：

天官符 **Heavenly Officer Charm**	寅 *Yin* **Tiger**	飛廉 **Flying Chaste**	卯 *Mao* **Rabbit**
地官符 **Earthly Officer Charm**	亥 *Hai* **Pig**	喪門 **Funeral Door**	酉 *You* **Rooster**
大煞 **Great Sha**	卯 *Mao* **Rabbit**	弔客 **Suspended Guest**	巳 *Si* **Snake**
大將軍 **Big General**	卯 *Mao* **Rabbit**	白虎 **White Tiger**	卯 *Mao* **Rabbit**
力士 **Strong Man**	坤 *Kun*	金神 **Golden God**	午 *Wu* **Horse**
蠶室 **Silkworm Room**	艮 *Gen*		未 *Wei* **Goat**
蠶官 **Silkworm Officer**	丑 *Chou* **Ox**		申 *Shen* **Monkey**
蠶命 **Silkworm Life**	寅 *Yin* **Tiger**		酉 *You* **Rooster**
歲刑 **Duke Punishment**	丑 *Chou* **Ox**	獨火 **Lonely Fire**	離 *Li*
黃幡 **Yellow Flag**	未 *Wei* **Goat**	五鬼 **Five Ghost**	酉 *You* **Rooster**
豹尾 **Leopard Tail**	丑 *Chou* **Ox**	破敗五鬼 **Destructive Five Ghost**	坎 *Kan*

Negative Repair / Renovation Sectors Diagram 修方凶位圖：

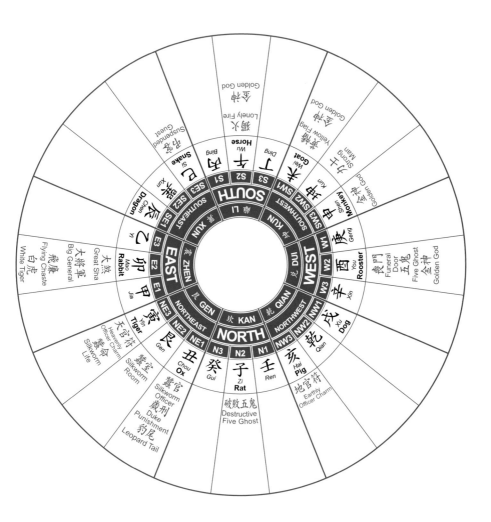

己未 (Ji Wei) Earth Goat

12-Month Auxiliary Stars Reference Table :
己未年十二月，開山立向修方星表

Positive Monthly Stars 吉星方

月 MONTH	寅 Tiger (Feb 4 - Mar 5) 正月 1st Month	卯 Rabbit (Mar 6 - Apr 4) 二月 2nd Month	辰 Dragon (Apr 5 - May 5) 三月 3rd Month	巳 Snake (May 6 - Jun 5) 四月 4th Month	午 Horse (Jun 6 - July 6) 五月 5th Month	未 Goat (July 7 - Aug 7) 六月 6th Month
天道 Heavenly Path	南 South	西南 Southwest	北 North	西 West	西北 Northwest	東 East
天德 Heavenly Virtue	丁 Ding Yin Fire	坤 Kun (申)	壬 Ren Yang Water	辛 Xin Yin Metal	乾 Qian (亥)	甲 Jia Yang Wood
天德合 Heavenly Virtue Combo	壬 Ren Yang Water	(巳)	丁 Ding Yin Fire	丙 Bing Yang Fire	(寅)	己 Ji Yin Earth
月德 Monthly Virtue	丙 Bing Yang Fire	甲 Jia Yang Wood	壬 Ren Yang Water	庚 Geng Yang Metal	丙 Bing Yang Fire	甲 Jia Yang Wood
月德合 Monthly Virtue Combo	辛 Xin Yin Metal	己 Ji Yin Earth	丁 Ding Yin Fire	乙 Yi Yin Wood	辛 Xin Yin Metal	己 Ji Yin Earth
月空 Month Emptiness	壬 Ren Yang Water	庚 Geng Yang Metal	丙 Bing Yang Fire	甲 Jia Yang Wood	壬 Ren Yang Water	庚 Geng Yang Metal
陽貴人 Yang Nobleman	乾 Qian	中 Middle	巽 Xun	震 Zhen	坤 Kun	坎 Kan
陰貴人 Yin Nobleman	坤 Kun	坎 Kan	離 Li	艮 Gen	兌 Dui	乾 Qian
飛天祿 Flying Heavenly Wealth	離 Li	艮 Gen	兌 Dui	乾 Qian	中 Middle	坎 Kan
飛天馬 Flying Heavenly Horse	艮 Gen	兌 Dui	乾 Qian	中 Middle	坎 Kan	離 Li

12-Month Auxiliary Stars Reference Table :
己未年十二月，開山立向修方星表

申 Monkey (Aug 8 - Sept 7) 七月 7th Month	酉 Rooster (Sept 8 - Oct 7) 八月 8th Month	戌 Dog (Oct 8 - Nov 6) 九月 9th Month	亥 Pig (Nov 7 - Dec 6) 十月 10th Month	子 Rat (Dec 7 - Jan 5) 十一月 11th Month	丑 Ox (Jan 6 - Feb 3) 十二月 12th Month	月 MONTH
北 North	東北 Northeast	南 South	東 East	東南 Southeast	西 West	天道 Heavenly Path
癸 Gui Yin Water	艮 Gen (寅)	丙 Bing Yang Fire	乙 Yi Yin Wood	巽 Xun (巳)	庚 Geng Yang Metal	天德 Heavenly Virtue
戊 Wu Yang Earth	(亥)	辛 Xin Yin Metal	庚 Geng Yang Metal	(申)	乙 Yi Yin Wood	天德合 Heavenly Virtue Combo
壬 Ren Yang Water	庚 Geng Yang Metal	丙 Bing Yang Fire	甲 Jia Yang Wood	壬 Ren Yang Water	庚 Geng Yang Metal	月德 Monthly Virtue
丁 Ding Yin Fire	乙 Yi Yin Wood	辛 Xin Yin Metal	己 Ji Yin Earth	丁 Ding Yin Fire	乙 Yi Yin Wood	月德合 Monthly Virtue Combo
丙 Bing Yang Fire	甲 Jia Yang Wood	壬 Ren Yang Water	庚 Geng Yang Metal	丙 Bing Yang Fire	甲 Jia Yang Wood	月空 Month Emptiness
離 Li	艮 Gen	兌 Dui	乾 Qian	中 Middle	坎 Kan	陽貴人 Yang Nobleman
中 Middle	坎 Kan	離 Li	艮 Gen	兌 Dui	乾 Qia	陰貴人 Yin Nobleman
離 Li	艮 Gen	兌 Dui	乾 Qia	中 Middle	巽 Xun	飛天祿 Flying Heavenly Wealth
艮 Gen	兌 Dui	乾 Qian	中 Middle	巽 Xun	震 Zhen	飛天馬 Flying Heavenly Horse

Monthly Purple White Stars 月紫白九星 ：

寅 Tiger (Feb 4 - Mar 5) 正月 1st Month

巽 SE	離 S	坤 SW
4 Green 四綠	9 Purple 九紫	2 Black 二黑
3 Jade 三碧 (震 E)	5 Yellow 五黃	7 Red 七赤 (兌 W)
8 White 八白	1 White 一白	6 White 六白
艮 NE	坎 N	乾 NW

卯 Rabbit (Mar 6 - Apr 4) 二月 2nd Month

巽 SE	離 S	坤 SW
3 Jade 三碧	8 White 八白	1 White 一白
2 Black 二黑 (震 E)	4 Green 四綠	6 White 六白 (兌 W)
7 Red 七赤	9 Purple 九紫	5 Yellow 五黃
艮 NE	坎 N	乾 NW

辰 Dragon (Apr 5 - May 5) 三月 3rd Month

巽 SE	離 S	坤 SW
2 Black 二黑	7 Red 七赤	9 Purple 九紫
1 White 一白 (震 E)	3 Jade 三碧	5 Yellow 五黃 (兌 W)
6 White 六白	8 White 八白	4 Green 四綠
艮 NE	坎 N	乾 NW

巳 Snake (May 6 - Jun 5) 四月 4th Month

巽 SE	離 S	坤 SW
1 White 一白	6 White 六白	8 White 八白
9 Purple 九紫 (震 E)	2 Black 二黑	4 Green 四綠 (兌 W)
5 Yellow 五黃	7 Red 七赤	3 Jade 三碧
艮 NE	坎 N	乾 NW

午 Horse (Jun 6 - July 6) 五月 5th Month

巽 SE	離 S	坤 SW
9 Purple 九紫	5 Yellow 五黃	7 Red 七赤
8 White 八白 (震 E)	1 White 一白	3 Jade 三碧 (兌 W)
4 Green 四綠	6 White 六白	2 Black 二黑
艮 NE	坎 N	乾 NW

未 Goat (July 7 - Aug 7) 六月 6th Month

巽 SE	離 S	坤 SW
8 White 八白	4 Green 四綠	6 White 六白
7 Red 七赤 (震 E)	9 Purple 九紫	2 Black 二黑 (兌 W)
3 Jade 三碧	5 Yellow 五黃	1 White 一白
艮 NE	坎 N	乾 NW

申 Monkey (Aug 8 - Sept 7) 七月 7th Month

巽 SE	離 S	坤 SW
7 Red 七赤	3 Jade 三碧	5 Yellow 五黃
6 White 六白 (震 E)	8 White 八白	1 White 一白 (兌 W)
2 Black 二黑	4 Green 四綠	9 Purple 九紫
艮 NE	坎 N	乾 NW

酉 Rooster (Sept 8 - Oct 7) 八月 8th Month

巽 SE	離 S	坤 SW
6 White 六白	2 Black 二黑	4 Green 四綠
5 Yellow 五黃 (震 E)	7 Red 七赤	9 Purple 九紫 (兌 W)
1 White 一白	3 Jade 三碧	8 White 八白
艮 NE	坎 N	乾 NW

戌 Dog (Oct 8 - Nov 6) 九月 9th Month

巽 SE	離 S	坤 SW
5 Yellow 五黃	1 White 一白	3 Jade 三碧
4 Green 四綠 (震 E)	6 White 六白	8 White 八白 (兌 W)
9 Purple 九紫	2 Black 二黑	7 Red 七赤
艮 NE	坎 N	乾 NW

亥 Pig (Nov 7 - Dec 6) 十月 10th Month

巽 SE	離 S	坤 SW
4 Green 四綠	9 Purple 九紫	2 Black 二黑
3 Jade 三碧 (震 E)	5 Yellow 五黃	7 Red 七赤 (兌 W)
8 White 八白	1 White 一白	6 White 六白
艮 NE	坎 N	乾 NW

子 Rat (Dec 7 - Jan 5) 十一月 11th Month

巽 SE	離 S	坤 SW
3 Jade 三碧	8 White 八白	1 White 一白
2 Black 二黑 (震 E)	4 Green 四綠	6 White 六白 (兌 W)
7 Red 七赤	9 Purple 九紫	5 Yellow 五黃
艮 NE	坎 N	乾 NW

丑 Ox (Jan 6 - Feb 3) 十二月 12th Month

巽 SE	離 S	坤 SW
2 Black 二黑	7 Red 七赤	9 Purple 九紫
1 White 一白 (震 E)	3 Jade 三碧	5 Yellow 五黃 (兌 W)
6 White 六白	8 White 八白	4 Green 四綠
艮 NE	坎 N	乾 NW

Qi Men Three Nobles 三奇 :

Three Nobles 三奇 / Seasons	乙 Yi	丙 Bing	丁 Ding
立春 **Coming of Spring** Feb 4 - Feb 18	離 Li	離 Li	坎 Kan
春分 **Spring Equinox** Mar 21 - Apr 4	巽 Xunn	巽 Xunn	中 **Middle**
立夏 **Coming of Summer** May 6 - May 20	中 **Middle**	中 **Middle**	乾 Qian
夏至 **Summer Solstice** Jun 22 - Jul 6	艮 Gen	艮 Gen	兌 Dui
立秋 **Coming of Autumn** Aug 8 - Aug 23	坎 Kan	坎 Kan	離 Li
秋分 **Autumn Equinox** Sept 23 - Oct 7	乾 Qian	乾 Qian	中 **Middle**
立冬 **Coming of Winter** Nov 7 - Nov 22	中 **Middle**	中 **Middle**	巽 Xunn
冬至 **Winter Solstice** Dec 22 - Jan 5	坤 Kun	坤 Kun	震 Zhen

Sectors to Avoid Opening Mountain 開山凶位 :

月 MONTH	月建 Month Establishment	月破 Month Destruction	月剋山家 Month Countering Sitting		陰府太歲 Yin Mansion Grand Duke	
寅 Tiger (Feb 4 - Mar 5) 正月 1st Month	寅 Yin Tiger	申 Shen Monkey	乾 Qian	兌 Dui	坎 Kan	坤 Kun
卯 Rabbit (Mar 6 - Apr 4) 二月 2nd Month	卯 Mao Rabbit	酉 You Rooster	亥 Hai Pig	丁 Ding Yin Fire	乾 Qian	離 Li
辰 Dragon (Apr 5 - May 5) 三月 3rd Month	辰 Chen Dragon	戌 Xu Dog	震 Zhen	巳 Si Snake	坤 Kun	震 Zhen
巳 Snake (May 6 - Jun 5) 四月 4th Month	巳 Si Snake	亥 Hai Pig	艮 Gen		巽 Xun	艮 Gen
午 Horse (Jun 6 - July 6) 五月 5th Month	午 Wu Horse	子 Zi Rat	–		乾 Qian	兌 Du
未 Goat (July 7 - Aug 7) 六月 6th Month	未 Wei Goat	丑 Chou Ox	–		坤 Kun	坎 Kan
申 Monkey (Aug 8 - Sept 7) 七月 7th Month	申 Shen Monkey	寅 Yin Tiger	水 Water	山 Mountain	離 Li	乾 Qian
酉 Rooster (Sept 8 - Oct 7) 八月 8th Month	酉 You Rooster	卯 Mao Rabbit	土 Earth		震 Zhen	坤 Kun
戌 Dog (Oct 8 - Nov 6) 九月 9th Month	戌 Xu Dog	辰 Chen Dragon	乾 Qian	兌 Dui	艮 Genn	巽 Xun
亥 Pig (Nov 7 - Dec 6) 十月 10th Month	亥 Hai Pig	巳 Si Snake	亥 Hai Pig	丁 Ding Yin Fire	兌 Duin	乾 Qian
子 Rat (Dec 7 - Jan 5) 十一月 11th Month	子 Zi Rat	午 Wu Horse	離 Li	丙 Bing Yang Fire	坎 Kan	坤 Kun
丑 Ox (Jan 6 - Feb 3) 十二月 12th Month	丑 Chou Ox	未 Wei Goat	壬 Ren Yang Water	乙 Yi Yin Wood	乾 Qian	離 Li

Negative Repair / Renovation Sectors 修方凶位 :

月 MONTH	天官符 Heavenly Officer Charm			地官符 Earth Officer Charm			小月建 Small Month Establishment		
寅 **Tiger** (Feb 4 - Mar 5) 正月 **1st Month**	中 Middle			中 Middle			丙 Bing Yang Fire	離 Li	丁 Ding Yin Fire
卯 **Rabbit** (Mar 6 - Apr 4) 二月 **2nd Month**	庚 Geng Yang Metal	兑 Dui	辛 Xin Yin Metal	辰 Chen Dragon	巽 Xun	巳 Si Snake	壬 Ren Yang Water	坎 Kan	癸 Gui Yin Water
辰 **Dragon** (Apr 5 - May 5) 三月 **3rd Month**	戌 Xu Dog	乾 Qian	亥 Hai Pig	甲 Jia Yang Wood	震 Zhen	乙 Yi Yin Wood	未 Wei Goat	坤 Kun	申 Shen Monkey
巳 **Snake** (May 6 - Jun 5) 四月 **4th Month**	中 Middle			未 Wei Goat	坤 Kun	申 Shen Monkey	甲 Jia Yang Wood	震 Zhen	乙 Yi Yin Wood
午 **Horse** (Jun 6 - July 6) 五月 **5th Month**	辰 Chen Dragon	巽 Xun	巳 Si Snake	壬 Ren Yang Water	坎 Kan	癸 Gui Yin Water	辰 Chen Dragon	巽 Xun	巳 Si Snake
未 **Goat** (July 7 - Aug 7) 六月 **6th Month**	甲 Jia Yang Wood	震 Zhen	乙 Yi Yin Wood	丙 Bing Yang Fire	離 Li	丁 Ding Yin Fire	中 Middle		
申 **Monkey** (Aug 8 - Sept 7) 七月 **7th Month**	未 Wei Goat	坤 Kun	申 Shen Monkey	丑 Chou Ox	艮 Gen	寅 Yin Tiger	戌 Xu Dog	乾 Qian	亥 Hai Pig
酉 **Rooster** (Sept 8 - Oct 7) 八月 **8th Month**	壬 Ren Yang Water	坎 Kan	癸 Gui Yin Water	庚 Geng Yang Metal	兑 Dui	辛 Xin Yin Metal	庚 Geng Yang Metal	兑 Dui	辛 Xin Yin Metal
戌 **Dog** (Oct 8 - Nov 6) 九月 **9th Month**	丙 Bing Yang Fire	離 Li	丁 Ding Yin Fire	戌 Xu Dog	乾 Qian	亥 Hai Pig	丑 Chou Ox	艮 Gen	寅 Yin Tiger
亥 **Pig** (Nov 7 - Dec 6) 十月 **10th Month**	丑 Chou Ox	艮 Gen	寅 Yin Tiger	中 Middle			丙 Bing Yang Fire	離 Li	丁 Ding Yin Fire
子 **Rat** (Dec 7 - Jan 5) 十一月 **11th Month**	庚 Geng Yang Metal	兑 Dui	辛 Xin Yin Metal	庚 Geng Yang Metal	兑 Dui	辛 Xin Yin Metal	壬 Ren Yang Water	坎 Kan	癸 Gui Yin Water
丑 **Ox** (Jan 6 - Feb 3) 十二月 **12th Month**	戌 Xu Dog	乾 Qian	亥 Hai Pig	戌 Xu Dog	乾 Qian	亥 Hai Pig	未 Wei Goat	坤 Kun	申 Shen Monkey

Negative Repair / Renovation Sectors 修方凶位 ：

月 MONTH	大月建 Big Month Establishment			飛大煞 Flying Great Sha			丙丁獨火 Bing Ding Lonely Fire	
寅 **Tiger** (Feb 4 - Mar 5) 正月 **1st Month**	中 Middle			戌 Xu Dog	乾 Qian	亥 Hai Pig	中 Middle	乾 Qian
卯 **Rabbit** (Mar 6 - Apr 4) 二月 **2nd Month**	辰 Chen Dragon	巽 Xun	巳 Si Snake	中 Middle			中 Middle	
辰 **Dragon** (Apr 5 - May 5) 三月 **3rd Month**	甲 Jia Yang Wood	震 Zhen	乙 Yi Yin Wood	庚 Geng Yang Metal	兌 Dui	辛 Xin Yin Metal	巽 Xun	中 Middle
巳 **Snake** (May 6 - Jun 5) 四月 **4th Month**	未 Wei Goat	坤 Kun	申 Shen Monkey	戌 Xu Dog	乾 Qian	亥 Hai Pig	震 Zhen	巽 Xun
午 **Horse** (Jun 6 - July 6) 五月 **5th Month**	壬 Ren Yang Water	坎 Kan	癸 Gui Yin Water	中 Middle			坤 Kun	震 Zhen
未 **Goat** (July 7 - Aug 7) 六月 **6th Month**	丙 Bing Yang Fire	離 Li	丁 Ding Yin Fire	辰 Chen Dragon	巽 Xun	巳 Si Snake	坎 Kan	坤 Kun
申 **Monkey** (Aug 8 - Sept 7) 七月 **7th Month**	丑 Chou Ox	艮 Gen	寅 Yin	甲 Jia Yang Wood	震 Zhen	乙 Yi Yin Wood	離 Li	坎 Kan
酉 **Rooster** (Sept 8 - Oct 7) 八月 **8th Month**	庚 Geng Yang Metal	兌 Dui	辛 Xin Yin Metal	未 Wei Goat	坤 Kun	申 Shen Monkey	艮 Gen	離 Li
戌 **Dog** (Oct 8 - Nov 6) 九月 **9th Month**	戌 Xu Dog	乾 Qian	亥 Hai Pig	壬 Ren Yang Water	坎 Kan	癸 Gui Yin Water	兌 Dui	艮 Gen
亥 **Pig** (Nov 7 - Dec 6) 十月 **10th Month**	中 Middle			丙 Bing Yang Fire	離 Li	丁 Ding Yin Fire	乾 Qian	兌 Dui
子 **Rat** (Dec 7 - Jan 5) 十一月 **11th Month**	辰 Chen Dragon	巽 Xun	巳 Si Snake	丑 Chou Ox	艮 Gen	寅 Yin	中 Middle	乾 Qian
丑 **Ox** (Jan 6 - Feb 3) 十二月 **12th Month**	甲 Jia Yang Wood	震 Zhen	乙 Yi Yin Wood	庚 Geng Yang Metal	兌 Dui	辛 Xin Yin Metal	中 Middle	

Negative Repair / Renovation Sectors 修方凶位 :

月 MONTH	月遊火 Month Wondering Fire	三煞 Monthly 3 Killings		
		劫煞 Robbery Sha	災煞 Calamity Sha	月煞 Month Sha
寅 Tiger (Feb 4 - Mar 5) 正月 1st Month	坤 Kun	亥 Hai Pig	子 Zi Rat	丑 Chou Ox
卯 Rabbit (Mar 6 - Apr 4) 二月 2nd Month	震 Zhen	申 Shen Monkey	酉 You Rooster	戌 Xu Dog
辰 Dragon (Apr 5 - May 5) 三月 3rd Month	巽 Xun	巳 Si Snake	午 Wu Horse	未 Wei Goat
巳 Snake (May 6 - Jun 5) 四月 4th Month	中 Middle	寅 Yin Tiger	卯 Mao Rabbit	辰 Chen Dragon
午 Horse (Jun 6 - July 6) 五月 5th Month	乾 Qian	亥 Hai Pig	子 Zi Rat	丑 Chou Ox
未 Goat (July 7 - Aug 7) 六月 6th Month	兌 Dui	申 Shen Monkey	酉 You Rooster	戌 Xu Dog
申 Monkey (Aug 8 - Sept 7) 七月 7th Month	艮 Gen	巳 Si Snake	午 Wu Horse	未 Wei Goat
酉 Rooster (Sept 8 - Oct 7) 八月 8th Month	離 Li	寅 Yin Tiger	卯 Mao Rabbit	辰 Chen Dragon
戌 Dog (Oct 8 - Nov 6) 九月 9th Month	坎 Kan	亥 Hai Pig	子 Zi Rat	丑 Chou Ox
亥 Pig (Nov 7 - Dec 6) 十月 10th Month	坤 Kun	申 Shen Monkey	酉 You Rooster	戌 Xu Dog
子 Rat (Dec 7 - Jan 5) 十一月 11th Month	震 Zhen	巳 Si Snake	午 Wu Horse	未 Wei Goat
丑 Ox (Jan 6 - Feb 3) 十二月 12th Month	巽 Xun	寅 Yin Tiger	卯 Mao Rabbit	辰 Chen Dragon

Negative Repair / Renovation Sectors 修方凶位 :

月 MONTH	月刑 Month Punishment	月害 Month Harm	月厭 Month Detest
寅 **Tiger** (Feb 4 - Mar 5) 正月 **1st Month**	巳 Si Snake	巳 Si Snake	戌 Xu Dog
卯 **Rabbit** (Mar 6 - Apr 4) 二月 **2nd Month**	子 Zi Rat	辰 Chen Dragon	酉 You Rooster
辰 **Dragon** (Apr 5 - May 5) 三月 **3rd Month**	辰 Chen Dragon	卯 Mao Rabbit	申 Shen Monkey
巳 **Snake** (May 6 - Jun 5) 四月 **4th Month**	申 Shen Monkey	寅 Yin Tiger	未 Wei Goat
午 **Horse** (Jun 6 - July 6) 五月 **5th Month**	午 Wu Horse	丑 Chou Ox	午 Wu Horse
未 **Goat** (July 7 - Aug 7) 六月 **6th Month**	丑 Chou Ox	子 Zi Rat	巳 Si Snake
申 **Monkey** (Aug 8 - Sept 7) 七月 **7th Month**	寅 Yin Tiger	亥 Hai Pig	辰 Chen Dragon
酉 **Rooster** (Sept 8 - Oct 7) 八月 **8th Month**	酉 You Rooster	戌 Xu Dog	卯 Mao Rabbit
戌 **Dog** (Oct 8 - Nov 6) 九月 **9th Month**	未 Wei Goat	酉 You Rooster	寅 Yin Tiger
亥 **Pig** (Nov 7 - Dec 6) 十月 **10th Month**	亥 Hai Pig	申 Shen Monkey	丑 Chou Ox
子 **Rat** (Dec 7 - Jan 5) 十一月 **11th Month**	卯 Mao Rabbit	未 Wei Goat	子 Zi Rat
丑 **Ox** (Jan 6 - Feb 3) 十二月 **12th Month**	戌 Xu Dog	午 Wu Horse	亥 Hai Pig

己酉 (Ji You)
Earth Rooster

己酉 (Ji You) Earth Rooster

Heavenly Stem 天干	己 Yin Earth (陰土)
Earthly Branch 地支	酉 Rooster (Yin Metal 陰金)
Hidden Stem 藏干	辛 Yin Metal (陰金)
Na Yin 納音	大驛土 Earth from the main roads
Grand Duke 太歲	酉 Rooster
Xuan Kong Five Element 玄空五行	3 木 Wood
Gua Name 卦名	☶ 火山旅 Travelling
Xuan Kong Period Luck 玄空卦運	8

Annual Positive Stars for Opening Mountain, Establishing Facing and Commencing Repairs 開山立向修方吉星：

歲德 Duke Virtue	甲 Jia Yang Wood
歲德合 Duke Virtue Combo	己 Ji Yin Earth
歲枝德 Duke Branch Virtue	寅 Yin Tiger
陽貴人 Yang Nobleman	子 Zi Rat
陰貴人 Yin Nobleman	申 Shen Monkey
歲祿 Duke Prosperous	午 Wu Horse
歲馬 Duke Horse	亥 Hai Pig
奏書 Decree	坤 Kun
博士 Professor	艮 Gen

Annual Negative Stars for Opening Mountain, Establishing Facing and Commencing Repairs 開山立向修方凶星：

太歲 Grand Duke	歲破 Year Breaker	三煞 Three Killings			坐煞向煞 Sitting Sha Facing Sha				浮天空亡 Floating Heaven Emptiness	
酉 You Rooster	卯 Mao Rabbit	寅 Yin Tiger	卯 Mao Rabbit	辰 Chen Dragon	甲 Jia Yang Wood	乙 Yi Yin Wood	庚 Geng Yang Metal	辛 Xin Yin Metal	乾 Qian	甲 Jia Yang Wood

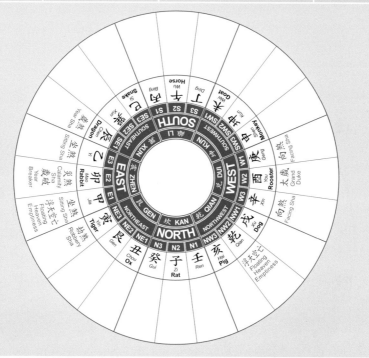

Annual San Yuan Purple White Stars 三元紫白九星：

上元 Upper Period Period 1, 2, 3			中元 Middle Period Period 4, 5, 6			下元 Lower Period Period 7, 8, 9		
巽SE	離S	坤SW	巽SE	離S	坤SW	巽SE	離S	坤SW
9	5	7	3	8	1	6	2	4
震E 8	1 己酉 Ji You Earth Rooster	兌W 3	震E 2	4 己酉 Ji You Earth Rooster	兌W 6	震E 5	7 己酉 Ji You Earth Rooster	兌W 9
4	6	2	7	9	5	1	3	8
艮NE	坎N	乾NW	艮NE	坎N	乾NW	艮NE	坎N	乾NW

Mountain Covering Yellow Path 蓋山黃道：

貪狼 *Tan Lang* **Greedy Wolf**				巨門 *Ju Men* **Huge Door**		武曲 *Wu Qu* **Military Arts**				文曲 *Wen Qu* **Literary Arts**	
離 *Li* S2	壬 *Ren* N1	寅 *Yin* NE3	戌 *Xu* NW1	乾 *Qian* NW2	甲 *Jia* E1	坎 *Kan* N2	癸 *Gui* N3	申 *Shen* SW3	辰 *Chen* SE1	艮 *Gen* NE2	丙 *Bing* S1

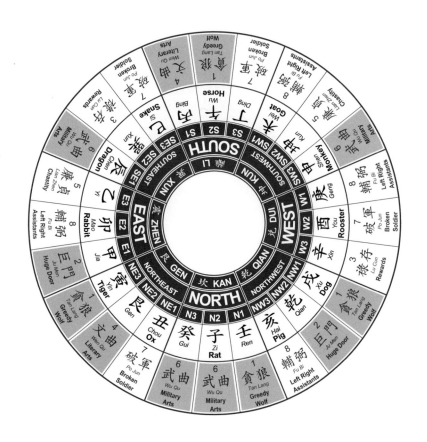

Heaven Penetrating Force 通天竅:			
三合前方 **Facing Three Harmony**	乾亥 Qian Hai	壬子 Ren Zi	癸丑 Gui Chou
三合後方 **Sitting Three Harmony**	巽巳 Xun Si	丙午 Bing Wu	丁未 Ding Wei

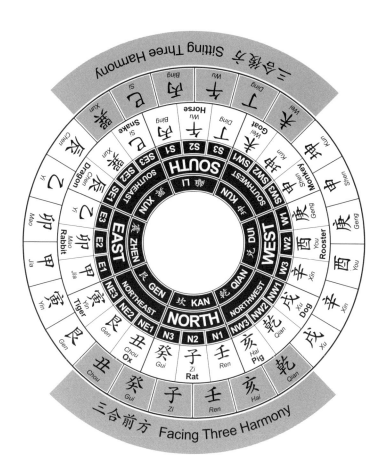

Moving Horse Six Ren Assessment 走馬六壬：

神后 *Shen Hou* **Holy Empress**	功曹 *Gong Cao* **Marshall**	天罡 *Tian Gang* **Heavenly Dipper**	勝光 *Sheng Guang* **Subliminal Bright**	傳送 *Chuan Song* **Great General**	河魁 *He Kui* **River Scholar**
甲卯 *Jia Mao*	巽巳 *Xun Si*	丁未 *Ding Wei*	庚酉 *Geng You*	乾亥 *Qian Hai*	癸丑 *Gui Chou*

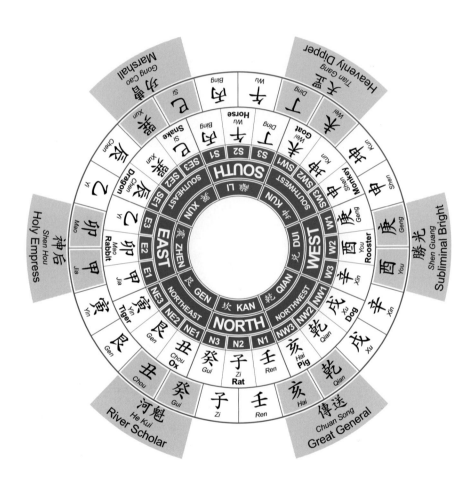

686

Four Advantages Three Cycles Star Plate 四利三元：

太陽 *Tai Yang* **Sun**	太陰 *Tai Yin* **Moon**	龍德 *Long De* **Dragon Virtue**	福德 *Fu De* **Fortune Virtue**
戌 *Xu* Dog	子 *Zi* Rat	辰 *Chen* Dragon	午 *Wu* Horse

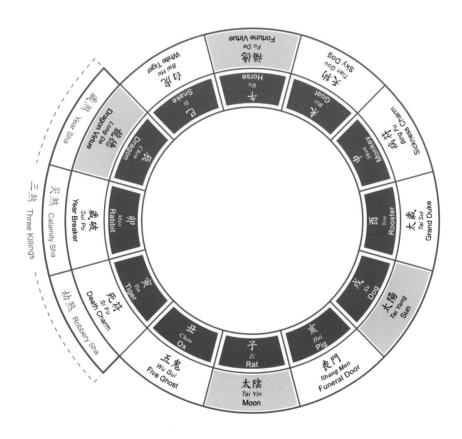

Negative Sectors For Opening Mountain 開山凶位：

年剋山家 Year Countering Sitting (冬至後 After Winter Solstice)

乾	亥	兌	丁
Qian	Hai	Dui	Ding
NW2	NW3	W2	S3

陰府太歲 Yin Fu Tai Sui **Yin Mansion Grand Duke**		六害 Liu Hai **Six Harm**	死符 Si Fu **Death Charm**	炙退 Zhi Tui **Roasting Star**
巽 Xun SE2	艮 Gen NE2	戌 Xu NW1	寅 Yin NE3	子 Zi N2

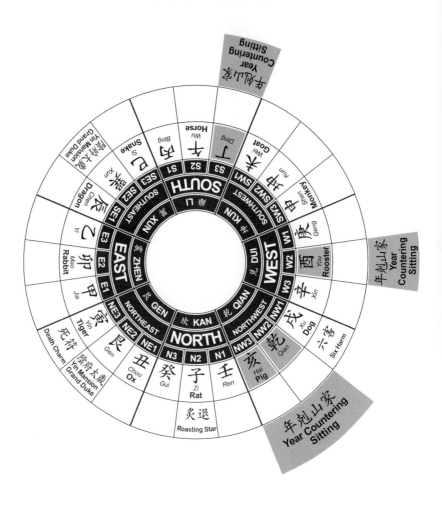

巡山羅喉 *Xun Shan Luo Hou* **Mountain Patrol Luo Hou Star**	病符 *Bing Fu* **Sickness Charm**
辛 *Xin* **W3**	申 *Shen* **SW3**

Negative Directions to Establish Facing 立向凶方：

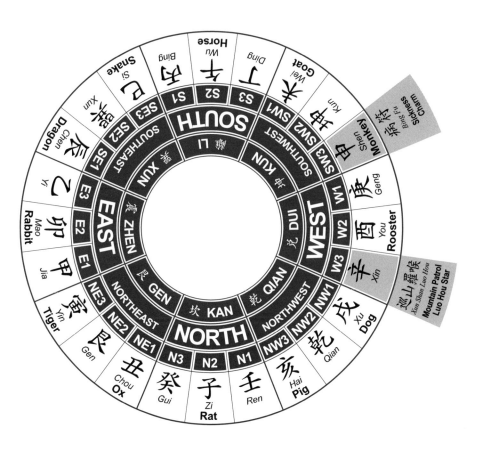

Negative Repair / Renovation Sectors Table 修方凶位表：

天官符 Heavenly Officer Charm	申 *Shen* **Monkey**	飛廉 Flying Chaste	亥 *Hai* **Pig**
地官符 Earthly Officer Charm	丑 *Chou* **Ox**	喪門 Funeral Door	亥 *Hai* **Pig**
大煞 Great Sha	酉 *You* **Rooster**	弔客 Suspended Guest	未 *Wei* **Goat**
大將軍 Big General	午 *Wu* **Horse**	白虎 White Tiger	巳 *Si* **Snake**
力士 Strong Man	乾 *Qian*	金神 Golden God	午 *Wu* **Horse** 未 *Wei* **Goat** 申 *Shen* **Monkey** 酉 *You* **Rooster**
蠶室 Silkworm Room	巽 *Xun*		
蠶官 Silkworm Officer	辰 *Chen* **Dragon**		
蠶命 Silkworm Life	巳 *Si* **Snake**		
歲刑 Duke Punishment	酉 *You* **Rooster**	獨火 Lonely Fire	坤 *Kun*
黃幡 Yellow Flag	丑 *Chou* **Ox**	五鬼 Five Ghost	未 *Wei* **Goat**
豹尾 Leopard Tail	未 *Wei* **Goat**	破敗五鬼 Destructive Five Ghost	坎 *Kan*

Negative Repair / Renovation Sectors Diagram 修方凶位圖：

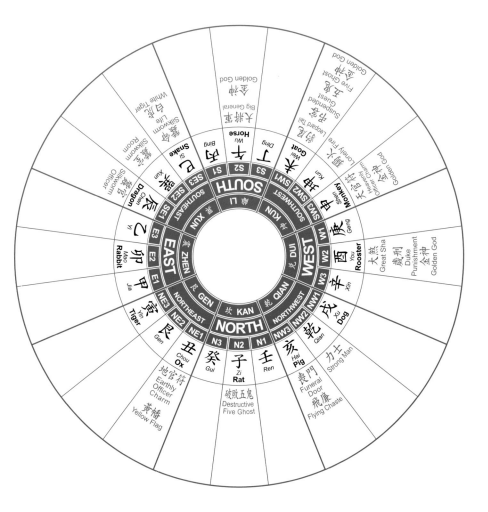

12-Month Auxiliary Stars Reference Table :
己酉年十二月，開山立向修方星表

Positive Monthly Stars 吉星方

月 MONTH	寅 Tiger (Feb 4 - Mar 5) 正月 1st Month	卯 Rabbit (Mar 6 - Apr 4) 二月 2nd Month	辰 Dragon (Apr 5 - May 5) 三月 3rd Month	巳 Snake (May 6 - Jun 5) 四月 4th Month	午 Horse (Jun 6 - July 6) 五月 5th Month	未 Goat (July 7 - Aug 7) 六月 6th Month
天道 Heavenly Path	南 South	西南 Southwest	北 North	西 West	西北 Northwest	東 East
天德 Heavenly Virtue	丁 Ding Yin Fire	坤 Kun (申)	壬 Ren Yang Water	辛 Xin Yin Metal	乾 Qian (亥)	甲 Jia Yang Wood
天德合 Heavenly Virtue Combo	壬 Ren Yang Water	(巳)	丁 Ding Yin Fire	丙 Bing Yang Fire	(寅)	己 Ji Yin Earth
月德 Monthly Virtue	丙 Bing Yang Fire	甲 Jia Yang Wood	壬 Ren Yang Water	庚 Geng Yang Metal	丙 Bing Yang Fire	甲 Jia Yang Wood
月德合 Monthly Virtue Combo	辛 Xin Yin Metal	己 Ji Yin Earth	丁 Ding Yin Fire	乙 Yi Yin Wood	辛 Xin Yin Metal	己 Ji Yin Earth
月空 Month Emptiness	壬 Ren Yang Water	庚 Geng Yang Metal	丙 Bing Yang Fire	甲 Jia Yang Wood	壬 Ren Yang Water	庚 Geng Yang Metal
陽貴人 Yang Nobleman	乾 Qian	中 Middle	巽 Xun	震 Zhen	坤 Kun	坎 Kan
陰貴人 Yin Nobleman	坤 Kun	坎 Kan	離 Li	艮 Gen	兌 Dui	乾 Qian
飛天祿 Flying Heavenly Wealth	離 Li	艮 Gen	兌 Dui	乾 Qian	中 Middle	坎 Kan
飛天馬 Flying Heavenly Horse	中 Middle	巽 Xun	震 Zhen	坤 Kun	坎 Kan	離 Li

12-Month Auxiliary Stars Reference Table :
己酉年十二月，開山立向修方星表

申 Monkey (Aug 8 - Sept 7)	酉 Rooster (Sept 8 - Oct 7)	戌 Dog (Oct 8 - Nov 6)	亥 Pig (Nov 7 - Dec 6)	子 Rat (Dec 7 - Jan 5)	丑 Ox (Jan 6 - Feb 3)	月 MONTH
七月 7th Month	八月 8th Month	九月 9th Month	十月 10th Month	十一月 11th Month	十二月 12th Month	
北 North	東北 Northeast	南 South	東 East	東南 Southeast	西 West	天道 Heavenly Path
癸 Gui Yin Water	艮 Gen (寅)	丙 Bing Yang Fire	乙 Yi Yin Wood	巽 Xun (巳)	庚 Geng Yang Metal	天德 Heavenly Virtue
戊 Wu Yang Earth	(亥)	辛 Xin Yin Metal	庚 Geng Yang Metal	(申)	乙 Yin Wood	天德合 Heavenly Virtue Combo
壬 Ren Yang Water	庚 Geng Yang Metal	丙 Bing Yang Fire	甲 Jia Yang Wood	壬 Ren Yang Water	庚 Geng Yang Metal	月德 Monthly Virtue
丁 Ding Yin Fire	乙 Yi Yin Wood	辛 Xin Yin Metal	己 Ji Yin Earth	丁 Ding Yin Fire	乙 Yi Yin Wood	月德合 Monthly Virtue Combo
丙 Bing Yang Fire	甲 Jia Yang Wood	壬 Ren Yang Water	庚 Geng Yang Metal	丙 Bing Yang Fire	甲 Jia Yang Wood	月空 Month Emptiness
離 Li	艮 Gen	兌 Dui	乾 Qian	中 Middle	坎 Kan	陽貴人 Yang Nobleman
中 Middle	坎 Kan	離 Li	艮 Gen	兌 Dui	乾 Qian	陰貴人 Yin Nobleman
離 Li	艮 Gen	兌 Dui	乾 Qian	中 Middle	巽 Xun	飛天祿 Flying Heavenly Wealth
艮 Gen	兌 Dui	乾 Qian	中 Middle	坎 Kan	離 Li	飛天馬 Flying Heavenly Horse

Monthly Purple White Stars 月紫白九星 :

寅 Tiger (Feb 4 - Mar 5) 正月 1st Month

巽 SE	離 S	坤 SW
7 Red 七赤	3 Jade 三碧	5 Yellow 五黃
震 E — 6 White 六白	8 White 八白	1 White 一白 — 兌 W
2 Black 二黑	4 Green 四綠	9 Purple 九紫
艮 NE	坎 N	乾 NW

卯 Rabbit (Mar 6 - Apr 4) 二月 2nd Month

巽 SE	離 S	坤 SW
6 White 六白	2 Black 二黑	4 Green 四綠
震 E — 5 Yellow 五黃	7 Red 七赤	9 Purple 九紫 — 兌 W
1 White 一白	3 Jade 三碧	8 White 八白
艮 NE	坎 N	乾 NW

辰 Dragon (Apr 5 - May 5) 三月 3rd Month

巽 SE	離 S	坤 SW
5 Yellow 五黃	1 White 一白	3 Jade 三碧
震 E — 4 Green 四綠	6 White 六白	8 White 八白 — 兌 W
9 Purple 九紫	2 Black 二黑	7 Red 七赤
艮 NE	坎 N	乾 NW

巳 Snake (May 6 - Jun 5) 四月 4th Month

巽 SE	離 S	坤 SW
4 Green 四綠	9 Purple 九紫	2 Black 二黑
震 E — 3 Jade 三碧	5 Yellow 五黃	7 Red 七赤 — 兌 W
8 White 八白	1 White 一白	6 White 六白
艮 NE	坎 N	乾 NW

午 Horse (Jun 6 - July 6) 五月 5th Month

巽 SE	離 S	坤 SW
3 Jade 三碧	8 White 八白	1 White 一白
震 E — 2 Black 二黑	4 Green 四綠	6 White 六白 — 兌 W
7 Red 七赤	9 Purple 九紫	5 Yellow 五黃
艮 NE	坎 N	乾 NW

未 Goat (July 7 - Aug 7) 六月 6th Month

巽 SE	離 S	坤 SW
2 Black 二黑	7 Red 七赤	9 Purple 九紫
震 E — 1 White 一白	3 Jade 三碧	5 Yellow 五黃 — 兌 W
6 White 六白	8 White 八白	4 Green 四綠
艮 NE	坎 N	乾 NW

申 Monkey (Aug 8 - Sept 7) 七月 7th Month

巽 SE	離 S	坤 SW
1 White 一白	6 White 六白	8 White 八白
震 E — 9 Purple 九紫	2 Black 二黑	4 Green 四綠 — 兌 W
5 Yellow 五黃	7 Red 七赤	3 Jade 三碧
艮 NE	坎 N	乾 NW

酉 Rooster (Sept 8 - Oct 7) 八月 8th Month

巽 SE	離 S	坤 SW
9 Purple 九紫	5 Yellow 五黃	7 Red 七赤
震 E — 8 White 八白	1 White 一白	3 Jade 三碧 — 兌 W
4 Green 四綠	6 White 六白	2 Black 二黑
艮 NE	坎 N	乾 NW

戌 Dog (Oct 8 - Nov 6) 九月 9th Month

巽 SE	離 S	坤 SW
8 White 八白	4 Green 四綠	6 White 六白
震 E — 7 Red 七赤	9 Purple 九紫	2 Black 二黑 — 兌 W
3 Jade 三碧	5 Yellow 五黃	1 White 一白
艮 NE	坎 N	乾 NW

亥 Pig (Nov 7 - Dec 6) 十月 10th Month

巽 SE	離 S	坤 SW
7 Red 七赤	3 Jade 三碧	5 Yellow 五黃
震 E — 6 White 六白	8 White 八白	1 White 一白 — 兌 W
2 Black 二黑	4 Green 四綠	9 Purple 九紫
艮 NE	坎 N	乾 NW

子 Rat (Dec 7 - Jan 5) 十一月 11th Month

巽 SE	離 S	坤 SW
6 White 六白	2 Black 二黑	4 Green 四綠
震 E — 5 Yellow 五黃	7 Red 七赤	9 Purple 九紫 — 兌 W
1 White 一白	3 Jade 三碧	8 White 八白
艮 NE	坎 N	乾 NW

丑 Ox (Jan 6 - Feb 3) 十二月 12th Month

巽 SE	離 S	坤 SW
5 Yellow 五黃	1 White 一白	3 Jade 三碧
震 E — 4 Green 四綠	6 White 六白	8 White 八白 — 兌 W
9 Purple 九紫	2 Black 二黑	7 Red 七赤
艮 NE	坎 N	乾 NW

Qi Men Three Nobles 三奇 :

Three Nobles 三奇 / Seasons	乙 Yi	丙 Bing	丁 Ding
立春 **Coming of Spring** Feb 4 - Feb 18	艮 Gen	艮 Gen	離 Li
春分 **Spring Equinox** Mar 21 - Apr 4	震 Zhen	震 Zhen	巽 Xun
立夏 **Coming of Summer** May 6 - May 20	巽 Xun	巽 Xun	中 **Middle**
夏至 **Summer Solstice** Jun 22 - Jul 6	離 Li	離 Li	艮 Gen
立秋 **Coming of Autumn** Aug 8 - Aug 23	坤 Kun	坤 Kun	坎 Kan
秋分 **Autumn Equinox** Sept 23 - Oct 7	兌 Dui	兌 Dui	乾 Qian
立冬 **Coming of Winter** Nov 7 - Nov 22	乾 Qian	乾 Qian	中 **Middle**
冬至 **Winter Solstice** Dec 22 - Jan 5	坎 Kan	坎 Kan	坤 Kun

Sectors to Avoid Opening Mountain 開山凶位 :

月 MONTH	月建 Month Establishment	月破 Month Destruction	月剋山家 Month Countering Sitting		陰府太歲 Yin Mansion Grand Duke	
寅 **Tiger** (Feb 4 - Mar 5) 正月 **1st Month**	寅 Yin **Tiger**	申 Shen **Monkey**	乾 Qian	兌 Dui	坎 Kan	坤 Kun
卯 **Rabbit** (Mar 6 - Apr 4) 二月 **2nd Month**	卯 Mao **Rabbit**	酉 You **Rooster**	亥 Hai	丁 Ding **Yin Fire**	乾 Qian	離 Li
辰 **Dragon** (Apr 5 - May 5) 三月 **3rd Month**	辰 Chen **Dragon**	戌 Xu **Dog**	震 Zhen	巳 Si **Snake**	坤 Kun	震 Zhen
巳 **Snake** (May 6 - Jun 5) 四月 **4th Month**	巳 Si **Snake**	亥 Hai **Pig**	艮 Gen		巽 Xun	艮 Gen
午 **Horse** (Jun 6 - July 6) 五月 **5th Month**	午 Wu **Horse**	子 Zi **Rat**	—		乾 Qian	兌 Dui
未 **Goat** (July 7 - Aug 7) 六月 **6th Month**	未 Wei **Goat**	丑 Chou **Ox**	—		坤 Kun	坎 Kan
申 **Monkey** (Aug 8 - Sept 7) 七月 **7th Month**	申 Shen **Monkey**	寅 Yin **Tiger**	水 **Water**	山 **Mountain**	離 Li	乾 Qian
酉 **Rooster** (Sept 8 - Oct 7) 八月 **8th Month**	酉 You **Rooster**	卯 Mao **Rabbit**	土 **Earth**		震 Zhen	坤 Kun
戌 **Dog** (Oct 8 - Nov 6) 九月 **9th Month**	戌 Xu **Dog**	辰 Chen **Dragon**	乾 Qian	兌 Dui	艮 Gen	巽 Xun
亥 **Pig** (Nov 7 - Dec 6) 十月 **10th Month**	亥 Hai **Pig**	巳 Si **Snake**	亥 Hai	丁 Ding **Yin Fire**	兌 Dui	乾 Qian
子 **Rat** (Dec 7 - Jan 5) 十一月 **11th Month**	子 Zi **Rat**	午 Wu **Horse**	離 Li	丙 Bing **Yang Fire**	坎 Kan	坤 Kun
丑 **Ox** (Jan 6 - Feb 3) 十二月 **12th Month**	丑 Chou **Ox**	未 Wei **Goat**	壬 Ren **Yang Water**	乙 Yi **Yin Wood**	乾 Qian	離 Li

Negative Repair / Renovation Sectors 修方凶位 :

月 MONTH	天官符 Heavenly Officer Charm			地官符 Earth Officer Charm			小月建 Small Month Establishment		
寅 **Tiger** (Feb 4 - Mar 5) 正月 **1st Month**	未 Wei Goat	坤 Kun	申 Shen Monkey	庚 Geng Yang Metal	兌 Dui	辛 Xin Yin Metal	丙 Bing Yang Fire	離 Li	丁 Ding Yin Fire
卯 **Rabbit** (Mar 6 - Apr 4) 二月 **2nd Month**	壬 Ren Yang Water	坎 Kan	癸 Gui Yin Water	戌 Xu Dog	乾 Qian	亥 Hai Pig	壬 Ren Yang Water	坎 Kan	癸 Gui Yin Water
辰 **Dragon** (Apr 5 - May 5) 三月 **3rd Month**	丙 Bing Yang Fire	離 Li	丁 Ding Yin Fire		中 Middle		未 Wei Goat	坤 Kun	申 Shen Monkey
巳 **Snake** (May 6 - Jun 5) 四月 **4th Month**	丑 Chou Ox	艮 Gen	寅 Yin Tiger	辰 Chen Dragon	巽 Xun	巳 Si Snake	甲 Jia Yang Wood	震 Zhen	乙 Yi Yin Wood
午 **Horse** (Jun 6 - July 6) 五月 **5th Month**	庚 Geng Yang Metal	兌 Dui	辛 Xin Yin Metal	甲 Jia Yang Wood	震 Zhen	乙 Yi Yin Wood	辰 Chen Dragon	巽 Xun	巳 Si Snake
未 **Goat** (July 7 - Aug 7) 六月 **6th Month**	戌 Xu Dog	乾 Qian	亥 Hai Pig	未 Wei Goat	坤 Kun	申 Shen Monkey		中 Middle	
申 **Monkey** (Aug 8 - Sept 7) 七月 **7th Month**		中 Middle		壬 Ren Yang Water	坎 Kan	癸 Gui Yin Water	戌 Xu Dog	乾 Qian	亥 Hai Pig
酉 **Rooster** (Sept 8 - Oct 7) 八月 **8th Month**	庚 Geng Yang Metal	兌 Dui	辛 Xin Yin Metal	丙 Bing Yang Fire	離 Li	丁 Ding Yin Fire	庚 Geng Yang Metal	兌 Dui	辛 Xin Yin Metal
戌 **Dog** (Oct 8 - Nov 6) 九月 **9th Month**	戌 Xu Dog	乾 Qian	亥 Hai Pig	丑 Chou Ox	艮 Gen	寅 Yin Tiger	丑 Chou Ox	艮 Gen	寅 Yin Tiger
亥 **Pig** (Nov 7 - Dec 6) 十月 **10th Month**		中 Middle		庚 Geng Yang Metal	兌 Dui	辛 Xin Yin Metal	丙 Bing Yang Fire	離 Li	丁 Ding Yin Fire
子 **Rat** (Dec 7 - Jan 5) 十一月 **11th Month**	辰 Chen Dragon	巽 Xun	巳 Si Snake	戌 Xu Dog	乾 Qian	亥 Hai Pig	壬 Ren Yang Water	坎 Kan	癸 Gui Yin Water
丑 **Ox** (Jan 6 - Feb 3) 十二月 **12th Month**	甲 Jia Yang Wood	震 Zhen	乙 Yi Yin Wood		中 Middle		未 Wei Goat	坤 Kun	申 Shen Monkey

Negative Repair / Renovation Sectors 修方凶位 :

月 MONTH	大月建 Big Month Establishment			飛大煞 Flying Great Sha			丙丁獨火 Bing Ding Lonely Fire	
寅 Tiger (Feb 4 - Mar 5) 正月 1st Month	丑 Chou Ox	艮 Gen	寅 Yin Tiger	甲 Jia Yang Wood	震 Zhen	乙 Yi Yin Wood	中 Middle	乾 Qian
卯 Rabbit (Mar 6 - Apr 4) 二月 2nd Month	庚 Geng Yang Metal	兌 Dui	辛 Xin Yin Metal	未 Wei Goat	坤 Kun	申 Shen Monkey	中 Middle	
辰 Dragon (Apr 5 - May 5) 三月 3rd Month	戊 Xu Dog	乾 Qian	亥 Hai Pig	壬 Ren Yang Water	坎 Kan	癸 Gui Yin Water	巽 Xun	中 Middle
巳 Snake (May 6 - Jun 5) 四月 4th Month	中 Middle			丙 Bing Yang Fire	離 Li	丁 Ding Yin Fire	震 Zhen	巽 Xun
午 Horse (Jun 6 - July 6) 五月 5th Month	辰 Chen Dragon	巽 Xun	巳 Si Snake	丑 Chou Ox	艮 Gen	寅 Yin Tiger	坤 Kun	震 Zhen
未 Goat (July 7 - Aug 7) 六月 6th Month	甲 Jia Yang Wood	震 Zhen	乙 Yi Yin Wood	庚 Geng Yang Metal	兌 Dui	辛 Xin Yin Metal	坎 Kan	坤 Kun
申 Monkey (Aug 8 - Sept 7) 七月 7th Month	未 Wei Goat	坤 Kun	申 Shen Monkey	戊 Xu Dog	乾 Qian	亥 Hai Pig	離 Li	坎 Kan
酉 Rooster (Sept 8 - Oct 7) 八月 8th Month	壬 Ren Yang Water	坎 Kan	癸 Gui Yin Water	中 Middle			艮 Gen	離 Li
戌 Dog (Oct 8 - Nov 6) 九月 9th Month	丙 Bing Yang Fire	離 Li	丁 Ding Yin Fire	庚 Geng Yang Metal	兌 Dui	辛 Xin Yin Metal	兌 Dui	艮 Gen
亥 Pig (Nov 7 - Dec 6) 十月 10th Month	丑 Chou Ox	艮 Gen	寅 Yin Tiger	戊 Xu Dog	乾 Qian	亥 Hai Pig	乾 Qian	兌 Dui
子 Rat (Dec 7 - Jan 5) 十一月 11th Month	庚 Geng Yang Metal	兌 Dui	辛 Xin Yin Metal	中 Middle			中 Middle	乾 Qian
丑 Ox (Jan 6 - Feb 3) 十二月 12th Month	戊 Xu Dog	乾 Qian	亥 Hai Pig	辰 Chen Dragon	巽 Xun	巳 Si Snake	中 Middle	

Negative Repair / Renovation Sectors 修方凶位 :

月 MONTH	月遊火 Month Wondering Fire	三煞 Monthly 3 Killings		
		劫煞 Robbery Sha	災煞 Calamity Sha	月煞 Month Sha
寅 **Tiger** (Feb 4 - Mar 5) 正月 **1st Month**	乾 Qian	亥 Hai **Pig**	子 Zi **Rat**	丑 Chou **Ox**
卯 **Rabbit** (Mar 6 - Apr 4) 二月 **2nd Month**	兌 Dui	申 Shen **Monkey**	酉 You **Rooster**	戌 Xu **Dog**
辰 **Dragon** (Apr 5 - May 5) 三月 **3rd Month**	艮 Gen	巳 Si **Snake**	午 Wu **Horse**	未 Wei **Goat**
巳 **Snake** (May 6 - Jun 5) 四月 **4th Month**	離 Li	寅 Yin **Tiger**	卯 Mao **Rabbit**	辰 Chen **Dragon**
午 **Horse** (Jun 6 - July 6) 五月 **5th Month**	坎 Kan	亥 Hai **Pig**	子 Zi **Rat**	丑 Chou **Ox**
未 **Goat** (July 7 - Aug 7) 六月 **6th Month**	坤 Kun	申 Shen **Monkey**	酉 You **Rooster**	戌 Xu **Dog**
申 **Monkey** (Aug 8 - Sept 7) 七月 **7th Month**	震 Zhen	巳 Si **Snake**	午 Wu **Horse**	未 Wei **Goat**
酉 **Rooster** (Sept 8 - Oct 7) 八月 **8th Month**	巽 Xun	寅 Yin **Tiger**	卯 Mao **Rabbit**	辰 Chen **Dragon**
戌 **Dog** (Oct 8 - Nov 6) 九月 **9th Month**	中 Middle	亥 Hai **Pig**	子 Zi **Rat**	丑 Chou **Ox**
亥 **Pig** (Nov 7 - Dec 6) 十月 **10th Month**	乾 Qian	申 Shen **Monkey**	酉 You **Rooster**	戌 Xu **Dog**
子 **Rat** (Dec 7 - Jan 5) 十一月 **11th Month**	兌 Dui	巳 Si **Snake**	午 Wu **Horse**	未 Wei **Goat**
丑 **Ox** (Jan 6 - Feb 3) 十二月 **12th Month**	艮 Gen	寅 Yin **Tiger**	卯 Mao **Rabbit**	辰 Chen **Dragon**

Negative Repair / Renovation Sectors 修方凶位 :

月 MONTH	月刑 Month Punishment	月害 Month Harm	月厭 Month Detest
寅 **Tiger** (Feb 4 - Mar 5) 正月 **1st Month**	巳 *Si* Snake	巳 *Si* Snake	戌 *Xu* Dog
卯 **Rabbit** (Mar 6 - Apr 4) 二月 **2nd Month**	子 *Zi* Rat	辰 *Chen* Dragon	酉 *You* Rooster
辰 **Dragon** (Apr 5 - May 5) 三月 **3rd Month**	辰 *Chen* Dragon	卯 *Mao* Rabbit	申 *Shen* Monkey
巳 **Snake** (May 6 - Jun 5) 四月 **4th Month**	申 *Shen* Monkey	寅 *Yin* Tiger	未 *Wei* Goat
午 **Horse** (Jun 6 - July 6) 五月 **5th Month**	午 *Wu* Horse	丑 *Chou* Ox	午 *Wu* Horse
未 **Goat** (July 7 - Aug 7) 六月 **6th Month**	丑 *Chou* Ox	子 *Zi* Rat	巳 *Si* Snake
申 **Monkey** (Aug 8 - Sept 7) 七月 **7th Month**	寅 *Yin* Tiger	亥 *Hai* Pig	辰 *Chen* Dragon
酉 **Rooster** (Sept 8 - Oct 7) 八月 **8th Month**	酉 *You* Rooster	戌 *Xu* Dog	卯 *Mao* Rabbit
戌 **Dog** (Oct 8 - Nov 6) 九月 **9th Month**	未 *Wei* Goat	酉 *You* Rooster	寅 *Yin* Tiger
亥 **Pig** (Nov 7 - Dec 6) 十月 **10th Month**	亥 *Hai* Pig	申 *Shen* Monkey	丑 *Chou* Ox
子 **Rat** (Dec 7 - Jan 5) 十一月 **11th Month**	卯 *Mao* Rabbit	未 *Wei* Goat	子 *Zi* Rat
丑 **Ox** (Jan 6 - Feb 3) 十二月 **12th Month**	戌 *Xu* Dog	午 *Wu* Horse	亥 *Hai* Pig

己亥 (Ji Hai)
Earth Pig

Heavenly Stem 天干	己 **Yin Earth (陰土)**
Earthly Branch 地支	亥 **Pig (Yin Water 陰水)**
Hidden Stem 藏干	壬 **Yang Water,** 甲 **Yang Wood**
Na Yin 納音	平地木 **Wood from the flatlands**
Grand Duke 太歲	亥 **Pig**
Xuan Kong Five Element 玄空五行	2 火 **Fire**
Gua Name 卦名	風地觀 **Observation**
Xuan Kong Period Luck 玄空卦運	2

Annual Positive Stars for Opening Mountain, Establishing Facing and Commencing Repairs 開山立向修方吉星：

歲德 **Duke Virtue**	甲 Jia **Yang Wood**
歲德合 **Duke Virtue Combo**	己 Ji **Yin Earth**
歲枝德 **Duke Branch Virtue**	辰 Chen **Dragon**
陽貴人 **Yang Nobleman**	子 Zi **Rat**
陰貴人 **Yin Nobleman**	申 Shen **Monkey**
歲祿 **Duke Prosperous**	午 Wu **Horse**
歲馬 **Duke Horse**	巳 Si **Snake**
奏書 **Decree**	乾 Qian
博士 **Professor**	巽 Xun

Annual Negative Stars for Opening Mountain, Establishing Facing and Commencing Repairs 開山立向修方凶星：

太歲 Grand Duke	歲破 Year Breaker	三煞 Three Killings			坐煞向煞 Sitting Sha Facing Sha				浮天空亡 Floating Heaven Emptiness	
亥 *Hai* Pig	巳 *Si* Snake	申 *Shen* Monkey	酉 *You* Rooster	戌 *Xu* Dog	庚 *Geng* Yang Metal	辛 *Xin* Yin Metal	甲 *Jia* Yang Wood	乙 *Yi* Yin Wood	乾 *Qian*	甲 *Jia* Yang Wood

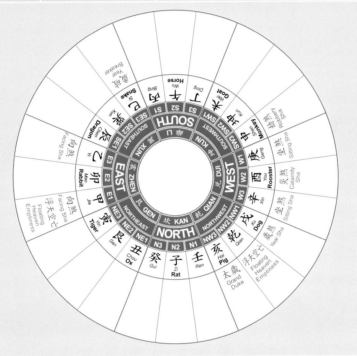

Annual San Yuan Purple White Stars 三元紫白九星：

上元 Upper Period Period 1, 2, 3			中元 Middle Period Period 4, 5, 6			下元 Lower Period Period 7, 8, 9		
巽SE	離S	坤SW	巽SE	離S	坤SW	巽SE	離S	坤SW
1	6	8	4	9	2	7	3	5
震E 9	2 己亥 *Ji Hai* Earth Pig	兌W 4	震E 3	5 己亥 *Ji Hai* Earth Pig	兌W 7	震E 6	8 己亥 *Ji Hai* Earth Pig	兌W 1
艮NE 5	坎N 7	乾NW 3	艮NE 8	坎N 1	乾NW 6	艮NE 2	坎N 4	乾NW 9

Mountain Covering Yellow Path 蓋山黃道：

貪狼 *Tan Lang* **Greedy Wolf**				巨門 *Ju Men* **Huge Door**		武曲 *Wu Qu* **Military Arts**				文曲 *Wen Qu* **Literary Arts**			
坎 *Kan* **N2**	癸 *Gui* **N3**	申 *Shen* **SW3**	辰 *Chen* **SE1**	坤 *Kun* **SW2**	乙 *Yi* **E3**	離 *Li* **S2**	壬 *Ren* **N1**	寅 *Yin* **NE3**	戌 *Xu* **NW1**	兌 *Dui* **W2**	丁 *Ding* **S3**	巳 *Si* **SE3**	丑 *Chou* **NE1**

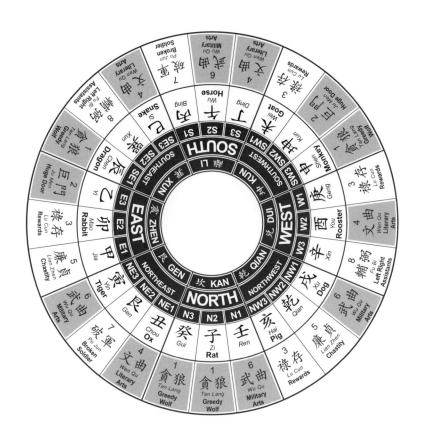

Heaven Penetrating Force 通天竅 :			
三合前方 **Facing Three Harmony**	巽巳 Xun Si	丙午 Bing Wu	丁未 Ding Wei
三合後方 **Sitting Three Harmony**	乾亥 Qian Hai	壬子 Ren Zi	癸丑 Gui Chou

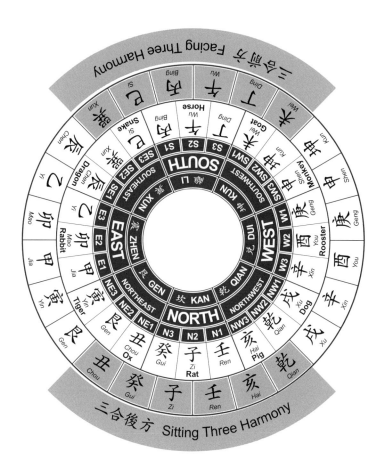

Moving Horse Six Ren Assessment 走馬六壬：

神后 Shen Hou **Holy Empress**	功曹 Gong Cao **Marshall**	天罡 Tian Gang **Heavenly Dipper**	勝光 Sheng Guang **Subliminal Bright**	傳送 Chuan Song **Great General**	河魁 He Kui **River Scholar**
癸丑 Gui Chou	甲卯 Jia Mao	巽巳 Xun Si	丁未 Ding Wei	庚酉 Geng You	乾亥 Qian Hai

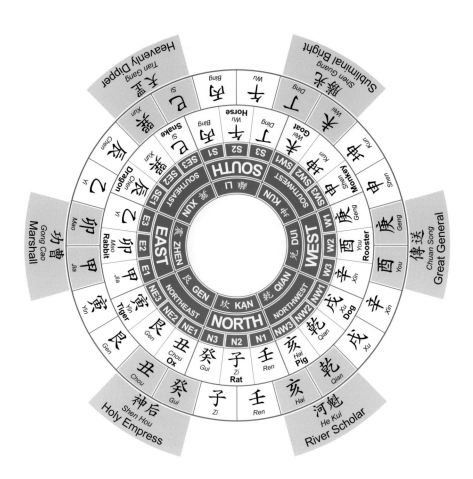

Four Advantages Three Cycles Star Plate 四利三元：

太陽 *Tai Yang* **Sun**	太陰 *Tai Yin* **Moon**	龍德 *Long De* **Dragon Virtue**	福德 *Fu De* **Fortune Virtue**
子 *Zi* Rat	寅 *Yin* Tiger	午 *Wu* Horse	申 *Shen* Monkey

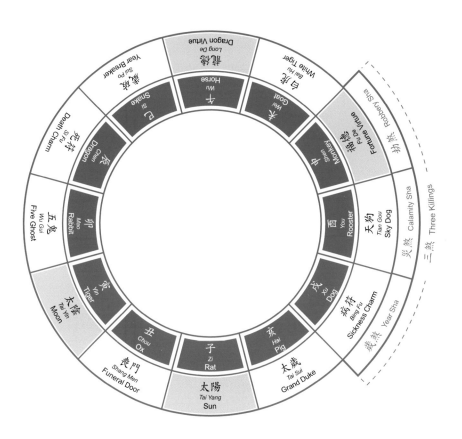

Negative Sectors For Opening Mountain 開山凶位：

年剋山家 Year Countering Sitting

震 Zhen **E2**	艮 Ge **NE2**	巳 Si **SE3**		
陰府太歲 Yin Fu Tai Sui **Yin Mansion Grand Duke**	六害 Liu Hai **Six Harm**	死符 Si Fu **Death Charm**	炙退 Zhi Tui **Roasting Star**	
巽 Xun **SE2**	艮 Ge **NE2**	申 Shen **SW3**	辰 Chen **SE1**	午 Wu **S2**

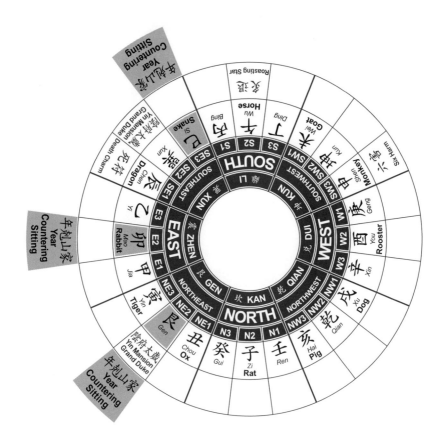

Negative Directions to Establish Facing 立向凶方:

巡山羅喉 *Xun Shan Luo Hou* **Mountain Patrol Luo Hou Star**	病符 *Bing Fu* **Sickness Charm**
壬 *Ren* **N1**	戌 *Xu* **NW1**

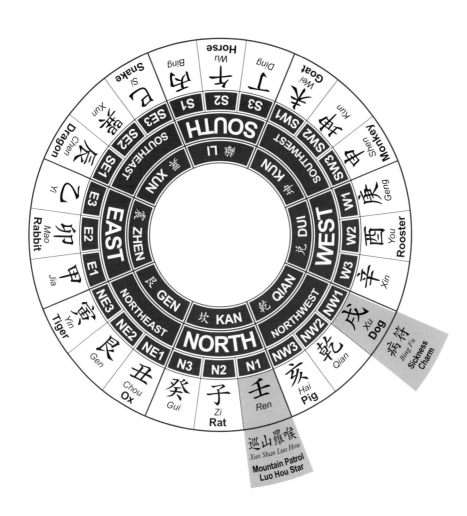

Negative Repair / Renovation Sectors Table 修方凶位表：

天官符 **Heavenly Officer Charm**	寅 *Yin* **Tiger**		飛廉 **Flying Chaste**	丑 *Chou* **Ox**
地官符 **Earthly Officer Charm**	卯 *Mao* **Rabbit**		喪門 **Funeral Door**	丑 *Chou* **Ox**
大煞 **Great Sha**	卯 *Mao* **Rabbit**		弔客 **Suspended Guest**	酉 *You* **Rooster**
大將軍 **Big General**	酉 *You* **Rooster**		白虎 **White Tiger**	未 *Wei* **Goat**
力士 **Strong Man**	艮 *Gen*		金神 **Golden God**	午 *Wu* **Horse**
蠶室 **Silkworm Room**	坤 *Kun*			未 *Wei* **Goat**
蠶官 **Silkworm Officer**	未 *Wei* **Goat**			申 *Shen* **Monkey**
蠶命 **Silkworm Life**	申 *Shen* **Monkey**			酉 *You* **Rooster**
歲刑 **Duke Punishment**	亥 *Hai* **Pig**		獨火 **Lonely Fire**	乾 *Qian*
黃幡 **Yellow Flag**	未 *Wei* **Goat**		五鬼 **Five Ghost**	巳 *Si* **Snake**
豹尾 **Leopard Tail**	丑 *Chou* **Ox**		破敗五鬼 **Destructive Five Ghost**	坎 *Kan*

Negative Repair / Renovation Sectors Diagram 修方凶位圖：

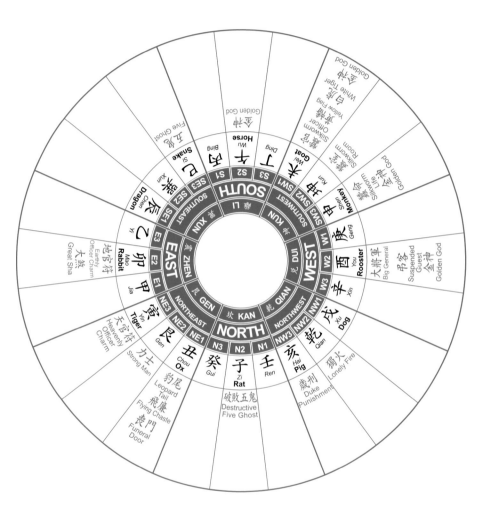

12-Month Auxiliary Stars Reference Table :
己亥年十二月，開山立向修方星表

Positive Monthly Stars 吉星方

月 MONTH	寅 Tiger (Feb 4 - Mar 5) 正月 1st Month	卯 Rabbit (Mar 6 - Apr 4) 二月 2nd Month	辰 Dragon (Apr 5 - May 5) 三月 3rd Month	巳 Snake (May 6 - Jun 5) 四月 4th Month	午 Horse (Jun 6 - July 6) 五月 5th Month	未 Goat (July 7 - Aug 7) 六月 6th Month
天道 Heavenly Path	南 South	西南 Southwest	北 North	西 West	西北 Northwest	東 East
天德 Heavenly Virtue	丁 Ding Yin Fire	坤 Kun （申）	壬 Ren Yang Water	辛 Xin Yin Metal	乾 Qian （亥）	甲 Jia Yang Wood
天德合 Heavenly Virtue Combo	壬 Ren Yang Water	（巳）	丁 Ding Yin Fire	丙 Bing Yang Fire	（寅）	己 Ji Yin Earth
月德 Monthly Virtue	丙 Bing Yang Fire	甲 Jia Yang Wood	壬 Ren Yang Water	庚 Geng Yang Metal	丙 Bing Yang Fire	甲 Jia Yang Wood
月德合 Monthly Virtue Combo	辛 Xin Yin Metal	己 Ji Yin Earth	丁 Ding Yin Fire	乙 Yi Yin Wood	辛 Xin Yin Metal	己 Ji Yin Earth
月空 Month Emptiness	壬 Ren Yang Water	庚 Geng Yang Metal	丙 Bing Yang Fire	甲 Jia Yang Wood	壬 Ren Yang Water	庚 Geng Yang Metal
陽貴人 Yang Nobleman	乾 Qian	中 Middle	巽 Xun	震 Zhen	坤 Kun	坎 Kan
陰貴人 Yin Nobleman	坤 Kun	坎 Kan	離 Li	艮 Gen	兌 Dui	乾 Qian
飛天祿 Flying Heavenly Wealth	離 Li	艮 Gen	兌 Dui	乾 Qian	中 Middle	坎 Kan
飛天馬 Flying Heavenly Horse	艮 Gen	兌 Dui	乾 Qian	中 Middle	坎 Kan	離 Li

12-Month Auxiliary Stars Reference Table :
己亥年十二月，開山立向修方星表

申 Monkey (Aug 8 - Sept 7) 七月 7th Month	酉 Rooster (Sept 8 - Oct 7) 八月 8th Month	戌 Dog (Oct 8 - Nov 6) 九月 9th Month	亥 Pig (Nov 7 - Dec 6) 十月 10th Month	子 Rat (Dec 7 - Jan 5) 十一月 11th Month	丑 Ox (Jan 6 - Feb 3) 十二月 12th Month	月 MONTH
北 North	東北 Northeast	南 South	東 East	東南 Southeast	西 West	天道 Heavenly Path
癸 Gui Yin Water	艮 Gen （寅）	丙 Bing Yang Fire	乙 Yi Yin Wood	巽 Xun （巳）	庚 Geng Yang Metal	天德 Heavenly Virtue
戊 Wu Yang Earth	（亥）	辛 Xin Yin Metal	庚 Geng Yang Metal	（申）	乙 Yi Yin Wood	天德合 Heavenly Virtue Combo
壬 Ren Yang Water	庚 Geng Yang Metal	丙 Bing Yang Fire	甲 Jia Yang Wood	壬 Ren Yang Water	庚 Geng Yang Metal	月德 Monthly Virtue
丁 Ding Yin Fire	乙 Yi Yin Wood	辛 Xin Yin Metal	己 Ji Yin Earth	丁 Ding Yin Fire	乙 Yi Yin Wood	月德合 Monthly Virtue Combo
丙 Bing Yang Fire	甲 Jia Yang Wood	壬 Ren Yang Water	庚 Geng Yang Metal	丙 Bing Yang Fire	甲 Jia Yang Wood	月空 Month Emptiness
離 Li	艮 Gen	兌 Dui	乾 Qian	中 Middle	坎 Kan	陽貴人 Yang Nobleman
中 Middle	坎 Kan	離 Li	艮 Gen	兌 Dui	乾 Qian	陰貴人 Yin Nobleman
離 Li	艮 Gen	兌 Dui	乾 Qian	中 Middle	巽 Xun	飛天祿 Flying Heavenly Wealth
艮 Gen	兌 Dui	乾 Qian	中 Middle	巽 Xun	震 Zhen	飛天馬 Flying Heavenly Horse

Monthly Purple White Stars 月紫白九星 :

寅 Tiger (Feb 4 - Mar 5) 正月 1st Month

SE 巽	S 離	SW 坤
1 White 一白	6 White 六白	8 White 八白
9 Purple 九紫 (E 震)	2 Black 二黑	4 Green 四綠 (W 兌)
5 Yellow 五黃	7 Red 七赤	3 Jade 三碧
NE 艮	N 坎	NW 乾

卯 Rabbit (Mar 6 - Apr 4) 二月 2nd Month

SE 巽	S 離	SW 坤
9 Purple 九紫	5 Yellow 五黃	7 Red 七赤
8 White 八白 (E 震)	1 White 一白	3 Jade 三碧 (W 兌)
4 Green 四綠	6 White 六白	2 Black 二黑
NE 艮	N 坎	NW 乾

辰 Dragon (Apr 5 - May 5) 三月 3rd Month

SE 巽	S 離	SW 坤
8 White 八白	4 Green 四綠	6 White 六白
7 Red 七赤 (E 震)	9 Purple 九紫	2 Black 二黑 (W 兌)
3 Jade 三碧	5 Yellow 五黃	1 White 一白
NE 艮	N 坎	NW 乾

巳 Snake (May 6 - Jun 5) 四月 4th Month

SE 巽	S 離	SW 坤
7 Red 七赤	3 Jade 三碧	5 Yellow 五黃
6 White 六白 (E 震)	8 White 八白	1 White 一白 (W 兌)
2 Black 二黑	4 Green 四綠	9 Purple 九紫
NE 艮	N 坎	NW 乾

午 Horse (Jun 6 - July 6) 五月 5th Month

SE 巽	S 離	SW 坤
6 White 六白	2 Black 二黑	4 Green 四綠
5 Yellow 五黃 (E 震)	7 Red 七赤	9 Purple 九紫 (W 兌)
1 White 一白	3 Jade 三碧	8 White 八白
NE 艮	N 坎	NW 乾

未 Goat (July 7 - Aug 7) 六月 6th Month

SE 巽	S 離	SW 坤
5 Yellow 五黃	1 White 一白	3 Jade 三碧
4 Green 四綠 (E 震)	6 White 六白	8 White 八白 (W 兌)
9 Purple 九紫	2 Black 二黑	7 Red 七赤
NE 艮	N 坎	NW 乾

申 Monkey (Aug 8 - Sept 7) 七月 7th Month

SE 巽	S 離	SW 坤
4 Green 四綠	9 Purple 九紫	2 Black 二黑
3 Jade 三碧 (E 震)	5 Yellow 五黃	7 Red 七赤 (W 兌)
8 White 八白	1 White 一白	6 White 六白
NE 艮	N 坎	NW 乾

酉 Rooster (Sept 8 - Oct 7) 八月 8th Month

SE 巽	S 離	SW 坤
3 Jade 三碧	8 White 八白	1 White 一白
2 Black 二黑 (E 震)	4 Green 四綠	6 White 六白 (W 兌)
7 Red 七赤	9 Purple 九紫	5 Yellow 五黃
NE 艮	N 坎	NW 乾

戌 Dog (Oct 8 - Nov 6) 九月 9th Month

SE 巽	S 離	SW 坤
2 Black 二黑	7 Red 七赤	9 Purple 九紫
1 White 一白 (E 震)	3 Jade 三碧	5 Yellow 五黃 (W 兌)
6 White 六白	8 White 八白	4 Green 四綠
NE 艮	N 坎	NW 乾

亥 Pig (Nov 7 - Dec 6) 十月 10th Month

SE 巽	S 離	SW 坤
1 White 一白	6 White 六白	8 White 八白
9 Purple 九紫 (E 震)	2 Black 二黑	4 Green 四綠 (W 兌)
5 Yellow 五黃	7 Red 七赤	3 Jade 三碧
NE 艮	N 坎	NW 乾

子 Rat (Dec 7 - Jan 5) 十一月 11th Month

SE 巽	S 離	SW 坤
9 Purple 九紫	5 Yellow 五黃	7 Red 七赤
8 White 八白 (E 震)	1 White 一白	3 Jade 三碧 (W 兌)
4 Green 四綠	6 White 六白	2 Black 二黑
NE 艮	N 坎	NW 乾

丑 Ox (Jan 6 - Feb 3) 十二月 12th Month

SE 巽	S 離	SW 坤
8 White 八白	4 Green 四綠	6 White 六白
7 Red 七赤 (E 震)	9 Purple 九紫	2 Black 二黑 (W 兌)
3 Jade 三碧	5 Yellow 五黃	1 White 一白
NE 艮	N 坎	NW 乾

Qi Men Three Nobles 三奇 :

Three Nobles 三奇 / Seasons	乙 *Yi*	丙 *Bing*	丁 *Ding*
立春 **Coming of Spring** Feb 4 - Feb 18	兑 *Dui*	兑 *Dui*	艮 *Gen*
春分 **Spring Equinox** Mar 21 - Apr 4	坤 *Kun*	坤 *Kun*	震 *Zhen*
立夏 **Coming of Summer** May 6 - May 20	震 *Zhen*	震 *Zhen*	巽 *Xun*
夏至 **Summer Solstice** Jun 22 - Jul 6	坎 *Kan*	坎 *Kan*	離 *Li*
立秋 **Coming of Autumn** Aug 8 - Aug 23	震 *Zhen*	震 *Zhen*	坤 *Kun*
秋分 **Autumn Equinox** Sept 23 - Oct 7	艮 *Gen*	艮 *Gen*	兑 *Dui*
立冬 **Coming of Winter** Nov 7 - Nov 22	兑 *Dui*	兑 *Dui*	乾 *Qian*
冬至 **Winter Solstice** Dec 22 - Jan 5	離 *Li*	離 *Li*	坎 *Kan*

Sectors to Avoid Opening Mountain 開山凶位：

月 MONTH	月建 Month Establishment	月破 Month Destruction	月剋山家 Month Countering Sitting		陰府太歲 Yin Mansion Grand Duke	
寅 **Tiger** (Feb 4 - Mar 5) 正月 **1st Month**	寅 *Yin* **Tiger**	申 *Shen* **Monkey**	乾 *Qian*	兌 *Dui*	坎 *Kan*	坤 *Kun*
卯 **Rabbit** (Mar 6 - Apr 4) 二月 **2nd Month**	卯 *Mao* **Rabbit**	酉 *You* **Rooster**	亥 *Hai* **Pig**	丁 *Ding* **Yin Fire**	乾 *Qian*	離 *Li*
辰 **Dragon** (Apr 5 - May 5) 三月 **3rd Month**	辰 *Chen* **Dragon**	戌 *Xu* **Dog**	震 *Zhen*	巳 *Si* **Snake**	坤 *Kun*	震 *Zhen*
巳 **Snake** (May 6 - Jun 5) 四月 **4th Month**	巳 *Si* **Snake**	亥 *Hai* **Pig**	艮 *Gen*		巽 *Xun*	艮 *Gen*
午 **Horse** (Jun 6 - July 6) 五月 **5th Month**	午 *Wu* **Horse**	子 *Zi* **Rat**	—		乾 *Qian*	兌 *Dui*
未 **Goat** (July 7 - Aug 7) 六月 **6th Month**	未 *Wei* **Goat**	丑 *Chou* **Ox**	—		坤 *Kun*	坎 *Kan*
申 **Monkey** (Aug 8 - Sept 7) 七月 **7th Month**	申 *Shen* **Monkey**	寅 *Yin* **Tiger**	水 **Water**	山 **Mountain**	離 *Li*	乾 *Qian*
酉 **Rooster** (Sept 8 - Oct 7) 八月 **8th Month**	酉 *You* **Rooster**	卯 *Mao* **Rabbit**	土 **Earth**		震 *Zhen*	坤 *Kun*
戌 **Dog** (Oct 8 - Nov 6) 九月 **9th Month**	戌 *Xu* **Dog**	辰 *Chen* **Dragon**	乾 *Qian*	兌 *Dui*	艮 *Gen*	巽 *Xun*
亥 **Pig** (Nov 7 - Dec 6) 十月 **10th Month**	亥 *Hai* **Pig**	巳 *Si* **Snake**	亥 *Hai* **Pig**	丁 *Ding* **Yin Fire**	兌 *Dui*	乾 *Qian*
子 **Rat** (Dec 7 - Jan 5) 十一月 **11th Month**	子 *Zi* **Rat**	午 *Wu* **Horse**	離 *Li*	丙 *Bing* **Yang Fire**	坎 *Kan*	坤 *Kun*
丑 **Ox** (Jan 6 - Feb 3) 十二月 **12th Month**	丑 *Chou* **Ox**	未 *Wei* **Goat**	壬 *Ren* **Yang Water**	乙 *Yi* **Yin Wood**	乾 *Qian*	離 *Li*

Negative Repair / Renovation Sectors 修方凶位 :

月 MONTH	天官符 Heavenly Officer Charm			地官符 Earth Officer Charm			小月建 Small Month Establishment		
寅 **Tiger** (Feb 4 - Mar 5) 正月 1st Month		中 Middle		戌 *Xu* Dog	乾 *Qian*	亥 *Hai* Pig	丙 *Bing* Yang Fire	離 *Li*	丁 *Ding* Yin Fire
卯 **Rabbit** (Mar 6 - Apr 4) 二月 2nd Month	庚 *Geng* Yang Metal	兑 *Dui*	辛 *Xin* Yin Metal		中 Middle		壬 *Ren* Yang Water	坎 *Kan*	癸 *Gui* Yin Water
辰 **Dragon** (Apr 5 - May 5) 三月 3rd Month	戌 *Xu* Dog	乾 *Qian*	亥 *Hai* Pig	庚 *Geng* Yang Metal	兑 *Dui*	辛 *Xin* Yin Metal	未 *Wei* Goat	坤 *Kun*	申 *Shen* Monkey
巳 **Snake** (May 6 - Jun 5) 四月 4th Month		中 Middle		戌 *Xu* Dog	乾 *Qian*	亥 *Hai* Pig	甲 *Jia* Yang Wood	震 *Zhen*	乙 *Yi* Yin Wood
午 **Horse** (Jun 6 - July 6) 五月 5th Month	辰 *Chen* Dragon	巽 *Xun*	巳 *Si* Snake		中 Middle		辰 *Chen* Dragon	巽 *Xun*	巳 *Si* Snake
未 **Goat** (July 7 - Aug 7) 六月 6th Month	甲 *Jia* Yang Wood	震 *Zhen*	乙 *Yi* Yin Wood	辰 *Chen* Dragon	巽 *Xun*	巳 *Si* Snake		中 Middle	
申 **Monkey** (Aug 8 - Sept 7) 七月 7th Month	未 *Wei* Goat	坤 *Kun*	申 *Shen* Monkey	甲 *Jia* Yang Wood	震 *Zhen*	乙 *Yi* Yin Wood	戌 *Xu* Dog	乾 *Qian*	亥 *Hai* Pig
酉 **Rooster** (Sept 8 - Oct 7) 八月 8th Month	壬 *Ren* Yang Water	坎 *Kan*	癸 *Gui* Yin Water	未 *Wei* Goat	坤 *Kun*	申 *Shen* Monkey	庚 *Geng* Yang Metal	兑 *Dui*	辛 *Xin* Yin Metal
戌 **Dog** (Oct 8 - Nov 6) 九月 9th Month	丙 *Bing* Yang Fire	離 *Li*	丁 *Ding* Yin Fire	壬 *Ren* Yang Water	坎 *Kan*	癸 *Gui* Yin Water	丑 *Chou* Ox	艮 *Gen*	寅 *Yin* Tiger
亥 **Pig** (Nov 7 - Dec 6) 十月 10th Month	丑 *Chou* Ox	艮 *Gen*	寅 *Yin* Tiger	丙 *Bing* Yang Fire	離 *Li*	丁 *Ding* Yin Fire	丙 *Bing* Yang Fire	離 *Li*	丁 *Ding* Yin Fire
子 **Rat** (Dec 7 - Jan 5) 十一月 11th Month	庚 *Geng* Yang Metal	兑 *Dui*	辛 *Xin* Yin Metal	丑 *Chou* Ox	艮 *Gen*	寅 *Yin* Tiger	壬 *Ren* Yang Water	坎 *Kan*	癸 *Gui* Yin Water
丑 **Ox** (Jan 6 - Feb 3) 十二月 12th Month	戌 *Xu* Dog	乾 *Qian*	亥 *Hai* Pig	庚 *Geng* Yang Metal	兑 *Dui*	辛 *Xin* Yin Metal	未 *Wei* Goat	坤 *Kun*	申 *Shen* Monkey

Negative Repair / Renovation Sectors 修方凶位 :

月 MONTH	大月建 Big Month Establishment			飛大煞 Flying Great Sha			丙丁獨火 Bing Ding Lonely Fire	
寅 Tiger (Feb 4 - Mar 5) 正月 1st Month	未 Wei Goat	坤 Kun	申 Shen Monkey	戌 Xu Dog	乾 Qian	亥 Hai Pig	中 Middle	乾 Qian
卯 Rabbit (Mar 6 - Apr 4) 二月 2nd Month	壬 Ren Yang Water	坎 Kan	癸 Gui Yin Water	中 Middle			中 Middle	
辰 Dragon (Apr 5 - May 5) 三月 3rd Month	丙 Bing Yang Fire	離 Li	丁 Ding Yin Fire	庚 Geng Yang Metal	兌 Dui	辛 Xin Yin Metal	巽 Xun	中 Middle
巳 Snake (May 6 - Jun 5) 四月 4th Month	丑 Chou Ox	艮 Gen	寅 Yin Tiger	戌 Xu Dog	乾 Qian	亥 Hai Pig	震 Zhen	巽 Xun
午 Horse (Jun 6 - July 6) 五月 5th Month	庚 Geng Yang Metal	兌 Dui	辛 Xin Yin Metal	中 Middle			坤 Kun	震 Zhen
未 Goat (July 7 - Aug 7) 六月 6th Month	戌 Xu Dog	乾 Qian	亥 Hai Pig	辰 Chen Dragon	巽 Xun	巳 Si Snake	坎 Kan	坤 Kun
申 Monkey (Aug 8 - Sept 7) 七月 7th Month	中 Middle			甲 Jia Yang Wood	震 Zhen	乙 Yi Yin Wood	離 Li	坎 Kan
酉 Rooster (Sept 8 - Oct 7) 八月 8th Month	辰 Chen Dragon	巽 Xun	巳 Si Snake	未 Wei Goat	坤 Kun	申 Shen Monkey	艮 Gen	離 Li
戌 Dog (Oct 8 - Nov 6) 九月 9th Month	甲 Jia Yang Wood	震 Zhen	乙 Yi Yin Wood	壬 Ren Yang Water	坎 Kan	癸 Gui Yin Water	兌 Dui	艮 Gen
亥 Pig (Nov 7 - Dec 6) 十月 10th Month	未 Wei Goat	坤 Kun	申 Shen Monkey	丙 Bing Yang Fire	離 Li	丁 Ding Yin Fire	乾 Qian	兌 Dui
子 Rat (Dec 7 - Jan 5) 十一月 11th Month	壬 Ren Yang Water	坎 Kan	癸 Gui Yin Water	丑 Chou Ox	艮 Gen	寅 Yin Tiger	中 Middle	乾 Qian
丑 Ox (Jan 6 - Feb 3) 十二月 12th Month	丙 Bing Yang Fire	離 Li	丁 Ding Yin Fire	庚 Geng Yang Metal	兌 Dui	辛 Xin Yin Metal	中 Middle	

Negative Repair / Renovation Sectors 修方凶位 :

月 MONTH	月遊火 Month Wondering Fire	三煞 Monthly 3 Killings		
		劫煞 Robbery Sha	災煞 Calamity Sha	月煞 Month Sha
寅 Tiger (Feb 4 - Mar 5) 正月 1st Month	坎 Kan	亥 Hai Pig	子 Zi Rat	丑 Chou Ox
卯 Rabbit (Mar 6 - Apr 4) 二月 2nd Month	坤 Kun	申 Shen Monkey	酉 You Rooster	戌 Xu Dog
辰 Dragon (Apr 5 - May 5) 三月 3rd Month	震 Zhen	巳 Si Snake	午 Wu Horse	未 Wei Goat
巳 Snake (May 6 - Jun 5) 四月 4th Month	巽 Xun	寅 Yin Tiger	卯 Mao Rabbit	辰 Chen Dragon
午 Horse (Jun 6 - July 6) 五月 5th Month	中 Middle	亥 Hai Pig	子 Zi Rat	丑 Chou Ox
未 Goat (July 7 - Aug 7) 六月 6th Month	乾 Qian	申 Shen Monkey	酉 You Rooster	戌 Xu Dog
申 Monkey (Aug 8 - Sept 7) 七月 7th Month	兌 Dui	巳 Si Snake	午 Wu Horse	未 Wei Goat
酉 Rooster (Sept 8 - Oct 7) 八月 8th Month	艮 Gen	寅 Yin Tiger	卯 Mao Rabbit	辰 Chen Dragon
戌 Dog (Oct 8 - Nov 6) 九月 9th Month	離 Li	亥 Hai Pig	子 Zi Rat	丑 Chou Ox
亥 Pig (Nov 7 - Dec 6) 十月 10th Month	坎 Kan	申 Shen Monkey	酉 You Rooster	戌 Xu Dog
子 Rat (Dec 7 - Jan 5) 十一月 11th Month	坤 Kun	巳 Si Snake	午 Wu Horse	未 Wei Goat
丑 Ox (Jan 6 - Feb 3) 十二月 12th Month	震 Zhen	寅 Yin Tiger	卯 Mao Rabbit	辰 Chen Dragon

Negative Repair / Renovation Sectors 修方凶位 :

月 MONTH	月刑 Month Punishment	月害 Month Harm	月厭 Month Detest
寅 **Tiger** (Feb 4 - Mar 5) 正月 **1st Month**	巳 Si Snake	巳 Si Snake	戌 Xu Dog
卯 **Rabbit** (Mar 6 - Apr 4) 二月 **2nd Month**	子 Zi Rat	辰 Chen Dragon	酉 You Rooster
辰 **Dragon** (Apr 5 - May 5) 三月 **3rd Month**	辰 Chen Dragon	卯 Mao Rabbit	申 Shen Monkey
巳 **Snake** (May 6 - Jun 5) 四月 **4th Month**	申 Shen Monkey	寅 Yin Tiger	未 Wei Goat
午 **Horse** (Jun 6 - July 6) 五月 **5th Month**	午 Wu Horse	丑 Chou Ox	午 Wu Horse
未 **Goat** (July 7 - Aug 7) 六月 **6th Month**	丑 Chou Ox	子 Zi Rat	巳 Si Snake
申 **Monkey** (Aug 8 - Sept 7) 七月 **7th Month**	寅 Yin Tiger	亥 Hai Pig	辰 Chen Dragon
酉 **Rooster** (Sept 8 - Oct 7) 八月 **8th Month**	酉 You Rooster	戌 Xu Dog	卯 Mao Rabbit
戌 **Dog** (Oct 8 - Nov 6) 九月 **9th Month**	未 Wei Goat	酉 You Rooster	寅 Yin Tiger
亥 **Pig** (Nov 7 - Dec 6) 十月 **10th Month**	亥 Hai Pig	申 Shen Monkey	丑 Chou Ox
子 **Rat** (Dec 7 - Jan 5) 十一月 **11th Month**	卯 Mao Rabbit	未 Wei Goat	子 Zi Rat
丑 **Ox** (Jan 6 - Feb 3) 十二月 **12th Month**	戌 Xu Dog	午 Wu Horse	亥 Hai Pig

庚子 (Geng Zi)
Metal Rat

Heavenly Stem 天干	庚 **Yang Metal (陽金)**
Earthly Branch 地支	子 **Rat (Yang Water 陽水)**
Hidden Stem 藏干	癸 **Yin Water**
Na Yin 納音	壁上土 **Earth on the walls**
Grand Duke 太歲	子 **Rat**
Xuan Kong Five Element 玄空五行	2 火 **Fire**
Gua Name 卦名	䷩ 風雷益 **Increasing**
Xuan Kong Period Luck 玄空卦運	**9**

Annual Positive Stars for Opening Mountain, Establishing Facing and Commencing Repairs 開山立向修方吉星：

歲德 **Duke Virtue**	庚 Geng **Yang Metal**	
歲德合 **Duke Virtue Combo**	乙 Yi **Yin Wood**	
歲枝德 **Duke Branch Virtue**	巳 Si **Snake**	
陽貴人 **Yang Nobleman**	丑 Chou **Ox**	
陰貴人 **Yin Nobleman**	未 Wei **Goat**	
歲祿 **Duke Prosperous**	申 Shen **Monkey**	
歲馬 **Duke Horse**	寅 Yin **Tiger**	
奏書 **Decree**	乾 Qian	
博士 **Professor**	巽 Xun	

Annual Negative Stars for Opening Mountain, Establishing Facing and Commencing Repairs 開山立向修方凶星：

太歲 Grand Duke	歲破 Year Breaker	三煞 Three Killings			坐煞向煞 Sitting Sha Facing Sha				浮天空亡 Floating Heaven Emptiness	
子 Zi Rat	午 Wu Horse	巳 Si Snake	午 Wu Horse	未 Wei Goat	丙 Bing Yang Fire	丁 Ding Yin Fire	壬 Ren Yang Water	癸 Gui Yin Water	兌 Dui	丁 Ding Yin Fire

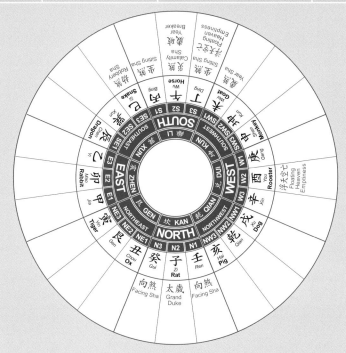

Annual San Yuan Purple White Stars 三元紫白九星：

上元 Upper Period
Period 1, 2, 3

巽SE	離S	坤SW
9	5	7
震E 8	1 庚子 Geng Zi Metal Rat	兌W 3
4	6	2
艮NE	坎N	乾NW

中元 Middle Period
Period 4, 5, 6

巽SE	離S	坤SW
3	8	1
震E 2	4 庚子 Geng Zi Metal Rat	兌W 6
7	9	5
艮NE	坎N	乾NW

下元 Lower Period
Period 7, 8, 9

巽SE	離S	坤SW
6	2	4
震E 5	7 庚子 Geng Zi Metal Rat	兌W 9
1	3	8
艮NE	坎N	乾NW

Mountain Covering Yellow Path 蓋山黃道：

貪狼 *Tan Lang* **Greedy Wolf**				巨門 *Ju Men* **Huge Door**				武曲 *Wu Qu* **Military Arts**		文曲 *Wen Qu* **Literary Arts**	
震 *Zhen* E2	庚 *Geng* W1	亥 *Hai* NW3	未 *Wei* SW1	兌 *Dui* W2	丁 *Ding* S3	巳 *Si* SE3	丑 *Chou* NE1	巽 *Xun* SE2	辛 *Xin* W3	坤 *Kun* SW2	乙 *Yi* E3

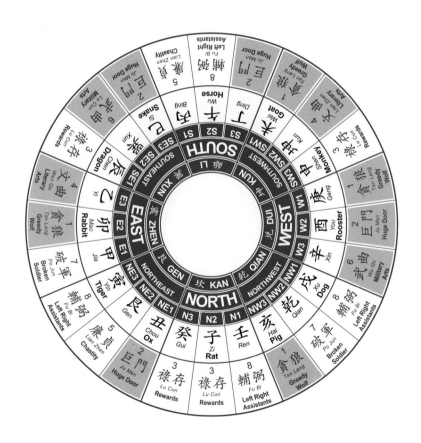

Heaven Penetrating Force 通天竅:			
三合前方 **Facing Three** **Harmony**	艮寅 Gen Yin	甲卯 Jia Mao	乙辰 Yi Chen
三合後方 **Sitting Three** **Harmony**	坤申 Kun Shen	庚酉 Geng You	辛戌 Xin Xu

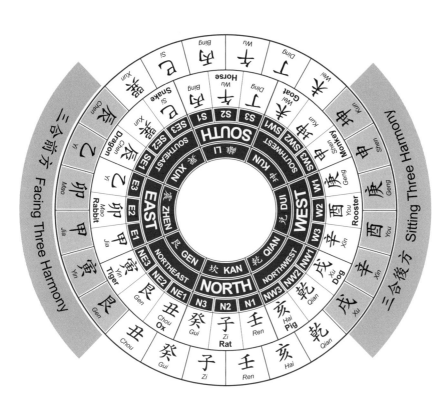

Moving Horse Six Ren Assessment 走馬六壬:

神后 Shen Hou Holy Empress	功曹 Gong Cao Marshall	天罡 Tian Gang Heavenly Dipper	勝光 Sheng Guang Subliminal Bright	傳送 Chuan Song Great General	河魁 He Kui River Scholar
壬子 Ren Zi	艮寅 Gen Yin	乙辰 Yi Chen	丙午 Bing Wu	坤申 Kun Shen	辛戌 Xin Xu

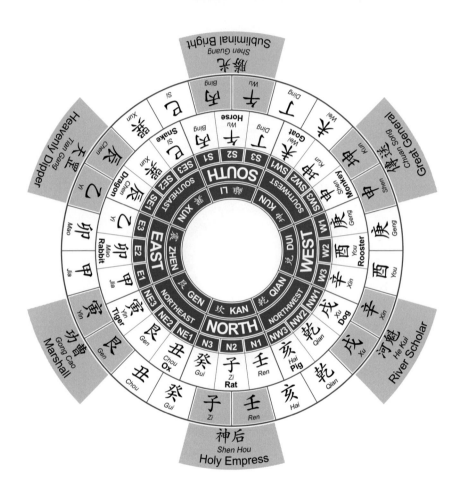

Four Advantages Three Cycles Star Plate 四利三元:

太陽 Tai Yang **Sun**	太陰 Tai Yin **Moon**	龍德 Long De **Dragon Virtue**	福德 Fu De **Fortune Virtue**
丑 Chou **Ox**	卯 Mao **Rabbit**	未 Wei **Goat**	酉 You **Rooster**

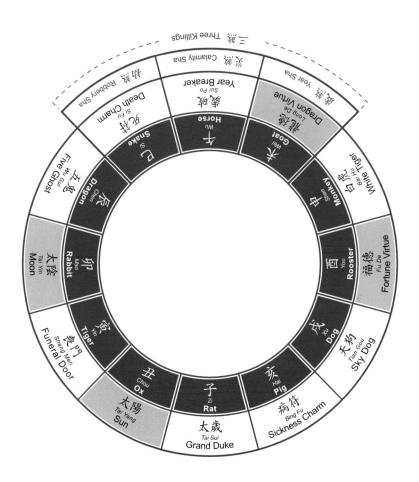

Negative Sectors For Opening Mountain 開山凶位：

年剋山家 Year Countering Sitting

乾	亥	兌	丁
Qian	*Hai*	*Dui*	*Ding*
NW2	**NW3**	**W2**	**S3**

陰府太歲 *Yin Fu Tai Sui* **Yin Mansion Grand Duke**		六害 *Liu Hai* **Six Harm**	死符 *Si Fu* **Death Charm**	炙退 *Zhi Tui* **Roasting Star**
乾 *Qian* **NW2**	兌 *Dui* **W2**	未 *Wei* **SW1**	巳 *Si* **SE3**	卯 *Mao* **E2**

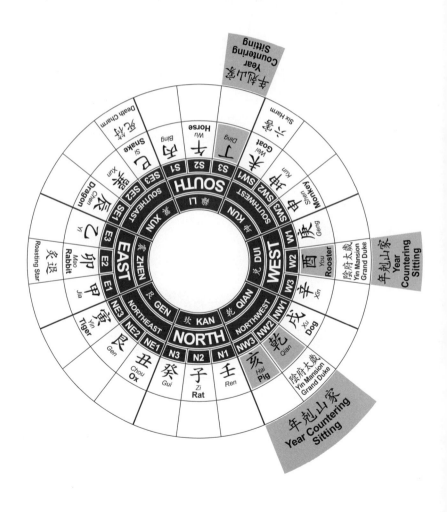

Negative Directions to Establish Facing 立向凶方：

巡山羅喉 *Xun Shan Luo Hou* **Mountain Patrol Luo Hou Star**	病符 *Bing Fu* **Sickness Charm**
癸 *Gui* **N3**	亥 *Hai* **NW3**

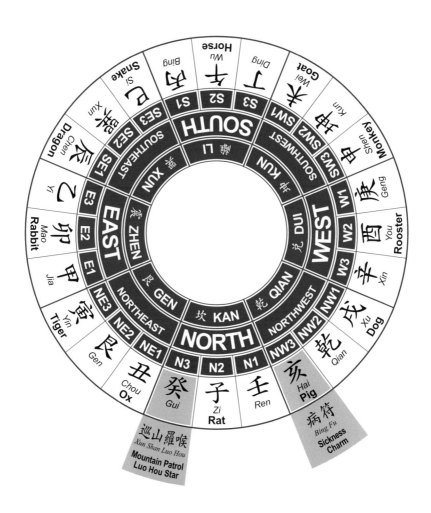

Negative Repair / Renovation Sectors Table 修方凶位表：

天官符 Heavenly Officer Charm	亥 Hai Pig	豹尾 Leopard Tail	戌 Xu Dog
地官符 Earthly Officer Charm	辰 Chen Dragon	飛廉 Flying Chaste	申 Shen Monkey
大煞 Great Sha	子 Zi Rat	喪門 Funeral Door	寅 Yin Tiger
大將軍 Big General	酉 You Rooster	弔客 Suspended Guest	戌 Xu Dog
力士 Strong Man	艮 Gen	白虎 White Tiger	申 Shen Monkey
蠶室 Silkworm Room	坤 Kun	金神 Golden God	辰 Chen Dragon 巳 Si Snake
蠶官 Silkworm Officer	未 Wei Goat		
蠶命 Silkworm Life	申 Shen Monkey	獨火 Lonely Fire	艮 Gen
歲刑 Duke Punishment	卯 Mao Rabbit	五鬼 Five Ghost	辰 Chen Dragon
黃幡 Yellow Flag	辰 Chen Dragon	破敗五鬼 Destructive Five Ghost	兌 Dui

Negative Repair / Renovation Sectors Diagram 修方凶位圖:

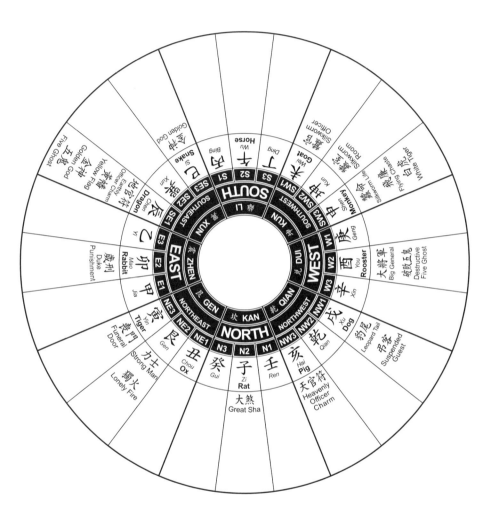

12-Month Auxiliary Stars Reference Table :
庚子年十二月，開山立向修方星表

Positive Monthly Stars 吉星方

月 MONTH	寅 Tiger (Feb 4 - Mar 5) 正月 1st Month	卯 Rabbit (Mar 6 - Apr 4) 二月 2nd Month	辰 Dragon (Apr 5 - May 5) 三月 3rd Month	巳 Snake (May 6 - Jun 5) 四月 4th Month	午 Horse (Jun 6 - July 6) 五月 5th Month	未 Goat (July 7 - Aug 7) 六月 6th Month
天道 Heavenly Path	南 South	西南 Southwest	北 North	西 West	西北 Northwest	東 East
天德 Heavenly Virtue	丁 Ding Yin Fire	坤 Kun （申）	壬 Ren Yang Water	辛 Xin Yin Metal	乾 Qian （亥）	甲 Jia Yang Wood
天德合 Heavenly Virtue Combo	壬 Ren Yang Water	（巳）	丁 Ding Yin Fire	丙 Bing Yang Fire	（寅）	己 Ji Yin Earth
月德 Monthly Virtue	丙 Bing Yang Fire	甲 Jia Yang Wood	壬 Ren Yang Water	庚 Geng Yang Metal	丙 Bing Yang Fire	甲 Jia Yang Wood
月德合 Monthly Virtue Combo	辛 Xin Yin Metal	己 Ji Yin Earth	丁 Ding Yin Fire	乙 Yi Yin Wood	辛 Xin Yin Metal	己 Ji Yin Earth
月空 Month Emptiness	壬 Ren Yang Water	庚 Geng Yang Metal	丙 Bing Yang Fire	甲 Jia Yang Wood	壬 Ren Yang Water	庚 Geng Yang Metal
陽貴人 Yang Nobleman	兌 Dui	乾 Qian	中 Middle	巽 Xun	震 Zhen	坤 Kun
陰貴人 Yin Nobleman	坎 Kan	離 Li	艮 Gen	兌 Dui	乾 Qian	中 Middle
飛天祿 Flying Heavenly Wealth	坤 Kun	坎 Kan	離 Li	艮 Gen	兌 Dui	乾 Qian
飛天馬 Flying Heavenly Horse	中 Middle	坎 Kan	離 Li	艮 Gen	兌 Dui	乾 Qian

12-Month Auxiliary Stars Reference Table :
庚子年十二月，開山立向修方星表

申 **Monkey** (Aug 8 - Sept 7) 七月 7th Month	酉 **Rooster** (Sept 8 - Oct 7) 八月 8th Month	戌 **Dog** (Oct 8 - Nov 6) 九月 9th Month	亥 **Pig** (Nov 7 - Dec 6) 十月 10th Month	子 **Rat** (Dec 7 - Jan 5) 十一月 11th Month	丑 **Ox** (Jan 6 - Feb 3) 十二月 12th Month	月 **MONTH**
北 North	東北 Northeast	南 South	東 East	東南 Southeast	西 West	天道 **Heavenly Path**
癸 Gui Yin Water	艮 Gen （寅）	丙 Bing Yang Fire	乙 Yi Yin Wood	巽 Xun （巳）	庚 Geng Yang Metal	天德 **Heavenly Virtue**
戊 Wu Yang Earth	（亥）	辛 Xin Yin Metal	庚 Geng Yang Metal	（申）	乙 Yi Yin Wood	天德合 **Heavenly Virtue Combo**
壬 Ren Yang Water	庚 Geng Yang Metal	丙 Bing Yang Fire	甲 Jia Yang Wood	壬 Ren Yang Water	庚 Geng Yang Metal	月德 **Monthly Virtue**
丁 Ding Yin Fire	乙 Yi Yin Wood	辛 Xin Yin Metal	己 Ji Yin Earth	丁 Ding Yin Fire	乙 Yi Yin Wood	月德合 **Monthly Virtue Combo**
丙 Bing Yang Fire	甲 Jia Yang Wood	壬 Ren Yang Water	庚 Geng Yang Metal	丙 Bing Yang Fire	甲 Jia Yang Wood	月空 **Month Emptiness**
坎 Kan	離 Li	艮 Gen	兌 Dui	乾 Qian	中 Middle	陽貴人 **Yang Nobleman**
坎 Kan	離 Li	艮 Gen	兌 Dui	乾 Qian	中 Middle	陰貴人 **Yin Nobleman**
中 Middle	坎 Kan	離 Li	艮 Gen	兌 Dui	乾 Qian	飛天祿 **Flying Heavenly Wealth**
中 Middle	巽 Xun	震 Zhen	坤 Kun	坎 Kan	離 Li	飛天馬 **Flying Heavenly Horse**

Monthly Purple White Stars 月紫白九星 :

寅 Tiger (Feb 4 - Mar 5) 正月 1st Month

巽 SE	離 S	坤 SW
7 Red 七赤	**3** Jade 三碧	**5** Yellow 五黃
6 White 六白	**8** White 八白	**1** White 一白
2 Black 二黑	**4** Green 四綠	**9** Purple 九紫
艮 NE	坎 N	乾 NW

(震 E / 兌 W)

卯 Rabbit (Mar 6 - Apr 4) 二月 2nd Month

巽 SE	離 S	坤 SW
6 White 六白	**2** Black 二黑	**4** Green 四綠
5 Yellow 五黃	**7** Red 七赤	**9** Purple 九紫
1 White 一白	**3** Jade 三碧	**8** White 八白
艮 NE	坎 N	乾 NW

(震 E / 兌 W)

辰 Dragon (Apr 5 - May 5) 三月 3rd Month

巽 SE	離 S	坤 SW
5 Yellow 五黃	**1** White 一白	**3** Jade 三碧
4 Green 四綠	**6** White 六白	**8** White 八白
9 Purple 九紫	**2** Black 二黑	**7** Red 七赤
艮 NE	坎 N	乾 NW

(震 E / 兌 W)

巳 Snake (May 6 - Jun 5) 四月 4th Month

巽 SE	離 S	坤 SW
4 Green 四綠	**9** Purple 九紫	**2** Black 二黑
3 Jade 三碧	**5** Yellow 五黃	**7** Red 七赤
8 White 八白	**1** White 一白	**6** White 六白
艮 NE	坎 N	乾 NW

(震 E / 兌 W)

午 Horse (Jun 6 - July 6) 五月 5th Month

巽 SE	離 S	坤 SW
3 Jade 三碧	**8** White 八白	**1** White 一白
2 Black 二黑	**4** Green 四綠	**6** White 六白
7 Red 七赤	**9** Purple 九紫	**5** Yellow 五黃
艮 NE	坎 N	乾 NW

(震 E / 兌 W)

未 Goat (July 7 - Aug 7) 六月 6th Month

巽 SE	離 S	坤 SW
2 Black 二黑	**7** Red 七赤	**9** Purple 九紫
1 White 一白	**3** Jade 三碧	**5** Yellow 五黃
6 White 六白	**8** White 八白	**4** Green 四綠
艮 NE	坎 N	乾 NW

(震 E / 兌 W)

申 Monkey (Aug 8 - Sept 7) 七月 7th Month

巽 SE	離 S	坤 SW
1 White 一白	**6** White 六白	**8** White 八白
9 Purple 九紫	**2** Black 二黑	**4** Green 四綠
5 Yellow 五黃	**7** Red 七赤	**3** Jade 三碧
艮 NE	坎 N	乾 NW

(震 E / 兌 W)

酉 Rooster (Sept 8 - Oct 7) 八月 8th Month

巽 SE	離 S	坤 SW
9 Purple 九紫	**5** Yellow 五黃	**7** Red 七赤
8 White 八白	**1** White 一白	**3** Jade 三碧
4 Green 四綠	**6** White 六白	**2** Black 二黑
艮 NE	坎 N	乾 NW

(震 E / 兌 W)

戌 Dog (Oct 8 - Nov 6) 九月 9th Month

巽 SE	離 S	坤 SW
8 White 八白	**4** Green 四綠	**6** White 六白
7 Red 七赤	**9** Purple 九紫	**2** Black 二黑
3 Jade 三碧	**5** Yellow 五黃	**1** White 一白
艮 NE	坎 N	乾 NW

(震 E / 兌 W)

亥 Pig (Nov 7 - Dec 6) 十月 10th Month

巽 SE	離 S	坤 SW
7 Red 七赤	**3** Jade 三碧	**5** Yellow 五黃
6 White 六白	**8** White 八白	**1** White 一白
2 Black 二黑	**4** Green 四綠	**9** Purple 九紫
艮 NE	坎 N	乾 NW

(震 E / 兌 W)

子 Rat (Dec 7 - Jan 5) 十一月 11th Month

巽 SE	離 S	坤 SW
6 White 六白	**2** Black 二黑	**4** Green 四綠
5 Yellow 五黃	**7** Red 七赤	**9** Purple 九紫
1 White 一白	**3** Jade 三碧	**8** White 八白
艮 NE	坎 N	乾 NW

(震 E / 兌 W)

丑 Ox (Jan 6 - Feb 3) 十二月 12th Month

巽 SE	離 S	坤 SW
5 Yellow 五黃	**1** White 一白	**3** Jade 三碧
4 Green 四綠	**6** White 六白	**8** White 八白
9 Purple 九紫	**2** Black 二黑	**7** Red 七赤
艮 NE	坎 N	乾 NW

(震 E / 兌 W)

Qi Men Three Nobles 三奇 :

Three Nobles 三奇 / Seasons	乙 Yi	丙 Bing	丁 Ding
立春 **Coming of Spring** Feb 4 - Feb 18	乾 Qian	兌 Dui	艮 Gen
春分 **Spring Equinox** Mar 21 - Apr 4	坎 Kan	坤 Kun	震 Zhen
立夏 **Coming of Summer** May 6 - May 20	坤 Kun	震 Zhen	巽 Xun
夏至 **Summer Solstice** Jun 22 - Jul 6	坤 Kun	坎 Kan	離 Li
立秋 **Coming of Autumn** Aug 8 - Aug 23	巽 Xun	震 Zhen	坤 Kun
秋分 **Autumn Equinox** Sept 23 - Oct 7	離 Li	艮 Gen	兌 Dui
立冬 **Coming of Winter** Nov 7 - Nov 22	艮 Gen	兌 Dui	乾 Qian
冬至 **Winter Solstice** Dec 22 - Jan 5	艮 Gen	離 Li	坎 Kan

Sectors to Avoid Opening Mountain 開山凶位：

月 MONTH	月建 Month Establishment	月破 Month Destruction	月剋山家 Month Countering Sitting		陰府太歲 Yin Mansion Grand Duke	
寅 **Tiger** (Feb 4 - Mar 5) 正月 **1st Month**	寅 *Yin* Tiger	申 *Shen* Monkey	乾 *Qian*	兌 *Dui*	坤 *Kun*	震 *Zhen*
卯 **Rabbit** (Mar 6 - Apr 4) 二月 **2nd Month**	卯 *Mao* Rabbit	酉 *You* Rooster	亥 *Hai* Pig	丁 *Ding* Yin Fire	巽 *Xun*	艮 *Gen*
辰 **Dragon** (Apr 5 - May 5) 三月 **3rd Month**	辰 *Chen* Dragon	戌 *Xu* Dog	震 *Zhen*	巳 *Si* Snake	乾 *Qian*	兌 *Dui*
巳 **Snake** (May 6 - Jun 5) 四月 **4th Month**	巳 *Si* Snake	亥 *Hai* Pig	艮 *Gen*		坤 *Kun*	坎 *Kan*
午 **Horse** (Jun 6 - July 6) 五月 **5th Month**	午 *Wu* Horse	子 *Zi* Rat	離 *Li* S2	丙 *Bing* Yang Fire	離 *Li*	乾 *Qian*
未 **Goat** (July 7 - Aug 7) 六月 **6th Month**	未 *Wei* Goat	丑 *Chou* Ox	壬 *Ren* Yang Water	乙 *Yi* Yin Wood	震 *Zhen*	坤 *Kun*
申 **Monkey** (Aug 8 - Sept 7) 七月 **7th Month**	申 *Shen* Monkey	寅 *Yin* Tiger	—		艮 *Gen*	巽 *Xun*
酉 **Rooster** (Sept 8 - Oct 7) 八月 **8th Month**	酉 *You* Rooster	卯 *Mao* Rabbit	—		兌 *Dui*	乾 *Qian*
戌 **Dog** (Oct 8 - Nov 6) 九月 **9th Month**	戌 *Xu* Dog	辰 *Chen* Dragon	乾 *Qian*	兌 *Dui*	坎 *Kan*	坤 *Kun*
亥 **Pig** (Nov 7 - Dec 6) 十月 **10th Month**	亥 *Hai* Pig	巳 *Si* Snake	亥 *Hai* Pig	丁 *Ding* Yin Fire	乾 *Qian*	離 *Li*
子 **Rat** (Dec 7 - Jan 5) 十一月 **11th Month**	子 *Zi* Rat	午 *Wu* Horse	水 Water	山 Mountain	坤 *Kun*	震 *Zhen*
丑 **Ox** (Jan 6 - Feb 3) 十二月 **12th Month**	丑 *Chou* Ox	未 *Wei* Goat	土 Earth		巽 *Xun*	艮 *Gen*

Negative Repair / Renovation Sectors 修方凶位 :

月 MONTH	天官符 Heavenly Officer Charm			地官符 Earth Officer Charm			小月建 Small Month Establishment		
寅 Tiger (Feb 4 - Mar 5) 正月 1st Month		中 Middle		庚 Geng Yang Metal	兌 Dui	辛 Xin Yin Metal		中 Middle	
卯 Rabbit (Mar 6 - Apr 4) 二月 2nd Month	辰 Chen Dragon	巽 Xun	巳 Si Snake	戌 Xu Dog	乾 Qian	亥 Hai Pig	戌 Xu Dog	乾 Qian	亥 Hai Pig
辰 Dragon (Apr 5 - May 5) 三月 3rd Month	甲 Jia Yang Wood	震 Zhen	乙 Yi Yin Wood		中 Middle		庚 Geng Yang Metal	兌 Dui	辛 Xin Yin Metal
巳 Snake (May 6 - Jun 5) 四月 4th Month	未 Wei Goat	坤 Kun	申 Shen Monkey	庚 Geng Yang Metal	兌 Dui	辛 Xin Yin Metal	丑 Chou Ox	艮 Gen	寅 Yin Tiger
午 Horse (Jun 6 - July 6) 五月 5th Month	壬 Ren Yang Water	坎 Kan	癸 Gui Yin Water	戌 Xu Dog	乾 Qian	亥 Hai Pig	丙 Bing Yang Fire	離 Li	丁 Ding Yin Fire
未 Goat (July 7 - Aug 7) 六月 6th Month	丙 Bing Yang Fire	離 Li	丁 Ding Yin Fire		中 Middle		壬 Ren Yang Water	坎 Kan	癸 Gui Yin Water
申 Monkey (Aug 8 - Sept 7) 七月 7th Month	丑 Chou Ox	艮 Gen	寅 Yin Tiger	辰 Chen Dragon	巽 Xun	巳 Si Snake	未 Wei Goat	坤 Kun	申 Shen Monkey
酉 Rooster (Sept 8 - Oct 7) 八月 8th Month	庚 Geng Yang Metal	兌 Dui	辛 Xin Yin Metal	甲 Jia Yang Wood	震 Zhen	乙 Yi Yin Wood	甲 Jia Yang Wood	震 Zhen	乙 Yi Yin Wood
戌 Dog (Oct 8 - Nov 6) 九月 9th Month	戌 Xu Dog	乾 Qian	亥 Hai Pig	未 Wei Goat	坤 Kun	申 Shen Monkey	辰 Chen Dragon	巽 Xun	巳 Si Snake
亥 Pig (Nov 7 - Dec 6) 十月 10th Month		中 Middle		壬 Ren Yang Water	坎 Kan	癸 Gui Yin Water		中 Middle	
子 Rat (Dec 7 - Jan 5) 十一月 11th Month	庚 Geng Yang Metal	兌 Dui	辛 Xin Yin Metal	丙 Bing Yang Fire	離 Li	丁 Ding Yin Fire	戌 Xu Dog	乾 Qian	亥 Hai Pig
丑 Ox (Jan 6 - Feb 3) 十二月 12th Month	戌 Xu Dog	乾 Qian	亥 Hai Pig	丑 Chou Ox	艮 Gen	寅 Yin Tiger	庚 Geng Yang Metal	兌 Dui	辛 Xin Yin Metal

Negative Repair / Renovation Sectors 修方凶位 :

月 MONTH	大月建 Big Month Establishment			飛大煞 Flying Great Sha			丙丁獨火 Bing Ding Lonely Fire	
寅 Tiger (Feb 4 - Mar 5) 正月 1st Month	丑 Chou Ox	艮 Gen	寅 Yin Tiger	戌 Xu Dog	乾 Qian	亥 Hai Pig	巽 Xun	中 Middle
卯 Rabbit (Mar 6 - Apr 4) 二月 2nd Month	庚 Geng Yang Metal	兌 Dui	辛 Xin Yin Metal	中 Middle			震 Zhen	巽 Xun
辰 Dragon (Apr 5 - May 5) 三月 3rd Month	戌 Xu Dog	乾 Qian	亥 Hai Pig	辰 Chen Dragon	巽 Xun	巳 Si Snake	坤 Kun	震 Zhen
巳 Snake (May 6 - Jun 5) 四月 4th Month	中 Middle			甲 Jia Yang Wood	震 Zhen	乙 Yi Yin Wood	坎 Kan	坤 Kun
午 Horse (Jun 6 - July 6) 五月 5th Month	辰 Chen Dragon	巽 Xun	巳 Si Snake	未 Wei Goat	坤 Kun	申 Shen Monkey	離 Li	坎 Kan
未 Goat (July 7 - Aug 7) 六月 6th Month	甲 Jia Yang Wood	震 Zhen	乙 Yi Yin Wood	壬 Ren Yang Water	坎 Kan	癸 Gui Yin Water	艮 Gen	離 Li
申 Monkey (Aug 8 - Sept 7) 七月 7th Month	未 Wei Goat	坤 Kun	申 Shen Monkey	丙 Bing Yang Fire	離 Li	丁 Ding Yin Fire	兌 Dui	艮 Gen
酉 Rooster (Sept 8 - Oct 7) 八月 8th Month	壬 Ren Yang Water	坎 Kan	癸 Gui Yin Water	丑 Chou Ox	艮 Gen	寅 Yin Tiger	乾 Qian	兌 Dui
戌 Dog (Oct 8 - Nov 6) 九月 9th Month	丙 Bing Yang Fire	離 Li	丁 Ding Yin Fire	庚 Geng Yang Metal	兌 Dui	辛 Xin Yin Metal	中 Middle	乾 Qian
亥 Pig (Nov 7 - Dec 6) 十月 10th Month	丑 Chou Ox	艮 Gen	寅 Yin Tiger	戌 Xu Dog	乾 Qian	亥 Hai Pig	中 Middle	
子 Rat (Dec 7 - Jan 5) 十一月 11th Month	庚 Geng Yang Metal	兌 Dui	辛 Xin Yin Metal	中 Middle			巽 Xun	中 Middle
丑 Ox (Jan 6 - Feb 3) 十二月 12th Month	戌 Xu Dog	乾 Qian	亥 Hai Pig	庚 Geng Yang Metal	兌 Dui	辛 Xin Yin Metal	震 Zhen	巽 Xun

Negative Repair / Renovation Sectors 修方凶位 :

月 MONTH	月遊火 Month Wondering Fire	三煞 Monthly 3 Killings		
		劫煞 Robbery Sha	災煞 Calamity Sha	月煞 Month Sha
寅 Tiger (Feb 4 - Mar 5) 正月 1st Month	艮 Gen	亥 Hai Pig	子 Zi Rat	丑 Chou Ox
卯 Rabbit (Mar 6 - Apr 4) 二月 2nd Month	離 Li	申 Shen Monkey	酉 You Rooster	戌 Xu Dog
辰 Dragon (Apr 5 - May 5) 三月 3rd Month	坎 Kan	巳 Si Snake	午 Wu Horse	未 Wei Goat
巳 Snake (May 6 - Jun 5) 四月 4th Month	坤 Kun	寅 Yin Tiger	卯 Mao Rabbit	辰 Chen Dragon
午 Horse (Jun 6 - July 6) 五月 5th Month	震 Zhen	亥 Hai Pig	子 Zi Rat	丑 Chou Ox
未 Goat (July 7 - Aug 7) 六月 6th Month	巽 Xun	申 Shen Monkey	酉 You Rooster	戌 Xu Dog
申 Monkey (Aug 8 - Sept 7) 七月 7th Month	中 Middle	巳 Si Snake	午 Wu Horse	未 Wei Goat
酉 Rooster (Sept 8 - Oct 7) 八月 8th Month	乾 Qian	寅 Yin Tiger	卯 Mao Rabbit	辰 Chen Dragon
戌 Dog (Oct 8 - Nov 6) 九月 9th Month	兌 Dui	亥 Hai Pig	子 Zi Rat	丑 Chou Ox
亥 Pig (Nov 7 - Dec 6) 十月 10th Month	艮 Gen	申 Shen Monkey	酉 You Rooster	戌 Xu Dog
子 Rat (Dec 7 - Jan 5) 十一月 11th Month	離 Li	巳 Si Snake	午 Wu Horse	未 Wei Goat
丑 Ox (Jan 6 - Feb 3) 十二月 12th Month	坎 Kan	寅 Yin Tiger	卯 Mao Rabbit	辰 Chen Dragon

庚子 (Geng Zi) Metal Rat

Negative Repair / Renovation Sectors 修方凶位 :

月 MONTH	月刑 Month Punishment	月害 Month Harm	月厭 Month Detest
寅 **Tiger** (Feb 4 - Mar 5) 正月 1st Month	巳 *Si* Snake	巳 *Si* Snake	戌 *Xu* Dog
卯 **Rabbit** (Mar 6 - Apr 4) 二月 2nd Month	子 *Zi* Rat	辰 *Chen* Dragon	酉 *You* Rooster
辰 **Dragon** (Apr 5 - May 5) 三月 3rd Month	辰 *Chen* Dragon	卯 *Mao* Rabbit	申 *Shen* Monkey
巳 **Snake** (May 6 - Jun 5) 四月 4th Month	申 *Shen* Monkey	寅 *Yin* Tiger	未 *Wei* Goat
午 **Horse** (Jun 6 - July 6) 五月 5th Month	午 *Wu* Horse	丑 *Chou* Ox	午 *Wu* Horse
未 **Goat** (July 7 - Aug 7) 六月 6th Month	丑 *Chou* Ox	子 *Zi* Rat	巳 *Si* Snake
申 **Monkey** (Aug 8 - Sept 7) 七月 7th Month	寅 *Yin* Tiger	亥 *Hai* Pig	辰 *Chen* Dragon
酉 **Rooster** (Sept 8 - Oct 7) 八月 8th Month	酉 *You* Rooster	戌 *Xu* Dog	卯 *Mao* Rabbit
戌 **Dog** (Oct 8 - Nov 6) 九月 9th Month	未 *Wei* Goat	酉 *You* Rooster	寅 *Yin* Tiger
亥 **Pig** (Nov 7 - Dec 6) 十月 10th Month	亥 *Hai* Pig	申 *Shen* Monkey	丑 *Chou* Ox
子 **Rat** (Dec 7 - Jan 5) 十一月 11th Month	卯 *Mao* Rabbit	未 *Wei* Goat	子 *Zi* Rat
丑 **Ox** (Jan 6 - Feb 3) 十二月 12th Month	戌 *Xu* Dog	午 *Wu* Horse	亥 *Hai* Pig

庚寅 (Geng Yin)
Metal Tiger

庚寅 (Geng Yin) Metal Tiger

Heavenly Stem 天干	庚 **Yang Metal** (陽金)
Earthly Branch 地支	寅 **Tiger (Yang Wood** 陽木**)**
Hidden Stem 藏干	甲 **Yang Wood,** 丙 **Yang Fire,** 戊 **Yang Earth**
Na Yin 納音	松柏木 **Wood from pine trees**
Grand Duke 太歲	寅 **Tiger**
Xuan Kong Five Element 玄空五行	3 木 **Wood**
Gua Name 卦名	☲ 離爲火 **Fire**
Xuan Kong Period Luck 玄空卦運	**1**

Annual Positive Stars for Opening Mountain, Establishing Facing and Commencing Repairs 開山立向修方吉星：

歲德 **Duke Virtue**	庚 *Geng* **Yang Metal**
歲德合 **Duke Virtue Combo**	乙 *Yi* **Yin Wood**
歲枝德 **Duke Branch Virtue**	未 *Wei* **Goat**
陽貴人 **Yang Nobleman**	丑 *Chou* **Ox**
陰貴人 **Yin Nobleman**	未 *Wei* **Goat**
歲祿 **Duke Prosperous**	申 *Shen* **Monkey**
歲馬 **Duke Horse**	申 *Shen* **Monkey**
奏書 **Decree**	艮 *Gen*
博士 **Professor**	坤 *Kun*

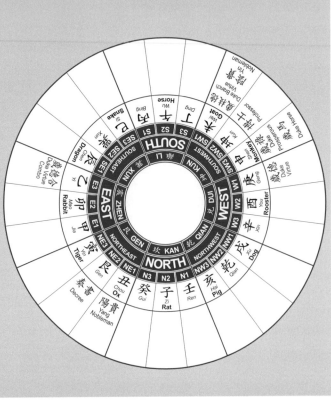

Annual Negative Stars for Opening Mountain, Establishing Facing and Commencing Repairs 開山立向修方凶星:

太歲 Grand Duke	歲破 Year Breaker	三煞 Three Killings			坐煞向煞 Sitting Sha Facing Sha				浮天空亡 Floating Heaven Emptiness	
寅 Yin Tiger	申 Shen Monkey	亥 Hai Pig	子 Zi Rat	丑 Chou Ox	壬 Ren Yang Water	癸 Gui Yin Water	丙 Bing Yang Fire	丁 Ding Yin Fire	兌 Dui	丁 Ding Yin Fire

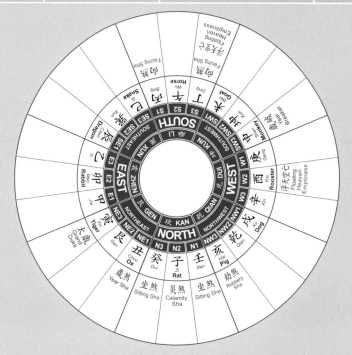

Annual San Yuan Purple White Stars 三元紫白九星:

	上元 Upper Period Period 1, 2, 3			中元 Middle Period Period 4, 5, 6			下元 Lower Period Period 7, 8, 9	
巽SE	離S	坤SW	巽SE	離S	坤SW	巽SE	離S	坤SW
1	6	8	4	9	2	7	3	5
震E 9	2 戊寅 Wu Yin Earth Tiger	兌W 4	震E 3	5 戊寅 Wu Yin Earth Tiger	兌W 7	震E 6	8 戊寅 Wu Yin Earth Tiger	兌W 1
艮NE 5	坎N 7	乾NW 3	艮NE 8	坎N 1	乾NW 6	艮NE 2	坎N 4	乾NW 9

Mountain Covering Yellow Path 蓋山黃道：

貪狼 Tan Lang **Greedy Wolf**		巨門 Ju Men **Huge Door**		武曲 Wu Qu **Military Arts**				文曲 Wen Qu **Literary Arts**			
艮 Gen NE2	丙 Bing S1	巽 Xun SE2	辛 Xin W3	兌 Dui W2	丁 Ding S3	巳 Si SE3	丑 Chou NE1	離 Li S2	壬 Ren N1	寅 Yin NE3	戌 Xu NW1

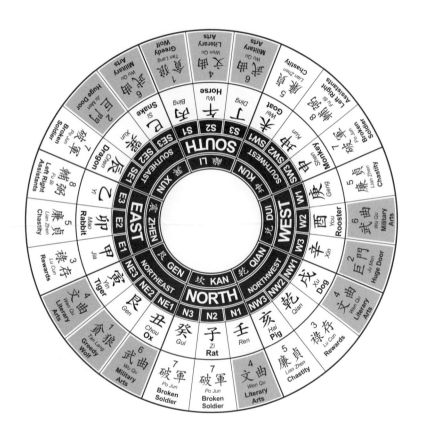

Heaven Penetrating Force 通天竅:

三合前方 **Facing Three Harmony**	坤申 Kun Shen	庚酉 Geng You	辛戌 Xin Xu
三合後方 **Sitting Three Harmony**	艮寅 Gen Yin	甲卯 Jia Mao	乙辰 Yi Chen

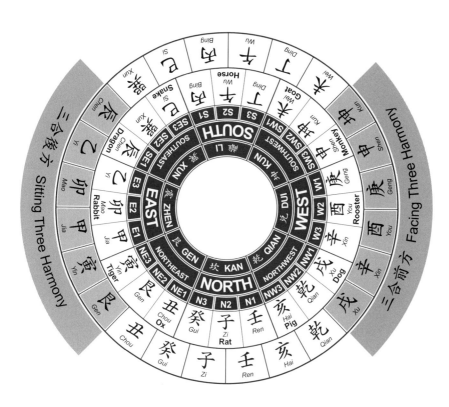

三合後方 Sitting Three Harmony

三合前方 Facing Three Harmony

Moving Horse Six Ren Assessment 走馬六壬：

神后 *Shen Hou* **Holy Empress**	功曹 *Gong Cao* **Marshall**	天罡 *Tian Gang* **Sky King**	勝光 *Sheng Guang* **Subliminal Bright**	傳送 *Chuan Song* **Great General**	河魁 *He Kui* **River Scholar**
辛戌 *Xin Xu*	壬子 *Ren Zi*	艮寅 *Gen Yin*	乙辰 *Yi Chen*	丙午 *Bing Wu*	坤申 *Kun Shen*

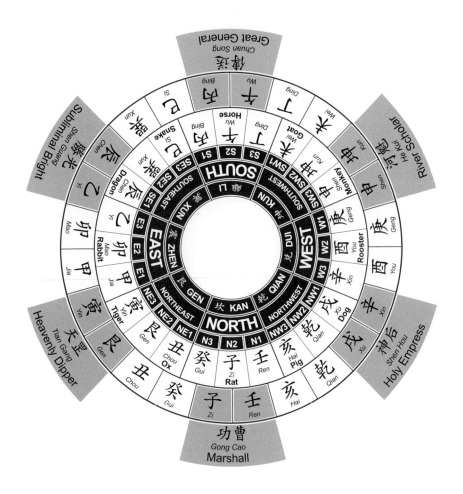

Four Advantages Three Cycles Star Plate 四利三元：

太陽 *Tai Yang* **Sun**	太陰 *Tai Yin* **Moon**	龍德 *Long De* **Dragon Virtue**	福德 *Fu De* **Fortune Virtue**
卯 *Mao* **Rabbit**	巳 *Si* **Snake**	酉 *You* **Rooster**	亥 *Hai* **Pig**

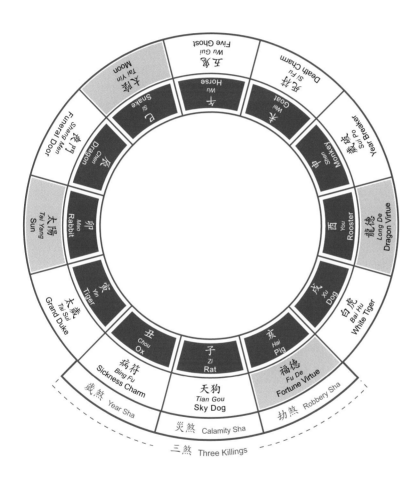

Negative Sectors For Opening Mountain 開山凶位：

年剋山家 Year Countering Sitting

離	壬	丙	乙
Li	*Ren*	*Bing*	*Yi*
S2	**N1**	**S1**	**E3**

陰府太歲	六害	死符	炙退
Yin Fu Tai Sui	*Liu Hai*	*Si Fu*	*Zhi Tui*
Yin Mansion Grand Duke	**Six Harm**	**Death Charm**	**Roasting Star**

乾	兌	巳	未	酉
Qian	*Dui*	*Si*	*Wei*	*You*
NW2	**W2**	**SE3**	**SW1**	**W2**

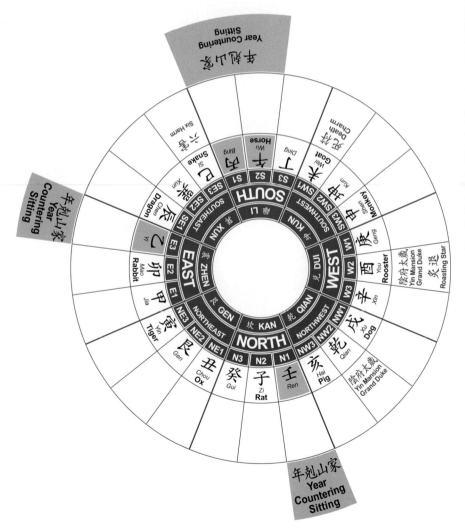

立向凶方: Negative Directions to Establish Facing	
巡山羅喉 *Xun Shan Luo Hou* **Mountain Patrol Luo Hou Star**	病符 *Bing Fu* **Sickness Charm**
甲 *Jia* **E1**	丑 *Chou* **NE1**

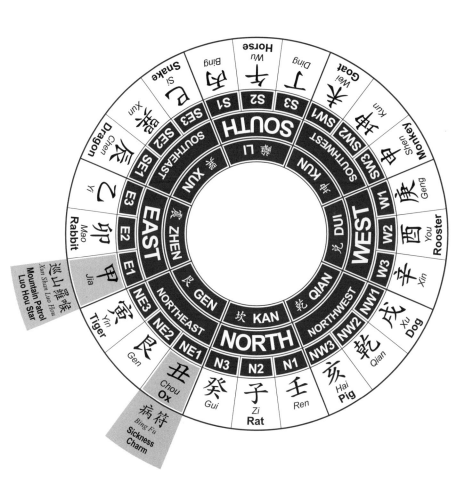

Negative Repair / Renovation Sectors Table 修方凶位表：

天官符 Heavenly Officer Charm	巳 *Si* Snake	豹尾 Leopard Tail	辰 *Chen* Dragon
地官符 Earthly Officer Charm	午 *Wu* Horse	飛廉 Flying Chaste	戌 *Xu* Dog
大煞 Great Sha	午 *Wu* Horse	喪門 Funeral Door	辰 *Chen* Dragon
大將軍 Big General	子 *Zi* Rat	弔客 Suspended Guest	子 *Zi* Rat
力士 Strong Man	巽 *Xun*	白虎 White Tiger	戌 *Xu* Dog
蠶室 Silkworm Room	乾 *Qian*	金神 Golden God	辰 *Chen* Dragon / 巳 *Si* Snake
蠶官 Silkworm Officer	戌 *Xu* Dog		
蠶命 Silkworm Life	亥 *Hai* Pig	獨火 Lonely Fire	震 *Zhen*
歲刑 Duke Punishment	巳 *Si* Snake	五鬼 Five Ghost	寅 *Yin* Tiger
黃幡 Yellow Flag	戌 *Xu* Dog	破敗五鬼 Destructive Five Ghost	兌 *Dui*

Negative Repair / Renovation Sectors Diagram 修方凶位圖：

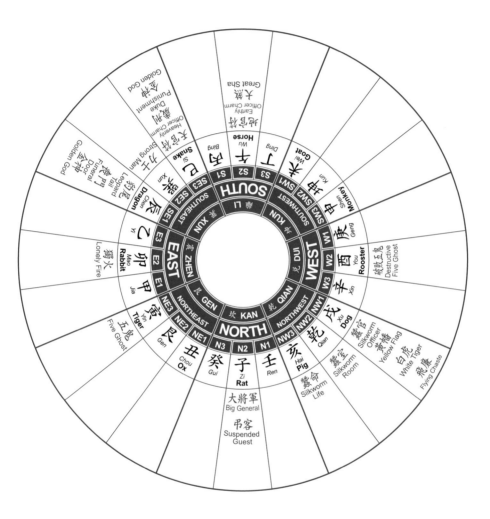

12-Month Auxiliary Stars Reference Table :
庚寅年十二月，開山立向修方星表

Positive Monthly Stars 吉星方

月 MONTH	寅 Tiger (Feb 4 - Mar 5) 正月 1st Month	卯 Rabbit (Mar 6 - Apr 4) 二月 2nd Month	辰 Dragon (Apr 5 - May 5) 三月 3rd Month	巳 Snake (May 6 - Jun 5) 四月 4th Month	午 Horse (Jun 6 - July 6) 五月 5th Month	未 Goat (July 7 - Aug 7) 六月 6th Month
天道 Heavenly Path	南 South	西南 Southwest	北 North	西 West	西北 Northwest	東 East
天德 Heavenly Virtue	丁 Ding Yin Fire	坤 Kun (申)	壬 Ren Yang Water	辛 Xin Yin Metal	乾 Qian (亥)	甲 Jia Yang Wood
天德合 Heavenly Virtue Combo	壬 Ren Yang Water	(巳)	丁 Ding Yin Fire	丙 Bing Yang Fire	(寅)	己 Ji Yin Earth
月德 Monthly Virtue	丙 Bing Yang Fire	甲 Jia Yang Wood	壬 Ren Yang Water	庚 Geng Yang Metal	丙 Bing Yang Fire	甲 Jia Yang Wood
月德合 Monthly Virtue Combo	辛 Xin Yin Metal	己 Ji Yin Earth	丁 Ding Yin Fire	乙 Yi Yin Wood	辛 Xin Yin Metal	己 Ji Yin Earth
月空 Month Emptiness	壬 Ren Yang Water	庚 Geng Yang Metal	丙 Bing Yang Fire	甲 Jia Yang Wood	壬 Ren Yang Water	庚 Geng Yang Metal
陽貴人 Yang Nobleman	兌 Dui	乾 Qian	中 Middle	巽 Xun	震 Zhen	坤 Kun
陰貴人 Yin Nobleman	坎 Kan	離 Li	艮 Gen	兌 Dui	乾 Qian	中 Middle
飛天祿 Flying Heavenly Wealth	坤 Kun	坎 Kan	離 Li	艮 Gen	兌 Dui	乾 Qian
飛天馬 Flying Heavenly Horse	坤 Kun	坎 Kan	離 Li	艮 Gen	兌 Dui	乾 Qian

12-Month Auxiliary Stars Reference Table :
庚寅年十二月，開山立向修方星表

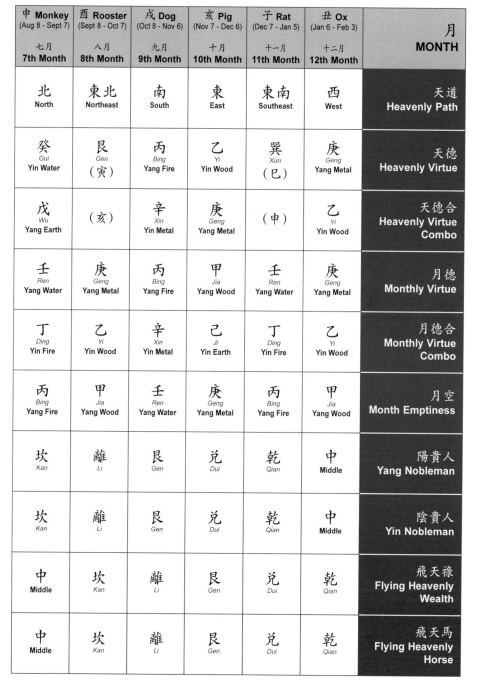

申 Monkey (Aug 8 - Sept 7) 七月 7th Month	酉 Rooster (Sept 8 - Oct 7) 八月 8th Month	戌 Dog (Oct 8 - Nov 6) 九月 9th Month	亥 Pig (Nov 7 - Dec 6) 十月 10th Month	子 Rat (Dec 7 - Jan 5) 十一月 11th Month	丑 Ox (Jan 6 - Feb 3) 十二月 12th Month	月 MONTH
北 North	東北 Northeast	南 South	東 East	東南 Southeast	西 West	天道 Heavenly Path
癸 Gui Yin Water	艮 Gen (寅)	丙 Bing Yang Fire	乙 Yi Yin Wood	巽 Xun (巳)	庚 Geng Yang Metal	天德 Heavenly Virtue
戊 Wu Yang Earth	(亥)	辛 Xin Yin Metal	庚 Geng Yang Metal	(申)	乙 Yi Yin Wood	天德合 Heavenly Virtue Combo
壬 Ren Yang Water	庚 Geng Yang Metal	丙 Bing Yang Fire	甲 Jia Yang Wood	壬 Ren Yang Water	庚 Geng Yang Metal	月德 Monthly Virtue
丁 Ding Yin Fire	乙 Yi Yin Wood	辛 Xin Yin Metal	己 Ji Yin Earth	丁 Ding Yin Fire	乙 Yi Yin Wood	月德合 Monthly Virtue Combo
丙 Bing Yang Fire	甲 Jia Yang Wood	壬 Ren Yang Water	庚 Geng Yang Metal	丙 Bing Yang Fire	甲 Jia Yang Wood	月空 Month Emptiness
坎 Kan	離 Li	艮 Gen	兌 Dui	乾 Qian	中 Middle	陽貴人 Yang Nobleman
坎 Kan	離 Li	艮 Gen	兌 Dui	乾 Qian	中 Middle	陰貴人 Yin Nobleman
中 Middle	坎 Kan	離 Li	艮 Gen	兌 Dui	乾 Qian	飛天祿 Flying Heavenly Wealth
中 Middle	坎 Kan	離 Li	艮 Gen	兌 Dui	乾 Qian	飛天馬 Flying Heavenly Horse

753

Monthly Purple White Stars 月紫白九星 :

寅 Tiger (Feb 4 - Mar 5) 正月 1st Month

巽 SE	離 S	坤 SW
1 White 一白	**6** White 六白	**8** White 八白
震 E **9** Purple 九紫	**2** Black 二黑	**4** Green 四綠 兌 W
5 Yellow 五黄	**7** Red 七赤	**3** Jade 三碧
艮 NE	坎 N	乾 NW

卯 Rabbit (Mar 6 - Apr 4) 二月 2nd Month

巽 SE	離 S	坤 SW
9 Purple 九紫	**5** Yellow 五黄	**7** Red 七赤
震 E **8** White 八白	**1** White 一白	**3** Jade 三碧 兌 W
4 Green 四綠	**6** White 六白	**2** Black 二黑
艮 NE	坎 N	乾 NW

辰 Dragon (Apr 5 - May 5) 三月 3rd Month

巽 SE	離 S	坤 SW
8 White 八白	**4** Green 四綠	**6** White 六白
震 E **7** Red 七赤	**9** Purple 九紫	**2** Black 二黑 兌 W
3 Jade 三碧	**5** Yellow 五黄	**1** White 一白
艮 NE	坎 N	乾 NW

巳 Snake (May 6 - Jun 5) 四月 4th Month

巽 SE	離 S	坤 SW
7 Red 七赤	**3** Jade 三碧	**5** Yellow 五黄
震 E **6** White 六白	**8** White 八白	**1** White 一白 兌 W
2 Black 二黑	**4** Green 四綠	**9** Purple 九紫
艮 NE	坎 N	乾 NW

午 Horse (Jun 6 - July 6) 五月 5th Month

巽 SE	離 S	坤 SW
6 White 六白	**2** Black 二黑	**4** Green 四綠
震 E **5** Yellow 五黄	**7** Red 七赤	**9** Purple 九紫 兌 W
1 White 一白	**3** Jade 三碧	**8** White 八白
艮 NE	坎 N	乾 NW

未 Goat (July 7 - Aug 7) 六月 6th Month

巽 SE	離 S	坤 SW
5 Yellow 五黄	**1** White 一白	**3** Jade 三碧
震 E **4** Green 四綠	**6** White 六白	**8** White 八白 兌 W
9 Purple 九紫	**2** Black 二黑	**7** Red 七赤
艮 NE	坎 N	乾 NW

申 Monkey (Aug 8 - Sept 7) 七月 7th Month

巽 SE	離 S	坤 SW
4 Green 四綠	**9** Purple 九紫	**2** Black 二黑
震 E **3** Jade 三碧	**5** Yellow 五黄	**7** Red 七赤 兌 W
8 White 八白	**1** White 一白	**6** White 六白
艮 NE	坎 N	乾 NW

酉 Rooster (Sept 8 - Oct 7) 八月 8th Month

巽 SE	離 S	坤 SW
3 Jade 三碧	**8** White 八白	**1** White 一白
震 E **2** Black 二黑	**4** Green 四綠	**6** White 六白 兌 W
7 Red 七赤	**9** Purple 九紫	**5** Yellow 五黄
艮 NE	坎 N	乾 NW

戌 Dog (Oct 8 - Nov 6) 九月 9th Month

巽 SE	離 S	坤 SW
2 Black 二黑	**7** Red 七赤	**9** Purple 九紫
震 E **1** White 一白	**3** Jade 三碧	**5** Yellow 五黄 兌 W
6 White 六白	**8** White 八白	**4** Green 四綠
艮 NE	坎 N	乾 NW

亥 Pig (Nov 7 - Dec 6) 十月 10th Month

巽 SE	離 S	坤 SW
1 White 一白	**6** White 六白	**8** White 八白
震 E **9** Purple 九紫	**2** Black 二黑	**4** Green 四綠 兌 W
5 Yellow 五黄	**7** Red 七赤	**3** Jade 三碧
艮 NE	坎 N	乾 NW

子 Rat (Dec 7 - Jan 5) 十一月 11th Month

巽 SE	離 S	坤 SW
9 Purple 九紫	**5** Yellow 五黄	**7** Red 七赤
震 E **8** White 八白	**1** White 一白	**3** Jade 三碧 兌 W
4 Green 四綠	**6** White 六白	**2** Black 二黑
艮 NE	坎 N	乾 NW

丑 Ox (Jan 6 - Feb 3) 十二月 12th Month

巽 SE	離 S	坤 SW
8 White 八白	**4** Green 四綠	**6** White 六白
震 E **7** Red 七赤	**9** Purple 九紫	**2** Black 二黑 兌 W
3 Jade 三碧	**5** Yellow 五黄	**1** White 一白
艮 NE	坎 N	乾 NW

Qi Men Three Nobles 三奇 :

Three Nobles 三奇 / Seasons	乙 Yi	丙 Bing	丁 Ding
立春 Coming of Spring Feb 4 - Feb 18	中 Middle	乾 Qian	兌 Dui
春分 Spring Equinox Mar 21 - Apr 4	離 Li	坎 Kan	坤 Kun
立夏 Coming of Summer May 6 - May 20	坎 Kan	坤 Kun	震 Zhen
夏至 Summer Solstice Jun 22 - Jul 6	震 Zhen	坤 Kun	坎 Kan
立秋 Coming of Autumn Aug 8 - Aug 23	中 Middle	巽 Xun	震 Zhen
秋分 Autumn Equinox Sept 23 - Oct 7	坎 Kan	離 Li	艮 Gen
立冬 Coming of Winter Nov 7 - Nov 22	離 Li	艮 Gen	兌 Dui
冬至 Winter Solstice Dec 22 - Jan 5	兌 Dui	艮 Gen	離 Li

庚寅 (Geng Yin) Metal Tiger

Sectors to Avoid Opening Mountain 開山凶位 :

月 MONTH	月建 Month Establishment	月破 Month Destruction	月剋山家 Month Countering Sitting		陰府太歲 Yin Mansion Grand Duke	
寅 **Tiger** (Feb 4 - Mar 5) 正月 **1st Month**	寅 *Yin* **Tiger**	申 *Shen* **Monkey**	乾 *Qian*	兌 *Dui*	坤 *Kun*	震 *Zhen*
卯 **Rabbit** (Mar 6 - Apr 4) 二月 **2nd Month**	卯 *Mao* **Rabbit**	酉 *You* **Rooster**	亥 *Hai* **Pig**	丁 *Ding* **Yin Fire**	巽 *Xun*	艮 *Gen*
辰 **Dragon** (Apr 5 - May 5) 三月 **3rd Month**	辰 *Chen* **Dragon**	戌 *Xu* **Dog**	震 *Zhen*	巳 *Si* **Snake**	乾 *Qian*	兌 *Dui*
巳 **Snake** (May 6 - Jun 5) 四月 **4th Month**	巳 *Si* **Snake**	亥 *Hai* **Pig**	艮 *Gen*		坤 *Kun*	坎 *Kan*
午 **Horse** (Jun 6 - July 6) 五月 **5th Month**	午 *Wu* **Horse**	子 *Zi* **Rat**	離 *Li*	丙 *Bing* **Yang Fire**	離 *Li*	乾 *Qian*
未 **Goat** (July 7 - Aug 7) 六月 **6th Month**	未 *Wei* **Goat**	丑 *Chou* **Ox**	壬 *Ren* **Yang Water**	乙 *Yi* **Yin Wood**	震 *Zhen*	坤 *Kun*
申 **Monkey** (Aug 8 - Sept 7) 七月 **7th Month**	申 *Shen* **Monkey**	寅 *Yin* **Tiger**	—		艮 *Gen*	巽 *Xun*
酉 **Rooster** (Sept 8 - Oct 7) 八月 **8th Month**	酉 *You* **Rooster**	卯 *Mao* **Rabbit**	—		兌 *Dui*	乾 *Qian*
戌 **Dog** (Oct 8 - Nov 6) 九月 **9th Month**	戌 *Xu* **Dog**	辰 *Chen* **Dragon**	乾 *Qian*	兌 *Dui*	坎 *Kan*	坤 *Kun*
亥 **Pig** (Nov 7 - Dec 6) 十月 **10th Month**	亥 *Hai* **Pig**	巳 *Si* **Snake**	亥 *Hai* **Pig**	丁 *Ding* **Yin Fire**	乾 *Qian*	離 *Li*
子 **Rat** (Dec 7 - Jan 5) 十一月 **11th Month**	子 *Zi* **Rat**	午 *Wu* **Horse**	水 **Water**	山 **Mountain**	坤 *Kun*	震 *Zhen*
丑 **Ox** (Jan 6 - Feb 3) 十二月 **12th Month**	丑 *Chou* **Ox**	未 *Wei* **Goat**	土 **Earth**		巽 *Xun*	艮 *Gen*

Negative Repair / Renovation Sectors 修方凶位 :

月 MONTH	天官符 Heavenly Officer Charm			地官符 Earth Officer Charm			小月建 Small Month Establishment		
寅 **Tiger** (Feb 4 - Mar 5) 正月 **1st Month**	丑 *Chou* Ox	艮 *Gen*	寅 *Yin* Tiger	丙 *Bing* Yang Fire	離 *Li*	丁 *Ding* Yin Fire	中 Middle		
卯 **Rabbit** (Mar 6 - Apr 4) 二月 **2nd Month**	庚 *Geng* Yang Metal	兌 *Dui*	辛 *Xin* Yin Metal	丑 *Chou* Ox	艮 *Gen*	寅 *Yin* Tiger	戌 *Xu* Dog	乾 *Qian*	亥 *Hai* Pig
辰 **Dragon** (Apr 5 - May 5) 三月 **3rd Month**	戌 *Xu* Dog	乾 *Qian*	亥 *Hai* Pig	庚 *Geng* Yang Metal	兌 *Dui*	辛 *Xin* Yin Metal	庚 *Geng* Yang Metal	兌 *Dui*	辛 *Xin* Yin Metal
巳 **Snake** (May 6 - Jun 5) 四月 **4th Month**	中 Middle			戌 *Xu* Dog	乾 *Qian*	亥 *Hai* Pig	丑 *Chou* Ox	艮 *Gen*	寅 *Yin* Tiger
午 **Horse** (Jun 6 - July 6) 五月 **5th Month**	庚 *Geng* Yang Metal	兌 *Dui*	辛 *Xin* Yin Metal	中 Middle			丙 *Bing* Yang Fire	離 *Li*	丁 *Ding* Yin Fire
未 **Goat** (July 7 - Aug 7) 六月 **6th Month**	戌 *Xu* Dog	乾 *Qian*	亥 *Hai* Pig	庚 *Geng* Yang Metal	兌 *Dui*	辛 *Xin* Yin Metal	壬 *Ren* Yang Water	坎 *Kan*	癸 *Gui* Yin Water
申 **Monkey** (Aug 8 - Sept 7) 七月 **7th Month**	中 Middle			戌 *Xu* Dog	乾 *Qian*	亥 *Hai* Pig	未 *Wei* Goat	坤 *Kun*	申 *Shen* Monkey
酉 **Rooster** (Sept 8 - Oct 7) 八月 **8th Month**	辰 *Chen* Dragon	巽 *Xun*	巳 *Si* Snake	中 Middle			甲 *Jia* Yang Wood	震 *Zhen*	乙 *Yi* Yin Wood
戌 **Dog** (Oct 8 - Nov 6) 九月 **9th Month**	甲 *Jia* Yang Wood	震 *Zhen*	乙 *Yi* Yin Wood	辰 *Chen* Dragon	巽 *Xun*	巳 *Si* Snake	辰 *Chen* Dragon	巽 *Xun*	巳 *Si* Snake
亥 **Pig** (Nov 7 - Dec 6) 十月 **10th Month**	未 *Wei* Goat	坤 *Kun*	申 *Shen* Monkey	甲 *Jia* Yang Wood	震 *Zhen*	乙 *Yi* Yin Wood	中 Middle		
子 **Rat** (Dec 7 - Jan 5) 十一月 **11th Month**	壬 *Ren* Yang Water	坎 *Kan*	癸 *Gui* Yin Water	未 *Wei* Goat	坤 *Kun*	申 *Shen* Monkey	戌 *Xu* Dog	乾 *Qian*	亥 *Hai* Pig
丑 **Ox** (Jan 6 - Feb 3) 十二月 **12th Month**	丙 *Bing* Yang Fire	離 *Li*	丁 *Ding* Yin Fire	壬 *Ren* Yang Water	坎 *Kan*	癸 *Gui* Yin Water	庚 *Geng* Yang Metal	兌 *Dui*	辛 *Xin* Yin Metal

Negative Repair / Renovation Sectors 修方凶位 :

月 MONTH	大月建 Big Month Establishment			飛大煞 Flying Great Sha			丙丁獨火 Bing Ding Lonely Fire	
寅 **Tiger** (Feb 4 - Mar 5) 正月 **1st Month**	未 Wei Goat	坤 Kun	申 Shen Monkey	丙 Bing Yang Fire	離 Li	丁 Ding Yin Fire	巽 Xun	中 Middle
卯 **Rabbit** (Mar 6 - Apr 4) 二月 **2nd Month**	壬 Ren Yang Water	坎 Kan	癸 Gui Yin Water	丑 Chou Ox	艮 Gen	寅 Yin Tiger	震 Zhen	巽 Xun
辰 **Dragon** (Apr 5 - May 5) 三月 **3rd Month**	丙 Bing Yang Fire	離 Li	丁 Ding Yin Fire	庚 Geng Yang Metal	兌 Dui	辛 Xin Yin Metal	坤 Kun	震 Zhen
巳 **Snake** (May 6 - Jun 5) 四月 **4th Month**	丑 Chou Ox	艮 Gen	寅 Yin Tiger	戌 Xu Dog	乾 Qian	亥 Hai Pig	坎 Kan	坤 Kun
午 **Horse** (Jun 6 - July 6) 五月 **5th Month**	庚 Geng Yang Metal	兌 Dui	辛 Xin Yin Metal	中 Middle			離 Li	坎 Kan
未 **Goat** (July 7 - Aug 7) 六月 **6th Month**	戌 Xu Dog	乾 Qian	亥 Hai Pig	庚 Geng Yang Metal	兌 Dui	辛 Xin Yin Metal	艮 Gen	離 Li
申 **Monkey** (Aug 8 - Sept 7) 七月 **7th Month**	中 Middle			戌 Xu Dog	乾 Qian	亥 Hai Pig	兌 Dui	艮 Gen
酉 **Rooster** (Sept 8 - Oct 7) 八月 **8th Month**	辰 Chen Dragon	巽 Xun	巳 Si Snake	中 Middle			乾 Qian	兌 Dui
戌 **Dog** (Oct 8 - Nov 6) 九月 **9th Month**	甲 Jia Yang Wood	震 Zhen	乙 Yi Yin Wood	辰 Chen Dragon	巽 Xun	巳 Si Snake	中 Middle	乾 Qian
亥 **Pig** (Nov 7 - Dec 6) 十月 **10th Month**	未 Wei Goat	坤 Kun	申 Shen Monkey	甲 Jia Yang Wood	震 Zhen	乙 Yi Yin Wood	中 Middle	
子 **Rat** (Dec 7 - Jan 5) 十一月 **11th Month**	壬 Ren Yang Water	坎 Kan	癸 Gui Yin Water	未 Wei Goat	坤 Kun	申 Shen Monkey	巽 Xun	中 Middle
丑 **Ox** (Jan 6 - Feb 3) 十二月 **12th Month**	丙 Bing Yang Fire	離 Li	丁 Ding Yin Fire	壬 Ren Yang Water	坎 Kan	癸 Gui Yin Water	震 Zhen	巽 Xun

Negative Repair / Renovation Sectors 修方凶位 :

月 MONTH	月遊火 Month Wondering Fire	三煞 Monthly 3 Killings		
		劫煞 Robbery Sha	災煞 Calamity Sha	月煞 Month Sha
寅 Tiger (Feb 4 - Mar 5) 正月 1st Month	震 Zhen	亥 Hai Pig	子 Zi Rat	丑 Chou Ox
卯 Rabbit (Mar 6 - Apr 4) 二月 2nd Month	巽 Xun	申 Shen Monkey	酉 You Rooster	戌 Xu Dog
辰 Dragon (Apr 5 - May 5) 三月 3rd Month	中 Middle	巳 Si Snake	午 Wu Horse	未 Wei Goat
巳 Snake (May 6 - Jun 5) 四月 4th Month	乾 Qian	寅 Yin Tiger	卯 Mao Rabbit	辰 Chen Dragon
午 Horse (Jun 6 - July 6) 五月 5th Month	兌 Dui	亥 Hai Pig	子 Zi Rat	丑 Chou Ox
未 Goat (July 7 - Aug 7) 六月 6th Month	艮 Gen	申 Shen Monkey	酉 You Rooster	戌 Xu Dog
申 Monkey (Aug 8 - Sept 7) 七月 7th Month	離 Li	巳 Si Snake	午 Wu Horse	未 Wei Goat
酉 Rooster (Sept 8 - Oct 7) 八月 8th Month	坎 Kan	寅 Yin Tiger	卯 Mao Rabbit	辰 Chen Dragon
戌 Dog (Oct 8 - Nov 6) 九月 9th Month	坤 Kun	亥 Hai Pig	子 Zi Rat	丑 Chou Ox
亥 Pig (Nov 7 - Dec 6) 十月 10th Month	震 Zhen	申 Shen Monkey	酉 You Rooster	戌 Xu Dog
子 Rat (Dec 7 - Jan 5) 十一月 11th Month	巽 Xun	巳 Si Snake	午 Wu Horse	未 Wei Goat
丑 Ox (Jan 6 - Feb 3) 十二月 12th Month	中 Middle	寅 Yin Tiger	卯 Mao Rabbit	辰 Chen Dragon

Negative Repair / Renovation Sectors 修方凶位 :

月 MONTH	月刑 Month Punishment	月害 Month Harm	月厭 Month Detest
寅 Tiger (Feb 4 - Mar 5) 正月 1st Month	巳 Si Snake	巳 Si Snake	戌 Xu Dog
卯 Rabbit (Mar 6 - Apr 4) 二月 2nd Month	子 Zi Rat	辰 Chen Dragon	酉 You Rooster
辰 Dragon (Apr 5 - May 5) 三月 3rd Month	辰 Chen Dragon	卯 Mao Rabbit	申 Shen Monkey
巳 Snake (May 6 - Jun 5) 四月 4th Month	申 Shen Monkey	寅 Yin Tiger	未 Wei Goat
午 Horse (Jun 6 - July 6) 五月 5th Month	午 Wu Horse	丑 Chou Ox	午 Wu Horse
未 Goat (July 7 - Aug 7) 六月 6th Month	丑 Chou Ox	子 Zi Rat	巳 Si Snake
申 Monkey (Aug 8 - Sept 7) 七月 7th Month	寅 Yin Tiger	亥 Hai Pig	辰 Chen Dragon
酉 Rooster (Sept 8 - Oct 7) 八月 8th Month	酉 You Rooster	戌 Xu Dog	卯 Mao Rabbit
戌 Dog (Oct 8 - Nov 6) 九月 9th Month	未 Wei Goat	酉 You Rooster	寅 Yin Tiger
亥 Pig (Nov 7 - Dec 6) 十月 10th Month	亥 Hai Pig	申 Shen Monkey	丑 Chou Ox
子 Rat (Dec 7 - Jan 5) 十一月 11th Month	卯 Mao Rabbit	未 Wei Goat	子 Zi Rat
丑 Ox (Jan 6 - Feb 3) 十二月 12th Month	戌 Xu Dog	午 Wu Horse	亥 Hai Pig

庚辰 (Geng Chen)
Metal Dragon

Heavenly Stem 天干	庚 Yang Metal (陽金)
Earthly Branch 地支	辰 Dragon (Yang Earth 陽土)
Hidden Stem 藏干	戊 Yang Earth, 乙 Yin Wood, 癸 Yin Water
Na Yin 納音	白臘金 Metal mold
Grand Duke 太歲	辰 Dragon
Xuan Kong Five Element 玄空五行	1 水 Water
Gua Name 卦名	䷊ 地天泰 Unity
Xuan Kong Period Luck 玄空卦運	9

Annual Positive Stars for Opening Mountain, Establishing Facing and Commencing Repairs 開山立向修方吉星:

歲德 Duke Virtue	庚 Geng Yang Metal
歲德合 Duke Virtue Combo	乙 Yi Yin Wood
歲枝德 Duke Branch Virtue	酉 You Rooster
陽貴人 Yang Nobleman	丑 Chou Ox
陰貴人 Yin Nobleman	未 Wei Goat
歲祿 Duke Prosperous	申 Shen Monkey
歲馬 Duke Horse	寅 Yin Tiger
奏書 Decree	艮 Gen
博士 Professor	坤 Kun

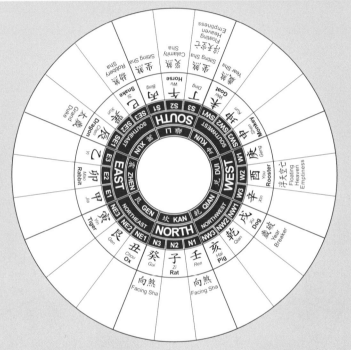

Annual Negative Stars for Opening Mountain, Establishing Facing and Commencing Repairs 開山立向修方凶星：

太歲 Grand Duke	歲破 Year Breaker	三煞 Three Killings			坐煞向煞 Sitting Sha Facing Sha				浮天空亡 Floating Heaven Emptiness	
辰 Chen Dragon	戌 Xu Dog	巳 Si Snake	午 Wu Horse	未 Wei Goat	丙 Bing Yang Fire	丁 Ding Yin Fire	壬 Ren Yang Water	癸 Gui Yin Water	兌 Dui	丁 Ding Yin Fire

Annual San Yuan Purple White Stars 三元紫白九星：

上元 Upper Period Period 1, 2, 3			中元 Middle Period Period 4, 5, 6			下元 Lower Period Period 7, 8, 9		
巽SE **2**	離S **7**	坤SW **9**	巽SE **5**	離S **1**	坤SW **3**	巽SE **8**	離S **4**	坤SW **6**
震E **1**	**3** 庚辰 Geng Chen Metal Dragon	兌W **5**	震E **4**	**6** 庚辰 Geng Chen Metal Dragon	兌W **8**	震E **7**	**9** 庚辰 Geng Chen Metal Dragon	兌W **2**
艮NE **6**	坎N **8**	乾NW **4**	艮NE **9**	坎N **2**	乾NW **7**	艮NE **3**	坎N **5**	乾NW **1**

Mountain Covering Yellow Path 蓋山黃道：

貪狼 *Tan Lang* **Greedy Wolf**				巨門 *Ju Men* **Huge Door**				武曲 *Wu Qu* **Military Arts**		文曲 *Wen Qu* **Literary Arts**			
兌	丁	巳	丑	震	庚	亥	未	艮	丙	坎	癸	申	辰
Duin	*Ding*	*Si*	*Chou*	*Zhen*	*Geng*	*Hai*	*Wei*	*Gen*	*Bing*	*Kan*	*Gui*	*Shen*	*Chen*
W2	S3	SE3	NE1	E2	W1	NW3	SW1	NE2	S1	N2	N3	SW3	SE1

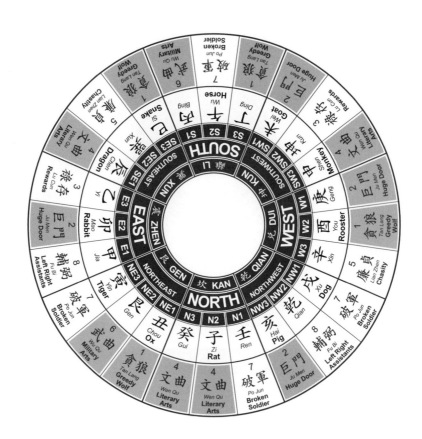

Heaven Penetrating Force 通天竅:

三合前方 **Facing Three Harmony**	艮寅 Gen Yin	甲卯 Jia Mao	乙辰 Yi Chen
三合後方 **Sitting Three Harmony**	坤申 Kun Shen	庚酉 Geng You	辛戌 Xin Xu

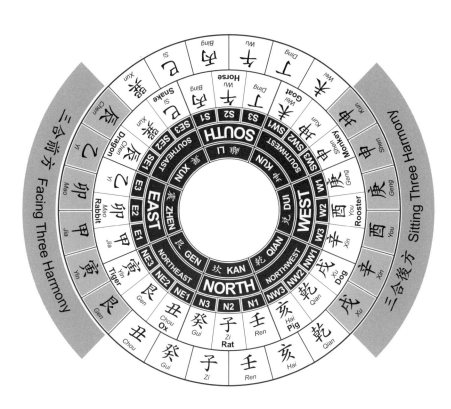

Moving Horse Six Ren Assessment 走馬六壬：

神后 *Shen Hou* **Holy Empress**	功曹 *Gong Cao* **Marshall**	天罡 *Tian Gang* **Heavenly Dipper**	勝光 *Sheng Guang* **Subliminal Bright**	傳送 *Chuan Song* **Great General**	河魁 *He Kui* **River Scholar**
坤申 *Kun Shen*	辛戌 *Xin Xu*	壬子 *Ren Zi*	艮寅 *Gen Yin*	乙辰 *Yi Chen*	丙午 *Bing Wu*

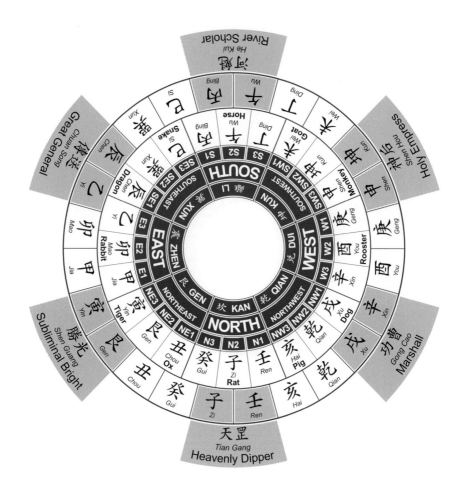

Four Advantages Three Cycles Star Plate 四利三元：			
太陽 *Tai Yang* **Sun**	太陰 *Tai Yin* **Moon**	龍德 *Long De* **Dragon Virtue**	福德 *Fu De* **Fortune Virtue**
巳 *Si* **Snake**	未 *Wei* **Goat**	亥 *Hai* **Pig**	丑 *Chou* **Ox**

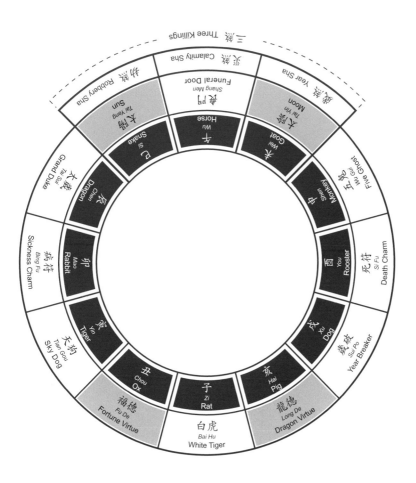

Negative Sectors For Opening Mountain 開山凶位：

年剋山家 Year Countering Sitting

震	艮	巳
Zhen	*Gen*	*Si*
E2	NE2	SE3

陰府太歲	六害	死符	炙退
Yin Fu Tai Sui	*Liu Hai*	*Si Fu*	*Zhi Tui*
Yin Mansion Grand Duke	**Six Harm**	**Death Charm**	**Roasting Star**

乾	兌	卯	酉	卯
Qian	*Dui*	*Mao*	*You*	*Mao*
NW2	W2	E2	W2	E2

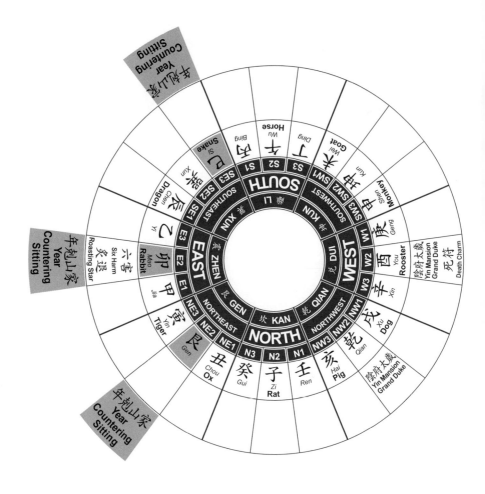

Negative Directions to Establish Facing 立向凶方：

巡山羅喉 Xun Shan Luo Hou **Mountain Patrol Luo Hou Star**	病符 Bing Fu **Sickness Charm**
巽 Xun **SE2**	卯 Mao **E2**

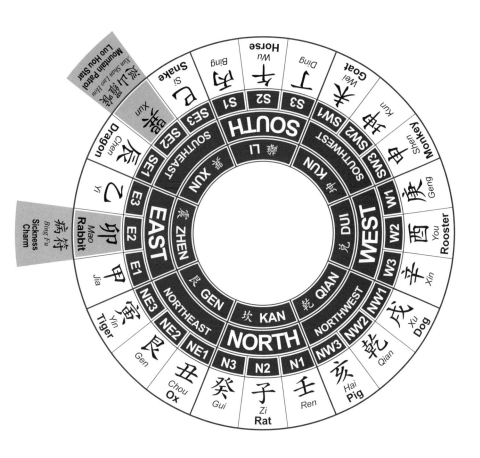

Negative Repair / Renovation Sectors Table 修方凶位表：

天官符 **Heavenly Officer Charm**	亥 *Hai* Pig		豹尾 **Leopard Tail**	戌 *Xu* Dog
地官符 **Earthly Officer Charm**	申 *Shen* Monkey		飛廉 **Flying Chaste**	午 *Wu* Horse
大煞 **Great Sha**	子 *Zi* Rat		喪門 **Funeral Door**	午 *Wu* Horse
大將軍 **Big General**	子 *Zi* Rat		吊客 **Suspended Guest**	寅 *Yin* Tiger
力士 **Strong Man**	巽 *Xun*		白虎 **White Tiger**	子 *Zi* Rat
蠶室 **Silkworm Room**	乾 *Qian*		金神 **Golden God**	辰 *Chen* Dragon
蠶官 **Silkworm Officer**	戌 *Xu* Dog			巳 *Si* Snake
蠶命 **Silkworm Life**	亥 *Hai* Pig		獨火 **Lonely Fire**	巽 *Xun*
歲刑 **Duke Punishment**	辰 *Chen* Dragon		五鬼 **Five Ghost**	子 *Zi* Rat
黃幡 **Yellow Flag**	辰 *Chen* Dragon		破敗五鬼 **Destructive Five Ghost**	兌 *Dui*

Negative Repair / Renovation Sectors Diagram 修方凶位圖 :

12-Month Auxiliary Stars Reference Table :
庚辰年十二月，開山立向修方星表

Positive Monthly Stars 吉星方

月 MONTH	寅 Tiger (Feb 4 - Mar 5) 正月 1st Month	卯 Rabbit (Mar 6 - Apr 4) 二月 2nd Month	辰 Dragon (Apr 5 - May 5) 三月 3rd Month	巳 Snake (May 6 - Jun 5) 四月 4th Month	午 Horse (Jun 6 - July 6) 五月 5th Month	未 Goat (July 7 - Aug 7) 六月 6th Month
天道 Heavenly Path	南 South	西南 Southwest	北 North	西 West	西北 Northwest	東 East
天德 Heavenly Virtue	丁 Ding Yin Fire	坤 Kun (申)	壬 Ren Yang Water	辛 Xin Yin Metal	乾 Qian (亥)	甲 Jia Yang Wood
天德合 Heavenly Virtue Combo	壬 Ren Yang Water	(巳)	丁 Ding Yin Fire	丙 Bing Yang Fire	(寅)	己 Ji Yin Earth
月德 Monthly Virtue	丙 Bing Yang Fire	甲 Jia Yang Wood	壬 Ren Yang Water	庚 Geng Yang Metal	丙 Bing Yang Fire	甲 Jia Yang Wood
月德合 Monthly Virtue Combo	辛 Xin Yin Metal	己 Ji Yin Earth	丁 Ding Yin Fire	乙 Yi Yin Wood	辛 Xin Yin Metal	己 Ji Yin Earth
月空 Month Emptiness	壬 Ren Yang Water	庚 Geng Yang Metal	丙 Bing Yang Fire	甲 Jia Yang Wood	壬 Ren Yang Water	庚 Geng Yang Metal
陽貴人 Yang Nobleman	兌 Dui	乾 Qian	中 Middle	巽 Xun	震 Zhen	坤 Kun
陰貴人 Yin Nobleman	坎 Kan	離 Li	艮 Gen	兌 Dui	乾 Qian	中 Middle
飛天祿 Flying Heavenly Wealth	坤 Kun	坎 Kan	離 Li	艮 Gen	兌 Dui	乾 Qian
飛天馬 Flying Heavenly Horse	中 Middle	坎 Kan	離 Li	艮 Gen	兌 Dui	乾 Qian

12-Month Auxiliary Stars Reference Table :
庚辰年十二月，開山立向修方星表

申 Monkey (Aug 8 - Sept 7) 七月 7th Month	酉 Rooster (Sept 8 - Oct 7) 八月 8th Month	戌 Dog (Oct 8 - Nov 6) 九月 9th Month	亥 Pig (Nov 7 - Dec 6) 十月 10th Month	子 Rat (Dec 7 - Jan 5) 十一月 11th Month	丑 Ox (Jan 6 - Feb 3) 十二月 12th Month	月 MONTH
北 North	東北 Northeast	南 South	東 East	東南 Southeast	西 West	天道 Heavenly Path
癸 Gui Yin Water	艮 Gen （寅）	丙 Bing Yang Fire	乙 Yi Yin Wood	巽 Xun （巳）	庚 Geng Yang Metal	天德 Heavenly Virtue
戊 Wu Yang Earth	（亥）	辛 Xin Yin Metal	庚 Geng Yang Metal	（申）	乙 Yi Yin Wood	天德合 Heavenly Virtue Combo
壬 Ren Yang Water	庚 Geng Yang Metal	丙 Bing Yang Fire	甲 Jia Yang Wood	壬 Ren Yang Water	庚 Geng Yang Metal	月德 Monthly Virtue
丁 Ding Yin Fire	乙 Yi Yin Wood	辛 Xin Yin Metal	己 Ji Yin Earth	丁 Ding Yin Fire	乙 Yi Yin Wood	月德合 Monthly Virtue Combo
丙 Bing Yang Fire	甲 Jia Yang Wood	壬 Ren Yang Water	庚 Geng Yang Metal	丙 Bing Yang Fire	甲 Jia Yang Wood	月空 Month Emptiness
坎 Kan	離 Li	艮 Gen	兌 Dui	乾 Qian	中 Middle	陽貴人 Yang Nobleman
坎 Kan	離 Li	艮 Gen	兌 Dui	乾 Qian	中 Middle	陰貴人 Yin Nobleman
中 Middle	坎 Kan	離 Li	艮 Gen	兌 Dui	乾 Qian	飛天祿 Flying Heavenly Wealth
中 Middle	巽 Xun	震 Zhen	坤 Kun	坎 Kan	離 Li	飛天馬 Flying Heavenly Horse

Monthly Purple White Stars 月紫白九星 :

寅 Tiger (Feb 4 - Mar 5) 正月 1st Month

巽 SE	離 S	坤 SW
4 Green 四綠	9 Purple 九紫	2 Black 二黑
震 E 3 Jade 三碧	5 Yellow 五黃	7 Red 七赤 兌 W
艮 NE 8 White 八白	1 White 一白 坎 N	6 White 六白 乾 NW

卯 Rabbit (Mar 6 - Apr 4) 二月 2nd Month

巽 SE	離 S	坤 SW
3 Jade 三碧	8 White 八白	1 White 一白
震 E 2 Black 二黑	4 Green 四綠	6 White 六白 兌 W
艮 NE 7 Red 七赤	9 Purple 九紫 坎 N	5 Yellow 五黃 乾 NW

辰 Dragon (Apr 5 - May 5) 三月 3rd Month

巽 SE	離 S	坤 SW
2 Black 二黑	7 Red 七赤	9 Purple 九紫
震 E 1 White 一白	3 Jade 三碧	5 Yellow 五黃 兌 W
艮 NE 6 White 六白	8 White 八白 坎 N	4 Green 四綠 乾 NW

巳 Snake (May 6 - Jun 5) 四月 4th Month

巽 SE	離 S	坤 SW
1 White 一白	6 White 六白	8 White 八白
震 E 9 Purple 九紫	2 Black 二黑	4 Green 四綠 兌 W
艮 NE 5 Yellow 五黃	7 Red 七赤 坎 N	3 Jade 三碧 乾 NW

午 Horse (Jun 6 - July 6) 五月 5th Month

巽 SE	離 S	坤 SW
9 Purple 九紫	5 Yellow 五黃	7 Red 七赤
震 E 8 White 八白	1 White 一白	3 Jade 三碧 兌 W
艮 NE 4 Green 四綠	6 White 六白 坎 N	2 Black 二黑 乾 NW

未 Goat (July 7 - Aug 7) 六月 6th Month

巽 SE	離 S	坤 SW
8 White 八白	4 Green 四綠	6 White 六白
震 E 7 Red 七赤	9 Purple 九紫	2 Black 二黑 兌 W
艮 NE 3 Jade 三碧	5 Yellow 五黃 坎 N	1 White 一白 乾 NW

申 Monkey (Aug 8 - Sept 7) 七月 7th Month

巽 SE	離 S	坤 SW
7 Red 七赤	3 Jade 三碧	5 Yellow 五黃
震 E 6 White 六白	8 White 八白	1 White 一白 兌 W
艮 NE 2 Black 二黑	4 Green 四綠 坎 N	9 Purple 九紫 乾 NW

酉 Rooster (Sept 8 - Oct 7) 八月 8th Month

巽 SE	離 S	坤 SW
6 White 六白	2 Black 二黑	4 Green 四綠
震 E 5 Yellow 五黃	7 Red 七赤	9 Purple 九紫 兌 W
艮 NE 1 White 一白	3 Jade 三碧 坎 N	8 White 八白 乾 NW

戌 Dog (Oct 8 - Nov 6) 九月 9th Month

巽 SE	離 S	坤 SW
5 Yellow 五黃	1 White 一白	3 Jade 三碧
震 E 4 Green 四綠	6 White 六白	8 White 八白 兌 W
艮 NE 9 Purple 九紫	2 Black 二黑 坎 N	7 Red 七赤 乾 NW

亥 Pig (Nov 7 - Dec 6) 十月 10th Month

巽 SE	離 S	坤 SW
4 Green 四綠	9 Purple 九紫	2 Black 二黑
震 E 3 Jade 三碧	5 Yellow 五黃	7 Red 七赤 兌 W
艮 NE 8 White 八白	1 White 一白 坎 N	6 White 六白 乾 NW

子 Rat (Dec 7 - Jan 5) 十一月 11th Month

巽 SE	離 S	坤 SW
3 Jade 三碧	8 White 八白	1 White 一白
震 E 2 Black 二黑	4 Green 四綠	6 White 六白 兌 W
艮 NE 7 Red 七赤	9 Purple 九紫 坎 N	5 Yellow 五黃 乾 NW

丑 Ox (Jan 6 - Feb 3) 十二月 12th Month

巽 SE	離 S	坤 SW
2 Black 二黑	7 Red 七赤	9 Purple 九紫
震 E 1 White 一白	3 Jade 三碧	5 Yellow 五黃 兌 W
艮 NE 6 White 六白	8 White 八白 坎 N	4 Green 四綠 乾 NW

Qi Men Three Nobles 三奇 :

Three Nobles 三奇 / Seasons	乙 Yi	丙 Bing	丁 Ding
立春 **Coming of Spring** Feb 4 - Feb 18	巽 Xun	中 Middle	乾 Qian
春分 **Spring Equinox** Mar 21 - Apr 4	艮 Gen	離 Li	坎 Kan
立夏 **Coming of Summer** May 6 - May 20	離 Li	坎 Kan	坤 Kun
夏至 **Summer Solstice** Jun 22 - Jul 6	巽 Xun	震 Zhen	坤 Kun
立秋 **Coming of Autumn** Aug 8 - Aug 23	乾 Qian	中 Middle	巽 Xun
秋分 **Autumn Equinox** Sept 23 - Oct 7	坤 Kun	坎 Kan	離 Li
立冬 **Coming of Winter** Nov 7 - Nov 22	坎 Kan	離 Li	艮 Gen
冬至 **Winter Solstice** Dec 22 - Jan 5	乾 Qian	兌 Dui	艮 Gen

Sectors to Avoid Opening Mountain 開山凶位 :

月 MONTH	月建 Month Establishment	月破 Month Destruction	月剋山家 Month Countering Sitting	陰府太歲 Yin Mansion Grand Duke	
寅 **Tiger** (Feb 4 - Mar 5) 正月 **1st Month**	寅 *Yin* **Tiger**	申 *Shen* **Monkey**	乾 *Qian* 兌 *Dui*	坤 *Kun*	震 *Zhen*
卯 **Rabbit** (Mar 6 - Apr 4) 二月 **2nd Month**	卯 *Mao* **Rabbit**	酉 *You* **Rooster**	亥 *Hai* **Pig** 丁 *Ding* **Yin Fire**	巽 *Xun*	艮 *Gen*
辰 **Dragon** (Apr 5 - May 5) 三月 **3rd Month**	辰 *Chen* **Dragon**	戌 *Xu* **Dog**	震 *Zhen* 巳 *Si* **Snake**	乾 *Qian*	兌 *Dui*
巳 **Snake** (May 6 - Jun 5) 四月 **4th Month**	巳 *Si* **Snake**	亥 *Hai* **Pig**	艮 *Gen*	坤 *Kun*	坎 *Kan*
午 **Horse** (Jun 6 - July 6) 五月 **5th Month**	午 *Wu* **Horse**	子 *Zi* **Rat**	離 *Li* 丙 *Bing* **Yang Fire**	離 *Li*	乾 *Qian*
未 **Goat** (July 7 - Aug 7) 六月 **6th Month**	未 *Wei* **Goat**	丑 *Chou* **Ox**	壬 *Ren* **Yang Water** 乙 *Yi* **Yin Wood**	震 *Zhen*	坤 *Kun*
申 **Monkey** (Aug 8 - Sept 7) 七月 **7th Month**	申 *Shen* **Monkey**	寅 *Yin* **Tiger**	—	艮 *Gen*	巽 *Xun*
酉 **Rooster** (Sept 8 - Oct 7) 八月 **8th Month**	酉 *You* **Rooster**	卯 *Mao* **Rabbit**	—	兌 *Dui*	乾 *Qian*
戌 **Dog** (Oct 8 - Nov 6) 九月 **9th Month**	戌 *Xu* **Dog**	辰 *Chen* **Dragon**	乾 *Qian* 兌 *Dui*	坎 *Kan*	坤 *Kun*
亥 **Pig** (Nov 7 - Dec 6) 十月 **10th Month**	亥 *Hai* **Pig**	巳 *Si* **Snake**	亥 *Hai* **Pig** 丁 *Ding* **Yin Fire**	乾 *Qian*	離 *Li*
子 **Rat** (Dec 7 - Jan 5) 十一月 **11th Month**	子 *Zi* **Rat**	午 *Wu* **Horse**	水 **Water** 山 **Mountain**	坤 *Kun*	震 *Zhen*
丑 **Ox** (Jan 6 - Feb 3) 十二月 **12th Month**	丑 *Chou* **Ox**	未 *Wei* **Goat**	土 **Earth**	巽 *Xun*	艮 *Gen*

Negative Repair / Renovation Sectors 修方凶位 :

月 MONTH	天官符 Heavenly Officer Charm			地官符 Earth Officer Charm			小月建 Small Month Establishment		
寅 **Tiger** (Feb 4 - Mar 5) 正月 **1st Month**	中 Middle			未 Wei Goat	坤 Kun	申 Shen Monkey	中 Middle		
卯 **Rabbit** (Mar 6 - Apr 4) 二月 **2nd Month**	辰 Chen Dragon	巽 Xun	巳 Si Snake	壬 Ren Yang Water	坎 Kan	癸 Gui Yin Water	戌 Xu Dog	乾 Qian	亥 Hai Pig
辰 **Dragon** (Apr 5 - May 5) 三月 **3rd Month**	甲 Jia Yang Wood	震 Zhen	乙 Yi Yin Wood	丙 Bing Yang Fire	離 Li	丁 Ding Yin Fire	庚 Geng Yang Metal	兑 Dui	辛 Xin Yin Metal
巳 **Snake** (May 6 - Jun 5) 四月 **4th Month**	未 Wei Goat	坤 Kun	申 Shen Monkey	丑 Chou Ox	艮 Gen	寅 Yin Tiger	丑 Chou Ox	艮 Gen	寅 Yin Tiger
午 **Horse** (Jun 6 - July 6) 五月 **5th Month**	壬 Ren Yang Water	坎 Kan	癸 Gui Yin Water	庚 Geng Yang Metal	兑 Dui	辛 Xin Yin Metal	丙 Bing Yang Fire	離 Li	丁 Ding Yin Fire
未 **Goat** (July 7 - Aug 7) 六月 **6th Month**	丙 Bing Yang Fire	離 Li	丁 Ding Yin Fire	戌 Xu Dog	乾 Qian	亥 Hai Pig	壬 Ren Yang Water	坎 Kan	癸 Gui Yin Water
申 **Monkey** (Aug 8 - Sept 7) 七月 **7th Month**	丑 Chou Ox	艮 Gen	寅 Yin Tiger	中 Middle			未 Wei Goat	坤 Kun	申 Shen Monkey
酉 **Rooster** (Sept 8 - Oct 7) 八月 **8th Month**	庚 Geng Yang Metal	兑 Dui	辛 Xin Yin Metal	庚 Geng Yang Metal	兑 Dui	辛 Xin Yin Metal	甲 Jia Yang Wood	震 Zhen	乙 Yi Yin Wood
戌 **Dog** (Oct 8 - Nov 6) 九月 **9th Month**	戌 Xu Dog	乾 Qian	亥 Hai Pig	戌 Xu Dog	乾 Qian	亥 Hai Pig	辰 Chen Dragon	巽 Xun	巳 Si Snake
亥 **Pig** (Nov 7 - Dec 6) 十月 **10th Month**	中 Middle			中 Middle			中 Middle		
子 **Rat** (Dec 7 - Jan 5) 十一月 **11th Month**	庚 Geng Yang Metal	兑 Dui	辛 Xin Yin Metal	辰 Chen Dragon	巽 Xun	巳 Si Snake	戌 Xu Dog	乾 Qian	亥 Hai Pig
丑 **Ox** (Jan 6 - Feb 3) 十二月 **12th Month**	戌 Xu Dog	乾 Qian	亥 Hai Pig	甲 Jia Yang Wood	震 Zhen	乙 Yi Yin Wood	庚 Geng Yang Metal	兑 Dui	辛 Xin Yin Metal

庚辰 (Geng Chen) Metal Dragon

Negative Repair / Renovation Sectors 修方凶位 :

月 MONTH	大月建 Big Month Establishment			飛大煞 Flying Great Sha			丙丁獨火 Bing Ding Lonely Fire	
寅 Tiger (Feb 4 - Mar 5) 正月 1st Month	中 Middle			戌 Xu Dog	乾 Qian	亥 Hai Pig	巽 Xun	中 Middle
卯 Rabbit (Mar 6 - Apr 4) 二月 2nd Month	辰 Chen Dragon	巽 Xun	巳 Si Snake	中 Middle			震 Zhen	巽 Xun
辰 Dragon (Apr 5 - May 5) 三月 3rd Month	甲 Jia Yang Wood	震 Zhen	乙 Yi Yin Wood	辰 Chen Dragon	巽 Xun	巳 Si Snake	坤 Kun	震 Zhen
巳 Snake (May 6 - Jun 5) 四月 4th Month	未 Wei Goat	坤 Kun	申 Shen Monkey	甲 Jia Yang Wood	震 Zhen	乙 Yi Yin Wood	坎 Kan	坤 Kun
午 Horse (Jun 6 - July 6) 五月 5th Month	壬 Ren Yang Water	坎 Kan	癸 Gui Yin Water	未 Wei Goat	坤 Kun	申 Shen Monkey	離 Li	坎 Kan
未 Goat (July 7 - Aug 7) 六月 6th Month	丙 Bing Yang Fire	離 Li	丁 Ding Yin Fire	壬 Ren Yang Water	坎 Kan	癸 Gui Yin Water	艮 Gen	離 Li
申 Monkey (Aug 8 - Sept 7) 七月 7th Month	丑 Chou Ox	艮 Gen	寅 Yin Tiger	丙 Bing Yang Fire	離 Li	丁 Ding Yin Fire	兌 Dui	艮 Gen
酉 Rooster (Sept 8 - Oct 7) 八月 8th Month	庚 Geng Yang Metal	兌 Dui	辛 Xin Yin Metal	丑 Chou Ox	艮 Gen	寅 Yin Tiger	乾 Qian	兌 Dui
戌 Dog (Oct 8 - Nov 6) 九月 9th Month	戌 Xu Dog	乾 Qian	亥 Hai Pig	庚 Geng Yang Metal	兌 Dui	辛 Xin Yin Metal	中 Middle	乾 Qian
亥 Pig (Nov 7 - Dec 6) 十月 10th Month	中 Middle			戌 Xu Dog	乾 Qian	亥 Hai Pig	中 Middle	
子 Rat (Dec 7 - Jan 5) 十一月 11th Month	辰 Chen Dragon	巽 Xun	巳 Si Snake	中 Middle			巽 Xun	中 Middle
丑 Ox (Jan 6 - Feb 3) 十二月 12th Month	甲 Jia Yang Wood	震 Zhen	乙 Yi Yin Wood	庚 Geng Yang Metal	兌 Dui	辛 Xin Yin Metal	震 Zhen	巽 Xun

Negative Repair / Renovation Sectors 修方凶位 :

月 MONTH	月遊火 Month Wondering Fire	三煞 Monthly 3 Killings		
		劫煞 Robbery Sha	災煞 Calamity Sha	月煞 Month Sha
寅 **Tiger** (Feb 4 - Mar 5) 正月 **1st Month**	巽 *Xun*	亥 *Hai* **Pig**	子 *Zi* **Rat**	丑 *Chou* **Ox**
卯 **Rabbit** (Mar 6 - Apr 4) 二月 **2nd Month**	中 **Middle**	申 *Shen* **Monkey**	酉 *You* **Rooster**	戌 *Xu* **Dog**
辰 **Dragon** (Apr 5 - May 5) 三月 **3rd Month**	乾 *Qian*	巳 *Si* **Snake**	午 *Wu* **Horse**	未 *Wei* **Goat**
巳 **Snake** (May 6 - Jun 5) 四月 **4th Month**	兌 *Dui*	寅 *Yin* **Tiger**	卯 *Mao* **Rabbit**	辰 *Chen* **Dragon**
午 **Horse** (Jun 6 - July 6) 五月 **5th Month**	艮 *Gen*	亥 *Hai* **Pig**	子 *Zi* **Rat**	丑 *Chou* **Ox**
未 **Goat** (July 7 - Aug 7) 六月 **6th Month**	離 *Li*	申 *Shen* **Monkey**	酉 *You* **Rooster**	戌 *Xu* **Dog**
申 **Monkey** (Aug 8 - Sept 7) 七月 **7th Month**	坎 *Kan*	巳 *Si* **Snake**	午 *Wu* **Horse**	未 *Wei* **Goat**
酉 **Rooster** (Sept 8 - Oct 7) 八月 **8th Month**	坤 *Kun*	寅 *Yin* **Tiger**	卯 *Mao* **Rabbit**	辰 *Chen* **Dragon**
戌 **Dog** (Oct 8 - Nov 6) 九月 **9th Month**	震 *Zhen*	亥 *Hai* **Pig**	子 *Zi* **Rat**	丑 *Chou* **Ox**
亥 **Pig** (Nov 7 - Dec 6) 十月 **10th Month**	巽 *Xun*	申 *Shen* **Monkey**	酉 *You* **Rooster**	戌 *Xu* **Dog**
子 **Rat** (Dec 7 - Jan 5) 十一月 **11th Month**	中 **Middle**	巳 *Si* **Snake**	午 *Wu* **Horse**	未 *Wei* **Goat**
丑 **Ox** (Jan 6 - Feb 3) 十二月 **12th Month**	乾 *Qian*	寅 *Yin* **Tiger**	卯 *Mao* **Rabbit**	辰 *Chen* **Dragon**

Negative Repair / Renovation Sectors 修方凶位 :

月 MONTH	月刑 Month Punishment	月害 Month Harm	月厭 Month Detest
寅 **Tiger** (Feb 4 - Mar 5) 正月 **1st Month**	巳 *Si* **Snake**	巳 *Si* **Snake**	戌 *Xu* **Dog**
卯 **Rabbit** (Mar 6 - Apr 4) 二月 **2nd Month**	子 *Zi* **Rat**	辰 *Chen* **Dragon**	酉 *You* **Rooster**
辰 **Dragon** (Apr 5 - May 5) 三月 **3rd Month**	辰 *Chen* **Dragon**	卯 *Mao* **Rabbit**	申 *Shen* **Monkey**
巳 **Snake** (May 6 - Jun 5) 四月 **4th Month**	申 *Shen* **Monkey**	寅 *Yin* **Tiger**	未 *Wei* **Goat**
午 **Horse** (Jun 6 - July 6) 五月 **5th Month**	午 *Wu* **Horse**	丑 *Chou* **Ox**	午 *Wu* **Horse**
未 **Goat** (July 7 - Aug 7) 六月 **6th Month**	丑 *Chou* **Ox**	子 *Zi* **Rat**	巳 *Si* **Snake**
申 **Monkey** (Aug 8 - Sept 7) 七月 **7th Month**	寅 *Yin* **Tiger**	亥 *Hai* **Pig**	辰 *Chen* **Dragon**
酉 **Rooster** (Sept 8 - Oct 7) 八月 **8th Month**	酉 *You* **Rooster**	戌 *Xu* **Dog**	卯 *Mao* **Rabbit**
戌 **Dog** (Oct 8 - Nov 6) 九月 **9th Month**	未 *Wei* **Goat**	酉 *You* **Rooster**	寅 *Yin* **Tiger**
亥 **Pig** (Nov 7 - Dec 6) 十月 **10th Month**	亥 *Hai* **Pig**	申 *Shen* **Monkey**	丑 *Chou* **Ox**
子 **Rat** (Dec 7 - Jan 5) 十一月 **11th Month**	卯 *Mao* **Rabbit**	未 *Wei* **Goat**	子 *Zi* **Rat**
丑 **Ox** (Jan 6 - Feb 3) 十二月 **12th Month**	戌 *Xu* **Dog**	午 *Wu* **Horse**	亥 *Hai* **Pig**

庚午 (Geng Wu)
Metal Horse

Heavenly Stem 天干	庚 Yang Metal (陽金)
Earthly Branch 地支	午 Horse (Yang Fire 陽火)
Hidden Stem 藏干	丁 Yin Fire, 己 Yin Earth
Na Yin 納音	路傍土 Earth from the road
Grand Duke 太歲	午 Horse
Xuan Kong Five Element 玄空五行	8 木 Wood
Gua Name 卦名	䷟ 雷風恆 Consistency
Xuan Kong Period Luck 玄空卦運	9

Annual Positive Stars for Opening Mountain, Establishing Facing and Commencing Repairs 開山立向修方吉星：

歲德 Duke Virtue	庚 Geng Yang Metal
歲德合 Duke Virtue Combo	乙 Yi Yin Wood
歲枝德 Duke Branch Virtue	亥 Hai Pig
陽貴人 Yang Nobleman	丑 Chou Ox
陰貴人 Yin Nobleman	未 Wei Goat
歲祿 Duke Prosperous	申 Shen Monkey
歲馬 Duke Horse	申 Shen Monkey
奏書 Decree	巽 Xun
博士 Professor	乾 Qian

Annual Negative Stars for Opening Mountain, Establishing Facing and Commencing Repairs 開山立向修方凶星：

太歲 Grand Duke	歲破 Year Breaker	三煞 Three Killings			坐煞向煞 Sitting Sha Facing Sha				浮天空亡 Floating Heaven Emptiness	
午 Wu Horse	子 Zi Rat	亥 Hai Pig	子 Zi Rat	丑 Chou Ox	壬 Ren Yang Water	癸 Gui Yin Water	丙 Bing Yang Fire	丁 Ding Yin Fire	兌 Dui	丁 Ding Yin Fire

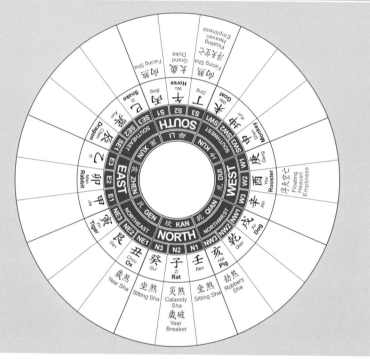

Annual San Yuan Purple White Stars 三元紫白九星：

上元 Upper Period Period 1, 2, 3			中元 Middle Period Period 4, 5, 6			下元 Lower Period Period 7, 8, 9		
巽SE **3**	離S **8**	坤SW **1**	巽SE **6**	離S **2**	坤SW **4**	巽SE **9**	離S **5**	坤SW **7**
震E **2**	**4** 庚午 Geng Wu Metal Horse	兌W **6**	震E **5**	**7** 庚午 Geng Wu Metal Horse	兌W **9**	震E **8**	**1** 庚午 Geng Wu Metal Horse	兌W **3**
艮NE **7**	坎N **9**	乾NW **5**	艮NE **1**	坎N **3**	乾NW **8**	艮NE **4**	坎N **6**	乾NW **2**

庚午 (Geng Wu) Metal Horse

Mountain Covering Yellow Path 蓋山黃道：

貪狼 *Tan Lang* **Greedy Wolf**		巨門 *Ju Men* **Huge Door**		武曲 *Wu Qu* **Military Arts**				文曲 *Wen Qu* **Literary Arts**	
巽 *Xun* SE2	辛 *Xin* W3	艮 *Gen* NE2	丙 *Bing* S1	震 *Zhen* E2	庚 *Geng* W1	亥 *Hai* NW3	未 *Wei* SW1	乾 *Qian* NW2	甲 *Jia* E1

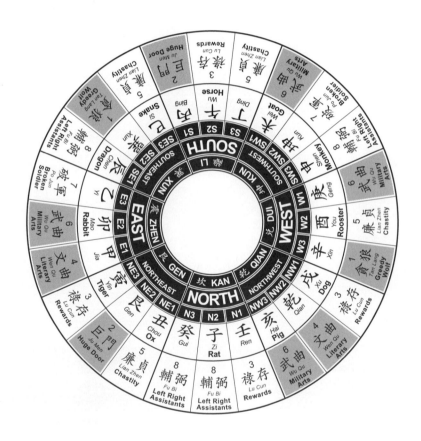

Heaven Penetrating Force 通天竅:

三合前方 Facing Three Harmony	坤申 Kun Shen	庚酉 Geng You	辛戌 Xin Xu
三合後方 Sitting Three Harmony	艮寅 Gen Yin	甲卯 Jia Mao	乙辰 Yi Chen

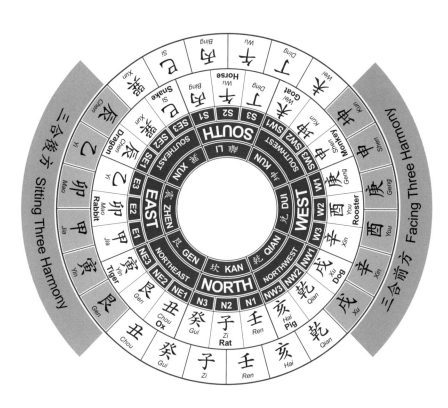

Moving Horse Six Ren Assessment 走馬六壬：

神后 Shen Hou Holy Empress	功曹 Gong Cao Marshall	天罡 Tian Gang Heavenly Dipper	勝光 Sheng Guang Subliminal Bright	傳送 Chuan Song Great General	河魁 He Kui River Scholar
丙午 Bing Wu	坤申 Kun Shen	辛戌 Xin Xu	壬子 Ren Zi	艮寅 Gen Yin	乙辰 Yi Chen

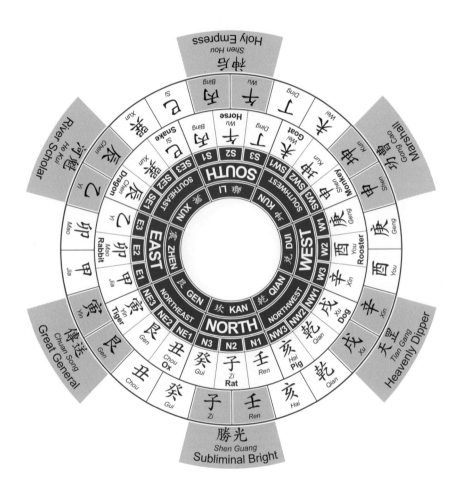

Four Advantages Three Cycles Star Plate 四利三元：

太陽 *Tai Yang* **Sun**	太陰 *Tai Yin* **Moon**	龍德 *Long De* **Dragon Virtue**	福德 *Fu De* **Fortune Virtue**
未 *Wei* **Goat**	酉 *You* **Rooster**	丑 *Chou* **Ox**	卯 *Mao* **Rabbit**

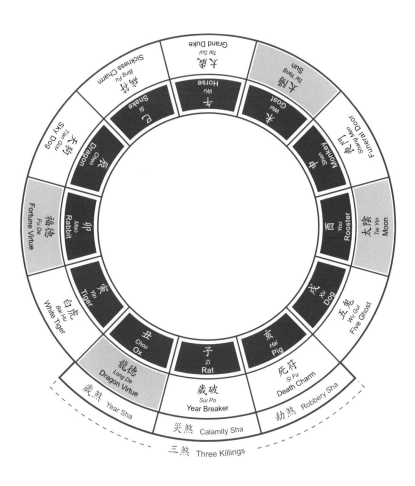

Negative Sectors For Opening Mountain 開山凶位:

年尅山家 Year Countering Sitting

乾 *Qian* **NW2**	亥 *Hai* **NW3**	兌 *Dui* **W2**	丁 *Ding* **S3**

陰府太歲 *Yin Fu Tai Sui* **Yin Mansion Grand Duke**		六害 *Liu Hai* **Six Harm**	死符 *Si Fu* **Death Charm**	炙退 *Zhi Tui* **Roasting Star**
乾 *Qian* **NW2**	兌 *Dui* **W2**	丑 *Chou* **NE1**	亥 *Hai* **NW3**	酉 *You* **W2**

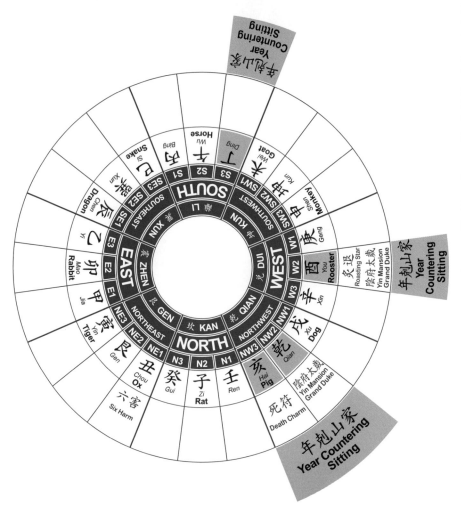

Negative Directions to Establish Facing 立向凶方：

巡山羅喉 *Xun Shan Luo Hou* **Mountain Patrol Luo Hou Star**	病符 *Bing Fu* **Sickness Charm**
丁 *Ding* **S3**	巳 *Si* **Snake**

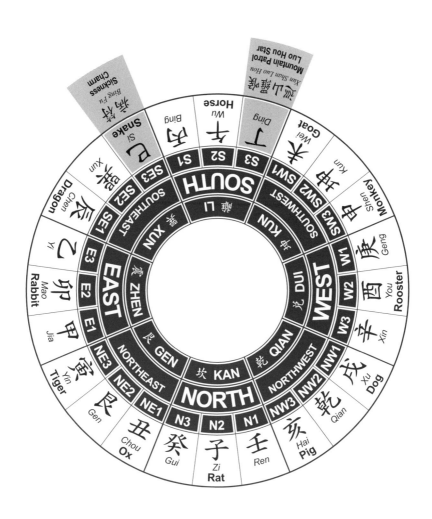

Negative Repair / Renovation Sectors Table 修方凶位表：

天官符 **Heavenly Officer Charm**	巳 Si Snake		豹尾 **Leopard Tail**	辰 Chen Dragon
地官符 **Earthly Officer Charm**	戌 Xu Dog		飛廉 **Flying Chaste**	寅 Yin Tiger
大煞 **Great Sha**	午 Wu Horse		喪門 **Funeral Door**	申 Shen Monkey
大將軍 **Big General**	卯 Mao Rabbit		弔客 **Suspended Guest**	辰 Chen Dragon
力士 **Strong Man**	坤 Kun		白虎 **White Tiger**	寅 Yin Tiger
蠶室 **Silkworm Room**	艮 Gen		金神 **Golden God**	辰 Chen Dragon
蠶官 **Silkworm Officer**	丑 Chou Ox			巳 Si Snake
蠶命 **Silkworm Life**	寅 Yin Tiger		獨火 **Lonely Fire**	兌 Dui
歲刑 **Duke Punishment**	午 Wu Horse		五鬼 **Five Ghost**	戌 Xu Dog
黃幡 **Yellow Flag**	戌 Xu Dog		破敗五鬼 **Destructive Five Ghost**	兌 Dui

Negative Repair / Renovation Sectors Diagram 修方凶位圖：

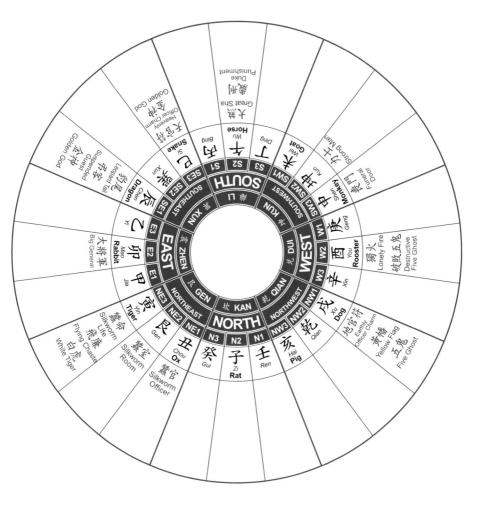

12-Month Auxiliary Stars Reference Table :
庚午年十二月，開山立向修方星表

Positive Monthly Stars 吉星方

月 MONTH	寅 Tiger (Feb 4 - Mar 5) 正月 1st Month	卯 Rabbit (Mar 6 - Apr 4) 二月 2nd Month	辰 Dragon (Apr 5 - May 5) 三月 3rd Month	巳 Snake (May 6 - Jun 5) 四月 4th Month	午 Horse (Jun 6 - July 6) 五月 5th Month	未 Goat (July 7 - Aug 7) 六月 6th Month
天道 Heavenly Path	南 South	西南 Southwest	北 North	西 West	西北 Northwest	東 East
天德 Heavenly Virtue	丁 Ding Yin Fire	坤 Kun	壬 Ren Yang Water	辛 Xin Yin Metal	乾 Qian	甲 Jia Yang Wood
天德合 Heavenly Virtue Combo	壬 Ren Yang Water	(巳)	丁 Ding Yin Fire	丙 Bing Yang Fire	(寅)	己 Ji Yin Earth
月德 Monthly Virtue	丙 Bing Yang Fire	甲 Jia Yang Wood	壬 Ren Yang Water	庚 Geng Yang Metal	丙 Bing Yang Fire	甲 Jia Yang Wood
月德合 Monthly Virtue Combo	辛 Xin Yin Metal	己 Ji Yin Earth	丁 Ding Yin Fire	乙 Yi Yin Wood	辛 Xin Yin Metal	己 Ji Yin Earth
月空 Month Emptiness	壬 Ren Yang Water	庚 Geng Yang Metal	丙 Bing Yang Fire	甲 Jia Yang Wood	壬 Ren Yang Water	庚 Geng Yang Metal
陽貴人 Yang Nobleman	兌 Duin	乾 Qian	中 Middle	巽 Xun	震 Zhen	坤 Kun
陰貴人 Yin Nobleman	坎 Kan	離 Li	艮 Gen	兌 Dui	乾 Qian	中 Middle
飛天祿 Flying Heavenly Wealth	坤 Kun	坎 Kan	離 Li	艮 Gen	兌 Dui	乾 Qian
飛天馬 Flying Heavenly Horse	坤 Kun	坎 Kan	離 Li	艮 Gen	兌 Dui	乾 Qian

12-Month Auxiliary Stars Reference Table :
庚午年十二月，開山立向修方星表

申 Monkey (Aug 8 - Sept 7) 七月 7th Month	酉 Rooster (Sept 8 - Oct 7) 八月 8th Month	戌 Dog (Oct 8 - Nov 6) 九月 9th Month	亥 Pig (Nov 7 - Dec 6) 十月 10th Month	子 Rat (Dec 7 - Jan 5) 十一月 11th Month	丑 Ox (Jan 6 - Feb 3) 十二月 12th Month	月 MONTH
北 North	東北 Northeast	南 South	東 East	東南 Southeast	西 West	天道 Heavenly Path
癸 Gui Yin Water	艮 Gen	丙 Bing Yang Fire	乙 Yi Yin Wood	巽 Xun	庚 Geng Yang Metal	天德 Heavenly Virtue
戊 Wu Yang Earth	（亥）	辛 Xin Yin Metal	庚 Geng Yang Metal	（申）	乙 Yi Yin Wood	天德合 Heavenly Virtue Combo
壬 Ren Yang Water	庚 Geng Yang Metal	丙 Bing Yang Fire	甲 Jia Yang Wood	壬 Ren Yang Water	庚 Geng Yang Metal	月德 Monthly Virtue
丁 Ding Yin Fire	乙 Yi Yin Wood	辛 Xin Yin Metal	己 Ji Yin Earth	丁 Ding Yin Fire	乙 Yi Yin Wood	月德合 Monthly Virtue Combo
丙 Bing Yang Fire	甲 Jia Yang Wood	壬 Ren Yang Water	庚 Geng Yang Metal	丙 Bing Yang Fire	甲 Jia Yang Wood	月空 Month Emptiness
坎 Kan	離 Li	艮 Gen	兌 Dui	乾 Qian	中 Middle	陽貴人 Yang Nobleman
坎 Kan	離 Li	艮 Gen	兌 Dui	乾 Qian	中 Middle	陰貴人 Yin Nobleman
中 Middle	坎 Kan	離 Li	艮 Gen	兌 Dui	乾 Qian	飛天祿 Flying Heavenly Wealth
中 Middle	坎 Kan	離 Li	艮 Gen	兌 Dui	乾 Qian	飛天馬 Flying Heavenly Horse

Monthly Purple White Stars 月紫白九星 :

寅 Tiger (Feb 4 - Mar 5) 正月 1st Month

巽 SE	離 S	坤 SW
7 Red 七赤	3 Jade 三碧	5 Yellow 五黄
6 White 六白 (震 E)	8 White 八白	1 White 一白 (兌 W)
2 Black 二黑	4 Green 四綠	9 Purple 九紫
艮 NE	坎 N	乾 NW

卯 Rabbit (Mar 6 - Apr 4) 二月 2nd Month

巽 SE	離 S	坤 SW
6 White 六白	2 Black 二黑	4 Green 四綠
5 Yellow 五黄 (震 E)	7 Red 七赤	9 Purple 九紫 (兌 W)
1 White 一白	3 Jade 三碧	8 White 八白
艮 NE	坎 N	乾 NW

辰 Dragon (Apr 5 - May 5) 三月 3rd Month

巽 SE	離 S	坤 SW
5 Yellow 五黄	1 White 一白	3 Jade 三碧
4 Green 四綠 (震 E)	6 White 六白	8 White 八白 (兌 W)
9 Purple 九紫	2 Black 二黑	7 Red 七赤
艮 NE	坎 N	乾 NW

巳 Snake (May 6 - Jun 5) 四月 4th Month

巽 SE	離 S	坤 SW
4 Green 四綠	9 Purple 九紫	2 Black 二黑
3 Jade 三碧 (震 E)	5 Yellow 五黄	7 Red 七赤 (兌 W)
8 White 八白	1 White 一白	6 White 六白
艮 NE	坎 N	乾 NW

午 Horse (Jun 6 - July 6) 五月 5th Month

巽 SE	離 S	坤 SW
3 Jade 三碧	8 White 八白	1 White 一白
2 Black 二黑 (震 E)	4 Green 四綠	6 White 六白 (兌 W)
7 Red 七赤	9 Purple 九紫	5 Yellow 五黄
艮 NE	坎 N	乾 NW

未 Goat (July 7 - Aug 7) 六月 6th Month

巽 SE	離 S	坤 SW
2 Black 二黑	7 Red 七赤	9 Purple 九紫
1 White 一白 (震 E)	3 Jade 三碧	5 Yellow 五黄 (兌 W)
6 White 六白	8 White 八白	4 Green 四綠
艮 NE	坎 N	乾 NW

申 Monkey (Aug 8 - Sept 7) 七月 7th Month

巽 SE	離 S	坤 SW
1 White 一白	6 White 六白	8 White 八白
9 Purple 九紫 (震 E)	2 Black 二黑	4 Green 四綠 (兌 W)
5 Yellow 五黄	7 Red 七赤	3 Jade 三碧
艮 NE	坎 N	乾 NW

酉 Rooster (Sept 8 - Oct 7) 八月 8th Month

巽 SE	離 S	坤 SW
9 Purple 九紫	5 Yellow 五黄	7 Red 七赤
8 White 八白 (震 E)	1 White 一白	3 Jade 三碧 (兌 W)
4 Green 四綠	6 White 六白	2 Black 二黑
艮 NE	坎 N	乾 NW

戌 Dog (Oct 8 - Nov 6) 九月 9th Month

巽 SE	離 S	坤 SW
8 White 八白	4 Green 四綠	6 White 六白
7 Red 七赤 (震 E)	9 Purple 九紫	2 Black 二黑 (兌 W)
3 Jade 三碧	5 Yellow 五黄	1 White 一白
艮 NE	坎 N	乾 NW

亥 Pig (Nov 7 - Dec 6) 十月 10th Month

巽 SE	離 S	坤 SW
7 Red 七赤	3 Jade 三碧	5 Yellow 五黄
6 White 六白 (震 E)	8 White 八白	1 White 一白 (兌 W)
2 Black 二黑	4 Green 四綠	9 Purple 九紫
艮 NE	坎 N	乾 NW

子 Rat (Dec 7 - Jan 5) 十一月 11th Month

巽 SE	離 S	坤 SW
6 White 六白	2 Black 二黑	4 Green 四綠
5 Yellow 五黄 (震 E)	7 Red 七赤	9 Purple 九紫 (兌 W)
1 White 一白	3 Jade 三碧	8 White 八白
艮 NE	坎 N	乾 NW

丑 Ox (Jan 6 - Feb 3) 十二月 12th Month

巽 SE	離 S	坤 SW
5 Yellow 五黄	1 White 一白	3 Jade 三碧
4 Green 四綠 (震 E)	6 White 六白	8 White 八白 (兌 W)
9 Purple 九紫	2 Black 二黑	7 Red 七赤
艮 NE	坎 N	乾 NW

Qi Men Three Nobles 三奇 :

Three Nobles 三奇 / Seasons	乙 Yi	丙 Bing	丁 Ding
立春 **Coming of Spring** Feb 4 - Feb 18	震 Zhen	巽 Xun	中 **Middle**
春分 **Spring Equinox** Mar 21 - Apr 4	兌 Dui	艮 Gen	離 Li
立夏 **Coming of Summer** May 6 - May 20	艮 Gen	離 Li	坎 Kan
夏至 **Summer Solstice** Jun 22 - Jul 6	中 **Middle**	巽 Xun	震 Zhen
立秋 **Coming of Autumn** Aug 8 - Aug 23	兌 Dui	乾 Qian	中 **Middle**
秋分 **Autumn Equinox** Sept 23 - Oct 7	震 Zhen	坤 Kun	坎 Kan
立冬 **Coming of Winter** Nov 7 - Nov 22	坤 Kun	坎 Kan	離 Li
冬至 **Winter Solstice** Dec 22 - Jan 5	中 **Middle**	乾 Qian	兌 Dui

Sectors to Avoid Opening Mountain 開山凶位 :

月 MONTH	月建 Month Establishment	月破 Month Destruction	月剋山家 Month Countering Sitting		陰府太歲 Yin Mansion Grand Duke	
寅 Tiger (Feb 4 - Mar 5) 正月 1st Month	寅 Yin Tiger	申 Shen Monkey	乾 Qian	兌 Dui	坤 Kun	震 Zhen
卯 Rabbit (Mar 6 - Apr 4) 二月 2nd Month	卯 Mao Rabbit	酉 You Rooster	亥 Hai Pig	丁 Ding Yin Fire	巽 Xun	艮 Gen
辰 Dragon (Apr 5 - May 5) 三月 3rd Month	辰 Chen Dragon	戌 Xu Dog	震 Zhen	巳 Si Snake	乾 Qian	兌 Dui
巳 Snake (May 6 - Jun 5) 四月 4th Month	巳 Si Snake	亥 Hai Pig	艮 Gen		坤 Kun	坎 Kan
午 Horse (Jun 6 - July 6) 五月 5th Month	午 Wu Horse	子 Zi Rat	離 Li	丙 Bing Yang Fire	離 Li	乾 Qian
未 Goat (July 7 - Aug 7) 六月 6th Month	未 Wei Goat	丑 Chou Ox	壬 Ren Yang Water	乙 Yi Yin Wood	震 Zhen	坤 Kun
申 Monkey (Aug 8 - Sept 7) 七月 7th Month	申 Shen Monkey	寅 Yin Tiger	–		艮 Gen	巽 Xun
酉 Rooster (Sept 8 - Oct 7) 八月 8th Month	酉 You Rooster	卯 Mao Rabbit	–		兌 Dui	乾 Qian
戌 Dog (Oct 8 - Nov 6) 九月 9th Month	戌 Xu Dog	辰 Chen Dragon	乾 Qian	兌 Dui	坎 Kan	坤 Kun
亥 Pig (Nov 7 - Dec 6) 十月 10th Month	亥 Hai Pig	巳 Si Snake	亥 Hai Pig	丁 Ding Yin Fire	乾 Qian	離 Li
子 Rat (Dec 7 - Jan 5) 十一月 11th Month	子 Zi Rat	午 Wu Horse	水 Water	山 Mountain	坤 Kun	震 Zhen
丑 Ox (Jan 6 - Feb 3) 十二月 12th Month	丑 Chou Ox	未 Wei Goat	土 Earth		巽 Xun	艮 Gen

Negative Repair / Renovation Sectors 修方凶位 :

月 MONTH	天官符 Heavenly Officer Charm			地官符 Earth Officer Charm			小月建 Small Month Establishment		
寅 **Tiger** (Feb 4 - Mar 5) 正月 **1st Month**	丑 *Chou* Ox	艮 *Gen*	寅 *Yin* Tiger	辰 *Chen* Dragon	巽 *Xun*	巳 *Si* Snake		中 Middle	
卯 **Rabbit** (Mar 6 - Apr 4) 二月 **2nd Month**	庚 *Geng* Yang Metal	兌 *Dui*	辛 *Xin* Yin Metal	甲 *Jia* Yang Wood	震 *Zhen*	乙 *Yi* Yin Wood	戌 *Xu* Dog	乾 *Qian*	亥 *Hai* Pig
辰 **Dragon** (Apr 5 - May 5) 三月 **3rd Month**	戌 *Xu* Dog	乾 *Qian*	亥 *Hai* Pig	未 *Wei* Goat	坤 *Kun*	申 *Shen* Monkey	庚 *Geng* Yang Metal	兌 *Dui*	辛 *Xin* Yin Metal
巳 **Snake** (May 6 - Jun 5) 四月 **4th Month**		中 Middle		壬 *Ren* Yang Water	坎 *Kan*	癸 *Gui* Yin Water	丑 *Chou* Ox	艮 *Gen*	寅 *Yin* Tiger
午 **Horse** (Jun 6 - July 6) 五月 **5th Month**	庚 *Geng* Yang Metal	兌 *Dui*	辛 *Xin* Yin Metal	丙 *Bing* Yang Fire	離 *Li*	丁 *Ding* Yin Fire	丙 *Bing* Yang Fire	離 *Li*	丁 *Ding* Yin Fire
未 **Goat** (July 7 - Aug 7) 六月 **6th Month**	戌 *Xu* Dog	乾 *Qian*	亥 *Hai* Pig	丑 *Chou* Ox	艮 *Gen*	寅 *Yin* Tiger	壬 *Ren* Yang Water	坎 *Kan*	癸 *Gui* Yin Water
申 **Monkey** (Aug 8 - Sept 7) 七月 **7th Month**		中 Middle		庚 *Geng* Yang Metal	兌 *Dui*	辛 *Xin* Yin Metal	未 *Wei* Goat	坤 *Kun*	申 *Shen* Monkey
酉 **Rooster** (Sept 8 - Oct 7) 八月 **8th Month**	辰 *Chen* Dragon	巽 *Xun*	巳 *Si* Snake	戌 *Xu* Dog	乾 *Qian*	亥 *Hai* Pig	甲 *Jia* Yang Wood	震 *Zhen*	乙 *Yi* Yin Wood
戌 **Dog** (Oct 8 - Nov 6) 九月 **9th Month**	甲 *Jia* Yang Wood	震 *Zhen*	乙 *Yi* Yin Wood		中 Middle		辰 *Chen* Dragon	巽 *Xun*	巳 *Si* Snake
亥 **Pig** (Nov 7 - Dec 6) 十月 **10th Month**	未 *Wei* Goat	坤 *Kun*	申 *Shen* Monkey	庚 *Geng* Yang Metal	兌 *Dui*	辛 *Xin* Yin Metal		中 Middle	
子 **Rat** (Dec 7 - Jan 5) 十一月 **11th Month**	壬 *Ren* Yang Water	坎 *Kan*	癸 *Gui* Yin Water	戌 *Xu* Dog	乾 *Qian*	亥 *Hai* Pig	戌 *Xu* Dog	乾 *Qian*	亥 *Hai* Pig
丑 **Ox** (Jan 6 - Feb 3) 十二月 **12th Month**	丙 *Bing* Yang Fire	離 *Li*	丁 *Ding* Yin Fire		中 Middle		庚 *Geng* Yang Metal	兌 *Dui*	辛 *Xin* Yin Metal

Negative Repair / Renovation Sectors 修方凶位 :

月 MONTH	大月建 Big Month Establishment			飛大煞 Flying Great Sha			丙丁獨火 Bing Ding Lonely Fire	
寅 **Tiger** (Feb 4 - Mar 5) 正月 **1st Month**	丑 *Chou* Ox	艮 *Gen*	寅 *Yin*	丙 *Bing* Yang Fire	離 *Li*	丁 *Ding* Yin Fire	巽 *Xun*	中 Middle
卯 **Rabbit** (Mar 6 - Apr 4) 二月 **2nd Month**	庚 *Geng* Yang Metal	兌 *Dui*	辛 *Xin* Yin Metal	丑 *Chou* Ox	艮 *Gen*	寅 *Yin*	震 *Zhen*	巽 *Xun*
辰 **Dragon** (Apr 5 - May 5) 三月 **3rd Month**	戌 *Xu* Dog	乾 *Qian*	亥 *Hai* Pig	庚 *Geng* Yang Metal	兌 *Dui*	辛 *Xin* Yin Metal	坤 *Kun*	震 *Zhen*
巳 **Snake** (May 6 - Jun 5) 四月 **4th Month**		中 Middle		戌 *Xu* Dog	乾 *Qian*	亥 *Hai* Pig	坎 *Kan*	坤 *Kun*
午 **Horse** (Jun 6 - July 6) 五月 **5th Month**	辰 *Chen* Dragon	巽 *Xun*	巳 *Si* Snake	中 Middle			離 *Li*	坎 *Kan*
未 **Goat** (July 7 - Aug 7) 六月 **6th Month**	甲 *Jia* Yang Wood	震 *Zhen*	乙 *Yi* Yin Wood	庚 *Geng* Yang Metal	兌 *Dui*	辛 *Xin* Yin Metal	艮 *Gen*	離 *Li*
申 **Monkey** (Aug 8 - Sept 7) 七月 **7th Month**	未 *Wei* Goat	坤 *Kun*	申 *Shen* Monkey	戌 *Xu* Dog	乾 *Qian*	亥 *Hai* Pig	兌 *Dui*	艮 *Gen*
酉 **Rooster** (Sept 8 - Oct 7) 八月 **8th Month**	壬 *Ren* Yang Water	坎 *Kan*	癸 *Gui* Yin Water	中 Middle			乾 *Qian*	兌 *Dui*
戌 **Dog** (Oct 8 - Nov 6) 九月 **9th Month**	丙 *Bing* Yang Fire	離 *Li*	丁 *Ding* Yin Fire	辰 *Chen* Dragon	巽 *Xun*	巳 *Si* Snake	中 Middle	乾 *Qian*
亥 **Pig** (Nov 7 - Dec 6) 十月 **10th Month**	丑 *Chou* Ox	艮 *Gen*	寅 *Yin*	甲 *Jia* Yang Wood	震 *Zhen*	乙 *Yi* Yin Wood	中 Middle	
子 **Rat** (Dec 7 - Jan 5) 十一月 **11th Month**	庚 *Geng* Yang Metal	兌 *Dui*	辛 *Xin* Yin Metal	未 *Wei* Goat	坤 *Kun*	申 *Shen* Monkey	巽 *Xun*	中 Middle
丑 **Ox** (Jan 6 - Feb 3) 十二月 **12th Month**	戌 *Xu* Dog	乾 *Qian*	亥 *Hai* Pig	壬 *Ren* Yang Water	坎 *Kan*	癸 *Gui* Yin Water	震 *Zhen*	巽 *Xun*

Negative Repair / Renovation Sectors 修方凶位 :

月 MONTH	月遊火 Month Wondering Fire	三煞 Monthly 3 Killings		
		劫煞 Robbery Sha	災煞 Calamity Sha	月煞 Month Sha
寅 **Tiger** (Feb 4 - Mar 5) 正月 **1st Month**	坤 *Kun*	亥 *Hai* Pig	子 *Zi* Rat	丑 *Chou* Ox
卯 **Rabbit** (Mar 6 - Apr 4) 二月 **2nd Month**	震 *Zhen*	申 *Shen* Monkey	酉 *You* Rooster	戌 *Xu* Dog
辰 **Dragon** (Apr 5 - May 5) 三月 **3rd Month**	巽 *Xun*	巳 *Si* Snake	午 *Wu* Horse	未 *Wei* Goat
巳 **Snake** (May 6 - Jun 5) 四月 **4th Month**	中 Middle	寅 *Yin* Tiger	卯 *Mao* Rabbit	辰 *Chen* Dragon
午 **Horse** (Jun 6 - July 6) 五月 **5th Month**	乾 *Qian*	亥 *Hai* Pig	子 *Zi* Rat	丑 *Chou* Ox
未 **Goat** (July 7 - Aug 7) 六月 **6th Month**	兌 *Dui*	申 *Shen* Monkey	酉 *You* Rooster	戌 *Xu* Dog
申 **Monkey** (Aug 8 - Sept 7) 七月 **7th Month**	艮 *Gen*	巳 *Si* Snake	午 *Wu* Horse	未 *Wei* Goat
酉 **Rooster** (Sept 8 - Oct 7) 八月 **8th Month**	離 *Li*	寅 *Yin* Tiger	卯 *Mao* Rabbit	辰 *Chen* Dragon
戌 **Dog** (Oct 8 - Nov 6) 九月 **9th Month**	坎 *Kan*	亥 *Hai* Pig	子 *Zi* Rat	丑 *Chou* Ox
亥 **Pig** (Nov 7 - Dec 6) 十月 **10th Month**	坤 *Kun*	申 *Shen* Monkey	酉 *You* Rooster	戌 *Xu* Dog
子 **Rat** (Dec 7 - Jan 5) 十一月 **11th Month**	震 *Zhen*	巳 *Si* Snake	午 *Wu* Horse	未 *Wei* Goat
丑 **Ox** (Jan 6 - Feb 3) 十二月 **12th Month**	巽 *Xun*	寅 *Yin* Tiger	卯 *Mao* Rabbit	辰 *Chen* Dragon

Negative Repair / Renovation Sectors 修方凶位 :

月 MONTH	月刑 Month Punishment	月害 Month Harm	月厭 Month Detest
寅 **Tiger** (Feb 4 - Mar 5) 正月 **1st Month**	巳 *Si* Snake	巳 *Si* Snake	戌 *Xu* Dog
卯 **Rabbit** (Mar 6 - Apr 4) 二月 **2nd Month**	子 *Zi* Rat	辰 *Chen* Dragon	酉 *You* Rooster
辰 **Dragon** (Apr 5 - May 5) 三月 **3rd Month**	辰 *Chen* Dragon	卯 *Mao* Rabbit	申 *Shen* Monkey
巳 **Snake** (May 6 - Jun 5) 四月 **4th Month**	申 *Shen* Monkey	寅 *Yin* Tiger	未 *Wei* Goat
午 **Horse** (Jun 6 - July 6) 五月 **5th Month**	午 *Wu* Horse	丑 *Chou* Ox	午 *Wu* Horse
未 **Goat** (July 7 - Aug 7) 六月 **6th Month**	丑 *Chou* Ox	子 *Zi* Rat	巳 *Si* Snake
申 **Monkey** (Aug 8 - Sept 7) 七月 **7th Month**	寅 *Yin* Tiger	亥 *Hai* Pig	辰 *Chen* Dragon
酉 **Rooster** (Sept 8 - Oct 7) 八月 **8th Month**	酉 *You* Rooster	戌 *Xu* Dog	卯 *Mao* Rabbit
戌 **Dog** (Oct 8 - Nov 6) 九月 **9th Month**	未 *Wei* Goat	酉 *You* Rooster	寅 *Yin* Tiger
亥 **Pig** (Nov 7 - Dec 6) 十月 **10th Month**	亥 *Hai* Pig	申 *Shen* Monkey	丑 *Chou* Ox
子 **Rat** (Dec 7 - Jan 5) 十一月 **11th Month**	卯 *Mao* Rabbit	未 *Wei* Goat	子 *Zi* Rat
丑 **Ox** (Jan 6 - Feb 3) 十二月 **12th Month**	戌 *Xu* Dog	午 *Wu* Horse	亥 *Hai* Pig

庚申 (Geng Shen)
Metal Monkey

Heavenly Stem 天干	庚 **Yang Metal** (陽金)
Earthly Branch 地支	申 **Monkey** (Yang Metal 陽金)
Hidden Stem 藏干	庚 **Yang Metal**, 壬 **Yang Water**, 戊 **Yang Earth**
Na Yin 納音	石榴木 **Wood from guava tree**
Grand Duke 太歲	申 **Monkey**
Xuan Kong Five Element 玄空五行	**7** 火 **Fire**
Gua Name 卦名	☵ 坎爲水 **Water**
Xuan Kong Period Luck 玄空卦運	**1**

Annual Positive Stars for Opening Mountain, Establishing Facing and Commencing Repairs 開山立向修方吉星：

歲德 **Duke Virtue**	庚 Geng **Yang Metal**	
歲德合 **Duke Virtue Combo**	乙 Yi **Yin Wood**	
歲枝德 **Duke Branch Virtue**	丑 Chou **Ox**	
陽貴人 **Yang Nobleman**	丑 Chou **Ox**	
陰貴人 **Yin Nobleman**	未 Wei **Goat**	
歲祿 **Duke Prosperous**	申 Shen **Monkey**	
歲馬 **Duke Horse**	寅 Yin **Tiger**	
奏書 **Decree**	坤 Kun	
博士 **Professor**	艮 Gen	

Annual Negative Stars for Opening Mountain, Establishing Facing and Commencing Repairs 開山立向修方凶星：

太歲 Grand Duke	歲破 Year Breaker	三煞 Three Killings			坐煞向煞 Sitting Sha Facing Sha				浮天空亡 Floating Heaven Emptiness	
申 Shen Monkey	寅 Yin Tiger	巳 Si Snake	午 Wu Horse	未 Wei Goat	丙 Bing Yang Fire	丁 Ding Yin Fire	壬 Ren Yang Water	癸 Gui Yin Water	兌 Dui	丁 Ding Yin Fire

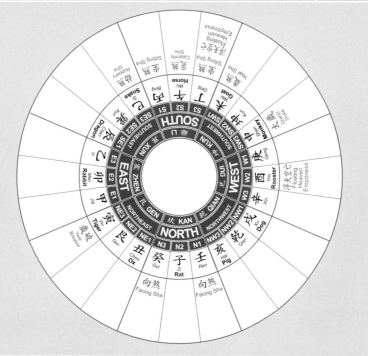

Annual San Yuan Purple White Stars 三元紫白九星：

上元 Upper Period Period 1, 2, 3			中元 Middle Period Period 4, 5, 6			下元 Lower Period Period 7, 8, 9		
巽SE **7**	離S **3**	坤SW **5**	巽SE **1**	離S **6**	坤SW **8**	巽SE **4**	離S **9**	坤SW **2**
震E **6**	**8** 庚申 Geng Shen Metal Monkey	兌W **1**	震E **9**	**2** 庚申 Geng Shen Metal Monkey	兌W **4**	震E **3**	**5** 庚申 Geng Shen Metal Monkey	兌W **7**
艮NE **2**	坎N **4**	乾NW **9**	艮NE **5**	坎N **7**	乾NW **3**	艮NE **8**	坎N **1**	乾NW **6**

Mountain Covering Yellow Path 蓋山黃道：

貪狼 Tan Lang **Greedy Wolf**		巨門 Ju Men **Huge Door**				武曲 Wu Qu **Military Arts**		文曲 Wen Qu **Literary Arts**			
坤 Kun SW2	乙 Yi E3	坎 Kan N2	癸 Gui N3	申 Shen SW3	辰 Chen SE1	乾 Qian NW2	甲 Jia E1	震 Zhen E2	庚 Geng W1	亥 Hai NW3	未 Wei SW1

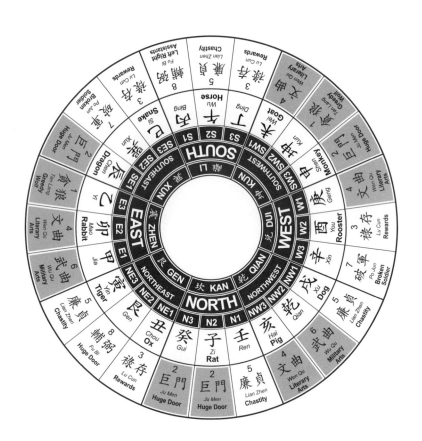

Heaven Penetrating Force 通天竅：

三合前方 **Facing Three Harmony**	艮寅 *Gen Yin*	甲卯 *Jia Mao*	乙辰 *Yi Chen*
三合後方 **Sitting Three Harmony**	坤申 *Kun Shen*	庚酉 *Geng You*	辛戌 *Xin Xu*

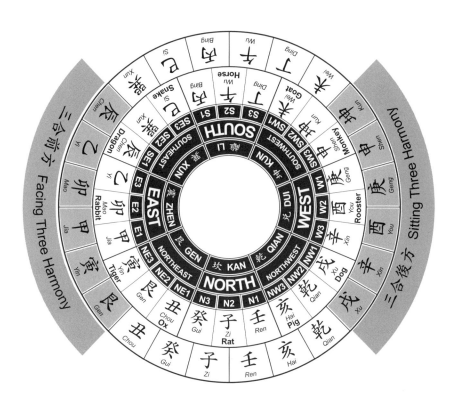

Moving Horse Six Ren Assessment 走馬六壬：

神后 Shen Hou **Holy Empress**	功曹 Gong Cao **Marshall**	天罡 Tian Gang **Heavenly Dipper**	勝光 Sheng Guang **Subliminal Bright**	傳送 Chuan Song **Great General**	河魁 He Kui **River Scholar**
乙辰 Yi Chen	丙午 Bing Wu	坤申 Kun Shen	辛戌 Xin Xu	壬子 Ren Zi	艮寅 Gen Yin

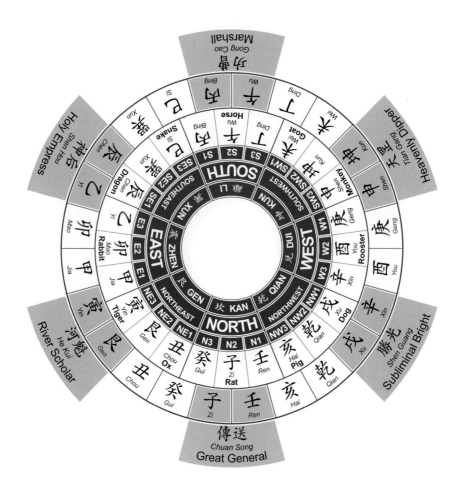

Four Advantages Three Cycles Star Plate 四利三元：

太陽 *Tai Yang* **Sun**	太陰 *Tai Yin* **Moon**	龍德 *Long De* **Dragon Virtue**	福德 *Fu De* **Fortune Virtue**
酉 *You* **Rooster**	亥 *Hai* **Pig**	卯 *Mao* **Rabbit**	巳 *Si* **Snake**

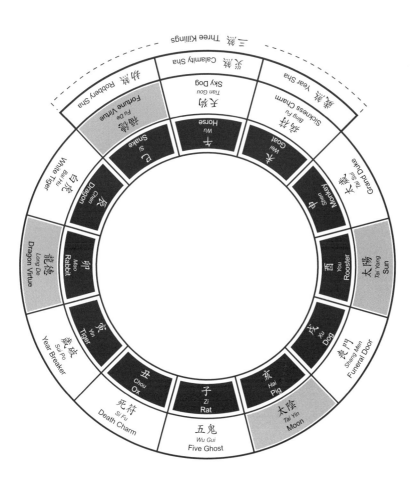

Negative Sectors For Opening Mountain 開山凶位：

年剋山家 Year Countering Sitting

離 Li S2	壬 Ren N1	丙 Bing S1	乙 Yi E3

陰府太歲 Yin Fu Tai Sui **Yin Mansion Grand Duke**	六害 Liu Hai **Six Harm**	死符 Si Fu **Death Charm**	炙退 Zhi Tui **Roasting Star**
乾 Qian NW2	兌 Dui W2	亥 Hai NW3	丑 Chou NE1	卯 Mao E2

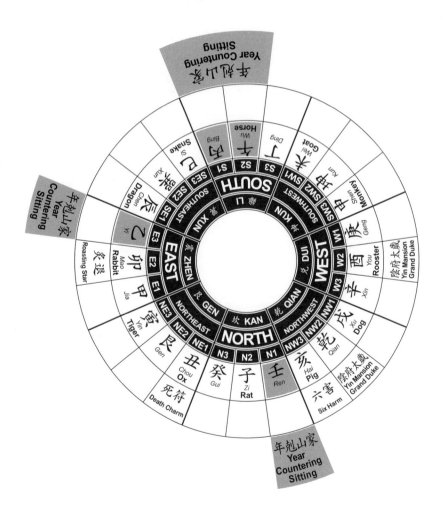

Negative Directions to Establish Facing 立向凶方:

巡山羅喉 *Xun Shan Luo Hou* **Mountain Patrol Luo Hou Star**	病符 *Bing Fu* **Sickness Charm**
庚 *Geng* **W1**	未 *Wei* **SW1**

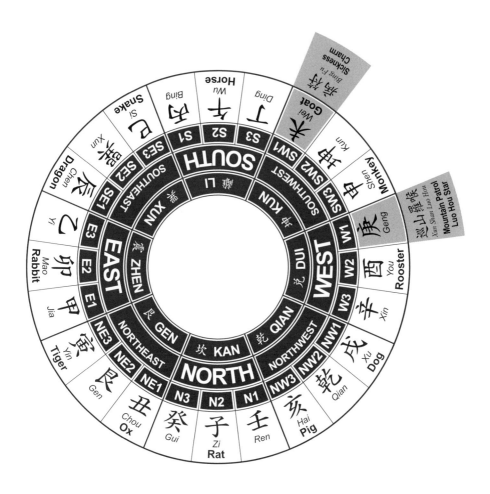

Negative Repair / Renovation Sectors Table 修方凶位表：

天官符 Heavenly Officer Charm	亥 *Hai* Pig		豹尾 Leopard Tail	戌 *Xu* Dog
地官符 Earthly Officer Charm	子 *Zi* Rat		飛廉 Flying Chaste	辰 *Chen* Dragon
大煞 Great Sha	子 *Zi* Rat		喪門 Funeral Door	戌 *Xu* Dog
大將軍 Big General	午 *Wu* Horse		弔客 Suspended Guest	午 *Wu* Horse
力士 Strong Man	乾 *Qian*		白虎 White Tiger	辰 *Chen* Dragon
蠶室 Silkworm Room	巽 *Xun*		金神 Golden God	辰 *Chen* Dragon 巳 *Si* Snake
蠶官 Silkworm Officer	辰 *Chen* Dragon			
蠶命 Silkworm Life	巳 *Si* Snake		獨火 Lonely Fire	離 *Li*
歲刑 Duke Punishment	寅 *Yin* Tiger		五鬼 Five Ghost	申 *Shen* Monkey
黃幡 Yellow Flag	辰 *Chen* Dragon		破敗五鬼 Destructive Five Ghost	兌 *Dui*

Negative Repair / Renovation Sectors Diagram 修方凶位圖：

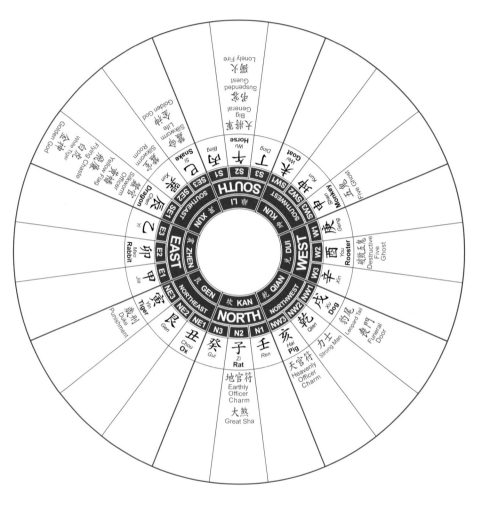

12-Month Auxiliary Stars Reference Table :
庚申年十二月，開山立向修方星表

Positive Monthly Stars 吉星方

月 MONTH	寅 Tiger (Feb 4 - Mar 5) 正月 1st Month	卯 Rabbit (Mar 6 - Apr 4) 二月 2nd Month	辰 Dragon (Apr 5 - May 5) 三月 3rd Month	巳 Snake (May 6 - Jun 5) 四月 4th Month	午 Horse (Jun 6 - July 6) 五月 5th Month	未 Goat (July 7 - Aug 7) 六月 6th Month
天道 Heavenly Path	南 South	西南 Southwest	北 North	西 West	西北 Northwest	東 East
天德 Heavenly Virtue	丁 Ding Yin Fire	坤 Kun (申)	壬 Ren Yang Water	辛 Xin Yin Metal	乾 Qian (亥)	甲 Jia Yang Wood
天德合 Heavenly Virtue Combo	壬 Ren Yang Water	(巳)	丁 Ding Yin Fire	丙 Bing Yang Fire	(寅)	己 Ji Yin Earth
月德 Monthly Virtue	丙 Bing Yang Fire	甲 Jia Yang Wood	壬 Ren Yang Water	庚 Geng Yang Metal	丙 Bing Yang Fire	甲 Jia Yang Wood
月德合 Monthly Virtue Combo	辛 Xin Yin Metal	己 Ji Yin Earth	丁 Ding Yin Fire	乙 Yi Yin Wood	辛 Xin Yin Metal	己 Ji Yin Earth
月空 Month Emptiness	壬 Ren Yang Water	庚 Geng Yang Metal	丙 Bing Yang Fire	甲 Jia Yang Wood	壬 Ren Yang Water	庚 Geng Yang Metal
陽貴人 Yang Nobleman	兌 Dui	乾 Qian	中 Middle	巽 Xun	震 Zhen	坤 Kun
陰貴人 Yin Nobleman	坎 Kan	離 Li	艮 Gen	兌 Dui	乾 Qian	中 Middle
飛天祿 Flying Heavenly Wealth	坤 Kun	坎 Kan	離 Lii	艮 Gen	兌 Dui	乾 Qian
飛天馬 Flying Heavenly Horse	中 Middle	坎 Kan	離 Li	艮 Gen	兌 Dui	乾 Qian

12-Month Auxiliary Stars Reference Table :
庚申年十二月，開山立向修方星表

申 Monkey (Aug 8 - Sept 7) 七月 7th Month	酉 Rooster (Sept 8 - Oct 7) 八月 8th Month	戌 Dog (Oct 8 - Nov 6) 九月 9th Month	亥 Pig (Nov 7 - Dec 6) 十月 10th Month	子 Rat (Dec 7 - Jan 5) 十一月 11th Month	丑 Ox (Jan 6 - Feb 3) 十二月 12th Month	月 MONTH
北 North	東北 Northeast	南 South	東 East	東南 Southeast	西 West	天道 Heavenly Path
癸 Gui Yin Water	艮 Gen (寅)	丙 Bing Yang Fire	乙 Yi Yin Wood	巽 Xun (巳)	庚 Geng Yang Metal	天德 Heavenly Virtue
戊 Wu Yang Earth	(亥)	辛 Xin Yin Metal	庚 Geng Yang Metal	(申)	乙 Yi Yin Wood	天德合 Heavenly Virtue Combo
壬 Ren Yang Water	庚 Geng Yang Metal	丙 Bing Yang Fire	甲 Jia Yang Wood	壬 Ren Yang Water	庚 Geng Yang Metal	月德 Monthly Virtue
丁 Ding Yin Fire	乙 Yi Yin Wood	辛 Xin Yin Metal	己 Ji Yin Earth	丁 Ding Yin Fire	乙 Yi Yin Wood	月德合 Monthly Virtue Combo
丙 Bing Yang Fire	甲 Jia Yang Wood	壬 Ren Yang Water	庚 Geng Yang Metal	丙 Bing Yang Fire	甲 Jia Yang Wood	月空 Month Emptiness
坎 Kan	離 Li	艮 Gen	兌 Dui	乾 Qian	中 Middle	陽貴人 Yang Nobleman
坎 Kan	離 Li	艮 Gen	兌 Dui	乾 Qian	中 Middle	陰貴人 Yin Nobleman
中 Middle	坎 Kan	離 Lii	艮 Gen	兌 Dui	乾 Qian	飛天祿 Flying Heavenly Wealth
中 Middle	巽 Xun	震 Zhen	坤 Kun	坎 Kan	離 Lii	飛天馬 Flying Heavenly Horse

Monthly Purple White Stars 月紫白九星 :

寅 Tiger (Feb 4 - Mar 5) 正月 1st Month

巽SE	離S	坤SW
1 White 一白	6 White 六白	8 White 八白
震E 9 Purple 九紫	2 Black 二黑	4 Green 四綠 兌W
艮NE 5 Yellow 五黃	坎N 7 Red 七赤	乾NW 3 Jade 三碧

卯 Rabbit (Mar 6 - Apr 4) 二月 2nd Month

巽SE	離S	坤SW
9 Purple 九紫	5 Yellow 五黃	7 Red 七赤
震E 8 White 八白	1 White 一白	3 Jade 三碧 兌W
艮NE 4 Green 四綠	坎N 6 White 六白	乾NW 2 Black 二黑

辰 Dragon (Apr 5 - May 5) 三月 3rd Month

巽SE	離S	坤SW
8 White 八白	4 Green 四綠	6 White 六白
震E 7 Red 七赤	9 Purple 九紫	2 Black 二黑 兌W
艮NE 3 Jade 三碧	坎N 5 Yellow 五黃	乾NW 1 White 一白

巳 Snake (May 6 - Jun 5) 四月 4th Month

巽SE	離S	坤SW
7 Red 七赤	3 Jade 三碧	5 Yellow 五黃
震E 6 White 六白	8 White 八白	1 White 一白 兌W
艮NE 2 Black 二黑	坎N 4 Green 四綠	乾NW 9 Purple 九紫

午 Horse (Jun 6 - July 6) 五月 5th Month

巽SE	離S	坤SW
6 White 六白	2 Black 二黑	4 Green 四綠
震E 5 Yellow 五黃	7 Red 七赤	9 Purple 九紫 兌W
艮NE 1 White 一白	坎N 3 Jade 三碧	乾NW 8 White 八白

未 Goat (July 7 - Aug 7) 六月 6th Month

巽SE	離S	坤SW
5 Yellow 五黃	1 White 一白	3 Jade 三碧
震E 4 Green 四綠	6 White 六白	8 White 八白 兌W
艮NE 9 Purple 九紫	坎N 2 Black 二黑	乾NW 7 Red 七赤

申 Monkey (Aug 8 - Sept 7) 七月 7th Month

巽SE	離S	坤SW
4 Green 四綠	9 Purple 九紫	2 Black 二黑
震E 3 Jade 三碧	5 Yellow 五黃	7 Red 七赤 兌W
艮NE 8 White 八白	坎N 1 White 一白	乾NW 6 White 六白

酉 Rooster (Sept 8 - Oct 7) 八月 8th Month

巽SE	離S	坤SW
3 Jade 三碧	8 White 八白	1 White 一白
震E 2 Black 二黑	4 Green 四綠	6 White 六白 兌W
艮NE 7 Red 七赤	坎N 9 Purple 九紫	乾NW 5 Yellow 五黃

戌 Dog (Oct 8 - Nov 6) 九月 9th Month

巽SE	離S	坤SW
2 Black 二黑	7 Red 七赤	9 Purple 九紫
震E 1 White 一白	3 Jade 三碧	5 Yellow 五黃 兌W
艮NE 6 White 六白	坎N 8 White 八白	乾NW 4 Green 四綠

亥 Pig (Nov 7 - Dec 6) 十月 10th Month

巽SE	離S	坤SW
1 White 一白	6 White 六白	8 White 八白
震E 9 Purple 九紫	2 Black 二黑	4 Green 四綠 兌W
艮NE 5 Yellow 五黃	坎N 7 Red 七赤	乾NW 3 Jade 三碧

子 Rat (Dec 7 - Jan 5) 十一月 11th Month

巽SE	離S	坤SW
9 Purple 九紫	5 Yellow 五黃	7 Red 七赤
震E 8 White 八白	1 White 一白	3 Jade 三碧 兌W
艮NE 4 Green 四綠	坎N 6 White 六白	乾NW 2 Black 二黑

丑 Ox (Jan 6 - Feb 3) 十二月 12th Month

巽SE	離S	坤SW
8 White 八白	4 Green 四綠	6 White 六白
震E 7 Red 七赤	9 Purple 九紫	2 Black 二黑 兌W
艮NE 3 Jade 三碧	坎N 5 Yellow 五黃	乾NW 1 White 一白

Qi Men Three Nobles 三奇 :

Three Nobles 三奇 / Seasons	乙 Yi	丙 Bing	丁 Ding
立春 **Coming of Spring** Feb 4 - Feb 18	艮 Gen	離 Li	坎 Kan
春分 **Spring Equinox** Mar 21 - Apr 4	震 Zhen	巽 Xun	中 **Middle**
立夏 **Coming of Summer** May 6 - May 20	巽 Xun	中 **Middle**	乾 Qian
夏至 **Summer Solstice** Jun 22 - Jul 6	離 Li	艮 Gen	兌 Dui
立秋 **Coming of Autumn** Aug 8 - Aug 23	坤 Kun	坎 Kan	離 Li
秋分 **Autumn Equinox** Sept 23 - Oct 7	兌 Dui	乾 Qian	中 **Middle**
立冬 **Coming of Winter** Nov 7 - Nov 22	乾 Qian	中 **Middle**	巽 Xun
冬至 **Winter Solstice** Dec 22 - Jan 5	坎 Kan	坤 Kun	震 Zhen

Sectors to Avoid Opening Mountain 開山凶位 :

月 MONTH	月建 Month Establishment	月破 Month Destruction	月剋山家 Month Countering Sitting		陰府太歲 Yin Mansion Grand Duke	
寅 **Tiger** (Feb 4 - Mar 5) 正月 **1st Month**	寅 *Yin* **Tiger**	申 *Shen* **Monkey**	乾 *Qian*	兌 *Dui*	坤 *Kun*	震 *Zhen*
卯 **Rabbit** (Mar 6 - Apr 4) 二月 **2nd Month**	卯 *Mao* **Rabbit**	酉 *You* **Rooster**	亥 *Hai* **Pig**	丁 *Ding* **Yin Fire**	巽 *Xun*	艮 *Gen*
辰 **Dragon** (Apr 5 - May 5) 三月 **3rd Month**	辰 *Chen* **Dragon**	戌 *Xu* **Dog**	震 *Zhen*	巳 *Si* **Snake**	乾 *Qian*	兌 *Dui*
巳 **Snake** (May 6 - Jun 5) 四月 **4th Month**	巳 *Si* **Snake**	亥 *Hai* **Pig**	艮 *Gen*		坤 *Kun*	坎 *Kan*
午 **Horse** (Jun 6 - July 6) 五月 **5th Month**	午 *Wu* **Horse**	子 *Zi* **Rat**	離 *Li*	丙 *Bing* **Yang Fire**	離 *Li*	乾 *Qian*
未 **Goat** (July 7 - Aug 7) 六月 **6th Month**	未 *Wei* **Goat**	丑 *Chou* **Ox**	壬 *Ren* **Yang Water**	乙 *Yi* **Yin Wood**	震 *Zhen*	坤 *Kun*
申 **Monkey** (Aug 8 - Sept 7) 七月 **7th Month**	申 *Shen* **Monkey**	寅 *Yin* **Tiger**	–		艮 *Gen*	巽 *Xun*
酉 **Rooster** (Sept 8 - Oct 7) 八月 **8th Month**	酉 *You* **Rooster**	卯 *Mao* **Rabbit**	–		兌 *Dui*	乾 *Qian*
戌 **Dog** (Oct 8 - Nov 6) 九月 **9th Month**	戌 *Xu* **Dog**	辰 *Chen* **Dragon**	乾 *Qian*	兌 *Dui*	坎 *Kan*	坤 *Kun*
亥 **Pig** (Nov 7 - Dec 6) 十月 **10th Month**	亥 *Hai* **Pig**	巳 *Si* **Snake**	亥 *Hai* **Pig**	丁 *Ding* **Yin Fire**	乾 *Qian*	離 *Li*
子 **Rat** (Dec 7 - Jan 5) 十一月 **11th Month**	子 *Zi* **Rat**	午 *Wu* **Horse**	水 **Water**	山 **Mountain**	坤 *Kun*	震 *Zhen*
丑 **Ox** (Jan 6 - Feb 3) 十二月 **12th Month**	丑 *Chou* **Ox**	未 *Wei* **Goat**	土 **Earth**		巽 *Xun*	艮 *Gen*

Negative Repair / Renovation Sectors 修方凶位 :

月 MONTH	天官符 Heavenly Officer Charm			地官符 Earth Officer Charm			小月建 Small Month Establishment		
寅 **Tiger** (Feb 4 - Mar 5) 正月 **1st Month**		中 Middle		戌 *Xu* Dog	乾 *Qian*	亥 *Hai* Pig		中 Middle	
卯 **Rabbit** (Mar 6 - Apr 4) 二月 **2nd Month**	辰 *Chen* Dragon	巽 *Xun*	巳 *Si* Snake		中 Middle		戌 *Xu* Dog	乾 *Qian*	亥 *Hai* Pig
辰 **Dragon** (Apr 5 - May 5) 三月 **3rd Month**	甲 *Jia* Yang Wood	震 *Zhen*	乙 *Yi* Yin Wood	辰 *Chen* Dragon	巽 *Xun*	巳 *Si* Snake	庚 *Geng* Yang Metal	兑 *Dui*	辛 *Xin* Yin Metal
巳 **Snake** (May 6 - Jun 5) 四月 **4th Month**	未 *Wei* Goat	坤 *Kun*	申 *Shen* Monkey	甲 *Jia* Yang Wood	震 *Zhen*	乙 *Yi* Yin Wood	丑 *Chou* Ox	艮 *Gen*	寅 *Yin* Tiger
午 **Horse** (Jun 6 - July 6) 五月 **5th Month**	壬 *Ren* Yang Water	坎 *Kan*	癸 *Gui* Yin Water	未 *Wei* Goat	坤 *Kun*	申 *Shen* Monkey	丙 *Bing* Yang Fire	離 *Li*	丁 *Ding* Yin Fire
未 **Goat** (July 7 - Aug 7) 六月 **6th Month**	丙 *Bing* Yang Fire	離 *Li*	丁 *Ding* Yin Fire	壬 *Ren* Yang Water	坎 *Kan*	癸 *Gui* Yin Water	壬 *Ren* Yang Water	坎 *Kan*	癸 *Gui* Yin Water
申 **Monkey** (Aug 8 - Sept 7) 七月 **7th Month**	丑 *Chou* Ox	艮 *Gen*	寅 *Yin* Tiger	丙 *Bing* Yang Fire	離 *Li*	丁 *Ding* Yin Fire	未 *Wei* Goat	坤 *Kun*	申 *Shen* Monkey
酉 **Rooster** (Sept 8 - Oct 7) 八月 **8th Month**	庚 *Geng* Yang Metal	兑 *Dui*	辛 *Xin* Yin Metal	丑 *Chou* Ox	艮 *Gen*	寅 *Yin* Tiger	甲 *Jia* Yang Wood	震 *Zhen*	乙 *Yi* Yin Wood
戌 **Dog** (Oct 8 - Nov 6) 九月 **9th Month**	戌 *Xu* Dog	乾 *Qian*	亥 *Hai* Pig	庚 *Geng* Yang Metal	兑 *Dui*	辛 *Xin* Yin Metal	辰 *Chen* Dragon	巽 *Xun*	巳 *Si* Snake
亥 **Pig** (Nov 7 - Dec 6) 十月 **10th Month**		中 Middle		戌 *Xu* Dog	乾 *Qian*	亥 *Hai* Pig		中 Middle	
子 **Rat** (Dec 7 - Jan 5) 十一月 **11th Month**	庚 *Geng* Yang Metal	兑 *Dui*	辛 *Xin* Yin Metal		中 Middle		戌 *Xu* Dog	乾 *Qian*	亥 *Hai* Pig
丑 **Ox** (Jan 6 - Feb 3) 十二月 **12th Month**	戌 *Xu* Dog	乾 *Qian*	亥 *Hai* Pig	庚 *Geng* Yang Metal	兑 *Dui*	辛 *Xin* Yin Metal	庚 *Geng* Yang Metal	兑 *Dui*	辛 *Xin* Yin Metal

Negative Repair / Renovation Sectors 修方凶位 :

月 MONTH	大月建 Big Month Establishment			飛大煞 Flying Great Sha			丙丁獨火 Bing Ding Lonely Fire	
寅 **Tiger** (Feb 4 - Mar 5) 正月 **1st Month**	未 Wei Goat	坤 Kun	申 Shen Monkey	戌 Xu Dog	乾 Qian	亥 Hai Pig	巽 Xun	中 Middle
卯 **Rabbit** (Mar 6 - Apr 4) 二月 **2nd Month**	壬 Ren Yang Water	坎 Kan	癸 Gui Yin Water	中 Middle			震 Zhen	巽 Xun
辰 **Dragon** (Apr 5 - May 5) 三月 **3rd Month**	丙 Bing Yang Fire	離 Li	丁 Ding Yin Fire	辰 Chen Dragon	巽 Xun	巳 Si Snake	坤 Kun	震 Zhen
巳 **Snake** (May 6 - Jun 5) 四月 **4th Month**	丑 Chou Ox	艮 Gen	寅 Yin Tiger	甲 Jia Yang Wood	震 Zhen	乙 Yi Yin Wood	坎 Kan	坤 Kun
午 **Horse** (Jun 6 - July 6) 五月 **5th Month**	庚 Geng Yang Metal	兌 Dui	辛 Xin Yin Metal	未 Wei Goat	坤 Kun	申 Shen Monkey	離 Li	坎 Kan
未 **Goat** (July 7 - Aug 7) 六月 **6th Month**	戌 Xu Dog	乾 Qian	亥 Hai Pig	壬 Ren Yang Water	坎 Kan	癸 Gui Yin Water	艮 Gen	離 Li
申 **Monkey** (Aug 8 - Sept 7) 七月 **7th Month**	中 Middle			丙 Bing Yang Fire	離 Li	丁 Ding Yin Fire	兌 Dui	艮 Gen
酉 **Rooster** (Sept 8 - Oct 7) 八月 **8th Month**	辰 Chen Dragon	巽 Xun	巳 Si Snake	丑 Chou Ox	艮 Gen	寅 Yin Tiger	乾 Qian	兌 Dui
戌 **Dog** (Oct 8 - Nov 6) 九月 **9th Month**	甲 Jia Yang Wood	震 Zhen	乙 Yi Yin Wood	庚 Geng Yang Metal	兌 Dui	辛 Xin Yin Metal	中 Middle	乾 Qian
亥 **Pig** (Nov 7 - Dec 6) 十月 **10th Month**	未 Wei Goat	坤 Kun	申 Shen Monkey	戌 Xu Dog	乾 Qian	亥 Hai Pig	中 Middle	
子 **Rat** (Dec 7 - Jan 5) 十一月 **11th Month**	壬 Ren Yang Water	坎 Kan	癸 Gui Yin Water	中 Middle			巽 Xun	中 Middle
丑 **Ox** (Jan 6 - Feb 3) 十二月 **12th Month**	丙 Bing Yang Fire	離 Li	丁 Ding Yin Fire	庚 Geng Yang Metal	兌 Dui	辛 Xin Yin Metal	震 Zhen	巽 Xun

Negative Repair / Renovation Sectors 修方凶位 :

月 MONTH	月遊火 Month Wondering Fire	三煞 Monthly 3 Killings		
		劫煞 Robbery Sha	災煞 Calamity Sha	月煞 Month Sha
寅 **Tiger** (Feb 4 - Mar 5) 正月 **1st Month**	兌 Dui	亥 Hai Pig	子 Zi Rat	丑 Chou Ox
卯 **Rabbit** (Mar 6 - Apr 4) 二月 **2nd Month**	艮 Gen	申 Shen Monkey	酉 You Rooster	戌 Xu Dog
辰 **Dragon** (Apr 5 - May 5) 三月 **3rd Month**	離 Li	巳 Si Snake	午 Wu Horse	未 Wei Goat
巳 **Snake** (May 6 - Jun 5) 四月 **4th Month**	坎 Kan	寅 Yin Tiger	卯 Mao Rabbit	辰 Chen Dragon
午 **Horse** (Jun 6 - July 6) 五月 **5th Month**	坤 Kun	亥 Hai Pig	子 Zi Rat	丑 Chou Ox
未 **Goat** (July 7 - Aug 7) 六月 **6th Month**	震 Zhen	申 Shen Monkey	酉 You Rooster	戌 Xu Dog
申 **Monkey** (Aug 8 - Sept 7) 七月 **7th Month**	巽 Xun	巳 Si Snake	午 Wu Horse	未 Wei Goat
酉 **Rooster** (Sept 8 - Oct 7) 八月 **8th Month**	中 Middle	寅 Yin Tiger	卯 Mao Rabbit	辰 Chen Dragon
戌 **Dog** (Oct 8 - Nov 6) 九月 **9th Month**	乾 Qian	亥 Hai Pig	子 Zi Rat	丑 Chou Ox
亥 **Pig** (Nov 7 - Dec 6) 十月 **10th Month**	兌 Dui	申 Shen Monkey	酉 You Rooster	戌 Xu Dog
子 **Rat** (Dec 7 - Jan 5) 十一月 **11th Month**	艮 Gen	巳 Si Snake	午 Wu Horse	未 Wei Goat
丑 **Ox** (Jan 6 - Feb 3) 十二月 **12th Month**	離 Li	寅 Yin Tiger	卯 Mao Rabbit	辰 Chen Dragon

Negative Repair / Renovation Sectors 修方凶位 :

月 MONTH	月刑 Month Punishment	月害 Month Harm	月厭 Month Detest
寅 **Tiger** (Feb 4 - Mar 5) 正月 **1st Month**	巳 Si **Snake**	巳 Si **Snake**	戌 Xu **Dog**
卯 **Rabbit** (Mar 6 - Apr 4) 二月 **2nd Month**	子 Zi **Rat**	辰 Chen **Dragon**	酉 You **Rooster**
辰 **Dragon** (Apr 5 - May 5) 三月 **3rd Month**	辰 Chen **Dragon**	卯 Mao **Rabbit**	申 Shen **Monkey**
巳 **Snake** (May 6 - Jun 5) 四月 **4th Month**	申 Shen **Monkey**	寅 Yin **Tiger**	未 Wei **Goat**
午 **Horse** (Jun 6 - July 6) 五月 **5th Month**	午 Wu **Horse**	丑 Chou **Ox**	午 Wu **Horse**
未 **Goat** (July 7 - Aug 7) 六月 **6th Month**	丑 Chou **Ox**	子 Zi **Rat**	巳 Si **Snake**
申 **Monkey** (Aug 8 - Sept 7) 七月 **7th Month**	寅 Yin **Tiger**	亥 Hai **Pig**	辰 Chen **Dragon**
酉 **Rooster** (Sept 8 - Oct 7) 八月 **8th Month**	酉 You **Rooster**	戌 Xu **Dog**	卯 Mao **Rabbit**
戌 **Dog** (Oct 8 - Nov 6) 九月 **9th Month**	未 Wei **Goat**	酉 You **Rooster**	寅 Yin **Tiger**
亥 **Pig** (Nov 7 - Dec 6) 十月 **10th Month**	亥 Hai **Pig**	申 Shen **Monkey**	丑 Chou **Ox**
子 **Rat** (Dec 7 - Jan 5) 十一月 **11th Month**	卯 Mao **Rabbit**	未 Wei **Goat**	子 Zi **Rat**
丑 **Ox** (Jan 6 - Feb 3) 十二月 **12th Month**	戌 Xu **Dog**	午 Wu **Horse**	亥 Hai **Pig**

庚戌 (Geng Xu)
Metal Dog

Heavenly Stem 天干	庚 Yang Metal (陽金)
Earthly Branch 地支	戌 Dog (Yang Earth 陽土)
Hidden Stem 藏干	戊 Yang Earth, 辛 Yin Metal , 丁 Yin Fire
Na Yin 納音	釵釧金 Metal from the Ornaments
Grand Duke 太歲	戌 Dog
Xuan Kong Five Element 玄空五行	9 金 Metal
Gua Name 卦名	䷋ 天地否 Stagnation
Xuan Kong Period Luck 玄空卦運	9

Annual Positive Stars for Opening Mountain, Establishing Facing and Commencing Repairs 開山立向修方吉星:

歲德 **Duke Virtue**	庚 Geng **Yang Metal**
歲德合 **Duke Virtue Combo**	乙 Yi **Yin Wood**
歲枝德 **Duke Branch Virtue**	卯 Mao **Rabbit**
陽貴人 **Yang Nobleman**	丑 Chou **Ox**
陰貴人 **Yin Nobleman**	未 Wei **Goat**
歲祿 **Duke Prosperous**	申 Shen **Monkey**
歲馬 **Duke Horse**	申 Shen **Monkey**
奏書 **Decree**	坤 Kun
博士 **Professor**	艮 Gen

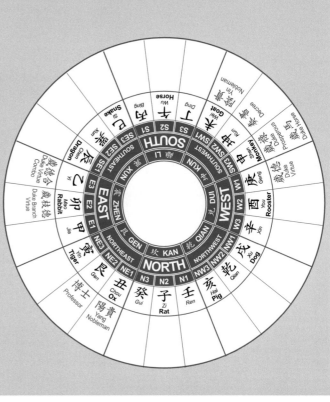

822

Annual Negative Stars for Opening Mountain, Establishing Facing and Commencing Repairs 開山立向修方凶星：

太歲 Grand Duke	歲破 Year Breaker	三煞 Three Killings			坐煞向煞 Sitting Sha Facing Sha				浮天空亡 Floating Heaven Emptiness	
戌 Xu Dog	辰 Chen Dragon	亥 Hai Pig	子 Zi Rat	丑 Chou Ox	壬 Ren Yang Water	癸 Gui Yin Water	丙 Bing Yang Fire	丁 Ding Yin Fire	兌 Dui	丁 Ding Yin Fire

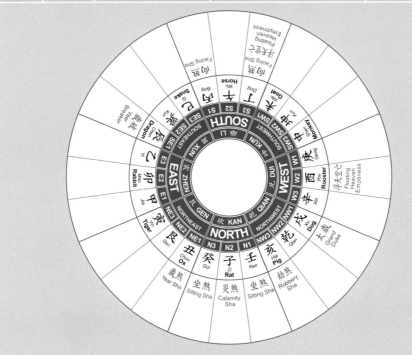

Annual San Yuan Purple White Stars 三元紫白九星：

上元 Upper Period Period 1, 2, 3		
巽SE **8**	離S **4**	坤SW **6**
震E **7**	**9** 庚戌 Geng Xu Metal Dog	兌W **2**
艮NE **3**	坎N **5**	乾NW **1**

中元 Middle Period Period 4, 5, 6		
巽SE **2**	離S **7**	坤SW **9**
震E **1**	**3** 庚戌 Geng Xu Metal Dog	兌W **5**
艮NE **6**	坎N **8**	乾NW **4**

下元 Lower Period Period 7, 8, 9		
巽SE **5**	離S **1**	坤SW **3**
震E **4**	**6** 庚戌 Geng Xu Metal Dog	兌W **8**
艮NE **9**	坎N **2**	乾NW **7**

Mountain Covering Yellow Path 蓋山黃道：

貪狼 *Tan Lang* **Greedy Wolf**				巨門 *Ju Men* **Huge Door**		武曲 *Wu Qu* **Military Arts**				文曲 *Wen Qu* **Literary Arts**			
坎 *Kan* N2	癸 *Gui* N3	申 *Shen* SW3	辰 *Chen* SE1	坤 *Kun* SW2	乙 *Yi* E3	離 *Li* S2	壬 *Ren* N1	寅 *Yin* NE3	戌 *Xu* NW1	兌 *Dui* W2	丁 *Ding* S3	巳 *Si* SE3	丑 *Chou* NE1

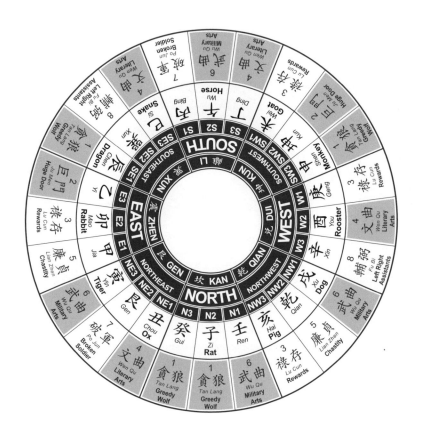

Heaven Penetrating Force 通天竅：

三合前方 Facing Three Harmony	坤申 Kun Shen	庚酉 Geng You	辛戌 Xin Xu
三合後方 Sitting Three Harmony	艮寅 Gen Yin	甲卯 Jia Mao	乙辰 Yi Chen

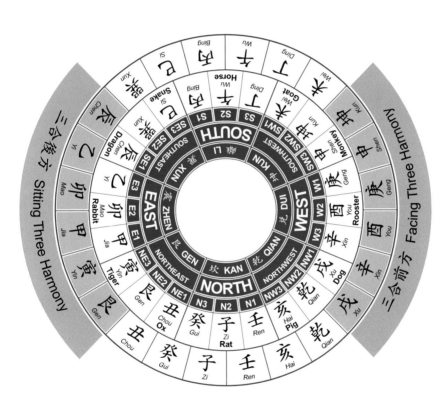

Moving Horse Six Ren Assessment 走馬六壬：

神后 Shen Hou **Holy Empress**	功曹 Gong Cao **Marshall**	天罡 Tian Gang **Heavenly Dipper**	勝光 Sheng Guang **Subliminal Bright**	傳送 Chuan Song **Great General**	河魁 He Kui **River Scholar**
艮寅 Gen Yin	乙辰 Yi Chen	丙午 Bing Wu	坤申 Kun Shen	辛戌 Xin Xu	壬子 Ren Zi

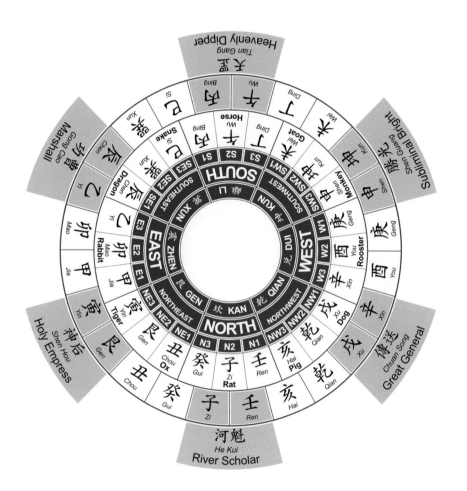

Four Advantages Three Cycles Star Plate 四利三元：

太陽 *Tai Yang* **Sun**	太陰 *Tai Yin* **Moon**	龍德 *Long De* **Dragon Virtue**	福德 *Fu De* **Fortune Virtue**
亥 *Hai* **Pig**	丑 *Chou* **Ox**	巳 *Si* **Snake**	未 *Wei* **Goat**

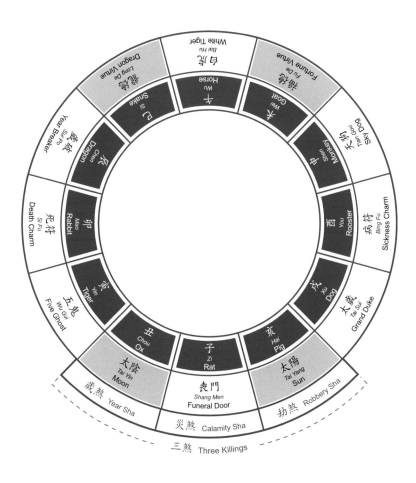

Negative Sectors For Opening Mountain 開山凶位：

年剋山家 Year Countering Sitting

震	艮	巳
Zhen	*Gen*	*Si*
E2	NE2	SE3

陰府太歲 *Yin Fu Tai Sui* **Yin Mansion Grand Duke**	六害 *Liu Hai* **Six Harm**	死符 *Si Fu* **Death Charm**	炙退 *Zhi Tui* **Roasting Star**
乾 *Qian* NW2 兑 *Dui* W2	酉 *You* W2	卯 *Mao* E2	酉 *You* W2

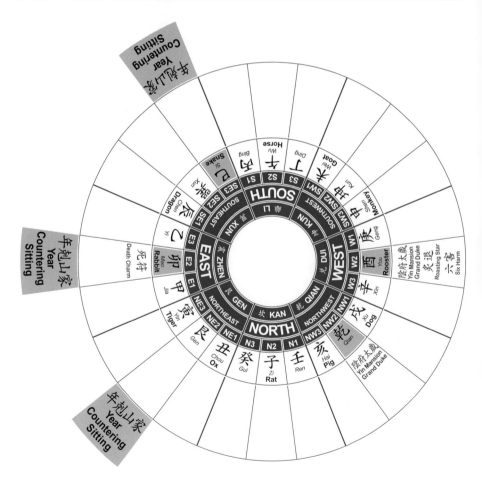

Negative Directions to Establish Facing 立向凶方：

巡山羅喉 *Xun Shan Luo Hou* **Mountain Patrol Luo Hou Star**	病符 *Bing Fu* **Sickness Charm**
乾 *Qian* **NW2**	酉 *You* **W2**

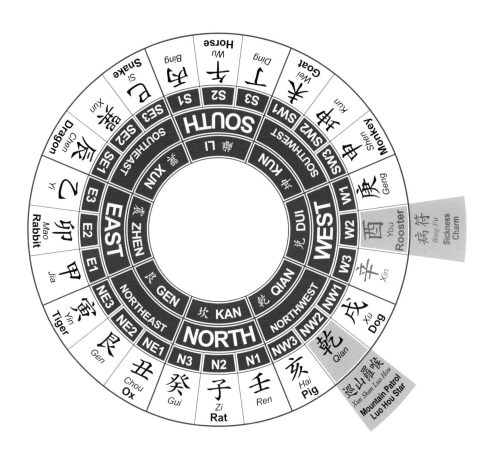

Negative Repair / Renovation Sectors Table 修方凶位表：

天官符 Heavenly Officer Charm	巳 *Si* Snake		豹尾 Leopard Tail	辰 *Chen* Dragon
地官符 Earthly Officer Charm	寅 *Yin* Tiger		飛廉 Flying Chaste	子 *Zi* Rat
大煞 Great Sha	午 *Wu* Horse		喪門 Funeral Door	子 *Zi* Rat
大將軍 Big General	午 *Wu* Horse		弔客 Suspended Guest	申 *Shen* Monkey
力士 Strong Man	乾 *Qian*		白虎 White Tiger	午 *Wu* Horse
蠶室 Silkworm Room	巽 *Xun*		金神 Golden God	辰 *Chen* Dragon 巳 *Si* Snake
蠶官 Silkworm Officer	辰 *Chen* Dragon			
蠶命 Silkworm Life	巳 *Si* Snake		獨火 Lonely Fire	乾 *Qian*
歲刑 Duke Punishment	未 *Wei* Goat		五鬼 Five Ghost	午 *Wu* Horse
黃幡 Yellow Flag	戌 *Xu* Dog		破敗五鬼 Destructive Five Ghost	兌 *Dui*

Negative Repair / Renovation Sectors Diagram 修方凶位圖：

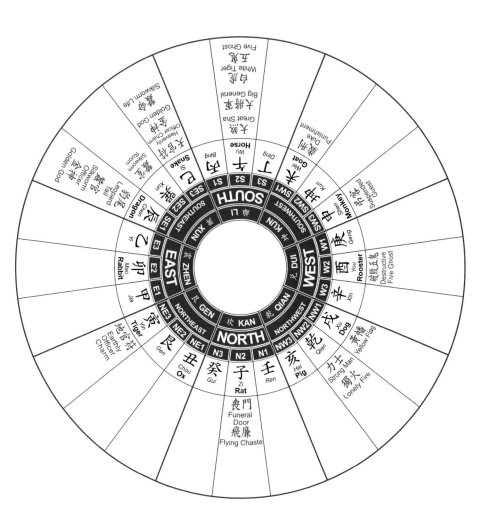

12-Month Auxiliary Stars Reference Table :
庚戌年十二月，開山立向修方星表

Positive Monthly Stars 吉星方

月 MONTH	寅 Tiger (Feb 4 - Mar 5) 正月 1st Month	卯 Rabbit (Mar 6 - Apr 4) 二月 2nd Month	辰 Dragon (Apr 5 - May 5) 三月 3rd Month	巳 Snake (May 6 - Jun 5) 四月 4th Month	午 Horse (Jun 6 - July 6) 五月 5th Month	未 Goat (July 7 - Aug 7) 六月 6th Month
天道 Heavenly Path	南 South	西南 Southwest	北 North	西 West	西北 Northwest	東 East
天德 Heavenly Virtue	丁 Ding Yin Fire	坤 Kun （申）	壬 Ren Yang Water	辛 Xin Yin Metal	乾 Qian （亥）	甲 Jia Yang Wood
天德合 Heavenly Virtue Combo	壬 Ren Yang Water	（巳）	丁 Ding Yin Fire	丙 Bing Yang Fire	（寅）	己 Ji Yin Earth
月德 Monthly Virtue	丙 Bing Yang Fire	甲 Jia Yang Wood	壬 Ren Yang Water	庚 Geng Yang Metal	丙 Bing Yang Fire	甲 Jia Yang Wood
月德合 Monthly Virtue Combo	辛 Xin Yin Metal	己 Ji Yin Earth	丁 Ding Yin Fire	乙 Yi Yin Wood	辛 Xin Yin Metal	己 Ji Yin Earth
月空 Month Emptiness	壬 Ren Yang Water	庚 Geng Yang Metal	丙 Bing Yang Fire	甲 Jia Yang Wood	壬 Ren Yang Water	庚 Geng Yang Metal
陽貴人 Yang Nobleman	兌 Dui	乾 Qian	中 Middle	巽 Xun	震 Zhen	坤 Kun
陰貴人 Yin Nobleman	坎 Kan	離 Li	艮 Gen	兌 Dui	乾 Qian	中 Middle
飛天祿 Flying Heavenly Wealth	坤 Kun	坎 Kan	離 Li	艮 Gen	兌 Dui	乾 Qian
飛天馬 Flying Heavenly Horse	坤 Kun	坎 Kan	離 Li	艮 Gen	兌 Dui	乾 Qian

12-Month Auxiliary Stars Reference Table :
庚戌年十二月，開山立向修方星表

申 Monkey (Aug 8 - Sept 7) 七月 7th Month	酉 Rooster (Sept 8 - Oct 7) 八月 8th Month	戌 Dog (Oct 8 - Nov 6) 九月 9th Month	亥 Pig (Nov 7 - Dec 6) 十月 10th Month	子 Rat (Dec 7 - Jan 5) 十一月 11th Month	丑 Ox (Jan 6 - Feb 3) 十二月 12th Month	月 MONTH
北 North	東北 Northeast	南 South	東 East	東南 Southeast	西 West	天道 Heavenly Path
癸 Gui Yin Water	艮 Gen (寅)	丙 Bing Yang Fire	乙 Yi Yin Wood	巽 Xun (巳)	庚 Geng Yang Metal	天德 Heavenly Virtue
戊 Wu Yang Earth	(亥)	辛 Xin Yin Metal	庚 Geng Yang Metal	(申)	乙 Yi Yin Wood	天德合 Heavenly Virtue Combo
壬 Ren Yang Water	庚 Geng Yang Metal	丙 Bing Yang Fire	甲 Jia Yang Wood	壬 Ren Yang Water	庚 Geng Yang Metal	月德 Monthly Virtue
丁 Ding Yin Fire	乙 Yi Yin Wood	辛 Xin Yin Metal	己 Ji Yin Earth	丁 Ding Yin Fire	乙 Yi Yin Wood	月德合 Monthly Virtue Combo
丙 Bing Yang Fire	甲 Jia Yang Wood	壬 Ren Yang Water	庚 Geng Yang Metal	丙 Bing Yang Fire	甲 Jia Yang Wood	月空 Month Emptiness
坎 Kan	離 Li	艮 Gen	兌 Dui	乾 Qian	中 Middle	陽貴人 Yang Nobleman
坎 Kan	離 Li	艮 Gen	兌 Dui	乾 Qian	中 Middle	陰貴人 Yin Nobleman
中 Middle	坎 Kan	離 Li	艮 Gen	兌 Dui	乾 Qian	飛天祿 Flying Heavenly Wealth
中 Middle	坎 Kan	離 Li	艮 Gen	兌 Dui	乾 Qian	飛天馬 Flying Heavenly Horse

Monthly Purple White Stars 月紫白九星 :

寅 Tiger (Feb 4 - Mar 5) 正月 1st Month

巽 SE	離 S	坤 SW
4 Green 四綠	**9** Purple 九紫	**2** Black 二黑
3 Jade 三碧 (震 E)	**5** Yellow 五黃	**7** Red 七赤 (兌 W)
8 White 八白	**1** White 一白	**6** White 六白
艮 NE	坎 N	乾 NW

卯 Rabbit (Mar 6 - Apr 4) 二月 2nd Month

巽 SE	離 S	坤 SW
3 Jade 三碧	**8** White 八白	**1** White 一白
2 Black 二黑 (震 E)	**4** Green 四綠	**6** White 六白 (兌 W)
7 Red 七赤	**9** Purple 九紫	**5** Yellow 五黃
艮 NE	坎 N	乾 NW

辰 Dragon (Apr 5 - May 5) 三月 3rd Month

巽 SE	離 S	坤 SW
2 Black 二黑	**7** Red 七赤	**9** Purple 九紫
1 White 一白 (震 E)	**3** Jade 三碧	**5** Yellow 五黃 (兌 W)
6 White 六白	**8** White 八白	**4** Green 四綠
艮 NE	坎 N	乾 NW

巳 Snake (May 6 - Jun 5) 四月 4th Month

巽 SE	離 S	坤 SW
1 White 一白	**6** White 六白	**8** White 八白
9 Purple 九紫 (震 E)	**2** Black 二黑	**4** Green 四綠 (兌 W)
5 Yellow 五黃	**7** Red 七赤	**3** Jade 三碧
艮 NE	坎 N	乾 NW

午 Horse (Jun 6 - July 6) 五月 5th Month

巽 SE	離 S	坤 SW
9 Purple 九紫	**5** Yellow 五黃	**7** Red 七赤
8 White 八白 (震 E)	**1** White 一白	**3** Jade 三碧 (兌 W)
4 Green 四綠	**6** White 六白	**2** Black 二黑
艮 NE	坎 N	乾 NW

未 Goat (July 7 - Aug 7) 六月 6th Month

巽 SE	離 S	坤 SW
8 White 八白	**4** Green 四綠	**6** White 六白
7 Red 七赤 (震 E)	**9** Purple 九紫	**2** Black 二黑 (兌 W)
3 Jade 三碧	**5** Yellow 五黃	**1** White 一白
艮 NE	坎 N	乾 NW

申 Monkey (Aug 8 - Sept 7) 七月 7th Month

巽 SE	離 S	坤 SW
7 Red 七赤	**3** Jade 三碧	**5** Yellow 五黃
6 White 六白 (震 E)	**8** White 八白	**1** White 一白 (兌 W)
2 Black 二黑	**4** Green 四綠	**9** Purple 九紫
艮 NE	坎 N	乾 NW

酉 Rooster (Sept 8 - Oct 7) 八月 8th Month

巽 SE	離 S	坤 SW
6 White 六白	**2** Black 二黑	**4** Green 四綠
5 Yellow 五黃 (震 E)	**7** Red 七赤	**9** Purple 九紫 (兌 W)
1 White 一白	**3** Jade 三碧	**8** White 八白
艮 NE	坎 N	乾 NW

戌 Dog (Oct 8 - Nov 6) 九月 9th Month

巽 SE	離 S	坤 SW
5 Yellow 五黃	**1** White 一白	**3** Jade 三碧
4 Green 四綠 (震 E)	**6** White 六白	**8** White 八白 (兌 W)
9 Purple 九紫	**2** Black 二黑	**7** Red 七赤
艮 NE	坎 N	乾 NW

亥 Pig (Nov 7 - Dec 6) 十月 10th Month

巽 SE	離 S	坤 SW
4 Green 四綠	**9** Purple 九紫	**2** Black 二黑
3 Jade 三碧 (震 E)	**5** Yellow 五黃	**7** Red 七赤 (兌 W)
8 White 八白	**1** White 一白	**6** White 六白
艮 NE	坎 N	乾 NW

子 Rat (Dec 7 - Jan 5) 十一月 11th Month

巽 SE	離 S	坤 SW
3 Jade 三碧	**8** White 八白	**1** White 一白
2 Black 二黑 (震 E)	**4** Green 四綠	**6** White 六白 (兌 W)
7 Red 七赤	**9** Purple 九紫	**5** Yellow 五黃
艮 NE	坎 N	乾 NW

丑 Ox (Jan 6 - Feb 3) 十二月 12th Month

巽 SE	離 S	坤 SW
2 Black 二黑	**7** Red 七赤	**9** Purple 九紫
1 White 一白 (震 E)	**3** Jade 三碧	**5** Yellow 五黃 (兌 W)
6 White 六白	**8** White 八白	**4** Green 四綠
艮 NE	坎 N	乾 NW

Qi Men Three Nobles 三奇 :

Three Nobles 三奇 / Seasons	乙 Yi	丙 Bing	丁 Ding
立春 **Coming of Spring** Feb 4 - Feb 18	兌 Dui	艮 Gen	離 Li
春分 **Spring Equinox** Mar 21 - Apr 4	坤 Kun	震 Zhen	巽 Xun
立夏 **Coming of Summer** May 6 - May 20	震 Zhen	巽 Xun	中 **Middle**
夏至 **Summer Solstice** Jun 22 - Jul 6	坎 Kan	離 Li	艮 Gen
立秋 **Coming of Autumn** Aug 8 - Aug 23	震 Zhen	坤 Kun	坎 Kan
秋分 **Autumn Equinox** Sept 23 - Oct 7	艮 Gen	兌 Dui	乾 Qian
立冬 **Coming of Winter** Nov 7 - Nov 22	兌 Dui	乾 Qian	中 **Middle**
冬至 **Winter Solstice** Dec 22 - Jan 5	離 Li	坎 Kan	坤 Kun

Sectors to Avoid Opening Mountain 開山凶位 :

月 MONTH	月建 Month Establishment	月破 Month Destruction	月尅山家 Month Countering Sitting		陰府太歲 Yin Mansion Grand Duke	
寅 **Tiger** (Feb 4 - Mar 5) 正月 **1st Month**	寅 Yin **Tiger**	申 Shen **Monkey**	乾 Qian	兌 Dui	坤 Kun	震 Zhen
卯 **Rabbit** (Mar 6 - Apr 4) 二月 **2nd Month**	卯 Mao **Rabbit**	酉 You **Rooster**	亥 Hai **Pig**	丁 Ding **Yin Fire**	巽 Xun	艮 Gen
辰 **Dragon** (Apr 5 - May 5) 三月 **3rd Month**	辰 Chen **Dragon**	戌 Xu **Dog**	震 Zhen	巳 Si **Snake**	乾 Qian	兌 Dui
巳 **Snake** (May 6 - Jun 5) 四月 **4th Month**	巳 Si **Snake**	亥 Hai **Pig**	艮 Gen		坤 Kun	坎 Kan
午 **Horse** (Jun 6 - July 6) 五月 **5th Month**	午 Wu **Horse**	子 Zi **Rat**	離 Li	丙 Bing **Yang Fire**	離 Li	乾 Qian
未 **Goat** (July 7 - Aug 7) 六月 **6th Month**	未 Wei **Goat**	丑 Chou **Ox**	壬 Ren **Yang Water**	乙 Yi **Yin Wood**	震 Zhen	坤 Kun
申 **Monkey** (Aug 8 - Sept 7) 七月 **7th Month**	申 Shen **Monkey**	寅 Yin **Tiger**	—		艮 Gen	巽 Xun
酉 **Rooster** (Sept 8 - Oct 7) 八月 **8th Month**	酉 You **Rooster**	卯 Mao **Rabbit**	—		兌 Dui	乾 Qian
戌 **Dog** (Oct 8 - Nov 6) 九月 **9th Month**	戌 Xu **Dog**	辰 Chen **Dragon**	乾 Qian	兌 Dui	坎 Kan	坤 Kun
亥 **Pig** (Nov 7 - Dec 6) 十月 **10th Month**	亥 Hai **Pig**	巳 Si **Snake**	亥 Hai **Pig**	丁 Ding **Yin Fire**	乾 Qian	離 Li
子 **Rat** (Dec 7 - Jan 5) 十一月 **11th Month**	子 Zi **Rat**	午 Wu **Horse**	水 **Water**	山 **Mountain**	坤 Kun	震 Zhen
丑 **Ox** (Jan 6 - Feb 3) 十二月 **12th Month**	丑 Chou **Ox**	未 Wei **Goat**	土 **Earth**		巽 Xun	艮 Gen

Negative Repair / Renovation Sectors 修方凶位 :

月 MONTH	天官符 Heavenly Officer Charm			地官符 Earth Officer Charm			小月建 Small Month Establishment		
寅 Tiger (Feb 4 - Mar 5) 正月 1st Month	丑 Chou Ox	艮 Gen	寅 Yin Tiger	中 Middle			中 Middle		
卯 Rabbit (Mar 6 - Apr 4) 二月 2nd Month	庚 Geng Yang Metal	兌 Dui	辛 Xin Yin Metal	庚 Geng Yang Metal	兌 Dui	辛 Xin Yin Metal	戌 Xu Dog	乾 Qian	亥 Hai Pig
辰 Dragon (Apr 5 - May 5) 三月 3rd Month	戌 Xu Dog	乾 Qian	亥 Hai Pig	戌 Xu Dog	乾 Qian	亥 Hai Pig	庚 Geng Yang Metal	兌 Dui	辛 Xin Yin Metal
巳 Snake (May 6 - Jun 5) 四月 4th Month	中 Middle			中 Middle			丑 Chou Ox	艮 Gen	寅 Yin Tiger
午 Horse (Jun 6 - July 6) 五月 5th Month	庚 Geng Yang Metal	兌 Dui	辛 Xin Yin Metal	辰 Chen Dragon	巽 Xun	巳 Si Snake	丙 Bing Yang Fire	離 Li	丁 Ding Yin Fire
未 Goat (July 7 - Aug 7) 六月 6th Month	戌 Xu Dog	乾 Qian	亥 Hai Pig	甲 Jia Yang Wood	震 Zhen	乙 Yi Yin Wood	壬 Ren Yang Water	坎 Kan	癸 Gui Yin Water
申 Monkey (Aug 8 - Sept 7) 七月 7th Month	中 Middle			未 Wei Goat	坤 Kun	申 Shen Monkey	未 Wei Goat	坤 Kun	申 Shen Monkey
酉 Rooster (Sept 8 - Oct 7) 八月 8th Month	辰 Chen Dragon	巽 Xun	巳 Si Snake	壬 Ren Yang Water	坎 Kan	癸 Gui Yin Water	甲 Jia Yang Wood	震 Zhen	乙 Yi Yin Wood
戌 Dog (Oct 8 - Nov 6) 九月 9th Month	甲 Jia Yang Wood	震 Zhen	乙 Yi Yin Wood	丙 Bing Yang Fire	離 Li	丁 Ding Yin Fire	辰 Chen Dragon	巽 Xun	巳 Si Snake
亥 Pig (Nov 7 - Dec 6) 十月 10th Month	未 Wei Goat	坤 Kun	申 Shen Monkey	丑 Chou Ox	艮 Gen	寅 Yin Tiger	中 Middle		
子 Rat (Dec 7 - Jan 5) 十一月 11th Month	壬 Ren Yang Water	坎 Kan	癸 Gui Yin Water	庚 Geng Yang Metal	兌 Dui	辛 Xin Yin Metal	戌 Xu Dog	乾 Qian	亥 Hai Pig
丑 Ox (Jan 6 - Feb 3) 十二月 12th Month	丙 Bing Yang Fire	離 Li	丁 Ding Yin Fire	戌 Xu Dog	乾 Qian	亥 Hai Pig	庚 Geng Yang Metal	兌 Dui	辛 Xin Yin Metal

Negative Repair / Renovation Sectors 修方凶位 :

月 MONTH	大月建 Big Month Establishment			飛大煞 Flying Great Sha			丙丁獨火 Bing Ding Lonely Fire	
寅 **Tiger** (Feb 4 - Mar 5) 正月 **1st Month**	中 Middle			丙 *Bing* **Yang Fire**	離 *Li*	丁 *Ding* **Yin Fire**	巽 *Xun*	中 Middle
卯 **Rabbit** (Mar 6 - Apr 4) 二月 **2nd Month**	辰 *Chen* **Dragon**	巽 *Xun*	巳 *Si* **Snake**	丑 *Chou* **Ox**	艮 *Gen*	寅 *Yin* **Tiger**	震 *Zhen*	巽 *Xun*
辰 **Dragon** (Apr 5 - May 5) 三月 **3rd Month**	甲 *Jia* **Yang Wood**	震 *Zhen*	乙 *Yi* **Yin Wood**	庚 *Geng* **Yang Metal**	兌 *Dui*	辛 *Xin* **Yin Metal**	坤 *Kun*	震 *Zhen*
巳 **Snake** (May 6 - Jun 5) 四月 **4th Month**	未 *Wei* **Goat**	坤 *Kun*	申 *Shen* **Monkey**	戌 *Xu* **Dog**	乾 *Qian*	亥 *Hai* **Pig**	坎 *Kan*	坤 *Kun*
午 **Horse** (Jun 6 - July 6) 五月 **5th Month**	壬 *Ren* **Yang Water**	坎 *Kan*	癸 *Gui* **Yin Water**	中 Middle			離 *Li*	坎 *Kan*
未 **Goat** (July 7 - Aug 7) 六月 **6th Month**	丙 *Bing* **Yang Fire**	離 *Li*	丁 *Ding* **Yin Fire**	庚 *Geng* **Yang Metal**	兌 *Dui*	辛 *Xin* **Yin Metal**	艮 *Gen*	離 *Li*
申 **Monkey** (Aug 8 - Sept 7) 七月 **7th Month**	丑 *Chou* **Ox**	艮 *Gen*	寅 *Yin* **Tiger**	戌 *Xu* **Dog**	乾 *Qian*	亥 *Hai* **Pig**	兌 *Dui*	艮 *Gen*
酉 **Rooster** (Sept 8 - Oct 7) 八月 **8th Month**	庚 *Geng* **Yang Metal**	兌 *Dui*	辛 *Xin* **Yin Metal**	中 Middle			乾 *Qian*	兌 *Dui*
戌 **Dog** (Oct 8 - Nov 6) 九月 **9th Month**	戌 *Xu* **Dog**	乾 *Qian*	亥 *Hai* **Pig**	辰 *Chen* **Dragon**	巽 *Xun*	巳 *Si* **Snake**	中 Middle	乾 *Qian*
亥 **Pig** (Nov 7 - Dec 6) 十月 **10th Month**	中 Middle			甲 *Jia* **Yang Wood**	震 *Zhen*	乙 *Yi* **Yin Wood**	中 Middle	
子 **Rat** (Dec 7 - Jan 5) 十一月 **11th Month**	辰 *Chen* **Dragon**	巽 *Xun*	巳 *Si* **Snake**	未 *Wei* **Goat**	坤 *Kun*	申 *Shen* **Monkey**	巽 *Xun*	中 Middle
丑 **Ox** (Jan 6 - Feb 3) 十二月 **12th Month**	甲 *Jia* **Yang Wood**	震 *Zhen*	乙 *Yi* **Yin Wood**	壬 *Ren* **Yang Water**	坎 *Kan*	癸 *Gui* **Yin Water**	震 *Zhen*	巽 *Xun*

Negative Repair / Renovation Sectors 修方凶位 ：

月 MONTH	月遊火 Month Wondering Fire	三煞 Monthly 3 Killings		
		劫煞 Robbery Sha	災煞 Calamity Sha	月煞 Month Sha
寅 Tiger (Feb 4 - Mar 5) 正月 1st Month	乾 Qian	亥 Hai Pig	子 Zi Rat	丑 Chou Ox
卯 Rabbit (Mar 6 - Apr 4) 二月 2nd Month	兌 Dui	申 Shen Monkey	酉 You Rooster	戌 Xu Dog
辰 Dragon (Apr 5 - May 5) 三月 3rd Month	艮 Gen	巳 Si Snake	午 Wu Horse	未 Wei Goat
巳 Snake (May 6 - Jun 5) 四月 4th Month	離 Li	寅 Yin Tiger	卯 Mao Rabbit	辰 Chen Dragon
午 Horse (Jun 6 - July 6) 五月 5th Month	坎 Kan	亥 Hai Pig	子 Zi Rat	丑 Chou Ox
未 Goat (July 7 - Aug 7) 六月 6th Month	坤 Kun	申 Shen Monkey	酉 You Rooster	戌 Xu Dog
申 Monkey (Aug 8 - Sept 7) 七月 7th Month	震 Zhen	巳 Si Snake	午 Wu Horse	未 Wei Goat
酉 Rooster (Sept 8 - Oct 7) 八月 8th Month	巽 Xun	寅 Yin Tiger	卯 Mao Rabbit	辰 Chen Dragon
戌 Dog (Oct 8 - Nov 6) 九月 9th Month	中 Middle	亥 Hai Pig	子 Zi Rat	丑 Chou Ox
亥 Pig (Nov 7 - Dec 6) 十月 10th Month	乾 Qian	申 Shen Monkey	酉 You Rooster	戌 Xu Dog
子 Rat (Dec 7 - Jan 5) 十一月 11th Month	兌 Dui	巳 Si Snake	午 Wu Horse	未 Wei Goat
丑 Ox (Jan 6 - Feb 3) 十二月 12th Month	艮 Gen	寅 Yin Tiger	卯 Mao Rabbit	辰 Chen Dragon

Negative Repair / Renovation Sectors 修方凶位 :

月 MONTH	月刑 Month Punishment	月害 Month Harm	月厭 Month Detest
寅 **Tiger** (Feb 4 - Mar 5) 正月 **1st Month**	巳 *Si* **Snake**	巳 *Si* **Snake**	戌 *Xu* **Dog**
卯 **Rabbit** (Mar 6 - Apr 4) 二月 **2nd Month**	子 *Zi* **Rat**	辰 *Chen* **Dragon**	酉 *You* **Rooster**
辰 **Dragon** (Apr 5 - May 5) 三月 **3rd Month**	辰 *Chen* **Dragon**	卯 *Mao* **Rabbit**	申 *Shen* **Monkey**
巳 **Snake** (May 6 - Jun 5) 四月 **4th Month**	申 *Shen* **Monkey**	寅 *Yin* **Tiger**	未 *Wei* **Goat**
午 **Horse** (Jun 6 - July 6) 五月 **5th Month**	午 *Wu* **Horse**	丑 *Chou* **Ox**	午 *Wu* **Horse**
未 **Goat** (July 7 - Aug 7) 六月 **6th Month**	丑 *Chou* **Ox**	子 *Zi* **Rat**	巳 *Si* **Snake**
申 **Monkey** (Aug 8 - Sept 7) 七月 **7th Month**	寅 *Yin* **Tiger**	亥 *Hai* **Pig**	辰 *Chen* **Dragon**
酉 **Rooster** (Sept 8 - Oct 7) 八月 **8th Month**	酉 *You* **Rooster**	戌 *Xu* **Dog**	卯 *Mao* **Rabbit**
戌 **Dog** (Oct 8 - Nov 6) 九月 **9th Month**	未 *Wei* **Goat**	酉 *You* **Rooster**	寅 *Yin* **Tiger**
亥 **Pig** (Nov 7 - Dec 6) 十月 **10th Month**	亥 *Hai* **Pig**	申 *Shen* **Monkey**	丑 *Chou* **Ox**
子 **Rat** (Dec 7 - Jan 5) 十一月 **11th Month**	卯 *Mao* **Rabbit**	未 *Wei* **Goat**	子 *Zi* **Rat**
丑 **Ox** (Jan 6 - Feb 3) 十二月 **12th Month**	戌 *Xu* **Dog**	午 *Wu* **Horse**	亥 *Hai* **Pig**

辛丑 (Xin Chou)
Metal Ox

Heavenly Stem 天干	辛 Yin Metal (陰金)
Earthly Branch 地支	丑 Ox (Yin Earth 陰土)
Hidden Stem 藏干	己 Yin Earth, 癸 Yin Water, 辛 Yin Metal
Na Yin 納音	壁上土 Earth on the walls
Grand Duke 太歲	丑 Ox
Xuan Kong Five Element 玄空五行	1 水 Water
Gua Name 卦名	䷣ 地火明夷 Dimming Light
Xuan Kong Period Luck 玄空卦運	3

Annual Positive Stars for Opening Mountain, Establishing Facing and Commencing Repairs 開山立向修方吉星：

歲德 Duke Virtue	丙 Bing Yang Fire	
歲德合 Duke Virtue Combo	辛 Xin Yin Metal	
歲枝德 Duke Branch Virtue	午 Wu Horse	
陽貴人 Yang Nobleman	寅 Yin Tiger	
陰貴人 Yin Nobleman	午 Wu Horse	
歲祿 Duke Prosperous	酉 You Rooster	
歲馬 Duke Horse	亥 Hai Pig	
奏書 Decree	乾 Qian	
博士 Professor	巽 Xun	

Annual Negative Stars for Opening Mountain, Establishing Facing and Commencing Repairs 開山立向修方凶星：

太歲 Grand Duke	歲破 Year Breaker	三煞 Three Killings			坐煞向煞 Sitting Sha Facing Sha				浮天空亡 Floating Heaven Emptiness	
丑 Chou Ox	未 Wei Goat	寅 Yin Tiger	卯 Mao Rabbit	辰 Chen Dragon	甲 Jia Yang Wood	乙 Yi Yin Wood	庚 Geng Yang Metal	辛 Xin Yin Metal	艮 Gen	丙 Bing Yang Fire

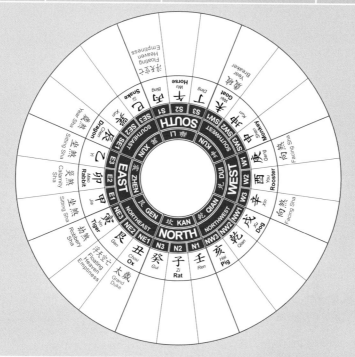

Annual San Yuan Purple White Stars 三元紫白九星：

上元 Upper Period Period 1, 2, 3			中元 Middle Period Period 4, 5, 6			下元 Lower Period Period 7, 8, 9		
巽SE	離S	坤SW	巽SE	離S	坤SW	巽SE	離S	坤SW
8	4	6	2	7	9	5	1	3
震E 7	9 辛丑 Xin Chou Metal Ox	2 兌W	震E 1	3 辛丑 Xin Chou Metal Ox	5 兌W	震E 4	6 辛丑 Xin Chou Metal Ox	8 兌W
3	5	1	6	8	4	9	2	7
艮NE	坎N	乾NW	艮NE	坎N	乾NW	艮NE	坎N	乾NW

Mountain Covering Yellow Path 蓋山黃道：

貪狼 Tan Lang **Greedy Wolf**		巨門 Ju Men **Huge Door**		武曲 Wu Qu **Military Arts**				文曲 Wen Qu **Literary Arts**			
艮 Gen NE2	丙 Bing S1	巽 Xun SE2	辛 Xin W3	兌 Dui W2	丁 Ding S3	巳 Si SE3	丑 Chou NE1	離 Li S2	壬 Ren N1	寅 Yin NE3	戌 Xu NW1

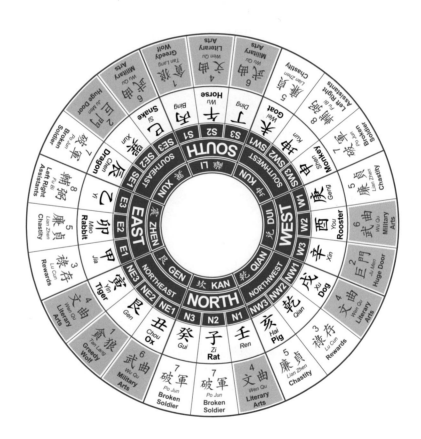

Heaven Penetrating Force 通天竅:			
三合前方 **Facing Three Harmony**	乾亥 *Qian Hai*	壬子 *Ren Zi*	癸丑 *Gui Chou*
三合後方 **Sitting Three Harmony**	巽巳 *Xun Si*	丙午 *Bing Wu*	丁未 *Ding Wei*

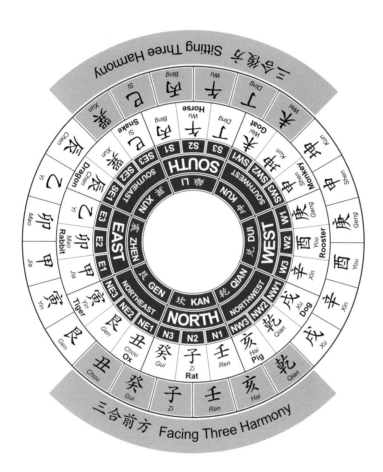

Moving Horse Six Ren Assessment 走馬六壬：

神后 Shen Hou Holy Empress	功曹 Gong Cao Marshall	天罡 Tian Gang Heavenly Dipper	勝光 Sheng Guang Subliminal Bright	傳送 Chuan Song Great General	河魁 He Kui River Scholar
乾亥 Qian Hai	癸丑 Gui Chou	甲卯 Jia Mao	巽巳 Xun Si	丁未 Ding Wei	庚酉 Geng You

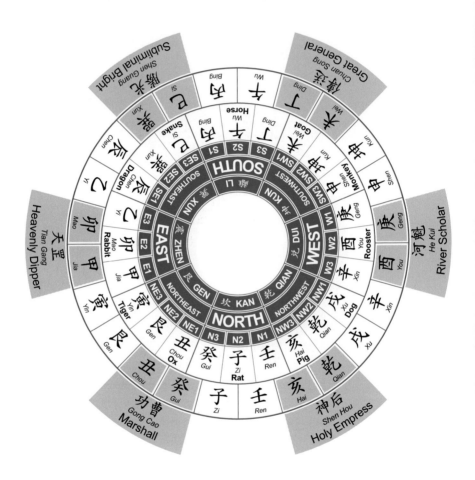

Four Advantages Three Cycles Star Plate 四利三元:

太陽 *Tai Yang* **Sun**	太陰 *Tai Yin* **Moon**	龍德 *Long De* **Dragon Virtue**	福德 *Fu De* **Fortune Virtue**
寅 *Yin* **Tiger**	辰 *Chen* **Dragon**	申 *Shen* **Monkey**	戌 *Xu* **Dog**

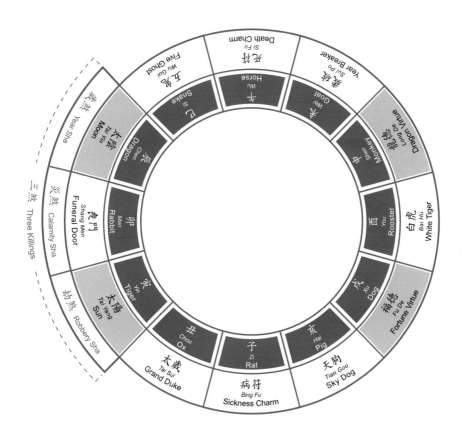

847

Negative Sectors For Opening Mountain 開山凶位：

年剋山家 Year Countering Sitting

甲	寅	辰	巽	戌	坎	辛	申	丑	癸	坤	庚	未
Jia	*Yin*	*Chen*	*Xun*	*Xu*	*Kan*	*Xin*	*Shen*	*Chou*	*Gui*	*Kun*	*Geng*	*Wei*
E1	NE3	SE1	SE2	NW1	N2	W3	SW3	NE1	N3	SW2	W1	SW1

陰府太歲 *Yin Fu Tai Sui* **Yin Mansion Grand Duke**		六害 *Liu Hai* **Six Harm**	死符 *Si Fu* **Death Charm**	炙退 *Zhi Tui* **Roasting Star**
坤 *Kun* SW2	坎 *Kan* N2	午 *Wu* S2	午 *Wu* S2	子 *Zi* N2

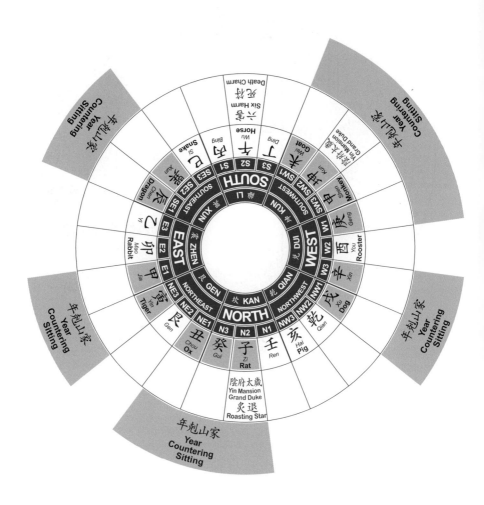

Negative Directions to Establish Facing 立向凶方：

巡山羅喉 *Xun Shan Luo Hou* **Mountain Patrol Luo Hou Star**	病符 *Bing Fu* **Sickness Charm**
艮 *Gen* **NE2**	子 *Zi* **N2**

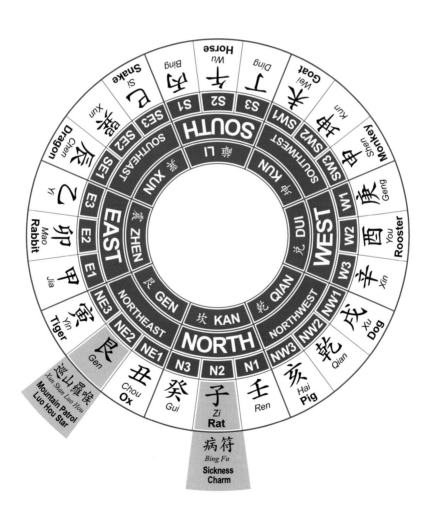

Negative Repair / Renovation Sectors Table 修方凶位表：

天官符 Heavenly Officer Charm	申 Shen Monkey	飛廉 Flying Chaste	酉 You Rooster
地官符 Earthly Officer Charm	巳 Si Snake	喪門 Funeral Door	卯 Mao Rabbit
大煞 Great Sha	酉 You Rooster	弔客 Suspended Guest	亥 Hai Pig
大將軍 Big General	酉 You Rooster	白虎 White Tiger	酉 You Rooster
力士 Strong Man	艮 Gen	金神 Golden God	寅 Yin Tiger / 卯 Mao Rabbit / 午 Wu Horse / 未 Wei Goat / 子 Zi Rat / 丑 Chou Ox
蠶室 Silkworm Room	坤 Kun		
蠶官 Silkworm Officer	未 Wei Goat		
蠶命 Silkworm Life	申 Shen Monkey		
歲刑 Duke Punishment	戌 Xu Dog	獨火 Lonely Fire	震 Zhen
黃幡 Yellow Flag	丑 Chou Ox	五鬼 Five Ghost	卯 Mao Rabbit
豹尾 Leopard Tail	未 Wei Goat	破敗五鬼 Destructive Five Ghost	乾 Qian

Negative Repair / Renovation Sectors Diagram 修方凶位圖：

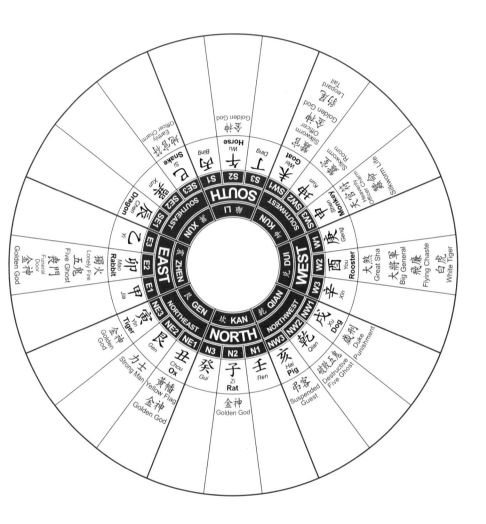

辛丑 (Xin Chou) Metal Ox

Positive Monthly Stars 吉星方

月 MONTH	寅 Tiger (Feb 4 - Mar 5) 正月 1st Month	卯 Rabbit (Mar 6 - Apr 4) 二月 2nd Month	辰 Dragon (Apr 5 - May 5) 三月 3rd Month	巳 Snake (May 6 - Jun 5) 四月 4th Month	午 Horse (Jun 6 - July 6) 五月 5th Month	未 Goat (July 7 - Aug 7) 六月 6th Month
天道 Heavenly Path	南 South	西南 Southwest	北 North	西 West	西北 Northwest	東 East
天德 Heavenly Virtue	丁 Ding Yin Fire	坤 Kun (申)	壬 Ren Yang Water	辛 Xin Yin Metal	乾 Qian (亥)	甲 Jia Yang Wood
天德合 Heavenly Virtue Combo	壬 Ren Yang Water	(巳)	丁 Ding Yin Fire	丙 Bing Yang Fire	(寅)	己 Ji Yin Earth
月德 Monthly Virtue	丙 Bing Yang Fire	甲 Jia Yang Wood	壬 Ren Yang Water	庚 Geng Yang Metal	丙 Bing Yang Fire	甲 Jia Yang Wood
月德合 Monthly Virtue Combo	辛 Xin Yin Metal	己 Ji Yin Earth	丁 Ding Yin Fire	乙 Yi Yin Wood	辛 Xin Yin Metal	己 Ji Yin Earth
月空 Month Emptiness	壬 Ren Yang Water	庚 Geng Yang Metal	丙 Bing Yang Fire	甲 Jia Yang Wood	壬 Ren Yang Water	庚 Geng Yang Metal
陽貴人 Yang Nobleman	中 Middle	坎 Kan	離 Li	艮 Gen	兌 Dui	乾 Qian
陰貴人 Yin Nobleman	離 Li	艮 Gen	兌 Dui	乾 Qian	中 Middle	坎 Kan
飛天祿 Flying Heavenly Wealth	震 Zhen	坤 Kun	坎 Kan	離 Li	艮 Gen	兌 Dui
飛天馬 Flying Heavenly Horse	中 Middle	巽 Xun	震 Zhen	坤 Kun	坎 Kan	離 Li

12-Month Auxiliary Stars Reference Table :
辛丑年十二月，開山立向修方星表

申 Monkey (Aug 8 - Sept 7) 七月 7th Month	酉 Rooster (Sept 8 - Oct 7) 八月 8th Month	戌 Dog (Oct 8 - Nov 6) 九月 9th Month	亥 Pig (Nov 7 - Dec 6) 十月 10th Month	子 Rat (Dec 7 - Jan 5) 十一月 11th Month	丑 Ox (Jan 6 - Feb 3) 十二月 12th Month	月 MONTH
北 North	東北 Northeast	南 South	東 East	東南 Southeast	西 West	天道 Heavenly Path
癸 Gui Yin Water	艮 Gen (寅)	丙 Bing Yang Fire	乙 Yi Yin Wood	巽 Xun (巳)	庚 Geng Yang Metal	天德 Heavenly Virtue
戊 Wu Yang Earth	(亥)	辛 Xin Yin Metal	庚 Geng Yang Metal	(申)	乙 Yi Yin Wood	天德合 Heavenly Virtue Combo
壬 Ren Yang Water	庚 Geng Yang Metal	丙 Bing Yang Fire	甲 Jia Yang Wood	壬 Ren Yang Water	庚 Geng Yang Metal	月德 Monthly Virtue
丁 Ding Yin Fire	乙 Yi Yin Wood	辛 Xin Yin Metal	己 Ji Yin Earth	丁 Ding Yin Fire	乙 Yi Yin Wood	月德合 Monthly Virtue Combo
丙 Bing Yang Fire	甲 Jia Yang Wood	壬 Ren Yang Water	庚 Geng Yang Metal	丙 Bing Yang Fire	甲 Jia Yang Wood	月空 Month Emptiness
中 Middle	巽 Xun	震 Zhen	坤 Kun	坎 Kan	離 Li	陽貴人 Yang Nobleman
離 Li	艮 Gen	兌 Dui	乾 Qian	中 Middle	巽 Xun	陰貴人 Yin Nobleman
乾 Qian	中 Middle	坎 Kan	離 Li	艮 Gen	兌 Dui	飛天祿 Flying Heavenly Wealth
艮 Gen	兌 Dui	乾 Qian	中 Middle	坎 Kan	離 Li	飛天馬 Flying Heavenly Horse

Monthly Purple White Stars 月紫白九星 :

寅 Tiger (Feb 4 - Mar 5) 正月 1st Month

巽SE	離S	坤SW
4 Green 四綠	9 Purple 九紫	2 Black 二黑
3 Jade 三碧	5 Yellow 五黃	7 Red 七赤
8 White 八白	1 White 一白	6 White 六白
艮NE	坎N	乾NW

震E / 兌W

卯 Rabbit (Mar 6 - Apr 4) 二月 2nd Month

巽SE	離S	坤SW
3 Jade 三碧	8 White 八白	1 White 一白
2 Black 二黑	4 Green 四綠	6 White 六白
7 Red 七赤	9 Purple 九紫	5 Yellow 五黃
艮NE	坎N	乾NW

震E / 兌W

辰 Dragon (Apr 5 - May 5) 三月 3rd Month

巽SE	離S	坤SW
2 Black 二黑	7 Red 七赤	9 Purple 九紫
1 White 一白	3 Jade 三碧	5 Yellow 五黃
6 White 六白	8 White 八白	4 Green 四綠
艮NE	坎N	乾NW

震E / 兌W

巳 Snake (May 6 - Jun 5) 四月 4th Month

巽SE	離S	坤SW
1 White 一白	6 White 六白	8 White 八白
9 Purple 九紫	2 Black 二黑	4 Green 四綠
5 Yellow 五黃	7 Red 七赤	3 Jade 三碧
艮NE	坎N	乾NW

震E / 兌W

午 Horse (Jun 6 - July 6) 五月 5th Month

巽SE	離S	坤SW
9 Purple 九紫	5 Yellow 五黃	7 Red 七赤
8 White 八白	1 White 一白	3 Jade 三碧
4 Green 四綠	6 White 六白	2 Black 二黑
艮NE	坎N	乾NW

震E / 兌W

未 Goat (July 7 - Aug 7) 六月 6th Month

巽SE	離S	坤SW
8 White 八白	4 Green 四綠	6 White 六白
7 Red 七赤	9 Purple 九紫	2 Black 二黑
3 Jade 三碧	5 Yellow 五黃	1 White 一白
艮NE	坎N	乾NW

震E / 兌W

申 Monkey (Aug 8 - Sept 7) 七月 7th Month

巽SE	離S	坤SW
7 Red 七赤	3 Jade 三碧	5 Yellow 五黃
6 White 六白	8 White 八白	1 White 一白
2 Black 二黑	4 Green 四綠	9 Purple 九紫
艮NE	坎N	乾NW

震E / 兌W

酉 Rooster (Sept 8 - Oct 7) 八月 8th Month

巽SE	離S	坤SW
6 White 六白	2 Black 二黑	4 Green 四綠
5 Yellow 五黃	7 Red 七赤	9 Purple 九紫
1 White 一白	3 Jade 三碧	8 White 八白
艮NE	坎N	乾NW

震E / 兌W

戌 Dog (Oct 8 - Nov 6) 九月 9th Month

巽SE	離S	坤SW
5 Yellow 五黃	1 White 一白	3 Jade 三碧
4 Green 四綠	6 White 六白	8 White 八白
9 Purple 九紫	2 Black 二黑	7 Red 七赤
艮NE	坎N	乾NW

震E / 兌W

亥 Pig (Nov 7 - Dec 6) 十月 10th Month

巽SE	離S	坤SW
4 Green 四綠	9 Purple 九紫	2 Black 二黑
3 Jade 三碧	5 Yellow 五黃	7 Red 七赤
8 White 八白	1 White 一白	6 White 六白
艮NE	坎N	乾NW

震E / 兌W

子 Rat (Dec 7 - Jan 5) 十一月 11th Month

巽SE	離S	坤SW
3 Jade 三碧	8 White 八白	1 White 一白
2 Black 二黑	4 Green 四綠	6 White 六白
7 Red 七赤	9 Purple 九紫	5 Yellow 五黃
艮NE	坎N	乾NW

震E / 兌W

丑 Ox (Jan 6 - Feb 3) 十二月 12th Month

巽SE	離S	坤SW
2 Black 二黑	7 Red 七赤	9 Purple 九紫
1 White 一白	3 Jade 三碧	5 Yellow 五黃
6 White 六白	8 White 八白	4 Green 四綠
艮NE	坎N	乾NW

震E / 兌W

Qi Men Three Nobles 三奇 ：

Three Nobles 三奇 / Seasons	乙 Yi	丙 Bing	丁 Ding
立春 **Coming of Spring** Feb 4 - Feb 18	中 Middle	乾 Qian	兌 Dui
春分 **Spring Equinox** Mar 21 - Apr 4	離 Li	坎 Kan	坤 Kun
立夏 **Coming of Summer** May 6 - May 20	坎 Kan	坤 Kun	震 Zhen
夏至 **Summer Solstice** Jun 22 - Jul 6	震 Zhen	坤 Kun	坎 Kan
立秋 **Coming of Autumn** Aug 8 - Aug 23	中 Middle	巽 Xun	震 Zhen
秋分 **Autumn Equinox** Sept 23 - Oct 7	坎 Kan	離 Li	艮 Gen
立冬 **Coming of Winter** Nov 7 - Nov 22	離 Li	艮 Gen	兌 Dui
冬至 **Winter Solstice** Dec 22 - Jan 5	兌 Dui	艮 Gen	離 Li

Sectors to Avoid Opening Mountain 開山凶位 :

月 MONTH	月建 Month Establishment	月破 Month Destruction	月剋山家 Month Countering Sitting		陰府太歲 Yin Mansion Grand Duke	
寅 **Tiger** (Feb 4 - Mar 5) 正月 **1st Month**	寅 *Yin* **Tiger**	申 *Shen* **Monkey**	—		乾 *Qian*	兌 *Dui*
卯 **Rabbit** (Mar 6 - Apr 4) 二月 **2nd Month**	卯 *Mao* **Rabbit**	酉 *You* **Rooster**	—		坤 *Kun*	坎 *Kan*
辰 **Dragon** (Apr 5 - May 5) 三月 **3rd Month**	辰 *Chen* **Dragon**	戌 *Xu* **Dog**	乾 *Qian*	兌 *Dui*	離 *Li*	乾 *Qian*
巳 **Snake** (May 6 - Jun 5) 四月 **4th Month**	巳 *Si* **Snake**	亥 *Hai* **Pig**	亥 *Hai* **Pig**	丁 *Ding* **Yin Fire**	震 *Zhen*	坤 *Kun*
午 **Horse** (Jun 6 - July 6) 五月 **5th Month**	午 *Wu* **Horse**	子 *Zi* **Rat**	離 *Li*	丙 *Bing* **Yang Fire**	艮 *Gen*	巽 *Xun*
未 **Goat** (July 7 - Aug 7) 六月 **6th Month**	未 *Wei* **Goat**	丑 *Chou* **Ox**	壬 *Ren* **Yang Water**	乙 *Yi* **Yin Wood**	兌 *Dui*	乾 *Qian*
申 **Monkey** (Aug 8 - Sept 7) 七月 **7th Month**	申 *Shen* **Monkey**	寅 *Yin* **Tiger**	震 *Zhen*	巳 *Si* **Snake**	坎 *Kan*	坤 *Kun*
酉 **Rooster** (Sept 8 - Oct 7) 八月 **8th Month**	酉 *You* **Rooster**	卯 *Mao* **Rabbit**	艮 *Gen*		乾 *Qian*	離 *Li*
戌 **Dog** (Oct 8 - Nov 6) 九月 **9th Month**	戌 *Xu* **Dog**	辰 *Chen* **Dragon**	—		坤 *Kun*	震 *Zhen*
亥 **Pig** (Nov 7 - Dec 6) 十月 **10th Month**	亥 *Hai* **Pig**	巳 *Si* **Snake**	—		巽 *Xun*	艮 *Gen*
子 **Rat** (Dec 7 - Jan 5) 十一月 **11th Month**	子 *Zi* **Rat**	午 *Wu* **Horse**	水 **Water**	山 **Mountain**	乾 *Qian*	兌 *Dui*
丑 **Ox** (Jan 6 - Feb 3) 十二月 **12th Month**	丑 *Chou* **Ox**	未 *Wei* **Goat**	土 **Earth**		坤 *Kun*	坎 *Kan*

Negative Repair / Renovation Sectors 修方凶位 :

月 MONTH	天官符 Heavenly Officer Charm			地官符 Earth Officer Charm			小月建 Small Month Establishment		
寅 **Tiger** (Feb 4 - Mar 5) 正月 **1st Month**	未 Wei Goat	坤 Kun	申 Shen Monkey	丑 Chou Ox	艮 Gen	寅 Yin Tiger	丙 Bing Yang Fire	離 Li	丁 Ding Yin Fire
卯 **Rabbit** (Mar 6 - Apr 4) 二月 **2nd Month**	壬 Ren Yang Water	坎 Kan	癸 Gui Yin Water	庚 Geng Yang Metal	兌 Dui	辛 Xin Yin Metal	壬 Ren Yang Water	坎 Kan	癸 Gui Yin Water
辰 **Dragon** (Apr 5 - May 5) 三月 **3rd Month**	丙 Bing Yang Fire	離 Li	丁 Ding Yin Fire	戊 Xu Dog	乾 Qian	亥 Hai Pig	未 Wei Goat	坤 Kun	申 Shen Monkey
巳 **Snake** (May 6 - Jun 5) 四月 **4th Month**	丑 Chou Ox	艮 Gen	寅 Yin Tiger		中 Middle		甲 Jia Yang Wood	震 Zhen	乙 Yi Yin Wood
午 **Horse** (Jun 6 - July 6) 五月 **5th Month**	庚 Geng Yang Metal	兌 Dui	辛 Xin Yin Metal	庚 Geng Yang Metal	兌 Dui	辛 Xin Yin Metal	辰 Chen Dragon	巽 Xun	巳 Si Snake
未 **Goat** (July 7 - Aug 7) 六月 **6th Month**	戊 Xu Dog	乾 Qian	亥 Hai Pig	戊 Xu Dog	乾 Qian	亥 Hai Pig		中 Middle	
申 **Monkey** (Aug 8 - Sept 7) 七月 **7th Month**		中 Middle			中 Middle		戊 Xu Dog	乾 Qian	亥 Hai Pig
酉 **Rooster** (Sept 8 - Oct 7) 八月 **8th Month**	庚 Geng Yang Metal	兌 Dui	辛 Xin Yin Metal	辰 Chen Dragon	巽 Xun	巳 Si Snake	庚 Geng Yang Metal	兌 Dui	辛 Xin Yin Metal
戌 **Dog** (Oct 8 - Nov 6) 九月 **9th Month**	戊 Xu Dog	乾 Qian	亥 Hai Pig	甲 Jia Yang Wood	震 Zhen	乙 Yi Yin Wood	丑 Chou Ox	艮 Gen	寅 Yin Tiger
亥 **Pig** (Nov 7 - Dec 6) 十月 **10th Month**		中 Middle		未 Wei Goat	坤 Kun	申 Shen Monkey	丙 Bing Yang Fire	離 Li	丁 Ding Yin Fire
子 **Rat** (Dec 7 - Jan 5) 十一月 **11th Month**	辰 Chen Dragon	巽 Xun	巳 Si Snake	壬 Ren Yang Water	坎 Kan	癸 Gui Yin Water	壬 Ren Yang Water	坎 Kan	癸 Gui Yin Water
丑 **Ox** (Jan 6 - Feb 3) 十二月 **12th Month**	甲 Jia Yang Wood	震 Zhen	乙 Yi Yin Wood	丙 Bing Yang Fire	離 Li	丁 Ding Yin Fire	未 Wei Goat	坤 Kun	申 Shen Monkey

Negative Repair / Renovation Sectors 修方凶位 :

月 MONTH	大月建 Big Month Establishment			飛大煞 Flying Great Sha			丙丁獨火 Bing Ding Lonely Fire	
寅 **Tiger** (Feb 4 - Mar 5) 正月 **1st Month**	中 Middle			甲 Jia Yang Wood	震 Zhen	乙 Yi Yin Wood	坤 Kun	震 Zhen
卯 **Rabbit** (Mar 6 - Apr 4) 二月 **2nd Month**	辰 Chen Dragon	巽 Xun	巳 Si Snake	未 Wei Goat	坤 Kun	申 Shen Monkey	坎 Kan	坤 Kun
辰 **Dragon** (Apr 5 - May 5) 三月 **3rd Month**	甲 Jia Yang Wood	震 Zhen	乙 Yi Yin Wood	壬 Ren Yang Water	坎 Kan	癸 Gui Yin Water	離 Li	坎 Kan
巳 **Snake** (May 6 - Jun 5) 四月 **4th Month**	未 Wei Goat	坤 Kun	申 Shen Monkey	丙 Bing Yang Fire	離 Li	丁 Ding Yin Fire	艮 Gen	離 Li
午 **Horse** (Jun 6 - July 6) 五月 **5th Month**	壬 Ren Yang Water	坎 Kan	癸 Gui Yin Water	丑 Chou Ox	艮 Gen	寅 Yin Tiger	兌 Dui	艮 Gen
未 **Goat** (July 7 - Aug 7) 六月 **6th Month**	丙 Bing Yang Fire	離 Li	丁 Ding Yin Fire	庚 Geng Yang Metal	兌 Dui	辛 Xin Yin Metal	乾 Qian	兌 Dui
申 **Monkey** (Aug 8 - Sept 7) 七月 **7th Month**	丑 Chou Ox	艮 Gen	寅 Yin Tiger	戌 Xu Dog	乾 Qian	亥 Hai Pig	中 Middle	乾 Qian
酉 **Rooster** (Sept 8 - Oct 7) 八月 **8th Month**	庚 Geng Yang Metal	兌 Dui	辛 Xin Yin Metal	中 Middle			中 Middle	
戌 **Dog** (Oct 8 - Nov 6) 九月 **9th Month**	戌 Xu Dog	乾 Qian	亥 Hai Pig	庚 Geng Yang Metal	兌 Dui	辛 Xin Yin Metal	巽 Xun	中 Middle
亥 **Pig** (Nov 7 - Dec 6) 十月 **10th Month**	中 Middle			戌 Xu Dog	乾 Qian	亥 Hai Pig	震 Zhen	巽 Xun
子 **Rat** (Dec 7 - Jan 5) 十一月 **11th Month**	辰 Chen Dragon	巽 Xun	巳 Si Snake	中 Middle			坤 Kun	震 Zhen
丑 **Ox** (Jan 6 - Feb 3) 十二月 **12th Month**	甲 Jia Yang Wood	震 Zhen	乙 Yi Yin Wood	辰 Chen Dragon	巽 Xun	巳 Si Snake	坎 Kan	坤 Kun

Negative Repair / Renovation Sectors 修方凶位：

月 MONTH	月遊火 Month Wondering Fire	三煞 Monthly 3 Killings		
		劫煞 Robbery Sha	災煞 Calamity Sha	月煞 Month Sha
寅 **Tiger** (Feb 4 - Mar 5) 正月 **1st Month**	艮 Gen	亥 Hai Pig	子 Zi Rat	丑 Chou Ox
卯 **Rabbit** (Mar 6 - Apr 4) 二月 **2nd Month**	離 Li	申 Shen Monkey	酉 You Rooster	戌 Xu Dog
辰 **Dragon** (Apr 5 - May 5) 三月 **3rd Month**	坎 Kan	巳 Si Snake	午 Wu Horse	未 Wei Goat
巳 **Snake** (May 6 - Jun 5) 四月 **4th Month**	坤 Kun	寅 Yin Tiger	卯 Mao Rabbit	辰 Chen Dragon
午 **Horse** (Jun 6 - July 6) 五月 **5th Month**	震 Zhen	亥 Hai Pig	子 Zi Rat	丑 Chou Ox
未 **Goat** (July 7 - Aug 7) 六月 **6th Month**	巽 Xun	申 Shen Monkey	酉 You Rooster	戌 Xu Dog
申 **Monkey** (Aug 8 - Sept 7) 七月 **7th Month**	中 Middle	巳 Si Snake	午 Wu Horse	未 Wei Goat
酉 **Rooster** (Sept 8 - Oct 7) 八月 **8th Month**	乾 Qian	寅 Yin Tiger	卯 Mao Rabbit	辰 Chen Dragon
戌 **Dog** (Oct 8 - Nov 6) 九月 **9th Month**	兌 Dui	亥 Hai Pig	子 Zi Rat	丑 Chou Ox
亥 **Pig** (Nov 7 - Dec 6) 十月 **10th Month**	艮 Gen	申 Shen Monkey	酉 You Rooster	戌 Xu Dog
子 **Rat** (Dec 7 - Jan 5) 十一月 **11th Month**	離 Li	巳 Si Snake	午 Wu Horse	未 Wei Goat
丑 **Ox** (Jan 6 - Feb 3) 十二月 **12th Month**	坎 Kan	寅 Yin Tiger	卯 Mao Rabbit	辰 Chen Dragon

Negative Repair / Renovation Sectors 修方凶位 :

月 MONTH	月刑 Month Punishment	月害 Month Harm	月厭 Month Detest
寅 **Tiger** (Feb 4 - Mar 5) 正月 **1st Month**	巳 *Si* Snake	巳 *Si* Snake	戌 *Xu* Dog
卯 **Rabbit** (Mar 6 - Apr 4) 二月 **2nd Month**	子 *Zi* Rat	辰 *Chen* Dragon	酉 *You* Rooster
辰 **Dragon** (Apr 5 - May 5) 三月 **3rd Month**	辰 *Chen* Dragon	卯 *Mao* Rabbit	申 *Shen* Monkey
巳 **Snake** (May 6 - Jun 5) 四月 **4th Month**	申 *Shen* Monkey	寅 *Yin* Tiger	未 *Wei* Goat
午 **Horse** (Jun 6 - July 6) 五月 **5th Month**	午 *Wu* Horse	丑 *Chou* Ox	午 *Wu* Horse
未 **Goat** (July 7 - Aug 7) 六月 **6th Month**	丑 *Chou* Ox	子 *Zi* Rat	巳 *Si* Snake
申 **Monkey** (Aug 8 - Sept 7) 七月 **7th Month**	寅 *Yin* Tiger	亥 *Hai* Pig	辰 *Chen* Dragon
酉 **Rooster** (Sept 8 - Oct 7) 八月 **8th Month**	酉 *You* Rooster	戌 *Xu* Dog	卯 *Mao* Rabbit
戌 **Dog** (Oct 8 - Nov 6) 九月 **9th Month**	未 *Wei* Goat	酉 *You* Rooster	寅 *Yin* Tiger
亥 **Pig** (Nov 7 - Dec 6) 十月 **10th Month**	亥 *Hai* Pig	申 *Shen* Monkey	丑 *Chou* Ox
子 **Rat** (Dec 7 - Jan 5) 十一月 **11th Month**	卯 *Mao* Rabbit	未 *Wei* Goat	子 *Zi* Rat
丑 **Ox** (Jan 6 - Feb 3) 十二月 **12th Month**	戌 *Xu* Dog	午 *Wu* Horse	亥 *Hai* Pig

辛卯 (Xin Mao)
Metal Rabbit

Heavenly Stem 天干	辛 Yin Metal (陰金)
Earthly Branch 地支	卯 Rabbit (Yin Wood 陰木)
Hidden Stem 藏干	乙 Yin Wood
Na Yin 納音	松柏木 Wood from pine trees
Grand Duke 太歲	卯 Rabbit
Xuan Kong Five Element 玄空五行	2 火 Fire
Gua Name 卦名	風澤中孚 Sincerity
Xuan Kong Period Luck 玄空卦運	3

Annual Positive Stars for Opening Mountain, Establishing Facing and Commencing Repairs 開山立向修方吉星：

歲德 Duke Virtue	丙 Bing Yang Fire
歲德合 Duke Virtue Combo	辛 Xin Yin Metal
歲枝德 Duke Branch Virtue	申 Shen Monkey
陽貴人 Yang Nobleman	寅 Yin Tiger
陰貴人 Yin Nobleman	午 Wu Horse
歲祿 Duke Prosperous	酉 You Rooster
歲馬 Duke Horse	巳 Si Snake
奏書 Decree	艮 Gen
博士 Professor	坤 Kun

Annual Negative Stars for Opening Mountain, Establishing Facing and Commencing Repairs 開山立向修方凶星:

太歲 Grand Duke	歲破 Year Breaker	三煞 Three Killings			坐煞向煞 Sitting Sha Facing Sha				浮天空亡 Floating Heaven Emptiness	
卯 *Mao* Rabbit	酉 *You* Rooster	申 *Shen* Monkey	酉 *You* Rooster	戌 *Xu* Dog	庚 *Geng* Yang Metal	辛 *Xin* Yin Metal	甲 *Jia* Yang Wood	乙 *Yi* Yin Wood	艮 *Gen*	丙 *Bing* Yang Fire

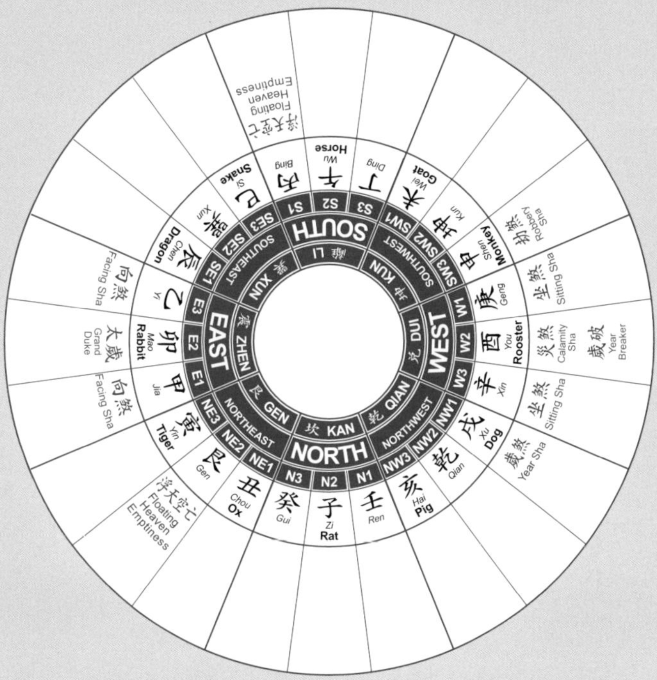

Annual San Yuan Purple White Stars 三元紫白九星:

上元 Upper Period — Period 1, 2, 3

巽SE	離S	坤SW
9	5	7
8	1 辛卯 Xin Mao Metal Rabbit	3
4	6	2
艮NE	坎N	乾NW

震 E (left), 兌 W (right)

中元 Middle Period — Period 4, 5, 6

巽SE	離S	坤SW
3	8	1
2	4 辛卯 Xin Mao Metal Rabbit	6
7	9	5
艮NE	坎N	乾NW

震 E (left), 兌 W (right)

下元 Lower Period — Period 7, 8, 9

巽SE	離S	坤SW
6	2	4
5	7 辛卯 Xin Mao Metal Rabbit	9
1	3	8
艮NE	坎N	乾NW

震 E (left), 兌 W (right)

Mountain Covering Yellow Path 蓋山黃道：

貪狼 *Tan Lang* **Greedy Wolf**		巨門 *Ju Men* **Huge Door**				武曲 *Wu Qu* **Military Arts**		文曲 *Wen Qu* **Literary Arts**	
乾 *Qian* NW2	甲 *Jia* E1	離 *Li* S2	壬 *Ren* N1	寅 *Yin* NE3	戌 *Xu* NW1	坤 *Kun* SW2	乙 *Yi* E3	巽 *Xun* SE2	辛 *Xin* W3

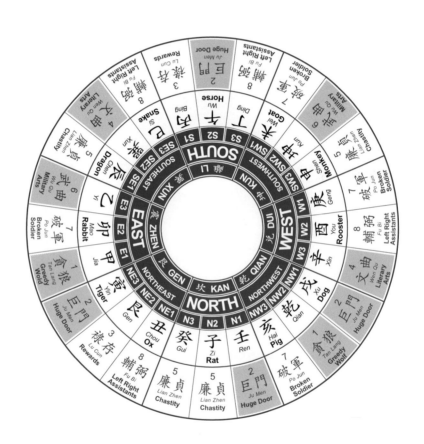

Heaven Penetrating Force 通天竅：

三合前方 **Facing Three Harmony**	巽巳 Xun Si	丙午 Bing Wu	丁未 Ding Wei
三合後方 **Sitting Three Harmony**	乾亥 Qian Hai	壬子 Ren Zi	癸丑 Gui Chou

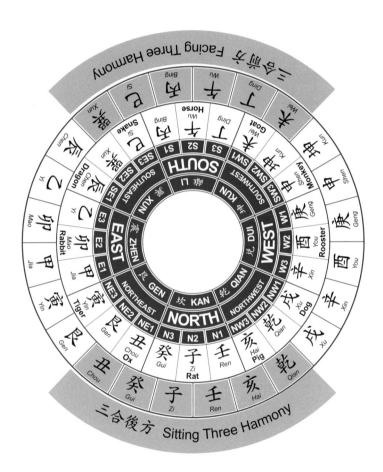

Moving Horse Six Ren Assessment 走馬六壬:

神后 *Shen Hou* **Holy Empress**	功曹 *Gong Cao* **Marshall**	天罡 *Tian Gang* **Heavenly Dipper**	勝光 *Sheng Guang* **Subliminal Bright**	傳送 *Chuan Song* **Great General**	河魁 *He Kui* **River Scholar**
庚酉 *Geng You*	乾亥 *Qian Hai*	癸丑 *Gui Chou*	甲卯 *Jia Mao*	巽巳 *Xun Si*	丁未 *Ding Wei*

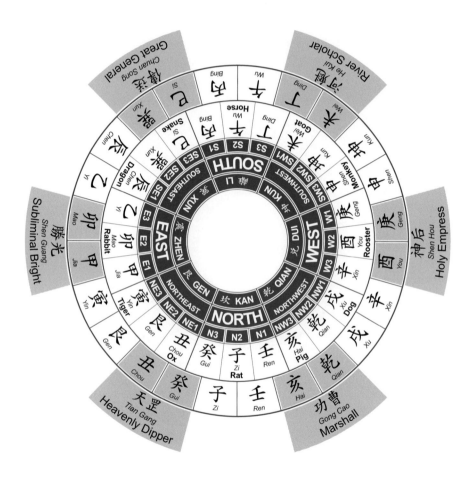

Four Advantages Three Cycles Star Plate 四利三元：

太陽 *Tai Yang* **Sun**	太陰 *Tai Yin* **Moon**	龍德 *Long De* **Dragon Virtue**	福德 *Fu De* **Fortune Virtue**
辰 *Chen* **Dragon**	午 *Wu* **Horse**	戌 *Xu* **Dog**	子 *Zi* **Rat**

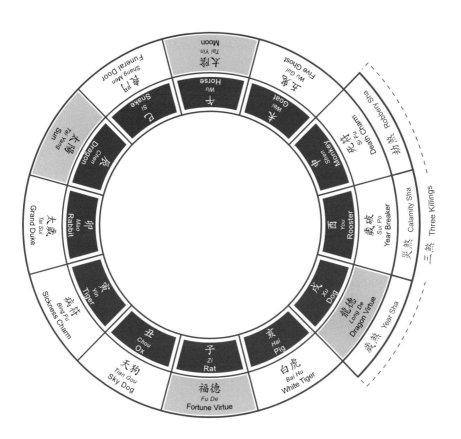

Negative Sectors For Opening Mountain 開山凶位：

年剋山家 Year Countering Sitting (冬至後 After Winter Solstice)

乾	亥	兌	丁
Qian	Hai	Dui	Ding
NW2	NW3	W2	S3

陰府太歲	六害	死符	炙退
Yin Fu Tai Sui	Liu Hai	Si Fu	Zhi Tui
Yin Mansion Grand Duke	**Six Harm**	**Death Charm**	**Roasting Star**

坤	坎	辰	申	午
Kun	Kan	Chen	Shen	Wu
SW2	N2	SE1	SW3	S2

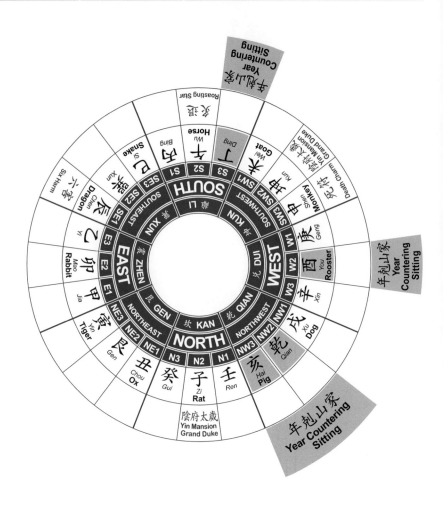

Negative Directions to Establish Facing 立向凶方：

巡山羅喉 *Xun Shan Luo Hou* **Mountain Patrol Luo Hou Star**	病符 *Bing Fu* **Sickness Charm**
乙 *Yi* **E3**	寅 *Yin* **NE3**

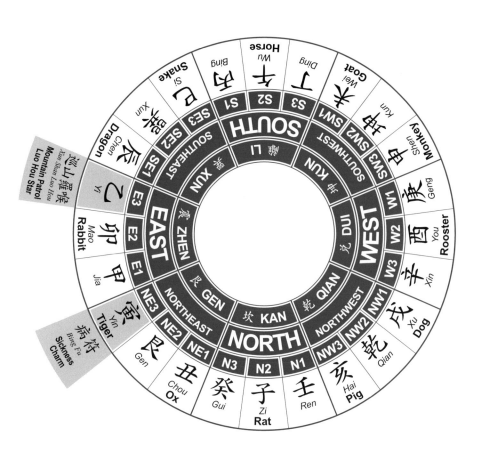

Negative Repair / Renovation Sectors Table 修方凶位表：

天官符 Heavenly Officer Charm	寅 Yin Tiger	飛廉 Flying Chaste	巳 Si Snake
地官符 Earthly Officer Charm	未 Wei Goat	喪門 Funeral Door	巳 Si Snake
大煞 Great Sha	卯 Mao Rabbit	弔客 Suspended Guest	丑 Chou Ox
大將軍 Big General	子 Zi Rat	白虎 White Tiger	亥 Hai Pig
力士 Strong Man	巽 Xun	金神 Golden God	寅 Yin Tiger / 卯 Mao Rabbit / 午 Wu Horse / 未 Wei Goat / 子 Zi Rat / 丑 Chou Ox
蠶室 Silkworm Room	乾 Qian		
蠶官 Silkworm Officer	戌 Xu Dog		
蠶命 Silkworm Life	亥 Hai Pig		
歲刑 Duke Punishment	子 Zi Rat	獨火 Lonely Fire	坎 Kan
黃幡 Yellow Flag	未 Wei Goat	五鬼 Five Ghost	丑 Chou Ox
豹尾 Leopard Tail	丑 Chou Ox	破敗五鬼 Destructive Five Ghost	乾 Qian

Negative Repair / Renovation Sectors Diagram 修方凶位圖：

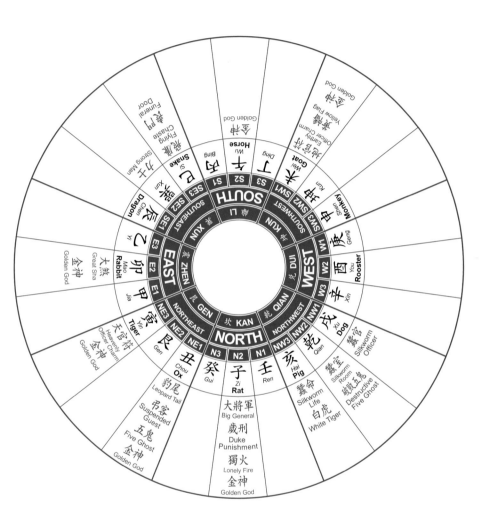

12-Month Auxiliary Stars Reference Table :
辛卯年十二月，開山立向修方星表

Positive Monthly Stars 吉星方

月 MONTH	寅 Tiger (Feb 4 - Mar 5) 正月 1st Month	卯 Rabbit (Mar 6 - Apr 4) 二月 2nd Month	辰 Dragon (Apr 5 - May 5) 三月 3rd Month	巳 Snake (May 6 - Jun 5) 四月 4th Month	午 Horse (Jun 6 - July 6) 五月 5th Month	未 Goat (July 7 - Aug 7) 六月 6th Month
天道 Heavenly Path	南 South	西南 Southwest	北 North	西 West	西北 Northwest	東 East
天德 Heavenly Virtue	丁 Ding Yin Fire	坤 Kun (申)	壬 Ren Yang Water	辛 Xin Yin Metal	乾 Qian (亥)	甲 Jia Yang Wood
天德合 Heavenly Virtue Combo	壬 Ren Yang Water	(巳)	丁 Ding Yin Fire	丙 Bing Yang Fire	(寅)	己 Ji Yin Earth
月德 Monthly Virtue	丙 Bing Yang Fire	甲 Jia Yang Wood	壬 Ren Yang Water	庚 Geng Yang Metal	丙 Bing Yang Fire	甲 Jia Yang Wood
月德合 Monthly Virtue Combo	辛 Xin Yin Metal	己 Ji Yin Earth	丁 Ding Yin Fire	乙 Yi Yin Wood	辛 Xin Yin Metal	己 Ji Yin Earth
月空 Month Emptiness	壬 Ren Yang Water	庚 Geng Yang Metal	丙 Bing Yang Fire	甲 Jia Yang Wood	壬 Ren Yang Water	庚 Geng Yang Metal
陽貴人 Yang Nobleman	中 Middle	坎 Kan	離 Li	艮 Gen	兌 Dui	乾 Qian
陰貴人 Yin Nobleman	離 Li	艮 Gen	兌 Dui	乾 Qian	中 Middle	坎 Kan
飛天祿 Flying Heavenly Wealth	震 Zhen	坤 Kun	坎 Kan	離 Li	艮 Gen	兌 Dui
飛天馬 Flying Heavenly Horse	艮 Gen	兌 Dui	乾 Qian	中 Middle	坎 Kan	離 Li

12-Month Auxiliary Stars Reference Table :
辛卯年十二月，開山立向修方星表

申 Monkey (Aug 8 - Sept 7) 七月 7th Month	酉 Rooster (Sept 8 - Oct 7) 八月 8th Month	戌 Dog (Oct 8 - Nov 6) 九月 9th Month	亥 Pig (Nov 7 - Dec 6) 十月 10th Month	子 Rat (Dec 7 - Jan 5) 十一月 11th Month	丑 Ox (Jan 6 - Feb 3) 十二月 12th Month	月 MONTH
北 North	東北 Northeast	南 South	東 East	東南 Southeast	西 West	天道 Heavenly Path
癸 Gui Yin Water	艮 Gen (寅)	丙 Bing Yang Fire	乙 Yi Yin Wood	巽 Xun (巳)	庚 Geng Yang Metal	天德 Heavenly Virtue
戊 Wu Yang Earth	(亥)	辛 Xin Yin Metal	庚 Geng Yang Metal	(申)	乙 Yi Yin Wood	天德合 Heavenly Virtue Combo
壬 Ren Yang Water	庚 Geng Yang Metal	丙 Bing Yang Fire	甲 Jia Yang Wood	壬 Ren Yang Water	庚 Geng Yang Metal	月德 Monthly Virtue
丁 Ding Yin Fire	乙 Yi Yin Wood	辛 Xin Yin Metal	己 Ji Yin Earth	丁 Ding Yin Fire	乙 Yi Yin Wood	月德合 Monthly Virtue Combo
丙 Bing Yang Fire	甲 Jia Yang Wood	壬 Ren Yang Water	庚 Geng Yang Metal	丙 Bing Yang Fire	甲 Jia Yang Wood	月空 Month Emptiness
中 Middle	巽 Xun	震 Zhen	坤 Kun	坎 Kan	離 Li	陽貴人 Yang Nobleman
離 Li	艮 Gen	兌 Dui	乾 Qian	中 Middle	巽 Xun	陰貴人 Yin Nobleman
乾 Qian	中 Middle	坎 Kan	離 Li	艮 Gen	兌 Dui	飛天祿 Flying Heavenly Wealth
艮 Gen	兌 Dui	乾 Qian	中 Middle	巽 Xun	震 Zhen	飛天馬 Flying Heavenly Horse

辛卯 (Xin Mao) Metal Rabbit

Monthly Purple White Stars 月紫白九星 :

寅 Tiger (Feb 4 - Mar 5) 正月 1st Month

巽 SE	離 S	坤 SW
7 Red 七赤	3 Jade 三碧	5 Yellow 五黃
震 E 6 White 六白	8 White 八白	1 White 一白 兌 W
艮 NE 2 Black 二黑	坎 N 4 Green 四綠	乾 NW 9 Purple 九紫

卯 Rabbit (Mar 6 - Apr 4) 二月 2nd Month

巽 SE	離 S	坤 SW
6 White 六白	2 Black 二黑	4 Green 四綠
震 E 5 Yellow 五黃	7 Red 七赤	9 Purple 九紫 兌 W
艮 NE 1 White 一白	坎 N 3 Jade 三碧	乾 NW 8 White 八白

辰 Dragon (Apr 5 - May 5) 三月 3rd Month

巽 SE	離 S	坤 SW
5 Yellow 五黃	1 White 一白	3 Jade 三碧
震 E 4 Green 四綠	6 White 六白	8 White 八白 兌 W
艮 NE 9 Purple 九紫	坎 N 2 Black 二黑	乾 NW 7 Red 七赤

巳 Snake (May 6 - Jun 5) 四月 4th Month

巽 SE	離 S	坤 SW
4 Green 四綠	9 Purple 九紫	2 Black 二黑
震 E 3 Jade 三碧	5 Yellow 五黃	7 Red 七赤 兌 W
艮 NE 8 White 八白	坎 N 1 White 一白	乾 NW 6 White 六白

午 Horse (Jun 6 - July 6) 五月 5th Month

巽 SE	離 S	坤 SW
3 Jade 三碧	8 White 八白	1 White 一白
震 E 2 Black 二黑	4 Green 四綠	6 White 六白 兌 W
艮 NE 7 Red 七赤	坎 N 9 Purple 九紫	乾 NW 5 Yellow 五黃

未 Goat (July 7 - Aug 7) 六月 6th Month

巽 SE	離 S	坤 SW
2 Black 二黑	7 Red 七赤	9 Purple 九紫
震 E 1 White 一白	3 Jade 三碧	5 Yellow 五黃 兌 W
艮 NE 6 White 六白	坎 N 8 White 八白	乾 NW 4 Green 四綠

申 Monkey (Aug 8 - Sept 7) 七月 7th Month

巽 SE	離 S	坤 SW
1 White 一白	6 White 六白	8 White 八白
震 E 9 Purple 九紫	2 Black 二黑	4 Green 四綠 兌 W
艮 NE 5 Yellow 五黃	坎 N 7 Red 七赤	乾 NW 3 Jade 三碧

酉 Rooster (Sept 8 - Oct 7) 八月 8th Month

巽 SE	離 S	坤 SW
9 Purple 九紫	5 Yellow 五黃	7 Red 七赤
震 E 8 White 八白	1 White 一白	3 Jade 三碧 兌 W
艮 NE 4 Green 四綠	坎 N 6 White 六白	乾 NW 2 Black 二黑

戌 Dog (Oct 8 - Nov 6) 九月 9th Month

巽 SE	離 S	坤 SW
8 White 八白	4 Green 四綠	6 White 六白
震 E 7 Red 七赤	9 Purple 九紫	2 Black 二黑 兌 W
艮 NE 3 Jade 三碧	坎 N 5 Yellow 五黃	乾 NW 1 White 一白

亥 Pig (Nov 7 - Dec 6) 十月 10th Month

巽 SE	離 S	坤 SW
7 Red 七赤	3 Jade 三碧	5 Yellow 五黃
震 E 6 White 六白	8 White 八白	1 White 一白 兌 W
艮 NE 2 Black 二黑	坎 N 4 Green 四綠	乾 NW 9 Purple 九紫

子 Rat (Dec 7 - Jan 5) 十一月 11th Month

巽 SE	離 S	坤 SW
6 White 六白	2 Black 二黑	4 Green 四綠
震 E 5 Yellow 五黃	7 Red 七赤	9 Purple 九紫 兌 W
艮 NE 1 White 一白	坎 N 3 Jade 三碧	乾 NW 8 White 八白

丑 Ox (Jan 6 - Feb 3) 十二月 12th Month

巽 SE	離 S	坤 SW
5 Yellow 五黃	1 White 一白	3 Jade 三碧
震 E 4 Green 四綠	6 White 六白	8 White 八白 兌 W
艮 NE 9 Purple 九紫	坎 N 2 Black 二黑	乾 NW 7 Red 七赤

Qi Men Three Nobles 三奇 :

Three Nobles 三奇 / Seasons	乙 Yi	丙 Bing	丁 Ding
立春 **Coming of Spring** Feb 4 - Feb 18	巽 Xun	中 **Middle**	乾 Qian
春分 **Spring Equinox** Mar 21 - Apr 4	艮 Gen	離 Li	坎 Kan
立夏 **Coming of Summer** May 6 - May 20	離 Li	坎 Kan	坤 Kun
夏至 **Summer Solstice** Jun 22 - Jul 6	巽 Xun	震 Zhen	坤 Kun
立秋 **Coming of Autumn** Aug 8 - Aug 23	乾 Qian	中 **Middle**	巽 Xun
秋分 **Autumn Equinox** Sept 23 - Oct 7	坤 Kun	坎 Kan	離 Li
立冬 **Coming of Winter** Nov 7 - Nov 22	坎 Kan	離 Li	艮 Gen
冬至 **Winter Solstice** Dec 22 - Jan 5	乾 Qian	兌 Dui	艮 Gen

辛卯 (Xin Mao) Metal Rabbit

Sectors to Avoid Opening Mountain 開山凶位 :

月 MONTH	月建 Month Establishment	月破 Month Destruction	月剋山家 Month Countering Sitting		陰府太歲 Yin Mansion Grand Duke	
寅 **Tiger** (Feb 4 - Mar 5) 正月 **1st Month**	寅 *Yin* **Tiger**	申 *Shen* **Monkey**	—		乾 *Qian*	兌 *Dui*
卯 **Rabbit** (Mar 6 - Apr 4) 二月 **2nd Month**	卯 *Mao* **Rabbit**	酉 *You* **Rooster**	—		坤 *Kun*	坎 *Kan*
辰 **Dragon** (Apr 5 - May 5) 三月 **3rd Month**	辰 *Chen* **Dragon**	戌 *Xu* **Dog**	乾 *Qian*	兌 *Dui*	離 *Li*	乾 *Qian*
巳 **Snake** (May 6 - Jun 5) 四月 **4th Month**	巳 *Si* **Snake**	亥 *Hai* **Pig**	亥 *Hai* **Pig**	丁 *Ding* **Yin Fire**	震 *Zhen*	坤 *Kun*
午 **Horse** (Jun 6 - July 6) 五月 **5th Month**	午 *Wu* **Horse**	子 *Zi* **Rat**	離 *Li*	丙 *Bing* **Yang Fire**	艮 *Gen*	巽 *Xun*
未 **Goat** (July 7 - Aug 7) 六月 **6th Month**	未 *Wei* **Goat**	丑 *Chou* **Ox**	壬 *Ren* **Yang Water**	乙 *Yi* **Yin Wood**	兌 *Dui*	乾 *Qian*
申 **Monkey** (Aug 8 - Sept 7) 七月 **7th Month**	申 *Shen* **Monkey**	寅 *Yin* **Tiger**	震 *Zhen*	巳 *Si* **Snake**	坎 *Kan*	坤 *Kun*
酉 **Rooster** (Sept 8 - Oct 7) 八月 **8th Month**	酉 *You* **Rooster**	卯 *Mao* **Rabbit**	艮 *Gen*		乾 *Qian*	離 *Li*
戌 **Dog** (Oct 8 - Nov 6) 九月 **9th Month**	戌 *Xu* **Dog**	辰 *Chen* **Dragon**	—		坤 *Kun*	震 *Zhen*
亥 **Pig** (Nov 7 - Dec 6) 十月 **10th Month**	亥 *Hai* **Pig**	巳 *Si* **Snake**	—		巽 *Xun*	艮 *Gen*
子 **Rat** (Dec 7 - Jan 5) 十一月 **11th Month**	子 *Zi* **Rat**	午 *Wu* **Horse**	水 **Water**	山 **Mountain**	乾 *Qian*	兌 *Dui*
丑 **Ox** (Jan 6 - Feb 3) 十二月 **12th Month**	丑 *Chou* **Ox**	未 *Wei* **Goat**	土 **Earth**		坤 *Kun*	坎 *Kan*

辛卯 (Xin Mao) Metal Rabbit

Negative Repair / Renovation Sectors 修方凶位 :

月 MONTH	天官符 Heavenly Officer Charm			地官符 Earth Officer Charm			小月建 Small Month Establishment		
寅 Tiger (Feb 4 - Mar 5) 正月 1st Month		中 Middle		壬 Ren Yang Water	坎 Kan	癸 Gui Yin Water	丙 Bing Yang Fire	離 Li	丁 Ding Yin Fire
卯 Rabbit (Mar 6 - Apr 4) 二月 2nd Month	庚 Geng Yang Metal	兌 Dui	辛 Xin Yin Metal	丙 Bing Yang Fire	離 Li	丁 Ding Yin Fire	壬 Ren Yang Water	坎 Kan	癸 Gui Yin Water
辰 Dragon (Apr 5 - May 5) 三月 3rd Month	戌 Xu Dog	乾 Qian	亥 Hai Pig	丑 Chou Ox	艮 Gen	寅 Yin Tiger	未 Wei Goat	坤 Kun	申 Shen Monkey
巳 Snake (May 6 - Jun 5) 四月 4th Month		中 Middle		庚 Geng Yang Metal	兌 Dui	辛 Xin Yin Metal	甲 Jia Yang Wood	震 Zhen	乙 Yi Yin Wood
午 Horse (Jun 6 - July 6) 五月 5th Month	辰 Chen Dragon	巽 Xun	巳 Si Snake	戌 Xu Dog	乾 Qian	亥 Hai Pig	辰 Chen Dragon	巽 Xun	巳 Si Snake
未 Goat (July 7 - Aug 7) 六月 6th Month	甲 Jia Yang Wood	震 Zhen	乙 Yi Yin Wood		中 Middle			中 Middle	
申 Monkey (Aug 8 - Sept 7) 七月 7th Month	未 Wei Goat	坤 Kun	申 Shen Monkey	庚 Geng Yang Metal	兌 Dui	辛 Xin Yin Metal	戌 Xu Dog	乾 Qian	亥 Hai Pig
酉 Rooster (Sept 8 - Oct 7) 八月 8th Month	壬 Ren Yang Water	坎 Kan	癸 Gui Yin Water	戌 Xu Dog	乾 Qian	亥 Hai Pig	庚 Geng Yang Metal	兌 Dui	辛 Xin Yin Metal
戌 Dog (Oct 8 - Nov 6) 九月 9th Month	丙 Bing Yang Fire	離 Li	丁 Ding Yin Fire		中 Middle		丑 Chou Ox	艮 Gen	寅 Yin Tiger
亥 Pig (Nov 7 - Dec 6) 十月 10th Month	丑 Chou Ox	艮 Gen	寅 Yin Tiger	辰 Chen Dragon	巽 Xun	巳 Si Snake	丙 Bing Yang Fire	離 Li	丁 Ding Yin Fire
子 Rat (Dec 7 - Jan 5) 十一月 11th Month	庚 Geng Yang Metal	兌 Dui	辛 Xin Yin Metal	甲 Jia Yang Wood	震 Zhen	乙 Yi Yin Wood	壬 Ren Yang Water	坎 Kan	癸 Gui Yin Water
丑 Ox (Jan 6 - Feb 3) 十二月 12th Month	戌 Xu Dog	乾 Qian	亥 Hai Pig	未 Wei Goat	坤 Kun	申 Shen Monkey	未 Wei Goat	坤 Kun	申 Shen Monkey

Negative Repair / Renovation Sectors 修方凶位 :

月 MONTH	大月建 Big Month Establishment			飛大煞 Flying Great Sha			丙丁獨火 Bing Ding Lonely Fire	
寅 **Tiger** (Feb 4 - Mar 5) 正月 **1st Month**	丑 Chou Ox	艮 Gen	寅 Yin Tiger	戌 Xu Dog	乾 Qian	亥 Hai Pig	坤 Kun	震 Zhen
卯 **Rabbit** (Mar 6 - Apr 4) 二月 **2nd Month**	庚 Geng Yang Metal	兌 Dui	辛 Xin Yin Metal	中 Middle			坎 Kan	坤 Kun
辰 **Dragon** (Apr 5 - May 5) 三月 **3rd Month**	戌 Xu Dog	乾 Qian	亥 Hai Pig	庚 Geng Yang Metal	兌 Dui	辛 Xin Yin Metal	離 Li	坎 Kan
巳 **Snake** (May 6 - Jun 5) 四月 **4th Month**	中 Middle			戌 Xu Dog	乾 Qian	亥 Hai Pig	艮 Gen	離 Li
午 **Horse** (Jun 6 - July 6) 五月 **5th Month**	辰 Chen Dragon	巽 Xun	巳 Si Snake	中 Middle			兌 Dui	艮 Gen
未 **Goat** (July 7 - Aug 7) 六月 **6th Month**	甲 Jia Yang Wood	震 Zhen	乙 Yi Yin Wood	辰 Chen Dragon	巽 Xun	巳 Si Snake	乾 Qian	兌 Dui
申 **Monkey** (Aug 8 - Sept 7) 七月 **7th Month**	未 Wei Goat	坤 Kun	申 Shen Monkey	甲 Jia Yang Wood	震 Zhen	乙 Yi Yin Wood	中 Middle	乾 Qian
酉 **Rooster** (Sept 8 - Oct 7) 八月 **8th Month**	壬 Ren Yang Water	坎 Kan	癸 Gui Yin Water	未 Wei Goat	坤 Kun	申 Shen Monkey	中 Middle	
戌 **Dog** (Oct 8 - Nov 6) 九月 **9th Month**	丙 Bing Yang Fire	離 Li	丁 Ding Yin Fire	壬 Ren Yang Water	坎 Kan	癸 Gui Yin Water	巽 Xun	中 Middle
亥 **Pig** (Nov 7 - Dec 6) 十月 **10th Month**	丑 Chou Ox	艮 Gen	寅 Yin Tiger	丙 Bing Yang Fire	離 Li	丁 Ding Yin Fire	震 Zhen	巽 Xun
子 **Rat** (Dec 7 - Jan 5) 十一月 **11th Month**	庚 Geng Yang Metal	兌 Dui	辛 Xin Yin Metal	丑 Chou Ox	艮 Gen	寅 Yin Tiger	坤 Kun	震 Zhen
丑 **Ox** (Jan 6 - Feb 3) 十二月 **12th Month**	戌 Xu Dog	乾 Qian	亥 Hai Pig	庚 Geng Yang Metal	兌 Dui	辛 Xin Yin Metal	坎 Kan	坤 Kun

Negative Repair / Renovation Sectors 修方凶位 :

月 MONTH	月遊火 Month Wondering Fire	三煞 Monthly 3 Killings		
		劫煞 Robbery Sha	災煞 Calamity Sha	月煞 Month Sha
寅 **Tiger** (Feb 4 - Mar 5) 正月 **1st Month**	巽 Xun	亥 Hai **Pig**	子 Zi **Rat**	丑 Chou **Ox**
卯 **Rabbit** (Mar 6 - Apr 4) 二月 **2nd Month**	中 **Middle**	申 Shen **Monkey**	酉 You **Rooster**	戌 Xu **Dog**
辰 **Dragon** (Apr 5 - May 5) 三月 **3rd Month**	乾 Qian	巳 Si **Snake**	午 Wu **Horse**	未 Wei **Goat**
巳 **Snake** (May 6 - Jun 5) 四月 **4th Month**	兌 Dui	寅 Yin **Tiger**	卯 Mao **Rabbit**	辰 Chen **Dragon**
午 **Horse** (Jun 6 - July 6) 五月 **5th Month**	艮 Gen	亥 Hai **Pig**	子 Zi **Rat**	丑 Chou **Ox**
未 **Goat** (July 7 - Aug 7) 六月 **6th Month**	離 Li	申 Shen **Monkey**	酉 You **Rooster**	戌 Xu **Dog**
申 **Monkey** (Aug 8 - Sept 7) 七月 **7th Month**	坎 Kan	巳 Si **Snake**	午 Wu **Horse**	未 Wei **Goat**
酉 **Rooster** (Sept 8 - Oct 7) 八月 **8th Month**	坤 Kun	寅 Yin **Tiger**	卯 Mao **Rabbit**	辰 Chen **Dragon**
戌 **Dog** (Oct 8 - Nov 6) 九月 **9th Month**	震 Zhen	亥 Hai **Pig**	子 Zi **Rat**	丑 Chou **Ox**
亥 **Pig** (Nov 7 - Dec 6) 十月 **10th Month**	巽 Xun	申 Shen **Monkey**	酉 You **Rooster**	戌 Xu **Dog**
子 **Rat** (Dec 7 - Jan 5) 十一月 **11th Month**	中 **Middle**	巳 Si **Snake**	午 Wu **Horse**	未 Wei **Goat**
丑 **Ox** (Jan 6 - Feb 3) 十二月 **12th Month**	乾 Qian	寅 Yin **Tiger**	卯 Mao **Rabbit**	辰 Chen **Dragon**

Negative Repair / Renovation Sectors 修方凶位 :

月 MONTH	月刑 Month Punishment	月害 Month Harm	月厭 Month Detest
寅 **Tiger** (Feb 4 - Mar 5) 正月 **1st Month**	巳 Si Snake	巳 Si Snake	戌 Xu Dog
卯 **Rabbit** (Mar 6 - Apr 4) 二月 **2nd Month**	子 Zi Rat	辰 Chen Dragon	酉 You Rooster
辰 **Dragon** (Apr 5 - May 5) 三月 **3rd Month**	辰 Chen Dragon	卯 Mao Rabbit	申 Shen Monkey
巳 **Snake** (May 6 - Jun 5) 四月 **4th Month**	申 Shen Monkey	寅 Yin Tiger	未 Wei Goat
午 **Horse** (Jun 6 - July 6) 五月 **5th Month**	午 Wu Horse	丑 Chou Ox	午 Wu Horse
未 **Goat** (July 7 - Aug 7) 六月 **6th Month**	丑 Chou Ox	子 Zi Rat	巳 Si Snake
申 **Monkey** (Aug 8 - Sept 7) 七月 **7th Month**	寅 Yin Tiger	亥 Hai Pig	辰 Chen Dragon
酉 **Rooster** (Sept 8 - Oct 7) 八月 **8th Month**	酉 You Rooster	戌 Xu Dog	卯 Mao Rabbit
戌 **Dog** (Oct 8 - Nov 6) 九月 **9th Month**	未 Wei Goat	酉 You Rooster	寅 Yin Tiger
亥 **Pig** (Nov 7 - Dec 6) 十月 **10th Month**	亥 Hai Pig	申 Shen Monkey	丑 Chou Ox
子 **Rat** (Dec 7 - Jan 5) 十一月 **11th Month**	卯 Mao Rabbit	未 Wei Goat	子 Zi Rat
丑 **Ox** (Jan 6 - Feb 3) 十二月 **12th Month**	戌 Xu Dog	午 Wu Horse	亥 Hai Pig

辛巳 (Xin Si)
Metal Snake

Heavenly Stem 天干	辛 Yin Metal (陰金)
Earthly Branch 地支	巳 Snake (Yin Fire 陰火)
Hidden Stem 藏干	丙 Yang Fire, 戊 Yang Earth, 庚 Yang Metal
Na Yin 納音	白臘金 Metal mold
Grand Duke 太歲	巳 Snake
Xuan Kong Five Element 玄空五行	3 木 Wood
Gua Name 卦名	☲☰ 火天大有 Great Reward
Xuan Kong Period Luck 玄空卦運	7

Annual Positive Stars for Opening Mountain, Establishing Facing and Commencing Repairs 開山立向修方吉星：

歲德 Duke Virtue	丙 Bing Yang Fire
歲德合 Duke Virtue Combo	辛 Xin Yin Metal
歲枝德 Duke Branch Virtue	戊 Xu Dog
陽貴人 Yang Nobleman	寅 Yin Tiger
陰貴人 Yin Nobleman	午 Wu Horse
歲祿 Duke Prosperous	酉 You Rooster
歲馬 Duke Horse	亥 Hai Pig
奏書 Decree	巽 Xun
博士 Professor	乾 Qian

Annual Negative Stars for Opening Mountain, Establishing Facing and Commencing Repairs 開山立向修方凶星：

太歲 Grand Duke	歲破 Year Breaker	三煞 Three Killings			坐煞向煞 Sitting Sha Facing Sha				浮天空亡 Floating Heaven Emptiness	
巳 Si Snake	亥 Hai Pig	寅 Yin Tiger	卯 Mao Rabbit	辰 Chen Dragon	甲 Jia Yang Wood	乙 Yi Yin Wood	庚 Geng Yang Metal	辛 Xin Yin Metal	艮 Gen	丙 Bing Yang Fire

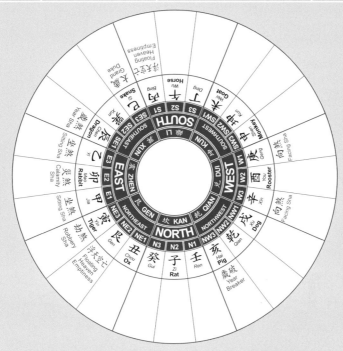

Annual San Yuan Purple White Stars 三元紫白九星：

上元 Upper Period Period 1, 2, 3			中元 Middle Period Period 4, 5, 6			下元 Lower Period Period 7, 8, 9		
巽SE 1	離S 6	坤SW 8	巽SE 4	離S 9	坤SW 2	巽SE 7	離S 3	坤SW 5
震E 9	2 辛巳 Xin Si Metal Snake	兌W 4	震E 3	5 辛巳 Xin Si Metal Snake	兌W 7	震E 6	8 辛巳 Xin Si Metal Snake	兌W 1
艮NE 5	坎N 7	乾NW 3	艮NE 8	坎N 1	乾NW 6	艮NE 2	坎N 4	乾NW 9

Mountain Covering Yellow Path 蓋山黃道：

貪狼 *Tan Lang* **Greedy Wolf**				巨門 *Ju Men* **Huge Door**				武曲 *Wu Qu* **Military Arts**		文曲 *Wen Qu* **Literary Arts**			
兌 *Dui* W2	丁 *Ding* S3	巳 *Si* SE3	丑 *Chou* NE1	震 *Zhen* E2	庚 *Geng* W1	亥 *Hai* NW3	未 *Wei* SW1	艮 *Gen* NE2	丙 *Bing* S1	癸 *Gui* N3	坎 *Kan* N2	申 *Shen* SW3	辰 *Chen* SE1

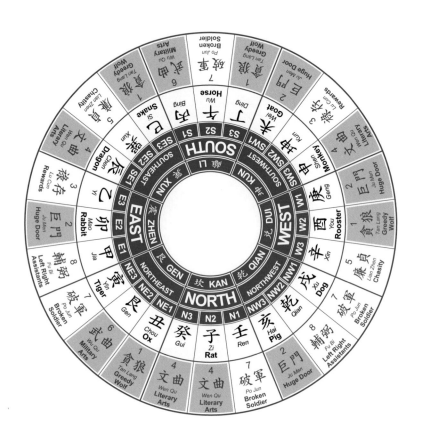

Heaven Penetrating Force 通天竅:

三合前方 **Facing Three Harmony**	乾亥 Qian Hai	壬子 Ren Zi	癸丑 Gui Chou
三合後方 **Sitting Three Harmony**	巽巳 Xun Si	丙午 Bing Wu	丁未 Ding Wei

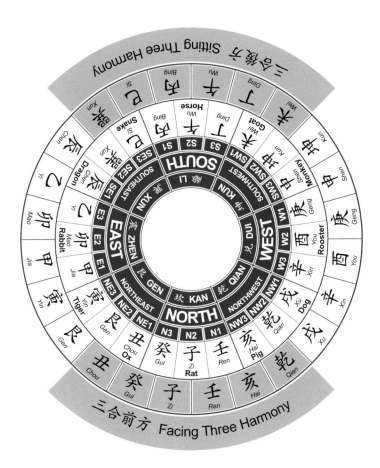

Moving Horse Six Ren Assessment 走馬六壬：

神后 *Shen Hou* **Holy Empress**	功曹 *Gong Cao* **Marshall**	天罡 *Tian Gang* **Heavenly Dipper**	勝光 *Sheng Guang* **Subliminal Bright**	傳送 *Chuan Song* **Great General**	河魁 *He Kui* **River Scholar**
丁未 _{*Ding Wei*}	庚酉 _{*Geng You*}	乾亥 _{*Qian Hai*}	癸丑 _{*Gui Chou*}	甲卯 _{*Jia Mao*}	巽巳 _{*Xun Si*}

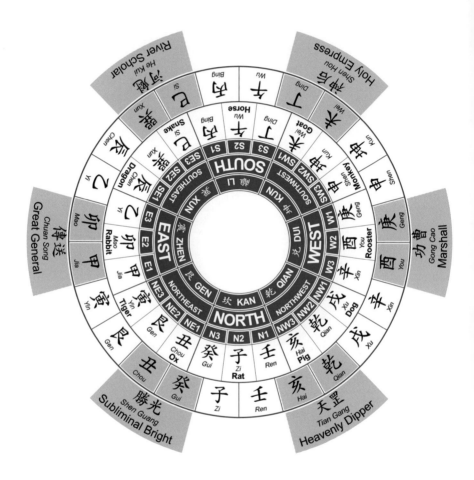

Four Advantages Three Cycles Star Plate 四利三元:

太陽 *Tai Yang* **Sun**	太陰 *Tai Yin* **Moon**	龍德 *Long De* **Dragon Virtue**	福德 *Fu De* **Fortune Virtue**
午 *Wu* **S2**	申 *Shen* **SW3**	子 *Zi* **N2**	寅 *Yin* **NE3**

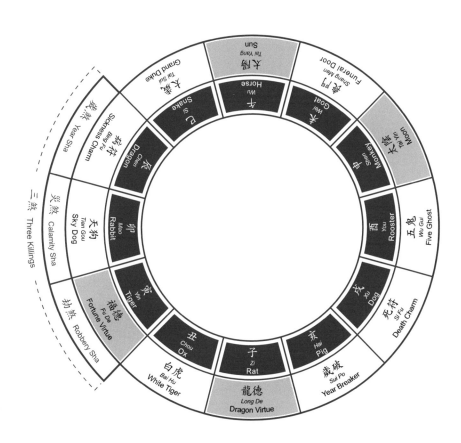

Negative Sectors For Opening Mountain 開山凶位:

年尅山家 Year Countering Sitting

離	壬	丙	乙
Li	Ren	Bing	Yi
S2	N1	S1	E3

陰府太歲	六害	死符	炙退
Yin Fu Tai Sui	Liu Hai	Si Fu	Zhi Tui
Yin Mansion Grand Duke	**Six Harm**	**Death Charm**	**Roasting Star**

坤	坎	寅	戌	子
Kun	Kan	Yin	Xu	Zi
SW2	N2	NE3	NW1	N2

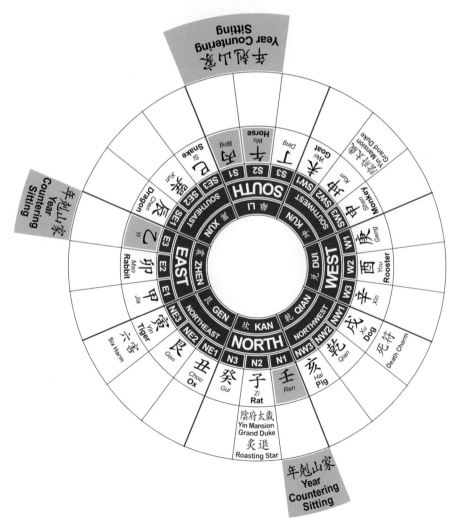

Negative Directions to Establish Facing 立向凶方：

巡山羅喉 *Xun Shan Luo Hou* **Mountain Patrol Luo Hou Star**	病符 *Bing Fu* **Sickness Charm**
丙 *Bing* **S1**	辰 *Chen* **SE1**

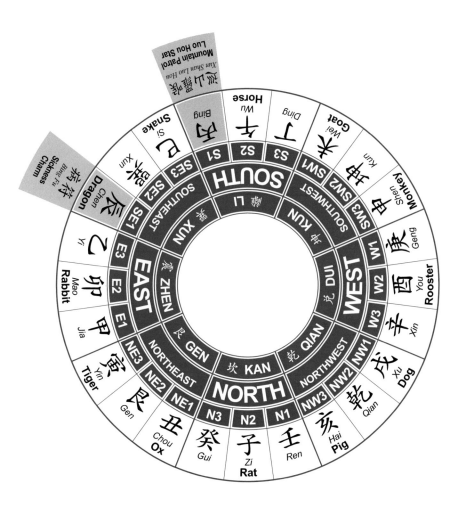

Negative Repair / Renovation Sectors Table 修方凶位表：

天官符 Heavenly Officer Charm	申 Shen Monkey	飛廉 Flying Chaste	未 Wei Goat
地官符 Earthly Officer Charm	酉 You Rooster	喪門 Funeral Door	未 Wei Goat
大煞 Great Sha	酉 You Rooster	弔客 Suspended Guest	卯 Mao Rabbit
大將軍 Big General	卯 Mao Rabbit	白虎 White Tiger	丑 Chou Ox
力士 Strong Man	坤 Kun	金神 Golden God	寅 Yin Tiger 卯 Mao Rabbit 午 Wu Horse 未 Wei Goat 子 Zi Rat 丑 Chou Ox
蠶室 Silkworm Room	艮 Gen		
蠶官 Silkworm Officer	丑 Chou Ox		
蠶命 Silkworm Life	寅 Yin Tige		
歲刑 Duke Punishment	申 Shen Monkey	獨火 Lonely Fire	巽 Xun
黃幡 Yellow Flag	丑 Chou Ox	五鬼 Five Ghost	亥 Hai Pig
豹尾 Leopard Tail	未 Wei Goat	破敗五鬼 Destructive Five Ghost	乾 Qian

Negative Repair / Renovation Sectors Diagram 修方凶位圖：

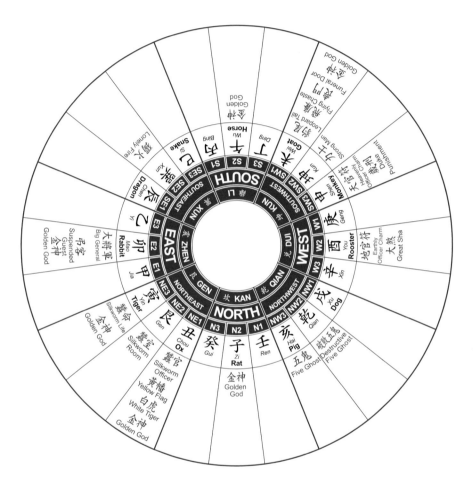

12-Month Auxiliary Stars Reference Table :
辛巳年十二月，開山立向修方星表

Positive Monthly Stars 吉星方

月 MONTH	寅 Tiger (Feb 4 - Mar 5) 正月 1st Month	卯 Rabbit (Mar 6 - Apr 4) 二月 2nd Month	辰 Dragon (Apr 5 - May 5) 三月 3rd Month	巳 Snake (May 6 - Jun 5) 四月 4th Month	午 Horse (Jun 6 - July 6) 五月 5th Month	未 Goat (July 7 - Aug 7) 六月 6th Month
天道 Heavenly Path	南 South	西南 Southwest	北 North	西 West	西北 Northwest	東 East
天德 Heavenly Virtue	丁 Ding Yin Fire	坤 Kun (申)	壬 Ren Yang Water	辛 Xin Yin Metal	乾 Qian (亥)	甲 Jia Yang Wood
天德合 Heavenly Virtue Combo	壬 Ren Yang Water	(巳)	丁 Ding Yin Fire	丙 Bing Yang Fire	(寅)	己 Ji Yin Earth
月德 Monthly Virtue	丙 Bing Yang Fire	甲 Jia Yang Wood	壬 Ren Yang Water	庚 Geng Yang Metal	丙 Bing Yang Fire	甲 Jia Yang Wood
月德合 Monthly Virtue Combo	辛 Xin Yin Metal	己 Ji Yin Earth	丁 Ding Yin Fire	乙 Yi Yin Wood	辛 Xin Yin Metal	己 Ji Yin Earth
月空 Month Emptiness	壬 Ren Yang Water	庚 Geng Yang Metal	丙 Bing Yang Fire	甲 Jia Yang Wood	壬 Ren Yang Water	庚 Geng Yang Metal
陽貴人 Yang Nobleman	中 Middle	坎 Kan	離 Li	艮 Gen	兌 Dui	乾 Qian
陰貴人 Yin Nobleman	離 Li	艮 Gen	兌 Dui	乾 Qian	中 Middle	坎 Kan
飛天祿 Flying Heavenly Wealth	震 Zhen	坤 Kun	坎 Kan	離 Li	艮 Gen	兌 Dui
飛天馬 Flying Heavenly Horse	中 Middle	巽 Xun	震 Zhen	坤 Kun	坎 Kan	離 Li

12-Month Auxiliary Stars Reference Table :
辛巳年十二月，開山立向修方星表

申 **Monkey** (Aug 8 - Sept 7) 七月 **7th Month**	酉 **Rooster** (Sept 8 - Oct 7) 八月 **8th Month**	戌 **Dog** (Oct 8 - Nov 6) 九月 **9th Month**	亥 **Pig** (Nov 7 - Dec 6) 十月 **10th Month**	子 **Rat** (Dec 7 - Jan 5) 十一月 **11th Month**	丑 **Ox** (Jan 6 - Feb 3) 十二月 **12th Month**	月 **MONTH**
北 North	東北 Northeast	南 South	東 East	東南 Southeast	西 West	天道 **Heavenly Path**
癸 Gui Yin Water	艮 Gen （寅）	丙 Bing Yang Fire	乙 Yi Yin Wood	巽 Xun （巳）	庚 Geng Yang Metal	天德 **Heavenly Virtue**
戊 Wu Yang Earth	（亥）	辛 Xin Yin Metal	庚 Geng Yang Metal	（申）	乙 Yi Yin Wood	天德合 **Heavenly Virtue Combo**
壬 Ren Yang Water	庚 Geng Yang Metal	丙 Bing Yang Fire	甲 Jia Yang Wood	壬 Ren Yang Water	庚 Geng Yang Metal	月德 **Monthly Virtue**
丁 Ding Yin Fire	乙 Yi Yin Wood	辛 Xin Yin Metal	己 Ji Yin Earth	丁 Ding Yin Fire	乙 Yi Yin Wood	月德合 **Monthly Virtue Combo**
丙 Bing Yang Fire	甲 Jia Yang Wood	壬 Ren Yang Water	庚 Geng Yang Metal	丙 Bing Yang Fire	甲 Jia Yang Wood	月空 **Month Emptiness**
中 Middle	巽 Xun	震 Zhen	坤 Kun	坎 Kan	離 Li	陽貴人 **Yang Nobleman**
離 Li	艮 Gen	兌 Dui	乾 Qian	中 Middle	巽 Xun	陰貴人 **Yin Nobleman**
乾 Qian	中 Middle	坎 Kan	離 Li	艮 Gen	兌 Dui	飛天祿 **Flying Heavenly Wealth**
艮 Gen	兌 Dui	乾 Qian	中 Middle	坎 Kan	離 Li	飛天馬 **Flying Heavenly Horse**

Monthly Purple White Stars 月紫白九星 :

寅 Tiger (Feb 4 - Mar 5) 正月 1st Month

巽SE	離S	坤SW
1 White 一白	6 White 六白	8 White 八白
9 Purple 九紫 (震E)	2 Black 二黑	4 Green 四綠 (兌W)
5 Yellow 五黃 (艮NE)	7 Red 七赤 (坎N)	3 Jade 三碧 (乾NW)

卯 Rabbit (Mar 6 - Apr 4) 二月 2nd Month

巽SE	離S	坤SW
9 Purple 九紫	5 Yellow 五黃	7 Red 七赤
8 White 八白 (震E)	1 White 一白	3 Jade 三碧 (兌W)
4 Green 四綠 (艮NE)	6 White 六白 (坎N)	2 Black 二黑 (乾NW)

辰 Dragon (Apr 5 - May 5) 三月 3rd Month

巽SE	離S	坤SW
8 White 八白	4 Green 四綠	6 White 六白
7 Red 七赤 (震E)	9 Purple 九紫	2 Black 二黑 (兌W)
3 Jade 三碧 (艮NE)	5 Yellow 五黃 (坎N)	1 White 一白 (乾NW)

巳 Snake (May 6 - Jun 5) 四月 4th Month

巽SE	離S	坤SW
7 Red 七赤	3 Jade 三碧	5 Yellow 五黃
6 White 六白 (震E)	8 White 八白	1 White 一白 (兌W)
2 Black 二黑 (艮NE)	4 Green 四綠 (坎N)	9 Purple 九紫 (乾NW)

午 Horse (Jun 6 - July 6) 五月 5th Month

巽SE	離S	坤SW
6 White 六白	2 Black 二黑	4 Green 四綠
5 Yellow 五黃 (震E)	7 Red 七赤	9 Purple 九紫 (兌W)
1 White 一白 (艮NE)	3 Jade 三碧 (坎N)	8 White 八白 (乾NW)

未 Goat (July 7 - Aug 7) 六月 6th Month

巽SE	離S	坤SW
5 Yellow 五黃	1 White 一白	3 Jade 三碧
4 Green 四綠 (震E)	6 White 六白	8 White 八白 (兌W)
9 Purple 九紫 (艮NE)	2 Black 二黑 (坎N)	7 Red 七赤 (乾NW)

申 Monkey (Aug 8 - Sept 7) 七月 7th Month

巽SE	離S	坤SW
4 Green 四綠	9 Purple 九紫	2 Black 二黑
3 Jade 三碧 (震E)	5 Yellow 五黃	7 Red 七赤 (兌W)
8 White 八白 (艮NE)	1 White 一白 (坎N)	6 White 六白 (乾NW)

酉 Rooster (Sept 8 - Oct 7) 八月 8th Month

巽SE	離S	坤SW
3 Jade 三碧	8 White 八白	1 White 一白
2 Black 二黑 (震E)	4 Green 四綠	6 White 六白 (兌W)
7 Red 七赤 (艮NE)	9 Purple 九紫 (坎N)	5 Yellow 五黃 (乾NW)

戌 Dog (Oct 8 - Nov 6) 九月 9th Month

巽SE	離S	坤SW
2 Black 二黑	7 Red 七赤	9 Purple 九紫
1 White 一白 (震E)	3 Jade 三碧	5 Yellow 五黃 (兌W)
6 White 六白 (艮NE)	8 White 八白 (坎N)	4 Green 四綠 (乾NW)

亥 Pig (Nov 7 - Dec 6) 十月 10th Month

巽SE	離S	坤SW
1 White 一白	6 White 六白	8 White 八白
9 Purple 九紫 (震E)	2 Black 二黑	4 Green 四綠 (兌W)
5 Yellow 五黃 (艮NE)	7 Red 七赤 (坎N)	3 Jade 三碧 (乾NW)

子 Rat (Dec 7 - Jan 5) 十一月 11th Month

巽SE	離S	坤SW
9 Purple 九紫	5 Yellow 五黃	7 Red 七赤
8 White 八白 (震E)	1 White 一白	3 Jade 三碧 (兌W)
4 Green 四綠 (艮NE)	6 White 六白 (坎N)	2 Black 二黑 (乾NW)

丑 Ox (Jan 6 - Feb 3) 十二月 12th Month

巽SE	離S	坤SW
8 White 八白	4 Green 四綠	6 White 六白
7 Red 七赤 (震E)	9 Purple 九紫	2 Black 二黑 (兌W)
3 Jade 三碧 (艮NE)	5 Yellow 五黃 (坎N)	1 White 一白 (乾NW)

Qi Men Three Nobles 三奇 :

Three Nobles 三奇 / Seasons	乙 Yi	丙 Bing	丁 Ding
立春 **Coming of Spring** Feb 4 - Feb 18	震 Zhen	巽 Xun	中 Middle
春分 **Spring Equinox** Mar 21 - Apr 4	兌 Dui	艮 Gen	離 Li
立夏 **Coming of Summer** May 6 - May 20	艮 Gen	離 Li	坎 Kan
夏至 **Summer Solstice** Jun 22 - Jul 6	中 Middle	巽 Xun	震 Zhen
立秋 **Coming of Autumn** Aug 8 - Aug 23	兌 Dui	乾 Qian	中 Middle
秋分 **Autumn Equinox** Sept 23 - Oct 7	震 Zhen	坤 Kun	坎 Kan
立冬 **Coming of Winter** Nov 7 - Nov 22	坤 Kun	坎 Kan	離 Li
冬至 **Winter Solstice** Dec 22 - Jan 5	中 Middle	乾 Qian	兌 Dui

辛巳 (Xin Si) Metal Snake

Sectors to Avoid Opening Mountain 開山凶位 :

月 MONTH	月建 Month Establishment	月破 Month Destruction	月剋山家 Month Countering Sitting		陰府太歲 Yin Mansion Grand Duke	
寅 **Tiger** (Feb 4 - Mar 5) 正月 **1st Month**	寅 *Yin* **Tiger**	申 *Shen* **Monkey**	—		乾 *Qian*	兌 *Dui*
卯 **Rabbit** (Mar 6 - Apr 4) 二月 **2nd Month**	卯 *Mao* **Rabbit**	酉 *You* **Rooster**	—		坤 *Kun*	坎 *Kan*
辰 **Dragon** (Apr 5 - May 5) 三月 **3rd Month**	辰 *Chen* **Dragon**	戌 *Xu* **Dog**	乾 *Qian*	兌 *Dui*	離 *Li*	乾 *Qian*
巳 **Snake** (May 6 - Jun 5) 四月 **4th Month**	巳 *Si* **Snake**	亥 *Hai* **Pig**	亥 *Hai* **Pig**	丁 *Ding* **Yin Fire**	震 *Zhen*	坤 *Kun*
午 **Horse** (Jun 6 - July 6) 五月 **5th Month**	午 *Wu* **Horse**	子 *Zi* **Rat**	離 *Li*	丙 *Bing* **Yang Fire**	艮 *Gen*	巽 *Xun*
未 **Goat** (July 7 - Aug 7) 六月 **6th Month**	未 *Wei* **Goat**	丑 *Chou* **Ox**	壬 *Ren* **Yang Water**	乙 *Yi* **Yin Wood**	兌 *Dui*	乾 *Qian*
申 **Monkey** (Aug 8 - Sept 7) 七月 **7th Month**	申 *Shen* **Monkey**	寅 *Yin* **Tiger**	震 *Zhen*	巳 *Si* **Snake**	坎 *Kan*	坤 *Kun*
酉 **Rooster** (Sept 8 - Oct 7) 八月 **8th Month**	酉 *You* **Rooster**	卯 *Mao* **Rabbit**	艮 *Gen*		乾 *Qian*	離 *Li*
戌 **Dog** (Oct 8 - Nov 6) 九月 **9th Month**	戌 *Xu* **Dog**	辰 *Chen* **Dragon**	—		坤 *Kun*	震 *Zhen*
亥 **Pig** (Nov 7 - Dec 6) 十月 **10th Month**	亥 *Hai* **Pig**	巳 *Si* **Snake**	—		巽 *Xun*	艮 *Gen*
子 **Rat** (Dec 7 - Jan 5) 十一月 **11th Month**	子 *Zi* **Rat**	午 *Wu* **Horse**	水 **Water**	山 **Mountain**	乾 *Qian*	兌 *Dui*
丑 **Ox** (Jan 6 - Feb 3) 十二月 **12th Month**	丑 *Chou* **Ox**	未 *Wei* **Goat**	土 **Earth**		坤 *Kun*	坎 *Kan*

Negative Repair / Renovation Sectors 修方凶位 :

月 MONTH	天官符 Heavenly Officer Charm			地官符 Earth Officer Charm			小月建 Small Month Establishment		
寅 Tiger (Feb 4 - Mar 5) 正月 1st Month	未 Wei Goat	坤 Kun	申 Shen Monkey	甲 Jia Yang Wood	震 Zhen	乙 Yi Yin Wood	丙 Bing Yang Fire	離 Li	丁 Ding Yin Fire
卯 Rabbit (Mar 6 - Apr 4) 二月 2nd Month	壬 Ren Yang Water	坎 Kan	癸 Gui Yin Water	未 Wei Goat	坤 Kun	申 Shen Monkey	壬 Ren Yang Water	坎 Kan	癸 Gui Yin Water
辰 Dragon (Apr 5 - May 5) 三月 3rd Month	丙 Bing Yang Fire	離 Li	丁 Ding Yin Fire	壬 Ren Yang Water	坎 Kan	癸 Gui Yin Water	未 Wei Goat	坤 Kun	申 Shen Monkey
巳 Snake (May 6 - Jun 5) 四月 4th Month	丑 Chou Ox	艮 Gen	寅 Yin Tiger	丙 Bing Yang Fire	離 Li	丁 Ding Yin Fire	甲 Jia Yang Wood	震 Zhen	乙 Yi Yin Wood
午 Horse (Jun 6 - July 6) 五月 5th Month	庚 Geng Yang Metal	兌 Dui	辛 Xin Yin Metal	丑 Chou Ox	艮 Gen	寅 Yin Tiger	辰 Chen Dragon	巽 Xun	己 Ji Yin Earth
未 Goat (July 7 - Aug 7) 六月 6th Month	戊 Xu Dog	乾 Qian	亥 Hai Pig	庚 Geng Yang Metal	兌 Dui	辛 Xin Yin Metal		中 Middle	
申 Monkey (Aug 8 - Sept 7) 七月 7th Month		中 Middle		戊 Xu Dog	乾 Qian	亥 Hai Pig	戊 Xu Dog	乾 Qian	亥 Hai Pig
酉 Rooster (Sept 8 - Oct 7) 八月 8th Month	庚 Geng Yang Metal	兌 Dui	辛 Xin Yin Metal		中 Middle		庚 Geng Yang Metal	兌 Dui	辛 Xin Yin Metal
戌 Dog (Oct 8 - Nov 6) 九月 9th Month	戊 Xu Dog	乾 Qian	亥 Hai Pig	庚 Geng Yang Metal	兌 Dui	辛 Xin Yin Metal	丑 Chou Ox	艮 Gen	寅 Yin Tiger
亥 Pig (Nov 7 - Dec 6) 十月 10th Month		中 Middle		戊 Xu Dog	乾 Qian	亥 Hai Pig	丙 Bing Yang Fire	離 Li	丁 Ding Yin Fire
子 Rat (Dec 7 - Jan 5) 十一月 11th Month	辰 Chen Dragon	巽 Xun	巳 Si Snake		中 Middle		壬 Ren Yang Water	坎 Kan	癸 Gui Yin Water
丑 Ox (Jan 6 - Feb 3) 十二月 12th Month	甲 Jia Yang Wood	震 Zhen	乙 Yi Yin Wood	辰 Chen Dragon	巽 Xun	巳 Si Snake	未 Wei Goat	坤 Kun	申 Shen Monkey

Negative Repair / Renovation Sectors 修方凶位 :

月 MONTH	大月建 Big Month Establishment			飛大煞 Flying Great Sha			丙丁獨火 Bing Ding Lonely Fire	
寅 **Tiger** (Feb 4 - Mar 5) 正月 **1st Month**	未 *Wei* Goat	坤 *Kun*	申 *Shen* Monkey	甲 *Jia* Yang Wood	震 *Zhen*	乙 *Yi* Yin Wood	坤 *Kun*	震 *Zhen*
卯 **Rabbit** (Mar 6 - Apr 4) 二月 **2nd Month**	壬 *Ren* Yang Water	坎 *Kan*	癸 *Gui* Yin Water	未 *Wei* Goat	坤 *Kun*	申 *Shen* Monkey	坎 *Kan*	坤 *Kun*
辰 **Dragon** (Apr 5 - May 5) 三月 **3rd Month**	丙 *Bing* Yang Fire	離 *Li*	丁 *Ding* Yin Fire	壬 *Ren* Yang Water	坎 *Kan*	癸 *Gui* Yin Water	離 *Li*	坎 *Kan*
巳 **Snake** (May 6 - Jun 5) 四月 **4th Month**	丑 *Chou* Ox	艮 *Gen*	寅 *Yin* Tiger	丙 *Bing* Yang Fire	離 *Li*	丁 *Ding* Yin Fire	艮 *Gen*	離 *Li*
午 **Horse** (Jun 6 - July 6) 五月 **5th Month**	庚 *Geng* Yang Metal	兌 *Dui*	辛 *Xin* Yin Metal	丑 *Chou* Ox	艮 *Gen*	寅 *Yin* Tiger	兌 *Dui*	艮 *Gen*
未 **Goat** (July 7 - Aug 7) 六月 **6th Month**	戊 *Xu* Dog	乾 *Qian*	亥 *Hai* Pig	庚 *Geng* Yang Metal	兌 *Dui*	辛 *Xin* Yin Metal	乾 *Qian*	兌 *Dui*
申 **Monkey** (Aug 8 - Sept 7) 七月 **7th Month**		中 Middle		戊 *Xu* Dog	乾 *Qian*	亥 *Hai* Pig	中 Middle	乾 *Qian*
酉 **Rooster** (Sept 8 - Oct 7) 八月 **8th Month**	辰 *Chen* Dragon	巽 *Xun*	巳 *Si* Snake		中 Middle			中 Middle
戌 **Dog** (Oct 8 - Nov 6) 九月 **9th Month**	甲 *Jia* Yang Wood	震 *Zhen*	乙 *Yi* Yin Wood	庚 *Geng* Yang Metal	兌 *Dui*	辛 *Xin* Yin Metal	巽 *Xun*	中 Middle
亥 **Pig** (Nov 7 - Dec 6) 十月 **10th Month**	未 *Wei* Goat	坤 *Kun*	申 *Shen* Monkey	戊 *Xu* Dog	乾 *Qian*	亥 *Hai* Pig	震 *Zhen*	巽 *Xun*
子 **Rat** (Dec 7 - Jan 5) 十一月 **11th Month**	壬 *Ren* Yang Water	坎 *Kan*	癸 *Gui* Yin Water		中 Middle		坤 *Kun*	震 *Zhen*
丑 **Ox** (Jan 6 - Feb 3) 十二月 **12th Month**	丙 *Bing* Yang Fire	離 *Li*	丁 *Ding* Yin Fire	辰 *Chen* Dragon	巽 *Xun*	巳 *Si* Snake	坎 *Kan*	坤 *Kun*

Negative Repair / Renovation Sectors 修方凶位 :

月 MONTH	月遊火 Month Wondering Fire	三煞 Monthly 3 Killings		
		劫煞 Robbery Sha	災煞 Calamity Sha	月煞 Month Sha
寅 Tiger (Feb 4 - Mar 5) 正月 1st Month	離 Li	亥 Hai Pig	子 Zi Rat	丑 Chou Ox
卯 Rabbit (Mar 6 - Apr 4) 二月 2nd Month	坎 Kan	申 Shen Monkey	酉 You Rooster	戌 Xu Dog
辰 Dragon (Apr 5 - May 5) 三月 3rd Month	坤 Kun	巳 Si Snake	午 Wu Horse	未 Wei Goat
巳 Snake (May 6 - Jun 5) 四月 4th Month	震 Zhen	寅 Yin Tiger	卯 Mao Rabbit	辰 Chen Dragon
午 Horse (Jun 6 - July 6) 五月 5th Month	巽 Xun	亥 Hai Pig	子 Zi Rat	丑 Chou Ox
未 Goat (July 7 - Aug 7) 六月 6th Month	中 Middle	申 Shen Monkey	酉 You Rooster	戌 Xu Dog
申 Monkey (Aug 8 - Sept 7) 七月 7th Month	乾 Qian	巳 Si Snake	午 Wu Horse	未 Wei Goat
酉 Rooster (Sept 8 - Oct 7) 八月 8th Month	兌 Dui	寅 Yin Tiger	卯 Mao Rabbit	辰 Chen Dragon
戌 Dog (Oct 8 - Nov 6) 九月 9th Month	艮 Gen	亥 Hai Pig	子 Zi Rat	丑 Chou Ox
亥 Pig (Nov 7 - Dec 6) 十月 10th Month	離 Li	申 Shen Monkey	酉 You Rooster	戌 Xu Dog
子 Rat (Dec 7 - Jan 5) 十一月 11th Month	坎 Kan	巳 Si Snake	午 Wu Horse	未 Wei Goat
丑 Ox (Jan 6 - Feb 3) 十二月 12th Month	坤 Kun	寅 Yin Tiger	卯 Mao Rabbit	辰 Chen Dragon

Negative Repair / Renovation Sectors 修方凶位 :

月 MONTH	月刑 Month Punishment	月害 Month Harm	月厭 Month Detest
寅 **Tiger** (Feb 4 - Mar 5) 正月 **1st Month**	巳 *Si* Snake	巳 *Si* Snake	戌 *Xu* Dog
卯 **Rabbit** (Mar 6 - Apr 4) 二月 **2nd Month**	子 *Zi* Rat	辰 *Chen* Dragon	酉 *You* Rooster
辰 **Dragon** (Apr 5 - May 5) 三月 **3rd Month**	辰 *Chen* Dragon	卯 *Mao* Rabbit	申 *Shen* Monkey
巳 **Snake** (May 6 - Jun 5) 四月 **4th Month**	申 *Shen* Monkey	寅 *Yin* Tiger	未 *Wei* Goat
午 **Horse** (Jun 6 - July 6) 五月 **5th Month**	午 *Wu* Horse	丑 *Chou* Ox	午 *Wu* Horse
未 **Goat** (July 7 - Aug 7) 六月 **6th Month**	丑 *Chou* Ox	子 *Zi* Rat	巳 *Si* Snake
申 **Monkey** (Aug 8 - Sept 7) 七月 **7th Month**	寅 *Yin* Tiger	亥 *Hai* Pig	辰 *Chen* Dragon
酉 **Rooster** (Sept 8 - Oct 7) 八月 **8th Month**	酉 *You* Rooster	戌 *Xu* Dog	卯 *Mao* Rabbit
戌 **Dog** (Oct 8 - Nov 6) 九月 **9th Month**	未 *Wei* Goat	酉 *You* Rooster	寅 *Yin* Tiger
亥 **Pig** (Nov 7 - Dec 6) 十月 **10th Month**	亥 *Hai* Pig	申 *Shen* Monkey	丑 *Chou* Ox
子 **Rat** (Dec 7 - Jan 5) 十一月 **11th Month**	卯 *Mao* Rabbit	未 *Wei* Goat	子 *Zi* Rat
丑 **Ox** (Jan 6 - Feb 3) 十二月 **12th Month**	戌 *Xu* Dog	午 *Wu* Horse	亥 *Hai* Pig

辛未 (Xin Wei)
Metal Goat

Heavenly Stem 天干	辛 Yin Metal (陰金)
Earthly Branch 地支	未 Goat (Yin Earth 陰土)
Hidden Stem 藏干	己 Yin Earth, 丁 Yin Fire, 乙 Yin Wood
Na Yin 納音	路傍土 Earth from the road
Grand Duke 太歲	未 Goat
Xuan Kong Five Element 玄空五行	9 金 Metal
Gua Name 卦名	䷅ 天水訟 Litigation
Xuan Kong Period Luck 玄空卦運	3

Annual Positive Stars for Opening Mountain, Establishing Facing and Commencing Repairs 開山立向修方吉星：

歲德 **Duke Virtue**	丙 *Bing* **Yang Fire**	
歲德合 **Duke Virtue Combo**	辛 *Xin* **Yin Metal**	
歲枝德 **Duke Branch Virtue**	子 *Zi* **Rat**	
陽貴人 **Yang Nobleman**	寅 *Yin* **Tiger**	
陰貴人 **Yin Nobleman**	午 *Wu* **Horse**	
歲祿 **Duke Prosperous**	酉 *You* **Rooster**	
歲馬 **Duke Horse**	巳 *Si* **Snake**	
奏書 **Decree**	巽 *Xun*	
博士 **Professor**	乾 *Qian*	

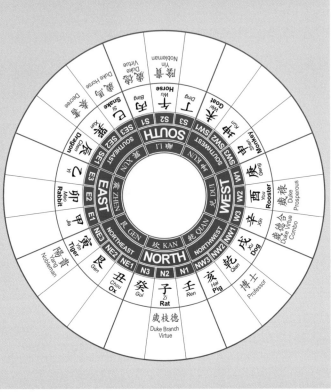

Annual Negative Stars for Opening Mountain, Establishing Facing and Commencing Repairs 開山立向修方凶星:

太歲 Grand Duke	歲破 Year Breaker	三煞 Three Killings			坐煞向煞 Sitting Sha Facing Sha				浮天空亡 Floating Heaven Emptiness	
未 Wei Goat	丑 Chou Ox	申 Shen Monkey	酉 You Rooster	戌 Xu Dog	庚 Geng Yang Metal	辛 Xin Yin Metal	甲 Jia Yang Wood	乙 Yi Yin Wood	艮 Gen	丙 Bing Yang Fire

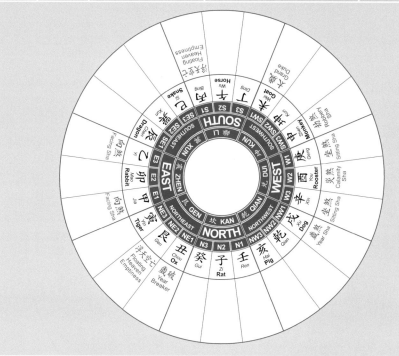

Annual San Yuan Purple White Stars 三元紫白九星:

上元 Upper Period
Period 1, 2, 3

巽SE	離S	坤SW
2	7	9
1	3 辛未 Xin Wei Metal Goat	5
6	8	4

震E ... 兌W
艮NE ... 坎N ... 乾NW

中元 Middle Period
Period 4, 5, 6

巽SE	離S	坤SW
5	1	3
4	6 辛未 Xin Wei Metal Goat	8
9	2	7

震E ... 兌W
艮NE ... 坎N ... 乾NW

下元 Lower Period
Period 7, 8, 9

巽SE	離S	坤SW
8	4	6
7	9 辛未 Xin Wei Metal Goat	2
3	5	1

震E ... 兌W
艮NE ... 坎N ... 乾NW

Mountain Covering Yellow Path 蓋山黃道：

貪狼	巨門	武曲	文曲
Tan Lang	Ju Men	Wu Qu	Wen Qu
Greedy Wolf	**Huge Door**	**Military Arts**	**Literary Arts**

坤	乙	坎	癸	申	辰	乾	甲	震	庚	亥	未
Kun	Yi	Kan	Gui	Shen	Chen	Qian	Jia	Zhen	Geng	Hai	Wei
SW2	E3	N2	N3	SW3	SE1	NW2	E1	E2	W1	NW3	SW1

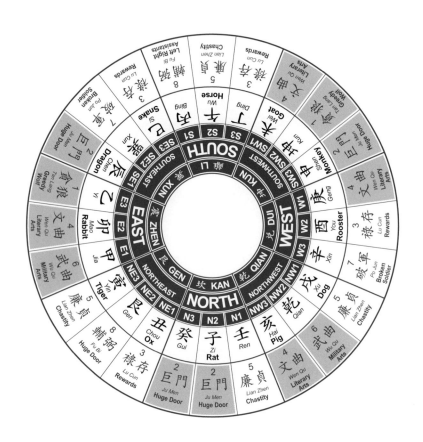

Heaven Penetrating Force 通天竅:

三合前方 **Facing Three Harmony**	巽巳 Xun Si	丙午 Bing Wu	丁未 Ding Wei
三合後方 **Sitting Three Harmony**	乾亥 Qian Hai	壬子 Ren Zi	癸丑 Gui Chou

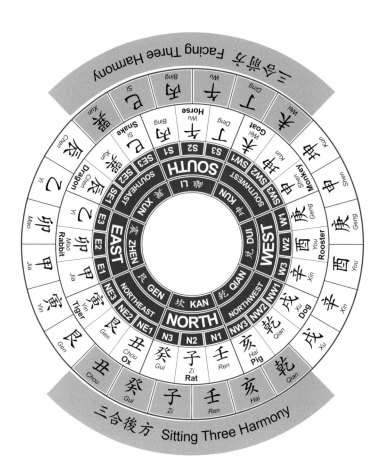

Moving Horse Six Ren Assessment 走馬六壬：

神后 Shen Hou Holy Empress	功曹 Gong Cao Marshall	天罡 Tian Gang Heavenly Dipper	勝光 Sheng Guang Subliminal Bright	傳送 Chuan Song Great General	河魁 He Kui River Scholar
巽巳 Xun Si	丁未 Ding Wei	庚酉 Geng You	乾亥 Qian Hai	癸丑 Gui Chou	甲卯 Jia Mao

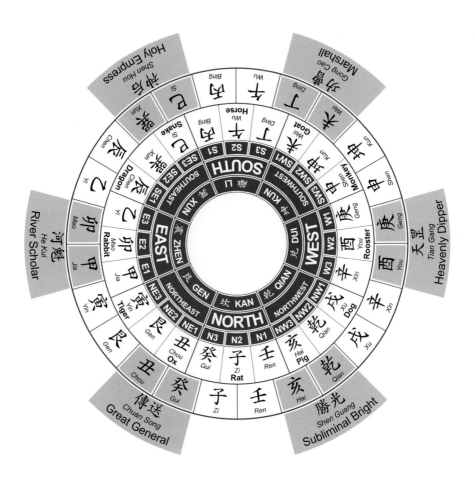

Four Advantages Three Cycles Star Plate 四利三元：

太陽 *Tai Yang* **Sun**	太陰 *Tai Yin* **Moon**	龍德 *Long De* **Dragon Virtue**	福德 *Fu De* **Fortune Virtue**
申 *Shen* **Monkey**	戌 *Xu* **Dog**	寅 *Yin* **Tiger**	辰 *Chen* **Dragon**

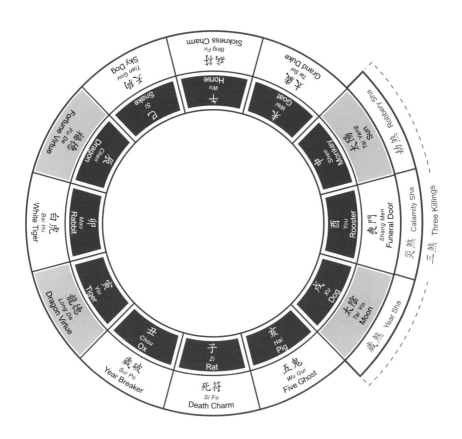

Negative Sectors For Opening Mountain 開山凶位:

年剋山家 Year Countering Sitting

震	艮	巳
Zhen	Gen	Si
E2	NE2	SE3

陰府太歲	六害	死符	炙退
Yin Fu Tai Sui	Liu Hai	Si Fu	Zhi Tui
Yin Mansion Grand Duke	**Six Harm**	**Death Charm**	**Roasting Star**

巽	艮	寅	戌	子
Xun	Gen	Yin	Xu	Zi
SE2	NE2	NE3	NW1	N2

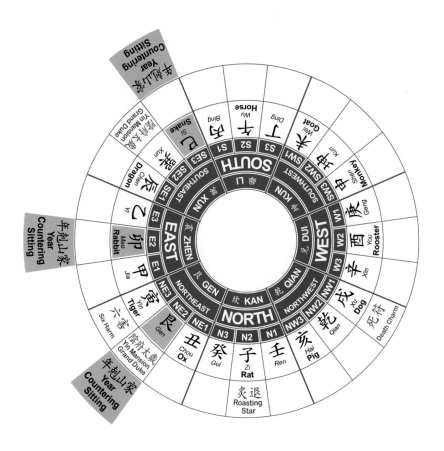

巡山羅喉 *Xun Shan Luo Hou* **Mountain Patrol Luo Hou Star**	病符 *Bing Fu* **Sickness Charm**
丙 *Bing* **S1**	辰 *Chen* **SE1**

Negative Directions to Establish Facing 立向凶方：

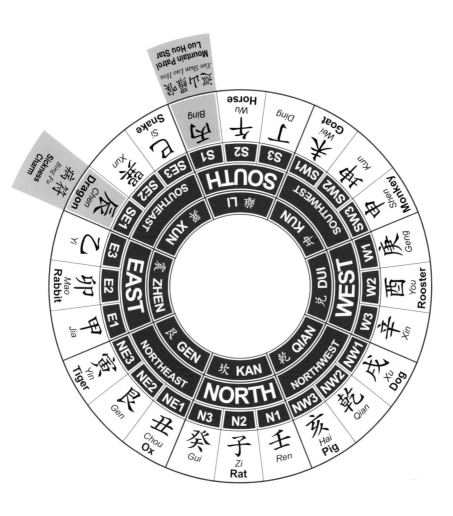

909

Negative Repair / Renovation Sectors Table 修方凶位表：

天官符 **Heavenly Officer Charm**	寅 Yin Tiger		飛廉 **Flying Chaste**	卯 Mao Rabbit
地官符 **Earthly Officer Charm**	亥 Hai Pig		喪門 **Funeral Door**	酉 You Rooster
大煞 **Great Sha**	卯 Mao Rabbit		弔客 **Suspended Guest**	巳 Si Snake
大將軍 **Big General**	卯 Mao Rabbit		白虎 **White Tiger**	卯 Mao Rabbit
力士 **Strong Man**	坤 Kun		金神 **Golden God**	寅 Yin Tiger 卯 Mao Rabbit 午 Wu Horse 未 Wei Goat 子 Zi Rat 丑 Chou Ox
蠶室 **Silkworm Room**	艮 Gen			
蠶官 **Silkworm Officer**	丑 Chou Ox			
蠶命 **Silkworm Life**	寅 Yin Tiger			
歲刑 **Duke Punishment**	丑 Chou Ox		獨火 **Lonely Fire**	離 Li
黃幡 **Yellow Flag**	未 Wei Goat		五鬼 **Five Ghost**	酉 You Rooster
豹尾 **Leopard Tail**	丑 Chou Ox		破敗五鬼 **Destructive Five Ghost**	乾 Qian

Negative Repair / Renovation Sectors Diagram 修方凶位圖：

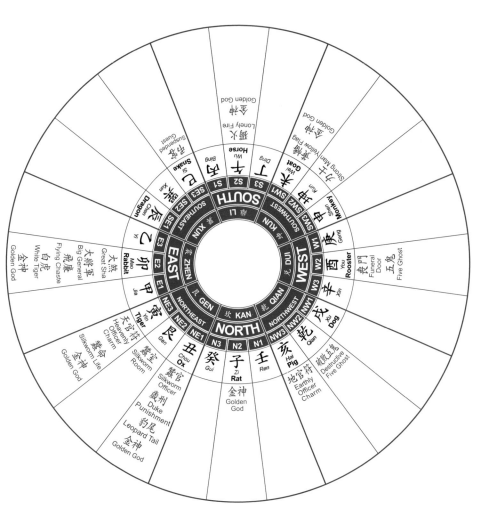

12-Month Auxiliary Stars Reference Table :
辛未年十二月，開山立向修方星表

Positive Monthly Stars 吉星方

月 MONTH	寅 Tiger (Feb 4 - Mar 5) 正月 1st Month	卯 Rabbit (Mar 6 - Apr 4) 二月 2nd Month	辰 Dragon (Apr 5 - May 5) 三月 3rd Month	巳 Snake (May 6 - Jun 5) 四月 4th Month	午 Horse (Jun 6 - July 6) 五月 5th Month	未 Goat (July 7 - Aug 7) 六月 6th Month
天道 Heavenly Path	南 South	西南 Southwest	北 North	西 West	西北 Northwest	東 East
天德 Heavenly Virtue	丁 Ding Yin Fire	坤 Kun (申)	壬 Ren Yang Water	辛 Xin Yin Metal	乾 Qian (亥)	甲 Jia Yang Wood
天德合 Heavenly Virtue Combo	壬 Ren Yang Water	(巳)	丁 Ding Yin Fire	丙 Bing Yang Fire	(寅)	己 Ji Yin Earth
月德 Monthly Virtue	丙 Bing Yang Fire	甲 Jia Yang Wood	壬 Ren Yang Water	庚 Geng Yang Metal	丙 Bing Yang Fire	甲 Jia Yang Wood
月德合 Monthly Virtue Combo	辛 Xin Yin Metal	己 Ji Yin Earth	丁 Ding Yin Fire	乙 Yi Yin Wood	辛 Xin Yin Metal	己 Ji Yin Earth
月空 Month Emptiness	壬 Ren Yang Water	庚 Geng Yang Metal	丙 Bing Yang Fire	甲 Jia Yang Wood	壬 Ren Yang Water	庚 Geng Yang Metal
陽貴人 Yang Nobleman	中 Middle	坎 Kan	離 Li	艮 Gen	兌 Dui	乾 Qian
陰貴人 Yin Nobleman	離 Li	艮 Gen	兌 Dui	乾 Qian	中 Middle	坎 Kan
飛天祿 Flying Heavenly Wealth	震 Zhen	坤 Kun	坎 Kan	離 Li	艮 Gen	兌 Dui
飛天馬 Flying Heavenly Horse	艮 Gen	兌 Dui	乾 Qian	中 Middle	坎 Kan	離 Li

12-Month Auxiliary Stars Reference Table :
辛未年十二月，開山立向修方星表

申 Monkey (Aug 8 - Sept 7) 七月 7th Month	酉 Rooster (Sept 8 - Oct 7) 八月 8th Month	戌 Dog (Oct 8 - Nov 6) 九月 9th Month	亥 Pig (Nov 7 - Dec 6) 十月 10th Month	子 Rat (Dec 7 - Jan 5) 十一月 11th Month	丑 Ox (Jan 6 - Feb 3) 十二月 12th Month	月 MONTH
北 North	東北 Northeast	南 South	東 East	東南 Southeast	西 West	天道 Heavenly Path
癸 Gui Yin Water	艮 Gen (寅)	丙 Bing Yang Fire	乙 Yi Yin Wood	巽 Xun (巳)	庚 Geng Yang Metal	天德 Heavenly Virtue
戊 Wu Yang Earth	(亥)	辛 Xin Yin Metal	庚 Geng Yang Metal	(申)	乙 Yi Yin Wood	天德合 Heavenly Virtue Combo
壬 Ren Yang Water	庚 Geng Yang Metal	丙 Bing Yang Fire	甲 Jia Yang Wood	壬 Ren Yang Water	庚 Geng Yang Metal	月德 Monthly Virtue
丁 Ding Yin Fire	乙 Yi Yin Wood	辛 Xin Yin Metal	己 Ji Yin Earth	丁 Ding Yin Fire	乙 Yi Yin Wood	月德合 Monthly Virtue Combo
丙 Bing Yang Fire	甲 Jia Yang Wood	壬 Ren Yang Water	庚 Geng Yang Metal	丙 Bing Yang Fire	甲 Jia Yang Wood	月空 Month Emptiness
中 Middle	巽 Xun	震 Zhen	坤 Kun	坎 Kan	離 Li	陽貴人 Yang Nobleman
離 Li	艮 Gen	兌 Dui	乾 Qian	中 Middle	巽 Xun	陰貴人 Yin Nobleman
乾 Qian	中 Middle	坎 Kan	離 Li	艮 Gen	兌 Dui	飛天祿 Flying Heavenly Wealth
艮 Gen	兌 Dui	乾 Qian	中 Middle	巽 Xun	震 Zhen	飛天馬 Flying Heavenly Horse

913

辛未 (Xin Wei) Metal Goat

Monthly Purple White Stars 月紫白九星：

寅 Tiger (Feb 4 - Mar 5) 正月 1st Month

巽 SE	離 S	坤 SW
4 Green 四綠	9 Purple 九紫	2 Black 二黑
3 Jade 三碧 (震 E)	5 Yellow 五黃	7 Red 七赤 (兌 W)
8 White 八白	1 White 一白	6 White 六白
艮 NE	坎 N	乾 NW

卯 Rabbit (Mar 6 - Apr 4) 二月 2nd Month

巽 SE	離 S	坤 SW
3 Jade 三碧	8 White 八白	1 White 一白
2 Black 二黑 (震 E)	4 Green 四綠	6 White 六白 (兌 W)
7 Red 七赤	9 Purple 九紫	5 Yellow 五黃
艮 NE	坎 N	乾 NW

辰 Dragon (Apr 5 - May 5) 三月 3rd Month

巽 SE	離 S	坤 SW
2 Black 二黑	7 Red 七赤	9 Purple 九紫
1 White 一白 (震 E)	3 Jade 三碧	5 Yellow 五黃 (兌 W)
6 White 六白	8 White 八白	4 Green 四綠
艮 NE	坎 N	乾 NW

巳 Snake (May 6 - Jun 5) 四月 4th Month

巽 SE	離 S	坤 SW
1 White 一白	6 White 六白	8 White 八白
9 Purple 九紫 (震 E)	2 Black 二黑	4 Green 四綠 (兌 W)
5 Yellow 五黃	7 Red 七赤	3 Jade 三碧
艮 NE	坎 N	乾 NW

午 Horse (Jun 6 - July 6) 五月 5th Month

巽 SE	離 S	坤 SW
9 Purple 九紫	5 Yellow 五黃	7 Red 七赤
8 White 八白 (震 E)	1 White 一白	3 Jade 三碧 (兌 W)
4 Green 四綠	6 White 六白	2 Black 二黑
艮 NE	坎 N	乾 NW

未 Goat (July 7 - Aug 7) 六月 6th Month

巽 SE	離 S	坤 SW
8 White 八白	4 Green 四綠	6 White 六白
7 Red 七赤 (震 E)	9 Purple 九紫	2 Black 二黑 (兌 W)
3 Jade 三碧	5 Yellow 五黃	1 White 一白
艮 NE	坎 N	乾 NW

申 Monkey (Aug 8 - Sept 7) 七月 7th Month

巽 SE	離 S	坤 SW
7 Red 七赤	3 Jade 三碧	5 Yellow 五黃
6 White 六白 (震 E)	8 White 八白	1 White 一白 (兌 W)
2 Black 二黑	4 Green 四綠	9 Purple 九紫
艮 NE	坎 N	乾 NW

酉 Rooster (Sept 8 - Oct 7) 八月 8th Month

巽 SE	離 S	坤 SW
6 White 六白	2 Black 二黑	4 Green 四綠
5 Yellow 五黃 (震 E)	7 Red 七赤	9 Purple 九紫 (兌 W)
1 White 一白	3 Jade 三碧	8 White 八白
艮 NE	坎 N	乾 NW

戌 Dog (Oct 8 - Nov 6) 九月 9th Month

巽 SE	離 S	坤 SW
5 Yellow 五黃	1 White 一白	3 Jade 三碧
4 Green 四綠 (震 E)	6 White 六白	8 White 八白 (兌 W)
9 Purple 九紫	2 Black 二黑	7 Red 七赤
艮 NE	坎 N	乾 NW

亥 Pig (Nov 7 - Dec 6) 十月 10th Month

巽 SE	離 S	坤 SW
4 Green 四綠	9 Purple 九紫	2 Black 二黑
3 Jade 三碧 (震 E)	5 Yellow 五黃	7 Red 七赤 (兌 W)
8 White 八白	1 White 一白	6 White 六白
艮 NE	坎 N	乾 NW

子 Rat (Dec 7 - Jan 5) 十一月 11th Month

巽 SE	離 S	坤 SW
3 Jade 三碧	8 White 八白	1 White 一白
2 Black 二黑 (震 E)	4 Green 四綠	6 White 六白 (兌 W)
7 Red 七赤	9 Purple 九紫	5 Yellow 五黃
艮 NE	坎 N	乾 NW

丑 Ox (Jan 6 - Feb 3) 十二月 12th Month

巽 SE	離 S	坤 SW
2 Black 二黑	7 Red 七赤	9 Purple 九紫
1 White 一白 (震 E)	3 Jade 三碧	5 Yellow 五黃 (兌 W)
6 White 六白	8 White 八白	4 Green 四綠
艮 NE	坎 N	乾 NW

Qi Men Three Nobles 三奇 :

Three Nobles 三奇 / Seasons	乙 Yi	丙 Bing	丁 Ding
立春 **Coming of Spring** Feb 4 - Feb 18	坤 Kun	震 Zhen	巽 Xun
春分 **Spring Equinox** Mar 21 - Apr 4	乾 Qian	兌 Dui	艮 Gen
立夏 **Coming of Summer** May 6 - May 20	兌 Dui	艮 Gen	離 Li
夏至 **Summer Solstice** Jun 22 - Jul 6	乾 Qian	中 Middle	巽 Xun
立秋 **Coming of Autumn** Aug 8 - Aug 23	艮 Gen	兌 Dui	乾 Qian
秋分 **Autumn Equinox** Sept 23 - Oct 7	巽 Xun	震 Zhen	坤 Kun
立冬 **Coming of Winter** Nov 7 - Nov 22	震 Zhen	坤 Kun	坎 Kan
冬至 **Winter Solstice** Dec 22 - Jan 5	巽 Xun	中 Middle	乾 Qian

Sectors to Avoid Opening Mountain 開山凶位 :

月 MONTH	月建 Month Establishment	月破 Month Destruction	月剋山家 Month Countering Sitting		陰府太歲 Yin Mansion Grand Duke	
寅 **Tiger** (Feb 4 - Mar 5) 正月 **1st Month**	寅 *Yin* **Tiger**	申 *Shen* **Monkey**	–		乾 *Qian*	兌 *Dui*
卯 **Rabbit** (Mar 6 - Apr 4) 二月 **2nd Month**	卯 *Mao* **Rabbit**	酉 *You* **Rooster**	–		坤 *Kun*	坎 *Kan*
辰 **Dragon** (Apr 5 - May 5) 三月 **3rd Month**	辰 *Chen* **Dragon**	戌 *Xu* **Dog**	乾 *Qian*	兌 *Dui*	離 *Li*	乾 *Qian*
巳 **Snake** (May 6 - Jun 5) 四月 **4th Month**	巳 *Si* **Snake**	亥 *Hai* **Pig**	亥 *Hai* **Pig**	丁 *Ding* **Yin Fire**	震 *Zhen*	坤 *Kun*
午 **Horse** (Jun 6 - July 6) 五月 **5th Month**	午 *Wu* **Horse**	子 *Zi* **Rat**	離 *Li*	丙 *Bing* **Yang Fire**	艮 *Gen*	巽 *Xun*
未 **Goat** (July 7 - Aug 7) 六月 **6th Month**	未 *Wei* **Goat**	丑 *Chou* **Ox**	壬 *Ren* **Yang Water**	乙 *Yi* **Yin Wood**	兌 *Dui*	乾 *Qian*
申 **Monkey** (Aug 8 - Sept 7) 七月 **7th Month**	申 *Shen* **Monkey**	寅 *Yin* **Tiger**	震 *Zhen*	巳 *Si* **Snake**	坎 *Kan*	坤 *Kun*
酉 **Rooster** (Sept 8 - Oct 7) 八月 **8th Month**	酉 *You* **Rooster**	卯 *Mao* **Rabbit**	艮 *Gen*		乾 *Qian*	離 *Li*
戌 **Dog** (Oct 8 - Nov 6) 九月 **9th Month**	戌 *Xu* **Dog**	辰 *Chen* **Dragon**	–		坤 *Kun*	震 *Zhen*
亥 **Pig** (Nov 7 - Dec 6) 十月 **10th Month**	亥 *Hai* **Pig**	巳 *Si* **Snake**	–		巽 *Xun*	艮 *Gen*
子 **Rat** (Dec 7 - Jan 5) 十一月 **11th Month**	子 *Zi* **Rat**	午 *Wu* **Horse**	水 **Water**	山 **Mountain**	乾 *Qian*	兌 *Dui*
丑 **Ox** (Jan 6 - Feb 3) 十二月 **12th Month**	丑 *Chou* **Ox**	未 *Wei* **Goat**	土 **Earth**		坤 *Kun*	坎 *Kan*

Negative Repair / Renovation Sectors 修方凶位 :

月 MONTH	天官符 Heavenly Officer Charm			地官符 Earth Officer Charm			小月建 Small Month Establishment		
寅 **Tiger** (Feb 4 - Mar 5) 正月 **1st Month**		中 Middle			中 Middle		丙 Bing Yang Fire	離 Li	丁 Ding Yin Fire
卯 **Rabbit** (Mar 6 - Apr 4) 二月 **2nd Month**	庚 Geng Yang Metal	兌 Dui	辛 Xin Yin Metal	辰 Chen Dragon	巽 Xun	巳 Si Snake	壬 Ren Yang Water	坎 Kan	癸 Gui Yin Water
辰 **Dragon** (Apr 5 - May 5) 三月 **3rd Month**	戊 Xu Dog	乾 Qian	亥 Hai Pig	甲 Jia Yang Wood	震 Zhen	乙 Yi Yin Wood	未 Wei Goat	坤 Kun	申 Shen Monkey
巳 **Snake** (May 6 - Jun 5) 四月 **4th Month**		中 Middle		未 Wei Goat	坤 Kun	申 Shen Monkey	甲 Jia Yang Wood	震 Zhen	乙 Yi Yin Wood
午 **Horse** (Jun 6 - July 6) 五月 **5th Month**	辰 Chen Dragon	巽 Xun	巳 Si Snake	壬 Ren Yang Water	坎 Kan	癸 Gui Yin Water	辰 Chen Dragon	巽 Xun	巳 Si Snake
未 **Goat** (July 7 - Aug 7) 六月 **6th Month**	甲 Jia Yang Wood	震 Zhen	乙 Yi Yin Wood	丙 Bing Yang Fire	離 Li	丁 Ding Yin Fire		中 Middle	
申 **Monkey** (Aug 8 - Sept 7) 七月 **7th Month**	未 Wei Goat	坤 Kun	申 Shen Monkey	丑 Chou Ox	艮 Gen	寅 Yin Tiger	戊 Xu Dog	乾 Qian	亥 Hai Pig
酉 **Rooster** (Sept 8 - Oct 7) 八月 **8th Month**	壬 Ren Yang Water	坎 Kan	癸 Gui Yin Water	庚 Geng Yang Metal	兌 Dui	辛 Xin Yin Metal	庚 Geng Yang Metal	兌 Dui	辛 Xin Yin Metal
戌 **Dog** (Oct 8 - Nov 6) 九月 **9th Month**	丙 Bing Yang Fire	離 Li	丁 Ding Yin Fire	戊 Xu Dog	乾 Qian	亥 Hai Pig	丑 Chou Ox	艮 Gen	寅 Yin Tiger
亥 **Pig** (Nov 7 - Dec 6) 十月 **10th Month**	丑 Chou Ox	艮 Gen	寅 Yin Tiger		中 Middle		丙 Bing Yang Fire	離 Li	丁 Ding Yin Fire
子 **Rat** (Dec 7 - Jan 5) 十一月 **11th Month**	庚 Geng Yang Metal	兌 Dui	辛 Xin Yin Metal	庚 Geng Yang Metal	兌 Dui	辛 Xin Yin Metal	壬 Ren Yang Water	坎 Kan	癸 Gui Yin Water
丑 **Ox** (Jan 6 - Feb 3) 十二月 **12th Month**	戊 Xu Dog	乾 Qian	亥 Hai Pig	戊 Xu Dog	乾 Qian	亥 Hai Pig	未 Wei Goat	坤 Kun	申 Shen Monkey

Negative Repair / Renovation Sectors 修方凶位 :

月 MONTH	大月建 Big Month Establishment			飛大煞 Flying Great Sha			丙丁獨火 Bing Ding Lonely Fire	
寅 **Tiger** (Feb 4 - Mar 5) 正月 **1st Month**		中 Middle		戌 *Xu* Dog	乾 *Qian*	亥 *Hai* Pig	坤 *Kun*	震 *Zhen*
卯 **Rabbit** (Mar 6 - Apr 4) 二月 **2nd Month**	辰 *Chen* Dragon	巽 *Xun*	巳 *Si* Snake		中 Middle		坎 *Kan*	坤 *Kun*
辰 **Dragon** (Apr 5 - May 5) 三月 **3rd Month**	甲 *Jia* Yang Wood	震 *Zhen*	乙 *Yi* Yin Wood	庚 *Geng* Yang Metal	兌 *Dui*	辛 *Xin* Yin Metal	離 *Li*	坎 *Kan*
巳 **Snake** (May 6 - Jun 5) 四月 **4th Month**	未 *Wei* Goat	坤 *Kun*	申 *Shen* Monkey	戌 *Xu* Dog	乾 *Qian*	亥 *Hai* Pig	艮 *Gen*	離 *Li*
午 **Horse** (Jun 6 - July 6) 五月 **5th Month**	壬 *Ren* Yang Water	坎 *Kan*	癸 *Gui* Yin Water		中 Middle		兌 *Dui*	艮 *Gen*
未 **Goat** (July 7 - Aug 7) 六月 **6th Month**	丙 *Bing* Yang Fire	離 *Li*	丁 *Ding* Yin Fire	辰 *Chen* Dragon	巽 *Xun*	巳 *Si* Snake	乾 *Qian*	兌 *Dui*
申 **Monkey** (Aug 8 - Sept 7) 七月 **7th Month**	丑 *Chou* Ox	艮 *Gen*	寅 *Yin* Tiger	甲 *Jia* Yang Wood	震 *Zhen*	乙 *Yi* Yin Wood	中 Middle	乾 *Qian*
酉 **Rooster** (Sept 8 - Oct 7) 八月 **8th Month**	庚 *Geng* Yang Metal	兌 *Dui*	辛 *Xin* Yin Metal	未 *Wei* Goat	坤 *Kun*	申 *Shen* Monkey		中 Middle
戌 **Dog** (Oct 8 - Nov 6) 九月 **9th Month**	戌 *Xu* Dog	乾 *Qian*	亥 *Hai* Pig	壬 *Ren* Yang Water	坎 *Kan*	癸 *Gui* Yin Water	巽 *Xun*	中 Middle
亥 **Pig** (Nov 7 - Dec 6) 十月 **10th Month**		中 Middle		丙 *Bing* Yang Fire	離 *Li*	丁 *Ding* Yin Fire	震 *Zhen*	巽 *Xun*
子 **Rat** (Dec 7 - Jan 5) 十一月 **11th Month**	辰 *Chen* Dragon	巽 *Xun*	巳 *Si* Snake	丑 *Chou* Ox	艮 *Gen*	寅 *Yin* Tiger	坤 *Kun*	震 *Zhen*
丑 **Ox** (Jan 6 - Feb 3) 十二月 **12th Month**	甲 *Jia* Yang Wood	震 *Zhen*	乙 *Yi* Yin Wood	庚 *Geng* Yang Metal	兌 *Dui*	辛 *Xin* Yin Metal	坎 *Kan*	坤 *Kun*

Negative Repair / Renovation Sectors 修方凶位 :

月 MONTH	月遊火 Month Wondering Fire	三煞 Monthly 3 Killings		
		劫煞 Robbery Sha	災煞 Calamity Sha	月煞 Month Sha
寅 Tiger (Feb 4 - Mar 5) 正月 1st Month	坤 Kun	亥 Hai Pig	子 Zi Rat	丑 Chou Ox
卯 Rabbit (Mar 6 - Apr 4) 二月 2nd Month	震 Zhen	申 Shen Monkey	酉 You Rooster	戌 Xu Dog
辰 Dragon (Apr 5 - May 5) 三月 3rd Month	巽 Xun	巳 Si Snake	午 Wu Horse	未 Wei Goat
巳 Snake (May 6 - Jun 5) 四月 4th Month	中 Middle	寅 Yin Tiger	卯 Mao Rabbit	辰 Chen Dragon
午 Horse (Jun 6 - July 6) 五月 5th Month	乾 Qian	亥 Hai Pig	子 Zi Rat	丑 Chou Ox
未 Goat (July 7 - Aug 7) 六月 6th Month	兌 Dui	申 Shen Monkey	酉 You Rooster	戌 Xu Dog
申 Monkey (Aug 8 - Sept 7) 七月 7th Month	艮 Gen	巳 Si Snake	午 Wu Horse	未 Wei Goat
酉 Rooster (Sept 8 - Oct 7) 八月 8th Month	離 Li	寅 Yin Tiger	卯 Mao Rabbit	辰 Chen Dragon
戌 Dog (Oct 8 - Nov 6) 九月 9th Month	坎 Kan	亥 Hai Pig	子 Zi Rat	丑 Chou Ox
亥 Pig (Nov 7 - Dec 6) 十月 10th Month	坤 Kun	申 Shen Monkey	酉 You Rooster	戌 Xu Dog
子 Rat (Dec 7 - Jan 5) 十一月 11th Month	震 Zhen	巳 Si Snake	午 Wu Horse	未 Wei Goat
丑 Ox (Jan 6 - Feb 3) 十二月 12th Month	巽 Xun	寅 Yin Tiger	卯 Mao Rabbit	辰 Chen Dragon

Negative Repair / Renovation Sectors 修方凶位 :

月 MONTH	月刑 Month Punishment	月害 Month Harm	月厭 Month Detest
寅 **Tiger** (Feb 4 - Mar 5) 正月 1st Month	巳 Si Snake	巳 Si Snake	戌 Xu Dog
卯 **Rabbit** (Mar 6 - Apr 4) 二月 2nd Month	子 Zi Rat	辰 Chen Dragon	酉 You Rooster
辰 **Dragon** (Apr 5 - May 5) 三月 3rd Month	辰 Chen Dragon	卯 Mao Rabbit	申 Shen Monkey
巳 **Snake** (May 6 - Jun 5) 四月 4th Month	申 Shen Monkey	寅 Yin Tiger	未 Wei Goat
午 **Horse** (Jun 6 - July 6) 五月 5th Month	午 Wu Horse	丑 Chou Ox	午 Wu Horse
未 **Goat** (July 7 - Aug 7) 六月 6th Month	丑 Chou Ox	子 Zi Rat	巳 Si Snake
申 **Monkey** (Aug 8 - Sept 7) 七月 7th Month	寅 Yin Tiger	亥 Hai Pig	辰 Chen Dragon
酉 **Rooster** (Sept 8 - Oct 7) 八月 8th Month	酉 You Rooster	戌 Xu Dog	卯 Mao Rabbit
戌 **Dog** (Oct 8 - Nov 6) 九月 9th Month	未 Wei Goat	酉 You Rooster	寅 Yin Tiger
亥 **Pig** (Nov 7 - Dec 6) 十月 10th Month	亥 Hai Pig	申 Shen Monkey	丑 Chou Ox
子 **Rat** (Dec 7 - Jan 5) 十一月 11th Month	卯 Mao Rabbit	未 Wei Goat	子 Zi Rat
丑 **Ox** (Jan 6 - Feb 3) 十二月 12th Month	戌 Xu Dog	午 Wu Horse	亥 Hai Pig

辛酉 (Xin You)
Metal Rooster

Heavenly Stem 天干	辛 Yin Metal (陰金)
Earthly Branch 地支	酉 Rooster (Yin Metal 陰金)
Hidden Stem 藏干	辛 Yin Metal
Na Yin 納音	石榴木 Wood from guava tree
Grand Duke 太歲	酉 Rooster
Xuan Kong Five Element 玄空五行	8 木 Wood
Gua Name 卦名	䷽ 雷山小過 Lesser Exceeding
Xuan Kong Period Luck 玄空卦運	3

Annual Positive Stars for Opening Mountain, Establishing Facing and Commencing Repairs 開山立向修方吉星:

歲德 Duke Virtue	丙 Bing Yang Fire
歲德合 Duke Virtue Combo	辛 Xin Yin Metal
歲枝德 Duke Branch Virtue	寅 Yin Tiger
陽貴人 Yang Nobleman	寅 Yin Tiger
陰貴人 Yin Nobleman	午 Wu Horse
歲祿 Duke Prosperous	酉 You Rooster
歲馬 Duke Horse	亥 Hai Pig
奏書 Decree	坤 Kun
博士 Professor	艮 Gen

Annual Negative Stars for Opening Mountain, Establishing Facing and Commencing Repairs 開山立向修方凶星:

太歲 Grand Duke	歲破 Year Breaker	三煞 Three Killings			坐煞向煞 Sitting Sha Facing Sha				浮天空亡 Floating Heaven Emptiness	
酉 You Rooster	卯 Mao Rabbit	寅 Yin Tiger	卯 Mao Rabbit	辰 Chen Dragon	甲 Jia Yang Wood	乙 Yi Yin Wood	庚 Geng Yang Metal	辛 Xin Yin Metal	艮 Gen	丙 Bing Yang Fire

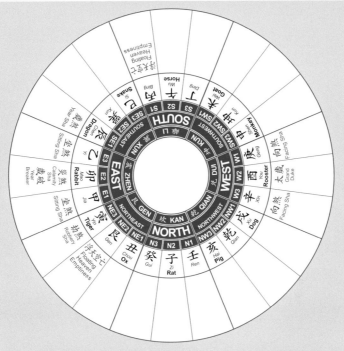

Annual San Yuan Purple White Stars 三元紫白九星:

上元 Upper Period Period 1, 2, 3			中元 Middle Period Period 4, 5, 6			下元 Lower Period Period 7, 8, 9		
巽SE 6	**離S** 2	**坤SW** 4	**巽SE** 9	**離S** 5	**坤SW** 7	**巽SE** 3	**離S** 8	**坤SW** 1
震E 5	7 辛酉 Xin You Metal Rooster	**兌W** 9	**震E** 8	1 辛酉 Xin You Metal Rooster	**兌W** 3	**震E** 2	4 辛酉 Xin You Metal Rooster	**兌W** 6
艮NE 1	**坎N** 3	**乾NW** 8	**艮NE** 4	**坎N** 6	**乾NW** 2	**艮NE** 7	**坎N** 9	**乾NW** 5

Mountain Covering Yellow Path 蓋山黃道：

貪狼 *Tan Lang* **Greedy Wolf**				巨門 *Ju Men* **Huge Door**		武曲 *Wu Qu* **Military Arts**				文曲 *Wen Qu* **Literary Arts**	
離 *Li* S2	壬 *Ren* N1	寅 *Yin* NE3	戌 *Xu* NW1	乾 *Qian* NW2	甲 *Jia* E1	坎 *Kan* N2	癸 *Gui* N3	申 *Shen* SW3	辰 *Chen* SE1	艮 *Gen* NE2	丙 *Bing* S1

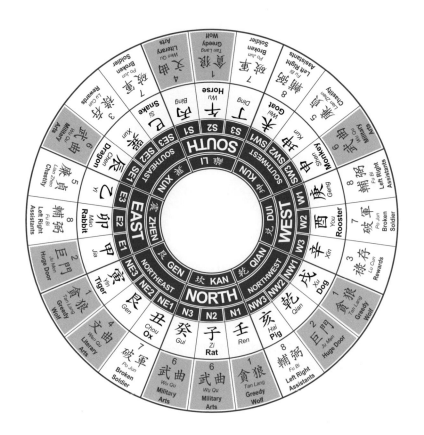

Heaven Penetrating Force 通天竅:

三合前方 Facing Three Harmony	乾亥 Qian Hai	壬子 Ren Zi	癸丑 Gui Chou
三合後方 Sitting Three Harmony	巽巳 Xun Si	丙午 Bing Wu	丁未 Ding Wei

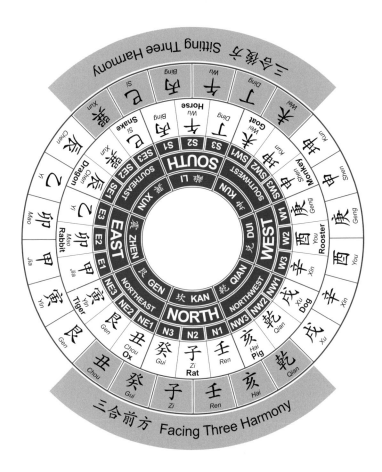

Moving Horse Six Ren Assessment 走馬六壬：

神后 *Shen Hou* **Holy Empress**	功曹 *Gong Cao* **Marshall**	天罡 *Tian Gang* **Heavenly Dipper**	勝光 *Sheng Guang* **Subliminal Bright**	傳送 *Chuan Song* **Great General**	河魁 *He Kui* **River Scholar**
甲卯 *Jia Mao*	巽巳 *Xun Si*	丁未 *Ding Wei*	庚酉 *Geng You*	乾亥 *Qian Hai*	癸丑 *Gui Chou*

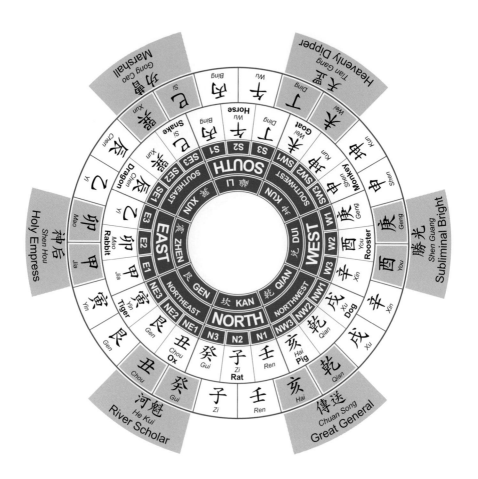

Four Advantages Three Cycles Star Plate 四利三元：

太陽 *Tai Yang* **Sun**	太陰 *Tai Yin* **Moon**	龍德 *Long De* **Dragon Virtue**	福德 *Fu De* **Fortune Virtue**
戌 *Xu* Dog	子 *Zi* Rat	辰 *Chen* Dragon	午 *Wu* Horse

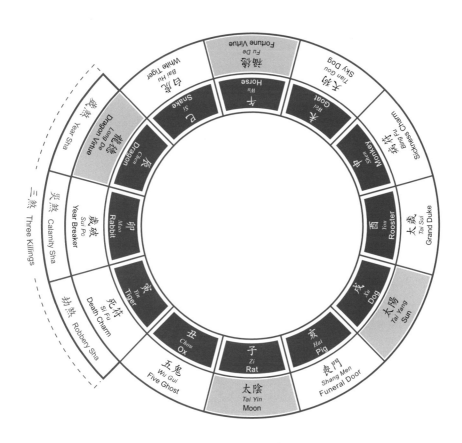

Negative Sectors For Opening Mountain 開山凶位：

年剋山家 Year Countering Sitting (冬至後 After Winter Solstice)

乾 Qian NW2	亥 Hai NW3	兌 Dui W2	丁 Ding S3

陰府太歲 Yin Fu Tai Sui **Yin Mansion Grand Duke**	六害 Liu Hai **Six Harm**	死符 Si Fu **Death Charm**	炙退 Zhi Tui **Roasting Star**
坤 Kun SW2 坎 Kan N2	戌 Xu NW1	寅 Yin NE3	子 Zi N2

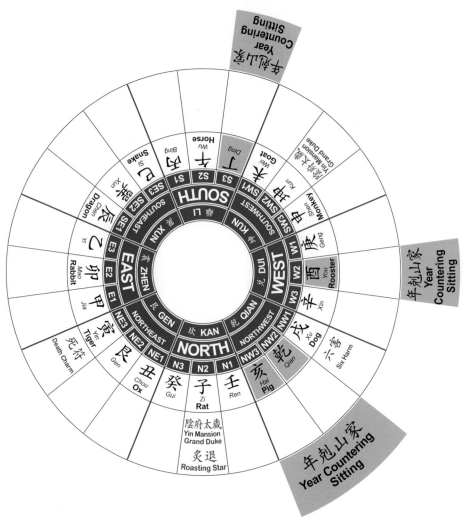

Negative Directions to Establish Facing 立向凶方:

巡山羅喉 *Xun Shan Luo Hou* **Mountain Patrol Luo Hou Star**	病符 *Bing Fu* **Sickness Charm**
辛 *Xin* **W3**	申 *Shen* **SW3**

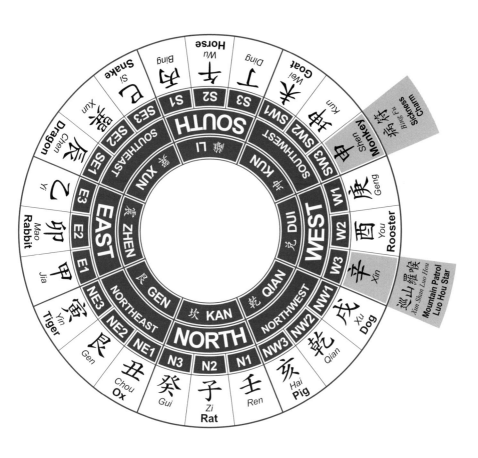

Negative Repair / Renovation Sectors Table 修方凶位表：

天官符 **Heavenly Officer Charm**	申 *Shen* Monkey		飛廉 **Flying Chaste**	亥 *Hai* Pig
地官符 **Earthly Officer Charm**	丑 *Chou* Ox		喪門 **Funeral Door**	亥 *Hai* Pig
大煞 **Great Sha**	酉 *You* Rooster		弔客 **Suspended Guest**	未 *Wei* Goat
大將軍 **Big General**	午 *Wu* Horse		白虎 **White Tiger**	巳 *Si* Snake
力士 **Strong Man**	乾 *Qian*		金神 **Golden God**	寅 *Yin* Tiger 卯 *Mao* Rabbit 午 *Wu* Horse 未 *Wei* Goat 子 *Zi* Rat 丑 *Chou* Ox
蠶室 **Silkworm Room**	巽 *Xun*			
蠶官 **Silkworm Officer**	辰 *Chen* Dragon			
蠶命 **Silkworm Life**	巳 *Si* Snake			
歲刑 **Duke Punishment**	酉 *You* Rooster		獨火 **Lonely Fire**	坤 *Kun*
黃幡 **Yellow Flag**	丑 *Chou* Ox		五鬼 **Five Ghost**	未 *Wei* Goat
豹尾 **Leopard Tail**	未 *Wei* Goat		破敗五鬼 **Destructive Five Ghost**	乾 *Qian*

Negative Repair / Renovation Sectors Diagram 修方凶位圖：

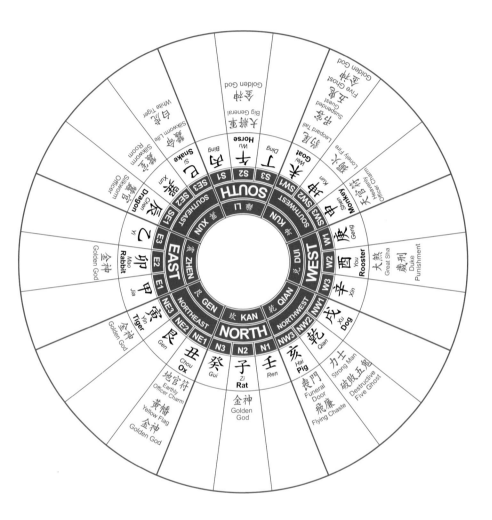

931

12-Month Auxiliary Stars Reference Table :
辛酉年十二月，開山立向修方星表

Positive Monthly Stars 吉星方

月 MONTH	寅 Tiger (Feb 4 - Mar 5) 正月 1st Month	卯 Rabbit (Mar 6 - Apr 4) 二月 2nd Month	辰 Dragon (Apr 5 - May 5) 三月 3rd Month	巳 Snake (May 6 - Jun 5) 四月 4th Month	午 Horse (Jun 6 - July 6) 五月 5th Month	未 Goat (July 7 - Aug 7) 六月 6th Month
天道 Heavenly Path	南 South	西南 Southwest	北 North	西 West	西北 Northwest	東 East
天德 Heavenly Virtue	丁 Ding Yin Fire	坤 Kun (申)	壬 Ren Yang Water	辛 Xin Yin Metal	乾 Qian (亥)	甲 Jia Yang Wood
天德合 Heavenly Virtue Combo	壬 Ren Yang Water	(巳)	丁 Ding Yin Fire	丙 Bing Yang Fire	(寅)	己 Ji Yin Earth
月德 Monthly Virtue	丙 Bing Yang Fire	甲 Jia Yang Wood	壬 Ren Yang Water	庚 Geng Yang Metal	丙 Bing Yang Fire	甲 Jia Yang Wood
月德合 Monthly Virtue Combo	辛 Xin Yin Metal	己 Ji Yin Earth	丁 Ding Yin Fire	乙 Yi Yin Wood	辛 Xin Yin Metal	己 Ji Yin Earth
月空 Month Emptiness	壬 Ren Yang Water	庚 Geng Yang Metal	丙 Bing Yang Fire	甲 Jia Yang Wood	壬 Ren Yang Water	庚 Geng Yang Metal
陽貴人 Yang Nobleman	中 Middle	坎 Kan	離 Li	艮 Gen	兌 Dui	乾 Qian
陰貴人 Yin Nobleman	離 Li	艮 Gen	兌 Dui	乾 Qian	中 Middle	坎 Kan
飛天祿 Flying Heavenly Wealth	震 Zhen	坤 Kun	坎 Kan	離 Li	艮 Gen	兌 Dui
飛天馬 Flying Heavenly Horse	中 Middle	巽 Xun	震 Zhen	坤 Kun	坎 Kan	離 Li

12-Month Auxiliary Stars Reference Table :
辛酉年十二月，開山立向修方星表

申 Monkey (Aug 8 - Sept 7)	酉 Rooster (Sept 8 - Oct 7)	戌 Dog (Oct 8 - Nov 6)	亥 Pig (Nov 7 - Dec 6)	子 Rat (Dec 7 - Jan 5)	丑 Ox (Jan 6 - Feb 3)	月 MONTH
七月 7th Month	八月 8th Month	九月 9th Month	十月 10th Month	十一月 11th Month	十二月 12th Month	
北 North	東北 Northeast	南 South	東 East	東南 Southeast	西 West	天道 Heavenly Path
癸 Gui Yin Water	艮 Gen (寅)	丙 Bing Yang Fire	乙 Yi Yin Wood	巽 Xun (巳)	庚 Geng Yang Metal	天德 Heavenly Virtue
戊 Wu Yang Earth	(亥)	辛 Xin Yin Metal	庚 Geng Yang Metal	(申)	乙 Yi Yin Wood	天德合 Heavenly Virtue Combo
壬 Ren Yang Water	庚 Geng Yang Metal	丙 Bing Yang Fire	甲 Jia Yang Wood	壬 Ren Yang Water	庚 Geng Yang Metal	月德 Monthly Virtue
丁 Ding Yin Fire	乙 Yi Yin Wood	辛 Xin Yin Metal	己 Ji Yin Earth	丁 Ding Yin Fire	乙 Yi Yin Wood	月德合 Monthly Virtue Combo
丙 Bing Yang Fire	甲 Jia Yang Wood	壬 Ren Yang Water	庚 Geng Yang Metal	丙 Bing Yang Fire	甲 Jia Yang Wood	月空 Month Emptiness
中 Middle	巽 Xun	震 Zhen	坤 Kun	坎 Kan	離 Li	陽貴人 Yang Nobleman
離 Li	艮 Gen	兌 Dui	乾 Qian	中 Middle	巽 Xun	陰貴人 Yin Nobleman
乾 Qian	中 Middle	坎 Kan	離 Li	艮 Gen	兌 Dui	飛天祿 Flying Heavenly Wealth
艮 Gen	兌 Dui	乾 Qian	中 Middle	坎 Kan	離 Li	飛天馬 Flying Heavenly Horse

933

Monthly Purple White Stars 月紫白九星 :

寅 Tiger (Feb 4 - Mar 5) 正月 1st Month

巽 SE	離 S	坤 SW
7 Red 七赤	3 Jade 三碧	5 Yellow 五黃
震 E — 6 White 六白	8 White 八白	1 White 一白 — 兌 W
艮 NE — 2 Black 二黑	4 Green 四緑	9 Purple 九紫 — 乾 NW

卯 Rabbit (Mar 6 - Apr 4) 二月 2nd Month

巽 SE	離 S	坤 SW
6 White 六白	2 Black 二黑	4 Green 四緑
震 E — 5 Yellow 五黃	7 Red 七赤	9 Purple 九紫 — 兌 W
艮 NE — 1 White 一白	3 Jade 三碧	8 White 八白 — 乾 NW

辰 Dragon (Apr 5 - May 5) 三月 3rd Month

巽 SE	離 S	坤 SW
5 Yellow 五黃	1 White 一白	3 Jade 三碧
震 E — 4 Green 四緑	6 White 六白	8 White 八白 — 兌 W
艮 NE — 9 Purple 九紫	2 Black 二黑	7 Red 七赤 — 乾 NW

巳 Snake (May 6 - Jun 5) 四月 4th Month

巽 SE	離 S	坤 SW
4 Green 四緑	9 Purple 九紫	2 Black 二黑
震 E — 3 Jade 三碧	5 Yellow 五黃	7 Red 七赤 — 兌 W
艮 NE — 8 White 八白	1 White 一白	6 White 六白 — 乾 NW

午 Horse (Jun 6 - July 6) 五月 5th Month

巽 SE	離 S	坤 SW
3 Jade 三碧	8 White 八白	1 White 一白
震 E — 2 Black 二黑	4 Green 四緑	6 White 六白 — 兌 W
艮 NE — 7 Red 七赤	9 Purple 九紫	5 Yellow 五黃 — 乾 NW

未 Goat (July 7 - Aug 7) 六月 6th Month

巽 SE	離 S	坤 SW
2 Black 二黑	7 Red 七赤	9 Purple 九紫
震 E — 1 White 一白	3 Jade 三碧	5 Yellow 五黃 — 兌 W
艮 NE — 6 White 六白	8 White 八白	4 Green 四緑 — 乾 NW

申 Monkey (Aug 8 - Sept 7) 七月 7th Month

巽 SE	離 S	坤 SW
1 White 一白	6 White 六白	8 White 八白
震 E — 9 Purple 九紫	2 Black 二黑	4 Green 四緑 — 兌 W
艮 NE — 5 Yellow 五黃	7 Red 七赤	3 Jade 三碧 — 乾 NW

酉 Rooster (Sept 8 - Oct 7) 八月 8th Month

巽 SE	離 S	坤 SW
9 Purple 九紫	5 Yellow 五黃	7 Red 七赤
震 E — 8 White 八白	1 White 一白	3 Jade 三碧 — 兌 W
艮 NE — 4 Green 四緑	6 White 六白	2 Black 二黑 — 乾 NW

戌 Dog (Oct 8 - Nov 6) 九月 9th Month

巽 SE	離 S	坤 SW
8 White 八白	4 Green 四緑	6 White 六白
震 E — 7 Red 七赤	9 Purple 九紫	2 Black 二黑 — 兌 W
艮 NE — 3 Jade 三碧	5 Yellow 五黃	1 White 一白 — 乾 NW

亥 Pig (Nov 7 - Dec 6) 十月 10th Month

巽 SE	離 S	坤 SW
7 Red 七赤	3 Jade 三碧	5 Yellow 五黃
震 E — 6 White 六白	8 White 八白	1 White 一白 — 兌 W
艮 NE — 2 Black 二黑	4 Green 四緑	9 Purple 九紫 — 乾 NW

子 Rat (Dec 7 - Jan 5) 十一月 11th Month

巽 SE	離 S	坤 SW
6 White 六白	2 Black 二黑	4 Green 四緑
震 E — 5 Yellow 五黃	7 Red 七赤	9 Purple 九紫 — 兌 W
艮 NE — 1 White 一白	3 Jade 三碧	8 White 八白 — 乾 NW

丑 Ox (Jan 6 - Feb 3) 十二月 12th Month

巽 SE	離 S	坤 SW
5 Yellow 五黃	1 White 一白	3 Jade 三碧
震 E — 4 Green 四緑	6 White 六白	8 White 八白 — 兌 W
艮 NE — 9 Purple 九紫	2 Black 二黑	7 Red 七赤 — 乾 NW

934

Qi Men Three Nobles 三奇 :

Three Nobles 三奇 / Seasons	乙 Yi	丙 Bing	丁 Ding
立春 **Coming of Spring** Feb 4 - Feb 18	兌 Dui	艮 Gen	離 Li
春分 **Spring Equinox** Mar 21 - Apr 4	坤 Kun	震 Zhen	巽 Xun
立夏 **Coming of Summer** May 6 - May 20	震 Zhen	巽 Xun	中 **Middle**
夏至 **Summer Solstice** Jun 22 - Jul 6	坎 Kan	離 Li	艮 Gen
立秋 **Coming of Autumn** Aug 8 - Aug 23	震 Zhen	坤 Kun	坎 Kan
秋分 **Autumn Equinox** Sept 23 - Oct 7	艮 Gen	兌 Dui	乾 Qian
立冬 **Coming of Winter** Nov 7 - Nov 22	兌 Dui	乾 Qian	中 **Middle**
冬至 **Winter Solstice** Dec 22 - Jan 5	離 Li	坎 Kan	坤 Kun

Sectors to Avoid Opening Mountain 開山凶位 :

月 MONTH	月建 Month Establishment	月破 Month Destruction	月剋山家 Month Countering Sitting		陰府太歲 Yin Charm Grand Duke	
寅 **Tiger** (Feb 4 - Mar 5) 正月 **1st Month**	寅 *Yin* **Tiger**	申 *Shen* **Monkey**	–		乾 *Qian*	兑 *Dui*
卯 **Rabbit** (Mar 6 - Apr 4) 二月 **2nd Month**	卯 *Mao* **Rabbit**	酉 *You* **Rooster**	–		坤 *Kun*	坎 *Kan*
辰 **Dragon** (Apr 5 - May 5) 三月 **3rd Month**	辰 *Chen* **Dragon**	戌 *Xu* **Dog**	乾 *Qian*	兑 *Dui*	離 *Li*	乾 *Qian*
巳 **Snake** (May 6 - Jun 5) 四月 **4th Month**	巳 *Si* **Snake**	亥 *Hai* **Pig**	亥 *Hai* **Pig**	丁 *Ding* **Yin Fire**	震 *Zhen*	坤 *Kun*
午 **Horse** (Jun 6 - July 6) 五月 **5th Month**	午 *Wu* **Horse**	子 *Zi* **Rat**	離 *Li*	丙 *Bing* **Yang Fire**	艮 *Gen*	巽 *Xun*
未 **Goat** (July 7 - Aug 7) 六月 **6th Month**	未 *Wei* **Goat**	丑 *Chou* **Ox**	壬 *Ren* **Yang Water**	乙 *Yi* **Yin Wood**	兑 *Dui*	乾 *Qian*
申 **Monkey** (Aug 8 - Sept 7) 七月 **7th Month**	申 *Shen* **Monkey**	寅 *Yin* **Tiger**	震 *Zhen*	巳 *Si* **Snake**	坎 *Kan*	坤 *Kun*
酉 **Rooster** (Sept 8 - Oct 7) 八月 **8th Month**	酉 *You* **Rooster**	卯 *Mao* **Rabbit**	艮 *Gen*		乾 *Qian*	離 *Li*
戌 **Dog** (Oct 8 - Nov 6) 九月 **9th Month**	戌 *Xu* **Dog**	辰 *Chen* **Dragon**	–		坤 *Kun*	震 *Zhen*
亥 **Pig** (Nov 7 - Dec 6) 十月 **10th Month**	亥 *Hai* **Pig**	巳 *Si* **Snake**	–		巽 *Xun*	艮 *Gen*
子 **Rat** (Dec 7 - Jan 5) 十一月 **11th Month**	子 *Zi* **Rat**	午 *Wu* **Horse**	水 **Water**	山 **Mountain**	乾 *Qian*	兑 *Dui*
丑 **Ox** (Jan 6 - Feb 3) 十二月 **12th Month**	丑 *Chou* **Ox**	未 *Wei* **Goat**	土 **Earth**		坤 *Kun*	坎 *Kan*

Negative Repair / Renovation Sectors 修方凶位 :

月 MONTH	天官符 Heavenly Officer Charm			地官符 Earth Officer Charm			小月建 Small Month Establishment		
寅 Tiger (Feb 4 - Mar 5) 正月 1st Month	未 Wei Goat	坤 Kun	申 Shen Monkey	庚 Geng Yang Metal	兌 Dui	辛 Xin Yin Metal	丙 Bing Yang Fire	離 Li	丁 Ding Yin Fire
卯 Rabbit (Mar 6 - Apr 4) 二月 2nd Month	壬 Ren Yang Water	坎 Kan	癸 Gui Yin Water	戌 Xu Dog	乾 Qian	亥 Hai Pig	壬 Ren Yang Water	坎 Kan	癸 Gui Yin Water
辰 Dragon (Apr 5 - May 5) 三月 3rd Month	丙 Bing Yang Fire	離 Li	丁 Ding Yin Fire	中 Middle			未 Wei Goat	坤 Kun	申 Shen Monkey
巳 Snake (May 6 - Jun 5) 四月 4th Month	丑 Chou Ox	艮 Gen	寅 Yin Tiger	辰 Chen Dragon	巽 Xun	巳 Si Snake	甲 Jia Yang Wood	震 Zhen	乙 Yi Yin Wood
午 Horse (Jun 6 - July 6) 五月 5th Month	庚 Geng Yang Metal	兌 Dui	辛 Xin Yin Metal	甲 Jia Yang Wood	震 Zhen	乙 Yi Yin Wood	辰 Chen Dragon	巽 Xun	巳 Si Snake
未 Goat (July 7 - Aug 7) 六月 6th Month	戌 Xu Dog	乾 Qian	亥 Hai Pig	未 Wei Goat	坤 Kun	申 Shen Monkey	中 Middle		
申 Monkey (Aug 8 - Sept 7) 七月 7th Month	中 Middle			壬 Ren Yang Water	坎 Kan	癸 Gui Yin Water	戌 Xu Dog	乾 Qian	亥 Hai Pig
酉 Rooster (Sept 8 - Oct 7) 八月 8th Month	庚 Geng Yang Metal	兌 Dui	辛 Xin Yin Metal	丙 Bing Yang Fire	離 Li	丁 Ding Yin Fire	庚 Geng Yang Metal	兌 Dui	辛 Xin Yin Metal
戌 Dog (Oct 8 - Nov 6) 九月 9th Month	戌 Xu Dog	乾 Qian	亥 Hai Pig	丑 Chou Ox	艮 Gen	寅 Yin Tiger	丑 Chou Ox	艮 Gen	寅 Yin Tiger
亥 Pig (Nov 7 - Dec 6) 十月 10th Month	中 Middle			庚 Geng Yang Metal	兌 Dui	辛 Xin Yin Metal	丙 Bing Yang Fire	離 Li	丁 Ding Yin Fire
子 Rat (Dec 7 - Jan 5) 十一月 11th Month	辰 Chen Dragon	巽 Xun	巳 Si Snake	戌 Xu Dog	乾 Qian	亥 Hai Pig	壬 Ren Yang Water	坎 Kan	癸 Gui Yin Water
丑 Ox (Jan 6 - Feb 3) 十二月 12th Month	甲 Jia Yang Wood	震 Zhen	乙 Yi Yin Wood	中 Middle			未 Wei Goat	坤 Kun	申 Shen Monkey

Negative Repair / Renovation Sectors 修方凶位 ：

月 MONTH	大月建 Big Month Establishment			飛大煞 Flying Great Sha			丙丁獨火 Bing Ding Lonely Fire	
寅 Tiger (Feb 4 - Mar 5) 正月 1st Month	丑 Chou Ox	艮 Gen	寅 Yin Tiger	甲 Jia Yang Wood	震 Zhen	乙 Yi Yin Wood	坤 Kun	震 Zhen
卯 Rabbit (Mar 6 - Apr 4) 二月 2nd Month	庚 Geng Yang Metal	兌 Dui	辛 Xin Yin Metal	未 Wei Goat	坤 Kun	申 Shen Monkey	坎 Kan	坤 Kun
辰 Dragon (Apr 5 - May 5) 三月 3rd Month	戌 Xu Dog	乾 Qian	亥 Hai Pig	壬 Ren Yang Water	坎 Kan	癸 Gui Yin Water	離 Li	坎 Kan
巳 Snake (May 6 - Jun 5) 四月 4th Month		中 Middle		丙 Bing Yang Fire	離 Li	丁 Ding Yin Fire	艮 Gen	離 Li
午 Horse (Jun 6 - July 6) 五月 5th Month	辰 Chen Dragon	巽 Xun	巳 Si Snake	丑 Chou Ox	艮 Gen	寅 Yin Tiger	兌 Dui	艮 Gen
未 Goat (July 7 - Aug 7) 六月 6th Month	甲 Jia Yang Wood	震 Zhen	乙 Yi Yin Wood	庚 Geng Yang Metal	兌 Dui	辛 Xin Yin Metal	乾 Qian	兌 Dui
申 Monkey (Aug 8 - Sept 7) 七月 7th Month	未 Wei Goat	坤 Kun	申 Shen Monkey	戌 Xu Dog	乾 Qian	亥 Hai Pig	中 Middle	乾 Qian
酉 Rooster (Sept 8 - Oct 7) 八月 8th Month	壬 Ren Yang Water	坎 Kan	癸 Gui Yin Water	中 Middle			中 Middle	
戌 Dog (Oct 8 - Nov 6) 九月 9th Month	丙 Bing Yang Fire	離 Li	丁 Ding Yin Fire	庚 Geng Yang Metal	兌 Dui	辛 Xin Yin Metal	巽 Xun	中 Middle
亥 Pig (Nov 7 - Dec 6) 十月 10th Month	丑 Chou Ox	艮 Gen	寅 Yin Tiger	戌 Xu Dog	乾 Qian	亥 Hai	震 Zhen	巽 Xun
子 Rat (Dec 7 - Jan 5) 十一月 11th Month	庚 Geng Yang Metal	兌 Dui	辛 Xin Yin Metal	中 Middle			坤 Kun	震 Zhen
丑 Ox (Jan 6 - Feb 3) 十二月 12th Month	戌 Xu Dog	乾 Qian	亥 Hai Pig	辰 Chen Dragon	巽 Xun	巳 Si Snake	坎 Kan	坤 Kun

Negative Repair / Renovation Sectors 修方凶位 :

月 MONTH	月遊火 Month Wondering Fire	三煞 Monthly 3 Killings		
		劫煞 Robbery Sha	災煞 Calamity Sha	月煞 Month Sha
寅 **Tiger** (Feb 4 - Mar 5) 正月 **1st Month**	乾 Qian	亥 Hai Pig	子 Zi Rat	丑 Chou Ox
卯 **Rabbit** (Mar 6 - Apr 4) 二月 **2nd Month**	兌 Dui	申 Shen Monkey	酉 You Rooster	戌 Xu Dog
辰 **Dragon** (Apr 5 - May 5) 三月 **3rd Month**	艮 Gen	巳 Si Snake	午 Wu Horse	未 Wei Goat
巳 **Snake** (May 6 - Jun 5) 四月 **4th Month**	離 Li	寅 Yin Tiger	卯 Mao Rabbit	辰 Chen Dragon
午 **Horse** (Jun 6 - July 6) 五月 **5th Month**	坎 Kan	亥 Hai Pig	子 Zi Rat	丑 Chou Ox
未 **Goat** (July 7 - Aug 7) 六月 **6th Month**	坤 Kun	申 Shen Monkey	酉 You Rooster	戌 Xu Dog
申 **Monkey** (Aug 8 - Sept 7) 七月 **7th Month**	震 Zhen	巳 Si Snake	午 Wu Horse	未 Wei Goat
酉 **Rooster** (Sept 8 - Oct 7) 八月 **8th Month**	巽 Xun	寅 Yin Tiger	卯 Mao Rabbit	辰 Chen Dragon
戌 **Dog** (Oct 8 - Nov 6) 九月 **9th Month**	中 Middle	亥 Hai Pig	子 Zi Rat	丑 Chou Ox
亥 **Pig** (Nov 7 - Dec 6) 十月 **10th Month**	乾 Qian	申 Shen Monkey	酉 You Rooster	戌 Xu Dog
子 **Rat** (Dec 7 - Jan 5) 十一月 **11th Month**	兌 Dui	巳 Si Snake	午 Wu Horse	未 Wei Goat
丑 **Ox** (Jan 6 - Feb 3) 十二月 **12th Month**	艮 Gen	寅 Yin Tiger	卯 Mao Rabbit	辰 Chen Dragon

Negative Repair / Renovation Sectors 修方凶位 ：

月 MONTH	月刑 Month Punishment	月害 Month Harm	月厭 Month Detest
寅 **Tiger** (Feb 4 - Mar 5) 正月 **1st Month**	巳 *Si* **Snake**	巳 *Si* **Snake**	戌 *Xu* **Dog**
卯 **Rabbit** (Mar 6 - Apr 4) 二月 **2nd Month**	子 *Zi* **Rat**	辰 *Chen* **Dragon**	酉 *You* **Rooster**
辰 **Dragon** (Apr 5 - May 5) 三月 **3rd Month**	辰 *Chen* **Dragon**	卯 *Mao* **Rabbit**	申 *Shen* **Monkey**
巳 **Snake** (May 6 - Jun 5) 四月 **4th Month**	申 *Shen* **Monkey**	寅 *Yin* **Tiger**	未 *Wei* **Goat**
午 **Horse** (Jun 6 - July 6) 五月 **5th Month**	午 *Wu* **Horse**	丑 *Chou* **Ox**	午 *Wu* **Horse**
未 **Goat** (July 7 - Aug 7) 六月 **6th Month**	丑 *Chou* **Ox**	子 *Zi* **Rat**	巳 *Si* **Snake**
申 **Monkey** (Aug 8 - Sept 7) 七月 **7th Month**	寅 *Yin* **Tiger**	亥 *Hai* **Pig**	辰 *Chen* **Dragon**
酉 **Rooster** (Sept 8 - Oct 7) 八月 **8th Month**	酉 *You* **Rooster**	戌 *Xu* **Dog**	卯 *Mao* **Rabbit**
戌 **Dog** (Oct 8 - Nov 6) 九月 **9th Month**	未 *Wei* **Goat**	酉 *You* **Rooster**	寅 *Yin* **Tiger**
亥 **Pig** (Nov 7 - Dec 6) 十月 **10th Month**	亥 *Hai* **Pig**	申 *Shen* **Monkey**	丑 *Chou* **Ox**
子 **Rat** (Dec 7 - Jan 5) 十一月 **11th Month**	卯 *Mao* **Rabbit**	未 *Wei* **Goat**	子 *Zi* **Rat**
丑 **Ox** (Jan 6 - Feb 3) 十二月 **12th Month**	戌 *Xu* **Dog**	午 *Wu* **Horse**	亥 *Hai* **Pig**

辛亥 (Xin Hai)
Metal Pig

Heavenly Stem 天干	辛 **Yin Metal (陰金)**
Earthly Branch 地支	亥 **Pig (Yin Water 陰水)**
Hidden Stem 藏干	壬 **Yang Water,** 甲 **Yang Wood**
Na Yin 納音	釵釧金 **Metal from the Ornaments**
Grand Duke 太歲	亥 **Pig**
Xuan Kong Five Element 玄空五行	**7** 火 **Fire**
Gua Name 卦名	水地比 **Alliance**
Xuan Kong Period Luck 玄空卦運	**7**

Annual Positive Stars for Opening Mountain, Establishing Facing and Commencing Repairs 開山立向修方吉星:

歲德 **Duke Virtue**	丙 Bing **Yang Fire**
歲德合 **Duke Virtue Combo**	辛 Xin **Yin Metal**
歲枝德 **Duke Branch Virtue**	辰 Chen **Dragon**
陽貴人 **Yang Nobleman**	寅 Yin **Tiger**
陰貴人 **Yin Nobleman**	午 Wu **Horse**
歲祿 **Duke Prosperous**	酉 You **Rooster**
歲馬 **Duke Horse**	巳 Si **Snake**
奏書 **Decree**	乾 Qian
博士 **Professor**	巽 Xun

Annual Negative Stars for Opening Mountain, Establishing Facing and Commencing Repairs 開山立向修方凶星：

太歲 Grand Duke	歲破 Year Breaker	三煞 Three Killings			坐煞向煞 Sitting Sha Facing Sha				浮天空亡 Floating Heaven Emptiness	
亥 Hai Pig	巳 Si Snake	申 Shen Monkey	酉 You Rooster	戌 Xu Dog	庚 Geng Yang Metal	辛 Xin Yin Metal	甲 Jia Yang Wood	乙 Yi Yin Wood	艮 Gen	丙 Bing Yang Fire

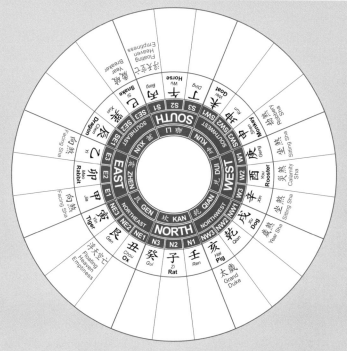

Annual San Yuan Purple White Stars 三元紫白九星：

上元 Upper Period — Period 1, 2, 3

巽SE	離S	坤SW
7	3	5
震E 6	**8** 辛亥 Xin Hai Metal Pig	1 兌W
2	4	9
艮NE	坎N	乾NW

中元 Middle Period — Period 4, 5, 6

巽SE	離S	坤SW
1	6	8
震E 9	**2** 辛亥 Xin Hai Metal Pig	4 兌W
5	7	3
艮NE	坎N	乾NW

下元 Lower Period — Period 7, 8, 9

巽SE	離S	坤SW
4	9	2
震E 3	**5** 辛亥 Xin Hai Metal Pig	7 兌W
8	1	6
艮NE	坎N	乾NW

Mountain Covering Yellow Path 蓋山黃道：

貪狼 Tan Lang **Greedy Wolf**				巨門 Ju Men **Huge Door**		武曲 Wu Qu **Military Arts**				文曲 Wen Qu **Literary Arts**			
坎 Kan N2	癸 Gui N3	申 Shen SW3	辰 Chen SE1	坤 Kun SW2	乙 Yi E3	離 Li S2	壬 Ren N1	寅 Yin NE3	戌 Xu NW1	兑 Dui W2	丁 Ding S3	巳 Si SE3	丑 Chou NE1

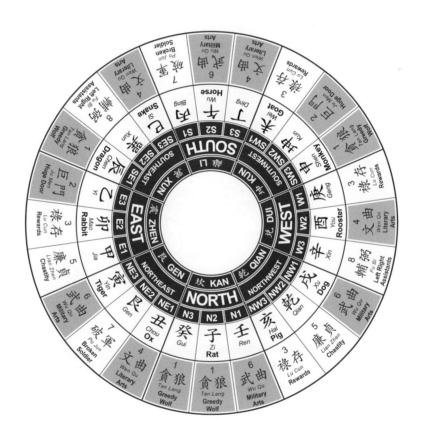

Heaven Penetrating Force 通天竅：			
三合前方 **Facing Three Harmony**	巽巳 Xun Si	丙午 Bing Wu	丁未 Ding Wei
三合後方 **Sitting Three Harmony**	乾亥 Qian Hai	壬子 Ren Zi	癸丑 Gui Chou

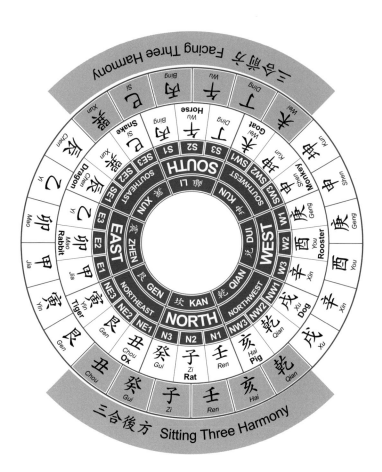

Moving Horse Six Ren Assessment 走馬六壬：

神后 *Shen Hou* **Holy Empress**	功曹 *Gong Cao* **Marshall**	天罡 *Tian Gang* **Heavenly Dipper**	勝光 *Sheng Guang* **Subliminal Bright**	傳送 *Chuan Song* **Great General**	河魁 *He Kui* **River Scholar**
癸丑 *Gui Chou*	甲卯 *Jia Mao*	巽巳 *Xun Si*	丁未 *Ding Wei*	庚酉 *Geng You*	乾亥 *Qian Hai*

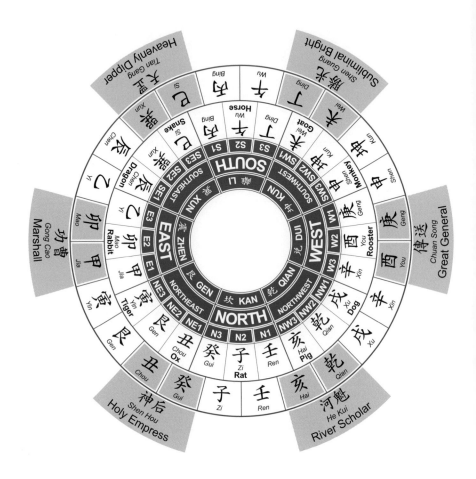

Four Advantages Three Cycles Star Plate 四利三元 :

太陽 *Tai Yang* **Sun**	太陰 *Tai Yin* **Moon**	龍德 *Long De* **Dragon Virtue**	福德 *Fu De* **Fortune Virtue**
子 *Zi* **Rat**	寅 *Yin* **Tiger**	午 *Wu* **Horse**	申 *Shen* **Monkey**

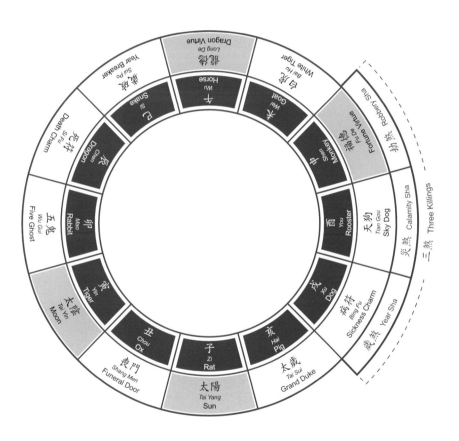

Negative Sectors For Opening Mountain 開山凶位：

年剋山家 Year Countering Sitting

離	壬	丙	乙
Li	Ren	Bing	Yi
S2	N1	S1	E3

陰府太歲 Yin Fu Tai Sui **Yin Mansion Grand Duke**		六害 Liu Hai **Six Harm**	死符 Si Fu **Death Charm**	炙退 Zhi Tui **Roasting Star**
坤 Kun SW2	坎 Kan N2	申 Shen SW3	辰 Chen SE1	午 Wu S2

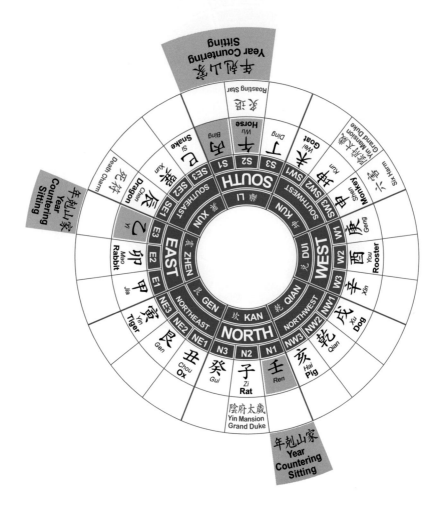

Negative Directions to Establish Facing 立向凶方：

巡山羅喉 *Xun Shan Luo Hou* **Mountain Patrol Luo Hou Star**	病符 *Bing Fu* **Sickness Charm**
壬 *Ren* **N1**	戌 *Xu* **NW1**

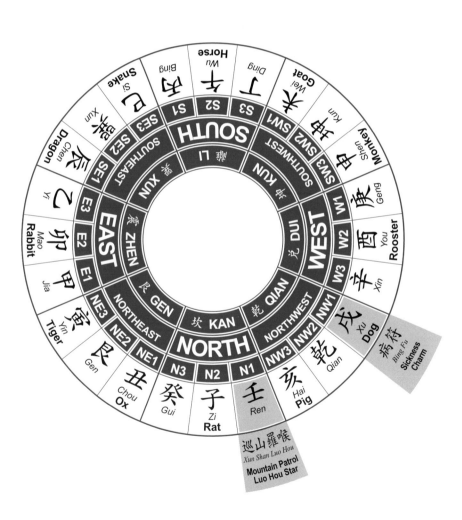

Negative Repair / Renovation Sectors Table 修方凶位表：

天官符 **Heavenly Officer Charm**	寅 *Yin* **Tiger**	飛廉 **Flying Chaste**	丑 *Chou* **Ox**
地官符 **Earthly Officer Charm**	卯 *Mao* **Rabbit**	喪門 **Funeral Door**	丑 *Chou* **Ox**
大煞 **Great Sha**	卯 *Mao* **Rabbit**	弔客 **Suspended Guest**	酉 *You* **Rooster**
大將軍 **Big General**	酉 *You* **Rooster**	白虎 **White Tiger**	未 *Wei* **Goat**
力士 **Strong Man**	艮 *Gen*	金神 **Golden God**	寅 *Yin* **Tiger** 卯 *Mao* **Rabbit** 午 *Wu* **Horse** 未 *Wei* **Goat** 子 *Zi* **Rat** 丑 *Chou* **Ox**
蠶室 **Silkworm Room**	坤 *Kun*		
蠶官 **Silkworm Officer**	未 *Wei* **Goat**		
蠶命 **Silkworm Life**	申 *Shen* **Monkey**		
歲刑 **Duke Punishment**	亥 *Hai* **Pig**	獨火 **Lonely Fire**	乾 *Qian*
黃幡 **Yellow Flag**	未 *Wei* **Goat**	五鬼 **Five Ghost**	巳 *Si* **Snake**
豹尾 **Leopard Tail**	丑 *Chou* **Ox**	破敗五鬼 **Destructive Five Ghost**	乾 *Qian*

Negative Repair / Renovation Sectors Diagram 修方凶位圖：

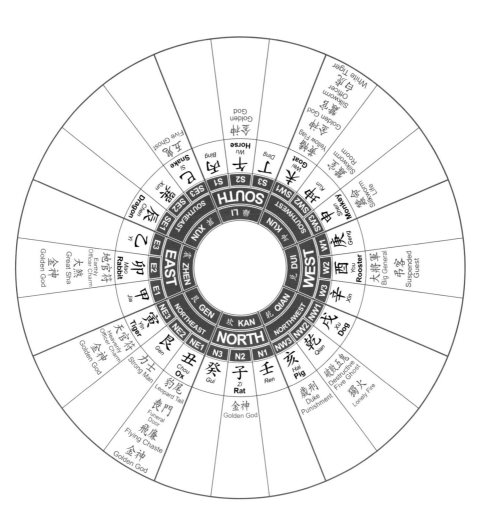

12-Month Auxiliary Stars Reference Table :
辛亥年十二月，開山立向修方星表

Positive Monthly Stars 吉星方

月 MONTH	寅 Tiger (Feb 4 - Mar 5) 正月 1st Month	卯 Rabbit (Mar 6 - Apr 4) 二月 2nd Month	辰 Dragon (Apr 5 - May 5) 三月 3rd Month	巳 Snake (May 6 - Jun 5) 四月 4th Month	午 Horse (Jun 6 - July 6) 五月 5th Month	未 Goat (July 7 - Aug 7) 六月 6th Month
天道 Heavenly Path	南 South	西南 Southwest	北 North	西 West	西北 Northwest	東 East
天德 Heavenly Virtue	丁 Ding Yin Fire	坤 Kun (申)	壬 Ren Yang Water	辛 Xin Yin Metal	乾 Qian (亥)	甲 Jia Yang Wood
天德合 Heavenly Virtue Combo	壬 Ren Yang Water	(巳)	丁 Ding Yin Fire	丙 Bing Yang Fire	(寅)	己 Ji Yin Earth
月德 Monthly Virtue	丙 Bing Yang Fire	甲 Jia Yang Wood	壬 Ren Yang Water	庚 Geng Yang Metal	丙 Bing Yang Fire	甲 Jia Yang Wood
月德合 Monthly Virtue Combo	辛 Xin Yin Metal	己 Ji Yin Earth	丁 Ding Yin Fire	乙 Yi Yin Wood	辛 Xin Yin Metal	己 Ji Yin Earth
月空 Month Emptiness	壬 Ren Yang Water	庚 Geng Yang Metal	丙 Bing Yang Fire	甲 Jia Yang Wood	壬 Ren Yang Water	庚 Geng Yang Metal
陽貴人 Yang Nobleman	中 Middle	坎 Kan	離 Li	艮 Gen	兌 Dui	乾 Qian
陰貴人 Yin Nobleman	離 Li	艮 Gen	兌 Dui	乾 Qian	中 Middle	坎 Kan
飛天祿 Flying Heavenly Wealth	震 Zhen	坤 Kun	坎 Kan	離 Li	艮 Gen	兌 Dui
飛天馬 Flying Heavenly Horse	艮 Gen	兌 Dui	乾 Qian	中 Middle	坎 Kan	離 Li

12-Month Auxiliary Stars Reference Table :
辛亥年十二月，開山立向修方星表

申 Monkey (Aug 8 - Sept 7) 七月 7th Month	酉 Rooster (Sept 8 - Oct 7) 八月 8th Month	戌 Dog (Oct 8 - Nov 6) 九月 9th Month	亥 Pig (Nov 7 - Dec 6) 十月 10th Month	子 Rat (Dec 7 - Jan 5) 十一月 11th Month	丑 Ox (Jan 6 - Feb 3) 十二月 12th Month	月 MONTH
北 North	東北 Northeast	南 South	東 East	東南 Southeast	西 West	天道 Heavenly Path
癸 Gui Yin Water	艮 Gen (寅)	丙 Bing Yang Fire	乙 Yi Yin Wood	巽 Xun (巳)	庚 Geng Yang Metal	天德 Heavenly Virtue
戊 Wu Yang Earth	(亥)	辛 Xin Yin Metal	庚 Geng Yang Metal	(申)	乙 Yi Yin Wood	天德合 Heavenly Virtue Combo
壬 Ren Yang Water	庚 Geng Yang Metal	丙 Bing Yang Fire	甲 Jia Yang Wood	壬 Ren Yang Water	庚 Geng Yang Metal	月德 Monthly Virtue
丁 Ding Yin Fire	乙 Yi Yin Wood	辛 Xin Yin Metal	己 Ji Yin Earth	丁 Ding Yin Fire	乙 Yi Yin Wood	月德合 Monthly Virtue Combo
丙 Bing Yang Fire	甲 Jia Yang Wood	壬 Ren Yang Water	庚 Geng Yang Metal	丙 Bing Yang Fire	甲 Jia Yang Wood	月空 Month Emptiness
中 Middle	巽 Xun	震 Zhen	坤 Kun	坎 Kan	離 Li	陽貴人 Yang Nobleman
離 Li	艮 Gen	兌 Dui	乾 Qian	中 Middle	巽 Xun	陰貴人 Yin Nobleman
乾 Qian	中 Middle	坎 Kan	離 Li	艮 Gen	兌 Dui	飛天祿 Flying Heavenly Wealth
艮 Gen	兌 Dui	乾 Qian	中 Middle	巽 Xun	震 Zhen	飛天馬 Flying Heavenly Horse

Monthly Purple White Stars 月紫白九星 :

寅 Tiger (Feb 4 - Mar 5) 正月 1st Month

巽 SE	離 S	坤 SW
1 White 一白	6 White 六白	8 White 八白
震 E 9 Purple 九紫	2 Black 二黑	4 Green 四綠 兌 W
艮 NE 5 Yellow 五黃	坎 N 7 Red 七赤	乾 NW 3 Jade 三碧

卯 Rabbit (Mar 6 - Apr 4) 二月 2nd Month

巽 SE	離 S	坤 SW
9 Purple 九紫	5 Yellow 五黃	7 Red 七赤
震 E 8 White 八白	1 White 一白	3 Jade 三碧 兌 W
艮 NE 4 Green 四綠	坎 N 6 White 六白	乾 NW 2 Black 二黑

辰 Dragon (Apr 5 - May 5) 三月 3rd Month

巽 SE	離 S	坤 SW
8 White 八白	4 Green 四綠	6 White 六白
震 E 7 Red 七赤	9 Purple 九紫	2 Black 二黑 兌 W
艮 NE 3 Jade 三碧	坎 N 5 Yellow 五黃	乾 NW 1 White 一白

巳 Snake (May 6 - Jun 5) 四月 4th Month

巽 SE	離 S	坤 SW
7 Red 七赤	3 Jade 三碧	5 Yellow 五黃
震 E 6 White 六白	8 White 八白	1 White 一白 兌 W
艮 NE 2 Black 二黑	坎 N 4 Green 四綠	乾 NW 9 Purple 九紫

午 Horse (Jun 6 - July 6) 五月 5th Month

巽 SE	離 S	坤 SW
6 White 六白	2 Black 二黑	4 Green 四綠
震 E 5 Yellow 五黃	7 Red 七赤	9 Purple 九紫 兌 W
艮 NE 1 White 一白	坎 N 3 Jade 三碧	乾 NW 8 White 八白

未 Goat (July 7 - Aug 7) 六月 6th Month

巽 SE	離 S	坤 SW
5 Yellow 五黃	1 White 一白	3 Jade 三碧
震 E 4 Green 四綠	6 White 六白	8 White 八白 兌 W
艮 NE 9 Purple 九紫	坎 N 2 Black 二黑	乾 NW 7 Red 七赤

申 Monkey (Aug 8 - Sept 7) 七月 7th Month

巽 SE	離 S	坤 SW
4 Green 四綠	9 Purple 九紫	2 Black 二黑
震 E 3 Jade 三碧	5 Yellow 五黃	7 Red 七赤 兌 W
艮 NE 8 White 八白	坎 N 1 White 一白	乾 NW 6 White 六白

酉 Rooster (Sept 8 - Oct 7) 八月 8th Month

巽 SE	離 S	坤 SW
3 Jade 三碧	8 White 八白	1 White 一白
震 E 2 Black 二黑	4 Green 四綠	6 White 六白 兌 W
艮 NE 7 Red 七赤	坎 N 9 Purple 九紫	乾 NW 5 Yellow 五黃

戌 Dog (Oct 8 - Nov 6) 九月 9th Month

巽 SE	離 S	坤 SW
2 Black 二黑	7 Red 七赤	9 Purple 九紫
震 E 1 White 一白	3 Jade 三碧	5 Yellow 五黃 兌 W
艮 NE 6 White 六白	坎 N 8 White 八白	乾 NW 4 Green 四綠

亥 Pig (Nov 7 - Dec 6) 十月 10th Month

巽 SE	離 S	坤 SW
1 White 一白	6 White 六白	8 White 八白
震 E 9 Purple 九紫	2 Black 二黑	4 Green 四綠 兌 W
艮 NE 5 Yellow 五黃	坎 N 7 Red 七赤	乾 NW 3 Jade 三碧

子 Rat (Dec 7 - Jan 5) 十一月 11th Month

巽 SE	離 S	坤 SW
9 Purple 九紫	5 Yellow 五黃	7 Red 七赤
震 E 8 White 八白	1 White 一白	3 Jade 三碧 兌 W
艮 NE 4 Green 四綠	坎 N 6 White 六白	乾 NW 2 Black 二黑

丑 Ox (Jan 6 - Feb 3) 十二月 12th Month

巽 SE	離 S	坤 SW
8 White 八白	4 Green 四綠	6 White 六白
震 E 7 Red 七赤	9 Purple 九紫	2 Black 二黑 兌 W
艮 NE 3 Jade 三碧	坎 N 5 Yellow 五黃	乾 NW 1 White 一白

Qi Men Three Nobles 三奇 :

Three Nobles 三奇 / Seasons	乙 Yi	丙 Bing	丁 Ding
立春 **Coming of Spring** Feb 4 - Feb 18	乾 Qian	兌 Dui	艮 Gen
春分 **Spring Equinox** Mar 21 - Apr 4	坎 Kan	坤 Kun	震 Zhen
立夏 **Coming of Summer** May 6 - May 20	坤 Kun	震 Zhen	巽 Xun
夏至 **Summer Solstice** Jun 22 - Jul 6	坤 Kun	坎 Kan	離 Li
立秋 **Coming of Autumn** Aug 8 - Aug 23	巽 Xun	震 Zhen	坤 Kun
秋分 **Autumn Equinox** Sept 23 - Oct 7	離 Li	艮 Gen	兌 Dui
立冬 **Coming of Winter** Nov 7 - Nov 22	艮 Gen	兌 Dui	乾 Qian
冬至 **Winter Solstice** Dec 22 - Jan 5	艮 Gen	離 Li	坎 Kan

Sectors to Avoid Opening Mountain 開山凶位 :

月 MONTH	月建 Month Establishment	月破 Month Destruction	月剋山家 Month Countering Sitting		陰府太歲 Yin Mansion Grand Duke	
寅 **Tiger** (Feb 4 - Mar 5) 正月 **1st Month**	寅 *Yin* **Tiger**	申 *Shen* **Monkey**	—		乾 *Qian*	兌 *Dui*
卯 **Rabbit** (Mar 6 - Apr 4) 二月 **2nd Month**	卯 *Mao* **Rabbit**	酉 *You* **Rooster**	—		坤 *Kun*	坎 *Kan*
辰 **Dragon** (Apr 5 - May 5) 三月 **3rd Month**	辰 *Chen* **Dragon**	戌 *Xu* **Dog**	乾 *Qian*	兌 *Dui*	離 *Li*	乾 *Qian*
巳 **Snake** (May 6 - Jun 5) 四月 **4th Month**	巳 *Si* **Snake**	亥 *Hai* **Pig**	亥 *Hai* **Pig**	丁 *Ding* **Yin Fire**	震 *Zhen*	坤 *Kun*
午 **Horse** (Jun 6 - July 6) 五月 **5th Month**	午 *Wu* **Horse**	子 *Zi* **Rat**	離 *Li*	丙 *Bing* **Yang Fire**	艮 *Gen*	巽 *Xun*
未 **Goat** (July 7 - Aug 7) 六月 **6th Month**	未 *Wei* **Goat**	丑 *Chou* **Ox**	壬 *Ren* **Yang Water**	乙 *Yi* **Yin Wood**	兌 *Dui*	乾 *Qian*
申 **Monkey** (Aug 8 - Sept 7) 七月 **7th Month**	申 *Shen* **Monkey**	寅 *Yin* **Tiger**	震 *Zhen*	巳 *Si* **Snake**	坎 *Kan*	坤 *Kun*
酉 **Rooster** (Sept 8 - Oct 7) 八月 **8th Month**	酉 *You* **Rooster**	卯 *Mao* **Rabbit**	艮 *Gen*		乾 *Qian*	離 *Li*
戌 **Dog** (Oct 8 - Nov 6) 九月 **9th Month**	戌 *Xu* **Dog**	辰 *Chen* **Dragon**	—		坤 *Kun*	震 *Zhen*
亥 **Pig** (Nov 7 - Dec 6) 十月 **10th Month**	亥 *Hai* **Pig**	巳 *Si* **Snake**	—		巽 *Xun*	艮 *Gen*
子 **Rat** (Dec 7 - Jan 5) 十一月 **11th Month**	子 *Zi* **Rat**	午 *Wu* **Horse**	水 **Water**	山 **Mountain**	乾 *Qian*	兌 *Dui*
丑 **Ox** (Jan 6 - Feb 3) 十二月 **12th Month**	丑 *Chou* **Ox**	未 *Wei* **Goat**	土 **Earth**		坤 *Kun*	坎 *Kan*

Negative Repair / Renovation Sectors 修方凶位 :

月 MONTH	天官符 Heavenly Officer Charm			地官符 Earth Officer Charm			小月建 Small Month Establishment		
寅 **Tiger** (Feb 4 - Mar 5) 正月 **1st Month**		中 Middle		戊 *Xu* Dog	乾 *Qian*	亥 *Hai* Pig	丙 *Bing* Yang Fire	離 *Li*	丁 *Ding* Yin Fire
卯 **Rabbit** (Mar 6 - Apr 4) 二月 **2nd Month**	庚 *Geng* Yang Metal	兌 *Dui*	辛 *Xin* Yin Metal		中 Middle		壬 *Ren* Yang Water	坎 *Kan*	癸 *Gui* Yin Water
辰 **Dragon** (Apr 5 - May 5) 三月 **3rd Month**	戊 *Xu* Dog	乾 *Qian*	亥 *Hai* Pig	庚 *Geng* Yang Metal	兌 *Dui*	辛 *Xin* Yin Metal	未 *Wei* Goat	坤 *Kun*	申 *Shen* Monkey
巳 **Snake** (May 6 - Jun 5) 四月 **4th Month**		中 Middle		戊 *Xu* Dog	乾 *Qian*	亥 *Hai* Pig	甲 *Jia* Yang Wood	震 *Zhen*	乙 *Yi* Yin Wood
午 **Horse** (Jun 6 - July 6) 五月 **5th Month**	辰 *Chen* Dragon	巽 *Xun*	巳 *Si* Snake		中 Middle		辰 *Chen* Dragon	巽 *Xun*	巳 *Si* Snake
未 **Goat** (July 7 - Aug 7) 六月 **6th Month**	甲 *Jia* Yang Wood	震 *Zhen*	乙 *Yi* Yin Wood	辰 *Chen* Dragon	巽 *Xun*	巳 *Si* Snake		中 Middle	
申 **Monkey** (Aug 8 - Sept 7) 七月 **7th Month**	未 *Wei* Goat	坤 *Kun*	申 *Shen* Monkey	甲 *Jia* Yang Wood	震 *Zhen*	乙 *Yi* Yin Wood	戊 *Xu* Dog	乾 *Qian*	亥 *Hai* Pig
酉 **Rooster** (Sept 8 - Oct 7) 八月 **8th Month**	壬 *Ren* Yang Water	坎 *Kan*	癸 *Gui* Yin Water	未 *Wei* Goat	坤 *Kun*	申 *Shen* Monkey	庚 *Geng* Yang Metal	兌 *Dui*	辛 *Xin* Yin Metal
戌 **Dog** (Oct 8 - Nov 6) 九月 **9th Month**	丙 *Bing* Yang Fire	離 *Li*	丁 *Ding* Yin Fire	壬 *Ren* Yang Water	坎 *Kan*	癸 *Gui* Yin Water	丑 *Chou* Ox	艮 *Gen*	寅 *Yin* Tiger
亥 **Pig** (Nov 7 - Dec 6) 十月 **10th Month**	丑 *Chou* Ox	艮 *Gen*	寅 *Yin* Tiger	丙 *Bing* Yang Fire	離 *Li*	丁 *Ding* Yin Fire	丙 *Bing* Yang Fire	離 *Li*	丁 *Ding* Yin Fire
子 **Rat** (Dec 7 - Jan 5) 十一月 **11th Month**	庚 *Geng* Yang Metal	兌 *Dui*	辛 *Xin* Yin Metal	丑 *Chou* Ox	艮 *Gen*	寅 *Yin* Tiger	壬 *Ren* Yang Water	坎 *Kan*	癸 *Gui* Yin Water
丑 **Ox** (Jan 6 - Feb 3) 十二月 **12th Month**	戊 *Xu* Dog	乾 *Qian*	亥 *Hai* Pig	庚 *Geng* Yang Metal	兌 *Dui*	辛 *Xin* Yin Metal	未 *Wei* Goat	坤 *Kun*	申 *Shen* Monkey

957

Negative Repair / Renovation Sectors 修方凶位 ：

月 MONTH	大月建 Big Month Establishment			飛大煞 Flying Great Sha			丙丁獨火 Bing Ding Lonely Fire	
寅 **Tiger** (Feb 4 - Mar 5) 正月 **1st Month**	未 *Wei* Goat	坤 *Kun*	申 *Shen* Monkey	戌 *Xu* Dog	乾 *Qian*	亥 *Hai* Pig	坤 *Kun*	震 *Zhen*
卯 **Rabbit** (Mar 6 - Apr 4) 二月 **2nd Month**	壬 *Ren* Yang Water	坎 *Kan*	癸 *Gui* Yin Water	中 Middle			坎 *Kan*	坤 *Kun*
辰 **Dragon** (Apr 5 - May 5) 三月 **3rd Month**	丙 *Bing* Yang Fire	離 *Li*	丁 *Ding* Yin Fire	庚 *Geng* Yang Metal	兌 *Dui*	辛 *Xin* Yin Metal	離 *Li*	坎 *Kan*
巳 **Snake** (May 6 - Jun 5) 四月 **4th Month**	丑 *Chou* Ox	艮 *Gen*	寅 *Yin* Tiger	戌 *Xu* Dog	乾 *Qian*	亥 *Hai* Pig	艮 *Gen*	離 *Li*
午 **Horse** (Jun 6 - July 6) 五月 **5th Month**	庚 *Geng* Yang Metal	兌 *Dui*	辛 *Xin* Yin Metal	中 Middle			兌 *Dui*	艮 *Gen*
未 **Goat** (July 7 - Aug 7) 六月 **6th Month**	戌 *Xu* Dog	乾 *Qian*	亥 *Hai* Pig	辰 *Chen* Dragon	巽 *Xun*	巳 *Si* Snake	乾 *Qian*	兌 *Dui*
申 **Monkey** (Aug 8 - Sept 7) 七月 **7th Month**	中 Middle			甲 *Jia* Yang Wood	震 *Zhen*	乙 *Yi* Yin Wood	中 Middle	乾 *Qian*
酉 **Rooster** (Sept 8 - Oct 7) 八月 **8th Month**	辰 *Chen* Dragon	巽 *Xun*	巳 *Si* Snake	未 *Wei* Goat	坤 *Kun*	申 *Shen* Monkey	中 Middle	
戌 **Dog** (Oct 8 - Nov 6) 九月 **9th Month**	甲 *Jia* Yang Wood	震 *Zhen*	乙 *Yi* Yin Wood	壬 *Ren* Yang Water	坎 *Kan*	癸 *Gui* Yin Water	巽 *Xun*	中 Middle
亥 **Pig** (Nov 7 - Dec 6) 十月 **10th Month**	未 *Wei* Goat	坤 *Kun*	申 *Shen* Monkey	丙 *Bing* Yang Fire	離 *Li*	丁 *Ding* Yin Fire	震 *Zhen*	巽 *Xun*
子 **Rat** (Dec 7 - Jan 5) 十一月 **11th Month**	壬 *Ren* Yang Water	坎 *Kan*	癸 *Gui* Yin Water	丑 *Chou* Ox	艮 *Gen*	寅 *Yin* Tiger	坤 *Kun*	震 *Zhen*
丑 **Ox** (Jan 6 - Feb 3) 十二月 **12th Month**	丙 *Bing* Yang Fire	離 *Li*	丁 *Ding* Yin Fire	庚 *Geng* Yang Metal	兌 *Dui*	辛 *Xin* Yin Metal	坎 *Kan*	坤 *Kun*

Negative Repair / Renovation Sectors 修方凶位 :

月 MONTH	月遊火 Month Wondering Fire	三煞 Monthly 3 Killings		
		劫煞 Robbery Sha	災煞 Calamity Sha	月煞 Month Sha
寅 Tiger (Feb 4 - Mar 5) 正月 1st Month	坎 Kan	亥 Hai Pig	子 Zi Rat	丑 Chou Ox
卯 Rabbit (Mar 6 - Apr 4) 二月 2nd Month	坤 Kun	申 Shen Monkey	酉 You Rooster	戌 Xu Dog
辰 Dragon (Apr 5 - May 5) 三月 3rd Month	震 Zhen	巳 Si Snake	午 Wu Horse	未 Wei Goat
巳 Snake (May 6 - Jun 5) 四月 4th Month	巽 Xun	寅 Yin Tiger	卯 Mao Rabbit	辰 Chen Dragon
午 Horse (Jun 6 - July 6) 五月 5th Month	中 Middle	亥 Hai Pig	子 Zi Rat	丑 Chou Ox
未 Goat (July 7 - Aug 7) 六月 6th Month	乾 Qian	申 Shen Monkey	酉 You Rooster	戌 Xu Dog
申 Monkey (Aug 8 - Sept 7) 七月 7th Month	兌 Dui	巳 Si Snake	午 Wu Horse	未 Wei Goat
酉 Rooster (Sept 8 - Oct 7) 八月 8th Month	艮 Gen	寅 Yin Tiger	卯 Mao Rabbit	辰 Chen Dragon
戌 Dog (Oct 8 - Nov 6) 九月 9th Month	離 Li	亥 Hai Pig	子 Zi Rat	丑 Chou Ox
亥 Pig (Nov 7 - Dec 6) 十月 10th Month	坎 Kan	申 Shen Monkey	酉 You Rooster	戌 Xu Dog
子 Rat (Dec 7 - Jan 5) 十一月 11th Month	坤 Kun	巳 Si Snake	午 Wu Horse	未 Wei Goat
丑 Ox (Jan 6 - Feb 3) 十二月 12th Month	震 Zhen	寅 Yin Tiger	卯 Mao Rabbit	辰 Chen Dragon

Negative Repair / Renovation Sectors 修方凶位 :

月 MONTH	月刑 Month Punishment	月害 Month Harm	月厭 Month Detest
寅 Tiger (Feb 4 - Mar 5) 正月 1st Month	巳 Si Snake	巳 Si Snake	戌 Xu Dog
卯 Rabbit (Mar 6 - Apr 4) 二月 2nd Month	子 Zi Rat	辰 Chen Dragon	酉 You Rooster
辰 Dragon (Apr 5 - May 5) 三月 3rd Month	辰 Chen Dragon	卯 Mao Rabbit	申 Shen Monkey
巳 Snake (May 6 - Jun 5) 四月 4th Month	申 Shen Monkey	寅 Yin Tiger	未 Wei Goat
午 Horse (Jun 6 - July 6) 五月 5th Month	午 Wu Horse	丑 Chou Ox	午 Wu Horse
未 Goat (July 7 - Aug 7) 六月 6th Month	丑 Chou Ox	子 Zi Rat	巳 Si Snake
申 Monkey (Aug 8 - Sept 7) 七月 7th Month	寅 Yin Tiger	亥 Hai Pig	辰 Chen Dragon
酉 Rooster (Sept 8 - Oct 7) 八月 8th Month	酉 You Rooster	戌 Xu Dog	卯 Mao Rabbit
戌 Dog (Oct 8 - Nov 6) 九月 9th Month	未 Wei Goat	酉 You Rooster	寅 Yin Tiger
亥 Pig (Nov 7 - Dec 6) 十月 10th Month	亥 Hai Pig	申 Shen Monkey	丑 Chou Ox
子 Rat (Dec 7 - Jan 5) 十一月 11th Month	卯 Mao Rabbit	未 Wei Goat	子 Zi Rat
丑 Ox (Jan 6 - Feb 3) 十二月 12th Month	戌 Xu Dog	午 Wu Horse	亥 Hai Pig

壬子 **(Ren Zi)**
Water Rat

Heavenly Stem 天干	壬 Yang Water (陽水)
Earthly Branch 地支	子 Rat (Yang Water 陽水)
Hidden Stem 藏干	癸 Yin Water
Na Yin 納音	桑柘木 Wood from mulberry tree
Grand Duke 太歲	子 Rat
Xuan Kong Five Element 玄空五行	8 木 Wood
Gua Name 卦名	震爲雷 Thunder
Xuan Kong Period Luck 玄空卦運	1

Annual Positive Stars for Opening Mountain, Establishing Facing and Commencing Repairs 開山立向修方吉星：

歲德 **Duke Virtue**	壬 *Ren* **Yang Water**	
歲德合 **Duke Virtue Combo**	丁 *Ding* **Yin Fire**	
歲枝德 **Duke Branch Virtue**	巳 *Si* **Snake**	
陽貴人 **Yang Nobleman**	卯 *Mao* **Rabbit**	
陰貴人 **Yin Nobleman**	巳 *Si* **Snake**	
歲祿 **Duke Prosperous**	亥 *Hai* **Pig**	
歲馬 **Duke Horse**	寅 *Yin* **Tiger**	
奏書 **Decree**	乾 *Qian*	
博士 **Professor**	巽 *Xun*	

Annual Negative Stars for Opening Mountain, Establishing Facing and Commencing Repairs 開山立向修方凶星：

太歲 Grand Duke	歲破 Year Breaker	三煞 Three Killings			坐煞向煞 Sitting Sha Facing Sha				浮天空亡 Floating Heaven Emptiness	
子 Zi Rat	午 Wu Horse	巳 Si Snake	午 Wu Horse	未 Wei Goat	丙 Bing Yang Fire	丁 Ding Yin Fire	壬 Ren Yang Water	癸 Gui Yin Water	乾 Qian	甲 Jia Yang Wood

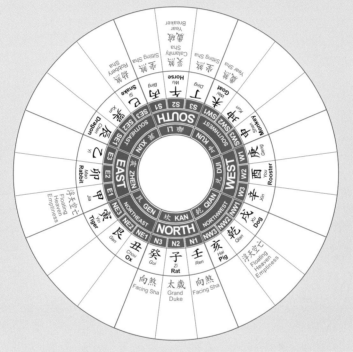

Annual San Yuan Purple White Stars 三元紫白九星：

上元 Upper Period Period 1, 2, 3			中元 Middle Period Period 4, 5, 6			下元 Lower Period Period 7, 8, 9		
巽SE	離S	坤SW	巽SE	離S	坤SW	巽SE	離S	坤SW
6	2	4	9	5	7	3	8	1
震E 5	7 壬子 Ren Zi Water Rat	兌W 9	震E 8	1 壬子 Ren Zi Water Rat	兌W 3	震E 2	4 壬子 Ren Zi Water Rat	兌W 6
1	3	8	4	6	2	7	9	5
艮NE	坎N	乾NW	艮NE	坎N	乾NW	艮NE	坎N	乾NW

Mountain Covering Yellow Path 蓋山黃道:

貪狼 Tan Lang Greedy Wolf				巨門 Ju Men Huge Door				武曲 Wu Qu Military Arts		文曲 Wen Qu Literary Arts	
震	庚	亥	未	兌	丁	巳	丑	巽	辛	坤	乙
Zhen	Geng	Hai	Wei	Dui	Ding	Si	Chou	Xun	Xin	Kun	Yi
E2	W1	NW3	SW1	W2	S3	SE3	NE1	SE2	W3	SW2	E3

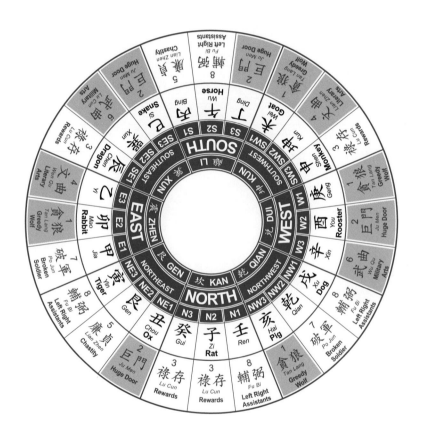

Heaven Penetrating Force 通天竅 :

三合前方 **Facing Three Harmony**	艮寅 Gen Yin	甲卯 Jia Mao	乙辰 Yi Chen
三合後方 **Sitting Three Harmony**	坤申 Kun Shen	庚酉 Geng You	辛戌 Xin Xu

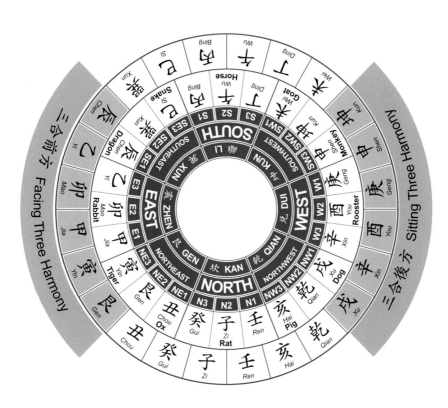

Moving Horse Six Ren Assessment 走馬六壬：

神后 *Shen Hou* **Holy Empress**	功曹 *Gong Cao* **Marshall**	天罡 *Tian Gang* **Heavenly Dipper**	勝光 *Sheng Guang* **Subliminal Bright**	傳送 *Chuan Song* **Great General**	河魁 *He Kui* **River Scholar**
壬子 *Ren Zi*	艮寅 *Gen Yin*	乙辰 *Yi Chen*	丙午 *Bing Wu*	坤申 *Kun Shen*	辛戌 *Xin Xu*

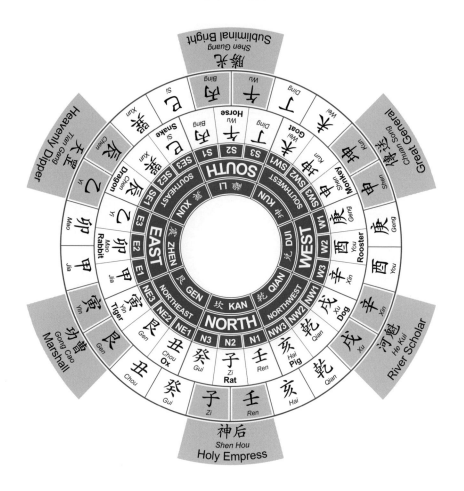

Four Advantages Three Cycles Star Plate 四利三元：

太陽 *Tai Yang* **Sun**	太陰 *Tai Yin* **Moon**	龍德 *Long De* **Dragon Virtue**	福德 *Fu De* **Fortune Virtue**
丑 *Chou* **Ox**	卯 *Mao* **Rabbit**	未 *Wei* **Goat**	酉 *You* **Rooster**

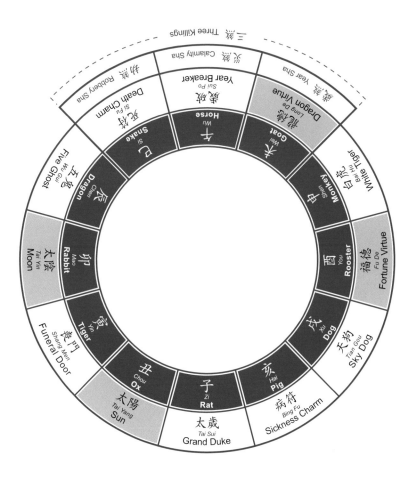

Negative Sectors For Opening Mountain 開山凶位：

年剋山家 Year Countering Sitting

乾	亥	兌	丁
Qian	Hai	Dui	Ding
NW2	NW3	W2	S3

陰府太歲 Yin Fu Tai Sui **Yin Mansion Grand Duke**	六害 Liu Hai **Six Harm**	死符 Si Fu **Death Charm**	炙退 Zhi Tui **Roasting Star**
離 　 乾 Li 　 Qian S2 　 NW2	未 Wei SW1	巳 Si SE3	卯 Mao E2

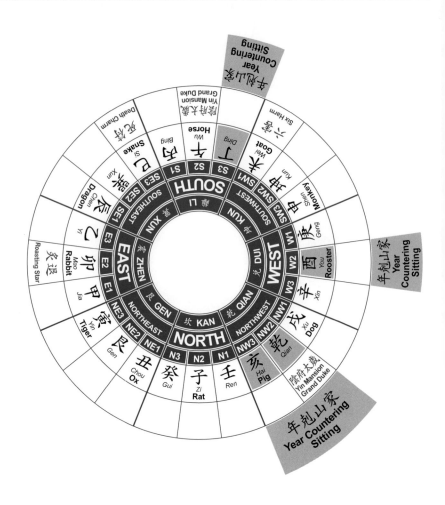

Negative Directions to Establish Facing 立向凶方：

巡山羅喉 *Xun Shan Luo Hou* **Mountain Patrol Luo Hou Star**	病符 *Bing Fu* **Sickness Charm**
癸 *Gui* **N3**	亥 *Hai* **NW3**

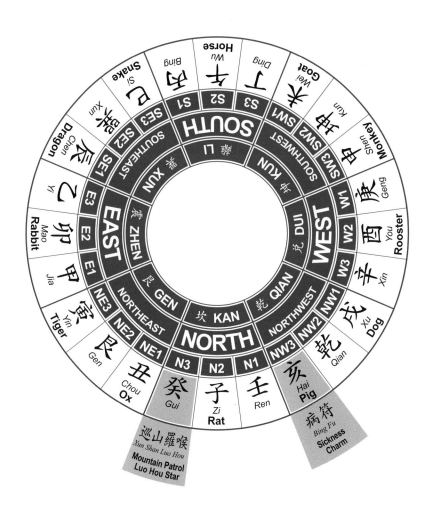

Negative Repair / Renovation Sectors Table 修方凶位表:

天官符 Heavenly Officer Charm	亥 *Hai* Pig		飛廉 Flying Chaste	申 *Shen* Monkey
地官符 Earthly Officer Charm	辰 *Chen* Dragon		喪門 Funeral Door	寅 *Yin* Tiger
大煞 Great Sha	子 *Zi* Rat		弔客 Suspended Guest	戌 *Xu* Dog
大將軍 Big General	酉 *You* Rooster		白虎 White Tiger	申 *Shen* Monkey
力士 Strong Man	艮 *Gen*		金神 Golden God	寅 *Yin* Tiger 卯 *Mao* Rabbit 戌 *Xu* Dog 亥 *Hai* Pig
蠶室 Silkworm Room	坤 *Kun*			
蠶官 Silkworm Officer	未 *Wei* Goat			
蠶命 Silkworm Life	申 *Shen* Monkey			
歲刑 Duke Punishment	卯 *Mao* Rabbit		獨火 Lonely Fire	艮 *Gen*
黃幡 Yellow Flag	辰 *Chen* Dragon		五鬼 Five Ghost	辰 *Chen* Dragon
豹尾 Leopard Tail	戌 *Xu* Dog		破敗五鬼 Destructive Five Ghost	巽 *Xun*

Negative Repair / Renovation Sectors Diagram 修方凶位圖:

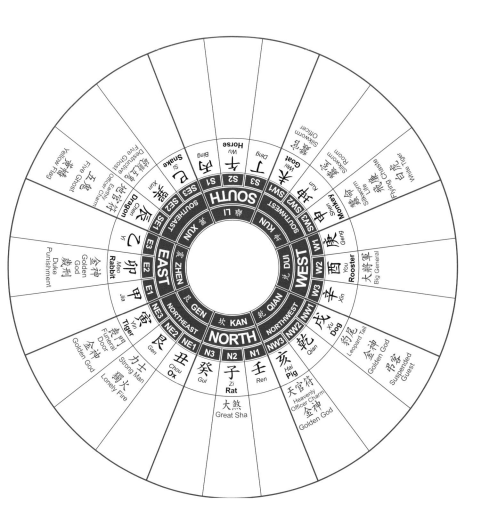

971

12-Month Auxiliary Stars Reference Table :
壬子年十二月，開山立向修方星表

Positive Monthly Stars 吉星方

月 MONTH	寅 Tiger (Feb 4 - Mar 5) 正月 1st Month	卯 Rabbit (Mar 6 - Apr 4) 二月 2nd Month	辰 Dragon (Apr 5 - May 5) 三月 3rd Month	巳 Snake (May 6 - Jun 5) 四月 4th Month	午 Horse (Jun 6 - July 6) 五月 5th Month	未 Goat (July 7 - Aug 7) 六月 6th Month
天道 Heavenly Path	南 South	西南 Southwest	北 North	西 West	西北 Northwest	東 East
天德 Heavenly Virtue	丁 Ding Yin Fire	坤 Kun (申)	壬 Ren Yang Water	辛 Xin Yin Metal	乾 Qian (亥)	甲 Jia Yang Wood
天德合 Heavenly Virtue Combo	壬 Ren Yang Water	(巳)	丁 Ding Yin Fire	丙 Bing Yang Fire	(寅)	己 Ji Yin Earth
月德 Monthly Virtue	丙 Bing Yang Fire	甲 Jia Yang Wood	壬 Ren Yang Water	庚 Geng Yang Metal	丙 Bing Yang Fire	甲 Jia Yang Wood
月德合 Monthly Virtue Combo	辛 Xin Yin Metal	己 Ji Yin Earth	丁 Ding Yin Fire	乙 Yi Yin Wood	辛 Xin Yin Metal	己 Ji Yin Earth
月空 Month Emptiness	壬 Ren Yang Water	庚 Geng Yang Metal	丙 Bing Yang Fire	甲 Jia Yang Wood	壬 Ren Yang Water	庚 Geng Yang Metal
陽貴人 Yang Nobleman	乾 Qian	中 Middle	坎 Kan	離 Li	艮 Gen	兌 Dui
陰貴人 Yin Nobleman	艮 Gen	兌 Dui	乾 Qian	中 Middle	坎 Kan	離 Li
飛天祿 Flying Heavenly Wealth	中 Middle	巽 Xun	震 Zhen	坤 Kun	坎 Kan	離 Li
飛天馬 Flying Heavenly Horse	中 Middle	坎 Kan	離 Li	艮 Gen	兌 Dui	乾 Qian

12-Month Auxiliary Stars Reference Table :
壬子年十二月，開山立向修方星表

申 Monkey (Aug 8 - Sept 7) 七月 7th Month	酉 Rooster (Sept 8 - Oct 7) 八月 8th Month	戌 Dog (Oct 8 - Nov 6) 九月 9th Month	亥 Pig (Nov 7 - Dec 6) 十月 10th Month	子 Rat (Dec 7 - Jan 5) 十一月 11th Month	丑 Ox (Jan 6 - Feb 3) 十二月 12th Month	月 MONTH
北 North	東北 Northeast	南 South	東 East	東南 Southeast	西 West	天道 Heavenly Path
癸 Gui Yin Water	艮 Gen (寅)	丙 Bing Yang Fire	乙 Yi Yin Wood	巽 Xun (巳)	庚 Geng Yang Metal	天德 Heavenly Virtue
戊 Wu Yang Earth	(亥)	辛 Xin Yin Metal	庚 Geng Yang Metal	(申)	乙 Yi Yin Wood	天德合 Heavenly Virtue Combo
壬 Ren Yang Water	庚 Geng Yang Metal	丙 Bing Yang Fire	甲 Jia Yang Wood	壬 Ren Yang Water	庚 Geng Yang Metal	月德 Monthly Virtue
丁 Ding Yin Fire	乙 Yi Yin Wood	辛 Xin Yin Metal	己 Ji Yin Earth	丁 Ding Yin Fire	乙 Yi Yin Wood	月德合 Monthly Virtue Combo
丙 Bing Yang Fire	甲 Jia Yang Wood	壬 Ren Yang Water	庚 Geng Yang Metal	丙 Bing Yang Fire	甲 Jia Yang Wood	月空 Month Emptiness
乾 Qian	中 Middle	巽 Xun	震 Zhen	坤 Kun	坎 Kan	陽貴人 Yang Nobleman
艮 Gen	兌 Dui	乾 Qian	中 Middle	巽 Xun	震 Zhen	陰貴人 Yin Nobleman
艮 Gen	兌 Dui	乾 Qian	中 Middle	坎 Kan	離 Li	飛天祿 Flying Heavenly Wealth
中 Middle	巽 Xun	震 Zhen	坤 Kun	坎 Kan	離 Li	飛天馬 Flying Heavenly Horse

Monthly Purple White Stars 月紫白九星 :

寅 Tiger (Feb 4 - Mar 5) 正月 1st Month

巽 SE	離 S	坤 SW
7 Red 七赤	3 Jade 三碧	5 Yellow 五黃
震 E 6 White 六白	8 White 八白	1 White 一白 兌 W
2 Black 二黑	4 Green 四綠	9 Purple 九紫
艮 NE	坎 N	乾 NW

卯 Rabbit (Mar 6 - Apr 4) 二月 2nd Month

巽 SE	離 S	坤 SW
6 White 六白	2 Black 二黑	4 Green 四綠
震 E 5 Yellow 五黃	7 Red 七赤	9 Purple 九紫 兌 W
1 White 一白	3 Jade 三碧	8 White 八白
艮 NE	坎 N	乾 NW

辰 Dragon (Apr 5 - May 5) 三月 3rd Month

巽 SE	離 S	坤 SW
5 Yellow 五黃	1 White 一白	3 Jade 三碧
震 E 4 Green 四綠	6 White 六白	8 White 八白 兌 W
9 Purple 九紫	2 Black 二黑	7 Red 七赤
艮 NE	坎 N	乾 NW

巳 Snake (May 6 - Jun 5) 四月 4th Month

巽 SE	離 S	坤 SW
4 Green 四綠	9 Purple 九紫	2 Black 二黑
震 E 3 Jade 三碧	5 Yellow 五黃	7 Red 七赤 兌 W
8 White 八白	1 White 一白	6 White 六白
艮 NE	坎 N	乾 NW

午 Horse (Jun 6 - July 6) 五月 5th Month

巽 SE	離 S	坤 SW
3 Jade 三碧	8 White 八白	1 White 一白
震 E 2 Black 二黑	4 Green 四綠	6 White 六白 兌 W
7 Red 七赤	9 Purple 九紫	5 Yellow 五黃
艮 NE	坎 N	乾 NW

未 Goat (July 7 - Aug 7) 六月 6th Month

巽 SE	離 S	坤 SW
2 Black 二黑	7 Red 七赤	9 Purple 九紫
震 E 1 White 一白	3 Jade 三碧	5 Yellow 五黃 兌 W
6 White 六白	8 White 八白	4 Green 四綠
艮 NE	坎 N	乾 NW

申 Monkey (Aug 8 - Sept 7) 七月 7th Month

巽 SE	離 S	坤 SW
1 White 一白	6 White 六白	8 White 八白
震 E 9 Purple 九紫	2 Black 二黑	4 Green 四綠 兌 W
5 Yellow 五黃	7 Red 七赤	3 Jade 三碧
艮 NE	坎 N	乾 NW

酉 Rooster (Sept 8 - Oct 7) 八月 8th Month

巽 SE	離 S	坤 SW
9 Purple 九紫	5 Yellow 五黃	7 Red 七赤
震 E 8 White 八白	1 White 一白	3 Jade 三碧 兌 W
4 Green 四綠	6 White 六白	2 Black 二黑
艮 NE	坎 N	乾 NW

戌 Dog (Oct 8 - Nov 6) 九月 9th Month

巽 SE	離 S	坤 SW
8 White 八白	4 Green 四綠	6 White 六白
震 E 7 Red 七赤	9 Purple 九紫	2 Black 二黑 兌 W
3 Jade 三碧	5 Yellow 五黃	1 White 一白
艮 NE	坎 N	乾 NW

亥 Pig (Nov 7 - Dec 6) 十月 10th Month

巽 SE	離 S	坤 SW
7 Red 七赤	3 Jade 三碧	5 Yellow 五黃
震 E 6 White 六白	8 White 八白	1 White 一白 兌 W
2 Black 二黑	4 Green 四綠	9 Purple 九紫
艮 NE	坎 N	乾 NW

子 Rat (Dec 7 - Jan 5) 十一月 11th Month

巽 SE	離 S	坤 SW
6 White 六白	2 Black 二黑	4 Green 四綠
震 E 5 Yellow 五黃	7 Red 七赤	9 Purple 九紫 兌 W
1 White 一白	3 Jade 三碧	8 White 八白
艮 NE	坎 N	乾 NW

丑 Ox (Jan 6 - Feb 3) 十二月 12th Month

巽 SE	離 S	坤 SW
5 Yellow 五黃	1 White 一白	3 Jade 三碧
震 E 4 Green 四綠	6 White 六白	8 White 八白 兌 W
9 Purple 九紫	2 Black 二黑	7 Red 七赤
艮 NE	坎 N	乾 NW

Qi Men Three Nobles 三奇 :

Three Nobles 三奇 / Seasons	乙 Yi	丙 Bing	丁 Ding
立春 **Coming of Spring** Feb 4 - Feb 18	中 Middle	乾 Qian	兑 Dui
春分 **Spring Equinox** Mar 21 - Apr 4	離 Li	坎 Kan	坤 Kun
立夏 **Coming of Summer** May 6 - May 20	坎 Kan	坤 Kun	震 Zhen
夏至 **Summer Solstice** Jun 22 - Jul 6	震 Zhen	坤 Kun	坎 Kan
立秋 **Coming of Autumn** Aug 8 - Aug 23	中 Middle	巽 Xun	震 Zhen
秋分 **Autumn Equinox** Sept 23 - Oct 7	坎 Kan	離 Li	艮 Gen
立冬 **Coming of Winter** Nov 7 - Nov 22	離 Li	艮 Gen	兑 Dui
冬至 **Winter Solstice** Dec 22 - Jan 5	兑 Dui	艮 Gen	離 Li

Sectors to Avoid Opening Mountain 開山凶位 :

月 MONTH	月建 Month Establishment	月破 Month Destruction	月剋山家 Month Countering Sitting		陰府太歲 Yin Mansion Grand Duke	
寅 **Tiger** (Feb 4 - Mar 5) 正月 **1st Month**	寅 *Yin* **Tiger**	申 *Shen* **Monkey**	—		離 *Li*	乾 *Qian*
卯 **Rabbit** (Mar 6 - Apr 4) 二月 **2nd Month**	卯 *Mao* **Rabbit**	酉 *You* **Rooster**	—		震 *Zhen*	坤 *Kun*
辰 **Dragon** (Apr 5 - May 5) 三月 **3rd Month**	辰 *Chen* **Dragon**	戌 *Xu* **Dog**	離 *Li* **S2**	丙 *Bing* **Yang Fire**	艮 *Gen*	巽 *Xun*
巳 **Snake** (May 6 - Jun 5) 四月 **4th Month**	巳 *Si* **Snake**	亥 *Hai* **Pig**	壬 *Ren* **Yang Water**	乙 *Yi* **Yin Wood**	兌 *Dui*	乾 *Qian*
午 **Horse** (Jun 6 - July 6) 五月 **5th Month**	午 *Wu* **Horse**	子 *Zi* **Rat**	水 **Water**	山 **Mountain**	坎 *Kan*	坤 *Kun*
未 **Goat** (July 7 - Aug 7) 六月 **6th Month**	未 *Wei* **Goat**	丑 *Chou* **Ox**	土 **Earth**		乾 *Qian*	離 *Li*
申 **Monkey** (Aug 8 - Sept 7) 七月 **7th Month**	申 *Shen* **Monkey**	寅 *Yin* **Tiger**	震 *Zhen*	巳 *Si* **Snake**	坤 *Kun*	震 *Zhen*
酉 **Rooster** (Sept 8 - Oct 7) 八月 **8th Month**	酉 *You* **Rooster**	卯 *Mao* **Rabbit**	艮 *Gen*		巽 *Xun*	艮 *Gen*
戌 **Dog** (Oct 8 - Nov 6) 九月 **9th Month**	戌 *Xu* **Dog**	辰 *Chen* **Dragon**	—		乾 *Qian*	兌 *Dui*
亥 **Pig** (Nov 7 - Dec 6) 十月 **10th Month**	亥 *Hai* **Pig**	巳 *Si* **Snake**	—		坤 *Kun*	坎 *Kan*
子 **Rat** (Dec 7 - Jan 5) 十一月 **11th Month**	子 *Zi* **Rat**	午 *Wu* **Horse**	—		離 *Li*	乾 *Qian*
丑 **Ox** (Jan 6 - Feb 3) 十二月 **12th Month**	丑 *Chou* **Ox**	未 *Wei* **Goat**	—		震 *Zhen*	坤 *Kun*

Negative Repair / Renovation Sectors 修方凶位 :

月 MONTH	天官符 Heavenly Officer Charm			地官符 Earth Officer Charm			小月建 Small Month Establishment		
寅 **Tiger** (Feb 4 - Mar 5) 正月 **1st Month**	中 Middle			庚 Geng **Yang Metal**	兌 Dui	辛 Xin **Yin Metal**	中 Middle		
卯 **Rabbit** (Mar 6 - Apr 4) 二月 **2nd Month**	辰 Chen **Dragon**	巽 Xun	巳 Si **Snake**	戌 Xu **Dog**	乾 Qian	亥 Hai **Pig**	戌 Xu **Dog**	乾 Qian	亥 Hai **Pig**
辰 **Dragon** (Apr 5 - May 5) 三月 **3rd Month**	甲 Jia **Yang Wood**	震 Zhen	乙 Yi **Yin Wood**	中 Middle			庚 Geng **Yang Metal**	兌 Dui	辛 Xin **Yin Metal**
巳 **Snake** (May 6 - Jun 5) 四月 **4th Month**	未 Wei **Goat**	坤 Kun	申 Shen **Monkey**	庚 Geng **Yang Metal**	兌 Dui	辛 Xin **Yin Metal**	丑 Chou **Ox**	艮 Gen	寅 Yin **Tiger**
午 **Horse** (Jun 6 - July 6) 五月 **5th Month**	壬 Ren **Yang Water**	坎 Kan	癸 Gui **Yin Water**	戌 Xu **Dog**	乾 Qian	亥 Hai **Pig**	丙 Bing **Yang Fire**	離 Li	丁 Ding **Yin Fire**
未 **Goat** (July 7 - Aug 7) 六月 **6th Month**	丙 Bing **Yang Fire**	離 Li	丁 Ding **Yin Fire**	中 Middle			壬 Ren **Yang Water**	坎 Kan	癸 Gui **Yin Water**
申 **Monkey** (Aug 8 - Sept 7) 七月 **7th Month**	丑 Chou **Ox**	艮 Gen	寅 Yin **Tiger**	辰 Chen **Dragon**	巽 Xun	巳 Si **Snake**	未 Wei **Goat**	坤 Kun	申 Shen **Monkey**
酉 **Rooster** (Sept 8 - Oct 7) 八月 **8th Month**	庚 Geng **Yang Metal**	兌 Dui	辛 Xin **Yin Metal**	甲 Jia **Yang Wood**	震 Zhen	乙 Yi **Yin Wood**	甲 Jia **Yang Wood**	震 Zhen	乙 Yi **Yin Wood**
戌 **Dog** (Oct 8 - Nov 6) 九月 **9th Month**	戌 Xu **Dog**	乾 Qian	亥 Hai **Pig**	未 Wei **Goat**	坤 Kun	申 Shen **Monkey**	辰 Chen **Dragon**	巽 Xun	巳 Si **Snake**
亥 **Pig** (Nov 7 - Dec 6) 十月 **10th Month**	中 Middle			壬 Ren **Yang Water**	坎 Kan	癸 Gui **Yin Water**	中 Middle		
子 **Rat** (Dec 7 - Jan 5) 十一月 **11th Month**	庚 Geng **Yang Metal**	兌 Dui	辛 Xin **Yin Metal**	丙 Bing **Yang Fire**	離 Li	丁 Ding **Yin Fire**	戌 Xu **Dog**	乾 Qian	亥 Hai **Pig**
丑 **Ox** (Jan 6 - Feb 3) 十二月 **12th Month**	戌 Xu **Dog**	乾 Qian	亥 Hai **Pig**	丑 Chou **Ox**	艮 Gen	寅 Yin **Tiger**	庚 Geng **Yang Metal**	兌 Dui	辛 Xin **Yin Metal**

Negative Repair / Renovation Sectors 修方凶位 :

月 MONTH	大月建 Big Month Establishment			飛大煞 Flying Great Sha			丙丁獨火 Bing Ding Lonely Fire	
寅 Tiger (Feb 4 - Mar 5) 正月 1st Month	丑 Chou Ox	艮 Gen	寅 Yin Tiger	戌 Xu Dog	乾 Qian	亥 Hai Pig	離 Li	坎 Kan
卯 Rabbit (Mar 6 - Apr 4) 二月 2nd Month	庚 Geng Yang Metal	兌 Dui	辛 Xin Yin Metal		中 Middle		艮 Gen	離 Li
辰 Dragon (Apr 5 - May 5) 三月 3rd Month	戌 Xu Dog	乾 Qian	亥 Hai Pig	辰 Chen Dragon	巽 Xun	巳 Si Snake	兌 Dui	艮 Gen
巳 Snake (May 6 - Jun 5) 四月 4th Month		中 Middle		甲 Jia Yang Wood	震 Zhen	乙 Yi Yin Wood	乾 Qian	兌 Dui
午 Horse (Jun 6 - July 6) 五月 5th Month	辰 Chen Dragon	巽 Xun	巳 Si Snake	未 Wei Goat	坤 Kun	申 Shen Monkey	中 Middle	乾 Qian
未 Goat (July 7 - Aug 7) 六月 6th Month	甲 Jia Yang Wood	震 Zhen	乙 Yi Yin Wood	壬 Ren Yang Water	坎 Kan	癸 Gui Yin Water	中 Middle	
申 Monkey (Aug 8 - Sept 7) 七月 7th Month	未 Wei Goat	坤 Kun	申 Shen Monkey	丙 Bing Yang Fire	離 Li	丁 Ding Yin Fire	巽 Xun	中 Middle
酉 Rooster (Sept 8 - Oct 7) 八月 8th Month	壬 Ren Yang Water	坎 Kan	癸 Gui Yin Water	丑 Chou Ox	艮 Gen	寅 Yin Tiger	震 Zhen	巽 Xun
戌 Dog (Oct 8 - Nov 6) 九月 9th Month	丙 Bing Yang Fire	離 Li	丁 Ding Yin Fire	庚 Geng Yang Metal	兌 Dui	辛 Xin Yin Metal	坤 Kun	震 Zhen
亥 Pig (Nov 7 - Dec 6) 十月 10th Month	丑 Chou Ox	艮 Gen	寅 Yin Tiger	戌 Xu Dog	乾 Qian	亥 Hai Pig	坎 Kan	坤 Kun
子 Rat (Dec 7 - Jan 5) 十一月 11th Month	庚 Geng Yang Metal	兌 Dui	辛 Xin Yin Metal		中 Middle		離 Li	坎 Kan
丑 Ox (Jan 6 - Feb 3) 十二月 12th Month	戌 Xu Dog	乾 Qian	亥 Hai Pig	庚 Geng Yang Metal	兌 Dui	辛 Xin Yin Metal	艮 Gen	離 Li

Negative Repair / Renovation Sectors 修方凶位 :

月 MONTH	月遊火 Month Wondering Fire	三煞 Monthly 3 Killings		
		劫煞 Robbery Sha	災煞 Calamity Sha	月煞 Month Sha
寅 Tiger (Feb 4 - Mar 5) 正月 1st Month	艮 Gen	亥 Hai Pig	子 Zi Rat	丑 Chou Ox
卯 Rabbit (Mar 6 - Apr 4) 二月 2nd Month	離 Li	申 Shen Monkey	酉 You Rooster	戌 Xu Dog
辰 Dragon (Apr 5 - May 5) 三月 3rd Month	坎 Kan	巳 Si Snake	午 Wu Horse	未 Wei Goat
巳 Snake (May 6 - Jun 5) 四月 4th Month	坤 Kun	寅 Yin Tiger	卯 Mao Rabbit	辰 Chen Dragon
午 Horse (Jun 6 - July 6) 五月 5th Month	震 Zhen	亥 Hai Pig	子 Zi Rat	丑 Chou Ox
未 Goat (July 7 - Aug 7) 六月 6th Month	巽 Xun	申 Shen Monkey	酉 You Rooster	戌 Xu Dog
申 Monkey (Aug 8 - Sept 7) 七月 7th Month	中 Middle	巳 Si Snake	午 Wu Horse	未 Wei Goat
酉 Rooster (Sept 8 - Oct 7) 八月 8th Month	乾 Qian	寅 Yin Tiger	卯 Mao Rabbit	辰 Chen Dragon
戌 Dog (Oct 8 - Nov 6) 九月 9th Month	兌 Dui	亥 Hai Pig	子 Zi Rat	丑 Chou Ox
亥 Pig (Nov 7 - Dec 6) 十月 10th Month	艮 Gen	申 Shen Monkey	酉 You Rooster	戌 Xu Dog
子 Rat (Dec 7 - Jan 5) 十一月 11th Month	離 Li	巳 Si Snake	午 Wu Horse	未 Wei Goat
丑 Ox (Jan 6 - Feb 3) 十二月 12th Month	坎 Kan	寅 Yin Tiger	卯 Mao Rabbit	辰 Chen Dragon

壬子 (Ren Zi) Water Rat

Negative Repair / Renovation Sectors 修方凶位 :

月 MONTH	月刑 Month Punishment	月害 Month Harm	月厭 Month Detest
寅 **Tiger** (Feb 4 - Mar 5) 正月 1st Month	巳 Si Snake	巳 Si Snake	戌 Xu Dog
卯 **Rabbit** (Mar 6 - Apr 4) 二月 2nd Month	子 Zi Rat	辰 Chen Dragon	酉 You Rooster
辰 **Dragon** (Apr 5 - May 5) 三月 3rd Month	辰 Chen Dragon	卯 Mao Rabbit	申 Shen Monkey
巳 **Snake** (May 6 - Jun 5) 四月 4th Month	申 Shen Monkey	寅 Yin Tiger	未 Wei Goat
午 **Horse** (Jun 6 - July 6) 五月 5th Month	午 Wu Horse	丑 Chou Ox	午 Wu Horse
未 **Goat** (July 7 - Aug 7) 六月 6th Month	丑 Chou Ox	子 Zi Rat	巳 Si Snake
申 **Monkey** (Aug 8 - Sept 7) 七月 7th Month	寅 Yin Tiger	亥 Hai Pig	辰 Chen Dragon
酉 **Rooster** (Sept 8 - Oct 7) 八月 8th Month	酉 You Rooster	戌 Xu Dog	卯 Mao Rabbit
戌 **Dog** (Oct 8 - Nov 6) 九月 9th Month	未 Wei Goat	酉 You Rooster	寅 Yin Tiger
亥 **Pig** (Nov 7 - Dec 6) 十月 10th Month	亥 Hai Pig	申 Shen Monkey	丑 Chou Ox
子 **Rat** (Dec 7 - Jan 5) 十一月 11th Month	卯 Mao Rabbit	未 Wei Goat	子 Zi Rat
丑 **Ox** (Jan 6 - Feb 3) 十二月 12th Month	戌 Xu Dog	午 Wu Horse	亥 Hai Pig

壬寅 (Ren Yin)
Water Tiger

Heavenly Stem 天干	壬 Yang Water (陽水)
Earthly Branch 地支	寅 Tiger (Yang Wood 陽木)
Hidden Stem 藏干	甲 Yang Wood, 丙 Yang Fire, 戊 Yang Earth
Na Yin 納音	金箔金 Metal from foils
Grand Duke 太歲	寅 Tiger
Xuan Kong Five Element 玄空五行	9 金 Metal
Gua Name 卦名	䷌ 天火同人 Fellowship
Xuan Kong Period Luck 玄空卦運	7

Annual Positive Stars for Opening Mountain, Establishing Facing and Commencing Repairs 開山立向修方吉星：

歲德 Duke Virtue	壬 Ren Yang Water
歲德合 Duke Virtue Combo	丁 Ding Yin Fire
歲枝德 Duke Branch Virtue	未 Wei Goat
陽貴人 Yang Nobleman	卯 Mao Rabbit
陰貴人 Yin Nobleman	巳 Si Snake
歲祿 Duke Prosperous	亥 Hai Pig
歲馬 Duke Horse	申 Shen Monkey
奏書 Decree	艮 Gen
博士 Professor	坤 Kun

Annual Negative Stars for Opening Mountain, Establishing Facing and Commencing Repairs 開山立向修方凶星：

太歲 Grand Duke	歲破 Year Breaker	三煞 Three Killings			坐煞向煞 Sitting Sha Facing Sha				浮天空亡 Floating Heaven Emptiness	
寅 Yin Tiger	申 Shen Monkey	亥 Hai Pig	子 Zi Rat	丑 Chou Ox	壬 Ren Yang Water	癸 Gui Yin Water	丙 Bing Yang Fire	丁 Ding Yin Fire	乾 Qian	甲 Jia Yang Wood

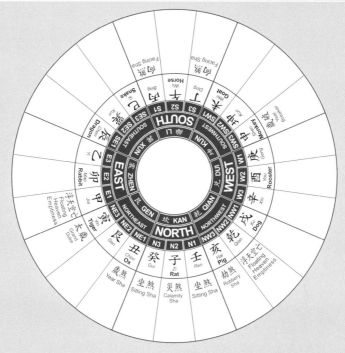

Annual San Yuan Purple White Stars 三元紫白九星：

上元 Upper Period — Period 1, 2, 3

巽SE	離S	坤SW
7	3	5
震E **6**	**8** 壬寅 *Ren Yin* **Water Tiger**	**1** 兌W
2	4	9
艮NE	坎N	乾NW

中元 Middle Period — Period 4, 5, 6

巽SE	離S	坤SW
1	6	8
震E **9**	**2** 壬寅 *Ren Yin* **Water Tiger**	**4** 兌W
5	7	3
艮NE	坎N	乾NW

下元 Lower Period — Period 7, 8, 9

巽SE	離S	坤SW
4	9	2
震E **3**	**5** 壬寅 *Ren Yin* **Water Tiger**	**7** 兌W
8	1	6
艮NE	坎N	乾NW

Mountain Covering Yellow Path 蓋山黃道：

貪狼 Tan Lang **Greedy Wolf**		巨門 Ju Men **Huge Door**		武曲 Wu Qu **Military Arts**				文曲 Wen Qu **Literary Arts**			
艮 Gen NE2	丙 Bing S1	巽 Xun SE2	辛 Xin W3	兌 Dui W2	丁 Ding S3	巳 Si SE3	丑 Chou NE1	離 Li S2	壬 Ren N1	寅 Yin NE3	戌 Xu NW1

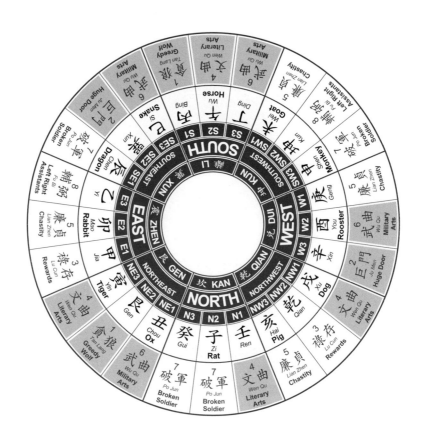

Heaven Penetrating Force 通天竅:

三合前方 **Facing Three Harmony**	坤申 *Kun Shen*	庚酉 *Geng You*	辛戌 *Xin Xu*
三合後方 **Sitting Three Harmony**	艮寅 *Gen Yin*	甲卯 *Jia Mao*	乙辰 *Yi Chen*

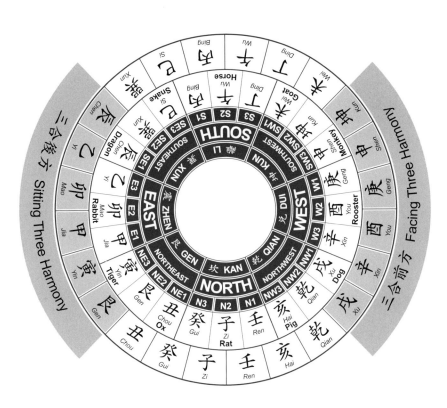

Moving Horse Six Ren Assessment 走馬六壬：					
神后 Shen Hou **Holy Empress**	功曹 Gong Cao **Marshall**	天罡 Tian Gang **Heavenly Dipper**	勝光 Sheng Guang **Subliminal Bright**	傳送 Chuan Song **Great General**	河魁 He Kui **River Scholar**
辛戌 Xin Xu	壬子 Ren Zi	艮寅 Gen Yin	乙辰 Yi Chen	丙午 Bing Wu	坤申 Kun Shen

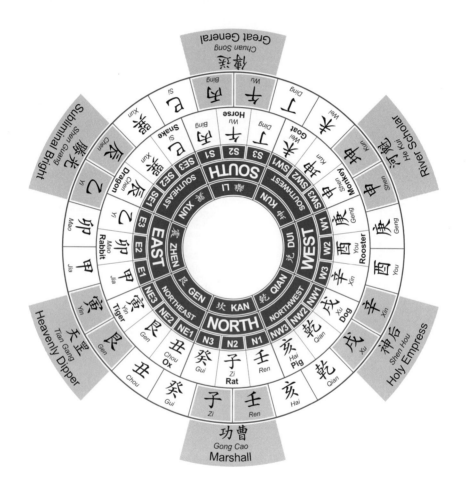

Four Advantages Three Cycles Star Plate 四利三元:

太陽 *Tai Yang* **Sun**	太陰 *Tai Yin* **Moon**	龍德 *Long De* **Dragon Virtue**	福德 *Fu De* **Fortune Virtue**
卯 *Mao* **Rabbit**	巳 *Si* **Snake**	酉 *You* **Rooster**	亥 *Hai* **Pig**

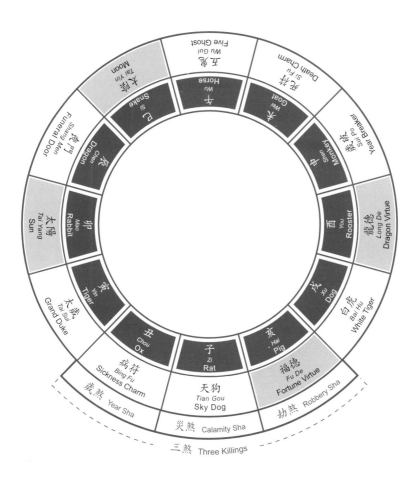

Negative Sectors For Opening Mountain 開山凶位:-

年剋山家 Year Countering Sitting（冬至後 After Winter Solstice）

乾 Qian NW2	亥 Hai NW3	兑 Dui W2	丁 Ding S3

陰府太歲 Yin Fu Tai Sui **Yin Mansion Grand Duke**	六害 Liu Hai **Six Harm**	死符 Si Fu **Death Charm**	炙退 Zhi Tui **Roasting Star**
離　　乾 Li　　Qian S2　　NW2	巳 Si SE3	未 Wei SW1	酉 You W2

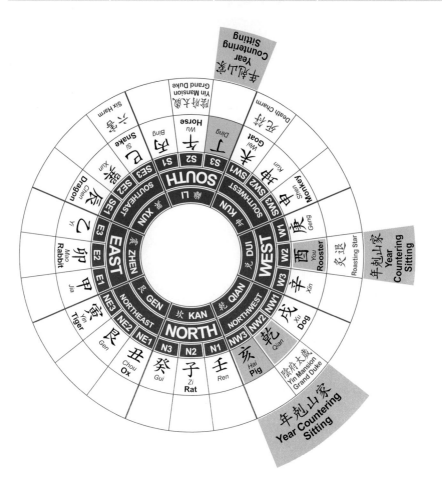

Negative Directions to Establish Facing 立向凶方：

巡山羅喉 *Xun Shan Luo Hou* **Mountain Patrol Luo Hou Star**	病符 *Bing Fu* **Sickness Charm**
甲 *Jia* **E1**	丑 *Chou* **NE1**

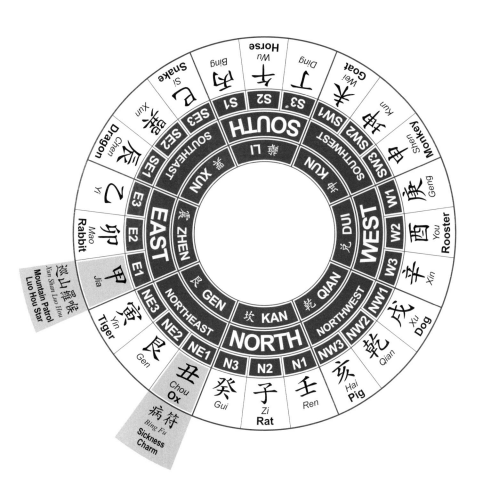

Negative Repair / Renovation Sectors Table 修方凶位表：

天官符 Heavenly Officer Charm	巳 Si Snake	飛廉 Flying Chaste	亥 Hai Pig
地官符 Earthly Officer Charm	午 Wu Horse	喪門 Funeral Door	辰 Chen Dragon
大煞 Great Sha	午 Wu Horse	弔客 Suspended Guest	子 Zi Rat
大將軍 Big General	子 Zi Rat	白虎 White Tiger	戌 Xu Dog
力士 Strong Man	巽 Xun	金神 Golden God	寅 Yin Tiger
蠶室 Silkworm Room	乾 Qian		卯 Mao Rabbit
蠶官 Silkworm Officer	戌 Xu Dog		戌 Xu Dog
蠶命 Silkworm Life	亥 Hai Pig		亥 Hai Pig
歲刑 Duke Punishment	巳 Si Snake	獨火 Lonely Fire	震 Zhen
黃幡 Yellow Flag	戌 Xu Dog	五鬼 Five Ghost	寅 Yin Tiger
豹尾 Leopard Tail	辰 Chen Dragon	破敗五鬼 Destructive Five Ghost	巽 Xun

Negative Repair / Renovation Sectors Diagram 修方凶位圖：

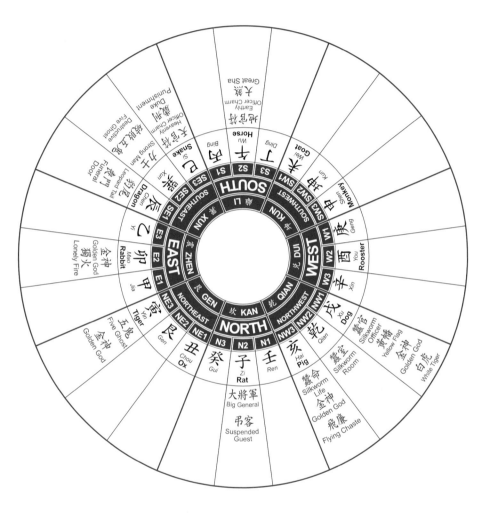

12-Month Auxiliary Stars Reference Table :
壬寅年十二月・開山立向修方星表

Positive Monthly Stars 吉星方

月 MONTH	寅 Tiger (Feb 4 - Mar 5) 正月 1st Month	卯 Rabbit (Mar 6 - Apr 4) 二月 2nd Month	辰 Dragon (Apr 5 - May 5) 三月 3rd Month	巳 Snake (May 6 - Jun 5) 四月 4th Month	午 Horse (Jun 6 - July 6) 五月 5th Month	未 Goat (July 7 - Aug 7) 六月 6th Month
天道 Heavenly Path	南 South	西南 Southwest	北 North	西 West	西北 Northwest	東 East
天德 Heavenly Virtue	丁 Ding Yin Fire	坤 Kun (申)	壬 Ren Yang Water	辛 Xin Yin Metal	乾 Qian (亥)	甲 Jia Yang Wood
天德合 Heavenly Virtue Combo	壬 Ren Yang Water	(巳)	丁 Ding Yin Fire	丙 Bing Yang Fire	(寅)	己 Ji Yin Earth
月德 Monthly Virtue	丙 Bing Yang Fire	甲 Jia Yang Wood	壬 Ren Yang Water	庚 Geng Yang Metal	丙 Bing Yang Fire	甲 Jia Yang Wood
月德合 Monthly Virtue Combo	辛 Xin Yin Metal	己 Ji Yin Earth	丁 Ding Yin Fire	乙 Yi Yin Wood	辛 Xin Yin Metal	己 Ji Yin Earth
月空 Month Emptiness	壬 Ren Yang Water	庚 Geng Yang Metal	丙 Bing Yang Fire	甲 Jia Yang Wood	壬 Ren Yang Water	庚 Geng Yang Metal
陽貴人 Yang Nobleman	乾 Qian	中 Middle	坎 Kan	離 Li	艮 Gen	兌 Dui
陰貴人 Yin Nobleman	艮 Gen	兌 Dui	乾 Qian	中 Middle	坎 Kan	離 Li
飛天祿 Flying Heavenly Wealth	中 Middle	巽 Xun	震 Zhen	坤 Kun	坎 Kan	離 Li
飛天馬 Flying Heavenly Horse	坤 Kun	坎 Kan	離 Li	艮 Gen	兌 Dui	乾 Qian

12-Month Auxiliary Stars Reference Table :
壬寅年十二月，開山立向修方星表

申 Monkey (Aug 8 - Sept 7) 七月 7th Month	酉 Rooster (Sept 8 - Oct 7) 八月 8th Month	戌 Dog (Oct 8 - Nov 6) 九月 9th Month	亥 Pig (Nov 7 - Dec 6) 十月 10th Month	子 Rat (Dec 7 - Jan 5) 十一月 11th Month	丑 Ox (Jan 6 - Feb 3) 十二月 12th Month	月 MONTH
北 North	東北 Northeast	南 South	東 East	東南 Southeast	西 West	天道 Heavenly Path
癸 Gui Yin Water	艮 Gen (寅)	丙 Bing Yang Fire	乙 Yi Yin Wood	巽 Xun (巳)	庚 Geng Yang Metal	天德 Heavenly Virtue
戊 Wu Yang Earth	(亥)	辛 Xin Yin Metal	庚 Geng Yang Metal	(申)	乙 Yi Yin Wood	天德合 Heavenly Virtue Combo
壬 Ren Yang Water	庚 Geng Yang Metal	丙 Bing Yang Fire	甲 Jia Yang Wood	壬 Ren Yang Water	庚 Geng Yang Metal	月德 Monthly Virtue
丁 Ding Yin Fire	乙 Yi Yin Wood	辛 Xin Yin Metal	己 Ji Yin Earth	丁 Ding Yin Fire	乙 Yi Yin Wood	月德合 Monthly Virtue Combo
丙 Bing Yang Fire	甲 Jia Yang Wood	壬 Ren Yang Water	庚 Geng Yang Metal	丙 Bing Yang Fire	甲 Jia Yang Wood	月空 Month Emptiness
乾 Qian	中 Middle	巽 Xun	震 Zhen	坤 Kun	坎 Kan	陽貴人 Yang Nobleman
艮 Gen	兌 Dui	乾 Qian	中 Middle	巽 Xun	震 Zhen	陰貴人 Yin Nobleman
艮 Gen	兌 Dui	乾 Qian	中 Middle	坎 Kan	離 Li	飛天祿 Flying Heavenly Wealth
中 Middle	坎 Kan	離 Li	艮 Gen	兌 Dui	乾 Qian	飛天馬 Flying Heavenly Horse

993

Monthly Purple White Stars 月紫白九星 :

寅 Tiger (Feb 4 - Mar 5) 正月 1st Month

巽 SE	離 S	坤 SW
1 White 一白	6 White 六白	8 White 八白
震 E — 9 Purple 九紫	2 Black 二黑	4 Green 四緑 — 兌 W
艮 NE — 5 Yellow 五黄	7 Red 七赤	3 Jade 三碧 — 乾 NW

卯 Rabbit (Mar 6 - Apr 4) 二月 2nd Month

巽 SE	離 S	坤 SW
9 Purple 九紫	5 Yellow 五黄	7 Red 七赤
震 E — 8 White 八白	1 White 一白	3 Jade 三碧 — 兌 W
艮 NE — 4 Green 四緑	6 White 六白	2 Black 二黑 — 乾 NW

辰 Dragon (Apr 5 - May 5) 三月 3rd Month

巽 SE	離 S	坤 SW
8 White 八白	4 Green 四緑	6 White 六白
震 E — 7 Red 七赤	9 Purple 九紫	2 Black 二黑 — 兌 W
艮 NE — 3 Jade 三碧	5 Yellow 五黄	1 White 一白 — 乾 NW

巳 Snake (May 6 - Jun 5) 四月 4th Month

巽 SE	離 S	坤 SW
7 Red 七赤	3 Jade 三碧	5 Yellow 五黄
震 E — 6 White 六白	8 White 八白	1 White 一白 — 兌 W
艮 NE — 2 Black 二黑	4 Green 四緑	9 Purple 九紫 — 乾 NW

午 Horse (Jun 6 - July 6) 五月 5th Month

巽 SE	離 S	坤 SW
6 White 六白	2 Black 二黑	4 Green 四緑
震 E — 5 Yellow 五黄	7 Red 七赤	9 Purple 九紫 — 兌 W
艮 NE — 1 White 一白	3 Jade 三碧	8 White 八白 — 乾 NW

未 Goat (July 7 - Aug 7) 六月 6th Month

巽 SE	離 S	坤 SW
5 Yellow 五黄	1 White 一白	3 Jade 三碧
震 E — 4 Green 四緑	6 White 六白	8 White 八白 — 兌 W
艮 NE — 9 Purple 九紫	2 Black 二黑	7 Red 七赤 — 乾 NW

申 Monkey (Aug 8 - Sept 7) 七月 7th Month

巽 SE	離 S	坤 SW
4 Green 四緑	9 Purple 九紫	2 Black 二黑
震 E — 3 Jade 三碧	5 Yellow 五黄	7 Red 七赤 — 兌 W
艮 NE — 8 White 八白	1 White 一白	6 White 六白 — 乾 NW

酉 Rooster (Sept 8 - Oct 7) 八月 8th Month

巽 SE	離 S	坤 SW
3 Jade 三碧	8 White 八白	1 White 一白
震 E — 2 Black 二黑	4 Green 四緑	6 White 六白 — 兌 W
艮 NE — 7 Red 七赤	9 Purple 九紫	5 Yellow 五黄 — 乾 NW

戌 Dog (Oct 8 - Nov 6) 九月 9th Month

巽 SE	離 S	坤 SW
2 Black 二黑	7 Red 七赤	9 Purple 九紫
震 E — 1 White 一白	3 Jade 三碧	5 Yellow 五黄 — 兌 W
艮 NE — 6 White 六白	8 White 八白	4 Green 四緑 — 乾 NW

亥 Pig (Nov 7 - Dec 6) 十月 10th Month

巽 SE	離 S	坤 SW
1 White 一白	6 White 六白	8 White 八白
震 E — 9 Purple 九紫	2 Black 二黑	4 Green 四緑 — 兌 W
艮 NE — 5 Yellow 五黄	7 Red 七赤	3 Jade 三碧 — 乾 NW

子 Rat (Dec 7 - Jan 5) 十一月 11th Month

巽 SE	離 S	坤 SW
9 Purple 九紫	5 Yellow 五黄	7 Red 七赤
震 E — 8 White 八白	1 White 一白	3 Jade 三碧 — 兌 W
艮 NE — 4 Green 四緑	6 White 六白	2 Black 二黑 — 乾 NW

丑 Ox (Jan 6 - Feb 3) 十二月 12th Month

巽 SE	離 S	坤 SW
8 White 八白	4 Green 四緑	6 White 六白
震 E — 7 Red 七赤	9 Purple 九紫	2 Black 二黑 — 兌 W
艮 NE — 3 Jade 三碧	5 Yellow 五黄	1 White 一白 — 乾 NW

Qi Men Three Nobles 三奇 :

Three Nobles 三奇 / Seasons	乙 Yi	丙 Bing	丁 Ding
立春 **Coming of Spring** Feb 4 - Feb 18	巽 Xun	中 Middle	乾 Qian
春分 **Spring Equinox** Mar 21 - Apr 4	艮 Gen	離 Li	坎 Kan
立夏 **Coming of Summer** May 6 - May 20	離 Li	坎 Kan	坤 Kun
夏至 **Summer Solstice** Jun 22 - Jul 6	巽 Xun	震 Zhen	坤 Kun
立秋 **Coming of Autumn** Aug 8 - Aug 23	乾 Qian	中 Middle	巽 Xun
秋分 **Autumn Equinox** Sept 23 - Oct 7	坤 Kun	坎 Kan	離 Li
立冬 **Coming of Winter** Nov 7 - Nov 22	坎 Kan	離 Li	艮 Gen
冬至 **Winter Solstice** Dec 22 - Jan 5	乾 Qian	兌 Dui	艮 Gen

Sectors to Avoid Opening Mountain 開山凶位 :

月 MONTH	月建 Month Establishment	月破 Month Destruction	月剋山家 Month Countering Sitting		陰府太歲 Yin Mansion Grand Duke	
寅 Tiger (Feb 4 - Mar 5) 正月 1st Month	寅 Yin Tiger	申 Shen Monkey	—		離 Li	乾 Qian
卯 Rabbit (Mar 6 - Apr 4) 二月 2nd Month	卯 Mao Rabbit	酉 You Rooster	—		震 Zhen	坤 Kun
辰 Dragon (Apr 5 - May 5) 三月 3rd Month	辰 Chen Dragon	戌 Xu Dog	離 Li	丙 Bing Yang Fire	艮 Gen	巽 Xun
巳 Snake (May 6 - Jun 5) 四月 4th Month	巳 Si Snake	亥 Hai Pig	壬 Ren Yang Water	乙 Yi Yin Wood	兌 Dui	乾 Qian
午 Horse (Jun 6 - July 6) 五月 5th Month	午 Wu Horse	子 Zi Rat	水 Water	山 Mountain	坎 Kan	坤 Kun
未 Goat (July 7 - Aug 7) 六月 6th Month	未 Wei Goat	丑 Chou Ox	土 Earth		乾 Qian	離 Li
申 Monkey (Aug 8 - Sept 7) 七月 7th Month	申 Shen Monkey	寅 Yin Tiger	震 Zhen	巳 Si Snake	坤 Kun	震 Zhen
酉 Rooster (Sept 8 - Oct 7) 八月 8th Month	酉 You Rooster	卯 Mao Rabbit	艮 Gen		巽 Xun	艮 Gen
戌 Dog (Oct 8 - Nov 6) 九月 9th Month	戌 Xu Dog	辰 Chen Dragon	—		乾 Qian	兌 Dui
亥 Pig (Nov 7 - Dec 6) 十月 10th Month	亥 Hai Pig	巳 Si Snake	—		坤 Kun	坎 Kan
子 Rat (Dec 7 - Jan 5) 十一月 11th Month	子 Zi Rat	午 Wu Horse	—		離 Li	乾 Qian
丑 Ox (Jan 6 - Feb 3) 十二月 12th Month	丑 Chou Ox	未 Wei Goat	—		震 Zhen	坤 Kun

Negative Repair / Renovation Sectors 修方凶位 :

月 MONTH	天官符 Heavenly Officer Charm			地官符 Earth Officer Charm			小月建 Small Month Establishment		
寅 Tiger (Feb 4 - Mar 5) 正月 1st Month	丑 Chou Ox	艮 Gen	寅 Yin Tiger	丙 Bing Yang Fire	離 Li	丁 Ding Yin Fire	中 Middle		
卯 Rabbit (Mar 6 - Apr 4) 二月 2nd Month	庚 Geng Yang Metal	兌 Dui	辛 Xin Yin Metal	丑 Chou Ox	艮 Gen	寅 Yin Tiger	戌 Xu Dog	乾 Qian	亥 Hai Pig
辰 Dragon (Apr 5 - May 5) 三月 3rd Month	戌 Xu Dog	乾 Qian	亥 Hai Pig	庚 Geng Yang Metal	兌 Dui	辛 Xin Yin Metal	庚 Geng Yang Metal	兌 Dui	辛 Xin Yin Metal
巳 Snake (May 6 - Jun 5) 四月 4th Month	中 Middle			戌 Xu Dog	乾 Qian	亥 Hai Pig	丑 Chou Ox	艮 Gen	寅 Yin Tiger
午 Horse (Jun 6 - July 6) 五月 5th Month	庚 Geng Yang Metal	兌 Dui	辛 Xin Yin Metal	中 Middle			丙 Bing Yang Fire	離 Li	丁 Ding Yin Fire
未 Goat (July 7 - Aug 7) 六月 6th Month	戌 Xu Dog	乾 Qian	亥 Hai Pig	庚 Geng Yang Metal	兌 Dui	辛 Xin Yin Metal	壬 Ren Yang Water	坎 Kan	癸 Gui Yin Water
申 Monkey (Aug 8 - Sept 7) 七月 7th Month	中 Middle			戌 Xu Dog	乾 Qian	亥 Hai Pig	未 Wei Goat	坤 Kun	申 Shen Monkey
酉 Rooster (Sept 8 - Oct 7) 八月 8th Month	辰 Chen Dragon	巽 Xun	巳 Si Snake	中 Middle			甲 Jia Yang Wood	震 Zhen	乙 Yi Yin Wood
戌 Dog (Oct 8 - Nov 6) 九月 9th Month	甲 Jia Yang Wood	震 Zhen	乙 Yi Yin Wood	辰 Chen Dragon	巽 Xun	巳 Si Snake	辰 Chen Dragon	巽 Xun	巳 Si Snake
亥 Pig (Nov 7 - Dec 6) 十月 10th Month	未 Wei Goat	坤 Kun	申 Shen Monkey	甲 Jia Yang Wood	震 Zhen	乙 Yi Yin Wood	中 Middle		
子 Rat (Dec 7 - Jan 5) 十一月 11th Month	壬 Ren Yang Water	坎 Kan	癸 Gui Yin Water	未 Wei Goat	坤 Kun	申 Shen Monkey	戌 Xu Dog	乾 Qian	亥 Hai Pig
丑 Ox (Jan 6 - Feb 3) 十二月 12th Month	丙 Bing Yang Fire	離 Li	丁 Ding Yin Fire	壬 Ren Yang Water	坎 Kan	癸 Gui Yin Water	庚 Geng Yang Metal	兌 Dui	辛 Xin Yin Metal

997

Negative Repair / Renovation Sectors 修方凶位 :

月 MONTH	大月建 Big Month Establishment			飛大煞 Flying Great Sha			丙丁獨火 Bing Ding Lonely Fire	
寅 **Tiger** (Feb 4 - Mar 5) 正月 **1st Month**	未 Wei Goat	坤 Kun	申 Shen Monkey	丙 Bing Yang Fire	離 Li	丁 Ding Yin Fire	離 Li	坎 Kan
卯 **Rabbit** (Mar 6 - Apr 4) 二月 **2nd Month**	壬 Ren Yang Water	坎 Kan	癸 Gui Yin Water	丑 Chou Ox	艮 Gen	寅 Yin Tiger	艮 Gen	離 Li
辰 **Dragon** (Apr 5 - May 5) 三月 **3rd Month**	丙 Bing Yang Fire	離 Li	丁 Ding Yin Fire	庚 Geng Yang Metal	兑 Dui	辛 Xin Yin Metal	兑 Dui	艮 Gen
巳 **Snake** (May 6 - Jun 5) 四月 **4th Month**	丑 Chou Ox	艮 Gen	寅 Yin Tiger	戊 Xu Dog	乾 Qian	亥 Hai Pig	乾 Qian	兑 Dui
午 **Horse** (Jun 6 - July 6) 五月 **5th Month**	庚 Geng Yang Metal	兑 Dui	辛 Xin Yin Metal	中 Middle			中 Middle	乾 Qian
未 **Goat** (July 7 - Aug 7) 六月 **6th Month**	戊 Xu Dog	乾 Qian	亥 Hai Pig	庚 Geng Yang Metal	兑 Dui	辛 Xin Yin Metal	中 Middle	
申 **Monkey** (Aug 8 - Sept 7) 七月 **7th Month**	中 Middle			戊 Xu Dog	乾 Qian	亥 Hai Pig	巽 Xun	中 Middle
酉 **Rooster** (Sept 8 - Oct 7) 八月 **8th Month**	辰 Chen Dragon	巽 Xun	巳 Si Snake	中 Middle			震 Zhen	巽 Xun
戌 **Dog** (Oct 8 - Nov 6) 九月 **9th Month**	甲 Jia Yang Wood	震 Zhen	乙 Yi Yin Wood	辰 Chen Dragon	巽 Xun	巳 Si Snake	坤 Kun	震 Zhen
亥 **Pig** (Nov 7 - Dec 6) 十月 **10th Month**	未 Wei Goat	坤 Kun	申 Shen Monkey	甲 Jia Yang Wood	震 Zhen	乙 Yi Yin Wood	坎 Kan	坤 Kun
子 **Rat** (Dec 7 - Jan 5) 十一月 **11th Month**	壬 Ren Yang Water	坎 Kan	癸 Gui Yin Water	未 Wei Goat	坤 Kun	申 Shen Monkey	離 Li	坎 Kan
丑 **Ox** (Jan 6 - Feb 3) 十二月 **12th Month**	丙 Bing Yang Fire	離 Li	丁 Ding Yin Fire	壬 Ren Yang Water	坎 Kan	癸 Gui Yin Water	艮 Gen	離 Li

Negative Repair / Renovation Sectors 修方凶位 :

月 MONTH	月遊火 Month Wondering Fire	三煞 Monthly 3 Killings		
		劫煞 Robbery Sha	災煞 Calamity Sha	月煞 Month Sha
寅 Tiger (Feb 4 - Mar 5) 正月 1st Month	震 Zhen	亥 Hai Pig	子 Zi Rat	丑 Chou Ox
卯 Rabbit (Mar 6 - Apr 4) 二月 2nd Month	巽 Xun	申 Shen Monkey	酉 You Rooster	戌 Xu Dog
辰 Dragon (Apr 5 - May 5) 三月 3rd Month	中 Middle	巳 Si Snake	午 Wu Horse	未 Wei Goat
巳 Snake (May 6 - Jun 5) 四月 4th Month	乾 Qian	寅 Yin Tiger	卯 Mao Rabbit	辰 Chen Dragon
午 Horse (Jun 6 - July 6) 五月 5th Month	兌 Dui	亥 Hai Pig	子 Zi Rat	丑 Chou Ox
未 Goat (July 7 - Aug 7) 六月 6th Month	艮 Gen	申 Shen Monkey	酉 You Rooster	戌 Xu Dog
申 Monkey (Aug 8 - Sept 7) 七月 7th Month	離 Li	巳 Si Snake	午 Wu Horse	未 Wei Goat
酉 Rooster (Sept 8 - Oct 7) 八月 8th Month	坎 Kan	寅 Yin Tiger	卯 Mao Rabbit	辰 Chen Dragon
戌 Dog (Oct 8 - Nov 6) 九月 9th Month	坤 Kun	亥 Hai Pig	子 Zi Rat	丑 Chou Ox
亥 Pig (Nov 7 - Dec 6) 十月 10th Month	震 Zhen	申 Shen Monkey	酉 You Rooster	戌 Xu Dog
子 Rat (Dec 7 - Jan 5) 十一月 11th Month	巽 Xun	巳 Si Snake	午 Wu Horse	未 Wei Goat
丑 Ox (Jan 6 - Feb 3) 十二月 12th Month	中 Middle	寅 Yin Tiger	卯 Mao Rabbit	辰 Chen Dragon

Negative Repair / Renovation Sectors 修方凶位 :

月 MONTH	月刑 Month Punishment	月害 Month Harm	月厭 Month Detest
寅 **Tiger** (Feb 4 - Mar 5) 正月 **1st Month**	巳 *Si* Snake	巳 *Si* Snake	戌 *Xu* Dog
卯 **Rabbit** (Mar 6 - Apr 4) 二月 **2nd Month**	子 *Zi* Rat	辰 *Chen* Dragon	酉 *You* Rooster
辰 **Dragon** (Apr 5 - May 5) 三月 **3rd Month**	辰 *Chen* Dragon	卯 *Mao* Rabbit	申 *Shen* Monkey
巳 **Snake** (May 6 - Jun 5) 四月 **4th Month**	申 *Shen* Monkey	寅 *Yin* Tiger	未 *Wei* Goat
午 **Horse** (Jun 6 - July 6) 五月 **5th Month**	午 *Wu* Horse	丑 *Chou* Ox	午 *Wu* Horse
未 **Goat** (July 7 - Aug 7) 六月 **6th Month**	丑 *Chou* Ox	子 *Zi* Rat	巳 *Si* Snake
申 **Monkey** (Aug 8 - Sept 7) 七月 **7th Month**	寅 *Yin* Tiger	亥 *Hai* Pig	辰 *Chen* Dragon
酉 **Rooster** (Sept 8 - Oct 7) 八月 **8th Month**	酉 *You* Rooster	戌 *Xu* Dog	卯 *Mao* Rabbit
戌 **Dog** (Oct 8 - Nov 6) 九月 **9th Month**	未 *Wei* Goat	酉 *You* Rooster	寅 *Yin* Tiger
亥 **Pig** (Nov 7 - Dec 6) 十月 **10th Month**	亥 *Hai* Pig	申 *Shen* Monkey	丑 *Chou* Ox
子 **Rat** (Dec 7 - Jan 5) 十一月 **11th Month**	卯 *Mao* Rabbit	未 *Wei* Goat	子 *Zi* Rat
丑 **Ox** (Jan 6 - Feb 3) 十二月 **12th Month**	戌 *Xu* Dog	午 *Wu* Horse	亥 *Hai* Pig

壬辰 (Ren Chen)
Water Dragon

壬辰 (Ren Chen) Water Dragon

Heavenly Stem 天干	壬 **Yang Water** (陽水)
Earthly Branch 地支	辰 **Dragon (Yang Earth** 陽土)
Hidden Stem 藏干	戊 **Yang Earth**, 乙 **Yin Wood**, 癸 **Yin Water**
Na Yin 納音	長流水 **Water flowing constantly**
Grand Duke 太歲	辰 **Dragon**
Xuan Kong Five Element 玄空五行	6 水 **Water**
Gua Name 卦名	☶ 山天大畜 **Big Livestock**
Xuan Kong Period Luck 玄空卦運	4

Annual Positive Stars for Opening Mountain, Establishing Facing and Commencing Repairs 開山立向修方吉星:

歲德 **Duke Virtue**	壬 *Ren* **Yang Water**	
歲德合 **Duke Virtue Combo**	丁 *Ding* **Yin Fire**	
歲枝德 **Duke Branch Virtue**	酉 *You* **Rooster**	
陽貴人 **Yang Nobleman**	卯 *Mao* **Rabbit**	
陰貴人 **Yin Nobleman**	巳 *Si* **Snake**	
歲祿 **Duke Prosperous**	亥 *Hai* **Pig**	
歲馬 **Duke Horse**	寅 *Yin* **Tiger**	
奏書 **Decree**	艮 *Gen*	
博士 **Professor**	坤 *Kun*	

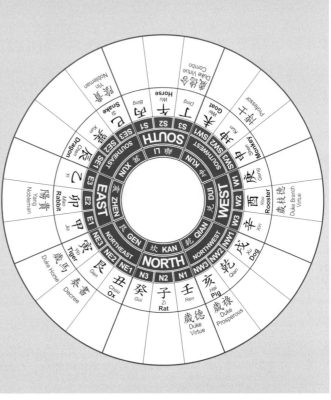

Annual Negative Stars for Opening Mountain, Establishing Facing and Commencing Repairs 開山立向修方凶星：

太歲 Grand Duke	歲破 Year Breaker	三煞 Three Killings			坐煞向煞 Sitting Sha Facing Sha				浮天空亡 Floating Heaven Emptiness	
辰 Chen Dragon	戌 Xu Dog	巳 Si Snake	午 Wu Horse	未 Wei Goat	丙 Bing Yang Fire	丁 Ding Yin Fire	壬 Ren Yang Water	癸 Gui Yin Water	乾 Qian	甲 Jia Yang Wood

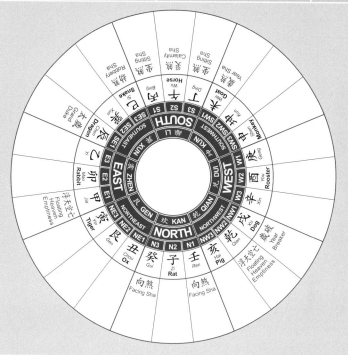

Annual San Yuan Purple White Stars 三元紫白九星：

上元 Upper Period Period 1, 2, 3			中元 Middle Period Period 4, 5, 6			下元 Lower Period Period 7, 8, 9		
巽SE 8	離S 4	坤SW 6	巽SE 2	離S 7	坤SW 9	巽SE 5	離S 1	坤SW 3
震E 7	9 壬辰 Ren Chen Water Dragon	兌W 2	震E 1	3 壬辰 Ren Chen Water Dragon	兌W 5	震E 4	6 壬辰 Ren Chen Water Dragon	兌W 8
艮NE 3	坎N 5	乾NW 1	艮NE 6	坎N 8	乾NW 4	艮NE 9	坎N 2	乾NW 7

Mountain Covering Yellow Path 蓋山黃道：

貪狼 *Tan Lang* **Greedy Wolf**				巨門 *Ju Men* **Huge Door**				武曲 *Wu Qu* **Military Arts**		文曲 *Wen Qu* **Literary Arts**			
兌 *Dui* W2	丁 *Ding* S3	巳 *Si* SE3	丑 *Chou* NE1	震 *Zhen* E2	庚 *Geng* W1	亥 *Hai* NW3	未 *Wei* SW1	艮 *Gen* NE2	丙 *Bing* S1	坎 *Kan* N2	癸 *Gui* N3	申 *Shen* SW3	辰 *Chen* SE1

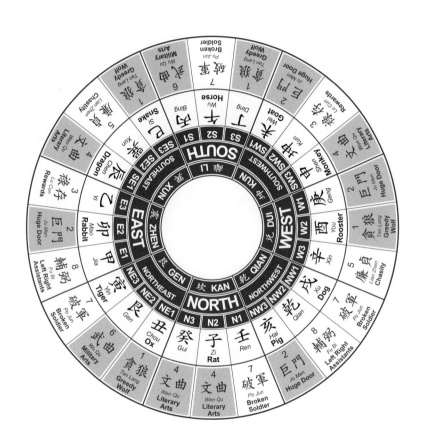

Heaven Penetrating Force 通天竅:			
三合前方 **Facing Three Harmony**	艮寅 Gen Yin	甲卯 Jia Mao	乙辰 Yi Chen
三合後方 **Sitting Three Harmony**	坤申 Kun Shen	庚酉 Geng You	辛戌 Xin Xu

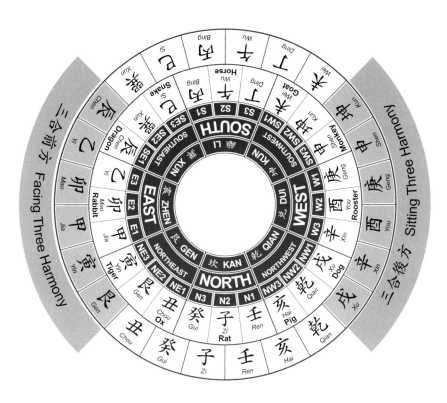

壬辰 (Ren Chen) Water Dragon

Moving Horse Six Ren Assessment 走馬六壬:

神后 Shen Hou **Holy Empress**	功曹 Gong Cao **Marshall**	天罡 Tian Gang **Heavenly Dipper**	勝光 Sheng Guang **Subliminal Bright**	傳送 Chuan Song **Great General**	河魁 He Kui **River Scholar**
坤申 Kun Shen	辛戌 Xin Xu	壬子 Ren Zi	艮寅 Gen Yin	乙辰 Yi Chen	丙午 Bing Wu

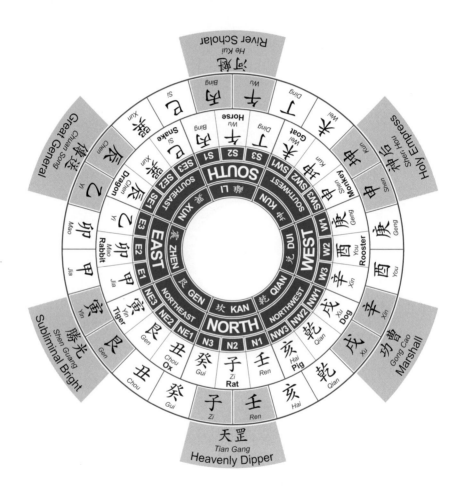

Four Advantages Three Cycles Star Plate 四利三元：

太陽 *Tai Yang* **Sun**	太陰 *Tai Yin* **Moon**	龍德 *Long De* **Dragon Virtue**	福德 *Fu De* **Fortune Virtue**
巳 *Si* **Snake**	未 *Wei* **Goat**	亥 *Hai* **Pig**	丑 *Chou* **Ox**

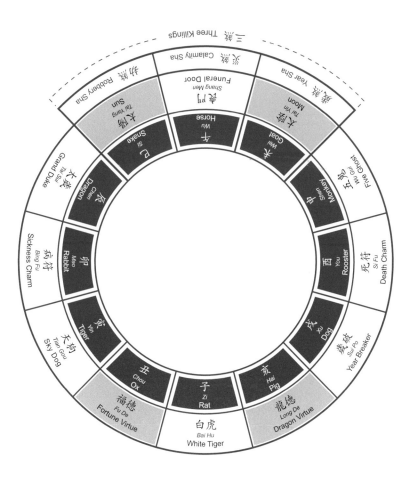

Negative Sectors For Opening Mountain 開山凶位：

年剋山家 Year Countering Sitting

甲 Jia E1	寅 Yin NE3	辰 Chen SE1	巽 Xun SE2	戌 Xu NW1	坎 Kan N2	辛 Xin W3	申 Shen SW3	丑 Chou NE1	癸 Gui N3	坤 Kun SW2	庚 Geng W1	未 Wei SW1

陰府太歲 Yin Fu Tai Sui **Yin Mansion Grand Duke**		六害 Liu Hai **Six Harm**	死符 Si Fu **Death Charm**	炙退 Zhi Tui **Roasting Star**
離 Li S2	乾 Qian NW2	卯 Mao E2	酉 You W2	卯 Mao E2

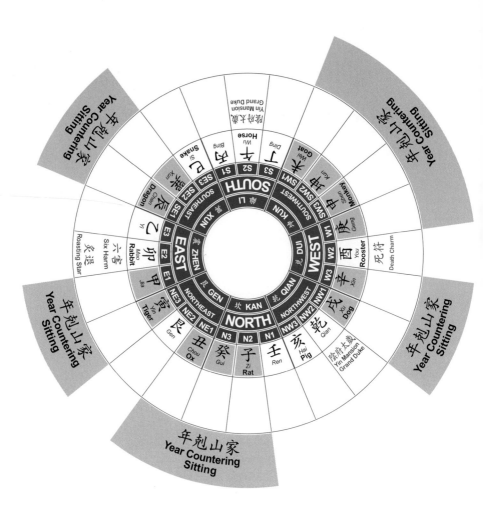

Negative Directions to Establish Facing 立向凶方：

巡山羅喉 *Xun Shan Luo Hou* **Mountain Patrol Luo Hou Star**	病符 *Bing Fu* **Sickness Charm**
巽 *Xun* **SE2**	卯 *Mao* **E2**

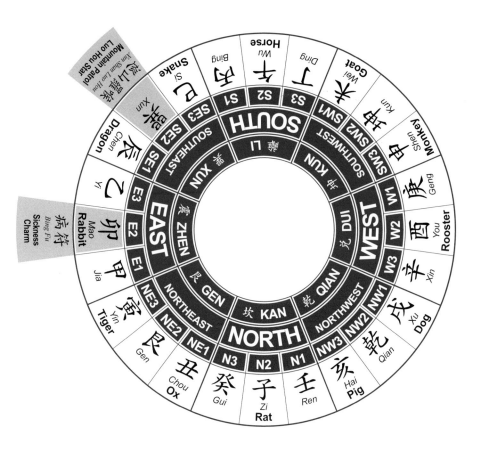

Negative Repair / Renovation Sectors Table 修方凶位表：

天官符 Heavenly Officer Charm	亥 *Hai* Pig		飛廉 Flying Chaste	午 *Wu* Horse
地官符 Earthly Officer Charm	申 *Shen* Monkey		喪門 Funeral Door	午 *Wu* Horse
大煞 Great Sha	子 *Zi* Rat		弔客 Suspended Guest	寅 *Yin* Tiger
大將軍 Big General	子 *Zi* Rat		白虎 White Tiger	子 *Zi* Rat
力士 Strong Man	巽 *Xun*		金神 Golden God	寅 *Yin* Tiger 卯 *Mao* Rabbit 戌 *Xu* Dog 亥 *Hai* Pig
蠶室 Silkworm Room	乾 *Qian*			
蠶官 Silkworm Officer	戌 *Xu* Dog			
蠶命 Silkworm Life	亥 *Hai* Pig			
歲刑 Duke Punishment	辰 *Chen* Dragon		獨火 Lonely Fire	巽 *Xun*
黃幡 Yellow Flag	辰 *Chen* Dragon		五鬼 Five Ghost	子 *Zi* Rat
豹尾 Leopard Tail	戌 *Xu* Dog		破敗五鬼 Destructive Five Ghost	巽 *Xun*

Negative Repair / Renovation Sectors Diagram 修方凶位圖：

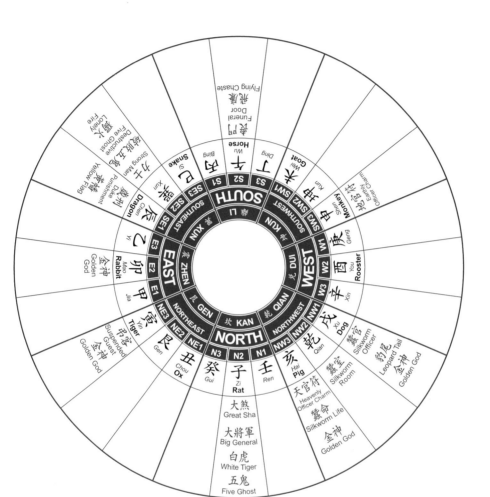

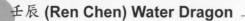

12-Month Auxiliary Stars Reference Table :
壬辰年十二月，開山立向修方星表

Positive Monthly Stars 吉星方

月 MONTH	寅 Tiger (Feb 4 - Mar 5) 正月 1st Month	卯 Rabbit (Mar 6 - Apr 4) 二月 2nd Month	辰 Dragon (Apr 5 - May 5) 三月 3rd Month	巳 Snake (May 6 - Jun 5) 四月 4th Month	午 Horse (Jun 6 - July 6) 五月 5th Month	未 Goat (July 7 - Aug 7) 六月 6th Month
天道 Heavenly Path	南 South	西南 Southwest	北 North	西 West	西北 Northwest	東 East
天德 Heavenly Virtue	丁 Ding Yin Fire	坤 Kun (申)	壬 Ren Yang Water	辛 Xin Yin Metal	乾 Qian (亥)	甲 Jia Yang Wood
天德合 Heavenly Virtue Combo	壬 Ren Yang Water	(巳)	丁 Ding Yin Fire	丙 Bing Yang Fire	(寅)	己 Ji Yin Earth
月德 Monthly Virtue	丙 Bing Yang Fire	甲 Jia Yang Wood	壬 Ren Yang Water	庚 Geng Yang Metal	丙 Bing Yang Fire	甲 Jia Yang Wood
月德合 Monthly Virtue Combo	辛 Xin Yin Metal	己 Ji Yin Earth	丁 Ding Yin Fire	乙 Yi Yin Wood	辛 Xin Yin Metal	己 Ji Yin Earth
月空 Month Emptiness	壬 Ren Yang Water	庚 Geng Yang Metal	丙 Bing Yang Fire	甲 Jia Yang Wood	壬 Ren Yang Water	庚 Geng Yang Metal
陽貴人 Yang Nobleman	乾 Qian	中 Middle	坎 Kan	離 Li	艮 Gen	兌 Dui
陰貴人 Yin Nobleman	艮 Gen	兌 Dui	乾 Qian	中 Middle	坎 Kan	離 Li
飛天祿 Flying Heavenly Wealth	中 Middle	巽 Xun	震 Zhen	坤 Kun	坎 Kan	離 Li
飛天馬 Flying Heavenly Horse	中 Middle	坎 Kan	離 Li	艮 Gen	兌 Dui	乾 Qian

12-Month Auxiliary Stars Reference Table :
壬辰年十二月，開山立向修方星表

申 Monkey (Aug 8 - Sept 7) 七月 7th Month	酉 Rooster (Sept 8 - Oct 7) 八月 8th Month	戌 Dog (Oct 8 - Nov 6) 九月 9th Month	亥 Pig (Nov 7 - Dec 6) 十月 10th Month	子 Rat (Dec 7 - Jan 5) 十一月 11th Month	丑 Ox (Jan 6 - Feb 3) 十二月 12th Month	月 MONTH
北 North	東北 Northeast	南 South	東 East	東南 Southeast	西 West	天道 Heavenly Path
癸 Gui Yin Water	艮 Gen (寅)	丙 Bing Yang Fire	乙 Yi Yin Wood	巽 Xun (巳)	庚 Geng Yang Metal	天德 Heavenly Virtue
戊 Wu Yang Earth	(亥)	辛 Xin Yin Metal	庚 Geng Yang Metal	(申)	乙 Yi Yin Wood	天德合 Heavenly Virtue Combo
壬 Ren Yang Water	庚 Geng Yang Metal	丙 Bing Yang Fire	甲 Jia Yang Wood	壬 Ren Yang Water	庚 Geng Yang Metal	月德 Monthly Virtue
丁 Ding Yin Fire	乙 Yi Yin Wood	辛 Xin Yin Metal	己 Ji Yin Earth	丁 Ding Yin Fire	乙 Yi Yin Wood	月德合 Monthly Virtue Combo
丙 Bing Yang Fire	甲 Jia Yang Wood	壬 Ren Yang Water	庚 Geng Yang Metal	丙 Bing Yang Fire	甲 Jia Yang Wood	月空 Month Emptiness
乾 Qian	中 Middle	巽 Xun	震 Zhen	坤 Kun	坎 Kan	陽貴人 Yang Nobleman
艮 Gen	兌 Dui	乾 Qian	中 Middle	巽 Xun	震 Zhen	陰貴人 Yin Nobleman
艮 Gen	兌 Dui	乾 Qian	中 Middle	巽 Xun	震 Zhen	飛天祿 Flying Heavenly Wealth
中 Middle	巽 Xun	震 Zhen	坤 Kun	坎 Kan	離 Li	飛天馬 Flying Heavenly Horse

Monthly Purple White Stars 月紫白九星 :

寅 Tiger (Feb 4 - Mar 5) 正月 1st Month

巽SE	離S	坤SW
4 Green 四綠	**9** Purple 九紫	**2** Black 二黑
震E **3** Jade 三碧	**5** Yellow 五黃	**7** Red 七赤 兌W
艮NE **8** White 八白	**1** White 一白 坎N	**6** White 六白 乾NW

卯 Rabbit (Mar 6 - Apr 4) 二月 2nd Month

巽SE	離S	坤SW
3 Jade 三碧	**8** White 八白	**1** White 一白
震E **2** Black 二黑	**4** Green 四綠	**6** White 六白 兌W
艮NE **7** Red 七赤	**9** Purple 九紫 坎N	**5** Yellow 五黃 乾NW

辰 Dragon (Apr 5 - May 5) 三月 3rd Month

巽SE	離S	坤SW
2 Black 二黑	**7** Red 七赤	**9** Purple 九紫
震E **1** White 一白	**3** Jade 三碧	**5** Yellow 五黃 兌W
艮NE **6** White 六白	**8** White 八白 坎N	**4** Green 四綠 乾NW

巳 Snake (May 6 - Jun 5) 四月 4th Month

巽SE	離S	坤SW
1 White 一白	**6** White 六白	**8** White 八白
震E **9** Purple 九紫	**2** Black 二黑	**4** Green 四綠 兌W
艮NE **5** Yellow 五黃	**7** Red 七赤 坎N	**3** Jade 三碧 乾NW

午 Horse (Jun 6 - July 6) 五月 5th Month

巽SE	離S	坤SW
9 Purple 九紫	**5** Yellow 五黃	**7** Red 七赤
震E **8** White 八白	**1** White 一白	**3** Jade 三碧 兌W
艮NE **4** Green 四綠	**6** White 六白 坎N	**2** Black 二黑 乾NW

未 Goat (July 7 - Aug 7) 六月 6th Month

巽SE	離S	坤SW
8 White 八白	**4** Green 四綠	**6** White 六白
震E **7** Red 七赤	**9** Purple 九紫	**2** Black 二黑 兌W
艮NE **3** Jade 三碧	**5** Yellow 五黃 坎N	**1** White 一白 乾NW

申 Monkey (Aug 8 - Sept 7) 七月 7th Month

巽SE	離S	坤SW
7 Red 七赤	**3** Jade 三碧	**5** Yellow 五黃
震E **6** White 六白	**8** White 八白	**1** White 一白 兌W
艮NE **2** Black 二黑	**4** Green 四綠 坎N	**9** Purple 九紫 乾NW

酉 Rooster (Sept 8 - Oct 7) 八月 8th Month

巽SE	離S	坤SW
6 White 六白	**2** Black 二黑	**4** Green 四綠
震E **5** Yellow 五黃	**7** Red 七赤	**9** Purple 九紫 兌W
艮NE **1** White 一白	**3** Jade 三碧 坎N	**8** White 八白 乾NW

戌 Dog (Oct 8 - Nov 6) 九月 9th Month

巽SE	離S	坤SW
5 Yellow 五黃	**1** White 一白	**3** Jade 三碧
震E **4** Green 四綠	**6** White 六白	**8** White 八白 兌W
艮NE **9** Purple 九紫	**2** Black 二黑 坎N	**7** Red 七赤 乾NW

亥 Pig (Nov 7 - Dec 6) 十月 10th Month

巽SE	離S	坤SW
4 Green 四綠	**9** Purple 九紫	**2** Black 二黑
震E **3** Jade 三碧	**5** Yellow 五黃	**7** Red 七赤 兌W
艮NE **8** White 八白	**1** White 一白 坎N	**6** White 六白 乾NW

子 Rat (Dec 7 - Jan 5) 十一月 11th Month

巽SE	離S	坤SW
3 Jade 三碧	**8** White 八白	**1** White 一白
震E **2** Black 二黑	**4** Green 四綠	**6** White 六白 兌W
艮NE **7** Red 七赤	**9** Purple 九紫 坎N	**5** Yellow 五黃 乾NW

丑 Ox (Jan 6 - Feb 3) 十二月 12th Month

巽SE	離S	坤SW
2 Black 二黑	**7** Red 七赤	**9** Purple 九紫
震E **1** White 一白	**3** Jade 三碧	**5** Yellow 五黃 兌W
艮NE **6** White 六白	**8** White 八白 坎N	**4** Green 四綠 乾NW

Qi Men Three Nobles 三奇 :

Three Nobles 三奇 / Seasons	乙 Yi	丙 Bing	丁 Ding
立春 **Coming of Spring** Feb 4 - Feb 18	震 Zhen	巽 Xun	中 Middle
春分 **Spring Equinox** Mar 21 - Apr 4	兌 Dui	艮 Gen	離 Li
立夏 **Coming of Summer** May 6 - May 20	艮 Gen	離 Li	坎 Kan
夏至 **Summer Solstice** Jun 22 - Jul 6	中 Middle	巽 Xun	震 Zhen
立秋 **Coming of Autumn** Aug 8 - Aug 23	兌 Dui	乾 Qian	中 Middle
秋分 **Autumn Equinox** Sept 23 - Oct 7	震 Zhen	坤 Kun	坎 Kan
立冬 **Coming of Winter** Nov 7 - Nov 22	坤 Kun	坎 Kan	離 Li
冬至 **Winter Solstice** Dec 22 - Jan 5	中 Middle	乾 Qian	兌 Dui

Sectors to Avoid Opening Mountain 開山凶位 :

月 MONTH	月建 Month Establishment	月破 Month Destruction	月剋山家 Month Countering Sitting		陰府太歲 Yin Mansion Grand Duke	
寅 **Tiger** (Feb 4 - Mar 5) 正月 **1st Month**	寅 Yin Tiger	申 Shen Monkey	—		離 Li	乾 Qian
卯 **Rabbit** (Mar 6 - Apr 4) 二月 **2nd Month**	卯 Mao Rabbit	酉 You Rooster	—		震 Zhen	坤 Kun
辰 **Dragon** (Apr 5 - May 5) 三月 **3rd Month**	辰 Chen Dragon	戌 Xu Dog	離 Li	丙 Bing **Yang Fire**	艮 Gen	巽 Xun
巳 **Snake** (May 6 - Jun 5) 四月 **4th Month**	巳 Si Snake	亥 Hai Pig	壬 Ren **Yang Water**	乙 Yi **Yin Wood**	兌 Dui	乾 Qian
午 **Horse** (Jun 6 - July 6) 五月 **5th Month**	午 Wu Horse	子 Zi Rat	水 Water	山 Mountain	坎 Kan	坤 Kun
未 **Goat** (July 7 - Aug 7) 六月 **6th Month**	未 Wei Goat	丑 Chou Ox	土 Earth		乾 Qian	離 Li
申 **Monkey** (Aug 8 - Sept 7) 七月 **7th Month**	申 Shen Monkey	寅 Yin Tiger	震 Zhen	巳 Si Snake	坤 Kun	震 Zhen
酉 **Rooster** (Sept 8 - Oct 7) 八月 **8th Month**	酉 You Rooster	卯 Mao Rabbit	艮 Gen		巽 Xun	艮 Gen
戌 **Dog** (Oct 8 - Nov 6) 九月 **9th Month**	戌 Xu Dog	辰 Chen Dragon	—		乾 Qian	兌 Dui
亥 **Pig** (Nov 7 - Dec 6) 十月 **10th Month**	亥 Hai Pig	巳 Si Snake	—		坤 Kun	坎 Kan
子 **Rat** (Dec 7 - Jan 5) 十一月 **11th Month**	子 Zi Rat	午 Wu Horse	—		離 Li	乾 Qian
丑 **Ox** (Jan 6 - Feb 3) 十二月 **12th Month**	丑 Chou Ox	未 Wei Goat	—		震 Zhen	坤 Kun

Negative Repair / Renovation Sectors 修方凶位 :

月 MONTH	天官符 Heavenly Officer Charm			地官符 Earth Officer Charm			小月建 Small Month Establishment		
寅 Tiger (Feb 4 - Mar 5) 正月 1st Month	中 Middle			未 Wei Goat	坤 Kun	申 Shen Monkey	中 Middle		
卯 Rabbit (Mar 6 - Apr 4) 二月 2nd Month	辰 Chen Dragon	巽 Xun	巳 Si Snake	壬 Ren Yang Water	坎 Kan	癸 Gui Yin Water	戌 Xu Dog	乾 Qian	亥 Hai Pig
辰 Dragon (Apr 5 - May 5) 三月 3rd Month	甲 Jia Yang Wood	震 Zhen	乙 Yi Yin Wood	丙 Bing Yang Fire	離 Li	丁 Ding Yin Fire	庚 Geng Yang Metal	兌 Dui	辛 Xin Yin Metal
巳 Snake (May 6 - Jun 5) 四月 4th Month	未 Wei Goat	坤 Kun	申 Shen Monkey	丑 Chou Ox	艮 Gen	寅 Yin Tiger	丑 Chou Ox	艮 Gen	寅 Yin Tiger
午 Horse (Jun 6 - July 6) 五月 5th Month	壬 Ren Yang Water	坎 Kan	癸 Gui Yin Water	庚 Geng Yang Metal	兌 Dui	辛 Xin Yin Metal	丙 Bing Yang Fire	離 Li	丁 Ding Yin Fire
未 Goat (July 7 - Aug 7) 六月 6th Month	丙 Bing Yang Fire	離 Li	丁 Ding Yin Fire	戌 Xu Dog	乾 Qian	亥 Hai Pig	壬 Ren Yang Water	坎 Kan	癸 Gui Yin Water
申 Monkey (Aug 8 - Sept 7) 七月 7th Month	丑 Chou Ox	艮 Gen	寅 Yin Tiger	中 Middle			未 Wei Goat	坤 Kun	申 Shen Monkey
酉 Rooster (Sept 8 - Oct 7) 八月 8th Month	庚 Geng Yang Metal	兌 Dui	辛 Xin Yin Metal	庚 Geng Yang Metal	兌 Dui	辛 Xin Yin Metal	甲 Jia Yang Wood	震 Zhen	乙 Yi Yin Wood
戌 Dog (Oct 8 - Nov 6) 九月 9th Month	戌 Xu Dog	乾 Qian	亥 Hai Pig	戌 Xu Dog	乾 Qian	亥 Hai Pig	辰 Chen Dragon	巽 Xun	巳 Si Snake
亥 Pig (Nov 7 - Dec 6) 十月 10th Month	中 Middle			中 Middle			中 Middle		
子 Rat (Dec 7 - Jan 5) 十一月 11th Month	庚 Geng Yang Metal	兌 Dui	辛 Xin Yin Metal	辰 Chen Dragon	巽 Xun	巳 Si Snake	戌 Xu Dog	乾 Qian	亥 Hai Pig
丑 Ox (Jan 6 - Feb 3) 十二月 12th Month	戌 Xu Dog	乾 Qian	亥 Hai Pig	甲 Jia Yang Wood	震 Zhen	乙 Yi Yin Wood	庚 Geng Yang Metal	兌 Dui	辛 Xin Yin Metal

壬辰 (Ren Chen) Water Dragon

Negative Repair / Renovation Sectors 修方凶位 ：

月 MONTH	大月建 Big Month Establishment			飛大煞 Flying Great Sha			丙丁獨火 Bing Ding Lonely Fire	
寅 **Tiger** (Feb 4 - Mar 5) 正月 **1st Month**	中 Middle			戌 Xu Dog	乾 Qian	亥 Hai Pig	離 Li	坎 Kan
卯 **Rabbit** (Mar 6 - Apr 4) 二月 **2nd Month**	辰 Chen Dragon	巽 Xun	巳 Si Snake	中 Middle			艮 Gen	離 Li
辰 **Dragon** (Apr 5 - May 5) 三月 **3rd Month**	甲 Jia Yang Wood	震 Zhen	乙 Yi Yin Wood	辰 Chen Dragon	巽 Xun	巳 Si Snake	兌 Dui	艮 Gen
巳 **Snake** (May 6 - Jun 5) 四月 **4th Month**	未 Wei Goat	坤 Kun	申 Shen Monkey	甲 Jia Yang Wood	震 Zhen	乙 Yi Yin Wood	乾 Qian	兌 Dui
午 **Horse** (Jun 6 - July 6) 五月 **5th Month**	壬 Ren Yang Water	坎 Kan	癸 Gui Yin Water	未 Wei Goat	坤 Kun	申 Shen Monkey	中 Middle	乾 Qian
未 **Goat** (July 7 - Aug 7) 六月 **6th Month**	丙 Bing Yang Fire	離 Li	丁 Ding Yin Fire	壬 Ren Yang Water	坎 Kan	癸 Gui Yin Water	中 Middle	
申 **Monkey** (Aug 8 - Sept 7) 七月 **7th Month**	丑 Chou Ox	艮 Gen	寅 Yin Tiger	丙 Bing Yang Fire	離 Li	丁 Ding Yin Fire	巽 Xun	中 Middle
酉 **Rooster** (Sept 8 - Oct 7) 八月 **8th Month**	庚 Geng Yang Metal	兌 Dui	辛 Xin Yin Metal	丑 Chou Ox	艮 Gen	寅 Yin Tiger	震 Zhen	巽 Xun
戌 **Dog** (Oct 8 - Nov 6) 九月 **9th Month**	戌 Xu Dog	乾 Qian	亥 Hai Pig	庚 Geng Yang Metal	兌 Dui	辛 Xin Yin Metal	坤 Kun	震 Zhen
亥 **Pig** (Nov 7 - Dec 6) 十月 **10th Month**	中 Middle			戌 Xu Dog	乾 Qian	亥 Hai Pig	坎 Kan	坤 Kun
子 **Rat** (Dec 7 - Jan 5) 十一月 **11th Month**	辰 Chen Dragon	巽 Xun	巳 Si Snake	中 Middle			離 Li	坎 Kan
丑 **Ox** (Jan 6 - Feb 3) 十二月 **12th Month**	甲 Jia Yang Wood	震 Zhen	乙 Yi Yin Wood	庚 Geng Yang Metal	兌 Dui	辛 Xin Yin Metal	艮 Gen	離 Li

Negative Repair / Renovation Sectors 修方凶位：

月 MONTH	月遊火 Month Wondering Fire	三煞 Monthly 3 Killings		
		劫煞 Robbery Sha	災煞 Calamity Sha	月煞 Month Sha
寅 **Tiger** (Feb 4 - Mar 5) 正月 **1st Month**	巽 *Xun*	亥 *Hai* **Pig**	子 *Zi* **Rat**	丑 *Chou* **Ox**
卯 **Rabbit** (Mar 6 - Apr 4) 二月 **2nd Month**	中 **Middle**	申 *Shen* **Monkey**	酉 *You* **Rooster**	戌 *Xu* **Dog**
辰 **Dragon** (Apr 5 - May 5) 三月 **3rd Month**	乾 *Qian*	巳 *Si* **Snake**	午 *Wu* **Horse**	未 *Wei* **Goat**
巳 **Snake** (May 6 - Jun 5) 四月 **4th Month**	兌 *Dui*	寅 *Yin* **Tiger**	卯 *Mao* **Rabbit**	辰 *Chen* **Dragon**
午 **Horse** (Jun 6 - July 6) 五月 **5th Month**	艮 *Gen*	亥 *Hai* **Pig**	子 *Zi* **Rat**	丑 *Chou* **Ox**
未 **Goat** (July 7 - Aug 7) 六月 **6th Month**	離 *Li*	申 *Shen* **Monkey**	酉 *You* **Rooster**	戌 *Xu* **Dog**
申 **Monkey** (Aug 8 - Sept 7) 七月 **7th Month**	坎 *Kan*	巳 *Si* **Snake**	午 *Wu* **Horse**	未 *Wei* **Goat**
酉 **Rooster** (Sept 8 - Oct 7) 八月 **8th Month**	坤 *Kun*	寅 *Yin* **Tiger**	卯 *Mao* **Rabbit**	辰 *Chen* **Dragon**
戌 **Dog** (Oct 8 - Nov 6) 九月 **9th Month**	震 *Zhen*	亥 *Hai* **Pig**	子 *Zi* **Rat**	丑 *Chou* **Ox**
亥 **Pig** (Nov 7 - Dec 6) 十月 **10th Month**	巽 *Xun*	申 *Shen* **Monkey**	酉 *You* **Rooster**	戌 *Xu* **Dog**
子 **Rat** (Dec 7 - Jan 5) 十一月 **11th Month**	中 **Middle**	巳 *Si* **Snake**	午 *Wu* **Horse**	未 *Wei* **Goat**
丑 **Ox** (Jan 6 - Feb 3) 十二月 **12th Month**	乾 *Qian*	寅 *Yin* **Tiger**	卯 *Mao* **Rabbit**	辰 *Chen* **Dragon**

Negative Repair / Renovation Sectors 修方凶位 ：

月 MONTH	月刑 Month Punishment	月害 Month Harm	月厭 Month Detest
寅 Tiger (Feb 4 - Mar 5) 正月 1st Month	巳 Si Snake	巳 Si Snake	戌 Xu Dog
卯 Rabbit (Mar 6 - Apr 4) 二月 2nd Month	子 Zi Rat	辰 Chen Dragon	酉 You Rooster
辰 Dragon (Apr 5 - May 5) 三月 3rd Month	辰 Chen Dragon	卯 Mao Rabbit	申 Shen Monkey
巳 Snake (May 6 - Jun 5) 四月 4th Month	申 Shen Monkey	寅 Yin Tiger	未 Wei Goat
午 Horse (Jun 6 - July 6) 五月 5th Month	午 Wu Horse	丑 Chou Ox	午 Wu Horse
未 Goat (July 7 - Aug 7) 六月 6th Month	丑 Chou Ox	子 Zi Rat	巳 Si Snake
申 Monkey (Aug 8 - Sept 7) 七月 7th Month	寅 Yin Tiger	亥 Hai Pig	辰 Chen Dragon
酉 Rooster (Sept 8 - Oct 7) 八月 8th Month	酉 You Rooster	戌 Xu Dog	卯 Mao Rabbit
戌 Dog (Oct 8 - Nov 6) 九月 9th Month	未 Wei Goat	酉 You Rooster	寅 Yin Tiger
亥 Pig (Nov 7 - Dec 6) 十月 10th Month	亥 Hai Pig	申 Shen Monkey	丑 Chou Ox
子 Rat (Dec 7 - Jan 5) 十一月 11th Month	卯 Mao Rabbit	未 Wei Goat	子 Zi Rat
丑 Ox (Jan 6 - Feb 3) 十二月 12th Month	戌 Xu Dog	午 Wu Horse	亥 Hai Pig

壬午 (Ren Wu)
Water Horse

Heavenly Stem 天干	壬 Yang Water (陽水)
Earthly Branch 地支	午 Horse (Yang Fire 陽火)
Hidden Stem 藏干	丁 Yin Fire, 己 Yin Earth
Na Yin 納音	楊柳木 Wood from willow tree
Grand Duke 太歲	午 Horse
Xuan Kong Five Element 玄空五行	2 火 Fire
Gua Name 卦名	䷸ 巽爲風 Wind
Xuan Kong Period Luck 玄空卦運	1

Annual Positive Stars for Opening Mountain, Establishing Facing and Commencing Repairs 開山立向修方吉星：

歲德 Duke Virtue	壬 Ren Yang Water
歲德合 Duke Virtue Combo	丁 Ding Yin Fire
歲枝德 Duke Branch Virtue	亥 Hai Pig
陽貴人 Yang Nobleman	卯 Mao Rabbit
陰貴人 Yin Nobleman	巳 Si Snake
歲祿 Duke Prosperous	亥 Hai Pig
歲馬 Duke Horse	申 Shen Monkey
奏書 Decree	巽 Xun
博士 Professor	乾 Qian

Annual Negative Stars for Opening Mountain, Establishing Facing and Commencing Repairs 開山立向修方凶星：

太歲 Grand Duke	歲破 Year Breaker	三煞 Three Killings			坐煞向煞 Sitting Sha Facing Sha				浮天空亡 Floating Heaven Emptiness	
午 Wu Horse	子 Zi Rat	亥 Hai Pig	子 Zi Rat	丑 Chou Ox	壬 Ren Yang Water	癸 Gui Yin Water	丙 Bing Yang Fire	丁 Ding Yin Fire	乾 Qian	甲 Jia Yang Wood

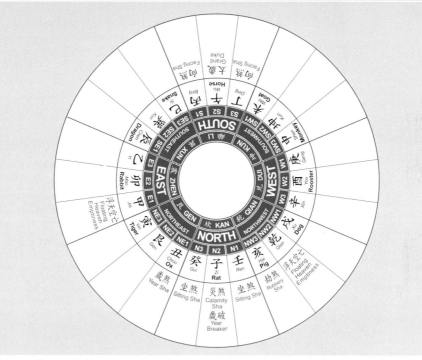

Annual San Yuan Purple White Stars 三元紫白九星：

上元 Upper Period — Period 1, 2, 3			中元 Middle Period — Period 4, 5, 6			下元 Lower Period — Period 7, 8, 9		
巽SE 9	離S 5	坤SW 7	巽SE 3	離S 8	坤SW 1	巽SE 6	離S 2	坤SW 4
震E 8	1 壬午 Ren Wu Water Horse	兌W 3	震E 2	4 壬午 Ren Wu Water Horse	兌W 6	震E 5	7 壬午 Ren Wu Water Horse	兌W 9
艮NE 4	坎N 6	乾NW 2	艮NE 7	坎N 9	乾NW 5	艮NE 1	坎N 3	乾NW 8

Mountain Covering Yellow Path 蓋山黃道：

貪狼 *Tan Lang* **Greedy Wolf**		巨門 *Ju Men* **Huge Door**		武曲 *Wu Qu* **Military Arts**				文曲 *Wen Qu* **Literary Arts**	
巽 *Xun* SE2	辛 *Xin* W3	艮 *Gen* NE2	丙 *Bing* S1	震 *Zhen* E2	庚 *Geng* W1	亥 *Hai* NW3	未 *Wei* SW1	乾 *Qian* NW2	甲 *Jia* E1

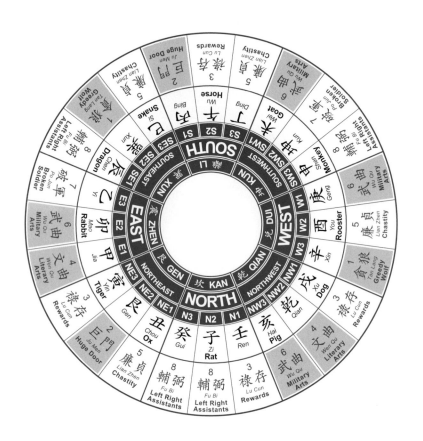

Heaven Penetrating Force 通天竅 :

三合前方 **Facing Three Harmony**	坤申 Kun Shen	庚酉 Geng You	辛戌 Xin Xu
三合後方 **Sitting Three Harmony**	艮寅 Gen Yin	甲卯 Jia Mao	乙辰 Yi Chen

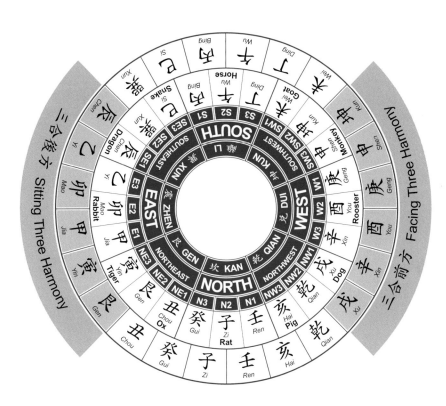

Moving Horse Six Ren Assessment 走馬六壬:

神后 Shen Hou Holy Empress	功曹 Gong Cao Marshall	天罡 Tian Gang Heavenly Dipper	勝光 Sheng Guang Subliminal Bright	傳送 Chuan Song Great General	河魁 He Kui River Scholar
丙午 Bing Wu	坤申 Kun Shen	辛戌 Xin Xu	壬子 Ren Zi	艮寅 Gen Yin	乙辰 Yi Chen

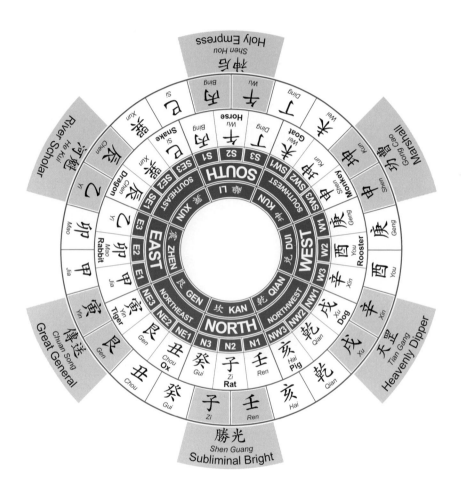

Four Advantages Three Cycles Star Plate 四利三元:

太陽 *Tai Yang* **Sun**	太陰 *Tai Yin* **Moon**	龍德 *Long De* **Dragon Virtue**	福德 *Fu De* **Fortune Virtue**
未 *Wei* **Goat**	酉 *You* **Rooster**	丑 *Chou* **Ox**	卯 *Mao* **Rabbit**

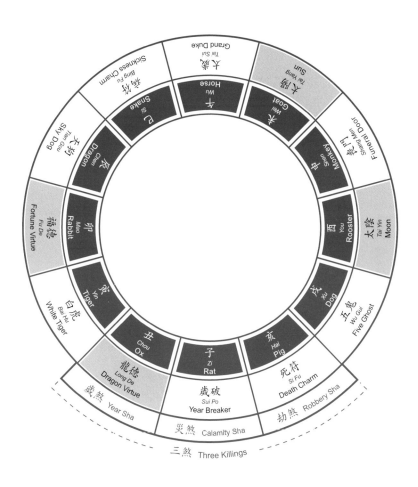

Negative Sectors For Opening Mountain 開山凶位：

年剋山家 Year Countering Sitting

乾	亥	兌	丁
Qian	Hai	Dui	Ding
NW2	NW3	W2	S3

陰府太歲 Yin Fu Tai Sui **Yin Mansion Grand Duke**	六害 Liu Hai **Six Harm**	死符 Si Fu **Death Charm**	炙退 Zhi Tui **Roasting Star**
離 Li S2 乾 Qian NW2	丑 Chou NE1	亥 Hai NW3	酉 You W2

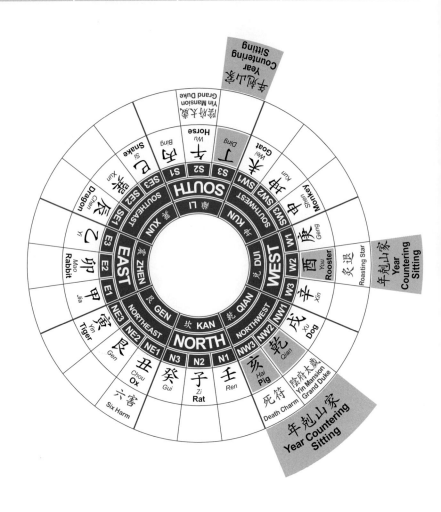

Negative Directions to Establish Facing 立向凶方：

巡山羅喉 *Xun Shan Luo Hou* **Mountain Patrol Luo Hou Star**	病符 *Bing Fu* **Sickness Charm**
丁 *Ding* **S3**	巳 *Si* **SE3**

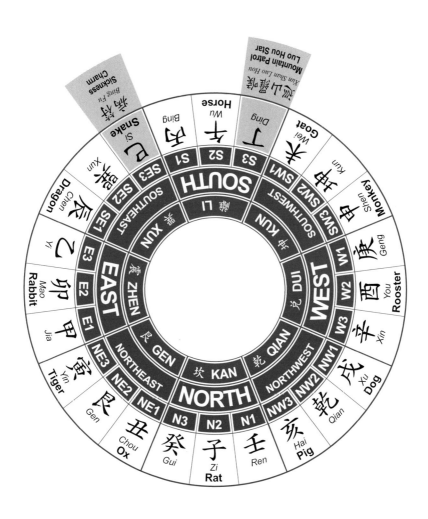

Negative Repair / Renovation Sectors Table 修方凶位表:

天官符 Heavenly Officer Charm	巳 Si Snake	飛廉 Flying Chaste	寅 Yin Tiger
地官符 Earthly Officer Charm	戌 Xu Dog	喪門 Funeral Door	申 Shen Monkey
大煞 Great Sha	午 Wu Horse	弔客 Suspended Guest	辰 Chen Dragon
大將軍 Big General	卯 Mao Rabbit	白虎 White Tiger	寅 Yin Tiger
力士 Strong Man	坤 Kun	金神 Golden God	寅 Yin Tiger
蠶室 Silkworm Room	艮 Gen		卯 Mao Rabbit
蠶官 Silkworm Officer	丑 Chou Ox		戌 Xu Dog
蠶命 Silkworm Life	寅 Yin Tiger		亥 Hai Pig
歲刑 Duke Punishment	午 Wu Horse	獨火 Lonely Fire	兌 Dui
黃幡 Yellow Flag	戌 Xu Dog	五鬼 Five Ghost	戌 Xu Dog
豹尾 Leopard Tail	辰 Chen Dragon	破敗五鬼 Destructive Five Ghost	巽 Xun

Negative Repair / Renovation Sectors Diagram 修方凶位圖：

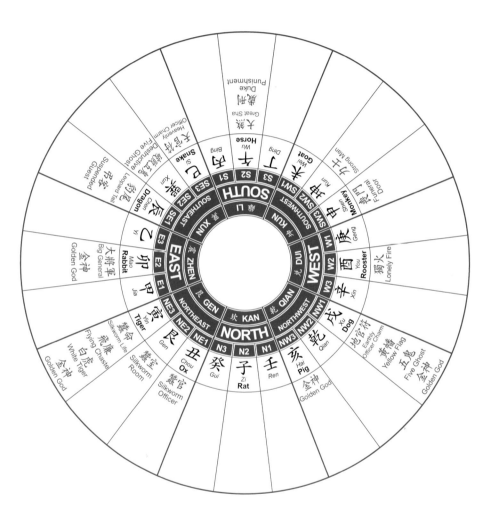

12-Month Auxiliary Stars Reference Table :
壬午年十二月，開山立向修方星表

Positive Monthly Stars 吉星方

月 MONTH	寅 Tiger (Feb 4 - Mar 5) 正月 1st Month	卯 Rabbit (Mar 6 - Apr 4) 二月 2nd Month	辰 Dragon (Apr 5 - May 5) 三月 3rd Month	巳 Snake (May 6 - Jun 5) 四月 4th Month	午 Horse (Jun 6 - July 6) 五月 5th Month	未 Goat (July 7 - Aug 7) 六月 6th Month
天道 Heavenly Path	南 South	西南 Southwest	北 North	西 West	西北 Northwest	東 East
天德 Heavenly Virtue	丁 Ding Yin Fire	坤 Kun (申)	壬 Ren Yang Water	辛 Xin Yin Metal	乾 Qian (亥)	甲 Jia Yang Wood
天德合 Heavenly Virtue Combo	壬 Ren Yang Water	(巳)	丁 Ding Yin Fire	丙 Bing Yang Fire	(寅)	己 Ji Yin Earth
月德 Monthly Virtue	丙 Bing Yang Fire	甲 Jia Yang Wood	壬 Ren Yang Water	庚 Geng Yang Metal	丙 Bing Yang Fire	甲 Jia Yang Wood
月德合 Monthly Virtue Combo	辛 Xin Yin Metal	己 Ji Yin Earth	丁 Ding Yin Fire	乙 Yi Yin Wood	辛 Xin Yin Metal	己 Ji Yin Earth
月空 Month Emptiness	壬 Ren Yang Water	庚 Geng Yang Metal	丙 Bing Yang Fire	甲 Jia Yang Wood	壬 Ren Yang Water	庚 Geng Yang Metal
陽貴人 Yang Nobleman	乾 Qian	中 Middle	坎 Kan	離 Li	艮 Gen	兌 Dui
陰貴人 Yin Nobleman	艮 Gen	兌 Dui	乾 Qian	中 Middle	坎 Kan	離 Li
飛天祿 Flying Heavenly Wealth	中 Middle	巽 Xun	震 Zhen	坤 Kun	坎 Kan	離 Li
飛天馬 Flying Heavenly Horse	坤 Kun	坎 Kan	離 Li	艮 Gen	兌 Dui	乾 Qian

12-Month Auxiliary Stars Reference Table :
壬午年十二月，開山立向修方星表

申 **Monkey** (Aug 8 - Sept 7) 七月 **7th Month**	酉 **Rooster** (Sept 8 - Oct 7) 八月 **8th Month**	戌 **Dog** (Oct 8 - Nov 6) 九月 **9th Month**	亥 **Pig** (Nov 7 - Dec 6) 十月 **10th Month**	子 **Rat** (Dec 7 - Jan 5) 十一月 **11th Month**	丑 **Ox** (Jan 6 - Feb 3) 十二月 **12th Month**	月 **MONTH**
北 North	東北 Northeast	南 South	東 East	東南 Southeast	西 West	天道 **Heavenly Path**
癸 *Gui* Yin Water	艮 *Gen* （寅）	丙 *Bing* Yang Fire	乙 *Yi* Yin Wood	巽 *Xun* （巳）	庚 *Geng* Yang Metal	天德 **Heavenly Virtue**
戊 *Wu* Yang Earth	（亥）	辛 *Xin* Yin Metal	庚 *Geng* Yang Metal	（申）	乙 *Yi* Yin Wood	天德合 **Heavenly Virtue Combo**
壬 *Ren* Yang Water	庚 *Geng* Yang Metal	丙 *Bing* Yang Fire	甲 *Jia* Yang Wood	壬 *Ren* Yang Water	庚 *Geng* Yang Metal	月德 **Monthly Virtue**
丁 *Ding* Yin Fire	乙 *Yi* Yin Wood	辛 *Xin* Yin Metal	己 *Ji* Yin Earth	丁 *Ding* Yin Fire	乙 *Yi* Yin Wood	月德合 **Monthly Virtue Combo**
丙 *Bing* Yang Fire	甲 *Jia* Yang Wood	壬 *Ren* Yang Water	庚 *Geng* Yang Metal	丙 *Bing* Yang Fire	甲 *Jia* Yang Wood	月空 **Month Emptiness**
乾 *Qian*	中 Middle	巽 *Xun*	震 *Zhen*	坤 *Kun*	坎 *Kan*	陽貴人 **Yang Nobleman**
艮 *Gen*	兌 *Dui*	乾 *Qian*	中 Middle	巽 *Xun*	震 *Zhen*	陰貴人 **Yin Nobleman**
艮 *Gen*	兌 *Dui*	乾 *Qian*	中 Middle	坎 *Kan*	離 *Li*	飛天祿 **Flying Heavenly Wealth**
中 Middle	坎 *Kan*	離 *Li*	艮 *Gen*	兌 *Dui*	乾 *Qian*	飛天馬 **Flying Heavenly Horse**

Monthly Purple White Stars 月紫白九星 :

寅 Tiger (Feb 4 - Mar 5) 正月 1st Month

巽 SE	離 S	坤 SW
7 Red 七赤	3 Jade 三碧	5 Yellow 五黃
震 E — 6 White 六白	8 White 八白	1 White 一白 — 兌 W
艮 NE — 2 Black 二黑	4 Green 四綠	9 Purple 九紫 — 乾 NW

卯 Rabbit (Mar 6 - Apr 4) 二月 2nd Month

巽 SE	離 S	坤 SW
6 White 六白	2 Black 二黑	4 Green 四綠
震 E — 5 Yellow 五黃	7 Red 七赤	9 Purple 九紫 — 兌 W
艮 NE — 1 White 一白	3 Jade 三碧	8 White 八白 — 乾 NW

辰 Dragon (Apr 5 - May 5) 三月 3rd Month

巽 SE	離 S	坤 SW
5 Yellow 五黃	1 White 一白	3 Jade 三碧
震 E — 4 Green 四綠	6 White 六白	8 White 八白 — 兌 W
艮 NE — 9 Purple 九紫	2 Black 二黑	7 Red 七赤 — 乾 NW

巳 Snake (May 6 - Jun 5) 四月 4th Month

巽 SE	離 S	坤 SW
4 Green 四綠	9 Purple 九紫	2 Black 二黑
震 E — 3 Jade 三碧	5 Yellow 五黃	7 Red 七赤 — 兌 W
艮 NE — 8 White 八白	1 White 一白	6 White 六白 — 乾 NW

午 Horse (Jun 6 - July 6) 五月 5th Month

巽 SE	離 S	坤 SW
3 Jade 三碧	8 White 八白	1 White 一白
震 E — 2 Black 二黑	4 Green 四綠	6 White 六白 — 兌 W
艮 NE — 7 Red 七赤	9 Purple 九紫	5 Yellow 五黃 — 乾 NW

未 Goat (July 7 - Aug 7) 六月 6th Month

巽 SE	離 S	坤 SW
2 Black 二黑	7 Red 七赤	9 Purple 九紫
震 E — 1 White 一白	3 Jade 三碧	5 Yellow 五黃 — 兌 W
艮 NE — 6 White 六白	8 White 八白	4 Green 四綠 — 乾 NW

申 Monkey (Aug 8 - Sept 7) 七月 7th Month

巽 SE	離 S	坤 SW
1 White 一白	6 White 六白	8 White 八白
震 E — 9 Purple 九紫	2 Black 二黑	4 Green 四綠 — 兌 W
艮 NE — 5 Yellow 五黃	7 Red 七赤	3 Jade 三碧 — 乾 NW

酉 Rooster (Sept 8 - Oct 7) 八月 8th Month

巽 SE	離 S	坤 SW
9 Purple 九紫	5 Yellow 五黃	7 Red 七赤
震 E — 8 White 八白	1 White 一白	3 Jade 三碧 — 兌 W
艮 NE — 4 Green 四綠	6 White 六白	2 Black 二黑 — 乾 NW

戌 Dog (Oct 8 - Nov 6) 九月 9th Month

巽 SE	離 S	坤 SW
8 White 八白	4 Green 四綠	6 White 六白
震 E — 7 Red 七赤	9 Purple 九紫	2 Black 二黑 — 兌 W
艮 NE — 3 Jade 三碧	5 Yellow 五黃	1 White 一白 — 乾 NW

亥 Pig (Nov 7 - Dec 6) 十月 10th Month

巽 SE	離 S	坤 SW
7 Red 七赤	3 Jade 三碧	5 Yellow 五黃
震 E — 6 White 六白	8 White 八白	1 White 一白 — 兌 W
艮 NE — 2 Black 二黑	4 Green 四綠	9 Purple 九紫 — 乾 NW

子 Rat (Dec 7 - Jan 5) 十一月 11th Month

巽 SE	離 S	坤 SW
6 White 六白	2 Black 二黑	4 Green 四綠
震 E — 5 Yellow 五黃	7 Red 七赤	9 Purple 九紫 — 兌 W
艮 NE — 1 White 一白	3 Jade 三碧	8 White 八白 — 乾 NW

丑 Ox (Jan 6 - Feb 3) 十二月 12th Month

巽 SE	離 S	坤 SW
5 Yellow 五黃	1 White 一白	3 Jade 三碧
震 E — 4 Green 四綠	6 White 六白	8 White 八白 — 兌 W
艮 NE — 9 Purple 九紫	2 Black 二黑	7 Red 七赤 — 乾 NW

Qi Men Three Nobles 三奇 :

Three Nobles 三奇 / Seasons	乙 Yi	丙 Bing	丁 Ding
立春 **Coming of Spring** Feb 4 - Feb 18	一	震 Zhen	巽 Xun
春分 **Spring Equinox** Mar 21 - Apr 4	乾 Qian	兌 Dui	艮 Gen
立夏 **Coming of Summer** May 6 - May 20	兌 Dui	艮 Gen	離 Li
夏至 **Summer Solstice** Jun 22 - Jul 6	乾 Qian	中 **Middle**	巽 Xun
立秋 **Coming of Autumn** Aug 8 - Aug 23	艮 Gen	兌 Dui	乾 Qian
秋分 **Autumn Equinox** Sept 23 - Oct 7	巽 Xun	震 Zhen	坤 Kun
立冬 **Coming of Winter** Nov 7 - Nov 22	震 Zhen	坤 Kun	坎 Kan
冬至 **Winter Solstice** Dec 22 - Jan 5	巽 Xun	中 **Middle**	乾 Qian

Sectors to Avoid Opening Mountain 開山凶位 :

月 MONTH	月建 Month Establishment	月破 Month Destruction	月剋山家 Month Countering Sitting		陰府太歲 Yin Mansion Grand Duke	
寅 **Tiger** (Feb 4 - Mar 5) 正月 **1st Month**	寅 Yin **Tiger**	申 Shen **Monkey**	—		離 Li	乾 Qian
卯 **Rabbit** (Mar 6 - Apr 4) 二月 **2nd Month**	卯 Mao **Rabbit**	酉 You **Rooster**	—		震 Zhen	坤 Kun
辰 **Dragon** (Apr 5 - May 5) 三月 **3rd Month**	辰 Chen **Dragon**	戌 Xu **Dog**	離 Li	丙 Bing **Yang Fire**	艮 Gen	巽 Xun
巳 **Snake** (May 6 - Jun 5) 四月 **4th Month**	巳 Si **Snake**	亥 Hai **Pig**	壬 Ren **Yang Water**	乙 Yi **Yin Wood**	兌 Dui	乾 Qian
午 **Horse** (Jun 6 - July 6) 五月 **5th Month**	午 Wu **Horse**	子 Zi **Rat**	水 **Water**	山 **Mountain**	坎 Kan	坤 Kun
未 **Goat** (July 7 - Aug 7) 六月 **6th Month**	未 Wei **Goat**	丑 Chou **Ox**	土 **Earth**		乾 Qian	離 Li
申 **Monkey** (Aug 8 - Sept 7) 七月 **7th Month**	申 Shen **Monkey**	寅 Yin **Tiger**	震 Zhen	巳 Si **Snake**	坤 Kun	震 Zhen
酉 **Rooster** (Sept 8 - Oct 7) 八月 **8th Month**	酉 You **Rooster**	卯 Mao **Rabbit**	艮 Gen		巽 Xun	艮 Gen
戌 **Dog** (Oct 8 - Nov 6) 九月 **9th Month**	戌 Xu **Dog**	辰 Chen **Dragon**	—		乾 Qian	兌 Dui
亥 **Pig** (Nov 7 - Dec 6) 十月 **10th Month**	亥 Hai **Pig**	巳 Si **Snake**	—		坤 Kun	坎 Kan
子 **Rat** (Dec 7 - Jan 5) 十一月 **11th Month**	子 Zi **Rat**	午 Wu **Horse**	—		離 Li	乾 Qian
丑 **Ox** (Jan 6 - Feb 3) 十二月 **12th Month**	丑 Chou **Ox**	未 Wei **Goat**	—		震 Zhen	坤 Kun

Negative Repair / Renovation Sectors 修方凶位 :

月 MONTH	天官符 Heavenly Officer Charm			地官符 Earth Officer Charm			小月建 Small Month Establishment		
寅 **Tiger** (Feb 4 - Mar 5) 正月 **1st Month**	丑 *Chou* Ox	艮 *Gen*	寅 *Yin* Tiger	辰 *Chen* Dragon	巽 *Xun*	巳 *Si* Snake	中 Middle		
卯 **Rabbit** (Mar 6 - Apr 4) 二月 **2nd Month**	庚 *Geng* Yang Metal	兌 *Dui*	辛 *Xin* Yin Metal	甲 *Jia* Yang Wood	震 *Zhen*	乙 *Yi* Yin Wood	戌 *Xu* Dog	乾 *Qian*	亥 *Hai* Pig
辰 **Dragon** (Apr 5 - May 5) 三月 **3rd Month**	戌 *Xu* Dog	乾 *Qian*	亥 *Hai* Pig	未 *Wei* Goat	坤 *Kun*	申 *Shen* Monkey	庚 *Geng* Yang Metal	兌 *Dui*	辛 *Xin* Yin Metal
巳 **Snake** (May 6 - Jun 5) 四月 **4th Month**		中 Middle		壬 *Ren* Yang Water	坎 *Kan*	癸 *Gui* Yin Water	丑 *Chou* Ox	艮 *Gen*	寅 *Yin* Tiger
午 **Horse** (Jun 6 - July 6) 五月 **5th Month**	庚 *Geng* Yang Metal	兌 *Dui*	辛 *Xin* Yin Metal	丙 *Bing* Yang Fire	離 *Li*	丁 *Ding* Yin Fire	丙 *Bing* Yang Fire	離 *Li*	丁 *Ding* Yin Fire
未 **Goat** (July 7 - Aug 7) 六月 **6th Month**	戌 *Xu* Dog	乾 *Qian*	亥 *Hai* Pig	丑 *Chou* Ox	艮 *Gen*	寅 *Yin* Tiger	壬 *Ren* Yang Water	坎 *Kan*	癸 *Gui* Yin Water
申 **Monkey** (Aug 8 - Sept 7) 七月 **7th Month**		中 Middle		庚 *Geng* Yang Metal	兌 *Dui*	辛 *Xin* Yin Metal	未 *Wei* Goat	坤 *Kun*	申 *Shen* Monkey
酉 **Rooster** (Sept 8 - Oct 7) 八月 **8th Month**	辰 *Chen* Dragon	巽 *Xun*	巳 *Si* Snake	戌 *Xu* Dog	乾 *Qian*	亥 *Hai* Pig	甲 *Jia* Yang Wood	震 *Zhen*	乙 *Yi* Yin Wood
戌 **Dog** (Oct 8 - Nov 6) 九月 **9th Month**	甲 *Jia* Yang Wood	震 *Zhen*	乙 *Yi* Yin Wood		中 Middle		辰 *Chen* Dragon	巽 *Xun*	巳 *Si* Snake
亥 **Pig** (Nov 7 - Dec 6) 十月 **10th Month**	未 *Wei* Goat	坤 *Kun*	申 *Shen* Monkey	庚 *Geng* Yang Metal	兌 *Dui*	辛 *Xin* Yin Metal		中 Middle	
子 **Rat** (Dec 7 - Jan 5) 十一月 **11th Month**	壬 *Ren* Yang Water	坎 *Kan*	癸 *Gui* Yin Water	戌 *Xu* Dog	乾 *Qian*	亥 *Hai* Pig	戌 *Xu* Dog	乾 *Qian*	亥 *Hai* Pig
丑 **Ox** (Jan 6 - Feb 3) 十二月 **12th Month**	丙 *Bing* Yang Fire	離 *Li*	丁 *Ding* Yin Fire		中 Middle		庚 *Geng* Yang Metal	兌 *Dui*	辛 *Xin* Yin Metal

Negative Repair / Renovation Sectors 修方凶位 :

月 MONTH	大月建 Big Month Establishment			飛大煞 Flying Great Sha			丙丁獨火 Bing Ding Lonely Fire	
寅 **Tiger** (Feb 4 - Mar 5) 正月 **1st Month**	丑 Chou Ox	艮 Gen	寅 Yin Tiger	丙 Bing Yang Fire	離 Li	丁 Ding Yin Fire	離 Li	坎 Kan
卯 **Rabbit** (Mar 6 - Apr 4) 二月 **2nd Month**	庚 Geng Yang Metal	兌 Dui	辛 Xin Yin Metal	丑 Chou Ox	艮 Gen	寅 Yin Tiger	艮 Gen	離 Li
辰 **Dragon** (Apr 5 - May 5) 三月 **3rd Month**	戌 Xu Dog	乾 Qian	亥 Hai Pig	庚 Geng Yang Metal	兌 Dui	辛 Xin Yin Metal	兌 Dui	艮 Gen
巳 **Snake** (May 6 - Jun 5) 四月 **4th Month**		中 Middle		戌 Xu Dog	乾 Qian	亥 Hai Pig	乾 Qian	兌 Dui
午 **Horse** (Jun 6 - July 6) 五月 **5th Month**	辰 Chen Dragon	巽 Xun	巳 Si Snake		中 Middle		中 Middle	乾 Qian
未 **Goat** (July 7 - Aug 7) 六月 **6th Month**	甲 Jia Yang Wood	震 Zhen	乙 Yi Yin Wood	庚 Geng Yang Metal	兌 Dui	辛 Xin Yin Metal	中 Middle	
申 **Monkey** (Aug 8 - Sept 7) 七月 **7th Month**	未 Wei Goat	坤 Kun	申 Shen Monkey	戌 Xu Dog	乾 Qian	亥 Hai Pig	巽 Xun	中 Middle
酉 **Rooster** (Sept 8 - Oct 7) 八月 **8th Month**	壬 Ren Yang Water	坎 Kan	癸 Gui Yin Water		中 Middle		震 Zhen	巽 Xun
戌 **Dog** (Oct 8 - Nov 6) 九月 **9th Month**	丙 Bing Yang Fire	離 Li	丁 Ding Yin Fire	辰 Chen Dragon	巽 Xun	巳 Si Snake	坤 Kun	震 Zhen
亥 **Pig** (Nov 7 - Dec 6) 十月 **10th Month**	丑 Chou Ox	艮 Gen	寅 Yin Tiger	甲 Jia Yang Wood	震 Zhen	乙 Yi Yin Wood	坎 Kan	坤 Kun
子 **Rat** (Dec 7 - Jan 5) 十一月 **11th Month**	庚 Geng Yang Metal	兌 Dui	辛 Xin Yin Metal	未 Wei Goat	坤 Kun	申 Shen Monkey	離 Li	坎 Kan
丑 **Ox** (Jan 6 - Feb 3) 十二月 **12th Month**	戌 Xu Dog	乾 Qian	亥 Hai Pig	壬 Ren Yang Water	坎 Kan	癸 Gui Yin Water	艮 Gen	離 Li

Negative Repair / Renovation Sectors 修方凶位 :

月 MONTH	月遊火 Month Wondering Fire	三煞 Monthly 3 Killings		
		劫煞 Robbery Sha	災煞 Calamity Sha	月煞 Month Sha
寅 Tiger (Feb 4 - Mar 5) 正月 1st Month	坤 Kun	亥 Hai Pig	子 Zi Rat	丑 Chou Ox
卯 Rabbit (Mar 6 - Apr 4) 二月 2nd Month	震 Zhen	申 Shen Monkey	酉 You Rooster	戌 Xu Dog
辰 Dragon (Apr 5 - May 5) 三月 3rd Month	巽 Xun	巳 Si Snake	午 Wu Horse	未 Wei Goat
巳 Snake (May 6 - Jun 5) 四月 4th Month	中 Middle	寅 Yin Tiger	卯 Mao Rabbit	辰 Chen Dragon
午 Horse (Jun 6 - July 6) 五月 5th Month	乾 Qian	亥 Hai Pig	子 Zi Rat	丑 Chou Ox
未 Goat (July 7 - Aug 7) 六月 6th Month	兑 Dui	申 Shen Monkey	酉 You Rooster	戌 Xu Dog
申 Monkey (Aug 8 - Sept 7) 七月 7th Month	艮 Gen	巳 Si Snake	午 Wu Horse	未 Wei Goat
酉 Rooster (Sept 8 - Oct 7) 八月 8th Month	離 Li	寅 Yin Tiger	卯 Mao Rabbit	辰 Chen Dragon
戌 Dog (Oct 8 - Nov 6) 九月 9th Month	坎 Kan	亥 Hai Pig	子 Zi Rat	丑 Chou Ox
亥 Pig (Nov 7 - Dec 6) 十月 10th Month	坤 Kun	申 Shen Monkey	酉 You Rooster	戌 Xu Dog
子 Rat (Dec 7 - Jan 5) 十一月 11th Month	震 Zhen	巳 Si Snake	午 Wu Horse	未 Wei Goat
丑 Ox (Jan 6 - Feb 3) 十二月 12th Month	巽 Xun	寅 Yin Tiger	卯 Mao Rabbit	辰 Chen Dragon

Negative Repair / Renovation Sectors 修方凶位 :

月 MONTH	月刑 Month Punishment	月害 Month Harm	月厭 Month Detest
寅 **Tiger** (Feb 4 - Mar 5) 正月 **1st Month**	巳 *Si* Snake	巳 *Si* Snake	戌 *Xu* Dog
卯 **Rabbit** (Mar 6 - Apr 4) 二月 **2nd Month**	子 *Zi* Rat	辰 *Chen* Dragon	酉 *You* Rooster
辰 **Dragon** (Apr 5 - May 5) 三月 **3rd Month**	辰 *Chen* Dragon	卯 *Mao* Rabbit	申 *Shen* Monkey
巳 **Snake** (May 6 - Jun 5) 四月 **4th Month**	申 *Shen* Monkey	寅 *Yin* Tiger	未 *Wei* Goat
午 **Horse** (Jun 6 - July 6) 五月 **5th Month**	午 *Wu* Horse	丑 *Chou* Ox	午 *Wu* Horse
未 **Goat** (July 7 - Aug 7) 六月 **6th Month**	丑 *Chou* Ox	子 *Zi* Rat	巳 *Si* Snake
申 **Monkey** (Aug 8 - Sept 7) 七月 **7th Month**	寅 *Yin* Tiger	亥 *Hai* Pig	辰 *Chen* Dragon
酉 **Rooster** (Sept 8 - Oct 7) 八月 **8th Month**	酉 *You* Rooster	戌 *Xu* Dog	卯 *Mao* Rabbit
戌 **Dog** (Oct 8 - Nov 6) 九月 **9th Month**	未 *Wei* Goat	酉 *You* Rooster	寅 *Yin* Tiger
亥 **Pig** (Nov 7 - Dec 6) 十月 **10th Month**	亥 *Hai* Pig	申 *Shen* Monkey	丑 *Chou* Ox
子 **Rat** (Dec 7 - Jan 5) 十一月 **11th Month**	卯 *Mao* Rabbit	未 *Wei* Goat	子 *Zi* Rat
丑 **Ox** (Jan 6 - Feb 3) 十二月 **12th Month**	戌 *Xu* Dog	午 *Wu* Horse	亥 *Hai* Pig

壬申 (Ren Shen)
Water Monkey

Heavenly Stem 天干	壬 Yang Water (陽水)
Earthly Branch 地支	申 Monkey (Yang Metal 陽金)
Hidden Stem 藏干	庚 Yang Metal, 壬 Yang Water, 戊 Yang Earth
Na Yin 納音	劍鋒金 Metal of the sword
Grand Duke 太歲	申 Monkey
Xuan Kong Five Element 玄空五行	1 水 Water
Gua Name 卦名	地水師 Officer
Xuan Kong Period Luck 玄空卦運	7

Annual Positive Stars for Opening Mountain, Establishing Facing and Commencing Repairs 開山立向修方吉星：

歲德 Duke Virtue	壬 Ren Yang Water
歲德合 Duke Virtue Combo	丁 Ding Yin Fire
歲枝德 Duke Branch Virtue	丑 Chou Ox
陽貴人 Yang Nobleman	卯 Mao Rabbit
陰貴人 Yin Nobleman	巳 Si Snake
歲祿 Duke Prosperous	亥 Hai Pig
歲馬 Duke Horse	寅 Yin Tiger
奏書 Decree	坤 Kun
博士 Professor	艮 Gen

Annual Negative Stars for Opening Mountain, Establishing Facing and Commencing Repairs 開山立向修方凶星:

太歲 Grand Duke	歲破 Year Breaker	三煞 Three Killings			坐煞向煞 Sitting Sha Facing Sha				浮天空亡 Floating Heaven Emptiness	
申 *Shen* Monkey	寅 *Yin* Tiger	巳 *Si* Snake	午 *Wu* Horse	未 *Wei* Goat	丙 *Bing* Yang Fire	丁 *Ding* Yin Fire	壬 *Ren* Yang Water	癸 *Gui* Yin Water	乾 *Qian*	甲 *Jia* Yang Wood

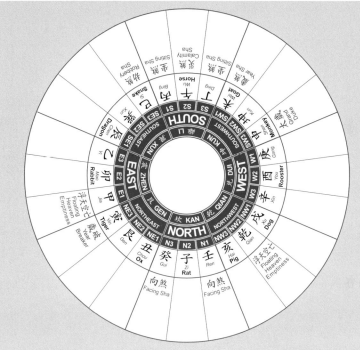

Annual San Yuan Purple White Stars 三元紫白九星:

上元 Upper Period Period 1, 2, 3	中元 Middle Period Period 4, 5, 6	下元 Lower Period Period 7, 8, 9

上元 Upper Period — Period 1, 2, 3

巽SE	離S	坤SW
1	6	8
震E 9	2 壬申 *Ren Shen* Water Monkey	4 兌W
5	7	3
艮NE	坎N	乾NW

中元 Middle Period — Period 4, 5, 6

巽SE	離S	坤SW
4	9	2
震E 3	5 壬申 *Ren Shen* Water Monkey	7 兌W
8	1	6
艮NE	坎N	乾NW

下元 Lower Period — Period 7, 8, 9

巽SE	離S	坤SW
7	3	5
震E 6	8 壬申 *Ren Shen* Water Monkey	1 兌W
2	4	9
艮NE	坎N	乾NW

Mountain Covering Yellow Path 蓋山黃道：

貪狼 *Tan Lang* **Greedy Wolf**		巨門 *Ju Men* **Huge Door**			武曲 *Wu Qu* **Military Arts**		文曲 *Wen Qu* **Literary Arts**			
坤 *Kun* SW2	乙 *Yi* E3	坎 *Kan* N2	癸 *Gui* N3	申 *Shen* SW3	辰 *Chen* SE1	乾 *Qian* NW2	甲 *Jia* E1	震 *Zhen* E2	庚 *Geng* W1	亥 *Hai* NW3	未 *Wei* SW1

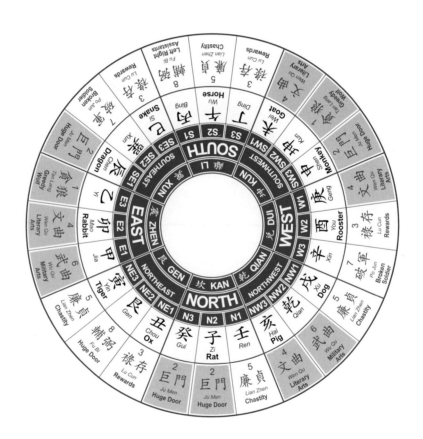

Heaven Penetrating Force 通天竅:

三合前方 Facing Three Harmony	艮寅 Gen Yin	甲卯 Jia Mao	乙辰 Yi Chen
三合後方 Sitting Three Harmony	坤申 Kun Shen	庚酉 Geng You	辛戌 Xin Xu

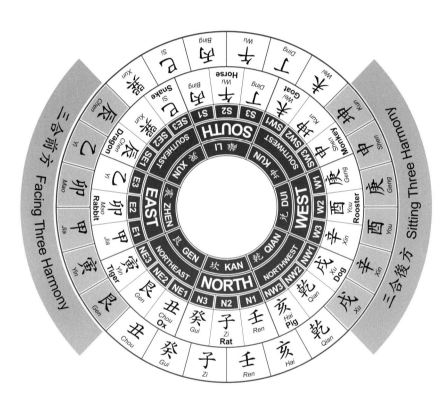

Moving Horse Six Ren Assessment 走馬六壬:

神后 *Shen Hou* **Holy Empress**	功曹 *Gong Cao* **Marshall**	天罡 *Tian Gang* **Heavenly Dipper**	勝光 *Sheng Guang* **Subliminal Bright**	傳送 *Chuan Song* **Great General**	河魁 *He Kui* **River Scholar**
乙辰 *Yi Chen*	丙午 *Bing Wu*	坤申 *Kun Shen*	辛卯 *Xin Mao*	壬子 *Ren Zi*	艮寅 *Gen Yin*

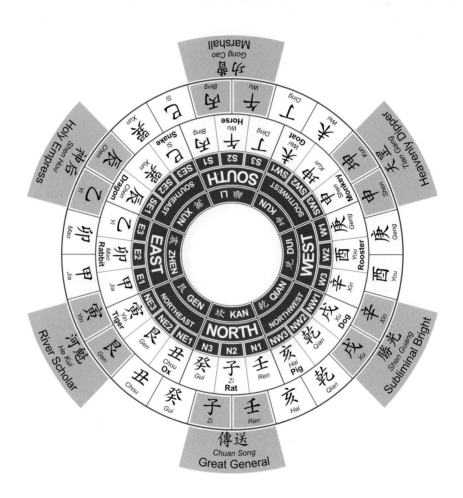

Four Advantages Three Cycles Star Plate 四利三元：

太陽 *Tai Yang* **Sun**	太陰 *Tai Yin* **Moon**	龍德 *Long De* **Dragon Virtue**	福德 *Fu De* **Fortune Virtue**
酉 *You* **Rooster**	亥 *Hai* **Pig**	卯 *Mao* **Rabbit**	巳 *Si* **Snake**

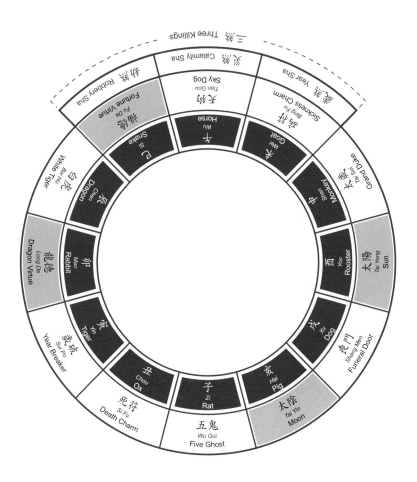

Negative Sectors For Opening Mountain 開山凶位：

年尅山家 Year Countering Sitting (冬至後 After Winter Solstice)

乾 Qian NW2	亥 Hai NW3	兌 Dui W2	丁 Ding S3

陰府太歲 Yin Fu Tai Sui **Yin Mansion Grand Duke**		六害 Liu Hai **Six Harm**	死符 Si Fu **Death Charm**	炙退 Zhi Tui **Roasting Star**
離 Li S2	乾 Qian NW2	亥 Hai NW3	丑 Chou NE1	卯 Mao E2

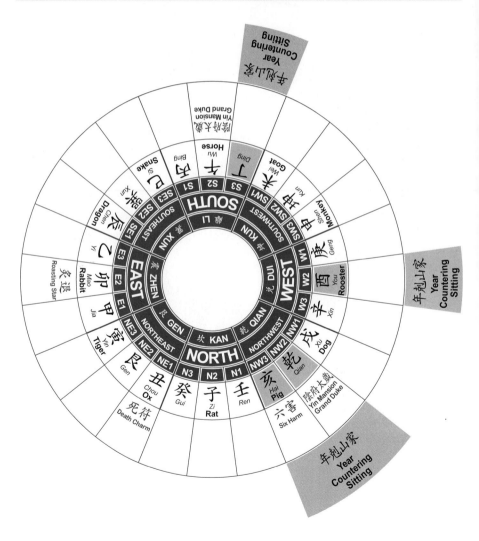

Negative Directions to Establish Facing 立向凶方：

巡山羅喉 *Xun Shan Luo Hou* **Mountain Patrol Luo Hou Star**	病符 *Bing Fu* **Sickness Charm**
庚 *Geng* **W1**	未 *Wei* **SW1**

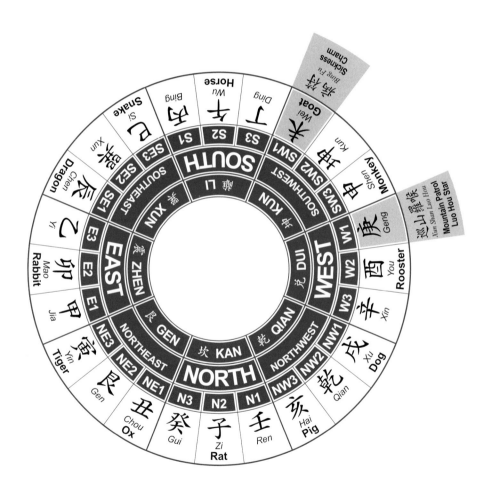

Negative Repair / Renovation Sectors Table 修方凶位表:

天官符 **Heavenly Officer Charm**	亥 *Hai* Pig		飛廉 **Flying Chaste**	辰 *Chen* Dragon
地官符 **Earthly Officer Charm**	子 *Zi* Rat		喪門 **Funeral Door**	戌 *Xu* Dog
大煞 **Great Sha**	子 *Zi* Rat		弔客 **Suspended Guest**	午 *Wu* Horse
大將軍 **Big General**	午 *Wu* Horse		白虎 **White Tiger**	辰 *Chen* Dragon
力士 **Strong Man**	乾 *Qian*		金神 **Golden God**	寅 *Yin* Tiger
蠶室 **Silkworm Room**	巽 *Xun*			卯 *Mao* Rabbit
蠶官 **Silkworm Officer**	辰 *Chen* Dragon			戌 *Xu* Dog
蠶命 **Silkworm Life**	巳 *Si* Snake			亥 *Hai* Pig
歲刑 **Duke Punishment**	寅 *Yin* Tiger		獨火 **Lonely Fire**	離 *Li*
黃幡 **Yellow Flag**	辰 *Chen* Dragon		五鬼 **Five Ghost**	申 *Shen* Monkey
豹尾 **Leopard Tail**	戌 *Xu* Dog		破敗五鬼 **Destructive Five Ghost**	巽 *Xun*

Negative Repair / Renovation Sectors Diagram 修方凶位圖：

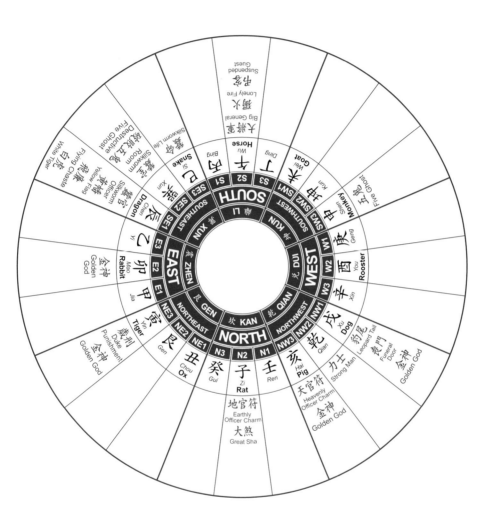

1051

12-Month Auxiliary Stars Reference Table :
壬申年十二月，開山立向修方星表

Positive Monthly Stars 吉星方

月 MONTH	寅 Tiger (Feb 4 - Mar 5) 正月 1st Month	卯 Rabbit (Mar 6 - Apr 4) 二月 2nd Month	辰 Dragon (Apr 5 - May 5) 三月 3rd Month	巳 Snake (May 6 - Jun 5) 四月 4th Month	午 Horse (Jun 6 - July 6) 五月 5th Month	未 Goat (July 7 - Aug 7) 六月 6th Month
天道 Heavenly Path	南 South	西南 Southwest	北 North	西 West	西北 Northwest	東 East
天德 Heavenly Virtue	丁 Ding Yin Fire	坤 Kun （申）	壬 Ren Yang Water	辛 Xin Yin Metal	乾 Qian （亥）	甲 Jia Yang Wood
天德合 Heavenly Virtue Combo	壬 Ren Yang Water	（巳）	丁 Ding Yin Fire	丙 Bing Yang Fire	（寅）	己 Ji Yin Earth
月德 Monthly Virtue	丙 Bing Yang Fire	甲 Jia Yang Wood	壬 Ren Yang Water	庚 Geng Yang Metal	丙 Bing Yang Fire	甲 Jia Yang Wood
月德合 Monthly Virtue Combo	辛 Xin Yin Metal	己 Ji Yin Earth	丁 Ding Yin Fire	乙 Yi Yin Wood	辛 Xin Yin Metal	己 Ji Yin Earth
月空 Month Emptiness	壬 Ren Yang Water	庚 Geng Yang Metal	丙 Bing Yang Fire	甲 Jia Yang Wood	壬 Ren Yang Water	庚 Geng Yang Metal
陽貴人 Yang Nobleman	乾 Qian	中 Middle	坎 Kan	離 Li	艮 Gen	兌 Dui
陰貴人 Yin Nobleman	艮 Gen	兌 Dui	乾 Qian	中 Middle	坎 Kan	離 Li
飛天祿 Flying Heavenly Wealth	中 Middle	巽 Xun	震 Zhen	坤 Kun	坎 Kan	離 Lii
飛天馬 Flying Heavenly Horse	中 Middle	坎 Kan	離 Li	艮 Gen	兌 Dui	乾 Qian

12-Month Auxiliary Stars Reference Table :
壬申年十二月，開山立向修方星表

申 Monkey (Aug 8 - Sept 7) 七月 7th Month	酉 Rooster (Sept 8 - Oct 7) 八月 8th Month	戌 Dog (Oct 8 - Nov 6) 九月 9th Month	亥 Pig (Nov 7 - Dec 6) 十月 10th Month	子 Rat (Dec 7 - Jan 5) 十一月 11th Month	丑 Ox (Jan 6 - Feb 3) 十二月 12th Month	月 MONTH
北 North	東北 Northeast	南 South	東 East	東南 Southeast	西 West	天道 Heavenly Path
癸 Gui Yin Water	艮 Gen （寅）	丙 Bing Yang Fire	乙 Yi Yin Wood	巽 Xun （巳）	庚 Geng Yang Metal	天德 Heavenly Virtue
戊 Wu Yang Earth	（亥）	辛 Xin Yin Metal	庚 Geng Yang Metal	（申）	乙 Yi Yin Wood	天德合 Heavenly Virtue Combo
壬 Ren Yang Water	庚 Geng Yang Metal	丙 Bing Yang Fire	甲 Jia Yang Wood	壬 Ren Yang Water	庚 Geng Yang Metal	月德 Monthly Virtue
丁 Ding Yin Fire	乙 Yi Yin Wood	辛 Xin Yin Metal	己 Ji Yin Earth	丁 Ding Yin Fire	乙 Yi Yin Wood	月德合 Monthly Virtue Combo
丙 Bing Yang Fire	甲 Jia Yang Wood	壬 Ren Yang Water	庚 Geng Yang Metal	丙 Bing Yang Fire	甲 Jia Yang Wood	月空 Month Emptiness
乾 Qian	中 Middle	巽 Xun	震 Zhen	坤 Kun	坎 Kan	陽貴人 Yang Nobleman
艮 Gen	兌 Dui	乾 Qian	中 Middle	巽 Xun	震 Zhen	陰貴人 Yin Nobleman
艮 Gen	兌 Dui	乾 Qian	中 Middle	坎 Kan	離 Lii	飛天祿 Flying Heavenly Wealth
中 Middle	巽 Xun	震 Zhen	坤 Kun	坎 Kan	離 Lii	飛天馬 Flying Heavenly Horse

Monthly Purple White Stars 月紫白九星：

寅 Tiger (Feb 4 - Mar 5) 正月 1st Month

巽 SE	離 S	坤 SW
1 White 一白	6 White 六白	8 White 八白
震 E — 9 Purple 九紫	2 Black 二黑	4 Green 四綠 — 兌 W
艮 NE — 5 Yellow 五黄	7 Red 七赤	3 Jade 三碧 — 乾 NW

卯 Rabbit (Mar 6 - Apr 4) 二月 2nd Month

巽 SE	離 S	坤 SW
9 Purple 九紫	5 Yellow 五黄	7 Red 七赤
震 E — 8 White 八白	1 White 一白	3 Jade 三碧 — 兌 W
艮 NE — 4 Green 四綠	6 White 六白	2 Black 二黑 — 乾 NW

辰 Dragon (Apr 5 - May 5) 三月 3rd Month

巽 SE	離 S	坤 SW
8 White 八白	4 Green 四綠	6 White 六白
震 E — 7 Red 七赤	9 Purple 九紫	2 Black 二黑 — 兌 W
艮 NE — 3 Jade 三碧	5 Yellow 五黄	1 White 一白 — 乾 NW

巳 Snake (May 6 - Jun 5) 四月 4th Month

巽 SE	離 S	坤 SW
7 Red 七赤	3 Jade 三碧	5 Yellow 五黄
震 E — 6 White 六白	8 White 八白	1 White 一白 — 兌 W
艮 NE — 2 Black 二黑	4 Green 四綠	9 Purple 九紫 — 乾 NW

午 Horse (Jun 6 - July 6) 五月 5th Month

巽 SE	離 S	坤 SW
6 White 六白	2 Black 二黑	4 Green 四綠
震 E — 5 Yellow 五黄	7 Red 七赤	9 Purple 九紫 — 兌 W
艮 NE — 1 White 一白	3 Jade 三碧	8 White 八白 — 乾 NW

未 Goat (July 7 - Aug 7) 六月 6th Month

巽 SE	離 S	坤 SW
5 Yellow 五黄	1 White 一白	3 Jade 三碧
震 E — 4 Green 四綠	6 White 六白	8 White 八白 — 兌 W
艮 NE — 9 Purple 九紫	2 Black 二黑	7 Red 七赤 — 乾 NW

申 Monkey (Aug 8 - Sept 7) 七月 7th Month

巽 SE	離 S	坤 SW
4 Green 四綠	9 Purple 九紫	2 Black 二黑
震 E — 3 Jade 三碧	5 Yellow 五黄	7 Red 七赤 — 兌 W
艮 NE — 8 White 八白	1 White 一白	6 White 六白 — 乾 NW

酉 Rooster (Sept 8 - Oct 7) 八月 8th Month

巽 SE	離 S	坤 SW
3 Jade 三碧	8 White 八白	1 White 一白
震 E — 2 Black 二黑	4 Green 四綠	6 White 六白 — 兌 W
艮 NE — 7 Red 七赤	9 Purple 九紫	5 Yellow 五黄 — 乾 NW

戌 Dog (Oct 8 - Nov 6) 九月 9th Month

巽 SE	離 S	坤 SW
2 Black 二黑	7 Red 七赤	9 Purple 九紫
震 E — 1 White 一白	3 Jade 三碧	5 Yellow 五黄 — 兌 W
艮 NE — 6 White 六白	8 White 八白	4 Green 四綠 — 乾 NW

亥 Pig (Nov 7 - Dec 6) 十月 10th Month

巽 SE	離 S	坤 SW
1 White 一白	6 White 六白	8 White 八白
震 E — 9 Purple 九紫	2 Black 二黑	4 Green 四綠 — 兌 W
艮 NE — 5 Yellow 五黄	7 Red 七赤	3 Jade 三碧 — 乾 NW

子 Rat (Dec 7 - Jan 5) 十一月 11th Month

巽 SE	離 S	坤 SW
9 Purple 九紫	5 Yellow 五黄	7 Red 七赤
震 E — 8 White 八白	1 White 一白	3 Jade 三碧 — 兌 W
艮 NE — 4 Green 四綠	6 White 六白	2 Black 二黑 — 乾 NW

丑 Ox (Jan 6 - Feb 3) 十二月 12th Month

巽 SE	離 S	坤 SW
8 White 八白	4 Green 四綠	6 White 六白
震 E — 7 Red 七赤	9 Purple 九紫	2 Black 二黑 — 兌 W
艮 NE — 3 Jade 三碧	5 Yellow 五黄	1 White 一白 — 乾 NW

Qi Men Three Nobles 三奇 :

Three Nobles 三奇 / Seasons	乙 Yi	丙 Bing	丁 Ding
立春 **Coming of Spring** Feb 4 - Feb 18	坎 Kan	坤 Kun	震 Zhen
春分 **Spring Equinox** Mar 21 - Apr 4	中 **Middle**	乾 Qian	兌 Dui
立夏 **Coming of Summer** May 6 - May 20	乾 Qian	兌 Dui	艮 Gen
夏至 **Summer Solstice** Jun 22 - Jul 6	兌 Dui	乾 Qian	中 **Middle**
立秋 **Coming of Autumn** Aug 8 - Aug 23	離 Li	艮 Gen	兌 Dui
秋分 **Autumn Equinox** Sept 23 - Oct 7	中 **Middle**	巽 Xun	震 Zhen
立冬 **Coming of Winter** Nov 7 - Nov 22	巽 Xun	震 Zhen	坤 Kun
冬至 **Winter Solstice** Dec 22 - Jan 5	震 Zhen	巽 Xun	中 **Middle**

Sectors to Avoid Opening Mountain 開山凶位 :

月 MONTH	月建 Month Establishment	月破 Month Destruction	月剋山家 Month Countering Sitting		陰府太歲 Yin Mansion Grand Duke	
寅 Tiger (Feb 4 - Mar 5) 正月 1st Month	寅 Yin Tiger	申 Shen Monkey	–		離 Li	乾 Qian
卯 Rabbit (Mar 6 - Apr 4) 二月 2nd Month	卯 Mao Rabbit	酉 You Rooster	–		震 Zhen	坤 Kun
辰 Dragon (Apr 5 - May 5) 三月 3rd Month	辰 Chen Dragon	戌 Xu Dog	離 Li	丙 Bing Yang Fire	艮 Gen	巽 Xun
巳 Snake (May 6 - Jun 5) 四月 4th Month	巳 Si Snake	亥 Hai Pig	壬 Ren Yang Water	乙 Yi Yin Wood	兌 Dui	乾 Qian
午 Horse (Jun 6 - July 6) 五月 5th Month	午 Wu Horse	子 Zi Rat	水 Water	山 Mountain	坎 Kan	坤 Kun
未 Goat (July 7 - Aug 7) 六月 6th Month	未 Wei Goat	丑 Chou Ox	土 Earth		乾 Qian	離 Li
申 Monkey (Aug 8 - Sept 7) 七月 7th Month	申 Shen Monkey	寅 Yin Tiger	震 Zhen	巳 Si Snake	坤 Kun	震 Zhen
酉 Rooster (Sept 8 - Oct 7) 八月 8th Month	酉 You Rooster	卯 Mao Rabbit	艮 Gen		巽 Xun	艮 Gen
戌 Dog (Oct 8 - Nov 6) 九月 9th Month	戌 Xu Dog	辰 Chen Dragon	–		乾 Qian	兌 Dui
亥 Pig (Nov 7 - Dec 6) 十月 10th Month	亥 Hai Pig	巳 Si Snake	–		坤 Kun	坎 Kan
子 Rat (Dec 7 - Jan 5) 十一月 11th Month	子 Zi Rat	午 Wu Horse	–		離 Li	乾 Qian
丑 Ox (Jan 6 - Feb 3) 十二月 12th Month	丑 Chou Ox	未 Wei Goat	–		震 Zhen	坤 Kun

Negative Repair / Renovation Sectors 修方凶位 :

月 MONTH	天官符 Heavenly Officer Charm			地官符 Earth Officer Charm			小月建 Small Month Establishment		
寅 **Tiger** (Feb 4 - Mar 5) 正月 1st Month	中 Middle			戌 Xu Dog	乾 Qian	亥 Hai Pig	中 Middle		
卯 **Rabbit** (Mar 6 - Apr 4) 二月 2nd Month	辰 Chen Dragon	巽 Xun	巳 Si Snake	中 Middle			戌 Xu Dog	乾 Qian	亥 Hai Pig
辰 **Dragon** (Apr 5 - May 5) 三月 3rd Month	甲 Jia Yang Wood	震 Zhen	乙 Yi Yin Wood	辰 Chen Dragon	巽 Xun	巳 Si Snake	庚 Geng Yang Metal	兌 Dui	辛 Xin Yin Metal
巳 **Snake** (May 6 - Jun 5) 四月 4th Month	未 Wei Goat	坤 Kun	申 Shen Monkey	甲 Jia Yang Wood	震 Zhen	乙 Yi Yin Wood	丑 Chou Ox	艮 Gen	寅 Yin Tiger
午 **Horse** (Jun 6 - July 6) 五月 5th Month	壬 Ren Yang Water	坎 Kan	癸 Gui Yin Water	未 Wei Goat	坤 Kun	申 Shen Monkey	丙 Bing Yang Fire	離 Li	丁 Ding Yin Fire
未 **Goat** (July 7 - Aug 7) 六月 6th Month	丙 Bing Yang Fire	離 Li	丁 Ding Yin Fire	壬 Ren Yang Water	坎 Kan	癸 Gui Yin Water	壬 Ren Yang Water	坎 Kan	癸 Gui Yin Water
申 **Monkey** (Aug 8 - Sept 7) 七月 7th Month	丑 Chou Ox	艮 Gen	寅 Yin Tiger	丙 Bing Yang Fire	離 Li	丁 Ding Yin Fire	未 Wei Goat	坤 Kun	申 Shen Monkey
酉 **Rooster** (Sept 8 - Oct 7) 八月 8th Month	庚 Geng Yang Metal	兌 Dui	辛 Xin Yin Metal	丑 Chou Ox	艮 Gen	寅 Yin Tiger	甲 Jia Yang Wood	震 Zhen	乙 Yi Yin Wood
戌 **Dog** (Oct 8 - Nov 6) 九月 9th Month	戌 Xu Dog	乾 Qian	亥 Hai Pig	庚 Geng Yang Metal	兌 Dui	辛 Xin Yin Metal	辰 Chen Dragon	巽 Xun	巳 Si Snake
亥 **Pig** (Nov 7 - Dec 6) 十月 10th Month	中 Middle			戌 Xu Dog	乾 Qian	亥 Hai Pig	中 Middle		
子 **Rat** (Dec 7 - Jan 5) 十一月 11th Month	庚 Geng Yang Metal	兌 Dui	辛 Xin Yin Metal	中 Middle			戌 Xu Dog	乾 Qian	亥 Hai Pig
丑 **Ox** (Jan 6 - Feb 3) 十二月 12th Month	戌 Xu Dog	乾 Qian	亥 Hai Pig	庚 Geng Yang Metal	兌 Dui	辛 Xin Yin Metal	庚 Geng Yang Metal	兌 Dui	辛 Xin Yin Metal

壬申 (Ren Shen) Water Monkey

Negative Repair / Renovation Sectors 修方凶位 :

月 MONTH	大月建 Big Month Establishment			飛大煞 Flying Great Sha			丙丁獨火 Bing Ding Lonely Fire	
寅 **Tiger** (Feb 4 - Mar 5) 正月 **1st Month**	未 *Wei* Goat	坤 *Kun*	申 *Shen* Monkey	戌 *Xu* Dog	乾 *Qian*	亥 *Hai* Pig	離 *Li*	坎 *Kan*
卯 **Rabbit** (Mar 6 - Apr 4) 二月 **2nd Month**	壬 *Ren* Yang Water	坎 *Kan*	癸 *Gui* Yin Water	中 Middle			艮 *Gen*	離 *Li*
辰 **Dragon** (Apr 5 - May 5) 三月 **3rd Month**	丙 *Bing* Yang Fire	離 *Li*	丁 *Ding* Yin Fire	辰 *Chen* Dragon	巽 *Xun*	巳 *Si* Snake	兌 *Dui*	艮 *Gen*
巳 **Snake** (May 6 - Jun 5) 四月 **4th Month**	丑 *Chou* Ox	艮 *Gen*	寅 *Yin* Tiger	甲 *Jia* Yang Wood	震 *Zhen*	乙 *Yi* Yin Wood	乾 *Qian*	兌 *Dui*
午 **Horse** (Jun 6 - July 6) 五月 **5th Month**	庚 *Geng* Yang Metal	兌 *Dui*	辛 *Xin* Yin Metal	未 *Wei* Goat	坤 *Kun*	申 *Shen* Monkey	中 Middle	乾 *Qian*
未 **Goat** (July 7 - Aug 7) 六月 **6th Month**	戌 *Xu* Dog	乾 *Qian*	亥 *Hai* Pig	壬 *Ren* Yang Water	坎 *Kan*	癸 *Gui* Yin Water	中 Middle	
申 **Monkey** (Aug 8 - Sept 7) 七月 **7th Month**	中 Middle			丙 *Bing* Yang Fire	離 *Li*	丁 *Ding* Yin Fire	巽 *Xun*	中 Middle
酉 **Rooster** (Sept 8 - Oct 7) 八月 **8th Month**	辰 *Chen* Dragon	巽 *Xun*	巳 *Si* Snake	丑 *Chou* Ox	艮 *Gen*	寅 *Yin* Tiger	震 *Zhen*	巽 *Xun*
戌 **Dog** (Oct 8 - Nov 6) 九月 **9th Month**	甲 *Jia* Yang Wood	震 *Zhen*	乙 *Yi* Yin Wood	庚 *Geng* Yang Metal	兌 *Dui*	辛 *Xin* Yin Metal	坤 *Kun*	震 *Zhen*
亥 **Pig** (Nov 7 - Dec 6) 十月 **10th Month**	未 *Wei* Goat	坤 *Kun*	申 *Shen* Monkey	戌 *Xu* Dog	乾 *Qian*	亥 *Hai* Pig	坎 *Kan*	坤 *Kun*
子 **Rat** (Dec 7 - Jan 5) 十一月 **11th Month**	壬 *Ren* Yang Water	坎 *Kan*	癸 *Gui* Yin Water	中 Middle			離 *Li*	坎 *Kan*
丑 **Ox** (Jan 6 - Feb 3) 十二月 **12th Month**	丙 *Bing* Yang Fire	離 *Li*	丁 *Ding* Yin Fire	庚 *Geng* Yang Metal	兌 *Dui*	辛 *Xin* Yin Metal	艮 *Gen*	離 *Li*

Negative Repair / Renovation Sectors 修方凶位 :

月 MONTH	月遊火 Month Wondering Fire	三煞 Monthly 3 Killings		
		劫煞 Robbery Sha	災煞 Calamity Sha	月煞 Month Sha
寅 **Tiger** (Feb 4 - Mar 5) 正月 **1st Month**	兑 *Dui*	亥 *Hai* Pig	子 *Zi* Rat	丑 *Chou* Ox
卯 **Rabbit** (Mar 6 - Apr 4) 二月 **2nd Month**	艮 *Gen*	申 *Shen* Monkey	酉 *You* Rooster	戌 *Xu* Dog
辰 **Dragon** (Apr 5 - May 5) 三月 **3rd Month**	離 *Li*	巳 *Si* Snake	午 *Wu* Horse	未 *Wei* Goat
巳 **Snake** (May 6 - Jun 5) 四月 **4th Month**	坎 *Kan*	寅 *Yin* Tiger	卯 *Mao* Rabbit	辰 *Chen* Dragon
午 **Horse** (Jun 6 - July 6) 五月 **5th Month**	坤 *Kun*	亥 *Hai* Pig	子 *Zi* Rat	丑 *Chou* Ox
未 **Goat** (July 7 - Aug 7) 六月 **6th Month**	震 *Zhen*	申 *Shen* Monkey	酉 *You* Rooster	戌 *Xu* Dog
申 **Monkey** (Aug 8 - Sept 7) 七月 **7th Month**	巽 *Xun*	巳 *Si* Snake	午 *Wu* Horse	未 *Wei* Goat
酉 **Rooster** (Sept 8 - Oct 7) 八月 **8th Month**	中 Middle	寅 *Yin* Tiger	卯 *Mao* Rabbit	辰 *Chen* Dragon
戌 **Dog** (Oct 8 - Nov 6) 九月 **9th Month**	乾 *Qian*	亥 *Hai* Pig	子 *Zi* Rat	丑 *Chou* Ox
亥 **Pig** (Nov 7 - Dec 6) 十月 **10th Month**	兑 *Dui*	申 *Shen* Monkey	酉 *You* Rooster	戌 *Xu* Dog
子 **Rat** (Dec 7 - Jan 5) 十一月 **11th Month**	艮 *Gen*	巳 *Si* Snake	午 *Wu* Horse	未 *Wei* Goat
丑 **Ox** (Jan 6 - Feb 3) 十二月 **12th Month**	離 *Li*	寅 *Yin* Tiger	卯 *Mao* Rabbit	辰 *Chen* Dragon

Negative Repair / Renovation Sectors 修方凶位 :

月 MONTH	月刑 Month Punishment	月害 Month Harm	月厭 Month Detest
寅 **Tiger** (Feb 4 - Mar 5) 正月 **1st Month**	巳 *Si* Snake	巳 *Si* Snake	戌 *Xu* Dog
卯 **Rabbit** (Mar 6 - Apr 4) 二月 **2nd Month**	子 *Zi* Rat	辰 *Chen* Dragon	酉 *You* Rooster
辰 **Dragon** (Apr 5 - May 5) 三月 **3rd Month**	辰 *Chen* Dragon	卯 *Mao* Rabbit	申 *Shen* Monkey
巳 **Snake** (May 6 - Jun 5) 四月 **4th Month**	申 *Shen* Monkey	寅 *Yin* Tiger	未 *Wei* Goat
午 **Horse** (Jun 6 - July 6) 五月 **5th Month**	午 *Wu* Horse	丑 *Chou* Ox	午 *Wu* Horse
未 **Goat** (July 7 - Aug 7) 六月 **6th Month**	丑 *Chou* Ox	子 *Zi* Rat	巳 *Si* Snake
申 **Monkey** (Aug 8 - Sept 7) 七月 **7th Month**	寅 *Yin* Tiger	亥 *Hai* Pig	辰 *Chen* Dragon
酉 **Rooster** (Sept 8 - Oct 7) 八月 **8th Month**	酉 *You* Rooster	戌 *Xu* Dog	卯 *Mao* Rabbit
戌 **Dog** (Oct 8 - Nov 6) 九月 **9th Month**	未 *Wei* Goat	酉 *You* Rooster	寅 *Yin* Tiger
亥 **Pig** (Nov 7 - Dec 6) 十月 **10th Month**	亥 *Hai* Pig	申 *Shen* Monkey	丑 *Chou* Ox
子 **Rat** (Dec 7 - Jan 5) 十一月 **11th Month**	卯 *Mao* Rabbit	未 *Wei* Goat	子 *Zi* Rat
丑 **Ox** (Jan 6 - Feb 3) 十二月 **12th Month**	戌 *Xu* Dog	午 *Wu* Horse	亥 *Hai* Pig

壬戌 (Ren Xu)
Water Dog

Heavenly Stem 天干	壬 Yang Water (陽水)
Earthly Branch 地支	戌 Dog (Yang Earth 陽土)
Hidden Stem 藏干	戊 Yang Earth, 辛 Yin Metal, 丁 Yin Fire
Na Yin 納音	大海水 Water from the sea
Grand Duke 太歲	戌 Dog
Xuan Kong Five Element 玄空五行	4 金 Metal
Gua Name 卦名	䷬ 澤地萃 Gathering
Xuan Kong Period Luck 玄空卦運	4

Annual Positive Stars for Opening Mountain, Establishing Facing and Commencing Repairs 開山立向修方吉星：

歲德 Duke Virtue	壬 Ren Yang Water
歲德合 Duke Virtue Combo	丁 Ding Yin Fire
歲枝德 Duke Branch Virtue	卯 Mao Rabbit
陽貴人 Yang Nobleman	卯 Mao Rabbit
陰貴人 Yin Nobleman	巳 Si Snake
歲祿 Duke Prosperous	亥 Hai Pig
歲馬 Duke Horse	申 Shen Monkey
奏書 Decree	坤 Kun
博士 Professor	艮 Gen

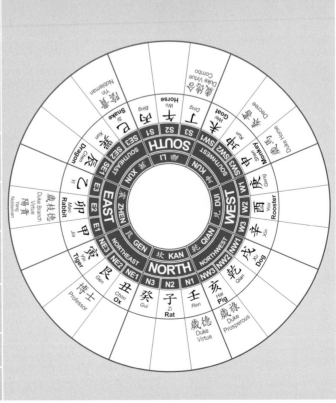

Annual Negative Stars for Opening Mountain, Establishing Facing and Commencing Repairs 開山立向修方凶星：

太歲 Grand Duke	歲破 Year Breaker	三煞 Three Killings			坐煞向煞 Sitting Sha Facing Sha				浮天空亡 Floating Heaven Emptiness	
戌 Xu Dog	辰 Chen Dragon	亥 Hai Pig	子 Zi Rat	丑 Chou Ox	壬 Ren Yang Water	癸 Gui Yin Water	丙 Bing Yang Fire	丁 Ding Yin Fire	乾 Qian	甲 Jia Yang Wood

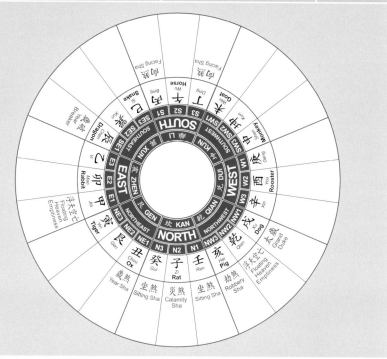

Annual San Yuan Purple White Stars 三元紫白九星：

上元 Upper Period Period 1, 2, 3

巽 SE	離 S	坤 SW
5	1	3
震 E 4	6 壬戌 Ren Xu Water Dog	8 兌 W
9	2	7
艮 NE	坎 N	乾 NW

中元 Middle Period Period 4, 5, 6

巽 SE	離 S	坤 SW
8	4	6
震 E 7	9 壬戌 Ren Xu Water Dog	2 兌 W
3	5	1
艮 NE	坎 N	乾 NW

下元 Lower Period Period 7, 8, 9

巽 SE	離 S	坤 SW
2	7	9
震 E 1	3 壬戌 Ren Xu Water Dog	5 兌 W
6	8	4
艮 NE	坎 N	乾 NW

Mountain Covering Yellow Path 蓋山黄道：

貪狼 *Tan Lang* **Greedy Wolf**				巨門 *Ju Men* **Huge Door**		武曲 *Wu Qu* **Military Arts**				文曲 *Wen Qu* **Literary Arts**			
坎 *Kan* N2	癸 *Gui* N3	申 *Shen* SW3	辰 *Chen* SE1	坤 *Kun* SW2	乙 *Yi* E3	離 *Li* S2	壬 *Ren* N1	寅 *Yin* NE3	戌 *Xu* NW1	兑 *Dui* W2	丁 *Ding* S3	巳 *Si* SE3	丑 *Chou* NE1

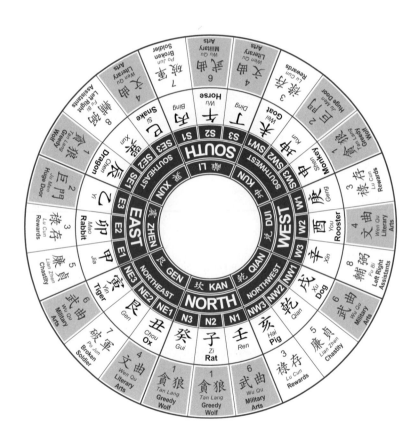

Heaven Penetrating Force 通天竅:

三合前方 Facing Three Harmony	坤申 *Kun Shen*	庚酉 *Geng You*	辛戌 *Xin Xu*
三合後方 Sitting Three Harmony	艮寅 *Gen Yin*	甲卯 *Jia Mao*	乙辰 *Yi Chen*

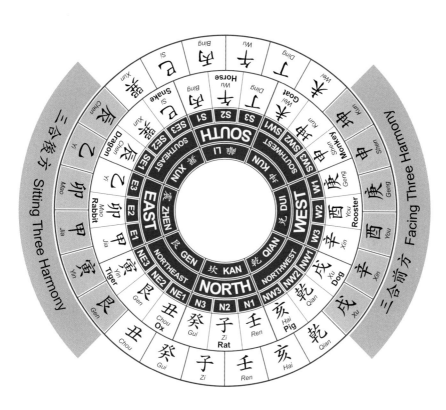

壬戌 (Ren Xu) Water Dog

神后 Shen Hou Holy Empress	功曹 Gong Cao Marshall	天罡 Tian Gang Heavenly Dipper	勝光 Sheng Guang Subliminal Bright	傳送 Chuan Song Great General	河魁 He Kui River Scholar
艮寅 Gen Yin	乙辰 Yi Chen	丙午 Bing Wu	坤申 Kun Shen	辛戌 Xin Xu	壬子 Ren Zi

Moving Horse Six Ren Assessment 走馬六壬：

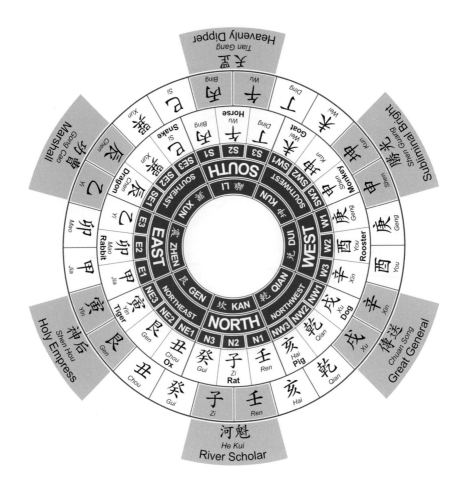

1066

Four Advantages Three Cycles Star Plate 四利三元：

太陽 Tai Yang **Sun**	太陰 Tai Yin **Moon**	龍德 Long De **Dragon Virtue**	福德 Fu De **Fortune Virtue**
亥 Hai **Pig**	丑 Chou **Ox**	巳 Si **Snake**	未 Wei **Goat**

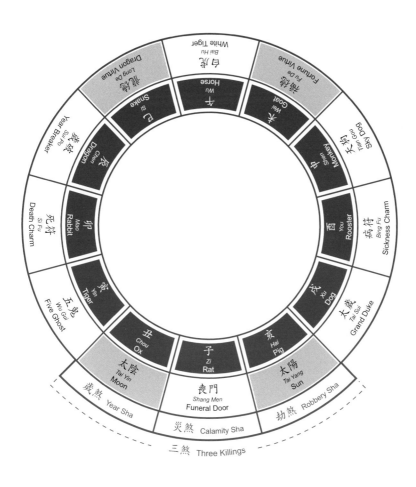

Negative Sectors For Opening Mountain 開山凶位：

年剋山家 Year Countering Sitting

甲 Jia E1	寅 Yin NE3	辰 Chen SE1	巽 Xun SE2	戌 Xu NW1	坎 Kan N2	辛 Xin W3	申 Shen SW3	丑 Chou NE1	癸 Gui N3	坤 Kun SW2	庚 Geng W1	未 Wei SW1

陰府太歲 Yin Fu Tai Sui **Yin Mansion Grand Duke**		六害 Liu Hai **Six Harm**	死符 Si Fu **Death Charm**	炙退 Zhi Tui **Roasting Star**
離 Li S2	乾 Qian NW2	酉 You W2	卯 Mao E2	酉 You W2

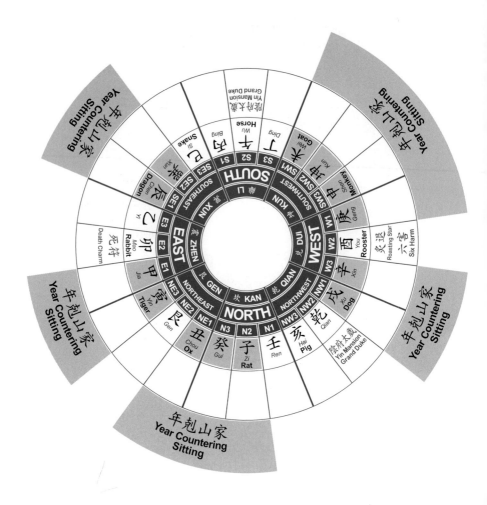

Negative Directions to Establish Facing 立向凶方：

巡山羅喉 *Xun Shan Luo Hou* **Mountain Patrol Luo Hou Star**	病符 *Bing Fu* **Sickness Charm**
乾 *Qian* **NW2**	酉 *You* **W2**

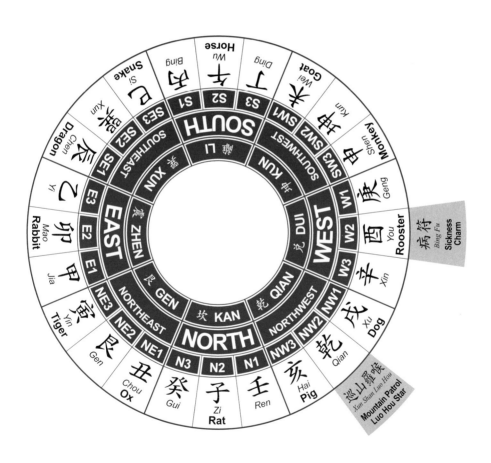

Negative Repair / Renovation Sectors Table 修方凶位表：

天官符 Heavenly Officer Charm	巳 Si Snake		飛廉 Flying Chaste	子 Zi Rat
地官符 Earthly Officer Charm	寅 Yin Tiger		喪門 Funeral Door	子 Zi Rat
大煞 Great Sha	午 Wu Horse		弔客 Suspended Guest	申 Shen Monkey
大將軍 Big General	午 Wu Horse		白虎 White Tiger	午 Wu Horse
力士 Strong Man	乾 Qian		金神 Golden God	寅 Yin Tiger
蠶室 Silkworm Room	巽 Xun			卯 Mao Rabbit
蠶官 Silkworm Officer	辰 Chen Dragon			戌 Xu Dog
蠶命 Silkworm Life	巳 Si Snake			亥 Hai Pig
歲刑 Duke Punishment	未 Wei Goat		獨火 Lonely Fire	乾 Qian
黃幡 Yellow Flag	戌 Xu Dog		五鬼 Five Ghost	午 Wu Horse
豹尾 Leopard Tail	辰 Chen Dragon		破敗五鬼 Destructive Five Ghost	巽 Xun

Negative Repair / Renovation Sectors Diagram 修方凶位圖：

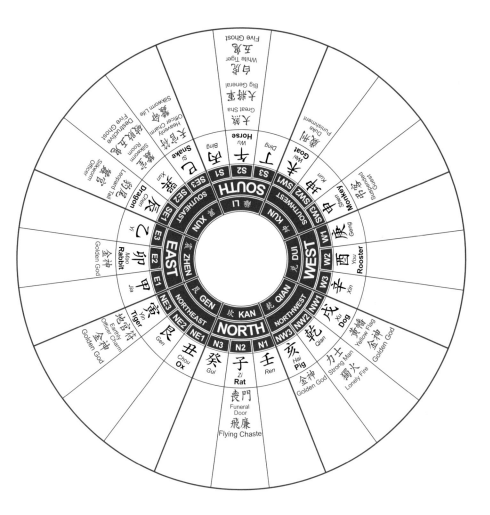

12-Month Auxiliary Stars Reference Table :
壬戌年十二月，開山立向修方星表

Positive Monthly Stars 吉星方

月 MONTH	寅 Tiger (Feb 4 - Mar 5) 正月 1st Month	卯 Rabbit (Mar 6 - Apr 4) 二月 2nd Month	辰 Dragon (Apr 5 - May 5) 三月 3rd Month	巳 Snake (May 6 - Jun 5) 四月 4th Month	午 Horse (Jun 6 - July 6) 五月 5th Month	未 Goat (July 7 - Aug 7) 六月 6th Month
天道 Heavenly Path	南 South	西南 Southwest	北 North	西 West	西北 Northwest	東 East
天德 Heavenly Virtue	丁 Ding Yin Fire	坤 Kun (申)	壬 Ren Yang Water	辛 Xin Yin Metal	乾 Qian (亥)	甲 Jia Yang Wood
天德合 Heavenly Virtue Combo	壬 Ren Yang Water	(巳)	丁 Ding Yin Fire	丙 Bing Yang Fire	(寅)	己 Ji Yin Earth
月德 Monthly Virtue	丙 Bing Yang Fire	甲 Jia Yang Wood	壬 Ren Yang Water	庚 Geng Yang Metal	丙 Bing Yang Fire	甲 Jia Yang Wood
月德合 Monthly Virtue Combo	辛 Xin Yin Metal	己 Ji Yin Earth	丁 Ding Yin Fire	乙 Yi Yin Wood	辛 Xin Yin Metal	己 Ji Yin Earth
月空 Month Emptiness	壬 Ren Yang Water	庚 Geng Yang Metal	丙 Bing Yang Fire	甲 Jia Yang Wood	壬 Ren Yang Water	庚 Geng Yang Metal
陽貴人 Yang Nobleman	乾 Qian	中 Middle	坎 Kan	離 Li	艮 Gen	兌 Dui
陰貴人 Yin Nobleman	艮 Gen	兌 Dui	乾 Qian	中 Middle	坎 Kan	離 Li
飛天祿 Flying Heavenly Wealth	中 Middle	巽 Xun	震 Zhen	坤 Kun	坎 Kan	離 Li
飛天馬 Flying Heavenly Horse	坤 Kun	坎 Kan	離 Li	艮 Gen	兌 Dui	乾 Qian

12-Month Auxiliary Stars Reference Table :
壬戌年十二月，開山立向修方星表

申 Monkey (Aug 8 - Sept 7)	酉 Rooster (Sept 8 - Oct 7)	戌 Dog (Oct 8 - Nov 6)	亥 Pig (Nov 7 - Dec 6)	子 Rat (Dec 7 - Jan 5)	丑 Ox (Jan 6 - Feb 3)	月 MONTH
七月 7th Month	八月 8th Month	九月 9th Month	十月 10th Month	十一月 11th Month	十二月 12th Month	
北 North	東北 Northeast	南 South	東 East	東南 Southeast	西 West	天道 Heavenly Path
癸 Gui Yin Water	艮 Gen (寅)	丙 Bing Yang Fire	乙 Yi Yin Wood	巽 Xun (巳)	庚 Geng Yang Metal	天德 Heavenly Virtue
戊 Wu Yang Earth	(亥)	辛 Xin Yin Metal	庚 Geng Yang Metal	(申)	乙 Yi Yin Wood	天德合 Heavenly Virtue Combo
壬 Ren Yang Water	庚 Geng Yang Metal	丙 Bing Yang Fire	甲 Jia Yang Wood	壬 Ren Yang Water	庚 Geng Yang Metal	月德 Monthly Virtue
丁 Ding Yin Fire	乙 Yi Yin Wood	辛 Xin Yin Metal	己 Ji Yin Earth	丁 Ding Yin Fire	乙 Yi Yin Wood	月德合 Monthly Virtue Combo
丙 Bing Yang Fire	甲 Jia Yang Wood	壬 Ren Yang Water	庚 Geng Yang Metal	丙 Bing Yang Fire	甲 Jia Yang Wood	月空 Month Emptiness
乾 Qian	中 Middle	巽 Xun	震 Zhen	坤 Kun	坎 Kan	陽貴人 Yang Nobleman
艮 Gen	兌 Dui	乾 Qian	中 Middle	巽 Xun	震 Zhen	陰貴人 Yin Nobleman
艮 Gen	兌 Dui	乾 Qian	中 Middle	坎 Kan	離 Li	飛天祿 Flying Heavenly Wealth
中 Middle	坎 Kan	離 Li	艮 Gen	兌 Dui	乾 Qian	飛天馬 Flying Heavenly Horse

Monthly Purple White Stars 月紫白九星 :

寅 Tiger (Feb 4 - Mar 5) 正月 1st Month

巽 SE	離 S	坤 SW
4 Green 四綠	9 Purple 九紫	2 Black 二黑
震 E — 3 Jade 三碧	5 Yellow 五黃	7 Red 七赤 — 兌 W
8 White 八白	1 White 一白	6 White 六白
艮 NE	坎 N	乾 NW

卯 Rabbit (Mar 6 - Apr 4) 二月 2nd Month

巽 SE	離 S	坤 SW
3 Jade 三碧	8 White 八白	1 White 一白
震 E — 2 Black 二黑	4 Green 四綠	6 White 六白 — 兌 W
7 Red 七赤	9 Purple 九紫	5 Yellow 五黃
艮 NE	坎 N	乾 NW

辰 Dragon (Apr 5 - May 5) 三月 3rd Month

巽 SE	離 S	坤 SW
2 Black 二黑	7 Red 七赤	9 Purple 九紫
震 E — 1 White 一白	3 Jade 三碧	5 Yellow 五黃 — 兌 W
6 White 六白	8 White 八白	4 Green 四綠
艮 NE	坎 N	乾 NW

巳 Snake (May 6 - Jun 5) 四月 4th Month

巽 SE	離 S	坤 SW
1 White 一白	6 White 六白	8 White 八白
震 E — 9 Purple 九紫	2 Black 二黑	4 Green 四綠 — 兌 W
5 Yellow 五黃	7 Red 七赤	3 Jade 三碧
艮 NE	坎 N	乾 NW

午 Horse (Jun 6 - July 6) 五月 5th Month

巽 SE	離 S	坤 SW
9 Purple 九紫	5 Yellow 五黃	7 Red 七赤
震 E — 8 White 八白	1 White 一白	3 Jade 三碧 — 兌 W
4 Green 四綠	6 White 六白	2 Black 二黑
艮 NE	坎 N	乾 NW

未 Goat (July 7 - Aug 7) 六月 6th Month

巽 SE	離 S	坤 SW
8 White 八白	4 Green 四綠	6 White 六白
震 E — 7 Red 七赤	9 Purple 九紫	2 Black 二黑 — 兌 W
3 Jade 三碧	5 Yellow 五黃	1 White 一白
艮 NE	坎 N	乾 NW

申 Monkey (Aug 8 - Sept 7) 七月 7th Month

巽 SE	離 S	坤 SW
7 Red 七赤	3 Jade 三碧	5 Yellow 五黃
震 E — 6 White 六白	8 White 八白	1 White 一白 — 兌 W
2 Black 二黑	4 Green 四綠	9 Purple 九紫
艮 NE	坎 N	乾 NW

酉 Rooster (Sept 8 - Oct 7) 八月 8th Month

巽 SE	離 S	坤 SW
6 White 六白	2 Black 二黑	4 Green 四綠
震 E — 5 Yellow 五黃	7 Red 七赤	9 Purple 九紫 — 兌 W
1 White 一白	3 Jade 三碧	8 White 八白
艮 NE	坎 N	乾 NW

戌 Dog (Oct 8 - Nov 6) 九月 9th Month

巽 SE	離 S	坤 SW
5 Yellow 五黃	1 White 一白	3 Jade 三碧
震 E — 4 Green 四綠	6 White 六白	8 White 八白 — 兌 W
9 Purple 九紫	2 Black 二黑	7 Red 七赤
艮 NE	坎 N	乾 NW

亥 Pig (Nov 7 - Dec 6) 十月 10th Month

巽 SE	離 S	坤 SW
4 Green 四綠	9 Purple 九紫	2 Black 二黑
震 E — 3 Jade 三碧	5 Yellow 五黃	7 Red 七赤 — 兌 W
8 White 八白	1 White 一白	6 White 六白
艮 NE	坎 N	乾 NW

子 Rat (Dec 7 - Jan 5) 十一月 11th Month

巽 SE	離 S	坤 SW
3 Jade 三碧	8 White 八白	1 White 一白
震 E — 2 Black 二黑	4 Green 四綠	6 White 六白 — 兌 W
7 Red 七赤	9 Purple 九紫	5 Yellow 五黃
艮 NE	坎 N	乾 NW

丑 Ox (Jan 6 - Feb 3) 十二月 12th Month

巽 SE	離 S	坤 SW
2 Black 二黑	7 Red 七赤	9 Purple 九紫
震 E — 1 White 一白	3 Jade 三碧	5 Yellow 五黃 — 兌 W
6 White 六白	8 White 八白	4 Green 四綠
艮 NE	坎 N	乾 NW

Qi Men Three Nobles 三奇 :

Three Nobles 三奇 / Seasons	乙 Yi	丙 Bing	丁 Ding
立春 **Coming of Spring** Feb 4 - Feb 18	乾 Qian	兌 Dui	艮 Gen
春分 **Spring Equinox** Mar 21 - Apr 4	坎 Kan	坤 Kun	震 Zhen
立夏 **Coming of Summer** May 6 - May 20	坤 Kun	震 Zhen	巽 Xun
夏至 **Summer Solstice** Jun 22 - Jul 6	坤 Kun	坎 Kan	離 Li
立秋 **Coming of Autumn** Aug 8 - Aug 23	巽 Xun	震 Zhen	坤 Kun
秋分 **Autumn Equinox** Sept 23 - Oct 7	離 Li	艮 Gen	兌 Dui
立冬 **Coming of Winter** Nov 7 - Nov 22	艮 Gen	兌 Dui	乾 Qian
冬至 **Winter Solstice** Dec 22 - Jan 5	艮 Gen	離 Li	坎 Kan

壬戌 (Ren Xu) Water Dog

Sectors to Avoid Opening Mountain 開山凶位 :

月 MONTH	月建 Month Establishment	月破 Month Destruction	月剋山家 Month Countering Sitting		陰府太歲 Yin Mansion Grand Duke	
寅 **Tiger** (Feb 4 - Mar 5) 正月 **1st Month**	寅 Yin Tiger	申 Shen Monkey	—		離 Li	乾 Qian
卯 **Rabbit** (Mar 6 - Apr 4) 二月 **2nd Month**	卯 Mao Rabbit	酉 You Rooster	—		震 Zhen	坤 Kun
辰 **Dragon** (Apr 5 - May 5) 三月 **3rd Month**	辰 Chen Dragon	戌 Xu Dog	離 Li	丙 Bing Yang Fire	艮 Gen	巽 Xun
巳 **Snake** (May 6 - Jun 5) 四月 **4th Month**	巳 Si Snake	亥 Hai Pig	壬 Ren Yang Water	乙 Yi Yin Wood	兌 Dui	乾 Qian
午 **Horse** (Jun 6 - July 6) 五月 **5th Month**	午 Wu Horse	子 Zi Rat	水 Water	山 Mountain	坎 Kan	坤 Kun
未 **Goat** (July 7 - Aug 7) 六月 **6th Month**	未 Wei Goat	丑 Chou Ox	土 Earth		乾 Qian	離 Li
申 **Monkey** (Aug 8 - Sept 7) 七月 **7th Month**	申 Shen Monkey	寅 Yin Tiger	震 Zhen	巳 Si Snake	坤 Kun	震 Zhen
酉 **Rooster** (Sept 8 - Oct 7) 八月 **8th Month**	酉 You Rooster	卯 Mao Rabbit	艮 Gen		巽 Xun	艮 Gen
戌 **Dog** (Oct 8 - Nov 6) 九月 **9th Month**	戌 Xu Dog	辰 Chen Dragon	—		乾 Qian	兌 Dui
亥 **Pig** (Nov 7 - Dec 6) 十月 **10th Month**	亥 Hai Pig	巳 Si Snake	—		坤 Kun	坎 Kan
子 **Rat** (Dec 7 - Jan 5) 十一月 **11th Month**	子 Zi Rat	午 Wu Horse	—		離 Li	乾 Qian
丑 **Ox** (Jan 6 - Feb 3) 十二月 **12th Month**	丑 Chou Ox	未 Wei Goat	—		震 Zhen	坤 Kun

Negative Repair / Renovation Sectors 修方凶位 :

月 MONTH	天官符 Heavenly Officer Charm			地官符 Earth Officer Charm			小月建 Small Month Establishment		
寅 Tiger (Feb 4 - Mar 5) 正月 1st Month	丑 Chou Ox	艮 Gen	寅 Yin Tiger	中 Middle			中 Middle		
卯 Rabbit (Mar 6 - Apr 4) 二月 2nd Month	庚 Geng Yang Metal	兑 Dui	辛 Xin Yin Metal	庚 Geng Yang Metal	兑 Dui	辛 Xin Yin Metal	戌 Xu Dog	乾 Qian	亥 Hai Pig
辰 Dragon (Apr 5 - May 5) 三月 3rd Month	戌 Xu Dog	乾 Qian	亥 Hai Pig	戌 Xu Dog	乾 Qian	亥 Hai Pig	庚 Geng Yang Metal	兑 Dui	辛 Xin Yin Metal
巳 Snake (May 6 - Jun 5) 四月 4th Month	中 Middle			中 Middle			丑 Chou Ox	艮 Gen	寅 Yin Tiger
午 Horse (Jun 6 - July 6) 五月 5th Month	庚 Geng Yang Metal	兑 Dui	辛 Xin Yin Metal	辰 Chen Dragon	巽 Xun	巳 Si Snake	丙 Bing Yang Fire	離 Li	丁 Ding Yin Fire
未 Goat (July 7 - Aug 7) 六月 6th Month	戌 Xu Dog	乾 Qian	亥 Hai Pig	甲 Jia Yang Wood	震 Zhen	乙 Yi Yin Wood	壬 Ren Yang Water	坎 Kan	癸 Gui Yin Water
申 Monkey (Aug 8 - Sept 7) 七月 7th Month	中 Middle			未 Wei Goat	坤 Kun	申 Shen Monkey	未 Wei Goat	坤 Kun	申 Shen Monkey
酉 Rooster (Sept 8 - Oct 7) 八月 8th Month	辰 Chen Dragon	巽 Xun	巳 Si Snake	壬 Ren Yang Water	坎 Kan	癸 Gui Yin Water	甲 Jia Yang Wood	震 Zhen	乙 Yi Yin Wood
戌 Dog (Oct 8 - Nov 6) 九月 9th Month	甲 Jia Yang Wood	震 Zhen	乙 Yi Yin Wood	丙 Bing Yang Fire	離 Li	丁 Ding Yin Fire	辰 Chen Dragon	巽 Xun	巳 Si Snake
亥 Pig (Nov 7 - Dec 6) 十月 10th Month	未 Wei Goat	坤 Kun	申 Shen Monkey	丑 Chou Ox	艮 Gen	寅 Yin Tiger	中 Middle		
子 Rat (Dec 7 - Jan 5) 十一月 11th Month	壬 Ren Yang Water	坎 Kan	癸 Gui Yin Water	庚 Geng Yang Metal	兑 Dui	辛 Xin Yin Metal	戌 Xu Dog	乾 Qian	亥 Hai Pig
丑 Ox (Jan 6 - Feb 3) 十二月 12th Month	丙 Bing Yang Fire	離 Li	丁 Ding Yin Fire	戌 Xu Dog	乾 Qian	亥 Hai Pig	庚 Geng Yang Metal	兑 Dui	辛 Xin Yin Metal

Negative Repair / Renovation Sectors 修方凶位 :

月 MONTH	大月建 Big Month Establishment			飛大煞 Flying Great Sha			丙丁獨火 Bing Ding Lonely Fire	
寅 **Tiger** (Feb 4 - Mar 5) 正月 **1st Month**	中 Middle			丙 *Bing* Yang Fire	離 *Li*	丁 *Ding* Yin Fire	離 *Li*	坎 *Kan*
卯 **Rabbit** (Mar 6 - Apr 4) 二月 **2nd Month**	辰 *Chen* Dragon	巽 *Xun*	巳 *Si* Snake	丑 *Chou* Ox	艮 *Gen*	寅 *Yin* Tiger	艮 *Gen*	離 *Li*
辰 **Dragon** (Apr 5 - May 5) 三月 **3rd Month**	甲 *Jia* Yang Wood	震 *Zhen*	乙 *Yi* Yin Wood	庚 *Geng* Yang Metal	兌 *Dui*	辛 *Xin* Yin Metal	兌 *Dui*	艮 *Gen*
巳 **Snake** (May 6 - Jun 5) 四月 **4th Month**	未 *Wei* Goat	坤 *Kun*	申 *Shen* Monkey	戌 *Xu* Dog	乾 *Qian*	亥 *Hai* Pig	乾 *Qian*	兌 *Dui*
午 **Horse** (Jun 6 - July 6) 五月 **5th Month**	壬 *Ren* Yang Water	坎 *Kan*	癸 *Gui* Yin Water	中 Middle			中 Middle	乾 *Qian*
未 **Goat** (July 7 - Aug 7) 六月 **6th Month**	丙 *Bing* Yang Fire	離 *Li*	丁 *Ding* Yin Fire	庚 *Geng* Yang Metal	兌 *Dui*	辛 *Xin* Yin Metal	中 Middle	
申 **Monkey** (Aug 8 - Sept 7) 七月 **7th Month**	丑 *Chou* Ox	艮 *Gen*	寅 *Yin* Tiger	戌 *Xu* Dog	乾 *Qian*	亥 *Hai* Pig	巽 *Xun*	中 Middle
酉 **Rooster** (Sept 8 - Oct 7) 八月 **8th Month**	庚 *Geng* Yang Metal	兌 *Dui*	辛 *Xin* Yin Metal	中 Middle			震 *Zhen*	巽 *Xun*
戌 **Dog** (Oct 8 - Nov 6) 九月 **9th Month**	戌 *Xu* Dog	乾 *Qian*	亥 *Hai* Pig	辰 *Chen* Dragon	巽 *Xun*	巳 *Si* Snake	坤 *Kun*	震 *Zhen*
亥 **Pig** (Nov 7 - Dec 6) 十月 **10th Month**	中 Middle			甲 *Jia* Yang Wood	震 *Zhen*	乙 *Yi* Yin Wood	坎 *Kan*	坤 *Kun*
子 **Rat** (Dec 7 - Jan 5) 十一月 **11th Month**	辰 *Chen* Dragon	巽 *Xun*	巳 *Si* Snake	未 *Wei* Goat	坤 *Kun*	申 *Shen* Monkey	離 *Li*	坎 *Kan*
丑 **Ox** (Jan 6 - Feb 3) 十二月 **12th Month**	甲 *Jiá* Yang Wood	震 *Zhen*	乙 *Yi* Yin Wood	壬 *Ren* Yang Water	坎 *Kan*	癸 *Gui* Yin Water	艮 *Gen*	離 *Li*

Negative Repair / Renovation Sectors 修方凶位 :

月 MONTH	月遊火 Month Wondering Fire	三煞 Monthly 3 Killings		
		劫煞 Robbery Sha	災煞 Calamity Sha	月煞 Month Sha
寅 **Tiger** (Feb 4 - Mar 5) 正月 **1st Month**	乾 Qian	亥 Hai Pig	子 Zi Rat	丑 Chou Ox
卯 **Rabbit** (Mar 6 - Apr 4) 二月 **2nd Month**	兌 Dui	申 Shen Monkey	酉 You Rooster	戌 Xu Dog
辰 **Dragon** (Apr 5 - May 5) 三月 **3rd Month**	艮 Gen	巳 Si Snake	午 Wu Horse	未 Wei Goat
巳 **Snake** (May 6 - Jun 5) 四月 **4th Month**	離 Li	寅 Yin Tiger	卯 Mao Rabbit	辰 Chen Dragon
午 **Horse** (Jun 6 - July 6) 五月 **5th Month**	坎 Kan	亥 Hai Pig	子 Zi Rat	丑 Chou Ox
未 **Goat** (July 7 - Aug 7) 六月 **6th Month**	坤 Kun	申 Shen Monkey	酉 You Rooster	戌 Xu Dog
申 **Monkey** (Aug 8 - Sept 7) 七月 **7th Month**	震 Zhen	巳 Si Snake	午 Wu Horse	未 Wei Goat
酉 **Rooster** (Sept 8 - Oct 7) 八月 **8th Month**	巽 Xun	寅 Yin Tiger	卯 Mao Rabbit	辰 Chen Dragon
戌 **Dog** (Oct 8 - Nov 6) 九月 **9th Month**	中 Middle	亥 Hai Pig	子 Zi Rat	丑 Chou Ox
亥 **Pig** (Nov 7 - Dec 6) 十月 **10th Month**	乾 Qian	申 Shen Monkey	酉 You Rooster	戌 Xu Dog
子 **Rat** (Dec 7 - Jan 5) 十一月 **11th Month**	兌 Dui	巳 Si Snake	午 Wu Horse	未 Wei Goat
丑 **Ox** (Jan 6 - Feb 3) 十二月 **12th Month**	艮 Gen	寅 Yin Tiger	卯 Mao Rabbit	辰 Chen Dragon

Negative Repair / Renovation Sectors 修方凶位 :

月 MONTH	月刑 Month Punishment	月害 Month Harm	月厭 Month Detest
寅 **Tiger** (Feb 4 - Mar 5) 正月 **1st Month**	巳 *Si* Snake	巳 *Si* Snake	戌 *Xu* Dog
卯 **Rabbit** (Mar 6 - Apr 4) 二月 **2nd Month**	子 *Zi* Rat	辰 *Chen* Dragon	酉 *You* Rooster
辰 **Dragon** (Apr 5 - May 5) 三月 **3rd Month**	辰 *Chen* Dragon	卯 *Mao* Rabbit	申 *Shen* Monkey
巳 **Snake** (May 6 - Jun 5) 四月 **4th Month**	申 *Shen* Monkey	寅 *Yin* Tiger	未 *Wei* Goat
午 **Horse** (Jun 6 - July 6) 五月 **5th Month**	午 *Wu* Horse	丑 *Chou* Ox	午 *Wu* Horse
未 **Goat** (July 7 - Aug 7) 六月 **6th Month**	丑 *Chou* Ox	子 *Zi* Rat	巳 *Si* Snake
申 **Monkey** (Aug 8 - Sept 7) 七月 **7th Month**	寅 *Yin* Tiger	亥 *Hai* Pig	辰 *Chen* Dragon
酉 **Rooster** (Sept 8 - Oct 7) 八月 **8th Month**	酉 *You* Rooster	戌 *Xu* Dog	卯 *Mao* Rabbit
戌 **Dog** (Oct 8 - Nov 6) 九月 **9th Month**	未 *Wei* Goat	酉 *You* Rooster	寅 *Yin* Tiger
亥 **Pig** (Nov 7 - Dec 6) 十月 **10th Month**	亥 *Hai* Pig	申 *Shen* Monkey	丑 *Chou* Ox
子 **Rat** (Dec 7 - Jan 5) 十一月 **11th Month**	卯 *Mao* Rabbit	未 *Wei* Goat	子 *Zi* Rat
丑 **Ox** (Jan 6 - Feb 3) 十二月 **12th Month**	戌 *Xu* Dog	午 *Wu* Horse	亥 *Hai* Pig

癸丑 (Gui Chou)
Water Ox

Heavenly Stem 天干	癸 Yin Water (陰水)
Earthly Branch 地支	丑 Ox (Yin Earth 陰土)
Hidden Stem 藏干	己 Yin Earth, 癸 Yin Water, 辛 Yin Metal
Na Yin 納音	桑柘木 Wood from mulberry tree
Grand Duke 太歲	丑 Ox
Xuan Kong Five Element 玄空五行	6 水 Water
Gua Name 卦名	䷕ 山火賁 Beauty
Xuan Kong Period Luck 玄空卦運	8

Annual Positive Stars for Opening Mountain, Establishing Facing and Commencing Repairs 開山立向修方吉星:

歲德 Duke Virtue	戊 Wu Yang Earth
歲德合 Duke Virtue Combo	癸 Gui Yin Water
歲枝德 Duke Branch Virtue	午 Wu Horse
陽貴人 Yang Nobleman	巳 Si Snake
陰貴人 Yin Nobleman	卯 Mao Rabbit
歲祿 Duke Prosperous	子 Zi Rat
歲馬 Duke Horse	亥 Hai Pig
奏書 Decree	乾 Qian
博士 Professor	巽 Xun

Annual Negative Stars for Opening Mountain, Establishing Facing and Commencing Repairs 開山立向修方凶星：

太歲 Grand Duke	歲破 Year Breaker	三煞 Three Killings			坐煞向煞 Sitting Sha Facing Sha				浮天空亡 Floating Heaven Emptiness	
丑 Chou Ox	未 Wei Goat	寅 Yin Tiger	卯 Mao Rabbit	辰 Chen Dragon	甲 Jia Yang Wood	乙 Yi Yin Wood	庚 Geng Yang Metal	辛 Xin Yin Metal	坤 Kun	乙 Yi Yin Wood

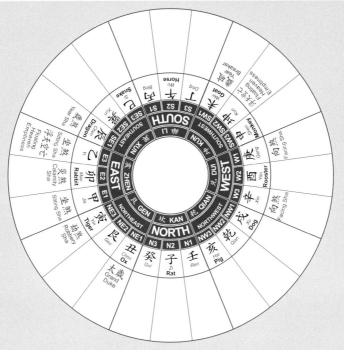

Annual San Yuan Purple White Stars 三元紫白九星：

上元 Upper Period — Period 1, 2, 3

巽SE	離S	坤SW
5	1	3
震E 4	6 癸丑 Gui Chou Water Ox	兌W 8
艮NE 9	坎N 2	乾NW 7

中元 Middle Period — Period 4, 5, 6

巽SE	離S	坤SW
8	4	6
震E 7	9 癸丑 Gui Chou Water Ox	兌W 2
艮NE 3	坎N 5	乾NW 1

下元 Lower Period — Period 7, 8, 9

巽SE	離S	坤SW
2	7	9
震E 1	3 癸丑 Gui Chou Water Ox	兌W 5
艮NE 6	坎N 8	乾NW 4

Mountain Covering Yellow Path 蓋山黃道：

貪狼 *Tan Lang* **Greedy Wolf**		巨門 *Ju Men* **Huge Door**		武曲 *Wu Qu* **Military Arts**				文曲 *Wen Qu* **Literary Arts**			
艮 *Gen* NE2	丙 *Bing* S1	巽 *Xun* SE2	辛 *Xin* W3	兌 *Dui* W2	丁 *Ding* S3	巳 *Si* SE3	丑 *Chou* NE1	離 *Li* S2	壬 *Ren* N1	寅 *Yin* NE3	戌 *Xu* NW1

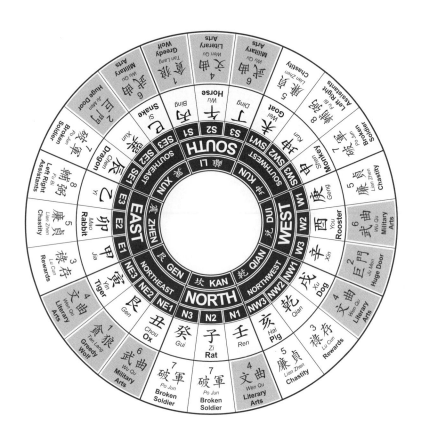

Heaven Penetrating Force 通天竅:			
三合前方 **Facing Three Harmony**	乾亥 Qian Hai	壬子 Ren Zi	癸丑 Gui Chou
三合後方 **Sitting Three Harmony**	巽巳 Xun Si	丙午 Bing Wu	丁未 Ding Wei

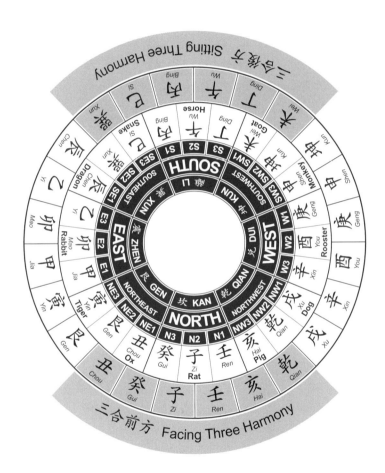

Moving Horse Six Ren Assessment 走馬六壬:

神后 *Shen Hou* **Holy Empress**	功曹 *Gong Cao* **Marshall**	天罡 *Tian Gang* **Heavenly Dipper**	勝光 *Sheng Guang* **Subliminal Bright**	傳送 *Chuan Song* **Great General**	河魁 *He Kui* **River Scholar**
乾亥 *Qian Hai*	癸丑 *Gui Chou*	甲卯 *Jia Mao*	巽巳 *Xun Si*	丁未 *Ding Wei*	庚酉 *Geng You*

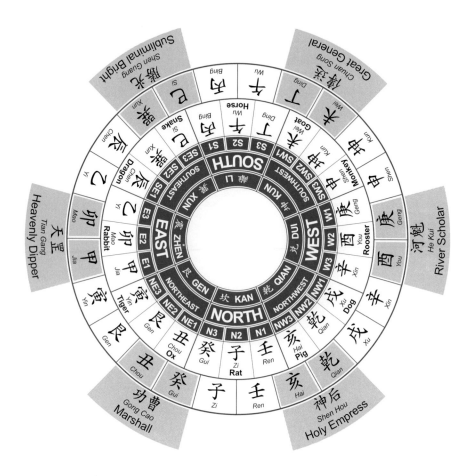

Four Advantages Three Cycles Star Plate 四利三元:

太陽 *Tai Yang* **Sun**	太陰 *Tai Yin* **Moon**	龍德 *Long De* **Dragon Virtue**	福德 *Fu De* **Fortune Virtue**
寅 *Yin* **Tiger**	辰 *Chen* **Dragon**	申 *Shen* **Monkey**	戌 *Xu* **Dog**

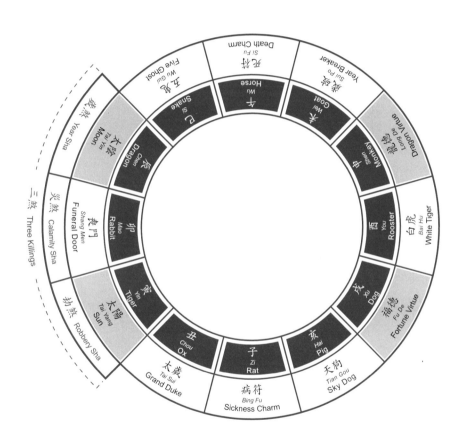

Negative Sectors For Opening Mountain 開山凶位：

年剋山家 Year Countering Sitting

甲	寅	辰	巽	戌	坎	辛	申	丑	癸	坤	庚	未
Jia	Yin	Chen	Xun	Xu	Kan	Xin	Shen	Chou	Gui	Kun	Geng	Wei
E1	NE3	SE1	SE2	NW1	N2	W3	SW3	NE1	N3	SW2	W1	SW1

陰府太歲 Yin Fu Tai Sui **Yin Mansion Grand Duke**		六害 Liu Hai **Six Harm**	死符 Si Fu **Death Charm**	炙退 Zhi Tui **Roasting Star**
震 Zhen E2	坤 Kun SW2	午 Wu S2	午 Wu S2	子 Zi N2

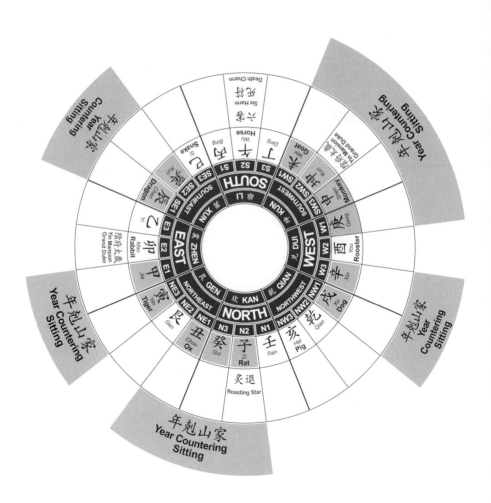

Negative Directions to Establish Facing 立向凶方：

巡山羅喉 *Xun Shan Luo Hou* **Mountain Patrol Luo Hou Star**	病符 *Bing Fu* **Sickness Charm**
艮 *Gen* **NE2**	子 *Zi* **N2**

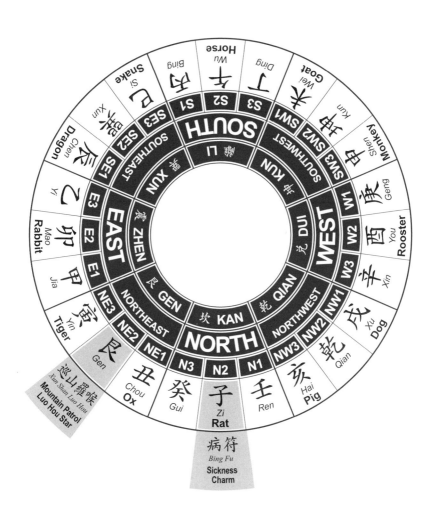

Negative Repair / Renovation Sectors Table 修方凶位表：

天官符 Heavenly Officer Charm	申 Shen Monkey	飛廉 Flying Chaste	酉 You Rooster
地官符 Earthly Officer Charm	巳 Si Snake	喪門 Funeral Door	卯 Mao Rabbit
大煞 Great Sha	酉 You Rooster	弔客 Suspended Guest	亥 Hai Pig
大將軍 Big General	酉 You Rooster	白虎 White Tiger	酉 You Rooster
力士 Strong Man	艮 Gen	金神 Golden God	申 Shen Monkey 酉 You Rooster 子 Zi Rat 丑 Chou Ox
蠶室 Silkworm Room	坤 Kun		
蠶官 Silkworm Officer	未 Wei Goat		
蠶命 Silkworm Life	申 Shen Monkey		
歲刑 Duke Punishment	戌 Xu Dog	獨火 Lonely Fire	震 Zhen
黃幡 Yellow Flag	丑 Chou Ox	五鬼 Five Ghost	卯 Mao Rabbit
豹尾 Leopard Tail	未 Wei Goat	破敗五鬼 Destructive Five Ghost	艮 Gen

Negative Repair / Renovation Sectors Diagram 修方凶位圖：

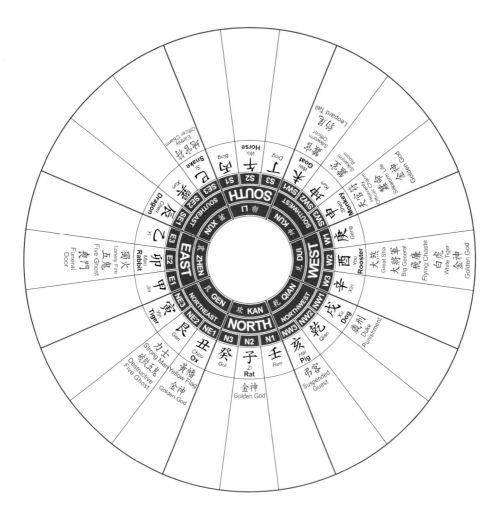

12-Month Auxiliary Stars Reference Table :
癸丑年十二月，開山立向修方星表

Positive Monthly Stars 吉星方

月 MONTH	寅 Tiger (Feb 4 - Mar 5) 正月 1st Month	卯 Rabbit (Mar 6 - Apr 4) 二月 2nd Month	辰 Dragon (Apr 5 - May 5) 三月 3rd Month	巳 Snake (May 6 - Jun 5) 四月 4th Month	午 Horse (Jun 6 - July 6) 五月 5th Month	未 Goat (July 7 - Aug 7) 六月 6th Month
天道 Heavenly Path	南 South	西南 Southwest	北 North	西 West	西北 Northwest	東 East
天德 Heavenly Virtue	丁 Ding Yin Fire	坤 Kun (申)	壬 Ren Yang Water	辛 Xin Yin Metal	乾 Qian (亥)	甲 Jia Yang Wood
天德合 Heavenly Virtue Combo	壬 Ren Yang Water	(巳)	丁 Ding Yin Fire	丙 Bing Yang Fire	(寅)	己 Ji Yin Earth
月德 Monthly Virtue	丙 Bing Yang Fire	甲 Jia Yang Wood	壬 Ren Yang Water	庚 Geng Yang Metal	丙 Bing Yang Fire	甲 Jia Yang Wood
月德合 Monthly Virtue Combo	辛 Xin Yin Metal	己 Ji Yin Earth	丁 Ding Yin Fire	乙 Yi Yin Wood	辛 Xin Yin Metal	己 Ji Yin Earth
月空 Month Emptiness	壬 Ren Yang Water	庚 Geng Yang Metal	丙 Bing Yang Fire	甲 Jia Yang Wood	壬 Ren Yang Water	庚 Geng Yang Metal
陽貴人 Yang Nobleman	艮 Gen	兌 Dui	乾 Qian	中 Middle	坎 Kan	離 Li
陰貴人 Yin Nobleman	乾 Qian	中 Middle	坎 Kan	離 Li	艮 Gen	兌 Dui
飛天祿 Flying Heavenly Wealth	乾 Qian	中 Middle	巽 Xun	震 Zhen	坤 Kun	坎 Kan
飛天馬 Flying Heavenly Horse	中 Middle	巽 Xun	震 Zhen	坤 Kun	坎 Kan	離 Li

12-Month Auxiliary Stars Reference Table :
癸丑年十二月，開山立向修方星表

申 Monkey (Aug 8 - Sept 7) 七月 **7th Month**	酉 Rooster (Sept 8 - Oct 7) 八月 **8th Month**	戌 Dog (Oct 8 - Nov 6) 九月 **9th Month**	亥 Pig (Nov 7 - Dec 6) 十月 **10th Month**	子 Rat (Dec 7 - Jan 5) 十一月 **11th Month**	丑 Ox (Jan 6 - Feb 3) 十二月 **12th Month**	月 **MONTH**
北 North	東北 Northeast	南 South	東 East	東南 Southeast	西 West	天道 **Heavenly Path**
癸 *Gui* Yin Water	艮 *Gen* (寅)	丙 *Bing* Yang Fire	乙 *Yi* Yin Wood	巽 *Xun* (巳)	庚 *Geng* Yang Metal	天德 **Heavenly Virtue**
戊 *Wu* Yang Earth	(亥)	辛 *Xin* Yin Metal	庚 *Geng* Yang Metal	(申)	乙 *Yi* Yin Wood	天德合 **Heavenly Virtue Combo**
壬 *Ren* Yang Water	庚 *Geng* Yang Metal	丙 *Bing* Yang Fire	甲 *Jia* Yang Wood	壬 *Ren* Yang Water	庚 *Geng* Yang Metal	月德 **Monthly Virtue**
丁 *Ding* Yin Fire	乙 *Yi* Yin Wood	辛 *Xin* Yin Metal	己 *Ji* Yin Earth	丁 *Ding* Yin Fire	乙 *Yi* Yin Wood	月德合 **Monthly Virtue Combo**
丙 *Bing* Yang Fire	甲 *Jia* Yang Wood	壬 *Ren* Yang Water	庚 *Geng* Yang Metal	丙 *Bing* Yang Fire	甲 *Jia* Yang Wood	月空 **Month Emptiness**
艮 *Gen*	兌 *Dui*	乾 *Qian*	中 **Middle**	巽 *Xun*	震 *Zhen*	陽貴人 **Yang Nobleman**
乾 *Qian*	中 **Middle**	巽 *Xun*	震 *Zhen*	坤 *Kun*	坎 *Kan*	陰貴人 **Yin Nobleman**
離 *Li*	艮 *Gen*	兌 *Dui*	乾 *Qian*	中 **Middle**	坎 *Kan*	飛天祿 **Flying Heavenly Wealth**
艮 *Gen*	兌 *Dui*	乾 *Qian*	中 **Middle**	坎 *Kan*	離 *Li*	飛天馬 **Flying Heavenly Horse**

Monthly Purple White Stars 月紫白九星 :

寅 Tiger (Feb 4 - Mar 5) 正月 1st Month

巽 SE	離 S	坤 SW	
4 Green 四綠	9 Purple 九紫	2 Black 二黑	
震 E 3 Jade 三碧	5 Yellow 五黃	7 Red 七赤	兌 W
8 White 八白	1 White 一白	6 White 六白	
艮 NE	坎 N	乾 NW	

卯 Rabbit (Mar 6 - Apr 4) 二月 2nd Month

巽 SE	離 S	坤 SW	
3 Jade 三碧	8 White 八白	1 White 一白	
震 E 2 Black 二黑	4 Green 四綠	6 White 六白	兌 W
7 Red 七赤	9 Purple 九紫	5 Yellow 五黃	
艮 NE	坎 N	乾 NW	

辰 Dragon (Apr 5 - May 5) 三月 3rd Month

巽 SE	離 S	坤 SW	
2 Black 二黑	7 Red 七赤	9 Purple 九紫	
震 E 1 White 一白	3 Jade 三碧	5 Yellow 五黃	兌 W
6 White 六白	8 White 八白	4 Green 四綠	
艮 NE	坎 N	乾 NW	

巳 Snake (May 6 - Jun 5) 四月 4th Month

巽 SE	離 S	坤 SW	
1 White 一白	6 White 六白	8 White 八白	
震 E 9 Purple 九紫	2 Black 二黑	4 Green 四綠	兌 W
5 Yellow 五黃	7 Red 七赤	3 Jade 三碧	
艮 NE	坎 N	乾 NW	

午 Horse (Jun 6 - July 6) 五月 5th Month

巽 SE	離 S	坤 SW	
9 Purple 九紫	5 Yellow 五黃	7 Red 七赤	
震 E 8 White 八白	1 White 一白	3 Jade 三碧	兌 W
4 Green 四綠	6 White 六白	2 Black 二黑	
艮 NE	坎 N	乾 NW	

未 Goat (July 7 - Aug 7) 六月 6th Month

巽 SE	離 S	坤 SW	
8 White 八白	4 Green 四綠	6 White 六白	
震 E 7 Red 七赤	9 Purple 九紫	2 Black 二黑	兌 W
3 Jade 三碧	5 Yellow 五黃	1 White 一白	
艮 NE	坎 N	乾 NW	

申 Monkey (Aug 8 - Sept 7) 七月 7th Month

巽 SE	離 S	坤 SW	
7 Red 七赤	3 Jade 三碧	5 Yellow 五黃	
震 E 6 White 六白	8 White 八白	1 White 一白	兌 W
2 Black 二黑	4 Green 四綠	9 Purple 九紫	
艮 NE	坎 N	乾 NW	

酉 Rooster (Sept 8 - Oct 7) 八月 8th Month

巽 SE	離 S	坤 SW	
6 White 六白	2 Black 二黑	4 Green 四綠	
震 E 5 Yellow 五黃	7 Red 七赤	9 Purple 九紫	兌 W
1 White 一白	3 Jade 三碧	8 White 八白	
艮 NE	坎 N	乾 NW	

戌 Dog (Oct 8 - Nov 6) 九月 9th Month

巽 SE	離 S	坤 SW	
5 Yellow 五黃	1 White 一白	3 Jade 三碧	
震 E 4 Green 四綠	6 White 六白	8 White 八白	兌 W
9 Purple 九紫	2 Black 二黑	7 Red 七赤	
艮 NE	坎 N	乾 NW	

亥 Pig (Nov 7 - Dec 6) 十月 10th Month

巽 SE	離 S	坤 SW	
4 Green 四綠	9 Purple 九紫	2 Black 二黑	
震 E 3 Jade 三碧	5 Yellow 五黃	7 Red 七赤	兌 W
8 White 八白	1 White 一白	6 White 六白	
艮 NE	坎 N	乾 NW	

子 Rat (Dec 7 - Jan 5) 十一月 11th Month

巽 SE	離 S	坤 SW	
3 Jade 三碧	8 White 八白	1 White 一白	
震 E 2 Black 二黑	4 Green 四綠	6 White 六白	兌 W
7 Red 七赤	9 Purple 九紫	5 Yellow 五黃	
艮 NE	坎 N	乾 NW	

丑 Ox (Jan 6 - Feb 3) 十二月 12th Month

巽 SE	離 S	坤 SW	
2 Black 二黑	7 Red 七赤	9 Purple 九紫	
震 E 1 White 一白	3 Jade 三碧	5 Yellow 五黃	兌 W
6 White 六白	8 White 八白	4 Green 四綠	
艮 NE	坎 N	乾 NW	

Qi Men Three Nobles 三奇 :

Three Nobles 三奇 / Seasons	乙 Yi	丙 Bing	丁 Ding
立春 **Coming of Spring** Feb 4 - Feb 18	巽 Xun	中 **Middle**	乾 Qian
春分 **Spring Equinox** Mar 21 - Apr 4	艮 Gen	離 Li	坎 Kan
立夏 **Coming of Summer** May 6 - May 20	離 Li	坎 Kan	坤 Kun
夏至 **Summer Solstice** Jun 22 - Jul 6	巽 Xun	震 Zhen	坤 Kun
立秋 **Coming of Autumn** Aug 8 - Aug 23	乾 Qian	中 **Middle**	巽 Xun
秋分 **Autumn Equinox** Sept 23 - Oct 7	坤 Kun	坎 Kan	離 Li
立冬 **Coming of Winter** Nov 7 - Nov 22	坎 Kan	離 Li	艮 Gen
冬至 **Winter Solstice** Dec 22 - Jan 5	乾 Qian	兌 Dui	艮 Gen

Sectors to Avoid Opening Mountain 開山凶位 :

月 MONTH	月建 Month Establishment	月破 Month Destruction	月剋山家 Month Countering Sitting		陰府太歲 Yin Charm Grand Duke	
寅 **Tiger** (Feb 4 - Mar 5) 正月 **1st Month**	寅 *Yin* Tiger	申 *Shen* Monkey	震 *Zhen*	巳 *Si* Snake	艮 *Gen*	巽 *Xun*
卯 **Rabbit** (Mar 6 - Apr 4) 二月 **2nd Month**	卯 *Mao* Rabbit	酉 *You* Rooster	艮 *Gen*		兌 *Dui*	乾 *Qian*
辰 **Dragon** (Apr 5 - May 5) 三月 **3rd Month**	辰 *Chen* Dragon	戌 *Xu* Dog	離 *Li* S2	丙 *Bing* Yang Fire	坎 *Kan*	坤 *Kun*
巳 **Snake** (May 6 - Jun 5) 四月 **4th Month**	巳 *Si* Snake	亥 *Hai* Pig	壬 *Ren* Yang Water	乙 *Yi* Yin Wood	乾 *Qian*	離 *Li*
午 **Horse** (Jun 6 - July 6) 五月 **5th Month**	午 *Wu* Horse	子 *Zi* Rat	–		坤 *Kun*	震 *Zhen*
未 **Goat** (July 7 - Aug 7) 六月 **6th Month**	未 *Wei* Goat	丑 *Chou* Ox	–		巽 *Xun*	艮 *Gen*
申 **Monkey** (Aug 8 - Sept 7) 七月 **7th Month**	申 *Shen* Monkey	寅 *Yin* Tiger	水 Water	山 Mountain	乾 *Qian*	兌 *Dui*
酉 **Rooster** (Sept 8 - Oct 7) 八月 **8th Month**	酉 *You* Rooster	卯 *Mao* Rabbit	土 Earth		坤 *Kun*	坎 *Kan*
戌 **Dog** (Oct 8 - Nov 6) 九月 **9th Month**	戌 *Xu* Dog	辰 *Chen* Dragon	震 *Zhen*	巳 *Si* Snake	離 *Li*	乾 *Qian*
亥 **Pig** (Nov 7 - Dec 6) 十月 **10th Month**	亥 *Hai* Pig	巳 *Si* Snake	艮 *Gen*		震 *Zhen*	坤 *Kun*
子 **Rat** (Dec 7 - Jan 5) 十一月 **11th Month**	子 *Zi* Rat	午 *Wu* Horse	–		艮 *Gen*	巽 *Xun*
丑 **Ox** (Jan 6 - Feb 3) 十二月 **12th Month**	丑 *Chou* Ox	未 *Wei* Goat	–		兌 *Dui*	乾 *Qian*

Negative Repair / Renovation Sectors 修方凶位 :

月 MONTH	天官符 Heavenly Officer Charm			地官符 Earth Officer Charm			小月建 Small Month Establishment		
寅 **Tiger** (Feb 4 - Mar 5) 正月 1st Month	未 Wei Goat	坤 Kun	申 Shen Monkey	丑 Chou Ox	艮 Gen	寅 Yin Tiger	丙 Bing Yang Fire	離 Li	丁 Ding Yin Fire
卯 **Rabbit** (Mar 6 - Apr 4) 二月 2nd Month	壬 Ren Yang Water	坎 Kan	癸 Gui Yin Water	庚 Geng Yang Metal	兑 Dui	辛 Xin Yin Metal	壬 Ren Yang Water	坎 Kan	癸 Gui Yin Water
辰 **Dragon** (Apr 5 - May 5) 三月 3rd Month	丙 Bing Yang Fire	離 Li	丁 Ding Yin Fire	戌 Xu Dog	乾 Qian	亥 Hai Pig	未 Wei Goat	坤 Kun	申 Shen Monkey
巳 **Snake** (May 6 - Jun 5) 四月 4th Month	丑 Chou Ox	艮 Gen	寅 Yin Tiger	中 Middle			甲 Jia Yang Wood	震 Zhen	乙 Yi Yin Wood
午 **Horse** (Jun 6 - July 6) 五月 5th Month	庚 Geng Yang Metal	兑 Dui	辛 Xin Yin Metal	庚 Geng Yang Metal	兑 Dui	辛 Xin Yin Metal	辰 Chen Dragon	巽 Xun	巳 Si Snake
未 **Goat** (July 7 - Aug 7) 六月 6th Month	戌 Xu Dog	乾 Qian	亥 Hai Pig	戌 Xu Dog	乾 Qian	亥 Hai Pig	中 Middle		
申 **Monkey** (Aug 8 - Sept 7) 七月 7th Month	中 Middle			中 Middle			戌 Xu Dog	乾 Qian	亥 Hai Pig
酉 **Rooster** (Sept 8 - Oct 7) 八月 8th Month	庚 Geng Yang Metal	兑 Dui	辛 Xin Yin Metal	辰 Chen Dragon	巽 Xun	巳 Si Snake	庚 Geng Yang Metal	兑 Dui	辛 Xin Yin Metal
戌 **Dog** (Oct 8 - Nov 6) 九月 9th Month	戌 Xu Dog	乾 Qian	亥 Hai Pig	甲 Jia Yang Wood	震 Zhen	乙 Yi Yin Wood	丑 Chou Ox	艮 Gen	寅 Yin Tiger
亥 **Pig** (Nov 7 - Dec 6) 十月 10th Month	中 Middle			未 Wei Goat	坤 Kun	申 Shen Monkey	丙 Bing Yang Fire	離 Li	丁 Ding Yin Fire
子 **Rat** (Dec 7 - Jan 5) 十一月 11th Month	辰 Chen Dragon	巽 Xun	巳 Si Snake	壬 Ren Yang Water	坎 Kan	癸 Gui Yin Water	壬 Ren Yang Water	坎 Kan	癸 Gui Yin Water
丑 **Ox** (Jan 6 - Feb 3) 十二月 12th Month	甲 Jia Yang Wood	震 Zhen	乙 Yi Yin Wood	丙 Bing Yang Fire	離 Li	丁 Ding Yin Fire	未 Wei Goat	坤 Kun	申 Shen Monkey

Negative Repair / Renovation Sectors 修方凶位 :

月 MONTH	大月建 Big Month Establishment			飛大煞 Flying Great Sha			丙丁獨火 Bing Ding Lonely Fire	
寅 **Tiger** (Feb 4 - Mar 5) 正月 **1st Month**	中 Middle			甲 Jia Yang Wood	震 Zhen	乙 Yi Yin Wood	兌 Dui	艮 Gen
卯 **Rabbit** (Mar 6 - Apr 4) 二月 **2nd Month**	辰 Chen Dragon	巽 Xun	巳 Si Snake	未 Wei Goat	坤 Kun	申 Shen Monkey	乾 Qian	兌 Dui
辰 **Dragon** (Apr 5 - May 5) 三月 **3rd Month**	甲 Jia Yang Wood	震 Zhen	乙 Yi Yin Wood	壬 Ren Yang Water	坎 Kan	癸 Gui Yin Water	中 Middle	乾 Qian
巳 **Snake** (May 6 - Jun 5) 四月 **4th Month**	未 Wei Goat	坤 Kun	申 Shen Monkey	丙 Bing Yang Fire	離 Li	丁 Ding Yin Fire	中 Middle	
午 **Horse** (Jun 6 - July 6) 五月 **5th Month**	壬 Ren Yang Water	坎 Kan	癸 Gui Yin Water	丑 Chou Ox	艮 Gen	寅 Yin Tiger	巽 Xun	中 Middle
未 **Goat** (July 7 - Aug 7) 六月 **6th Month**	丙 Bing Yang Fire	離 Li	丁 Ding Yin Fire	庚 Geng Yang Metal	兌 Dui	辛 Xin Yin Metal	震 Zhen	巽 Xun
申 **Monkey** (Aug 8 - Sept 7) 七月 **7th Month**	丑 Chou Ox	艮 Gen	寅 Yin Tiger	戌 Xu Dog	乾 Qian	亥 Hai Pig	坤 Kun	震 Zhen
酉 **Rooster** (Sept 8 - Oct 7) 八月 **8th Month**	庚 Geng Yang Metal	兌 Dui	辛 Xin Yin Metal	中 Middle			坎 Kan	坤 Kun
戌 **Dog** (Oct 8 - Nov 6) 九月 **9th Month**	戌 Xu Dog	乾 Qian	亥 Hai Pig	庚 Geng Yang Metal	兌 Dui	辛 Xin Yin Metal	離 Li	坎 Kan
亥 **Pig** (Nov 7 - Dec 6) 十月 **10th Month**	中 Middle			戌 Xu Dog	乾 Qian	亥 Hai Pig	艮 Gen	離 Li
子 **Rat** (Dec 7 - Jan 5) 十一月 **11th Month**	辰 Chen Dragon	巽 Xun	巳 Si Snake	中 Middle			兌 Dui	艮 Gen
丑 **Ox** (Jan 6 - Feb 3) 十二月 **12th Month**	甲 Jia Yang Wood	震 Zhen	乙 Yi Yin Wood	辰 Chen Dragon	巽 Xun	巳 Si Snake	乾 Qian	兌 Dui

Negative Repair / Renovation Sectors 修方凶位 :

月 MONTH	月遊火 Month Wondering Fire	三煞 Monthly 3 Killings		
		劫煞 Robbery Sha	災煞 Calamity Sha	月煞 Month Sha
寅 Tiger (Feb 4 - Mar 5) 正月 1st Month	艮 Gen	亥 Hai Pig	子 Zi Rat	丑 Chou Ox
卯 Rabbit (Mar 6 - Apr 4) 二月 2nd Month	離 Li	申 Shen Monkey	酉 You Rooster	戌 Xu Dog
辰 Dragon (Apr 5 - May 5) 三月 3rd Month	坎 Kan	巳 Si Snake	午 Wu Horse	未 Wei Goat
巳 Snake (May 6 - Jun 5) 四月 4th Month	坤 Kun	寅 Yin Tiger	卯 Mao Rabbit	辰 Chen Dragon
午 Horse (Jun 6 - July 6) 五月 5th Month	震 Zhen	亥 Hai Pig	子 Zi Rat	丑 Chou Ox
未 Goat (July 7 - Aug 7) 六月 6th Month	巽 Xun	申 Shen Monkey	酉 You Rooster	戌 Xu Dog
申 Monkey (Aug 8 - Sept 7) 七月 7th Month	中 Middle	巳 Si Snake	午 Wu Horse	未 Wei Goat
酉 Rooster (Sept 8 - Oct 7) 八月 8th Month	乾 Qian	寅 Yin Tiger	卯 Mao Rabbit	辰 Chen Dragon
戌 Dog (Oct 8 - Nov 6) 九月 9th Month	兌 Dui	亥 Hai Pig	子 Zi Rat	丑 Chou Ox
亥 Pig (Nov 7 - Dec 6) 十月 10th Month	艮 Gen	申 Shen Monkey	酉 You Rooster	戌 Xu Dog
子 Rat (Dec 7 - Jan 5) 十一月 11th Month	離 Li	巳 Si Snake	午 Wu Horse	未 Wei Goat
丑 Ox (Jan 6 - Feb 3) 十二月 12th Month	坎 Kan	寅 Yin Tiger	卯 Mao Rabbit	辰 Chen Dragon

Negative Repair / Renovation Sectors 修方凶位 :

月 MONTH	月刑 Month Punishment	月害 Month Harm	月厭 Month Detest
寅 **Tiger** (Feb 4 - Mar 5) 正月 **1st Month**	巳 Si Snake	巳 Si Snake	戌 Xu Dog
卯 **Rabbit** (Mar 6 - Apr 4) 二月 **2nd Month**	子 Zi Rat	辰 Chen Dragon	酉 You Rooster
辰 **Dragon** (Apr 5 - May 5) 三月 **3rd Month**	辰 Chen Dragon	卯 Mao Rabbit	申 Shen Monkey
巳 **Snake** (May 6 - Jun 5) 四月 **4th Month**	申 Shen Monkey	寅 Yin Tiger	未 Wei Goat
午 **Horse** (Jun 6 - July 6) 五月 **5th Month**	午 Wu Horse	丑 Chou Ox	午 Wu Horse
未 **Goat** (July 7 - Aug 7) 六月 **6th Month**	丑 Chou Ox	子 Zi Rat	巳 Si Snake
申 **Monkey** (Aug 8 - Sept 7) 七月 **7th Month**	寅 Yin Tiger	亥 Hai Pig	辰 Chen Dragon
酉 **Rooster** (Sept 8 - Oct 7) 八月 **8th Month**	酉 You Rooster	戌 Xu Dog	卯 Mao Rabbit
戌 **Dog** (Oct 8 - Nov 6) 九月 **9th Month**	未 Wei Goat	酉 You Rooster	寅 Yin Tiger
亥 **Pig** (Nov 7 - Dec 6) 十月 **10th Month**	亥 Hai Pig	申 Shen Monkey	丑 Chou Ox
子 **Rat** (Dec 7 - Jan 5) 十一月 **11th Month**	卯 Mao Rabbit	未 Wei Goat	子 Zi Rat
丑 **Ox** (Jan 6 - Feb 3) 十二月 **12th Month**	戌 Xu Dog	午 Wu Horse	亥 Hai Pig

癸卯 (Gui Mao)
Water Rabbit

Heavenly Stem 天干	癸 Yin Water (陰水)
Earthly Branch 地支	卯 Rabbit (Yin Wood 陰木)
Hidden Stem 藏干	乙 Yin Wood
Na Yin 納音	金箔金 Metal from foils
Grand Duke 太歲	卯 Rabbit
Xuan Kong Five Element 玄空五行	8 木 Wood
Gua Name 卦名	䷵ 雷澤歸妹 Marrying Maiden
Xuan Kong Period Luck 玄空卦運	7

Annual Positive Stars for Opening Mountain, Establishing Facing and Commencing Repairs 開山立向修方吉星：

歲德 Duke Virtue	戊 Wu Yang Earth
歲德合 Duke Virtue Combo	癸 Gui Yin Water
歲枝德 Duke Branch Virtue	申 Shen Monkey
陽貴人 Yang Nobleman	巳 Si Snake
陰貴人 Yin Nobleman	卯 Mao Rabbit
歲祿 Duke Prosperous	子 Zi Rat
歲馬 Duke Horse	巳 Si Snake
奏書 Decree	艮 Gen
博士 Professor	坤 Kun

Annual Negative Stars for Opening Mountain, Establishing Facing and Commencing Repairs 開山立向修方凶星：

太歲 Grand Duke	歲破 Year Breaker	三煞 Three Killings			坐煞向煞 Sitting Sha Facing Sha				浮天空亡 Floating Heaven Emptiness	
卯 Mao Rabbit	酉 You Rooster	申 Shen Monkey	酉 You Rooster	戌 Xu Dog	庚 Geng Yang Metal	辛 Xin Yin Metal	甲 Jia Yang Wood	乙 Yi Yin Wood	坤 Kun	乙 Yi Yin Wood

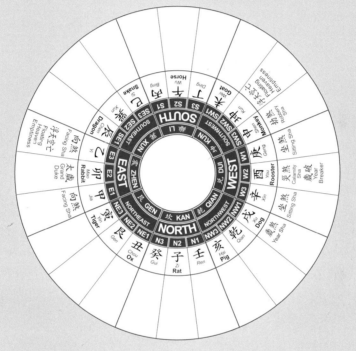

Annual San Yuan Purple White Stars 三元紫白九星：

上元 Upper Period Period 1, 2, 3			中元 Middle Period Period 4, 5, 6			下元 Lower Period Period 7, 8, 9		
巽SE	離S	坤SW	巽SE	離S	坤SW	巽SE	離S	坤SW
6	2	4	9	5	7	3	8	1
震E 5	7 癸卯 Gui Mao Water Rabbit	兌W 9	震E 8	1 癸卯 Gui Mao Water Rabbit	兌W 3	震E 2	4 癸卯 Gui Mao Water Rabbit	兌W 6
艮NE 1	坎N 3	乾NW 8	艮NE 4	坎N 6	乾NW 2	艮NE 7	坎N 9	乾NW 5

Mountain Covering Yellow Path 蓋山黃道:

貪狼 *Tan Lang* **Greedy Wolf**		巨門 *Ju Men* **Huge Door**				武曲 *Wu Qu* **Military Arts**		文曲 *Wen Qu* **Literary Arts**	
乾 *Qian* NW2	甲 *Jia* E1	離 *Li* S1	壬 *Ren* N1	寅 *Yin* NE3	戌 *Xu* NW1	坤 *Kun* SW2	乙 *Yi* E3	巽 *Xun* SE2	辛 *Xin* W3

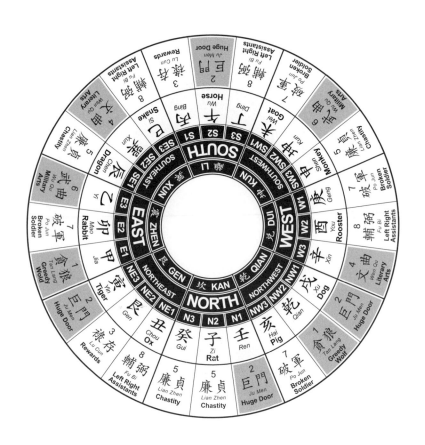

Heaven Penetrating Force 通天竅:

三合前方 Facing Three Harmony	巽巳 Xun Si	丙午 Bing Wu	丁未 Ding Wei
三合後方 Sitting Three Harmony	乾亥 Qian Hai	壬子 Ren Zi	癸丑 Gui Chou

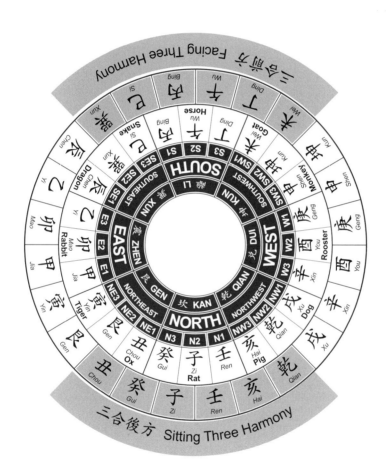

Moving Horse Six Ren Assessment 走馬六壬：

神后 Shen Hou Holy Empress	功曹 Gong Cao Marshall	天罡 Tian Gang Heavenly Dipper	勝光 Sheng Guang Subliminal Bright	傳送 Chuan Song Great General	河魁 He Kui River Scholar
庚酉 Geng You	乾亥 Qian Hai	癸丑 Gui Chou	甲卯 Jia mao	巽巳 Xun Si	丁未 Ding Wei

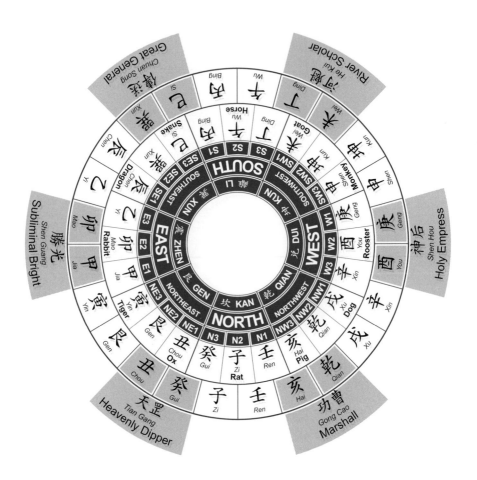

Four Advantages Three Cycles Star Plate 四利三元：

太陽 *Tai Yang* **Sun**	太陰 *Tai Yin* **Moon**	龍德 *Long De* **Dragon Virtue**	福德 *Fu De* **Fortune Virtue**
辰 *Chen* Dragon	午 *Wu* Horse	戌 *Xu* Dog	子 *Zi* Rat

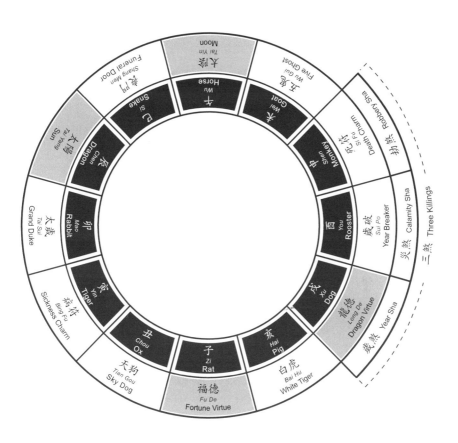

Negative Sectors For Opening Mountain 開山凶位：

年剋山家 Year Countering Sitting

乾	亥	兌	丁
Qian	*Hai*	*Dui*	*Ding*
NW2	NW3	W2	S3

陰府太歲 *Yin Fu Tai Sui* **Yin Mansion Grand Duke**	六害 *Liu Hai* **Six Harm**	死符 *Si Fu* **Death Charm**	炙退 *Zhi Tui* **Roasting Star**
震 *Zhen* E2 坤 *Kun* SW2	辰 *Chen* SE1	申 *Shen* SW3	午 *Wu* S2

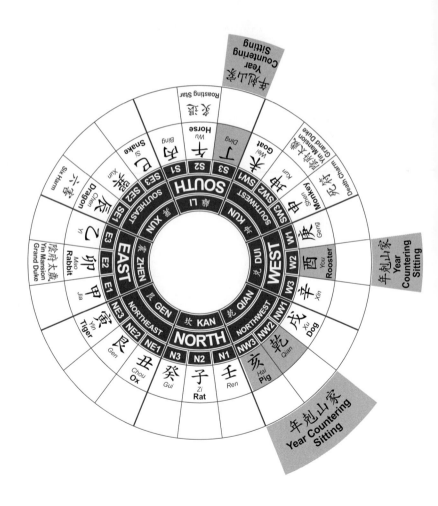

Negative Directions to Establish Facing 立向凶方：

巡山羅喉 *Xun Shan Luo Hou* **Mountain Patrol Luo Hou Star**	病符 *Bing Fu* **Sickness Charm**
乙 *Yi* **E3**	寅 *Yin* **NE3**

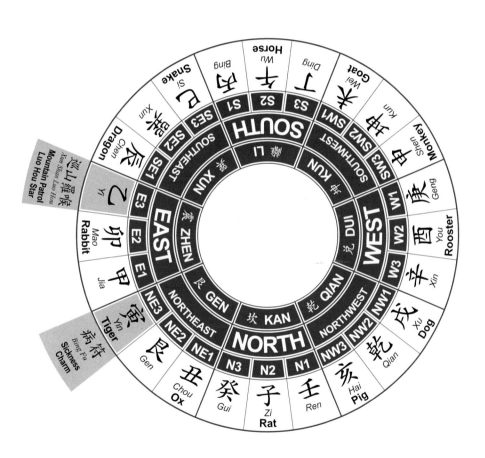

癸卯 (Gui Mao) Water Rabbit

天官符 Heavenly Officer Charm	寅 *Yin* Tiger		飛廉 Flying Chaste	巳 *Si* Snake
地官符 Earthly Officer Charm	未 *Wei* Goat		喪門 Funeral Door	巳 *Si* Snake
大煞 Great Sha	卯 *Mao* Rabbit		弔客 Suspended Guest	丑 *Chou* Ox
大將軍 Big General	子 *Zi* Rat		白虎 White Tiger	亥 *Hai* Pig
力士 Strong Man	巽 *Xun*		金神 Golden God	申 *Shen* Monkey
蠶室 Silkworm Room	乾 *Qian*			酉 *You* Rooster
蠶官 Silkworm Officer	戌 *Xu* Dog			子 *Zi* Rat
蠶命 Silkworm Life	亥 *Hai* Pig			丑 *Chou* Ox
歲刑 Duke Punishment	子 *Zi* Rat		獨火 Lonely Fire	坎 *Kan*
黃幡 Yellow Flag	未 *Wei* Goat		五鬼 Five Ghost	丑 *Chou* Ox
豹尾 Leopard Tail	丑 *Chou* Ox		破敗五鬼 Destructive Five Ghost	艮 *Gen*

Negative Repair / Renovation Sectors Diagram 修方凶位圖:

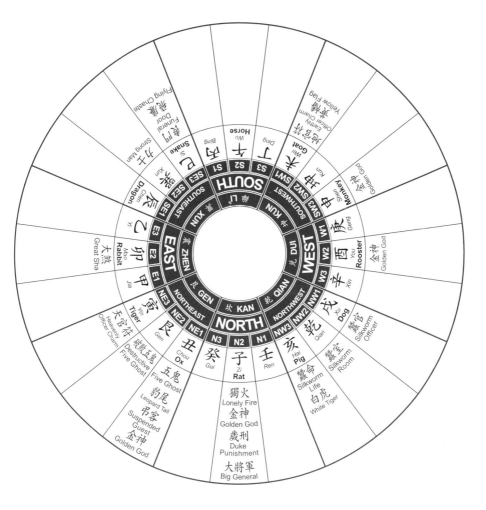

12-Month Auxiliary Stars Reference Table :
癸卯年十二月，開山立向修方星表

Positive Monthly Stars 吉星方

月 MONTH	寅 Tiger (Feb 4 - Mar 5) 正月 1st Month	卯 Rabbit (Mar 6 - Apr 4) 二月 2nd Month	辰 Dragon (Apr 5 - May 5) 三月 3rd Month	巳 Snake (May 6 - Jun 5) 四月 4th Month	午 Horse (Jun 6 - July 6) 五月 5th Month	未 Goat (July 7 - Aug 7) 六月 6th Month
天道 Heavenly Path	南 South	西南 Southwest	北 North	西 West	西北 Northwest	東 East
天德 Heavenly Virtue	丁 Ding Yin Fire	坤 Kun (申)	壬 Ren Yang Water	辛 Xin Yin Metal	乾 Qian (亥)	甲 Jia Yang Wood
天德合 Heavenly Virtue Combo	壬 Ren Yang Water	(巳)	丁 Ding Yin Fire	丙 Bing Yang Fire	(寅)	己 Ji Yin Earth
月德 Monthly Virtue	丙 Bing Yang Fire	甲 Jia Yang Wood	壬 Ren Yang Water	庚 Geng Yang Metal	丙 Bing Yang Fire	甲 Jia Yang Wood
月德合 Monthly Virtue Combo	辛 Xin Yin Metal	己 Ji Yin Earth	丁 Ding Yin Fire	乙 Yi Yin Wood	辛 Xin Yin Metal	己 Ji Yin Earth
月空 Month Emptiness	壬 Ren Yang Water	庚 Geng Yang Metal	丙 Bing Yang Fire	甲 Jia Yang Wood	壬 Ren Yang Water	庚 Geng Yang Metal
陽貴人 Yang Nobleman	艮 Gen	兌 Dui	乾 Qian	中 Middle	坎 Kan	離 Li
陰貴人 Yin Nobleman	乾 Qian	中 Middle	坎 Kan	離 Li	艮 Gen	兌 Dui
飛天祿 Flying Heavenly Wealth	乾 Qian	震 Zhen	巽 Xun	震 Zhen	坤 Kun	坎 Kan
飛天馬 Flying Heavenly Horse	艮 Gen	兌 Dui	乾 Qian	中 Middle	坎 Kan	離 Li

癸卯 (Gui Mao) Water Rabbit

12-Month Auxiliary Stars Reference Table :
癸卯年十二月，開山立向修方星表

申 Monkey (Aug 8 - Sept 7) 七月 7th Month	酉 Rooster (Sept 8 - Oct 7) 八月 8th Month	戌 Dog (Oct 8 - Nov 6) 九月 9th Month	亥 Pig (Nov 7 - Dec 6) 十月 10th Month	子 Rat (Dec 7 - Jan 5) 十一月 11th Month	丑 Ox (Jan 6 - Feb 3) 十二月 12th Month	月 MONTH
北 North	東北 Northeast	南 South	東 East	東南 Southeast	西 West	天道 Heavenly Path
癸 Gui Yin Water	艮 Gen （寅）	丙 Bing Yang Fire	乙 Yi Yin Wood	巽 Xun （巳）	庚 Geng Yang Metal	天德 Heavenly Virtue
戊 Wu Yang Earth	（亥）	辛 Xin Yin Metal	庚 Geng Yang Metal	（申）	乙 Yi Yin Wood	天德合 Heavenly Virtue Combo
壬 Ren Yang Water	庚 Geng Yang Metal	丙 Bing Yang Fire	甲 Jia Yang Wood	壬 Ren Yang Water	庚 Geng Yang Metal	月德 Monthly Virtue
丁 Ding Yin Fire	乙 Yi Yin Wood	辛 Xin Yin Metal	己 Ji Yin Earth	丁 Ding Yin Fire	乙 Yi Yin Wood	月德合 Monthly Virtue Combo
丙 Bing Yang Fire	甲 Jia Yang Wood	壬 Ren Yang Water	庚 Geng Yang Metal	丙 Bing Yang Fire	甲 Jia Yang Wood	月空 Month Emptiness
艮 Gen	兌 Dui	乾 Qian	中 Middle	巽 Xun	震 Zhen	陽貴人 Yang Nobleman
乾 Qian	中 Middle	巽 Xun	震 Zhen	坤 Kun	坎 Kan	陰貴人 Yin Nobleman
離 Li	艮 Gen	兌 Dui	乾 Qian	中 Middle	坎 Kan	飛天祿 Flying Heavenly Wealth
艮 Gen	兌 Dui	乾 Qian	中 Middle	巽 Xun	震 Zhen	飛天馬 Flying Heavenly Horse

1113

Monthly Purple White Stars 月紫白九星 :

寅 Tiger (Feb 4 - Mar 5) 正月 1st Month

巽 SE	離 S	坤 SW	
7 Red 七赤	**3** Jade 三碧	**5** Yellow 五黃	
6 White 六白	**8** White 八白	**1** White 一白	震 E ... 兌 W
2 Black 二黑	**4** Green 四綠	**9** Purple 九紫	
艮 NE	坎 N	乾 NW	

卯 Rabbit (Mar 6 - Apr 4) 二月 2nd Month

巽 SE	離 S	坤 SW	
6 White 六白	**2** Black 二黑	**4** Green 四綠	
5 Yellow 五黃	**7** Red 七赤	**9** Purple 九紫	震 E ... 兌 W
1 White 一白	**3** Jade 三碧	**8** White 八白	
艮 NE	坎 N	乾 NW	

辰 Dragon (Apr 5 - May 5) 三月 3rd Month

巽 SE	離 S	坤 SW	
5 Yellow 五黃	**1** White 一白	**3** Jade 三碧	
4 Green 四綠	**6** White 六白	**8** White 八白	震 E ... 兌 W
9 Purple 九紫	**2** Black 二黑	**7** Red 七赤	
艮 NE	坎 N	乾 NW	

巳 Snake (May 6 - Jun 5) 四月 4th Month

巽 SE	離 S	坤 SW	
4 Green 四綠	**9** Purple 九紫	**2** Black 二黑	
3 Jade 三碧	**5** Yellow 五黃	**7** Red 七赤	震 E ... 兌 W
8 White 八白	**1** White 一白	**6** White 六白	
艮 NE	坎 N	乾 NW	

午 Horse (Jun 6 - July 6) 五月 5th Month

巽 SE	離 S	坤 SW	
3 Jade 三碧	**8** White 八白	**1** White 一白	
2 Black 二黑	**4** Green 四綠	**6** White 六白	震 E ... 兌 W
7 Red 七赤	**9** Purple 九紫	**5** Yellow 五黃	
艮 NE	坎 N	乾 NW	

未 Goat (July 7 - Aug 7) 六月 6th Month

巽 SE	離 S	坤 SW	
2 Black 二黑	**7** Red 七赤	**9** Purple 九紫	
1 White 一白	**3** Jade 三碧	**5** Yellow 五黃	震 E ... 兌 W
6 White 六白	**8** White 八白	**4** Green 四綠	
艮 NE	坎 N	乾 NW	

申 Monkey (Aug 8 - Sept 7) 七月 7th Month

巽 SE	離 S	坤 SW	
1 White 一白	**6** White 六白	**8** White 八白	
9 Purple 九紫	**2** Black 二黑	**4** Green 四綠	震 E ... 兌 W
5 Yellow 五黃	**7** Red 七赤	**3** Jade 三碧	
艮 NE	坎 N	乾 NW	

酉 Rooster (Sept 8 - Oct 7) 八月 8th Month

巽 SE	離 S	坤 SW	
9 Purple 九紫	**5** Yellow 五黃	**7** Red 七赤	
8 White 八白	**1** White 一白	**3** Jade 三碧	震 E ... 兌 W
4 Green 四綠	**6** White 六白	**2** Black 二黑	
艮 NE	坎 N	乾 NW	

戌 Dog (Oct 8 - Nov 6) 九月 9th Month

巽 SE	離 S	坤 SW	
8 White 八白	**4** Green 四綠	**6** White 六白	
7 Red 七赤	**9** Purple 九紫	**2** Black 二黑	震 E ... 兌 W
3 Jade 三碧	**5** Yellow 五黃	**1** White 一白	
艮 NE	坎 N	乾 NW	

亥 Pig (Nov 7 - Dec 6) 十月 10th Month

巽 SE	離 S	坤 SW	
7 Red 七赤	**3** Jade 三碧	**5** Yellow 五黃	
6 White 六白	**8** White 八白	**1** White 一白	震 E ... 兌 W
2 Black 二黑	**4** Green 四綠	**9** Purple 九紫	
艮 NE	坎 N	乾 NW	

子 Rat (Dec 7 - Jan 5) 十一月 11th Month

巽 SE	離 S	坤 SW	
6 White 六白	**2** Black 二黑	**4** Green 四綠	
5 Yellow 五黃	**7** Red 七赤	**9** Purple 九紫	震 E ... 兌 W
1 White 一白	**3** Jade 三碧	**8** White 八白	
艮 NE	坎 N	乾 NW	

丑 Ox (Jan 6 - Feb 3) 十二月 12th Month

巽 SE	離 S	坤 SW	
5 Yellow 五黃	**1** White 一白	**3** Jade 三碧	
4 Green 四綠	**6** White 六白	**8** White 八白	震 E ... 兌 W
9 Purple 九紫	**2** Black 二黑	**7** Red 七赤	
艮 NE	坎 N	乾 NW	

Qi Men Three Nobles 三奇 :

Three Nobles 三奇 / Seasons	乙 Yi	丙 Bing	丁 Ding
立春 **Coming of Spring** Feb 4 - Feb 18	震 Zhen	巽 Xun	中 **Middle**
春分 **Spring Equinox** Mar 21 - Apr 4	兌 Dui	艮 Gen	離 Li
立夏 **Coming of Summer** May 6 - May 20	艮 Gen	離 Li	坎 Kan
夏至 **Summer Solstice** Jun 22 - Jul 6	中 **Middle**	巽 Xun	震 Zhen
立秋 **Coming of Autumn** Aug 8 - Aug 23	兌 Dui	乾 Qian	中 **Middle**
秋分 **Autumn Equinox** Sept 23 - Oct 7	震 Zhen	坤 Kun	坎 Kan
立冬 **Coming of Winter** Nov 7 - Nov 22	坤 Kun	坎 Kan	離 Li
冬至 **Winter Solstice** Dec 22 - Jan 5	中 **Middle**	乾 Qian	兌 Dui

癸卯 (Gui Mao) Water Rabbit

Sectors to Avoid Opening Mountain 開山凶位 :

月 MONTH	月建 Month Establishment	月破 Month Destruction	月剋山家 Month Countering Sitting		陰府太歲 Yin Mansion Grand Duke	
寅 **Tiger** (Feb 4 - Mar 5) 正月 **1st Month**	寅 *Yin* Tiger	申 *Shen* Monkey	震 *Zhen*	巳 *Si* Snake	艮 *Gen*	巽 *Xun*
卯 **Rabbit** (Mar 6 - Apr 4) 二月 **2nd Month**	卯 *Mao* Rabbit	酉 *You* Rooster	艮 *Gen*		兌 *Dui*	乾 *Qian*
辰 **Dragon** (Apr 5 - May 5) 三月 **3rd Month**	辰 *Chen* Dragon	戌 *Xu* Dog	離 *Li*	丙 *Bing* Yang Fire	坎 *Kan*	坤 *Kun*
巳 **Snake** (May 6 - Jun 5) 四月 **4th Month**	巳 *Si* Snake	亥 *Hai* Pig	壬 *Ren* Yang Water	乙 *Yi* Yin Wood	乾 *Qian*	離 *Li*
午 **Horse** (Jun 6 - July 6) 五月 **5th Month**	午 *Wu* Horse	子 *Zi* Rat	–		坤 *Kun*	震 *Zhen*
未 **Goat** (July 7 - Aug 7) 六月 **6th Month**	未 *Wei* Goat	丑 *Chou* Ox	–		巽 *Xun*	艮 *Gen*
申 **Monkey** (Aug 8 - Sept 7) 七月 **7th Month**	申 *Shen* Monkey	寅 *Yin* Tiger	水 Water	山 Mountain	乾 *Qian*	兌 *Dui*
酉 **Rooster** (Sept 8 - Oct 7) 八月 **8th Month**	酉 *You* Rooster	卯 *Mao* Rabbit	土 Earth		坤 *Kun*	坎 *Kan*
戌 **Dog** (Oct 8 - Nov 6) 九月 **9th Month**	戌 *Xu* Dog	辰 *Chen* Dragon	震 *Zhen*	巳 *Si* Snake	離 *Li*	乾 *Qian*
亥 **Pig** (Nov 7 - Dec 6) 十月 **10th Month**	亥 *Hai* Pig	巳 *Si* Snake	艮 *Gen*		震 *Zhen*	坤 *Kun*
子 **Rat** (Dec 7 - Jan 5) 十一月 **11th Month**	子 *Zi* Rat	午 *Wu* Horse	–		艮 *Gen*	巽 *Xun*
丑 **Ox** (Jan 6 - Feb 3) 十二月 **12th Month**	丑 *Chou* Ox	未 *Wei* Goat	–		兌 *Dui*	乾 *Qian*

Negative Repair / Renovation Sectors 修方凶位 :

月 MONTH	天官符 Heavenly Officer Charm			地官符 Earth Officer Charm			小月建 Small Month Establishment		
寅 **Tiger** (Feb 4 - Mar 5) 正月 **1st Month**		中 Middle		壬 *Ren* Yang Water	坎 *Kan*	癸 *Gui* Yin Water	丙 *Bing* Yang Fire	離 *Li*	丁 *Ding* Yin Fire
卯 **Rabbit** (Mar 6 - Apr 4) 二月 **2nd Month**	庚 *Geng* Yang Metal	兌 *Dui*	辛 *Xin* Yin Metal	丙 *Bing* Yang Fire	離 *Li*	丁 *Ding* Yin Fire	壬 *Ren* Yang Water	坎 *Kan*	癸 *Gui* Yin Water
辰 **Dragon** (Apr 5 - May 5) 三月 **3rd Month**	戌 *Xu* Dog	乾 *Qian*	亥 *Hai* Pig	丑 *Chou* Ox	艮 *Gen*	寅 *Yin* Tiger	未 *Wei* Goat	坤 *Kun*	申 *Shen* Monkey
巳 **Snake** (May 6 - Jun 5) 四月 **4th Month**		中 Middle		庚 *Geng* Yang Metal	兌 *Dui*	辛 *Xin* Yin Metal	甲 *Jia* Yang Wood	震 *Zhen*	乙 *Yi* Yin Wood
午 **Horse** (Jun 6 - July 6) 五月 **5th Month**	辰 *Chen* Dragon	巽 *Xun*	巳 *Si* Snake	戌 *Xu* Dog	乾 *Qian*	亥 *Hai* Pig	辰 *Chen* Dragon	巽 *Xun*	巳 *Si* Snake
未 **Goat** (July 7 - Aug 7) 六月 **6th Month**	甲 *Jia* Yang Wood	震 *Zhen*	乙 *Yi* Yin Wood		中 Middle			中 Middle	
申 **Monkey** (Aug 8 - Sept 7) 七月 **7th Month**	未 *Wei* Goat	坤 *Kun*	申 *Shen* Monkey	庚 *Geng* Yang Metal	兌 *Dui*	辛 *Xin* Yin Metal	戌 *Xu* Dog	乾 *Qian*	亥 *Hai* Pig
酉 **Rooster** (Sept 8 - Oct 7) 八月 **8th Month**	壬 *Ren* Yang Water	坎 *Kan*	癸 *Gui* Yin Water	戌 *Xu* Dog	乾 *Qian*	亥 *Hai* Pig	庚 *Geng* Yang Metal	兌 *Dui*	辛 *Xin* Yin Metal
戌 **Dog** (Oct 8 - Nov 6) 九月 **9th Month**	丙 *Bing* Yang Fire	離 *Li*	丁 *Ding* Yin Fire		中 Middle		丑 *Chou* Ox	艮 *Gen*	寅 *Yin* Tiger
亥 **Pig** (Nov 7 - Dec 6) 十月 **10th Month**	丑 *Chou* Ox	艮 *Gen*	寅 *Yin* Tiger	辰 *Chen* Dragon	巽 *Xun*	巳 *Si* Snake	丙 *Bing* Yang Fire	離 *Li*	丁 *Ding* Yin Fire
子 **Rat** (Dec 7 - Jan 5) 十一月 **11th Month**	庚 *Geng* Yang Metal	兌 *Dui*	辛 *Xin* Yin Metal	甲 *Jia* Yang Wood	震 *Zhen*	乙 *Yi* Yin Wood	壬 *Ren* Yang Water	坎 *Kan*	癸 *Gui* Yin Water
丑 **Ox** (Jan 6 - Feb 3) 十二月 **12th Month**	戌 *Xu* Dog	乾 *Qian*	亥 *Hai* Pig	未 *Wei* Goat	坤 *Kun*	申 *Shen* Monkey	未 *Wei* Goat	坤 *Kun*	申 *Shen* Monkey

癸卯 (Gui Mao) Water Rabbit

Negative Repair / Renovation Sectors 修方凶位 :

月 MONTH	大月建 Big Month Establishment			飛大煞 Flying Great Sha			丙丁獨火 Bing Ding Lonely Fire	
寅 Tiger (Feb 4 - Mar 5) 正月 1st Month	丑 Chou Ox	艮 Gen	寅 Yin Tiger	戌 Xu Dog	乾 Qian	亥 Hai Pig	兌 Dui	艮 Gen
卯 Rabbit (Mar 6 - Apr 4) 二月 2nd Month	庚 Geng Yang Metal	兌 Dui	辛 Xin Yin Metal		中 Middle		乾 Qian	兌 Dui
辰 Dragon (Apr 5 - May 5) 三月 3rd Month	戌 Xu Dog	乾 Qian	亥 Hai Pig	庚 Geng Yang Metal	兌 Dui	辛 Xin Yin Metal	中 Middle	乾 Qian
巳 Snake (May 6 - Jun 5) 四月 4th Month		中 Middle		戌 Xu Dog	乾 Qian	亥 Hai Pig		中 Middle
午 Horse (Jun 6 - July 6) 五月 5th Month	辰 Chen Dragon	巽 Xun	巳 Si Snake		中 Middle		巽 Xun	中 Middle
未 Goat (July 7 - Aug 7) 六月 6th Month	甲 Jia Yang Wood	震 Zhen	乙 Yi Yin Wood	辰 Chen Dragon	巽 Xun	巳 Si Snake	震 Zhen	巽 Xun
申 Monkey (Aug 8 - Sept 7) 七月 7th Month	未 Wei Goat	坤 Kun	申 Shen Monkey	甲 Jia Yang Wood	震 Zhen	乙 Yi Yin Wood	坤 Kun	震 Zhen
酉 Rooster (Sept 8 - Oct 7) 八月 8th Month	壬 Ren Yang Water	坎 Kan	癸 Gui Yin Water	未 Wei Goat	坤 Kun	申 Shen Monkey	坎 Kan	坤 Kun
戌 Dog (Oct 8 - Nov 6) 九月 9th Month	丙 Bing Yang Fire	離 Li	丁 Ding Yin Fire	壬 Ren Yang Water	坎 Kan	癸 Gui Yin Water	離 Li	坎 Kan
亥 Pig (Nov 7 - Dec 6) 十月 10th Month	丑 Chou Ox	艮 Gen	寅 Yin Tiger	丙 Bing Yang Fire	離 Li	丁 Ding Yin Fire	艮 Gen	離 Li
子 Rat (Dec 7 - Jan 5) 十一月 11th Month	庚 Geng Yang Metal	兌 Dui	辛 Xin Yin Metal	丑 Chou Ox	艮 Gen	寅 Yin Tiger	兌 Dui	艮 Gen
丑 Ox (Jan 6 - Feb 3) 十二月 12th Month	戌 Xu Dog	乾 Qian	亥 Hai Pig	庚 Geng Yang Metal	兌 Dui	辛 Xin Yin Metal	乾 Qian	兌 Dui

1118

Negative Repair / Renovation Sectors 修方凶位 ：

月 MONTH	月遊火 Month Wondering Fire	三煞 Monthly 3 Killings		
		劫煞 Robbery Sha	災煞 Calamity Sha	月煞 Month Sha
寅 Tiger (Feb 4 - Mar 5) 正月 1st Month	巽 Xun	亥 Hai Pig	子 Zi Rat	丑 Chou Ox
卯 Rabbit (Mar 6 - Apr 4) 二月 2nd Month	中 Middle	申 Shen Monkey	酉 You Rooster	戌 Xu Dog
辰 Dragon (Apr 5 - May 5) 三月 3rd Month	乾 Qian	巳 Si Snake	午 Wu Horse	未 Wei Goat
巳 Snake (May 6 - Jun 5) 四月 4th Month	兑 Dui	寅 Yin Tiger	卯 Mao Rabbit	辰 Chen Dragon
午 Horse (Jun 6 - July 6) 五月 5th Month	艮 Gen	亥 Hai Pig	子 Zi Rat	丑 Chou Ox
未 Goat (July 7 - Aug 7) 六月 6th Month	離 Li	申 Shen Monkey	酉 You Rooster	戌 Xu Dog
申 Monkey (Aug 8 - Sept 7) 七月 7th Month	坎 Kan	巳 Si Snake	午 Wu Horse	未 Wei Goat
酉 Rooster (Sept 8 - Oct 7) 八月 8th Month	坤 Kun	寅 Yin Tiger	卯 Mao Rabbit	辰 Chen Dragon
戌 Dog (Oct 8 - Nov 6) 九月 9th Month	震 Zhen	亥 Hai Pig	子 Zi Rat	丑 Chou Ox
亥 Pig (Nov 7 - Dec 6) 十月 10th Month	巽 Xun	申 Shen Monkey	酉 You Rooster	戌 Xu Dog
子 Rat (Dec 7 - Jan 5) 十一月 11th Month	中 Middle	巳 Si Snake	午 Wu Horse	未 Wei Goat
丑 Ox (Jan 6 - Feb 3) 十二月 12th Month	乾 Qian	寅 Yin Tiger	卯 Mao Rabbit	辰 Chen Dragon

Negative Repair / Renovation Sectors 修方凶位 :

月 MONTH	月刑 Month Punishment	月害 Month Harm	月厭 Month Detest
寅 **Tiger** (Feb 4 - Mar 5) 正月 **1st Month**	巳 *Si* Snake	巳 *Si* Snake	戌 *Xu* Dog
卯 **Rabbit** (Mar 6 - Apr 4) 二月 **2nd Month**	子 *Zi* Rat	辰 *Chen* Dragon	酉 *You* Rooster
辰 **Dragon** (Apr 5 - May 5) 三月 **3rd Month**	辰 *Chen* Dragon	卯 *Mao* Rabbit	申 *Shen* Monkey
巳 **Snake** (May 6 - Jun 5) 四月 **4th Month**	申 *Shen* Monkey	寅 *Yin* Tiger	未 *Wei* Goat
午 **Horse** (Jun 6 - July 6) 五月 **5th Month**	午 *Wu* Horse	丑 *Chou* Ox	午 *Wu* Horse
未 **Goat** (July 7 - Aug 7) 六月 **6th Month**	丑 *Chou* Ox	子 *Zi* Rat	巳 *Si* Snake
申 **Monkey** (Aug 8 - Sept 7) 七月 **7th Month**	寅 *Yin* Tiger	亥 *Hai* Pig	辰 *Chen* Dragon
酉 **Rooster** (Sept 8 - Oct 7) 八月 **8th Month**	酉 *You* Rooster	戌 *Xu* Dog	卯 *Mao* Rabbit
戌 **Dog** (Oct 8 - Nov 6) 九月 **9th Month**	未 *Wei* Goat	酉 *You* Rooster	寅 *Yin* Tiger
亥 **Pig** (Nov 7 - Dec 6) 十月 **10th Month**	亥 *Hai* Pig	申 *Shen* Monkey	丑 *Chou* Ox
子 **Rat** (Dec 7 - Jan 5) 十一月 **11th Month**	卯 *Mao* Rabbit	未 *Wei* Goat	子 *Zi* Rat
丑 **Ox** (Jan 6 - Feb 3) 十二月 **12th Month**	戌 *Xu* Dog	午 *Wu* Horse	亥 *Hai* Pig

癸巳 (Gui Si)
Water Snake

癸巳 (Gui Si) Water Snake

Heavenly Stem 天干	癸 Yin Water (陰水)
Earthly Branch 地支	巳 Snake (Yin Fire 陰火)
Hidden Stem 藏干	丙 Yang Fire, 戊 Yang Earth, 庚 Yang Metal
Na Yin 納音	長流水 Water flowing constantly
Grand Duke 太歲	巳 Snake
Xuan Kong Five Element 玄空五行	4 金 Metal
Gua Name 卦名	䷪ 澤天夬 Eliminating
Xuan Kong Period Luck 玄空卦運	6

Annual Positive Stars for Opening Mountain, Establishing Facing and Commencing Repairs 開山立向修方吉星：

歲德 Duke Virtue	戊 Wu Yang Earth	
歲德合 Duke Virtue Combo	癸 Gui Yin Water	
歲枝德 Duke Branch Virtue	戊 Xu Dog	
陽貴人 Yang Nobleman	巳 Si Snake	
陰貴人 Yin Nobleman	卯 Mao Rabbit	
歲祿 Duke Prosperous	子 Zi Rat	
歲馬 Duke Horse	亥 Hai Pig	
奏書 Decree	巽 Xun	
博士 Professor	乾 Qian	

Annual Negative Stars for Opening Mountain, Establishing Facing and Commencing Repairs 開山立向修方凶星：

太歲 Grand Duke	歲破 Year Breaker	三煞 Three Killings			坐煞向煞 Sitting Sha Facing Sha				浮天空亡 Floating Heaven Emptiness	
巳 *Si* Snake	亥 *Hai* Pig	寅 *Yin* Tiger	卯 *Mao* Rabbit	辰 *Chen* Dragon	甲 *Jia* Yang Wood	乙 *Yi* Yin Wood	庚 *Geng* Yang Metal	辛 *Xin* Yin Metal	坤 *Kun*	乙 *Yi* Yin Wood

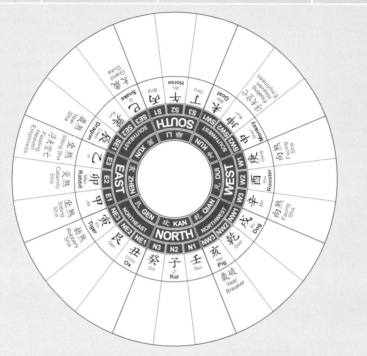

Annual San Yuan Purple White Stars 三元紫白九星：

上元 Upper Period Period 1, 2, 3			中元 Middle Period Period 4, 5, 6			下元 Lower Period Period 7, 8, 9		
巽SE 7	離S 3	坤SW 5	巽SE 1	離S 6	坤SW 8	巽SE 4	離S 9	坤SW 2
震E 6	8 癸巳 *Gui Si* Water Snake	兌W 1	震E 9	2 癸巳 *Gui Si* Water Snake	兌W 4	震E 3	5 癸巳 *Gui Si* Water Snake	兌W 7
艮NE 2	坎N 4	乾NW 9	艮NE 5	坎N 7	乾NW 3	艮NE 8	坎N 1	乾NW 6

Mountain Covering Yellow Path 蓋山黃道:

貪狼 Tan Lang Greedy Wolf				巨門 Ju Men Huge Door				武曲 Wu Qu Military Arts		文曲 Wen Qu Literary Arts			
兌	丁	巳	丑	震	庚	亥	未	艮	丙	坎	癸	申	辰
Dui	Ding	Si	Chou	Zhen	Geng	Hai	Wei	Gen	Bing	Kan	Gui	Shen	Chen
W2	S3	SE3	NE1	E2	W1	NW3	SW1	NE2	S1	N2	N3	SW3	SE1

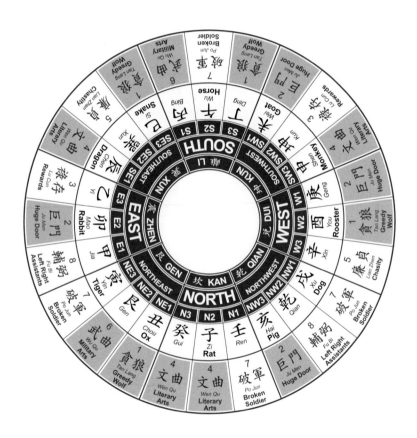

Heaven Penetrating Force 通天竅:

三合前方 **Facing Three Harmony**	乾亥 Qian Hai	壬子 Ren Zi	癸丑 Gui Chou
三合後方 **Sitting Three Harmony**	巽巳 Xun Si	丙午 Bing Wu	丁未 Ding Wei

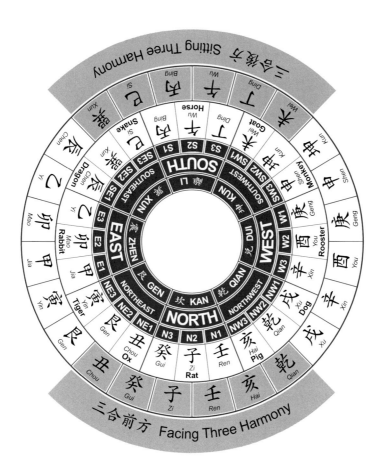

癸巳 (Gui Si) Water Snake

神后 *Shen Hou* **Holy Empress**	功曹 *Gong Cao* **Marshall**	天罡 *Tian Gang* **Heavenly Dipper**	勝光 *Sheng Guang* **Subliminal Bright**	傳送 *Chuan Song* **Great General**	河魁 *He Kui* **River Scholar**
丁未 *Ding Wei*	庚酉 *Geng You*	乾亥 *Qian Hai*	癸丑 *Gui Chou*	甲卯 *Jia Mao*	巽巳 *Xun Si*

Moving Horse Six Ren Assessment 走馬六壬:

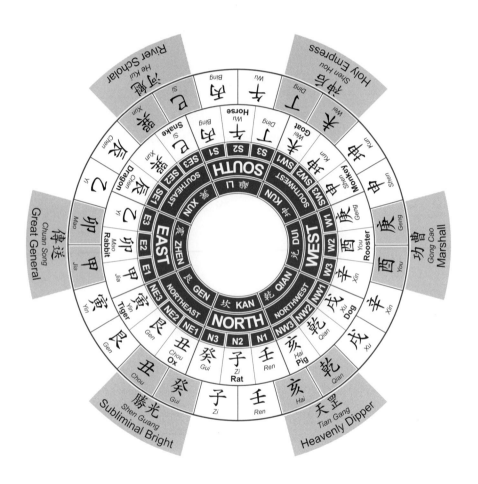

Four Advantages Three Cycles Star Plate 四利三元:

太陽 *Tai Yang* **Sun**	太陰 *Tai Yin* **Moon**	龍德 *Long De* **Dragon Virtue**	福德 *Fu De* **Fortune Virtue**
午 *Wu* S2	申 *Shen* SW3	子 *Zi* N2	寅 *Yin* NE3

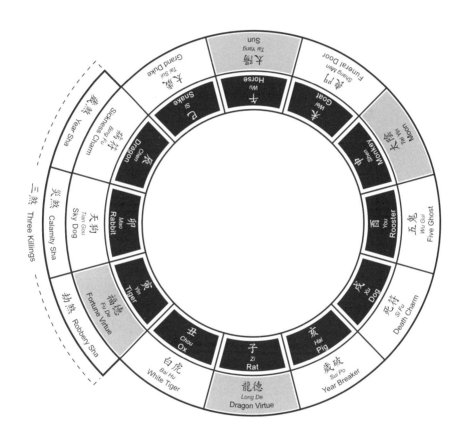

Negative Sectors For Opening Mountain 開山凶位：

年尅山家 Year Countering Sitting

震	艮	巳
Zhen	Gen	Si
E2	NE2	SE3

陰府太歲	六害	死符	炙退
Yin Fu Tai Sui	Liu Hai	Si Fu	Zhi Tui
Yin Mansion Grand Duke	**Six Harm**	**Death Charm**	**Roasting Star**
震	坤	寅	戌	子
Zhen	Kun	Yin	Xu	Zi
E2	SW2	NE3	NW1	N2

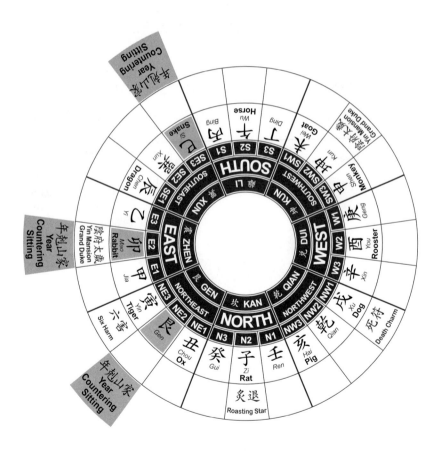

Negative Directions to Establish Facing 立向凶方：

巡山羅喉 *Xun Shan Luo Hou* **Mountain Patrol Luo Hou Star**	病符 *Bing Fu* **Sickness Charm**
丙 *Bing* **S1**	辰 *Chen* **SE1**

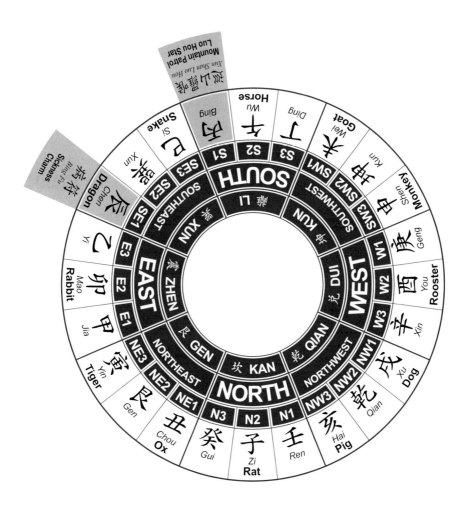

Negative Repair / Renovation Sectors Table 修方凶位表：

天官符 **Heavenly Officer Charm**	申 *Shen* **Monkey**	飛廉 **Flying Chaste**	未 *Wei* **Goat**
地官符 **Earthly Officer Charm**	酉 *You* **Rooster**	喪門 **Funeral Door**	未 *Wei* **Goat**
大煞 **Great Sha**	酉 *You* **Rooster**	弔客 **Suspended Guest**	卯 *Mao* **Rabbit**
大將軍 **Big General**	卯 *Mao* **Rabbit**	白虎 **White Tiger**	丑 *Chou* **Ox**
力士 **Strong Man**	坤 *Kun*	金神 **Golden God**	申 *Shen* **Monkey** 酉 *You* **Rooster** 子 *Zi* **Rat** 丑 *Chou* **Ox**
蠶室 **Silkworm Room**	艮 *Gen*		
蠶官 **Silkworm Officer**	丑 *Chou* **Ox**		
蠶命 **Silkworm Life**	寅 *Yin* **Tiger**		
歲刑 **Duke Punishment**	申 *Shen* **Monkey**	獨火 **Lonely Fire**	巽 *Xun*
黃幡 **Yellow Flag**	丑 *Chou* **Ox**	五鬼 **Five Ghost**	亥 *Hai* **Pig**
豹尾 **Leopard Tail**	未 *Wei* **Goat**	破敗五鬼 **Destructive Five Ghost**	艮 *Gen*

Negative Repair / Renovation Sectors Diagram 修方凶位圖：

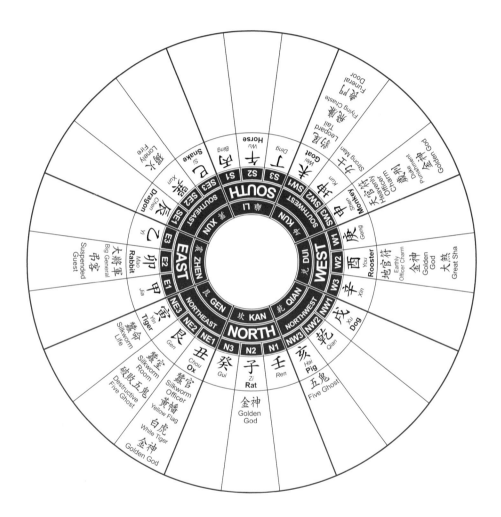

12-Month Auxiliary Stars Reference Table :
癸巳年十二月，開山立向修方星表

Positive Monthly Stars 吉星方

月 MONTH	寅 Tiger (Feb 4 - Mar 5) 正月 1st Month	卯 Rabbit (Mar 6 - Apr 4) 二月 2nd Month	辰 Dragon (Apr 5 - May 5) 三月 3rd Month	巳 Snake (May 6 - Jun 5) 四月 4th Month	午 Horse (Jun 6 - July 6) 五月 5th Month	未 Goat (July 7 - Aug 7) 六月 6th Month
天道 Heavenly Path	南 South	西南 Southwest	北 North	西 West	西北 Northwest	東 East
天德 Heavenly Virtue	丁 Ding Yin Fire	坤 Kun (申)	壬 Ren Yang Water	辛 Xin Yin Metal	乾 Qian (亥)	甲 Jia Yang Wood
天德合 Heavenly Virtue Combo	壬 Ren Yang Water	(巳)	丁 Ding Yin Fire	丙 Bing Yang Fire	(寅)	己 Ji Yin Earth
月德 Monthly Virtue	丙 Bing Yang Fire	甲 Jia Yang Wood	壬 Ren Yang Water	庚 Geng Yang Metal	丙 Bing Yang Fire	甲 Jia Yang Wood
月德合 Monthly Virtue Combo	辛 Xin Yin Metal	己 Ji Yin Earth	丁 Ding Yin Fire	乙 Yi Yin Wood	辛 Xin Yin Metal	己 Ji Yin Earth
月空 Month Emptiness	壬 Ren Yang Water	庚 Geng Yang Metal	丙 Bing Yang Fire	甲 Jia Yang Wood	壬 Ren Yang Water	庚 Geng Yang Metal
陽貴人 Yang Nobleman	艮 Gen	兌 Dui	乾 Qian	中 Middle	坎 Kan	離 Li
陰貴人 Yin Nobleman	乾 Qian	中 Middle	坎 Kan	離 Li	艮 Gen	兌 Dui
飛天祿 Flying Heavenly Wealth	乾 Qian	中 Middle	巽 Xun	震 Zhen	坤 Kun	坎 Kan
飛天馬 Flying Heavenly Horse	中 Middle	巽 Xun	震 Zhen	坤 Kun	坎 Kan	離 Li

12-Month Auxiliary Stars Reference Table :
癸巳年十二月，開山立向修方星表

申 Monkey (Aug 8 - Sept 7) 七月 7th Month	酉 Rooster (Sept 8 - Oct 7) 八月 8th Month	戌 Dog (Oct 8 - Nov 6) 九月 9th Month	亥 Pig (Nov 7 - Dec 6) 十月 10th Month	子 Rat (Dec 7 - Jan 5) 十一月 11th Month	丑 Ox (Jan 6 - Feb 3) 十二月 12th Month	月 MONTH
北 North	東北 Northeast	南 South	東 East	東南 Southeast	西 West	天道 Heavenly Path
癸 Gui Yin Water	艮 Gen (寅)	丙 Bing Yang Fire	乙 Yi Yin Wood	巽 Xun (巳)	庚 Geng Yang Metal	天德 Heavenly Virtue
戊 Wu Yang Earth	(亥)	辛 Xin Yin Metal	庚 Geng Yang Metal	(申)	乙 Yi Yin Wood	天德合 Heavenly Virtue Combo
壬 Ren Yang Water	庚 Geng Yang Metal	丙 Bing Yang Fire	甲 Jia Yang Wood	壬 Ren Yang Water	庚 Geng Yang Metal	月德 Monthly Virtue
丁 Ding Yin Fire	乙 Yi Yin Wood	辛 Xin Yin Metal	己 Ji Yin Earth	丁 Ding Yin Fire	乙 Yi Yin Wood	月德合 Monthly Virtue Combo
丙 Bing Yang Fire	甲 Jia Yang Wood	壬 Ren Yang Water	庚 Geng Yang Metal	丙 Bing Yang Fire	甲 Jia Yang Wood	月空 Month Emptiness
艮 Gen	兌 Dui	乾 Qian	中 Middle	巽 Xun	震 Zhen	陽貴人 Yang Nobleman
乾 Qian	中 Middle	巽 Xun	震 Zhen	坤 Kun	坎 Kan	陰貴人 Yin Nobleman
離 Li	艮 Gen	兌 Dui	乾 Qian	中 Middle	坎 Kan	飛天祿 Flying Heavenly Wealth
艮 Gen	兌 Dui	乾 Qian	中 Middle	坎 Kan	離 Li	飛天馬 Flying Heavenly Horse

癸巳 (Gui Si) Water Snake

Monthly Purple White Stars 月紫白九星 :

寅 Tiger (Feb 4 - Mar 5) 正月 1st Month

巽SE	離S	坤SW
1 White 一白	**6** White 六白	**8** White 八白
9 Purple 九紫	**2** Black 二黑	**4** Green 四綠
5 Yellow 五黃	**7** Red 七赤	**3** Jade 三碧
艮NE	坎N	乾NW

震E — 兌W

卯 Rabbit (Mar 6 - Apr 4) 二月 2nd Month

巽SE	離S	坤SW
9 Purple 九紫	**5** Yellow 五黃	**7** Red 七赤
8 White 八白	**1** White 一白	**3** Jade 三碧
4 Green 四綠	**6** White 六白	**2** Black 二黑
艮NE	坎N	乾NW

震E — 兌W

辰 Dragon (Apr 5 - May 5) 三月 3rd Month

巽SE	離S	坤SW
8 White 八白	**4** Green 四綠	**6** White 六白
7 Red 七赤	**9** Purple 九紫	**2** Black 二黑
3 Jade 三碧	**5** Yellow 五黃	**1** White 一白
艮NE	坎N	乾NW

震E — 兌W

巳 Snake (May 6 - Jun 5) 四月 4th Month

巽SE	離S	坤SW
7 Red 七赤	**3** Jade 三碧	**5** Yellow 五黃
6 White 六白	**8** White 八白	**1** White 一白
2 Black 二黑	**4** Green 四綠	**9** Purple 九紫
艮NE	坎N	乾NW

震E — 兌W

午 Horse (Jun 6 - July 6) 五月 5th Month

巽SE	離S	坤SW
6 White 六白	**2** Black 二黑	**4** Green 四綠
5 Yellow 五黃	**7** Red 七赤	**9** Purple 九紫
1 White 一白	**3** Jade 三碧	**8** White 八白
艮NE	坎N	乾NW

震E — 兌W

未 Goat (July 7 - Aug 7) 六月 6th Month

巽SE	離S	坤SW
5 Yellow 五黃	**1** White 一白	**3** Jade 三碧
4 Green 四綠	**6** White 六白	**8** White 八白
9 Purple 九紫	**2** Black 二黑	**7** Red 七赤
艮NE	坎N	乾NW

震E — 兌W

申 Monkey (Aug 8 - Sept 7) 七月 7th Month

巽SE	離S	坤SW
4 Green 四綠	**9** Purple 九紫	**2** Black 二黑
3 Jade 三碧	**5** Yellow 五黃	**7** Red 七赤
8 White 八白	**1** White 一白	**6** White 六白
艮NE	坎N	乾NW

震E — 兌W

酉 Rooster (Sept 8 - Oct 7) 八月 8th Month

巽SE	離S	坤SW
3 Jade 三碧	**8** White 八白	**1** White 一白
2 Black 二黑	**4** Green 四綠	**6** White 六白
7 Red 七赤	**9** Purple 九紫	**5** Yellow 五黃
艮NE	坎N	乾NW

震E — 兌W

戌 Dog (Oct 8 - Nov 6) 九月 9th Month

巽SE	離S	坤SW
2 Black 二黑	**7** Red 七赤	**9** Purple 九紫
1 White 一白	**3** Jade 三碧	**5** Yellow 五黃
6 White 六白	**8** White 八白	**4** Green 四綠
艮NE	坎N	乾NW

震E — 兌W

亥 Pig (Nov 7 - Dec 6) 十月 10th Month

巽SE	離S	坤SW
1 White 一白	**6** White 六白	**8** White 八白
9 Purple 九紫	**2** Black 二黑	**4** Green 四綠
5 Yellow 五黃	**7** Red 七赤	**3** Jade 三碧
艮NE	坎N	乾NW

震E — 兌W

子 Rat (Dec 7 - Jan 5) 十一月 11th Month

巽SE	離S	坤SW
9 Purple 九紫	**5** Yellow 五黃	**7** Red 七赤
8 White 八白	**1** White 一白	**3** Jade 三碧
4 Green 四綠	**6** White 六白	**2** Black 二黑
艮NE	坎N	乾NW

震E — 兌W

丑 Ox (Jan 6 - Feb 3) 十二月 12th Month

巽SE	離S	坤SW
8 White 八白	**4** Green 四綠	**6** White 六白
7 Red 七赤	**9** Purple 九紫	**2** Black 二黑
3 Jade 三碧	**5** Yellow 五黃	**1** White 一白
艮NE	坎N	乾NW

震E — 兌W

Qi Men Three Nobles 三奇 :

Three Nobles 三奇 Seasons	乙 Yi	丙 Bing	丁 Ding
立春 **Coming of Spring** Feb 4 - Feb 18	坤 Kun	震 Zhen	巽 Xun
春分 **Spring Equinox** Mar 21 - Apr 4	乾 Qian	兌 Dui	艮 Gen
立夏 **Coming of Summer** May 6 - May 20	兌 Dui	艮 Gen	離 Li
夏至 **Summer Solstice** Jun 22 - Jul 6	乾 Qian	中 **Middle**	巽 Xun
立秋 **Coming of Autumn** Aug 8 - Aug 23	艮 Gen	兌 Dui	乾 Qian
秋分 **Autumn Equinox** Sept 23 - Oct 7	巽 Xun	震 Zhen	坤 Kun
立冬 **Coming of Winter** Nov 7 - Nov 22	震 Zhen	坤 Kun	坎 Kan
冬至 **Winter Solstice** Dec 22 - Jan 5	巽 Xun	中 **Middle**	乾 Qian

Sectors to Avoid Opening Mountain 開山凶位：

月 MONTH	月建 Month Establishment	月破 Month Destruction	月剋山家 Month Countering Sitting		陰府太歲 Yin Mansion Grand Duke	
寅 Tiger (Feb 4 - Mar 5) 正月 1st Month	寅 Yin Tiger	申 Shen Monkey	震 Zhen	巳 Si Snake	艮 Gen	巽 Xun
卯 Rabbit (Mar 6 - Apr 4) 二月 2nd Month	卯 Mao Rabbit	酉 You Rooster	艮 Gen		兌 Dui	乾 Qian
辰 Dragon (Apr 5 - May 5) 三月 3rd Month	辰 Chen Dragon	戌 Xu Dog	離 Li	丙 Bing Yang Fire	坤 Kun	坎 Kan
巳 Snake (May 6 - Jun 5) 四月 4th Month	巳 Si Snake	亥 Hai Pig	壬 Ren Yang Water	乙 Yi Yin Wood	乾 Qian	離 Li
午 Horse (Jun 6 - July 6) 五月 5th Month	午 Wu Horse	子 Zi Rat	–		坤 Kun	震 Zhen
未 Goat (July 7 - Aug 7) 六月 6th Month	未 Wei Goat	丑 Chou Ox	–		巽 Xun	艮 Gen
申 Monkey (Aug 8 - Sept 7) 七月 7th Month	申 Shen Monkey	寅 Yin Tiger	水 Water	山 Mountain	乾 Qian	兌 Dui
酉 Rooster (Sept 8 - Oct 7) 八月 8th Month	酉 You Rooster	卯 Mao Rabbit	土 Earth		坤 Kun	坎 Kan
戌 Dog (Oct 8 - Nov 6) 九月 9th Month	戌 Xu Dog	辰 Chen Dragon	震 Zhen	巳 Si Snake	離 Li	乾 Qian
亥 Pig (Nov 7 - Dec 6) 十月 10th Month	亥 Hai Pig	巳 Si Snake	艮 Gen		震 Zhen	坤 Kun
子 Rat (Dec 7 - Jan 5) 十一月 11th Month	子 Zi Rat	午 Wu Horse	–		艮 Gen	巽 Xun
丑 Ox (Jan 6 - Feb 3) 十二月 12th Month	丑 Chou Ox	未 Wei Goat	–		兌 Dui	乾 Qian

Negative Repair / Renovation Sectors 修方凶位 :

月 MONTH	天官符 Heavenly Officer Charm			地官符 Earth Officer Charm			小月建 Small Month Establishment		
寅 **Tiger** (Feb 4 - Mar 5) 正月 **1st Month**	未 Wei Goat	坤 Kun	申 Shen Monkey	甲 Jia Yang Wood	震 Zhen	乙 Yi Yin Wood	丙 Bing Yang Fire	離 Li	丁 Ding Yin Fire
卯 **Rabbit** (Mar 6 - Apr 4) 二月 **2nd Month**	壬 Ren Yang Water	坎 Kan	癸 Gui Yin Water	未 Wei Goat	坤 Kun	申 Shen Monkey	壬 Ren Yang Water	坎 Kan	癸 Gui Yin Water
辰 **Dragon** (Apr 5 - May 5) 三月 **3rd Month**	丙 Bing Yang Fire	離 Li	丁 Ding Yin Fire	壬 Ren Yang Water	坎 Kan	癸 Gui Yin Water	未 Wei Goat	坤 Kun	申 Shen Monkey
巳 **Snake** (May 6 - Jun 5) 四月 **4th Month**	丑 Chou Ox	艮 Gen	寅 Yin Tiger	丙 Bing Yang Fire	離 Li	丁 Ding Yin Fire	甲 Jia Yang Wood	震 Zhen	乙 Yi Yin Wood
午 **Horse** (Jun 6 - July 6) 五月 **5th Month**	庚 Geng Yang Metal	兌 Dui	辛 Xin Yin Metal	丑 Chou Ox	艮 Gen	寅 Yin Tiger	辰 Chen Dragon	巽 Xun	巳 Si Snake
未 **Goat** (July 7 - Aug 7) 六月 **6th Month**	戊 Xu Dog	乾 Qian	亥 Hai Pig	庚 Geng Yang Metal	兌 Dui	辛 Xin Yin Metal		中 Middle	
申 **Monkey** (Aug 8 - Sept 7) 七月 **7th Month**		中 Middle		戊 Xu Dog	乾 Qian	亥 Hai Pig	戊 Xu Dog	乾 Qian	亥 Hai Pig
酉 **Rooster** (Sept 8 - Oct 7) 八月 **8th Month**	庚 Geng Yang Metal	兌 Dui	辛 Xin Yin Metal		中 Middle		庚 Geng Yang Metal	兌 Dui	辛 Xin Yin Metal
戌 **Dog** (Oct 8 - Nov 6) 九月 **9th Month**	戊 Xu Dog	乾 Qian	亥 Hai Pig	庚 Geng Yang Metal	兌 Dui	辛 Xin Yin Metal	丑 Chou Ox	艮 Gen	寅 Yin Tiger
亥 **Pig** (Nov 7 - Dec 6) 十月 **10th Month**		中 Middle		戊 Xu Dog	乾 Qian	亥 Hai Pig	丙 Bing Yang Fire	離 Li	丁 Ding Yin Fire
子 **Rat** (Dec 7 - Jan 5) 十一月 **11th Month**	辰 Chen Dragon	巽 Xun	巳 Si Snake		中 Middle		壬 Ren Yang Water	坎 Kan	癸 Gui Yin Water
丑 **Ox** (Jan 6 - Feb 3) 十二月 **12th Month**	甲 Jia Yang Wood	震 Zhen	乙 Yi Yin Wood	辰 Chen Dragon	巽 Xun	巳 Si Snake	未 Wei Goat	坤 Kun	申 Shen Monkey

Negative Repair / Renovation Sectors 修方凶位 :

月 MONTH	大月建 Big Month Establishment			飛大煞 Flying Great Sha			丙丁獨火 Bing Ding Lonely Fire	
寅 Tiger (Feb 4 - Mar 5) 正月 1st Month	未 Wei Goat	坤 Kun	申 Shen Monkey	甲 Jia Yang Wood	震 Zhen	乙 Yi Yin Wood	兌 Dui	艮 Gen
卯 Rabbit (Mar 6 - Apr 4) 二月 2nd Month	壬 Ren Yang Water	坎 Kan	癸 Gui Yin Water	未 Wei Goat	坤 Kun	申 Shen Monkey	乾 Qian	兌 Dui
辰 Dragon (Apr 5 - May 5) 三月 3rd Month	丙 Bing Yang Fire	離 Li	丁 Ding Yin Fire	壬 Ren Yang Water	坎 Kan	癸 Gui Yin Water	中 Middle	乾 Qian
巳 Snake (May 6 - Jun 5) 四月 4th Month	丑 Chou Ox	艮 Gen	寅 Yin Tiger	丙 Bing Yang Fire	離 Li	丁 Ding Yin Fire	中 Middle	
午 Horse (Jun 6 - July 6) 五月 5th Month	庚 Geng Yang Metal	兌 Dui	辛 Xin Yin Metal	丑 Chou Ox	艮 Gen	寅 Yin Tiger	巽 Xun	中 Middle
未 Goat (July 7 - Aug 7) 六月 6th Month	戊 Xu Dog	乾 Qian	亥 Hai Pig	庚 Geng Yang Metal	兌 Dui	辛 Xin Yin Metal	震 Zhen	巽 Xun
申 Monkey (Aug 8 - Sept 7) 七月 7th Month		中 Middle		戊 Xu Dog	乾 Qian	亥 Hai Pig	坤 Kun	震 Zhen
酉 Rooster (Sept 8 - Oct 7) 八月 8th Month	辰 Chen Dragon	巽 Xun	巳 Si Snake		中 Middle		坎 Kan	坤 Kun
戌 Dog (Oct 8 - Nov 6) 九月 9th Month	甲 Jia Yang Wood	震 Zhen	乙 Yi Yin Wood	庚 Geng Yang Metal	兌 Dui	辛 Xin Yin Metal	離 Li	坎 Kan
亥 Pig (Nov 7 - Dec 6) 十月 10th Month	未 Wei Goat	坤 Kun	申 Shen Monkey	戊 Xu Dog	乾 Qian	亥 Hai Pig	艮 Gen	離 Li
子 Rat (Dec 7 - Jan 5) 十一月 11th Month	壬 Ren Yang Water	坎 Kan	癸 Gui Yin Water		中 Middle		兌 Dui	艮 Gen
丑 Ox (Jan 6 - Feb 3) 十二月 12th Month	丙 Bing Yang Fire	離 Li	丁 Ding Yin Fire	辰 Chen Dragon	巽 Xun	巳 Si Snake	乾 Qian	兌 Dui

Negative Repair / Renovation Sectors 修方凶位 :

月 MONTH	月遊火 Month Wondering Fire	三煞 Monthly 3 Killings		
		劫煞 Robbery Sha	災煞 Calamity Sha	月煞 Month Sha
寅 **Tiger** (Feb 4 - Mar 5) 正月 **1st Month**	離 Li	亥 Hai Pig	子 Zi Rat	丑 Chou Ox
卯 **Rabbit** (Mar 6 - Apr 4) 二月 **2nd Month**	坎 Kan	申 Shen Monkey	酉 You Rooster	戌 Xu Dog
辰 **Dragon** (Apr 5 - May 5) 三月 **3rd Month**	坤 Kun	巳 Si Snake	午 Wu Horse	未 Wei Goat
巳 **Snake** (May 6 - Jun 5) 四月 **4th Month**	震 Zhen	寅 Yin Tiger	卯 Mao Rabbit	辰 Chen Dragon
午 **Horse** (Jun 6 - July 6) 五月 **5th Month**	巽 Xun	亥 Hai Pig	子 Zi Rat	丑 Chou Ox
未 **Goat** (July 7 - Aug 7) 六月 **6th Month**	中 Middle	申 Shen Monkey	酉 You Rooster	戌 Xu Dog
申 **Monkey** (Aug 8 - Sept 7) 七月 **7th Month**	乾 Qian	巳 Si Snake	午 Wu Horse	未 Wei Goat
酉 **Rooster** (Sept 8 - Oct 7) 八月 **8th Month**	兌 Dui	寅 Yin Tiger	卯 Mao Rabbit	辰 Chen Dragon
戌 **Dog** (Oct 8 - Nov 6) 九月 **9th Month**	艮 Gen	亥 Hai Pig	子 Zi Rat	丑 Chou Ox
亥 **Pig** (Nov 7 - Dec 6) 十月 **10th Month**	離 Li	申 Shen Monkey	酉 You Rooster	戌 Xu Dog
子 **Rat** (Dec 7 - Jan 5) 十一月 **11th Month**	坎 Kan	巳 Si Snake	午 Wu Horse	未 Wei Goat
丑 **Ox** (Jan 6 - Feb 3) 十二月 **12th Month**	坤 Kun	寅 Yin Tiger	卯 Mao Rabbit	辰 Chen Dragon

Negative Repair / Renovation Sectors 修方凶位 :

月 MONTH	月刑 Month Punishment	月害 Month Harm	月厭 Month Detest
寅 **Tiger** (Feb 4 - Mar 5) 正月 **1st Month**	巳 *Si* **Snake**	巳 *Si* **Snake**	戌 *Xu* **Dog**
卯 **Rabbit** (Mar 6 - Apr 4) 二月 **2nd Month**	子 *Zi* **Rat**	辰 *Chen* **Dragon**	酉 *You* **Rooster**
辰 **Dragon** (Apr 5 - May 5) 三月 **3rd Month**	辰 *Chen* **Dragon**	卯 *Mao* **Rabbit**	申 *Shen* **Monkey**
巳 **Snake** (May 6 - Jun 5) 四月 **4th Month**	申 *Shen* **Monkey**	寅 *Yin* **Tiger**	未 *Wei* **Goat**
午 **Horse** (Jun 6 - July 6) 五月 **5th Month**	午 *Wu* **Horse**	丑 *Chou* **Ox**	午 *Wu* **Horse**
未 **Goat** (July 7 - Aug 7) 六月 **6th Month**	丑 *Chou* **Ox**	子 *Zi* **Rat**	巳 *Si* **Snake**
申 **Monkey** (Aug 8 - Sept 7) 七月 **7th Month**	寅 *Yin* **Tiger**	亥 *Hai* **Pig**	辰 *Chen* **Dragon**
酉 **Rooster** (Sept 8 - Oct 7) 八月 **8th Month**	酉 *You* **Rooster**	戌 *Xu* **Dog**	卯 *Mao* **Rabbit**
戌 **Dog** (Oct 8 - Nov 6) 九月 **9th Month**	未 *Wei* **Goat**	酉 *You* **Rooster**	寅 *Yin* **Tiger**
亥 **Pig** (Nov 7 - Dec 6) 十月 **10th Month**	亥 *Hai* **Pig**	申 *Shen* **Monkey**	丑 *Chou* **Ox**
子 **Rat** (Dec 7 - Jan 5) 十一月 **11th Month**	卯 *Mao* **Rabbit**	未 *Wei* **Goat**	子 *Zi* **Rat**
丑 **Ox** (Jan 6 - Feb 3) 十二月 **12th Month**	戌 *Xu* **Dog**	午 *Wu* **Horse**	亥 *Hai* **Pig**

癸未 Gui Wei
(Water Goat)

Heavenly Stem 天干	癸 **Yin Water (陰水)**
Earthly Branch 地支	未 **Goat (Yin Earth 陰土)**
Hidden Stem 藏干	己 **Yin Earth, 丁 Yin Fire, 乙 Yin Wood**
Na Yin 納音	楊柳木 **Wood from willow tree**
Grand Duke 太歲	未 **Goat**
Xuan Kong Five Element 玄空五行	4 金 **Metal**
Gua Name 卦名	䷲ 澤水困 **Trap**
Xuan Kong Period Luck 玄空卦運	8

Annual Positive Stars for Opening Mountain, Establishing Facing and Commencing Repairs 開山立向修方吉星：

歲德 **Duke Virtue**	戊 Wu **Yang Earth**	
歲德合 **Duke Virtue Combo**	癸 Gui **Yin Water**	
歲枝德 **Duke Branch Virtue**	子 Zi **Rat**	
陽貴人 **Yang Nobleman**	巳 Si **Snake**	
陰貴人 **Yin Nobleman**	卯 Mao **Rabbit**	
歲祿 **Duke Prosperous**	子 Zi **Rat**	
歲馬 **Duke Horse**	巳 Si **Snake**	
奏書 **Decree**	巽 Xun	
博士 **Professor**	乾 Qian	

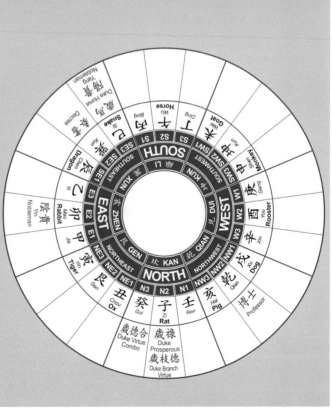

Annual Negative Stars for Opening Mountain, Establishing Facing and Commencing Repairs 開山立向修方凶星：

太歲 Grand Duke	歲破 Year Breaker	三煞 Three Killings			坐煞向煞 Sitting Sha Facing Sha				浮天空亡 Floating Heaven Emptiness	
未 Wei Goat	丑 Chou Ox	申 Shen Monkey	酉 You Rooster	戌 Xu Dog	庚 Geng Yang Metal	辛 Xin Yin Metal	甲 Jia Yang Wood	乙 Yi Yin Wood	坤 Kun	乙 Yi Yin Wood

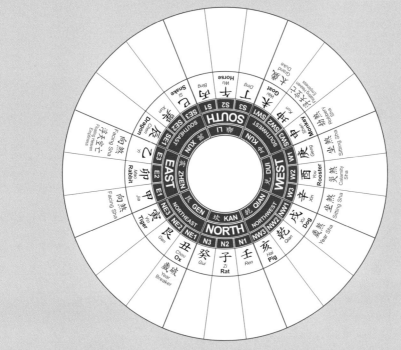

Annual San Yuan Purple White Stars 三元紫白九星：

上元 Upper Period Period 1, 2, 3			中元 Middle Period Period 4, 5, 6			下元 Lower Period Period 7, 8, 9		
巽SE **8**	離S **4**	坤SW **6**	巽SE **2**	離S **7**	坤SW **9**	巽SE **5**	離S **1**	坤SW **3**
震E **7**	**9** 癸未 Gui Wei Water Goat	兑W **2**	震E **1**	**3** 癸未 Gui Wei Water Goat	兑W **5**	震E **4**	**6** 癸未 Gui Wei Water Goat	兑W **8**
艮NE **3**	坎N **5**	乾NW **1**	艮NE **6**	坎N **8**	乾NW **4**	艮NE **9**	坎N **2**	乾NW **7**

Mountain Covering Yellow Path 蓋山黃道：

貪狼 *Tan Lang* **Greedy Wolf**		巨門 *Ju Men* **Huge Door**				武曲 *Wu Qu* **Military Arts**		文曲 *Wen Qu* **Literary Arts**			
坤 *Kun* SW2	乙 *Yi* E3	坎 *Kan* N2	癸 *Gui* N3	申 *Shen* SW3	辰 *Chen* SE1	乾 *Qian* NW2	甲 *Jia* E1	震 *Zhen* E2	庚 *Geng* W1	亥 *Hai* NW3	未 *Wei* SW1

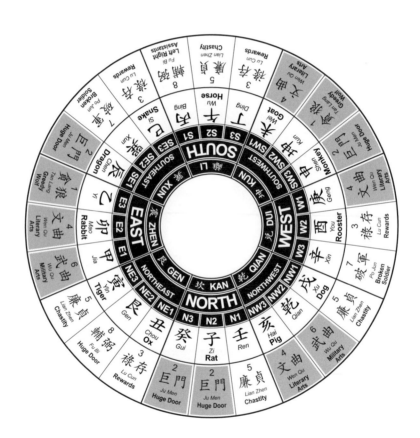

Heaven Penetrating Force 通天竅:

三合前方 **Facing Three Harmony**	巽巳 Xun Si	丙午 Bing Wu	丁未 Ding Wei
三合後方 **Sitting Three Harmony**	乾亥 Qian Hai	壬子 Ren Zi	癸丑 Gui Chou

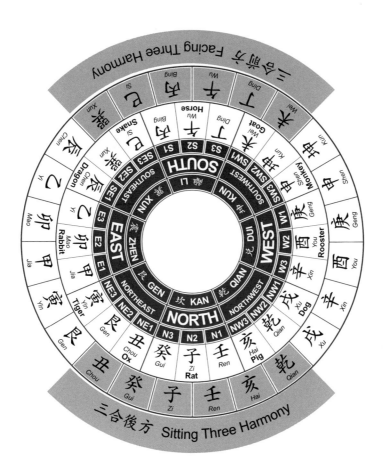

Moving Horse Six Ren Assessment 走馬六壬：					
神后 *Shen Hou* **Holy Empress**	功曹 *Gong Cao* **Marshall**	天罡 *Tian Gang* **Heavenly Dipper**	勝光 *Sheng Guang* **Subliminal Bright**	傳送 *Chuan Song* **Great General**	河魁 *He Kui* **River Scholar**
巽巳 *Xun Si*	丁未 *Ding Wei*	庚酉 *Geng You*	乾亥 *Qian Hai*	癸丑 *Gui Chou*	甲卯 *Jia Mao*

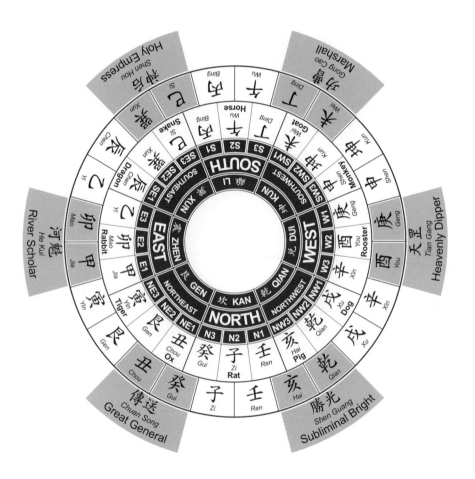

Four Advantages Three Cycles Star Plate 四利三元：

太陽 *Tai Yang* **Sun**	太陰 *Tai Yin* **Moon**	龍德 *Long De* **Dragon Virtue**	福德 *Fu De* **Fortune Virtue**
申 *Shen* **Monkey**	戌 *Xu* **Dog**	寅 *Yin* **Tiger**	辰 *Chen* **Dragon**

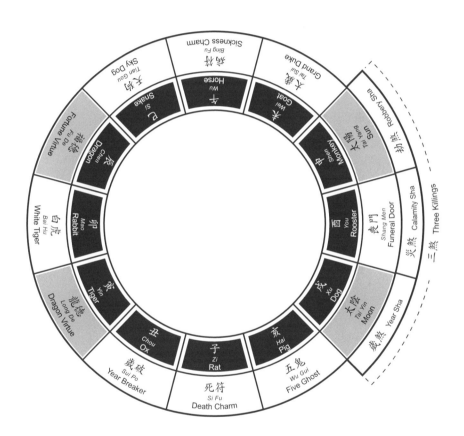

Negative Sectors For Opening Mountain 開山凶位：

年剋山家 Year Countering Sitting

甲 Jia E1	寅 Yin NE3	辰 Chen SE1	巽 Xun SE2	戌 Xu NW1	坎 Kan N2	申 Shen SW3	辛 Xin W3	丑 Chou NE1	癸 Gui N3	坤 Kun SW2	庚 Geng W1	未 Wei SW1

陰府太歲 Yin Fu Tai Sui **Yin Mansion Grand Duke**		六害 Liu Hai **Six Harm**	死符 Si Fu **Death Charm**	炙退 Zhi Tui **Roasting Star**
震 Zhen E2	坤 Kun SW2	子 Zi N2	子 Zi N2	午 Wu S2

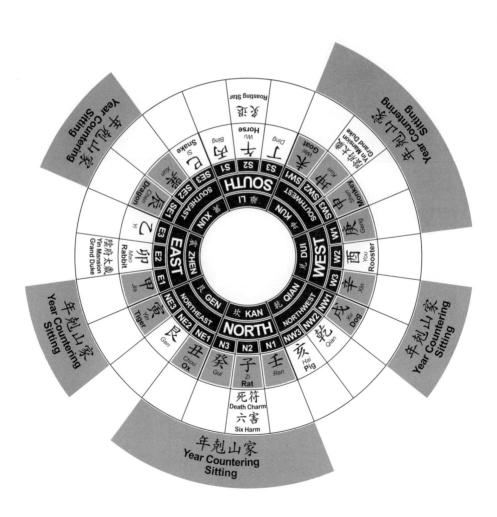

Negative Directions to Establish Facing 立向凶方：	
巡山羅喉 *Xun Shan Luo Hou* **Mountain Patrol Luo Hou Star**	病符 *Bing Fu* **Sickness Charm**
坤 *Kun* **SW2**	午 *Wu* **S2**

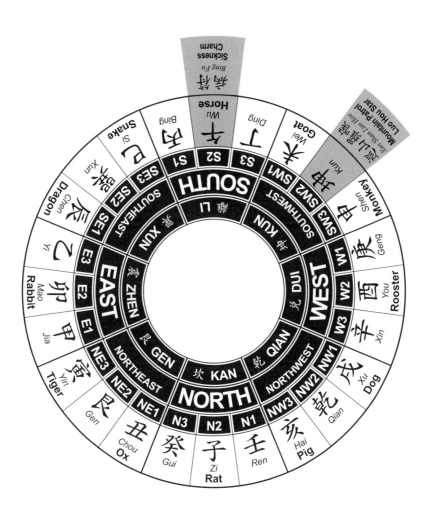

Negative Repair / Renovation Sectors Table 修方凶位表：

天官符 **Heavenly Officer Charm**	寅 Yin Tiger	飛廉 **Flying Chaste**	卯 Mao Rabbit
地官符 **Earthly Officer Charm**	亥 Hai Pig	喪門 **Funeral Door**	酉 You Rooster
大煞 **Great Sha**	卯 Mao Rabbit	弔客 **Suspended Guest**	巳 Si Snake
大將軍 **Big General**	卯 Mao Rabbit	白虎 **White Tiger**	卯 Mao Rabbit
力士 **Strong Man**	坤 Kun	金神 **Golden God**	申 Shen Monkey
蠶室 **Silkworm Room**	艮 Gen		酉 You Rooster
蠶官 **Silkworm Officer**	丑 Chou Ox		子 Zi Rat
蠶命 **Silkworm Life**	寅 Yin Tiger		丑 Chou Ox
歲刑 **Duke Punishment**	丑 Chou Ox	獨火 **Lonely Fire**	離 Li
黃幡 **Yellow Flag**	未 Wei Goat	五鬼 **Five Ghost**	酉 You Rooster
豹尾 **Leopard Tail**	丑 Chou Ox	破敗五鬼 **Destructive Five Ghost**	艮 Gen

Negative Repair / Renovation Sectors Diagram 修方凶位圖：

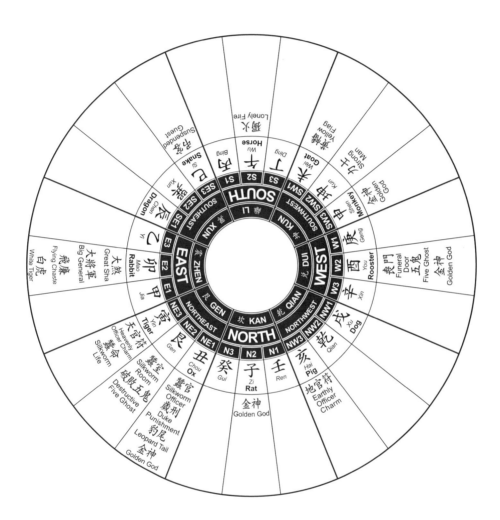

12-Month Auxiliary Stars Reference Table :
癸未年十二月，開山立向修方星表

Positive Monthly Stars 吉星方

月 MONTH	寅 Tiger (Feb 4 - Mar 5) 正月 1st Month	卯 Rabbit (Mar 6 - Apr 4) 二月 2nd Month	辰 Dragon (Apr 5 - May 5) 三月 3rd Month	巳 Snake (May 6 - Jun 5) 四月 4th Month	午 Horse (Jun 6 - July 6) 五月 5th Month	未 Goat (July 7 - Aug 7) 六月 6th Month
天道 Heavenly Path	南 South	西南 Southwest	北 North	西 West	西北 Northwest	東 East
天德 Heavenly Virtue	丁 Ding Yin Fire	坤 Kun (申)	壬 Ren Yang Water	辛 Xin Yin Metal	乾 Qian (亥)	甲 Jia Yang Wood
天德合 Heavenly Virtue Combo	壬 Ren Yang Water	(巳)	丁 Ding Yin Fire	丙 Bing Yang Fire	(寅)	己 Ji Yin Earth
月德 Monthly Virtue	丙 Bing Yang Fire	甲 Jia Yang Wood	壬 Ren Yang Water	庚 Geng Yang Metal	丙 Bing Yang Fire	甲 Jia Yang Wood
月德合 Monthly Virtue Combo	辛 Xin Yin Metal	己 Ji Yin Earth	丁 Ding Yin Fire	乙 Yi Yin Wood	辛 Xin Yin Metal	己 Ji Yin Earth
月空 Month Emptiness	壬 Ren Yang Water	庚 Geng Yang Metal	丙 Bing Yang Fire	甲 Jia Yang Wood	壬 Ren Yang Water	庚 Geng Yang Metal
陽貴人 Yang Nobleman	艮 Gen	兌 Dui	乾 Qian	中 Middle	坎 Kan	離 Li
陰貴人 Yin Nobleman	乾 Qian	中 Middle	坎 Kan	離 Li	艮 Gen	兌 Dui
飛天祿 Flying Heavenly Wealth	乾 Qian	中 Middle	巽 Xun	震 Zhen	坤 Kun	坎 Kan
飛天馬 Flying Heavenly Horse	艮 Gen	兌 Dui	乾 Qian	中 Middle	坎 Kan	離 Li

12-Month Auxiliary Stars Reference Table :
癸未年十二月，開山立向修方星表

申 Monkey (Aug 8 - Sept 7) 七月 7th Month	酉 Rooster (Sept 8 - Oct 7) 八月 8th Month	戌 Dog (Oct 8 - Nov 6) 九月 9th Month	亥 Pig (Nov 7 - Dec 6) 十月 10th Month	子 Rat (Dec 7 - Jan 5) 十一月 11th Month	丑 Ox (Jan 6 - Feb 3) 十二月 12th Month	月 MONTH
北 North	東北 Northeast	南 South	東 East	東南 Southeast	西 West	天道 Heavenly Path
癸 Gui Yin Water	艮 Gen (寅)	丙 Bing Yang Fire	乙 Yi Yin Wood	巽 Xun (巳)	庚 Geng Yang Metal	天德 Heavenly Virtue
戊 Wu Yang Earth	(亥)	辛 Xin Yin Metal	庚 Geng Yang Metal	(申)	乙 Yi Yin Wood	天德合 Heavenly Virtue Combo
壬 Ren Yang Water	庚 Geng Yang Metal	丙 Bing Yang Fire	甲 Jia Yang Wood	壬 Ren Yang Water	庚 Geng Yang Metal	月德 Monthly Virtue
丁 Ding Yin Fire	乙 Yi Yin Wood	辛 Xin Yin Metal	己 Ji Yin Earth	丁 Ding Yin Fire	乙 Yi Yin Wood	月德合 Monthly Virtue Combo
丙 Bing Yang Fire	甲 Jia Yang Wood	壬 Ren Yang Water	庚 Geng Yang Metal	丙 Bing Yang Fire	甲 Jia Yang Wood	月空 Month Emptiness
艮 Gen	兌 Dui	乾 Qian	中 Middle	巽 Xun	震 Zhen	陽貴人 Yang Nobleman
乾 Qian	中 Middle	巽 Xun	震 Zhen	坤 Kun	坎 Kan	陰貴人 Yin Nobleman
離 Li	艮 Gen	兌 Dui	乾 Qian	中 Middle	坎 Kan	飛天祿 Flying Heavenly Wealth
艮 Gen	兌 Dui	乾 Qian	中 Middle	巽 Xun	震 Zhen	飛天馬 Flying Heavenly Horse

Monthly Purple White Stars 月紫白九星 :

寅 Tiger (Feb 4 - Mar 5) 正月 1st Month

巽SE	離S	坤SW
4 Green 四綠	**9** Purple 九紫	**2** Black 二黑
震E **3** Jade 三碧	**5** Yellow 五黃	**7** Red 七赤 兌W
8 White 八白	**1** White 一白	**6** White 六白
艮NE	坎N	乾NW

卯 Rabbit (Mar 6 - Apr 4) 二月 2nd Month

巽SE	離S	坤SW
3 Jade 三碧	**8** White 八白	**1** White 一白
震E **2** Black 二黑	**4** Green 四綠	**6** White 六白 兌W
7 Red 七赤	**9** Purple 九紫	**5** Yellow 五黃
艮NE	坎N	乾NW

辰 Dragon (Apr 5 - May 5) 三月 3rd Month

巽SE	離S	坤SW
2 Black 二黑	**7** Red 七赤	**9** Purple 九紫
震E **1** White 一白	**3** Jade 三碧	**5** Yellow 五黃 兌W
6 White 六白	**8** White 八白	**4** Green 四綠
艮NE	坎N	乾NW

巳 Snake (May 6 - Jun 5) 四月 4th Month

巽SE	離S	坤SW
1 White 一白	**6** White 六白	**8** White 八白
震E **9** Purple 九紫	**2** Black 二黑	**4** Green 四綠 兌W
5 Yellow 五黃	**7** Red 七赤	**3** Jade 三碧
艮NE	坎N	乾NW

午 Horse (Jun 6 - July 6) 五月 5th Month

巽SE	離S	坤SW
9 Purple 九紫	**5** Yellow 五黃	**7** Red 七赤
震E **8** White 八白	**1** White 一白	**3** Jade 三碧 兌W
4 Green 四綠	**6** White 六白	**2** Black 二黑
艮NE	坎N	乾NW

未 Goat (July 7 - Aug 7) 六月 6th Month

巽SE	離S	坤SW
8 White 八白	**4** Green 四綠	**6** White 六白
震E **7** Red 七赤	**9** Purple 九紫	**2** Black 二黑 兌W
3 Jade 三碧	**5** Yellow 五黃	**1** White 一白
艮NE	坎N	乾NW

申 Monkey (Aug 8 - Sept 7) 七月 7th Month

巽SE	離S	坤SW
7 Red 七赤	**3** Jade 三碧	**5** Yellow 五黃
震E **6** White 六白	**8** White 八白	**1** White 一白 兌W
2 Black 二黑	**4** Green 四綠	**9** Purple 九紫
艮NE	坎N	乾NW

酉 Rooster (Sept 8 - Oct 7) 八月 8th Month

巽SE	離S	坤SW
6 White 六白	**2** Black 二黑	**4** Green 四綠
震E **5** Yellow 五黃	**7** Red 七赤	**9** Purple 九紫 兌W
1 White 一白	**3** Jade 三碧	**8** White 八白
艮NE	坎N	乾NW

戌 Dog (Oct 8 - Nov 6) 九月 9th Month

巽SE	離S	坤SW
5 Yellow 五黃	**1** White 一白	**3** Jade 三碧
震E **4** Green 四綠	**6** White 六白	**8** White 八白 兌W
9 Purple 九紫	**2** Black 二黑	**7** Red 七赤
艮NE	坎N	乾NW

亥 Pig (Nov 7 - Dec 6) 十月 10th Month

巽SE	離S	坤SW
4 Green 四綠	**9** Purple 九紫	**2** Black 二黑
震E **3** Jade 三碧	**5** Yellow 五黃	**7** Red 七赤 兌W
8 White 八白	**1** White 一白	**6** White 六白
艮NE	坎N	乾NW

子 Rat (Dec 7 - Jan 5) 十一月 11th Month

巽SE	離S	坤SW
3 Jade 三碧	**8** White 八白	**1** White 一白
震E **2** Black 二黑	**4** Green 四綠	**6** White 六白 兌W
7 Red 七赤	**9** Purple 九紫	**5** Yellow 五黃
艮NE	坎N	乾NW

丑 Ox (Jan 6 - Feb 3) 十二月 12th Month

巽SE	離S	坤SW
2 Black 二黑	**7** Red 七赤	**9** Purple 九紫
震E **1** White 一白	**3** Jade 三碧	**5** Yellow 五黃 兌W
6 White 六白	**8** White 八白	**4** Green 四綠
艮NE	坎N	乾NW

Qi Men Three Nobles 三奇 :

Three Nobles 三奇 / Seasons	乙 Yi	丙 Bing	丁 Ding
立春 **Coming of Spring** Feb 4 - Feb 18	坎 Kan	坤 Kun	震 Zhen
春分 **Spring Equinox** Mar 21 - Apr 4	中 **Middle**	乾 Qian	兌 Dui
立夏 **Coming of Summer** May 6 - May 20	乾 Qian	兌 Dui	艮 Gen
夏至 **Summer Solstice** Jun 22 - Jul 6	兌 Dui	乾 Qian	中 **Middle**
立秋 **Coming of Autumn** Aug 8 - Aug 23	離 Li	艮 Gen	兌 Dui
秋分 **Autumn Equinox** Sept 23 - Oct 7	中 **Middle**	巽 Xun	震 Zhen
立冬 **Coming of Winter** Nov 7 - Nov 22	巽 Xun	震 Zhen	坤 Kun
冬至 **Winter Solstice** Dec 22 - Jan 5	震 Zhen	巽 Xun	中 **Middle**

Sectors to Avoid Opening Mountain 開山凶位 :

月 MONTH	月建 Month Establishment	月破 Month Destruction	月剋山家 Month Countering Sitting		陰府太歲 Yin Mansion Grand Duke	
寅 **Tiger** (Feb 4 - Mar 5) 正月 **1st Month**	寅 Yin **Tiger**	申 Shen **Monkey**	震 Zhen	巳 Si **Snake**	艮 Gen	巽 Xun
卯 **Rabbit** (Mar 6 - Apr 4) 二月 **2nd Month**	卯 Mao **Rabbit**	酉 You **Rooster**	艮 Gen		兌 Dui	乾 Qian
辰 **Dragon** (Apr 5 - May 5) 三月 **3rd Month**	辰 Chen **Dragon**	戌 Xu **Dog**	離 Li	丙 Bing **Yang Fire**	坎 Kan	坤 Kun
巳 **Snake** (May 6 - Jun 5) 四月 **4th Month**	巳 Si **Snake**	亥 Hai **Pig**	壬 Ren **Yang Water**	乙 Yi **Yin Wood**	乾 Qian	離 Li
午 **Horse** (Jun 6 - July 6) 五月 **5th Month**	午 Wu **Horse**	子 Zi **Rat**	—		坤 Kun	震 Zhen
未 **Goat** (July 7 - Aug 7) 六月 **6th Month**	未 Wei **Goat**	丑 Chou **Ox**	—		巽 Xun	艮 Gen
申 **Monkey** (Aug 8 - Sept 7) 七月 **7th Month**	申 Shen **Monkey**	寅 Yin **Tiger**	水 Water	山 Mountain	乾 Qian	兌 Dui
酉 **Rooster** (Sept 8 - Oct 7) 八月 **8th Month**	酉 You **Rooster**	卯 Mao **Rabbit**	土 Earth		坤 Kun	坎 Kan
戌 **Dog** (Oct 8 - Nov 6) 九月 **9th Month**	戌 Xu **Dog**	辰 Chen **Dragon**	震 Zhen	巳 Si **Snake**	離 Li	乾 Qian
亥 **Pig** (Nov 7 - Dec 6) 十月 **10th Month**	亥 Hai **Pig**	巳 Si **Snake**	艮 Gen		震 Zhen	坤 Kun
子 **Rat** (Dec 7 - Jan 5) 十一月 **11th Month**	子 Zi **Rat**	午 Wu **Horse**	—		艮 Gen	巽 Xun
丑 **Ox** (Jan 6 - Feb 3) 十二月 **12th Month**	丑 Chou **Ox**	未 Wei **Goat**	—		兌 Dui	乾 Qian

Negative Repair / Renovation Sectors 修方凶位 :

月 MONTH	天官符 Heavenly Officer Charm			地官符 Earth Officer Charm			小月建 Small Month Establishment		
寅 **Tiger** (Feb 4 - Mar 5) 正月 **1st Month**		中 Middle			中 Middle		丙 Bing Yang Fire	離 Li	丁 Ding Yin Fire
卯 **Rabbit** (Mar 6 - Apr 4) 二月 **2nd Month**	庚 Geng Yang Metal	兌 Dui	辛 Xin Yin Metal	辰 Chen Dragon	巽 Xun	巳 Si Snake	壬 Ren Yang Water	坎 Kan	癸 Gui Yin Water
辰 **Dragon** (Apr 5 - May 5) 三月 **3rd Month**	戊 Xu Dog	乾 Qian	亥 Hai Pig	甲 Jia Yang Wood	震 Zhen	乙 Yi Yin Wood	未 Wei Goat	坤 Kun	申 Shen Monkey
巳 **Snake** (May 6 - Jun 5) 四月 **4th Month**		中 Middle		未 Wei Goat	坤 Kun	申 Shen Monkey	甲 Jia Yang Wood	震 Zhen	乙 Yi Yin Wood
午 **Horse** (Jun 6 - July 6) 五月 **5th Month**	辰 Chen Dragon	巽 Xun	巳 Si Snake	壬 Ren Yang Water	坎 Kan	癸 Gui Yin Water	辰 Chen Dragon	巽 Xun	巳 Si Snake
未 **Goat** (July 7 - Aug 7) 六月 **6th Month**	甲 Jia Yang Wood	震 Zhen	乙 Yi Yin Wood	丙 Bing Yang Fire	離 Li	丁 Ding Yin Fire		中 Middle	
申 **Monkey** (Aug 8 - Sept 7) 七月 **7th Month**	未 Wei Goat	坤 Kun	申 Shen Monkey	丑 Chou Ox	艮 Gen	寅 Yin Tiger	戊 Xu Dog	乾 Qian	亥 Hai Pig
酉 **Rooster** (Sept 8 - Oct 7) 八月 **8th Month**	壬 Ren Yang Water	坎 Kan	癸 Gui Yin Water	庚 Geng Yang Metal	兌 Dui	辛 Xin Yin Metal	庚 Geng Yang Metal	兌 Dui	辛 Xin Yin Metal
戌 **Dog** (Oct 8 - Nov 6) 九月 **9th Month**	丙 Bing Yang Fire	離 Li	丁 Ding Yin Fire	戊 Xu Dog	乾 Qian	亥 Hai Pig	丑 Chou Ox	艮 Gen	寅 Yin Tiger
亥 **Pig** (Nov 7 - Dec 6) 十月 **10th Month**	丑 Chou Ox	艮 Gen	寅 Yin Tiger		中 Middle		丙 Bing Yang Fire	離 Li	丁 Ding Yin Fire
子 **Rat** (Dec 7 - Jan 5) 十一月 **11th Month**	庚 Geng Yang Metal	兌 Dui	辛 Xin Yin Metal	庚 Geng Yang Metal	兌 Dui	辛 Xin Yin Metal	壬 Ren Yang Water	坎 Kan	癸 Gui Yin Water
丑 **Ox** (Jan 6 - Feb 3) 十二月 **12th Month**	戊 Xu Dog	乾 Qian	亥 Hai Pig	戊 Xu Dog	乾 Qian	亥 Hai Pig	未 Wei Goat	坤 Kun	申 Shen Monkey

Negative Repair / Renovation Sectors 修方凶位 :

月 MONTH	大月建 Big Month Establishment			飛大煞 Flying Great Sha			丙丁獨火 Bing Ding Lonely Fire	
寅 Tiger (Feb 4 - Mar 5) 正月 1st Month		中 Middle		戌 Xu Dog	乾 Qian	亥 Hai Pig	兌 Dui	艮 Gen
卯 Rabbit (Mar 6 - Apr 4) 二月 2nd Month	辰 Chen Dragon	巽 Xun	巳 Si Snake		中 Middle		乾 Qian	兌 Dui
辰 Dragon (Apr 5 - May 5) 三月 3rd Month	甲 Jia Yang Wood	震 Zhen	乙 Yi Yin Wood	庚 Geng Yang Metal	兌 Dui	辛 Xin Yin Metal	中 Middle	乾 Qian
巳 Snake (May 6 - Jun 5) 四月 4th Month	未 Wei Goat	坤 Kun	申 Shen Monkey	戌 Xu Dog	乾 Qian	亥 Hai Pig		中 Middle
午 Horse (Jun 6 - July 6) 五月 5th Month	壬 Ren Yang Water	坎 Kan	癸 Gui Yin Water		中 Middle		巽 Xun	中 Middle
未 Goat (July 7 - Aug 7) 六月 6th Month	丙 Bing Yang Fire	離 Li	丁 Ding Yin Fire	辰 Chen Dragon	巽 Xun	巳 Si Snake	震 Zhen	巽 Xun
申 Monkey (Aug 8 - Sept 7) 七月 7th Month	丑 Chou Ox	艮 Gen	寅 Yin Tiger	甲 Jia Yang Wood	震 Zhen	乙 Yi Yin Wood	坤 Kun	震 Zhen
酉 Rooster (Sept 8 - Oct 7) 八月 8th Month	庚 Geng Yang Metal	兌 Dui	辛 Xin Yin Metal	未 Wei Goat	坤 Kun	申 Shen Monkey	坎 Kan	坤 Kun
戌 Dog (Oct 8 - Nov 6) 九月 9th Month	戌 Xu Dog	乾 Qian	亥 Hai Pig	壬 Ren Yang Water	坎 Kan	癸 Gui Yin Water	離 Li	坎 Kan
亥 Pig (Nov 7 - Dec 6) 十月 10th Month		中 Middle		丙 Bing Yang Fire	離 Li	丁 Ding Yin Fire	艮 Gen	離 Li
子 Rat (Dec 7 - Jan 5) 十一月 11th Month	辰 Chen Dragon	巽 Xun	巳 Si Snake	丑 Chou Ox	艮 Gen	寅 Yin	兌 Dui	艮 Gen
丑 Ox (Jan 6 - Feb 3) 十二月 12th Month	甲 Jia Yang Wood	震 Zhen	乙 Yi Yin Wood	庚 Geng Yang Metal	兌 Dui	辛 Xin Yin Metal	乾 Qian	兌 Dui

Negative Repair / Renovation Sectors 修方凶位 :

月 MONTH	月遊火 Month Wondering Fire	三煞 Monthly 3 Killings		
		劫煞 Robbery Sha	災煞 Calamity Sha	月煞 Month Sha
寅 **Tiger** (Feb 4 - Mar 5) 正月 **1st Month**	坤 Kun	亥 Hai Pig	子 Zi Rat	丑 Chou Ox
卯 **Rabbit** (Mar 6 - Apr 4) 二月 **2nd Month**	震 Zhen	申 Shen Monkey	酉 You Rooster	戌 Xu Dog
辰 **Dragon** (Apr 5 - May 5) 三月 **3rd Month**	巽 Xun	巳 Si Snake	午 Wu Horse	未 Wei Goat
巳 **Snake** (May 6 - Jun 5) 四月 **4th Month**	中 Middle	寅 Yin Tiger	卯 Mao Rabbit	辰 Chen Dragon
午 **Horse** (Jun 6 - July 6) 五月 **5th Month**	乾 Qian	亥 Hai Pig	子 Zi Rat	丑 Chou Ox
未 **Goat** (July 7 - Aug 7) 六月 **6th Month**	兌 Dui	申 Shen Monkey	酉 You Rooster	戌 Xu Dog
申 **Monkey** (Aug 8 - Sept 7) 七月 **7th Month**	艮 Gen	巳 Si Snake	午 Wu Horse	未 Wei Goat
酉 **Rooster** (Sept 8 - Oct 7) 八月 **8th Month**	離 Li	寅 Yin Tiger	卯 Mao Rabbit	辰 Chen Dragon
戌 **Dog** (Oct 8 - Nov 6) 九月 **9th Month**	坎 Kan	亥 Hai Pig	子 Zi Rat	丑 Chou Ox
亥 **Pig** (Nov 7 - Dec 6) 十月 **10th Month**	坤 Kun	申 Shen Monkey	酉 You Rooster	戌 Xu Dog
子 **Rat** (Dec 7 - Jan 5) 十一月 **11th Month**	震 Zhen	巳 Si Snake	午 Wu Horse	未 Wei Goat
丑 **Ox** (Jan 6 - Feb 3) 十二月 **12th Month**	巽 Xun	寅 Yin Tiger	卯 Mao Rabbit	辰 Chen Dragon

Negative Repair / Renovation Sectors 修方凶位 :

月 MONTH	月刑 Month Punishment	月害 Month Harm	月厭 Month Detest
寅 **Tiger** (Feb 4 - Mar 5) 正月 **1st Month**	巳 *Si* **Snake**	巳 *Si* **Snake**	戌 *Xu* **Dog**
卯 **Rabbit** (Mar 6 - Apr 4) 二月 **2nd Month**	子 *Zi* **Rat**	辰 *Chen* **Dragon**	酉 *You* **Rooster**
辰 **Dragon** (Apr 5 - May 5) 三月 **3rd Month**	辰 *Chen* **Dragon**	卯 *Mao* **Rabbit**	申 *Shen* **Monkey**
巳 **Snake** (May 6 - Jun 5) 四月 **4th Month**	申 *Shen* **Monkey**	寅 *Yin* **Tiger**	未 *Wei* **Goat**
午 **Horse** (Jun 6 - July 6) 五月 **5th Month**	午 *Wu* **Horse**	丑 *Chou* **Ox**	午 *Wu* **Horse**
未 **Goat** (July 7 - Aug 7) 六月 **6th Month**	丑 *Chou* **Ox**	子 *Zi* **Rat**	巳 *Si* **Snake**
申 **Monkey** (Aug 8 - Sept 7) 七月 **7th Month**	寅 *Yin* **Tiger**	亥 *Hai* **Pig**	辰 *Chen* **Dragon**
酉 **Rooster** (Sept 8 - Oct 7) 八月 **8th Month**	酉 *You* **Rooster**	戌 *Xu* **Dog**	卯 *Mao* **Rabbit**
戌 **Dog** (Oct 8 - Nov 6) 九月 **9th Month**	未 *Wei* **Goat**	酉 *You* **Rooster**	寅 *Yin* **Tiger**
亥 **Pig** (Nov 7 - Dec 6) 十月 **10th Month**	亥 *Hai* **Pig**	申 *Shen* **Monkey**	丑 *Chou* **Ox**
子 **Rat** (Dec 7 - Jan 5) 十一月 **11th Month**	卯 *Mao* **Rabbit**	未 *Wei* **Goat**	子 *Zi* **Rat**
丑 **Ox** (Jan 6 - Feb 3) 十二月 **12th Month**	戌 *Xu* **Dog**	午 *Wu* **Horse**	亥 *Hai* **Pig**

癸酉 (Gui You)
Water Rooster

Heavenly Stem 天干	癸 **Yin Water (陰水)**
Earthly Branch 地支	酉 **Rooster (Yin Metal 陰金)**
Hidden Stem 藏干	辛 **Yin Metal**
Na Yin 納音	劍鋒金 **Metal of the sword**
Grand Duke 太歲	酉 **Rooster**
Xuan Kong Five Element 玄空五行	2 火 **Fire**
Gua Name 卦名	䷴ 風山漸 **Gradual Progress**
Xuan Kong Period Luck 玄空卦運	7

Annual Positive Stars for Opening Mountain, Establishing Facing and Commencing Repairs 開山立向修方吉星：

歲德 **Duke Virtue**	戊 *Wu* **Yang Earth**
歲德合 **Duke Virtue Combo**	癸 *Gui* **Yin Water**
歲枝德 **Duke Branch Virtue**	寅 *Yin* **Tiger**
陽貴人 **Yang Nobleman**	巳 *Si* **Snake**
陰貴人 **Yin Nobleman**	卯 *Mao* **Rabbit**
歲祿 **Duke Prosperous**	子 *Zi* **Rat**
歲馬 **Duke Horse**	亥 *Hai* **Pig**
奏書 **Decree**	坤 *Kun*
博士 **Professor**	艮 *Gen*

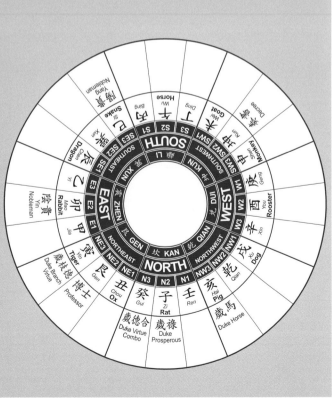

Annual Negative Stars for Opening Mountain, Establishing Facing and Commencing Repairs 開山立向修方凶星：

太歲 Grand Duke	歲破 Year Breaker	三煞 Three Killings			坐煞向煞 Sitting Sha Facing Sha				浮天空亡 Floating Heaven Emptiness	
酉 You Rooster	卯 Mao Rabbit	寅 Yin Tiger	卯 Mao Rabbit	辰 Chen Dragon	甲 Jia Yang Wood	乙 Yi Yin Wood	庚 Geng Yang Metal	辛 Xin Yin Metal	坤 Kun	乙 Yi Yin Wood

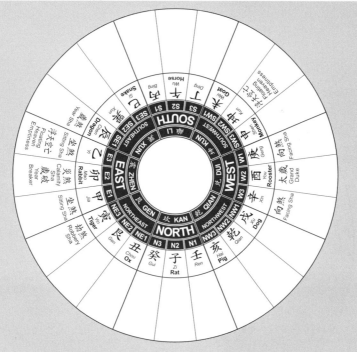

Annual San Yuan Purple White Stars 三元紫白九星：

上元 Upper Period Period 1, 2, 3			中元 Middle Period Period 4, 5, 6			下元 Lower Period Period 7, 8, 9		
巽SE **9**	離S **5**	坤SW **7**	巽SE **3**	離S **8**	坤SW **1**	巽SE **6**	離S **2**	坤SW **4**
震E **8**	**1** 癸酉 Gui You Water Rooster	兌W **3**	震E **2**	**4** 癸酉 Gui You Water Rooster	兌W **6**	震E **5**	**7** 癸酉 Gui You Water Rooster	兌W **9**
艮NE **4**	坎N **6**	乾NW **2**	艮NE **7**	坎N **9**	乾NW **5**	艮NE **1**	坎N **3**	乾NW **8**

Mountain Covering Yellow Path 蓋山黃道：

貪狼 Tan Lang **Greedy Wolf**				巨門 Ju Men **Huge Door**		武曲 Wu Qu **Military Arts**				文曲 Wen Qu **Literary Arts**	
離 Li **S2**	壬 Ren **N1**	寅 Yin **NE3**	戌 Xu **NW1**	乾 Qian **NW2**	甲 Jia **E1**	坎 Kan **N2**	癸 Gui **N3**	申 Shen **SW3**	辰 Chen **SE1**	艮 Gen **NE2**	丙 Bing **S1**

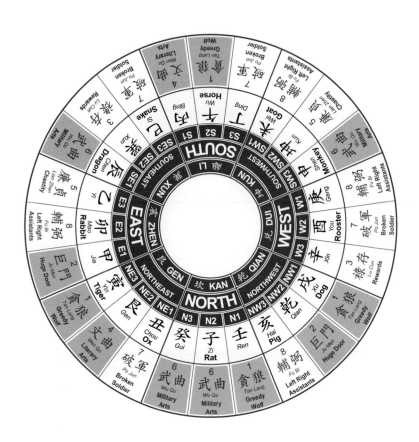

Heaven Penetrating Force 通天竅：

三合前方 **Facing Three Harmony**	乾亥 Qian Hai	壬子 Ren Zi	癸丑 Gui Chou
三合後方 **Sitting Three Harmony**	巽巳 Xun Si	丙午 Bing Wu	丁未 Ding Wei

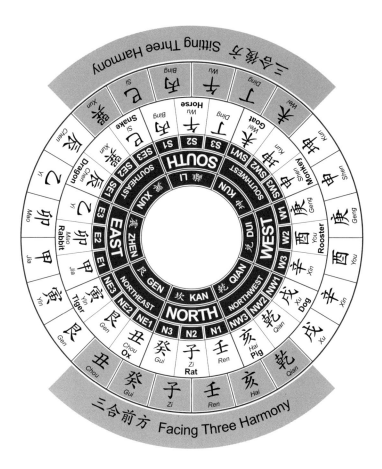

Moving Horse Six Ren Assessment 走馬六壬：

神后 *Shen Hou* **Holy Empress**	功曹 *Gong Cao* **Marshall**	天罡 *Tian Gang* **Heavenly Dipper**	勝光 *Sheng Guang* **Subliminal Bright**	傳送 *Chuan Song* **Great General**	河魁 *He Kui* **River Scholar**
甲卯 *Jia Mao*	巽巳 *Xun Si*	丁未 *Ding Wei*	庚酉 *Geng You*	乾亥 *Qian Hai*	癸丑 *Gui Chou*

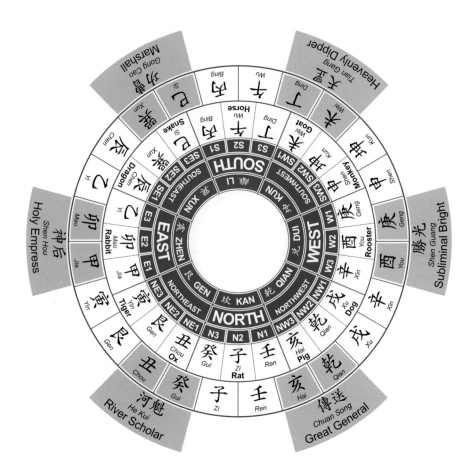

Four Advantages Three Cycles Star Plate 四利三元：

太陽 *Tai Yang* **Sun**	太陰 *Tai Yin* **Moon**	龍德 *Long De* **Dragon Virtue**	福德 *Fu De* **Fortune Virtue**
戌 *Xu* Dog	子 *Zi* Rat	辰 *Chen* Dragon	午 *Wu* Horse

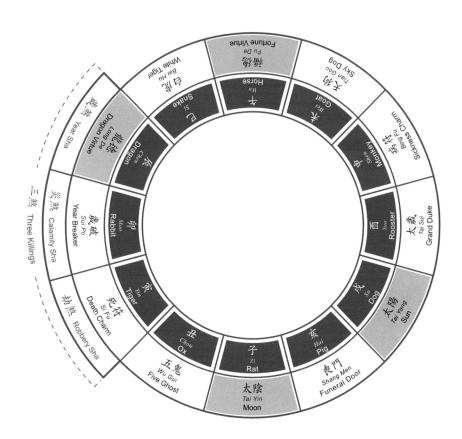

Negative Sectors For Opening Mountain 開山凶位:

年剋山家 Year Countering Sitting

乾 Qian NW2	亥 Hai NW3	兌 Dui W2	丁 Ding S3

陰府太歲 Yin Fu Tai Sui **Yin Mansion Grand Duke**		六害 Liu Hai **Six Harm**	死符 Si Fu **Death Charm**	炙退 Zhi Tui **Roasting Star**
震 Zhen E2	坤 Kun SW2	寅 Yin NE3	寅 Yin NE3	子 Zi N2

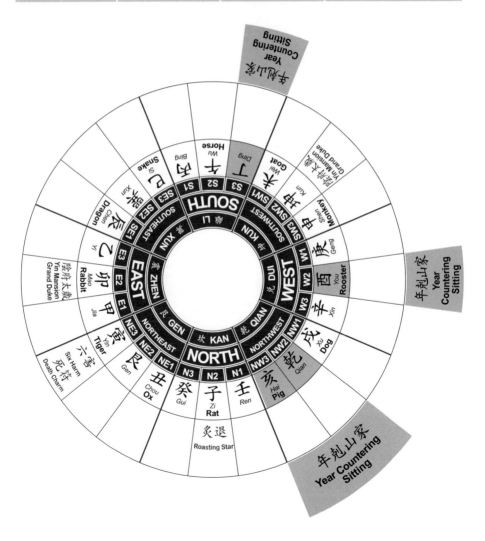

Negative Directions to Establish Facing 立向凶方：

巡山羅睺 *Xun Shan Luo Hou* **Mountain Patrol Luo Hou Star**	病符 *Bing Fu* **Sickness Charm**
辛 *Xin* **W3**	申 *Shen* **SW3**

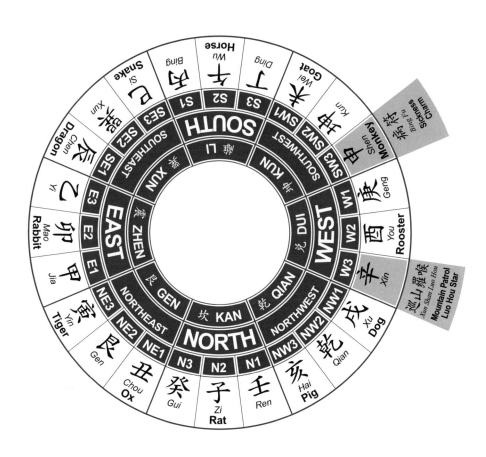

Negative Repair / Renovation Sectors Table 修方凶位表：

天官符 Heavenly Officer Charm	申 Shen Monkey	飛廉 Flying Chaste	亥 Hai Pig
地官符 Earthly Officer Charm	丑 Chou Ox	喪門 Funeral Door	亥 Hai Pig
大煞 Great Sha	酉 You Rooster	弔客 Suspended Guest	未 Wei Goat
大將軍 Big General	午 Wu Horse	白虎 White Tiger	巳 Si Snake
力士 Strong Man	乾 Qian	金神 Golden God	申 Shen Monkey
蠶室 Silkworm Room	巽 Xun		酉 You Rooster
蠶官 Silkworm Officer	辰 Chen Dragon		子 Zi Rat
蠶命 Silkworm Life	巳 Si Snake		丑 Chou Ox
歲刑 Duke Punishment	酉 You Rooster	獨火 Lonely Fire	坤 Kun
黃幡 Yellow Flag	丑 Chou Ox	五鬼 Five Ghost	未 Wei Goat
豹尾 Leopard Tail	未 Wei Goat	破敗五鬼 Destructive Five Ghost	艮 Gen

Negative Repair / Renovation Sectors Diagram 修方凶位圖：

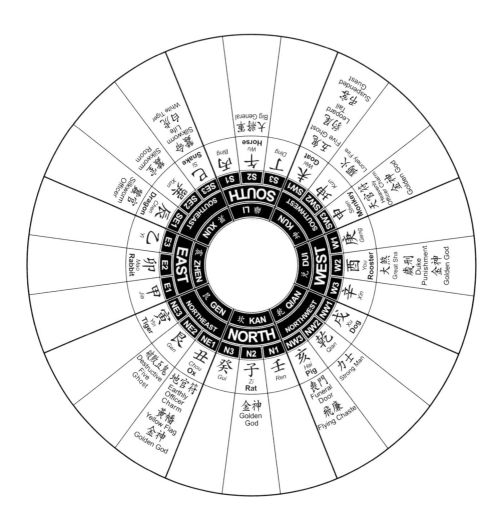

12-Month Auxiliary Stars Reference Table :
癸酉年十二月，開山立向修方星表

Positive Monthly Stars 吉星方

月 **MONTH**	寅 **Tiger** (Feb 4 - Mar 5) 正月 **1st Month**	卯 **Rabbit** (Mar 6 - Apr 4) 二月 **2nd Month**	辰 **Dragon** (Apr 5 - May 5) 三月 **3rd Month**	巳 **Snake** (May 6 - Jun 5) 四月 **4th Month**	午 **Horse** (Jun 6 - July 6) 五月 **5th Month**	未 **Goat** (July 7 - Aug 7) 六月 **6th Month**
天道 **Heavenly Path**	南 South	西南 Southwest	北 North	西 West	西北 Northwest	東 East
天德 **Heavenly Virtue**	丁 Ding Yin Fire	坤 Kun (申)	壬 Ren Yang Water	辛 Xin Yin Metal	乾 Qian (亥)	甲 Jia Yang Wood
天德合 **Heavenly Virtue Combo**	壬 Ren Yang Water	(巳)	丁 Ding Yin Fire	丙 Bing Yang Fire	(寅)	己 Ji Yin Earth
月德 **Monthly Virtue**	丙 Bing Yang Fire	甲 Jia Yang Wood	壬 Ren Yang Water	庚 Geng Yang Metal	丙 Bing Yang Fire	甲 Jia Yang Wood
月德合 **Monthly Virtue Combo**	辛 Xin Yin Metal	己 Ji Yin Earth	丁 Ding Yin Fire	乙 Yi Yin Wood	辛 Xin Yin Metal	己 Ji Yin Earth
月空 **Month Emptiness**	壬 Ren Yang Water	庚 Geng Yang Metal	丙 Bing Yang Fire	甲 Jia Yang Wood	壬 Ren Yang Water	庚 Geng Yang Metal
陽貴人 **Yang Nobleman**	艮 Gen	兌 Dui	乾 Qian	中 Middle	坎 Kan	離 Li
陰貴人 **Yin Nobleman**	乾 Qian	中 Middle	坎 Kan	離 Li	艮 Gen	兌 Dui
飛天祿 **Flying Heavenly Wealth**	乾 Qian	中 Middle	巽 Xun	震 Zhen	坤 Kun	坎 Kan
飛天馬 **Flying Heavenly Horse**	中 Middle	巽 Xun	震 Zhen	坤 Kun	坎 Kan	離 Li

12-Month Auxiliary Stars Reference Table :
癸酉年十二月，開山立向修方星表

申 **Monkey** (Aug 8 - Sept 7)	酉 **Rooster** (Sept 8 - Oct 7)	戌 **Dog** (Oct 8 - Nov 6)	亥 **Pig** (Nov 7 - Dec 6)	子 **Rat** (Dec 7 - Jan 5)	丑 **Ox** (Jan 6 - Feb 3)	月 **MONTH**
七月 **7th Month**	八月 **8th Month**	九月 **9th Month**	十月 **10th Month**	十一月 **11th Month**	十二月 **12th Month**	
北 North	東北 Northeast	南 South	東 East	東南 Southeast	西 West	天道 **Heavenly Path**
癸 Gui Yin Water	艮 Gen (寅)	丙 Bing Yang Fire	乙 Yi Yin Wood	巽 Xun (巳)	庚 Geng Yang Metal	天德 **Heavenly Virtue**
戊 Wu Yang Earth	(亥)	辛 Xin Yin Metal	庚 Geng Yang Metal	(申)	乙 Yi Yin Wood	天德合 **Heavenly Virtue Combo**
壬 Ren Yang Water	庚 Geng Yang Metal	丙 Bing Yang Fire	甲 Jia Yang Wood	壬 Ren Yang Water	庚 Geng Yang Metal	月德 **Monthly Virtue**
丁 Ding Yin Fire	乙 Yi Yin Wood	辛 Xin Yin Metal	己 Ji Yin Earth	丁 Ding Yin Fire	乙 Yi Yin Wood	月德合 **Monthly Virtue Combo**
丙 Bing Yang Fire	甲 Jia Yang Wood	壬 Ren Yang Water	庚 Geng Yang Metal	丙 Bing Yang Fire	甲 Jia Yang Wood	月空 **Month Emptiness**
艮 Gen	兌 Dui	乾 Qian	中 **Middle**	巽 Xun	震 Zhen	陽貴人 **Yang Nobleman**
乾 Qian	中 **Middle**	巽 Xun	震 Zhen	坤 Kun	坎 Kan	陰貴人 **Yin Nobleman**
離 Li	艮 Gen	兌 Dui	乾 Qian	中 **Middle**	坎 Kan	飛天祿 **Flying Heavenly Wealth**
艮 Gen	兌 Dui	乾 Qian	中 **Middle**	坎 Kan	離 Li	飛天馬 **Flying Heavenly Horse**

1173

Monthly Purple White Stars 月紫白九星 :

寅 Tiger (Feb 4 - Mar 5) 正月 1st Month

巽 SE	離 S	坤 SW
7 Red 七赤	3 Jade 三碧	5 Yellow 五黃
震 E — 6 White 六白	8 White 八白	1 White 一白 — 兌 W
2 Black 二黑	4 Green 四綠	9 Purple 九紫
艮 NE	坎 N	乾 NW

卯 Rabbit (Mar 6 - Apr 4) 二月 2nd Month

巽 SE	離 S	坤 SW
6 White 六白	2 Black 二黑	4 Green 四綠
震 E — 5 Yellow 五黃	7 Red 七赤	9 Purple 九紫 — 兌 W
1 White 一白	3 Jade 三碧	8 White 八白
艮 NE	坎 N	乾 NW

辰 Dragon (Apr 5 - May 5) 三月 3rd Month

巽 SE	離 S	坤 SW
5 Yellow 五黃	1 White 一白	3 Jade 三碧
震 E — 4 Green 四綠	6 White 六白	8 White 八白 — 兌 W
9 Purple 九紫	2 Black 二黑	7 Red 七赤
艮 NE	坎 N	乾 NW

巳 Snake (May 6 - Jun 5) 四月 4th Month

巽 SE	離 S	坤 SW
4 Green 四綠	9 Purple 九紫	2 Black 二黑
震 E — 3 Jade 三碧	5 Yellow 五黃	7 Red 七赤 — 兌 W
8 White 八白	1 White 一白	6 White 六白
艮 NE	坎 N	乾 NW

午 Horse (Jun 6 - July 6) 五月 5th Month

巽 SE	離 S	坤 SW
3 Jade 三碧	8 White 八白	1 White 一白
震 E — 2 Black 二黑	4 Green 四綠	6 White 六白 — 兌 W
7 Red 七赤	9 Purple 九紫	5 Yellow 五黃
艮 NE	坎 N	乾 NW

未 Goat (July 7 - Aug 7) 六月 6th Month

巽 SE	離 S	坤 SW
2 Black 二黑	7 Red 七赤	9 Purple 九紫
震 E — 1 White 一白	3 Jade 三碧	5 Yellow 五黃 — 兌 W
6 White 六白	8 White 八白	4 Green 四綠
艮 NE	坎 N	乾 NW

申 Monkey (Aug 8 - Sept 7) 七月 7th Month

巽 SE	離 S	坤 SW
1 White 一白	6 White 六白	8 White 八白
震 E — 9 Purple 九紫	2 Black 二黑	4 Green 四綠 — 兌 W
5 Yellow 五黃	7 Red 七赤	3 Jade 三碧
艮 NE	坎 N	乾 NW

酉 Rooster (Sept 8 - Oct 7) 八月 8th Month

巽 SE	離 S	坤 SW
9 Purple 九紫	5 Yellow 五黃	7 Red 七赤
震 E — 8 White 八白	1 White 一白	3 Jade 三碧 — 兌 W
4 Green 四綠	6 White 六白	2 Black 二黑
艮 NE	坎 N	乾 NW

戌 Dog (Oct 8 - Nov 6) 九月 9th Month

巽 SE	離 S	坤 SW
8 White 八白	4 Green 四綠	6 White 六白
震 E — 7 Red 七赤	9 Purple 九紫	2 Black 二黑 — 兌 W
3 Jade 三碧	5 Yellow 五黃	1 White 一白
艮 NE	坎 N	乾 NW

亥 Pig (Nov 7 - Dec 6) 十月 10th Month

巽 SE	離 S	坤 SW
7 Red 七赤	3 Jade 三碧	5 Yellow 五黃
震 E — 6 White 六白	8 White 八白	1 White 一白 — 兌 W
2 Black 二黑	4 Green 四綠	9 Purple 九紫
艮 NE	坎 N	乾 NW

子 Rat (Dec 7 - Jan 5) 十一月 11th Month

巽 SE	離 S	坤 SW
6 White 六白	2 Black 二黑	4 Green 四綠
震 E — 5 Yellow 五黃	7 Red 七赤	9 Purple 九紫 — 兌 W
1 White 一白	3 Jade 三碧	8 White 八白
艮 NE	坎 N	乾 NW

丑 Ox (Jan 6 - Feb 3) 十二月 12th Month

巽 SE	離 S	坤 SW
5 Yellow 五黃	1 White 一白	3 Jade 三碧
震 E — 4 Green 四綠	6 White 六白	8 White 八白 — 兌 W
9 Purple 九紫	2 Black 二黑	7 Red 七赤
艮 NE	坎 N	乾 NW

Qi Men Three Nobles 三奇 :

Three Nobles 三奇 / Seasons	乙 Yi	丙 Bing	丁 Ding
立春 **Coming of Spring** Feb 4 - Feb 18	離 Li	坎 Kan	坤 Kun
春分 **Spring Equinox** Mar 21 - Apr 4	巽 Xun	中 Middle	乾 Qian
立夏 **Coming of Summer** May 6 - May 20	中 Middle	乾 Qian	兌 Dui
夏至 **Summer Solstice** Jun 22 - Jul 6	艮 Gen	兌 Dui	乾 Qian
立秋 **Coming of Autumn** Aug 8 - Aug 23	坎 Kan	離 Li	艮 Gen
秋分 **Autumn Equinox** Sept 23 - Oct 7	乾 Qian	中 Middle	巽 Xun
立冬 **Coming of Winter** Nov 7 - Nov 22	中 Middle	巽 Xun	震 Zhen
冬至 **Winter Solstice** Dec 22 - Jan 5	坤 Kun	震 Zhen	巽 Xun

Sectors to Avoid Opening Mountain 開山凶位 :

月 MONTH	月建 Month Establishment	月破 Month Destruction	月剋山家 Month Countering Sitting		陰府太歲 Yin Mansion Grand Duke	
寅 Tiger (Feb 4 - Mar 5) 正月 1st Month	寅 Yin Tiger	申 Shen Monkey	震 Zhen	巳 Si Snake	艮 Gen	巽 Xun
卯 Rabbit (Mar 6 - Apr 4) 二月 2nd Month	卯 Mao Rabbit	酉 You Rooster	艮 Gen		兌 Dui	乾 Qian
辰 Dragon (Apr 5 - May 5) 三月 3rd Month	辰 Chen Dragon	戌 Xu Dog	離 Li	丙 Bing Yang Fire	坎 Kan	坤 Kun
巳 Snake (May 6 - Jun 5) 四月 4th Month	巳 Si Snake	亥 Hai Pig	壬 Ren Yang Water	乙 Yi Yin Wood	乾 Qian	離 Li
午 Horse (Jun 6 - July 6) 五月 5th Month	午 Wu Horse	子 Zi Rat	–		坤 Kun	震 Zhen
未 Goat (July 7 - Aug 7) 六月 6th Month	未 Wei Goat	丑 Chou Ox	–		巽 Xun	艮 Gen
申 Monkey (Aug 8 - Sept 7) 七月 7th Month	申 Shen Monkey	寅 Yin Tiger	水 Water	山 Mountain	乾 Qian	兌 Dui
酉 Rooster (Sept 8 - Oct 7) 八月 8th Month	酉 You Rooster	卯 Mao Rabbit	土 Earth		坤 Kun	坎 Kan
戌 Dog (Oct 8 - Nov 6) 九月 9th Month	戌 Xu Dog	辰 Chen Dragon	震 Zhen	巳 Si Snake	離 Li	乾 Qian
亥 Pig (Nov 7 - Dec 6) 十月 10th Month	亥 Hai Pig	巳 Si Snake	艮 Gen		震 Zhen	坤 Kun
子 Rat (Dec 7 - Jan 5) 十一月 11th Month	子 Zi Rat	午 Wu Horse	–		艮 Gen	巽 Xun
丑 Ox (Jan 6 - Feb 3) 十二月 12th Month	丑 Chou Ox	未 Wei Goat	–		兌 Dui	乾 Qian

Negative Repair / Renovation Sectors 修方凶位 :

月 MONTH	天官符 Heavenly Officer Charm			地官符 Earth Officer Charm			小月建 Small Month Establishment		
寅 **Tiger** (Feb 4 - Mar 5) 正月 1st Month	未 Wei Goat	坤 Kun	申 Shen Monkey	庚 Geng Yang Metal	兌 Dui	辛 Xin Yin Metal	丙 Bing Yang Fire	離 Li	丁 Ding Yin Fire
卯 **Rabbit** (Mar 6 - Apr 4) 二月 2nd Month	壬 Ren Yang Water	坎 Kan	癸 Gui Yin Water	戊 Xu Dog	乾 Qian	亥 Hai Pig	壬 Ren Yang Water	坎 Kan	癸 Gui Yin Water
辰 **Dragon** (Apr 5 - May 5) 三月 3rd Month	丙 Bing Yang Fire	離 Li	丁 Ding Yin Fire	中 Middle			未 Wei Goat	坤 Kun	申 Shen Monkey
巳 **Snake** (May 6 - Jun 5) 四月 4th Month	丑 Chou Ox	艮 Gen	寅 Yin Tiger	辰 Chen Dragon	巽 Xun	巳 Si Snake	甲 Jia Yang Wood	震 Zhen	乙 Yi Yin Wood
午 **Horse** (Jun 6 - July 6) 五月 5th Month	庚 Geng Yang Metal	兌 Dui	辛 Xin Yin Metal	甲 Jia Yang Wood	震 Zhen	乙 Yi Yin Wood	辰 Chen Dragon	巽 Xun	己 Ji Yin Earth
未 **Goat** (July 7 - Aug 7) 六月 6th Month	戊 Xu Dog	乾 Qian	亥 Hai Pig	未 Wei Goat	坤 Kun	申 Shen Monkey	中 Middle		
申 **Monkey** (Aug 8 - Sept 7) 七月 7th Month	中 Middle			壬 Ren Yang Water	坎 Kan	癸 Gui Yin Water	戊 Xu Dog	乾 Qian	亥 Hai Pig
酉 **Rooster** (Sept 8 - Oct 7) 八月 8th Month	庚 Geng Yang Metal	兌 Dui	辛 Xin Yin Metal	丙 Bing Yang Fire	離 Li	丁 Ding Yin Fire	庚 Geng Yang Metal	兌 Dui	辛 Xin Yin Metal
戌 **Dog** (Oct 8 - Nov 6) 九月 9th Month	戊 Xu Dog	乾 Qian	亥 Hai Pig	丑 Chou Ox	艮 Gen	寅 Yin Tiger	丑 Chou Ox	艮 Gen	寅 Yin Tiger
亥 **Pig** (Nov 7 - Dec 6) 十月 10th Month	中 Middle			庚 Geng Yang Metal	兌 Dui	辛 Xin Yin Metal	丙 Bing Yang Fire	離 Li	丁 Ding Yin Fire
子 **Rat** (Dec 7 - Jan 5) 十一月 11th Month	辰 Chen Dragon	巽 Xun	巳 Si Snake	戊 Xu Dog	乾 Qian	亥 Hai Pig	壬 Ren Yang Water	坎 Kan	癸 Gui Yin Water
丑 **Ox** (Jan 6 - Feb 3) 十二月 12th Month	甲 Jia Yang Wood	震 Zhen	乙 Yi Yin Wood	中 Middle			未 Wei Goat	坤 Kun	申 Shen Monkey

Negative Repair / Renovation Sectors 修方凶位 :

月 MONTH	大月建 Big Month Establishment			飛大煞 Flying Great Sha			丙丁獨火 Bing Ding Lonely Fire	
寅 **Tiger** (Feb 4 - Mar 5) 正月 **1st Month**	丑 *Chou* Ox	艮 *Gen*	寅 *Yin* Tiger	甲 *Jia* Yang Wood	震 *Zhen*	乙 *Yi* Yin Wood	兑 *Dui*	艮 *Gen*
卯 **Rabbit** (Mar 6 - Apr 4) 二月 **2nd Month**	庚 *Geng* Yang Metal	兑 *Dui*	辛 *Xin* Yin Metal	未 *Wei* Goat	坤 *Kun*	申 *Shen* Monkey	乾 *Qian*	兑 *Dui*
辰 **Dragon** (Apr 5 - May 5) 三月 **3rd Month**	戌 *Xu* Dog	乾 *Qian*	亥 *Hai* Pig	壬 *Ren* Yang Water	坎 *Kan*	癸 *Gui* Yin Water	中 Middle	乾 *Qian*
巳 **Snake** (May 6 - Jun 5) 四月 **4th Month**		中 Middle		丙 *Bing* Yang Fire	離 *Li*	丁 *Ding* Yin Fire		中 Middle
午 **Horse** (Jun 6 - July 6) 五月 **5th Month**	辰 *Chen* Dragon	巽 *Xun*	巳 *Si* Snake	丑 *Chou* Ox	艮 *Gen*	寅 *Yin* Tiger	巽 *Xun*	中 Middle
未 **Goat** (July 7 - Aug 7) 六月 **6th Month**	甲 *Jia* Yang Wood	震 *Zhen*	乙 *Yi* Yin Wood	庚 *Geng* Yang Metal	兑 *Dui*	辛 *Xin* Yin Metal	震 *Zhen*	巽 *Xun*
申 **Monkey** (Aug 8 - Sept 7) 七月 **7th Month**	未 *Wei* Goat	坤 *Kun*	申 *Shen* Monkey	戌 *Xu* Dog	乾 *Qian*	亥 *Hai* Pig	坤 *Kun*	震 *Zhen*
酉 **Rooster** (Sept 8 - Oct 7) 八月 **8th Month**	壬 *Ren* Yang Water	坎 *Kan*	癸 *Gui* Yin Water		中 Middle		坎 *Kan*	坤 *Kun*
戌 **Dog** (Oct 8 - Nov 6) 九月 **9th Month**	丙 *Bing* Yang Fire	離 *Li*	丁 *Ding* Yin Fire	庚 *Geng* Yang Metal	兑 *Dui*	辛 *Xin* Yin Metal	離 *Li*	坎 *Kan*
亥 **Pig** (Nov 7 - Dec 6) 十月 **10th Month**	丑 *Chou* Ox	艮 *Gen*	寅 *Yin* Tiger	戌 *Xu* Dog	乾 *Qian*	亥 *Hai* Tiger	艮 *Gen*	離 *Li*
子 **Rat** (Dec 7 - Jan 5) 十一月 **11th Month**	庚 *Geng* Yang Metal	兑 *Dui*	辛 *Xin* Yin Metal		中 Middle		兑 *Dui*	艮 *Gen*
丑 **Ox** (Jan 6 - Feb 3) 十二月 **12th Month**	戌 *Xu* Dog	乾 *Qian*	亥 *Hai* Pig	辰 *Chen* Dragon	巽 *Xun*	巳 *Si* Snake	乾 *Qian*	兑 *Dui*

Negative Repair / Renovation Sectors 修方凶位 ：

月 MONTH	月遊火 Month Wondering Fire	三煞 Monthly 3 Killings		
		劫煞 Robbery Sha	災煞 Calamity Sha	月煞 Month Sha
寅 Tiger (Feb 4 - Mar 5) 正月 1st Month	乾 Qian	亥 Hai Pig	子 Zi Rat	丑 Chou Ox
卯 Rabbit (Mar 6 - Apr 4) 二月 2nd Month	兌 Dui	申 Shen Monkey	酉 You Rooster	戌 Xu Dog
辰 Dragon (Apr 5 - May 5) 三月 3rd Month	艮 Gen	巳 Si Snake	午 Wu Horse	未 Wei Goat
巳 Snake (May 6 - Jun 5) 四月 4th Month	離 Li	寅 Yin Tiger	卯 Mao Rabbit	辰 Chen Dragon
午 Horse (Jun 6 - July 6) 五月 5th Month	坎 Kan	亥 Hai Pig	子 Zi Rat	丑 Chou Ox
未 Goat (July 7 - Aug 7) 六月 6th Month	坤 Kun	申 Shen Monkey	酉 You Rooster	戌 Xu Dog
申 Monkey (Aug 8 - Sept 7) 七月 7th Month	震 Zhen	巳 Si Snake	午 Wu Horse	未 Wei Goat
酉 Rooster (Sept 8 - Oct 7) 八月 8th Month	巽 Xun	寅 Yin Tiger	卯 Mao Rabbit	辰 Chen Dragon
戌 Dog (Oct 8 - Nov 6) 九月 9th Month	中 Middle	亥 Hai Pig	子 Zi Rat	丑 Chou Ox
亥 Pig (Nov 7 - Dec 6) 十月 10th Month	乾 Qian	申 Shen Monkey	酉 You Rooster	戌 Xu Dog
子 Rat (Dec 7 - Jan 5) 十一月 11th Month	兌 Dui	巳 Si Snake	午 Wu Horse	未 Wei Goat
丑 Ox (Jan 6 - Feb 3) 十二月 12th Month	艮 Gen	寅 Yin Tiger	卯 Mao Rabbit	辰 Chen Dragon

Negative Repair / Renovation Sectors 修方凶位 :

月 MONTH	月刑 Month Punishment	月害 Month Harm	月厭 Month Detest
寅 Tiger (Feb 4 - Mar 5) 正月 1st Month	巳 Si Snake	巳 Si Snake	戌 Xu Dog
卯 Rabbit (Mar 6 - Apr 4) 二月 2nd Month	子 Zi Rat	辰 Chen Dragon	酉 You Rooster
辰 Dragon (Apr 5 - May 5) 三月 3rd Month	辰 Chen Dragon	卯 Mao Rabbit	申 Shen Monkey
巳 Snake (May 6 - Jun 5) 四月 4th Month	申 Shen Monkey	寅 Yin Tiger	未 Wei Goat
午 Horse (Jun 6 - July 6) 五月 5th Month	午 Wu Horse	丑 Chou Ox	午 Wu Horse
未 Goat (July 7 - Aug 7) 六月 6th Month	丑 Chou Ox	子 Zi Rat	巳 Si Snake
申 Monkey (Aug 8 - Sept 7) 七月 7th Month	寅 Yin Tiger	亥 Hai Pig	辰 Chen Dragon
酉 Rooster (Sept 8 - Oct 7) 八月 8th Month	酉 You Rooster	戌 Xu Dog	卯 Mao Rabbit
戌 Dog (Oct 8 - Nov 6) 九月 9th Month	未 Wei Goat	酉 You Rooster	寅 Yin Tiger
亥 Pig (Nov 7 - Dec 6) 十月 10th Month	亥 Hai Pig	申 Shen Monkey	丑 Chou Ox
子 Rat (Dec 7 - Jan 5) 十一月 11th Month	卯 Mao Rabbit	未 Wei Goat	子 Zi Rat
丑 Ox (Jan 6 - Feb 3) 十二月 12th Month	戌 Xu Dog	午 Wu Horse	亥 Hai Pig

癸亥 (Gui Hai)
Water Pig

Heavenly Stem 天干	癸 **Yin Water (**陰水**)**
Earthly Branch 地支	亥 **Pig (Yin Water** 陰水**)**
Hidden Stem 藏干	壬 **Yang Water,** 甲 **Yang Wood**
Na Yin 納音	大海水 **Water from the sea**
Grand Duke 太歲	亥 **Pig**
Xuan Kong Five Element 玄空五行	6 水 **Water**
Gua Name 卦名	山地剝 **Peel**
Xuan Kong Period Luck 玄空卦運	**6**

Annual Positive Stars for Opening Mountain, Establishing Facing and Commencing Repairs 開山立向修方吉星:

歲德 **Duke** **Virtue**	戊 *Wu* **Yang Earth**	
歲德合 **Duke Virtue** **Combo**	癸 *Gui* **Yin Water**	
歲枝德 **Duke Branch** **Virtue**	辰 *Chen* **Dragon**	
陽貴人 **Yang** **Nobleman**	巳 *Si* **Snake**	
陰貴人 **Yin** **Nobleman**	卯 *Mao* **Rabbit**	
歲祿 **Duke** **Prosperous**	子 *Zi* **Rat**	
歲馬 **Duke** **Horse**	巳 *Si* **Snake**	
奏書 **Decree**	乾 *Qian*	
博士 **Professor**	巽 *Xun*	

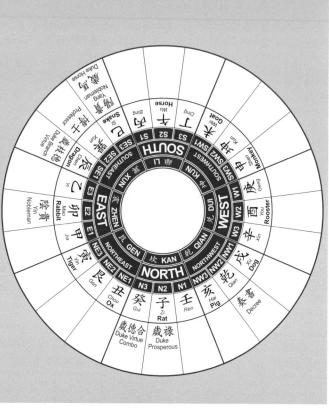

Annual Negative Stars for Opening Mountain, Establishing Facing and Commencing Repairs 開山立向修方凶星:

太歲 Grand Duke	歲破 Year Breaker	三煞 Three Killings			坐煞向煞 Sitting Sha Facing Sha				浮天空亡 Floating Heaven Emptiness	
亥 Hai Pig	巳 Si Snake	申 Shen Monkey	酉 You Rooster	戌 Xu Dog	庚 Geng Yang Metal	辛 Xin Yin Metal	甲 Jia Yang Wood	乙 Yi Yin Wood	坤 Kun	乙 Yi Yin Wood

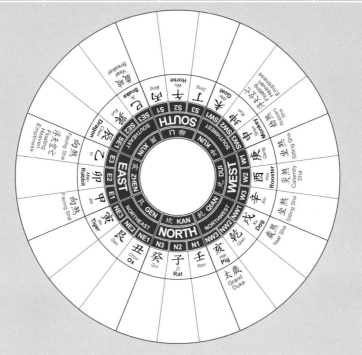

Annual San Yuan Purple White Stars 三元紫白九星:

上元 Upper Period Period 1, 2, 3			中元 Middle Period Period 4, 5, 6			下元 Lower Period Period 7, 8, 9		
巽SE **4**	離S **9**	坤SW **2**	巽SE **7**	離S **3**	坤SW **5**	巽SE **1**	離S **6**	坤SW **8**
震E **3**	**5** 癸亥 Gui Hai Water Pig	兌W **7**	震E **6**	**8** 癸亥 Gui Hai Water Pig	兌W **1**	震E **9**	**2** 癸亥 Gui Hai Water Pig	兌W **4**
艮NE **8**	坎N **1**	乾NW **6**	艮NE **2**	坎N **4**	乾NW **9**	艮NE **5**	坎N **7**	乾NW **3**

Mountain Covering Yellow Path 蓋山黃道：

貪狼 *Tan Lang* **Greedy Wolf**				巨門 *Ju Men* **Huge Door**		武曲 *Wu Qu* **Military Arts**				文曲 *Wen Qu* **Literary Arts**			
坎 *Kan* N2	癸 *Gui* N3	申 *Shen* SW3	辰 *Chen* SE1	坤 *Kun* SW2	乙 *Yi* E3	離 *Li* S2	壬 *Ren* N1	寅 *Yin* NE3	戌 *Xu* NW1	兌 *Dui* W2	丁 *Ding* S3	巳 *Si* SE3	丑 *Chou* NE1

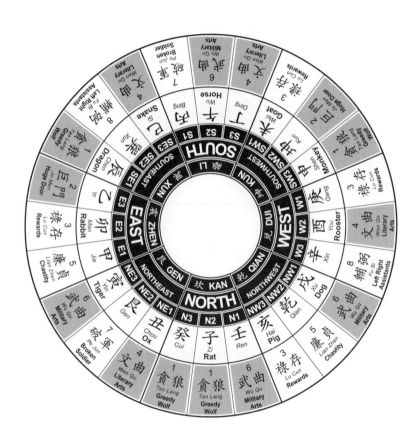

Heaven Penetrating Force 通天竅:

三合前方 **Facing Three Harmony**	巽巳 Xun Si	丙午 Bing Wu	丁未 Ding Wei
三合後方 **Sitting Three Harmony**	乾亥 Qian Hai	壬子 Ren Zi	癸丑 Gui Chou

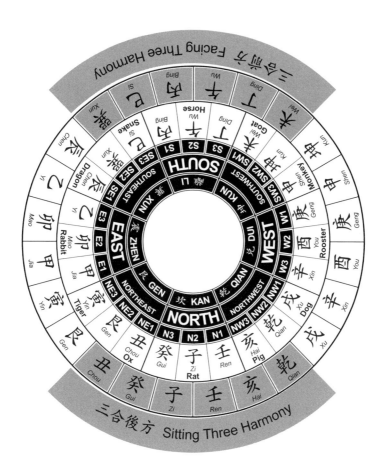

Moving Horse Six Ren Assessment 走馬六壬：					
神后 *Shen Hou* **Holy Empress**	功曹 *Gong Cao* **Marshall**	天罡 *Tian Gang* **Heavenly Dipper**	勝光 *Sheng Guang* **Subliminal Bright**	傳送 *Chuan Song* **Great General**	河魁 *He Kui* **River Scholar**
癸丑 *Gui Chou*	甲卯 *Jia Mao*	巽巳 *Xun Si*	丁未 *Ding Wei*	庚酉 *Geng You*	乾亥 *Qian Hai*

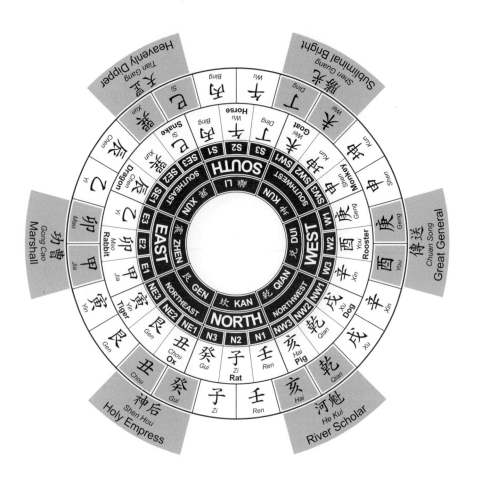

Four Advantages Three Cycles Star Plate 四利三元：

太陽 *Tai Yang* **Sun**	太陰 *Tai Yin* **Moon**	龍德 *Long De* **Dragon Virtue**	福德 *Fu De* **Fortune Virtue**
子 *Zi* **Rat**	寅 *Yin* **Tiger**	午 *Wu* **Horse**	申 *Shen* **Monkey**

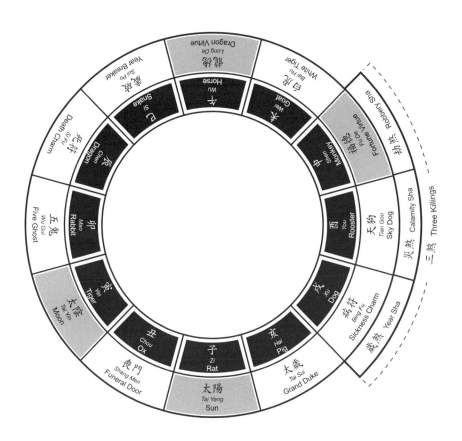

Negative Sectors For Opening Mountain 開山凶位：

年剋山家 Year Countering Sitting

震	艮	巳
Zhen	*Gen*	*Si*
E2	NE2	SE3

陰府太歲 *Yin Fu Tai Sui* **Yin Mansion Grand Duke**	六害 *Liu Hai* **Six Harm**	死符 *Si Fu* **Death Charm**	炙退 *Zhi Tui* **Roasting Star**
震 　　坤 *Zhen*　　*Kun* E2　　　SW2	申 *Shen* SW3	辰 *Chen* SE1	午 *Wu* S2

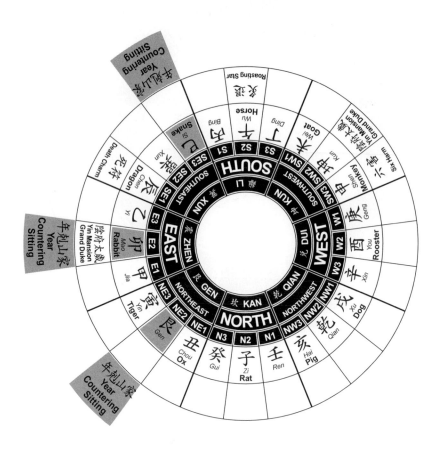

Negative Directions to Establish Facing 立向凶方：

巡山羅喉 *Xun Shan Luo Hou* **Mountain Patrol Luo Hou Star**	病符 *Bing Fu* **Sickness Charm**
壬 *Ren* **N1**	戌 *Xu* **NW1**

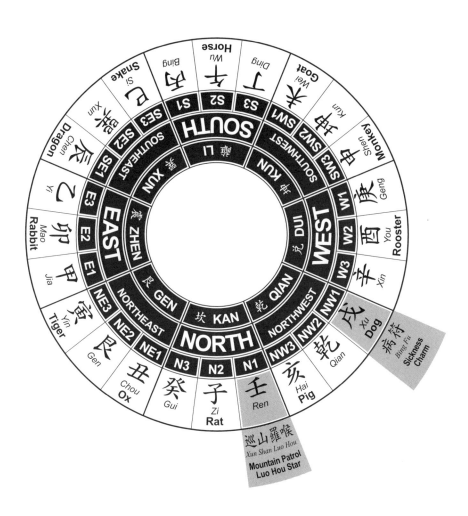

Negative Repair / Renovation Sectors Table 修方凶位表：

天官符 **Heavenly Officer Charm**	寅 *Yin* **Tiger**	飛廉 **Flying Chaste**	丑 *Chou* **Ox**
地官符 **Earthly Officer Charm**	卯 *Mao* **Rabbit**	喪門 **Funeral Door**	丑 *Chou* **Ox**
大煞 **Great Sha**	卯 *Mao* **Rabbit**	弔客 **Suspended Guest**	酉 *You* **Rooster**
大將軍 **Big General**	酉 *You* **Rooster**	白虎 **White Tiger**	未 *Wei* **Goat**
力士 **Strong Man**	艮 *Gen*	金神 **Golden God**	申 *Shen* **Monkey**
蠶室 **Silkworm Room**	坤 *Kun*		酉 *You* **Rooster**
蠶官 **Silkworm Officer**	未 *Wei* **Goat**		子 *Zi* **Rat**
蠶命 **Silkworm Life**	申 *Shen* **Monkey**		丑 *Chou* **Ox**
歲刑 **Duke Punishment**	亥 *Hai* **Pig**	獨火 **Lonely Fire**	乾 *Qian*
黃幡 **Yellow Flag**	未 *Wei* **Goat**	五鬼 **Five Ghost**	巳 *Si* **Snake**
豹尾 **Leopard Tail**	丑 *Chou* **Ox**	破敗五鬼 **Destructive Five Ghost**	艮 *Gen*

Negative Repair / Renovation Sectors Diagram 修方凶位圖：

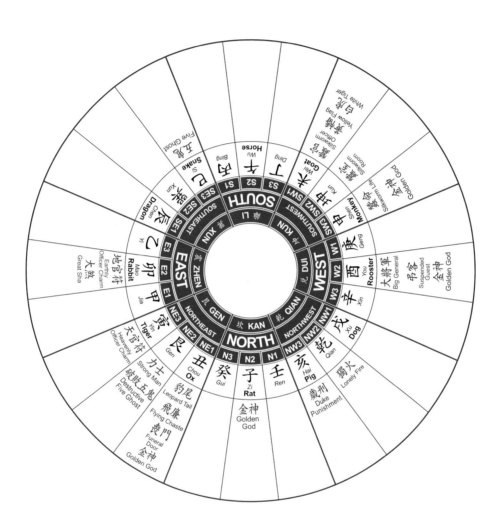

12-Month Auxiliary Stars Reference Table :
癸亥年十二月，開山立向修方星表

Positive Monthly Stars 吉星方

月 MONTH	寅 Tiger (Feb 4 - Mar 5) 正月 1st Month	卯 Rabbit (Mar 6 - Apr 4) 二月 2nd Month	辰 Dragon (Apr 5 - May 5) 三月 3rd Month	巳 Snake (May 6 - Jun 5) 四月 4th Month	午 Horse (Jun 6 - July 6) 五月 5th Month	未 Goat (July 7 - Aug 7) 六月 6th Month
天道 Heavenly Path	南 South	西南 Southwest	北 North	西 West	西北 Northwest	東 East
天德 Heavenly Virtue	丁 Ding Yin Fire	坤 Kun (申)	壬 Ren Yang Water	辛 Xin Yin Metal	乾 Qian (亥)	甲 Jia Yang Wood
天德合 Heavenly Virtue Combo	壬 Ren Yang Water	(巳)	丁 Ding Yin Fire	丙 Bing Yang Fire	(寅)	己 Ji Yin Earth
月德 Monthly Virtue	丙 Bing Yang Fire	甲 Jia Yang Wood	壬 Ren Yang Water	庚 Geng Yang Metal	丙 Bing Yang Fire	甲 Jia Yang Wood
月德合 Monthly Virtue Combo	辛 Xin Yin Metal	己 Ji Yin Earth	丁 Ding Yin Fire	乙 Yi Yin Wood	辛 Xin Yin Metal	己 Ji Yin Earth
月空 Month Emptiness	壬 Ren Yang Water	庚 Geng Yang Metal	丙 Bing Yang Fire	甲 Jia Yang Wood	壬 Ren Yang Water	庚 Geng Yang Metal
陽貴人 Yang Nobleman	艮 Gen	兌 Dui	乾 Qian	中 Middle	坎 Kan	離 Li
陰貴人 Yin Nobleman	乾 Qian	中 Middle	坎 Kan	離 Li	艮 Gen	兌 Dui
飛天祿 Flying Heavenly Wealth	乾 Qian	中 Middle	巽 Xun	震 Zhen	坤 Kun	坎 Kan
飛天馬 Flying Heavenly Horse	艮 Gen	兌 Dui	乾 Qian	中 Middle	坎 Kan	離 Li

12-Month Auxiliary Stars Reference Table :
癸亥年十二月，開山立向修方星表

申 Monkey (Aug 8 - Sept 7) 七月 7th Month	酉 Rooster (Sept 8 - Oct 7) 八月 8th Month	戌 Dog (Oct 8 - Nov 6) 九月 9th Month	亥 Pig (Nov 7 - Dec 6) 十月 10th Month	子 Rat (Dec 7 - Jan 5) 十一月 11th Month	丑 Ox (Jan 6 - Feb 3) 十二月 12th Month	月 MONTH
北 North	東北 Northeast	南 South	東 East	東南 Southeast	西 West	天道 Heavenly Path
癸 Gui Yin Water	艮 Gen (寅)	丙 Bing Yang Fire	乙 Yi Yin Wood	巽 Xun (巳)	庚 Geng Yang Metal	天德 Heavenly Virtue
戊 Wu Yang Earth	(亥)	辛 Xin Yin Metal	庚 Geng Yang Metal	(申)	乙 Yi Yin Wood	天德合 Heavenly Virtue Combo
壬 Ren Yang Water	庚 Geng Yang Metal	丙 Bing Yang Fire	甲 Jia Yang Wood	壬 Ren Yang Water	庚 Geng Yang Metal	月德 Monthly Virtue
丁 Ding Yin Fire	乙 Yi Yin Wood	辛 Xin Yin Metal	己 Ji Yin Earth	丁 Ding Yin Fire	乙 Yi Yin Wood	月德合 Monthly Virtue Combo
丙 Bing Yang Fire	甲 Jia Yang Wood	壬 Ren Yang Water	庚 Geng Yang Metal	丙 Bing Yang Fire	甲 Jia Yang Wood	月空 Month Emptiness
艮 Gen	兌 Dui	乾 Qian	中 Middle	巽 Xun	震 Zhen	陽貴人 Yang Nobleman
乾 Qian	中 Middle	巽 Xun	震 Zhen	坤 Kun	坎 Kan	陰貴人 Yin Nobleman
離 Li	艮 Gen	兌 Dui	乾 Qian	中 Middle	坎 Kan	飛天祿 Flying Heavenly Wealth
艮 Gen	兌 Dui	乾 Qian	中 Middle	巽 Xun	震 Zhen	飛天馬 Flying Heavenly Horse

Monthly Purple White Stars 月紫白九星 :

寅 Tiger (Feb 4 - Mar 5) 正月 1st Month

巽 SE	離 S	坤 SW
1 White 一白	**6** White 六白	**8** White 八白
震 E **9** Purple 九紫	**2** Black 二黑	**4** Green 四綠 兌 W
艮 NE **5** Yellow 五黃	坎 N **7** Red 七赤	乾 NW **3** Jade 三碧

卯 Rabbit (Mar 6 - Apr 4) 二月 2nd Month

巽 SE	離 S	坤 SW
9 Purple 九紫	**5** Yellow 五黃	**7** Red 七赤
震 E **8** White 八白	**1** White 一白	**3** Jade 三碧 兌 W
艮 NE **4** Green 四綠	坎 N **6** White 六白	乾 NW **2** Black 二黑

辰 Dragon (Apr 5 - May 5) 三月 3rd Month

巽 SE	離 S	坤 SW
8 White 八白	**4** Green 四綠	**6** White 六白
震 E **7** Red 七赤	**9** Purple 九紫	**2** Black 二黑 兌 W
艮 NE **3** Jade 三碧	坎 N **5** Yellow 五黃	乾 NW **1** White 一白

巳 Snake (May 6 - Jun 5) 四月 4th Month

巽 SE	離 S	坤 SW
7 Red 七赤	**3** Jade 三碧	**5** Yellow 五黃
震 E **6** White 六白	**8** White 八白	**1** White 一白 兌 W
艮 NE **2** Black 二黑	坎 N **4** Green 四綠	乾 NW **9** Purple 九紫

午 Horse (Jun 6 - July 6) 五月 5th Month

巽 SE	離 S	坤 SW
6 White 六白	**2** Black 二黑	**4** Green 四綠
震 E **5** Yellow 五黃	**7** Red 七赤	**9** Purple 九紫 兌 W
艮 NE **1** White 一白	坎 N **3** Jade 三碧	乾 NW **8** White 八白

未 Goat (July 7 - Aug 7) 六月 6th Month

巽 SE	離 S	坤 SW
5 Yellow 五黃	**1** White 一白	**3** Jade 三碧
震 E **4** Green 四綠	**6** White 六白	**8** White 八白 兌 W
艮 NE **9** Purple 九紫	坎 N **2** Black 二黑	乾 NW **7** Red 七赤

申 Monkey (Aug 8 - Sept 7) 七月 7th Month

巽 SE	離 S	坤 SW
4 Green 四綠	**9** Purple 九紫	**2** Black 二黑
震 E **3** Jade 三碧	**5** Yellow 五黃	**7** Red 七赤 兌 W
艮 NE **8** White 八白	坎 N **1** White 一白	乾 NW **6** White 六白

酉 Rooster (Sept 8 - Oct 7) 八月 8th Month

巽 SE	離 S	坤 SW
3 Jade 三碧	**8** White 八白	**1** White 一白
震 E **2** Black 二黑	**4** Green 四綠	**6** White 六白 兌 W
艮 NE **7** Red 七赤	坎 N **9** Purple 九紫	乾 NW **5** Yellow 五黃

戌 Dog (Oct 8 - Nov 6) 九月 9th Month

巽 SE	離 S	坤 SW
2 Black 二黑	**7** Red 七赤	**9** Purple 九紫
震 E **1** White 一白	**3** Jade 三碧	**5** Yellow 五黃 兌 W
艮 NE **6** White 六白	坎 N **8** White 八白	乾 NW **4** Green 四綠

亥 Pig (Nov 7 - Dec 6) 十月 10th Month

巽 SE	離 S	坤 SW
1 White 一白	**6** White 六白	**8** White 八白
震 E **9** Purple 九紫	**2** Black 二黑	**4** Green 四綠 兌 W
艮 NE **5** Yellow 五黃	坎 N **7** Red 七赤	乾 NW **3** Jade 三碧

子 Rat (Dec 7 - Jan 5) 十一月 11th Month

巽 SE	離 S	坤 SW
9 Purple 九紫	**5** Yellow 五黃	**7** Red 七赤
震 E **8** White 八白	**1** White 一白	**3** Jade 三碧 兌 W
艮 NE **4** Green 四綠	坎 N **6** White 六白	乾 NW **2** Black 二黑

丑 Ox (Jan 6 - Feb 3) 十二月 12th Month

巽 SE	離 S	坤 SW
8 White 八白	**4** Green 四綠	**6** White 六白
震 E **7** Red 七赤	**9** Purple 九紫	**2** Black 二黑 兌 W
艮 NE **3** Jade 三碧	坎 N **5** Yellow 五黃	乾 NW **1** White 一白

Qi Men Three Nobles 三奇 :

Three Nobles 三奇 / Seasons	乙 Yi	丙 Bing	丁 Ding
立春 **Coming of Spring** Feb 4 - Feb 18	中 Middle	乾 Qian	兑 Dui
春分 **Spring Equinox** Mar 21 - Apr 4	離 Li	坎 Kan	坤 Kunn
立夏 **Coming of Summer** May 6 - May 20	坎 Kan	坤 Kun	震 Zhen
夏至 **Summer Solstice** Jun 22 - Jul 6	震 Zhen	坤 Kun	坎 Kan
立秋 **Coming of Autumn** Aug 8 - Aug 23	中 Middle	巽 Xun	震 Zhen
秋分 **Autumn Equinox** Sept 23 - Oct 7	坎 Kan	離 Li	艮 Gen
立冬 **Coming of Winter** Nov 7 - Nov 22	離 Li	艮 Gen	兑 Dui
冬至 **Winter Solstice** Dec 22 - Jan 5	兑 Dui	艮 Gen	離 Li

Sectors to Avoid Opening Mountain 開山凶位 :

月 MONTH	月建 Month Establishment	月破 Month Destruction	月剋山家 Month Countering Sitting		陰府太歲 Yin Mansion Grand Duke	
寅 **Tiger** (Feb 4 - Mar 5) 正月 **1st Month**	寅 *Yin* **Tiger**	申 *Shen* **Monkey**	震 *Zhen*	巳 *Si* **Snake**	艮 *Gen*	巽 *Xun*
卯 **Rabbit** (Mar 6 - Apr 4) 二月 **2nd Month**	卯 *Mao* **Rabbit**	酉 *You* **Rooster**	艮 *Gen*		兌 *Dui*	乾 *Qian*
辰 **Dragon** (Apr 5 - May 5) 三月 **3rd Month**	辰 *Chen* **Dragon**	戌 *Xu* **Dog**	離 *Li*	丙 *Bing* **Yang Fire**	坎 *Kan*	坤 *Kun*
巳 **Snake** (May 6 - Jun 5) 四月 **4th Month**	巳 *Si* **Snake**	亥 *Hai* **Pig**	壬 *Ren* **Yang Water**	乙 *Yi* **Yin Wood**	乾 *Qian*	離 *Li*
午 **Horse** (Jun 6 - July 6) 五月 **5th Month**	午 *Wu* **Horse**	子 *Zi* **Rat**	—		坤 *Kun*	震 *Zhen*
未 **Goat** (July 7 - Aug 7) 六月 **6th Month**	未 *Wei* **Goat**	丑 *Chou* **Ox**	—		巽 *Xun*	艮 *Gen*
申 **Monkey** (Aug 8 - Sept 7) 七月 **7th Month**	申 *Shen* **Monkey**	寅 *Yin* **Tiger**	水 **Water**	山 **Mountain**	乾 *Qian*	兌 *Dui*
酉 **Rooster** (Sept 8 - Oct 7) 八月 **8th Month**	酉 *You* **Rooster**	卯 *Mao* **Rabbit**	土 **Earth**		坤 *Kun*	坎 *Kan*
戌 **Dog** (Oct 8 - Nov 6) 九月 **9th Month**	戌 *Xu* **Dog**	辰 *Chen* **Dragon**	震 *Zhen*	巳 *Si* **Snake**	離 *Li*	乾 *Qian*
亥 **Pig** (Nov 7 - Dec 6) 十月 **10th Month**	亥 *Hai* **Pig**	巳 *Si* **Snake**	艮 *Gen*		震 *Zhen*	坤 *Kun*
子 **Rat** (Dec 7 - Jan 5) 十一月 **11th Month**	子 *Zi* **Rat**	午 *Wu* **Horse**	—		艮 *Gen*	巽 *Xun*
丑 **Ox** (Jan 6 - Feb 3) 十二月 **12th Month**	丑 *Chou* **Ox**	未 *Wei* **Goat**	—		兌 *Dui*	乾 *Qian*

Negative Repair / Renovation Sectors 修方凶位 :

月 MONTH	天官符 Heavenly Officer Charm			地官符 Earth Officer Charm			小月建 Small Month Establishment		
寅 **Tiger** (Feb 4 - Mar 5) 正月 **1st Month**		中 Middle		戌 Xu Dog	乾 Qian	亥 Hai Pig	丙 Bing Yang Fire	離 Li	丁 Ding Yin Fire
卯 **Rabbit** (Mar 6 - Apr 4) 二月 **2nd Month**	庚 Geng Yang Metal	兌 Dui	辛 Xin Yin Metal		中 Middle		壬 Ren Yang Water	坎 Kan	癸 Gui Yin Water
辰 **Dragon** (Apr 5 - May 5) 三月 **3rd Month**	戌 Xu Dog	乾 Qian	亥 Hai Pig	庚 Geng Yang Metal	兌 Dui	辛 Xin Yin Metal	未 Wei Goat	坤 Kun	申 Shen Monkey
巳 **Snake** (May 6 - Jun 5) 四月 **4th Month**		中 Middle		戌 Xu Dog	乾 Qian	亥 Hai Pig	甲 Jia Yang Wood	震 Zhen	乙 Yi Yin Wood
午 **Horse** (Jun 6 - July 6) 五月 **5th Month**	辰 Chen Dragon	巽 Xun	巳 Si Snake		中 Middle		辰 Chen Dragon	巽 Xun	巳 Si Snake
未 **Goat** (July 7 - Aug 7) 六月 **6th Month**	甲 Jia Yang Wood	震 Zhen	乙 Yi Yin Wood	辰 Chen Dragon	巽 Xun	巳 Si Snake		中 Middle	
申 **Monkey** (Aug 8 - Sept 7) 七月 **7th Month**	未 Wei Goat	坤 Kun	申 Shen Monkey	甲 Jia Yang Wood	震 Zhen	乙 Yi Yin Wood	戌 Xu Dog	乾 Qian	亥 Hai Pig
酉 **Rooster** (Sept 8 - Oct 7) 八月 **8th Month**	壬 Ren Yang Water	坎 Kan	癸 Gui Yin Water	未 Wei Goat	坤 Kun	申 Shen Monkey	庚 Geng Yang Metal	兌 Dui	辛 Xin Yin Metal
戌 **Dog** (Oct 8 - Nov 6) 九月 **9th Month**	丙 Bing Yang Fire	離 Li	丁 Ding Yin Fire	壬 Ren Yang Water	坎 Kan	癸 Gui Yin Water	丑 Chou Ox	艮 Gen	寅 Yin Tiger
亥 **Pig** (Nov 7 - Dec 6) 十月 **10th Month**	丑 Chou Ox	艮 Gen	寅 Yin Tiger	丙 Bing Yang Fire	離 Li	丁 Ding Yin Fire	丙 Bing Yang Fire	離 Li	丁 Ding Yin Fire
子 **Rat** (Dec 7 - Jan 5) 十一月 **11th Month**	庚 Geng Yang Metal	兌 Dui	辛 Xin Yin Metal	丑 Chou Ox	艮 Gen	寅 Yin Tiger	壬 Ren Yang Water	坎 Kan	癸 Gui Yin Water
丑 **Ox** (Jan 6 - Feb 3) 十二月 **12th Month**	戌 Xu Dog	乾 Qian	亥 Hai Pig	庚 Geng Yang Metal	兌 Dui	辛 Xin Yin Metal	未 Wei Goat	坤 Kun	申 Shen Monkey

Negative Repair / Renovation Sectors 修方凶位 :

月 MONTH	大月建 Big Month Establishment			飛大煞 Flying Great Sha			丙丁獨火 Bing Ding Lonely Fire	
寅 **Tiger** (Feb 4 - Mar 5) 正月 **1st Month**	未 Wei Goat	坤 Kun	申 Shen Monkey	戌 Xu Dog	乾 Qian	亥 Hai Pig	兌 Dui	艮 Gen
卯 **Rabbit** (Mar 6 - Apr 4) 二月 **2nd Month**	壬 Ren Yang Water	坎 Kan	癸 Gui Yin Water		中 Middle		乾 Qian	兌 Dui
辰 **Dragon** (Apr 5 - May 5) 三月 **3rd Month**	丙 Bing Yang Fire	離 Li	丁 Ding Yin Fire	庚 Geng Yang Metal	兌 Dui	辛 Xin Yin Metal	中 Middle	乾 Qian
巳 **Snake** (May 6 - Jun 5) 四月 **4th Month**	丑 Chou Ox	艮 Gen	寅 Yin Tiger	戌 Xu Dog	乾 Qian	亥 Hai Pig		中 Middle
午 **Horse** (Jun 6 - July 6) 五月 **5th Month**	庚 Geng Yang Metal	兌 Dui	辛 Xin Yin Metal		中 Middle		巽 Xun	中 Middle
未 **Goat** (July 7 - Aug 7) 六月 **6th Month**	戌 Xu Dog	乾 Qian	亥 Hai Pig	辰 Chen Dragon	巽 Xun	巳 Si Snake	震 Zhen	巽 Xun
申 **Monkey** (Aug 8 - Sept 7) 七月 **7th Month**		中 Middle		甲 Jia Yang Wood	震 Zhen	乙 Yi Yin Wood	坤 Kun	震 Zhen
酉 **Rooster** (Sept 8 - Oct 7) 八月 **8th Month**	辰 Chen Dragon	巽 Xun	巳 Si Snake	未 Wei Goat	坤 Kun	申 Shen Monkey	坎 Kan	坤 Kun
戌 **Dog** (Oct 8 - Nov 6) 九月 **9th Month**	甲 Jia Yang Wood	震 Zhen	乙 Yi Yin Wood	壬 Ren Yang Water	坎 Kan	癸 Gui Yin Water	離 Li	坎 Kan
亥 **Pig** (Nov 7 - Dec 6) 十月 **10th Month**	未 Wei Goat	坤 Kun	申 Shen Monkey	丙 Bing Yang Fire	離 Li	丁 Ding Yin Fire	艮 Gen	離 Li
子 **Rat** (Dec 7 - Jan 5) 十一月 **11th Month**	壬 Ren Yang Water	坎 Kan	癸 Gui Yin Water	丑 Chou Ox	艮 Gen	寅 Yin Tiger	兌 Dui	艮 Gen
丑 **Ox** (Jan 6 - Feb 3) 十二月 **12th Month**	丙 Bing Yang Fire	離 Li	丁 Ding Yin Fire	庚 Geng Yang Metal	兌 Dui	辛 Xin Yin Metal	乾 Qian	兌 Dui

Negative Repair / Renovation Sectors 修方凶位 :

月 MONTH	月遊火 Month Wondering Fire	三煞 Monthly 3 Killings		
		劫煞 Robbery Sha	災煞 Calamity Sha	月煞 Month Sha
寅 **Tiger** (Feb 4 - Mar 5) 正月 **1st Month**	坎 Kan	亥 Hai Pig	子 Zi Rat	丑 Chou Ox
卯 **Rabbit** (Mar 6 - Apr 4) 二月 **2nd Month**	坤 Kun	申 Shen Monkey	酉 You Rooster	戌 Xu Dog
辰 **Dragon** (Apr 5 - May 5) 三月 **3rd Month**	震 Zhen	巳 Si Snake	午 Wu Horse	未 Wei Goat
巳 **Snake** (May 6 - Jun 5) 四月 **4th Month**	巽 Xun	寅 Yin Tiger	卯 Mao Rabbit	辰 Chen Dragon
午 **Horse** (Jun 6 - July 6) 五月 **5th Month**	中 Middle	亥 Hai Pig	子 Zi Rat	丑 Chou Ox
未 **Goat** (July 7 - Aug 7) 六月 **6th Month**	乾 Qian	申 Shen Monkey	酉 You Rooster	戌 Xu Dog
申 **Monkey** (Aug 8 - Sept 7) 七月 **7th Month**	兌 Dui	巳 Si Snake	午 Wu Horse	未 Wei Goat
酉 **Rooster** (Sept 8 - Oct 7) 八月 **8th Month**	艮 Gen	寅 Yin Tiger	卯 Mao Rabbit	辰 Chen Dragon
戌 **Dog** (Oct 8 - Nov 6) 九月 **9th Month**	離 Li	亥 Hai Pig	子 Zi Rat	丑 Chou Ox
亥 **Pig** (Nov 7 - Dec 6) 十月 **10th Month**	坎 Kan	申 Shen Monkey	酉 You Rooster	戌 Xu Dog
子 **Rat** (Dec 7 - Jan 5) 十一月 **11th Month**	坤 Kun	巳 Si Snake	午 Wu Horse	未 Wei Goat
丑 **Ox** (Jan 6 - Feb 3) 十二月 **12th Month**	震 Zhen	寅 Yin Tiger	卯 Mao Rabbit	辰 Chen Dragon

Negative Repair / Renovation Sectors 修方凶位 :

月 MONTH	月刑 Month Punishment	月害 Month Harm	月厭 Month Detest
寅 Tiger (Feb 4 - Mar 5) 正月 1st Month	巳 Si Snake	巳 Si Snake	戌 Xu Dog
卯 Rabbit (Mar 6 - Apr 4) 二月 2nd Month	子 Zi Rat	辰 Chen Dragon	酉 You Rooster
辰 Dragon (Apr 5 - May 5) 三月 3rd Month	辰 Chen Dragon	卯 Mao Rabbit	申 Shen Monkey
巳 Snake (May 6 - Jun 5) 四月 4th Month	申 Shen Monkey	寅 Yin Tiger	未 Wei Goat
午 Horse (Jun 6 - July 6) 五月 5th Month	午 Wu Horse	丑 Chou Ox	午 Wu Horse
未 Goat (July 7 - Aug 7) 六月 6th Month	丑 Chou Ox	子 Zi Rat	巳 Si Snake
申 Monkey (Aug 8 - Sept 7) 七月 7th Month	寅 Yin Tiger	亥 Hai Pig	辰 Chen Dragon
酉 Rooster (Sept 8 - Oct 7) 八月 8th Month	酉 You Rooster	戌 Xu Dog	卯 Mao Rabbit
戌 Dog (Oct 8 - Nov 6) 九月 9th Month	未 Wei Goat	酉 You Rooster	寅 Yin Tiger
亥 Pig (Nov 7 - Dec 6) 十月 10th Month	亥 Hai Pig	申 Shen Monkey	丑 Chou Ox
子 Rat (Dec 7 - Jan 5) 十一月 11th Month	卯 Mao Rabbit	未 Wei Goat	子 Zi Rat
丑 Ox (Jan 6 - Feb 3) 十二月 12th Month	戌 Xu Dog	午 Wu Horse	亥 Hai Pig

About Joey Yap

Joey Yap is the Founder and Master Trainer of the Mastery Academy of Chinese Metaphysics, a global organisation devoted to the worldwide teaching of Feng Shui, BaZi, Mian Xiang, Yi Jing and other Chinese Metaphysics subjects. Joey is also the Chief Consultant of Yap Global Consulting, an international Feng Shui and Chinese Astrology consulting firm offering audit and consultation services to corporations and individuals all over the world.

Joey received his formal education in Malaysia and Australia. He has combined the best of Eastern learning and Western education systems in the teaching methodology practiced at the Academy. Students of the Mastery Academy study traditional syllabuses of Chinese Metaphysics but through Western-style modular programs that are structured and systematic, enabling individuals to easily and quickly learn, grasp and master complex Chinese Metaphysics subjects like Feng Shui and BaZi. These unique structured learning systems are also utilized by Mastery Academy instructors all over the world to teach BaZi and Feng Shui.

The Mastery Academy is also the first international educational organisation to fully utilize the benefits of the Internet to promote continuous education, encourage peer-to-peer learning, enable mentoring and distance learning. Students interact with each other live, and continue to learn and improve their knowledge.

Joey Yap is also the bestselling author of various books, including *Stories and Lessons on Feng Shui*, *BaZi – The Destiny Code* and its sequel, *BaZi – The Destiny Code Revealed*, *Mian Xiang – Discover Face Reading*, *Feng Shui for Homebuyers – Exterior*, *Feng Shui for Homebuyers – Interior*, and *The Art of Date Selection – Personal Date Selection*, which topped the Malaysian MPH bookstores' bestseller lists. He has recently released *Even More Stories and Lessons on Feng Shui* and *Walking the Dragons*, a travelogue of China from a Feng Shui perspective. He is also the producer of the first comprehensive reference source of Chinese Metaphysics, *The Chinese Metaphysics Compendium*, a compilation of all the essential formulas and applications known and practiced in Chinese Metaphysics today.

Besides being a regular guest of various radio and TV talk shows, Joey is also a regular columnist for a national newspaper and various magazines in Malaysia. He has hosted his own TV series, *Discover Feng Shui with Joey Yap*, on Malaysia's 8TV channel in 2005; a popular program that focused on heightening awareness of Feng Shui and Chinese Metaphysics among the general public.

A firm believer in innovation being the way forward, Joey has released the **BaZi Ming Pan 2.0 software**, which allows users to generate configurable, detailed BaZi charts, and has recently released the **Xuan Kong Flying Stars Feng Shui Software**, a professional and interactive application to aid in the practice and study of Xuan Kong Feng Shui.

Author's personal website: www.joeyyap.com | www.fengshuilogy.com
Academy website: www.masteryacademy.com | www.masteryjournal.com |
www.maelearning.com

EDUCATION
The Mastery Academy of Chinese Metaphysics:
the first choice for practitioners and aspiring students of the
art and science of Chinese Classical Feng Shui and Astrology.

For thousands of years, Eastern knowledge has been passed from one generation to another through the system of discipleship. A venerated master would accept suitable individuals at a young age as his disciples, and informally through the years, pass on his knowledge and skills to them. His disciples in turn, would take on their own disciples, as a means to perpetuate knowledge or skills.

This system served the purpose of restricting the transfer of knowledge to only worthy honourable individuals and ensuring that outsiders or Westerners would not have access to thousands of years of Eastern knowledge, learning and research.

However, the disciple system has also resulted in Chinese Metaphysics and Classical Studies lacking systematic teaching methods. Knowledge garnered over the years has not been accumulated in a concise, systematic manner, but scattered amongst practitioners, each practicing his/her knowledge, art and science, in isolation.

The disciple system, out of place in today's modern world, endangers the advancement of these classical fields that continue to have great relevance and application today.

At the Mastery Academy of Chinese Metaphysics, our Mission is to bring Eastern Classical knowledge in the fields of metaphysics, Feng Shui and Astrology sciences and the arts to the world. These Classical teachings and knowledge, previously shrouded in secrecy and passed on only through the discipleship system, are adapted into structured learning, which can easily be understood, learnt and mastered. Through modern learning methods, these renowned ancient arts, sciences and practices can be perpetuated while facilitating more extensive application and understanding of these classical subjects.

The Mastery Academy espouses an educational philosophy that draws from the best of the East and West. It is the world's premier educational institution for the study of Chinese Metaphysics Studies offering a wide range and variety of courses, ensuring that students have the opportunity to pursue their preferred field of study and enabling existing practitioners and professionals to gain cross-disciplinary knowledge that complements their current field of practice.

Courses at the Mastery Academy have been carefully designed to ensure a comprehensive yet compact syllabus. The modular nature of the courses enables students to immediately begin to put their knowledge into practice while pursuing continued study of their field and complementary fields. Students thus have the benefit of developing and gaining practical experience in tandem with the expansion and advancement of their theoretical knowledge.

Students can also choose from a variety of study options, from a distance learning program, the Homestudy Series, that enables study at one's own pace or intensive foundation courses and compact lecture-based courses, held in various cities around the world by Joey Yap or our licensed instructors. The Mastery Academy's faculty and make-up is international in nature, thus ensuring that prospective students can attend courses at destinations nearest to their country of origin or with a licensed Mastery Academy instructor in their home country.

The Mastery Academy provides 24x7 support to students through its Online Community, with a variety of tools, documents, forums and e-learning materials to help students stay at the forefront of research in their fields and gain invaluable assistance from peers and mentoring from their instructors.

TM

MASTERY ACADEMY
OF CHINESE METAPHYSICS

www.masteryacademy.com

MALAYSIA
19-3, The Boulevard
Mid Valley City
59200 Kuala Lumpur, Malaysia
Tel   : +603-2284 8080
Fax   : +603-2284 1218
Email : info@masteryacademy.com

SINGAPORE
14, Robinson Road # 13-00
Far East Finance Building
Singapore 048545
Tel   : +65-6494 9147
Email : singapore@masteryacademy.com

AUSTRALIA
Unit 3 / 61 Belmont Avenue,
Belmont WA 6104.
Australia.
Tel   : +618-9467 3626
Fax   : +618-9479 3388
Email : australia@masteryacademy.com

Australia, Austria, Canada, China, Croatia, Cyprus, Czech Republic, Denmark, France, Germany, Greece, Hungary, India, Italy, Kazakhstan, Malaysia, Netherlands (Holland), New Zealand, Philippines, Poland, Russian Federation, Singapore, Slovenia, South Africa, Switzerland, Turkey, U.S.A., Ukraine, United Kingdom

Introducing...
The Mastery Academy's E-Learning Center!

The Mastery Academy's goal has always been to share authentic knowledge of Chinese Metaphysics with the whole world.

Nevertheless, we do recognize that distance, time, and hotel and traveling costs – amongst many other factors – could actually hinder people from enrolling for a classroom-based course. But with the advent and amazing advance of IT today, NOT any more!

With this in mind, we have invested heavily in IT, to conceive what is probably the first and only E-Learning Center in the world today that offers a full range of studies in the field of Chinese Metaphysics.

Convenient   Study from Your   Easy Enrollment
                Own Home

The Mastery Academy's E-Learning Center

Now, armed with your trusty computer or laptop, and Internet access, knowledge of classical Feng Shui, BaZi (Destiny Analysis) and Mian Xiang (Face Reading) are but a literal click away!

Study at your own pace, and interact with your Instructor and fellow students worldwide, from anywhere in the world. With our E-Learning Center, knowledge of Chinese Metaphysics is brought DIRECTLY to you in all its clarity – topic-by-topic, and lesson-by-lesson; with illustrated presentations and comprehensive notes expediting your learning curve!

Your education journey through our E-Learning Center may be done via any of the following approaches:

1. Online Courses

There are 3 Programs available: our Online Feng Shui Program, Online BaZi Program, and Online Mian Xiang Program. Each Program consists of several Levels, with each Level consisting of many Lessons in turn. Each Lesson contains a pre-recorded video session on the topic at hand, accompanied by presentation-slides and graphics as well as downloadable tutorial notes that you can print and file for future reference.

Video Lecture

Presentation Slide

Downloadable Notes

2. MA Live!

MA Live!, as its name implies, enables LIVE broadcasts of Joey Yap's courses and seminars – right to your computer screen. Students will not only get to see and hear Joey talk on real-time 'live', but also participate and more importantly, TALK to Joey via the MA Live! interface. All the benefits of a live class, minus the hassle of actually having to attend one!

How It Works

Our Live Classes   You at Home

3. Video-On-Demand (VOD)

Get immediate streaming-downloads of the Mastery Academy's wide range of educational DVDs, right on your computer screen. No more shipping costs and waiting time to be incurred!

Instant VOD Online

Choose From Our list of Available VODs!   Click "Play" on Your PC

Welcome to **www.maelearning.com**; the web portal of our E-Learning Center, and YOUR virtual gateway to Chinese Metaphysics!

Mastery Academy around the world

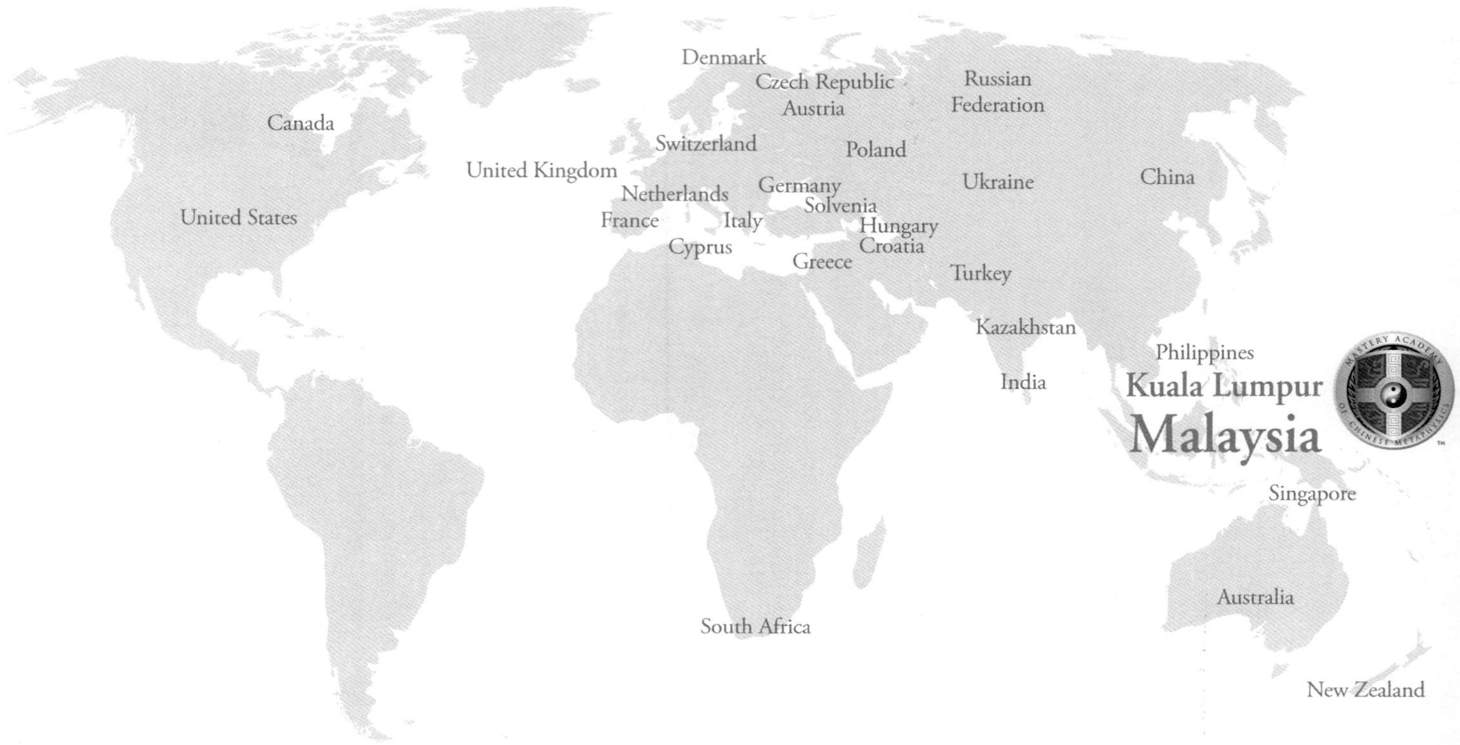

Canada

United States

Denmark
Czech Republic
Austria
United Kingdom
Switzerland
Poland
Germany
Netherlands
Solvenia
Hungary
France
Italy
Cyprus
Greece
Croatia

Russian
Federation

Ukraine

Turkey

Kazakhstan

India

South Africa

China

Philippines

Kuala Lumpur
Malaysia

Singapore

Australia

New Zealand

YAP GLOBAL CONSULTING

Joey Yap & Yap Global Consulting

Headed by Joey Yap, Yap Global Consulting (YGC) is a leading international consulting firm specializing in Feng Shui, Mian Xiang (Face Reading) and BaZi (Destiny Analysis) consulting services worldwide. Joey - an internationally renowned Master Trainer, Consultant, Speaker and best-selling Author - has dedicated his life to the art and science of Chinese Metaphysics.

YGC has its main offices in Kuala Lumpur and Australia, and draws upon its diverse reservoir of strength from a group of dedicated and experienced consultants based in more than 30 countries, worldwide.

As the pioneer in blending established, classical Chinese Metaphysics techniques with the latest approach in consultation practices, YGC has built its reputation on the principles of professionalism and only the highest standards of service. This allows us to retain the cutting edge in delivering Feng Shui and Destiny consultation services to both corporate and personal clients, in a simple and direct manner, without compromising on quality.

Across Industries: Our Portfolio of Clients

Our diverse portfolio of both corporate and individual clients from all around the world bears testimony to our experience and capabilities.

Virtually every industry imaginable has benefited from our services - ranging from academic and financial institutions, real-estate developers and multinational corporations, to those in the leisure and tourism industry. Our services are also engaged by professionals, prominent business personalities, celebrities, high-profile politicians and people from all walks of life.

YAP GLOBAL CONSULTING

Name (Mr./Mrs./Ms.):

Contact Details

Tel: _____ Fax: _____

Mobile : _____

E-mail: _____

What Type of Consultation Are You Interested In?

☐ Feng Shui ☐ BaZi ☐ Date Selection ☐ Yi Jing

Please tick if applicable:

☐ Are you a Property Developer looking to engage Yap Global Consulting?

☐ Are you a Property Investor looking for tailor-made packages to suit your investment requirements?

Please attach your name card here.

Thank you for completing this form.
Please fax it back to us at:

Singapore	**Australia**	**Malaysia & the rest of the world**
Tel : +65-6494 9147	Fax: +618-9479 3388	Fax: +603-2284 2213
	Tel : +618-9467 3626	Tel : +603-2284 1213

Feng Shui Consultations

For Residential Properties
- Initial Land/Property Assessment
- Residential Feng Shui Consultations
- Residential Land Selection
- End-to-End Residential Consultation

For Commercial Properties
- Initial Land/Property Assessment
- Commercial Feng Shui Consultations
- Commercial Land Selection
- End-to-End Commercial Consultation

For Property Developers
- End-to-End Consultation
- Post-Consultation Advisory Services
- Panel Feng Shui Consultant

For Property Investors
- Your Personal Feng Shui Consultant
- Tailor-Made Packages

For Memorial Parks & Burial Sites
- Yin House Feng Shui

BaZi Consultations

Personal Destiny Analysis
- Personal Destiny Analysis for Individuals
- Children's BaZi Analysis
- Family BaZi Analysis

Strategic Analysis for Corporate Organizations
- Corporate BaZi Consultations
- BaZi Analysis for Human Resource Management

Entrepreneurs & Business Owners
- BaZi Analysis for Entrepreneurs

Career Pursuits
- BaZi Career Analysis

Relationships
- Marriage and Compatibility Analysis
- Partnership Analysis

For Everyone
- Annual BaZi Forecast
- Your Personal BaZi Coach

Date Selection Consultations

- **Marriage Date Selection**
- **Caesarean Birth Date Selection**
- **House-Moving Date Selection**
- **Renovation & Groundbreaking Dates**

- **Signing of Contracts**
- **Official Openings**
- **Product Launches**

Yi Jing Assessment

A Time-Tested, Accurate Science

- With a history predating 4 millennia, the Yi Jing - or Classic of Change - is one of the oldest Chinese texts surviving today. Its purpose as an oracle, in predicting the outcome of things, is based on the variables of Time, Space and Specific Events.

- A Yi Jing Assessment provides specific answers to any specific questions you may have about a specific event or endeavor. This is something that a Destiny Analysis would not be able to give you.

Basically, what a Yi Jing Assessment does is focus on only ONE aspect or item at a particular point in your life, and give you a calculated prediction of the details that will follow suit, if you undertake a particular action. It gives you an insight into a situation, and what course of action to take in order to arrive at a satisfactory outcome at the end of the day.

Please Contact YGC for a personalized Yi Jing Assessment!

Tel: +603-2284 1213   Email: consultation@joeyyap.com

INVITING US TO YOUR CORPORATE EVENTS

Many reputable organizations and institutions have worked closely with YGC to build a synergistic business relationship by engaging our team of consultants, led by Joey Yap, as speakers at their corporate events. Our seminars and short talks are always packed with audiences consisting of clients and associates of multinational and public-listed companies as well as key stakeholders of financial institutions.

We tailor our seminars and talks to suit the anticipated or pertinent group of audience. Be it a department, subsidiary, your clients or even the entire corporation, we aim to fit your requirements in delivering the intended message(s).

CHINESE METAPHYSICS REFERENCE SERIES

The Chinese Metaphysics Reference Series is a collection of reference texts, source material, and educational textbooks to be used as supplementary guides by scholars, students, researchers, teachers and practitioners of Chinese Metaphysics.

These comprehensive and structured books provide fast, easy reference to aid in the study and practice of various Chinese Metaphysics subjects including Feng Shui, BaZi, Yi Jing, Zi Wei, Liu Ren, Ze Ri, Ta Yi, Qi Men and Mian Xiang.

The Chinese Metaphysics Compendium

At over 1,000 pages, the *Chinese Metaphysics Compendium* is a unique one-volume reference book that compiles all the formulas relating to Feng Shui, BaZi (Four Pillars of Destiny), Zi Wei (Purple Star Astrology), Yi Jing (I-Ching), Qi Men (Mystical Doorways), Ze Ri (Date Selection), Mian Xiang (Face Reading) and other sources of Chinese Metaphysics.

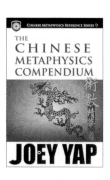

It is presented in the form of easy-to-read tables, diagrams and reference charts, all of which are compiled into one handy book. This first-of-its-kind compendium is presented in both English and the original Chinese, so that none of the meanings and contexts of the technical terminologies are lost.

The only essential and comprehensive reference on Chinese Metaphysics, and an absolute must-have for all students, scholars, and practitioners of Chinese Metaphysics.

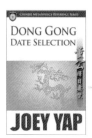

Dong Gong Date Selection

Xuan Kong Da Gua Ten Thousand Year Calendar

Xuan Kong Da Gua Reference Book

The Ten Thousand Year Calendar
(Professional Edition)

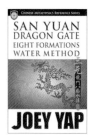

San Yuan Dragon Gate Eight Formations Water Method

Plum Blossoms Divination Reference Book

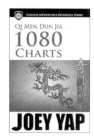

Qi Men Dun Jia 1080 Charts

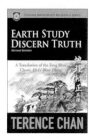

Earth Study Discern Truth Volume Two

Educational Tools & Software

Xuan Kong Flying Stars Feng Shui Software
The Essential Application for Enthusiasts and Professionals

The Xuan Kong Flying Stars Feng Shui Software is a brand-new application by Joey Yap that will assist you in the practice of Xuan Kong Feng Shui with minimum fuss and maximum effectiveness. Superimpose the Flying Stars charts over your house plans (or those of your clients) to clearly demarcate the 9 Palaces. Use it to help you create fast and sophisticated chart drawings and presentations, as well as to assist professional practitioners in the report-writing process before presenting the final reports for your clients. Students can use it to practice their Xuan Kong Feng Shui skills and knowledge, and it can even be used by designers and architects!

Some of the highlights of the software include:
- Natal Flying Stars
- Monthly Flying Stars
- 81 Flying Stars Combinations
- Dual-View Format
- Annual Flying Stars
- Flying Stars Integration
- 24 Mountains

All charts will be are printable and configurable, and can be saved for future editing. Also, you'll be able to export your charts into most image file formats like jpeg, bmp, and gif.

The Xuan Kong Flying Stars Feng Shui Software can make your Feng Shui practice simpler and more effective, garnering you amazing results with less effort!

Mini Feng Shui Compass

This Mini Feng Shui Compass with the accompanying Companion Booklet written by leading Feng Shui and Chinese Astrology Master Trainer Joey Yap is a must-have for any Feng Shui enthusiast.

The Mini Feng Shui Compass is a self-aligning compass that is not only light at 100gms but also built sturdily to ensure it will be convenient to use anywhere. The rings on the Mini Feng Shui Compass are bi-lingual and incorporate the 24 Mountain Rings that is used in your traditional Luo Pan.

The comprehensive booklet included will guide you in applying the 24 Mountain Directions on your Mini Feng Shui Compass effectively and the 8 Mansions Feng Shui to locate the most auspicious locations within your home, office and surroundings. You can also use the Mini Feng Shui Compass when measuring the direction of your property for the purpose of applying Flying Stars Feng Shui.

Educational Tools & Software

BaZi Ming Pan Software Version 2.0
Professional Four Pillars Calculator for Destiny Analysis

The BaZi Ming Pan Version 2.0 Professional Four Pillars Calculator for Destiny Analysis is the most technically advanced software of its kind in the world today. It allows even those without any knowledge of BaZi to generate their own BaZi Charts, and provides virtually every detail required to undertake a comprehensive Destiny Analysis.

This Professional Four Pillars Calculator allows you to even undertake a day-to-day analysis of your Destiny. What's more, all BaZi Charts generated by this software are fully printable and configurable! Designed for both enthusiasts and professional practitioners, this state-of-the-art software blends details with simplicity, and is capable of generating 4 different types of BaZi charts: **BaZi Professional Charts, BaZi Annual Analysis Charts, BaZi Pillar Analysis Charts and BaZi Family Relationship Charts.**

Additional references, configurable to cater to all levels of BaZi knowledge and usage, include:
• Dual Age & Bilingual Option (Western & Chinese) • Na Yin narrations • 12 Life Stages evaluation • Death & Emptiness • Gods & Killings • Special Days • Heavenly Virtue Nobles

This software also comes with a Client Management feature that allows you to save and trace clients' records instantly, navigate effortlessly between BaZi charts, and file your clients' information in an organized manner.

The BaZi Ming Pan Version 2.0 Calculator sets a new standard by combining the best of BaZi and technology.

Joey Yap Feng Shui Template Set

Directions are the cornerstone of any successful Feng Shui audit or application. The **Joey Yap Feng Shui Template Set** is a set of three templates to simplify the process of taking directions and determining locations and positions, whether it's for a building, a house, or an open area such as a plot of land, all with just a floor plan or area map.

The Set comprises 3 basic templates: The Basic Feng Shui Template, 8 Mansions Feng Shui Template, and the Flying Stars Feng Shui Template.

With bi-lingual notations for these directions; both in English and the original Chinese, the **Joey Yap Feng Shui Template Set** comes with its own Booklet that gives simple yet detailed instructions on how to make use of the 3 templates within.

• Easy-to-use, simple, and straightforward
• Small and portable; each template measuring only 5" x 5"
• Additional 8 Mansions and Flying Stars Reference Rings
• Handy companion booklet with usage tips and examples

Accelerate Your Face Reading Skills With Joey Yap's Face Reading Revealed DVD Series

Mian Xiang, the Chinese art of Face Reading, is an ancient form of physiognomy and entails the use of the face and facial characteristics to evaluate key aspects of a person's life, luck and destiny. In his Face Reading DVDs series, Joey Yap shows you how the facial features reveal a wealth of information about a person's luck, destiny and personality.

Mian Xiang also tell us the talents, quirks and personality of an individual. Do you know that just by looking at a person's face, you can ascertain his or her health, wealth, relationships and career? Let Joey Yap show you how the 12 Palaces can be utilised to reveal a person's inner talents, characteristics and much more.

Each facial feature on the face represents one year in a person's life. Your face is a 100-year map of your life and each position reveals your fortune and destiny at a particular age as well as insights and information about your personality, skills, abilities and destiny.

Using Mian Xiang, you will also be able to plan your life ahead by identifying, for example, the right business partner and knowing the sort of person that you need to avoid. By knowing their characteristics through the facial features, you will be able to gauge their intentions and gain an upper hand in negotiations.

Do you know what moles signify? Do they bring good or bad luck? Do you want to build better relationships with your partner or family members or have your ever wondered why you seem to be always bogged down by trivial problems in your life?

In these highly entertaining DVDs, Joey will help you answer all these questions and more. You will be able to ascertain the underlying meaning of moles, birthmarks or even the type of your hair in Face Reading. Joey will also reveal the guidelines to help you foster better and stronger relationships with your loved ones through Mian Xiang.

Feng Shui for Homebuyers DVD Series

Best-selling Author, and international Master Trainer and Consultant Joey Yap reveals in these DVDs the significant Feng Shui features that every homebuyer should know when evaluating a property.

Joey will guide you on how to customise your home to maximise the Feng Shui potential of your property and gain the full benefit of improving your health, wealth and love life using the 9 Palace Grid. He will show you how to go about applying the classical applications of the Life Gua and House Gua techniques to get attuned to your Sheng Qi (positive energies).

In these DVDs, you will also learn how to identify properties with good Feng Shui features that will help you promote a fulfilling life and achieve your full potential. Discover how to avoid properties with negative Feng Shui that can bring about detrimental effects to your health, wealth and relationships.

Joey will also elaborate on how to fix the various aspects of your home that may have an impact on the Feng Shui of your property and give pointers on how to tap into the positive energies to support your goals.

Discover Feng Shui with Joey Yap (TV Series)

Discover Feng Shui with Joey Yap: Set of 4 DVDs

Informative and entertaining, classical Feng Shui comes alive in *Discover Feng Shui with Joey Yap!*

Dying to know how you can use Feng Shui to improve your house or office, but simply too busy attend for formal classes?

You have the questions. Now let Joey personally answer them in this 4-set DVD compilation! Learn how to ensure the viability of your residence or workplace, Feng Shui-wise, without having to convert it into a Chinese antiques' shop. Classical Feng Shui is about harnessing the natural power of your environment to improve quality of life. It's a systematic and subtle metaphysical science.

And that's not all. Joey also debunks many a myth about classical Feng Shui, and shares with viewers Face Reading tips as well!

Own the series that national channel 8TV did a re-run of in 2005, today!

Annual Releases

Chinese Astrology for 2009

This information-packed annual guide to the Chinese Astrology for 2009 goes way beyond the conventional 'animal horoscope' book. To begin with, author Joey Yap includes a personalized outlook for 2009 based on the individual's BaZi Day Pillar (Jia Zi) and a 12-month micro-analysis for each of the 60 Day Pillars – in addition to the annual outlook for all 12 animal signs and the 12-month outlook for each animal sign in 2009. Find out what awaits you in 2009 from the four key aspects of Health, Wealth, Career and Relationships…with Joey Yap's **Chinese Astrology for 2009**!

Feng Shui for 2009

Maximize the Qi of the Year of the Earth Rat for your home and office, with Joey Yap's **Feng Shui for 2009** book. Learn how to tap into the positive sectors of the year, and avoid the negative ones and those with the Annual Afflictions, as well as ascertain how the annual Flying Stars affect your property by comparing them against the Eight Mansions (Ba Zhai) for 2009. Flying Stars enthusiasts will also find this book handy, as it includes the monthly Flying Stars charts for the year, accompanied by detailed commentaries on what sectors to use and avoid – to enable you to optimize your Academic, Relationships and Wealth Luck in 2009.

Tong Shu Diary 2009

Organize your professional and personal lives with the **Tong Shu Diary 2009**, with a twist… it also allows you to determine the most suitable dates on which you can undertake important activities and endeavors throughout the year! This compact Diary integrates the Chinese Solar and Lunar Calendars with the universal lingua franca of the Gregorian Calendar.

Tong Shu Monthly Planner 2009

Tailor-made for the Feng Shui or BaZi enthusiast in you, or even professional Chinese Metaphysics consultants who want a compact planner with useful information incorporated into it. In the **Tong Shu Monthly Planner 2009**, you will find the auspicious and inauspicious dates for the year marked out for you, alongside the most suitable activities to be undertaken on each day. As a bonus, there is also a reference section containing all the monthly Flying Stars charts and Annual Afflictions for 2009.

Tong Shu Desktop Calendar 2009

Get an instant snapshot of the suitable and unsuitable activities for each day of the Year of the Earth Rat, with the icons displayed on this lightweight Desktop Calendar. Elegantly presenting the details of the Chinese Solar Calendar in the form of the standard Gregorian one, the **Tong Shu Desktop Calendar 2009** is perfect for Chinese Metaphysics enthusiasts and practitioners alike. Whether it a business launching or meeting, ground breaking ceremony, travel or house-moving that you have in mind, this Calendar is designed to fulfill your information needs.

Tong Shu Year Planner 2009

This one-piece Planner presents you all the essential information you need for significant activities or endeavors…with just a quick glance! In a nutshell, it allows you to identify the favorable and unfavorable days, which will in turn enable you to schedule your year's activities so as to make the most of good days, and avoid the ill-effects brought about by inauspicious ones.

Continue Your Journey with Joey Yap's Books

Walking the Dragons

Walking the Dragons is a guided tour through the classical landform Feng Shui of ancient China, an enchanting collection of deeply-researched yet entertaining essays rich in historical detail.

Compiled in one book for the first time from Joey Yap's Feng Shui Mastery Excursion Series, the book highlights China's extensive, vibrant history with astute observations on the Feng Shui of important sites and places. Learn the landform formations of Yin Houses (tombs and burial places), as well as mountains, temples, castles, and villages.

It demonstrates complex Feng Shui theories and principles in easy-to-understand, entertaining language and is the perfect addition to the bookshelf of a Feng Shui or history lover. Anyone, whether experienced in Feng Shui or new to the practice, will be able to enjoy the insights shared in this book. Complete with gorgeous full-colour pictures of all the amazing sights and scenery, it's the next best thing to having been there yourself!

Your Aquarium Here

Your Aquarium Here is a simple, practical, hands-on Feng Shui book that teaches you how to incorporate a Water feature – an aquarium – for optimal Feng Shui benefit, whether for personal relationships, wealth, or career. Designed to be comprehensive yet simple enough for a novice or beginner, *Your Aquarium Here* provides historical and factual information about the role of Water in Feng Shui, and provides a step-by-step guide to installing and using an aquarium.

The book is the first in the **Fengshuilogy Series**, a series of matter-of-fact and useful Feng Shui books designed for the person who wants to do fuss-free Feng Shui. Not everyone who wants to use Feng Shui is an expert or a scholar! This series of books are just the kind you'd want on your bookshelf to gain basic, practical knowledge of the subject. Go ahead and Feng Shui-It-Yourself – *Your Aquarium Here* eliminates all the fuss and bother, but maintains all the fun and excitement, of authentic Feng Shui application!

The Art of Date Selection: Personal Date Selection

In today's modern world, it is not good enough to just do things effectively – we need to do them efficiently, as well. From the signing of business contracts and moving into a new home, to launching a product or even tying the knot; everything has to move, and move very quickly too. There is a premium on Time, where mistakes can indeed be costly.

The notion of doing the Right Thing, at the Right Time and in the Right Place is the very backbone of Date Selection. Because by selecting a suitable date specially tailored to a specific activity or endeavor, we infuse it with the most positive energies prevalent in our environment during that particular point in time; and that could well make the difference between 'make-and-break'! With the *Art of Date Selection: Personal Date Selection*, learn simple, practical methods you can employ to select not just good dates, but personalized good dates. Whether it's a personal activity such as a marriage or professional endeavor such as launching a business, signing a contract or even acquiring assets, this book will show you how to pick the good dates and tailor them to suit the activity in question, as well as avoid the negative ones too!

The Art of Date Selection: Feng Shui Date Selection

Date Selection is the Art of selecting the most suitable date, where the energies present on the day support the specific activities or endeavors we choose to undertake on that day. Feng Shui is the Chinese Metaphysical study of the Physiognomy of the Land – landforms and the Qi they produce, circulate and conduct. Hence, anything that exists on this Earth is invariably subject to the laws of Feng Shui. So what do we get when Date Selection and Feng Shui converge?

Feng Shui Date Selection, of course! Say you wish to renovate your home, or maybe buy or rent one. Or perhaps, you're a developer, and wish to know WHEN is the best date possible to commence construction works on your project. In any case – and all cases – you certainly wish to ensure that your endeavors are well supported by the positive energies present on a good day, won't you? And this is where Date Selection supplements the practice of Feng Shui. At the end of the day, it's all about making the most of what's good, and minimizing what's bad.

(Available Soon)

Continue Your Journey with Joey Yap's Books

Feng Shui For Homebuyers - Exterior

Best selling Author and international Feng Shui Consultant, Joey Yap, will guide you on the various important features in your external environment that have a bearing on the Feng Shui of your home. For homeowners, those looking to build their own home or even investors who are looking to apply Feng Shui to their homes, this book provides valuable information from the classical Feng Shui theories and applications.

This book will assist you in screening and eliminating unsuitable options with negative FSQ (Feng Shui Quotient) should you acquire your own land or if you are purchasing a newly built home. It will also help you in determining which plot of land to select and which to avoid when purchasing an empty parcel of land.

Feng Shui for Homebuyers - Interior

A book every homeowner or potential house buyer should have. The Feng Shui for Homebuyers (Interior) is an informative reference book and invaluable guide written by best selling Author and international Feng Shui Consultant, Joey Yap.

This book provides answers to the important questions of what really does matter when looking at the internal Feng Shui of a home or office. It teaches you how to analyze your home or office floor plans and how to improve their Feng Shui. It will answer all your questions about the positive and negative flow of Qi within your home and ways to utilize them to your maximum benefit.

Providing you with a guide to calculating your Life Gua and House Gua to fine-tune your Feng Shui within your property, Joey Yap focuses on practical, easily applicable ideas on what you can implement internally in a property.

Feng Shui for Apartment Buyers - Home Owners

Finding a good apartment or condominium is never an easy task but who do you ensure that is also has good Feng Shui? And how exactly do you apply Feng Shui to an apartment or condominium or high-rise residence?

These questions and more are answered by renowned Feng Shui Consultant and Master Trainer Joey Yap in **Feng Shui for Apartment Buyers - Home Owners**. Joey answers the key questions about Feng Shui and apartments, then guides you through the bare basics like taking a direction and super-imposing a Flying Stars chart onto a floor plan. Joey also walks you through the process of finding an apartment with favorable Feng Shui, sharing with you some of the key methods and techniques that are employed by professional Feng Shui consultants in assesing apartment Feng Shui.

In his trademark straight-to-the-point manner, Joey shares with you the Feng Shui do's and dont's when it comes to finding an apartment with favorable Feng Shui and which is conducive for home living.

The Ten Thousand Year Calendar

The Ten Thousand Year Calendar or 萬年曆 Wan Nian Li is a regular reference book and an invaluable tool used by masters, practitioners and students of Feng Shui, BaZi (Four Pillars of Destiny), Chinese Zi Wei Dou Shu Astrology (Purple Star), Yi Jing (I-Ching) and Date Selection specialists.

JOEY YAP's Ten Thousand Year Calendar provides the Gregorian (Western) dates converted into both the Chinese Solar and Lunar calendar in both the English and Chinese language.

It also includes a comprehensive set of key Feng Shui and Chinese Astrology charts and references, including Xuan Kong Nine Palace Flying Star Charts, Monthly and Daily Flying Stars, Water Dragon Formulas Reference Charts, Zi Wei Dou Shu (Purple Star) Astrology Reference Charts, BaZi (Four Pillars of Destiny) Heavenly Stems, Earthly Branches and all other related reference tables for Chinese Metaphysical Studies.

Continue Your Journey with Joey Yap's Books

Stories and Lessons on Feng Shui (English & Chinese versions)

Stories and Lessons on Feng Shui is a compilation of essays and stories written by leading Feng Shui and Chinese Astrology trainer and consultant Joey Yap about Feng Shui and Chinese Astrology.

In this heart-warming collection of easy to read stories, find out why it's a myth that you should never have Water on the right hand side of your house, the truth behind the infamous 'love' and 'wealth' corners and that the sudden death of a pet fish is really NOT due to bad luck!

More Stories and Lessons on Feng Shui

Finally, the long-awaited sequel to *Stories & Lessons on Feng Shui*!

If you've read the best-selling Stories & Lessons on Feng Shui, you won't want to miss this book. And even if you haven't read *Stories & Lessons on Feng Shui*, there's always a time to rev your Feng Shui engine up.

The time is NOW.

And the book? *More Stories & Lessons on Feng Shui* – the 2nd compilation of the most popular articles and columns penned by Joey Yap; **specially featured in national and international publications, magazines and newspapers.**

All in all, *More Stories & Lessons on Feng Shui* is a delightful chronicle of Joey's articles, thoughts and vast experience - as a professional Feng Shui consultant and instructor - that have been purposely refined, edited and expanded upon to make for a light-hearted, interesting yet educational read. And with Feng Shui, BaZi, Mian Xiang and Yi Jing all thrown into this one dish, there's something for everyone...so all you need to serve or accompany *More Stories & Lessons on Feng Shui* with is your favorite cup of tea or coffee!

Even More Stories and Lessons on Feng Shui

In this third release in the Stories and Lessons series, Joey Yap continues his exploration on the study and practice of Feng Shui in the modern age through a series of essays and personal anecdotes. Debunking superstition, offering simple and understandable "Feng Shui-It-Yourself" tips, and expounding on the history and origins of classical Feng Shui, Joey takes readers on a journey that is always refreshing and exciting.

Besides 'behind-the-scenes' revelations of actual Feng Shui audits, there are also chapters on how beginners can easily and accurately incorporate Feng Shui practice into their lives, as well as travel articles that offer proof that when it comes to Feng Shui, the Qi literally knows no boundaries.

In his trademark lucid and forthright style, Joey covers themes and topics that will strike a chord with all readers who have an interest in Feng Shui.

Mian Xiang - Discover Face Reading

Need to identify a suitable business partner? How about understanding your staff or superiors better? Or even choosing a suitable spouse? These mind boggling questions can be answered in Joey Yap's introductory book to Face Reading titled *Mian Xiang – Discover Face Reading*. This book will help you discover the hidden secrets in a person's face.

Mian Xiang – Discover Face Reading is comprehensive book on all areas of Face Reading, covering some of the most important facial features, including the forehead, mouth, ears and even the philtrum above your lips. This book will help you analyse not just your Destiny but help you achieve your full potential and achieve life fulfillment.

Continue Your Journey with Joey Yap's Books

BaZi - The Destiny Code (English & Chinese versions)

Leading Chinese Astrology Master Trainer Joey Yap makes it easy to learn how to unlock your Destiny through your BaZi with this book. BaZi or Four Pillars of Destiny is an ancient Chinese science which enables individuals to understand their personality, hidden talents and abilities as well as their luck cycle, simply by examining the information contained within their birth data. *The Destiny Code* is the first book that shows readers how to plot and interpret their own Destiny Charts and lays the foundation for more in-depth BaZi studies. Written in a lively entertaining style, the Destiny Code makes BaZi accessible to the layperson. Within 10 chapters, understand and appreciate more about this astoundingly accurate ancient Chinese Metaphysical science.

BaZi - The Destiny Code Revealed

In this follow up to Joey Yap's best-selling *The Destiny Code*, delve deeper into your own Destiny chart through an understanding of the key elemental relationships that affect the Heavenly Stems and Earthly Branches. Find out how Combinations, Clash, Harm, Destructions and Punishments bring new dimension to a BaZi chart. Complemented by extensive real-life examples, *The Destiny Code Revealed* takes you to the next level of BaZi, showing you how to unlock the Codes of Destiny and to take decisive action at the right time, and capitalise on the opportunities in life.

Xuan Kong: Flying Stars Feng Shui

Xuan Kong Flying Stars Feng Shui is an essential introductory book to the subject of Xuan Kong Fei Xing, a well-known and popular system of Feng Shui, written by International Feng Shui Master Trainer Joey Yap.

In his down-to-earth, entertaining and easy to read style, Joey Yap takes you through the essential basics of Classical Feng Shui, and the key concepts of Xuan Kong Fei Xing (Flying Stars). Learn how to fly the stars, plot a Flying Star chart for your home or office and interpret the stars and star combinations. Find out how to utilise the favourable areas of your home or office for maximum benefit and learn 'tricks of the trade' and 'trade secrets' used by Feng Shui practitioners to enhance and maximise Qi in your home or office.

An essential integral introduction to the subject of Classical Feng Shui and the Flying Stars System of Feng Shui!

Xuan Kong Flying Stars: Structures and Combinations

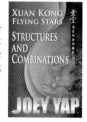

Delve deeper into Flying Stars through a greater understanding of the 81 Combinations and the influence of the Annual and Monthly Stars on the Base, Sitting and Facing Stars in this 2nd book in the Xuan Kong Feng Shui series. Learn how Structures like the Combination of 10, Up the Mountain and Down the River, Pearl and Parent String Structures are used to interpret a Flying Star chart.

(Available Soon)

Xuan Kong Flying Stars: Advanced Techniques

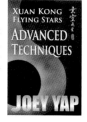

Take your knowledge of Xuan Kong Flying Stars to a higher level and learn how to apply complex techniques and advanced formulas such as Castle Gate Technique, Seven Star Robbery Formation, Advancing the Dragon Formation and Replacement Star technique amongst others. Joey Yap also shows you how to use the Life Palace technique to combine Gua Numbers with Flying Star numbers and utilise the predictive facets of Flying Stars Feng Shui.

(Available Soon)

Elevate Your Feng Shui Skills With Joey Yap's Home Study Course And Educational DVDs

Xuan Kong Vol.1
An Advanced Feng Shui Home Study Course

Learn the Xuan Kong Flying Star Feng Shui system in just 20 lessons! Joey Yap's specialised notes and course work have been written to enable distance learning without compromising on the breadth or quality of the syllabus. Learn at your own pace with the same material students in a live class would use. The most comprehensive distance learning course on Xuan Kong Flying Star Feng Shui in the market. Xuan Kong Flying Star Vol.1 comes complete with a special binder for all your course notes.

Feng Shui for Period 8 - (DVD)

Don't miss the Feng Shui Event of the next 20 years! Catch Joey Yap LIVE and find out just what Period 8 is all about. This DVD boxed set zips you through the fundamentals of Feng Shui and the impact of this important change in the Feng Shui calendar. Joey's entertaining, conversational style walks you through the key changes that Period 8 will bring and how to tap into Wealth Qi and Good Feng Shui for the next 20 years.

Xuan Kong Flying Stars Beginners Workshop - (DVD)

Take a front row seat in Joey Yap's Xuan Kong Flying Stars workshop with this unique LIVE RECORDING of Joey Yap's Xuan Kong Flying Stars Feng Shui workshop, attended by over 500 people. This DVD program provides an effective and quick introduction of Xuan Kong Feng Shui essentials for those who are just starting out in their study of classical Feng Shui. Learn to plot your own Flying Star chart in just 3 hours. Learn 'trade secret' methods, remedies and cures for Flying Stars Feng Shui. This boxed set contains 3 DVDs and 1 workbook with notes and charts for reference.

BaZi Four Pillars of Destiny Beginners Workshop - (DVD)

Ever wondered what Destiny has in store for you? Or curious to know how you can learn more about your personality and inner talents? BaZi or Four Pillars of Destiny is an ancient Chinese science that enables us to understand a person's hidden talent, inner potential, personality, health and wealth luck from just their birth data. This specially compiled DVD set of Joey Yap's BaZi Beginners Workshop provides a thorough and comprehensive introduction to BaZi. Learn how to read your own chart and understand your own luck cycle. This boxed set contains 3 DVDs and 1 workbook with notes and reference charts.

Interested in learning MORE about Feng Shui? Advance Your Feng Shui Knowledge with the Mastery Academy Courses.

Feng Shui Mastery Series™
LIVE COURSES (MODULES ONE TO FOUR)

Feng Shui Mastery – Module One
Beginners Course

Designed for students seeking an entry-level intensive program into the study of Feng Shui , Module One is an intensive foundation course that aims not only to provide you with an introduction to Feng Shui theories and formulas and equip you with the skills and judgments to begin practicing and conduct simple Feng Shui audits upon successful completion of the course. Learn all about Forms, Eight Mansions Feng Shui and Flying Star Feng Shui in just one day with a unique, structured learning program that makes learning Feng Shui quick and easy!

Feng Shui Mastery – Module Two
Practitioners Course

Building on the knowledge and foundation in classical Feng Shui theory garnered in M1, M2 provides a more advanced and in-depth understanding of Eight Mansions, Xuan Kong Flying Star and San He and introduces students to theories that are found only in the classical Chinese Feng Shui texts. This 3-Day Intensive course hones analytical and judgment skills, refines Luo Pan (Chinese Feng Shui compass) skills and reveals 'trade secret' remedies. Module Two covers advanced Forms Analysis, San He's Five Ghost Carry Treasure formula, Advanced Eight Mansions and Xuan Kong Flying Stars and equips you with the skills needed to undertake audits and consultations for residences and offices.

Feng Shui Mastery – Module Three
Advanced Practitioners Course

Module Three is designed for Professional Feng Shui Practitioners. Learn advanced topics in Feng Shui and take your skills to a cutting edge level. Be equipped with the knowledge, techniques and confidence to conduct large scale audits (like estate and resort planning). Learn how to apply different systems appropriately to remedy situations or cases deemed inauspicious by one system and reconcile conflicts in different systems of Feng Shui. Gain advanced knowledge of San He (Three Harmony) systems and San Yuan (Three Cycles) systems, advanced Luan Tou (Forms Feng Shui) and specialist Water Formulas.

Feng Shui Mastery – Module Four
Master Course

The graduating course of the Feng Shui Mastery (FSM) Series, this course takes the advanced practitioner to the Master level. Power packed M4 trains students to 'walk the mountains' and identify superior landform, superior grade structures and make qualitative evaluations of landform, structures, Water and Qi and covers advanced and exclusive topics of San He, San Yuan, Xuan Kong, Ba Zhai, Luan Tou (Advanced Forms and Water Formula) Feng Shui. Master Internal, External and Luan Tou (Landform) Feng Shui methodologies to apply Feng Shui at every level and undertake consultations of every scale and magnitude, from houses and apartments to housing estates, townships, shopping malls and commercial districts.

BaZi Mastery – Module One
Intensive Foundation Course

This Intensive One Day Foundation Course provides an introduction to the principles and fundamentals of BaZi (Four Pillars of Destiny) and Destiny Analysis methods such as Ten Gods, Useful God and Strength of Qi. Learn how to plot a BaZi chart and interpret your Destiny and your potential. Master BaZi and learn to capitalize on your strengths, minimize risks and downturns and take charge of your Destiny.

BaZi Mastery – Module Two
Practical BaZi Applications

BaZi Module Two teaches students advanced BaZi analysis techniques and specific analysis methods for relationship luck, health evaluation, wealth potential and career potential. Students will learn to identify BaZi chart structures, sophisticated methods for applying the Ten Gods, and how to read Auxiliary Stars. Students who have completed Module Two will be able to conduct professional BaZi readings.

BaZi Mastery – Module Three
Advanced Practitioners Program

Designed for the BaZi practitioner, learn how to read complex cases and unique events in BaZi charts and perform Big and Small assessments. Discover how to analyze personalities and evaluate talents precisely, as well as special formulas and classical methodologies for BaZi from classics such as Di Tian Sui and Qiong Tong Bao Jian.

BaZi Mastery – Module Four
Master Course in BaZi

The graduating course of the BaZi Mastery Series, this course takes the advanced practitioner to the Masters' level. BaZi M4 focuses on specialized techniques of BaZi reading, unique special structures and advance methods from ancient classical texts. This program includes techniques on date selection and ancient methodologies from the Qiong Tong Bao Jian and Yuan Hai Zi Ping classics.

Xuan Kong Mastery – Module One
Advanced Foundation Program

This course is for the experienced Feng Shui professionals who wish to expand their knowledge and skills in the Xuan Kong system of Feng Shui, covering important foundation methods and techniques from the Wu Chang and Guang Dong lineages of Xuan Kong Feng Shui.

Xuan Kong Mastery – Module Two A
Advanced Xuan Kong Methodologies

Designed for Feng Shui practitioners seeking to specialise in the Xuan Kong system, this program focuses on methods of application and Joey Yap's unique Life Palace and Shifting Palace Methods, as well as methods and techniques from the Wu Chang lineage.

Xuan Kong Mastery – Module Two B
Purple White

Explore in detail and in great depth the star combinations in Xuan Kong. Learn how each different combination reacts or responds in different palaces, under different environmental circumstances and to whom in the property. Learn methods, theories and techniques extracted from ancient classics such as Xuan Kong Mi Zhi, Xuan Kong Fu, Fei Xing Fu and Zi Bai Jue.

Xuan Kong Mastery – Module Three
Advanced Xuan Kong Da Gua

This intensive course focuses solely on the Xuan Kong Da Gua system covering the theories, techniques and methods of application of this unique 64-Hexagram based system of Xuan Kong including Xuan Kong Da Gua for landform analysis.

Walk the Mountains! Learn Feng Shui in a Practical and Hands-on Program

Feng Shui Mastery Excursion Series™: CHINA

Learn landform (Luan Tou) Feng Shui by walking the mountains and chasing the Dragon's vein in China. This Program takes the students in a study tour to examine notable Feng Shui landmarks, mountains, hills, valleys, ancient palaces, famous mansions, houses and tombs in China. The Excursion is a 'practical' hands-on course where students are shown to perform readings using the formulas they've learnt and to recognize and read Feng Shui Landform (Luan Tou) formations.

Read about China Excursion here:
http://www.masteryacademy.com/Education/schoolfengshui/fengshuimasteryexcursion.asp

Mian Xiang Mastery Series™
LIVE COURSES (MODULES ONE AND TWO)

Mian Xiang Mastery – Module One
Basic Face Reading

A person's face is their fortune – learn more about the ancient Chinese art of Face Reading. In just one day, be equipped with techniques and skills to read a person's face and ascertain their character, luck, wealth and relationship luck.

Mian Xiang Mastery – Module Two
Practical Face Reading

Mian Xiang Module Two covers face reading techniques extracted from the ancient classics Shen Xiang Quan Pian and Shen Xiang Tie Guan Dau. Gain a greater depth and understanding of Mian Xiang and learn to recognize key structures and characteristics in a person's face.

Yi Jing Mastery Series™
LIVE COURSES (MODULES ONE AND TWO)

Yi Jing Mastery – Module One
Traditional Yi Jing

'Yi', relates to change. Change is the only constant in life and the universe, without exception to this rule. The Yi Jing is hence popularly referred to as the Book or Classic of Change. Discoursed in the language of Yin and Yang, the Yi Jing is one of the oldest Chinese classical texts surviving today. With Traditional Yi Jing, learnn how this Classic is used to divine the outcomes of virtually every facet of life; from your relationships to seeking an answer to the issues you may face in your daily life.

Yi Jing Mastery – Module Two
Plum Blossom Numerology

Shao Yong, widely regarded as one of the greatest scholars of the Sung Dynasty, developed Mei Hua Yi Shu (Plum Blossom Numerology) as a more advanced means for divination purpose using the Yi Jing. In Plum Blossom Numerology, the results of a hexagram are interpreted by referring to the Gua meanings, where the interaction and relationship between the five elements, stems, branches and time are equally taken into consideration. This divination method, properly applied, allows us to make proper decisions whenever we find ourselves in a predicament.

Ze Ri Mastery Series Module 1
Personal and Feng Shui Date Selection

The Mastery Academy's Date Selection Mastery Series Module 1 is specifically structured to provide novice students with an exciting introduction to the Art of Date Selection. Learn the rudiments and tenets of this intriguing metaphysical science. What makes a good date, and what makes a bad date? What dates are suitable for which activities, and what dates simply aren't? And of course, the mother of all questions: WHY aren't all dates created equal. All in only one Module – Module 1!

Ze Ri Mastery Series Module 2
Xuan Kong Da Gua Date Selection

In Module 2, discover advanced Date Selection techniques that will take your knowledge of this Art to a level equivalent to that of a professional's! This is the Module where Date Selection infuses knowledge of the ancient metaphysical science of Feng Shui and BaZi (Chinese Astrology, or Four Pillars of Destiny). Feng Shui, as a means of maximizing Human Luck (i.e. our luck on Earth), is often quoted as the cure to BaZi, which allows us to decipher our Heaven (i.e. inherent) Luck. And one of the most potent ways of making the most of what life has to offer us is to understand our Destiny, know how we can use the natural energies of our environment for our environments and MOST importantly, WHEN we should use these energies and for WHAT endeavors!

You will learn specific methods on how to select suitable dates, tailored to specific activities and events. More importantly, you will also be taught how to suit dates to a person's BaZi (Chinese Astrology, or Four Pillars of Destiny), in order to maximize his or her strengths, and allow this person to surmount any challenges that lie in wait. Add in the factor of 'place', and you would have satisfied the notion of 'doing the right thing, at the right time and in the right place'! A basic knowledge of BaZi and Feng Shui will come in handy in this Module, although these are not pre-requisites to successfully undergo Module 2.

Feng Shui for Life

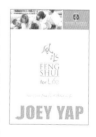

Feng Shui for life is a 5-day course designed for the Feng Shui beginner to learn how to apply practical Feng Shui in day-to-day living. It is a culmination of powerful tools and techniques that allows you to gain quick proficiency in Classical Feng Shui. Discover quick tips on analysing your own BaZi, how to apply Feng Shui solutions for your own home, how to select auspicious dates for important activities, as well as simple and useful Face Reading techniques and practical Water Formulas. This is a complete beginner's course that is suitable for anyone with an interest in applying practical, real-world Feng Shui for life! Enhance every aspect of your life – your health, wealth, and relationships – using these easy-to-apply Classical Feng Shui methods.

Mastery Academy courses are conducted around the world. Find out when will Joey Yap be in your area by visiting **www.masteryacademy.com** or call our office at **+603-2284 8080**.